Beginning Java Databases

Kevin Mukhar
Todd Lauinger
John Carnell

with

James R. de Carli
Mark Mamone
Nitin Nanda
Damon Payne
Joel Peach
Ron Phillips
David Shanes
Sakhr Youness

Wrox Press Ltd. ®

Beginning Java Databases

Published by Wrox Press Ltd,
Arden House, 1102 Warwick Road, Acocks Green,
Birmingham, B27 6BH, UK
Printed in the United States
ISBN 1-861004-37-0

Trademark Acknowledgements

Credits

Authors
Kevin Mukhar
Todd Lauinger
John Carnell

Contributing Authors
James R. de Carli
Mark Mamone
Nitin Nanda
Damon Payne
Joel Peach
Ron Phillips
David Shanes
Sakhr Youness

Additional Material
Thomas Kyte
Piyush Khanna

Technical Architect
Tony Davis

Technical Editors
Helen Callaghan
John Chapman
Mankee Cheng
Mohammed Rfaquat
Mark Waterhouse

Category Managers
Louay Fatoohi
Paul Cooper

Author Agent
Velimir Ilic

Project Administrators
Claire Robinson
Chandima Nethisinghe

Cover Design
Dawn Chellingworth

Technical Reviewers
Danny Ayers
John Bell
Thomas Bishop
Jim W. Brzowski
Chris Crane
Jeremy Crosbie
Brian Higdon
Bjarki Holm
Rahul Kumthekar
Thomas Kyte
Rick Leander
Jim MacIntosh
Vinay Menon
Jason Montgomery
Faisal Nazir
Stéphane Osmont
Phil Powers-deGeorge
David Schultz
Keyur Shah
Joe Sam Shirah
Andrew Watt
Paul Wilt

Production Manager
Simon Hardware

Production Coordinator
Emma Eato

Production Assistants
Paul Grove
Natalie O'Donnell

Indexers
Adrian Axinte
Michael Brinkman
Martin Brooks
Andrew Criddle

Proofreader
Chris Smith

About the Authors

Kevin Mukhar

Kevin Mukhar started programming as a teenager, beginning with COBOL on a teletype terminal. He also programmed on HP calculators and on one of the first home PCs, the Commodore 64. Unfortunately, he didn't realize how much he enjoyed programming and so, only took one programming course in college. He graduated from the University of Washington with a BA degree in Mathematics, and received a commission from the U S Air Force. While in the Air Force, he continued programming as hobby, learning several languages including Pascal, FORTRAN, assembly, C, and dBase. This experience enabled him to get a software development job when he left the Air Force.

Since becoming a professional software developer, he has programmed a client-server based training system in C and C++. He then worked on a large-scale data management system using an Oracle database to manage terabytes of binary data. The front-end was developed as a web application employing C++ and Java. This was followed by an all-Java system for dynamically finding and displaying data from distributed data repositories. His latest job is developing Java intranet web applications using J2EE technologies. The web applications provide customer management for a company with millions of customers.

His heroes are Steve McConnell (http://www.construx.com/stevemcc/), Philip Greenspun (http://philip.greenspun.com/), and Ron Jeffries (http://c2.com/cgi/wiki?RonJeffries).

Kevin thanks Dave Johnson for reawakening his desire to be a writer and providing the help to get started. He also thanks the editors and reviewers at Wrox Press for taking his sorry prose, and helping to turn it into clear explanations.

Kevin dedicates his chapters to his wife Anne.

Todd Lauinger

Todd Lauinger is a freelance instructor, mentor, conference speaker, and published author. He is currently employed as a Software Construction Fellow at Best Buy Co., Inc., working there to establish a common infrastructure for all Java-related software development activities in the enterprise. Todd has his Masters degree in Software Engineering, along with over 10 years of experience developing large, mission-critical software systems for engineering and business organizations. Outside of work he enjoys spending time with his wife hiking, biking, blading, and playing volleyball.

I would like to dedicate my efforts in this book to my Lord and Savior, who gave me the opportunity and gifts to do so. I thank my precious wife Teri, without whose support, encouragement, and patience I would never been able to put those gifts into action. All my love!

John Carnell

John Carnell has had an obsession with computers since he was 12 years old working on his Commodore 64. That obsession never waned and he is currently working as a Senior Systems Architect for Workscape, a leading provider of HR and employee benefits self-service solutions. John's favorite topic of discussion, much to his wife's chagrin, is component-based, n-tier architectures. John has extensive experience with Microsoft, Oracle, and Java n-tier solutions. He lives in Waukesha, Wisconsin with his wife Janet and his two pups Ladybug and Ginger. John can be reached at john_carnell@yahoo.com.

To my wife Janet: We all have defining moments in our life. Mine was when I was 18 years old sitting on a tennis court in the pouring rain, huddled underneath my jacket with you. It was at that point I realized you were something wonderfully new and different. Eleven years later, you still amaze and surprise me. Thank you for all your love and support over the years. I am what you helped make me: a better man. I love you.

James R. de Carli

James R de Carli's background within the computer industry spans writing, teaching, and application development.

With more than two-dozen certification exams under his belt, James has earned several technical certifications, including Microsoft Certified Systems Engineer (MCSE), Microsoft Certified Solutions Developer (MCSD), and Microsoft Certified Database Administrator (MCDBA). In addition, James holds a Master's degree in Computer and Information Sciences, and a Bachelor's degree in Mathematics and Statistics.

James has made numerous contributions to various technical magazines and has co-authored two books, Professional JavaScript and Professional ASP Data Access, both from Wrox Press. Today, he works as Director, Website Architecture and Development, for SiteShell Corporation, a Connecticut-based Internet media provider. He is also an Assistant Professor at Fairfield University where he teaches graduate-level Software Engineering courses. James spent many years as an instructor for a Microsoft Authorized Training and Education Center, and was also a Senior Consultant for a Microsoft Solution Provider Partner.

James lives in Connecticut with his wife Catherine and their three sons, Kenneth, Robert, and Daniel.

Mark Mamone

Mark Mamone is a Technical Design Authority with Syntegra, a global Consulting and Systems Integration house, currently designing and implementing J2EE and Microsoft .NET solutions for global e-commerce systems. Mark has worked professionally in the IT industry for some 13 years for companies such as Thomas Cook, ABN AMRO, and Royal Mail. His recent accomplishments have been a WAP gateway for a global logistics company and the definition of the Microsoft eFramework for use on new projects within Syntegra.

I'd like to dedicate this book to Julie, James, and Cameron, for, without their understanding, drive and support, it would never have been finished. I'd also like to thank my mum and dad, without the purchase of my first computer, the Commodore VIC-20, my career may never have followed this path.

Nitin Nanda

Nitin Nanda works as Associate Project Manager in R & D center of Quark, Inc. based at Chandigarh, India. Here he is responsible for managing R&D of a suite of products targeted for the print catalog market. These products use RMI and CORBA as the underlying protocol for middle-tier development.

He has co-authored the book, *Professional Java Data* for Wrox Press, and has contributed articles in premier Java magazines like *Java World*, *Java Developer's Journal*, and *Java Report*. Off-hours, he spends time in the publication and translation of books into English, the words of Sri Ramakrishna, India's great spiritual saint (http://www.kathamrita.org/).

Nitin would like to acknowledge his thanks to his Guru (spiritual preceptor) Ishwar Devi Gupta, who taught him the fundamental truths of life towards keeping a balance of both physical science and spirit!

Damon Payne

Damon moved to Milwaukee, Wisconsin last year where he lives now. He currently works for Cornerstone Consulting, Inc. His professional expertise lies mostly in developing thin-client web applications using Java and XML technologies. Damon's other professional interests include wireless applications, object databases, and open source software development.

When he is not at a computer, Damon enjoys playing in his WRX, electronic music, and playing the guitar. He also takes martial arts lessons and regularly goes to the gym in a feeble attempt to not look like a programmer.

I'd like to thank John Carnell for encouraging my interest in technical writing and sticking his neck out by giving my name to Wrox.

Joel Peach

Joel Peach is Vice President of Consulting Services, and co-founder of Tracer Information Systems in Columbus, OH. He is a Java-certified programmer with extensive experience implementing distributed Java enterprise applications using the J2EE platform and of course... databases!

You can e-mail him at jpeach@traceris.com.

Joel would like to acknowledge Tom Acree for taking a young hack and helping to turn him into a developer; Sarah Camper and Chet Cady for their encouragement, support and not laughing when he said he was going to be a writer some day; Tony Davis, Vel Ilic at Wrox for terrific authoring support. (We made it! Let's get some sleep.) And every developer, too numerous to name, that he's had the pleasure of calling a colleague.

For Gina Lynch, thank you for being cool enough to let me temporarily neglect you to pursue an opportunity that's almost as wonderful as you.

Ron Phillips

Ron Phillips has been designing and developing commercial software tools for over 10 years, with commercial IDEs, languages, compilers, and software design tools to his credit. He is active in the IT community, and has spoken at numerous industry conferences in the USA and Europe. His current research efforts focus on loose federations in distributed systems and architectural pattern mining.

David Shanes

David Shanes is a Senior Software Engineer at Predicate Logic Software Systems, Inc. in San Diego, California where he is involved with middle-tier Java development for U S Space and Naval Warfare Systems Center projects. David has been working with Java since 1996 and has extensive experience in object-oriented design and development, Java, database, multi-threaded, and network programming.

David received his Bachelor of Science degree in Computer Science from the United States Naval Academy in 1988, and is currently working on the thesis for his Master's Degree in Computer Science from San Diego State University.

David's interests include biking, roller-skating, sailing, and spending time with his wife and two children.

To my wonderful wife Mindy, and our little ones Joshua and Jessica who always make me laugh, I would like to thank you for being so supportive of me, for letting me be ambitious and for loving me unconditionally. I love you with all of my heart.

I would like to thank my mom for all her guidance and patience when I was growing up (have I stopped?) and my in-laws for being there when we need you.

Finally, I would like to dedicate this to my dad who worked his whole life to provide for us. Thank you for showing me the meaning of hard work and integrity and for always holding mom's hand. I miss you dad.

Sakhr Youness

Sakhr Youness is a senior architect at Commerce One, Inc. He is a professional engineer (PE) and a Microsoft-certified solution developer (MCSD) who has more than ten years of experience in data modeling, business-to-business (B2B) applications, client-server, and database application development. As a senior software architect and technical consultant, he designed, developed, or participated in developing a number of online business-to-business and client-server applications related to the automotive, banking, and engineering industries.

Mr. Youness is the author of the Wrox book, *Professional Data Warehousing with SQL Server 7.0 and OLAP Services*, published in January 2000. He is also the main author of the *SQL Unleashed* book, published by Sams Publishing in November 1999. He also contributed to many other books, including *Beginning SQL Programming*, *Professional SQL Server 2000 Programming*, both from Wrox Press, and *SQL Server 7.0 Programming Unleashed*, from Sams Publishing. He also participated in the technical reviews of more than a dozen books for Macmillan and Wrox Press, spanning several topics in Oracle 8, SQL Server 7, Visual Basic 6, and Visual Studio 98.

Mr. Youness enjoys going out with his wife, Nada, and two young daughters, Maya and Jenna. Among his hobbies are swimming, playing basketball, reading, and watching sporting events. He can be reached by e-mail at: syouness@home.com.

I would like to dedicate this to my family members, Nada, Maya, and Jenna. I would like to thank the Wrox 'family' for giving me the chance to write and work with a wonderful team.

akarta
JAVA

Table of Contents

akarta
JAVA

Introduction

In Java we have a versatile, robust programming language that is adaptable to a range of different environments, be it on a middle-tier application server or a client browser. Regardless of if what sort of application you are developing and where your code will run, your application will almost certainly need to make use of data that is stored in some form of database. Relational databases are the data store of choice in the vast majority of businesses, and have also evolved enormously over the recent years, into powerful and feature-rich data-management systems.

This book aims to teach you how to use these two powerful technologies to build successful Java database applications. The basic goals of this book are as follows:

- Provide an understanding of the design and operation of the relational database and of the language that it understands, SQL.
- Give a thorough grounding in JDBC fundamentals.
- Teach the reader how to produce production-quality data-persistent programs, even at the introductory level. We hope that this book is one that an aspiring programmer can use to improve knowledge of Java and good object-oriented design, in writing effective database applications.
- Give the reader an appreciation of how to tackle Object-Relational mapping and of the Java mapping frameworks that may provide the right solution for their application.
- Demonstrate how the above knowledge may be applied in an enterprise environment, where Java programs may need to interface with other versatile technologies such as XML.

Who is This Book For?

Although this is a Wrox *Beginning...* series book, it could not seriously attempt to teach from the ground up each of its three core subject areas: Java, JDBC, and databases. We know Wrox books are usually big, but not that big!

Instead, this book assumes that the reader has a reasonable grasp of the fundamentals of the Java programming language and aims to build on this, elucidating the core Java features in direct relation to database programming. This basic knowledge of Java is the only prerequisite for this book. If you know little or nothing about relational databases or the JDBC Application Programming Interface, then this book will teach you what you need to know to start building effective database-driven Java applications.

So, in a sense this book may be considered a "second-level" *Beginning...* book. It is ideal for the Java programmer who has completed a foundational title, such as Ivor Horton's *Beginning Java 2* (ISBN: 1-861003-66-8), or equivalent, and now wishes (or is being called on) to put their Java skills to use in a database-based project.

If you are not familiar with Java, but have migrated from a language such as C or C++, then the code explanations given in the text should enable you to understand and work through the code examples.

What is Covered in This Book?

Conceptually, the book breaks down into five distinct sections. We start with a foundational section covering the basics of SQL and relational databases, and follow it with a section devoted to explaining the workings of the JDBC API. Subsequent chapters build on theses foundations, challenging your Java skills as we add complexity to our Java programs and explore the integration of Java and databases with other technologies, such as XML and XSLT.

Following is a brief description of the chapter structure within each section. Every chapter in every section contains well-explained code examples – ones that you can actually run, as opposed to just code snippets – that will clearly demonstrate the issues being discussed.

Section I: Java, SQL, and Databases

In order to build effective Java database applications, you must have a solid understanding of what a relational database is, how it works and of the language that it understands, namely Structured Query Language (SQL).

Chapter 1 sets the scene. We introduce the fundamental concepts behind Relational Database Management Systems (RDBMSs), and take a high-level look at how and why we would want to marry Java and relational databases using SQL and the JDBC API. We describe how to install the Cloudscape RDBMS and set up the Music Store database that will store and persist our data for all of the examples in this book.

Chapter 2 gets you up and running. We describe some of the basic JDBC concepts and terminology, and look at some of the fundamental Java objects that JDBC provides to allow you to retrieve data from database. We also look at basic error-handling techniques in your code.

By this stage we have already written a few basic SQL statements to retrieve data from a database table, but the power of SQL extends far beyond this. **Chapter 3** and **Chapter 4** take an in-depth look at SQL. In Chapter 3, we look at how we can query and manipulate the data that is already contained in the database using the SQL `SELECT` statement. In Chapter 4, we focus on the creation and modification of tables and how to create new rows of data in these tables, as well as how to modify and delete them.

At the heart of your successful application will be a well-designed database. The data that your application needs must be stored efficiently and in a manner that ensures the integrity of the data. In **Chapter 5** we describe how to correctly organize your data into tables and define relationship between them. We also take a high-level look at some of the other database objects that we can incorporate in our design to provide useful functionality, including stored **procedures**, **views,** and **triggers**.

In **Chapter 6** we put into practice many of the concepts covered in the previous two chapters, by designing and building the Music Store database that is used throughout the book. Based on an understanding of the requirements of our fictional Music Store business, we design and build the tables and then implement some support queries, views, and procedures that could provide some of the required functionality of the system.

Section II: Exploring JDBC

You have a firm grasp of relational database design, and in particular of our Music Store database, and you understand how to utilize the power of the SQL programming language to query and modify data. It is now time to start designing and building some Java programs that can interface with the database (and SQL) through the **JDBC API**. JDBC provides a whole host of Java objects that we can use to send data between our Java classes and the database. Here you'll learn about the core JDBC classes and interfaces that you'll need to use in developing your applications.

Chapter 7 starts this section, with a broad overview of some of the decisions you will need to make before building a Java database application. How will you model your Java application? What strategy will you use to map that model to the database? What JDBC driver will you use? This chapter gives guidance on these issues and also discusses the crucial question of how exactly you need to use data in your application.

Chapter 8 is where we start using JDBC in earnest. Before our application can do anything, it will need to establish a connection to the database. So that is where we start. We discuss the JDBC `Connection` interface and show how to implement a `ConnectionFactory` class that encapsulates the connection code and can be used all of our applications.

Chapter 9 looks in detail at the `Statement` and the `ResultSet` interfaces. We look at how to use `Statement` objects to execute data query and modification commands in SQL. We then discuss the `ResultSet` object, which stores any data that is returned from our queries. We show how to navigate through our `ResultSet` data, and how to update data in our tables, through the `ResultSet`.

Sometimes, when you develop an application, we may not necessarily know the structure or type of the data that your application needs to use. If you wish to port your application between databases, you need a way to find out this information. JDBC allows you to make use of meta data (information about the data) for just this purpose. **Chapter 10** explores the meta data interfaces that JDBC provides.

While `ResultSets` are a very useful object for data retrieval, they need to maintain a permanent connection to the database. In **Chapter 11**, we discuss an alternative – the `RowSet` interface. A `RowSet` object has the advantage that it can be detached from the database and sent across a network. We look at the three versions of Rowset objects that we can create, `CahchedRowSet`, `JdbcRowSet`, and `WebRowSet`, and why each interface might be useful to us.

When a SQL statement is sent to the database, the database needs to spend time compiling that statement and working out a "plan" for its execution, which is then stored in a special data area. Often, we will resend SQL queries that we have used before; the columns are the same, the tables are the same – only the data is different. If we are smart, we will not make the database perform all that compilation work over again and store an entirely new plan. **Chapter 12** discusses the `PreparedStatment` interface that provides a means to create a reusable SQL statement – once the database has compiled it the first time, it can use the same execution plan over and over again.

A database is much more than just a storage place – it is a programming platform in its own right where you can build procedures and functions to enforce security, data integrity, and the business rules of your application. In **Chapter 13** we look at how to create these stored procedures, and then call them from our Java code using the `CallableStatement` interface.

Chapter 14 discussed the important topic of **transactions**. We look at what a transaction is, and at the properties that they must exhibit. We discuss the different mechanisms that databases use to ensure that transactions occurring simultaneously in the database do not interfere with each other. In this context, we touch on the complex issues of locking, concurrency, and transaction isolation levels. We include clear examples of how to control transactions through JDBC.

Section III: Object Relational Mapping

This is where we start to challenge your Java programming skills, and your grasp of the concepts learned in the first two sections, as we build complexity into our Java applications. We look at the difficulties we face when the carefully constructed object-model for our Java application "clashes" with the design of relational database. We see how we can use a Java framework and JDBC to map these more complex applications to our database.

Java is an object-oriented software development language using a set of objects to accomplish work. Relational databases use a relational, table-based model. As your Java application grows in complexity you will find that the two designs start to 'clash'. In **Chapter 15**, we build an application the uses a simple "one-class-to-one-table" mapping and then, conceptually, add complexity to our application (such as hierarchical object relationships) and look at the sort of problems we are going to encounter when mapping one model to the other.

Following on from the previous chapter, **Chapter 16** uses an open source framework called Java Layered Frameworks to map Java objects to a relational database. We will look at how this framework can alleviate some of the difficulties discussed in the previous chapter. The framework is reasonably complex but you will learn a lot from investigating how it works.

As your Java database application gets more complex, the need to log the activities of your application becomes more and more of a necessity, as does the ability to successfully debug it. This is the subject of **Chapter 17**. Some of the techniques we will look at are logging to `System.out` and `System.err`, running local and remote interactive debuggers, and instrumenting your applications.

Section IV: Java and Databases in the Enterprise

Essentially, this section supplies a taster of how you can apply your new skills in the enterprise application development arena. We'll see how we can adapt some of our Java classes to work in the Java 2 Enterprise Edition framework and look at how we can exploit the components and services that this provides. We'll look at how you can build flexible and sophisticated Java database applications that interface with the data interchange and transformation technologies, XML and XSLT.

New with the JDBC 2.0 API comes the `DataSource` object. With our connection code stored in a `DataSource`, we can change the connection parameters all in one place, without having to recompile our application. This can add a great deal of flexibility and portability to our code. In **Chapter 18** we investigate this feature, and look at how it enables us to use advanced features such as connection pooling and distributed transactions in our applications.

Chapter 19 demonstrate how you can employ the skills that you have learnt so far to build Java database applications suitable for use in an enterprise scenario. We focus on the features and components provided in the Enterprise Edition of the Java 2 platform (J2EE). We have designed our classes carefully, so it is a relatively easy task to adapt them for this new environment. We show how to adapt a previously developed class for the web, using **Java Server Pages**. We then delve in to the advanced topic of Enterprise JavaBeans (EJBs). Again, we adapt a previously developed class and deploy it as an EJB.

Chapter 20 shows how our applications can incorporate use of XML – a self-describing markup language that has revolutionized the way in which we transfer data and share it between applications. In this chapter, we look at how we can map relational data to XML.

Once you have your data in XML format, there are many ways that you can transform it, depending on the requirements of your application. We can transform it to HTMK for a browser, to a text format, or just to a different XML format. In **Chapter 21**, take a look at XSLT – the principal means of processing XML. We look at how XML and XSLT can be implemented practically and applied to the Music Store application that we have been using throughout the book.

As the final chapter in this section, and indeed the book, **Chapter 22** ties together a lot of the knowledge you've gained so far. It describes some of the issues to consider when developing fully-production-standard Java database applications. First, we have a section describing potential architectures for your application. After this, we implement a framework know as the Model-View-Controller that incorporates use of open source projects such as Tomcat, JBoss, Xalan, and Xerces to demonstrate how to build a fully functional web-enabled, enterprise database application using Java.

Section V: Appendices

The purpose of the appendices is to bring you up to speed with XML and to guide you in the setup of the various pieces of software that the book uses, and to let you know where you can get help, if required.

Appendix A demonstrates how to set up and access the Music Store database on a variety of RDBMSs, including Oracle, Cloudscape, and Microsoft Access.

Appendix B contains instructions and hints on how to set up the JBoss application server and the Tomcat web server.

Since the final three chapters of the book require some knowledge of XML, we have provided an XML primer in **Appendix C**.

Finally, if you need help and guidance when you are reading through this book then **Appendix D** will point you in the right direction to get advice.

What You Need to Use This Book

In order to put into practice the theories discussed in the majority of this book, all that is required is the Java Development Kit (JDK) and a database with a suitable JDBC driver.

In this book we have used JDK 1.3, which is available from the Sun web site (http://java.sun.com). The two databases that the book uses extensively are Cloudscape and Oracle, although with a little tweaking you should be able to get the code working on the database of your choice. Chapter 1 of this book shows you how to obtain and install Cloudscape, while Appendix A shows you how to obtain and install a copy of Personal Oracle 8i on your computer.

As our code examples get more advanced, and as we begin to diversify the subject matter to include more technologies, there will be new software that will need to be installed and set up. At each relevant point in the text, instructions are given regarding where to get this software and how to get it up and running. Examples of this software include the open source, Java Layered Frameworks implementation for the object-relational mapping chapters, Xalan and Xerces parsers for the XML and XSLT chapters, and JBoss and Tomcat for the web-enabled enterprise applications towards the end of the book.

Conventions

In order to help you understand and follow what is going on throughout this text, and to maintain consistency, we have used a number of different styles of text and layout. Here are some examples of these, and what they mean:

> *Background is a style that is used to display some information aside from the general discussion, such as advice, hints, and other sideline information.*

When **important words** are introduced for the first time, they are displayed in a bold format to stand out from the page.

Words that appear on the screen in menus and windows, such as File or Open, are displayed in a similar style in which they would be viewed.

Keys that you would press, such as *Ctrl-C* and *Enter*, are displayed in italics.

Next, there are three styles we use to display code. The first is used when we are referring to code within the main body of the text. In this case, use a format called `code in text`.

```
The second is used when there are full pieces of standalone code you can run, or
when there is code that is new or important to take in.
```

```
This type of formatting is used when there are snippets of code, or code that you
have seen before.
```

```
Sometimes, you may see some old bits of code, like this section here,
interspersed with a new section, where the code is highlighted in a gray box.
```

The code foreground style is also used when command lines are shown, with the output of a command being displayed in code background. An example of this is:

```
> javac input.java
This is the output from the command.
```

Important pieces of information come highlighted in boxes like this.

Try It Out – An Example For You to Try

After introducing and learning a new concept, there is a *Try It Out* section to demonstrate how to use it. These pieces of code are full examples and include instructions on how to execute them properly.

How It Works

After a *Try It Out* section, there is usually a *How It Works* section that does what its heading suggests. Here, we explain the important, underlying mechanics of how the code works as it does. This will help you relate what you have just done with what you have just learnt.

Downloading the Sourcecode

As you work through the examples in this book, you may decide that you want to type in all the code by hand. Many readers prefer this because it is a good way to get familiar with the coding techniques that are being used.

Whether you want to type the code in or not, we have made all the sourcecode for this book available at our web site at the following address, http://www.wrox.com/. Click on the Java link towards the top of the page, and find this book towards the top of the list of Java book.

If you are one of those readers who likes to type in the code, you can use our files to check the results you should be getting – they should be your first stop if you think you might have typed in an error. If you're one of those readers who do not like typing, then downloading the sourcecode from our web site is a must!

Either way, it'll help you with updates and debugging.

Tell us What You Think

We have tried to make this book as accurate and enjoyable as possible, but what really matters is what the book actually does for you. Please let us know your views, either by returning the reply card in the back of the book, or by contacting us via e-mail at feedback@wrox.com.

Errata

We have made every effort to make sure that there are no errors in the text or the code. However, to err is human, and as such, we recognize the need to keep you informed of any mistakes as they are spotted and corrected. Errata sheets are available for all our books at http://www.wrox.com/. If you find an error that hasn't already been reported, please let us know.

Our web site acts as a focus for other information and support, including the code from all our books, sample chapters, previews of forthcoming titles, and articles and opinions on related topics. For more details on obtaining support, finding out about errata, and providing us with feedback, you can look at Appendix D.

akarta
JAVA
Java

Setting Up Your Java Environment

Throughout this book, we will be showing examples of code to compile and run. In order to do this, there are a few settings you will need to make sure of. First and foremost, you need to make sure that your Java installation has been configured and set up properly.

Installing the JDK

For this book, we are using the Sun Microsystems JDK1.3, which we will assume is installed in `C:\jdk1.3`. This is the value that we will set in our `JAVA_HOME` variable. If you have your JDK in a different place, you need to make sure that your `JAVA_HOME` variable points to the right place. If you don't already have the kit, then it can be obtained from http://www.java.sun.com/j2se/.

Setting the JAVA_HOME Variable

There are several ways to set your `JAVA_HOME` variable, and this depends on what system your computer runs. If you have Windows 9x, include the following line in your `autoexec.bat` file:

```
SET JAVA_HOME=C:\jdk1.3
```

Any changes you make to your `autoexec.bat` file will only take effect once you restart your computer. This is because the `autoexec.bat` file is only read when your computer starts up. If you are running Windows NT or Windows 2000, you can set environment variables in the following manner:

1. Right-click the My Computer icon on the desktop
2. Select Properties
3. Select the Advanced tab
4. Click the Environment Variables button
5. In the bottom half of the screen, under System Variables, click New

6. Now, set the Variable Name to be JAVA_HOME, and the Variable Value to point to your JDK installation (say, C:\jdk1.3)

7. Click OK on the New System Variable dialog, and OK on the Environment Variables dialog, and OK on the System Properties dialog

When you open a new command window, the additions you made to your environment variables will take effect – if you already have a command window open, the new variable won't be available there.

The next things to check on are your PATH and CLASSPATH settings.

Setting Your PATH

In order to be able to run the Java compiler javac, and the Java run time java, your computer needs to know where to look for them. To make sure that you *don't* get the following message when you type javac at the command line:

```
'javac' is not recognized as an internal or external command, operable program or
batch file.
```

you will need to add the bin directory of your JDK to your PATH. This means that when you type a command at the prompt, the system will look in the \bin directory of your JDK installation for the program you want. Again, there are several ways to do this depending on your operating system.

If you're using Windows 9x, you can add the following line to your autoexec.bat file:

```
SET PATH=%PATH%;%JAVA_HOME%\bin
```

This will have effect of adding (for our setting of JAVA_HOME) C:\jdk1.3\bin to the end of our PATH variable, which will mean that our system will look in the C:\jdk1.3\bin directory when we try to run commands.

It is important to separate values with a semi-colon (;) so that the system knows where one directory ends and another begins.

If you're running Windows 2000, go to the Environment Variables dialog (My Computer | Properties | Advanced | Environment Variables), select path (might be capitalized), and click the Edit button. Scroll to the end of the Variable Value box, and add the following:

```
;%JAVA_HOME%\bin
```

Once you've clicked OK as before, this will have the same effect as altering the autoexec.bat file; the addition of C:\jdk1.3\bin to your PATH variable. Now when you type javac or java at the command prompt, you should get a list of valid options for the command, like the following screenshot:

```
C:\WINNT\System32\cmd.exe
C:\>javac
Usage: javac <options> <source files>
where possible options include:
  -g                         Generate all debugging info
  -g:none                    Generate no debugging info
  -g:{lines,vars,source}     Generate only some debugging info
  -O                         Optimize; may hinder debugging or enlarge class file
  -nowarn                    Generate no warnings
  -verbose                   Output messages about what the compiler is doing
  -deprecation               Output source locations where deprecated APIs are used
  -classpath <path>          Specify where to find user class files
  -sourcepath <path>         Specify where to find input source files
  -bootclasspath <path>      Override location of bootstrap class files
  -extdirs <dirs>            Override location of installed extensions
  -d <directory>             Specify where to place generated class files
  -encoding <encoding>       Specify character encoding used by source files
  -target <release>          Generate class files for specific VM version

C:\>java
Usage: java [-options] class [args...]
           (to execute a class)
   or  java -jar [-options] jarfile [args...]
           (to execute a jar file)

where options include:
    -cp -classpath <directories and zip/jar files separated by ;>
                  set search path for application classes and resources
    -D<name>=<value>
                  set a system property
    -verbose[:class|gc|jni]
                  enable verbose output
    -version      print product version and exit
    -showversion  print product version and continue
    -? -help      print this help message
    -X            print help on non-standard options

C:\>
```

Setting Your CLASSPATH

In order to be able to compile and run many of the examples in this book, you will need to have not only a Java compiler, but also a variety of class files and JAR files. In a similar fashion to the system variable PATH, which tells the system where to look for programs to execute, CLASSPATH is used by Java to locate classes.

The CLASSPATH variable can contain both directories and JAR files, although any JAR files you want in your classpath have to be added explicitly. There are a couple of ways to use the CLASSPATH variable. First, you can set a CLASSPATH variable to include all the files you want. This can be achieved by declaring a variable CLASSPATH (as above for JAVA_HOME and PATH), and setting it to point to the directories you want. For Windows 9x, you can add the following to your autoexec.bat file:

```
SET CLASSPATH=%CLASSPATH%;%JAVA-HOME%\lib
```

Under Windows 2000, you can locate the CLASSPATH variable on the Environment Variables dialog, and add the following:

```
;%JAVA_HOME%\lib
```

Each time you need extra files in your classpath, you can add them to your variable, either through the ways already shown, or by setting it at the command prompt like this:

```
SET CLASSPATH=%CLASSPATH%;c:\java\lib\useful.jar
```

Here, we are adding the `c:\java\lib\useful.jar` file to our classpath. This method is useful when we are adding JAR files (and directories) that we will be using frequently, to our classpath.

The other way to use the classpath varies, depending on how we make additions to it. As before, we declare our `CLASSPATH` variable. This time, rather than making additions to it, we use it as a starting point for the -classpath option when running `javac` or `java`. As an example, here is a command in which we set the classpath at the same time in which we call `javac`:

```
> javac -classpath %CLASSPATH%;c:\java\lib\jndi.jar;. RunSomething.java
```

Here, we are adding two things to the classpath for the duration of this call to `javac`:

- The `c:\java\lib\jndi.jar` file
- The current directory, indicated by the dot (`.`)

Using this method, although slower to type, has one distinct advantage over the other method – it makes for quicker compilation of the class. This is because `javac` will look through all the directories and all the JAR files in the classpath when it comes to compile a class. The more you have in your classpath, then the longer that search will take.

How you decide to set and use your classpath is entirely up to you, as long as you make sure that you have the files you need in your classpath.

Directory Structure for the Examples

To simplify things, all the examples in this book will be run from one directory, `C:\BegJavaDB`. Each chapter will have its own sub directory; these are named `Ch01`, `Ch02`, and so on.

In addition, for convenience, we will store all the JAR files we come across in one place as well, `c:\java\lib`. In order to reduce typing time, we can set up an environment variable to point to this directory, calling it something short like `JLIB`. This can be set in the same way that we set `JAVA_HOME` earlier.

Let's assume that we have a JAR file called `jndi.jar`, and it is stored in the `C:\java\lib` directory. We then set our `JLIB` variable to point to the `C:\java\lib` directory. Using this new variable, we can add new JAR files to our classpath at run time in the following manner:

```
> javac -classpath %CLASSPATH%;.;%JLIB%\jndi.jar RunSomething.java
```

As before, we are including both the current directory (this time specified in between `%CLASSPATH%` and `%JLIB%\jndi.jar`), and `c:\java\lib\jndi.jar`. The `javac` command will evaluate the `%JLIB%` to the contents of the `JLIB` variable, `c:\java\lib`.

In general, there are instructions in the text to demonstrate where particular code examples should be saved within the `C:BegJavaDB\` directory structure. Often, there are `package` declarations at the start of a piece of Java code. This means that the relevant script should be saved in that sub-directory within the chapter sub-directory. For instance, if we had the following section of code at the start of a `.java` file:

```
package results;

import java.sql.*;
import java.io.*;
import connections.*;

public class ScrollingDemo {
    .
    .
    .
```

then we would instantly recognize the fact that this file should be saved as `ScrollingDemo.java` in a directory called `results`, within the relevant chapter folder.

Also, some of the code throughout the book is reused in many of the demonstrations. For example, the `ConnectionFactory` class developed in Chapter 8, *Connecting to a Database* is reused in numerous chapters. This is contained in the `connections` sub-folder and is called by the `import connections.*` statement at the start of a piece of Java script. You need to make sure, if possible, that there is a folder named `connections` containing the `ConnectionFactory` class in the directory you are working in, or at least that your classpath points to a location where there *is* a `connections` directory containing a copy of the `ConnectionFactory` class.

Relational Databases and Java

Data is the foundation of all but the most trivial application development. Whether the application is a video game storing a user's score in memory or an accounting package saving a customer's order, it will need to load, manipulate, and store data in some form or another. The relational database, although not the only option, is currently by far the most common means of storing this data.

In this chapter we will:

- Give a foundation in the basics of relational databases
- Introduce the Structured Query language (SQL), the standard programming interface for retrieving and manipulating data in relational databases
- Introduce the JDBC Application Programming Interface, through which Java supports relational databases (and thus the ability to execute SQL commands from our Java programs)
- Install the Cloudscape database and the sample Music Store database that we will use throughout this book

Persisting Data

The Java language defines a vast array of data structures with which we can store information in our programs, from the simple variable to arrays, vectors, and nodes. The idea behind **persisting** that data is simple: your program has knowledge about some kind of information or data at one point in time and you want to be able to access that same information and maybe even update it or delete it at a point of time in the future.

Almost any kind of program you could mention will involve some kind of persistent data – even those you might not immediately associate with the need for data storage, until you start to think about it. Consider, for example, what happens when you request a web page from you browser (say, http://www.wrox.com). Your request will go through a 'naming server' that will convert your URL into an IP address, by performing a database lookup. The data needed to do this conversion database must be persistent and is continuously updated.

If your program handles only small amounts of data, then you may be able to simply store that data in a text file on disk, or make use of Java's object serialization. However, if it handles a significant amount of data, then it is likely to store that data in a relational database. Let's briefly consider the first two of these options before moving on to discuss the need to write Java applications that are driven by a relational database.

Persistence in Java

There are several ways that we can persist data in Java. Some of the examples include utilizing flat files, serializing objects and using a database. Depending on the amount and type of data that you need to persist, you might choose a different implementation.

Flat Files

We can write to and read from flat files that are stored in the file system on disk. This is a viable option when all you need to store are some configuration settings, a text document to be printed out later, or an XML document for transfer to some other part of the world. For a very small set of data that is not updated very often, the overhead of something as complex as a database might be excessive.

If you have more than a small set of static data, a flat file implementation might be too costly. If the data is going to be queried, then traversing through a file to search for records to read and/or update data can be very expensive in terms of memory and application time. Also, there is not a natural way to relate the information between different files. Of course you could create some sort of key into another file, but trying to query against multiple flat files would be very inefficient.

If you have to deal with updating or deleting the data in files then you need to deal with ways to control access to the files to avoid locking problems. This is a much more difficult problem than it sounds like. If you lock the whole file so that one user can update a record in that file, you can take a very serious performance hit. Trying to figure out which record in a flat file is going to be updated and locking that one only is not an easy task either.

Sometimes, you may want to store more complex data. For example, you may wish to store the state of your application at a given point in time so that a user can return to the application at some future time and find it in the state in which it was left. In such a scenario, a flat file would be very costly. You would have to go through all of the active objects that contained any data that needed to be persisted and put it in a format that could be written to disk and then read it back into memory later. This also creates a maintenance problem. Any time that you add new functionality into your classes, you need to ensure that the mechanism that you used to persist the data to disk is updated to reflect those changes.

Object Serialization

To handle the case when you need to store the state of your system, Java has the option of making your objects **serializable**. Making an object serializable simply means that you want to be able to write the object out over some stream and read it back in later. Examples of streaming are sending the output to a file on your disk or over a network connection to another computer. When you define your classes, you simply have your class implement the `java.io.Serializable` interface.

Once you have implemented the interface, you are now abstracted away from having to know about how the file I/O is going to work or the format of the files. You do not even need to worry about any changes to the structure of the object since that will all be taken care of for you. If you change the structure of your Java class, because you implemented the serializable interface, Java will take care of ensuring that any new variables and methods are added when the object is written out and that they are repopulated when the object is read in.

Java's object is commonly implemented in distributed programming and is very useful when you wish to store an object's state and then recreate a copy of that object in a different application. Instead of having to make several remote method calls to populate the data in the remote object, you can just stream the remote object over the network to another computer where it can be recreated. However, again, it is only really effective for handling small amounts of data – it is not a good implementation in general for overall persistence.

Relational Databases

The persistence mechanism that we use exclusively in this book is the relational database. A database is really a collection of entities, or objects. These objects control how the data is stored and how it is managed.

In a relational database the basic data storage entity is a **table**. Each entity will have a specific set of attributes (or properties) that define the sort of data that is stored in that entity. In the diagram below, the attributes of our `CustomerAddress` table are `NAME`, `ADDRESS`, and `TEL#`. In the relational database we refer to these attributes as columns or **fields**. If we take our object analogy further, then each instance of our entity will have identical attributes but will be uniquely characterized by the values of these attributes. In the database, an instance of our object is analogous to a row, or **record**, in the table. The following diagram illustrates a table and its associated nomenclature:

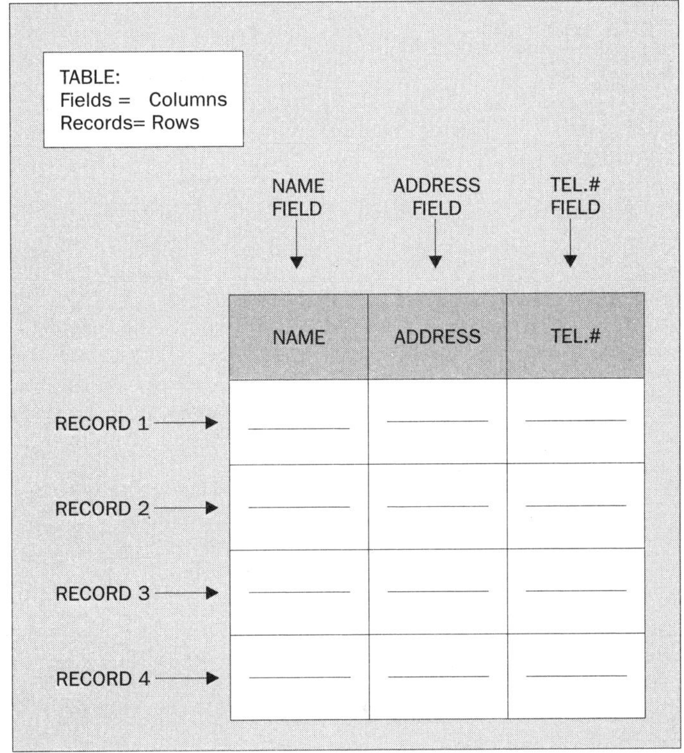

- **Field** – A single attribute of information, represented as a column in a table.
- **Record** – A set of attribute values, represented as a row in a table.
- **Table** – A collection of fields and records of data.

Relational Associations

When designing our relational database, we take care to define our tables so that they only store specific, well-defined data. For example, we would not want our `CustomerAddress` table to store information about the orders that that customer had made. Instead we would have a separate table, `CustomerOrders`, which stores the order information. Of course, if this is the case, then we need a mechanism by which to relate a customer to the orders they have placed, and vice versa.

When we were talking about flat files, we discussed how difficult it would be to try to implement any kind of relationship. However, a relational database we can do this very easily, simply by defining some special **key** fields in our tables:

- A **primary key** – A field or group of fields in a table that can be used to uniquely identify each record in a table
- A **foreign key** – A field in a table that is used to relate a record in that table to a specific record in another table

These concepts are discussed in far greater detail in Chapters 4 and 5 of this book, but for now the following diagram should give you the idea:

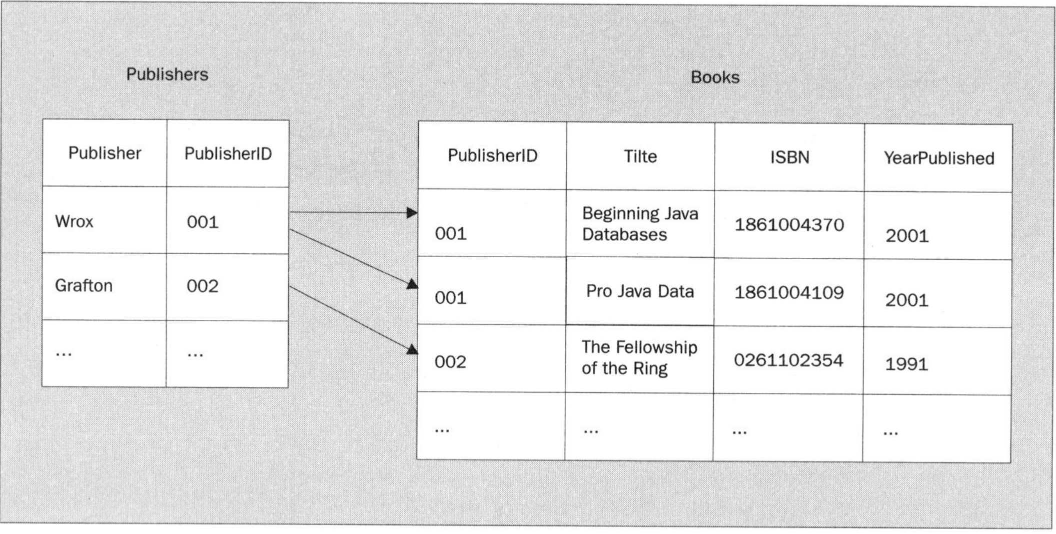

In our `Publishers` table on the left, each publisher is given a unique identifier – a **PublisherID**. The `PublisherID` field is the primary key field in the `Publishers` table. Once we have defined this column as a primary key (you'll see how to do that in Chapter 4) then no two rows will be allowed to have the same value in this column. Once Wrox has been assigned a value of 001 for this field, no other publisher will be allowed to use that value. Now, one publisher can publish many books, so the `Books` table on the right stores information on each title. In the `Books` table the `PublisherId` column is a Foreign Key. The values here 'point' to specific values in the `PublisherID` field in the `Publishers` table. We can immediately see that two books are listed as being published by Wrox and one by Grafton.

By defining our tables and the data they can store carefully, and by creating relationships between tables as necessary, we can store our data efficiently and in a manner that ensures that it will not become corrupted by subsequent modifications. For example, what would happen if someone deleted the Wrox row from the `Publishers` table? We would no longer be able to identify who had published the two books in the `Books` table. In fact, once the PK-FK relationship has been established, the database will not allow you to do this. In order to remove the Wrox row, you would first have to delete all of the dependant rows in the `Books` table.

OK, now you now a little about what a relational database is, where do you get one? There is a vast array of relational database products available to you. There are commercial enterprise-scale databases like Oracle, Microsoft SQL Server, and Sybase SQL Server. There are commercial desktop databases like Microsoft Access. There are also open source databases such as MySQL, PostGreSQL, and Interbase that can very easily handle large applications and are free. Cloudscape is another database resource that is free for developmental use (but you must purchase a Cloudscape Deployment License to deploy it).

These relational database products are referred to as Relational Database Management Systems (RDBMSs), while the database is the set of data that is managed by the RDBMS. Many of these RDBMSs have evolved through several versions and are, therefore, very mature, sophisticated, and feature-rich. They provide a comprehensive system for storing and managing your data in a secure and efficient manner. Over the past ten years they have grown massively in popularity and at least a proportion of the data required by any corporation is likely to reside in a relational database of some form.

There are many reasons for the popularity of the RDBMS, and we will discuss some of these a little later, but perhaps the single most powerful factor in their favor is that, regardless of the database vendor, all relational databases present a standard programming interface: a standard means to retrieve and modify data in that database. In other words there is one language that all relational databases understand, namely Structured Query Language (SQL).

Structured Query Language

SQL is a computer language for communication with databases. The communicating parties are typically a 'front end' which sends a SQL Statement across a connection to a 'backend' that holds the data. That statement contains instructions to create, read, modify, or delete data. Unlike procedural languages such as Java, SQL is a declarative language. This means that instead of specifying *how* to perform a particular task, you simply tell SQL *what* you want to achieve and let the DBMS decide the best way to go about it.

The commercial acceptance of SQL was precipitated by the formation of SQL Standards committees by the American National Standards Institute and the International Standards Organization in 1986 and 1987. Two years later, they published a specification known as SQL-89. An improvement and expansion (to some 600 pages) to the standard gave the world SQL-92. We now have the third generation standard, SQL-99. The existence of standards is important for the general portability of SQL statements. As such, the SQL language is non-proprietary (open) language, meaning it is not owned or controlled by any single company.

The ANSI SQL group has published three standards over the years:

- SQL-89 (SQL-1)
- SQL-92 (SQL-2)
- SQL-99 (SQL-3)

The vast majority of the language has not changed through these updates. We can all profit from the fact that almost all of the code we wrote to SQL standards of 1989 is still perfectly usable.

Most DBMS are designed to meet the SQL-92 standard. Since many of the advanced features of SQL-92 have yet to be implemented by DBMS vendors, there has been little pressure for a new version of the standard. Nevertheless, a SQL-99 standard was developed to address advanced issues in SQL. All of the core functions of SQL, such as adding, reading, and modifying data, are the same. As of early 2001, no vendor has implemented the SQL-99 standard.

As its name suggests, SQL includes syntax for executing queries. We can ask questions of the database and have the results returned. In addition to reading data from a database we can insert new records, delete records, and update existing records. Reading data is the most common task. An ANSI SQL statement requesting a list of names of all members of your society that live in New York, such as the following, can be sent from a Java application to an Oracle database:

```
SELECT * FROM Members WHERE City = 'New York';
```

This will select all society members from the `Members` table of the database whose city of residence (as listed in the `City` column) is New York. If the database is later changed to IBM's DB2, the SQL statement is still valid. The SQL language offers many permutations of the request, including the ability to return the names in various orders, only the first or last few names, a list of names without duplicates, and various other requests where people require specific information from their database.

Records can be created in a database using SQL. A form page on a web site can gather information from a visitor and then put that data into a SQL statement. The SQL statement will instruct the database to insert a new record. Since SQL is universally accepted, the same SQL statement could, for example, be used for clerks who create new records from, say, a Java application on their local network.

Data can also be changed using SQL. As in the examples above, a front-end user interface such as a web page can accept changes to data and send them via a SQL statement to the database. But there does not have to be direct user interaction. A DB2 database running on an IBM mainframe could have a procedure to connect to another corporate mainframe running Sybase. The IBM can generate and send a SQL statement to modify the data in certain records in the Sybase database. Although the systems are from different vendors and have different ways of storing and using data, they both understand the SQL statement.

Although SQL is a standard, every DBMS vendor wants to differentiate their DBMS product. So if you look at the feature set of each DBMS product you see that not only does the product support ANSI-SQL but it also offers extra features, enhancements or extensions, that are available only from individual vendors. For example, most vendors offer a field type that auto-increments even though this is not described in the SQL standards. These additions to ANSI-SQL are generally proprietary and will not work if you try to use them on competitor's SQL products.

There are three areas where there is current development in SQL standards. The first entails improving Internet access to data, particularly to meet the needs of the emerging XML standards. The second is integration with Java, either through JDBC or through internal implementation. Last, the groups that establish SQL standards are considering how to integrate object-based programming models. As a Java developer dealing with databases all these three areas offer interesting possibilities for the future.

How Java Interacts with Databases

While there might exist a standard language for querying a relational database, these databases are anything but standard. Every relational database vendor provides its own API and a set of development tools for building applications with its database. These development tools provide an easy path to quickly building simple and fast database applications, but they are proprietary. Applications written with them often end with business rules and logic that cannot easily be moved to another database platform. What is needed here is a development language that can fulfill two basic development needs:

- Build database applications irrespective of the hardware platform the database is running on. Developers need to be able to write database applications that can be run on any hardware platform. (Intel, Sun, AS/400, etc.)
- Give the developer the ability to build applications that will run on a variety of database platforms. A developer should be able to write their application once and run it against another database with very little reworking.

These two requirements are easily filled by the Java programming language. Java is platform-independent and provides a common database Application Programming Interface called JDBC. JDBC allows the developer to write applications using a common API that is database-independent. The software developer writes to the API and not the underlying database.

JDBC

In the previous SQL section, we talked about how SQL was a standard database language, which meant that we could send the same SQL statement from a Java application to virtually any relational database and it would still be valid. This, of course raises the obvious question of how exactly we send and execute SQL statements from our Java program. A large proportion of this book is given over to the most common mechanism for connecting Java and databases: the JDBC API.

Java is designed to be platform-independent. A pure Java program written for a Windows machine will run without recompilation on a Solaris Sparc, an Apple Macintosh, or any platform with the appropriate Java virtual machine. JDBC extends this to databases. If you write a Java program with JDBC, given the appropriate database driver, that program will run against any database without having to recompile the Java code. Without JDBC, your Java code would need to run platform-specific native database code, thus violating the Java motto of Write Once, Run Anywhere.

JDBC allows you to write Java code, and leave the platform (database) specific code to the driver.

The reason that your Java JDBC code is portable between databases is because the database-specific code is contained in a Java class known as the **driver**. In the event you change databases, you simply change the driver used by your Java code and you are immediately ready to run against the new database. The JDBC API was designed to work with as wide a range of relational databases as possible.

The JDBC API makes it very easy to write code to access relational databases by providing a whole range of Java classes and interfaces that encapsulate specific functionality. We can use:

- A `DriverManager` class to load a driver
- A `Connection` object (by which we mean an instance of a class that implements the `Connection` interface) to establish a connection to the database
- A `Statement` object to encapsulate our SQL statements and send them to the database for execution
- A `ResultSet` object in which to retrieve the results of our queries

And so on. We will discover the full details of the JDBC API in section II of this book.

There are various other methods by which we can access a database using Java, which are either out-of-scope for this book or are covered in the final section of this book *(Java and Databases in the Enterprise).* We briefly discuss a few of these here.

SQLJ

SQLJ is a facility whereby you can embed static SQL statements directly in Java code. A SQLJ program is a Java program that contains static embedded SQL code. This is in contrast to the JDBC API where we execute dynamic SQL queries.

Let's consider what we mean by this for a moment. In JDBC our SQL statements are stored in character strings that are built by the program at run time and sent to the database for processing. The following SQL statement is a perfect example of dynamic SQL:

```
SELECT * FROM Authors
```

This is known as a dynamic SQL statement because the database server must dynamically process the text of the statement at execution time. With SQLJ we embed the SQL directly in the Java program and that SQL is known at compile time (hence the term, static).

SQLJ can greatly simplify our code. Instead of using the JDBC API to open connections, create statements, call methods to execute SQL, and parse through a resultset, you can write just a few lines of embedded SQL and achieve the same result. However, SQLJ lacks the flexibility and power of JDBC – which is still by far the most common mean of accessing a database through Java.

The goal of SQLJ is to allow a tighter integration between Java and databases. You can find more about SQLJ at http://www.sqlj.org. Many of the bigger database vendors have some support for SQLJ, but they have yet to come up with a set of standards so you will encounter various implementations.

> *SQLJ is not covered in this book. For further details, see* Professional Java Data, *Wrox Press, 1-861004-10-9.*

EJB

Enterprise JavaBeans, or **EJBs**, provide another way to access data from a database in enterprise applications. EJBs are an important component of the Java2 Enterprise Edition framework.

The EJB specification supports special type of Javabeans that are housed in a **container** in an Application Server. The two main types of bean are **session** beans and **entity** beans. Session beans interact with the user by handling the user's request and either sending back what the user asked for or forwarding the request on to another bean for action.

Entity beans are used to interact with the database. There are two implementations of entity beans, **Container-Managed Persistence (CMP)** and **Bean-Managed Persistence (BMP)**. With CMP, the container in which the EJB is deployed is responsible for ensuring that the data is persisted to the database. In the case of BMP, the EJB developer is responsible for ensuring that the data within the bean is persisted to the database. Entity beans allow you to directly access the data in the database without having to worry about some of the details of JDBC and SQL programming. We cover this topic in Chapter 19 of this book.

JDO

Java Data Objects (JDO) is a forthcoming addition to the Java API that is currently being developed at Sun. You can browse the available information on JDO by visiting Sun's web site at http://java.sun.com/products/jdbc/related.html where you should also find the current status. You can also visit the JDO home page at http://access1.sun.com.jdo.

JDO is being designed as an API that is complementary to JDBC. The goal of JDO is to add a layer of transparency to remove the Java programmer from any database-specific implementation details. The Java programmer interacts with the database using Java, not SQL. The advantage of JDBC is that it provides more direct control over the underlying database. While this added level over JDBC will allow the Java programmer to concentrate more on Java development and less on the intricacies of programming in SQL, its added level of indirection will result in a performance hit that will have to be assessed once the JDO API is available for testing.

JDO will not have any affect on the way that EJB developers access databases. EJB developers access database information through the use of a connection pool and do not directly access JDBC, which is handled with entity beans. JDO can be thought of as a way to access the database through JDBC that is different from the way that EJBs access a database.

Features of an RDBMS

A database management system (DBMS) as mentioned above is a suite of programs that allow the construction of databases and applications that use them. Let's recap and expand on the specific responsibilities of a DBMS:

- **Creation of the database** itself, usually in one or more files stored on the hard disk of a computer system. Some systems will manage one large file and create one or more databases inside it. Users need not worry about the low-level structure of these files as the DBMS provides all of the access developers and users need.
- **Provide query and update facilities**. A DBMS will have a method of asking for data that matches certain criteria, such as all orders made by a particular customer that have not yet been delivered. Before the widespread introduction of the SQL standard the way that queries like this were performed varied from system to system.
- **Keep an audit trail**. A DBMS will keep a log of all the changes to the data for a period of time. This can be used to investigate access violations, but perhaps even more importantly can be used to reconstruct data in the event of a fault in the system, perhaps an unscheduled power down. Typically a data backup and log of transactions since the backup can be used to restore the database in case of disk failure.

- **Managing the security of the database.** A DBMS will provide access controls so that only authorized users can manipulate the data held in the database and the structure of the database itself (the attributes, tables, and indexes). Typically, there will be a hierarchy of users defined for any particular database, from a 'superuser' (the DBA, or database administrator) who can change anything, through to users with permissions to add or delete data, down to users who are only able to read data. The DBMS will have facilities to add and delete users, and specify which features of the database system they are able to use.

On top of these basic services, certain RDBMSs – certainly enterprise-level systems such as Oracle and Microsoft SQL Server – will provide a whole host of services and support. Let's have a look at some of these here.

Transactions

When we define a transaction we group together a series of events that must all complete successfully before their results are made permanent. Either all of the changes performed by the transaction should be carried out successfully or they should all fail and the database returned to the state it was in before the transaction began. The purpose of transactions in the database is to take the database from one consistent state to the next.

The classic example is that of a bank account transfer. Let us say that you have an account at a bank and you transferred money from your savings account to your checking account to cover a check you just wrote for that new laptop. Behind the scenes the ATM application may execute two SQL `UPDATE` statements – the first to remove the requested amount from the savings account and the second to deposit that same amount into your checking account. However what happens if, say, the system crashes after the first SQL statement has executed but before the second? You would be justifiably outraged if the money was taken out of your savings account and not put in your checking account. Transactions in a database allow you to group these two statements together so that either they are both completed or neither of them is completed. If your money is withdrawn from savings, but cannot be deposited in checking then the database should simply return your savings account to its original state.

The manner in which a database supports transactions varies from vendor to vendor and is quite a complex subject – one that we discuss in detail in Chapter 14. Suffice it to say here that transactions are one of the core features of a database and one of those that really set a database apart from a file system. Again, this is complicated functionality that would be extremely difficult to write in a non-database implementation. Why redo all of this work when it is taken care of for you by a database? If we mark a series of operations as belonging to a transaction, the database will record the actions and their effects, and if one (even the last) fails for some reason, the whole series of actions will be undone, or rolled back, returning the database to the state it was in before we started the transaction.

Concurrent Access

If a database is used in several applications, or is accessed concurrently by several users at the same time, the DBMS will make sure that each users request is processed without impacting on the others. Another way of putting this is to say that the DBMS must ensure that concurrently occurring transactions do not interfere with each other.

Again, the way that this is implemented varies tremendously from database to database. Most databases employ, to a greater or lesser degree, **locking** controls. These are a complex topic that we only really scratch the surface of in this book (in Chapter 14) but, by way of a simple example, consider a transaction that is calculating the total value of a store's stock as listed in an `Inventory` table. While this calculation is progressing, a second transaction wishes to register the arrival of new stock by inserting new rows or updating the quantity column for a particular row in the `Inventory` table. Immediately we can see a potential conflict here. Should our first transaction be able to "see" the activity of the second? How do we ensure a consistent result?

One solution would be to place a lock on the `Inventory` table for the duration of the first transaction. This would mean that the second transaction would simply have to wait for the first one to finish. Of course the obvious problem here is that nobody can access the `Inventory` table for the duration of that transaction. The more you lock resources in this manner, the poorer will be the performance of your application and the fewer concurrent users it will support. The more powerful databases can deal with this situation by only locking one row at a time, or even (in the case of Oracle) without having to lock anything at all.

If you have ever done any multithreaded programming, you have dealt with exactly this issue. You may have critical sections of your code that you want only one thread to access and you want that thread to run until it has completed its tasks. You do not want your thread stopped and another thread given the opportunity to possibly change the same data until your thread is done. Any other thread that needs access to that section of code has to wait until it can acquire the lock. In this case, we mark sections of code as critical and use the Java reserved word 'synchronized'. The larger the section of code that you make synchronized, the greater the degradation in performance you will have.

Remember again, that locking is implemented and controlled by the database so that you do not have to worry about it and you do not need code all over your program to support it.

Proprietary Procedural Languages

Enterprise databases, such as Oracle and Microsoft SQL Server, provide procedural extensions to the SQL language so that you can write powerful programs, incorporating procedural logic, in their respective database servers. In Oracle this programming language is called PL/SQL. In SQL Server it is called Transact-SQL.

What this essentially means is that these databases will allow us to implement some of our business logic in the database itself. We can write procedures that perform certain calculations, apply business rules, or perform actions to protect the integrity of our data, and store them on the database server. When you are writing code that performs data-intensive operations, it can be a considerable performance advantage. The fact that the code is stored on the database with the data on which it is operating cuts down on network traffic considerably. The fact that the business logic is written in the native, optimized language of the database means that it will execute very quickly. We will cover **stored procedures** in Chapters 5, 6, and 13.

Choice of RDBMS for this Book

As you progress through this book you will find numerous code examples that you can try out for yourself. With some tweaking you will be able to run most of the examples in the book on any database for which there is a sufficiently featured JDBC driver available. However, the databases that we have chosen to focus on in this book are **Cloudscape** and **Oracle**. There were a number of criteria on which this decision was based, including ease of availability and setup of the RDBMS itself and of sufficiently capable JDBC drivers. We avoided using databases where only the JDBC-ODBC Bridge driver was easily available.

Cloudscape

Cloudscape is a 100% pure Java RDBMS that is available for free from http://www.cloudscape.com/, although you will have to fill in a registration form. It also comes bundled as part of the J2EE SDK 1.2.1, available from http://java.sun.com/j2ee/. It supports the SQL-92 and JDBC standards and is fully featured, with transaction support and row-level locking. The documentation presents performance results for up to 350 users (http://www.cloudscape.com/products/whitepapers.jsp).

Other factors in its favor include:

- **Free developer license** – The use of Cloudscape is free for the purposes of this book. Refer to the Cloudscape license agreement for specific restrictions regarding the use of the database.
- **Relatively small download** – To obtain a database with comparable features, the size of the download would most likely exceed 300MB. The Cloudscape installation file is less than 12MB (for the Java-based installation).
- **Simple installation** – Using the Java-based installer, and following the instructions below, the database can be up and running in a matter of minutes.
- **Full set of GUI-based administration tools** – While learning the basics of the JDBC API, it is important that the database can be administered as easily as possible so as not to get in the way of learning the concepts being presented.

The only points that may count against it are that the currently available drivers do not support some of the latest JDBC 2.0 functionality, such as updateable `ResulSets` and the documentation is not as extensive you will find for better established databases such as Oracle or Microsoft SQL Server.

Since this database really is rather easy to set up, we're gong to run through the installation now. This will mean that, if you are happy to work along with this database, you will be set up to work through the majority of the code examples in this book.

Installing Cloudscape

The Cloudscape RDBMS is available for free from http://www.cloudscape.com/, although you will have to fill in a registration form.

> *Cloudscape also comes bundled as part of the J2EE SDK 1.2.1, available from http://java.sun.com/j2ee/. This package also contains the classes needed to run EJBs, JSPs, and servlets, but does weigh in at around 16 MB.*

For this book, we have used version 3.6.4. Cloudscape comes as a ZIP file, 10.9 MB in size. Once this is downloaded, you can extract it to a suitable directory. If you extract to the root directory (`C:\`), using the Use Folder Names setting in WinZip (or GZIP), you should end up with a directory structure like this:

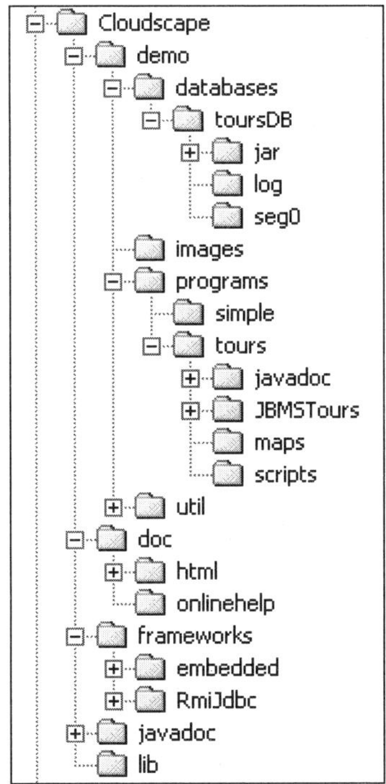

Congratulations, you now have Cloudscape installed on your system. The main files we'll be interested in using are `cloudscape.jar`, and `tools.jar`, both located in the `C:\cloudscape\lib` directory. The `cloudscape.jar` file contains JDBC drivers and the classes that provide database functionality, so we will need this in the classpath when we come to run any programs that connect to the database.

As we saw in the introduction, there are several ways of making sure that the `cloudscape.jar` file is in your classpath. You can add it to your classpath, either using the My Computer | Properties | Advanced | Environment Variables method detailed in the introduction, or by running a command such as the following:

```
set classpath=%CLASSPATH%;C:\cloudscape\lib\cloudscape.jar
```

This will have much the same effect. Alternatively, you can add it to your classpath through the `-classpath` and `-cp` options for `javac` and `java`, respectively. If you're going to do this, it might be a good idea to copy the JAR file to a central directory for archives to be included in your classpath, say, `C:\java\lib`. Then, you can reference this directory with an environment variable, like this:

```
set JLIB=c:\java\lib
```

Then, reference the JAR file as follows:

```
java -cp .;%JLIB%\cloudscape.jar SomeClass
```

Thus, we can include the JDBC drivers contained in the `cloudscape.jar` file when we need them.

Other Useful Things with Cloudscape

Cloudscape comes complete with a wealth of documentation, for which this set of instructions are no replacement. To get you started, however, we will take a quick look at two of the more frequently used tools that come with Cloudscape: Cloudview, and ij.

Using Cloudview

Cloudview is a graphical interface to Cloudscape databases, allowing you to create a database, fill it with tables, and populate the tables with data. Cloudview is a Java program that connects to the database using JDBC (the very drivers we'll use throughout this book), and is a good example of what you can do with JDBC.

To run Cloudview, type the following command:

```
java -cp
    .;%CLASSPATH%;c:\cloudscape\lib\cloudscape.jar;c:\cloudscape\lib\tool.jar
        COM.cloudscape.tools.cview
```

This will launch Cloudview, which will then enable us to rummage around in any Cloudscape database we can find on our system. Cloudview with a database open looks like the following screenshot:

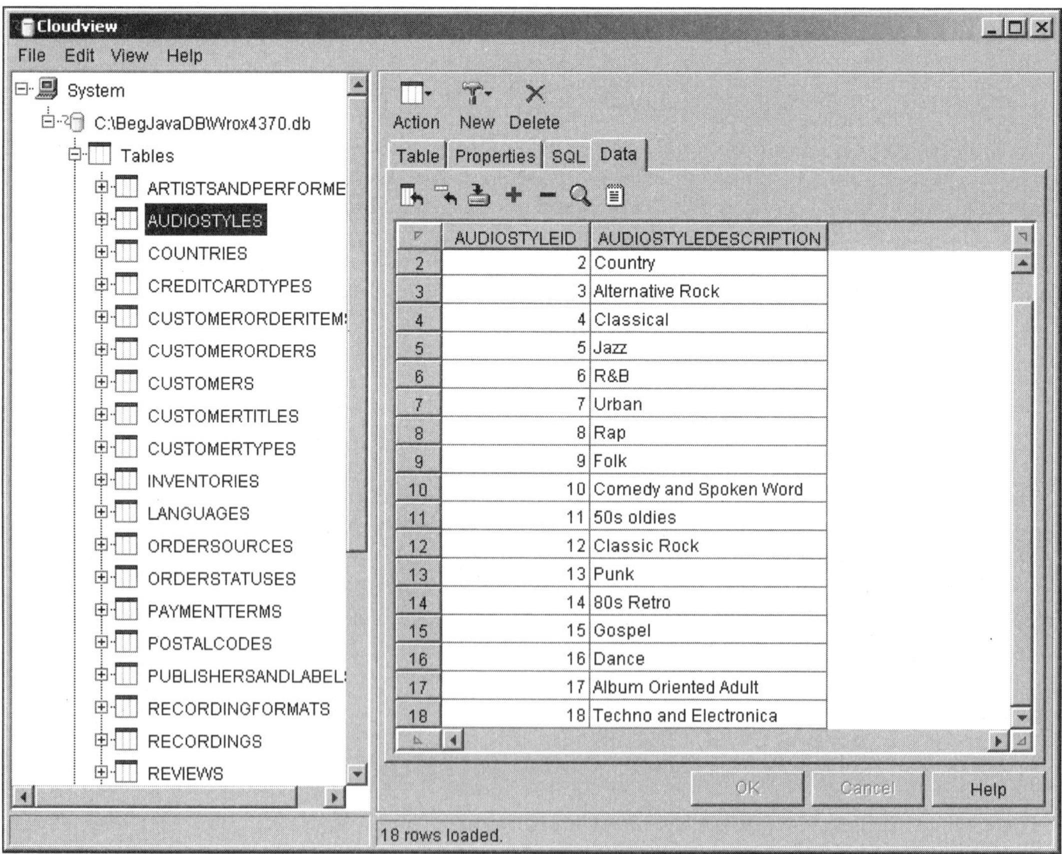

Using ij

`ij` is a command line tool used for issuing SQL statements against a database. To set ourselves up to use this we need to run the `ij` utility. We're going to issue a SQL statement against the `toursDB` database that comes pre-installed with Cloudscape. In order to do this, we need to set the `cloudscape.system.home` variable to point to the directory where this database is stored (using the `-D` command). In our case, we set this variable to point to the `\cloudscape\demo\databases` directory. If no system home is specified, Cloudscape will assume that the current directory is the system home directory. Therefore, you can omit this variable if running the utility from the `\cloudscape\demo\databases` directory. We'll run the following command from the `c:\cloudscape\lib` directory:

```
> java -Dcloudscape.system.home=C:\Cloudscape\demo\databases -classpath
        cloudscape.jar;tools.jar COM.cloudscape.tools.ij
```

Now we have a different command prompt:

```
ij>
```

Connect to the database:

```
ij> connect 'jdbc:cloudscape:toursDB';
```

Execute a SQL statement:

```
ij> select * from people;
```

Upon completion of the previous 5 steps, your screens should look something like this:

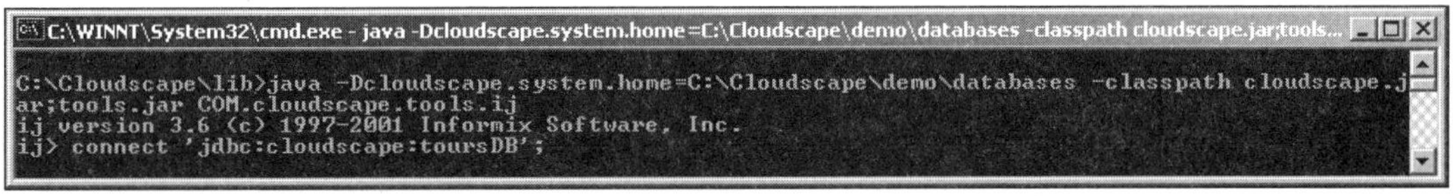

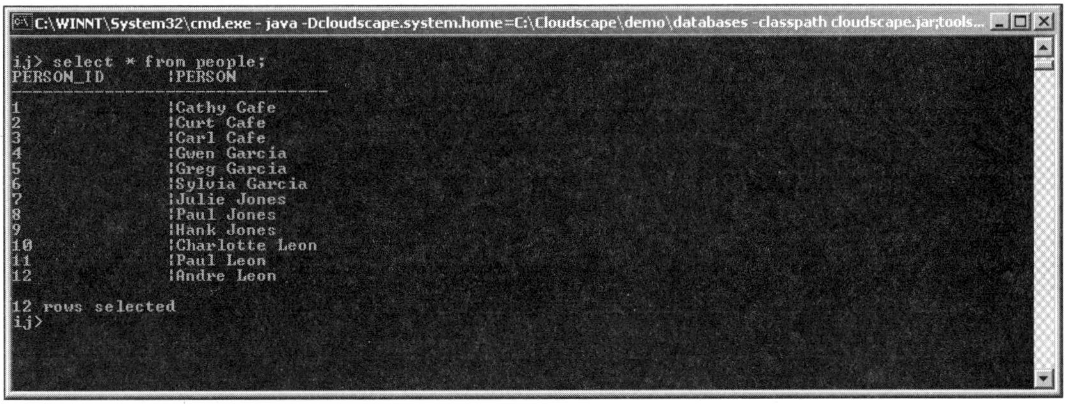

```
C:\WINNT\System32\cmd.exe - java -Dcloudscape.system.home=C:\Cloudscape\demo\databases -classpath cloudscape.jar;tools...

C:\Cloudscape\lib>java -Dcloudscape.system.home=C:\Cloudscape\demo\databases -classpath cloudscape.j
ar;tools.jar COM.cloudscape.tools.ij
ij version 3.6 (c) 1997-2001 Informix Software, Inc.
ij> connect 'jdbc:cloudscape:toursDB';
```

```
C:\WINNT\System32\cmd.exe - java -Dcloudscape.system.home=C:\Cloudscape\demo\databases -classpath cloudscape.jar;tools...

ij> select * from people;
PERSON_ID       |PERSON
--------------------------------
1               |Cathy Cafe
2               |Curt Cafe
3               |Carl Cafe
4               |Gwen Garcia
5               |Greg Garcia
6               |Sylvia Garcia
7               |Julie Jones
8               |Paul Jones
9               |Hank Jones
10              |Charlotte Leon
11              |Paul Leon
12              |Andre Leon

12 rows selected
ij>
```

Exit the ij utility by pressing *Ctrl-C*.

Installing the Sample Database

The problem domain we focus on for the applications in this book, is that of a Music Store owner wishing to maintain an inventory of stock in her various stores, with the ability to search the databases by a variety of criteria, and offer various services to her customers.

> *The Music Store application is described in detail in Chapters 5 and 6.*

Once you have Cloudscape on your system, you're ready to add the sample Music Store database, `Wrox4370.db`. This database is available along with the rest of the code in the book from http://www.wrox.com/. Go to Java at the top of the page, find this book in the list (it will be near to the top), and click on `Download`. This will take you to the code download page for this book.

Once you have the `Wrox4370.db` ZIP file downloaded, you can extract it to your computer. Make sure that the directory structure inside the ZIP file is maintained, but other than that you can put it pretty much anywhere you like on your computer. Many of the examples assume that you've saved the Cloudscape database in the `C:\wrox\database\Wrox4370.db` folder. In this case, the name of the database that you will need to supply as part of the JDBC connection information will be:

```
c:/wrox/database/Wrox4370.db.
```

Notice that we use slashes (/) rather than back-slashes (\). This is because Java reads directory structures using slashes as separators. If you were to save the database to some other directory, say `C:\cloudsape\data\Wrox4370.db`, then the name of the database for JDBC purposes would be:

```
c:/cloudscape/data/Wrox4370.db
```

Alternatively, you can store the database in `C:\Wrox4370.db`, and the name will be:

```
Wrox4370.db
```

That's it; you might want to fire up Cloudview to have a quick look around the database at the sample data.

Oracle

Oracle offers one of the world's most widely deployed DBMS, currently named Oracle 9i. Oracle has established itself as a leader for web sites with very high traffic. The explosion of data access requests from the web has pushed Oracle to further increase speed, capacity and reliability.

You can check out Oracle DBMS products at:

http://www.oracle.com/ip/deploy/database/index.html.

Furthermore, you can try out all Oracle software by downloading it from their Technet site, http://technet.oracle.com. You will need to register for this service, but it is free. The software is available for download under a strict development-only license. If you need to use the database for any commercial purpose then you must buy a full license. There are four distributions of the oracle database, ranging from the Oracle Lite version, designed for mobile computing, through a desktop version (Personal Oracle) up to the full-featured enterprise edition for large-scale high-end data processing.

We have used Oracle in this book when the Cloudscape JDBC drivers do not support particular JDBC 2.0 functionality and as a more appropriate choice for demonstrating Java technology that is totally geared towards enterprise-level applications, such as Enterprise JavaBeans (Chapters 19 and 22).

We demonstrate how to install Personal Oracle on your computer, and set up the Music Store database in Appendix A.

Microsoft SQL Server

The flagship database management system from Microsoft is SQL Server (versions 7 and 2000). The product is optimized to run on Windows NT (or Windows 2000) and has done well in speed tests against competing products.

For product information on Microsoft SQL Server 7 or 2000, visit http://www.microsoft.com/sql/productinfo/prodover.htm.

IBM

IBM offers the DB2 family of products, which run on the hardware and operating systems of both IBM and non-IBM machines, including a developer's kit for their products on Linux platforms. The *DB2 Universal Version 7* includes features that move more operations to memory and thus improve performance.

Go to http://www-4.ibm.com/software/data/db2/ for information on IBM's DB2.

Open Source Databases

There are several open source databases available for you to try out. The databases are generally distributed under a GNU General Public License, which means that the software is free and can be used, modified, and shared without restriction (always check the exact terms of the license) and will also come with the source code.

The most widely used open source database currently is **MySQL**. It has gained a reputation for being reliable and very fast. It can handle very large data sets and is very stable. By some it is considered only suitable for mainly read-only applications, as it does not support transactions. The latest version of MySQL at the time of release of this book is 3.23. Also, a new database was being developed that does have transaction support (MySQL-Max 3.23). You can check out this database at www.mysql.com and there is a very useful FAQ site at:

http://www.bitbybit.dk/mysqlfaq/faq.html#ch4_1_0

Another open source database that is considered a more enterprise-level database and is currently gaining in popularity is PostgreSQL. You can check this database out at http://www.postgresql.org/.

Desktop Databases

You do not need to buy and maintain a Data Server in order to have a backend. Several desktop applications can support SQL requests and will run in memory space on your laptop.

Probably the best-known desktop database is Microsoft Access, which is easy to learn, with a nice graphical drag and drop interface that translates to SQL. However, it was not designed to scale to more then a few users at once. The only JDBC driver that is readily available for the Access database is the JDBC-ODBC Bridge.

> **The Music Store database is also supplied as an mdb file for the Access database. See Appendix A for setup instructions.**

Microsoft also offers the MSDE (Microsoft Data Engine) which is essentially the Microsoft SQL Server data engine without the rest of the DBMS features (such as Query Analyzer), and without the ability to scale beyond a few users. You can use MSDE to manage your data and to run SQL statements against that data but you do not have the tools for performance monitoring, replication, security, and other features found in SQL Server. MSDE is, at the time of this writing, a free download from www.microsoft.com. It also ships with editions of Microsoft Office 2000, which include Access (Microsoft Office 2000 Premium or Developer Editions).

Oracle offers a Personal Edition that can be installed on a desktop – see Appendix A for full details on this.

The RDBMS that you choose to use, outside the context of this book, will of course depend very much on the type of application you wish to build, how many users it needs to support, the range of functionality you expect from the server, and so on.

There is no quick and easy way to make the decision about which RDBMS to choose. You must simply evaluate the needs of your application against the capabilities of the available and viable databases on offer and make some basic judgments and tradeoffs based around such considerations as:

- Feature set required: do you need transaction support? Stored Procedures?
- How many users are you hoping to support?
- Cost
- Complexity to administer
- How much information is available? Do you require IT support?

An enterprise database, such as Oracle, is fully-featured and very powerful, but does come at a price, both in terms of cost and complexity to administer. A desktop database such as Access will be cheap and very easy to use but is only really suitable for applications that need to support only a few users. A third option may be to "go open source" and choose a database such as MySQL or PostgreSQL. This option will be cheap (free, in fact!) but may have drawbacks in terms of feature set and IT support. A database such as Cloudscape is well featured and may also provide a viable alternative.

Summary

Java is a portable and very powerful object-oriented programming language. Relational database management systems allow you to store all of the data required by your Java applications in an efficient and well-defined manner. In addition, they provide means to write business logic and store it directly on the database server, can enforce the transactional integrity, and provide in-built mechanisms for the support of multiple users. All of these things are provided for 'free' by the database, thus removing the need to deal with them in you Java code.

The goal of this book is to show you how to use these two powerful technologies together to write effective database-driven applications. In this chapter we have taken the first small step along this road. We have given a preview of the relational databases and introduced the main technologies that we will use in our Java programs throughout this book: namely SQL and JDBC.

Furthermore, we have actually installed an RDBMS (Cloudscape) and set up the sample database that will be used as a base for all of the programs we build in this book. You are now ready to move on and see JDBC in action for the first time.

Basic JDBC Techniques

The basic goal of this chapter is to present a high-level overview of the JDBC API, and how it can be used to connect Java programs to relational databases.

In this chapter, the basic goal is to get you to the stage where you can connect to your database using JDBC, get some information out from a table in the database, and include basic error handling in your code. As you progress further on in the book, the JDBC API will be described in far greater detail, but here we will discuss:

- The different versions of JDBC and what major functionality was introduced with each version
- How to load a `Driver` class and register it with `DriverManager`
- How to make a connection with cloudscape and Oracle databases using the `getConnection()` method
- Passing a query to the database using the `Statement` object
- Getting the data back from the database using a `Resultset` object
- How to get meta data from the database using `getMetaData()` method
- How to put all it together in a simple program to get data from selected columns in a database table and also how to get the all the data from the table
- Basic error handling techniques in your JDBC code

JDBC Concepts and Terminology

To make sure we have a common understanding of the jargon, we will first take a look at database terminology. Firstly, in general, **data access** is the process of retrieving or manipulating data that is taken from a remote or local **data source**. Data sources don't have to be relational – they can come in a variety of different forms. Some common examples of data sources that you might access are:

- ❑ A remote relational database on a server, for example, Oracle
- ❑ A local relational database on your computer, for example, Personal Oracle or Cloudscape
- ❑ A text file on your computer
- ❑ A spreadsheet
- ❑ A remote mainframe/midrange host providing data access
- ❑ An online information service (Dow Jones, etc.)

JDBC is, by definition, an interface to **relational** data sources. While it is conceivable that non-relational sources may be accessible through JDBC, we will be concentrating on relational databases in this book. If you haven't met relational databases before, you should still be able to follow the discussion. The structure of relational databases is logical and fairly easy to learn, and we provide a comprehensive tutorial on it in Chapter 5.

The Java Database Connectivity (JDBC) library provides the means for executing SQL statements to access and operate on a relational database. JDBC was designed as an object-oriented, Java-based application programming interface (API) for database access, and is intended to be a standard to which Java developers and database vendors could adhere.

JDBC is based on other standard program-database interfaces – largely the X/Open SQL CLI (Call-Level Interface) specification, but knowledge of these standards isn't necessary to use JDBC. However, if you've programmed database access before, you should be able to draw on that experience when using JDBC.

The library is implemented in the `java.sql` package. It is a set of classes and interfaces that provide a uniform API for access to a broad range of databases.

SQL and JDBC

The computer industry is burdened with many languages and standards, most of which are unintelligible to each other. Here and there, true standards have emerged, and in these cases, it is well worth the time of any programmer to learn them. **Structured Query Language**, or **SQL** as we commonly call it (which is pronounced as Ess-Que-Ell or as *sequel*, depending on who you talk to) has over the last ten years, emerged as the standard language for programmers to talk with databases through a Database Management System (DBMS). Oracle, Microsoft SQL Server, Cloudscape, MySQL, IBM's DB2, Sybase, and virtually every other DBMS sold in the last five years use SQL. This is the core strength of SQL: its universal acceptance by database vendors. There has been a lot of talk and marketing about 'write once, run anywhere' languages like Java. For database programmers, understanding SQL is the ticket to 'learn once, profit anywhere'.

SQL has many capabilities, but the most common needs in business are to:

- ❑ Read existing data
- ❑ Create new records holding data
- ❑ Change existing data
- ❑ Delete data

Knowledge of SQL is becoming necessary for almost every IT professional. And as the development of basic web sites becomes common among non-programmers, a grasp of SQL will help them to integrate data into their HTML pages. Its emergence was a major step forward in the drive to separate code from data.

However, before our Java programs can make use of SQL to retrieve the data they need from a DBMS, it is obviously necessary to make a connection between the program and the database and to establish an interface through which the two can interact. This is where JDBC comes in.

The JDBC library was designed as an interface for executing SQL statements, and not as a high-level abstraction layer for data access. So, although it wasn't designed to automatically map Java classes to rows in a database, it allows large scale applications to be written to the JDBC interface without worrying too much about which database will be deployed with the application. A JDBC application is well insulated from the particular characteristics of the database system being used, and therefore doesn't have to be re-engineered for specific databases. From the user's point of view, the Java application looks something like this:

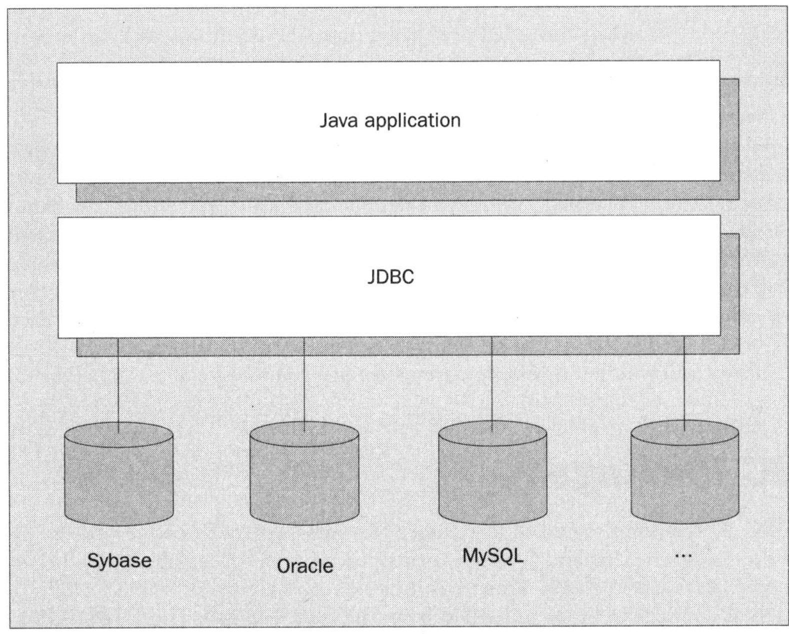

JDBC manages this by having an implementation of the JDBC interface for each specific database – a **driver**. This handles the mapping of Java method calls in the JDBC classes to the database API. We'll learn more about this later on.

JDBC is a Java API (Application Programming Interface) that documents a standard framework for dealing with tabular and, generally, relational data. It consists of a set of classes and interfaces written in the Java Programming language that provides a standard API for tool/database developers to access relational databases.

The JDBC API was designed as an interface for executing SQL statements and supports all dialects of SQL.

Relating JDBC to ODBC

One of the fundamental principles of JDBC's design was to make it practical to build JDBC drivers based on other database APIs. There is a very close mapping between the JDBC architecture and API, and their ODBC counterparts, fundamentally because they are all based on the same standard, the SQL X/Open CLI; but JDBC is a lot easier to use. Because of their common ancestry, they share some important conceptual components:

Driver Manager	Loads database drivers, and manages the connections between the application and the driver.
Driver	Translates API calls into operations for a specific data source.
Connection	A session between an application and a database.
Statement	A SQL statement to perform a query or update operation.
Metadata	Information about returned data, the database, and the driver.
Result Set	Logical set of columns and rows of data returned by executing a statement.

The basic point is that JDBC was built on ODBC but, in addition, provides all of the benefits of a pure Java API, as discussed in Chapter 1, portability being a key issue. JDBC maintains Java's goal of being a 'write once, run anywhere' platform. When you write a database application, you want the code itself to be portable if you were to move it to another platform. Additionally, you want to be able to replace the original persistent data store that you used with another and not require any sourcecode changes. This loose coupling is of great value to a developer. A system engineer, network engineer, or database administrator can change the persistent store that your driver points to and everything will ideally work. The extent to which the data store can be changed is dependent on the type of JDBC driver that your application is using and whether or not you are using any vendor-specific extensions that are not standard.

The JDBC Package

The core JDBC API, containing all of the classes and interfaces we need for accessing data stores, is provided in the `java.sql` package, which forms part of Java's class library in the same manner as `java.io`, `java.util`, and so on. Thus, it is included in the current release of the JDK, Standard Edition, which of course can be downloaded from the Sun web site. The JDBC API specifies interfaces to be implemented by database providers that allow Java developers to access those data sources through JDBC without having to know any specific details of a particular vendor's database

At the time publishing, the current release of the API was JDBC 2.0, although JDBC 3.0 was in final draft form and some of the important advances are covered in this book.

Bear in mind that only the JDBC technology-enabled driver bundled with the JDK 1.1.x or Java 2 Platform releases is the JDBC-ODBC Bridge, and there are numerous reasons why use of this driver should be avoided, unless there is no alternative (see Chapter 7). So, in addition to installing the JDK, you will also need to install a driver it before you can connect to a database.

JDBC Versions

Let's take a quick look at the evolution of JDBC through the version releases.

JDBC 1.x

The initial Java Database Connectivity (JDBC) specification was intended to provide simplified access for Java developers to execute SQL statements to access and operate on a relational database.

Originally distributed as an 'add in', JDBC 1.x was soon integrated into the standard JDK. It provided the basic framework for data access, consisting primarily of the core interfaces listed in the previous section (`DriverManager`, `Connection`, `Statement`, `ResultSet`, and so on).

JDBC 2.0

With this, the current release, the API now comes in two parts:

- The JDBC 2.0 Core API, implemented in the `java.sql` package, which is included in the Java 2 SDK, Standard Edition
- The JDBC 2.0 Optional Package API, implemented in the `javax.sql` package, which is available separately from http://java.sun.com/products/jdbc/download.htm, or as part of the Java 2 SDK, Enterprise Edition

The JDBC 2.0 Core API

The core API was changed little from the JDBC1.0 release. A few classes were added, but the major changes came in the form of enhancements to existing interfaces and classes and better performance. Using JDBC 2.0, you can access practically any data source possible. Your data can be stored in a fully relational database, a spreadsheet, or even a flat file.

The new features in JDBC 2.0 can, essentially, be divided into two categories: New functionality and new support for advanced data types. The new functionality features that were introduced include:

- **Scrollable result sets** – result sets have always allowed you to move forward through the records. Now with the introduction of scrollable result sets, you can move backwards through the result set as well to either an exact location or to a location relative to the current cursor position. This is covered in Chapter 9.
- **Updateable result sets** – prior to JDBC 2.0 updates were performed using SQL statements. Now, the `ResultSet` object has a series of methods of the form `updateXXXX()`, where the `XXXX` corresponds to the different data types. We cover updateable result sets in Chapter 9.
- **Batch updates** – these allow you to mark a series of updates to the database as a group that will be sent to the database and executed as a single group instead of sending each update one at a time. This can have considerable performance benefits in terms of reduced network traffic. We cover these in Chapter 14.
- **Performance tuning** additions allow you to fine tune details about retrieving rows.

The support for new advanced data types extends to cover those in the SQL99 specification. We can now store, retrieve, and modify new SQL data types that are essentially objects (for example `BLOB`, `CLOB`, `ARRAY`). More details about exactly what these data types are can be found at the JDBC web site at http://java.sun.com/j2se/1.3/docs/guide/jdbc/spec2/jdbc2.1.frame.html

The JDBC 2.0 Optional Package API

This extension API adds functionality that is particularly required for enterprise applications.

The functionality added by this package includes:

- **DataSources** – The `DataSource` interface attempts to provide a more flexible architecture for creating and using database connections. It hides the connection details so that you, as the client programmer, never need to worry about the connection URL, host, port, etc. This feature is covered in Chapter 18.
- **JNDI** – the Java Naming and Directory Interface is an API that provides an interface to naming and directory services. A naming service acts like a repository on the network that can be accessed to look up information. This allows you to remove any dependencies in your application on a particular JDBC driver or JDBC URL.
- **Connection Pooling** – Each time a resource connects with a database, it creates a physical database connection. In JDBC this translates to creating a specific `Connection` object. A database connection incurs overhead – it requires resources to create the connection, maintain it, and then release it when it is no longer required. By using a connection pool for reserving and returning pooled connection objects, this overhead of separately creating and destroying can be largely avoided. Since one of the most expensive operations using JDBC will be establishing your database connection, this can offer significant performance benefits.
- **Rowsets** – With a `Rowset` object we can pass data across a network. We have a whole chapter devoted to this important new functionality, Chapter 11.
- **Distributed Transactions** – in addition to handling transactions involving a single connection to a single database, we can now handle transactions that span multiple data sources or multiple connections. This advanced topic is covered briefly in Chapter 14.

JDBC 3.0

At the time of this writing, the JDBC 3.0 specification was in final draft form. The JDBC API is 3.0 is due to ship as part of J2SE (Java 2 Standard Edition) 1.4 which is planned for release in the fourth quarter of 2001. In this release, both the core API, found in the `java.sql.*` package, and the optional API, found in the `javax.sql.*` package will be included in the Standard Edition release.

There are some very significant enhancements to JDBC 3.0. Here are some of the changes that are proposed. There is the new notion of a 'savepoint', which can be used to mark parts of a transaction so that the transaction can be rolled back to a given point (see Chapter 14). There are additional configuration parameters that control how connection pools can reuse prepared statements. There are more configuration parameters that control how connection pools are managed. You can even query prepared statements for their meta data and learn all about the properties that need to be passed in and their types.

It also focuses more closely on SQL99 support, which has been finalized since the completion of the JDBC 2.x specification. In addition, the 3.0 specification provides a migration path for database vendors to migrate their JDBC products towards the Java Connectors architecture, which in turn simplifies data access to relational and non-relational enterprise information systems. The JDBC home page (http://java.sun.com/products/jdbc/index.html) is a great place to get the latest information on the 3.0 specification.

How JDBC Works

The previous section, *Relating JDBC to ODBC*, hinted at the basic components of the JDBC API that would allow you to connect to a database and retrieve and manipulate data in your programs. It is now time to look at them in more detail.

The JDBC architecture is based on a collection of Java interfaces and classes that together enable you to connect to data sources, to create and execute SQL statements, and to retrieve and modify data in a database. These operations are illustrated in the figure below:

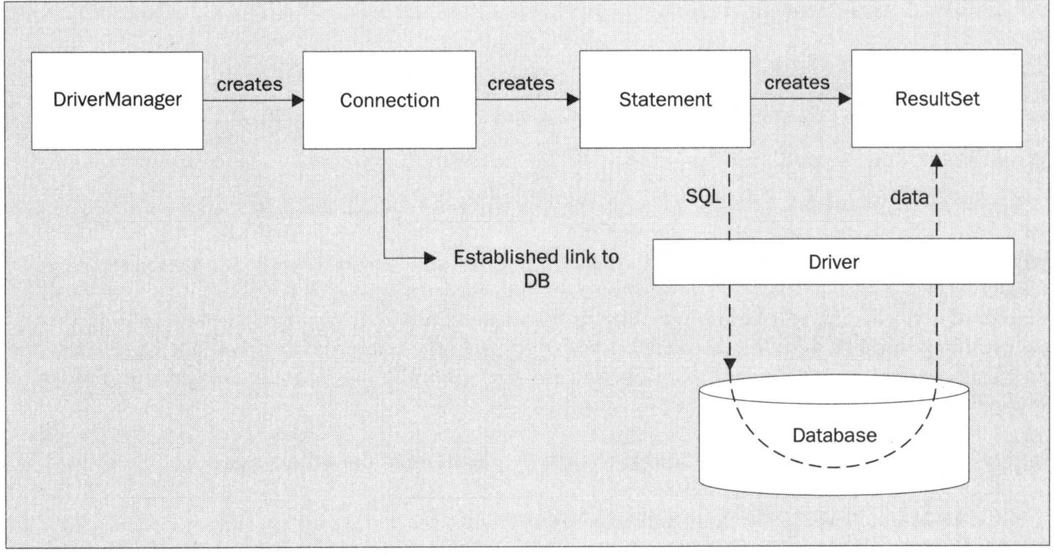

Each of the boxes in the illustration represents a JDBC class or interface that has a fundamental role in accessing a relational database. All your work with JDBC will begin with the `DriverManager` class, which is responsible for establishing connections to the data sources, accessed through the JDBC drivers.

Basic information regarding the four different types of driver that are available can be found in Chapter 7.

JDBC database drivers are defined by classes that implement the `Driver` interface. A JDBC driver understands how to convert SQL requests for a particular database. Without an appropriate driver, we cannot connect to the database in the first place, and JDBC is one of the few areas of the Java programming language that depends vendor-specific products – each RDBMS has a specific set of drivers that can be used to communicate with that database. So one of the first things your program must do is to load the appropriate driver that will allow your Java classes to communicate with your particular database.

Delving a little deeper into the previous diagram, we can describe a basic JDBC program as involving the following steps:

- Import the necessary classes
- Load the JDBC driver
- Identify the data source
- Allocate a `Connection` object
- Allocate a `Statement` object
- Execute a query using the `Statement` object
- Retrieve data from the returned `ResultSet` object
- Close the `ResultSet` object
- Close the `Statement` object
- Close the `Connection` object

We will now work towards implementing a simple program that illustrates these essential elements.

Setting up

One final piece of business before we jump in: you can simply read through the examples in this chapter, but you'll be a lot further ahead if you work with the examples as you read. It will enhance your comprehension significantly to build and run the examples, and noodle around with them a bit with your own experimentation.

In order to work through the code in this chapter, you will need the following:

- JDK 1.2, or later, development environment
- Access to a database with appropriate driver
- The source code files from the Wrox web site (unless you need the typing practice)
- The sample `music store` schema on your database, which is part of the sourcecode download

We've used the Cloudscape database throughout most of this chapter, which comes bundled with the J2EE development kit published by Sun, and can also be downloaded from www.cloudscape.com. However, with a bit of tweaking, these examples will work with any JDBC-compliant data source.

Even with the JDBC API and the database installed, you may still need to set up the appropriate JDBC driver for your database. All of the examples in this chapter use the Cloudscape driver – `COM.cloudscape.core.JDBCDriver` – to access the database.

If you're working with a database other than Cloudscape you will need to obtain an appropriate JDBC driver for it, if you do not already have one. An up-to-date list of suitable drivers for various databases can be found at http://www.javasoft.com/products/jdbc/jdbc.drivers.html. This topic is discussed in much more detail in Chapter 7.

You'll also need to set up the example music store database, which stores information about the music store's customers, their orders, and information on the recordings sold by the store, the artists, genres, albums, and reviews (see Chapter 5, for full details). We have provided several means for you to set up and use this database:

- A `Wrox4370.db` file for the Cloudscape database
- A set of SQL scripts to load and populate the database on Oracle
- A script to create a `Music.mdf` file for SQL Server 2000
- A `Music.mdb` file for the Access database

Details of how to get the music store tables created and populated in each of these environments are given in Appendix A.

It is quite common for database systems not to support all of the SQL capabilities defined by the ANSI standard. If you have no luck getting the sample database up and running first time around, try reading on in this chapter and then re-reading your driver and database documentation before having another go.

Loading a Driver

The first logical step that your program must take in order to connect to a relational database, via JDBC, is to load the appropriate JDBC driver and obtain a connection to the database. In order to do this, we use the JDBC `java.sql.DriverManager` class. The `DriverManager` class implements the `java.sql.Driver` interface.

> *The `Driver` interface is only really used directly by people who need to write their own custom drivers. The `DriverManager` class will deal with the `Driver` methods for us, behind the scenes.*

There are two ways in which to load a `Driver` class and register it with the `DriverManager`:

- Using the `Class.forName()` method
- Identifying the `Driver` class in the `jdbc.drivers` system property

We will focus on the first method here (details of the second method can be found in Chapter 7).

Basically, we can load the driver explicitly by calling the static `forName()` method in the `Class` class, and passing a `String` object, containing the driver class name, as an argument. For example:

```
Class.forName("COM.cloudscape.core.JDBCDriver ");  // Load the Cloudscape driver
```

The `forName()` method can throw an exception of type `ClassNotFoundException` if the driver class cannot be found, and this must be caught. Therefore, a call to the function has to appear in a `try` block with an appropriate `catch` block.

Each `Driver` class will typically create an instance of itself when it is loaded, and register that instance automatically by calling the `RegisterDriver` method of the `DriverManager` class. Some programmers prefer to force the issue by explicitly calling the `newInstance()` method on the class object:

```
Class.forName("COM.cloudscape.core.JDBCDriver ").newInstance();
```

However, you should be aware that this will often create a second, superfluous object.

You don't need to create `DriverManager` objects (in fact you can't because the constructor is declared `private`), and all the methods in the `DriverManager` class are `static` so they operate on the whole class, not on specific instances.

There are `DriverManager` class methods that can be used to determine which drivers have been loaded, as well as methods that register or unregister drivers 'on the fly'. However, for the most part, you will only need to use one method of the `DriverManager` class, and that is `getConnection()`.

Establishing a Connection

Once we have loaded and registered a driver, we need to explicitly establish a connection to our database, in order to access the required data. An object of a class that implements the `Connection` interface – in other words, a `Connection` object, represents a connection to a specific data source. The `Connection` object essentially establishes a context in which you can create and execute SQL commands.

When you need a connection to a JDBC driver, you don't create a new object encapsulating the connection yourself – you ask the `DriverManager` to do it for you. The `DriverManager` class provides several `static` methods for creating objects that implement the `Connection` interface, which we will get to in a moment, and that encapsulate a connection to a database. These are all overloaded versions of the `getConnection()` method.

There are actually three overloaded forms of the `getConnection()` method in the `DriverManager` class that return a `Connection` object (see Chapter 8), but we will just consider the simplest case here, whereby we can obtain a `Connection` object that represents a session for our database with the following statement:

```
Connection databaseConnection = DriverManager.getConnection(sourceURL);
```

The argument, `sourceURL`, is a `String` object defining the URL that identifies where the database is located. Note that this is a `String` object specifying the URL, not an object of the `java.net.URL` class.

URLs and JDBC

A URL (Uniform Resource Locator) describes an electronic resource, such as a World Wide Web page, or a file on an FTP server, in a manner that uniquely identifies that resource. URLs play a central role in networked application development in Java. JDBC uses URLs to identify the locations of both drivers and data sources. JDBC URLs have the format:

```
jdbc:<subprotocol>:<data source identifier>
```

The scheme `jdbc` indicates that the URL refers to a JDBC data source. The `<sub-protocol>:` identifies which JDBC driver to use. For example, the JDBC-ODBC Bridge (included with the J2SE, used to access ODBC data sources) uses the driver identifier `odbc`. The Cloudscape driver uses the identifier `cloudscape`.

The JDBC driver dictates the format of `<data source identifier>`. In our example, the Cloudscape driver simply uses the Cloudscape database name. In order to use the driver with the music store database, you would create a URL with the format:

```
jdbc:cloudscape:Wrox4370.db
```

`Wrox4370.db`, as you may have guessed, is simply the name of that database. It's important to note that each database type (Cloudscape, Oracle, and so on.) will use a different URL form. The reason for that is that each database needs different information to identify exactly what database we're after. In the case of a database server, the database server name would be included in the URL so the driver would know which machine to talk to in order to create a connection. In the first case, we're using Cloudscape as an embedded server, so the database name is in fact a directory name that the Cloudscape classes will look for immediately in the directory where our code is executing.

The URL may also include – depending on the data source – information about the user and password. In our case, it's not required. You will see, however, when you look at the code, there are also JDBC API calls to specify username and password so you can identify the user programmatically.

Let's exercise the `getConnection()` method in a working example.

Try It Out – Making a Connection

We will write a minimal JDBC program that creates a `Connection` object. In this instance, the connection will be established using only the URL for the data source. This is the code for Cloudscape.

Create the following `MakingTheConnection` class:

```
import java.sql.*;

public class MakingTheConnection {
  public static void main(String[] args) {

    // Load the driver
    try {

      // Load the driver class
      Class.forName("COM.cloudscape.core.JDBCDriver");

      // Define the data source for the driver
      String sourceURL = "jdbc:cloudscape:Wrox4370.db";

      // Create a connection through the DriverManager
      Connection databaseConnection =
        DriverManager.getConnection(sourceURL);

      // We made it!
      System.out.println("Connection established successfully!");

      // close connection
      databaseConnection.close();
    }
      catch (ClassNotFoundException cnfe) {
      System.err.println(cnfe);
    }
      catch (SQLException sqle) {
      System.err.println(sqle);
    }
  }
}
```

Save this in a directory where you've created or downloaded the `wrox4370.db` database (which contains the `Music store` tables). Save the file as `MakingTheConnection.java` and then compile the class:

```
> javac MakingTheConnection.java
```

Run the class (making sure to set the classpath to include the directory); you should get a message saying:

```
Connection established successfully!
```

How It Works

Naturally we need to import the classes and interfaces for the JDBC library. These classes are defined in the `java.sql` package:

```
import java.sql.*;
```

The `forName()` method call at the beginning of the method `main()` causes the Java interpreter's class loader to load the class for the driver specified by the argument, in this case the `COM.cloudscape.core.JDBCDriver` driver. As we said earlier, the `forName()` method will throw a `ClassNotFoundException` if the driver class cannot be found, and this exception must be caught:

```
  public static void main(String[] args) {

    // Load the driver
    try {

      // Load the driver class
      Class.forName("COM.cloudscape.core.JDBCDriver");
```

When the `Driver` class is loaded, the class loader will determine if the `Driver` class has any `static` initialization code, implemented in the class's static method, which must be completed before our code actually uses the driver. If it does, it will execute the `static` initialization code immediately after the class has been loaded. That is how the `Driver` class is able to instantiate itself, and register the instance that is created with the `DriverManager` object. It can also execute other initialization code that may be required, such as loading a dynamic link library if the driver uses native methods for instance, and since this all happens when the class is loaded, it is guaranteed to happen before any other driver methods get called.

We then identify our data source in the `sourceURL String` and pass it as an argument to the `getConnection()` method:

```
      // Define the data source for the driver
      String sourceURL = "jdbc:cloudscape:Wrox4370.db";

      // Create a connection through the DriverManager
      Connection databaseConnection =
        DriverManager.getConnection(sourceURL);
```

If we successfully connect, we print a message then close the connection:

```
      // We made it!
      System.out.println("Connection established successfully!");

      // close connection
      databaseConnection.close();
    }
```

Most JDBC methods handle errors by throwing an exception of the type `SQLException`, and the `getConnection()` method of the `DriverManager` class does exactly that, so we also have a `catch` block that handles the `SQLException` exception. In this example, a simple message will be displayed in the event of a problem loading the JDBC driver or creating a `Connection` to the data source.

```
      catch (ClassNotFoundException cnfe) {
      System.err.println(cnfe);
    }
      catch (SQLException sqle) {
      System.err.println(sqle);
    }
  }
}
```

Connecting to Other Databases

With a little bit of tweaking, the above code, and indeed all of the code in this chapter, will run against databases other than Cloudscape.

Let's consider what modifications are required if you are using an Oracle database (chapters in this book dealing with more advanced features database access from Java, or exploiting functionality that, say, the cloudscape JDBC drivers do not support, will generally use Oracle).

Appendix A gives details of how to create a new user (called `beg`) and install the Music Store tables in that user's account. Assuming that you have followed these instructions, the following code demonstrates the changes required in your code in order to connect to the Oracle database.

Try It Out – Connecting to Oracle

Before trying out the code, you will need to make sure that you have Oracle's JDBC drivers in your classpath. The code to make a connection to Oracle is very similar to the code above:

```
import java.sql.*;

public class MakingTheConnection {
  public static void main(String[] args) {

    // Load the driver
    try {

      // Load the driver class
      Class.forName("oracle.jdbc.driver.OracleDriver");

      // Define the data source for the driver
      String sourceURL = "jdbc:oracle:thin:@server:1521:databasename";
      String user = "beg";
      String password = "java";

      // Create a connection through the DriverManager
      Connection databaseConnection =
        DriverManager.getConnection(sourceURL, user, password);
```

```
            // We made it!
            System.out.println("Connection established successfully!");

            // close connection
            databaseConnection.close();
         }
            catch (ClassNotFoundException cnfe) {
            System.err.println(cnfe);
         }
            catch (SQLException sqle) {
            System.err.println(sqle);
         }
      }
   }
```

This is compiled and run in the same manner as for the earlier example.

How It Works

In the `Class.forName()` method, we now load the class for the Oracle driver:

```
Class.forName("oracle.jdbc.driver.OracleDriver");
```

We identify the data source as a `sourceURL String`:

```
String sourceURL = "jdbc:oracle:thin:@server:1521:databasename";
```

The `sourceURL` is slightly different from the one used for Cloudscape. Here we are using Oracle's `thin` JDBC driver, which is a type 4 driver (details on the different types of drivers are given in Chapter 7). The next difference is the `@` notation. The information provided after "@" tells the driver how to find the database. Oracle databases typically reside on a remote server and not on your own machine (unless you are using Personal Oracle) so the driver needs be told the name (or IP address) of the server on which to look for music store. If the database *is* on your own machine, replace `server` with `localhost`. The port on which the Oracle JDBC drivers listen is `1521`, (these change with different drivers and databases, for instance in if you use MySQL this would be `3306`). The `databasename` is used to identify the particular database we want to connect to as our data source.

In Oracle's terminology, a database is simply a collection of files, including the files that actually store the data. In order to get the database up and running it must be mounted and opened by an instance – a set of Oracle process and memory structures. Suffice it to say that for all our intents and purposes they are the same thing and any reference to a database in this book will mean an instance in Oracle.

To access any table you need a user and password that will allow you to do so. Here we define these, we our user is `beg` whom we created earlier:

```
String user = "beg";
String password = "java";
```

Next, we pass all these arguments to the `getConnection()` method:

```
DriverManager.getConnection(sourceURL, user, password);
```

The rest of the code is the same as above; we print a statement, close the connection and then handle the errors.

If you are running against an Access or SQL Server database, you can connect to the Music Store database through the JDBC-ODBC bridge driver (assuming you have set up the appropriate database driver – see Chapter 7), then the code to load the driver and identify the data source would simply be as follows:

```
// Load the driver class
Class.forName("sun.jdbc.odbc.JdbcOdbcDriver");

// This defines the data source for the driver
String sourceURL = "jdbc:odbc:music";

// Create connection through the DriverManager
Connection databaseConnection = DriverManager.getConnection(sourceURL);
```

Let's now move on to briefly discuss the JDBC `Statement` and `ResultSet` objects that allow us to send SQL statements to the database and retrieve the results.

Statements and ResultSets

The `Statement` interface provides methods for executing SQL statements and retrieving the results. Since `Statement` is an interface, you cannot create a `Statement` object directly. That is, you can't instantiate a `Statement` in the normal way you would when dealing with a class:

```
Statement statement = new Statement(); //won't compile
```

If you try the above, you'll get the compilation error message: "`interface java.sql.Statement is an interface. It can't be instantiated.`" Objects of classes that implement the `Statement` interface (referred to as `Statement` objects in the rest of the chapter) are obtained by calling the `createStatement()` method of a valid `Connection` object:

```
Statement statement = connection.createStatement();
```

When a `Statement` object is created, it provides a workspace for you to create a SQL query, execute it, and retrieve any results that are returned.

You can also assemble multiple SQL statements into a batch, and submit them for processing as a batch to the database, as we shall see in Chapter 14.

Once you have created a `Statement` object, you can use it to execute a SQL query by calling on&of the execute methods of your `Statement` object:

- `executeQuery()` – for SQL statements that retrieve data from the database in a single `ResultSet` object.
- `executeUpdate()` – to execute queries that do not return a `ResultSet`. For example, SQL DML statements (`INSERT`, `UPDATE`, and `DELETE`) as well as SQL DDL (Data Definition Language) statements like `CREATE TABLE`, `DROP TABLE`, and `ALTER TABLE`. The return value of `executeUpdate()` is an integer (referred to as the update count) that indicates the number of rows that were affected. For statements such as `CREATE TABLE` or `DROP TABLE`, which do not operate on rows, the return value of `executeUpdate()` is always zero.
- `execute()` – to execute statements that return more than one result set, more than one update count, or a combination of the two.

In our example, we wish to retrieve data rows from the database, so we will use the `executeQuery()` method. We pass as the argument to this method, a `String` object containing the text of our SQL query.

The resultset from the query is returned as an object of type `ResultSet`. For instance, if we have a `Statement` object, `statement`, we could write:

```
ResultSet results = statement.executeQuery(
                                   "SELECT lastname, firstname FROM authors");
```

This will execute the `SELECT` statement that appears in the argument and will retrieve the names of all the authors from a table called `authors` into a `ResultSet` object called `results`.

> **There are actually two further interfaces that inherit from the `java.sql.Statement` interface. These 'sub-interfaces' are the `java.sql.PreparedStatement` and `java.sql.CallableStatement`, discussed in Chapter 12 and Chapter 13, respectively. They provide methods to deal with parameters and to execute dynamic SQL. With these three interfaces, we have a means to execute almost any legal SQL statement.**

Now let's discuss the `ResultSet` object in a little more detail. The results of executing an SQL query are returned in the form of an object that implements the `ResultSet` interface, and that contains the table produced by the SQL query. The `ResultSet` object contains something called a **cursor** that you can manipulate to refer to any particular row in the resultset. This initially points to a position immediately preceding the first row. Calling the `next()` method for the `ResultSet` object will move the cursor to the next position. A cursor remains valid until the `ResultSet` object or its parent `Statement` object is closed.

The `ResultSet` object called `results`, from the previous code snippet, will have a cursor that moves **forward only** (and also cannot be updated). This is the default type of `ResultSet` object returned by `executeQuery()`.

This is the only cursor movement possible with drivers that implement the JDBC 1.0 API. With JDBC 2.0-compatible driver we can create scrollable cursors and make use of other navigational methods.

Usually you will want to process rows from a result set in a loop, and you have a couple of ways to do this. Both the `next()` and `previous()` methods return `true` if the move is to a valid row, and `false` if you fall off the end, so you can use this to control a `while` loop. You could process all the rows in a resultset with the following loop:

```
while(resultset.next()){
   // Process the row...
}
```

This assumes `resultset` is the object returned as a result of executing a query and the `resultset` object starts out in its default state with the cursor set to one before the first row. You can also use the `isLast()` or `isFirst()` methods to test whether you have reached the end or the beginning of the resultset.

Now we know how to get at the rows in a resultset, let's look into how we access the fields in a row.

Accessing Data in a Resultset

Using the `ResultSet` reference, you can retrieve the value of any column for the current row (as specified by the cursor) by name or by position. You can also determine information about the columns such as the number of columns returned, or the data types of columns. The `ResultSet` interface declares the following basic methods for retrieving column data for the current row as Java types:

`getAsciiStream()`	`getTimestamp()`	`getTime()`
`getBoolean()`	`getBinaryStream()`	`getString()`
`getDate()`	`getBytes()`	`getByte()`
`getInt()`	`getFloat()`	`getDouble()`
`getShort()`	`getObject()`	`getLong()`

Note that this is not a comprehensive list, but it is not likely you will need to know about the others. For a full list of the methods available take a look at the documentation for the `ResultSet` interface. There are overloaded versions of each of the methods shown above that provide two ways of identifying the column containing the data. The column can be selected by passing the SQL column name as a `String` argument, or by passing an index value for the column of type `int`, where the first column has the index value 1. Note that column names are not case sensitive so `ArtistName` is the same as `artistname`.

The `getDate()`, `getTime()`, and `getTimestamp()` methods return objects of type `Date`, `Time`, and `TimeStamp` respectively. The `getAsciiStream()` method returns an object of type `InputStream` that you can use to read the data as a stream of ASCII characters. This is primarily for use with values of the SQL type `LONGVARCHAR`, which can be very long strings that you would want to read piecemeal. Most of the basic data access methods are very flexible in converting from SQL data types to Java data types. For instance if you use `getInt()` on a field of type `CHAR`, the method will attempt to parse the characters assuming they specify an integer. Equally, you can read numeric SQL types using the `getString()` method.

With all these methods, an absence of a value – a SQL `NULL` – is returned as the equivalent of zero, or `null` if an object reference is returned. Thus a `NULL` boolean field will return `false` and a `NULL` numeric field will return 0. If a database access error occurs when executing a `getXXX()` method for a ResultSet, an exception of type `SQLException` will be thrown.

Together, the `Connection`, `Statement` and `ResultSet` classes and interfaces make up the bulk of the JDBC components that you will be working with. Let's now put them into action with a simple code example.

Try It Out – Using a Connection

We'll do something useful with the `Connection` object created by changing our `MakingTheConnection` class into a new class for accessing the music store database. You can alter the code from the earlier example to that shown overleaf:

```
import java.sql.*;

public class MakingAStatement {
  public static void main(String[] args) {

    // Load the driver
    try {

      // Load the driver class
      Class.forName("COM.cloudscape.core.JDBCDriver");

      // This defines the data source for the driver
      String sourceURL =
        new String("jdbc:cloudscape:C:/wrox/database/Wrox4370.db");

      // Create connection through the DriverManager
      Connection databaseConnection =
        DriverManager.getConnection(sourceURL);

      Statement statement = databaseConnection.createStatement();

      ResultSet artistNames =
        statement.executeQuery("SELECT artistid, artistname " +
                               "FROM artistsandperformers");

      // Output the resultset data
      while (artistNames.next()) {
        System.out.println(artistNames.getInt("artistid") + " "
                           + artistNames.getString("artistname"));
      }

      // close connection
      databaseConnection.close();

    } catch (ClassNotFoundException cnfe) {
      System.err.println(cnfe);
    } catch (SQLException sqle) {
      System.err.println(sqle);
    }
  }
}
```

You can save this as `MakingAStatement.java`. Compile the class and then execute it as follow:

```
> java -classpath .;%JLIB%\cloudscape.jar MakingAStatement
```

This program will list all the artist IDs and names, with the ID followed by the name on each line:

```
100 10,000 Maniacs
101 Aerosmith
102 Alanis Morissette
103 Babyface
104 Billy Joel
105 Toni Braxton
106 Garth Brooks
107 Peter Gabriel
108 Everything But The Girl
109 Candy Skins
110 Various Artists
```

```
111 Eric Clapton
112 Bryan Ferry
113 Aaron Neville
114 Taj Mahal
115 Jewel
116 Marvin Gaye
117 The Iguanas
118 Dorthy Moore
119 J.J. Cale
120 Thomas Newman
121 Tori Amos
```

How It Works

Once the connection has been established by the `getConnection()` method call, the next step is to create a `Statement` object that enables you to execute a SQL statement and retrieve the results. To create a `Statement` object we simply call the `createStatement()` method for the `Connection` object.

Once we have created the `statement` object, we execute a SQL query against the connected database by passing a `String` object as the argument to the `executeQuery()` method for the `statement` object. The `executeQuery()` method returns an object that implements the `ResultSet` interface. As the name implies, the `ResultSet` interface enables you to get at information that was retrieved by the query. You can think of the `ResultSet` interface as providing row-at-a-time access to a virtual table of results. The `ResultSet` object provides an internal **cursor** or logical pointer to keep track of its current row. When the `ResultSet` is first returned, the cursor is positioned just before the first row of data.

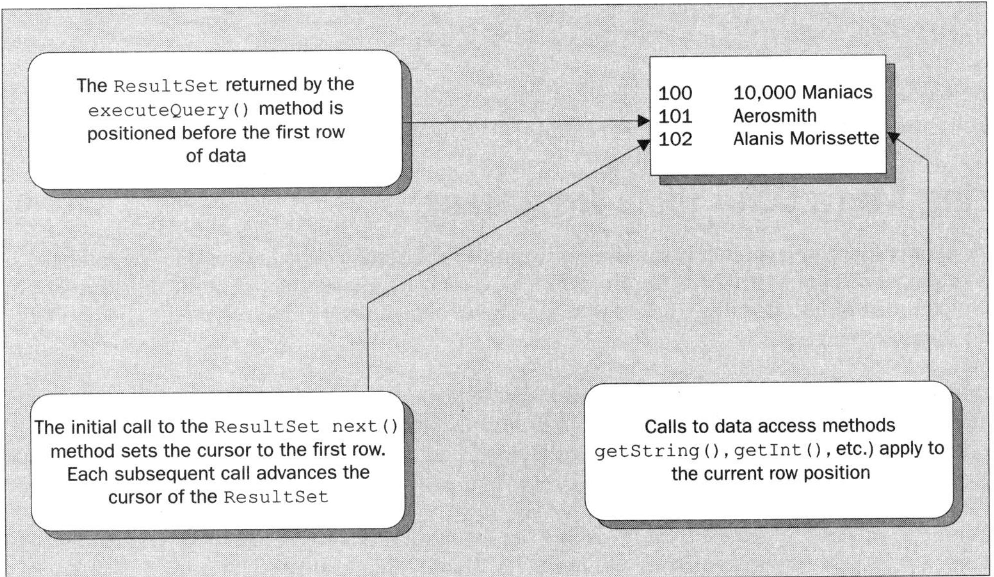

After executing the query and before any column data can be accessed, the row position needs to be advanced by calling the `next()` method, and we do this in the `while` loop condition. The `next()` method advances the row position and returns a `boolean` value that indicates if the `ResultSet` is positioned at a valid row (`true`), or that there are no more rows (`false`). Thus our `while` loop continues until we have output the data from all the rows that are in the resultset, `artistNames`.

Within the `while` loop, we access the data in the columns using the `getString()` method for the `ResultSet` object. In both cases we use the column names to reference the column. Accessing the columns by name has the advantage that you don't need to know the order of the columns. On the other hand you do need to know the column names. If you wanted to process the columns by their index position, you would just use the index values 1 and 2 to refer to data in the first and second columns respectively. Using the column position is slightly faster than using the column name since there is no additional overhead in matching a column name to determine a particular column position. It can also be more convenient to refer to columns using their position when you want to identify the column by means of an expression.

Note that in spite of the illustration above, the rows in the resultset are not ordered. If you want to output the rows in `artistname` order, you need to change the SQL statement to sort the rows, as follows:

```
ResultSet artistNames = statement.executeQuery(
   "SELECT artistid, artistname FROM artistsandperformers ORDER BY artistname");
```

The rows in the resultset will be sorted in `artistname` order, by default this is in an ascending sequence. To sort in descending sequence you should add the keyword `DESC` to the end of the SQL statement. You can sort on multiple columns by separating the column names by commas. The sorting applies to the columns successively from left to right, so if you specify the sort columns as `artistname, artistid` in the `SELECT` statement then the rows in the resultset will be ordered by `artistname`, and where two names are the same, by the artist's identifier. For instance, if we want the rows in the resultset `artistNames` to be sorted in descending sequence, we could write:

```
ResultSet authorNames = statement.executeQuery(
          "SELECT artistid, artistname FROM artistsandperformers ORDER BY
artistname DESC, artistid DESC");
```

Note that we must supply the `DESC` keyword for each column name that we want it to apply to. If you omit it for a column the default ascending sequence will apply.

Getting Meta Data for a Resultset

Meta data is a jargon term that is sometimes intimidating. Meta data is data about the database and the data that is stored in the database. Table definitions, view definitions, constraints, index definitions, permissions, stored procedures, and so on are all meta data and are often referred to by another jargon term: **database schema**.

With the JDBC API, Java database programmers can access and manipulate database meta data as well as the data stored in a database. The JDBC API also provides access to meta data, for both the `Connection` object and for the `ResultSet` object. One common and useful application is a query that reads the column definitions for a table.

The `getMetaData()` method for a `ResultSet` object returns a reference to an object of type `ResultSetMetaData` that encapsulates the meta data for the resultset. The `ResultSetMetaData` interface declares methods that enable you to get items of meta data for the resultset.

The `getColumnCount()` method returns the number of columns in the resultset as a value of type `int`. For each column, you can get the column name and column type by calling the `getColumnName()` and `getColumnType()` methods respectively. In both cases you specify the column by its index value. The column name is returned as a `String` object and the column type is returned as an `int` value that identifies the SQL type. The `Types` class in the `java.sql` package defines public fields of type `int` that identify the SQL types, and the names of these class data members are the same as the SQL types they represent – such as `CHAR`, `VARCHAR`, `DOUBLE`, `INT`, `TIME`, and so on. Thus you could list the names of the columns in a resultset that were of type `CHAR` with the following code:

```
ResultSetMetaData metadata = results.getMetaData();
int columns = metadata.getColumnCount();               // Get number of columns

for(int i = 1 ; i<= columns ; i++)                           // For each column
  if(metadata.getColumnType(i) == Types.CHAR)                // if it is CHAR
     System.out.println(metadata.getColumnName(i));          // display the name
```

You could output the data value of each row of a `ResultSet` object, `results`, that were of SQL type `CHAR` with the following code:

```
ResultSetMetaData metadata = results.getMetaData();
int columns = metadata.getColumnCount();                // Get number of columns

int row = 0;                                            // Row number
while(results.next()){                                  // For each row

  System.out.print("\nRow "+(++row)+":");               // increment row count
  for(int i = 1 ; i<= columns ; i++)                    // For each column
    if(metadata.getColumnType(i) == Types.CHAR)         // if it is CHAR display it
      System.out.print(" "+results.getString(i));
}
```

You can also get the type name for a column as a `String` by calling the `getColumnTypeName()` method with the column number as the argument. Another very useful method is `getColumnDisplaySize()`, which returns the normal maximum number of characters required to display the data stored in the column. You pass the index number of the column that you are interested in as the argument. The return value is type `int`. You can use this to help format the output of column data. We'll work with meta data a bit more later in the chapter.

The Essential JDBC Program

We now have all the pieces to make up the essential JDBC program, which will initialize the environment, create `Connection` and `Statement` objects, and retrieve data by both position and column name.

Try It Out – Putting It All Together

This example will use another table in the music store application. This table, called `recordings`, stores information on recordings including the `recordingid`, the `recordingtitle`, and the `catalognumber`. Our application will execute two queries, one that selects specific columns by name, and another that selects all columns. First we will define the application class in outline, with the data members and the `main()` function and the other methods in the class:

```
import java.sql.*;

public class EssentialJDBC {

  public static void main(String[] args) {
    EssentialJDBC SQLExample =
      new EssentialJDBC();   // Create application object

    SQLExample.getResultsByColumnName();
    SQLExample.getResultsByColumnPosition();
    SQLExample.getAllColumns();
    SQLExample.closeConnection();
  }

  public EssentialJDBC() {
    try {
      Class.forName("COM.cloudscape.core.JDBCDriver");
      connection = DriverManager.getConnection(sourceURL);
      statement = connection.createStatement();
    } catch (SQLException sqle) {
      System.err.println("Error creating connection");
    } catch (ClassNotFoundException cnfe) {
      System.err.println(cnfe.toString());
    }
  }

  void getResultsByColumnName() {

    // Execute wildcard query and output selected columns...
    try {
      ResultSet recordingResults = statement.executeQuery(queryWildcard);
      int row = 0;

      while (recordingResults.next()) {
        System.out.println("Row " + (++row) + ") "
                         + recordingResults.getString("recordingid")
                         + " "
                         + recordingResults.getString("recordingtitle")
                         + " , "
                         + recordingResults.getString("catalognumber"));
      }

      recordingResults.close();
    } catch (SQLException sqle) {
      System.err.println("\nSQLException-------------------\n");
      System.err.println("SQLState: " + sqle.getSQLState());
      System.err.println("Message : " + sqle.getMessage());
    }

  }

  void getResultsByColumnPosition() {

    // Execute ID and name query and output results...
    try {
      ResultSet recordingResults = statement.executeQuery(queryIDAndName);

      int row = 0;
      while (recordingResults.next()) {
        System.out.print("\nRow " + (++row) + ") ");
        for (int i = 1; i <= 3; i++) {
```

```
          System.out.print((i > 1 ? ", " : " ")
                          + recordingResults.getString(i));
        }
      }
      recordingResults.close();   // Close the result set
    } catch (SQLException ex) {
      System.err.println("\nSQLException-------------------\n");
      System.err.println("SQLState: " + ex.getSQLState());
      System.err.println("Message : " + ex.getMessage());
    }

  }

  void getAllColumns() {

    // Execute wildcard query and output all columns...
    try {
      ResultSet recordingResults = statement.executeQuery(queryWildcard);

      ResultSetMetaData metadata = recordingResults.getMetaData();
      int columns = metadata.getColumnCount();   // Column count
      int row = 0;
      while (recordingResults.next()) {
        System.out.print("\nRow " + (++row) + ") ");
        for (int i = 1; i <= columns; i++) {
          System.out.print((i > 1 ? ", " : " ")
                          + recordingResults.getString(i));
        }
      }

      recordingResults.close();                     // Close the result set
    } catch (SQLException ex) {
      System.err.println("\nSQLException-------------------\n");
      System.err.println("SQLState: " + ex.getSQLState());
      System.err.println("Message : " + ex.getMessage());
    }

  }

  // Close the connection
  void closeConnection() {
    if (connection != null) {
      try {
        connection.close();
        connection = null;
      } catch (SQLException ex) {
        System.out.println("\nSQLException-------------------\n");
        System.out.println("SQLState: " + ex.getSQLState());
        System.out.println("Message : " + ex.getMessage());
      }
    }
  }

  Connection connection;
  Statement statement;
  String sourceURL = "jdbc:cloudscape:Wrox4370.db";
  String queryIDAndName =
    "SELECT recordingid, recordingtitle, catalognumber FROM recordings";
  String queryWildcard = "SELECT * FROM recordings";   // Select all columns
}
```

Save and compile the class and then execute it as follows:

```
>java -classpath .;%JLIB%/cloudscape.jar EssentialJDBC
```

You should see the following output:

```
Row 1) 1000 Space I'm In , 2064-24370-2
Row 2) 1001 Phenomenon Soundtrack , 9362-46360-2
Row 3) 1002 Little Earthquakes , 7567-82358-2
Row 4) 1003 Crucify , 82399-2
Row 5) 1004 Big Time , GAIL3 12
Row 6) 1005 US , GAHN2 07

Row 1)  1000, Space I'm In, 2064-24370-2
Row 2)  1001, Phenomenon Soundtrack, 9362-46360-2
Row 3)  1002, Little Earthquakes, 7567-82358-2
Row 4)  1003, Crucify, 82399-2
Row 5)  1004, Big Time, GAIL3 12
Row 6)  1005, US, GAHN2 07

Row 1)  1000, Space I'm In, 112, 2064-24370-2, 1, 1991-05-23, 1, 14.99, null
Row 2)  1001, Phenomenon Soundtrack, 108, 9362-46360-2, 1, 1996-08-23, 1, 15.99,
null
Row 3)  1002, Little Earthquakes, 103, 7567-82358-2, 1, 1991-10-02, 1, 14.99, null
Row 4)  1003, Crucify, 103, 82399-2, 1, 1992-03-21, 1, 9.99, null
Row 5)  1004, Big Time, 107, GAIL3 12, 1, 1987-06-21, 1, 9.99, null
Row 6)  1005, US, 107, GAHN2 07, 1, 1992-09-29, 1, 18.97, null
```

How It Works

The `EssentialJDBC` class provides a `main()` method to declare and allocate an `EssentialJDBC` object by calling the class constructor. It then calls the `getResultsByColumnName()`, the `getResultsByColumnPosition()`, and the `getAllColumns()` methods of the new object. Finally we call a `closeConnection()` method here that closes the connection when we are done:

```
public static void main(String[] args) {
  EssentialJDBC SQLExample =
    new EssentialJDBC();    // Create application object

  SQLExample.getResultsByColumnName();
  SQLExample.getResultsByColumnPosition();
  SQLExample.getAllColumns();
  SQLExample.closeConnection();
}
```

Next, we can fill in the details of the constructor for the class. The constructor initializes member variables, and loads the `Cloudscape driver` class. The data source is identified by a URL in the form, `jdbc:driver_name:datasource`. The driver defines the data source identifier format. In the case of the Cloudscape driver, the source is the database name. It then creates a `Connection` object by calling the static `getConnection()` method of the `DriverManager` class. It then uses the `Connection` object to create a `Statement` object that will be used for executing queries.

```
public EssentialJDBC(){
  try{
    Class.forName("COM.cloudscape.core.JDBCDriver");
    connection = DriverManager.getConnection(sourceURL);
```

```
      statement = connection.createStatement();
    }
    catch(SQLException sqle){
      System.err.println("Error creating connection");
    }
    catch(ClassNotFoundException cnfe){
      System.err.println(cnfe.toString());
    }
  }
```

The bulk of the work is done in the three getXXX() methods. All three use the same Statement object to execute a SQL query. The difference between the three methods is how they retrieve the returned data.

The getResultsByColumnName() method executes the wildcard form of a SQL SELECT statement where the column names are specified by an (*) and the column ordering of the returned results is determined by the database engine. This query is executed by calling the executeQuery() method of the Statement object and this method returns the data in a ResultSet object. Since the column ordering is unknown ahead of time, we retrieve data by explicitly specifying the column names. A while loop with a call to next() as the condition will iterate through all the rows starting at the first.

The column data is retrieved as strings and written to the standard output stream. Finally, the ResultSet is closed. Note that the garbage collection of Java will handle this automatically anyway, but calling close() explicitly ensures that the resources used by the ResultSet object will be cleaned up sooner:

```
  void getResultsByColumnName(){
  // Execute wildcard query and output selected columns...
    try{
      ResultSet recordingResults = statement.executeQuery(queryWildcard);
      int row = 0;

      while(recordingResults.next())
      System.out.println("Row " + (++row) + ") "+
                 recordingResults.getString("recordingid")+ " " +
                 recordingResults.getString("recordingtitle")+ " , "+
                 recordingResults.getString("catalognumber"));

      recordingResults.close();
    }
    catch (SQLException sqle){
      System.err.println ("\nSQLException------------------\n");
      System.err.println ("SQLState: " + sqle.getSQLState());
      System.err.println ("Message : " + sqle.getMessage());
    }
  }
```

The SQLException handling code here doesn't provide very elegant error handling for this program, but we are obliged to catch this exception.

The getResultsByColumnPosition() method executes a SELECT that explicitly specifies the columns required by name so the column ordering in the result set is the same as the sequence of column names in the SELECT statement. We can therefore use the column position index values to retrieve the data from the ResultSet. Like the previous method, the column data is retrieved as strings and printed to the console for each row returned. Finally, the ResultSet object is closed as before.

```
void getResultsByColumnPosition(){
// Execute ID and name query and output results...
  try{
    ResultSet recordingResults = statement.executeQuery(queryIDAndName);

    int row = 0;
    while (recordingResults.next()){
      System.out.print("\nRow " + (++row) + ") ");
      for(int i = 1 ; i<=3 ; i++)
        System.out.print((i>1?", ":" ")+recordingResults.getString(i));
    }
    recordingResults.close();                    // Close the result set
     }
  catch (SQLException ex){
    System.err.println("\nSQLException-------------------\n");
    System.err.println("SQLState: " + ex.getSQLState());
    System.err.println("Message : " + ex.getMessage());
  }
}
```

The `getAllColumns()` method uses the wildcard form of `SELECT` statement to retrieve a result set containing all columns from the `authors` table – the entire table in other words. The method gets the count of the number of columns by means of the `ResultSetMetaData` object for the `ResultSet` object created as a result of the query. This is used to output however many columns there are in the result set. In general we won't necessarily know how many columns are returned in the resultset, but we can implement the method so that it will deal with any number of columns as well as any number of rows:

```
void getAllColumns(){
// Execute wildcard query and output all columns...
  try{
    ResultSet recordingResults = statement.executeQuery(queryWildcard);

    ResultSetMetaData metadata = recordingResults.getMetaData();
    int columns = metadata.getColumnCount();          // Column count
    int row = 0;
    while (recordingResults.next()){
      System.out.print("\nRow " + (++row) + ") ");
      for(int i = 1 ; i<=columns ; i++)
        System.out.print((i>1?", ":" ")+ recordingResults.getString(i));
    }

    recordingResults.close();                         // Close the result set
  }
  catch (SQLException ex){
    System.err.println("\nSQLException-------------------\n");
    System.err.println("SQLState: " + ex.getSQLState());
    System.err.println("Message : " + ex.getMessage());
  }
}
```

Next we have our `close()` method. Notice that this method tests the value of the connection to ensure that we don't try to close a `null` connection:

```
  void closeConnection() {
    if (connection != null) {
      try {
        connection.close();
        connection = null;
      } catch (SQLException ex) {
        System.out.println("\nSQLException-------------------\n");
        System.out.println("SQLState: " + ex.getSQLState());
        System.out.println("Message : " + ex.getMessage());
      }
    }
  }
```

The final section of code defines all of the variables for connecting to and querying the database:

```
  Connection connection;
  Statement statement;
  String sourceURL = "jdbc:cloudscape:Wrox4370.db";
  String queryIDAndName =
    "SELECT recordingid, recordingtitle, catalognumber FROM recordings";
  String queryWildcard = "SELECT * FROM recordings";    // Select all columns
}
```

Running the `EssentialJDBC` program produces three sets of results. The first two sets are the same and consist of the ID, title, and catalog number from the `recordings` table. The third set lists all columns from the recordings. Although the additional columns are Null, you can see that we get them all in this case.

Handling Errors

Most programmers would like to be able to ignore the issue of errors, warnings, and exceptions that occur in their JDBC applications. After all, since they write perfect code, then everything will work OK, right?! Unfortunately, life is a bit less predictable than that, and you need to take some extra steps in all of your JDBC applications to handle conditions that generate warnings or errors. In this section, you'll see how to build mechanisms to trap errors, how to use the extra facilities built into JDBC to get detailed warning and error information from the data source, and how to gracefully recover from JDBC exceptions. The first place where we get some extra help is from the `SQLException` class.

SQLException

Most of the examples that you have seen so far have just output the basic exception that is thrown when an error occurred:

```
try
{
  //do JDBC stuff
}
catch(SQLException sqle)
{
  System.err.println(sqle);
}
```

This invokes the `toString()` method for the exception object and displays the result. Every method of every JDBC class and interface can throw a `SQLException`. Using the `SQLException` exception in this way is a pretty broad-brush approach to handling errors in JDBC, and it is possible to do a little better.

In order to do useful things with the `SQLException`, you need to know that there are three important pieces of information available from the exception object that is thrown. How you use these pieces of information depends on what is possible in the context of your application.

The Exception Message

The boiler-plate information that you get with just about any exception is a string that describes the exception, and as you have seen, is returned by the `getMessage()` method of the exception object. For the examples that we've presented so far, this is the most useful piece of information. This string, however, varies, depending on the JDBC driver that you're using, so while this information is useful for humans as an indication of why things are not working out as they should, it is difficult for programs to make decisions based on this information. For that you need to use something a little different.

SQL State

There is another piece of information that is available when an error occurs, the **SQL state**, which can be used within a program to make decisions about how best to proceed. The SQL state is a string that contains a state as defined by the X/Open SQL standard. The SQL state value can be obtained from the `SQLException` by calling the `getSQLState()` method.

The X/Open standard defines the SQL state as a five-character string that consists of two parts. The first two characters of the string define the **class** of the state. For example, the characters `01` represent the SQL state `success with warning`. Class here is merely a classification – it's nothing to do with class types.

The next three characters define the subclass of the state. The X/Open standard defines specific subclasses, and also provides the value `000` as a general subclass. Specific implementations may define state subclasses of their own using the values `900` through `ZZZ` where the standard does not provide a specific subclass.

The following table shows a partial list of the SQL state strings defined in the X/Open standard. When these state codes are set, they may not be directly attributable to your JDBC code, but may reflect an error occurring in the underlying driver or database. For example, if you are using the JDBC-ODBC Bridge, a SQL state can reflect an error occurring at the ODBC driver level.

Class	Subclass	Description
`01`		Success with warning
	`002`	Disconnect error
	`004`	String data, right truncation
	`006`	Privilege not revoked
`02`	`000`	No data
`07`		Dynamic SQL error
	`001`	Using-clause does not match dynamic parameters
	`006`	Restricted data type attribute violation

Class	Subclass	Description
	008	Invalid descriptor count
08		Connection exception
	001	Server rejected the connection
	002	Connection name in use
	003	Connection does not exist
	004	Client unable to establish connection
	007	Transaction state unknown
	S01	Communication failure
21		Cardinality violation
	S01	Insert value list does not match column list
	S02	Degree of derived table does not match column list
22		Data exception
	001	String data, right truncation
	003	Numeric value out of range
	005	Error in assignment
	012	Divide by zero
23	000	Integrity constraint violation
24	000	Invalid cursor state
25	000	Invalid transaction state
	S02	Transaction still active
	S03	Transaction is rolled back
2D	000	Invalid transaction termination
34	000	Invalid cursor name
37	000	Syntax error or access violation
40	000	Transaction rollback
	001	Statement completion unknown
42	000	Syntax error or access violation
HZ	000-ZZZ	RDA(Remote Data Access) errors
S0		Invalid name

Table continued on following page

Class	Subclass	Description
	001	Base table or view already exists
	002	Base table not found
	011	Index already exists
	012	Index not found
	021	Column already exists
S1		Call Level Interface specific
	001	Memory allocation error
	002	Invalid column number
	003	Program type out of range
	004	SQL data type out of range
	008	Operation canceled
	009	Invalid argument value
	010	Function sequence error
	012	Invalid transaction operation code
	013	Memory management error
	015	No cursor name available
	900-ZZZ	Implementation defined

The SQL state string is a very useful piece of information if you want to programmatically handle exceptions. As you can see from the table, the subclasses indicate specific problems that in many cases may be recoverable. Using the SQL state value, you can make decisions in your program as to whether it is possible to recover from an exception or not.

For example, if your application creates tables, an exception indicating SQL state `S0001` means that the table already exists. Depending on your application, this may not represent a fatal error, and your program can continue. Most of the examples so far, though, haven't been that smart. Most of the examples terminated when an exception was thrown. It would obviously be possible, though, to code the example to use the SQL state information and allow the program to continue with the output operation depending on the severity of the exception.

Vendor Error Code

The third piece of information that you can get from the `SQLException` is a vendor-specific error code. This value is returned as an integer, and it's meaning is completely defined by the driver vendor. This value can be obtained by calling the `getErrorCode()` method of the `SQLException`.

Let's use an example to take a look at the additional information we can get when an exception is thrown.

Try It Out – Extracting information from SQLException

In this example, we will intentionally create errors in the executed SQL statements to generate exceptions, and then extract the message, vendor code, and SQL state from the exception. In order to generate the exception, I've misspelled the name of the table in the variable, `theStatement`.

```
import java.sql.*;

public class ExtractSQLExceptionInfo {
  public static void main(String[] args) {
    String url = "jdbc:cloudscape:Wrox4370.db";
    String driver = "COM.cloudscape.core.JDBCDriver";

    String username = "guest";
    String password = "guest";

    String theStatement =
      "SELECT recordingid, recordingtitle, coverimagefilespec FROM rekordings";

    // intentional misspelling to generate exception


    try {
      Class.forName(driver);
      Connection connection = DriverManager.getConnection(url, username,
              password);
      Statement queryRecordings = connection.createStatement();
      ResultSet theResults = queryRecordings.executeQuery(theStatement);
      queryRecordings.close();
    } catch (ClassNotFoundException cnfe) {
      System.err.println(cnfe);
    } catch (SQLException sqle) {
      String sqlMessage = sqle.getMessage();
      String sqlState = sqle.getSQLState();
      int vendorCode = sqle.getErrorCode();
      System.err.println("Exception occurred:");
      System.err.println("Message: " + sqlMessage);
      System.err.println("SQL state: " + sqlState);
      System.err.println("Vendor code: " + vendorCode
                         + "\n----------------");
    }
  }
}
```

When I ran this example, it produced the following:

```
Exception occurred:
Message: Table 'REKORDINGS' does not exist.
SQL state: 42X05
Vendor code: 30000
----------------
```

How It Works

In the `SQLException` exception handler, instead of simply displaying the string representation of the exception, we extract the message, the SQL state, and the vendor-specific error code. In this simple example, the information is formatted and displayed on the screen. In a more sophisticated application, you might want to decide how the program proceeds based on the information, and log this information to a file to help you troubleshoot your application.

The message returned is quite self-explanatory. The text will vary, of course, from driver to driver, hence the importance of the SQL state value. If you look back to the previous table, you will see that the SQL state reported in this exception corresponds to the SQL state 'Base table not found', which correctly identifies the problem. Lastly, the vendor code that was returned indicates the driver vendor's numeric code for the exception.

Chaining SQL Exceptions

When a SQL exception is thrown, there may be more than one exception object associated with the error that caused the exception to be thrown. In order to handle this situation, the `SQLException` may be linked to another in a chain of exceptions:

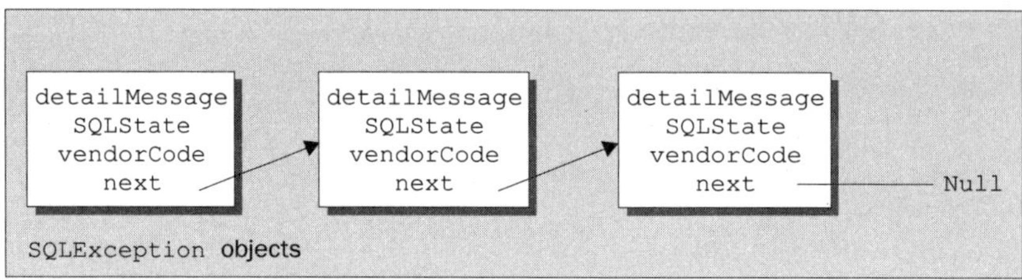

A `SQLException` object is essentially a node in a linked list. The `SQLException` class defines the `setNextException()` method for JDBC drivers and applications – the code throwing the exception in other words – to link a new exception to the chain. When a `catch` block in your program catches an exception of type `SQLException`, it is always the first node in a chain of one or more exception objects. You can call the `getNextException()` method for the `SQLException` that is passed to a `catch` block to obtain the next exception object in the chain, if one exists. This method returns either a reference to the next `SQLException` object in the chain, or Null if there are no more exceptions.

Thus, when your program catches an `SQLException`, you should always use the `getNextException()` method in a loop to get all of the exceptions. The code fragment below illustrates a simple technique for looping:

```
try
{
  // call a method that can throw SQLException
  theProgram.doSQLQuery();
}
catch(SQLException sqle)
{
  do                              // loop through each exception
  {
   // do something with each exception
   System.err.println("Exception occurred:\nMessage: " + sqle.getMessage());
   System.err.println("SQL state: " + sqle.getSQLState());
   System.err.println("Vendor code: " + sqle.getErrorCode() + "\n");

  }while((sqle = sqle.getNextException()) != null);
}
```

In the `do-while` loop, we output information from the exception object, `sqle`, which is passed to the `catch` block on the first iteration. The loop condition stores the references returned by the `getNextException()` for the `sqle` object back in `sqle`, and if it is not Null, the loop continues. In this way we iterate through all the exceptions in the chain, outputting the information from each.

The next example shows the mechanics of how an application can loop through a chain of SQLException objects in its exception handling. This technique is useful for troubleshooting problems and extracting the full scope of information that is provided in the exceptions.

Try It Out – Chaining SQLExceptions

We'll make a simple change to the ExtractSQLExceptionInfo program to loop through the linked list of exceptions, and display the exception information:

```
import java.sql.*;

public class TryChainedSQLExceptionInfo
{
  public static void main(String[] args)
  {
     String url = "jdbc:cloudscape:Wrox4370.db";
    String driver = "COM.cloudscape.core.JDBCDriver";

    String username = "guest";
    String password = "guest";

      String theStatement =
            "SELECT recordingid, recordingtitle, coverimagefilespec FROM
rekordings";

    try
    {
      Class.forName(driver);
      Connection connection = DriverManager.getConnection(url, username,
password);
      Statement queryRecordings = connection.createStatement();
      ResultSet theResults =  queryRecordings.executeQuery(theStatement);
      queryRecordings.close();
    }
    catch (ClassNotFoundException cnfe)
    {
     System.err.println(cnfe);
    }
    catch (SQLException sqle)
    {
      do // loop through each exception
      {
        // do something with each exception
        System.err.println("Exception occurred:\nMessage: " + sqle.getMessage());
        System.err.println("SQL state: " + sqle.getSQLState());
        System.err.println("Vendor code: " + sqle.getErrorCode() +
                "\n----------------");
      } while((sqle = sqle.getNextException()) != null);
    }
  }
}
```

In order to create an error condition, I set up two processes to directly access the music store database at the same time. Cloudscape treats this as an error condition when two applications accessing the same database in 'embedded' (non client-server) mode. When I ran the program I got:

```
Exception occurred:
Message: Failed to start database 'Wrox4370.db', see the next exception for
details.
SQL state: XJ040
Vendor code: 40000
----------------
Exception occurred:
Message: Another instance of cloudscape may have already booted the database
w:\Wrox\JavaDB\Wrox4370.db.
SQL state: XSDB6
Vendor code: 45000
----------------
```

How It Works

This example demonstrates how to use the code we saw earlier to handle chains of `SQLException` objects.

As soon as a connection is attempted, the database throws an exception indicating that something is wrong. The text of the exception suggests that there is another exception in the chain. Sure enough, when the next exception in the chain is examined, it provides the exact source of the problem.

SQLWarnings

JDBC provides a means of obtaining warning information from JDBC objects. Sometimes, conditions may arise that may not be serious enough to throw an exception, but do merit the program being signaled that all is not completely well. Warnings are represented by objects of type `SQLWarning`, and a `SQLWarning` object is silently appended to a JDBC object when an operation using the object causes something odd to occur.

The `SQLWarning` class is derived from `SQLException`, therefore it inherits the ability of the `SQLException` objects to define a message, a `SQLState` code, and a vendor code. A `SQLWarning` object can also be chained to one or more other `SQLWarning` objects. The techniques described in the previous section for traversing `SQLException` object chains apply just as well to `SQLWarning` object chains. In most respects, the `SQLWarning` looks a lot like `SQLException`, except for one very important distinction: you have to ask for a `SQLWarning` object explicitly. If you don't ask, you won't get.

The `ResultSet`, `Connection`, and `Statement` interfaces all declare the `getWarnings()` method, which returns a `SQLWarning` object if warnings are present, and Null otherwise.

To better understand how `SQLWarning` objects arise, consider one special class of warnings – data truncation. There is nothing preventing an application from retrieving data from a column as a Java type that is not particularly suitable for the SQL type – for example, accessing a floating-point column as an integer type. Of course, this can and probably will, result in data loss. This sort of thing will cause a `SQLWarning` object to be chained to the `ResultSet` object that requested the inappropriate data conversion. In order to detect this, the application can call the `getWarnings()` method of the `ResultSet` object.

Since data truncation is a particularly common type of warning, JDBC provides a `DataTruncation` class that is itself derived from `SQLWarning`. Let's give it a go.

Try It Out – Using SQLWarning

This example is basically the same code as the previous example, except that here we intentionally retrieve floating-point values from the `Recordings` table as integers, in order to force a warning. Any warnings arising from data access operations are detected by the `checkForWarning()` method that we have added to the class. Here's the code:

```
import java.sql.*;

public class TrySQLWarning {
  public static void main(String[] args) {
    String url = "jdbc:cloudscape:Wrox4370.db";
    String driver = "COM.cloudscape.core.JDBCDriver";

    String username = "guest";
    String password = "guest";

    String theStatement =
      "SELECT recordingid, recordingtitle, listprice FROM recordings";


    try {
      Class.forName(driver);
      Connection connection = DriverManager.getConnection(url, username,
              password);
      Statement queryRecordings = connection.createStatement();

      ResultSet theResults = queryRecordings.executeQuery(theStatement);
      while (theResults.next()) {
        int id, price;
        String title;

        id = theResults.getInt("recordingid");
        checkForWarning(theResults.getWarnings());

        title = theResults.getString("recordingtitle");
        checkForWarning(theResults.getWarnings());

        price = theResults.getInt("listprice");
        checkForWarning(theResults.getWarnings());

        System.out.println(id + ", " + title + ", " + price);
      }

      queryRecordings.close();
    } catch (ClassNotFoundException cnfe) {
      System.out.println(cnfe);
    } catch (SQLException sqle) {
      do   // loop through each exception
       {

        // do something with each exception
        System.err.println("Exception occurred:\nMessage: "
                    + sqle.getMessage());
        System.err.println("SQL state: " + sqle.getSQLState());
        System.err.println("Vendor code: " + sqle.getErrorCode()
                    + "\n----------------");
      } while ((sqle = sqle.getNextException()) != null);
    }
  }
```

```
    static boolean checkForWarning(SQLWarning w) {
      if (w == null) {
        return false;
      }
      do {
        System.err.println("Warning:\nMessage: " + w.getMessage());
        System.err.println("SQL state: " + w.getSQLState());
        System.err.println("Vendor code: " + w.getErrorCode()
                          + "\n----------------");
      } while ((w = w.getNextWarning()) != null);
      return true;
    }
  }
```

At the time of writing, the Cloudscape database does not generate warning information for the data truncation error in this example.

How It Works

Since `SQLWarning` objects are just attached to the `ResultSet` object when unusual conditions arise, the code needs to check the `ResultSet` object after extracting each value to find out if any warnings were produced. The `ResultSet.getWarnings()` method returns a `SQLWarning` object if any warnings were generated, and Null otherwise. The value returned by the method call is passed to our `checkForWarning()` method, which checks for a non-Null value, and iterates through the chain of `SQLWarning` objects in the way we have seen applied to a chain of `SQLException` objects. For each warning the method outputs the message, the SQL state, and the vendor code. The method also returns a Boolean value that is True if there was a warning, just in case the calling method needs to know about it. As you can see, we don't make use of this in our code.

Summary

In this chapter we introduced some of the main interfaces that compose the JDBC API, including the `Connection`, `Statement`, and `ResultSet` interfaces.

We did not fully explain how these interfaces are defined or the extent of the functionality that they encapsulate but we covered enough so that you should now be able to load a JDBC driver, connect to a Cloudscape or Oracle database, and retrieve column data into a `ResultSet` object. In our essential JDBC program we saw several ways to retrieve this column data, including use of `ResultSet` meta data, to help us deal with situations where we do not know the number of columns we are dealing with.

We discussed basic error handling techniques in you code, and we will be taking a look at more sophisticated techniques for debugging and logging your applications in Chapter 17.

The programs in this chapter executed some fairly basic SQL statements in the database, with little explanation of how that SQL worked. Over the coming chapters we take a step back form the JDBC interface to take a look at full power of the SQL programming language in data retrieval and manipulation, and in actually defining and creating the Music Store database model that we have used in this chapter.

SQL Queries and Data Manipulation

In applications that use a database, we need to be able to do things such as get at data and manipulate it. **Structured Query Language** (**SQL**) is considered the defacto standard data access language for database systems. All major relational database management systems (RDBMS), such as those from Cloudscape, IBM, Oracle, and Microsoft, support SQL. When you are developing a database-enhanced web site, you will need to use SQL.

The SQL language includes commands for selecting, altering, and deleting data. It also allows you to create, change, and delete objects, such as tables. Given its power, SQL is a relatively simple to use language, and the best part is that there is a well-defined standard that is universally accepted. If you learn SQL for one relational database product, then you will be able to use SQL in just about any other relational database product. Having said this, however, most vendors will make additions to ANSI SQL in order to provide better performance, so you need to check that the database you are using supports the commands you want to issue.

There are ways other than SQL in which an application can access data in a database. Products such as Microsoft's ActiveX Data Objects (ADO) make it possible for a developer to perform virtually all database-related tasks without knowing SQL, but it often comes with a price – slower performance. This is due to a number of factors, including having to convert the data into the product's object model. For maximum performance, SQL is generally the best choice.

In this chapter, we will begin with a short history of SQL, describe the versions of it that are in use today, and what it is exactly, and then move on to look at how to use SQL to acquire data, including how to specify what records are to be acted upon – in individual tables as well as from multiple tables. Also, we will see how SQL may be used to consolidate information by using a variety of **joins**.

A Brief History of SQL

Originally, SQL (which some people pronounce as *Es-Que-El* and some pronounce as *sequel*) was a language designed and implemented at IBM Research for a relational database system called *SYSTEM R*. The language soon became very popular and many commercial vendors were developing their own variations of the language. Due to this widespread use, there have been efforts made to standardize the language. To date, there have been four major versions of SQL approved by the **A**merican **N**ational **S**tandards **I**nstitute (**ANSI**) and the **I**nternational **S**tandards **O**rganization (**ISO**):

- **SQL-86** – Defined in 1986 as a standard that defined the common features of the most important DBMS products at the time.
- **SQL-89** – A superset of SQL-86 that added a small number of new features, such as support for certain multi-set operations.
- **SQL-92** (a.k.a. **SQL-2** and **International Standard Database Language SQL**) – Completed in 1992 and includes extra data types and a number of other features, including additional ways to relate tables called **outer joins**.
- **SQL-99** (a.k.a. **SQL-3**) – Approved in December of 1999, and formalized many features that had been available in many databases through proprietary implementations. This version included support for many of the statements commonly found in procedural languages such as Visual Basic and C++. It also added support for international character sets and new data types.

You can purchase downloadable copies of the five-document SQL-3 standard, ISO/IEC 9075-1:1999 through ISO/IEC 9075-5:1999, at https://webstore.ansi.org/.

As suggested by the number of years between the releases of the major versions, these standards don't happen overnight. Between each major version, a series of minor additions and amendments are made. Currently, enhancements are being made concerning such topics as object-language bindings, online analytical processing, management of external data, and time-based operations. The next major release is expected around 2003.

Virtually all RDBMSs fully support SQL-2, and the major vendors support much of what is defined in SQL-3. Although SQL-3 was only recently approved, it was first developed in 1995, and most of the major vendors have been adding support for the new version based upon the proposal. Unfortunately, without an official standard, each vendor implemented many of the proposed changes differently. You should see a greater adherence to the SQL-3 standard in the next major releases from the major RDBMS vendors.

Although each vendor may have some minor differences in how they implement SQL-3 features, SQL is almost universally supported. The similarities between versions are so strong that if you learn any one vendor's version, you will be able to work with the other major vendors' versions with little difficulty. Even with such strong support for SQL among many vendors, you should still strive to learn the intricacies of the exact RDBMS you are working with. By doing so, you will be better positioned to construct more robust and scalable applications.

At the time of this writing, the most recent version of Cloudscape, version 3.6, does not yet fully support all the new SQL-3 features.

What is in SQL?

Historically, SQL has been a declarative language, unlike procedural languages such as C, C++, Java, and Visual Basic. In these procedural languages, your code provides statements on *how* to process information. In the SQL language, statements describe *what* information gets processed and allow the database engine to determine the best method for getting that information.

As its name suggests, SQL includes syntax for executing queries. We can ask questions of the database and have the results returned. In addition to extracting data from a database we can insert new records, delete records and update existing records. The query and update commands together form the **Data Manipulation Language** (**DML**) component of SQL. There are only four basic statements in the DML component: `SELECT`, `UPDATE`, `DELETE`, and `INSERT`. We'll see how these command work in the next section. There is also a **Data Definition Language** (**DDL**) component of SQL that is used to create new tables and other objects. The main DDL statements in SQL are `CREATE TABLE`, `ALTER TABLE`, `DROP TABLE`, `CREATE INDEX`, and `DROP INDEX`. These are looked at in a little more detail in the next chapter. A third language component, the **Data Control Language** (**DCL**), is used to manage who has authorization and ownership rights for the objects in the database, with statements such as `GRANT` and `REVOKE`. The DCL also contains procedural control statements, for constructs such as loops and conditions, as well as for managing how to treat failures of statements with commands such as `COMMIT` and `ROLLBACK`. We'll take a look at some DDL and DCL statements later in this chapter.

The SQL commands may be issued directly to the database using a query tool such as Microsoft SQL Server's oSQL or Query Analyzer, Oracle's SQL Worksheet, or Cloudscape's Cloudview. Also, SQL commands may be executed via a programming language such as Visual Basic Script, Visual Basic for Applications, or C++.

SQL relies heavily on set theory to define what records should be processed. Having a strong emphasis on set theory doesn't imply that SQL is devoid of procedural commands, like those in Java, that allow you to govern the order of the processing and other logic. SQL does contain most of the typical constructs that you would find in most modern languages, like `while` loops, `if`, and `case` statements. Even with these procedural features though, the basis of the language is telling the RDBMS what needs to be done and the RDBMS figures out the best way to do it.

SQL and Set Theory

The typical SQL command to access data uses English-like statements that define a set of records to be acquired, as well as what information should be returned from this set. The syntax requires that we define the set by specifying what conditions any given record must meet in order to be considered part of that set.

To illustrate how SQL uses set theory, let's consider a simple SQL statement. In the next section, we will delve into the exact usage of the syntax, but until then, let's consider the set of records this SQL statement defines. The following SQL statement retrieves the names of all cities from a subset of records found in the `Locations` table where the `State` field contains a value of `MA` and whose `Population` field has a value greater than `10000`:

```
SELECT City
  FROM Locations
 WHERE ((State ='MA')
   AND (Population > 10000))
```

Unless otherwise noted, the examples of SQL in this chapter have been written using the SQL-3 and are not written in any RDBMS-specific SQL implementation. Since there are some differences in SQL implementations from vendor to vendor, some minor editing to these examples may be needed so that these examples will work with your specific RDBMS. You will need to check your RDBMS's documentation for details on syntax.

Graphically, this query can be displayed as follows:

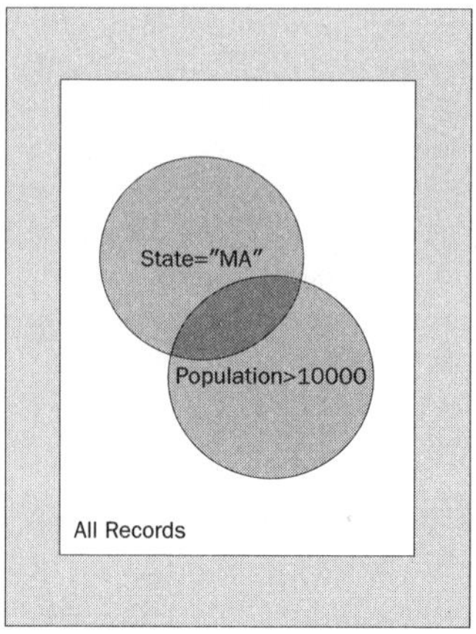

This type of graphic is called a **Venn diagram**. The rectangle with all of its contents represents all records – the 'universe' of records. The upper circle represents the set of all records where the `State` field has a value of `MA`. The lower circle represents the set of all records where the `Population` field is greater than 10000. The dark gray area where the two circles overlap represent the subset of records where the `State` field has a value of `MA` *and* where the `Population` field is greater than 10000. In other words, this gray area represents records that meet *both* conditions.

To represent a set of data that satisfies at least one of a number of conditions, we use an `OR` condition. Suppose we wanted to select records where the `State` is either `MA` or the state is `IL`. The following SQL will return those records for us:

```
SELECT City
  FROM Locations
 WHERE ((State ='MA')
    OR (State ='IL'))
```

Using a Venn diagram, this selection would be represented as follows:

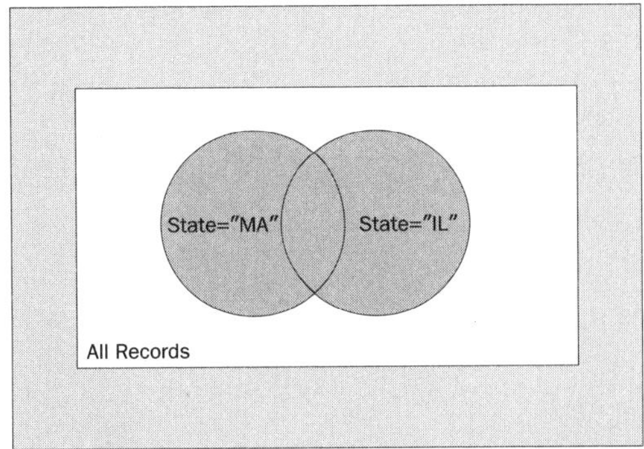

As with the previous illustration, the gray area represents the set of records that will be returned – in this case the entirety of both circles. It is interesting to note that with Venn diagrams, even if a compound condition, such as an OR condition, can produce only an empty set, then that empty set is still displayed. Such is the case here. Although it is impossible for a city to be located in two different states at the same time, the Venn diagram still shows the overlapping area to denote those records that meet this condition.

We can use SQL to produce a set of records where the State field has a value of MA, or the Population field is greater than 10000, or both:

```
SELECT City
  FROM Locations
 WHERE ((State ='MA')
    OR (Population > 10000))
```

For a record to be included in the resulting set, it must meet *either* condition or *both* conditions. Since a record will be included in the resultset if it meets both requirements, the SQL OR operator is sometimes known as an **inclusive or**.

We can even combine AND and OR conditions, such as in the following:

```
SELECT City
  FROM Locations
 WHERE ((State ='MA') AND (Population > 10000))
    OR ((State ='IL') AND (Population > 10000))
```

Using a bit of Boolean algebra, we can rewrite this statement more simply as:

```
SELECT City
  FROM Locations
 WHERE ((State ='MA') OR (State ='IL'))
   AND (Population > 10000)
```

Regardless of which of the two above forms is used, each can be graphically represented as the following:

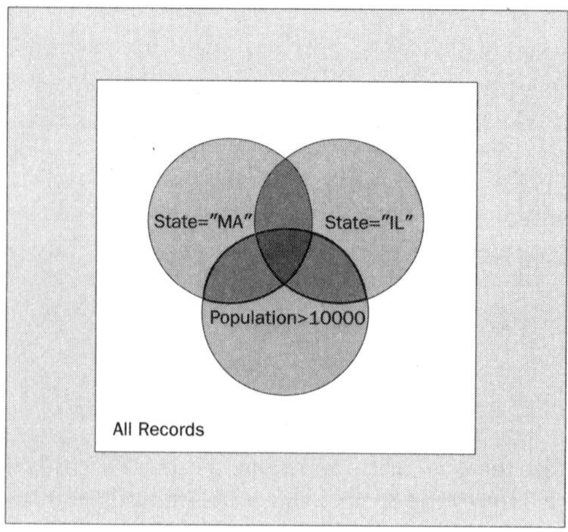

Where two circles overlap denotes records that meet two conditions – the AND portion of our WHERE clause. The overlapping areas that are denoted with the thick black borders represent the set of records returned by our query. As noted before, there is a section of the diagram where no records could possibly exist. The exact center of the diagram, denoted by the very dark gray, contains an empty set.

Accessing Data Using SELECT

When we want to obtain information from a database, we issue what is called a **query**. Queries created using SQL are constructed very much like questions are constructed in the English language. In English, when we ask a question the basic structure of the sentence is generally the same. For example, consider the following questions:

- What are the birthdays of each of our customers?
- Which restaurants offer Sunday brunch?
- How many modems were sold in the month of July 2001?

In each case, we are requesting information by name. When phrasing a question in SQL, we need to be very specific about which columns of data are to be returned, as well as under what conditions that data should be pulled from the table.

Basic Structure of the SELECT Statement

Since SQL is not nearly as flexible as the English language, the format of a question in SQL must be phrased in some exact format. To ask a question in SQL, we use the SELECT statement, which takes the following general form:

```
  SELECT column1[, column2, ..., columnN]
    FROM table1[, table2, ..., tableN]
   WHERE condition
GROUP BY column1[, column1, ..., columnN]
ORDER BY column1[, column1, ..., columnN];
```

The `SELECT` clause of the statement identifies which fields (or calculations) are to be returned. The statement uses the `FROM` clause to identify the table (or tables in more advanced `SELECT` statements) from which the data will be obtained. The `WHERE` clause allows us to specify restrictions limiting which rows of the table will be selected, and the `ORDER BY` clause is used to sort the resulting records.

Although the SQL-3 standard does not require the use of a terminating semicolon, in some implementations of SQL, a semicolon must be placed at the end of the statement. This is one example of the differences between different vendors' versions of SQL. Some other differences may be less apparent. You should check the documentation that accompanies your RDBMS to see if it contains a section comparing its version of SQL with the ANSI standard for further details.

Specifying the Columns

In its simplest form, the `SELECT` statement is used to return all the rows from all records in a given table. Rather than specifying in the `SELECT` clause which columns to return, as was shown in our above examples, we can use an asterisk character (`*`) to select all columns in the table. Let's assume that we have a table called `Recordings` that describes various music albums and CDs our music store sells. To list all of the information we have in our `Recordings` table, we could issue the following command:

```
SELECT * FROM Recordings
```

The results of this query might look similar to the following:

RecordingID	RecordingTitle	Publisher ID	Catalog Number	Release Date	List Price
1000	Space I'm In	112	2064-24370-2	1991-05-23	14.99
1001	Phenomenon Soundtrack	108	9362-46360-2	1996-08-23	15.99
1002	Little Earthquakes	103	7567-82358-2	1991-10-02	14.99
1003	Crucify	103	82399-2	1992-03-21	9.99
1004	Big Time	107	GAIL3 12	1987-06-21	9.99
1005	Us	107	GAHN2 07	1992-09-29	18.97

The order in which the columns appear in the output is determined by the database. To specify the order of the columns, you could explicitly list each field, separated by commas after the keyword `SELECT`. When the columns are listed explicitly, you are not required to list every field. If we specify particular columns rather than the asterisk, only those columns will be returned. For example, if we are interested in only the release date of each recording (and the name of the recording so we can make sense of the release dates), we could use the statement:

```
SELECT RecordingTitle, ReleaseDate
  FROM Recordings
```

Since we want to find out the release dates of all recordings, there are no restrictions to the query, so the `WHERE` clause is not used. This statement will return all the values of the `RecordingTitle` and `ReleaseDate` in a columnar layout:

RecordingTitle	ReleaseDate
Space I'm In	1991-05-23
Phenomenon Soundtrack	1996-08-23
Little Earthquakes	1991-10-02
Crucify	1992-03-21
Big Time	1987-06-21
Us	1992-09-29

Try It Out – Using the SELECT Statement

To demonstrate how to use SQL, we will use the database described, in part, in Chapter 5 on *Relational Database Design Concepts*. This database was designed for the fictitious music retailer. This company is planning to open up a chain of retail stores across North America and Europe as well as allowing customers to make purchase via an Internet web site.

Let's use the `SELECT` statement to find out what information is stored in some of the tables in our Music Store example. Specifically, determine the following:

- Which cities do we have listed in the `PostalCodes` table?
- What are the `FirstName`, `LastName`, and `EmailAddress` values for all of our customers?

If you are using Cloudscape as your database, start the database and open Cloudview. In order to execute your SQL statements, you will need to first select the database icon found in the left panel. Select the database tab to display the SQL command window. Type into this command window the first SQL statement that will display the cities we have listed in the `PostalCodes` table:

```
SELECT City FROM PostalCodes
```

and then hit the Execute button:

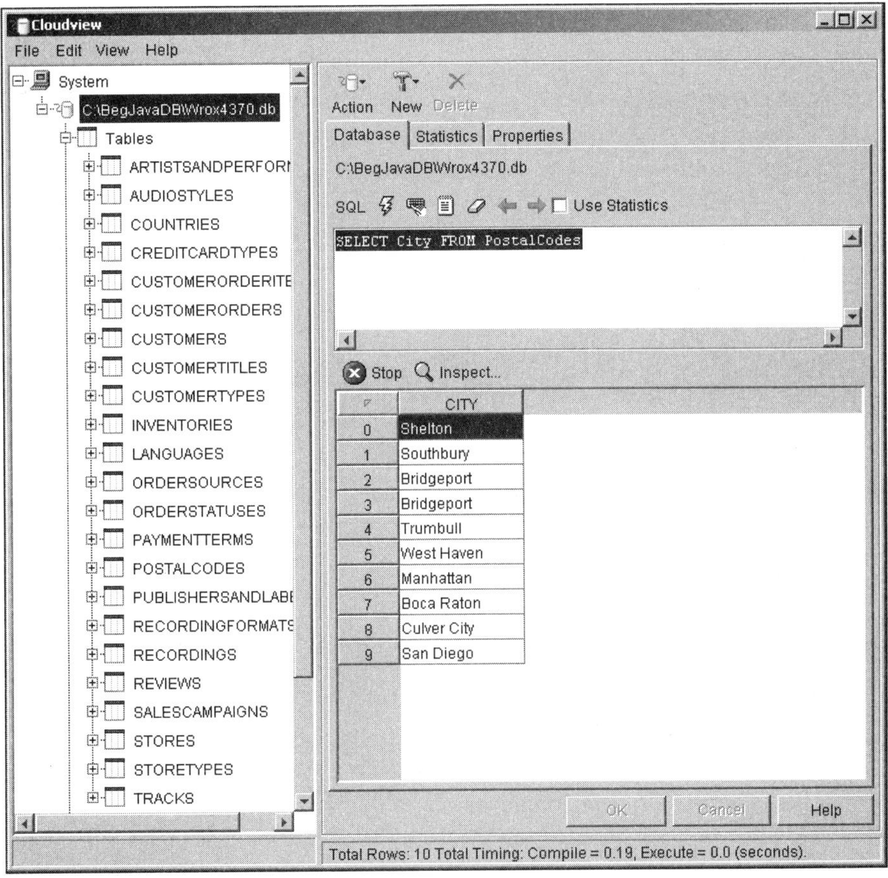

In the results pane of Cloudview, you will see 10 city names listed.

To determine the values of `FirstName`, `LastName`, and `EmailAddress` for all of our customers, we issue the SQL statement:

```
SELECT CustomerFirstName, CustomerLastName, EmailAddress
  FROM Customers
```

as illustrated overleaf:

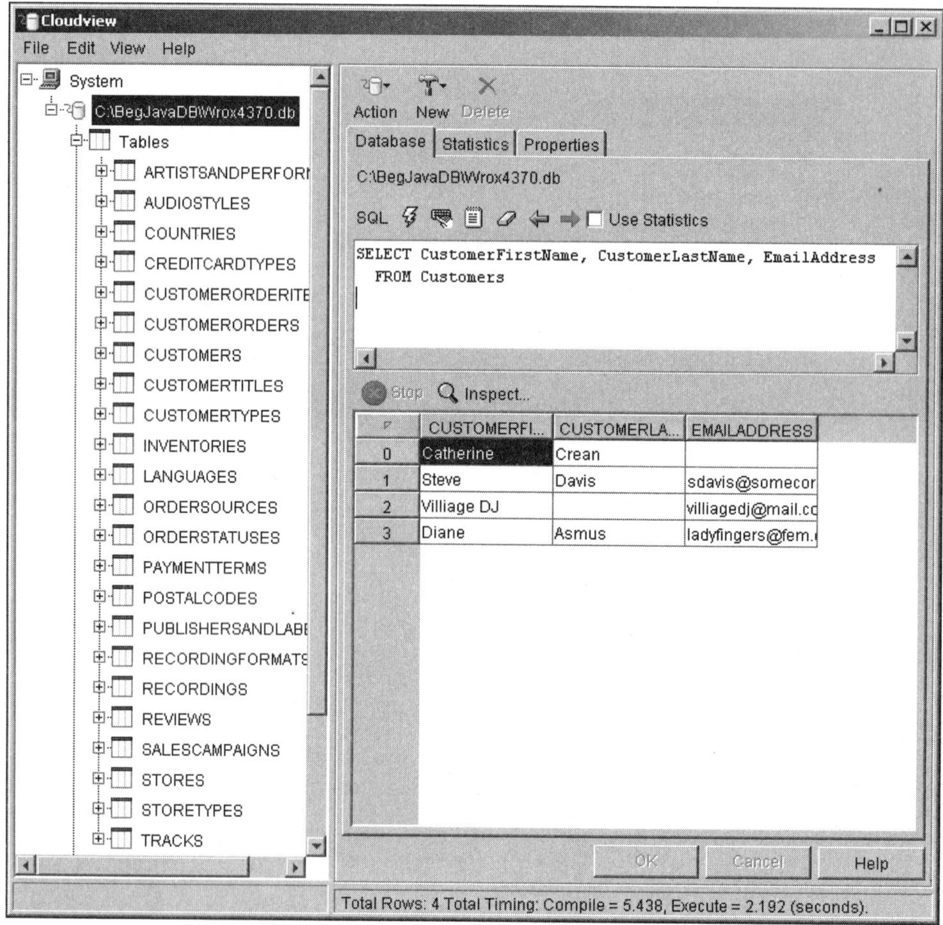

Selecting Unique Records

It is common to ask questions about which values in a table are unique. For example, you may wish to find out what products were sold in a given month. You might not want to list any particular product more than once, so we need some way to remove duplicate values so that only unique results are returned.

To eliminate duplicates from the result set of a query, we add the `DISTINCT` keyword, as in this statement, which requests the values of the `ListPrice` field found in our `Recordings` table:

```
SELECT DISTINCT ListPrice
  FROM Recordings
```

This query would produce:

ListPrice
14.99
15.99
9.99
18.97

To better illustrate how the DISTINCT keyword works, let's compare these results with what would be produced if we didn't include it:

```
SELECT ListPrice
  FROM Recordings
```

This statement would produce the following results:

ListPrice
14.99
15.99
14.99
9.99
9.99
18.97

Notice that six rows were returned – one for each record. The statement:

```
SELECT ListPrice
  FROM Recordings
```

is interpreted as 'select the value of the ListPrice field for every record in the Recordings table.' However, what if we wanted to ask the question, 'What are the list prices found in the Recordings table?', which should return each list price only once regardless of how often a list price is duplicated in the table. To do so, we use the DISTINCT keyword.

Formatting SQL

The SQL language allows for a great deal of flexibility when adding whitespace in commands. SQL requires that the keywords must be separated by at least one space character or carriage return. Any additional space characters and carriage returns will be ignored. Therefore, the following three statements are considered identical:

```
SELECT RecordingTitle FROM Recordings
```

```
SELECT RecordingTitle
```

```
    FROM Recordings
```

```
SELECT
  RecordingTitle
FROM
  Recordings
```

Having the option of placing extra spaces and carriage returns allows us to format the text of the commands for easier reading. So when you have a fairly long SQL statement, feel free to break it apart on several lines to make it more readable.

Also, most RDBMSs allow you to use either upper or lowercase with the keywords, and with the names of the database objects. For readability, you should be consistent in using case. Case-sensitivity is a configurable option with many databases, so check your product's documentation.

The safest approach is to type your keywords and object names using the same case as is described in your documentation or as you have used when you named your objects. This way, regardless of how the system is configured, you shouldn't run into case-sensitivity issues. For example, if you name a table `CustomerOrders`, then do not refer to this table using `customerorders` or `CUSTOMERORDERS`, but rather as `CustomerOrders`. Similarly, if your RDBMS's documentation shows that a function is named `rand()`, then refer to it as `rand()`, and not `Rand()` or `RAND()`.

Case-sensitivity is not limited to names and keywords. Some databases allow you to configure them so that data is case-sensitive. It is also worth noting that most database systems run significantly faster when they are configured to be case-sensitive. Unfortunately, this increase in performance is often negated by the additional code required when case-insensitive queries are needed. This is most common with queries that are required to search for records that contain specific values. If you used a case-sensitive database, these queries would require that you search for uppercase, lowercase, and combinations of upper and lowercase text values.

Calculations

When using the `SELECT` statement, we can have the database compute formulas and calculations based on our data. By using basic mathematical operators such as +, -, *, and /, we can construct most of the formulae we may need. The SQL-3 standard defines a limited number of functions as well (although most RDBMSs include many additional functions) to allow you to create robust and sophisticated calculations.

Building Formulae

To create a calculation, simply enter a formula rather than a column name in the `SELECT` statement. If the calculation is to operate on certain fields, you may include those fields as if they were variables in the formula. When the query is executed, the formula will be computed for each row selected from the database and a table of results will be returned.

To illustrate this, consider the situation where we wanted to calculate the cost of purchasing a number of products. We could use a statement similar to the following:

```
SELECT Quantity * PricePerItem
  FROM CustomerOrderItems
```

Here, the formula (often referred to as the **expression**) is the portion of the statement between the `SELECT` and `FROM` keywords. When the RDBMS processes this expression, it performs a calculation on a record-by-record basis. The values from the first record's `Quantity` and `PricePerItem` fields are used to produce the first value returned by the statement. Next, the values from the second record are applied to this statement to produce the second returned value. Then the RDBMS uses the values from the third record, and so on. If the `CustomerOrderItems` table contained the following three records:

OrderID	...	Quantity	PricePer Item	...
1001	...	1	15.65	...
1002	...	2	9.99	...
1003	...	1	9.99	...

then the resulting set of the above SQL statement would produce the following:

15.65
19.98
9.99

As with any other programming language, we can create more complex formulae using a variety of operators. Here is a chart of these operators, in order of decreasing precedence:

Operator Symbol	Name	Comments
( )	Parentheses	Used to force the order of calculations. For example, under normal precedence 8 – 4 / 2 would equal 6. If we wanted to force subtraction of the 4 from the 8 before dividing by 2, we would use parentheses in the calculation: (8 – 4) / 2, which would yield the value of 2.
+	Positive	
-	Negative	
*	Multiplication	
/	Division	
+	Addition	
-	Subtraction	
`|` or `+`	Concatenate	For example `"John"	" "	"Smith"` would yield `"John Smith"`.

Individual RDBMS will offer operators beyond those explicitly defined in the SQL standard. Commonly offered operators include:

Operator Symbol	Name	Comments
%	Modulo	Returns the integer remainder of a division. For example, 11 % 5 would equal 1 because the remainder of 11 divided by 5 is 1. This function is useful when calculating intervals.
^	Exponentiation	Raises a number to a power. For example, 2^3 would yield 8.

Try It Out – Using Calculations with the SELECT Statement

Some countries apply a value added tax on all purchases. Assuming that a 4.5% tax was applied to every order that has been placed, let's determine for each ordered item, the total price and the amount of this tax. In addition, name the total price calculated column `TotalPrice` and the amount of the tax `VAT`.

For this example, the SQL statement we need to execute is:

```
SELECT
  OrderID,
  Quantity * PricePerItem As TotalPrice,
  (Quantity * PricePerItem) * 0.045 As VAT
FROM
  CustomerOrderItems
```

and the resulting screenshot appears as follows:

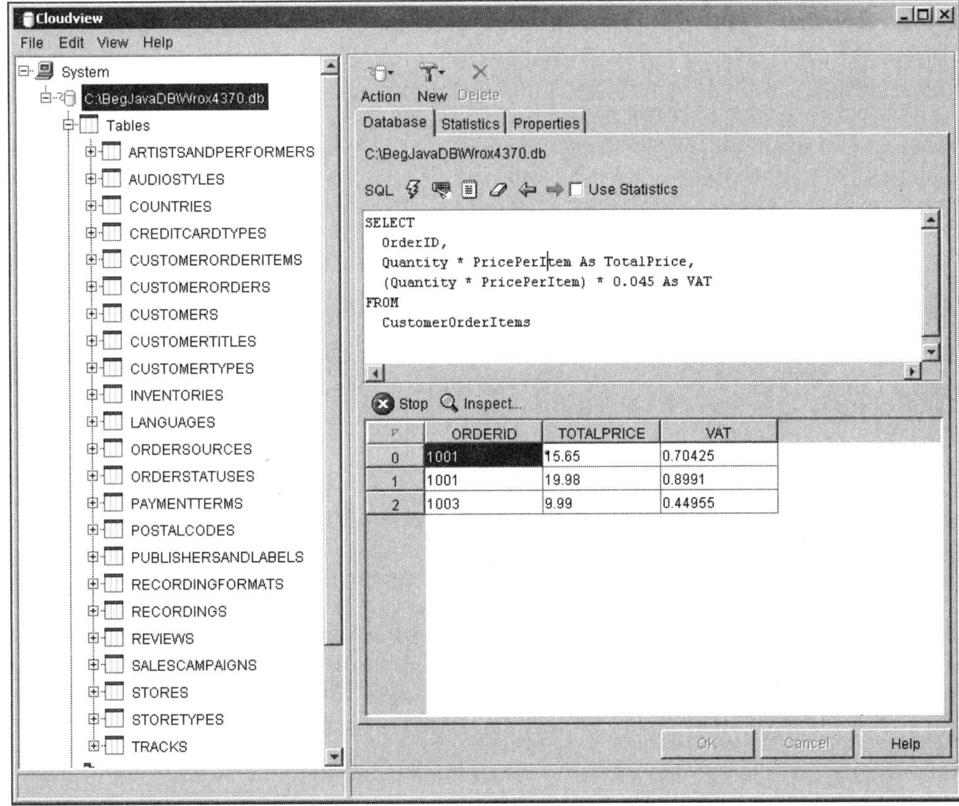

How It Works – Using Calculations with the SELECT Statement

Since we wish to compute this tax on an item-by-item basis, we will need to reference the `CustomerOrderItems` table. This means that we use `FROM CustomerOrderItems` as part of our `SELECT` statement.

The 4.5% tax rate will need to be applied to the total price for each item. Therefore, we will need to determine the total price by multiplying the quantity ordered by the price per item. The amount of the tax will be 0.045 multiplied by the total price. Therefore, our calculation will need to be `(Quantity * PricePerItem) * 0.045`.

In addition, since we need to display the amount of tax per order, we will need to include the `OrderID` with each result.

Putting this all together, we arrive at our solution:

```
SELECT
  OrderID,
  Quantity * PricePerItem As TotalPrice,
  (Quantity * PricePerItem) * 0.045 As VAT
FROM
  CustomerOrderItems
```

Specifying Column Names

Notice that the column returned in the last but one example is unnamed. Some database systems will supply a default name such as `column1` or `SQLCol1`. Other RDBMSs will generate a name based upon the field used in the expression, such as `MinOfQtyOnHand` when calculating the minimum value of the `QtyOnHand` field. Most systems simply will not name the column at all. If you wish to provide a name to any column in the resulting set of records, you may do so by using the `AS` keyword followed by the desired name. For example, if we wanted to name the resulting column `TotalPrice` we would write the query as:

```
SELECT Quantity * PricePerItem As TotalPrice
  FROM CustomerOrderItems
```

Now the results of this query would have the resulting column named appropriately:

TotalPrice
15.65
19.98
9.99

Of course, you can't assign column names that are reserved words in SQL or in the RDBMS, but most common sense names will be accepted. Most RDBMSs have some restrictions on column names, but if you stick with letters and numbers, you will not have any problems. You can include some other characters such as a dollar sign (`$`) or tilde (~), but it is generally not recommended. Recent usability research suggests that the easiest for the eye to read is all lowercase names with the first letter of each word capitalized. Also, you should try to use names that are not likely to become reserved words in future versions of SQL by taking care to avoid identifiers beginning with `CURRENT_`, `SESSION_`, `SYSTEM_`, or `TIMEZONE_`, ending in `_LENGTH`, or starting with an underscore.

Programming Concerns With Specifying Column Names

Specifying column names can be very important when programming, especially with regards to readability of code, as well as performance.

Most programmatic tools for database access, such as ADO and JBDC, will return the name of each column in the result set. These names can then be used by the programmer as a convenient way of referencing each column. If your SQL statements do not provide column names, then the application programmer will need to know, in advance, the exact position of each column in the result set (in other words, its ordinal position in the resultset). Although it is usually not a tremendous issue for the programmer to obtain this information, it does make the coding less obvious. When code is less than obvious, there is an increased likelihood that mistakes will happen. On the other hand, there is generally a performance gain when you refer to each column by its ordinal position rather than using the name of the column.

If your application's code is referencing columns in a loop, then the repeated performance gain by using the ordinal position can be substantial. If the application only references the columns once, then the difference in performance will probably be insignificant.

Functions in Expressions

When constructing formulae in SQL, most RDBMSs provide a wide-range of functions that may be included. Some of these functions are to be used with an individual value such as a field's value or some constant. For example, the `UPPER` function provides a mechanism to convert a string to its uppercase equivalent. Other functions are designed to operate on all rows in a resultset. The `SUM` function is one such function; it is used to add values found in more than one record.

Commonly Available Functions

Although the SQL standard does not explicitly define many of these functions, they have become ubiquitous among the major database vendors. As always, consult with your RDBMS documentation for the specifics.

Mathematical Functions	**Description**
`ABS(X)`	Returns the absolute value of `X`.
`CEIL(X)`	Returns the smallest integer greater than or equal to the given numeric expression.
`FLOOR(X)`	Returns the largest integer less than or equal to the given numeric expression.
`MOD(X,Y)`	Returns the remainder of `X/Y`.
`POWER(X,Y)`	Returns `X` to the power of `Y`.
`ROUND(X,Y)`	Rounds `X` to `Y` decimal places. If `Y` is omitted, `X` is rounded to the nearest integer.
`SIGN(X)`	Returns `-1` when `X` is negative, a `0` when `X` is zero, or `+1` when `X` is positive.
`SQRT(X)`	Returns the square root of `X`.

Character Functions	**Description**
`LEFT(`*`string`*`,X)`	Returns the leftmost `X` characters of the string.
`RIGHT(`*`string`*`,X)`	Returns the rightmost `X` characters of the string.
`UPPER(`*`string`*`)`	Converts the string to all uppercase letters.
`LOWER(`*`string`*`)`	Converts the string to all lowercase letters.
`LENGTH(`*`string`*`)`	Returns the number of characters in the string.

Table continued on following page

Character Functions	Description
string || *string* *string* + *string*	Combines the two strings of text into one, concatenated string, where the first string is immediately followed by the second.
SUBSTR(*string*,X,Y)	Extracts Y letters from the string beginning at position X.
NVL(*expression*,*value*) ISNULL(*expression*,*value*)	If the expression passed is a Null, then value is returned, otherwise the value of the expression is returned.

Date Functions	Description
DateAdd(*unitsoftime*,*X*,*date*)	Adds X number of *unitsoftime* to date. The *unitsoftime* may be 'year', 'month', 'week', 'day', 'hour', 'minute', or 'second'.
Year(*date*) DatePart(*year*,*date*)	Returns the year of the given date.
Month(*date*) DatePart(*month*,*date*)	Returns the month of the year (1 - 12) of the given date.
Day(*date*) DatePart(*day*,*date*)	Returns the day of the month (1 -31) of the given date.
Weekday(*date*) DatePart(*weekday*,*date*)	Returns the day of the week (1-7) of the given date.
Sysdate Getdate() Current_Date	Returns today's date.

Aggregate Functions

The SQL standard also defines a number of functions that operate based upon the values in fields among multiple records:

- MIN
- MAX
- COUNT
- AVG

Such functions are called **aggregate functions**. These functions do not re-compute their values once for each record. Rather, they operate based upon values throughout the table. Let's take a look at each of these functions in turn.

The MIN function returns the minimum value for some expression. This expression may be a field name or formula, but may not contain other aggregate functions. An example of using this function is to find the earliest value in the ReleaseDate field in the Recordings table using:

```
SELECT MIN(ReleaseDate) AS EarliestRelease
  FROM Recordings
```

This SQL statement returns:

EarliestRelease
1987-06-21

and is determined by comparing the value of each record's ReleaseDate field to determine which value was the smallest.

Similar to the MIN function, the MAX function finds the largest value. An example is:

```
SELECT MAX(ReleaseDate) AS LatestRelease
  FROM Recordings
```

This statement returns:

LatestRelease
1996-08-23

The COUNT function may be used to determine the number of records in a table. Rather than specifying some particular field when using the COUNT function, use an asterisk:

```
SELECT COUNT(*) AS NumberOfRecordings
  FROM Recordings
```

which returns the following:

NumberOfRecordings
6

This COUNT(*) query is particularly useful in many situations. It is often advantageous to determine if a table has any records of interest before attempting to process those records. Most RDBMSs have optimized their query engines to process a query using the COUNT(*) function as quickly as possible, and will most likely be the fastest single query you will find against any single table. You should do some testing to see if, in your particular application and RDBMS, the time taken by making two queries will provide increased performance since there are many factors influencing access speed such as volume of data and availability of indexes.

The AVG function is used to compute an average value – specifically, the arithmetic mean value:

```
SELECT AVG(Quantity * PricePerItem) As AvgTotalPrice
  FROM CustomerOrderItems
```

which returns:

AvgTotalPrice
15.20...

Although the SQL-3 standard does not provide for a function that computes the median value of a set of values, some RDBMSs do provide such a function. Check your systems' documentation to see if its implementation of SQL supports such a function.

Using Multiple Aggregate Functions

We can also obtain more than one statistic in a single query by listing each statistical function separated by commas:

```
SELECT MIN(ReleaseDate) AS EarliestRelease,
       MAX(ReleaseDate) AS LatestRelease
  FROM Recordings
```

which returns:

EarliestRelease	LatestRelease
1987-06-21	1996-08-23

It should be pointed out that these return results do not correspond to any given record in the database. Although the values returned are derived from data found in the database tables, these results exist only in the returned resultset.

SQL Data Types

SQL, like many other languages, requires that you store data in objects of a known data type. A data type, regardless of the language, defines what types of data values can be stored by an object of that type. Every data value belongs to at least one data type and some belong to several data types. For example, the value of one can be considered a 'numeric' data type as well as an 'integer' data type. All items in SQL that can be referenced by name, such as fields and variables, must have a declared type.

SQL-3 defines a rich collection of data types. These data types may be summarized as follows:

Data type group	Specific data types
Character String Types	The data types CHARACTER, CHARACTER VARYING, and CHARACTER LARGE OBJECT are collectively referred to as character string types. A character string is a sequence of characters. A character string has a length, which is the number of characters in the sequence. The length is 0 (zero) or a positive integer.
Binary String Types	The data type BINARY LARGE OBJECT is referred to as the binary string type and the values of binary string types are referred to as binary strings.
Bit String Types	The data types BIT and BIT VARYING are collectively referred to as bit string types. A bit string is a sequence of bits, each having the value of 0 (zero) or 1 (one). A bit string has a length, which is the number of bits in the string. The length is 0 (zero) or a positive integer.
Boolean Types	The data type BOOLEAN comprises the distinct truth values, True and False. Unless prohibited by a NOT NULL constraint, the BOOLEAN data type also supports the unknown truth value as the Null value.
Numeric Types	The data types NUMERIC, DECIMAL, INTEGER, and SMALLINT are collectively referred to as exact numeric types. The data types FLOAT, REAL, and DOUBLE PRECISION are collectively referred to as approximate numeric types. Exact numeric types and approximate numeric types are collectively referred to as numeric types. Values of numeric types are referred to as numbers.
Temporal Types	The data types TIME, TIMESTAMP, and DATE are collectively referred to as datetime types. The data type INTERVAL is referred to as an interval type. Values of these types may include the following information: YEAR – Year (0001-9999) MONTH – Month within year (0-11) DAY – Day within month (0-31) HOUR – Hour within day (0-23) MINUTE – Minute within hour (0-59) SECOND – Second within minute and possibly fraction of a second within minute (0-59.999...)
Nulls	SQL-3 also defines a Null value, which is a special value that is used to indicate the absence of any data value. When an object (variable, field, and so on) is declared, its data type is specified as well as if the object will allow Null values to be stored, regardless of data type.

You will find that different RDBMSs may name these data types differently from the SQL-3 standard. Usually, the RDBMS will support a SQL-standard data type through the use of aliases. For example, Microsoft SQL Server 2000 uses `varchar` rather than `CHARACTER VARYING` to specify variable length character strings. If you specify `CHARACTER VARYING` with Microsoft SQL Server 2000, the data type will be mapped to a `varchar`.

Below, we list some of the most common data types as implemented by Cloudscape, Microsoft SQL Server, and Oracle:

SQL-3 Data Type	Cloudscape	Microsoft SQL Server	Oracle
`BOOLEAN`	`boolean`	`bit`	`number`
`BIT`	`bit`	`bit`	`number`
`INTEGER`	`integer`	`integer`	`integer`
`DECIMAL`	`decimal`	`decimal`	`number`
`FLOAT`	`float` or `real`	`float` or `real`	`float`
`DOUBLE PRECISION`	`float` or `real`	`float` or `real`	`number`
`DATE`	`date`	`datetime`	`date`
`CHAR`	`char`	`char`	`char`
`VARCHAR`	`varchar`	`varchar`	`varchar` or `varchar2`

The following table shows the SQL-3 data types as implemented in Java and JDBC meta data:

SQL-3 Data Type	Compile-Time Java Type	JDBC Meta Data Type java.sql.Types	Description
`BOOLEAN`	`java.lang.Boolean`	`BIT`	Truth values True, False, and Null.
`BIT`	`Byte[]`	`BINARY`	Values of 0 or 1.
`INTEGER`	`java.lang.Integer`	`INTEGER`	Integer values.
`DECIMAL`	`java.math.BigDecimal`	`DECIMAL`	Fixed single precision real values.

SQL-3 Data Type	Compile-Time Java Type	JDBC Meta Data Type java.sql.Types	Description
FLOAT	java.lang.Float or java.lang.Double	REAL or DOUBLE	Floating precision real values.
DOUBLE PRECISION	java.lang.Double	DOUBLE	Fixed double precision real values.
DATE	java.sql.Date	DATE	Date and time data.
CHAR	java.lang.String	CHAR	Fixed-length non-Unicode character data.
VARCHAR	java.lang.String	VARCHAR	Variable-length non-Unicode character data.

The different RDBMSs will also support data types that are not defined by the formal SQL standard. Some of these 'non-standard' data types were developed to provide additional functionality and features. Others were developed as specific implementations of SQL data types, such as Microsoft SQL Server's `MONEY` data type, which is a special case of a `REAL`. Others are simply different from the SQL standards, such as Microsoft SQL Server's use of the name `datetime` rather than `DATE`.

Data Types and Calculations

Obviously, you can't construct a formula using incompatible data types, such as dividing a text value by some number, and get a meaningful result. When you do attempt to use such a formula, your RDBMS will return an error message. To illustrate such an error message, consider what would be returned if we attempt to execute the following nonsensical query:

```
SELECT ArtistName + ArtistID
  FROM ArtistsAndPerformers
```

Here we are attempting to add the value of a text field (`RecordingTitle`) with a numeric field (`RecordingID`). The RDBMS makes an attempt at converting the `ArtistName` values into some numeric data types that can be added. When it finds non-numeric text values in this field, it produces and error such as:

```
Database access resulted in SQL exception:
SQLState , Error code 30000, Message:
Type INTEGER does not recognize the format of the string '10,000 Maniacs'.
```

or:

```
Syntax error converting the nvarchar value '10,000 Maniacs' to a column of data
type int.
```

The exact message that you get back will vary from RDBMS to RDBMS, but the message will inform you of a problem with the data type that was expected.

Some data types are considered **compatible**. That is, they are easily converted to the same data type. For instance, we can add the value 2.1 (a real number) to 3 (an integer number). The query engine examines the two data types used and converts one value into the data type of the other. In this example, the value 3 is converted into the real number value of 3.0 and the result of the expression is a real number. In general, this conversion is performed on the least precise data type.

If we want to explicitly convert a value to a particular data type, we can use a conversion function. The most commonly used conversion function is named `CAST`. This function takes the form:

```
CAST(expression AS datatype)
```

For example, to convert the integer value of a field called `NumberOfRecordings` into a variable length character string, we may use:

```
CAST(NumberOfRecordings AS varchar(5))
```

Sometimes, it is not obvious when we would need to explicitly perform a conversion. Consider the following `SELECT` statement:

```
SELECT QtyOnHand / 2 AS HalfOfQty
  FROM Inventories
```

This statement will perform a simple calculation to determine half the amount of inventory on hand for each product. To determine what this statement should return, let's first assume that the `Inventories` table contains the following records:

ProductID	StoreID	QtyOnHand
1003	3	5
1003	4	5
1003	5	0
1003	6	4
1001	4	15
1001	5	22
1002	9	1
1004	5	4
1005	3	1

You would expect that the results of this `SELECT` statement would return values such as 2.5, 2, 7.5, 11, 0.5, and so on. Surprisingly, this query returns the values 2, 2, 0, 2, 7, 11, 0, 2, and 0. The reason for this is because the `QtyOnHand` field is defined to contain only integer values and the value 2 found in the denominator is an integer. When the query engine determines the data type of the resulting column, it too will be an integer. Since integers can't hold any digits to the right of the decimal point, they are discarded.

To alleviate this problem, we must make sure that the value we are dividing by is a real number. To do this, we may use the CAST function:

```
SELECT QtyOnHand / CAST(2 AS float) AS HalfOfQty
  FROM Inventories
```

Although this statement does produce the correct results, there is a simpler and more efficient way to get the same result. All we need to do is make sure that the denominator is written explicitly as a real number:

```
SELECT QtyOnHand / 2.0 AS HalfOfQty
  FROM Inventories
```

Sorting Data

Unless we specify otherwise, the records returned from a SELECT statement will be displayed in their 'natural order'. This means that the records are displayed in the order in which the RDBMS found them. If the RDBMS allows for a table to be set up so that its records are saved in a particular sequence, then the returned records will also be presented in that sequence. Otherwise, the order of the records will be in an order determined by the RDBMS, and this order may even vary between SELECT statements.

If we wish to have the resulting records from a SELECT statement be presented in some specific order, we can add the ORDER BY clause to the SELECT statement. This clause allows you to specify some field or fields and/or some calculation that will be used to sort the results. Using our example above to select the recordings in order of release, we can add an ORDER BY clause to sort the results by the ReleaseDate field:

```
SELECT RecordingTitle, PublisherID, ReleaseDate
  FROM Recordings
 ORDER BY ReleaseDate
```

The records returned would be presented as:

RecordingTitle	PublisherID	ReleaseDate
Big Time	107	1987-06-21
Space I'm In	112	1991-05-23
Little Earthquakes	103	1991-10-02
Crucify	103	1992-03-21
Us	107	1992-09-29
Phenomenon Soundtrack	108	1996-08-23

As you can see, the data is presented in ascending order. If we wished to sort the results with the earliest release date first, we add the DESCENDING (or DESC) modifier:

```
SELECT RecordingTitle, PublisherID, ReleaseDate
  FROM Recordings
 ORDER BY ReleaseDate DESC
```

This query will return the following results:

RecordingTitle	PublisherID	ReleaseDate
Phenomenon Soundtrack	108	1996-08-23
Us	107	1992-09-29
Crucify	103	1992-03-21
Little Earthquakes	103	1991-10-02
Space I'm In	112	1991-05-23
Big Time	107	1987-06-21

We can explicitly state that sequencing is to be in ascending order by using `ASCENDING` (or `ASC`). Since ascending order is the default, unless you are sorting in descending order, there is little reason to include this modifier, except perhaps, to make the statements more clear about precisely what sorting is being used.

If two records possess the same value in the field used to sort by, you may include additional fields for sub-sorting, provided that each field is separated by a comma. Therefore, to get a listing of our `Recordings`, sorted by `PublisherID`, and then by `RecordingTitle`, we could use:

```
SELECT RecordingTitle, PublisherID, ReleaseDate
  FROM Recordings
 ORDER BY PublisherID, RecordingTitle
```

RecordingTitle	PublisherID	ReleaseDate
Crucify	103	1992-03-21
Little Earthquakes	103	1991-10-02
Big Time	107	1987-06-21
Us	107	1992-09-29
Phenomenon Soundtrack	108	1996-08-23
Space I'm In	112	1991-05-23

We can use both the `ASC` and `DESC` keywords when we are sorting by more than one column. By doing so, we can sort by one column in one direction, and then sub-sort rows in the other direction. For example, the following query will produce the same results, but all recordings from the same publisher will be sorted in descending order by `RecordingTitle`:

```
SELECT RecordingTitle, PublisherID, ReleaseDate
  FROM Recordings
 ORDER BY PublisherID ASC, RecordingTitle DESC
```

The resultset that this query produces is:

RecordingTitle	PublisherID	ReleaseDate
Little Earthquakes	103	1991-10-02
Crucify	103	1992-03-21
Us	107	1992-09-29
Big Time	107	1987-06-21
Phenomenon Soundtrack	108	1996-08-23
Space I'm In	112	1991-05-23

Obviously, the query engine will have to perform extra work to sort the results. This extra work may well cause significant reductions in performance if the resultset is large, so do not idly use the `ORDER BY` clause unless there is a good reason for returning the records in a particular order. When this clause is used, the query engine will attempt to utilize an appropriate index to sort the records faster, if an index is available. If you know that certain columns will be used frequently for sorting, you may consider creating indexes on those columns. However, even adding an index may not help in the end. Since indexes must be maintained when data is added, deleted, or changed, they incur a certain amount of overhead. By adding too many indexes, you may speed up your queries but slow down other activities in the database.

Try It Out – Sorting with the SELECT Statement

The owner of the Music Store would like to start sending promotional e-mail messages to their customers. They want to send these messages out in an order that is based upon the customer's postal code. For this marketing effort, they need a list of existing customers' first and last names, their e-mail addresses as well as their postal code. They also inform you that they wish to send e-mail messages to those customers with the highest postal codes first and lowest postal codes last. For all customers having the same postal code, they would like the list to be in alphabetical order by last name.

The resulting SQL statement should be:

```
SELECT CustomerPostalCode, CustomerFirstName, CustomerLastName, EmailAddress
  FROM Customers
 ORDER BY CustomerPostalCode DESC, EmailAddress ASC
```

This statement should produce results similar to the following illustration:

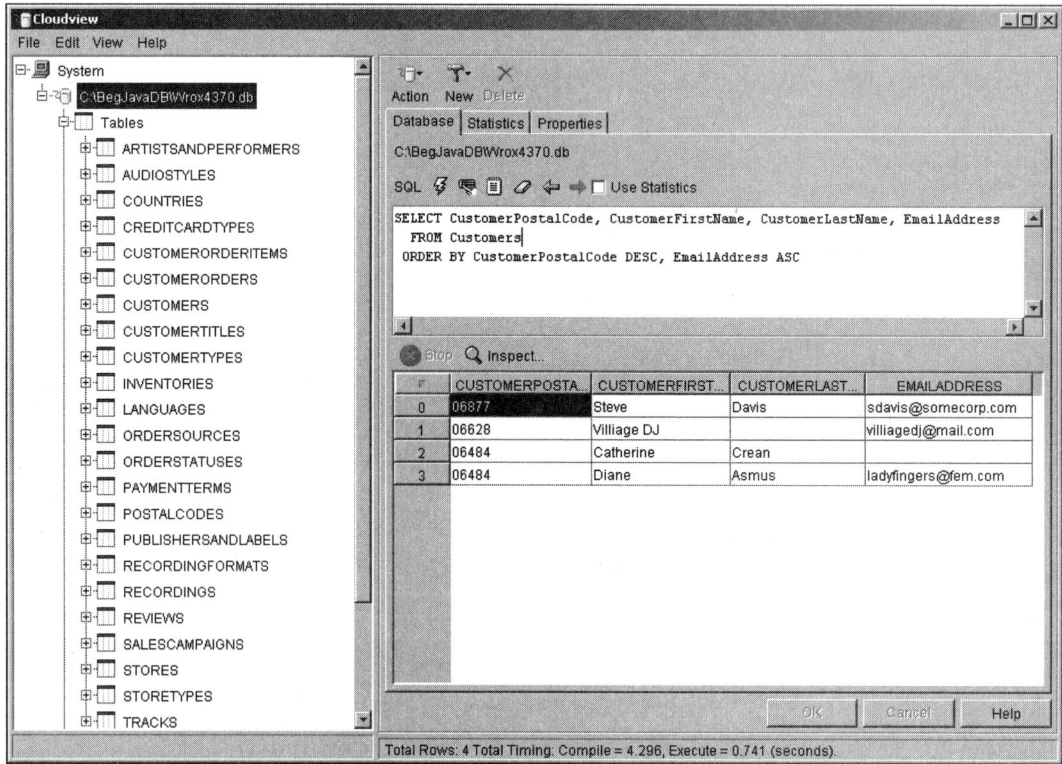

How It Works – Sorting with the SELECT Statement

The requirements for this query dictate that we display the customer's first and last name, as well as their postal code and their e-mail address. To do this, so we will need to include the `CustomerFirstName`, `CustomerLastName`, `EmailAddress`, and `PostalCode` from the `Customers` table. Therefore, the `FROM` clause is `FROM Customers`. The sequence of the rows in the result set must be in descending order, so we must use an `ORDER BY` clause that lists the `CustomerPostalCode` with the `DESC` keyword. Due to the requirement that we sort all records with the same postal code by the customer's last name, we will need to include in the `ORDER BY` clause the notation to sort by `CustomerLastName` *after* sorting by `CustomerPostalCode`.

Obtaining Only the First n Records

We can extend the idea of sorting our results to find out which of our recordings came out first, to make queries such as, 'Which are the three oldest `Recordings`?' Rather than having the query engine return all results, we can have only the required records returned. This is done by adding a modifier to the `SELECT` clause called a **predicate**.

The `TOP` *n* predicate may be added immediately after the `SELECT` keyword to restrict the result to the first *n* records. For example, this statement restricts the results to 3 records:

```
SELECT TOP 3 RecordingTitle, PublisherID, ReleaseDate
  FROM Recordings
 ORDER BY ReleaseDate
```

The records returned would be as follows:

RecordingTitle	PublisherID	ReleaseDate
Big Time	107	1987-06-21
Space I'm In	112	1991-05-23
Little Earthquakes	103	1991-10-02

These particular records are chosen because this resultset was ordered using `ORDER BY ReleaseDate`. If a different set columns were used in the `ORDER BY` clause, then the first records presented in that other sequence would be returned. For example, if we execute the same query as above, but using a sort order based on `PublisherID`, we would get:

RecordingTitle	PublisherID	ReleaseDate
Crucify	103	1992-03-21
Little Earthquakes	103	1991-10-02
Big Time	107	1987-06-21

There are a few other interesting comments on sorting that are worth mentioning. You can use the `TOP` predicate without an `ORDER BY` clause, but the records presented will not be in any particular order (unless the records are stored in a particular sequence). If you add a percent symbol (`%`) immediately after the number in the `TOP` predicate, you will limit the results to the top *n*`%` of the records processed. By using this version of the `TOP` predicate, you can construct queries that ask questions such as, 'Which students are in the top 10% of their class?', and 'Which products account for the top 15% of sales?'

Note that not all databases support the `TOP n` predicate.

Applying Conditions to a SELECT Statement

With most database applications, we often are more concerned with certain subsets of the data, rather than every record in a table. To restrict the data selection to particular records, we add the `WHERE` clause to the `SELECT` statement, which sets the criteria to be used to acquire records. The `WHERE` clause must immediately follow the `FROM` clause in the statement. For example, if we want to know which customers live in the city of Hartford, we could phrase the `SELECT` statement as:

```
SELECT CustomerLastName, CustomerFirstName
  FROM Customers
 WHERE CustomerCity = 'Hartford'
```

The database would scan through all records in the `Customers` table to find those that had a value of `Hartford` in the `City` column. From these records, only the values of each record's `CustomerLastName` and `CustomerFirstName` fields will be returned. Note that we use an apostrophe character to delineate text. Some RDBMSs also support the use of the quote double character, but you will hardly ever go wrong by using the apostrophe.

Cloudscape does not support the use of a quote character for delineating text. Instead, use an apostrophe.

If the data we are searching for includes an apostrophe, such as in the title of the album 'Space I'm In', we should use a pair of apostrophe characters to indicate a literal apostrophe in the string. For example:

```
SELECT *
  FROM Recordings
 WHERE RecordingTitle ='Space I''m In'
```

If we wish to construct a condition that references a numeric field, no delimiters are needed. If, for instance, we are asking, 'Which recordings are in Spanish?' and we know that the `Recordings` table will have a value of `2` in the `LanguageID` column for any recording that is in Spanish, we could write the SQL statement like this:

```
SELECT TOP 3 RecordingTitle
  FROM Recordings
 WHERE LanguageID = 2
```

When specifying the search criteria, SQL provides operators that are common to most other languages:

Operator	Meaning/Use
=	Equal to
>	Greater than
<	Less than
>=	Greater than or equal to
<=	Less than or equal to
<>	Not equal to
NOT	Boolean Negation
AND	Boolean And
OR	Boolean Or

In addition, many database systems will provide alternative notation for these operators that are not strictly the SQL standard. It is worth noting some of these operators since translating between the various dialects of SQL is commonplace:

Operator	Meaning
!	Not
!=	Not equal to
!<	Not less than
!>	Not greater than

Specifying Multiple Conditions

It is also possible to use more than one condition in our `SELECT` statements. To construct the question, 'How many copies of recording 1003 are in stock in Store 3?', we need to specify more than one condition in the `WHERE` clause. The first condition is that the recording must have a `ProductID` of 1003. The question specifically asks for the number of recordings for a specific store, so we need to add to the `WHERE` clause a second condition.

SQL allows the `AND`, and the `OR` operators, so that we can produce multiple conditions to be considered. In order to have the database return some statistic, we need to specify which statistic, and which column the statistic will describe. SQL supports the aggregate functions of `SUM`, `COUNT`, `AVERAGE`, `MIN`, and `MAX`. Therefore, the SQL statement equivalent to our earlier question might be phrased as the following:

```
SELECT SUM(QtyOnHand) AS TotalQty
  FROM Inventories
 WHERE ProductID = 1003 AND StoreID = 3
```

The result would contain a single column with a single value, since we are asking for a single statistic:

TotalQty
5

We can change the query to ask for the stock of two particular recordings. To do so, we would specify the `ProductID`s of the two recordings using an `OR` operator:

```
SELECT SUM(QtyOnHand) AS TotalQty
  FROM Inventories
 WHERE (ProductID = 1003 OR ProductID = 1005)
   AND StoreID = 3
```

The SQL language also provides a `NOT` operator so that we can exclude certain records. If we wanted to determine the quantity of stock for all products except for these two recordings, we can add a slight modification to our query:

```
SELECT SUM(QtyOnHand) AS TotalQty
  FROM Inventories
 WHERE NOT (ProductID = 1003 OR ProductID = 1005)
   AND StoreID = 3
```

It is sometime easier (and perhaps faster) to use Boolean algebra to rewrite statements that use `AND`s, `OR`s, and `NOT`s. When we need to construct a condition in the form (NOT *ConditionA* And NOT *ConditionB)* we can use **DeMorgan's Theorem** from the rules of sentential calculus to rewrite the condition as NOT (*ConditionA* OR *ConditionB).* Similarly, if we have a condition in the form (NOT *ConditionA* OR NOT *ConditionB),* it can be rewritten as NOT (*ConditionA* AND *ConditionB).* For example, if someone is not tall and thin then they are either short or fat (or both).

If we were asking for the stock levels of many different products, we can use an abbreviated notation when specifying the stock numbers. This is done using the `IN` operator. When using this operator, each value must be separated with a comma, and the entire set of acceptable values should be enclosed in parentheses:

```
SELECT SUM(QtyOnHand) AS TotalQty
  FROM Inventories
 WHERE ProductID IN (1003,1005)
```

Most database systems will internally convert a `WHERE` clause that uses the `IN` operator into a `WHERE` clause that uses a series of `OR` operators. The time required for this conversion is not great, but extra time *is* required. Therefore, to increase performance, consider using the `OR` operator rather than the `IN` operator when you know in advance what values you are searching for.

We may also use the `NOT` operator together with the `IN` operator. By using the two operators together, we can select all records except those contained in a defined set. For example, consider the following statement that provides the sum of the quantities on hand for all products except those with certain `ProductIDs`:

```
SELECT SUM(QtyOnHand) AS TotalQty
  FROM Inventories
 WHERE ProductID NOT IN (1003,1005)
```

If we again wanted to ask a similar question to before, but include all recordings that have a `ProductID` between 1003 and 1005, we could use the following statement that utilizes inequality operators to limit the range of `ProductIDs`:

```
SELECT Sum(QtyOnHand) AS TotalQty
  FROM Inventories
 WHERE (ProductID >= 1003 AND ProductID <= 1005)
```

As an alternative to specifying an upper and lower bound for the `ProductID` field by using inequality operators, SQL provides the `BETWEEN` statement. This statement still requires that upper and lower bounds be specified. For example, we could rewrite the above query as follows:

```
SELECT Sum(QtyOnHand) AS TotalQty
  FROM Inventories
 WHERE ProductID BETWEEN 1003 AND 1005
```

Notice that we get the same results, because `BETWEEN` is inclusive of the values specified.

As with using the `IN` operator, when processing the query, most database systems will convert bounds specified by the `BETWEEN` keyword into a pair of conditions using inequality operators and an `AND` operator. So, functionally they are equivalent but the `BETWEEN` operator takes a small amount of additional effort. For speed purposes, avoid using the `BETWEEN` operator if possible.

Try It Out – Selecting Records with the SELECT Statement

The owner of the music store would like a SQL statement that will display the track list for a recording, provided that the `RecordingID` of the recording is known. The listing should display each track's title and track number in the order it appears on the recording. For development purposes, use the value of 1005 for the `RecordingID`.

Based upon these requirements, the SQL statement should read:

```
SELECT TrackNumber, TrackTitle
  FROM Tracks
 WHERE RecordingID = 1005
 ORDER BY TrackNumber
```

This query should produce a resultset similar to that displayed here:

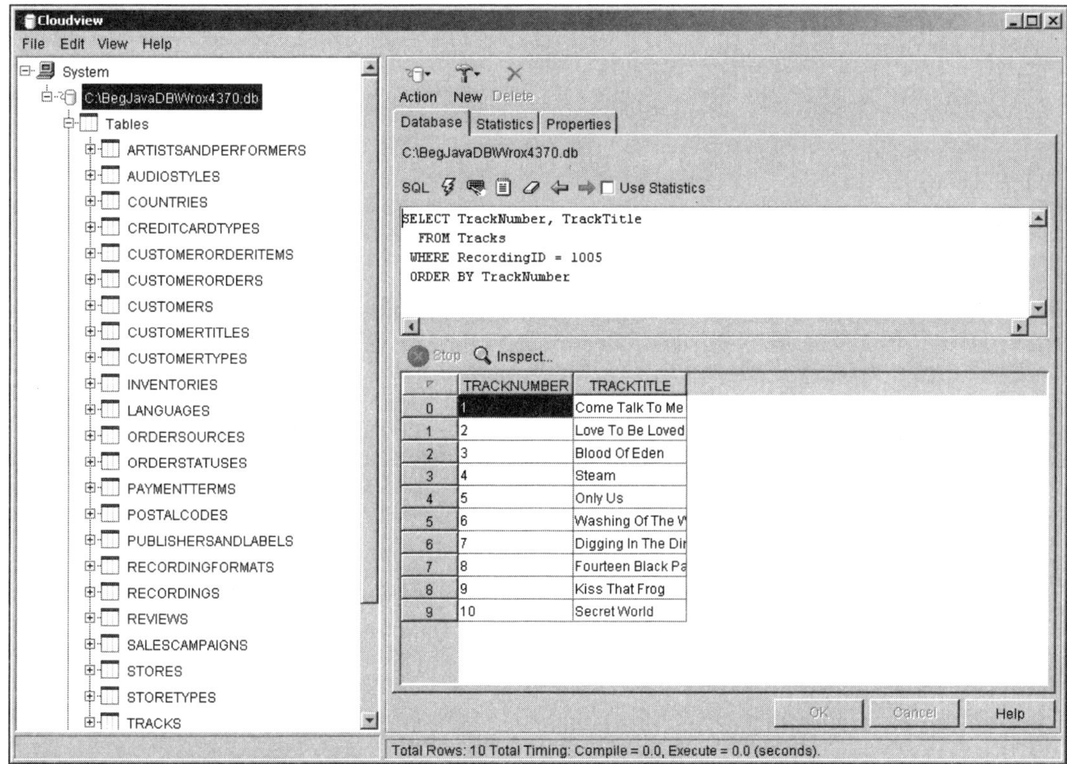

How It Works – Selecting Records with the SELECT Statement

Since the query will display information about tracks of recordings, we needed to include the table named `Tracks` in the `FROM` clause of our `SELECT` statement. We will need only to display the `TrackNumber` and `TrackTitle` fields in the select list. Due to the sequencing requirements, an `ORDER BY` clause specifying `TrackNumber` will be needed. Since we are limiting the tracks to only those of a specific recording, namely recording 1005, we will need to use a `WHERE` clause that restricts record selection to only those records with a `RecordingID` of 1005.

Fuzzy Searches

There is another interesting operator that may be used to select multiple records; the `LIKE` operator. This operator allows you to use wildcard characters for pattern-matching of strings. Such searches are often called **fuzzy searches**. Fuzzy searches are much more flexible than using the = and <> comparison operators.

Let's say we wanted to see the names of all artists whose names began with the letter `T`. To do this, we need to use a wildcard character with the `LIKE` keyword:

```
SELECT ArtistName
  FROM ArtistsAndPerformers
 WHERE ArtistName LIKE 'T%'
```

The percent sign (`%`) is used to represent any possible character (number, letter, or punctuation) or set of characters that might appear after the character `T`. This query returns the following:

ARTISTNAME
Toni Braxton
Taj Mahal
The Iguanas
Thomas Newman
Tori Amos

If we wanted to find all artists whose name started with `To` then we would need to use this `WHERE` clause:

```
SELECT ArtistName
  FROM ArtistsAndPerformers
 WHERE ArtistName LIKE 'To%'
```

which returns:

ARTISTNAME
Toni Braxton
Tori Amos

Notice the case used. In the above example, we explicitly used a capitalized `T`. This may, or may not, be required with the database system you are using. Case-sensitivity is often a configurable option with databases, so check your product's documentation.

In a similar fashion, we can use wildcards to search other parts of the data and not just the starting characters. For example, to restrict the selection to artists whose names end in `on`, we would use:

```
SELECT ArtistName
  FROM ArtistsAndPerformers
 WHERE ArtistName LIKE '%on'
```

which returns:

ArtistName
Toni Braxton
Eric Clapton

To return all artists that have the text The as part of their name, we would use the % wildcard character at the start and end of the text, like so:

```
SELECT ArtistName
  FROM ArtistsAndPerformers
 WHERE ArtistName LIKE '%The%'
```

which returns all records have The included anywhere in the artist's name:

ArtistName
Everything But The Girl
The Iguanas

It is interesting to note that this query returns The Iguanas, which has the text The at the start. Therefore, the first % specified represents a zero-length string.

Other characters may be used with the LIKE command for other pattern matching. The following table describes the characters that are common in most implementations of SQL:

Character(s)	Purpose	WHERE clause example
%	Any string of zero or more characters.	WHERE City LIKE '%new%' Finds all city names with the word new anywhere in the name (New Haven, Newtown, Old NewCastle, Agnew, and so on).
_ (underscore)	Any single character.	WHERE State LIKE 'C_' Finds all two-letter state abbreviations that starts with a C (CA, CO, CT, and so on).
[ ]	Any single character within the specified range ([a-f]) or set ([abcdef]).	WHERE Fname LIKE '[a-h]ean' Finds the first name of Dean but not Jean. WHERE Lname LIKE 'Sm[iy]th' Finds last names Smith and Smyth.
[^]	Any single character not within the specified range ([^a-f]) or set ([^abcdef]).	WHERE StockCode LIKE '[^k-m]%' Finds all product codes that do not begin with a k, l, or m.

There are some important performance considerations when using pattern matching. If the column we are scanning is indexed, the query engine of most RDBMSs will use the index with the LIKE operation such as:

```
LIKE Lname='smith'
```

or:

```
LIKE Lname='smith%'
```

However, if we look for these two operations, the index will not be used and therefore performance will suffer. This is fairly sensible behavior, since the index won't be much use if we have a wildcard at the start of our search term.

Special Considerations for Null Values

Most RDBMSs will store a special value called a **Null value** when the data is unknown or unavailable. Null values should not be confused with a zero (which is a legitimate number), a zero-length string (a string data type with no characters), or the space character. The SQL-3 standard defines a Null as:

> *... a special value that is used to indicate the absence of any data value...*

Null values are usually ignored when using aggregate functions such as MIN, MAX, or AVG as well as when including a WHERE clause that searches for specific values. In fact, many RDBMSs will not allow you to use a WHERE clause that specifies a Null value for a field. For example, the following would produce an error under Cloudscape:

```
SELECT *
  FROM Tracks
 WHERE SampleFilespec = Null
```

This can pose a problem for us when we need to find fields with Null values. Fortunately, we have a couple of options to get around this. Let's take a look at these.

Handling Nulls

The way we get around this issue with Null entries is to either use a function that converts Null values to some other value, or use some function specifically made to check for a Null. Almost universally supported amongst RDBMSs, the IS function may be used.

To select records based upon a field being Null, simply use the following syntax in the WHERE clause:

```
WHERE fieldname IS Null
```

Using this function, we can modify the above example to make a more efficient SQL statement that will achieve the same results:

```
SELECT *
  FROM Tracks
 WHERE SampleFilespec IS Null
```

We may also detect when a value isn't Null. To do this we simply use the NOT operator with IS, such as:

```
SELECT *
  FROM Tracks
 WHERE SampleFilespec IS NOT Null
```

The SQL-3 standard defines a **Null-call function** that is a SQL-invoked function defined to return the Null value if any of its input arguments is the Null value. The exact functions to use may differ from RDBMS to RDBMS, so you should consult the documentation. For example, Microsoft SQL Server 2000 provides a Null-call function named `ISNULL`.

The `ISNULL` function is used to substitute Null values with other values. Its syntax is:

```
ISNULL(check_expression, replacement_value)
```

This function will only substitute the *`replacement_value`* for the *`check_expression`* if the *`check_expression`* is Null. Otherwise, the value of the *`check_expression`* is returned. Here is an example to illustrate this function:

```
SELECT *
  FROM Tracks
 WHERE ISNULL(SampleFilespec, 'n/a') = 'n/a'
```

Using Groupings with Statistical Functions

As we have seen, SQL provides a number of aggregate functions that are used to calculate statistics from our data. Although we can use a `WHERE` clause in the `SELECT` statement to limit the rows used to compute the statistics, it is more common that we compute these statistics on collections of our data. If we needed to find the total sales for each of a number of stores, we could approach this by issuing one query for each store.

A more efficient approach is to issue a single query that groups the records based upon the different stores, and then calculates the required statistics on each group. To cause the `SELECT` statement to group similar records, we use the `GROUP BY` clause along with instructions on how the database query should organize the selected records.

To see how this works, let's assume that we have the following `Inventories` table:

ProductId	StoreId	QtyOnHand
1003	3	5
1003	4	5
1003	5	0
1003	6	4

Table continued on following page

ProductId	StoreId	QtyOnHand
1001	4	15
1001	5	22
1002	9	1
1004	5	4
1005	3	1

To find out the quantity of products on hand from each store, try this SQL statement:

```
SELECT StoreID, Sum(QtyOnHand) AS TotalQuantity
  FROM Inventories
 GROUP BY StoreID
 ORDER BY StoreID
```

This query produces:

StoreId	Total Quantity
3	6
4	20
5	26
6	4
9	1

As we saw earlier, we can request multiple statistics in a single query. To compute the total and average quantities on hand for all stores, we could use:

```
SELECT
  StoreID,
  Sum(QtyOnHand) AS TotalQuantity,
  Avg(QtyOnHand) AS AverageQuantity
  FROM Inventories
 GROUP BY StoreID
 ORDER BY StoreID
```

which returns:

StoreId	TotalQuantity	AverageQuantity
3	6	3
4	20	10
5	26	8
6	4	4
9	1	1

If the ORDER BY clause is not specified, groups returned using the GROUP BY clause are not in any particular order. Due to this fact, you will usually use the ORDER BY clause to specify a particular ordering of the data when the GROUP BY clause is used. As was mentioned above, the query engine will have to perform extra work to sort the results and cause a hit to performance. Therefore, do not idly use the ORDER BY clause unless there is a good reason for returning the records in a particular order.

Fields Restrictions with GROUP BY

There are some important comments to mention when using the GROUP BY clause. Any field listed in the SELECT clause that is not used in an aggregate function must be listed in the GROUP BY clause. Therefore, the first of the following statements would be legal, while the second statement would not:

```
SELECT
  ArtistID,
  RecordingId,
  Count(TrackNumber) AS TotalQuantity
  FROM tracks
 GROUP BY ArtistID, RecordingId
 ORDER BY ArtistID, RecordingId
```

```
SELECT
  ArtistID,
  RecordingId,
  Count(TrackNumber) AS TotalQuantity
  FROM tracks
 GROUP BY ArtistID
 ORDER BY ArtistID
```

This second statement would produce an error message. The error message itself will differ, from database to database. Here are a couple of examples of the error messages that you might see.

From Cloudscape 3.6:

```
Database access resulted in SQL exception:
SQLState , Error code 30000, Message:
Column reference 'RecordingId' is invalid. For a SELECT with a GROUP BY, the
SELECT list may only contain grouping columns and valid aggregate expressions.
```

From Microsoft SQL Server 2000:

```
Server: Msg 8118, Level 16, State 1, Line 1
Column 'RecordingID' is invalid in the select list because it is not contained in
either an aggregate function or the GROUP BY clause.
```

Using HAVING with GROUP BY

You may include a search condition for a group by adding the `HAVING` clause to the `SELECT` statement. The `HAVING` clause acts like a `WHERE` clause, but for the grouped records. The `HAVING` clause is used to determine which groups of records will be returned.

To understand how the `HAVING` clause is used, consider the following data:

CountryName	Region	PercentGrowthRate
USA	North America	9
Canada	North America	8
Mexico	North America	4
Egypt	Middle East	1
Saudi Arabia	Middle East	3
Taiwan	Asia	6
India	Asia	3
Australia	Pacific	7
Philippines	Pacific	2
UK	Europe	7
France	Europe	6
Spain	Europe	5
Germany	Europe	5

We can compute the average `PercentGrowthRate` for each region:

```
SELECT
  Region,
  AVG(PercentGrowthRate) As AvergeGrowthRate
  FROM Performance
 GROUP BY Region
```

Region	AverageGrowthRate
North America	7.00
Middle East	2.00
Asia	4.50
Pacific	4.50
Europe	5.75

Let's assume that we want to find out the names of those regions and their average growth rates of those regions that have at least a 5% average growth. To accomplish this, we need to first compute what the average growth rate is for each of the regions. Only after we know each region's average growth rate can we determine which regions will be included in our resultset. The query used to produce the desired results would use a GROUP BY clause to first compute the average growth rate and also use a HAVING clause to filter out those unwanted regions:

```
SELECT
  Region,
  AVG(PercentGrowthRate) As AvergeGrowthRate
  FROM Performance
 GROUP BY Region
HAVING
  AVG(PercentGrowthRate) > 5.0
```

WHERE vs. HAVING

It is common for people to confuse the use of the WHERE and HAVING clauses. This is understandable since both are used to reduce the number of rows that are returned, but there is a fundamental difference between these two clauses that is important to understand.

This difference is that the WHERE clause selects *rows* from the table (or some other supplier of rows, such as a view) whereas the HAVING clause selects *groups* that have been constructed from those original rows. This means that the elimination of rows from the HAVING clause will occur *after* the WHERE clause has processed.

To illustrate the use of the HAVING clause with a WHERE clause, let's step through what happens to produce the resultset for the following query:

```
SELECT
  ArtistId,
  RecordingId,
  COUNT(TrackNumber) AS CountOfTracks
  FROM Tracks
 WHERE ArtistId IN (107, 109, 111)
 GROUP BY ArtistId, RecordingId
HAVING COUNT(TrackNumber) <= 5
 ORDER BY ArtistId, RecordingId
```

First, let's look at what the query would produce without using either the WHERE or HAVING clauses (as the following query demonstrates):

```
SELECT
  RecordingId,
  ArtistId,
  COUNT(TrackNumber) AS CountOfTracks
  FROM Tracks
 GROUP BY RecordingId, ArtistId
 ORDER BY RecordingId, ArtistId
```

which returns the following 16 rows:

RecordingID	ArtistID	CountOfTracks
1000	109	12
1001	111	1
1001	112	1
1001	113	1
1001	114	1
1001	115	1
1001	107	1
1001	116	1
1001	117	1
1001	118	1
1001	119	1
1001	120	1
1002	121	12
1003	121	5
1004	107	5
1005	107	10

Now let's consider the same query, but with using a `WHERE` clause to include only those tracks that were by artists with an `ArtistID` value of 107, 109, or 111:

```
SELECT
  RecordingId,
  ArtistId,
  COUNT(TrackNumber) AS CountOfTracks
  FROM Tracks
 WHERE ArtistId IN (107, 109, 111)
 GROUP BY ArtistId, RecordingId
 ORDER BY ArtistId, RecordingId
```

This generates a much smaller subset of rows:

RecordingID	Artist ID	CountOf Tracks
1001	107	1
1004	107	5
1005	107	10
1000	109	12
1001	111	1

Next, let's add the `HAVING` clause to the query:

```
SELECT
  ArtistId,
  RecordingId,
  COUNT(TrackNumber) AS CountOfTracks
  FROM Tracks
 WHERE ArtistId IN (107, 109, 111)
 GROUP BY ArtistId, RecordingId
HAVING COUNT(TrackNumber) <= 5
 ORDER BY ArtistId, RecordingId
```

As the RDBMS processes the query, it first produces a temporary resultset that contains the five records displayed above. Then the RDBMS uses the `HAVING` clause to examine each row of this temporary resultset and eliminates any row that did not have a `CountOfTracks` value that is five or less:

RecordingID	ArtistID	CountOf Tracks
1001	107	1
1004	107	5
1001	111	1

The important thing to note here is that the `WHERE` clause culls down the number of rows that are processed by the `GROUP BY` clause. It is only *after* the groups have been composed will the `HAVING` clause be applied.

It is interesting to note that although the same set of results often can be produced by using either a query with a `WHERE` clause or a query with a `HAVING` clause, there is a significant difference in the amount of work required to process the query. For example, the following query produces the same resultset as above:

```
SELECT
  ArtistId,
  RecordingId,
  COUNT(TrackNumber) AS CountOfTracks
  FROM Tracks
 GROUP BY ArtistId, RecordingId
HAVING
```

```
   COUNT(TrackNumber) <= 5 and (ArtistId IN (107, 109, 111))
  ORDER BY ArtistId, RecordingId
```

This second query takes much longer to process than our original query since every record in the table is first grouped before the final resultset is determined. In the original query, the WHERE clause greatly reduced the number of records that were created to begin with, so that the HAVING clause had less to process.

Try It Out – Using Groups

In this example, the owner of the Music Store wants to be able to determine the total inventory levels at each of their locations, in other words, the total number of recordings at each location. We will develop a single SQL statement that will display the total number of recordings for each location.

This is the SQL statement we should use to satisfy the requirements:

```
SELECT StoreID, SUM(QtyOnHand) AS TotalOnHand
  FROM Inventories
 GROUP BY StoreID
```

This query should produce results similar to the following:

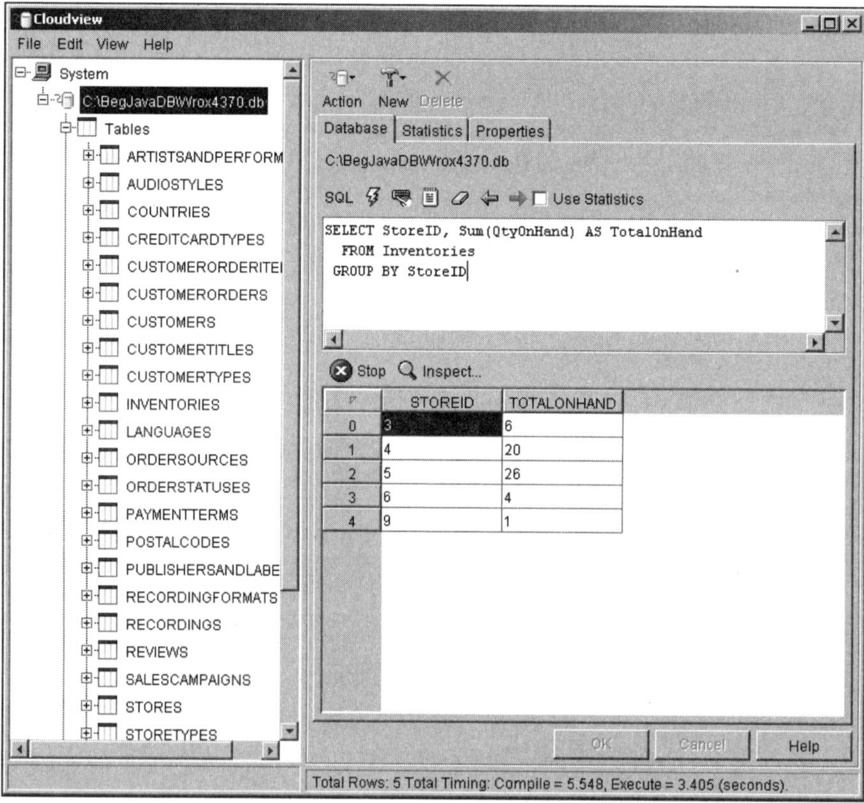

How It Works – Using Groups

The required query needs to determine the number of recordings, so it obtains records from the `Inventories` table. Since we are to determine a value for each location, we will need to include the `StoreID` field in the `SELECT` list, as well as in the `GROUP BY` clause. Since we are to compute the total number of recordings, we will need to use the aggregate function, `SUM`.

Queries Using Multiple Tables

It is a commonplace need to draw information from more than one table. When we specify more than one table in a `SELECT` statement, it is said that the tables are being **joined**.

Typically, in order for two tables to be joined, they need to share some common information. For instance, the `Customers` table may include such fields as `Name`, `Address`, `PostalCode`, and a `PostalCodes` table may contain the fields `PostalCode`, `City`, and `State`. Each table holds a `PostalCode` field that may be used to relate the two tables. In this case, the `PostalCode` field in the `Customers` table is a foreign key that references the primary key of the `PostalCodes` table, which is the `PostalCode` field. When you query against two tables, the database's query engine may not know implicitly which columns should be used for the join. When you construct the query, you must explicitly state which tables are being used and which fields hold the common information.

The data model used in our Music Store database uses two tables for storing orders from customers. The first table, `CustomerOrders`, holds information about when the order was made and who placed it, but not what items were ordered. Since any given order may be for more than one item, the items ordered are stored in a related table called `CustomerOrderItems`, as the following illustration shows:

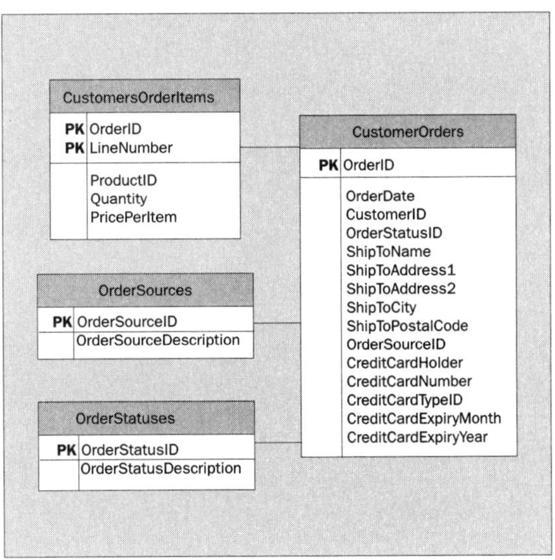

In order to get a listing of each order and the items contained in that order, we need to join the two tables. The common field to relate these tables together is the `OrderID` column. Therefore, our query would look something like the following:

```
SELECT
  CustomerOrders.OrderID,
  CustomerOrders.OrderDate,
  CustomerOrderItems.ProductID,
  CustomerOrderItems.Quantity,
  CustomerOrderItems.PricePerItem,
  Total = CustomerOrderItems.Quantity * CustomerOrderItems.PricePerItem
  FROM
  CustomerOrders INNER JOIN CustomerOrderItems
    ON
      (CustomerOrders.OrderID =
       CustomerOrderItems.OrderID)
```

Notice that the `FROM` clause now lists the names of the two tables being joined along with the keywords `INNER` and `JOIN` and an `ON` operator that specifies the columns from each table used for referencing. Both tables have a field named `OrderID`, so in the `SELECT` clause of the statement, we need to explicitly state from which table the `OrderID` value would be drawn. If a field used in the query is unique between the two tables, you don't need to explicitly specify the table name. Therefore our SQL code becomes a bit simpler to read:

```
SELECT
  CustomerOrders.OrderID,
  OrderDate,
  ProductID,
  Quantity,
  PricePerItem,
  Total = Quantity * PricePerItem
  FROM
  CustomerOrders INNER JOIN CustomerOrderItems
    ON
      (CustomerOrders.OrderID =
       CustomerOrderItems.OrderID)
```

Often the two tables will have fields that use the same name, so having to type in the table name frequently can become arduous. To further simplify the query, we could use aliases for the tables:

```
SELECT
  CO.OrderID,
  OrderDate,
  ProductID,
  Quantity,
  PricePerItem,
  Total = Quantity * PricePerItem
  FROM
  CustomerOrders AS CO
    INNER JOIN CustomerOrderItems AS COI
  ON (CO.OrderID = COI.OrderID)
```

Most RDBMSs will allow you to simply use the keyword `JOIN` and assume an inner join.

Alternative Syntax for Inner Joins

It should be noted that this syntax of using the keyword `JOIN` and the `ON` operator was introduced with SQL-2. Some RDBMSs that have been around for a while may still have code that uses the pre-SQL-2 syntax. In addition, some of us will still need to work with much older RDBMSs, so knowing how this older syntax is used is worthwhile. This older syntax does not use the `JOIN` keyword and simply lists each table to be referenced in the `FROM` clause, separated by a comma with the `JOIN` condition being presented in the `WHERE` clause:

```
SELECT
  CO.OrderID,
  OrderDate,
  ProductID,
  Quantity,
  PricePerItem,
  Total = Quantity * PricePerItem
FROM
  CustomerOrders AS CO,
  CustomerOrderItems AS COI
WHERE
  CO.OrderID = COI.OrderID
```

This syntax works by first performing a join between the two tables, matching each record in the first table with every record in the second. Next, the `WHERE` clause filters out all records that do not have matching `OrderID` fields.

Since this approach requires that every record in each table is joined, the database requires quite a bit of extra resources to process the information, which often results in slower performance. If your RDBMS supports both versions of the syntax, you should test each version to see which one provides the best performance. There is often a significant difference in speed between the two versions, and usually, the newer `JOIN...ON` syntax is substantially faster.

How Inner Joins Work

Regardless of the syntax used, the process of joining tables is conceptually the same. When performing the join described above, only those records that have an `OrderID` value found in both tables will be presented in the results. To better understand how inner joins work, consider the following sample tables and a `SELECT` statement that queries both of them:

TableA		**TableB**	
ColumnA1	**ColumnA2**	**ColumnB1**	**ColumnB2**
1	A	A	Blue
2	A	B	Green
3	C	C	Yellow

Table continued on following page

4	D	D	Black
5	A	F	Orange
6	H	G	White
7	A	I	Red
8	Null		

```
SELECT *
  FROM TableA JOIN TableB
  ON (TableA.ColumnA2 = TableB.ColumnB1)
```

The above syntax works on Cloudscape as it is. However, for a version of the syntax that works on Oracle, we can use the following SQL statement for the same results:

```
SELECT *
  FROM TableA, TableB
 WHERE TableA.ColumnA2 = TableB.ColumnB1;
```

As the query engine processes the query, it starts with the first table listed in the statement, in this case `TableA`. The first record of `TableA` is referenced and the value of its `ColumnA2` field is sought in `ColumnB1` field of `TableB`. Since the value, `A` is found in both of the joining columns, the first record of the resultset is determined:

ColumnA1	ColumnA2	ColumnB1	ColumnB2
1	A	A	Blue

Now the second record in `TableA` is referenced and the value of its `ColumnA2` field is looked for in `TableB`. Again, a match is found and a new record for the resultset is generated:

ColumnA1	ColumnA2	ColumnB1	ColumnB2
1	A	A	Blue
2	A	A	Blue

This process continues with the third, fourth, and fifth records of `TableA` to produce the following:

ColumnA1	ColumnA2	ColumnB1	ColumnB2
1	A	A	Blue
2	A	A	Blue
3	C	C	Yellow
4	D	D	Black
5	A	A	Blue

When the sixth record of TableA is referenced, a corresponding record is not found in TableB since no record in TableB has a value of H in ColumnB1. With the lack of a matching record in TableB, the query engine skips this sixth record in TableA and the resultset is not added to.

The process continues with the seventh record in TableA, matching to it a record in TableB, and adding a new record into the resultset. When the eighth record of TableA is processed, we again cannot find a match in TableB, so this record is also discarded. The result displayed will be the following:

ColumnA1	ColumnA2	ColumnB1	ColumnB2
1	A	A	Blue
2	A	A	Blue
3	C	C	Yellow
4	D	D	Black
5	A	A	Blue
7	A	A	Blue

Notice that not just the records from TableA were discarded; three records in TableB were also ignored. This is again due to the behavior of inner joins to select only the records that are common between the two tables.

Try It Out – Queries that Join Tables

The owner of the Music Store would like to enhance the SQL statement created earlier, which displays the track list for a recording, provided that its RecordingID is known. This new query should still display each track's title and track number in the order the track appears on the recording. What is different with this query is that it must also display the recording's title. As before, for development purposes, use the value of 1005 for the RecordingID.

The resulting SQL statement should be similar to:

```
SELECT R.RecordingID, R.RecordingTitle, T.TrackNumber, T.TrackTitle
  FROM Recordings As R INNER JOIN Tracks As T
    ON R.RecordingID = T.RecordingID
 WHERE R.RecordingID = 1005
 ORDER BY T.TrackNumber
```

This query returns results similar to the following:

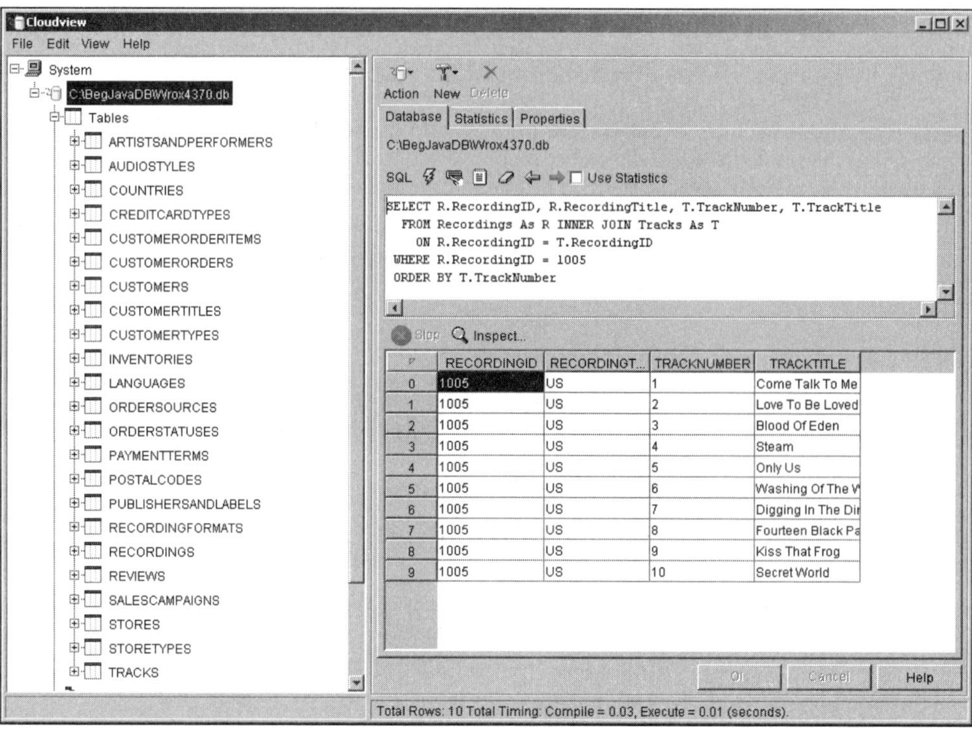

How It Works

As with the first version of this query, the track information will be provided by the `Tracks` table. To obtain the title of the recording, we will need to reference the `Recordings` table. The `RecordingID` field exists in both tables and should be used for the `JOIN` condition in the query.

Cross Joins

Cross joins, also called **Cartesian joins**, are joins that combine every record from one table with every record of a second table.

The syntax for the SQL-2 and later standards is much like the inner join, except you use the keyword `CROSS` rather than `INNER`, and you do not specify which fields to join by. Without a `JOIN` condition specifying how the records in the two tables are to be matched, any record from the first table may be matched with any record in the second table. For example:

```
SELECT * FROM TableA CROSS JOIN TableB
```

When you use the pre-SQL-2 syntax for joins using a `WHERE` clause, you are actually performing a cross join and then filtering the resulting records using the condition set in the `WHERE` clause. This means that you may also use this pre-SQL-2 syntax for cross joins:

```
SELECT * FROM TableA, TableB
```

As with inner joins, this is the syntax to use with Oracle.

How Cross Joins Work

To see how cross joins work, let's assume that `TableA` and `TableB` contain the following fields and values:

TableA	**TableB**
ColumnFromA	**ColumnFromB**
1	A
2	B
3	C
4	

Executing the query:

```
SELECT * FROM TableA CROSS JOIN TableB
ORDER BY ColumnFromA, ColumnFromB
```

would produce records that were every combination of records from the two source tables:

ColumnFromA	**ColumnFromB**
1	A
1	B
1	C
2	A
2	B
2	C
3	A
3	B
3	C
4	A
4	B
4	C

There are many situations where a cross join is needed. For example, a clothing retailer may need to associate each item with all available sizes or colors. If the retailer has a table of item numbers (often called **SKUs**, for **S**tock **K**eeping **U**nit), and a table of colors, you can produce a resultset that shows every combination of SKUs and colors:

```
SELECT Inventory.SKU, Attributes.Color
FROM Inventory CROSS JOIN Attributes
```

Since each record from the first table is matched with every record in the second table, the number of records in the resultset will be equal to the number of records in the first table multiplied by the number of records from the second table. Therefore, in our above example, if there were 100 SKUs and 5 colors, the resultset would contain 500 records.

Since a combination of every record between the two tables will be generated, depending upon how many records are in each table, this type of join can produce a large number of resulting rows.

Outer Joins

There will be occasions when you need to obtain *all* records from one table and the matching records from the second table, if available. Such a join is called an **outer join**. There are three types of outer joins:

- **Right outer join**
- **Left outer join**
- **Full outer join**

Left Outer Join

Left joins work very much like inner joins except that all records in the first (left) table that meet the `WHERE` clause condition are returned, regardless of whether a matching record is found in the second (right) table. For example, if we were to issue the following SQL statement on our previous `TableA` and `TableB`, each with two columns:

```
SELECT *
  FROM TableA LEFT OUTER JOIN TableB
    ON (TableA.ColumnA2 = TableB.ColumnB1)
```

The resultset would be displayed as follows:

ColumnA1	ColumnA2	ColumnB1	ColumnB2
1	A	A	Blue
2	A	A	Blue
3	C	C	Yellow
4	D	D	Black
5	A	A	Blue
6	H	Null	Null
7	A	A	Blue
8	Null	Null	Null

Notice that when a matching record was not found in the right-side table, Null values are assigned.

Many RDBMSs, such as Microsoft's SQL Server, do not require the keyword `OUTER`*. Other RDBMS, such as Cloudscape require that this keyword is explicitly mentioned.*

Right Outer Join

Right outer joins work exactly as do left outer joins, except that all records from the right-side table are returned, and values from the left table are provided if a matching record is found. The following SQL statement:

```
SELECT *
  FROM TableA RIGHT OUTER JOIN TableB
    ON (TableA.ColumnA2 = TableB.ColumnB1)
```

returns the following resultset:

ColumnA1	ColumnA2	ColumnB1	ColumnB2
1	A	A	Blue
2	A	A	Blue
5	A	A	Blue
7	A	A	Blue
Null	Null	B	Green
3	C	C	Yellow
4	D	D	Black
Null	Null	F	Orange
Null	Null	G	White
Null	Null	I	Red

Full Outer Join

A full outer join acts like a double-ended left and right join. All records from both tables are returned (assuming they meet the `WHERE` clause requirement) and Null values are used for columns where a matching record was not found. Full outer joins are relatively uncommon, but under certain circumstances, provide a convenient way to select results that you might otherwise have to add a significant amount of additional code to produce.

Take, for instance, the situation where you are assigning players to teams. You want to make sure that every player is assigned to a team and that every team has players assigned to it. To determine the current player assignments, you could perform a series of queries, including one query to find out which team each player was assigned to, and a second to find out which players have been assigned to each team. Then, you would need to compare these two resultsets. This process could get somewhat complicated and require your application to run additional algorithms to verify the assignments of players and teams. As an alternative, full outer joins may be used as a relatively easy and complete solution.

To illustrate how full outer joins work, let's see what results from the following query:

```
SELECT *
  FROM TableA FULL OUTER JOIN TableB
    ON (TableA.ColumnA2 = TableB.ColumnB1)
```

Like left joins, all records from the left table, `TableA`, will be represented in the resultset. Similarly, like right joins, all records from the right table, `TableB`, will also be represented. If any record in `TableA` does not have a corresponding record in `TableB`, the columns that `TableB` provides will have Null values. Similarly, if any record in `TableB` does not have a corresponding record in `TableA`, the columns that `TableA` provides will have Null values. The result of our query will produce:

ColumnA1	ColumnA2	ColumnB1	ColumnB2
1	A	A	Blue
2	A	A	Blue
3	C	C	Yellow
4	D	D	Black
5	A	A	Blue
6	H	Null	Null
7	A	A	Blue
8	Null	Null	Null
Null	Null	B	Green
Null	Null	F	Orange
Null	Null	G	White
Null	Null	I	Red

Alternative Syntax for Outer Joins

As with inner joins, you may use an alternative syntax for outer joins. It is important to recognize this alternative syntax, due to the number of older applications that use it.

Like the older syntax for inner joins, the old syntax for outer joins lists in the `FROM` clause each table to be referenced, and the `JOIN` condition is presented in the `WHERE` clause. What differs with the outer join syntax is that rather than using an equals sign as the comparison operator in the `WHERE` clause, use += for left outer joins and =+ for right outer joins.

The following are examples of outer joins using the pre-SQL-2 syntax. First is the left outer join:

```
SELECT *
  FROM TableA, TableB
 WHERE TableA.ColumnA2 += TableB.ColumnB1
```

and then the right outer join:

```
SELECT *
  FROM TableA, TableB
 WHERE TableA.ColumnA2 =+ TableB.ColumnB1
```

Try It Out – Using Outer Joins

The owner of the Music Store would like to keep track of how many items have been removed from inventory for each store. Each store in the company should be listed in this query, regardless of whether the store had any change in inventory levels. Also, the query should display each store's description and ID in addition to the number of items sold.

In this case, we can use the following SQL statement:

```
SELECT S.StoreID, S.StoreDescription, Sum(COI.Quantity) As QtySold
  FROM Stores AS S LEFT OUTER JOIN CustomerOrderItems AS COI
    ON S.StoreID = COI.ProvidingStore
 GROUP BY S.StoreID, S.StoreDescription
```

which produces the following resultset:

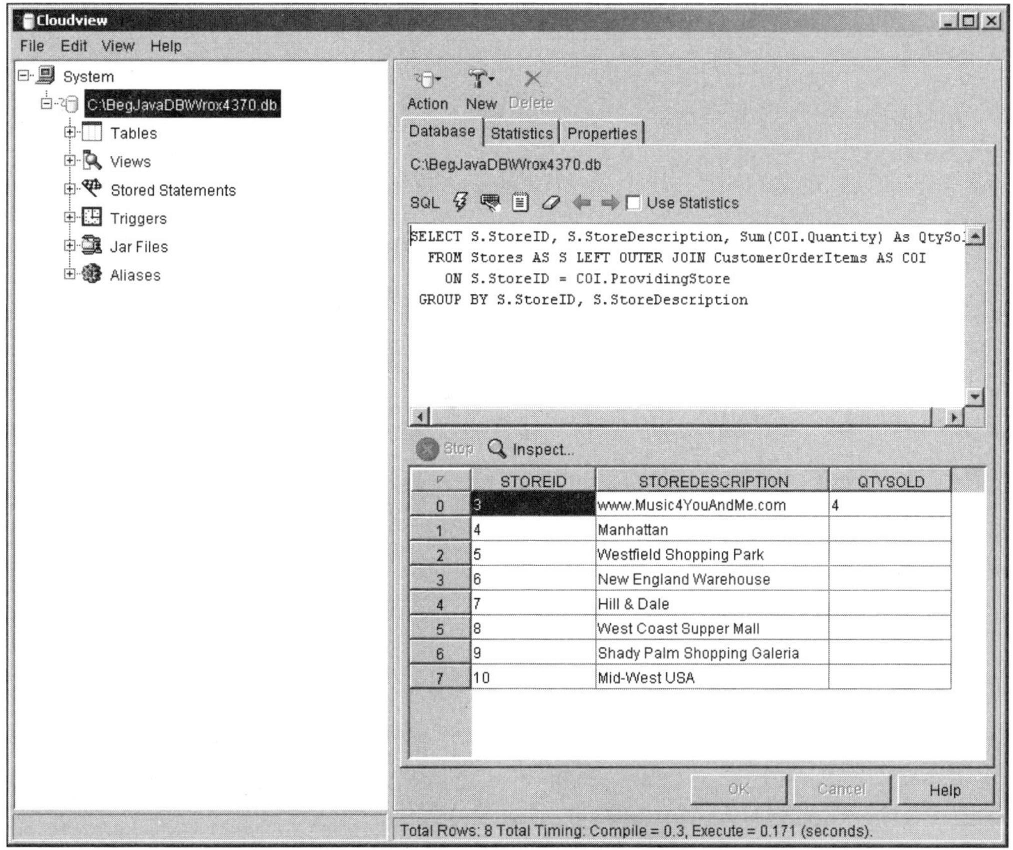

How It Works

The first requirement for this query is that it must count the number of items sold by each store. Therefore we need to use the SUM function in a grouping and reference the CustomerOrderItems table. Since the fields to be listed include the store's description, we also need to reference the Stores table. We must list each store, regardless if they had any sales, so we will need to perform a left join with the 'left table' being Stores. These two tables both contain the StoreID field, so we can use that field for our JOIN condition.

Using Dynamic Tables

When we use the FROM clause of a SELECT statement, what we are doing is identifying the source of the records for the query. We generally think of these sources as being tables, but they need not be. Views may be used just as tables are in most queries, and are often used for security purposes. As we know, views are objects that are defined with SQL statements to acquire data for us on the fly. If we can use dynamically acquired data from a view, why can't we use it from other sources that produce sets of records?

There are many situations where the information that you need to use is not found in any particular table, such as when you need to query against the results of a prior query. You could take the approach of issuing one query and saving the results in a table, then issuing a second query and saving those results as well, and then performing a third query that joins the first two tables. Not only is this inefficient (especially if done from the client side), but there are timing issues as well. How accurate will your data be? What if someone makes changes to the data in between the time the first query is executed and the second? Most database systems allow you to **lock** these tables so that they can't be altered while you are issuing the series of queries. Unfortunately, by doing so, you risk impacting on other operations in the database.

One way to solve this problem is to use queries rather than tables in the FROM clause of the SELECT statement. SQL statements like these are considered a type of nested query (or sub-query) and the results produced by these nested queries are often referred to as **dynamic tables**.

Consider the following SQL code that calculates the fraction of sales for each store in the entire company:

```
SELECT A.ProvidingStore, A.SalesForStore/B.SalesForFirm
    AS FractionOfSales
  FROM (SELECT ProvidingStore,
               SUM(Quantity*PricePerItem)
            AS SalesForStore
          FROM CustomerOrderItems
         GROUP BY ProvidingStore
       ) AS A
  CROSS JOIN
    (SELECT
          SUM(Quantity*PricePerItem)
         AS SalesForFirm
       FROM CustomerOrderItems
    ) AS B
ORDER BY A.ProvidingStore
```

This query computes the total sales for each store, as well as for all stores combined. The first sub-query calculates the store-by-store sales, therefore generating a dynamic table with as many rows as we have stores with sales. The second sub-query produces a single row dynamic table that represents the total sales for all stores. Since this second dynamic table does not have a column that we can use for a `JOIN` condition, we need to perform a cross join. The result is that each store's total sales gets divided by the total sales for the company as a whole.

Summary

The defacto standard language for accessing database is SQL. When you construct an application that uses a database, it is almost a certainty that you will use SQL to access the database. In this chapter, we looked at the use of SQL statements to access and manipulate information contained within a database.

We have concentrated on the `SELECT` statement to gain access to information, and massage it into a form we require. We started off with the basic mechanics of the statement and then moved on to using it in conjunction with calculations, sorting, applying conditions, and grouping data.

In those actions, we needed to specify what records are to be acted upon, so we discussed using `JOIN` conditions in the `WHERE` clause of the `SELECT` statement. By using inner, left outer, right outer, full outer, and cross joins we have a great deal of power over what is selected and how information from different tables can be combined.

JAVA
Java

Creating Tables and Modifying Data with SQL

Having thoroughly investigated the power of SQL for data querying, it is now time to move on to discuss how we actually create, alter, and delete tables and other objects in the database, and how we can insert new rows into these tables, delete them or modify, existing rows.

The SQL command that allows us to work on the actual objects in a database (tables etc.) are the `CREATE`, `ALTER`, and `DROP` commands. These commands fall into that component of SQL known as **Data Definition Language** (**DDL**). Some of the database activities that can be performed with these commands mostly fall outside the jurisdiction of the developer, such as creating and managing the database itself, but others are a better fit for the role of the developer, including:

- Tables (including associated constraints)
- Indexes
- Sequences (in Oracle)
- Views
- Stored Procedures
- Triggers

In this chapter we will focus only on the first of the bullet points above, covering the later points as we delve deeper into database design over the coming two chapters.

After completing our discussion of DDL, we will move back into the realm of DML, and discuss how to add, delete and modify data in the table rows using the `INSERT`, `UPDATE`, and `DELETE` commands. Finally we cover transactional processing in brief. For a more detailed look at *Transactions* and related topics, refer to Chapter 14, later in the book.

Creating and Changing Tables Using SQL

All tables within a database must be created at some point. As the application is used, there may be a need to add to or change these tables. Most modern RDBMSs have easy to use utilities with nice graphical interfaces that make table creation and maintenance convenient. As easy-to-use as these utilities may be, there are many times that you need to create or alter tables with SQL, especially within stored procedures.

This section will cover how you can approach table generation and update through the use of SQL. As always, there are variations in notation and data types between RDBMSs, so you will need to check with your database vendor's documentation to confirm some of the specific syntax used here.

Creating Tables

The SQL **Data Definition Language** (**DDL**) provides the `CREATE TABLE` command for generating empty tables. Here is the most basic syntax:

```
CREATE TABLE tablename (
  columnName1 datatype
    {identity | null | not null}
  [, columnName2 ...]
)
```

The `CREATE TABLE` command in its most basic form allows us to create a table of a specific name, to identify the column names in the table, and to specify the type of data that each column will hold (the data type). Optionally, we can set limits on the size of the data that may be stored in a particular column.

Let's take a look at the basic `CREATE TABLE` command for the `Reviews` table in our Music Store database:

```
CREATE TABLE Reviews (
  ReviewID        INT NOT NULL,
  RecordingID     INT NOT NULL,
  ReviewerName    VARCHAR(40) NOT NULL,
  ReviewText      VARCHAR(5000),
  Rating          INT,
  ReviewDate      DATE NOT NULL
)
```

In the above statement, the `VARCHAR(40)` data type defines a variable length string that may contain up to 40 characters, while `VARCHAR(5000)` defines a variable length string of up to 5000 characters. `INT` and `DATE` specify integer and date/time data types, respectively.

The SQL-2 standard defined a limited number of data types. In the years since, additional data types have been widely adopted, although the names used for them differ slightly from RDBMS to RDBMS. The most common data types found are:

- `CHAR(x)` – A fixed length string of characters, where `x` is a number designating the number of characters. If the data to be saved has fewer characters than `x`, the data will be padded with spaces.
- `VARCHAR(x)` – A variable length string of characters, where `x` is a number designating the maximum number of characters allowed (maximum length) in the column.

- `INTEGER` – Integer values. These may be positive, negative, or zero, and the values do not store digits to the right of the decimal point.
- `DECIMAL(x, y)` or `NUMERIC(x, y)` – Real numbers, where `x` is the maximum length in digits of the decimal numbers in this column, and `y` is the maximum number of digits allowed after the decimal point. The maximum value of a `NUMERIC(4,2)` field would be `99.99`.
- `DATE` or `DATETIME` – A date column in an RDBMS-specific format.
- `BOOLEAN` – A column that can hold only two values; `TRUE` or `FALSE`.

Following is a table showing how the names of some of the common data types vary from database to database:

SQL-3 Data Type	Cloudscape	Oracle	Transact-SQL (SQL Server)	MS Access
BOOLEAN	boolean	number	Bit	Yes/No
BIT	bit	number	Bit	NA
INTEGER	integer	integer/ number	Int	Number/Integer
DECIMAL	decimal	number	Decimal	Number/Decimal
FLOAT	float or real	float	Float	Number/Single
DOUBLE PRECISION	float or real	number	Real	Number/Double
DATE	date	date	Datetime	Date/Time
CHAR	char	char	Char or nChar	Text
VARCHAR	varchar	varchar or varchar2	Varchar or nVarchar	Text

So, in an Oracle database, for example, our `CREATE TABLE` might look slightly different:

```
CREATE TABLE REVIEWS (
       REVIEWID            NUMBER NOT NULL,
       RECORDINGID         NUMBER NOT NULL,
       REVIEWERNAME        VARCHAR2(40) NOT NULL,
       REVIEWTEXT          VARCHAR2(3000) NULL,
       RATING              NUMBER NULL,
       REVIEWDATE          DATE NOT NULL
);
```

To make sure that our SQL code can be as widely used as possible, there are some general guidelines we should follow for names when creating a table. The name of the table should:

- Be less than 64 characters long
- Start with a letter
- Not contain spaces or most symbols

Some RDBMSs allow longer names or different symbols to be included, so you should consult your vendor's documentation for specifics. Still, if you keep your table names less than 64 characters long, and include only alphanumeric characters, your names will be acceptable to most RDBMSs.

When defining a table, in addition to declaring column names and data types, you may also declare other properties that specify data integrity restrictions. These additional properties include such things as check constraints, primary keys, foreign keys, and default values. In fact, we have already declared one special type of constraint in our `Reviews` table: the `NOT NULL` constraint.

This constraint simply specifies that a column cannot contain a Null value. If a column is defined as `NOT NULL` and a user attempts to load it with `NULL`, then the database will return an error. So, in our `Reviews` table the `ReviewID`, `RecordingID`, and `ReviewDate` columns all prohibit Null values from being saved in the column.

As mentioned above, we can also the `CREATE TABLE` command to include a variety of other constraints, such as primary key, foreign key and so on. Let's take a quick look at some of these now.

Primary Key Constraint

This constraint defines a column as the primary key. If a column is a designated as primary key then each row must have a unique value in this column. Here, we define the PK for our `Reviews` table:

```
CREATE TABLE Reviews (
  ReviewID       INT CONSTRAINT PK_ReviewID Primary key,
  RecordingID    INT NOT NULL,
  ReviewerName   VARCHAR(40) NOT NULL,
  ReviewText    VARCHAR(5000),
  Rating         INT,
  ReviewDate     DATE NOT NULL
)
```

The `CONSTRAINT` keyword is followed by the name of the constraint (`PK_ReviewID`) and the type of constraint.

Foreign Key Constraint

This constraint defines a column as a foreign key. When a column is defined as an FK, you will not be able to add a new row to a table without it pointing to an existing row in the table it references by the FK. Let's now look at how we establish this referential relationship between the `Reviews` table and the `Recordings` table:

```
CREATE TABLE Reviews (
  ReviewID       INT CONSTRAINT PK_ReviewID Primary key,
  RecordingID    INT CONSTRAINT FK_Reviews_Recordings REFERENCES Recordings,
  ReviewerName   VARCHAR(40) NOT NULL,
  ReviewText     VARCHAR(5000),
  Rating         INT,
  ReviewDate     DATE NOT NULL
)
```

We place a constraint on the `RecordingID` column of the `Reviews` table (called `FK_Reviews_Recordings`) and, using the `REFERENCES` keyword, specify that any value in this column must also exist in the PK of a parent table – in this case the `Recordings` table.

The CHECK Constraint

In order to demonstrate this constraint, suppose that the only people who were allowed to enter reviews into the database were Jenny and Paul. This is how that could be achieved:

```
CREATE TABLE Reviews (
  ReviewID        INT CONSTRAINT PK_ReviewID Primary key,
  RecordingID     INT NOT NULL,
  ReviewerName    VARCHAR(40) NOT NULL
      CONSTRAINT CHK_Reviewer CHECK (ReviewerName IN ('Jenny', 'Paul')),
  ReviewText      VARCHAR(5000),
  Rating          INT,
  ReviewDate      DATE NOT NULL
)
```

We create a `CHECK` constraint (called `CHK_Reviewer`) on the `ReviewerName` column, which uses the `IN` keyword to ensure that the column can contain one of only two possible values.

Default Values

If we do not enter a value for a column the database normally fills it with a `NULL`. We use the `DEFAULT` keyword to tell the database that, in an absence of an assigned value, it should use the default value instead:

```
CREATE TABLE Reviews (
  ReviewID        INT CONSTRAINT PK_ReviewID Primary key,
  RecordingID     INT NOT NULL,
  ReviewerName    VARCHAR(40) NOT NULL,
  ReviewText      VARCHAR(5000) DEFAULT 'Great Record',
  Rating          INT,
  ReviewDate      DATE NOT NULL
)
```

Altering Tables Using SQL

Sometimes, the original database design overlooked some item of data that needed to be stored nor after a time some business requirement changed. In these situations, you will need to change a table, either by adding or removing column, or by changing some of the properties of the table.

To make changes to table using SQL, we may use the `ALTER TABLE` command. The `ALTER TABLE` command is very similar to `CREATE TABLE`, and follows a very similar syntax. The same command is used to add, change, or delete objects (columns, constraints, and so on) in a table.

Many people use the `ALTER TABLE` command as a matter of course when defining various constraints on a table. They use the `CREATE TABLE` in a basic format, including only the `NOT NULL` constraint and, perhaps, any default values that are required. All other data integrity constraints are then added using the `ALTER TABLE` command. If you view the SQL script, which can be used to create the Music Store tables in Oracle, you will see that this is exactly the approach taken there (see Appendix A)

Adding New Columns and Deleting Columns

To add a new column to an existing table we can use the syntax:

```
ALTER TABLE table
  ADD newcolumnname <column_definition>
```

So, if our initial Reviews table did not have a Ratings column, then we could add one as follows:

```
ALTER TABLE Reviews
  ADD Ratings INT
```

Similarly, we can remove columns from a table:

```
ALTER TABLE table
  DROP columnname
```

Here is the SQL to remove the Ratings column:

```
ALTER TABLE Reviews
  DROP Ratings
```

There are similar approaches to changing the data type for a column and to add, remove, or alter constraints on columns, but such actions are more typically performed using one of the many graphical tools provided by the RDBMS.

Modifying Columns

Most of today's relational databases systems allow you to modify the definition of an existing column in a table. To do so, use the ALTER TABLE command, which has the general syntax of:

```
ALTER TABLE table
  ALTER COLUMN columnname
    <new_column_definition>
```

For example, the following will change the Ratings column so that Null values are not allowed:

```
ALTER TABLE Reviews
  ALTER COLUMN Ratings INT NOT NULL
```

The ALTER TABLE statement is one of the few SQL statements where you are likely to find differences in syntax from RDBMS to RDBMS. One noteworthy example of such a difference is that Cloudscape 3.6 uses the keyword MODIFY rather than the keywords ALTER COLUMN in the ALTER TABLE statement.

It is uncommon to find a recent RDBMS that does not support altering the definition of a column, but you may come across older systems that have this limitation. For those RDBMSs, follow the basic procedure outlined here:

1. Create a new table with the new column definition.
2. Use the INSERT command to copy the records from the old table to the new table.
3. Delete the old table using the DROP TABLE statement.
4. Rename the new table so that it uses the old table's name.

Adding Constraints

As we discussed in Chapter 5 on *Relational Database Design Concepts*, constraints define rules regarding the values allowed in columns. Constraints are the preferred mechanism for enforcing integrity. Widely supported constraint types allow us to define a column's behavior concerning Null values, uniqueness of data, and keys, as well as ways to limit which values may be stored. As with changing column definitions, the SQL command used is `ALTER TABLE`.

There are two types of constraints; those that act upon a single column, and those that act on multiple columns or the table itself. Having a column reject Null values is an example of a column-level constraint. The definition of a multi-column primary key is an example of a table-level constraint.

Column-level constraints are added when you define or modify the column, such as when you use the `CREATE TABLE` or `ALTER TABLE ADD COLUMN` statements. Table-level constraints are added using `ALTER TABLE ADD CONSTRAINT`.

The general syntax for altering a table to add a constraint is:

```
ALTER TABLE table
  ADD CONSTRAINT constraintname
    <constraint_type> <constraint_definition>
```

where `<constraint_type>` can be any one of the following:

- `CHECK`
- `PRIMARY KEY`
- `FOREIGN KEY`
- `UNIQUE`

Of course, the `<constraint_definition>` portion of the syntax will vary depending upon the type of constraint.

Adding a Primary Key

Working from our first basic definition of the `Reviews` table:

```
CREATE TABLE Reviews (
  ReviewID        INT NOT NULL,
  RecordingID     INT NOT NULL,
  ReviewerName    VARCHAR(40) NOT NULL,
  ReviewText      VARCHAR(5000),
  Rating          INT,
  ReviewDate      DATE NOT NULL
)
```

We can alter the table to define the `ReviewID` column as a primary key as follows:

```
ALTER TABLE Reviews
   ADD CONSTRAINT PK_ReviewID PRIMARY KEY (ReviewID)
```

It is worth noting that it is not strictly necessary to name your constraints. For example, the following SQL would work equally as well:

```
ALTER TABLE Reviews
   ADD PRIMARY KEY (ReviewID)
```

Here, the database will assign its own name to the constraint. In Oracle, the name will be of the form SYS_Cxxxxx (where xxxxx is a number). When I tried this in Cloudscape, I found that my primary key was named 9a4840c2-00e7-ccd5-9ba5-00c0a8016300. If a referential integrity problem arises, we get a cryptic error message that gives us a mumbo-jumbo constraint name. When we put in the constraints separately, we have the privilege of naming the constraint in a meaningful way.

Since the ALTER TABLE statement does vary somewhat in syntax between RDBMSs, you should check your documentation for the exact usage of this statement.

With most RDBMSs, when creating a primary key in a CREATE TABLE or ALTER TABLE ADD COLUMN statement, you automatically make all columns in a primary key non-Nullable. ALTER TABLE ADD CONSTRAINT does *not* do this, so the columns it references when defining a primary key constraint must already be NOT NULL.

Adding a Foreign Key

Here is how we could alter our basic Reviews table structure to define the RecordingID column as a foreign key:

```
ALTER TABLE Reviews
   ADD CONSTRAINT FK_Reviews_Recordings
   FOREIGN KEY (RecordingID) REFERENCES Recordings
```

In a sense this syntax is much clearer, since we can now use the FOREIGN KEY keyword. The referenced column must be a PK column or a UNIQUE column of that table.

When adding a FOREIGN KEY or CHECK constraint to an existing table, most RDBMSs will check the table to make sure existing rows satisfy the constraint. If any row is invalid, an error is thrown and the constraint is not added.

Dropping Constraints

The ALTER TABLE DROP CONSTRAINT statement drops a named constraint on an existing table. For example, to drop the CHECK constraint we added previously, we could use the following statement:

```
ALTER TABLE Reviews
  DROP CONSTRAINT CHK_Reviewer
```

When you drop a PRIMARY KEY or UNIQUE constraint and there may be FOREIGN KEY constraints referencing that PRIMARY KEY or UNIQUE constraint. Most RDBMSs will provide you with two options for dealing with this; drop all referencing foreign key constraints, or abort the dropping of the constraint. You will need to check your RDBMS's documentation for the exact behavior.

Dropping Tables

It is important that after you no longer need the new table you removed it from the database. To do so, use the DROP TABLE command. This command takes a single argument; the name of the table to be removed:

```
Drop Table Reviews
```

Be careful when using `DROP TABLE`*, however, because the database won't give you any warning that it is about to delete the table.*

Remember, if we have defined foreign-key relationships between our tables, then this will dictate the order in which we can drop them. For example, if we try to drop our `Recordings` table, we may get the following sort of error message (this one was generated in Cloudscape):

```
Database access resulted in SQL exception:

SQLState , Error code 30000, Message:

Operation 'DROP CONSTRAINT' cannot be performed on object 'PK_RECORDINGS' because
CONSTRAINT ' FK_REVIEWS_RECORDINGS ' is dependent on that object.
```

If we were allowed to drop the parent table then all of the records in the child table would become orphaned and the referential integrity of the database would be compromised.

Adding, Deleting, and Changing Data

There are three major functions of a database management system. The first of these functions is to provide a structured way of storing data. Another of these functions is to provide a mechanism for searching and describing the data stored in the database. The last major function is to get the data into the database and manipulate it.

Adding Data to Tables

The `INSERT` statement may be used to add rows of data to a table. The command requires that you specify the destination of the new records (either a table or, in some cases a view) as well as the data. If you are not providing data to every field in the table, you will also be required to specify which fields are to be populated with the data.

The `INSERT` statement takes the following general form:

```
INSERT INTO tablename (col1, col2, ..., colX)
  VALUES (val1, val2, ..., valX)
```

To insert a new record in all fields of the `Employee` table, we could use the following:

```
INSERT INTO Reviews (ReviewID, RecordingID, ReviewerName, ReviewText, Rating,
ReviewDate)
VALUES (
1000,
1005,
'Lance Trickey',
'Another uplifting release from Peter Gabriel',
5,
'2001-04-25')
```

Bear in mind that if you still have our previous CHECK constraint, CHK_Reviewer, in place then the above code will violate that constraint and you will receive an error message:

```
The check constraint 'CHK_REVIEWER' was violated while performing an INSERT or
UPDATE on table 'APP.REVIEWS3'
```

If you are certain of the order of the columns in the table, then you do not need to list the column names:

```
INSERT INTO Reviews

VALUES (
1000,
1005,
'Jenny',
'Another uplifting release from Peter Gabriel',
5,
'2001-04-25')
```

However, this is not really recommended practice. The first method is much clearer and also means that you can list the fields to be populated in any order. If the identifier of the table, in this case the ReviewID field, were generated automatically, we would not want to specify its value. For example, in Cloudscape we can enable the Auto Increment property of a column, and set an initial value and step increment for the field value. In this case our INSERT statement would look as follows:

```
INSERT INTO Reviews
(RecordingID, ReviewerName, ReviewText, Rating, ReviewDate)

VALUES (
1005,
'Jenny',
'Another uplifting release from Peter Gabriel',
5,
'2001-04-25')
```

Beware of date formats when inserting data. While the above may work in one database, another may be expecting a date of a different format, such as '20-JUL-01'. In Oracle you can find out the correct format with the following command:

```
SELECT SYSDATE FROM DUAL;
```

Dual is a special table that contains one column, called dummy (data type: varchar2) and one row, of value x. It provides a very convenient way of testing functions and so on.

Multiple Row Inserts

An INSERT statement may be used in conjunction with the SELECT statement. The syntax is virtually the same, except that the VALUES clause is replaced with the SELECT statement. We could use these two statements together to copy data from one table to another:

```
INSERT INTO WhatsHot
SELECT * FROM Reviews
WHERE Rating>3
```

There is a noteworthy detail concerning this technique, namely, the columns returned by the SELECT statement must match the exact order and data types of the fields listed in the INSERT portion of the statement.

Using the above method, we had to create the WhatsHot table first. Some databases, such as Oracle, provide an alternative method whereby we can effectively create a 'copy' of a table:

```
CREATE TABLE Whatshot AS (SELECT *
    FROM Reviews
   WHERE Rating>3);
```

Regardless of the method we try, it is possible that we will not be allowed to use the command. In order to be able to create tables in a given database, we need to have security permissions. In addition, some databases by default will explicitly prohibit these commands because these types of 'bulk inserts' are very costly to perform, and can cause inaccuracies with the database statistics. In Microsoft SQL Server and Sybase SQL Server, use the db_options command to view and set the ability to use bulk inserts. Check your RDBMS's documentation for details.

Deleting Data from Tables

In order to remove records from a table using SQL, the DELETE statement may be used. This statement takes the general form:

```
DELETE
FROM tablename
WHERE conditions
```

To remove all records in the Reviews table that are older than a certain date, we could use:

```
Delete
  From Reviews
WHERE ReviewDate <= '2001-01-01'
```

The WHERE clause of this statement uses the same syntax found in the SELECT statement. As with the SELECT statement, if the WHERE clause is omitted, the query engine will select all records in the table. Therefore, if you wish to purge an entire table of records simply use the statement:

```
DELETE FROM tablename
```

DELETE versus TRUNCATE

Sybase SQL Server and Microsoft SQL Server offer another method, called the TRUNCATE TABLE statement, for purging all rows from a table. It operates like a DELETE statement without a WHERE clause, and therefore can only be used to remove all records from a table. This statement offers some advantages over using the DELETE statement, but it also has some drawbacks.

The DELETE statement removes records one at a time and the action is recorded in transaction logs by the server. Since each deletion is recorded individually, it is possible to undo the deletion. When the TRUNCATE TABLE statement is used, the records are removed and the action is not recorded in the logs. The advantage to not recording the deletion of individual records is that TRUNCATE TABLE statement is extremely fast and does not cause the transaction logs to grow. The disadvantage of using TRUNCATE TABLE is that if you issue this command mistakenly, you can't undo the action. Just hope that you have a good backup on tape. We'll see more about transactions shortly, and then come back to them in Chapter 14.

DELETE and Foreign Keys

Another important note about using the DELETE statement concerns foreign key dependencies. If you have foreign key relationships defined between two tables, you may be prevented from deleting certain records.

Foreign keys are used to establish and enforce a relationship between two tables. When a foreign key is defined, it associates one or more columns that hold a table's primary key values to a column or columns in a second table.

Recall that earlier we defined a foreign key relationship between the Reviews table and the Recordings table.

```
CREATE TABLE Reviews (
  ReviewID        INT CONSTRAINT PK_ReviewID Primary key,
  RecordingID     INT CONSTRAINT FK_Reviews_Recordings REFERENCES Recordings,
  ReviewerName    VARCHAR(40) NOT NULL,
  ReviewText      VARCHAR(5000),
  Rating          INT,
  ReviewDate      DATE NOT NULL
)
```

Having entered our Peter Gabriel review, if we now try to delete the parent recording:

```
DELETE FROM Recordings
WHERE RecordingTitle = 'US'
```

We will receive an error message along the lines that we have "caused a violation of foreign key constraint".

Updating Data in Tables

To change the values of columns in a table, we can use the UPDATE statement. The general format of this statement is:

```
UPDATE targettablename
SET field1 = newvalue1, field2 = newvalue2
WHERE conditions
```

To demonstrate the use of the UPDATE statement, consider the SQL statement below. It changes the Rating field to 80% of the original Rating for *all* reviews of the Peter Gabriel recording:

```
UPDATE REVIEWS
SET Rating = Rating * 0.8
WHERE RecordingID = 1005
```

Transactional Processing

In many commercial and corporate applications, there is the need to perform a series of operations. If any single operation fails, then the entire series of operations cannot be used. Take for instance, a transfer of funds from a savings account to a checking account. For this to happen, a withdrawal needs to be made from one account, and a deposit into the other. If, for any reason, we are unable to perform one of these actions, we need to cancel both, and be able to return the database to the state it was in before the actions started.

Through the **Data Control Language** (**DCL**) component of SQL, we have a mechanism to group such operations into what are called **transactions**. All database systems that support transactions must have a way to explicitly tell the system that a transaction is beginning (although the syntax used may vary from RDBMS to RBDMS). There is also a statement that will identify the end of the transaction, specifying if the entire transaction was a success or a failure. If successful, all of the actions taken between the command that started the transaction and the command that ended it will be saved to the database. If the transaction was not successful, then the state of the records prior to the start of the transaction will be reinstated.

This section presents a very brief coverage of transactions. For more details, please refer to Chapter 14.

With Cloudscape, transactions are handled through JDBC methods, not by SQL commands.

This is the command for marking the start of a transaction in Sybase SQL Server and Microsoft SQL Server:

```
BEGIN TRANSACTION
```

In oracle there is no `BEGIN TRANSACTION` statement. A transaction implicitly begins with the first statement that modifies data.

Once a transaction has started, we then have the sequence of SQL statements that perform the required operations. If these statements execute without incident, then we can save the results of the operations with the `COMMIT` statement for Oracle, or the `COMMIT TRANSACTION` statement for the Microsoft and Sybase products.

If an error is raised before the `COMMIT` command is invoked, all of the changes made will be reversed or **rolled back**. You can explicitly cause the transaction to roll back by issuing the `ROLLBACK` command (in Oracle) or `ROLLBACK TRANSACTION` (in Microsoft and Sybase SQL Servers).

Therefore, if we issue a block of SQL statements by wrapping them in a transaction, we can ensure that they *all* are executed or *none* are. For example, the following group of SQL statements define a transaction that we can use to purge our database of old reviews. If an error occurs during the `DELETE` command, then not only is the `DELETE` operation canceled, the insertion of records into the `NewReviews` table will be reversed:

```
BEGIN TRANSACTION

  INSERT INTO NewReviews
    SELECT *
    FROM Reviews
    WHERE ReviewDate >= '2001-01-01'

  DELETE FROM Reviews
    WHERE ReviewDate < '2001-01-01'

COMMIT TRANSACTION
```

Transactions are possible because the RDBMS keeps track of every change that takes place in the database; when a record is inserted into a table, a record is deleted, or a value is updated in some column. This record is kept in a **transaction log**. If the transaction fails, the database is able to reconstruct the values of the database before the transaction by reading this log. It is this transaction log that is used to undo the changes to the database if the transaction is rolled back.

Summary

In this chapter, we have looked in more detail at the DDL component of the SQL language that allows us to create, alter, and drop database objects. We have also looked at how to add, modify, and delete rows of table data.

We can combine what we learned from the previous chapter about `JOIN` conditions with the statements discussed in this chapter, to define which records we wish to act upon. This gives us a powerful mechanism with which we can control what is selected and how data from differing tables can be manipulated.

Acquiring, deleting, and changing data are not the only actions we need to perform when working with databases. Having the ability to create and destroy tables provides us with mechanisms to consolidate data for faster, and more efficient, operations. We saw how to use SQL to create, destroy, and modify constraints for both column and table-level control of data validation.

With the combined information covered in this and the previous chapter, we should now be able to construct flexible and powerful SQL commands that can be used in an application to access and control the information contained in a database, as well as the database itself. After we have looked in more detail at the concepts surrounding database design, you will put this knowledge into practice in a case study, where we will actually demonstrate how build and populate our Music Store database.

akarta
JAVA
Java

Relational Database Design Concepts

It is very likely that when developing an application that uses a database, you will do more than just access the information from the database. Since it is commonplace for application developers to also be responsible for designing the database as well, an understanding of database design concepts is in order. Even if you are not responsible for constructing the database, knowing what makes for a good database design can help you in coming up with better strategies for accessing that data.

A well-designed structure for your database can make the crucial difference between creating a 'successful' database application and one that is, shall we say, 'less than successful.' A poor design will cause performance problems, integrity problems, and functionality limitations, and even the best program code in the world can't help much. A solid design will go a long way in avoiding these problems and make it much, much easier to code the application that uses the database. The importance of database design cannot be stressed highly enough.

In today's marketplace, a wide range of tools are available that make creating a database really easy. Many database products provide wizards that step you through the database creation process, allowing you to produce a database in a matter of a few minutes. Unfortunately, most wizard-generated applications are sufficient only for low volume, and relatively simple, data access. For many professional applications, especially for high volume Internet access, we need a database that is efficient, flexible, and fast enough to handle many users. To create such a database, the human touch is usually required.

Database design is not rocket science and if you follow some basic rules and guidelines, it is not difficult to produce a good quality design. Of course, the final design will depend on a great many factors, including the type of database with which you are working, the nature of the information that you are trying to organize, and the business rules that you need to apply. The main focus of this chapter is to discuss what makes for a good database design and the concepts used to construct databases so that they are fast and efficient. In the very next chapter we will put the concepts learned here into practice as we design and build the Music Store database that is used throughout this book.

Understanding How Things Are Done

With all applications, the ultimate goal is to effectively, and efficiently, build and implement a solution that meets the business needs. The starting points for an effective database design are always the same:

- Understand what are the goals for the business in developing the application
- Determine what information and processes are needed to meet these goals

A considerable amount of research on the business needs must be conducted before you can begin designing the architecture of the system. This architecture will describe the data that needs to be stored as well as how the various parts of the business interact. There are a number of steps in the development of the business system:

- Research the business goals and processes
- Develop a model that represents what needs to be done
- Figure out what approaches we can take to meet these needs
- Implement these approaches by actually using a database system, such as Cloudscape or Oracle, to code the objects use to store and manipulate the required data

The first step in the process listed leads us to a **conceptual design** for our model.

The Conceptual Design

Understanding the business needs is sometimes the most difficult task in this stage of development, especially since most business operations have a certain degree of complexity to them. Although there are many specific reasons that make understanding the business difficult, such as logistics, industry specializations, and legal issues to name a few, these reasons can be generalized as 'complexity.' The key to dealing with complexity is to come up with a model that represents the business as simple system.

To do this, we break the design project into its constituent parts so that it is easier to understand the processes required. For all these parts, we try to describe each as simply as possible by eliminating unnecessary details. This way, we can more easily concentrate our efforts on what is important.

Don't try to determine every last detail about the business operations at this stage. Details will come later. If you try to collect every minute detail now, you risk getting bogged down in the details.

Let's consider our Music Store database application again. Our client owns several successful music stores and is looking to expand still further. However, before she can do so she realizes the urgent need for a database in which she can keep an accurate record of all of her inventory in the various stores. In broad terms we could identify the following goals that our database design must enable and facilitate in this scenario:

- Save information regarding all **recordings** stocked by her stores, with a mechanism for flexibly searching this data, say by song title, artist, or album name
- Keep an accurate track of **inventories** in any **store**
- Store information about **customer orders** so that she can accurately track the progress of these orders
- Store information about **customers** so that she can inform them when an order is available, ship the order if necessary and even start to understand more about their buying habits

Just from the highlighted nouns in the above list, we can start to see some of the most significant pieces of information required for the business. These highlighted words, such as customers, customer orders, and store, represent important data items, or **entities**, in our system.

Entities, Attributes, and Values

An entity represents some object in reality, such as a person or a thing. Entities, as objects, represent a class of 'things'. If you consider the `Customers` entity, then each instance of that object will represent a specific `Customer`.

Each instance of our `Customers` entity will have identical attributes that define the meaning of that entity. Consider the following collection of attributes:

- Customer First Name
- Customer Last Name
- Postal Address
- E-mail Address
- Phone Number

Each of these attributes will store values, and these values are generally different from one `Customer` instance to another. One instance of `Customer` could store the values 'Diane', 'Asmus', '23 Lakeside Drive', 'dasmus@myemail.com', '013-456-143'. Another instance will store completely different values in each attribute. Regardless of the actual values that may be stored in these attributes, collectively, these attributes define an instance of an entity that describes `Customers`.

In a similar fashion, instances of a `Recordings` entity will hold attributes such as 'recording title', 'release date', 'recording format', and so on, and each instance will have attribute values that uniquely define a specific recording. Our recording entity may look as follows:

The process outlined above describes (albeit in a simplified manner) the process that will lead you to an understanding of roughly what entities are required in your system and to start building up a picture of these entities.

The goal of this exercise is to come up with a meaningful representation of the system, with the various entities identified and an understanding of what services those portions will provide. The result of this effort is the conceptual design. The conceptual design will not describe *how* things are done, but rather *what* needs to be done.

The next step is to consider how these entities will coexist and this leads us in to the next stage: the **logical design**.

Developing the Logical Design

Once you have a conceptual design you can then start paying more attention to the details of our business processes represented in our model. We need to concentrate not only on *what* needs to be done in the business, but also *how* things are done in the business. The result of this will be the **logical design**.

The logical design will be a very detailed specification of all entities. A logical design has to include more than just what was considered in the conceptual design. It has to include interactions between entities, as well as all the processing of the application such as any maintenance or auditing features. It has to take account of specific features of the chosen database engine (Oracle, Cloudscape, SQL Server). It should consider the skills of the development team, strategies that may be used in building the product, and possible configuration issues.

Interactions and Relationships Between Entities

Now that we have determined some of the entities that are required, we need to consider how these entities will coexist and interact. For example, how does the customer interact with the catalog of recordings? How do recordings and tracks relate? The answers to such questions may require you to add additional information that you didn't think about at first. Again, don't try to get too detailed; just enough detail to be confident in the design. Later on in the process, you will review these entities and their interactions and refine them.

One common technique used to determine how the entities interact identifies verbs used in our narratives. Consider a phrase such as, 'Customers *order* Recordings'. Pictorially, we can represent such relationships as follows:

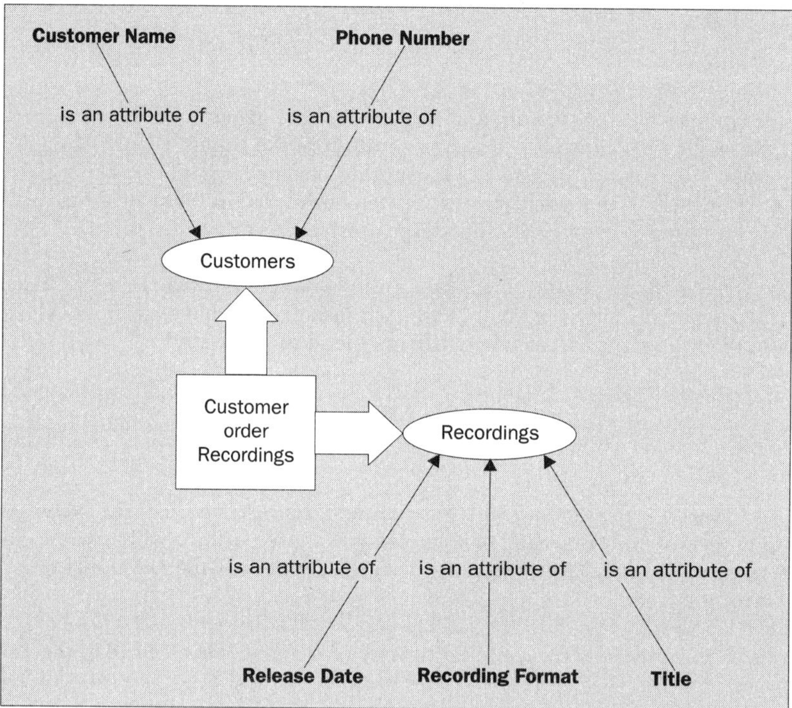

What we have here is a rather crude **Entity Relationship diagram** (or **ER diagram**), which identifies details about the entities required for various business functions and how the entities may reference each other. Since this chapter is concerned with the fundamentals and concepts of relational database design, I do not at this stage want us to get too sidetracked into the full details of an ER diagram for our Music Store database – we will save that for the case study in Chapter 6.

The general form of the key phases that will help us identify relationship between entities and build up our full ER diagram is 'Noun *verb* Noun'. Other key phrases that will help you may include: 'Record Labels *produce* Recordings', and 'Tracks *are made by* Recording Artists'. Sometimes, you may need to rewrite the phrases to fit this general form. For instance, 'Tracks *are made by* Recording Artists' could be rewritten as 'Recording Artists *create* Tracks.

As you investigate the relationships between your entities, your understanding of the model will evolve and a property of an entity may actually be recognized as a potential entity in its own right. In our music store example, a recording can come in numerous formats (Compact Disc, DVD, Cassette tape, video, and so on). Rather than record these values of the `RecordingFormat` attribute for *every* instance of our `Recordings` entity (every recording) it may make sense to have a separate `RecordingFormat` entity that stores all of the valid types of recordings. We would then establish the appropriate relationship between the two entities.

You will also come to appreciate the **cardinality** that exists between your entities. Cardinality refers to any restrictions in the number of instances of an entity that may be related to (contained in) another entity. The key phrases to look for to identify cardinality include words such as 'contains', 'comprises', and 'is made up of.'

For example, an order is composed of one or more items being purchased. The fact that one instance of an order can have one or more instances of items in that order is an example of the cardinality between the two entities. A further example is the fact that a recording is made up of a number of tracks.

After we determine the major entities, some of their properties, and their interactions and relationships, we continue our discussions with the client. Let them see early drafts of your work and allow them to help you fill in any missing information. Another great practice when designing a database (or any other type of application for that matter) is to enlist the aid of other developers to bounce problems and ideas off of. Hold a meeting with them and explain the objectives of the application, the major obstacles, the known business process, and your proposed design. Let them look things over, evaluate what has been done, and provide you with feedback.

Keep cycling through these activities – researching the business, identifying the components, identifying relationships, business review, peer review, and refining the model – until a clear and understandable model of the system is developed.

What you will have at the end of the process is a high-level picture. Now, up to this point you may have been surprised to see barely a mention of the words **table**, **record**, **field** (or even database!). At the end of the above process we would have a high-level view of the entities that will comprise your system and how they interact, but how do we implement these entities, attributes, and relationships in our database? That is what we will now move on to discuss.

Entities and Relationships in the Database

The reason that we avoided using terms such as field or record when describing the components of our model is because those terms really refer to implementation specifics of the database product that is used. If we implement our model in, say, an Oracle database then our **entity** would be represented as a **table** and our **attributes** implemented as **fields** in that table. Each **instance** of our entity would be a **record** in a table.

However, if we used some spreadsheet application, then our entities are implemented as a worksheet and our attributes as columns in the worksheet.

In a general sense, databases are simply devices for information storage and retrieval. They can take many forms and do not have to be created with computer programs such as Oracle, Microsoft SQL Server, or Microsoft Access. In fact, it is quite common for people to not use any of these database systems for their first database. This is often because most people, when developing their first database, do not actually think of it *as* a database. Phone lists stored in a word processing document, clients listed in some contact management software, and a check register kept in a spreadsheet are all such examples.

In fact, it is quite typical for a person's first databases to be a simple list or spreadsheet that has relatively few pieces of information for each entry. When the information is displayed or printed, it looks like one big table. These examples are called **flat-file** databases. The term 'flat', comes from the fact that these tables are very two-dimensional – a certain number of columns wide with the number of records in the table defining its length.

Many small single-user applications are successfully built on flat-file databases. When our music store owner first started out in business, she may have very happily got by with recording her orders on a simple spreadsheet. Her model may have consisted of a single `CustomerOrder` entity that may have looked something like the following:

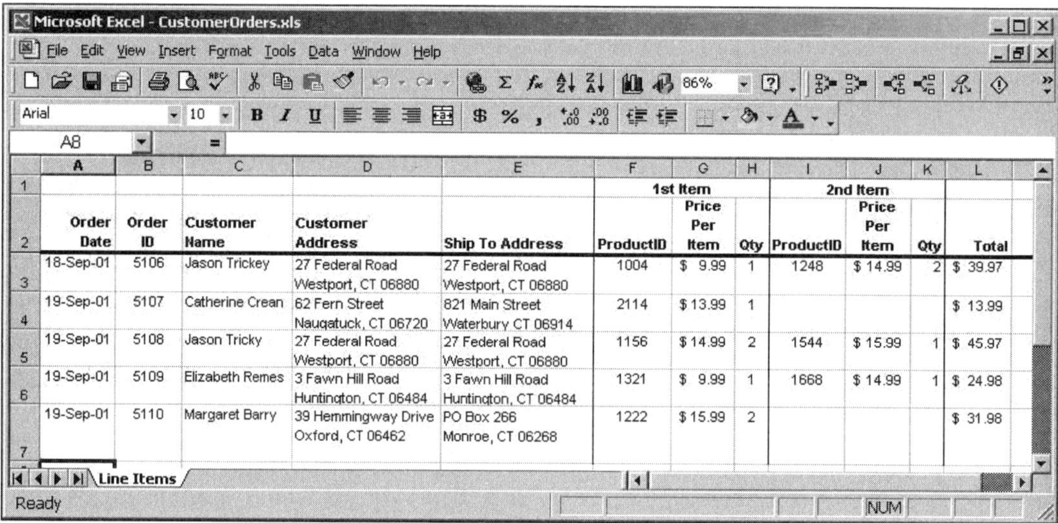

Order Date	Order ID	Customer Name	Customer Address	Ship To Address	1st Item ProductID	1st Item Price Per Item	1st Item Qty	2nd Item ProductID	2nd Item Price Per Item	2nd Item Qty	Total
18-Sep-01	5106	Jason Trickey	27 Federal Road Westport, CT 06880	27 Federal Road Westport, CT 06880	1004	$ 9.99	1	1248	$ 14.99	2	$ 39.97
19-Sep-01	5107	Catherine Crean	62 Fern Street Naugatuck, CT 06720	821 Main Street Waterbury CT 06914	2114	$ 13.99	1				$ 13.99
19-Sep-01	5108	Jason Tricky	27 Federal Road Westport, CT 06880	27 Federal Road Westport, CT 06880	1156	$ 14.99	2	1544	$ 15.99	1	$ 45.97
19-Sep-01	5109	Elizabeth Remes	3 Fawn Hill Road Huntington, CT 06484	3 Fawn Hill Road Huntington, CT 06484	1321	$ 9.99	1	1668	$ 14.99	1	$ 24.98
19-Sep-01	5110	Margaret Barry	39 Hemmingway Drive Oxford, CT 06462	PO Box 266 Monroe, CT 06268	1222	$ 15.99	2				$ 31.98

However, as her business grew and she had to store and retrieve larger volumes of data, she would have found that these types of databases were too inefficient and prone to developing errors.

One problem is with a limitation on the data; this system does not allow for more than two items to be ordered in a single order. Although more columns could be added, doing so would require recoding how the total cost is computed.

Other problems with this spreadsheet approach concern redundant data between records. Consider the need to type in the customer's name with each item purchased, regardless if the buyer is a returning customer. Not only is this tedious to do, but is also prone to typing errors. Notice that the name of the customer, Jason Trickey, is spelled differently in orders 5106 and 5108. Furthermore, if Jason Trickey (or Tricky!) moves address then we have potential four places where we need to modify that address, again making the system much more prone to the introduction of errors.

In addition, when storing data a consideration should be made of how much disk space you are willing to provide to the application. Although hard disk space is relatively inexpensive to purchase, it still costs money, so storage efficiencies are often a concern.

In order to address these problems we need to give more thought to how the entities are defined. In order to address the data repetition problem, perhaps we need one entity to represent customers and another separate entity to represent their orders. In relational database parlance, we would refer to this as creating a **lookup table** for the customers. Each customer would be assigned a customer number on their first purchase and that number would be used to identify the customer each time they placed an order. In our data model, we would need to keep the information for each customer's number (by using a `Customers` table) separate from the information kept on customer orders (by using an `Orders` table).

This may look something like the following:

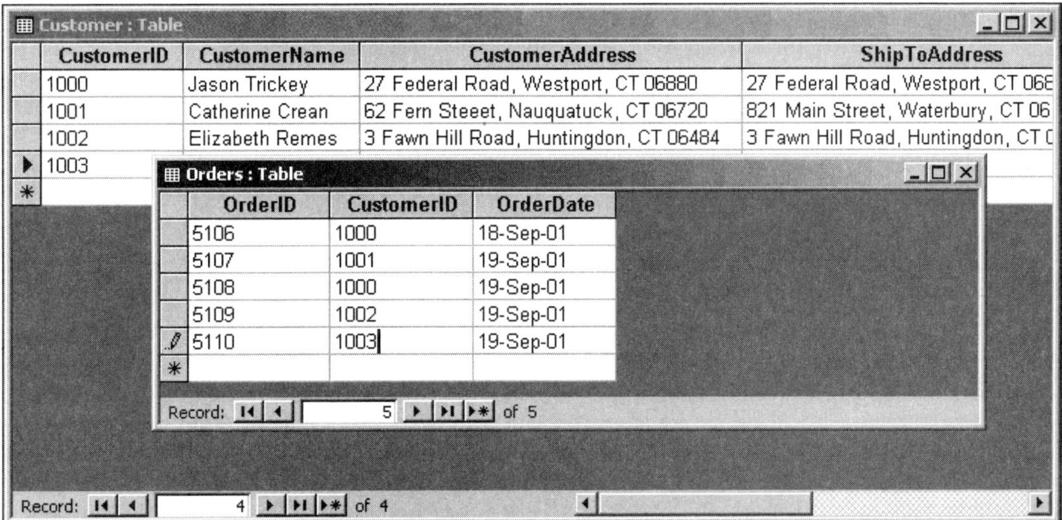

Customer : Table

CustomerID	CustomerName	CustomerAddress	ShipToAddress
1000	Jason Trickey	27 Federal Road, Westport, CT 06880	27 Federal Road, Westport, CT 068
1001	Catherine Crean	62 Fern Steeet, Nauquatuck, CT 06720	821 Main Street, Waterbury, CT 06
1002	Elizabeth Remes	3 Fawn Hill Road, Huntingdon, CT 06484	3 Fawn Hill Road, Huntingdon, CT
1003			

Record: 4 of 4

Orders : Table

OrderID	CustomerID	OrderDate
5106	1000	18-Sep-01
5107	1001	19-Sep-01
5108	1000	19-Sep-01
5109	1002	19-Sep-01
5110	1003	19-Sep-01

Record: 5 of 5

The Customers table contains relevant details of all existing customers (company name, address, etc.). A particular field in this table, called Customer ID, uniquely identifies each customer. A second table, the Orders table, contains a field that is populated by the same Customer ID (Customer) and thus a relationship exists between the two. Since customers, such as Jason Trickey, can place more than one order, a one-to-many relationship exists between the Customers and the Orders table.

This approach offers a number of improvements. Firstly, the chances of typographical errors decrease since fewer characters are entered for a customer number than are with the customer's full name. Secondly, each customer's full name is recorded only once so the *overall* amount of space required is reduced.

Of course, in order for this approach to work we need a means of relating the information in each of these tables. The key to this relationship is the customer number. As long as you know the customer number from an entry in the Orders table, you can search through the Customers table to find the appropriate customer entry, and therefore find out every detail stored about that customer. Databases that organize data in a series of related tables are, of course, **relational databases**.

Defining Relationships

Dr. E.F. Codd described the solution to the above problems in his concept of the Relational Database. In a nutshell, his ideas were two-fold:

- As much as possible, divide data into smaller tables with strict rules for what data they can contain.
- Create relationships between the tables that allow the DBMS to look from one table to another to assemble the complete set of results.

In a relational database, being able to match related records between two tables is essential. From Chapter 1, and from our exploration of SQL in Chapter 4, we are already very familiar with the concept of **key** fields and how to implement them.

Primary Keys

In a relational database, we never record information about something we cannot identify. To distinguish each row in the table, we define a **primary key** (**PK**).

The primary key may be selected from one or more of the columns in the table. The only requirements for what column or columns are used for the primary key is that they must uniquely distinguish each row in the table from every other row, and that there are no missing value in the column(s) that make up the primary key.

It should be noted that, since the purpose of a primary key is to uniquely identify every row of a table, missing values (called ***Null*** *values) should not be allowed in any of the columns composing the primary key. In fact, database systems will not allow you to include a 'nullable column' as part of the primary key.*

If no single column or set of columns, meet these requirements, then a new column may be created for this purpose. If there are columns already in the table that you can guarantee to be unique, then they should be used rather than taking up additional space for a new column. If a new column is to be created, then the values in this column will typically be in some sequence, such as an order number or employee ID, which increments by a value of one with each new row.

If you have a choice of which column(s) to use for the primary key, it is generally best to choose the most concise column(s), in other words, those with the smallest usable data type. Since most database systems process numbers more efficiently than characters strings, consider using numbers for this column, preferably an integer value. Integer values are stored very efficiently in most database systems. Also, the column(s) used for the primary key should be ones that change very infrequently or not at all. The best type of primary key is a single column that contains integer values that never change. In the example given earlier, the `CustomerID` field in the `Customers` table is an excellent choice of PK field.

With some tables, there may not be a single unique column. In these cases, we define the primary key to be some combination of two or more columns that *together* will be unique. A common example of this in the United States is to use both a person's social security number *and* their last name. Although it is not widely known, social security numbers are not unique and are re-issued every so many years. Obviously, a person's last name is not unique. Although neither piece of information is unique, if we use a combination of the two, the probability of two people having the same social security number and last name is small, so together they are 'sufficiently unique'.

In our Music Store model, we need to be able to record how many of each product is currently in stock for any given store. Therefore, the `Inventories` table has to store the `ProductID`, the `StoreID`, and the quantity on hand. In this situation, no single column would uniquely identify any given row of the `Inventories` table:

ProductID	StoreID	QtyOnHand
1003	3	5
1003	4	5
1003	5	0
1003	6	4
1001	4	15
1001	5	22
1002	9	1
1004	5	4
1005	3	1

To resolve this issue, we use more than one column to define the primary key; we use `ProductID` and `StoreID`. When more than one column is used for a key, that key is said to be a **composite key**.

A Note on Ordering Columns

It should be noted that when defining the key, the order of the columns could greatly affect performance. This is due to the algorithms used by RDBMSs to physically store the records of a table and the algorithms used to search these tables. The most common algorithm for storing records is based on a sorted order of the primary key. The algorithms used for searching vary greatly depending upon such factors as the RDBMS itself, the structure of the tables, and the data being searched for.

In general, if the table is expected to be large, you want to order the columns so the column that is most likely to contain the fewest duplicate values is listed first. If the table is expected to be small, then order the columns so the column that is most likely to contain the fewest duplicate values is listed last. What is considered 'small' and what is considered 'large' is somewhat of a judgment call, but here is one useful guideline. 'Small' can be considered to be less than or equal to the number of rows in a table the RDBMS will likely hold in cache memory. This is usually in the magnitude of a few dozen to a few hundred rows. 'Large' could be considered any number of rows greater than what is considered "small." Of course, you should conduct some experiments to compare how different orders of columns for the PK will affect the performance.

Foreign Keys

A foreign key is a column holding data that is able to point to a unique column in another table. So, if we want our `Order` records to be linked to our `Customer` records, the `Orders` table will need a foreign key field, in this case also called `CustomerID`, that points to the PK field in the `Customers` table.

The RDBMS can then read data in the `CustomerID` field of the `Orders` table and go over and match the Order record to one, and only one, Customer record using the `Customer` table's Primary key field of `CustomerID`:

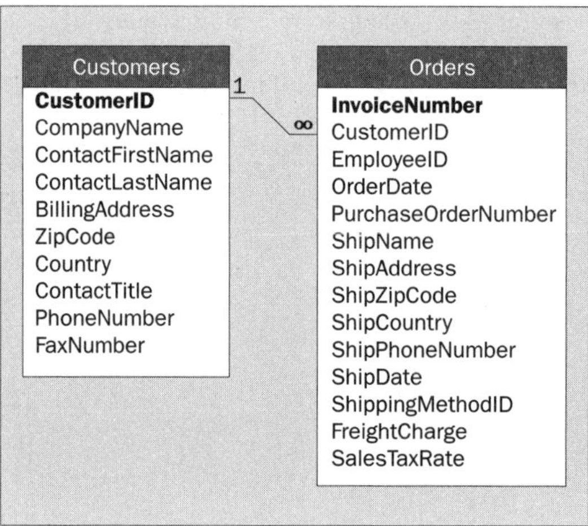

The above is a common way of diagramming the relationship of two tables (and is also commonly referred to as an ER diagram, for reasons that I hope are clear from the preceding discussion in this chapter).

Since it is possible that any one customer will place more than one order, there will exist any number of rows in the `Orders` table for a customer. When a single row in one table can be related to more than one row in a second table, the relationship between the tables is called a one-to-many relationship. This relationship is denoted in the above ER diagram by the line connecting the two tables with the 1 and infinity ∞ symbols. The counting of the number of rows that may be matched between tables denotes the cardinality of the relationship. This is another term with which you are already familiar, and hopefully you are beginning to see how our somewhat abstract design concepts are actually implemented in the database. The cardinality value of the `Customer` table in this relationship is 'one' while the value of the cardinality of the `Orders` table in this relationship is 'many'.

Although there may be a relationship between tables, it is possible that some rows in one table will not match any rows in the related table. This would happen if a customer had not yet placed any orders (therefore having no rows in the `Orders` table), but was still listed in the `Customers` table. Since it is possible for zero rows to match, a cardinality of zero is possible. In some circumstances, only a single row in one table will be match with one and only one row in the related table.

One-to-One Relationships

One-to-one (**1:1**) relationships require that one and only one row in a table can be matched with a single row in its related table. This type of cardinality is not common in many relational databases, but will happen on occasion depending upon business rules. For example, suppose the business rules for your application states that a sales representative will service one and only one corporate client. In this case, the sales representative's row in a `SalesReps` table will be matched with only one particular customer in a `Clients` table. Similarly, each company listed in the `Clients` table will be matched with one and only one sales representative in the `SalesRep` table. In our Music Store example, there are no 1:1 relationships between tables.

In many ER Diagramming tools, one-to-one relationships are denoted with simply a single line connecting the two entities, while other tools add a '1' next to the line as a notation. In the following example, we are displaying a 1:1 relationship that joins patients to beds in a hospital.

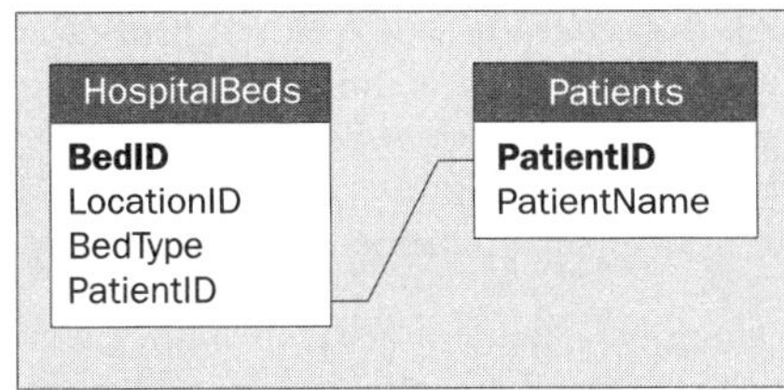

It is possible that a patient is found in the `Patients` table but a corresponding bed assignment was not recorded. This would be possible for ambulatory patients who do not need to be admitted overnight or when patient information is first being entered into the database. In these situations, we have a '**1:0-or-1**' relationship or a 'cardinality of zero or one.' Although some diagramming tools explicitly denote these relationships, many diagramming tools assume that 1:1 and 1:0-or-1 relations are the same.

One-to-Many Relationships

One-to-many (1:M) relationships allow one row in a table to be related to one or more rows in the related table. For an example of a one-to-many relationship, look back at the first illustration of this section that shows the relationship between `Customers` and `Orders`. Any one customer found in a `Customers` table may be matched with one or more invoices in an `Orders` table. This relationship could also be described as one or more invoices can be matched with only one customer. Many-to-one relationships are the same as one-to-many relationships, except for a matter of perspective.

Many-to-many (**M:M**) relationships are also provided for in ER Diagrams. With these types of relationships, multiple rows in one table match multiple rows in the related table. As with one-to-one relationships, these are not as common as one-to-many relationships are in most business applications, but when they are needed, they are often difficult to work with and are inefficient.

When a situation arises when a many-to-many relationship is needed, often a new intermediary table is used to link the two tables. This new table is often called a **junction** table. The idea behind a junction table is to record every combination of records that match in the tables with the M:M relationship. This junction table is designed to hold the primary keys of other tables. Both of the original tables are then linked to the junction table in a many-to-one relationship.

If you have downloaded the complete Music Store database model as part of the code download and examined the tables, you will find that our model has a number of 1:M relationships. The `Customers` table possesses such a relationship with the `CustomerOrders` table since any one customer may place any number of orders. The foreign key used from the `CustomerOrders` table is the `CustomerID` field and this field references primary key of `Customer`. Having this relationship makes sense for the music store business, since you want to make sure that you have a valid `CustomerID` created for each customer before the order can be fulfilled.

Referential Integrity

By defining our relationships in the manner discussed in the previous sections, we are effectively informing the database which tables are involved in the relationships and which FK relates to which PK. Once we have done this we are in a position to take advantage of the referential integrity that a relational database offers.

With referential integrity enabled, the database will seek to ensure that data in related tables remains consistent. First, let's consider what can happen without referential integrity. Suppose we created an order in the `Orders` table but attached it to an invalid `CustomerID`. How would we dispatch the order? Our `CustomerID` won't find a match in the `Customers` table so we won't be able to find the customer's address! In effect, the new order record is orphaned – it has no parent record.

Referential integrity ensures that values are consistent between entities. This is usually achived in databases by requiring that the value stored in one column of an entity is a value that also exists in some related entity. It is a simple rule: 'If B references A, then A must exist.' In a nutshell, this means that when populating a record of a table with a foreign key, such as `CustomerID`, the primary key of the linked table must have a matching value. In this way, we can preserve the defined relationships between tables when rows are entered or deleted.

Some examples of how RI can ensure data integrity include:

- Preventing orders being taken from nonexistent customers
- Preventing the deletion of an employee record if there exists a corresponding entry in an `EmployeeSchedule` table
- Automatically changing the records in related tables when the primary table is updated (it is worth noting that, in general, you should never update a PK field)

As an example of this last point, say we updated a `CustomerID` in the `Customers` table and that customer had placed 100 orders. We would have to update every one of these order records with the new `CustomerID` field value – any we missed would become orphaned.

With referential integrity enforced, you may have the option to 'cascade update related fields' or to 'cascade delete related fields':

- Cascade update: If a field value in a table's primary key is changed then the database will automatically scan all related tables and related foreign key field values will be updated accordingly. Therefore, when we update a `CustomerID` value (say from 100 to 101) in the `Customers` table, the `CustomerID` field values for all orders generated by that customer will change from 100 to 101 as well.
- Cascade delete: When you delete a record, the database will delete all related records in related tables. You should take extra care when deleting records in the primary table. For example, if we delete a customer from the `Customers` table, all relating orders in the `Orders` table will be deleted as well (whether you wanted to or not). Some databases have an 'on delete set Null' clause that handles this problem, allowing you to keep the legacy data.

Under most RDBMSs, you can set referential integrity only when certain conditions are met. Since we are comparing values between two tables when the tables are related, the fields that are being referenced must be of the same or 'compatible' data types and size. Compatible data types are those that contain the same types of values although the precision of the data may differ. For example, it is possible to join an `integer` field with a `real` number field, or a `character` field whose maximum width is 20 with another `character` field whose maximum width is 25. Another condition that is required for referential integrity is that the matching column from the primary table be uniquely identifiable, by either its primary key or candidate key. The last condition is that both tables in the reference belong to the same database.

One significant advantage of defining RI rules in the database is that once the rules are established, the burden of enforcing these rules is removed from your application's code. Your application does not have to explicitly check for conditions that violate referential integrity. Instead, the RDBMS will raise an error to inform you when an attempt to violate the rules has been made. Your application will still need to check for and respond to the error, but the majority of the work is done by the database where such errors are more efficiently handled.

By having these rules as part of the database and not in the application, more than one application may be written for the same database and use the same rules. If the logic for RI were contained in the application only and some business rule changed, then updates would be required to all applications that use that database.

To illustrate this, consider the scenario where a company uses Visual Basic to develop an order entry system for use by its sales department. The database used requires that orders may be placed only for those products in its inventory. The developers decide to put code in the Visual Basic application to ensure that this rule is followed. Some time later, the company develops a web site that allows customers to place orders directly. The same business rule concerning what products may be ordered is to be used. Since the code for this business rule is not in the database, the company would have to duplicate this logic for the web site. By having the logic in two places, you need to maintain two sets of code and risk having inconsistencies between the two versions. If the business rules logic were located in the database, where both applications could access it, then the business rules are more easily maintained and are guaranteed to be consistent.

The Normalization Process

Dr Codd and his followers went far beyond simply splitting up tables and creating relationships: they developed rules for how to define tables, columns, and records so that there cannot be a duplication of information or a failure in the logical relationships. The rules are named **Normal Forms** and are part of the **Normalization** process.

Normalization applies successive sets of tests (called rules) to a database design that will identify types of data integrity problems and applying corrective measures if any entities fail to meet any of these sets of rules. In database design jargon, when an entity is tested against these rules, it is said that these rules are being *applied* to the entity.

The process of applying rules to the entities and taking any required corrective action results in simplifying the structure of the database entities by removing duplications in the data items stored. By using these normalization rules, we can more clearly identify relationships between the different entities in our model, and help ensure that our data is consistent between entities.

If an entity passes the first set of rules for normalization, it is said to be in **first normal form**, or **1NF** for short. If an entity is already 1NF and certain additional rules are applied to it, it is said to be in **second normal form** (**2NF**). As more and more rules are applied, entities may reach higher forms, such as **third normal form** (**3NF**), the **Boyce-Codd normal form** (BCNF), **fourth normal form** (4NF), **fifth normal form** (5NF), and **domain/key normal form** (DKNF).

In the broadest sense, there are three basic steps in normalization:

1. Elimination of redundant attributes and/or redundant rows
2. Removal of derived data
3. Making certain that each table represents only one single business entity

When normalization is applied to the tables of a database, not all tables will necessarily be normalized to the same level or degree. Some tables may be in 3NF while others are in 4NF, and yet others in 2NF. Having tables normalized to different degrees is OK; our goal is to have a fast, efficient, and meaningful design. Normalization helps in achieving these goals, but normalization can be overdone in some cases.

With each increasing form of normalcy there are tradeoffs between efficiencies in storage and performance, so we should strive to have an 'appropriate' amount of normalization based upon the particular needs of the application. In many commercial applications, tables end up being in 3NF or 4NF in order to obtain reasonable performance for queries.

However, you should be aware that, for certain applications, there is a danger that you may compromise the integrity of your data if you do not normalize to 4NF or 5NF. Although our Music Store application does not provide an environment for the discussion of rules above third normal form, we nevertheless cover them here with the exception of the most restrictive level of all – DKNF). By doing so we hope you will be better able to spot certain scenarios that may call for further normalization, when working on more complex applications and designs.

Once we discuss the normalization process, we'll have a good understanding of the issues involved in normalization, so we'll wait until then to have a discussion about how far you should normalize your tables. In that discussion, we'll evaluate the trade-offs and benefits that should be considered.

First Normal Form

The goal of having a table in first normal form concerns being able to clearly distinguish data in different rows and in different columns. For a table to be in first normal form, each row must be identified, all columns in the table should be atomic, and each column must be unique. What do we mean by identified, atomic, and unique? To understand how these terms are used in database theory, consider the following discussion. We have already covered identification, with our discussion of primary keys, so let's consider the other two requirements.

Atomic Values

For a column to be **atomic**, it should contain one piece of information only. It should not contain any data that resembles a list or a collection.

To illustrate the requirement of being 'atomic', consider the 'Ship ToAddress' column in the spreadsheet example above. This column contained four items of data in one field:

- A street address
- A city
- A state
- A ZIP code

Having more than one item of data grouped together makes operations such as selecting and sorting very arduous. For instance, if you wanted to sort the data by postal code, you would first need to extract the postal code value from the rest of the data for each record before the sort order can be determined. The extra work required to extract the postal code would make coming up with a sorting command difficult and would take extra time and consume more resources.

To resolve this problem, the first normal form rules require that each of these items of data must be in their own column; a column for street address, a column for city, a column for state, and a column for postal code.

Another common example of this is grouping both the first and last name into a single column. In our original Microsoft Excel spreadsheet, we did just that – included a single column for the customer's name. To ensure that our `Customers` table contains only atomic values, we need to store the customer's first name separately from their last name, so we define the `CustomerFirstName` and `CustomerLastName` fields.

Unique Columns

This requirement concerns having every column in a table storing information that is different from each of the other columns in that table. In other words, the table should contain no redundant columns. This requirement should not be confused with having unique values within a column, as is required for PKs.

For an illustration, again consider our Music Store example using the Microsoft Excel spreadsheet. This system allows for only two items to be purchased with one order. The information for the first product is saved in the `ProductID`, `Price Per Item`, and `Qty` fields under the group `1st Item`. The information for the second product is saved in columns with the same name but under the group `2nd Item`. Clearly, these two sets of columns are redundant and this approach wastes space when only one item is ordered.

To resolve this problem, we eliminate the `2nd Item` set of columns and, instead, insert the second item as a new row. By having one row for each line item, we use only the space we need and we are able to add any number of line items to the order. This approach offers another advantage – more than two items can be purchased with a single order.

To make sure that we can match each row in the `CustomerOrders` table with the correct (in other words, related) rows in the `CustomerOrderItems` table, we need to store some common information in each table. As we know, each order will have a unique `OrderID` value. If we include the `OrderID` for each row in the `CustomerOrderItems` table as well, then we can then properly relate these two tables.

This is the `Orders` table:

OrderID	CustomerID	...
2140	101	...
2141	184	...
2142	101	...

and now the `CustomerOrderItems` table:

OrderID	LineNumber	ProductID	Quantity	PricePerItem	...
2140	1	1002	1	9.99	...
2140	2	1005	2	12.99	...
2141	1	1001	1	12.99k	...
2142	1	1000	1	9.99	...
2142	2	1002	1	9.99	
2142	3	1003	2	15.99	...

It is also worth noting that the CustomerOrderItem table includes a LineNumber column. To understand why this column is needed consider the following. Any one customer may order more than one product at a time, so for any single row in the CustomerOrders table, there will be one or more related rows in the CustomerOrderItems table. This implies that the OrderID column cannot, by itself, be the primary key. Since no other column in this table could be used for the PK, we are forced to add another column. The values stored in this new column, LineNumber, need not have any real meaning except that they are values that can be used to uniquely identify any given row in the table.

Traditionally, merchants issuing paper invoices would refer to each item listed on an invoice as a 'line item' since the paperwork usually displayed each product ordered on its own line, and these lines were often numbered. The approach taken in the data model is to mimic this paper system, so the values found in the LineNumber column will have a value of 1 for the first item listed in a given order, a value to 2 for the second item listed, 3 for the third, and so on.

Try It Out – Normalizing to 1NF

Given what we currently know about the entities for our music store, determine which of the following items should be included in a 1NF table that will store information about the customers. Feel free to add additional data items as needed and to ignore those items that should not be included in the Customer entity:

- CustomerName
- CustomerTitle
- CustomerPostalAddress
- CreditCardHolderName
- CreditCardNumber
- CreditCardType
- CreditCardExpiryDate
- EmailAddress
- CountryAbbrev
- CountryName

How It Works

In order for the Customer entity to be in 1NF, we need to select only those data items that are identifiable, atomic, and unique. In addition, the data items selected should all have something to do with the customers themselves. As we examine each data item listed, we should realize the following:

- The CustomerName attribute should be decomposed into CustomerFirstName and CustomerLastName
- The CustomerPostalAddress attribute should be decomposed into CustomerAddress, CustomerCity, CustomerState, CustomerCountry, and CustomerPostalCode
- The CreditCardExpiryDate attribute should be decomposed into CreditCardExpiryMonth and CreditCardExpiryYear
- There is no single attribute or combination of attributes that will be guaranteed to be unique, so a new attribute will need to be created

- `CountryAbbrev` and `CountryName` are not both needed
- Since it is possible that the credit card may not be issued to the customer using the same spelling as their full name (or perhaps the card is issued in a company's name), we store both the customer's full name and the name that the card was issued under

Therefore, our first attempt at producing a `Customer` entity should yield:

```
CustomerID (PK)
CustomerTitle
CustomerFirstName
CustomerLastName
CustomerAddress
CustomerCity
CustomerState
CustomerCountry
CustomerPostalCode
EmailAddress
CreditCardHolderName
CreditCardNumber
CreditCardType
CreditCardExpiryMonth
CreditCardExpiryYear
```

Second Normal Form

Storing duplicate data unnecessarily will take up disk space, slow down performance, and may cause issues when trying to change or delete data. Part of the goal of normalization is to eliminate redundant data and the second normal form is applied to help ensure that redundant data does not exist.

For an entity to be in second normal form (2NF), it must pass two tests. The first test is that it must already be in first normal form. The second test is that all attributes that are not part of the primary key are dependent upon that key. In more mathematical terms, the entity has no partial key dependencies.

To illustrate this, consider the following movie schedule:

Theater	Movie	ShowingTime	Telephone
Empire Theater	Atlantis: The Lost Empire	5:30 PM	(203) 555-1111
Empire Theater	Atlantis: The Lost Empire	7:30 PM	(203) 555-1111
Empire Theater	Bridget Jones's Diary	7:30 PM	(203) 555-1111
Royal Heights	Bridget Jones's Diary	7:30 PM	(860) 221-9876
Empire Theater	Ghosts of Mars	9:00 PM	(203) 555-1111

This entity describes what movies are played at what times at certain theaters. In this entity, the primary key is composed of the `Theater` and the `Movie` fields. Since the same movie can be shown at different times and at different theaters, we need to know both the theater and the movie before we can determine the show time. It said that there is a functional dependency between the `ShowingTime` field and the two fields of the primary key. This is usually denoted as:

```
(Theater, Movie) • (ShowingTime)
```

While it can be read as '*Theater* and *Movie* determine *ShowingTime.*' The `Telephone` field violates the 2NF rule since it is an attribute of the theater and is independent of the movie being played.

To resolve this, remove the `Telephone` attribute from this entity forming a new entity that describes each theater, called `ShowingTimes`:

Theater	Movie	ShowingTime
Empire Theater	Atlantis: The Lost Empire	5:30 PM
Empire Theater	Atlantis: The Lost Empire	7:30 PM
Empire Theater	Bridget Jones's Diary	7:30 PM
Royal Heights	Bridget Jones's Diary	7:30 PM
Empire Theater	Ghosts of Mars	9:00 PM

and an entity called `Theaters`, which contains the telephone numbers of the respective theaters:

Theater	Telephone
Royal Heights	(860) 221-9876
Empire Theater	(203) 555-1111

Try It Out – Normalizing to 2NF

Let's take another look at our Music Store example and determine if the following entities are all in 2NF:

CustomerOrders	CustomerOrderItems	Customers
`OrderID (PK)`	`OrderID (PK)`	`CustomerID (PK)`
`OrderDate`	`LineNumber (PK)`	`CustomerTitle`
`CustomerID`	`ProductCode`	`CustomerFirstName`
`ShipToAddress`	`ProductDescription`	`CustomerLastName`
`ShipToCity`	`Price`	`CustomerAddress`
`ShipToState`	`Qty`	`CustomerCity`
`ShipToPostalCode`	`Discount`	`CustomerState`

Table continued on following page

CustomerOrders	CustomerOrderItems	Customers
		CustomerCountry
		CustomerPostalCode
		EmailAddress
		CreditCardHolderName
		CreditCardNumber
		CreditCardType
		CreditCardExpiryMonth
		CreditCardExpiryYear

For each entity, determine if each attribute is dependent upon the primary key. Since the primary key is used to identify each row in the entity, each attribute in a given entity must be dependent upon that key. In other words, each attribute must describe the entity that the primary key represents. Do any of these entities violate 2NF? If so, how would you alter the entity to make it 2NF?

How It Works

One technique for determining if an attribute is dependent upon the primary key is to ask the question, 'Does this attribute directly describe the primary key for each attribute in the table?' For example, 'Does `OrderDate` directly describe the `OrderID`?' Since the primary key identifies each order, it is easier to answer the question if we restate the question as, 'Does `OrderDate` directly describe the `Order`.' The answer is, of course, yes. The `OrderDate` describes when the order was placed. 'Does `CustomerID` describe the `Order`?' Yes, the `CustomerID` describes which customer placed the order. If we continue through the `Orders` table, we shall find that we can answer yes for every attribute, so the `Orders` entity is in 2NF.

With the `CustomerOrderItems` entity, we have a compound primary key that is composed of both `OrderID` and `LineNumber`. This is needed since multiple products may be order in a single order. The `LineNumber` attribute will contain a value of 1 for the first item order for a given order. It will have a value of 2 for the second item, and so on. Therefore, the primary key identifies the item of the order. When we ask our questions, we state them such as 'Does `ProductCode` describe the 1st item purchased in the order?' When we answer these questions, we find that this entity is also in 2NF. Similarly, we find that the `Customers` table is also in 2NF.

Third Normal Form

The requirements for third normal form (3NF) are similar to those for second normal form in that it considers functional dependencies. Where the rules for 2NF required that each column is dependent upon the primary key, the rules for the 3NF require that each attribute be dependent on the primary key only and not any other attributes.

An entity is considered to be in third normal form if it is already in second normal form and all attributes that are not part of the primary key are dependent entirely on the primary key. In other words, every column in the table must be dependent upon the primary key, the whole key, and nothing but the key. If a column describes some non-key column, it should be removed and placed into a different table.

Let us again take a look at our music store example and apply the rules for 3NF. Starting with the `CustomerOrderItems`, let's make sure that each column in the table that isn't part of the primary key directly describes the key, `OrderID`, and `LineNumber` (in other words, the line item).

ProductCode identifies the product that is being order for the line item, so that column looks good. The next column is ProductDescription. Although you can think of this column as identifying the product that is being ordered, in actuality, ProductDescription describes the product, which we identify by its ProductCode value. If the product were changed for this line item (which we identify with the ProductCode), then ProductDescription column would change accordingly. Therefore, ProductDescription is dependent upon ProductCode, not the primary key, so this violates our rule for 3NF.

To remedy this violation, we do not include ProductDescription in the CustomerOrderItems table, but rather, store this column in a different table, one that describes each product that is sold. This new table, Products, can use the ProductCode column as a primary key. Since the CustomerOrderItems table will still contain the ProductCode column, we can relate the two tables.

After applying 3NF rules to our schema, the resulting entities would be:

CustomerOrders	**CustomerOrderItems**	**Products**	**Customers**
OrderID (PK)	OrderID (PK)	ProductCode (PK)	CustomerID (PK)
OrderDate	LineNumber (PK)	ProductDescription	CustomerTitle
CustomerID	ProductCode	Price	CustomerFirstName
ShipToAddress	Qty		CustomerLastName
ShipToCity	Discount		CustomerAddress
ShipToState			CustomerCity
ShipToPostalCode			CustomerState
			CustomerCountry
			CustomerPostalCode
			EmailAddress
			CreditCardHolderName
			CreditCardNumber
			CreditCardNumber
			CreditCardType
			CreditCardExpiryMonth
			CreditCardExpiryYear

As we shall see in the next section, the remaining normal forms deal with composite key situations. Therefore, we need only to evaluate the CustomerOrderItems table to see if it violates these higher forms.

Boyce-Codd Normal Form

When Edgar F. Codd initially developed the normal forms, he envisioned five of them. As we know, he numbered these forms 1 through 5. Later on, a group of researchers from IBM, which included Raymond Boyce, discovered that there was a problem with some tables in 3NF and a stricter version of 3NF was developed. Since there was already a form called 4th Normal form, it was decided to name this form after the people who developed it, hence the name Boyce-Codd Normal Form (BCNF).

It should be noted that tables that are in 3NF are usually also in BCNF. Only under special circumstances, which we will describe next, will a table in 3NF not also be in BCNF.

Although the earlier normal forms address dependencies of columns with the primary key, the Boyce-Codd Normal form (BCNF) deals with dependencies within keys. The BCNF is concerned with what fields may be selected to make up the primary key of a 3NF table. To understand this form, we first need to define a couple of terms. If each row in a table can be uniquely described by more than one set of fields, you have your choice which set of fields will be compose the primary key. Each set of fields that you may choose from is called a **candidate key**. If the keys contain more than one field, it is said to be a **composite key**. If each of the candidate keys shares some of the same fields, it is said that they are both "composite and overlapping."

A table is said to be in BCNF if it is already in 3NF and there are no dependencies within the fields that compose the candidate keys. The BCNF differs from the 3NF only when there is more than one candidate key and these keys are composite and overlapping.

To illustrate the need for the BCNF, consider a financial application where you need to keep track of loans across a number of banks for a variety of people. A Borrower table could be constructed that contains the columns `BankNumber`, `LoanNumber`, `CustomerID`, and `Amount`. This table could have it's primary key selected from the following functional dependencies:

- (BankNumber, LoanNumber, CustomerID) Amount
- (BankNumber, LoanNumber) CustomerID and Amount
- (CustomerID, LoanNumber) BankNumber and Amount

Since each of these candidate keys contains more than one column, they are all composite keys. Also, each key uses the `LoanNumber` column, so they are also overlapping. Although this table is in 3NF, there is a redundancy problem, such as for each customer associated with a loan, we must repeat the bank name and amount of the loan. We can eliminate this redundancy by decomposing the table into two tables that are each in BCNF. One table that describes the loans themselves and a second table describing which customers are associated with each loan:

- BankLoan table: LoanNumber, BankNumber and Amount
- CustomerLoan table: LoanNumber and CustomerID

This works because no single bank will issue two loans with the same loan number, and no single customer will get the same loan number from two different banks.

Fourth Normal Form

Our rules of normalization so far resolved redundancies among columns in a table, but these rules did not address all types of redundancies. Tables in the fourth normal form resolve problems that arise from tables having composite primary keys, but still possess redundant data between rows.

In order to describe a table in 4NF, consider the following scenario that illustrates the problems that 4NF tables resolve. Suppose we are asked to add to a university database a table that contains, for each course, a list of all teachers who are qualified to teach the course and a list of all the textbooks required for the course. In this scenario, the required text for a course is dictated by the course, not the teacher.

CourseNumber	TeacherID	RequiredText
SW460	101	Instant JavaScript
SW460	101	Professional JavaScript
SW460	77	Instant JavaScript
SW460	77	Professional JavaScript
SW481	101	Professional ASP Data Access
SW524	77	Professional Active Server Pages 3.0

The primary key for this table is a composite of each of the three fields. There are no non-key columns. The table is in at least 3NF.

There is a redundancy between rows worth noting: every `CourseNumber` of `SW460` uses `Instant JavaScript` and `Professional JavaScript` as the `RequiredTexts`. Tables that allow such redundancies can lead to problems when updating it. For example, the addition of one new textbook requires the insertion of a new row for each teacher who teaches the course and the addition of a new qualified teacher requires the insertion of a new row for each textbook on the list. These problems are due to the fact that the list of `TeacherIDs` and the list of `RequiredTexts` are each dependent on `CourseNumber` but `TeacherID` and `RequiredText` are not. In other words, the lists of qualified teachers and texts both depend on Course but have nothing to do with each other.

The solution for this problem is to decompose this table into two new tables. One table will define which teachers are qualified for which course, and the second table will define which texts are required for each course. These new tables will be in fourth normal form.

CourseNumber	TeacherID
SW460	101
SW460	77
SW481	101
SW524	77

CourseNumber	RequiredText
SW460	Instant JavaScript
SW460	Professional JavaScript
SW481	Professional ASP Data Access
SW524	Professional Active Server Pages 3.0

Fifth Normal Form

The fifth normal form was developed to address problems that may arise when you query a 4NF table, edit the values returned, and then need to apply those changed values back into the table. Depending upon the key used for the table, it may be impossible to determine which rows in the table the query came from. The aim of the fifth normal form is to decompose 4NF tables such that you can relate these new tables to get back the original table's data without losing any information.

To illustrate why a 5NF table is needed, we'll consider what would happen when a 4NF is queried twice and then results of those two queries are used to recreate the original 4NF table. Rather than constructing an actual SQL statement for the queries, we'll decompose the table to show the information that would be acquired by those queries. By doing so, we'll see what data could be lost when we recreate the original table. The example uses the following 4NF table that describes online auctions. In this example, any given seller may place their goods to be auctioned off on any number of online auction sites. A buyer also may place bids on any number of auction sites:

AuctionSite	Seller	Buyer
CyberAuction	Barbara Curry	Kara Russell
CyberAuction	James Conrad	Stephanie Vanin
HighBid	Barbara Curry	Stephanie Vanin
CyberAuction	Barbara Curry	Stephanie Vanin

Let's see what happens when we decompose this 4NF table into two tables using (`AuctionSite,Seller`) and (`AuctionSite,Buyer`).

The following tables are `AuctionSeller`:

AuctionSite	Seller
CyberAuction	Barbara Curry
CyberAuction	James Conrad
HighBid	Barbara Curry

and `AuctionBuyer`:

AuctionSite	Buyer
CyberAuction	Kara Russell
CyberAuction	Stephanie Vanin
HighBid	Stephanie Vanin

Now let's see what happens when we join these tables. For this join, let us relate the two tables using `AuctionSite`. The first record from `AuctionSeller` is from Barbara Curry using CyberAuction. This record matches up with two records from `AuctionBuyer`, those for Kara Russell and Stephanie Vanin, to produce:

AuctionSite	Seller	Buyer
CyberAuction	Barbara Curry	Kara Russell
CyberAuction	Barbara Curry	Stephanie Vanin

So far, so good. These records match exactly with our original table. Now let us consider the second record of `AuctionSeller`, which produces:

AuctionSite	Seller	Buyer
CyberAuction	James Conrad	Kara Russell
CyberAuction	James Conrad	Stephanie Vanin

Here is a problem: James Conrad never sold anything to Kara Russell using CyberAuction! Therefore, these two tables are not in 5NF. In most cases, the problem is that we chose the wrong columns for the primary key in one or both of the tables, or we need to use more than two tables. The solution in our auction example is to decompose our original table into three tables: (`AuctionSite,Seller`), (`AuctionSite,Buyer`), and (`Seller,Buyer`) as follows.

The first is `AuctionSeller`:

AuctionSite	Seller
CyberAuction	Barbara Curry
CyberAuction	James Conrad
HighBid	Barbara Curry

Next is `AuctionBuyer`:

AuctionSite	Buyer
CyberAuction	Kara Russell
CyberAuction	Stephanie Vanin
HighBid	Stephanie Vanin

Finally we have table `SellerBuyer`:

Seller	Buyer
Barbara Curry	Kara Russell
James Conrad	Stephanie Vanin
Barbara Curry	Stephanie Vanin

When we join these tables, we do so two at a time. The result of any two tables being joined will produce some false rows, but when this result is joined with the third table, these data anomalies will disappear. The following is `AuctionSellerBuyer`, which is `AuctionSeller` joined with `AuctionBuyer`:

AuctionSite	Seller	Buyer
CyberAuction	Barbara Curry	Kara Russell
CyberAuction	Barbara Curry	Stephanie Vanin
CyberAuction	James Conrad	Kara Russell
CyberAuction	James Conrad	Stephanie Vanin
HighBids	Barbara Curry	Stephanie Vanin

Now let us walk through the joining of table `AuctionSellerBuyer` with table `SellerBuyer`. We will match records from both tables that share the same (`Seller, Buyer`) values. The first record of `AuctionSellerBuyer`, Barbara Curry selling to Kara Russell using CyberAuction has a match in `SellerBuyer`, so the following record is produced:

AuctionSite	Seller	Buyer
CyberAuction	Barbara Curry	Kara Russell

Similarly for the second record in `AuctionSellerBuyer`, our resulting table becomes:

AuctionSite	Seller	Buyer
CyberAuction	Barbara Curry	Kara Russell
CyberAuction	Barbara Curry	Stephanie Vanin

When we come to the third record of `AuctionSellerBuyer`, we find no corresponding record in `SellerBuyer`. Therefore our resulting table is left unchanged.

We continue with the fourth record of James Conrad selling to Stephanie Vanin using CyberAuctions and find matching values in `SellerBuyer` to produce:

AuctionSite	Seller	Buyer
CyberAuction	Barbara Curry	Kara Russell
CyberAuction	Barbara Curry	Stephanie Vanin
CyberAuction	James Conrad	Stephanie Vanin

Finally, we match the record in `AuctionSellerBuyer` of Barbara Curry selling to Stephanie Vanin using HighBid to a record in `SellerBuyer` to produce a table containing the same records as our original 4NF table!

AuctionSite	Seller	Buyer
CyberAuction	Barbara Curry	Kara Russell
CyberAuction	Barbara Curry	Stephanie Vanin
CyberAuction	James Conrad	Stephanie Vanin
HighBid	Barbara Curry	Stephanie Vanin

Although the order of the records may not be the same between our 4NF table and our result, such differences are not considered in relational theory. As long as the two tables contain the same records, regardless of the order, we can consider them to be the same. Therefore, the tables `AuctionSeller`, `AuctionBuyer`, and `SellerBuyer` are all considered to be in 5NF.

How Far Should You Normalize?

When you normalize tables, you are able to better organize the data and reduce the amount of storage required. Although these benefits are very important, there are situations where the benefits of normalized tables are outweighed by the reduction in performance. Whenever more than one table needs to be joined, additional processing power must be expended. If the number of tables being joined is small or the tables themselves hold few rows, this hit to performance is negligible, but when many tables are involved with a large number of rows, the execution time can increase significantly. What is needed is the 'optimal degree' of normalization.

But what is the optimal degree of normalization? You really can't know for sure until you get some test data in the database and you start running some stress tests and calculate some empirical performance measurements (see later). When coming up with the initial logical design, it is generally a good practice to normalize each table as much as possible. If all of your tables are in 5NF, the design is sound and will work well for applications that use it. If you find that there is a significant enough performance hit to justify not to using 5NF tables, you can always 'flatten' the tables easily to make them a lower degree of normalcy.

It is quite true that a large number of databases in business today rarely go beyond 3NF. The argument for stopping at 3NF usually deals with simplifying queries to increase the speed. While it may be true that a query that uses fewer tables may be faster, there will be occasions when you risk introducing data anomalies if you do so. We either have to live with these anomalies or we have to write additional code to deal with them. Sometimes the errors introduced by these anomalies are inconsequential, and sometimes they are not. Keep in mind that any additional code written will need to be duplicated in every application that uses the database.

You need to carefully consider the impact of how far you normalize. Many would argue that a slightly slower application that is 100 percent accurate is preferable to a slightly faster application that is 97 percent accurate.

Using Summary Tables

A common violation of the normalization rules comes with the use of summary tables. **Summary tables** are tables that contain aggregations or calculations on another table. Examples of the use of summary tables include:

- Calculating last year's sales statistics from individual stores of a national retailer on a region-by-region basis and store these statistics in a new table for use in enterprise reporting queries
- Copying the daily records for a single department from some table into a new table

A strong case can be made in favor of the first example and, indeed, RDBMSs such As Oracle provide special features for just such a reason (called materialized views). They are used in a data warehousing scenario and can increase by many orders of magnitude the speed of enterprise-level calculations that access a large number of rows.

The second example is more typical and is often problematic. In the first example, the values are from last year, so they will not ever need to be updated. In the second example, a simple **view** can be defined in the database that would accomplish the same result but not need the extra processing and disk space required to generate a new table each day.

Under most circumstances, the use of summary tables is only acceptable if all of the following conditions are met:

1. The processing required to compute the statistics is exceptionally burdensome or time consuming to perform repeatedly

2. There is little or no chance that the statistics would ever change, such as with historical values, or the effort required to recalculate those statistics is trivial

3. Storage space for the additional tables will always be available

It should be stressed that this recommendation against using summary tables does not always apply in every circumstance. There are some very good reasons for the duplication of data in a summary table, but these are almost always due to technology – such as when data is being transferred between databases for purposes of replication or data warehousing – or some business rule – such as telephone companies are prohibited by law from retaining certain information about telephone traffic, except in the aggregate.

Data Integrity

One of the key aspects of designing our entities according to the rules of normalization is to arrive at a well-organized set of entities where the data contained in them will not be susceptible to anomalies. In other words, we are striving to preserve our data integrity.

As we continue our discussion of developing a logical design, we must consider how data integrity can be ensured through the design of the entities in our data model. After we have identified the entities for our design, our next step is to organize their attributes so that each piece of data is stored once, and it is stored in the correct place. Without this data integrity will be lost. One crucial technique for designing our entities with data integrity is the process of **normalization**.

By designing our entities carefully, correctly defining relationships and normalizing appropriately, we are ensuring both entity integrity and referential integrity. We have entity integrity because every row of data can be properly identified, and the information contained in any given row represents a meaningful collection of data. We have referential integrity because data values will be consistent between entities.

There is a further type of integrity that we haven't explicitly covered and that is **domain** integrity. This type of integrity is concerned with the actual values of data in a given column, rather than with having valid data between columns and between rows.

For each attribute of our entity we need to ask such questions as:

- What kind of data is it? Numeric? Text? Date?
- What are the limits to the size of the data? What ranges of values will it need to hold?
- Is the data value dependent upon other values? Is the data value derived? If so, how?
- What are valid values? How do we test for valid values?

In order to ensure domain integrity, a database system provides various **Integrity Constraints** that we can use to validate the data being stored in the columns. These constraints are the ones that we covered in our discussion of creating tables in Chapter 4. In brief summary, we have (in addition to the PK and FK constraints):

- Nullability constraints – specifies that the column does or does not accept Null values. Null values indicate no value is stored in the column. This is not the same as having a numeric value of zero or a zero-length string, both of which are valid values. Null is a special value used by the database system to indicate that a value has not been supplied (just like in Java). Allowing Null values can cause issues when performing queries, and so they are often not allowed. This doesn't mean that you should always avoid the use of Null values. There are situations where you really do need to use Null values; if for example, the information is to be identified as being unavailable. If you do want to avoid using Null, you can do so by specifying a default value that will be used in place of storing a Null. Also, most RDBMSs allow you to specify whether columns will allow Nulls.
- A `UNIQUE` constraint – specifies that the value entered cannot be the same as an existing value in the same column. An example of this would be to make sure that only one customer is assigned to a given seat on an airline flight.
- `CHECK` constraints – provides a validation rule that is applied to the data before it can be stored in the column, such as limiting the value of a person's age to only positive numbers.

When developing your tables, try to avoid Null values whenever possible. When a table contains too many columns that allow Null values, it is often hard to normalize. When examining the business rules for an entity, you can usually define some default value that can be used in place of a Null. This is not to say that Nulls are inherently bad – they have their place and may be very useful – it is just that their use can be overdone.

Physical Design and Tuning

When you finish building the logical model and it has been reviewed and accepted by all the interested parties, you will need to actually construct the database. The construction of the database will require that you decide upon all of the details for column data types and constraints, physical storage assignments, and other physical properties of the database. This detailed design, which defines exactly how the database will be implemented on your target database system, is called the **physical design**.

> **We will implement the physical design of our Music Store database in the next chapter.**

The physical design requires that you get very, very specific. You will need to decide whether to use an integer or real number for a column, or if the column should contain variable-length data or fixed-length data. Other decisions, such as what will be the physical ordering of the rows in of the table, if any, and what mechanisms will be used to assist searches in the table. By implementing these specific details, you turn your columns into 'fields', and the rows into 'records.' The actual implementation requires that you invoke the commands required to construct the database your design describes. This can be done by manually entering the specifications for each object that is defined, or by using some CASE tool.

If you are using an ER Diagramming program such as Microsoft Visio (http://www.microsoft.com/office/visio/) or CA ERwin (http://www.cai.com/), you can choose the Generate Database option to produce a definition of the database's physical structure and, optionally, execute that definition in the RDBMS to generate the database itself. Most of the better-known ER Diagramming tools can generate a design for servers (Oracle, SQL Server, and so on), desktop databases (Paradox, Access, FoxPro), the Visual Basic Access Engine, or a generic SQL database. They recognize product-specific features such as cascading referential integrity in Access or Transact-SQL triggers (SQL Server) and exploit those features when generating the physical design. As clever as these products may be, don't expect that everything will generate properly or in the optimal manner. For example, Cloudscape allows various properties to be assigned to each table, such as the size of each page of data, which are not considered when you use these ER Diagramming tools.

Once the database is generated in the database system, you can then start refining the design. First, you will need to load into the database test data that will reasonably represent production data. After this is done, you can then consider such things as index creation and (possibly) de-normalization of tables. Technically, some of this work should have been done during the logical design phase, but in reality, much of this work needs to be done after some empirical testing.

Using Indexes

An **index** is used in a database to speed up the referencing of data. In the same way that an index of a book provides you with a fast way to locate a particular topic, a database index provides a series of "pointers" which identify particular blocks of data in the database. In a book, all of the important words should be listed, along with the page numbers that deal with each one of those topics. The index is in alphabetical order, for easy reference. In databases, an index specifies the order of each record in a table if you want to reference it by some column (or columns).

Supposing we frequently use the `LastName` field of the `Customers` table for searching using a `WHERE` clause. In such a situation, we could build an index based on the `LastName` field in the table. Now, when we run our query, the records of the last names in the index are scanned, and, as scanning these requires fewer resources than scanning the actual contents of a table, our query will run much faster.

Indexes are critical to the operation of most databases. A well-placed index will improve the performance of searches and joins in a database significantly, often by several orders of magnitude. However, indexing can be a double-edged sword. When entering data into an indexed table, not only does the table have to be updated, but the index also has to be updated. This requires resources, so, if we are in a situation where a lot of updates have to be done, having the table indexed can actually slow down performance.

We create an index using the `CREATE INDEX` statement. This can actually be a rather complex statement since there are many different options in building a database index. However, to create the basic index on our `LastName` column, the statement would look as follows:

```
CREATE INDEX IDX_CustLastname
ON Customers(Lastname);
```

There are three basic types of index:

- **Clustered index** – this type of index forces the table to physically sequence the records. This way, when you issue a query against the table, the records returned will be presented in this physical order. Obviously, if this type of index causes the records in the table to be placed on disk in some physical order, you can have only one index of this type for any single table. When the index orders the records in the most commonly-used sort order, then significant performance gains may be achieved.
- **Non-clustered index** – works by keeping track of the order of the records if that table was sorted by a particular column or columns. When the database engine processes a query against a table with an index, that index can be used, often increasing the performance of the query several fold.
- **Unique index** – used when we do not want any duplicate values in the field or fields within the index. A primary key is an example of a unique index.

While indexes can greatly improve performance of applications, they are not appropriate for every column. Creating too many indexes can actually hurt performance. This is because with every index created, there is some overhead required for storage and maintenance. Index maintenance will negatively impact on operations such as insertions of new records in a table or changing the values of fields included in keys. What we need is an *appropriate* number of indexes – not too many to degrade performance, but enough that they are available when needed.

So how many indexes should a table have? There really is no correct answer since different tables will have differing numbers of columns and differing contents. A better question to ask is "Which columns should be indexed?" To answer this, we need to consider each table one-by-one as well as how the tables reference each other. First, consider which columns *not* to index. Most RDBMSs will create an index for every primary key and for every field with a Uniqueness constraint, so these columns should not require indexes. One of the main benefits of an index is to quickly find the desired rows without having to perform lots of disk I/O, which has a considerable impact on performance. If the table will contain only a small number of rows, the RDBMS will be able to store the entire table in memory, so having an index will not reduce the amount of disk I/O. Also, avoid placing an index on a column whose values do not vary much. For example, a Gender field that stores only 'M' or 'F' would not be a good candidate for an index. A similar case can be made against columns that contain a significant number of Null values.

Once you have eliminated from consideration all of the columns that are not good candidates for an index, we should consider which of the remaining columns would offer the most benefit if indexed. The fields that are used by query statements to join tables make excellent candidates for indexing. In most cases, joins are made between the first table's primary key and the second table's foreign key. Since primary keys are already indexed, all you need to do is index the foreign key field(s). Other excellent candidates are those fields that are often used as part of the selection criteria of queries or those fields that are often used to sort the results of a query.

There are a few other considerations when choosing fields for indexes. Fields that are updated less frequently typically make better index candidates that fields that have their values changed often. Also, when given a choice of two equally qualified fields, it is often better to use numeric values over string values, and shorter data types over longer ones.

You may also create indexes that include more than one field. These composite indexes can be useful when you don't have a wide variation of values in any of the candidate fields. Composite indexes can also improve performance when a query retrieves only the fields contained in the index. Just keep in mind that there are usually limits to the number of fields that may be included in a composite index as well as limits on the total length of the data contained in a composite query.

Once the indexes have been created, you should regularly administer them. For a variety of reasons, indexes can become corrupt, inaccurate, or inefficiently organized over time. If a table is subject to a great deal of updating and deleting, the indexes may become 'scattered' or 'uncondensed.' When this happens, the gains from using indexes decrease. To correct these problems, the index will need to be rebuilt. Most database systems offer commands that will reconstruct an index. You can also reconstruct an index by dropping it and then creating it again. You may wish to consider establishing a regular schedule of rebuilding the indexes in your database.

Using Views and Stored Procedures

As sophisticated as constraints are, there are often many places in the database that require additional programming logic. Centralizing this logic in the database is almost always preferable to requiring the applications that use the database to implement the logic. Today's modern database systems offer a range of commands that you would find in any high-level language for developing this logic, such as conditional statements, and looping and constructs. Views and Stored Procedures provide a means to execute the logic.

A view is one of several ways to store SQL statements. Once a view is created, you can use it almost as if it were a table itself, since the SQL statements that define the view select and return rows. There are many advantages to using views. They can help simplify queries, isolate application logic, add additional security, and since they can include logic in their definitions, views can provide ways to incorporate business logic.

Stored procedures are functions that, like views, contain a mixture of SQL commands and program logic. Unlike views, stored procedures can accept and return parameters. Stored procedures are also complied on the server for faster execution.

Views

A **view** is a stored query. Views are often referred to as virtual tables. You define the output of a query as a view, in the following fashion:

```
CREATE OR REPLACE VIEW ViewName
AS
SELECT columnlist
FROM TableName
WHERE Conditions
```

Once the view is created, you can query it just as if you were querying the base table. They do not store actual data; rather they contain data from the table for which the query is built.

Views are commonly used to hide information from unauthorized users. In such a case, a view consists of some, but not all, of the base table's columns, and the user has permission to use the view but not the underlying table. When nesting multiple queries, views come in handy to encapsulate data into one view.

To see how views may be of use, imagine that you had an employee table that contained records of all employees, including those no longer with the firm. Assume that the table contains a field named `Active`, which distinguishes current employees from past employees. When we query this table, we can restrict the results to only current employees by specifying some selection criteria. Naturally, most of the interaction with this table will be for current employees only, so we will need to explicitly specify the active employees every time we query the database. To simplify things, we can create a view that is designed to always select active employees. Once we have the view defined, we can reference it as if it were a table itself.

Although this example is fairly trivial, we can see how using a view can shield end users from having to know certain details about the table we draw information from. You may also use views to prevent users from accessing sensitive information. If we did not want users to be able to access all fields from the `Employees` table, such as the `Salary` field, we can use the view to return only particular columns. We could also use a view to perform calculations, translations of data, or acquire data from multiple sources.

If you code your applications to use only views, you are providing the ability to change the names of tables or to use different tables in the future. By implementing views, if you needed to change the name of a table, you can hide the renaming of the table by updating only the views that your application uses. If you didn't use views and a table name changed, you would be forced to modify your application's source code, recompile it and then redistribute the application.

View Drawbacks

There are some drawbacks and limitations with using views. Most of these are specific to the RDBMS, but the most common is the inability to post changes using a view if that view draws information from more than one table.

Another common issue with views concerns **phantom rows**. Phantom rows are rows that are selected by a view because initially they meet some condition for inclusion, and then are edited so that they longer meet these requirements, but the view does not refresh properly to reflect this change. Similarly, phantom rows could happen because a record did not initially meet the view's selection requirements and later was edited to meet them and the view did not refresh properly.

For example, one user, Lance, queries the database using a view that selects only employees in the marketing department. This query returns an employee named Caroline Kunkle. Just after Lance's query has completes, another user updates Caroline Kunkle's employee record to reflect her transfer to a new position outside the marketing department. In some RDBMSs, Lance's view would not dynamically update to exclude this employee.

Stored Procedures

Like views, stored procedures will contain statements and may return a set of records from the database. Views, at the most basic level, act as filters for existing information that must be accessed as part of a query statement. Stored procedures are much more dynamic and offer a number of performance advantages. Unlike views, stored procedures can accept arguments when they are invoked and may return a set of records, a return code, or an output argument that may be used outside the stored procedure to access data.

One of the most important advantages of stored procedures is that they are compiled when they are created and stored within the database ready to be executed. For most database systems, executing precompiled routines is several times faster than executing similar commands sent to it as SQL statements. When a SQL statement is received by a database system, the statement is parsed, analyzed, and then the database engine evaluates the most efficient approach for executing the statement. All of this takes time. By using a stored procedure, most of this work is done at compilation time. Using stored procedures can also reduce network traffic since only the call to the stored procedure and parameter values need to be transmitted.

For example, consider the processing required for placing an order for a product. A check needs to be made to see if the quantity ordered of the product is available. If it is not, then the quantity not available needs to be placed on back order and the order updated accordingly. If these actions were taken on the client side, then several queries would be required, causing many round trips to the server. If this logic was all part of a single order request stored procedure, network traffic would be reduced and the operation would be significantly faster.

Like views, stored procedures can shield users from knowing the details of the tables in the database. This may be done for security reasons or to make using business functions easier. Also, the internal logic of a stored procedure may be updated without affecting the code of the applications that use them, thus making maintenance easier. We'll cover stored procedures in more depth in Chapter 13.

Triggers

In many cases, integrity constraints will be able to enforce most data integrity rules in a database, but there may be certain business rules that are too complex for simple constraints. **Triggers** are compiled procedures stored in the database that are associated with a table and some condition for when the procedure should be executed (fired). Most RDBMSs will allow a trigger to be executed when data is added, deleted, or changed in a table. You can specify a trigger (or triggers, in some RDBMSs) to be fired when data is added, another trigger for when data is deleted, and yet another for when data is updated.

Consider the scenario of an online auction site where bidders and sellers can change their user ID no more than once a month. In order for this business rule to apply, the current data must be compared with the date of the last time the user ID was modified. We would be unable to enforce this rule with simple constraints. To do so, we need some procedure to execute that will check if the required amount of time has elapsed and to update a `LastModifiedDate` field if the user is allowed to make the change. Another scenario is when a student graduates from a university. The business rule states that when a student leaves the university, their student row is moved from the `Students` table into the `Alumni` table.

Triggers are useful in a number of ways. First of all, they provide logic inside the database so as to relieve the application from having to execute a series of commands to perform a single operation. This approach is generally much faster for the application since it will reduce the number of calls to the database and therefore reduce network traffic.

Secondly, the statements that fire within a trigger are treated as a single transaction that can be rolled back from within the trigger. If a severe error is detected, the entire transaction automatically rolls back. We'll talk more about *Transactions* in Chapter 14.

A third benefit comes from the fact that triggers can be defined to fire before and after attempts are made to modify a table. Triggers can disallow or roll back changes that violate referential integrity, thereby canceling the attempted data modification.

Performance Tuning

Much of the work done up to this point has been theoretical: we analyze entities relations, evaluate columns for indexes, and determine data types. Even if we are very careful and have thought of every possible option, we are bound to miss something. Usually, what we missed becomes apparent when the application goes live. The trick is to make sure we have tested the application sufficiently that whatever we miss is relatively harmless and minor. It is also very likely that, in spite of our best efforts with the logical design, some the decisions made do not provide the performance that we expected. The best way to shake out performance problems before going live with the database is to do some empirical testing.

After testing and analyzing the database and the server itself, you should be able to resolve most issues through one or more of the following actions:

- Further normalization of tables to eliminate duplicate data
- The de-normalization of some tables to reduce the time required for joins
- The creation, modification, or removal of indexes
- Redistributing various database objects across physical devices
- Adding additional hardware, especially memory and fast-access disk drives

Stress Testing

One effective way to test the application is to stress test it. Stress testing will often make design flaws obvious. The first requirement of stress testing is data; lots of data. Many of the ER Diagramming tools available will be able to generate sample test data if you cannot obtain a sufficient amount of real-world data to test against. It's also possible to write cross-join queries that will produce large amounts of data from a relatively small amount of test data. With a large enough data set to work with you will be able to use performance analysis tools to optimize your stored procedures, views, and queries substantially. Many of these tools will not only time the execution of your routines, but breakdown this time statement-by-statement to help identify bottlenecks.

Performance monitoring tools tend to fall into certain categories: analysis; system monitoring; and error trapping. Each has a different focus, each is valuable, and they often are most useful when used together. All of the major RDBMS vendors provide such tools with their products, so you should check the product documentation to see what utilities are included. It is also worth browsing through the CDs that the RDBMS is installed from since some tools might not be automatically installed when you install the database server software.

Microsoft Windows NT and Windows 2000 also provides the Performance Monitor utility that may be used to track a variety of variables on the server that can be useful in getting a better understanding of how the database is responding. The Performance Monitor can be found under Control Panel | Administrative Tools | Performance. By using Performance Monitor, you can track real-time statistics such as CPU utilization, disk I/O, and network throughput. There are literally hundreds of items of information that can be tracked, although the most important to start with deal with memory, user connections, disk I/O, processor, and locking. Once you have tracked these items over a period of time, you will be able to establish patterns of behavior. Only after you have a good baseline of operations will you be able to best judge the impact of changes that you implement.

There are also many good third-party products available for stress testing. The Benchmark Factory product from Quest Software (http://www.quest.com/benchmark_factory/) can be used to simulate a load of thousands of users connected to your database for several hours for rigorous load testing. Mercury Interactive (http://www-heva.mercuryinteractive.com/) offer a number of highly regarded products such as LoadRunner, TestDirector, and TestSuite which may be of tremendous use in testing large scale applications. Active Measurement and eMeasure from Bluecurve Software (now owned by Redhat, see http://www.redhat.com/products/software/performance_mgmt/emeasure.html for eMeasure) are also worth looking at, as is Rational Suite PerformanceStudio from Rational Software (http://www.rational.com/).

Query and Procedure Optimization

An important aspect to a database application's performance is the efficiency of the code using it. The various SQL statements and stored procedures used by the RDBMS can be analyzed and bottlenecks may be found. Examples of tools to do this include Oracle's SQL Trace and Microsoft's Query Analyzer. In addition, most RDBMSs support a `SHOW PLAN` or `EXPLAIN PLAN` SQL command that gives details of what the database query engine is doing when it executes a SQL statement.

The usefulness of tools like these cannot be overstated. Analyzing the queries and code won't make them faster, but the analysis will give you insight into what needs to be adjusted to make execution faster. With the right tool, some experimentation, and some patience, SQL statements and stored procedures can see a substantial increase in performance – sometimes making the code run several times faster.

Creating and Maintaining Statistics

Most modern RDBMSs use what is called a cost-based query optimizer to determine how best to execute a query. The optimizer analyzes the various alternative methods that may be used to execute the query and determines which one is 'optimal.' It is this optimal execution plan that is used and saved for later reference.

This begs the question, 'How does the optimizer compare the various ways a query may be executed and determine which one is optimal?' The exact process will vary from RDBMS to RDBMS, but each follows the same general approach. The optimizer parses the statements into discrete steps that require a particular type of action: sorting records, searching through tables, matching records between tables, and so on. At each step, the optimizer determines if there is more than one way to execute the action. For example, should a table been scanned using an index, and if so, which index. As each step is examined, the various alternative approaches are evaluated based upon an estimate of CPU and I/O usage and other factors such as the physical layout of the tables. The greater the usage, the higher the 'cost.' The optimizer chooses the least expensive execution path to process the query.

The next question that arises from this explanation is, 'How does the optimizer estimate the usage/cost at each step?' Again, this varies with each RDBMS, but they all base these estimates on a set of statistics stored for the database. These statistics include such things as the number of rows in the table, a measure of uniqueness of the values in an index, and the distribution of data stored on disk.

Statistics are usually generated and updated automatically, but over time you may find that the statistics are less representative of the data they describe. This is due to the fact the some of the statistics are computed based upon a sampling of the data and not all of the data. Also, certain database operations, such as bulk inserts, deletes, and updates that affect large numbers of records may make these statistics less accurate. When the statistics are inaccurate, the query optimizer will base its decisions on faulty information and the most optimal plan may not be used.

To alleviate this problem, periodically you should manually regenerate the statistics used. This is especially true after loading test data into the system. Most database systems provide an `UPDATE STATISTICS` command that regenerates the statistics. If your RDBMS doesn't have such a command, or you are not able to find it, try dropping and rebuilding the various indexes in the database to force at least some of the statistics to be regenerated.

Summary

There are many reasons why applications suffer from poor performance. A poorly designed database should not be one of them. To construct a fast, efficient database, a good design is essential. All good designs start with an understanding of the business process that we are modeling. By enlisting the aid of key stakeholders and the knowledge of co-workers, you start constructing a conceptual design. The conceptual design identifies the major entities used in the database and the relationships between these entities to describe what needs to be modeled.

After you are confident enough in the conceptual design, begin working on the logical design. The logical design describes how things are done and provides details on the mechanics of the database by specifying such things as data types, keys, calculations, and data integrity rules. One major aspect of the logical design is the organization of the data into tables. Using the rules for normalization, we can efficiently store and access the information without risking data loss. After the tables have been structured, we then apply data integrity rules and enforce business practices through the use of constraints and triggers.

With a detailed logical design in hand, we generate the statements that define our objects and execute these statements to physically generate the database. After loading the database with meaningful test data, we double-check our work through stress testing. We also begin to tune the database, by adding additional indexes and by generating statistics.

The end result will be a fast, flexible, and efficient database that will be able to keep up the demands of today's web-based industries.

Case Study: Designing the Music Store Database

In this chapter, we will begin the design and development of the database used in the book. The database is used to organize the business in a music store. The case study focuses on what is labeled as 'Phase I' of the development: keeping track of the inventory in multiple stores. Once the design is done, the database is built in Oracle 8i to show you how the implementation of the design in an industrial-strength database is done.

In this chapter we will look at:

- Business description and client requirements
- Database design approaches
- Good programming practices
- Building the database schema objects
- Quality testing the database design
- Finalizing the database design
- Using the database (views, queries, and stored procedures)

Problem Statement

Our client opened her dream music store a few years ago. The store did well, despite the slow start at the time, and started to build up a loyal customer base of both individuals and businesses. In fact, the initial store did so well that she leased a neighboring shop and expanded her business.

With imminent plans to open further stores in different parts of the city and the city's suburbs, the owner realized that her business could not expand much further than it had, and might actually suffer and go out of her control, unless she did something to organize it. Up to now she had ordered all of the stock and kept inventory details in a tattered old log book. She realized that she needed to start organizing her inventory properly. Doing so would allow her to have minimal margin stock and make sure she could react quickly to market needs.

She knew that she needed to have a database for keeping an accurate record of what music albums existed where in her stores. She also wanted her database to handle everyday transactions in her stores, allowing her to check items to customers and update the inventory as some of the items are sold. She set about talking to a database designer and expert, about helping her build the systems he needs.

Gathering the Requirements

The first step in the design of the Music Store database is what is known as 'requirements gathering'. As we discussed in the previous chapter, we need to obtain enough information so that we clearly understand the business needs that are driving the development of the database application. We then need to develop a database model that will meet these requirements.

The first step in this process is to interview the music store owner and find out more details about the way she conducts her business now, what problems she is faced with, and what she wants the database to do for her in terms of alleviating these problems. We would also interview her employees, asking them about how they did their work and what would be a better way to make their work easier if the database system were to be used.

Having done this, we need to start documenting these requirements, as we understand them and then present them to the owner for further discussion and ultimate approval. The requirements can be grouped in to two phases:

- Phase I deals with establishing a database that can be used to hold the inventory data relating to music records in the different stores and allows the owner to search and maintain these records. The database has to be designed in a way that makes it possible to modify the design in Phase II and expand on it with minimal impact on existing data.
- Phase II takes the design a step further, allowing the owner and her employees to store data related to any customer transaction in the database. Phase II has the potential to become the basis for a web-based application.

In the initial development phase, we are going to focus only on the Phase I requirements, which as a result of the interview process are documented as follows:

- Store and ensure the integrity of all of the data needed for the day-to-day running of her stores.
- Add, edit, and delete records in any of the tables in the system. For example, ability to add, edit, or delete a recording (album).
- Allow for flexible criteria-based searching of the records. The criteria would be song title, artist, or album name. This searching is needed since many customers come asking for a song, sometimes without knowing the artist or the album name, for instance.
- List store information with the ability to apply filters, such as showing the stores in a particular postal code area.
- List record details in a given store with the ability to apply filters to the list. For instance, a filter would only show records for a certain artist.
- List recordings available in a given store so that she knows where to get a recording for a customer if it does not exist in the visited store.

- If a customer asks about an item that does not exist in stock, it would be nice if the customer can be notified when the item becomes available. To do this, some customer information has to be stored, including e-mail address, and maybe a phone number.
- Provide the ability to categorize customers based on some criteria, such as whether they are individuals, a profit making organization, or a non-profit organization. The owner wants to establish a customer loyalty program with discount incentives for volume and repeat customers based on the categories they belong to.
- Allow customers to provide their reviews of the recording in a way that makes such reviews available for other customers.

We will not discuss the Phase II requirements in detail in this case study. However, it is important that we document these requirements and implement our design so that the database can be smoothly expanded to fulfill these needs:

- The owner is intrigued by the idea of being able to track customers' interests and make recommendations of titles that might interest them. Therefore, she wants to be able to track what titles where obtained by customers and maybe link such events to other customer attributes.
- She supports local bands and regularly advertises their gigs and plays their songs in-store. She has been in discussion with a few bands and would love to be able to let users download and hear samples of their music. The database should support storing large binary data representing such music samples (MP3 files, say).
- Ultimately the owner hopes that her database will support transactions over the Internet.

The next step is to take our requirement list and start to develop the database entities that will satisfy these requirements and the relationships that must be established between these entities. In the previous chapter, we described this as the process of 'developing the logical design'.

Designing the Music Store: the Logical Design

In order to start establishing the database entities that our system will require, we need to examine the business operations related to each of the Phase I objectives. One way to do this is to run through various scenarios describing possible actions that will occur during the fulfillment of each of the objectives.

To determine what entities will be included in our data model, we should ask ourselves other questions:

- What information will need to be kept in the database?
- How would we best group these items of information?
- What business actions need to be performed and what data will be involved in these actions?
- Which of these actions will be handled by the database and which by the application using that database?

Try it Out – Determining Entities for the Music Store Data Model

To illustrate this, consider the following requirement:

- Allow for flexible criteria-based search of the records. The criteria would be song title, artist, or album name. This search is needed since many customers come asking for a song, sometimes without knowing the artist or the album name, for instance.

The owner describes the following scenario that frequently occurs when a customer visits the store to make a purchase:

1. A **customer** visits a branch of the store, wishing to purchase a song that they just heard on the radio. They heard the DJ mention the title of the song but not who the performer was.

2. The owner searches the database by **track** title. The search results include two **recordings** by different **artists** that contain tracks with that that name.

3. Following an off-key rendition of the song's chorus, the owner is able to identify the required recording, and the name of the artist. She then checks to see if she has the recording in **stock** and in what **format** it is available.

4. If the recording is in stock in the visited store, the customer makes the purchase. If the recording is currently out-of-stock or is available at another branch, the owner offers to **order** the title or have it sent over from the other store.

5. If the customer would like to order the item, the owner takes minimal **customer details**, such as the customer's name and phone number or e-mail address, and promises to notify the customer when the recording arrives.

As you can see, various data items have been identified in **bold**. Some of these items will end up being represented as entities. Each of these potential entities will have specific associated properties. Below is a list of the major entities along with specific data about these entities:

- **Customer** – contains properties such as name, e-mail address and phone number
- **Track** – has properties such as title, artist, and music genre
- **Recording** – a collection of tracks; a recording may be audio compact disc, cassette tape, or DVD
- **Stock inventory**– will have properties such as the number of a specific recording that are in stock and the store in which it is held
- **Order** – will have properties such as the identity of the customer who placed the order, the date the item was ordered and so on.

All of these entities will be represented in the database data model. If we look forward to the time when orders can be placed on-line, we would be able to identify entities that may or may not be represented in the data model. For example, an **order form** used to place and order is likely to be a construct of the user interface to allow the customer to enter information. The information that the customer enters will be saved, but the order form itself will not be saved. A **shopping cart** could conceivably be represented in the data model, but there are alternatives to doing so, such as saving its information on the customer's computer using cookies. The number of items that will be in a shopping cart will usually be relatively small, so saving the shopping cart information outside the database is a reasonable approach.

As a result of gathering the requirements, we are able to identify many entities that are candidate for building as tables in the database. These entities will satisfy all of the phase I requirements and also take due account of phase II requirements:

Recordings	RecordingFormats
Tracks	ArtistsAndPerformers
AudioStyles	PublishersAndLabels
Languages	Inventories
PostalCode	Countries
StoreTypes	Stores
Reviews	Customers
CustomerOrders	CustomerOrderItems
OrderStatuses	OrderSources
CustomerTypes	CustomerTitles
CreditCardTypes	PaymentTerms
SalesCampaigns	

Most of these entities are candidates to be represented as tables in our schema. However, before we start building these entities, we need to establish how they must interact to satisfy our requirements and the sorts of relationships that must exist between them

Establishing the Interactions between Entities

In the previous chapter, we discussed at a high level how to determine the relationships between entities in the system, and the cardinality of these relationships - the number of instances of an entity that may be related to (contained in) another entity. Let's now take a look at this in more practical detail and see how we might perform this exercise for our Music Store entities.

Try it Out – Interactions and Relationships in the Music Store Model

We need to determine the relationships and interactions of the various entities in our model. Based upon our discussions about the Music Store so far, what interactions can you find? Are there any new entities that may need to be created? What is the cardinality between any two entities?

As with identifying the entities before, it is often useful to rewrite the narrative so that the interactions and relationships between the entities become more obvious. We will try to rephrase the narrative so that we can recognize these relationships and interactions based upon the verbs we use. For example, here is one example of a partial rewriting of the previous narrative:

> The owner and employees will *search* through the music store database to find the **recordings** that a customer wishes to purchase or *order*. The searches may reference either the recordings or the **tracks** that *comprise* those recordings. For example, we may search for a track by the artist that performed on that track, or for a recording by its title. We can also search for the record label that published the recording. Any given recording may *be* one of the following standards; audio compact discs, cassette tapes, or DVDs. The customer may *place* an order for one or more recordings at one time. The customer must *supply* sufficient information so that they may be notified of a recording's availability.

In this passage, we can easily identify a number of relationships and interactions (you can probably find more):

- **Users** *search* **the database**
- **Artists** *perform* on **tracks**.
- **Publishers** *publish* **recordings**.
- **Tracks** *comprise* **recordings**.
- **Orders** *are composed of* one or more **recordings**.
- **Recordings** will *belong to* any one **recording type**.
- **Customers** *place* **orders**
- **Customers** *supply* **information**

Using this information we can take a pen and paper and come up with a first draft of a portion of our data model:

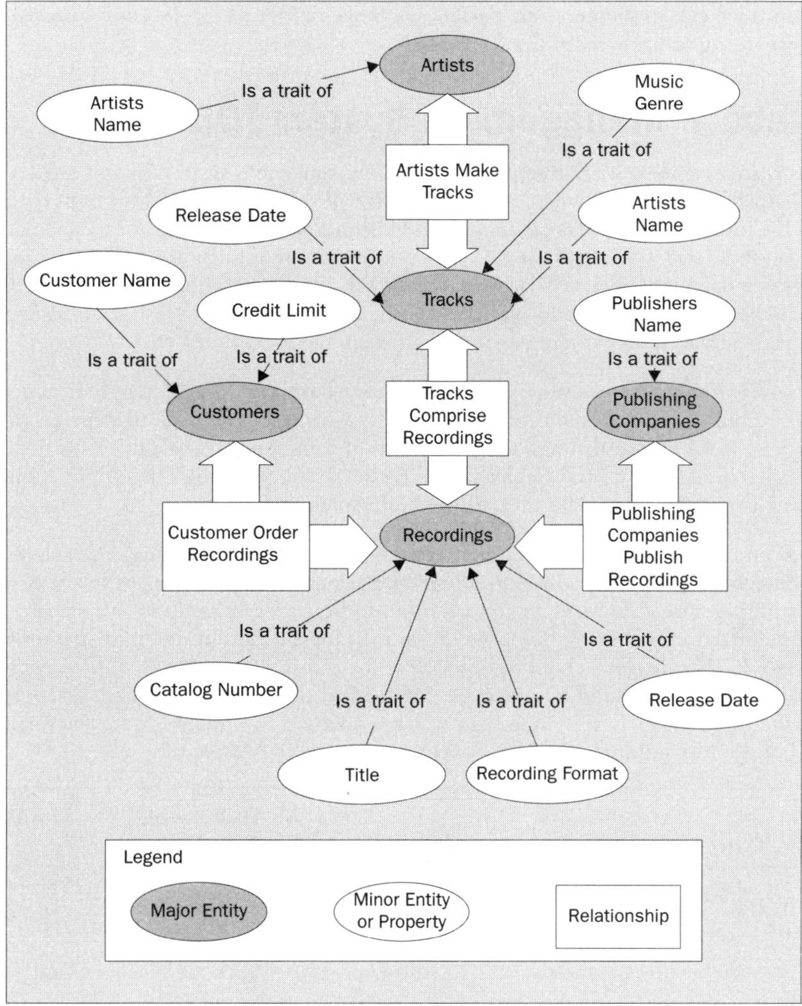

Of course, much more work is required in order to drill down into the full details of the entities and their relationships, but this is an excellent start. Having repeated this process for each section of your data model, you are then ready to move on to converting this model into concrete tables in the database, with the fields and properties that will accurately present our model.

After researching published case studies as guidance in the initial design, you are ready to move on to the physical design of the database.

Designing the Music Store: the Physical Design

Based on the requirements gathered so far, we are now going to formulate the full Entity-Relationship diagrams for our Music Store. We need to keep track of entities like customers, recordings, tracks, languages, countries, recording formats, and so on. We also need to fully define how these entities relate to each other.

However, before we can implement our design, we have an important decision to make. On what RDBMS are we going to implement the database?

What Database Management System (DBMS)?

Since the music store business is relatively small right now, one could say, "Why not use a small, cheap DBMS?" Well, this makes sense if we know the business will remain small and may not require any special data needs in the future. Such needs may include establishing business intelligence, data marts, data mining, etc. A simple business may be able to use an Open Source database, such as mySQL or Cloudscape, or a small desktop-type database, such as Microsoft Access; but a business with the potential of the music store must assess whether it will derive sufficient benefit from an industrial-strength DBMS, such as Oracle, DB2, or Microsoft SQL Server, such that these benefits outweigh the extra initial cost.

Certainly, phase I of the development, with a small user base and limited need for concurrent access, is well suited to a small, "desktop" database such as Microsoft Access or Cloudscape or an open source option. However, if we glance through the phase II requirements we see a need for database that can support multiple concurrent transactions against the database, will allow the application to scale to a large user base, can easily store data in multimedia formats and so on.

We have decided in this case study to implement the Music Store database on Oracle 8i. The SQL examples in the chapter can be applied to other DBMS's with simple changes to the data type or the syntax. For example, the SQL Server's equivalent to Oracle's `varchar2` is `nVarchar` or `varchar`. For ease of reference in converting the table definitions for a different database, we present again the table first shown in the previous chapter, describing the main differences in data types between the major DBMS's on the market and Cloudscape. Syntactical differences may include something like the semi-colon used to end Oracle statements, or using sequences in Oracle for automatically incrementing fields instead of identity columns (in SQL Server), counters (in MS Access), etc.

SQL-3 Data Type	Cloudscape	Oracle	Transact-SQL (SQL Server)	MS Access
BOOLEAN	boolean	number	Bit	Yes/No
BIT	bit	number	Bit	NA
INTEGER	integer	Integer or number	Int	Number/Integer
DECIMAL	decimal	number	Decimal	Number/Decimal
FLOAT	float or real	float	Float	Number/Single
DOUBLE PRECISION	float or real	number	Real	Number/Double
DATE	date	date	Datetime	Date/Time
CHAR	char	char	Char or nChar	Text
VARCHAR	varchar	varchar or varchar2	Varchar or nVarchar	Text

Full scripts to create the database in Oracle are provided, as part of the code download for this book. We also provide a script, along with the actual database files for creating the database on Cloudscape. We also provide an `mdb` and `mdf` file for Access and SQL Server respectively.

One more thing to mention is that if you wish to test out the code in this chapter, you will need to have some familiarity with an Oracle client tool, such as SQL*Plus that allows you to connect to the database and issue SQL statements. If you are using Cloudscape, then you could use the `ij` tool (see Chapter 1).

Naming Conventions

Before you actually start creating the schema objects, it's vitally important to decide on a naming scheme and stick with it. The rules we set for ourselves can be summarized as:

- Physical table names will be the same as the logical names with no underscores separating the words composing the name; for example, the customer orders table would be named `CustomerOrders`.
- If the name is composed of more than one word, we will **not** have spaces; instead, we'll use upper case for the first letter of each of these component words. For example, the table storing artist information is called `ArtistsAndPerformers`.
- Constraints will be identified by a prefix, followed by the name of the constraint. For example a Primary key on the `StoreID` column of the `Stores` table will be denoted `PK_StoreID`. View names will be prefixed with `vw`; for instance, a view showing all families and their children in a certain city would be called `vwCityFamilyChildren`.

Designing the Database

Since we are presenting a case study that shows you how to use the information you gained in the previous chapters, it is best if we use pencil and paper (or any software that helps you draw diagrams, such as Microsoft Visio) to design the database schema and write the script to create it in a text editor. It is useful to note, however, that there are many database design tools that you may use.

The most notable and popular of database design tools is Computer Associate's ERwin (http://www.cai.com/products/alm/erwin.htm). This tool can be used to create a logical design of the database, along with a physical design, then generate a script to create the database in many database management systems, including SQL Server, MS Access, Oracle, DB2, etc. Oracle provides a tool that allows us to build database designs and create a database from such designs: Oracle Designer 2000. Other tools that can be used in the design include, Microsoft Visual Studio, Rational software, etc.

In this section, we will look at some of the things you need to know about entity relation diagrams (ERD), without concerning ourselves with how you draw them. The sections that follow will walk you through building the data model for our case study.

In our ER diagrams we can designate three types of relationships:

- An identifying relationship (represented with a solid line with one dark circle at one end)
- A many-to-many relationship (represented with a solid line with a dark circle at either end)
- A non-identifying relationship (represented with a dashed line with one dark circle at one end)

An **identifying** relationship is a relationship between two tables where the foreign key relating one of them to the other is part of the primary key of first table. A **non-identifying** relationship is a relationship between two tables where the foreign key relating one of them to the other **is not** part of the primary key of first table.

As an example, if we were to link two tables, `Customers` and `CustomerOrders`, the `CustomerID` field in the `Customers` table will be a foreign key in the `CustomerOrders` table. If the primary key of the `CustomerOrders` table is comprised of one field, `OrderID`, then the relationship between the two tables is non-identifying; however, if the primary key in the `CustomerOrders` table were comprised of the `CustomerID` and some other fields, then the relationship would be an identifying one, because the foreign key, `CustomerID` is part of the primary key of the `CustomerOrders` table.

The following sections will walk you through building the data model for our case study. It is up to you whether you want to use a drawing tool to build this diagram or not. Either way, the result will be the same for our purposes. In this case study, we will be normalizing the data model as much as possible. In reality, the model might not be normalized to this extent, especially if the database were to be used for reporting purposes, as we will discuss as we walk through the ER diagrams.

The ERD Diagrams

To make it easier to build the model, let's divide it in to "subject areas". Subject areas are used to group related tables so that they can be represented in a "mini" ERD to make it easier to zoom onto their relationships and interactions.

Stores Subject Area

Each store is located in a geographical area with a particular postal code. The postal code may be related to a country, in case the music store business expands overseas. A store can also be of a particular type and can hold a certain amount of inventory. The inventory is related to the products being sold, namely the recordings. The diagram below shows how the relationships between the `Stores`, `Recordings`, `StoreTypes`, `PostalCodes`, `Inventories`, and `Countries` entities are represented:

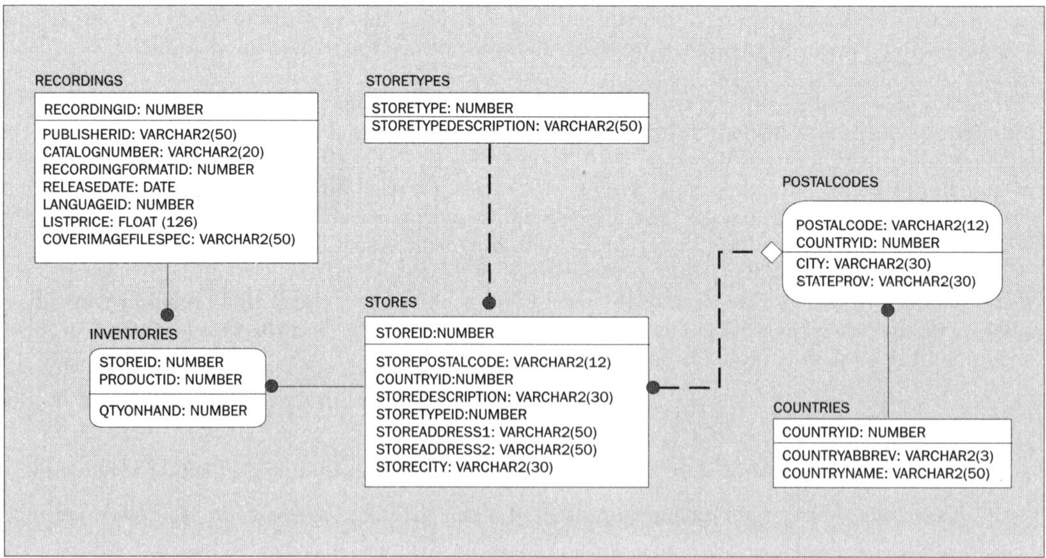

In the diagram above, the broken lines indicate a **non-identifying relationship**. A non-identifying relationship is a relationship between two tables where the foreign key relating one of them to the other is not part of the primary key of that table. For instance in our example, the field `PostalCode` is a foreign key in the `Stores` table and links this table to the `PostalCodes` table. However, this foreign key is not part of the primary key, nor an alternate key in the table `Stores`. Therefore, the relation between the two tables, `Stores` and `PostalCodes`, is a non-identifying relationship.

The open dots on the end of a relationship line indicate the "one" side of a one-to-many relationship (although are not always used), while the dark dots on the end of a relationship line indicate the "many" side. For instance, the relationship between `Stores` and `Inventories` is a one-to-many relationship with the `Inventories` table on the "many" side (a store will contain many inventory items); therefore, we see that the dark dot is located at the `Inventory` side. This relationship can be expressed in English as: "one store may have many inventory items in it, but any single inventory item can only exist in one store."

> **Notice that `STORES` and `RECORDINGS` are related in a many-to-many relationship, which is expressed in terms of two one-to-many relationships between the `STORES` table and the `INVENTORIES` table, and between the `RECORDINGS` table and the `INVENTORIES` table. The `INVENTORIES` table is called in this case the** cross table **or** normalizing table

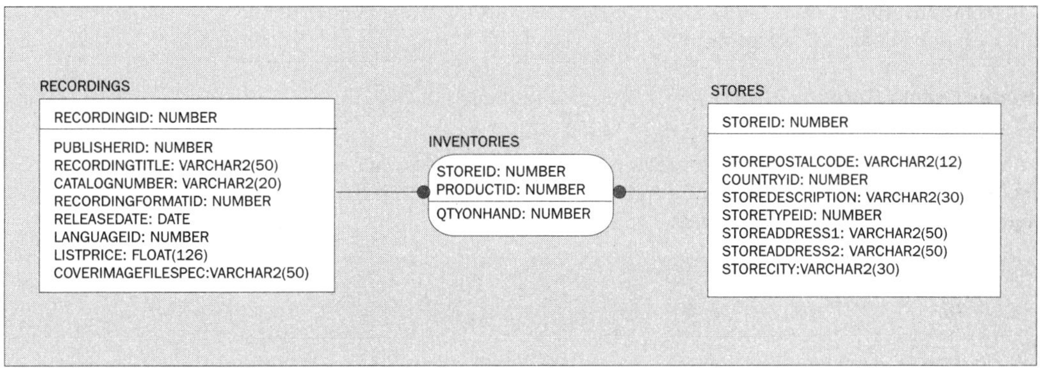

In this subject area, you can see that we took the postal codes, and countries out and put them in their own tables. Well, this is OK as long as the database is used for transactional purposes, in which case normalization is a good thing. But if the database were to be used for reporting purposes, denormalizing the model by including the country and postal code in the store table makes more sense. This is because building queries that span several joins and tables is more difficult, and, generally speaking, the performance of such queries will be much less than if the query were to target one table.

Recordings Subject Area

In this subject area, the `Recordings` entity is the central entity. This entity corresponds to the physical table, `Recordings`, and stores data about the products sold and dealt with each store. For example, this table stores information about recording title, publisher, catalog number, format, release data, language, list price, etc. Many of these attributes are stored in separate tables, as the following diagram shows; hence, the following tables can be seen as part of this subject area: `RecordingFormats`, `Reviews` (a table that holds reviews for a given recording), `CustomerOrderItems`, `AudioStyles`, `Languages`, `Tracks` (a table that holds information on all the tracks in each recording), `ArtistsAndPerformers`, `PublishersAndLabels`, `Inventories`, and, of course, `Recordings`:

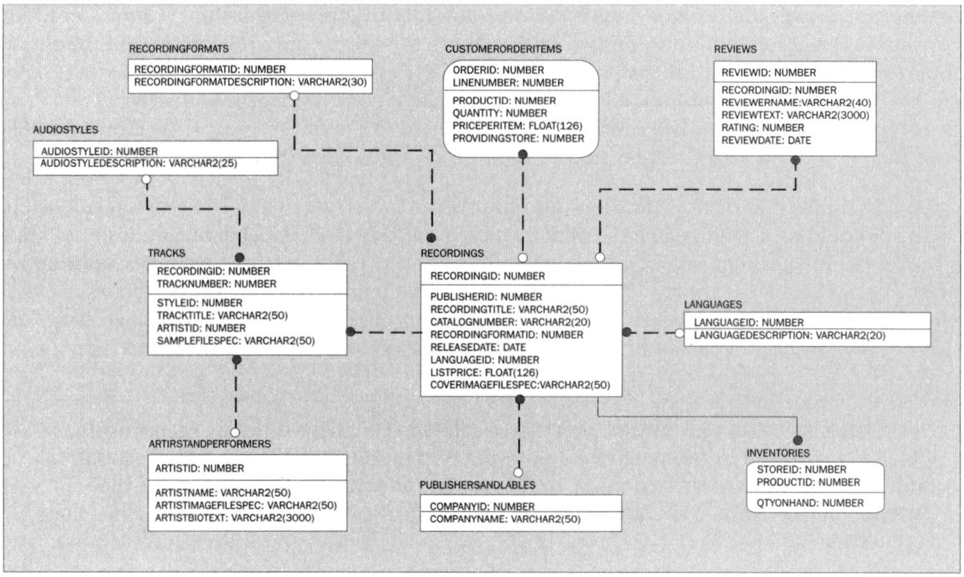

The relationship between the `Recordings` table and the `CustomerOrderItems` table is described in the next subject area description.

Customer Orders Subject Area

This subject area describes the relations between the `CustomerOrders` entity and the entities related to it. Of special interest here is the relationship between customer orders and recordings. This relationship is another example of a many-to-many relationship that is broken down into two one-to-many relations through the `CustomerOrderItems` entity:

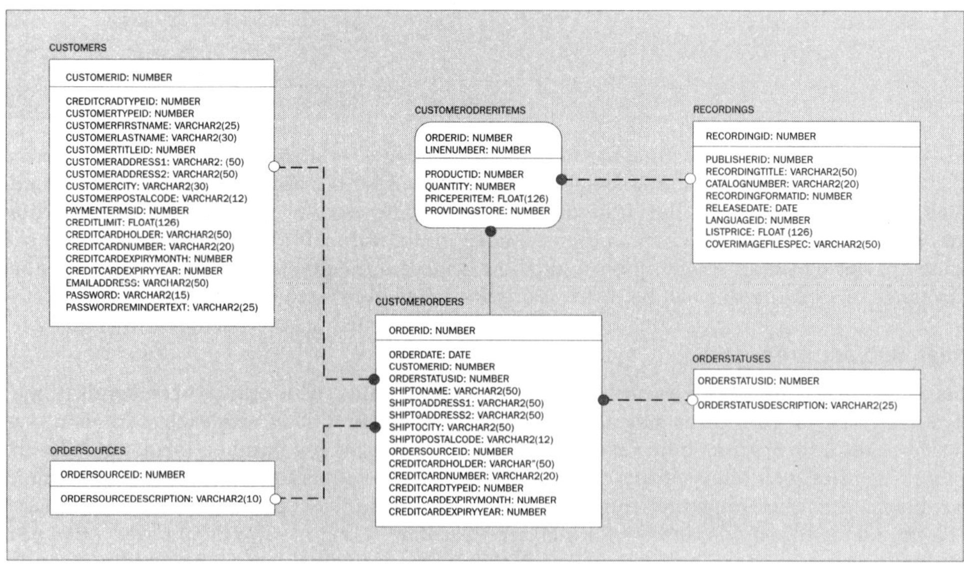

Customer Subject Area

This subject area shows the `Customers` entity and how it relates to other entities, such as customer types, titles, credit card types, payment terms, and customer orders. The `CustomerOrders` entity is the linkage between this subject area and the customer orders subject area.

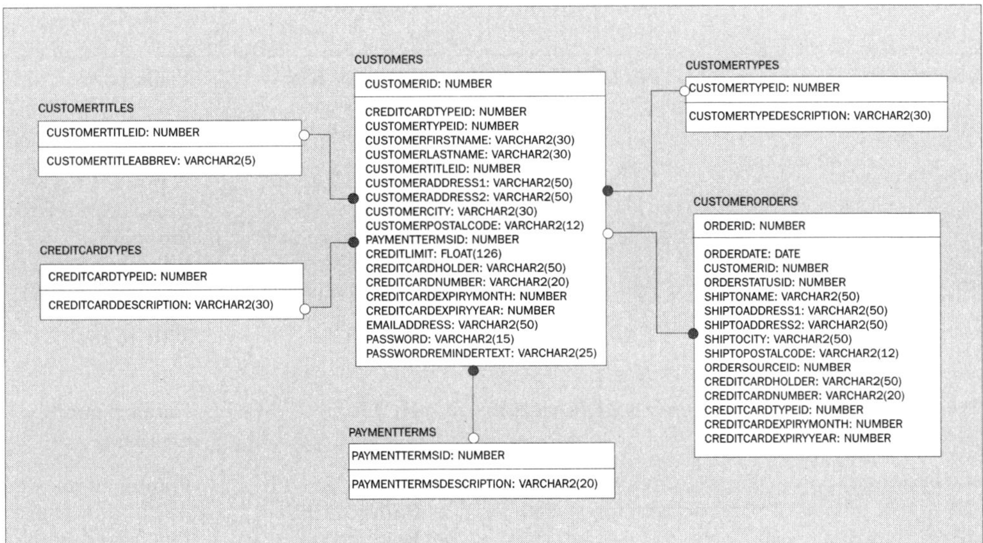

Data Model Tables

This section discusses a few of the data model tables in more detail showing the fields in these tables, along with their data types, and any constraints that apply to them or to the tables as a whole.

The scripts needed to create all of the tables for the Music Store database is available as part of the code download (along with scripts to drop all of the tables and populate all of the tables). Remember to create all the tables in the database so that you can follow through in following chapters. Remember also, that the data types here are for the Oracle database and you may need to adjust some of them to suit your particular database, using the table supplied earlier as a guide.

You will notice that in our scripts we use the `ALTER TABLE` statement to add the primary key constraint. This makes the statement somewhat independent of the dialect you want to create the table with (except for the data types and the semi-colon as mentioned earlier). We also add foreign key constraints in a similar manner.

Recordings Subject Area Tables

We will create all tables in this subject area except the `Inventories` table (which itself requires that the `PostalCode`, `StoreTypes` and `Stores` tables be created first) and the `Reviews` table, which we covered extensively in Chapter 4. We will defer creating the `CustomerOrderItems` table until we discuss the Customer Orders subject area.

Recordings

The Recordings table is the central table in the database for storing information about for the products offered by the Music Store:

Field Name	Data Type (and Size)	Constraints	Description
RecordingID	NUMBER	Primary Key – may use a sequence	Primary key
PublisherID	NUMBER	Not NULL, FK Points to the publisher in the PublisherAnd Labels table	A pointer to the CompanyID field in the table PublishersAndL abels
RecordingTitle	VARCHAR2(50)	Not NULL	Title of the recording
CatalogNumber	VARCHAR2(50)	NULL	Catalog number for recording
RecordingFormatID	NUMBER	Not NULL, FK Points to the RecordingFor mats table	Pointer to the RecordingForma tsID field in the RecordingsForm ats table
ReleaseDate	DATE	NULL	Date of release of recording
LanguageID	NUMBER	Not NULL, FK Points to the language in the Language table	Pointer to the Language table
ListPrice	FLOAT	NULL	Price of recording
CoverImageFileSpec	VARCHAR2(50)	NULL	Path to an image file shown on the recording case

Note that because Recordings is a central table and our database has been normalized, the table references data in surrounding tables rather than all data being stored in the one table. The referenced tables must exist before the reference can be established, so in order to create the Recordings table, you must first create the Languages, PublishersAndLabels and RecordingFormats tables. We will not discuss these tables, but provide the script to create them here so that you may work through and create the Recordings table:

```
CREATE TABLE Languages (
       LanguageID            NUMBER NOT NULL,
       LanguageDescription   VARCHAR2(20) NOT NULL
```

```
);
ALTER TABLE LANGUAGES
   ADD CONSTRAINT PK_Languages Primary Key (LanguageID);

CREATE TABLE PublishersAndLabels (
       COMPANYID                NUMBER NOT NULL,
       COMPANYNAME              VARCHAR2(50) NOT NULL
);

ALTER TABLE PublishersAndLabels
   ADD CONSTRAINT PK_PublishersAndLabels Primary Key (CompanyID);

CREATE TABLE RecordingFormats (
       RecordingFormatID    NUMBER NOT NULL,
       RecordingFormatDescription VARCHAR2(30) NOT NULL);

ALTER TABLE RecordingFormats
   ADD CONSTRAINT PK_RecordingFormats Primary Key (RecordingFormatID);
```

The script to create the `Recordings` table is:

```
CREATE TABLE Recordings (
       PublisherID              NUMBER NOT NULL,
       RecordingID              NUMBER NOT NULL,
       RecordingTitle           VARCHAR2(50) NULL,
       CatalogNumber            VARCHAR2(20) NULL,
       RecordingFormatID        NUMBER DEFAULT 1 NOT NULL,
       ReleaseDate              DATE NULL,
       LanguageID               NUMBER DEFAULT 1 NOT NULL,
       ListPrice                FLOAT(126) NULL,
       CoverImageFileSpec       VARCHAR2(50) NULL
);

ALTER TABLE Recordings
       ADD CONSTRAINT PK_RecordingID PRIMARY KEY (RecordingID);

ALTER TABLE RECORDINGS
   ADD CONSTRAINT FK_Recordings_Languages Foreign Key (LanguageID)
   REFERENCES Languages (LanguageID);

ALTER TABLE Recordings
 ADD CONSTRAINT FK_Recordings_PubsAndLabels Foreign Key (PublisherID)
   REFERENCES PublishersAndLabels (CompanyID);

ALTER TABLE Recordings
ADD CONSTRAINT FK_Recordings_RecordingFormats Foreign Key(RecordingFormatID)
   REFERENCES RecordingFormats (RecordingFormatID);
```

AudioStyles

This table stores the different styles of audio recordings, such as Classical, Rap, Techno and Electronica, etc. and helps in queries that need to pull artists or orders that produce Rock music, for instance. This table along with others linked to it, such as `Tracks`, `Recordings`, `Orders`, etc., can help identify the best selling styles and the least selling ones.

Field Name	Data Type (and Size)	Constraints	Description
`AudioStyleID`	NUMBER	Primary Key – may use a sequence	Primary Key
`AudioStyleDescription`	VARCHAR2(25)	None	

The script to create this table is:

```
CREATE TABLE AudioStyles (
       AudioStyleID           NUMBER NOT NULL,
       AudioStyleDescription VARCHAR2(25) NOT NULL
);

ALTER TABLE AudioStyles
       ADD CONSTRAINT PK_AudioStyleID PRIMARY KEY (AudioStyleID);
```

ArtistsAndPerformers

This table serves as a repository of the artist and performers for which the store has records. It can help the owner identify what records exist for a particular artist in a certain store. The table also stores an image and a short bio of the artist that, in the future, can be displayed on her web site.

Field Name	Data Type (and Size)	Constraints	Description
`ArtistID`	NUMBER	Primary Key – may use a sequence	Primary Key
`ArtistName`	VARCHAR2(50)	None	Name of artist
`ArtistImageFileSpec`	VARCHAR2(50)	None	Path to image file of artist
`ArtistBioText`	VARCHAR2(3000)	None	Artist bio

The script to create this table is:

```
CREATE TABLE ArtistsAndPerformers (
       ArtistID               NUMBER NOT NULL,
       ArtistName             VARCHAR2(50) NOT NULL,
       ArtistImageFileSpec    VARCHAR2(50) NULL,
       ArtistBioText          VARCHAR2(3000) NULL
);

ALTER TABLE ArtistsAndPerformers
    ADD CONSTRAINT PK_ArtistsAndPerformers Primary Key (ArtistID);
```

Tracks

Here we store all of the relevant information for individual tracks. Notice that a field is included that points to an audio sample of a given track (a phase II requirement):

Field Name	Data Type (and Size)	Constraints	Description
`RecordingID`	NUMBER	Part of composite Primary Key – FK referencing the Recording table	References the `RecordingID` field in the `Recordings` table
`TrackNumber`	NUMBER	Part of composite Primary Key	Indicated the number of the track on the recording
`StyleID`	NUMBER	Foreign key for `AudioStyles table`	A pointer to the table `AudioStyle`
`TrackTitle`	VARCHAR2(50)	None	Title of the individual track within the recording
`ArtistID`	NUMBER	Not NULL, FK points to the `ArtistsAndPerformers` table	References the `ArtistID` field in the `ArtistsAndPerformers` table
`SampleFileSpec`	VARCHAR2(50)	None	Path to a file including a sample of the track

The SQL script needed to create this table is:

```
CREATE TABLE TRACKS (
       RecordingID            NUMBER NOT NULL,
       StyleID                NUMBER NULL,
       TrackNumber            NUMBER NOT NULL,
       TrackTitle             VARCHAR2(50) NULL,
       ArtistID               NUMBER NULL,
       SampleFileSpec         VARCHAR2(50) NULL
);

ALTER TABLE TRACKS
   ADD CONSTRAINT PK_Tracks Primary Key (RecordingID, TrackNumber);

ALTER TABLE TRACKS
   ADD CONSTRAINT FK_Tracks_ArtistsAndPerformers Foreign Key (ArtistID)
   REFERENCES ArtistsAndPerformers (ArtistID);

ALTER TABLE TRACKS
```

```
    ADD CONSTRAINT FK_Tracks_AudioStyles Foreign Key (StyleID)
    REFERENCES AudioStyles (AudioStyleID);

ALTER TABLE TRACKS
    ADD CONSTRAINT FK_Tracks_Recordings Foreign Key (Recordingid)
    REFERENCES Recordings (RecordingID);
```

Reviews

We discussed this table in some detail in Chapter 4, so we will simply present the script here:

```
CREATE TABLE Reviews (
  ReviewID        NUMBER NOT NULL,
  RecordingID     NUMBER NOT NULL,
  ReviewerName    VARCHAR2(40) NOT NULL,
  ReviewerText    VARCHAR2(1000),
  Rating          NUMBER,
  ReviewDate      DATE NOT NULL
);

ALTER TABLE Reviews
    ADD CONSTRAINT PK_ReviewID PRIMARY KEY (ReviewID);

ALTER TABLE Reviews
    ADD CONSTRAINT FK_Reviews_Recordings FOREIGN KEY (RecordingID)
    REFERENCES Recordings (RecordingID);
```

Stores Subject Area Tables

Here, the central table is the `Stores` table, which holds the core details of the various retail outlets of the Music Store business. For the same reasons discussed previously, we will need to create the `StoreTypes`, and `PostalCodes` tables before we can create the stores table (and will need to create the `Countries` tables before creating `PostalCodes`. We will not discuss these tables here, but provide the scripts to create them:

```
CREATE TABLE Countries (
       CountryID             NUMBER NOT NULL,
       CountryAbbrev         VARCHAR2(3) NULL,
       CountryName           VARCHAR2(50) NOT NULL
);

ALTER TABLE Countries
       ADD CONSTRAINT PK_Countries Primary Key (CountryID);


CREATE TABLE PostalCodes (
       PostalCode            VARCHAR2(12) NOT NULL,
       City                  VARCHAR2(30) NOT NULL,
       StateProv             VARCHAR2(30) NOT NULL,
       CountryID             NUMBER DEFAULT 1 NOT NULL
);

ALTER TABLE POSTALCODES
```

```
        ADD CONSTRAINT PK_PostalCodes Primary Key (PostalCode, CountryID);

ALTER TABLE POSTALCODES
        ADD CONSTRAINT FK_PostalCodes_Countries Foreign Key (CountryID)
        REFERENCES Countries (CountryID);


CREATE TABLE StoreTypes (
        StoreTypeID          NUMBER NOT NULL,
        StoreTypeDescription VARCHAR2(50) NOT NULL
);

ALTER TABLE StoreTypes
        ADD CONSTRAINT PK_StoreTypes Primary Key (StoreTypeID);
```

Stores

Here is the table describing the `Stores` table:

Field Name	Data Type (and Size)	Constraints	Description
`StorePostalCode`	VARCHAR2(12)	Cannot contain Null values	Postal code of a store. Part of a composite foreign key that references the `PostalCodes` table
`StoreID`	NUMBER	Primary key – may use a sequence	Primary key
`StoreDescription`	VARCHAR2(30)	Cannot contain Null values	The name of the store
`CountryID`	NUMBER	Cannot contain Null values. FK. If no value is supplied, default will be 1 (meaning the store is in the US)	Part of a composite foreign key that references the `PostalCodes` table
`StoreTypeID`	NUMBER	Cannot contain Null values. FK. If no value is supplied, default will be 1 (meaning the store is Brick&Mortar)	Pointer to the `StoreTypeID` field in the `StoreTypes` table

StoreAddress1	VARCHAR2(50)	Store address
StoreAddress2	VARCHAR2(50)	Store address
StoreCity	VARCHAR2(30)	City in which store is located

Here is the script to create the Stores table:

```
CREATE TABLE Stores (
       StorePostalCode      VARCHAR2(12) NOT NULL,
       StoreID              NUMBER NOT NULL,
       StoreDescription     VARCHAR2(30) NOT NULL,
       CountryID            NUMBER DEFAULT 1 NOT NULL,
       StoreTypeID          NUMBER DEFAULT 1 NOT NULL,
       StoreAddress1        VARCHAR2(50),
       StoreAddress2        VARCHAR2(50),
       StoreCity            VARCHAR2(30)
);

ALTER TABLE Stores
       ADD CONSTRAINT PK_Stores Primary Key (StoreID);

ALTER TABLE Stores
       ADD CONSTRAINT FK_Stores_StoreTypes Foreign Key (StoreTypeID)
       REFERENCES StoreTypes(StoreTypeID);

ALTER TABLE STORES
      ADD CONSTRAINT
      FK_Stores_PostalCodes Foreign Key (StorePostalCode, CountryID)
      REFERENCES PostalCodes(PostalCode, CountryID);
```

Note that since the PostalCodes table has a composite primary key, we must reference both components of the PK in any FK that points at this table.

Inventories

The Inventories table is important as it provides the link over to our Recordings table, as described previously:

```
CREATE TABLE Inventories (
       ProductID            NUMBER NOT NULL,
       StoreID              NUMBER NOT NULL,
       QtyOnHand            NUMBER DEFAULT 0 NOT NULL
);

ALTER TABLE Inventories
       ADD CONSTRAINT PK_Inventories Primary Key (StoreID, ProductID);

ALTER TABLE Inventories
       ADD CONSTRAINT FK_Inventories_Recordings Foreign Key (ProductID)
       REFERENCES Recordings(RecordingID) ;
```

```
ALTER TABLE Inventories
       ADD CONSTRAINT FK_Inventories_Stores Foreign Key (StoreID)
       REFERENCES Stores (StoreID);
```

Customer Subject Area Tables

The central table here is the `Customers` table. However in order to create these tables, we first need to create its four "subsidiary" tables:

- `CustomerTypes` – This table allows categorization of customers based on different criteria. For instance, based on this table, we can query the database for all customers belonging to a particular type, such as educational institutions, individual, etc. This table will be a tremendous help in the long term as the owner starts mining the data to find about any trends.
- `CustomerTitles` – This table serves as a lookup table for the `Customers` table and is linked to it in a one-to-many relationship, with the `Customers` table on the "many" side. This means that if a new title is added in the future, or one is theoretically changed, you can make the addition or change in the look-up table without affecting the `Customers` table.
- `PaymentTerms` – This table is another lookup table that is used to lookup values of payment terms, such as "cash only". Again, the fact that such values are kept in a lookup table, rather than the `Customer` table that is related to it, means that we can change the values for multiple customers by changing one record in this table. This table will help the owner and her staff to identify a default payment term for each customer they deal with.
- `CreditCardTypes` – This table is another lookup table that is used to lookup values of credit card types, such as "visa". This table will help to identify a default credit card type for each customer.

Here is the script to create these tables:

```
/* The CustomerTypes table */
CREATE TABLE CustomerTypes (
       CustomerTypeID          NUMBER NOT NULL,
       CustomerTypeDescription VARCHAR2(30) NOT NULL
);

ALTER TABLE CustomerTypes
   ADD CONSTRAINT PK_CustomerTypes Primary Key (CustomerTypeID);

/* The CustomerTitles table */
CREATE TABLE CustomerTitles (
       CustomerTitleID      NUMBER NOT NULL,
       CUstomerTitleAbbrev  VARCHAR2(5) NOT NULL
);

ALTER TABLE CustomerTitles
   ADD CONSTRAINT PK_CustomerTitles Primary Key (CustomerTitleID);

/* The PaymentTerms table */
CREATE TABLE PaymentTerms(
       PaymentTermsID           NUMBER NOT NULL,
       PaymentTermsDescription   VARCHAR2(25) NOT NULL
);
```

```
ALTER TABLE PaymentTerms
ADD CONSTRAINT PK_PaymentTerms Primary Key (PaymentTermsID);

/* The CreditCardTypes table */
CREATE TABLE CreditCardTypes (
       CreditCardTypeID      NUMBER NOT NULL,
       CreditCardDescription VARCHAR2(30) NOT NULL
);

ALTER TABLE CreditCardTypes
ADD CONSTRAINT PK_CreditCardTypes Primary Key (CreditCardTypeID);
```

Customers

This is an important table that allows the owner to keep track of her customers and provide them with a better service. As mentioned in the requirements section, the owner wants to be able to notify customers of any titles they had requested and were not available once such titles become available. This table allows her to store customer information, such as email address, phone number, etc., to allow such notifications. This table actually takes account of some of the phase II requirement and, in the long term, will help the owner to conduct analysis on the data she is collecting to improve her business and make it more competitive.

Field Name	Data Type (and Size)	Constraints	Description
`CustomerID`	NUMBER	Primary key	Primary key
`CreditCardTypeID`	NUMBER	Not NULL, FK Foreign key for `CreditCard Type` table	References `CreditCardType ID` in `CreditCardType` table
`CustomerTypeID`	NUMBER	Foreign key for `CustomerTy pe` table	A pointer to the table `CustomerTypeID`
`CustomerFirstName`	VARCHAR2(25)	None	Customer's first name
`CustomerLastName`	VARCHAR2(30)	None	Customer's last name
`CustomerTitleID`	NUMBER	Foreign key for `Customer Title` table	References `CustomerTitle ID` field
`CustomerAddress1`	VARCHAR2(50)	None	

Field Name	Data Type (and Size)	Constraints	Description
CustomerAddress2	VARCHAR2(50)	None	
CustomerCity	VARCHAR2(30)	None	
CustomerPostalCode	VARCHAR2(12)	None	
PaymentTermID	NUMBER	Foreign key for PaymentTerm table	References PaymentTermsID field
CreditLimit	FLOAT(126)	None	
CreditCardHolder	VARCHAR2(50)	Not NULL	Name appearing on credit card
CreditCardNumber	VARCHAR2(20)	Not NULL	
CreditCardExpiryMonth	NUMBER	Not NULL	
CreditCardExpiryYear	NUMBER	Not Null	
EmailAddress	VARCHAR2(50)	None	
Password	VARCHAR2(15)	None	
PasswordReminderText	VARCHAR2(25)	None	

The SQL script needed to create this table is:

```
CREATE TABLE CUSTOMERS (
       CustomerID              NUMBER NOT NULL,
       CreditCardTypeID        NUMBER NULL,
       CustomerTypeID          NUMBER DEFAULT 0 NOT NULL,
       CustomerFirstName       VARCHAR2(25) NULL,
       CustomerLastName        VARCHAR2(30) NULL,
       CUstomerTitleID         NUMBER NULL,
       CUstomerAddress1        VARCHAR2(50) NULL,
       CustomerAddress2        VARCHAR2(50) NULL,
       CustomerCity            VARCHAR2(30) NULL,
       CustomerPostalCode      VARCHAR2(12) NULL,
       PaymentTermsID          NUMBER DEFAULT 0 NOT NULL,
       CreditLimit             FLOAT(126) NULL,
       CreditCardHolder        VARCHAR2(50) NULL,
       CreditCardNumber        VARCHAR2(20) NULL,
       CreditCardexpiryMonth   NUMBER NULL,
       CreditCardExpiryYear    NUMBER NULL,
       EmailAddress            VARCHAR2(50) NULL,
       Password                VARCHAR2(15) NULL,
       PasswordReminderText    VARCHAR2(25) NULL
);

ALTER TABLE Customers
```

```
    ADD CONSTRAINT PK_Customers Primary Key (CustomerID);

ALTER TABLE Customers
    ADD CONSTRAINT FK_Customers_CCTypes Foreign Key (CreditCardTypeID)
    REFERENCES CreditCardTypes (CreditCardTypeID);

ALTER TABLE CUSTOMERS
    ADD CONSTRAINT FK_Customers_CustTitles Foreign Key (CustomerTitleID)
    REFERENCES CustomerTitles (CustomerTitleID);

ALTER TABLE Customers
    ADD CONSTRAINT FK_Customers_CustTypes Foreign Key (CustomerTypeID)
    REFERENCES CustomerTypes (CustomerTypeID);

ALTER TABLE CUSTOMERS
    ADD CONSTRAINT FK_Customers_PayTerms Foreign Key (PaymentTermsID)
    REFERENCES PaymentTerms (PaymentTermsID);
```

Customer Orders Subject Area Tables

Here our central table is the `CustomerOrders` table. This table has foreign keys that point to the following tables:

- `OrderSources` – a lookup table that allows categorization of orders based on the means used to place them. Some orders are placed over the phone, others are placed in person at the store, and in the future some will be placed online. This would also help the owner conduct some analysis on the data collected in the database.
- `OrderStatuses` – this table serves to store the possible status of an order. It helps allow changing such statuses descriptions without changing multiple records in the `Orders` table. This table, along with the `Orders` table, facilitates tracking and updating the status of an order.

Here are the scripts to create them:

```
CREATE TABLE OrderSources (
       OrderSourceID            NUMBER NOT NULL,
       OrderSourceDescription   VARCHAR2(10) NOT NULL
);

ALTER TABLE OrderSources
   ADD CONSTRAINT PK_OrderSources Primary Key (OrderSourceID);

CREATE TABLE OrderStatuses (
       OrderStatusID            NUMBER NOT NULL,
       OrderStatusDescription   VARCHAR2(25) NOT NULL
);

ALTER TABLE OrderStatuses
   ADD CONSTRAINT PK_OrderStatuses Primary Key (OrderStatusID);
```

CustomerOrders

This is where data about customer orders is stored. It includes the status of such orders, what line items are in the order, where to ship the order, etc.

Field Name	Data Type (and Size)	Constraints	Description
OrderID	NUMBER	Primary key	Primary key
OrderDate	DATE	Not NULL	Defaults to the system date (sysdate)
CustomerID	NUMBER	Foreign key for Customer table	A pointer to CustomerID field in the Customer table
OrderStatusID	NUMBER	Foreign key for Order Statuses table	A pointer to OrderStatusID
ShipToName	VARCHAR2(50)	None	Customer's last name
ShiptoAddress1	VARCHAR2(50)	None	
ShiptoAddress2	VARCHAR2(50)	None	
ShiptoCity	VARCHAR2(30)	None	
ShiptoPostalCode	VARCHAR2(12)	None	
OrderSourceID	NUMBER	Foreign key for OrderSources table	References OrderSourceID field
CreditCardHolder	VARCHAR2(50)	Not NULL	Name appearing on credit card
CreditCardNumber	VARCHAR2(20)	Not NULL	
CreditCardTypeID	NUMBER	Not NULL - Foreign key for CreditCard Types table	References CreditCardType ID field
CreditCardExpiry Month	NUMBER	Not NULL	
CreditCardExpiry Year	NUMBER	Not NULL	

The SQL script needed to create this table is:

```
CREATE TABLE CustomerOrders (
        OrderID                 NUMBER NOT NULL,
        OrderDate               DATE DEFAULT SYSDATE NOT NULL,
        CustomerID              NUMBER NOT NULL,
        OrderStatusID           NUMBER DEFAULT 0 NOT NULL,
        ShipToName              VARCHAR2(50) NULL,
        ShipToaddress1          VARCHAR2(50) NULL,
```

```
        ShipToAddress2        VARCHAR2(50) NULL,
        ShipToCity            VARCHAR2(50) NULL,
        ShipToPostalCode      VARCHAR2(12) NULL,
        OrderSourceID         NUMBER NOT NULL,
        CreditCardHolder      VARCHAR2(50) NULL,
        CreditCardNumber      VARCHAR2(20) NULL,
        CreditCardTypeID      NUMBER NULL,
        CreditCardExpiryMonth NUMBER NULL,
        CreditCardExpiryYear  NUMBER NULL
);

ALTER TABLE CustomerOrders
   ADD CONSTRAINT PK_CustomerOrders Primary Key (OrderID);

ALTER TABLE CustomerOrders
   ADD CONSTRAINT FK_CustOrders_CCTypes Foreign Key (CreditCardTypeID)
   REFERENCES CreditCardTypes (CreditCardTypeID);

ALTER TABLE CustomerOrders
   ADD CONSTRAINT FK_CustOrders_Customers Foreign Key (CustomerID)
   REFERENCES Customers (CustomerID);

ALTER TABLE CustomerOrders
   ADD CONSTRAINT FK_CustOrders_OrderSources Foreign Key (OrderSourceID)
   REFERENCES OrderSources (OrderSourceID);

ALTER TABLE CustomerOrders
   ADD CONSTRAINT FK_CustOrders_OrderStatuses Foreign Key (OrderStatusID)
   REFERENCES OrderStatuses (OrderStatusID);
```

CustomerOrderItems

Finally, we create the table that provides the vital link between the `Recordings` table and the `CustomerOrders` table:

```
CREATE TABLE CUstomerOrderItems (
       OrderID               NUMBER NOT NULL,
       ProductID             NUMBER NULL,
       LineNumber            NUMBER DEFAULT 1 NOT NULL,
       Quantity              NUMBER NOT NULL,
       PricePerItem          FLOAT(126) NOT NULL,
       ProvidingStore        NUMBER DEFAULT 3 NOT NULL
);

ALTER TABLE CustomerOrderItems
   ADD CONSTRAINT PK_CustomerOrderItems Primary Key (OrderID, LineNumber);

ALTER TABLE CustomerOrderItems
       ADD CONSTRAINT FK_CustOrdItems_Recordings Foreign Key (ProductID)
       REFERENCES Recordings (RecordingID);

ALTER TABLE CustomerOrderItems
   ADD CONSTRAINT FK_CustOrdItems_CustOrders Foreign Key (OrderID)
   REFERENCES CustomerOrders (OrderID);
```

Populating the Tables with Sample Data

Well, now we have the physical structure of the database all ready for us, how do we use it? Well, the very first thing we need to do is populate the tables with some sample data and test the design. There are many ways to do this. For example, we can write a quick graphical interface to enter the data, or we can use SQL data manipulation language (DML) commands, namely the `INSERT` statement, to populate the tables. In this case study, we'll adopt the latter approach, building on the knowledge of the SQL DML that you gained in Chapter 3 .

Inserting Values

When inserting values in the tables of our schema, it is important to do so in the right order because of the foreign key/primary key relations and the referential integrity among many of these tables. For instance, you will not be able to insert any records in the `Customer` table unless values have already been inserted in all the tables that provide foreign keys to the `Customer` table. Hence, you have to populate the tables: `CustomerTypes`, `CustomerTitles`, `CreditCardTypes`, and `PaymentTerms` before you can populate the `Customer` table. Similarly, in order to populate the `PostalCode` table, you have to populate the `Countries` tables first because the later table lends `CountryID` as a foreign key into the first one.

Not only the sequence in which you populate your tables matters, but also the accuracy of the values of the foreign key fields. Such values have to exist, or referential integrity will be violated. For instance, if you try to insert a record in the `PostalCode` table with a value of 22 for the `CountryID` field (which does not exist in the `Countries` table), you will get an error indicating that you violated the referential integrity between the two tables: `Countries` and `PostalCodes`.

```
INSERT INTO PostalCodes (
  PostalCode,
  City,
  StateProv,
  CountryID)
VALUES (
  '06484',
  'Shelton',
  'CT',
  22);
```

The Oracle error message is:

```
INSERT INTO PostalCodes (
*
ERROR at line 1:
ORA-02291: integrity constraint (SYOUNESS.SYS_C001699) violated - parent key
not found
```

A script will be available (as part of the code download for this book) to populate all the tables. The recommended sequence for populating the tables is as follows:

Suggested Order	Table	Relations
1	`Countries`	Needed to populate `PostalCodes`
2	`PostalCodes`	Needed to populate `Stores` (and maybe `Customers`)
3	`StoreTypes`	Needed to populate `Stores`
4	`Stores`	Needed to populate `Inventories`
5	`CustomerTitles`	Needed to populate `Customers`
6	`CustomerTypes`	Needed to populate `Customers`
7	`PaymentTerms`	Needed to populate `Customers`
8	`CreditCardTypes`	Needed to populate `Customers`
9	`Customers`	Needed to populate `CustomerOrders`
10	`OrderResources`	Needed to populate `CustomerOrders`
11	`OrderStatuses`	Needed to populate `CustomerOrders`
12	`CustomerOrders`	Needed to populate `CustomerOrderItems`
13	`AudioStyles`	Needed to populate `Tracks`
14	`ArtsAndPerformers`	Needed to populate `Tracks`
15	`PublishersAndLabels`	Needed to populate `Recordings`
16	`RecordingFormats`	Needed to populate `Recordings`
17	`Languages`	Needed to populate `Recordings`
18	`Recordings`	Needed to populate `Tracks`, `Reviews`, `CustomerOrderItems`, and `Inventories`
19	`Tracks`	
20	`CustomerOrderItems`	
21	`Reviews`	
22	`Inventories`	
23	`SalesCampaigns`	Stand-alone table

An important aspect of populating tables with data is ensuring that we obtain a unique identifying value for each row in the primary key column. Different databases achieve this in different ways. Many databases use an automumbering strategy, but Oracle requires you to create a specific database object in order to safely populate numeric primary keys: namely, the **Sequence**.

Using Sequences

In many cases, primary key values are set automatically using **sequences** in Oracle. A sequence is a system counter that can be used to obtain unique values by making sure the new values will follow the particular sequence.

Here is how we would create a sequence for the Countries table:

```
CREATE SEQUENCE seqCountries INCREMENT BY 1 START WITH 1 NOCYCLE;
```

Every time a sequence is used it is incremented by the increment value, which defaults to 1 if not specified. Even a simple statement such as the following will increment the sequence and the next insert will assign a value of 2 to the primary key (given the previous statement is the very first use of the sequence):

```
SELECT seqCountries.NextVal from DUAL;
```

Note here that Oracle does not allow us to use `SELECT` statements without a table. Since sequences are independent of any table, we use the `DUAL` table. The `DUAL` table is a system table, used for when we have no table of our own to select the information from. To demonstrate this in action, let's insert some data into our Countries table:

```
INSERT INTO Countries (CountryID,CountryAbbrev,CountryName) VALUES
(seqCountries.NextVal,'USA','United States');

INSERT INTO Countries (CountryID,CountryAbbrev,CountryName) VALUES
(seqCountries.NextVal,'CA','Canada');

INSERT INTO Countries (CountryID,CountryAbbrev,CountryName) VALUES
(seqCountries.NextVal,'MEX','Mexico');
```

Our `Countries` table now looks like this:

```
COUNTRYID      COUNTRYABBREV     COUNTRYNAME
--------------------------------------------
1              USA               United States
2              CA                Canada
3              MEX               Mexico
```

Let's now move on to the `PostalCodes` table, which has a PK field, `CountryID`, that points at `Countries.CountryID`:

```
INSERT INTO PostalCodes (PostalCode, City, StateProv, CountryID)
VALUES ('10022','Manhattan','NY', 1);
```

Notice that we supply the FK files with a value of `1`. At the moment, we can only enter stores that exist in USA, Canada or Mexico. If we attempted to supply a value of `4`, say, in the FK field, we would get an error, unless we first added a row to the `Countries` table that also had a PK field value of `4`.

We did not need to create a sequence for the PostalCodes table, since the PK in this table is not numerical.

Using Autonumbered Columns

Many databases allow you to use automatically incremented number for numerical primary keys. For instance, SQL Server provides identity columns, MS Access provides autonumber columns, and Cloudscape provides the autoincrement constraint for INT columns.

The information in this section also applies to the way automatically generated columns work in Access, and in Cloudscape. Here, the user must define how he or she wants the PK to autoincrement when defining the table. So, for example, in Cloudscape our definition of the Countries table might look as follows:

```
CREATE TABLE COUNTRIES
   (
      COUNTRYID INT DEFAULT AUTOINCREMENT INITIAL 1 INCREMENT 1 NOT NULL,
      COUNTRYABBREV VARCHAR(3),
      COUNTRYNAME VARCHAR(50) NOT NULL
   )
```

Now, when a user inserts a row into the COUNTRIES table, she does not specify the value of the primary key in the insert statement, rather, she leaves it to the database engine to determine the value and insert it:

```
INSERT INTO Countries (CountryAbbrev, CountryName)
VALUES ('USA','United States')
```

Updating Values

Similar to inserting values, updating values in the tables can be done in many ways: a graphical user interface that takes care of the logic involved, or simple `UPDATE` SQL statements. Just like in the `INSERT` case, care must be taken in the update statements so that only valid foreign key values are used in order to prevent referential integrity constraints between the tables being compromised.

The following is an example that shows how one can reduce the inventory of a certain title in a certain store, when a purchase is made:

```
DECLARE
  v_StoreID NUMBER;
  v_ProductID NUMBER;

BEGIN
V_StoreID := 3;
V_ProductID := 1;
UPDATE Inventories
SET QTYONHAND = QTYONHAND - 1
WHERE StoreID = v_StoreID AND
   ProductID = v_ProductID;
END;
```

In the real world, the script above would be placed in a stored procedure or function, and the values of the `StoreID` and `ProductID` passed as parameters to the procedure.

Deleting Values

Deleting values from the tables can be done using graphical interfaces, or through `DELETE` statements. Many systems implement what is called "logical deletes" to avoid losing the records for good. They do this by assigning a certain value of a "flag" field. For example, if the `Tracks` table had a field called "`deleted`" with possible values True or False, assigning the value True means the record has to be dealt with as if it is deleted. In this case, all queries dealing with the `Tracks` table have to take this into account adding a condition in the `WHERE` clause to check for this field. As an example:

```
SELECT  *
FROM  Tracks
WHERE  Deleted = False;
```

Ignoring this condition in the `WHERE` clause will result in showing all records including the deleted ones.

> **With relational database management systems (RDBMSs), such as Oracle, tables are linked by relations and such relations create what is called referential integrity that helps, as the name implies, maintain the integrity of the data in the database.Also, such relations insure that no "orphan" records exist in a table after the related tables in the parent table are deleted. This last point is referred to as** cascading deletes. **In other words, if you delete a record in a table, all related records in tables linked to it in foreign key relationships will be deleted. The same thing also applies to updates.**

Building Supporting Queries, Views, and Stored Procedures

Now that the database has been populated, let's take a quick look at how we can build some database objects that could fulfill useful functions in the Music Store. Please remember that all of the code presented here will be Oracle specific.

Building an Inventories View

In this section, we will show how to store information based on certain criteria provided by the user. We will build a view that can be used as a basis for several queries allowing for passing different criteria in the `WHERE` clause. This view becomes useful especially because of the level to which the database is normalized. Such normalization makes it more difficult (or at least more tedious) to issue queries that span several table joins, not to mention that the performance of such queries will be less than if they had to span fewer table joins (as in the case of denormalized databases that are used for reporting purposes, such as data marts and data warehouses).

So, given the above explanation, let's build the view. In the view we are concerned with listing the store id, address, country, city, state or province, type, the description associated with it, and most importantly, the inventories in the stores. Having all this information available in a view allows us to issue simple queries to retrieve partial sets based on certain criteria, such as listing the inventories in a particular store, or the inventory of a certain recording in stores in a certain city, etc.

```
CREATE OR REPLACE VIEW vwStoreInventories
AS
SELECT  s.StoreID,
    s.StoreCity,
    c.CountryName,
    s.StorePostalCode,
    st.StoreTypeDescription,
    s.StoreDescription,
    s.StoreAddress1,
    s.StoreAddress2,
    i.QtyOnHand,
    r.RecordingTitle
FROM  Stores s,
    PostalCodes p,
    Countries c,
    StoreTypes st,
    Inventories I,
    Recordings r
WHERE  s.StoreTypeID = st.StoreTypeID AND
    s.StorePostalCode = p.PostalCode AND
    s.CountryID = p.CountryID AND
    p.CountryID = c.CountryID AND
    s.StoreID = i.StoreID AND
    r.RecordingID = i.ProductID
```

As an example of using this view, let's list all stores that have no stock in hand for the title `Crucify`:

```
SELECT   STOREDESCRIPTION,
    STOREPOSTALCODE,
    STORECITY
FROM     vwStoreInventories
WHERE   RecordingTitle = 'Crucify' AND
    QTYONHAND = 0 OR
    RECORDINGTITLE <> 'Crucify';
```

The result will look something like this:

STOREDESCRIPTION	STOREPOSTALCODE	STORECITY
Westfield Shopping Park	06601	Bridgeport
Manhattan	10022	New York
Westfield Shopping Park	06601	Bridgeport
Shady Palm Shopping Galeria	33487	Boca Raton
Westfield Shopping Park	06601	Bridgeport

Having carried out the complex six table join in the view definition, our query to find out which stores have no stock of `Crucify` is relatively simple. The real bonus is that we can issues different queries against this view, and each time we are spared the complex table joining operation. Another example of using this view would allow us to list all stores that have a certain record title in their inventories. The query to do so is:

```
SELECT   STOREDESCRIPTION,
    STOREPOSTALCODE,
    STORECITY,
    QTYONHAND
FROM     vwStoreInventories
WHERE   RecordingTitle = 'Phenomenon Soundtrack' AND
    QTYONHAND > 0;
```

And the result will look something like this:

STOREDESCRIPTION	STOREPOSTAL CODE	STORECITY	QTYONHAND
Manhattan	10022	New York	15
Westfield Shopping Park	06601	Bridgeport	22

A Stored Procedure for Entering Inventory Values

In this section, we will fulfill one of the requirements of the database: easily enter data into the database. As an example, every time new recordings become available in a store, we want to update the database with these new recordings. The table that will be affected in this case is the `Inventories` table.

Of course, based on whether the store has ever had the particular recording, the action could be inserting a new record or updating an existing one. In other words, if the store has never had the recording in question, then we have to insert a new record in the `Inventories` table with the new quantity on hand. If, on the other hand, the store already has some of the recording in question, or maybe does not have any at the time, but had some in the past, a record already exists in the `Inventories` table linking the store with the recording, and all we need to do is update the record to reflect the new quantity on hand.

The following stored procedure accomplishes this task. In the beginning, the procedure checks for a record in the inventories table with the store and recording in question. If the record is found, it updates it by adding the new quantity to that on hand. If the record does not exist, it inserts a new record with the new quantity as the quantity on hand:

```
CREATE OR REPLACE PROCEDURE pr_UpdateInventory(
    p_TitleID IN Inventories.ProductID%Type,
    p_StoreID IN Inventories.StoreID%Type,
    p_QTY IN Inventories.QTYOnHand%Type)
AS
  RecCount NUMBER;

BEGIN

  SELECT  COUNT(*)
  INTO  RecCount
  FROM  Inventories
  WHERE  StoreID = p_StoreID AND
    ProductID = p_TitleID;

  IF RecCount > 0 THEN
```

```
      UPDATE Inventories
      SET QTYONHAND = QTYONHAND + p_QTY
      WHERE StoreID = p_StoreID AND
         ProductID = p_TitleID;
   ELSE
      INSERT INTO Inventories(
        StoreID,
        ProductID,
        QTYONHAND)
      VALUES(p_StoreID,
        P_TitleID,
        P_QTY);
   END IF;
END pr_UpdateInventory;
```

To use this procedure in PL/SQL, we need to use a code block similar to the one below, which updates the inventory for store id 1 with title id 2 with a new quantity on hand of 20 units:

```
BEGIN
  pr_UpdateInventory (1, 2, 20);
END;
```

Using a Trigger to Generate Sequence Values

Triggers are parameter-less procedures that are triggered (fired) either before or after inserting, updating or deleting rows from a table. Because they are fired by the event and not by choice they cannot have parameters.

Triggers are used for a variety of reasons, but a common simple application of a trigger in Oracle is to automatically generate sequence number for you. Here is the trigger that could perform this task on the `Countries` table:

```
CREATE OR REPLACE TRIGGER Countries_key
BEFORE
INSERT ON Countries
FOR EACH ROW
DECLARE X NUMBER;
BEGIN
     SELECT seqCountries.NEXTVAL INTO X FROM DUAL;
     :new.CountryID := X;
END;
/
```

Now, when we come to insert a new row into our `Countries` table, we can just issue the following command:

```
INSERT INTO Countries (CountryAbbrev, CountryName) VALUES
('BRA','Brazil');
```

The trigger will ensure that a unique value is assigned to the `CountryID` field.

Summary

In this chapter, you saw to design and create the Music Store database used in the book. We started right at the beginning, with the requirements gathering stage and we saw how to transform these requirements into a data model that would satisfy the needs of the business.

Having established some of our data model entities, we investigated the relationships that must exist between them and then went on to build Entity-Relationship diagrams. We then took a detailed look at the how to build these tables and populate them with data.

Finally, we took a whirlwind look at some of the database objects that could potentially be very useful in the Music Store application (we will be discussing stored procedures in much more detail in Chapter 13).

The scripts to create the database in Oracle and Cloudscape are provided as part of the code download for the book. Also, a fully populated Access database is also provided along with a dump file that you can recover in a SQL Server database to create the database with the data used to populate it.

This chapter concludes our detailed look at database design and SQL. It is now time to move on and look at how we can use SQL to retrieve and modify data from our Java applications, using the JDBC API.

akarta
JAVA
Java

Overview of JDBC Application Development

Earlier on in the book, in Chapter 2, *Basic JDBC Techniques*, we looked at the basic features of the JDBC API and built a few simple programs that could connect to a database and retrieve data. However, before we move on to investigate the JDBC API in full detail, we need to consider some of the broader issues and decisions that you will need to tackle in developing your JDBC application:

- How will you define and model the classes required for your Java application? In this book we will model our classes using **Unified Modeling Languag**e (UML) diagrams. This chapter covers the very basics of UML for modeling, objects, classes, relationships and so on.
- What sort of basic architecture will be used? We look at some typical scenarios of using JDBC applications in 2-tier and 3-tier models.
- What JDBC driver will suit the needs of your application's architecture and programming requirements? We discuss the four different types of JDBC driver that are availiable and discuss when each might be an appropriate choice.
- OK, you have decided on a driver, can connect to your chosen database, and can pass relational data to and from the database to your Java classes. But exactly how are you going to use this relational data in your application? Will you simply make use of the JDBC `ResultSet` object? Or will you populate a Java object from the `ResultSet`? Or pass the data around as XML? The section on *Using Relational Data in Your Application* addresses some of these issues.
- Finally, we take a more detailed look at possible mapping strategies that can be used to map between objects and relational data, in particular at the strategy favored in this book, whereby our Java object handles its own data extraction from a `ResultSet` object.

Object Modeling

In Chapter 3, *Relational Database Design Concepts*, we discussed how to take a problem domain (in this case a Music Store application) and from this, define a set of entities (or objects) that would satisfy the data requirements of our application. In order to communicate this model graphically we presented a simple Entity-Relationship (ER) diagram and it was this diagram that was used as a basis to build the actual database.

A similar process is followed when modeling the 'entities' that will compose your Java application and satisfy the data retrieval and manipulation requirements. In Java database programming, the designer starts by identifying the Java objects that will be used in the system. One way to identify objects in the system is to look at the tables in the database. That is, each table in the database is a candidate class. There can be many objects of each class, each of which represents a set of data from the tables (usually, a single row). So, for example, we can build a `Stores` Java class, and each instance of that class will represent one retail outlet for our Music Store application. As your Java application grows, this simple relationship breaks down, as we will see in Chapter 15, but it provides a good starting point.

Once you've identified the possible classes, you model the classes to determine if they are correct and if the relationships between the classes make sense. You then need a consistent and clear way to represent these classes to fellow developers. At various points in this book, we will be showing graphical representations of Java classes. In order to do this consistently with other sources, we shall use the **U**nified **M**odeling **L**anguage (**UML**). We do not use this tool extensively in this book, so the purpose of this section is simply to give you a quick taste and to provide enough information so that you can recognize and interpret these diagrams when they appear in the text.

As you would imagine from its name, UML is a language for modeling. Specifically, UML defines a way of drawing diagrams to represent various aspects of programming. UML, although used only to represent classes in this book, has a much broader range of application. Here are the types of diagram that UML supports:

- **Class diagrams** – Represent the static structure of classes, interfaces, and relationships in an object model.
- **Use case diagrams** – Represent the functions of a system from the perspective of users.
- **Object diagrams** – Illustrate objects and links.
- **Collaboration diagrams** – Illustrate interactions (in other words, messages) between objects using a spatial representation.
- **Sequence diagrams** – Focus on the chronology of interactions among objects.
- **Statechart diagrams** – Express the behaviors of a class in terms of object state.
- **Activity diagrams** – Specify the behavior of an operation (a method) as a set of actions.
- **Component diagrams** – Display the physical components of a software system.
- **Deployment diagrams** – Show the physical deployment of components on particular pieces of hardware.

Although the other diagrams are important in their place, they are not used in depth in this book. For a detailed exposure of these, see *Instant UML, Wrox Press, 1861000871.*

As with most diagrams, UML diagrams help to present a large amount of simple information quickly. Let's see the general form of a class diagram:

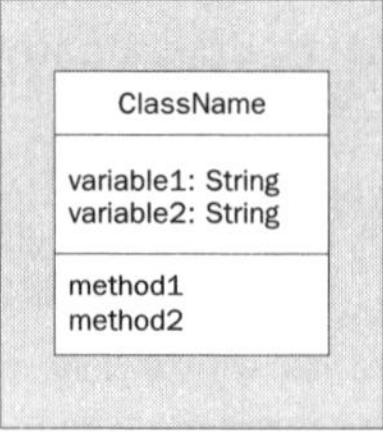

The rectangle representing the class is divided into three compartments with the top one showing the class name, the second showing the attributes, and the third showing the methods.

UML defines three visibility levels for attributes and methods:

- **Public** – The element is visible to all clients of the class. This is represented by a plus (+).
- **Protected** – The element is visible to all subclasses of the class. This is represented by a hash (#).
- **Private** – The element is visible only to the class. This is represented by a minus (-).

Since Java allows us to define methods and variables without a visibility setting, we can omit the UML visibility representation for unsigned methods. Let's look at a simple example to see how this fits together:

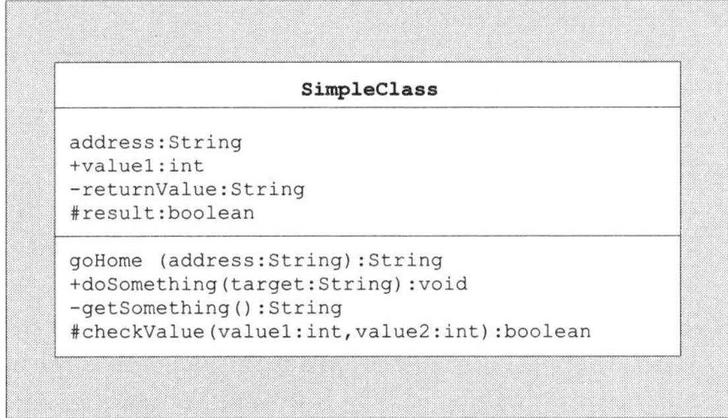

What does the diagram show us? Well, it is a class diagram for a class called `simpleClass`, which declares four variables and four methods. Let's see the Java declarations that match this UML class diagram:

```
public class simpleClass {

  String address;
  public int value1;
  private String returnValue;
  protected boolean result;

  String goHome(String address) {
  // leave the office and head for home
  }

  public void doSomething(String target) {
  // do something interesting
  }

  private String getSomething() {
  // go to the shops and get something
  }

  protected boolean checkValue(int value1, int value2) {
  // check the two values
  }
}
```

As you can see, it is really simple. We have not shown any code for the methods, but the UML diagram wouldn't show the business logic anyway. See how the variable declaration in the UML diagram maps to the variable declaration in the Java code (or, more strictly, how the UML represents the Java code). Let's compare the declaration for the `boolean` variable `result`, in UML:

```
#result:boolean
```

and in Java:

```
protected boolean result;
```

Now the `doSomething()` method, first in UML:

```
+doSomething(target:String):void
```

and in Java:

```
public void doSomething(String target) {
// do something interesting
}
```

There are a couple of other important aspects of UML that we will see in this book: **inheritance** and **interfaces**. Since we will often see the two together, we might as well demonstrate them as a pair. Here is our `simpleClass` class inheriting from a simple interface, named `simpleInterface`:

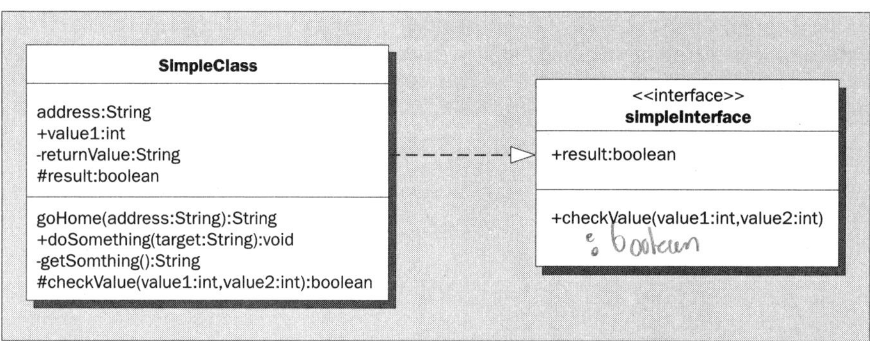

The `simpleClass` part of the diagram hasn't changed much, so we'll focus on the interface part. The first thing to understand is the notation that this is an interface, which is:

```
<< interface >>
```

When we see a UML diagram of a Java class that contains the `<< interface >>` tag, we shouldn't expect there to be any implementation to the methods it declares. As you can see, the rest of the diagram is much the same as a class diagram; the class name, variables, and methods are all the same.

The other thing to understand from this diagram is the notation for inheritance, which is an arrow extending from one class (`simpleClass`) to the class it inherits from (`simpleInterface`). In Java, there are two types of inheritance: **extending**, and **implementing**. Since the above diagram shows a class inheriting from an interface, we have a *dashed line* representing **implementing**. The following diagram shows an extending line:

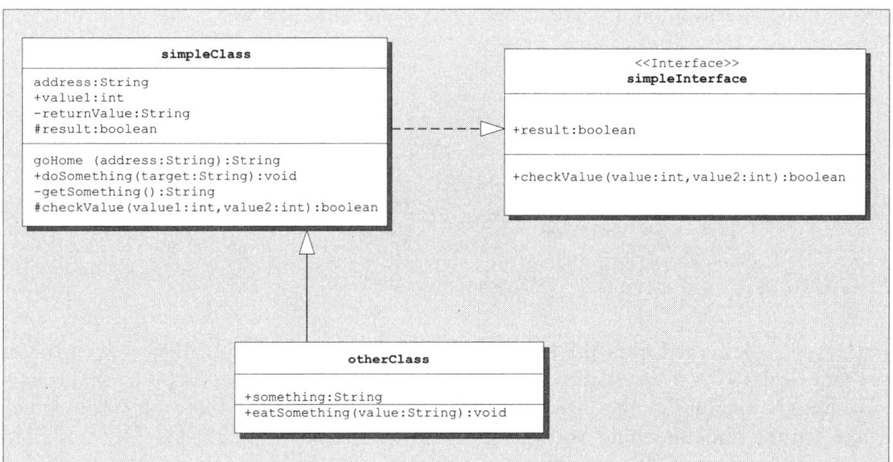

Notice that the line from `otherClass` to `simpleClass` is solid – this is the UML representation of one class **extending** another.

UML is an important part of **C**omputer-**A**ssisted **S**oftware **E**ngineering (**CASE**) tools. CASE tools for object modeling have become increasingly sophisticated. UML tools typically have very interactive GUI interfaces. Many generate code skeletons for Java. Some can even reverse engineer UML diagrams from existing Java code.

While this list is not exhaustive, here are some UML CASE tools to consider:

- MicroGold WithClass 2000

  http://www.microgold.com

- Popkin System Architect 2001

  http://www.popkin.com/products/sa2001/systemarchitect.htm

- Rational Rose

  http://www.rational.com/products/rose/index.jsp

- Together Enterprise

  http://www.togethersoft.com/together/togetherE.html

- WebGain StructureBuilder

  http://www.webgain.com/products/structure_builder

As was said earlier, this was not meant to be a detailed look at UML, but rather its aim was to give you a little bit of background on what it is used for, and how it is used.

Application Scenarios

In this section, we will look at some typical scenarios in which you would be developing Java applications interacting with databases, using the Java API. When exploring the core JDBC functionality in this book, we use simple 2-tier console applications, in which a Java class loads the JDBC driver and talks directly to the RDBMS. Graphically, this looks something like this:

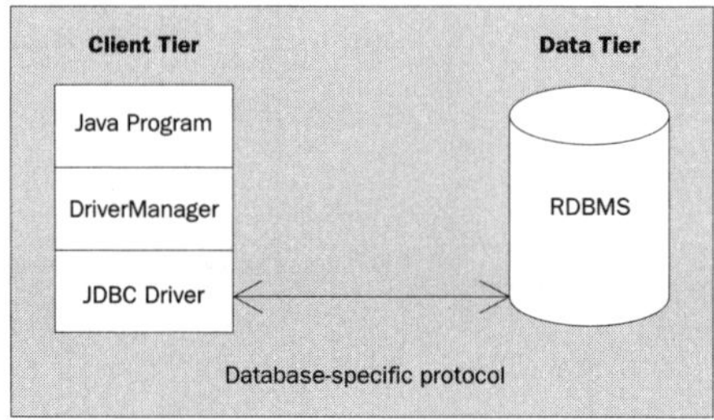

A user's queries are delivered from the client to the database via an RDBMS-specific protocol, and results are sent back to the user via the same protocol. The database can be on a local host or it may be another machine belonging to the same network, and this includes the Internet. In other words, it does not *have* to be on the same machine, or even in the same country. This simple 2-tier, or client-server, configuration covers most of the examples you will see in this book.

Good coding practice dictates building applications comprising well-defined, reusable components. This makes it easy to turn what was a simple 2-tier application into a more functional n-tier web application for database access. To create a more flexible way to access information on a database server, we can utilize a middle tier, or **application server**, with which to send users' commands and queries. This means that the client tier, which may be running a Java applet or a web browser for example, communicates with Java components housed in the application server, which will then use JDBC to pass the clients' requests to the database in the data tier. Again this will be via a database-specific protocol. When the database returns the results of the commands, this process will happen in reverse. There are many advantages of using a physical 3-tier model for data access, and these include:

- Performance increases, as there is a dedicated server processing the Java code. The client does not have to contend with the rigorous task of converting the user's commands into JDBC code.
- Deploying and maintaining applications involving the extensive use of database access is simplified.
- Security is increased, especially over web access, where sensitive data can and should be subject to restricted viewing and modification.

A simple diagram of this kind of set up appears opposite:

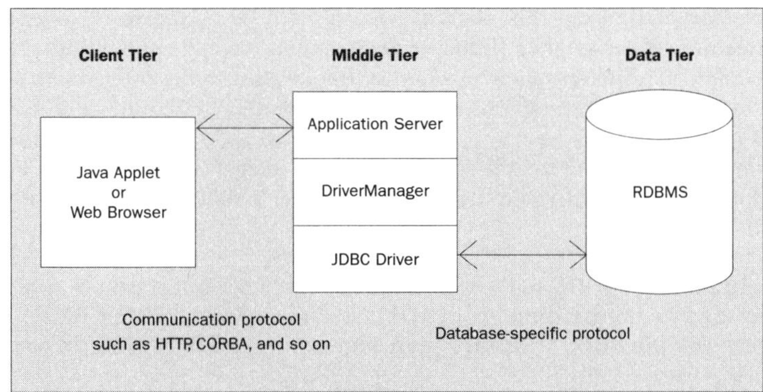

Another reason for using a physical 3-tier model is obviously the ability to effectively use Java in the middle tier. With the advent of technologies such as **E**nterprise **J**ava**B**eans (**EJB**), **J**ava**S**erver **P**ages (**JSP**), and **servlets**, together with the fact that many enterprise-level applications already use Java in one form or another, using Java in the middle tier makes a great deal of sense. The JDBC 2.0 API introduces enterprise features that can be leveraged in the application-server tier (these features are covered in Chapters 18 and 14, respectively):

- **Connection pooling** – This is a very similar concept to **thread pooling** whereby a number of clients can share the same server resources.
- **Distributed transactions** – Also known as **global transactions** and means parts of the same transaction can occur in different databases and possibly in different locations.

A key point to remember is that whether you're developing a console application, a GUI client or a web application using Servlets, JSP and EJB, the step involved in building a successful Java database application are essentially the same. In this book, we have put the emphasis on designing good, well-defined Java classes. Once you have encapsulated your JDBC code in a Java class, it should be a relatively simple job to add in additional applet-specific code and embed that in a web page. If your classes are built along well-defined functional boundaries, then it should be relatively painless to convert a data-centric class in to an EJB or a presentation-oriented class into a JSP-bean pattern and so on, as we demonstrate in Chapter 19.

Choosing a Driver

Another of your important design decisions, when planning a Java database application, will be the choice of JDBC driver that will enable your JDBC classes to communicate with the database. JDBC drivers are divided into **four** types or levels. Each type defines a JDBC driver implementation with increasingly higher levels of platform independence, performance, and deployment administration. The four types are:

- **Type 1**: JDBC-ODBC Bridge
- **Type 2**: Native-API/partly Java driver
- **Type 3**: Net-protocol/all-Java driver
- **Type 4**: Native-protocol/all-Java driver

There are questions that arise from this, such as what type of JDBC driver is suited for what kind of application architecture. What level of JDBC driver is suited for our application? The type of driver depends on quite a few parameters, such as whether the application is Internet or intranet-based, whether it needs to support heterogeneous databases, the number of concurrent users, and so on.

In this short section, we will attempt to address some of these issues. Understanding a little of how drivers are built, and their limitations, will help you to decide which driver is most appropriate for your application.

> **There are a number of JDBC drivers available. As we mentioned earlier, the best source of up-to-date information about JDBC drivers is from the Sun JDBC drivers page on their web site http://industry.java.sun.com/products/jdbc/drivers.**

Throughout this book, we have used the Cloudscape and Oracle databases to demonstrate the features of the JDBC API. In both cases we have chosen to use the available type 4 drivers. You should bear in mind, of course, that just beacuse the drivers are of the same type, it does not mean that they have the same capabilites. To give just one example, the Oracle type 4 driver supports updatable `ResultSet` objects, whereas the Cloudscape driver currently does not. You should always check your driver documentation to make sure that it supports the functionality you require for your particular application.

Type 1: JDBC-ODBC Bridge Driver

The JDBC-ODBC Bridge is a type 1 JDBC driver that translates JDBC operations into C language ODBC APIs, and the ODBC calls are then passed to the appropriate ODBC driver for the back-end data store. Its architecture is shown in figure below:

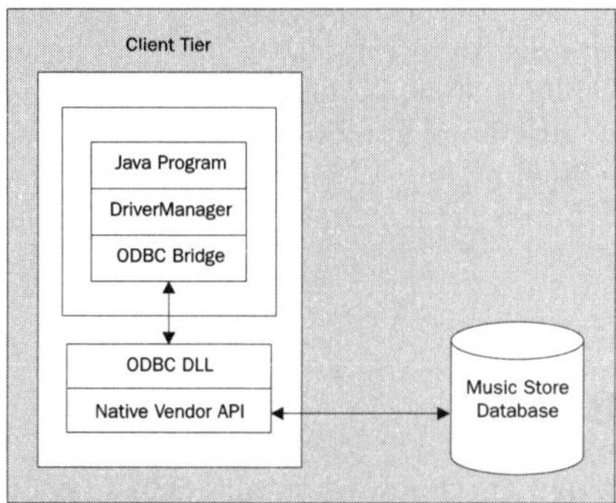

The Bridge implements JDBC for any database for which an ODBC driver is available. The Bridge is implemented as the `sun.jdbc.odbc` Java package and contains a native library used to access ODBC. It is a joint development of Merant (http://www.merant.com) and Java Software (http://www.javasoft.com). The Bridge is implemented in Java and uses Java native methods to call ODBC. This is presently available on Windows as well as Solaris.

Advantages of the Bridge Driver

Often, people's first encounter with a JDBC driver is with the JDBC-ODBC Bridge, simply beacuse this is the driver that is distributed as part of the Java 2 SDK, Standard Edition, as the package `sun.jdbc.odbc.JdbcOdbcDriver`. There is no other configuration required for the Bridge.

It also has the advantage of working with a huge number of ODBC drivers (but it only works under the Microsoft Windows and Sun Solaris operating systems). ODBC, which predates JDBC, is widely used by developers to connect to databases in a non-Java environment. So, type 1 drivers may be useful for those companies that have an ODBC driver already installed on client machines. It might be typically used for Windows-based machines running business applications. Of course, it may be the only way to gain access to some low-end desktop databases, such as MS Access, dBase, and Paradox.

On the face of it, the lack of complexity in the setup and the fact that it can allow you to access virtually any database you could name, make this a good choice of driver. However there are many reasons why its use is discouraged and, in fact, we have generally avoided its use in this book.

Drawbacks of the Bridge

If you visit the JDBC FAQ site, http://java.sun.com/products/jdbc/faq.html, you'll find listed there numerous reasons why the use of the bridge is discouraged. Basically it is only recommended for use in prototyping efforts and for cases where no other JDBC technology-based driver exists. If possible, we must use a JDBC driver instead of the Bridge and an ODBC driver. This completely eliminates the client configuration required by ODBC. It also eliminates the potential that the JVM could be corrupted by an error in the ODBC native code invoked by the Bridge using JNI.

The following bullets summarize some of the drawbacks of the Bridge driver:

- Performance – As you might have guessed from the number of layers and translations that have to occur, using the bridge is far from the most efficient option in terms of performance.
- By using the JDBC-ODBC Bridge, the user is limited by the functionality of the underlying ODBC driver. Moreover, the JDBC-ODBC Bridges limit themselves to the subset of functionality provided by all databases. By providing lowest common denominator functionality, they preclude users from exploiting database specific advances such as performance and scalability improvements.
- When an application development reaches some advanced stage, for example, when it needs to support multi-threading, the JDBC-ODBC Bridge poses a few problems. The Bridge assumes that ODBC drivers are able to handle multi-threaded access. If we need to use multi-threading and the ODBC package does not support it, the client program will have to implement locking.
- The Bridge driver does not work well with applets. The ODBC driver and native connectivity interface must already be installed on the client machine. Thus, any advantage of using Java applets in an intranet environment is lost, since the deployment problems of traditional applications remain.
- Most browsers do not natively support the Bridge. Since the Bridge is an optional component of the Java 2 SDK, Standard Edition, it may not be provided by a browser. Even if it is provided, only trusted applets (those allowed to write to files) will be able to use the Bridge. This is required in order to preserve the security of the applet sandbox. Finally, even if the applet is trusted, ODBC and the DBMS client library must be configured on each client.

Type 2: Native-API/Partly-Java Driver

Type 2 drivers, of which Oracle's JDBC/OCI driver is an example, is use Java's Native Methods Interface to convert the JDBC database requests into database-specific calls for databases such as SQL Server, Informix, Oracle, or Sybase, as depicted in the figure below:

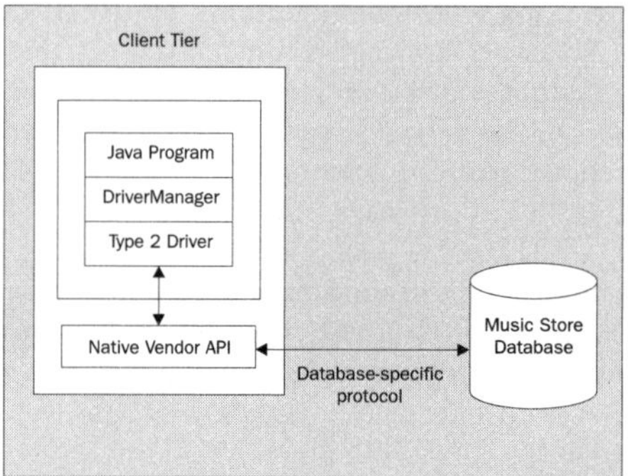

The type 2 driver, residing on the client tier along with the application, communicates directly with the database server. Therefore it requires that some binary code be present on the client machine. While type 2 drivers typically offer significantly better performance than the JDBC-ODBC Bridge, they still suffer from the same deployment problem in that the native connectivity interface must already be installed on the client machine. The JDBC driver requires a vendor-supplied library to translate JDBC functions into the DBMS's specific query language. These drivers are usually written in some combination of Java and C/C++, since the driver must use a layer of C to make calls to the vendor libraries that are written in C.

Pros

- The type 2 driver offers significantly better performance than the JDBC-ODBC Bridge since the JDBC calls are not converted to ODBC calls, but directly to native API calls.

Cons

- The vendor database library needs to be loaded on each client machine. Consequently, type 2 drivers cannot be used for the Internet. Type 2 drivers show lower performance than type 3 and type 4 drivers.
- A type 2 driver also uses the Java Native Interface, which is not consistently implemented between different vendors of JVMs so it isn't usually very portable across platforms.

Type 3: Net-Protocol/All-Java Driver

JDBC type 3 drivers are implemented in a three-tiered approach whereby the JDBC database requests are translated into a database-independent network protocol and forwarded to the middle-tier server. The middle-tier server then translates the request to the database-specific native-connectivity interface and passes the request to the database server. If the middle-tier server is written in Java, it can use a type 1 or a type 2 JDBC driver to do this, which means that it is very flexible architecturally.

The overall architecture consists of three tiers: the JDBC client and driver, middleware, and the database(s) being accessed:

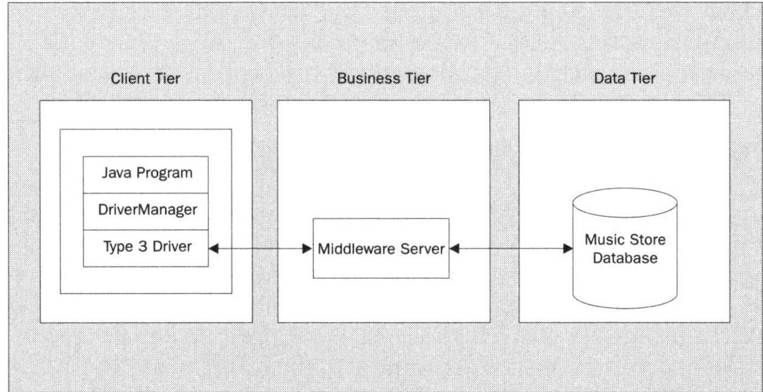

The small JDBC driver (usually few hundred KB in size) executes on the client and implements the logic needed to pass SQL commands over the network to the JDBC server, receive the data back from the server, and manage the connection. Type 3 drivers allow for client deployment on the Internet.

The middleware server component can be implemented as a native component, or alternatively written in Java. Native implementations connect to the database server using either a vendor's client library or ODBC. The server has to be configured for the database(s) being accessed. This could involve setting port numbers, database-specific environment variables, database-specific parameters (logging, translation), and other parameters that the server may require. If the middleware server is written in Java, it can use any JDBC-compliant driver to communicate with the DBMS via the database vendor's proprietary protocol. The JDBC server manages multiple connections to the database, as well as exception and status events resulting from SQL execution. It also packages the data for transmission over the network to JDBC clients.

Pros

- The net-protocol/all-Java driver has a component on the middle-tier server, so there is no need for any vendor database library to be present on client machines.
- Type 3 drivers are best suited for Internet/intranet-based, concurrent user, data-intensive applications, where a large number of concurrent data operations such as queries, searches, and so on, are expected and scalability and performance is a major factor. There are many opportunities to optimize portability, performance, and scalability.
- The net protocol can be designed to make the client JDBC driver very small and fast to load, which is ideally suited for Internet deployment.
- Additionally, a type 3 driver typically provides support for features such as caching (connections, query results, and so on), load balancing, and advanced system administration such as logging and auditing.
- Most 3-tier web database applications involve security, firewalls, and proxies and type 3 drivers generally provide these features.

Cons

- Type 3 drivers require database-specific coding to be done in the middle tier.
- Additionally, traversing the recordset may take longer, since the data comes through the backend server.

We do not cover the tpye 3 driver in this book but there are several third party vendors like MERANT, i-net Software, OpenLink, and so on, that supply them. For a comprehensive list of vendors that provide type 3 drivers, refer to following URL, http://industry.java.sun.com/products/jdbc/drivers.

Type 4: Native-Protocol/All-Java Driver

This class of driver, of which Oracle's thin driver and the Cloudscape driver are examples, communicates directly to the database server using the server's native protocol. These drivers can be written entirely in Java and can provide for just-in-time delivery of applets, achieve platform independence, and eliminate deployment administration issues. However, this driver is specific to a particular database vendor, say Oracle. When the database needs to be changed to a different vendor product, the same JDBC driver cannot be used. Instead, the driver needs to replaced and also the client program, or its setting, to be able to utilize a different connection string for loading the driver.

These drivers translate JDBC directly into the native protocol without the use of ODBC or native APIs, so they can provide very high-performance database access. These drivers might only be made available from the DBMS vendors due to the fact that the knowledge of protocol lies with the vendor.

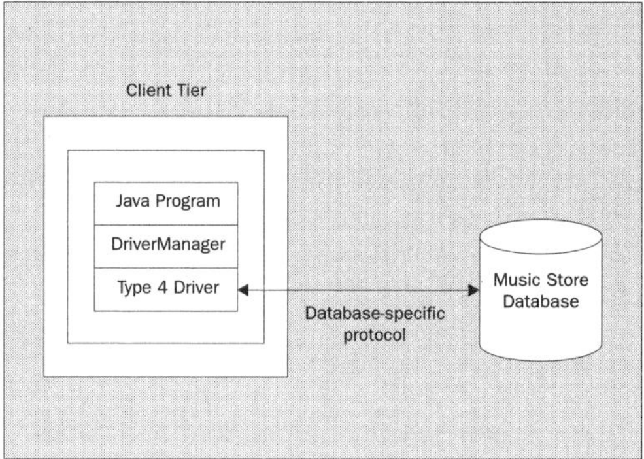

Pros

- Since type 4 JDBC drivers don't have to translate database requests to ODBC or a native connectivity interface, or to pass the request on to another server, performance is typically quite good. Moreover, the native-protocol/all-Java driver boasts better performance than types 1 and 2.
- Also, there is no need to install special software on the client or server. Further, these drivers can be downloaded dynamically.

Cons

- With type 4 drivers, the user needs a different driver for each database.

There are several third-party vendors like Ashna Inc., i-net Software, NetDirect, and so on, that supply type 4 drivers. For a comprehensive list of vendors that provide type 4 drivers, refer to the same URL as given previously.

Application Architectures

There are a variety of possible architectures for enterprise-wide database applications. It really depends on the application requirements. Each JDBC driver type is better suited to a particular architecture. Choosing the right driver is important because it has a direct impact on the application performance.

The JDBC-ODBC Bridge should be considered only a transitional solution since it doesn't support all the features of Java, and the user is limited by the functionality of the underlying ODBC driver. Large-scale applications should use any of the type 2, type 3, or type 4 drivers.

For intranet applications it would be useful to consider type 2 drivers, but type 2 drivers, like the JDBC-ODBC Bridge, require that code (that is, the vendor library) be installed on each client. Thus, they have the same software maintenance problems as the Bridge. However, type 2 drivers are faster than type 1 because the extra layer of translation to ODBC is removed. Since type 3 and type 4 drivers show significantly better performance than type 2 drivers, and the trend is towards the development of more robust pure-Java drivers though, it might be useful to evaluate type 3 or type 4 for intranet solutions too.

For Internet-related applications, there is no option but to use type 3 or type 4 drivers. Type 3 drivers are best suited to environments that need to provide connectivity to a variety of DBMS servers and heterogeneous databases. Type 3 drivers suit multi-user data-intensive applications, where a large number of concurrent data operations such as queries, searches, and so on, are expected, and scalability and performance is a major factor. The server can provide logging and administration facilities, and load balancing features, and can support catalog and query caches. In addition to the aforementioned issues, most 3-tier web database applications involve security, firewalls, and proxies. Type 3 drivers address these issues. For example, the Weblogic application server can be used as middleware to handle the multi-transaction management as well as all database calls to avoid the client library having to be installed on every client-tier machine.

However, a type 3 driver is not a good choice for servlets, since data access is done at the servlet level, not the client level.

Type 4 drivers are generally aimed at the workgroup level. These drivers can provide just-in-time delivery of applets. Since these drivers translate JDBC calls directly into the native protocol without the use of ODBC or native APIs, they can provide very high-performance database access.

Network Protocol for Windows NT and 98

It is possible to connect the JDBC driver to databases like Oracle through a variety of network protocols like TCP/IP, named pipes, and others. On Windows 95 and Windows 98 operating systems, the default network library installed is the TCP/IP socket's Net-Library. This is because Windows 95 and Windows 98 do not support server-side named pipes. Windows 95 and Windows 98 operating systems can use named pipes as clients, but not as servers. Windows NT is currently the only platform that can create server ends of named pipes.

Most JDBC drivers like Oracle's JDBC/OCI type 2 JDBC driver, provide support both for TCP/IP and named pipes. If we want to support an application both for Windows NT and 98/95 though, we must use TCP/IP as the connecting protocol. This can be indicated in the URL of the JDBC driver connection string. Though named pipes is also a protocol available to connect to databases, it must not be used if we want to provide a solution both for NT and 98/95.

Considerations for Selecting JDBC Drivers

Suppose we have a design decision to make between two JDBC drivers. The architecture of the application, for example, is intranet-based and can use either of Oracle's type 2 or type 4 drivers. In that scenario, we might look into following parameters while selecting the appropriate JDBC driver:

- Memory footprint
- Database connection time
- Data retrieval time
- Data retrieval and traversal time
- Stored procedure execution time
- Concurrent query execution time
- Data insertion time

Memory footprint is the size of the JDBC driver `.jar` file. This is a vital parameter for Internet-based applications since greater size means larger download time. The database connection time is the average connection time it takes for the JDBC driver to connect to the database. Lower **database connection time** means higher application performance.

Data retrieval time is the time taken to execute a SQL `SELECT` query. **Data retrieval and traversal time** is the time taken to execute the query and also to scroll through the resultset for a fixed number of records. The `SELECT` and the data retrieval are often two separate actions, with the latter taking the bulk of the time, depending on transport. The data retrieval and traversal time is higher for type 3 drivers since all the data comes to the client program through a middle-tier server. This is an important parameter in deciding the performance of a JDBC driver.

The **stored procedure execution time** is the time it takes to execute the stored procedure, via a JDBC driver for a varying number of times. This test could be performed using the `CallableStatement` interface.

The **concurrent query execution time** is determined by starting a predefined number of threads, with the `Connection` object shared by all the threads. Each of the threads must create a `Statement` object and execute a query with fixed number of records. Time for executing such a query with concurrent access can be logged into a log file and performance ascertained.

Data insertion time is defined as the time it takes to insert a fixed number of records into a database with the SQL `INSERT` statement. This parameter helps in determining the time it takes to insert records using a certain JDBC driver.

Using Relational Data in Your Application

Reading the upcoming chapters will give you a solid understanding of the mechanics of database access using Java. Now that you have learned the basics of relational databases you are ready to learn how to access them using the Java language. As you discover how to tap into the data with Java, you will need to make some decisions about the best way to obtain the data and represent it to the rest of your application.

- Will you access the data right where you need it, in a servlet or JSP page?
- Will you access the data via a set of specialized data-aware components?
- Will you manipulate the data in its simplest Java form, a `ResultSet`?
- Will you pass the data around to application components as a disconnected `RowSet`?
- Will you convert the data into Java data objects, JavaBeans, or go one-step further and represent it as XML?

These considerations are at the heart of application data design. While there are no hard and fast rules for application data representation, by understanding which approaches are available and their associated strengths and weaknesses, you will be able to make rational design decisions that best fit into the context of your application.

This section assumes that a piece of code has already executed a query or stored procedure and the data results exist in the form of a `ResultSet` object. We shall cover the details of obtaining and using a `ResultSet` in Chapter 9, *Using Statements and Resultsets*, but with the basic understanding that a resultset represents data returned from a query, we will cover the following approaches for data representation and manipulation:

- Using a `ResultSet`
- Using a `RowSet`
- Transforming the `ResultSet` into a Java object
- Transforming the `ResultSet` into an XML representation

First, we begin with a brief detour to consider how the data gets into our application system.

Where Does the Data Originate?

This may seem like a silly question, as your first intuition is probably to answer, 'In the database of course.' While this is quite true, we must address the deeper issue of where data originates *inside our application*. In most applications, the data enters the system in one of two places:

- Directly where it is needed (for example, a client application, servlet, or JSP)
- In a set of components whose primary responsibility is to get data in and out of the database, typically referred to as a **data-persistence tier**

At first glance, there may not seem to be much of distinction between these two approaches. However, this decision can be one of the most important in terms of its impact on your application's development time, scalability, and maintainability.

Direct Data Access

It seems rather intuitive to get the data where you need it. After all, if you have a JSP that's displaying customer information, why not load the customer information in that JSP? If you have an applet that is displaying database data in a tabular format, why not make a direct call to the database from the applet?

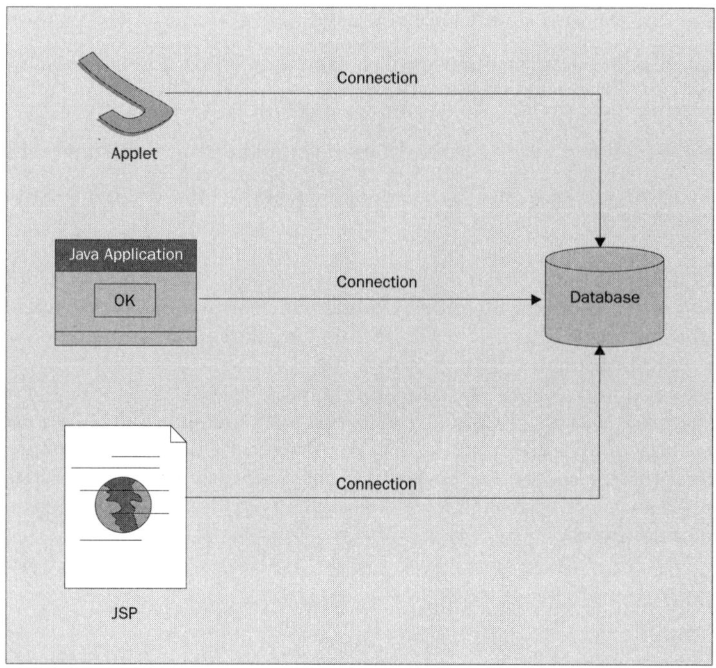

Something to notice about this technique is that it requires the database access code to be present in each object that pulls data from the database. Imagine if each type of client had a copy of the SQL to retrieve data from the `Recordings` table and we decided to change the name of one of the database columns. Updating the configuration of all of the client applications could be a maintenance nightmare if the application was widely deployed.

Each client to the data also has its own connection to the database, as well as all the resources needed to support both the connection and data retrieval. We will see shortly how this can have a negative impact on the scalability of your application.

Another factor to consider is that each client to the database must now deal with a potentially complex database interaction. Databases typically represent data in a normalized fashion that does not always map well into an object-oriented paradigm. In the above configuration, data clients are left to manage the intricacies of the data by themselves. This configuration is commonly known as a 2-tier, or client-server architecture.

Creating a Data-Persistence Tier

A common alternative to direct database access is to create a tier of objects that have the responsibility for communicating with the database. This makes the architecture into a 3-tier architecture. These objects manage all of the SQL, connections, and transactions needed to create, modify, and delete data in the database. Other programs interact with this object tier to request database operations. The following diagram illustrates how the tiers fit together:

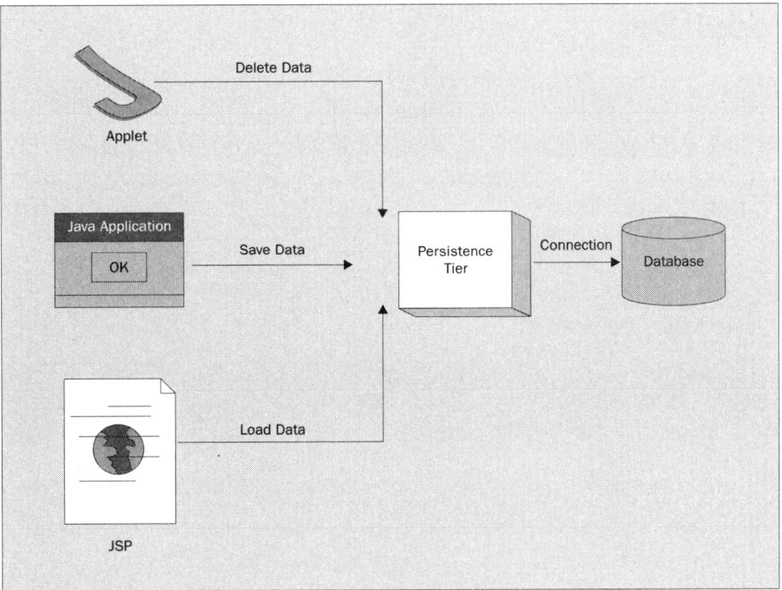

By localizing database access to the persistence tier, you have the potential to circumvent all of the downsides to the direct access approach. A persistence tier provides a centralized point of management for all configuration information required to move data between the database and the application. The persistence tier can also better manage precious database resources via pooling of connection objects, and caching of data. By taking over database access management, it allows the data clients (and developers) to focus on doing useful things with more useful representations of the data. Additionally, such a persistence tier can give stricter control over access to the database.

Another feature worth noting is that a persistence tier effectively isolates client applications from the underlying storage mechanism. If all the clients see is the interface of a persistence tier, we can take advantage of providing them access not only to an RDBMS, but also to a nearly endless list of directory services, legacy systems, and data sources. In Chapter 19, *J2EE and Java Database Applications*, you will see how Java provides this capability as part of the Java 2, Enterprise Edition platform.

Constructing a persistence layer requires either a pre-existing framework (such as EJB), or the careful construction of a framework that meets your specific needs. In either case an extra measure of planning that is not usually required for direct data access will be needed.

Choosing Your Approach

While the use of direct data access or a persistence tier has a set of tradeoffs that need be considered, you should hold off on making a design decision until you understand how the various means of data representation can affect it. Once you have considered all of your options and weighed them against any existing constraints you will be able to gain a measure of confidence that you are making a decision that is appropriate to your situation.

Now to consider the more common, architecture-independent approaches for representing database data in an application.

Using a ResultSet

Nearly all data retrieved from a database query or stored procedure will start out in this form. The `ResultSet` is the most basic way in Java to represent relational data retrieved from a query or stored procedure. It provides a row-by-row view of the data and method calls that are used to return the data.

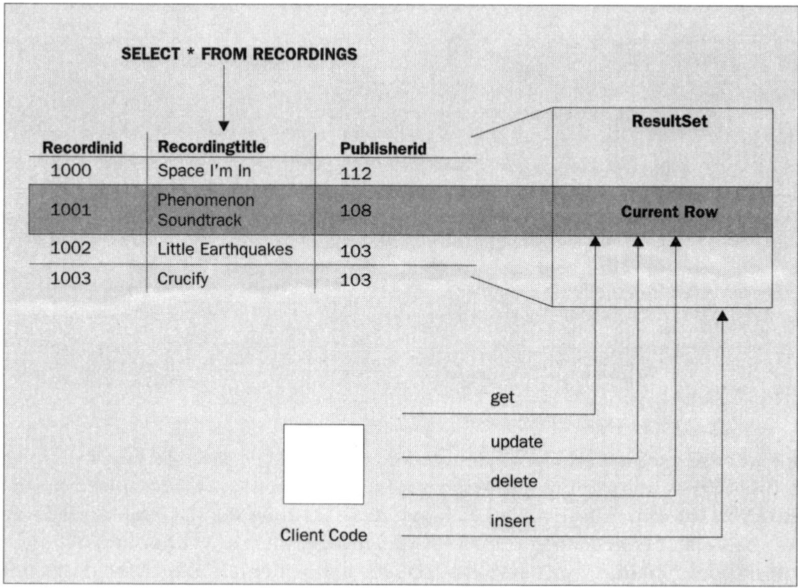

Although the data will typically be accessed 'line-by-line' in a sequential fashion, JDBC 2.0 is robust enough to support both forward and reverse traversal through the `ResultSet` as well as jumping to a numbered row. Additionally, the `ResultSet` can be used to insert, update, and delete data in the returned rows.

Advantages

As you can see, the `ResultSet` provides robust access to the data. This is the simplest object-based view into the data that Java provides. Since it is relatively easy to obtain a `ResultSet` from a database query, this approach often is the quickest to implement for simple examples, application prototypes, and quick 'throw-away' utility applications. An example of such an application is one that is used to dump out a table's contents for debugging purposes.

Consider a simple GUI application that allows a user to view the results of a database query in a `JTable`. Perhaps we have standard reports we want to provide to the user in this fashion, or perhaps we are using this technique as part of our debugging tool set to see what data is actually in the database. It would be a tool not unlike Oracle's SQL Advantage, or Cloudview that ships with the Cloudscape database.

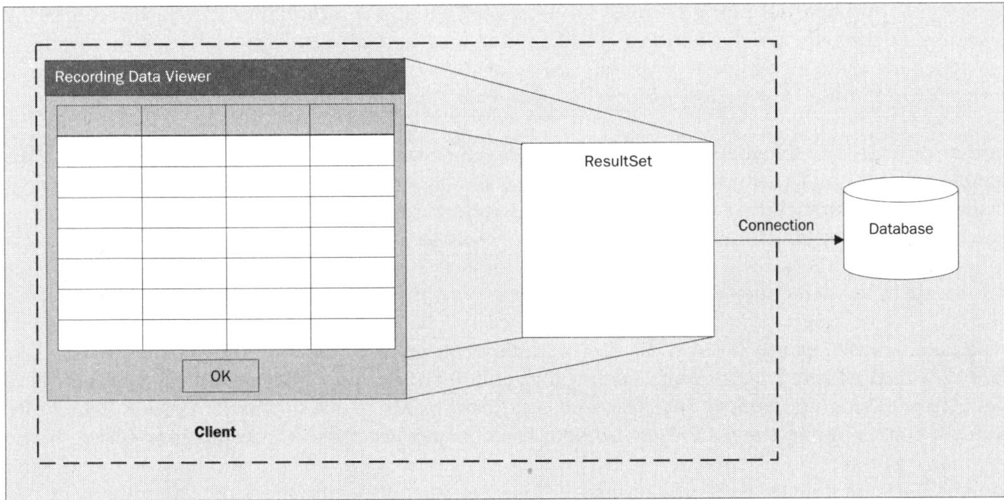

In this sample application, a graphical component like a `JTable` directly presents the data contained in a `ResultSet` query. Changes can be made to the data represented in table cells, and can be immediately sent to the database or can be batched until a 'Save' command is issued.

Using a `ResultSet` also keeps you from having to load many data objects into memory. If the `JTable` above only displayed 25 rows at a time, you could request only the rows you need from the `ResultSet` at that time, and later get more (such as when the user hit 'Page Down'). Since the `ResultSet` is typically implemented as a connection to an open result on the database server, the data in the `ResultSet` will only exist in your virtual machine when you request it.

With all of the flexibility this approach is capable of, you might say to yourself, 'Why would I ever use data in my application with anything other than a `ResultSet`?' As full-featured as a `ResultSet` may seem, there are some limitations to this approach that you should be aware of.

Limitations

One of the first limiting considerations for the `ResultSet` approach is that when deployed on a large scale (say 500 users), it may not make the most efficient use of certain resources. Each user getting the data will need to obtain their own connection to the database, then execute their own query, and finally get their own copy of the data back.

Databases typically charge by the number of client access licenses. When multiple users are accessing the data in this way, there are two choices:

- Buy enough licenses to cover concurrent access by all of the deployed clients
- Buy a handful of licenses and make the database control the number of people allowed to access the data concurrently

The first approach is usually limited by the cost of database access licenses. Most database vendors charge a licensing fee based on the number of concurrent clients the database will support. This cost may be trivial if the application is deployed to a handful of users, but it can become prohibitively expensive at the enterprise level.

The second approach is limiting because it makes inefficient use of precious database resources. Instead of running queries, the database has to spend time managing licenses. This can result in a poor experience for users who have to wait for their queries to execute, and others whose queries timeout because the database is busy doing things besides fetching their data.

Another downside to this method is that the `ResultSet` must be used in the same virtual machine that created it. The `ResultSet` object relies on an active connection to the database and cannot be serialized to a remote client such as an applet or wireless device. In order to get to the data, the `ResultSet`, and of course the database query and connection, would have to be created in the remote application. Thus a `ResultSet` can only be part of a persistence-tier solution if the client applications are running in the same memory space.

In the data viewer example above, the user maintains an open connection the entire time they are working with the `ResultSet`. This was listed as an advantage above because it can prevent data objects from taking up memory space in your application. There is a downside as well. When one client is using a connection to the database, another client cannot use the same connection. Since the number of available connections is constrained by database licenses, when all connections are in use, other clients will not be able to access the database. This means that during the 5, 10, 30 minutes or more that several users are looking at the data, another might have to wait for a connection to free up.

An approach where each client prepares their own query and maintains the `ResultSet` may work quite well on a very small scale, but as the application size increases, this method is one of the first to run out of gas.

Using a RowSet

As you can probably see, the scarcity of database resources, and need to have the connection opened in the same virtual machine as the `ResultSet` can put a damper on our efforts to scale and distribute an application. Fortunately, JDBC 2.0 improves the picture somewhat through the introduction of an extension to the `ResultSet` interface: the `RowSet` interface.

Advantages

You will learn the details of using `RowSet` in Chapter 11 on *Using Rowsets*, but it functions almost identically to `ResultSet` (in fact, the `RowSet` interface inherits from `ResultSet`) with a few notable improvements:

- `RowSets` encapsulate information needed to connect to a database
- `RowSet` implementations are serializable

By encapsulating the information needed to connect to a database, a `RowSet` can exist outside the context of a `Connection` object. Normally an open `ResultSet` requires an open `Connection`. With a `RowSet`, the data can be retrieved and the database disconnected. You can then manipulate the data and reconnect when you are ready to apply all of the changes.

Because the connection information is maintained internally, a `RowSet` can be serialized after it is disconnected. This means you can run the queries in a persistence-tier component, and ship the `RowSet` over the network to a client. Whether you send the `RowSet` to a PDA, an applet, or even another object in the same virtual machine, this is a great step toward centralizing your data access. Centralizing your data access means maintaining less database configuration information in each client.

Limitations

Even though the RowSet may have been generated in a persistence tier, when you give it to a client, you are giving them the ability to directly modify the data in the database. Because the RowSet encapsulates all of the information necessary to reconnect to the data source and update the data, there is no convenient way to force the client to resubmit the RowSet to a persistence layer and enforce business rules on the changes.

There is also a concurrency issue. Due to its disconnected nature, it is entirely possible for a user to retrieve a RowSet remotely, make changes, and when it comes to updating the database find that someone else has already updated that information before the original RowSet is reconnected. A JSP or servlet application might allow the user to interact with data that is stale if they do not update frequently enough.

The returned result can hog system memory if it is large when the RowSet is disconnected. Since a regular ResultSet maintains a connection to the database, many driver implementations retrieve data on demand only. Because a RowSet can be viewed in its entirety while disconnected, all of the data is loaded into memory.

RowSet support can be another potential limitation. RowSet is just an interface and you'll need a concrete implementation in order to use it. Sun currently only provides pre-release implementations via its developer connection. (Note: there is a plan to include RowSet implementations in the upcoming 1.4 release of the JDK.)

ResultSets and RowSets can't always model the complex nature of application data. Traditional database design emphasizes normalization of data so that it may be stored in related tables. Java makes use of compositional and behavioral patterns that make objects functionally oriented rather than data-centric. A good example is when hierarchical data is being accessed.

In the Java object world, a hierarchy of objects is represented by a tree structure. A common beginning approach to storing a hierarchy in the database involves the use of a self-referencing table where each node stores the key of its parent node, which in turn is modeled as a row in the same table. The parent of the root node is usually set to null. The following diagram illustrates a simple case of this:

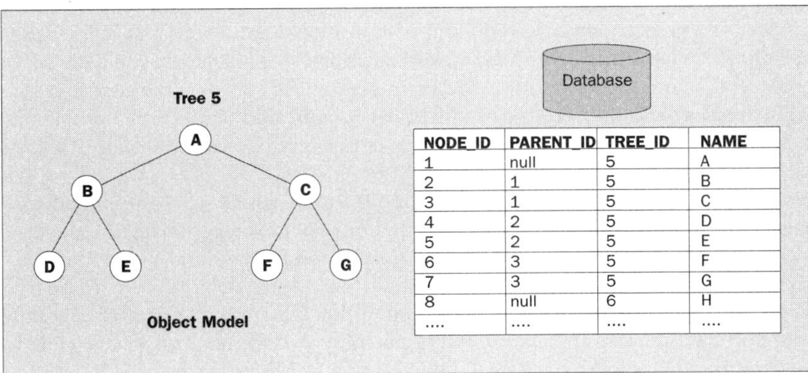

NODE_ID	PARENT_ID	TREE_ID	NAME
1	null	5	A
2	1	5	B
3	1	5	C
4	2	5	D
5	2	5	E
6	3	5	F
7	3	5	G
8	null	6	H
....	....	....	....

In this case, dealing with a ResultSet or RowSet representation of the tree, each client must jump around in the ResultSet to access the data relative to its position in the tree. It would be much more natural and user-friendly, to allow a persistence-tier component to read in the ResultSet and convert it into a Java tree object, such as a linked list, for the client to use. More on Java value objects next.

Transforming a ResultSet into a Java Value Object

If we stop for a moment and consider the above approaches, we will find that they share a few common limitations.

- Access to data must usually be decentralized and can be difficult to maintain and control
- They do not provide an elegant way to manage scarce database resources
- Some data is poorly represented by a `ResultSet` or requires multiple `ResultSet` instances to represent completely

A common approach to solve these issues, and in fact one you'll see used extensively in this book, is to create a Java object representation from the data in a `ResultSet`.

Advantages

Java value objects are typically managed by a persistence tier. The persistence tier contains all of the necessary information about the data-to-object mapping (such as database table and column names) and can manage the SQL necessary to insert, update, retrieve, and delete the underlying data in the database. Clients to the persistence tier only interact with the data via these objects.

This approach not only allows the clients to be isolated from potential complexities of database code, but also centralizes the management of that database code. This is easier to maintain since any changes to the way the object is generated from the database happen behind the interface to the persistence tier. It is also easier to support new clients to the data since they will request an object from the persistence tier instead of needing to be programmed with database access code.

For example, we may create a value object in an e-commerce application that represents data about a product we sell in our catalog. This same object could be used when the customer is browsing, ordering the item, and when the product information is sent off to the fulfillment house. Each of these separate functions could execute using a Java value object instead of having the same messy database access code in three locations.

A Java object gives you greater power to represent compositional and functional relationships of objects. Instead of dealing with a customer `ResultSet`, and an address `ResultSet`, the data can be encapsulated as a `Customer` object containing one or more `Address` objects. Of course some components still need to interact with the database and the two `ResultSets`, but a dedicated persistence tier that has the responsibility to manage information going in and out of the database can now perform this function.

This persistence tier provides a convenient location on top of which a business platform can be built and used to enforce business rules. Additionally the tier provides a centralized location for access so data objects can be cached for quick access and a minimized use of database resources.

The objects can also be made serializable. They can be loaded from the database, serialized, and sent to the client for modification. Now instead of making arbitrary modifications to the underlying data, the client must submit the Java object back to the persistence tier for storage.

A striking advantage of this approach is that it lets application builders stick to the framework of how objects interact instead of getting bogged down in the complexities of database interaction at all levels.

Limitations

Although the value object approach seems to be getting more robust there are definitely some tradeoffs you should be aware of. The first is that Java value objects can hog your memory resources if you're creating objects from a particularly large `ResultSet`.

Since the object will typically be designed to contain the data from a single row in a `ResultSet`, extracting several rows will require several objects: one object for each row, in fact. Recall from our discussion of using a `ResultSet` that they typically rely on their connection to the database to retrieve data on demand and do not fill up the Java memory space with their results. Java objects on the other hand will usually be packed into some kind of collection before being passed to the client. Imagine the logjam this approach could create if you needed to access a `ResultSet` with several hundred rows.

The second consideration is that adding a data tier to an application's design involves another layer of complexity that must be planned for. You must map out the structure for your objects and the relationships between them. Then you must decide which queries will be needed to build your objects. If you want to enforce business rules, you need to plan for them as well.

The extra overhead of planning and design may not produce any noticeable benefits if the application being developed is a prototype or small in nature. Take this consideration with a grain of salt however because most big software projects started out as successful little software projects. More information on the specifics of object-relational mapping can be found in Chapter 15, *Object-Relational Mapping Concepts*.

Transforming the ResultSet into an XML Representation

One potential drawback to all of the above approaches is that they require the data to be accessed and manipulated in a Java environment. Meanwhile, the software industry at large is moving to make data platform- and language-agnostic and to find neutral ways to represent data. The introduction and adoption of the **eXtensible Markup Language** (**XML**) was a giant leap in this direction. XML standardized the platform-independent representation of data.

Advantages

By marking up data into XML format, we are able to represent hierarchical and relational data structures in what is essentially a string format. This string may then be sent from a data-access tier to local clients, remote clients, and with an access protocol like SOAP, to clients in systems that aren't even implemented in Java!

The transformation to XML can be accomplished rather easily. An implementation of `RowSet` scheduled to ship with the 1.4 JDK called `WebRowSet` (available now as an early-access release) will provide the capability to transform a database result into XML with minimal programming.

XML can also be easily transformed into a presentation format via XSLT. (More complete information on XML can be found in Appendix C and on XSLT in Chapter 21). XSLT is a script-like style transformation that can be used, for instance, to make an XML representation into an HTML page. If you want to use the same data to create a text report, no problem, just apply a different XSLT.

Limitations

While XML representation doesn't incur quite the same design and planning overhead as creating Java value objects, application run-time performance may be a consideration. Making use of XML means parsing text, and no matter how you slice it, parsing text to retrieve a value will take longer than making a Java call to a 'getter' method. Although there have been some improvements in ease-of-use, the Java API for XML Parsing (JAXP) can still be intimidating for those unused to it.

Something else to consider is that XML provides only a representation of the data. It does not provide a means to act on data, and provides little help in the way of applying business rules on the data. Basic structural rules can be represented (for example, an `<employee>` **must** contain **one** `<address>`) and there is some field-level validation support provided by an accompanying document (an XML Schema), but it often cannot address the complex requirements of most business applications (such as transaction support).

In many cases where XML data support is not an application requirement, it can make an excellent "add-on" to make data available to external systems the application was never originally designed to support.

Making Tough Decisions Easier

At the beginning of this section we explored approaches to design by asking questions about the approaches we had at our disposal. Now that you know some of the advantages and disadvantages to each of the above approaches, making an application data-design decision can best be put in terms of questions about your application constraints. At the simplest, this means getting to the Who, What, Where, When, and Why of your data needs.

- How many users will need to access and manipulate data at the same time?
- Will the users be accessing and manipulating the data from different locations?
- Should we centralize data access to make it more efficient via caching?
- Does the data access need to be centralized so that business rules can be applied?
- Can the data be made more functional by transforming it into a Java object?
- What types of applications platforms will need to access the data and will transforming the data to XML facilitate this?

As you continue to learn the ins and outs of programming databases in Java, each design situation will provide you with a unique context to answer these questions and develop the right design for your application.

Object-Relational Mapping

Regardless of application architecture, we need to carefully consider how we are going to map our Java object model to the tables of our relational database, and vice-versa. In order to do this effectively, we need to look at the SQL data types and understand how they map to the Java data types in your program.

Mapping Between Java and SQL Data Types

In all of the examples we saw in Chapter 2 on *Basic JDBC Techniques*, all of the data extracted from a resultset was retrieved as a `String`. You'll certainly need to get other types of data, and as you will see in Chapter 9, the `ResultSet` object provides a number of methods for retrieving different data types.

The SQL standard defines a set of data types that do not map one-for-one with those in Java. As you write applications that move data from SQL to Java and back, you'll have to take into account how JDBC performs that mapping. That is, you need to know the Java data type you require to represent a given SQL data type, and vice versa.

The `Types` class in the `java.sql` package defines constants of type `int` that represent each of the SQL types supported. The name given to the data member storing each constant is the same as that of the corresponding SQL type. When you retrieve the SQL type of a table column, by calling the `getColumnType()` method, for a `ResultSet` object for instance, the SQL type is returned as one of the constants defined in the `Types` class.

When you are retrieving data from a JDBC data source, the `ResultSet` implementation will map the SQL data onto Java data types. The table below shows the SQL-to-Java mappings:

SQL Data Type	Java Data Type
CHAR	String
VARCHAR	String
LONGVARCHAR	String
NUMERIC	java.math.BigDecimal
DECIMAL	java.math.BigDecimal
BIT	boolean
TINYINT	byte
SMALLINT	short
INTEGER	int
BIGINT	long
REAL	float
FLOAT	double
DOUBLE	double
BINARY	byte[]
VARBINARY	byte[]
LONGVARBINARY	byte[]
DATE	java.sql.Date
TIME	java.sql.Time
TIMESTAMP	java.sql.Timestamp

Note that the last three are Java class types defined in the `java.sql` package. The `Date`, `Time`, and `Timestamp` classes that accommodate the requirements of the SQL types are derived from the `Date` class that is defined in the `java.util` package.

Conversely, when you are relating data types from Java to SQL the following mappings apply:

Java Data Type	SQL Data Type
`String`	`VARCHAR,LONGVARCHAR`
`java.math.BigDecimal`	`NUMERIC`
`boolean`	`BIT`
`byte`	`TINYINT`
`short`	`SMALLINT`
`int`	`INTEGER`
`long`	`BIGINT`
`float`	`REAL`
`double`	`DOUBLE`
`byte[]`	`VARBINARY,LONGVARBINARY`
`Java.sql.Date`	`DATE`
`Java.sql.Time`	`TIME`
`Java.sql.Timestamp`	`TIMESTAMP`

Note that some databases implement `INTEGER` data types as `NUMERIC`. When accessing `INTEGER` elements through the JDBC, it is important to associate the JDBC data type with the internal data type actually stored in the database.

Most likely, you will know ahead of time what the SQL type is for the data you are accessing in a database. When this is not the case, you can easily determine the SQL type for each column in a resultset by calling the `getColumnType()` method for the `ResultSetMetaData` object. You can then compare the return value with the constants defined in the `Types` class to select the `getXxx()` method for the `ResultSet` object that is appropriate for retrieving the data.

Mapping Relational Data onto Java Objects

In Chapter 2, you saw how you could get the basic attribute data from a JDBC `ResultSet` object. Since Java is object-oriented, you won't want to deal with individual data items such as a recording ID and title in many cases – you will want to work with `Recording` objects that represent the recordings. That's what we'll focus on now, and in the process, you'll get some more experience with the `Statement` and `ResultSet` interfaces.

The way that information is handled at the object level is usually different from the way data is stored in a relational database. In the world of objects, the underlying principle is to make those objects exhibit the same characteristics (information and behavior) as their real-world counterparts – in other words, objects function at the level of the conceptual model. Relational databases, on the other hand, work at the data-model level. Relational databases store information using normalized forms, whereas conceptual objects like orders and customers can be decomposed into a number of tables. So how do you deal with the problem of mapping objects to relational data models?

Sometimes there is a straightforward relationship between the columns in a table and the member variables in an object. In that case, the mapping task consists simply of matching the data types of the database with those of Java. The following figure shows this simple application-level SQL-to-object mapping:

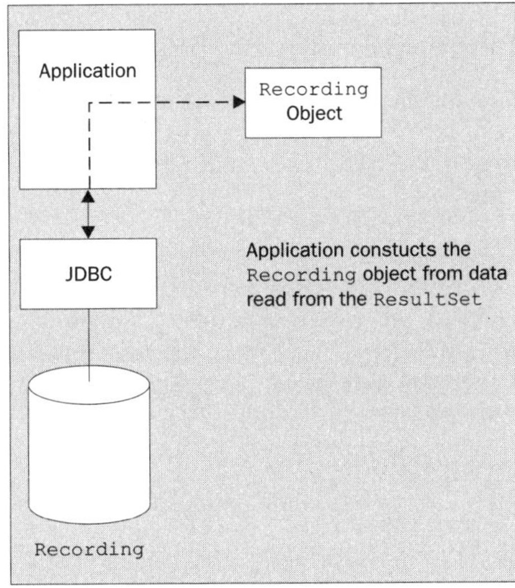

Try It Out – A Simple Mapping from SQL Rows to Java Objects

1. The `recordings` table in the sample database is a good example of a simple mapping. This table has the following definition:

Column	Data Type	Description
`Recordingid`	`int`	Unique identifier for each recording.
`Recordingtitle`	`varchar(50)`	Title of the recording.
`Publisherid`	`Int`	Unique ID for the publisher of the recording – a foreign key to the `publishersandlabels` table.
`Catalognumber`	`Varchar(20)`	Publisher's catalog number.

Table continued on following page

Column	Data Type	Description
`Recordingformatid`	`Int`	Unique ID for the type of recording. This is a foreign key to the `recordingformats` table.
`Releasedate`	`Date`	Date of release.
`Languageid`	`Int`	Unique ID for the recording's language. This is a foreign key to the `languages` table.
`Listprice`	`Double precision`	List price of the recording.

2. Let's define a Java class for the recordings. Take a look back at the table, which shows you how to map data types from SQL to Java. Based on those mappings, we can define the member variables for a `Recording` class, and add a constructor, member access methods, and a `toString()` method.

```
import java.sql.Date;

public class Recording {
  public Recording(int recordingId, String title, int publisherId,
                   String catalogNumber, int recordingFormat,
                   Date releaseDate, int languageId, double price) {

    this.recordingId = recordingId;
    this.title = title;
    this.publisherId = publisherId;
    this.catalogNumber = catalogNumber;
    this.recordingFormat = recordingFormat;
    this.releaseDate = releaseDate;
    this.languageId = languageId;
    this.price = price;
  }

  public int getId() {
    return recordingId;
  }

  public String getTitle() {
    return title;
  }

  public int getPublisherId() {
    return publisherId;
  }

  public String getCatalogNumber() {
    return catalogNumber;
  }

  public int getRecordingFormat() {
```

```
    return recordingFormat;
  }

  public Date getReleaseDate() {
    return releaseDate;
  }

  public double getPrice() {
    return price;
  }

  public String toString() {
    return new String("recording ID: " + Integer.toString(recordingId) +
                      "\ntitle       : " + title + "\npublisherId   : " +
                      Integer.toString(publisherId) +
                      "\ncatalogNumber : " + catalogNumber +
                      "\nrecording format :" + recordingFormat +
                      "\nrelease date :" + releaseDate.toString() +
                      "\nprice : " +
                      java.text.NumberFormat.getCurrencyInstance()
                        .format(price));
  }

  int recordingId;
  String title;
  int publisherId;
  String catalogNumber;
  int recordingFormat;
  Date releaseDate;
  int languageId;
  double price;
}
```

3. Next, we need to get the data from the database into the `Recording` object. Our first strategy for doing this is pretty basic – the application class will create the `Connection`, `Statement`, and `ResultSet`, and read the data from the database. The `Recording` class constructor will be called using each row of data read. For this example, we will use an SQL statement that is a literal string in the code, rather than creating a `PreparedStatement`.

```
import java.sql.*;

public class TrySimpleMapping {
  public static void main(String[] args) {
    TrySimpleMapping SQLtoJavaExample;
    try {
      SQLtoJavaExample = new TrySimpleMapping();
      SQLtoJavaExample.listRecordings();
    } catch (SQLException sqle) {
      System.err.println(sqle);
    } catch (ClassNotFoundException cnfe) {
      System.err.println(cnfe);
    }
  }
```

```
  public TrySimpleMapping() throws SQLException, ClassNotFoundException {
    Class.forName(driverName);
    connection = DriverManager.getConnection(sourceURL, user, password);
  }

  public void listRecordings() throws SQLException {
    Recording recording;

    String query =
      "SELECT recordingid, recordingtitle, publisherid, catalognumber,
recordingformatid, releasedate, languageid, listprice from recordings";

    Statement statement = connection.createStatement();
    ResultSet recordings = statement.executeQuery(query);

    while (recordings.next()) {
      int id = recordings.getInt(1);
      String title = recordings.getString(2);
      int publisherId = recordings.getInt(3);
      String catalogNumber = recordings.getString(4);
      int recordingFormat = recordings.getInt(5);
      Date releaseDate = recordings.getDate(6);
      int languageId = recordings.getInt(7);
      double listPrice = recordings.getDouble(8);

      recording = new Recording(id, title, publisherId, catalogNumber,
                                recordingFormat, releaseDate, languageId,
                                listPrice);

      System.out.println("\n" + recording);
    }
    recordings.close();
    connection.close();
  }

  Connection connection;
  String driverName = "COM.cloudscape.core.JDBCDriver";
  String sourceURL = "jdbc:cloudscape:Wrox4370.db";
  String user = "guest";
  String password = "guest";
}
```

You should get the following output:

```
recording ID: 1000
title     : Space I'm In
publisherId  : 112
catalogNumber : 2064-24370-2
recording format :1
release date :1991-05-23
price : $14.99

recording ID: 1001
```

```
title     : Phenomenon Soundtrack
publisherId  : 108
catalogNumber : 9362-46360-2
recording format :1
release date :1996-08-23
price : $15.99

recording ID: 1002
title     : Little Earthquakes
publisherId  : 103
catalogNumber : 7567-82358-2
recording format :1
release date :1991-10-02
price : $14.99

recording ID: 1003
title     : Crucify
publisherId  : 103
catalogNumber : 82399-2
recording format :1
release date :1992-03-21
price : $9.99

recording ID: 1004
title     : Big Time
publisherId  : 107
catalogNumber : GAIL3 12
recording format :1
release date :1987-06-21
price : $9.99

recording ID: 1005
title     : US
publisherId  : 107
catalogNumber : GAHN2 07
recording format :1
release date :1992-09-29
price : $18.97
```

How It Works

Everything in this example should look pretty familiar, but there are just a couple of new things we need to cover.

Note first that there is an extra step after the data is read, which creates the `Recording` object by calling its constructor with that data. Also, in the `while` loop, as each row is read from the `ResultSet`, the application uses the appropriate `getXXX()` method of the `ResultSet` object to perform the mapping from SQL to Java data types. In each of these method calls, the argument is the index value to select the column. Since the query selects the columns by name, the columns in the resultset will be in the same sequence as the column names in the SQL query. In order to display the data for each `Recording` object, we simply call `System.out.println()` and pass it the `Recording` object reference. This will automatically invoke the `toString()` method for the object. Note that in the output, the literal 'Null', would appear where there are Null values in the database. In this example there were no Null values, but this practice keeps you from running into Null pointer exceptions by gracefully handling Null values.

> **This example uses a data source that does not require a username or password. If you need a username and password to access that data source, simply modify the code in the `TrySimpleMapping` constructor to use the appropriate driver, URL, and `getConnection()` method of the `DriverManager`.**

A Better Mapping Strategy

As you saw, the simple strategy we have just seen does in fact transfer the data between the relational database and the Java objects successfully (and this approach can be used in reverse to get data back to the database, as we'll see shortly). It does, however, leave quite a lot to be desired because the movement of data between the database and the Java object is left completely to the application code.

A better, more object-oriented strategy would be to make the `Recording` class handle its own data extraction from a `ResultSet` object. To do this we could add a `static` factory method (a method that manufactures `Recording` objects) to the `Recording` class that will synthesize `Recording` objects from data in the database. The code calling the factory method must still do the work of creating the `Connection` and `Statement` objects, and use the `Statement` object to execute the query that retrieves the data. It will also need to ensure that the `ResultSet` contains the columns required for populating the `Recording` object.

The following figure shows this encapsulated SQL-to-object mapping.

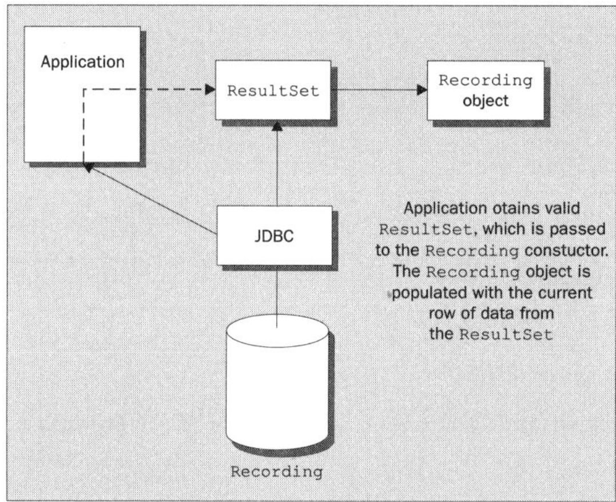

We need to establish an implied 'contract' between this factory method and any code that calls it:

- The current row of the `ResultSet` object that is passed to the factory method must be positioned at a valid row
- The `ResultSet` must contain all the columns from the `Recording` table

We can implement the factory method in the `Recording` class as:

```
public static Recording fromResults(ResultSet recordings)
      throws SQLException
   {

      int id             = recordings.getInt(1);
    String title       = recordings.getString(2);
    int publisherId    = recordings.getInt(3);
    String catalogNumber     = recordings.getString(4);
    int recordingFormat = recordings.getInt(5);
    Date releaseDate = recordings.getDate(6);
    int languageId = recordings.getInt(7);
    double listPrice = recordings.getDouble(8);

    Recording recording = new Recording(id, title, publisherId, catalogNumber,
                          recordingFormat, releaseDate, languageId, listPrice);

    return recording;
      }
```

Here, we access the columns by name; so there is no dependency on the order in which they are retrieved in the query. This gives a little added flexibility to the application – to use the wildcard notation for instance. The only requirement is that all the columns should be present in the `ResultSet` object. If any are not, an exception of type `SQLException` will be thrown, and this will need to be caught by the calling method. Of course, the `Recording.java` file must now have an import statement added for the `java.sql` package.

We can see this in action with another example.

Try it Out – Encapsulated Mapping of SQL Rows to Java Objects

We just need to create the application class. This class is nearly identical to `TrySimpleMapping`, except that there is less code in the `listRecordings()` method.

```
import java.sql.*;

public class TryEncapsulatedMapping {
  Connection databaseConnection;
  String driverName;
  String sourceURL;

  public static void main(String[] args) {
    TryEncapsulatedMapping SQLtoJavaExample;
    try {
      SQLtoJavaExample = new TryEncapsulatedMapping();
      SQLtoJavaExample.listRecordings();
    } catch (SQLException sqle) {
      System.out.println("SQL Exception: " + sqle);
    } catch (ClassNotFoundException cnfe) {
      System.out.println(cnfe.toString());
    }
  }
```

```
    public TryEncapsulatedMapping()
            throws SQLException, ClassNotFoundException {
      driverName = "COM.cloudscape.core.JDBCDriver";
      sourceURL = "jdbc:cloudscape:Wrox4370.db";

      Class.forName(driverName);
      databaseConnection = DriverManager.getConnection(sourceURL);
    }

    public void listRecordings() throws SQLException {

      Recording aRecording;
      String query =
        "SELECT recordingid, recordingtitle, publisherid, catalognumber,
        recordingformatid, releasedate, languageid, listprice from recordings";

      Statement statement = databaseConnection.createStatement();
      ResultSet recordings = statement.executeQuery(query);

      while (recordings.next()) {
        aRecording = Recording.fromResults(recordings);
        System.out.println("\n" + aRecording.toString());
      }

      recordings.close();
      databaseConnection.close();
    }
  }
```

When you run the example, you should get results exactly as those from the previous example.

How It Works

All we have really done in this example is pushed the work of extracting Java types from the `ResultSet` to the class that is using the data. Instead of reading from the `ResultSet` and instantiating a new `Recording` object for each row in the `listRecordings()` method, we just call the static `fromResults()` method of the `Recording` class, which will create a new `Recording` object from the data in the current row of the `ResultSet`.

This approach is better than the previous example because the class itself is responsible for ensuring that the correct mapping is performed between the database and the Java object. That way, applications don't have to duplicate that logic, and don't have the opportunity to attempt bad mappings (such as converting an SQL `REAL` type to an `int`). The mapping is also independent of the sequence of columns in the resultset. Encapsulation of the mapping from the database data to the class object is important for ensuring that classes can be reused easily within, and between applications. So, although it's a little more work than the simple mapping method, it is well worth it.

Summary

Over the course of this chapter, we have looked at some of the issues that will need to be considered in all real-world JDBC applications. We have:

- Taken a brief look at the use of UML diagrams to represent the classes that compose our application
- Briefly discussed some of the different application scenarios in which your JDBC skills will be put to use
- Assessed the four types of JDBC driver that are available
- Looked at the different ways in which you might use data in your applications
- Discussed basic strategies for mapping between the worlds of object programming and relational data; we look at more advanced mapping strategies in Section III of this book

You are now in a good position to move on and examine the capability of the JDBC API in much more detail and to start developing more complex and sophisticated JDBC applications.

akarta JAVA
Java

Connecting to a Database

Central to every database program is a way for the code to make a connection to the database and then execute SQL statements. The `Connection` interface in JDBC defines the methods for creating and using connections to the database.

To demonstrate how to use a connection, we will develop a class that uses a JDBC `Connection` object to connect to a database, and sends a SQL `INSERT` string to the database using a `Statement` object. While the `Connection` interface represents connections to a database, it is the `Statement` interface that defines the class that sends SQL to the database. The `Connection` interface has methods for creating `Statement` objects. In the course of developing the class, we will create a flexible implementation for creating, using, and managing database resources.

Even though the example class developed in this chapter will illustrate some best practices to use in your JDBC programs, it still obtains a connection to a database using the same technique as almost every example JDBC program: a driver is registered and a URL is passed to a method that returns a connection. In the section on `DataSources`, we look at a more flexible architecture for getting a connection to a database.

Just as the connection is central to JDBC programming, this chapter will provide the central foundation to many of the following chapters. We will:

- Discuss how to register a driver and get a database connection
- Use a database connection in a class
- Create a portable connection class for managing database resources
- Briefly introduce the concept of `DataSource` objects for getting a connection in a networked environment

The main focus is on connections and how to establish them and use them; therefore, we will only be showing simplistic examples of data access. Later chapters will expand on the simple one-row methods demonstrated here.

The DriverManager Class

As stated above, a database connection is central to every JDBC program. But `Connection` is an interface and thus can't be instantiated by calling a constructor method. You obtain a connection by calling a method that returns a `Connection` object. That method, `getConnection()`, belongs to the `DriverManager` class.

> *If `Connection` is an interface, how can the above paragraph refer to a `Connection` object? The answer is that when the `getConnection()` method is called, it must return an object of some concrete class that implements the `Connection` interface. We use the phrase "`Connection` object" instead of the more awkward "instance of a class that implements the `Connection` interface."*

In the UML diagram below, we show the relationship between the `DriverManager` class and the `Connection` interface, and the methods of each that will be covered in this chapter.

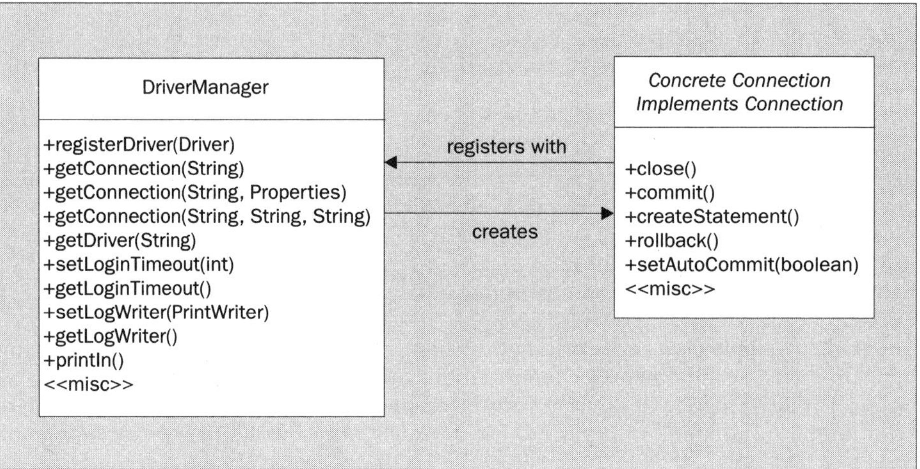

In Chapter 2 we discussed the use of a call to `Class.forName()` to cause the Java Virtual Machine to load the driver class. This method takes a `String` parameter that is the fully qualified class name of the vendor-specific driver class. We saw that, for the Cloudscape database, the code was as follows:

```
//Load the Driver class
Class.forName("COM.cloudscape.core.JDBCDriver ");
```

The fully qualified class name above is '`COM.cloudscape.core.JDBCDriver`.'

> *The term 'fully qualified class name' is just a fancy way to say 'the package specification and the class name.' In the example, `COM.cloudscape.core` is the package, and `JDBCDriver` is the class name.*

If you are developing for the MySQL database, the fully qualified class name is `org.gjt.mm.mysql.Driver`. So, to use the MySQL driver, the equivalent code would be as follows:

```
      Class.forName("org.gjt.mm.mysql.Driver");
```

For an Oracle database, we would use:

```
      Class.forName("oracle.jdbc.driver.OracleDriver");
```

The driver class name will be different for every database. The documentation for the driver will provide the driver class name. Sun keeps a list of available drivers at http://java.sun.com/products/jdbc/drivers.

There is actually a second way to load the appropriate driver class, and that is to add the driver classname to a list of possible drivers that the `DriverManager` class loads. This list is kept as a `java.lang.System` property with the name `jdbc.drivers`. When the `DriverManager` class is loaded, it will attempt to load any JDBC driver that has been identified in the `jdbc.drivers` system property.

The system properties are actually stored in a `Properties` object. The `Properties` class, defined in the `java.util` package, associates values with keys in a map, and the contents of the map define a set of system properties. In general, each key is supplied as a `String` and the value corresponding to a key can be any valid object. Thus you can use a `Properties` object to supply as much information as is required by your driver – or anything else that interacts with the system properties for that matter. You just set the key/value pairs for the `Properties` object that are needed.

You can set the `jdbc.drivers` system property by calling the `setProperty()` method for the `System` class, for example:

```
  System.setProperty("jdbc.drivers", "COM.cloudscape.core.JDBCDriver");
```

The first argument is the key for the property to be set and the second argument is the value. This statement identifies the Cloudscape JDBC driver in the system property. If you want to specify multiple drivers in the system property value, you should separate the driver names within the string by colons.

If the security manager permits it, you can obtain a reference to the `Properties` object for your system by calling the static `getProperties()` method for the `System` class. If there is no `Properties` object defined containing the system properties, one will be created with a default set of properties. The `Properties` class defines a `list()` method that you can use to list all your system properties as follows:

```
public class ListProps
{
   public static void main(String args[])
   {
      System.getProperties().list(System.out);    // List all properties
   }
}
```

Running this simple program lists out all of your system properties (only the first twelve of my system properties are shown here):

```
C:\WINDOWS\System32\cmd.exe
C:\BegJavaDB\Ch08>java -cp . ListProps
-- listing properties --
java.runtime.name=Java(TM) 2 Runtime Environment, Stand...
sun.boot.library.path=c:\jdk1.3\jre\bin
java.vm.version=1.3.0-C
java.vm.vendor=Sun Microsystems Inc.
java.vendor.url=http://java.sun.com/
path.separator=;
java.vm.name=Java HotSpot(TM) Client VM
file.encoding.pkg=sun.io
java.vm.specification.name=Java Virtual Machine Specification
user.dir=C:\BegJavaDB\Ch06
java.runtime.version=1.3.0-C
java.awt.graphicsenv=sun.awt.Win32GraphicsEnvironment
```

The `Properties` class also defines a `setProperty()` method, so once you have a `Properties` object, you can set properties directly by calling this method for the object.

If a security manager is in effect and a security policy has been set up on your system, you may not be allowed to set the system property. In that case the `setProperty()` call with throw an exception of type `SecurityException`. In this situation, and in any situation where there is any doubt, it is safest to use the `Class.forName()` call.

When the driver class is loaded, either with `Class.forName()` or through the system properties, the driver class is required by the JDBC specification to register itself with the `DriverManager`. It does this by calling the `DriverManager.registerDriver(Driver)` method. For that reason, it is totally unnecessary for your application to explicitly call the `registerDriver(Driver)` method (because the driver class does this itself).

The only time that you are likely to come into contact with the `Driver` object is when you install it. Your applications need not ever interact directly with the `Driver` object itself since the `DriverManager` class takes care of communicating with it. When you call the `getConnection()` method of the `DriverManager` class, it iterates through the drivers that are registered with the `DriverManager`, and asks each one in turn if it can handle the URL that you have passed to it. The first driver that can satisfy the connection defined by the URL creates a `Connection` object, which is passed back to the application by way of the `DriverManager`.

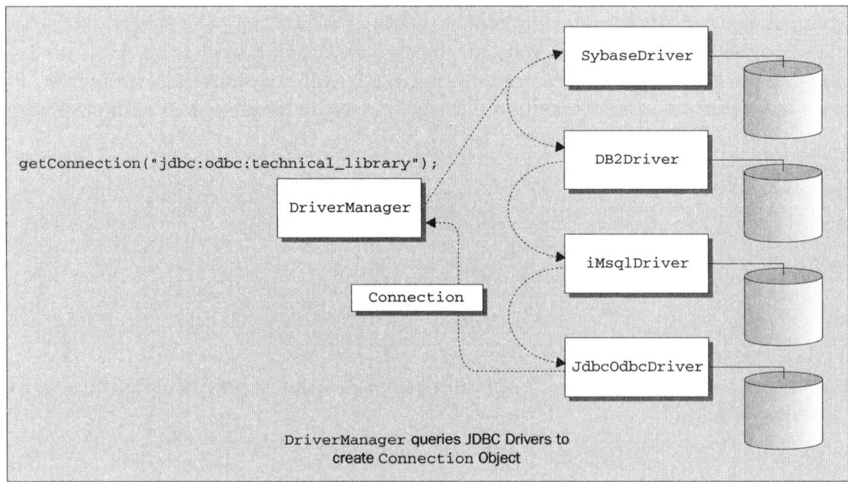

`DriverManager` queries JDBC Drivers to create `Connection` Object

There are occasions, however, when you may want to query a specific driver for information, such as its version number. For example, you may know that a particular feature that your program makes use of wasn't incorporated into a driver until version 2.1. You can query the driver to get the version number so your program can handle an earlier version intelligently.

In order to get the `Driver` object, you call the static `getDriver()` method of the `DriverManager` class, passing the URL of the data source to it as the argument. If the `DriverManager` finds a driver that can accommodate the data source, a reference to a `Driver` object encapsulating it is returned. The code fragment below illustrates testing the version of a JDBC driver, looking for versions that are 1.1 or greater.

```
// Load the driver class
Class.forName("COM.cloudscape.core.JDBCDriver");

// Define the data source for the driver
String sourceURL = "jdbc:cloudscape:Wrox4370.db";

// Test for driver version
int verMajor;
float verComplete;
float verPreferred;

// Set the minimum preferred version
verPreferred = 1.1f;

// Set the driver
Driver theDriver = DriverManager.getDriver(sourceURL);

// Get the version number to the left of the decimal point,
// e.g. 1 out of 1.0
verMajor = theDriver.getMajorVersion();

/* Make a float of the complete version number by adding
   the minor number (to the right of the decimal point,
   e.g. 1108 out of 1.1108)  on to verMajor
*/
verComplete = Float.parseFloat(verMajor + "." +
                              theDriver.getMinorVersion());

// Test to see if we have a suitable version of the driver
if(verComplete >= verPreferred)
    System.out.println("Version " + verComplete + " found");
    //Make the connection...
else
    System.out.println("Required version of driver (" +
                verPreferred + ") not found");
    // Otherwise drop out...
```

In practice you could do a lot more that just output messages depending on the version of the driver that is available. Your program might choose to operate differently to account for the limitations of an earlier version for instance.

The getConnection() Method

Once we have loaded our driver, the next step is to create a Connection object in order to actually establish a link to the database. Within a session represented by a particular Connection object, we can execute our SQL statements, and the results will be returned via that connection.

As we discussed in Chapter 2, we establish our connection with a call to the getConnection() method of the DriverManager class. We looked at the simplest form of the getConnection() method:

```
Connection DBConnection = DriverManager.getConnection(sourceURL);
```

The method call above takes a single String parameter. That string contains all of the parameters needed to make the connection, including username and password. So, for our Cloudscape driver we had the code:

```
    // Define the data source for the driver
    String sourceURL = "jdbc:cloudscape:Wrox4370.db";

    // Create a connection through the DriverManager
   Connection DBConnection = DriverManager.getConnection(sourceURL);
```

The code constructs a JDBC URL for the database and uses the URL to get a connection to the database from the DriverManager class. The URL for each database will vary depending on the database and the driver. However, all URLs will have the general form jdbc:<subprotocol>:<subname>, with the <subprotocol> identifying the machine or server and <subname> identifying the database and providing additional information needed to make the connection. Let's consider the URL for an Oracle driver:

```
    //Create a url for the database
    String url = "jdbc:oracle:thin:@localhost:1521:orcl";
    //connect to the database
    Connection DBConnection =
        DriverManager.getConnection(url, "wrox", "jdbc");
```

In this example, the <subprotocol> is oracle and the <subname> is translated by the driver to mean 'using the thin driver, connect to the database on the localhost at port 1521 with Service Name orcl.' The thin driver is Oracle's Type 4 driver. The Oracle Type 4 driver makes a network connection to the port given in the URL. Port 1521 is the default port used by Oracle for connections. Other drivers will generally use different ports (Cloudscape uses port 1099), and the port is usually configurable. Consult your database or driver documentation for more information on the format of the JDBC URL for that database.

You'll also notice that, in the code snippet above, the database requires a user name and password in order to gain access to it, so we use the second form of the getConnection() method:

```
Connection DBConnection =
    DriverManager.getConnection(sourceURL, myUserName, myPassword);
```

All three arguments here are of type String; 'wrox' is the username and 'jdbc' is the password. If we were developing for MySQL, our equivalent code would look as follows:

```
//Create a url for the database and...
String url = "jdbc:mysql://localhost/MusicStore?user=wrox&password=jdbc";
```

```
//...connect to the database
Connection DBConnection = DriverManager.getConnection(url);
```

In this URL, `jdbc` is again the protocol, `mysql` is the `<subprotocol>`, and the `<subname>` tells the driver to connect to the MySQL database named `MusicStore` on the `localhost` using the database username `wrox` and the password `jdbc`. Note also, that we pass the username and password as part of the URL. Consult your driver documentation to find the correct URL for your database, as not all drivers support this method of authentication.

In some cases, however, the username and password may not be enough to establish a connection and more information is required or allowed to create the connection. In order to accommodate those situations, the `DriverManager` class provides another `getConnection()` method that accepts a `Properties` object as an argument. The basic form of this method is as follows:

```
Connection DBConnection = DriverManager.getConnection(SourceURL, prop);
```

Where *`prop`* is an instance of the `java.util.Properties` class. To supply the properties required by your JDBC driver, you can create a `Properties` object using the default class constructor, and then set the properties that you need by calling its `setProperty()` method.

> *Properties, as you may recall, are tag name-value pairs that allow you to associate a value with a given name. For example, you can assign your user ID to the tag value "username".*

The properties that can be set for this version of `getConnection()` are dependent on the database and driver you're dealing with. For example, Cloudscape lists the following attributes that can be set with a `Properties` object:

autocommit	dataEncryption	password
bootPassword	encryptionProvider	shutdown
create	encryptionAlgorithm	unicode
current	locale	upgrade
databaseName	logDevice	user

In general, at least the username and password need to be set. The code fragment below illustrates using a `Properties` object to create a connection to a Cloudscape database:

```
import java.util.Properties;

// ...

  String driverName = "COM.cloudscape.core.JDBCDriver";
  String sourceURL = "jdbc.odbc:Wrox4370.db";

  try
  {
    Class.forName (driverName);
```

```
    Properties prop = new Properties();
    prop.setProperty("user", "ItIsMe");
    prop.setProperty("password", "abracadabra");
    Connection databaseConnection = DriverManager.getConnection(sourceURL,
                                                                 prop);
  }
  catch(ClassNotFoundException cnfe)
  {
    System.err.println("Error loading " + driverName);
  }
  catch(SQLException sqle)
  {
    System.err.println(sqle);
  }
```

Note that the `Properties` class is imported from the `java.util` package. While this pretty much covers everything that most developers will ever do with the `DriverManager` class, there are other methods that may be useful. Let's take a look at two of these now.

Setting the Login Timeout

The `DriverManager` class provides a pair of methods for the login timeout period. These allow you to specify a timeout period (in seconds) that limits the time that a driver is prepared to wait for logging in to the database. The two methods are:

```
public static void setLoginTimeout(int seconds)
public static int getLoginTimeout()
```

The default timeout depends on the data source. Specifying a non-default timeout period can be useful for troubleshooting applications that are having difficulty connecting to a remote database server. For example, if your application is trying to connect to a very busy server, the applications might appear to have hung. You can tell the `DriverManager` to fail the connection attempt by specifying a timeout period. The code fragment below tells the `DriverManager` to fail the login attempt after 60 seconds:

```
String driverName = "COM.cloudscape.core.JDBCDriver";
String sourceURL = "jdbc:cloudscape:Wrox4370.db";

try {
  Class.forName(driverName);

  // fail after 60 seconds
  DriverManager.setLoginTimeout(60);

  Connection databaseConnection = DriverManager.getConnection(sourceURL);
} catch(ClassNotFoundException cnfe) {
  System.err.println("Error loading " + driverName);
} catch(SQLException sqle) {
  System.err.println(sqle);
}
```

Naturally, in a real-world application you'd never want to subject the user to a 60 second timeout – the user would have given up long before the timeout expired. This can be helpful, however, in identifying if the problem is related to a timeout failure or some other problem.

Logging JDBC Driver Operations

A good way to find out what JDBC calls are doing is to enable JDBC tracing. The JDBC trace contains a detailed listing of the activity occurring in the system that is related to JDBC operations.

If you use the DriverManager facility to establish your database connection, you use the DriverManager.setLogWriter() method to enable tracing of JDBC operations.

The DriverManager class provides a pair of methods to control JDBC tracing. These allow you to set, or reroute, the PrintWriter that the driver uses to log information. The two methods are:

```
public static void setLogWriter(PrintWriter out);
```

```
public static PrintWriter getLogWriter();
```

You can disable logging by passing a null argument to the setLogWriter() method.

Your application can print to the PrintWriter stream using the static println() method defined in the DriverManager class. Just pass a String object as an argument containing the message you want to record in the log. This method is typically used by JDBC drivers, but it may prove useful for debugging or logging database-related errors or events.

Try It Out – Logging JDBC Driver Operations

The following source code is a simple class that demonstrates using a LogWriter to trace JDBC activity:

```
import java.sql.*;
import java.io.*;

public class LogTester {
  public static void main(String[] args) {
    try {
      DriverManager
        .println("User Message: No LogWriter. This won't be seen");
      PrintWriter log = new PrintWriter(System.out, true);
      DriverManager.setLogWriter(log);
      DriverManager.println("User Message: LogWriter set");

      DriverManager.println("User Message: Loading Driver");
      Class.forName("COM.cloudscape.core.JDBCDriver");
      DriverManager.setLoginTimeout(60);

      DriverManager.println("User Message: Getting connection");
      String url = "jdbc:cloudscape:c:/wrox/database/Wrox4370.db";
      Connection connection = DriverManager.getConnection(url);

      DriverManager.println("User Message: Setting AutoCommit and closing");
      connection.setAutoCommit(false);
      connection.close();
    } catch (Exception e) {
      e.printStackTrace();
    }
  }
}
```

We should save this Java file as `LogTester.java`, in the `C:\BegJavaDB\Ch06` directory. We can then compile it using the following command:

```
> javac LogTester.java
```

We can then run the file as follows:

```
> java -classpath .;%JLIB%\cloudscape.jar LogTester
```

Note the addition of the `cloudscape.jar` file from `C:\java\lib`; this is the JAR file that contains the Cloudscape driver, which we are using to connect to the Cloudscape database.

Compiling and running this class should produce output similar to this:

```
C:\WINDOWS\System32\cmd.exe
Microsoft Windows 2000 [Version 5.00.2195]
(C) Copyright 1985-2000 Microsoft Corp.

C:\BegJavaDB\Ch08>javac LogTester.java

C:\BegJavaDB\Ch08>java -classpath .;%JLIB%\cloudscape.jar LogTester
User Message: LogWriter set
User Message: Loading Driver

DriverManager.getDriver("jdbc:cloudscape:")
DriverManager.initialize: jdbc.drivers = null
JDBC DriverManager initialized
getDriver: no suitable driver
registerDriver: driver[className=c8e.cs.c,c8e.cs.c@52068d]
User Message: Getting connection
DriverManager.getConnection("jdbc:cloudscape:c:/wrox/database/Wrox4370.db")

    trying driver[className=c8e.cs.c,c8e.cs.c@52068d]
getConnection returning driver[className=c8e.cs.c,c8e.cs.c@52068d]
User Message: Setting AutoCommit and closing

C:\BegJavaDB\Ch08>_
```

How It Works

The class starts by importing the `java.sql` and the `java.io` packages. The `java.sql` package provides the JDBC functionality; the `java.io` package provides the output stream for logging. Note that these packages are part of the JDK, so as long as have our `CLASSPATH` variable set to point at the `lib` directory of our JDK installation, they will be found when we compile.

The class contains several calls to the `DriverManager.println()` method. The string passed with each call to this method includes the substring `"User Message."` This allows user logging to be easily distinguished from logging performed by the `DriverManager` and the `Driver`. However, the first call to `DriverManager.println()` will not be printed to a log because the code has not yet set the `LogWriter`:

```
import java.sql.*;
import java.io.*;

public class LogTester {
  public static void main(String[] args) {
```

```
    try {
      DriverManager
        .println("User Message: No LogWriter. This won't be seen");
```

The class creates a `PrintWriter` using the `System.out` output stream. All strings printed to this `PrintWriter` will go to `System.out`. This `PrintWriter` is then passed to the `setLogWriter()` method.

```
      PrintWriter log = new PrintWriter(System.out, true);
      DriverManager.setLogWriter(log);
      DriverManager.println("User Message: LogWriter set");
```

The example loads the Cloudscape driver; if you are using a different database, you will need to change the driver name (which will also change the output you see), and also include a different JAR file when you run the class. After setting the login timeout, the class gets a connection to the database, sets the autocommit mode, and finally closes the connection.

```
      DriverManager.println("User Message: Loading Driver");
      Class.forName("COM.cloudscape.core.JDBCDriver");
      DriverManager.setLoginTimeout(60);

      DriverManager.println("User Message: Getting connection");
      String url = "jdbc:cloudscape:c:/wrox/database/Wrox4370.db";
      Connection connection = DriverManager.getConnection(url);

      DriverManager.println("User Message: Setting AutoCommit and closing");
      connection.setAutoCommit(false);
      connection.close();
```

You can see that the driver does not log every detail of what is occurring (such as setting the timeout).

Connections

Now that we have discussed how to establish a connection to our database, it is time to start putting that connection to work.

There are three main areas that fall under the control of our `Connection` object:

- Creating `Statement`, `PreparedStatement`, and `CallableStatement` objects. The `Statement` interface will be discussed in more detail in the next chapter, whereas the `PreparedStatement` and `CallableStatement` interfaces are described in Chapters 12 and 13, respectively.
- Controlling **transactions**. This is such an important issue when building database-driven applications that we devote a full chapter to the subject: Chapter 14, *Transactions.*
- Obtaining `DatabaseMetadata` objects. We briefly mentioned use of meta data in Chapter 2, *Basic JDBC Techniques*, but will discuss this in more detail in Chapter 10.

In this chapter we introduce the basics of getting and using a `Connection`. We will start by developing a `Store` class for the Music Store database.

The Store Class

Starting in this chapter, and through subsequent chapters, we build some of the core JDBC functionality needed to satisfy the data requirements of our Music Store application. We will not be building pretty GUIs, as we want to maintain a strong database focus. Our aim is to code well-designed, reusable data and connection classes that can be easily used in a variety of different environments.

Imagine, if you will, that you are a member of the development team assigned to develop the components of the system that will talk to the database system.

Let's quickly review the requirements for the Music Store application. The Music Store application and database will:

- Store details of all recordings in stock and the quantity in stock.
- Provide the ability to search the database by a variety of criteria (by artist, song title, album name, and so on). Ultimately, this search facility will be self-service in the store, with a facility for customers to be able to post reviews of recordings.
- Store minimal customer information in order that customers may be notified by e-mail or phone when their order arrives.
- Provide the ability to keep track of stock in a central database and be able to tell which recordings were in which store.
- Provide the ability to track customer information for a customer loyalty discount scheme.

As a junior developer on the team, your first assigned task is to develop a simple class that will allow the owner to maintain the details of her retail outlets.

As discussed in Chapter 7, *Overview of JDBC Application Development*, one way to develop a database application is to map each database table to a Java class. A database table becomes a Java class in the application. Each column in the table becomes a member variable in the class. The rows of the table correspond to instances of the class.

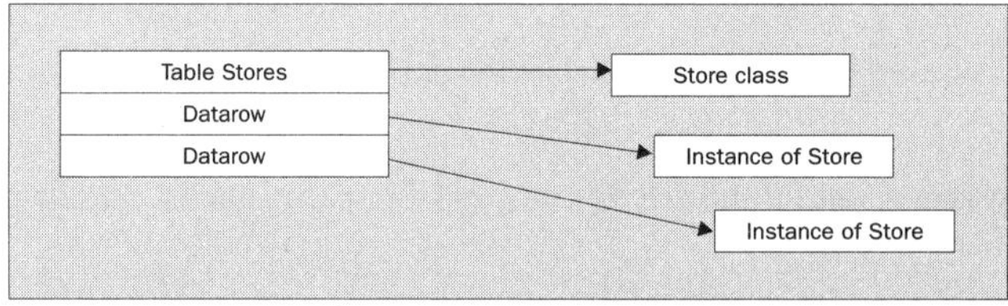

The first thing you do is to define and test the SQL statement that the Java class must send to be executed in the database in order for a row describing a new retail outlet to be inserted:

```
insert into stores (StoreDescription, StoreTypeID,
                    StoreAddress1,StoreAddress2, StoreCity,
                    StorePostalCode)
values ('Independent Records and Tapes', 1, '123 E. Bijou St.',
        '', 'Colorado Springs', '80903')
```

You can execute the SQL above in the SQL tool of your choice. For example, Cloudscape provides an interactive JDBC tool called 'ij' (see Chapter 1) and all versions of Oracle come with the SQL*PLUS tool. Here's the result of sending the SQL statement to the Music Store Cloudscape database using ij:

```
ij version 3.6 (c) 1997-2001 Informix Software, Inc.
ij> connect 'jdbc:cloudscape:c:\wrox\database\Wrox4370.db';
ij> insert into stores (STOREDESCRIPTION, STORETYPEID, STOREADDRESS1,
STOREADDRESS2, STORECITY, STOREPOSTALCODE) VALUES ('Independent Records and
Tapes', 1, '123 E. Bijou St.', '', 'Colorado Springs', '80903');

1 row inserted/updated/deleted
```

You may have noticed that the `Stores` table defines a `STOREID` column, but the SQL above does not insert a value for that column. The reason is that the `Stores` table definition in the Music Store Cloudscape database defines that column as an auto-increment column. The database automatically generates and inserts a value for that column when the row is inserted. You may need to generate or insert this value explicitly depending on the database you are using. For example, in Oracle the `INSERT` statement would look as follows:

```
INSERT INTO stores
                  (StoreId, StoreDescription, StoreTypeID, StoreAddress1,
                   StoreAddress2, StoreCity, StorePostalCode)
        VALUES Storeid_SEQ.NEXTVAL, toreDescription, StoreTypeId,
               StoreAddress1, StoreAddress2,
               StoreCity, StorePostalCode
```

Note the addition of the value for the `StoreId` column, which is generated by a database object called a `SEQUENCE` (see Appendix A). The following example will use the Cloudscape database, but the equivalent code for Oracle can be downloaded from the Wrox web site.

Try It Out – Implementing the Store Class create() Method

1. In order to run this example you will need to have a database installed and running and to have created the Music Store tables. It also assumes that you have loaded the tables with data. If you have not loaded the data but wish to complete this example, you will need first to insert a row into the `StoreTypes` table so that the PK-FK relationship between this table and the `Stores` table is not violated when you add a new row to `Stores`:

```
insert into storetypes (StoreTypeID, StoreTypeDescription)
values (1, 'Brick & Morter');
```

Note that these are the values we'll be using later, and are already present in the database if you have loaded the data.

2. Create the following `Store01.java` class that will map to the `Stores` table in the Music Store database. (The name `Store01` is used to indicate that this is the first version of the class. Later versions will add functionality or improve existing functionality.) You can download the full code from the Wrox web site.

Here is the SQL we will use for the Cloudscape database:

```
INSERT INTO stores
                   (StoreDescription, StoreTypeID, StoreAddress1,
                    StoreAddress2, StoreCity, StorePostalCode)
        VALUES StoreDescription, StoreTypeId,
               StoreAddress1, StoreAddress2,
               StoreCity, StorePostalCode
```

Here is the code for `Store01`:

```
// BegJavaDB/Ch08/connections/Store01.java
package connections;

import java.sql.*;

/**
 * A class to represent a retail store in the Music system.
 */
public class Store01 {
  int storeId;
  String storeDescription = "";
  int storeTypeId;
  String storeAddress1 = "";
  String storeAddress2 = "";
  String storeCity = "";
  String storePostalCode = "";

  // constructor
  public Store01() {}

  // constructor
  public Store01(String description, int typeId, String address1,
                 String address2, String city, String postalCode) {
    storeDescription = description;
    storeTypeId = typeId;
    storeAddress1 = address1;
    storeAddress2 = address2;
    storeCity = city;
    storePostalCode = postalCode;
  }

  /**
   * Create an entry in the database for this object.
   */
  public boolean create() {
    int result = 0;
    Connection connection = null;
    Statement statement = null;

    try {

      // Load the Driver class file, and create an instance of the class
```

```
      // Creating an instance causes the driver to register with the
      // DriverManager
      Class.forName("COM.cloudscape.core.JDBCDriver");

      // Create a url for the database and...
      String url = "jdbc:cloudscape:c:/wrox/database/Wrox4370.db";

      // ...connect to the database
      connection = DriverManager.getConnection(url);

      statement = connection.createStatement();
      String sql = "INSERT INTO stores " +
                   "(StoreDescription, StoreTypeID, StoreAddress1, " +
                   "StoreAddress2, StoreCity, StorePostalCode) " +
                   "VALUES ('" + getStoreDescription() + "', " +
                   getStoreTypeId() + ", " + "'" + getStoreAddress1() +
                   "', " + "'" + getStoreAddress2() + "', " + "'" +
                   getStoreCity() + "', " + "'" + getStorePostalCode() +
                   "')";
      result = statement.executeUpdate(sql);
    } catch (Exception e) {
      e.printStackTrace();
    } finally {
      try {
        if (statement != null) {
          statement.close();
        }
        if (connection != null) {
          connection.close();
        }
      } catch (SQLException sqle) {
        sqle.printStackTrace();
      }
    }

    return (result == 1);
  }

  public int getStoreId() {
    return storeId;
  }

  public String getStoreDescription() {
    return storeDescription;
  }
  public void setStoreDescription(String v) {
    storeDescription = v;
  }

  public String getStoreAddress1() {
    return storeAddress1;
  }
  public void setStoreAddress1(String v) {
    storeAddress1 = v;
```

```
    }

    public String getStoreAddress2() {
      return storeAddress2;
    }
    public void setStoreAddress2(String v) {
      storeAddress2 = v;
    }

    public int getStoreTypeId() {
      return storeTypeId;
    }
    public void setStoreTypeId(int v) {
      storeTypeId = v;
    }

    public String getStoreCity() {
      return storeCity;
    }
    public void setStoreCity(String v) {
      storeCity = v;
    }

    public String getStorePostalCode() {
      return storePostalCode;
    }
    public void setStorePostalCode(String v) {
      storePostalCode = v;
    }
  }
```

3. Save the class in the `C:\BegJavaDB\Ch08\connections` directory (you can replace the '`C:\BegJavaDB\Ch08`' part of the path with the directory of your choice, as long as the last part of the path matches the package specification '`connections`' for the class). Navigate to the `Ch08` directory and compile the class using the following command:

```
> javac connections/Store01.java
```

Alternatively if you are using an IDE, compile the source using your IDE.

4. In order to check that our class works, we need to write a simple test driver that will create an instance of the `Store01` class with the information for a record, and call the `create()` method to insert that row into the `Stores` table. Create the following `TestStore01.java` class, save it in the same directory as the `Store01.java` class, and compile it:

```
package connections;

public class TestStore01 {
  public static void main(String[] args) {
    String description = "Bricks & Morter";
    int typeId = 1;
    String address1 = "123 E. Bijou St.";
    String address2 = "";
```

```
    String city = "Colorado Springs";
    String postalCode = "80903";

    Store01 store = new Store01(description, typeId, address1,
                                address2, city, postalCode);
    boolean result = store.create();
    if (result) {
      System.out.println("Store created successfully");
    } else {
      System.out.println("Store NOT created");
    }
  }
}
```

You can compile `TestStore01` in much the same way as `Store01`, except that you'll need to make sure that the `connections` directory (and hence the `connections` package) can be found in the classpath:

```
> javac -classpath . connections/TestStore01.java
```

Note that changes in the SQL to work on Oracle won't need to be reflected in the test driver code.

5. Execute the `Store01` class as follows:

```
> java -classpath .;%JLIB%\cloudscape.jar connections.TestStore01
```

If the test program executes without errors, you will see the "Store created successfully" message:

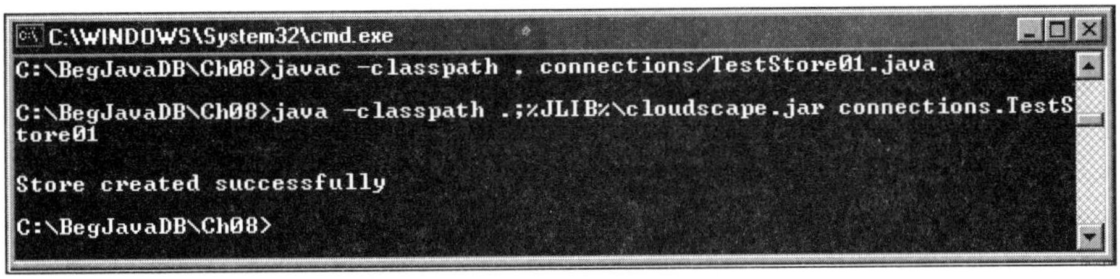

```
C:\BegJavaDB\Ch08>javac -classpath . connections/TestStore01.java

C:\BegJavaDB\Ch08>java -classpath .;%JLIB%\cloudscape.jar connections.TestS
tore01

Store created successfully

C:\BegJavaDB\Ch08>
```

You can also log in to the database and manually display the table to verify the row was inserted. Overleaf is the view of the table using the Cloudscape `cview` tool.

See Chapter 1 and consult your Cloudscape documentation for information on how to run the cview tool.

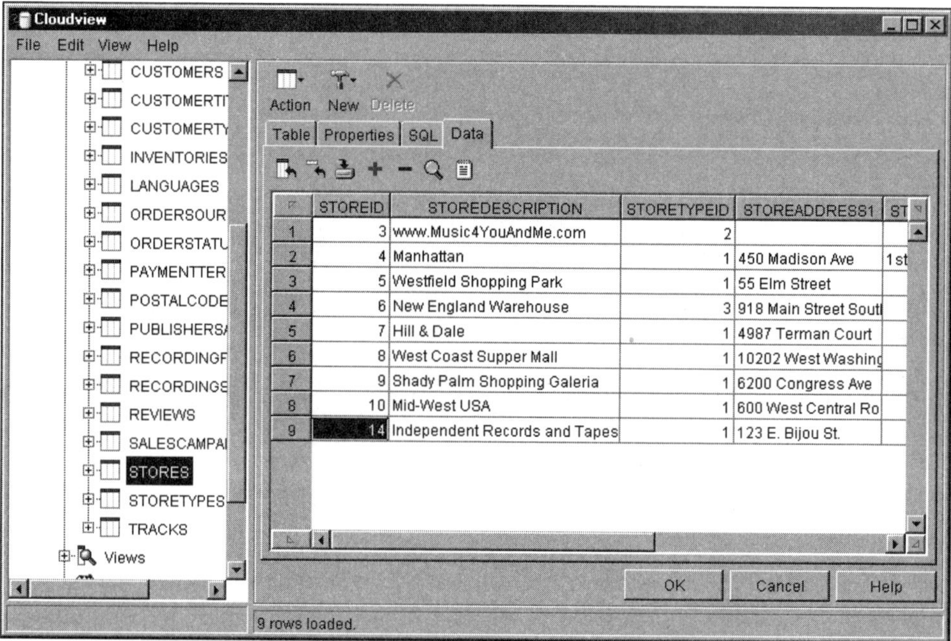

If the test program is unsuccessful, you will need to determine and fix the problem. Here are some common problems:

- Class Not Found error message – Your classpath does not include the correct paths or JAR libraries or ZIP libraries. Ensure the classpath includes the complete path and JAR name of the driver library.
- Connection refused – Is the database running? Is the URL used by the create method correct?
- Other error – Is the SQL string correct? Does the SQL violate any primary key or foreign key constraints?

How It Works

Let's now step through the code and discuss what it does and how it works. First we define a new package and import the classes and interfaces for the JDBC library. Putting classes into packages allows you to better manage the classes and helps avoid name conflicts between different classes. For this class, we've created a package that reflects that this example class is part of the connections chapter:

```
// BegJavaDB/Ch08/connections/Store01.java
package connections;

import java.sql.*;
```

Recall that this class represents a row in the `Stores` table. Thus, the class will need member variables that correspond to each column in the table to store the information that will become a record in the table:

```
public class Store01 {
  int storeId;
  String storeDescription = "";
  int storeTypeId;
  String storeAddress1 = "";
  String storeAddress2 = "";
  String storeCity = "";
  String storePostalCode = "";
```

And two constructors; one is a no-argument constructor, the other is a constructor that sets the initial values of the member variables:

```
  //constructor
  public Store01() {}

  //constructor
  public Store01 (String description, int typeId, String address1,
                  String address2, String city, String postalCode) {
    storeDescription = description;
    storeTypeId = typeId;
    storeAddress1 = address1;
    storeAddress2 = address2;
    storeCity = city;
    storePostalCode = postalCode;
  }
```

Next, we implement the `create()` method that will insert a new row in the `Stores` table. It will return a `boolean` to let the user of the class know if the entry was created. The `create()` method starts by defining local variables for the SQL return code, the `Connection`, and the `Statement`:

```
  public boolean create() {
    int result = 0;
    Connection connection = null;
    Statement statement = null;
```

Next come the lines of code that establish our connection to the database:

```
    try {
      //Load the Driver class file, and create an instance of the class
      //Creating an instance causes the driver to register with the
      //DriverManager
      Class.forName("COM.cloudscape.core.JDBCDriver");

      //Create a url for the database and...
      String url = "jdbc:cloudscape:c:/wrox/database/Wrox4370.db";

      //...connect to the database
      connection = DriverManager.getConnection(url);
```

If you are using a database other than Cloudscape or a different driver, then you will need to modify these lines of code as appropriate (see the *DriverManager* section for guidance).

Using the `Connection` object, the code calls the `createStatement()` method to get a `Statement` object. The `Statement` interface is discussed in more detail later in this book; for now, you only need to know that the `Statement` interface defines methods for sending SQL to the database. Then the `create()` method constructs an SQL statement that inserts a row into the `Stores` table and uses the `Statement` object to pass the SQL to the database:

```
statement = connection.createStatement();
String sql = "INSERT INTO stores " +
             "(StoreDescription, StoreTypeID, StoreAddress1, " +
             "StoreAddress2, StoreCity, StorePostalCode) " +
             "VALUES ('" + getStoreDescription() + "', " +
             getStoreTypeId() + ", " + "'" + getStoreAddress1() +
             "', " + "'" + getStoreAddress2() + "', " + "'" +
             getStoreCity() + "', " + "'" + getStorePostalCode() +
             "')";
```

This is where we would need to make changes if we were to use this class in conjunction with an Oracle database. The changes are entirely in the SQL code, so the Java remains unchanged. The return value return value `executeUpdate()` method of the is the number of rows affected by the SQL; since we are inserting a single row, the expected value is `1`. Any other value signals that the insert failed:

```
result = statement.executeUpdate(sql);
```

If any exceptions are thrown, the `catch` block prints the stack trace from the exception:

```
} catch (Exception e) {
  e.printStackTrace();
```

In the `finally` block, the method closes the `statement` and `connection`. The method calls are put into a `finally` block to ensure they are called regardless of what else occurs in the method. Since the `close()` methods can also throw a `SQLException`, we have another `try-catch` block surrounding the `close()` method calls:

```
} finally {
  try {
    if (statement != null) {
      statement.close();
    }
    if (connection != null) {
      connection.close();
    }
  } catch (SQLException sqle) {
    sqle.printStackTrace();
  }
}
```

The last action of the `create()` method is to return the value of evaluating `result == 1`. If one row was updated, then this evaluates to `true`, and the method returns `true`. Another other value for `result` means the insert failed, and `false` is returned:

```
    return (result == 1);
  }
```

One of the biggest mistakes of developers – beginner or experienced – is to leave `statements` or `connections` open. Always put calls to the `close()` methods in a `finally` block to ensure that resources will be closed regardless of what happens in the method, and always ensure you close resources in the opposite order to that in which they were opened. If you don't, the time you find the problem is when your code is deployed and hundreds of frustrated users can't use your system because it's starved for connection resources.

Finally the class ends with accessors and mutators (or getters and setters) for the member variables:

```
    public int getStoreId() {
      return storeId;
    }

    public String getStoreDescription() {
      return storeDescription;
    }
    public void setStoreDescription(String v) {
      storeDescription = v;
    }
  }
```

Finally, let's briefly discuss the test driver class, `TestStore01`. The test driver sets some variables with the data that will be inserted into the `Stores` table. It then creates an instance of the `Store01` class with that data and calls the `create()` method. The return value of the `create()` method is used to determine whether the `create()` call succeeded or failed, and the appropriate message is printed:

```
    public static void main(String[] args) {
      String description = "Independent Records and Tapes";
      int typeId = 1;
      String address1 = "123 E. Bijou St.";
      String address2 = "";
      String city = "Colorado Springs";
      String postalCode = "80903";

      Store01 store = new Store01(description, typeId, address1,
                                  address2, city, postalCode);
      boolean result = store.create();
      if (result) {
        System.out.println("Store created successfully");
      } else {
        System.out.println("Store NOT created");
      }
    }
```

In the `Store01.create()` method above, only two methods of the `Connection` interface were used. The `createStatement()` method obtained a `Statement` object and the `close()` method closed the `Connection` object.

The code above also did not perform any explicit transaction management. Each SQL statement that is sent to the database is executed and committed immediately. There may be times when you don't want the database to automatically commit the SQL. When you do not want the SQL to be automatically committed, you disable the `autocommit` with a call to:

```
connection.setAutoCommit(false);
```

When autocommit is disabled, you must explicitly save changes to the database by calling the commit() method:

```
connection.commit();
```

If you do not want to save changes, you can tell the database to discard the changes by calling:

```
connection.rollback ();
```

These Connection interface methods for performing transaction management will be covered further in Chapter 14, *Transactions.*

The Store Class, Continued

Now that we've implemented the create() method to insert data into the database, we will want to implement a method to get Store data from the database. Here is the SQL we would want to use to get the information from the database:

```
select * from stores where StoreID= + id
```

Here's the first draft of a method that finds a single row from the Store class based on the primary key for the Stores table, storeid:

```
  public boolean findByPrimaryKey(String id) {
    if (id == null || id.equals("")) {
      errorMessage = "Invalid value of [" + id + "] for Store Id";
      return false;
    }

    boolean result = false;
    Connection connection = null;
    Statement statement = null;
    ResultSet resultSet = null;

    try {
      //Load the Driver class file, and create an instance of the class
      //Creating an instance causes the driver to register with the
      //DriverManager
      Class.forName("COM.cloudscape.core.JDBCDriver");

      //Create a url for the database and...
      String url = "jdbc:cloudscape:c:\wrox\database\Wrox4370.db";

      //...connect to the database
      connection = DriverManager.getConnection(url);
      statement = connection.createStatement();

      String sql = "select * from stores where StoreID=" + id;
      resultSet = statement.executeQuery(sql);
```

```
        if (resultSet.next()) {
          result = true;
          setStoreId(resultSet.getInt("StoreID"));
          //additional code to set the member variables not shown
        }
      } catch (Exception e) {
        errorMessage = e.getMessage();
        e.printStackTrace();
      } finally {
        try {
          if (resultSet != null) {
            resultSet.close();
          }
          if (statement != null) {
            statement.close();
          }
          if (connection != null) {
            connection.close();
          }
        } catch (SQLException sqle) {
          sqle.printStackTrace();
        }
      }
      return result;
    }
```

This method is similar to the `create()` method. It loads the driver, gets a connection to the database, uses the connection to create a `Statement`. The `Statement` is used to send a SQL query to the database. The result of the query is returned in a `ResultSet` object, from which the code will extract each column value and set the member variables of the `Store` object. Finally, the method closes the `ResultSet`, `Statement`, and `Connection` resources.

There is one other thing to note about this implementation: its simplicity. Although inserting a single row into a database is not uncommon, the chances of needing to extract a single row of data are fairly slim. Here, we deliberately keep things simple in order to maintain the focus on connections. In later chapters, when we come to focus on `Statements` and `ResultSets`, we will develop classes that can handle multiple database rows.

Problems with the Store01 Class

You are pleased with your first efforts and arrange a meeting with your team to discuss progress. While generally pleased with your code, the meeting throws up several suggestions for improvements.

Closing Resources

First, look at the code for closing the `ResultSet`, `Statement`, and `Connection` objects:

```
      } finally {
        try {
          if (resultSet != null) {
            resultSet.close();
```

```
      }
      if (statement != null) {
        statement.close();
      }
      if (connection != null) {
        connection.close();
      }
    } catch (SQLException sqle) {
      sqle.printStackTrace();
    }
  }
```

Recall that we put that code into a `finally` block to ensure it gets called regardless of what occurs in the `try` block. The problem is that it is possible for the code to skip over the `statement.close()` or `connection.close()` method calls. This would occur if the call to `resultSet.close()` or `statement.close()` throws an exception. If one of those calls throws an exception, the thread of execution jumps into the `catch` block, skipping over the following calls. You could put a separate `try-catch` block around every `close()` method, but remember that this code will be in `create()`, `retrieve()`, `update()`, and `delete()` and any other class methods that will be talking to the database. We don't want identical `try-catch` blocks wherever the code needs to close a resource. A better solution is to define separate `close()` methods like this:

```
void close(ResultSet rset) {
  try {
    if (rset != null) rset.close();
  } catch (Exception e) {
    e.printStackTrace();
  }
}
```

> **If you read the Javadoc for `ResultSet`, you will find that it says the `ResultSet` is closed automatically when the `Statement` that generated the ResultSet is closed or re-executed. You might be tempted, then, to rely on closing or re-executing the `Statement` to close the `ResultSet`. However the JDBC specification states, "The resources held by the `ResultSet` object may not be released until garbage collection runs again, so it is a good practice to explicitly close `ResultSet` objects when they are no longer needed."**

If we put those `close()` methods into the `Store` class, we'll end up putting them into every class that accesses the database. This is the same problem that we have with the code that loads the driver and creates a connection; this issue is discussed in the next section.

Duplicate Connection Code

Looking at the code for `create()` and `findByPrimaryKey()` in the source code above, you can see that there is code duplication between the two methods: both methods load the driver, get a connection, and get a statement, and close the statement and connection. Loading the driver only needs to occur once. Every time you need to change the driver or URL parameters for the connection, you'll need to do it in two places. "Not so bad," you think, "it's just two methods in one class." However, remember that in a large system you'll have dozens or hundreds of classes. Do all the team members want to duplicate the connection code over and over again? Do you want to go through hundreds of classes looking for JDBC code that needs to be modified?

The solution is to create a single class to manage the connection and associated resources. Every object in the system that needs a connection to the database will use this one class. Here's a class diagram showing the class that we will create to do this:

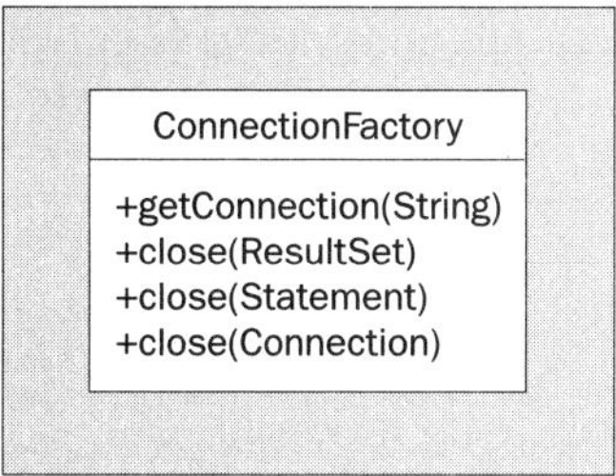

Try it Out – Writing a ConnectionFactory

Here's the source code that implements the class diagram shown above:

```
package connections;

import java.sql.*;

public class ConnectionFactory {
  private static ConnectionFactory ref = new ConnectionFactory();
  private ConnectionFactory() {
    try {
      Class.forName("COM.cloudscape.core.JDBCDriver");
    } catch (ClassNotFoundException e) {
      System.out.println("ERROR: exception loading driver class");
    }
  }

  public static Connection getConnection() throws SQLException {
    String url = "jdbc:cloudscape:c:/wrox/database/Wrox4370.db";
    return DriverManager.getConnection(url);
  }

  public static void close(ResultSet rs) {
    try {
      rs.close();
    } catch (Exception ignored) {}
  }
```

```
    public static void close(Statement stmt) {
      try {
        stmt.close();
      } catch (Exception ignored) {}
    }

    public static void close(Connection conn) {
      try {
        conn.close();
      } catch (Exception ignored) {}
    }
  }
```

How it Works

The class above is the implementation of a purely static class. All of its methods are static, and so no instance of the class is ever needed. Every method can be referenced by using just the class name as compared to calling a method using a variable:

```
  //call method using class name
  Connection DBConnection = ConnectionFactory.getConnection();
```

Even if a caller wanted an instance of the class, no instance can be created because the constructor is private.

When the class is loaded, the virtual machine initializes the static member variable. This variable is initialized by calling the private constructor, and assigning the reference to the variable:

```
    private static ConnectionFactory ref = new ConnectionFactory();
```

Since no instance of the class is actually needed (all the methods are static), the only reason for the static variable is to call the constructor to load the driver. There are other techniques that could have been used to load the driver; this technique was chosen because it is straightforward and easily comprehended.

Users of the class will call the `getConnection()` method to get a connection to the database. When a class needs to release a resource, it will call one of the `close()` methods. Since the `ConnectionFactory` class handles all the details of getting the connection, users of the class do not need to know any of the connection parameters. Note also, that we've hard coded the driver name and connection URL. We will deal with this shortly. If you are using a different database or driver, you will want to change those values so that they are appropriate for your environment.

Using the ConnectionFactory

Our next job is to rewrite our storeclass so that it uses the `ConnectionFactory` class. Instead of having connection code in every data class we create, all of our classes will now get a connection from the `ConnectionFactory` class.

Try It Out – Modifying the Store Class to use ConnectionFactory

1. Create the following `Store02.java` class. The new sections of code are highlighted.

```
// BegJavaDB/Ch08/connections/Store02.java
package connections;

import java.sql.*;

/**
 * A class to represent a retail store in the Music system.
 */
public class Store02 {
  int storeId;
  String storeDescription = "";
  int storeTypeId;
  String storeAddress1 = "";
  String storeAddress2 = "";
  String storeCity = "";
  String storePostalCode = "";

  Connection connection;
  Statement statement;
  ResultSet resultSet;

  // constructor
  public Store02() {}

  // constructor
  public Store02(String description, int typeId, String address1,
                 String address2, String city, String postalCode) {
    storeDescription = description;
    storeTypeId = typeId;
    storeAddress1 = address1;
    storeAddress2 = address2;
    storeCity = city;
    storePostalCode = postalCode;
  }

  private Statement getStatement() throws SQLException {
    connection = ConnectionFactory.getConnection();
    return connection.createStatement();
  }

  /**
   * Create an entry in the database for this object.
   */
  public boolean create() {
    int result = 0;

    try {
      statement = getStatement();
      String sql = "insert into stores " +
                   "(StoreDescription, StoreTypeID, StoreAddress1, " +
```

```
                  "StoreAddress2, StoreCity, StorePostalCode) " +
                  "values ('" + storeDescription + "', " + storeTypeId +
                  ", " + "'" + storeAddress1 + "', " + "'" +
                  storeAddress2 + "', " + "'" + storeCity + "', " + "'" +
                  storePostalCode + "')";
      result = statement.executeUpdate(sql);
    } catch (Exception e) {
      e.printStackTrace();
    } finally {
      close();
    }

    return (result == 1);
  }

  /**
   * Retrieve the entry for the given store id from the database. Return
   * true if the entry is found. Return false if the entry is not
   * found in the database.
   */
  public boolean findByPrimaryKey(String id) {
    if (id == null || id.equals("")) {
      return false;
    }

    boolean result = false;

    try {
      statement = getStatement();
      String sql = "select * from stores " + "where StoreID=" + id;
      resultSet = statement.executeQuery(sql);
      if (resultSet.next()) {
        result = true;
        setStoreId(resultSet.getInt("StoreID"));
        storeDescription = resultSet.getString("StoreDescription");
        storeTypeId = resultSet.getInt("StoreTypeID");
        storeAddress1 = resultSet.getString("StoreAddress1");
        storeAddress2 = resultSet.getString("StoreAddress2");
        storeCity = resultSet.getString("StoreCity");
        storePostalCode = resultSet.getString("StorePostalCode");
      }
    } catch (Exception e) {
      e.printStackTrace();
    } finally {
      close();
    }
    return result;
  }

  void close() {
    ConnectionFactory.close(resultSet);
    ConnectionFactory.close(statement);
    ConnectionFactory.close(connection);
  }
```

```
public String toString() {
  return "Name      : " + storeDescription + "\n" + "Store Id : " +
         storeId + "\n" + "Address  : " + storeAddress1 + "\n" +
         "          : " + storeAddress2 + "\n" + "          : " +
         storeCity + ", " + storePostalCode;
}

public int getStoreId() {
  return storeId;
}
private void setStoreId(int v) {
  this.storeId = v;
}

public String getStoreDescription() {
  return storeDescription;
}
public void setStoreDescription(String v) {
  storeDescription = v;
}

public String getStoreAddress1() {
  return storeAddress1;
}
public void setStoreAddress1(String v) {
  storeAddress1 = v;
}

public String getStoreAddress2() {
  return storeAddress2;
}
public void setStoreAddress2(String v) {
  storeAddress2 = v;
}

public int getStoreTypeId() {
  return storeTypeId;
}
public void setStoreTypeId(int v) {
  storeTypeId = v;
}

public String getStoreCity() {
  return storeCity;
}
public void setStoreCity(String v) {
  storeCity = v;
}

public String getStorePostalCode() {
  return storePostalCode;
}
public void setStorePostalCode(String v) {
```

```
      storePostalCode = v;
    }
  }
```

2. Save the code in the same directory as the `ConnectionFactory` class and the `Store01` class.

3. Use the `TestStore02` class below to test the `ConnectionFactory` and `Store02` classes. Notice that the `id` that we're using here is the same as the `id` of the row we created earlier in the chapter. You could also combine this test driver with `TestStore01` to first create a row and then retrieve that same row using a different `Store` object:

```
package connections;

public class TestStore02 {
  public static void main(String[] args) {
    String id = "14";
    Store02 store = new Store02();
    boolean result = store.findByPrimaryKey(id);
    if (result) {
      System.out.println("Store retrieve");
      System.out.println("Store details: \n" + store.toString());
    } else {
      System.out.println("Store NOT retrieved");
    }
  }
}
```

4. Compile this class as follows from the `C:\BegJavaDB\Ch08` directory, and notice that both the `Store02` and `ConnectionFactory` classes will also compile if you haven't already done so:

```
> javac -classpath . connections/TestStore02.java
```

Then run the class as follows:

```
> java -classpath .;%JLIB%\cloudscape.jar connections.TestStore02
```

You should see results similar to those below:

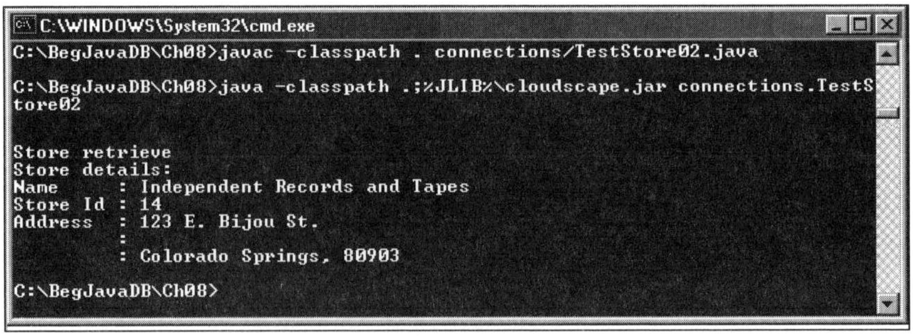

```
C:\WINDOWS\System32\cmd.exe
C:\BegJavaDB\Ch08>javac -classpath . connections/TestStore02.java

C:\BegJavaDB\Ch08>java -classpath .;%JLIB%\cloudscape.jar connections.TestS
tore02

Store retrieve
Store details:
Name      : Independent Records and Tapes
Store Id  : 14
Address   : 123 E. Bijou St.
          :
          : Colorado Springs, 80903

C:\BegJavaDB\Ch08>
```

How It Works

Most of this code will be familiar to you, so we will only discuss the new portions.

We start by adding a new method to the store class, `Store02: getStatement()`. This method uses the `ConnectionFactory` class to get a connection object. The `getStatement()` method calls the `getConnection()` method of our `ConnectionFactory`. Then `getStatement()` uses the `Connection` to create a `Statement` object. The method does not catch any exceptions, but simply allows them to propagate out of the method to the caller:

```
private Statement getStatement() throws SQLException {
  connection = ConnectionFactory.getConnection();
  return connection.createStatement();
}
```

In both the `create()` and `findByPrimaryKey()` methods, the various JDBC calls to load the driver and get the connection have been replaced by a single call to `getStatement()`:

```
statement = getStatement();
```

After the `Statement` is obtained, the two methods insert or query the database just as they did before. The SQL string is created and passed to the database using either `executeUpdate()` or `executeQuery()`. When each method completes, a `finally` block calls a new method named `close()`. The `close()` method calls the `ConnectionFactory` methods to release those resources:

```
void close() {
  ConnectionFactory.close(resultSet);
  ConnectionFactory.close(statement);
  ConnectionFactory.close(connection);
}
```

Now that the connection parameters are no longer hard-coded into the `Store` class, you can use this class with any database by simply changing just the single `ConnectionFactory` class. This change would also be effective for every other class that used the `ConnectionFactory`.

Implementing for Flexibility

Even with all the connection code in a single class, it is soon pointed out that the code still isn't as flexible as it could be. What happens, for example, if the Music Store owner decides to go open source and use a MySQL database instead of Cloudscape?

We have adapted the code so that changes will only need to be made in one place, but the connection parameters are hard-coded into a class file; to make the change you need to load the code into an editor, make the change, compile the change, deploy the class file, and restart the application. This would not be an issue for you, the developer. However, suppose you were developing a database browser application that allowed a user to view the contents of any arbitrary database. You would want the user of this application to be able to easily configure the application to talk to their database. Hard coding the parameters into a class file would not be the way to provide this flexibility.

If you were to use the `ConnectionFactory` in a real-world application that need configuration flexibility, you would want to put the connection parameters into some kind of configuration file, property file, or resource bundle. When the `ConnectionFactory` was loaded, it would read the configuration file in preparation for creating connections. Changing the `ConnectionFactory` to connect to a different database would be as easy as editing the text file that contained the configuration parameters.

For this book, we will continue to use the `ConnectionFactory` as created above with the hard-coded connection parameters. First, our `MusicStore` database is intended for a single client (the Music Store owner) whose database will seldom, if ever, change. Thus, we do not need a great deal of flexibility in connecting to different databases. The other reason is that by using the `ConnectionFactory` as is, we are free to concentrate on the important JDBC issues, and not worry about reading a configuration file.

DataSources

In the previous section we looked at a way to make your JDBC classes more flexible by providing a single source for connections, and optionally storing the connection parameters in a configuration file. There is a similar method of providing connections that uses a class called a `DataSource`.

`DataSource` was introduced as part of the `javax.sql` optional package of JDBC 2.0. The `DataSource` interface attempts to provide a more flexible architecture for creating and using database connections. As you will see, by using a `DataSource` to obtain a connection, you can access different databases without a single change in your client code. The `DataSource` hides the connection details so that you, as the client programmer, never need to worry about the connection URL, host, port, etc.

Directory Overview

A `DataSource` is usually obtained by performing a lookup in a **context**. At its simplest, context is just a means to associate a name with a resource. One implementation of a context is a directory. There are numerous implementations of directory services and protocols. There is Active Directory, X.500, Lightweight Directory Access Protocol (LDAP), and your computer's directory (which associates a name with a file resource).

On the server side of the connection, some code will create a `DataSource` instance, and then **bind** that instance to the directory. Binding is the action that tells a directory that a particular name is associated with a particular resource. For example, in a telephone directory, information (a resource) about your address and phone number is associated with your name.

Another example is when you created the `Store01.java` file in the file system of your computer. When you did that, you caused a collection of bytes to be written to some media such as the hard drive; at the same time, you told the operating system to associate (bind) that collection of bytes with the name `Store01.java`. Thus, anyone that has access to the hard drive can get the collection of bytes by giving the name "`Store01.java`" to the operating system.

Just as JDBC provides a vendor-neutral interface to numerous databases, Java has provided a vendo-neutral interface to directory services: the Java Naming and Directory Interface (JNDI). This API provides a common set of functions for accessing directories. The details of talking to a particular directory are provided by directory-specific libraries, in a similar fashion to JDBC drivers.

Using a DataSource

A DataSource is similar to the DriverManager in that it provides methods for obtaining a connection to a database. In fact, the basic method for obtaining a connection has the same name: getConnection().

Before any client code can get a connection form a DataSource, however, a DataSource object must be created and bound to a directory. The exact steps will be different for every directory and database. This step will likely be performed by the database administrator. The DataSource will be created with parameters for connecting to the database, and then the DataSource will be bound to a directory.

Here is a code snippet showing how that might be accomplished programmatically for a Cloudscape database.

```
//create the context, env is an object which contains information
//about the particular context
Context context = new InitialContext(env);

//Create a Cloudscape BasicDataSource object
BasicDataSource csDataSource = new BasicDataSource();

//set the connection parameters
csDataSource.setDatabaseName("c:/wrox/database/Wrox4370.db");

//bind the DataSource with the name
context.bind("jdbc/cloudscape", csDataSource);
```

Now, whatever directory the Context object refers to, has associated the name "jdbc/cloudscape" with the Cloudscape BasicDataSource object that knows how to connect to the database "c:/wrox/database/Wrox4370.db." Any client that has access to the same directory context and knows the correct name can then obtain a DataSource by performing a lookup in the directory, as shown in the following snippet:

```
Context context = new InitialContext(env);
DataSource dataSource = (DataSource) context.lookup(bindName);
Connection connection = dataSource.getConnection();
```

Using a DataSource to get a connection, the JDBC client code doesn't need to know anything about the database. It simply performs a directory lookup and obtains a connection from the DataSource it gets from the directory. Using a DataSource, a database administrator could change anything about the database such as the connection URL, username, password, etc. By simply changing and rebinding the DataSource, the change would be completely transparent to the JDBC client code. As soon as the client code performs a lookup, it will automatically get the connection without knowing that anything about the connection had changed.

Summary

In this chapter, we began developing a Store class for the Music Store application. In version 1 of the class, we implemented a method to create a row in a database; in version 2, we implemented the first method to find and retrieve a row. In later chapters we will add more functionality to this class as we explore more features of JDBC.

The store class is designed to be easily used in various ways in the Music Store application. We could combine it with a servlet to provide a view of the database for users. Users could enter information into an HTML form; the servlet would extract data from the form, and use it to create, delete, or retrieve store information using the `Store` class. We could easily modify the `Store` class to be either a session or entity Enterprise JavaBean (EJB). An EJB often represents a record of information from a database, exactly the design we've used for the `Store` class.

The class we've developed at this point uses a `ConnectionFactory` class to obtain database connections. Another technique that was briefly introduced was using a `DataSource` to get a connection. `DataSources` are explored in more detail in Chapter 18.

With the `Connection`, the `Store` class was able to get a `Statement` object. The statement object is used to pass SQL to a database and return the results to the caller. This chapter mentioned, but did not explore in any detail the `executeUpdate()` and `executeQuery()` methods. The `Statement` object and its subclasses will be explored in more detail in later chapters.

The connections created in this chapter automatically committed all changes to the database as soon as the SQL was executed. In the *Transactions* chapter, we will look to finer control of when and if changes are saved to the database.

akarta JAVA

Java

Using Statements and ResultSets

In this chapter, we look in more detail at the JDBC interfaces that allow us to send SQL to, and get data from, a database. We have already seen these interfaces in the previous chapter, *Connecting to a Database.* These interfaces are `Statement` and `ResultSet`. We will utilize and build on some of the classes we have already used previously and look at:

- How we can create and execute a `Statement` object
- The sorts of things we can do with a `Statement` object, such as manipulating and modifying data
- How to use the `ResultSet` interface to get results from a query, and especially how we can control the amount and type of data we receive
- What we can do with the `ResultSet` object such as navigating though it, and incorporating more flexibility by creating scrollable and updatable varieties

Using Statement Objects

In previous chapters, we have been using basic `Statement` objects to `SELECT`, `INSERT`, and `DELETE` data from our database. It is now time to take a broader look at the functionality provided by the `Statement` interface, and expand the discussion into the realm of executing SQL `UPDATE` commands against the database.

As we have discussed, the `Statement` interface defines a set of methods implemented by a `Statement` object, which is returned to your program by the `Connection` object. We can see the relationship between the two interfaces in the class diagram overleaf.

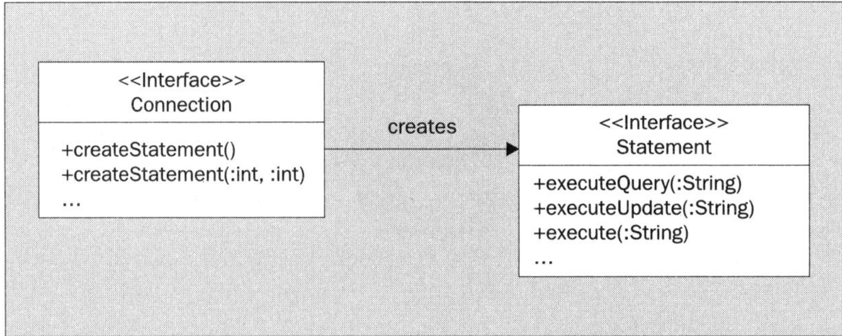

So far we have always obtained the `Statement` object by calling the `createStatement()` method of the `Connection` interface without any parameters (more on this later in the chapter):

```
try
{
  Statement queryStatement = connection.createStatement();
  // ...
}
catch(SQLException sqle)
{
  System.err.println(sqle);
}
```

Like pretty much every other method defined by JDBC, this code must be within a `try` clause, and include a `catch` statement for a `SQLException`.

Once the `Statement` has been created, defining the query is as simple as building a `String` containing a valid SQL statement, and then passing that statement as the argument to one of the `execute` methods of the `Statement` object. The SQL query can be a literal, or it can be a `String` value that you build dynamically at run-time.

In conjunction with its sub-interfaces, `PreparedStatement` and `CallableStatement`, the `Statement` interface provides a means to execute almost any legal SQL.

> *PreparedStatement is covered in Chapter 12. CallableStatement is covered in Chapter 13.*
>
> *'Legal SQL' means SQL as defined by the standards SQL-92 or SQL-99. The JDBC 2.0 and 3.0 specifications require that compliant JDBC drivers support SQL-92 fully, and support a subset of SQL-99. The specifications define which features of SQL-99 are required. You can get the JDBC specifications at* http://java.sun.com/products/jdbc.

So, the `Statement` object can be used to create, retrieve, update, and delete, known as CRUD, data from a table. It can be used to pass DDL statements such as `CREATE TABLE` or `CREATE USER`. Let's now take a slightly more detailed look at executing `UPDATE` commands with the `Statement` object.

Executing a Statement

As we've discussed, the two primary methods in the `Statement` interface for executing SQL statements are the `executeUpdate()` method and the `executeQuery()` method. The `executeQuery()` method is used whenever you want to retrieve data from the database. For almost every other kind of SQL statement, your code should use the `executeUpdate()` method.

In the previous chapter, we coded a `create()` method that we used to insert a new row into the `Stores` table. In our `create()` method, we built and executed the following SQL:

```
statement = connection.createStatement();
String sql = "INSERT INTO stores " +
          "(STOREID, StoreDescription, StoreTypeID, StoreAddress1, " +
          "StoreAddress2, StoreCity, StorePostalCode) " +
          "VALUES (Storeid_SEQ.NEXTVAL, '" + getStoreDescription() + "', " +
          getStoreTypeId() + ", " + "'" + getStoreAddress1() +
          "', " + "'" + getStoreAddress2() + "', " + "'" +
          getStoreCity() + "', " + "'" + getStorePostalCode() +
          "')";
```

We then called the `executeUpdate()` method of the `Statement` object in order to send this SQL to the database:

```
result = statement.executeUpdate(sql);
```

The `executeUpdate()` method returns an `int`. The return value represents the number of rows modified by the SQL statement. Since the SQL in the `create()` method only inserts a single row, we expect the return value to be either `1` (1 row affected, so the insert was successful) or `0` (no rows updated, so insert failed).

Likewise, if a class needed to query a database, the code would construct the SQL `SELECT` statement, and pass that SQL to the database using the `executeQuery()` method. The `executeQuery()` method returns an object to the caller. This object is a `ResultSet` object and it contains the results, if any, of the query. Whether or not any rows are returned by the query, the `executeQuery()` method will always return a non-Null `ResultSet`. Later in the chapter, we will show how to determine whether any rows were returned in the `ResultSet`.

From our `retrieve()` method in Chapter 8, we built and executed our query as follows:

```
String sql = "select * from stores " + "where StoreID=" + id;
resultSet = statement.executeQuery(sql);
if (resultSet.next()) {
  result = true;
  setStoreId(resultSet.getInt("StoreID"));
```

Our query in this case searched by primary key, so we retrieved a single row. Of course, we can also execute queries that may return multiple rows:

```
Statement statement = connection.createStatement();
String sql = "select * from stores where storeid > 2453";
ResultSet resultSet = statement.executeQuery(sql);
```

If you create the `Statement` object as shown above using the no-argument `createStatement()` method, then `executeQuery()` will return the default `ResultSet` object, which has a cursor that moves forward only. Your code will only be able to traverse the `ResultSet` from the first returned row to the last returned row, by use of the `next()` method, with no way to go backwards, or jump to a specific row. It is possible to create a scrollable `ResultSet`; this topic is covered in the *Using ResultSet Objects* section later in this chapter.

A third method for executing statements is the `executeBatch()` method. With `executeQuery()` and `executeUpdate()`, these methods send a single SQL statement to the database where it is immediately executed. The `executeBatch()` method sends a set of SQL statements to the database at the same time. The statements are all executed and the results of each statement are returned as update counts in an array to the caller. Since `executeBatch()` returns an array of update counts, it can be used with any SQL except `SELECT` statements.

There is one other `execute` method in the statement class: the `execute()` method. Normally, your code would want to use either the `executeQuery()` or `executeUpdate()` method but there are special circumstances when you might wish to use the `execute()` method, such as when the SQL being executed could return multiple resultsets, multiple update counts, or a combination of resultsets and update counts. This is a rare situation, so you can ignore this method except in the following circumstances:

- You are dynamically executing unknown SQL, for example, SQL that was entered at run-time by a user
- You are executing a stored procedure that you know returns multiple values. See Chapter 13 for more information about stored procedures

Using the methods `getResultSet()`, `getUpdateCount()`, and `getMoreResults()` of the `Statement` class, your code can get the multiple return values of the `execute()` method. Consult the JDBC Javadoc for more information on how to use these methods; http://java.sun.com/j2se/1.3/docs/api/java/sql/Statement.html#execute(java.lang.String).

Modifying Data Using a Statement

In the previous chapter, we used `Statement` objects in order to insert data into a table, and retrieve data from a table. We did this in the `Store` class, which mapped to the `Stores` table in the Music Store database. The next major function that needs to be implemented is the ability to change the data in a table. Once again, we'll use a `Statement` object to update the data in the `Stores` table.

Try It Out – The update() Method of the Store Class

Let's add an `update()` method to the `Store` class, so that we can update one of the rows in the `Stores` table in our database.

1. Open up the `Store02` class that we built in Chapter 8 (if you have not worked through that chapter but want to try out the code here, then you can download the file from the Wrox web site, http://www.wrox.com. We will only walk through the new portions of code here, but you can find a full explanation of the `Store02` class in the previous chapter).

2. Save the `Store02.java` source as `Store03.java`. The class is in the `connections` package, so save the source in a directory named `connections`. The directory above the `connections` directory must be part of the classpath. If it is not, you will need to adjust the classpath appropriately.

3. The `Store` class obtains a connection through the `ConnectionFactory` class that we developed in the previous chapter. Save the source file for that class in the same directory as the `Store03.java` file. Again, if you haven't worked through that chapter, you can download the `ConnectionFactory.java` source from http://www.wrox.com.

4. Insert the following method into the `Store03.java` file. Note that the only other change that is needed is to rename the class and constructors:

```
// connections/Store03.java
package connections;

import java.sql.*;

/**
 * A class to represent a retail store in the Music system.
 */
public class Store03 {
  int storeId;
  String storeDescription = "";
  int storeTypeId;
  String storeAddress1 = "";
  String storeAddress2 = "";
  String storeCity = "";
  String storePostalCode = "";

  Connection connection;
  Statement statement;
  ResultSet resultSet;

  // constructor
  public Store03() {}

  // constructor
  public Store03(String description, int typeId, String address1,
                 String address2, String city, String postalCode) {
    storeDescription = description;
    storeTypeId = typeId;
    storeAddress1 = address1;
    storeAddress2 = address2;
    storeCity = city;
    storePostalCode = postalCode;
  }

  private Statement getStatement() throws SQLException {
    connection = ConnectionFactory.getConnection();
    return connection.createStatement();
  }
```

```
  /**
   * Update the Stores table entry for this object. This method
   * updates every column for the given store, regardless of whether
   * the data was actually changed or not.
   */
  public boolean update() {
    int result = 0;

    try {
      statement = getStatement();

      String sql = "update stores set " + "StoreDescription='"
                   + getStoreDescription() + "', " + "StoreTypeId="
                   + getStoreTypeId() + ", " + "StoreAddress1='"
                   + getStoreAddress1() + "', " + "StoreAddress2='"
                   + getStoreAddress2() + "', " + "StoreCity='"
                   + getStoreCity() + "', " + "StorePostalCode='"
                   + getStorePostalCode() + "' " + "where StoreID="
                   + getStoreId();
      result = statement.executeUpdate(sql);
    } catch (Exception e) {
      e.printStackTrace();
    }
    finally {
      close();
    }
    return (result == 1);
  }

  //rest of class (create(), setters and getters, etc.) as before

}
```

5. The `update()` method can be tested with the following test driver, `testStore03`:

```
package connections;

public class TestStore03 {
  public static void main(String[] args) {
    int id = 3;
    Store03 store = new Store03();
    boolean result = store.findByPrimaryKey("3");
    if (result) {
      System.out.println("Store retrieved successfully");
      System.out.println(store.toString());
    } else {
      System.out.println("Store NOT retrieved successfully");
      return;
    }

    System.out.println("Updating local data for store");
    store.setStoreAddress1("1370 Denny Way");
    store.setStoreCity("Seattle");
    store.setStorePostalCode("98001");
```

```
      System.out.println("Attempting to update database");
      result = store.update();
      if (result) {
        System.out.println("Store updated successfully");
      } else {
        System.out.println("Store NOT updated successfully");
        return;
      }

      // retrieve again to show update
      store = new Store03();
      store.findByPrimaryKey("3");
      System.out.println(store.toString());
    }
  }
```

6. This program is designed to run against the Music Store database that you can download from the Wrox web site. To run the program, set your classpath to point to the correct directories, and then execute the test class. For example, if you have the database installed as `C:\BegJavaDB\Wrox4370.db`, Cloudscape installed in `C:\Cloudscape`, and the class files `ConnectionFactory`, `Store03`, and `TestStore03` installed in the directory `C:\BegJavaDB\Ch09\connections`, you would use the following commands to run the program:

```
> set classpath=c:\Cloudscape\lib\cloudscape.jar;c:\BegJavaDB\Ch09
> java connections.TestStore03
```

When this program is executed, you should see output similar to the following:

```
Store retrieved successfully
Name     : www.Music4YouAndMe.com
Store Id : 3
Address  : null
         : null
         : null, null
Updating local data for store
Attempting to update database
Store updated successfully
Name     : www.Music4YouAndMe.com
Store Id : 3
Address  : 1370 Denny Way
         : null
         : Seattle, 98001
```

How It Works

The `TestStore03` program starts by creating a `store` instance and using it to retrieve one specific row from the Music Store database. Recall that the `findByPrimaryKey()` method will retrieve one row from the database, the row with the primary key that matches the input parameter. Then, the method uses the data from the row to populate the member variables. When the `toString()` method is called, this prints the values of the variables (and thus, the data retrieved from the table). The test program then changes three of the member variables of the object by calling the setter methods for those variables; then it calls the `update()` method.

As with the `create()` and `retrieve()` methods from the previous chapter, one of the first steps in the `update()` method is to get a reference to a `Statement` object:

```
statement = getStatement();
```

The `update()` method does this by calling `getStatement()`. The `statement` variable is defined as a class member at the top of the source file. The `getStatement()` method gets a connection from the `ConnectionFactory` class. It then uses the connection to create a `Statement` object as shown below:

```
private Statement getStatement() throws SQLException {
  connection = ConnectionFactory.getConnection();
  return connection.createStatement();
}
```

The `update()` method then constructs a SQL `UPDATE` string:

```
String sql = "update stores set " + "StoreDescription='"
           + getStoreDescription() + "', " + "StoreTypeId="
           + getStoreTypeId() + ", " + "StoreAddress1='"
           + getStoreAddress1() + "', " + "StoreAddress2='"
           + getStoreAddress2() + "', " + "StoreCity='"
           + getStoreCity() + "', " + "StorePostalCode='"
           + getStorePostalCode() + "' " + "where StoreID="
           + getStoreId();
```

With the new values passed to the `Store03` object by the test class, the line of code above creates a SQL `UPDATE` statement that looks like this (whitespace added for readability):

```
update stores set
  StoreDescription='www.Music4YouAndMe.com',
  StoreTypeId=2,
  StoreAddress1='1370 Denny Way',
  StoreAddress2='',
  StoreCity='Seattle',
  StorePostalCode='98001'
where StoreID=3
```

The SQL string that is generated assigns a value for each column in the table, whether the value held by the object has been changed or not.

Notice that in the SQL statement, each string value is enclosed in single quotes. To achieve that, we placed single quotes directly into the line of code that creates the SQL. There was no need to escape the quotes with a backslash, as we need to do when we need to insert double quotes into a string literal. It is important that you include those single quotes when sending string literals to the database. The double quotes used in the sourcecode are not part of the SQL and are not sent to the database.

The SQL `UPDATE` string that was created is then passed to the database using the `executeUpdate()` method of the `Statement`:

```
result = statement.executeUpdate(sql);
```

As usual, we have a catch block to deal with any SQLException, and a finally block to close the Statement and Connection resources we used. The finally block has a line of code that calls the Store03 method, close(). This method closes the Statement and Connection with the help of the ConnectionFactory. The last step in the method is to check the return value from the update. The Store class can only update the single row that it represents, so the return value should be 1; any other return value is an error. The method returns True if the result equals 1; it returns False otherwise.

The test program then creates a new instance of the store class and calls the findByPrimaryKey() method to retrieve the row that was updated.

```
store = new Store03();
store.findByPrimaryKey("3");
System.out.println(store.toString());
```

The code creates a new instance because if it had reused the existing instance, we could not be sure if the data displayed with toString() was the data retrieved from the table, or if it was the pre-existing data. The code calls toString() so you can see what was retrieved. If you look at the complete sourcecode for the class, you can see that the toString() method is implemented to print all the member variables of the class.

Further Enhancements

While the Store class does a good job of meeting the basic requirements and design developed in Chapter 8, there is still more functionality that could be implemented if this class were being developed for a real application. Unfortunately, we won't be implementing any further enhancements in this book. As we move on to other topics and other chapters, we will also be developing other classes. In the next few pages, though, we will look at a summary of some of the enhancements that could be made. The topics we will review are:

- Using the class to update multiple rows in the Stores table.
- Changing the update() method to selectively update table columns.
- Providing additional findByXXX methods.

Updating Multiple Rows

Our Store class follows a design whereby it maps to one table in the database (the Stores table) and one instance of that class corresponds to one row in the table. This is the same mapping strategy that was presented in the *Overview of JDBC Application Development* in Chapter 7. Each instance of the class stores a set of variables that can fully define exactly one row in the Stores table.

This has worked well enough for us so far, but it does have obvious limitations. There are situations where our application might wish to issue a single UPDATE command that will modify multiple rows, based on some criteria other than the primary key (StoreId). For example, suppose we wanted to make a change to the database for all the stores with a given store description. The SQL for that is trivial:

```
UPDATE stores SET ... WHERE storedescription='some_description'
```

However, the update() method presented as part of the Store03 class can't perform this update. There are various ways we could approach this problem:

- Add additional methods to the Store class (updateByStoreDescription(), for example) to handle the desired updates (and deletes and inserts)
- Implement a class that acts as a collection of stores
- Put the enhanced functionality into a different class
- Allow users to enter SQL into the application

There may be additional approaches not listed above. The approach you take will depend on the requirements of your system. For example, if there are many variations in the format of the SQL that might be executed in the database, you might choose the last option. On the other hand, you might decide that all interactions with a table occur through a single class. In this case, you might choose the first approach.

If you took the second approach, the collection idea, you might also be able to use batch processing. When updating a number of rows based in the same criteria, you will want to use a single SQL statement. However, there are times when each change will depend on different criteria. One situation where this occurs is when you are inserting rows into a table. This is a time when you do need to execute SQL for each row. Let's assume the store class has been modified to have a method that returns the SQL string used to insert a row into a table:

```
public String getInsertSql() {
      return "insert into stores " +
        "(StoreDescription, StoreTypeID, StoreAddress1, " +
        "StoreAddress2, StoreCity, StorePostalCode) " +
        "values ('" + storeDescription + "', " +
        storeTypeId + ", " +
        "'" + storeAddress1 + "', " +
        "'" + storeAddress2 + "', " +
        "'" + storeCity + "', " +
        "'" + storePostalCode + "')";
}
```

We will also assume that the class that acts as a collection of stores is called StoreCollection. The StoreCollection class will keep the list of stores in some kind of collection class; we'll assume it's a Vector. Instead of calling the executeUpdate() method for each store we want to insert, we'll add the SQL INSERT string to the statement using the addBatch() method. This adds the SQL to the batch of statements, but does not send the statement to the database:

```
// Disable autocommit
connection.setAutoCommit(false);

// v is the vector that holds store instances.
for (int i = 0; i < v.size(); i++) {
  Store03 store = v.elementAt(i);
  statement.addBatch(store.getInsertSql());
}

// When all the statements have been added, we execute them using:
int[] results = statement.executeBatch();
```

Calling executeBatch causes the Statement to send all the statements in the batch to the database where they are executed. After the statements have been executed, the code can decide whether to undo the changes, or make them permanent.

The ability to undo or commit changes is covered in detail in Chapter 14, Transactions.

Selectively Updating Columns

If you look at the SQL `UPDATE` statement in the `Store03` class, you will see that the code sets the values for all the columns in the row, whether they have been changed or no:

```
String sql = "update stores set " + "StoreDescription='"
            + getStoreDescription() + "', " + "StoreTypeId="
            + getStoreTypeId() + ", " + "StoreAddress1='"
            + getStoreAddress1() + "', " + "StoreAddress2='"
            + getStoreAddress2() + "', " + "StoreCity='"
            + getStoreCity() + "', " + "StorePostalCode='"
            + getStorePostalCode() + "' " + "where StoreID="
            + getStoreId();
```

At some point, we may decide that we really only want to update the rows that have changed. One reason for doing this is to improve database concurrency. Suppose we have the following situation in the database:

Time	User A	User B
T0	Reads a row from `Stores` table.	Reads the same row from `Stores` table.
T1		Updates the row previously selected. Commits changes.
T2	Updates the row previously selected. Commits changes. Any changes made by Transaction B are lost.	

In the situation above, user A overwrites the changes made by user B. B's update is lost. This is known, not surprisingly, as a **lost update**. The more columns we change in the row, the more likely we are to conflict with some other user. By updating only the columns that have new values, we can reduce the risk of a lost update.

Modifying only the changed columns does not eliminate the lost update problem; it only reduces the chances of it occurring. How to prevent lost updates is discussed in Chapter 14.

How might you change the code to update only columns with new data? You might try leaving the fields of the object empty, and letting the user enter only the fields that need to be updated. The problem here is that the user might want to clear a field. If you determine the SQL based on which fields have non-empty values, the user would have no way to clear a column value.

One approach would be to keep a set of flags, one flag for each member variable in the class. As each member variable is changed through a setter method, the setter sets the flag. When it is time to create the SQL statement, the class could examine the flags and only include the columns for which the flag is set.

There are, of course, other ways of dealing with this issue. The approach you take, if needed, will depend on your preferences and the requirements of your application.

Additional findByXXX Methods

The `Store03` class has only one way to retrieve store data, and this method retrieves only a single row. However, our application may need other ways to search for and retrieve store data. For example, we may need to search by store type or store postal code.

To provide this functionality, we would first modify the `findByPrimaryKey()` method. This method contains the code that parses the query results. This code would be moved to its own method. This allows any `findByXXX` method to perform its query and then call common code to create objects from the query results. It also allows other classes to create objects by passing a valid `ResultSet` to the method. This method might look like this:

```
public class Store {

  // ...same methods as in the Store03 class

  public static Store fromResults(ResultSet rset) {
    Store store = new Store();
    store.setStoreId(rset.getInt("StoreID"));
    store.setStoreDescription(rset.getString("StoreDescription"));
    store.setStoreTypeId(rset.getInt("StoreTypeID"));
    store.setStoreAddress1(rset.getString("StoreAddress1"));
    store.setStoreAddress2(rset.getString("StoreAddress2"));
    store.setStoreCity(rset.getString("StoreCity"));
    store.setStorePostalCode(rset.getString("StorePostalCode"));

    return store;
  }
}
```

It is these `findByXXX` methods that make our application useful. While it is important to be able to insert, update, and delete rows in the database, the usefulness of the database application is the ability to get data out of the database. Since it is difficult to discuss `Statement` objects without also mentioning `ResultSet` objects, we have already been introduced to them. In the second part of this chapter we look at the latter objects in more detail.

Using ResultSet Objects

Now that we have a good understanding of the `Statement` interface, it is time to dig a little deeper into the details of getting the data back from the query. In this section, we'll add to what you already know about the `ResultSet` interface and object. We will explore the `getXXX()` methods in more depth and look at some of the special SQL data types and how they are handled.

A `ResultSet` object is an object that encapsulates the data returned by a query. The `Store03` class that has been developed in this chapter has already used a `ResultSet` object. The `ResultSet` object was returned from the `executeQuery()` method. In the illustration opposite, we show a class diagram for the `ResultSet` interface and its relationship to the `Statement` interface:

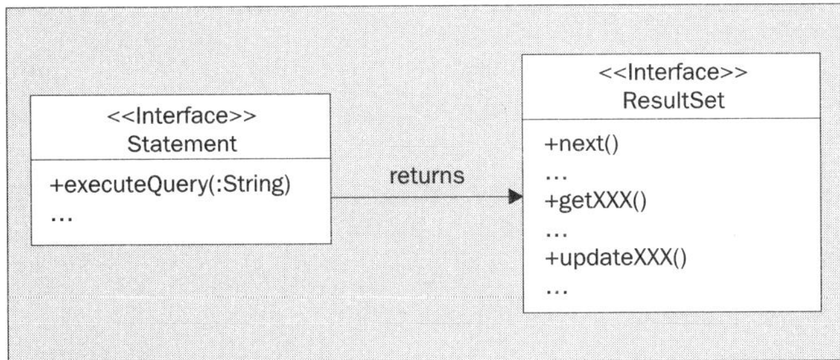

To save space, the diagram shows only three methods in the `ResultSet` interface. In actual fact, it has many methods. It has a number of different methods for moving through the rows of the `ResultSet`; this is represented by the `next()` method in the diagram. It also has methods for getting the column values of the rows in the `ResultSet`; this is represented by the `getXXX()` method in the diagram. The last set of methods in the diagram are the methods represented by the `updateXXX()` method. These are the methods that provide the ability to modify a table through the `ResultSet`.

Retrieving Column Data for Specified Data Types

After retrieving the results of a query in a `ResultSet` object, we need to determine whether or not any rows were returned by the query. When a statement returns a resultset, it will always be non-Null. However, it may or may not contain any rows. The only way to determine if there are any rows in the resultset is to attempt to move to a row. This is normally performed by calling the `next()` method. If the resultset contains one or more rows, `next()` will move to the first row, and return True. If there are no rows in the resultset, the first call to `next()` will return False.

After moving to the first row, the `retrieve()` method of the `Store03` class then extracted the column data from the row. Here are the first two lines of that code again:

```
setStoreId(resultSet.getInt("StoreID"));
storeDescription = resultSet.getString("StoreDescription");
```

In theory, we could retrieve all the data from the `Stores` table as `String` types because all the data in that table can be represented with a `String`. However, the `ResultSet` interface provides methods for working with a variety of data types and retrieving data as a Java type that is more consistent with the original SQL type.

Most of these methods work alike, and come in two overloaded forms. One form specifies the column by the column name:

```
xxxvalue ResultSet.getXxx(String columnName)
```

The form used in the `Store` class uses a `String` parameter, corresponding to the column name, to get the data for that column. The code below gets the `int` value of the `StoreId` column:

```
setStoreId(resultSet.getInt("StoreID"));
```

The other form specifies the column name by its index position, the first position index being 1:

```
xxxvalue ResultSet.getXxx(int columnPosition)
```

So, if we know that the `StoreID` column is the first column, the code can be written as:

```
setStoreId(resultSet.getInt(1));
```

The first column is index 1. With SQL, all column numbering begins at 1 and not 0. Likewise, row numbering starts with 1. The first column is 1 and the first row is 1.

For flexibility, though, if you can use the column name as the input parameter, you should. If you hard-code the column number into your code, you'll have problems as soon as the database analysts change the schema of the database tables so that the column numbers change.

The mechanics of calling these methods is quite straightforward, but to use these methods effectively, you need to understand the possible mappings between Java data types and SQL data types in both directions.

The following table illustrates the mappings between SQL data types and the appropriate `ResultSet` `getXXX()` methods. To decide which `getXXX()` method you should use, look in the table for the method that maps the column data type to the Java type you will use. The 'preferred' method for a type is indicated with the 'tick' symbol. This means that it is the closest mapping to the SQL type. Other methods may also work, however, and these are indicated by the plus/minus symbol:

`ResultSet` method to SQL Data Type Mapping

	TINYINT	SMALLINT	INTEGER	BIGINT	REAL	FLOAT	DOUBLE	DECIMAL	NUMERIC	BIT	CHAR	VARCHAR	LONGVARCHAR	BINARY	VARBINARY	LONGVARBINARY	DATE	TIME	TIMESTAMP
getByte()	✓	±	±	±	±	±	±	±	±	±	±	±	±						
getShort()	±	✓	±	±	±	±	±	±	±	±	±	±	±						
getInt	±	±	✓	±	±	±	±	±	±	±	±	±	±						
getLong()	±	±	±	✓	±	±	±	±	±	±	±	±	±						
getFloat()	±	±	±	±	✓	±	±	±	±	±	±	±	±						
getDouble()	±	±	±	±	±	✓	✓	±	±	±	±	±	±						
getBigDecimal()	±	±	±	±	±	±	±	✓	✓	±	±	±	±						
getBoolean()	±	±	±	±	±	±	±	±	±	✓	±	±	±						
getString()	±	±	±	±	±	±	±	±	±	±	✓	✓	±	±	±	±	±	±	±
getBytes()														✓	✓	±			
getDate()											±	±	±				✓		
getTime()											±	±	±					✓	±
getTimeStamp()											±	±	±				±		✓
getAsciiStraem()											±	±	✓	±	±	±			
getUnicodeStream()											±	±	✓	±	±	±			
getBinaryStream()														±	✓	✓			
getObject()	±	±	±	±	±	±	±	±	±	±	±	±	±	±	±	±	±	±	±

Working with Null Values

As we have already said, Null is a special value in the world of SQL. It is not the same thing as an empty string for text columns, nor is it the same thing as zero for a numeric field. Null means that no data is defined for a column value within a relation.

When the column data for a row is a SQL Null, the `getXXX` method returns a value that is appropriate for the return type. For all the `getXXX` methods that return an object, `getDate()` for example, the methods return a Java Null for SQL Null. All of the `getXXX` numeric methods, `getFloat()` for example, return the value 0 for SQL Null. The `getBoolean()` method returns False for SQL Null.

Let's take a look at the `Recordings` table, which has a `Coverimagefilespec` column that points to an image file – this may or may not have values assigned. In order to determine which recordings do not have an image of the recording cover stored, you could use the query:

```
SELECT recordingid FROM recordings WHERE coverimagefilespec IS NULL
```

This query will return the ID for each recording without a cover image.

The `ResultSet` interface provides a method for testing a column value within a resultset to determine if it is Null. The `wasNull()` method returns a Boolean value that is True if the last column read from the `ResultSet` object was a Null, and False if it was some other value.

You will need to use the ability to detect a Null value for a field in your code unless you created your tables with every column defined as not Null, which would tell the database that it must never allow a Null value in any column. However, that's not always a practicable or desirable way to design tables.

Let's consider a simple example that selects and displays the recording ID, title, and cover image filename for each row in the `Recordings` table. If any of these values are not assigned a value, the code could throw a `NullPointerException` when the program attempts to display the value. In order to avoid that sort of bad program behavior, this example will use the `wasNull()` method of the `ResultSet` to check for empty fields. Notice that the `wasNull()` method is called after the value is retrieved from the `ResultSet`.

Try It Out – Testing for Null Values in the ResultSet

Here is the code for the example:

```
package results;

import java.sql.*;
import connections.*;

public class TestNullValues {
  public static void main(String[] args) {
    String sql = "SELECT recordingid, recordingtitle, coverimagefilespec "
               + "FROM recordings";
    Connection connection = null;
    Statement queryRecordings = null;
    ResultSet results = null;

    try {
```

```
      connection = ConnectionFactory.getConnection();
      queryRecordings = connection.createStatement();
      results = queryRecordings.executeQuery(sql);

      String title, coverimagefilespec;
      int id;
      while (results.next()) {
        id = results.getInt("RECORDINGID");
        title = results.getString("RECORDINGTITLE");
        coverimagefilespec = results.getString("COVERIMAGEFILESPEC");
        if (results.wasNull()) {
          coverimagefilespec = "[no cover graphic]";
        }
        System.out.println(id + ", " + title.trim() + ", "
                           + coverimagefilespec.trim());
      }
    } catch (Exception e) {
      e.printStackTrace();
    }
    finally {
      ConnectionFactory.close(results);
      ConnectionFactory.close(queryRecordings);
      ConnectionFactory.close(connection);
    }
  }
}
```

Compiling and running this code produces the following results:

```
1000, Space I'm In, [no cover graphic]
1001, Phenomenon Soundtrack, [no cover graphic]
1002, Little Earthquakes, [no cover graphic]
1003, Crucify, [no cover graphic]
1004, Big Time, [no cover graphic]
1005, US, [no cover graphic]
```

How It Works

The code for this program again uses the `ConnectionFactory` class that was introduced in Chapter 8. Using this class, we get a connection to the database. For most of the examples in this chapter, this will be the Cloudscape Music Store database. With the connection we get a `Statement`, and then use the `Statement` to execute a query.

After the SQL statement is executed, the values for the recording ID, title and cover image are extracted into local variables. Since the value for `Coverimagefilespec` can be Null in the table, we call the `wasNull()` method immediately after retrieving that column from `results` to test if the value read was a Null value. If so, we store a literal value in the `coverimagefilespec` variable so outputting the report will work without throwing an exception. If we allowed `comerimagefilespec` to remain Null, a `NullPointerException` would be thrown when the code tried to call `coverimagefilespec.trim()`.

Working with Special Data Types

In addition to providing access methods for standard Java data types, the JDBC `java.sql` package also defines some special data types to accommodate the characteristics of particular SQL types.

Date

The `java.sql.Date` class defines the object that is returned by the `ResultSet.getDate()` method. This class subclasses the `Date` class defined in the `java.util` package, so all of the methods for that class can be applied against this class. The `java.sql.Date` class overrides many of these methods, and provides a static `valueOf()` method that converts a string representation (*yyyy-mm-dd* form) of a date into a `Date` object.

Time

Like `java.sql.Date`, the `java.sql.Time` class is a subclass of the `java.util.Date` class, and provides a static `valueOf()` method that returns a `Time` object from a string representation (*hh:mm:ss* form) of time into a `Time` object.

Timestamp

The `java.sql.Timestamp` class also subclasses `java.util.Date`, but provides additional support for SQL timestamps with support for nanoseconds (`java.util.Date` only supports time to the nearest millisecond). The static `valueOf()` method creates a `Timestamp` object from a string representation (*yyyy-mm-dd hh:mm:ss.fffffffff* form). It also overloads accessor methods and comparison methods (`before()`, `after()`) to support nanoseconds.

Big Numbers

The SQL `NUMERIC` and `DECIMAL` types are mapped to the Java `BigDecimal` class type. This class is defined in the `java.math` package along with the `BigInteger` class. A `BigInteger` object defines an integer of arbitrary precision, with negative values in 2's complement form. A `BigDecimal` object defines a decimal value of arbitrary precision that can be positive or negative. A `BigDecimal` object is implemented as an arbitrary precision, signed integer – a `BigInteger` object, plus a scale value that specifies the number of digits to the right of the decimal point. Thus the value of a `BigDecimal` object is the integer value divided by 10 ^ *scale*.

To read a column value of either `NUMERIC` or `DECIMAL` SQL type as a Java `BigDecimal` object, you use the `getBigDecimal()` method for the `ResultSet` object.

The `BigInteger` and `BigDecimal` classes are worth taking the time to look into. They are very useful for applications that require a large number of digits of precision, such as security keys, very large monetary values, and so forth. The `BigInteger` and `BigDecimal` classes provide mathematical methods for addition, subtraction, multiplication, and division, as well as comparison methods, and methods for returning their values as standard Java types. Additionally, `BigInteger` objects support bit-wise and shift operations. The `BigDecimal` class provides methods for tailoring the rounding behavior in arithmetic operations.

Like Java `String` objects, the value of a `BigInteger` or `BigDecimal` object is immutable. That is, once an object has been created, you can't change its value. When you apply arithmetic operations to `BigInteger` and `BigDecimal` objects using their methods, such as `multiply()` and `divide()`, you always get a new object as a result, in much the same way as you get a new `String` object when you use the `concat()` or `substring()` methods of `String`.

Consider the difficulties you might have if you had to compute very large sums and needed a great deal of accuracy. Suppose you had to accurately calculate the product of the following two floating-point numbers:

```
987654234625762356235623462346234623462.35632456234567890
```

and:

```
989823452323562466437643763467437343654 7.34586558
```

You might be tempted to write the following code:

```
class BigMultiplication {
  public static void main(String[] args) {
    Double d1 =
      Double
        .valueOf("987654234625762356235623462346234623462.35632456234567890");
    Double d2 =
      Double.valueOf("9898234523235624664376437634674373436547.34586558");
    Double d3 = d1.doubleValue() * d2.doubleValue();
    System.out.println(Double.toString(d3));
  }
}
```

and then be very disappointed when your code produced the result:

```
9.776033242192577E74
```

Considering the number of digits of precision you entered originally for the factors, you would probably find this unacceptable. Of course, the problem is that the precision for values type `double` is fixed, and limited to the number of digits that you see above.

Try It Out – The BigDecimal Class

We can do the calculation using `BigDecimal` objects as follows:

```
import java.math.*;

public class TestBigDecimal {
  public static void main(String[] args) {
    BigDecimal bn1 =
      new
        BigDecimal("987654234625762356235623462346234623462.35632456234567890");
    BigDecimal bn2 =
      new BigDecimal("9898234523235624664376437634674373436547.34586558");
    BigDecimal bn3 = bn1.multiply(bn2);
    System.out.println(bn3);
  }
}
```

When you compile and run the code the program prints the result:

```
977603324219257863723893512231480785031019252779047208595196675768219339448.773313
5102106926932422620
```

How It Works

The BigDecimal class has remarkable capabilities. It can support numbers of virtually limitless precision. The precision and scale are both 32-bit signed integer values, so they can be as large as 2,147,483,647 digits – and that's a huge number of decimal digits! In our example, we create two BigDecimal objects, bn1 and bn2, representing the original values that we want to multiply. We multiply them using the multiply() method for bn1, and store the reference to the BigDecimal object that is returned containing the result in bn3. We can use this in a println() method call since the BigDecimal class implements the toString() method to print the current value of the object.

The BigInteger class is just as impressive – it provides the same arbitrary precision characteristics for integer values. Of course, there is a price to pay for that precision. Computations using the BigInteger and BigDecimal classes are noticeably slower than their counterparts using native Java types.

The BigInteger and BigDecimal classes manage digits as objects in a vector, so to get the flexibility of unlimited precision, you have to trade-off computing time for operations on the numbers. Nonetheless, this class is invaluable for many applications.

In Chapter 12, we'll learn how to use the PreparedStatement and ResultSet interfaces to read and write some of the SQL3 types such as LOBs and Streams. However, let's now look at how we can move around in our ResultSet.

Constraining the Resultset

In general, you will not normally know how much data will be returned from executing a query. In our Music Store sample database, there isn't any possibility of getting into difficulties because of the volume of data, but with production databases you may need some controls. Getting a million rows back from a SELECT operation could be an embarrassment, particularly since a substantial amount of time and memory will be involved. The Statement interface allows you to set constraints on the consequences of executing a query. You can limit the number of rows in the ResultSet objects that are returned, as well as specifying the maximum field size. You can also limit the amount of time for executing a query.

Maximum Number of Rows

The JDBC driver may impose a limitation on how many rows may be returned by a query, and you may wish to impose your limit on how many rows are returned in a resultset. The Statement interface defines the methods getMaxRows() and setMaxRows() that allow you to query and set the maximum rows returned in the ResultSet object, respectively. The value 0 is defined as no limit.

A particular JDBC driver may default to a practical limit on the number of rows in a resultset, or may even have implementation restrictions that limit the returned rows. To determine the row limit in effect, you can call the getMaxRows() method for your Statement object:

```
Statement statement = connection.createStatement();
int maxRows = statement.getMaxRows();
```

When you wish to limit the number of rows returned from a query in an application, to prevent an extremely lengthy query process for example, you can call setMaxRows() to limit the number of returned rows:

```
SQLStatement.setMaxRows(30);
```

It is important to note that, when the maximum row count is set to a non-zero value (zero being unlimited), you will not get any indication when the data that would have been returned is truncated. If the total number of rows exceeds the maximum value, the maximum number of rows is returned in the resultset, and any remaining rows that meet the query criteria will be silently left behind.

Try It Out – Limited and Unlimited Row Count Query

Enter this simple program that performs a query with and without a maximum row count:

```
package results;

import java.sql.*;
import connections.*;

public class MaxRows {
  public static void main(String[] args) {
    Connection conn = null;
    Statement stmt = null;
    ResultSet rset = null;

    try {
      conn = ConnectionFactory.getConnection();
      stmt = conn.createStatement();
      rset = stmt.executeQuery("SELECT * FROM tracks");

      int count = 0;
      while (rset.next()) {
        count++;
      }
      System.out.println("Unconstrained query returned " + count + " rows");

      stmt.setMaxRows(5);
      rset = stmt.executeQuery("SELECT * FROM tracks");

      count = 0;
      while (rset.next()) {
        count++;
      }
      System.out.println("Constrained query returned " + count + " rows");

    } catch (Exception e) {
      e.printStackTrace();
    }
    finally {
      ConnectionFactory.close(rset);
      ConnectionFactory.close(stmt);
      ConnectionFactory.close(conn);
    }
  }
}
```

When executed, this program should give an output similar to the following:

```
Unconstrained query returned 64 rows
Constrained query returned 5 rows
```

How It Works

Using the ConnectionFactory class, we get a connection to the database. The Statement object created from the Connection does not have a constraint on the number of rows returned by a query. Thus the query returned all the rows in the Tracks table in my Music Store database. There were 64 tracks when I ran the program. When the Statement was constrained to return only 5 rows, the query returned that number of rows.

Maximum Field Size

The Statement interface also enables you to query and set the maximum field size that applies to all column values returned in a ResultSet. Querying this value will tell you if the JDBC driver imposes a practical or absolute limit on the size of the columns returned. The value 0 is defined as no limit.

To determine the maximum field size for statement results, simply call the getMaxFieldSize() method of the Statement interface:

```
Statement statement = connection.createStatement();
int maxFieldSize = statement.getMaxFieldSize();
```

The value returned is the maximum number of bytes permitted for any field returned in a resultset. Like the maximum row method pair, there is a corresponding setMaxFieldSize() method to set the maximum field size:

```
SQLStatement.setMaxFieldSize(4096);
```

Note that the setMaxFieldSize() only applies to columns with the following SQL data types:

BINARY	VARBINARY	LONGVARBINARY
CHAR	VARCHAR	LONGVARCHAR

A note on the above data types: the length limits on these types may vary by your particular database vendor, but in general, the following limits apply:

BINARY, CHAR, VARBINARY, and VARCHAR are limited in length by the upper-bound of a signed 32-bit integer – specifically, 2,147,483,647. LONGVARBINARY and LONGVARCHAR have no fixed limit.

Any bytes in a field in excess of the maximum will be silently discarded.

Query Timeout

Depending on your JDBC driver and the database to which it is attached, there may be an execution timeout period after which a query will fail, and the executeQuery() method will throw an exception. You can check the value for the timeout period with the getQueryTimeout() method for a Statement object, or set the timeout period (for instance, if you want a query to fail after a fixed time period) using the setQueryTimeout() method. The timeout period is defined in seconds and a timeout value of 0 indicates that there is no limit on the time that a query can take.

Try It Out – Query Constraints

Here is a simple program that will test the default query constraints for your JDBC driver:

```
package results;

import java.sql.*;
import connections.*;

public class TestDriverInfo {
  public static void main(String[] args) {
    Connection conn = null;
    Statement stmt = null;

    try {
      conn = ConnectionFactory.getConnection();
      stmt = conn.createStatement();

      int maxRows = stmt.getMaxRows();
      System.out.println("Maximum rows : " + maxRows);

      int maxFieldSize = stmt.getMaxFieldSize();
      System.out.println("Maximum fieldsize : " + maxFieldSize);

      int queryTimeout = stmt.getQueryTimeout();
      System.out.println("Query timeout : " + queryTimeout);
    } catch (Exception e) {
      e.printStackTrace();
    }
    finally {
      ConnectionFactory.close(stmt);
      ConnectionFactory.close(conn);
    }
  }
}
```

Running this with Cloudscape should result in the following output:

```
Maximum rows : 0
Maximum fieldsize : 0
SQL Exception: Feature not implemented: getQueryTimeout.
        at c8e.l.h._uv(Unknown Source)
        at c8e.l.h._uv(Unknown Source)
        at c8e.l.h.notImplemented(Unknown Source)
        at c8e.l.i.getQueryTimeout(Unknown Source)
        at results.TestDriverInfo.main(TestDriverInfo.java:21)
```

You can see that the number of rows that can be returned is unlimited, as is the field size. Notice that an exception was caught in trying to get the query timeout value. As the exception says, this is not implemented by the Cloudscape driver.

How It Works

This code is pretty simple. It gets a `Connection` from the `ConnectionFactory` class and uses it to create a `Statement`. Using that `Statement` object, the values for the maximum number of rows returned by a query, the maximum column size returned by a query, and the value of the query timeout are retrieved. All three methods providing this information will throw an exception of type `SQLException` if the information is not available – as is the case with the Cloudscape and the query timeout.

In this section, we have looked at various ways to get the column data from the rows returned by a query. To get to any row, though, we need to be able to move through the `ResultSet` object; that is the topic of the next section.

Moving Through a ResultSet

Here's a snippet of code from the `retrieve()` method:

```
resultSet = statement.executeQuery(sql);
if (resultSet.next()) {
  result = true;
  setStoreId(resultSet.getInt("StoreID"));
  storeDescription = resultSet.getString("StoreDescription");
```

When the `executeQuery()` method returns a `ResultSet`, the *cursor* is positioned *prior* to the first row of data.

> ***Cursor** is a database term. It generally refers to the set of rows returned by a query. When a cursor is positioned at a row, we mean that we are accessing a particular row in the set.*

To get to the first row of data, you must call the `next()` method. Each time you need to get the next row of data, you call `next()` again. The `next()` method returns a Boolean value. If there is another row of data, the cursor is positioned at that row and the method returns True. If there are no more rows of data, then the `next()` method returns False.

The `ResultSet` interface provides other methods for navigating the `ResultSet`, including:

- `previous()` – moves to previous row
- `first()` – moves to first row
- `last()` – moves to last row
- `absolute(int n)` – moves to the nth row in the `ResultSet`
- `relative(int n)` – moves n rows from the current row

None of these methods, however, could be used with the `ResultSet` as it is returned in the `retrieve()` method. The reason for this is that when we created our `Statement` object, we used the parameter-less version of the `createStatement()` method:

```
return connection.createStatement();
```

When you create a `Statement` using the parameter-less constructor, the `Statement` object will produce a `ResultSet` object of type forward-only (and read-only; in other words, non-updatable). The only valid method for traversing a `ResultSet` of type forward-only is the `next()` method. In the case of our `retrieve()` method, this is not a problem because only a single result row is expected, so there is no need to move backwards in the `ResultSet` or jump to a specific row in it.

Let's look in to this in a little more detail and find out how we create a **scrollable ResultSet**.

Creating a Scrollable ResultSet Object

In order to create a scrollable `ResultSet` object, we need to use another form of the `createStatement()` method (newly available with JDBC 2.0):

```
Statement createStatement(int resultSetType, int resultSetConcurrency)
```

The `resultSetType` parameter determines the type of `ResultSet` that will be produced (scrollable or non-scrollable), and the `resultSetConcurrency` parameter determines the concurrency level.

The `int` parameters that you pass in the method are static constants defined in the `ResultSet` class. Possible values for the `resultSetType` parameter are:

- `ResultSet.TYPE_FORWARD_ONLY`
- `ResultSet.TYPE_SCROLL_INSENSITIVE`
- `ResultSet.TYPE_SCROLL_SENSITIVE`

and possible values for the `resultSetConcurrency` parameter are:

- `CONCUR_READ_ONLY`
- `CONCUR_UPDATABLE`

Your database driver may, or may not, support scrolling and updating. Check your driver documentation to determine the details.

The outcome of setting either of these values for the `resultSetConcurrency` parameter is pretty self-explanatory. Setting the value to `CONCUR_UPDATABLE` will mean that the database can be updated through the `ResultSet`. Setting the value to `CONCUR_READ_ONLY` (which is the default) will produce a read-only `ResultSet`, and you will need to perform updates by sending SQL through the `Statement` object. We will be looking at updatable `ResultSets` in the next section, so let's concentrate on setting the `ResultSet` type here.

If you specify `TYPE_FORWARD_ONLY`, then you will create a `Statement` object that produces a forward-only `ResultSet`. This is the default value – when you create a `Statement` with the no-argument `createStatement()` method, the `ResultSet` defaults to `TYPE_FORWARD_ONLY`.

The other two possible values create a `Statement` that produces a scrollable `ResultSet`. With a scrollable `ResultSet`, the cursor can be programmatically moved forwards and backwards through the `ResultSet`. The scroll-insensitive `ResultSet` is not affected by changes made to the underlying database while it is open. For example, if a scroll-insensitive `ResultSet` is created as the result of query, and a separate transaction changes one of the rows in the underlying database, that change is not seen in the `ResultSet`. A scroll-sensitive `ResultSet` can see changes to the underlying database, provided those changes are visible to the transaction that contains the `ResultSet`. *Transactions* are covered in more detail in Chapter 14.

> **Although a JDBC 2.0 driver provides the capability to scroll forward and backward, you should be careful when using this feature. For example, the Oracle driver provides this capability by caching the results in memory. For an extremely large query result, this could lead to a shortage of memory.**

When you create the statement with either `ResultSet.TYPE_SCROLL_INSENSITIVE` or `ResultSet.TYPE_SCROLL_SENSITIVE`, you can use any of the methods `next()`, `previous()`, `first()`, `last()`, `absolute()`, or `relative()` to move through the `ResultSet`. The full set of methods that can be used to move the cursor through a scrollable `ResultSet` or check the position of the cursor in the `ResultSet` are as follows:

`boolean next()`	`boolean previous()`	`boolean first()`
`boolean last()`	`void afterLast()`	`void beforeFirst()`
`boolean absolute(int row)`	`boolean relative(int rows)`	
`boolean isFirst()`	`boolean isBeforeFirst()`	`boolean isLast()`
`boolean isAfterLast()`	`int getRow()`	
`void moveToInsertRow()`	`void moveToCurrentRow()`	

Most of the methods above are self-explanatory (you can consult the Java documentation for more information). Two of the not-so-obvious methods are `moveToInsertRow()` and `moveToCurrentRow()`.

- The method `moveToInsertRow()` moves to a special row that is used for inserting a row of data into the table. After moving to insert the row, the code should call the `updateXXX` methods to update the column values, and then calls `insertRow()` to actually write the data to the database. If the code moves the `ResultSet` to some other row before `insertRow()` is called, the row is not inserted into the database and the updates to the insert row are discarded.
- The `moveToCurrentRow()` method moves the `ResultSet` back to the last position before `moveToInsertRow()` was called. You can also leave the insert row by calling `first()`, `last()`, `beforeFirst()`, `afterLast()`, `absolute()`, `previous()`, or `relative()`.

Try It Out – Using a Scrollable ResultSet

With a simple program, we can demonstrate some of the methods for moving through a result set. The program below is designed to query the `Tracks` table of the Music Store database. You may need to modify it if you want to use it with a different table or a different database.

1. Create the following `ScrollingDemo.java` class:

```
package results;

import java.sql.*;
import java.io.*;
import connections.*;

public class ScrollingDemo {
  public static void main(String[] args) {
    Connection conn = null;
    Statement stmt = null;
    ResultSet rset = null;

    try {
      conn = ConnectionFactory.getConnection();
      stmt = conn.createStatement(ResultSet.TYPE_SCROLL_INSENSITIVE,
                                  ResultSet.CONCUR_READ_ONLY);
      String sql = "SELECT * FROM tracks "
                 + "ORDER BY recordingid, tracknumber";
      rset = stmt.executeQuery(sql);

      if (rset.next()) {
        rset.beforeFirst();
        boolean done = false;
        BufferedReader in =
          new BufferedReader(new InputStreamReader(System.in));
        while (!done) {
          System.out.print("\nType F (first), N (next), P (previous), "
                           + "L (last), Q (quit) : ");
          String s = in.readLine();
          boolean result = false;
          if (s.equalsIgnoreCase("F")) {
            result = rset.first();
          } else if (s.equalsIgnoreCase("N")) {
            result = rset.next();
          } else if (s.equalsIgnoreCase("P")) {
            result = rset.previous();
          } else if (s.equalsIgnoreCase("L")) {
            result = rset.last();
          } else if (s.equalsIgnoreCase("Q")) {
            done = true;
          }
          if (done) {
            break;
          }
          if (result) {
            System.out.println("cursor moved to row " + rset.getRow());
```

```
            System.out.println("Record Id : " + rset.getInt(1)
                               + ", Track Number : " + rset.getInt(2)
                               + ", Track Title : " + rset.getString(3));
          } else {
            System.out.println("Could not move cursor");
          }
        }
        in.close();
      } else {
        System.out.println("ResultSet contained no rows");
      }
    } catch (Exception e) {
      e.printStackTrace();
    }
    finally {
      ConnectionFactory.close(rset);
      ConnectionFactory.close(stmt);
      ConnectionFactory.close(conn);
    }
  }
}
```

2. Save the class in the `results` directory and compile it using something similar to the following command at the prompt:

```
C:\BegJavaDB\Ch09>javac -classpath . results/ScrollingDemo.java
```

3. The program can be run with the following command (change as necessary for your environment):

```
C:\BegJavaDB\Ch09>java results.ScrollingDemo
```

which will produce output similar to the following:

```
Type F (first), N (next), P (previous), L (last), Q (quit) : f
cursor moved to row 1
Record Id : 1000, Track Number : 1, Track Title : So Easy

Type F (first), N (next), P (previous), L (last), Q (quit) : p
Could not move cursor

Type F (first), N (next), P (previous), L (last), Q (quit) : l
cursor moved to row 55
Record Id : 1005, Track Number : 10, Track Title : Secret World

Type F (first), N (next), P (previous), L (last), Q (quit) : p
cursor moved to row 54
Record Id : 1005, Track Number : 9, Track Title : Kiss That Frog

Type F (first), N (next), P (previous), L (last), Q (quit) : n
cursor moved to row 55
Record Id : 1005, Track Number : 10, Track Title : Secret World
```

```
Type F (first), N (next), P (previous), L (last), Q (quit) : n
Could not move cursor

Type F (first), N (next), P (previous), L (last), Q (quit) : q

Process results.ScrollingDemo finished
```

How It Works

The class consists of a single `main()` method that creates a scrollable `ResultSet` as described earlier in the section. After obtaining a connection from the `ConnectionFactory` class, the `createStatement(int, int)` method is called to create a `Statement`. Using the `ResultSet.TYPE_SCROLL_INSENSITIVE` parameter creates a `Statement` that returns a scrollable `ResultSet`.

```
conn = ConnectionFactory.getConnection();
conn.setAutoCommit(false);
stmt = conn.createStatement(ResultSet.TYPE_SCROLL_INSENSITIVE,
                            ResultSet.CONCUR_READ_ONLY);
String sql = "SELECT * FROM tracks "
           + "ORDER BY recordingid, tracknumber";
rset = stmt.executeQuery(sql);
```

The program then calls the `next()` method to determine whether any rows are in the `ResultSet`. If `next()` returns True, the program repositions the cursor to before the first row and starts waiting for user input. The program accepts user input from the keyboard using a `BufferedReader` created from the `System.in` stream. The program reads the input into a `String` variable and then compares the variable against a set of values. If the string matches one of the values, the program calls a movement method of the `ResultSet`. If the movement was successful (returned True), then the program prints the first three columns of the current row. If the user tries to move past the last row, or before the first row, the method returns False, and the program reports that it was unable to move the cursor. When the user types `Q`, the program terminates.

The program only uses some of the cursor movement methods of the `ResultSet`. You may wish to add these methods to the program to experiment with their use. Another interesting experiment that you may wish to try is to see what happens when you change the `createStatement()` method call like this:

```
stmt = conn.createStatement(ResultSet.TYPE_FORWARD_ONLY,
                            ResultSet.CONCUR_READ_ONLY);
```

Modifying Data Using a ResultSet

Previously in this chapter, we modified an existing row in the `Stores` table using a `Statement` object only. This worked fine because we have only been dealing with a single row from the database. However, in the broader scheme of things, there will be times when we will want to retrieve multiple rows and take actions upon those rows. For example, our Music Store application will need to:

- Query the `Tracks` table for all the tracks belonging to a given recording
- Query the `Recordings` table for all recordings by a given artist
- Query the `Stores` table for all stores with a given store type, and so on

If the user of our application wishes to view certain rows and then select one or more of them for modification using only a `Statement` object, then the code will have to do something like this:

1. Use the `Statement` object to execute a query and get a `ResultSet`.
2. Navigate through the `ResultSet` to the desired row.
3. Use the `Statement` object to execute an update.
4. Loop back to step 1, until finished.

In other words: using a `Statement`, we would need to execute a query, execute an update, execute a query, execute an update, and so on. The reason that the code would have to execute the query again is because when the `Statement` object is used to execute another SQL statement, any open `ResultSet` is closed. Only a single `ResultSet` per `Statement` can be open – executing another SQL statement with the `Statement` closes the `ResultSet`. After the `Statement` executes the update, the original `ResultSet` can no longer be used. Prior to JDBC 2.0, the only way to update a database was through a `Statement` object.

Starting with JDBC 2.0, there is a more effective method; we can update the database through the `ResultSet` object. Although a table can be modified using a non-scrolling `ResultSet` (one that moves forward only), code that updates the `ResultSet` will also be likely to use a scrolling `ResultSet` for moving through the `ResultSet`. With a `TYPE_FORWARD_ONLY ResultSet`, we would start at the first row, use `next()` to move to each subsequent row, and update the desired row when the cursor was positioned at that row. We would not be able to insert new rows with a non-scrolling `ResultSet` because there is no way to move to the insert row. With a scrollable `ResultSet`, we could move forwards or backwards to any desired row and update that row, or move to the insert row and create a new row.

Creating an Updatable ResultSet

As we have already discussed, in order to create an updatable `ResultSet`, we need to supply the appropriate value for the `resultSetConcurrency` parameter of the `createStatement()` method:

```
Statement createStatement(int resultSetType, int resultSetConcurrency)
```

The valid values for this parameter are `CONCUR_READ_ONLY` and `CONCUR_UPDATABLE`, and by supplying the latter we can produce an updatable `ResultSet` object.

> *You should note that the Cloudscape 3.6.1 database that we have used for certain sections of this book does not support an updatable `ResultSet`. If you try to create an updatable `ResultSet` with the Cloudscape driver, the code will throw an exception. The only `ResultSet` allowed is `CONCUR_READ_ONLY`. You should consult your driver documentation to determine if your driver supports an updatable `ResultSet`.*

In addition to calling the `createStatement()` method with the correct parameters, the SQL statement that queries the database must adhere to some requirements. The SQL `SELECT` must:

- Reference only one table
- Not contain a `join` or `group by` clause
- Select the primary key as one of the columns

Methods for Updating a ResultSet

JDBC 2.0 defines numerous methods for updating the columns in a `ResultSet` object. After creating an updatable `ResultSet` and navigating to the desired row, you can update a given column value with the following methods. When you are inserting a new row, you navigate to a special insert row, and use the same methods:

`updateString()`	`updateBoolean()`	`updateByte()`
`updateShort()`	`updateInt()`	`updateLong()`
`updateFloat()`	`updateDouble()`	`updateBigDecimal()`
`updateBytes()`	`updateDate()`	`updateTime()`
`updateTimeStamp()`	`updateAsciiStream()`	`updateCharacterStream()`
`updateBinaryStream()`	`updateNull()`	`updateObject()`

Each of the methods above comes in two overloaded forms. You can update a particular column based on the column number, or the column name. Columns are numbered starting with 1, in the same order in which they appear in the SQL `SELECT`, if columns were selected explicitly by name (`SELECT col1, col2, col3 FROM` ...). If the SQL `SELECT` was a `select *` ..., then the columns are numbered in the same order as their sequence in the table. So for example, in the `Stores` table, the `StoreDescription` column is the second column, and its type maps to a JDBC `String`. Either of the following method calls could be used to update the `StoreDescription` column in a particular row:

```
resultSet.updateString(2, aString);  // use the column number

resultSet.updateString("StoreDescription", aString); //  use the column name
```

For any given column, you use the `updateXXX` method that is appropriate for the column type. After the desired columns have been changed, the code *must* call the method `updateRow()` or `insertRow()` for the changes to be written to the database:

- Call `updateRow()` when the code is changing an existing row in the `ResultSet`.
- Call `insertRow()` only after updating the columns in the insert row, a special row in the `ResultSet`.

When you insert a new row, the row is NOT part of the `ResultSet`. *When you move to a different row, you will no longer be able to see the values you inserted as part of the new row. To see the new row, you must execute a query that selects the new row.*

Try It Out – Using a Scrollable and Updatable ResultSet

Now, let's add the ability to update and insert rows to the `ScrollingDemo` program from the previous section of this chapter:

When this chapter was written, Cloudscape did not support an updatable `ResultSet`, so for this example, an Oracle database was used.

1. Create the following `UpdatingDemo.java` source. This program is created by adding functionality to the `ScrollingDemo.java` source from the previous section:

```
package results;

import java.sql.*;
import java.io.*;
import connections.*;

public class UpdatingDemo {
  public static void main(String[] args) {
    Connection conn = null;
    Statement stmt = null;
    ResultSet rset = null;

    try {
      conn = ConnectionFactory.getConnection();
      stmt = conn.createStatement(ResultSet.TYPE_SCROLL_SENSITIVE,
                                  ResultSet.CONCUR_UPDATABLE);
      String sql = "SELECT recordingid, tracknumber, tracktitle "
                 + "FROM tracks ORDER BY recordingid, tracknumber";
      rset = stmt.executeQuery(sql);

      // if (rset.next()) {
      // rset.beforeFirst();
      boolean done = false;
      BufferedReader inr =
        new BufferedReader(new InputStreamReader(System.in));
      while (!done) {
        System.out.print("\nType F (first), N (next), P (previous), "
                         + "L (last), Q (quit), I (insert), U (update) : ");
        String s = inr.readLine();
        boolean result = false;
        if (s.equalsIgnoreCase("F")) {
          result = rset.first();
        } else if (s.equalsIgnoreCase("N")) {
          result = rset.next();
        } else if (s.equalsIgnoreCase("P")) {
          result = rset.previous();
        } else if (s.equalsIgnoreCase("L")) {
          result = rset.last();
        } else if (s.equalsIgnoreCase("Q")) {
          done = true;
        } else if (s.equalsIgnoreCase("U")) {
          updateRow(rset, inr, false);
```

```
        } else if (s.equalsIgnoreCase("I")) {
          rset.moveToInsertRow();
          updateRow(rset, inr, true);
        }
        if (done) {
          break;
        }
        if (result) {
          System.out.println("cursor moved to row " + rset.getRow());
          System.out.println("Record Id : " + rset.getInt(1)
                             + ", Track Number : " + rset.getInt(2)
                             + ", Track Title : " + rset.getString(3));
        } else {
          if (!s.equalsIgnoreCase("U") &&!s.equalsIgnoreCase("I")) {
            System.out.println("Could not move cursor");
          }
        }
      }
      inr.close();

      // } else {
      // System.out.println("ResultSet contained no rows");
      // }
    } catch (Exception e) {
      e.printStackTrace();
    }
    finally {
      ConnectionFactory.close(rset);
      ConnectionFactory.close(stmt);
      ConnectionFactory.close(conn);
    }
  }

  public static void updateRow(ResultSet rset, BufferedReader inr,
                               boolean insert) throws SQLException,
                               IOException {
    System.out.print("Enter Recording Id: ");
    String recordId = inr.readLine();
    rset.updateInt("RECORDINGID", Integer.parseInt(recordId));

    System.out.print("Enter Track Number: ");
    String trackNumber = inr.readLine();
    rset.updateInt("TRACKNUMBER", Integer.parseInt(trackNumber));

    System.out.print("Enter Track Title: ");
    String trackTitle = inr.readLine();
    rset.updateString("TRACKTITLE", trackTitle);

    System.out.print("Enter Y to commit the change, "
                     + "or any other key to stop the update: ");
    String choice = inr.readLine();
    if (choice.equalsIgnoreCase("Y")) {
      if (insert) {
        rset.insertRow();
        rset.moveToCurrentRow();
```

```
        } else {
          rset.updateRow();
        }
      }
    }
  }
```

2. Save this class in the `c:\BegJavaDB\Ch09\results` directory and compile it.

3. Create the table in the database. The following SQL will create the table and insert some initial rows of data:

```
create table tracks (
  recordingid int,
  tracknumber int,
  tracktitle varchar2(50)
);

INSERT INTO tracks VALUES (1000, 1, 'So Easy');
INSERT INTO tracks VALUES (1000, 2, 'Submarine Soing');
INSERT INTO tracks VALUES (1000, 3, 'Black and Blue');
```

Notice that the script above misspells the title of the second track. We will correct that when we run the program.

4. Change the `ConnectionFactory` class to connect to the database. Here are the changes I made to connect to my Oracle database:

```
package connections;

import java.sql.*;

public class ConnectionFactory {
  private static ConnectionFactory ref = new ConnectionFactory();
  private ConnectionFactory() {
    try {
      Class.forName("COM.cloudscape.core.JDBCDriver");
      // Class.forName("oracle.jdbc.driver.OracleDriver");
    } catch (ClassNotFoundException e) {
      System.out.println("ERROR: exception loading driver class");
    }
  }

  public static Connection getConnection() throws SQLException {
    String url = "jdbc:cloudscape:c:/BegJavaDB/Wrox4370.db";
    //String url = "jdbc:oracle:thin@dbserver:1521:database";
    return DriverManager.getConnection("url", "beg", "java");
  }

  // ... rest of class as before (See Chapter 8)
```

```
}
```

You will need to change the URL for your system, and also the driver string if you are using a different database.

5. The program can be run with the following command (change as necessary for your environment):

```
C:\BegJavaDB\Ch09>java results.UpdatingDemo
```

6. Execute the program and try inserting or changing some rows. Here is what I did when I ran the program. I went to the track 'Submarine Song' and corrected the title; then I inserted a new row:

```
Type F (first), N (next), P (previous), L (last), Q (quit), I (insert), U (update)
: n
cursor moved to row 1
Record Id : 1000, Track Number : 1, Track Title : So Easy

Type F (first), N (next), P (previous), L (last), Q (quit), I (insert), U (update)
: n
cursor moved to row 2
Record Id : 1000, Track Number : 2, Track Title : Submarine Soing

Type F (first), N (next), P (previous), L (last), Q (quit), I (insert), U (update)
: u
Enter Recording Id: 1000
Enter Track Number: 2
Enter Track Title: Submarine Song
Enter Y to commit the change, or any other key to stop the update: y

Type F (first), N (next), P (previous), L (last), Q (quit), I (insert), U (update)
: n
cursor moved to row 3
Record Id : 1000, Track Number : 3, Track Title : Black and Blue

Type F (first), N (next), P (previous), L (last), Q (quit), I (insert), U (update)
: p
cursor moved to row 2
Record Id : 1000, Track Number : 2, Track Title : Submarine Song

Type F (first), N (next), P (previous), L (last), Q (quit), I (insert), U (update)
: i
Enter Recording Id: 1001
Enter Track Number: 1
Enter Track Title: The First Cut
Enter Y to commit the change, or any other key to stop the update: y

Type F (first), N (next), P (previous), L (last), Q (quit), I (insert), U (update)
: q

Process results.UpdatingDemo finished
```

How It Works

This program creates a scrollable, updatable ResultSet. Like the ScrollingDemo class we saw earlier on, the program provides the ability for the user to scroll to any row in the ResultSet. By creating the statement with the correct parameter, ResultSet.CONCUR_UPDATABLE, the ResultSet is also updatable. Notice also that the SQL SELECT statement in this class identified the columns by name.

The program looks for two additional input selections from the user. Whether the user wants to update an existing row, or insert a new row, the code is almost identical. One difference is that if the user wants to insert a row, the code must first move the cursor to a special row used for inserts. This is done with the moveToInsertRow() method:

```
} else if (s.equalsIgnoreCase("U")) {
  updateRow(rset, inr, false);
} else if (s.equalsIgnoreCase("I")) {
  rset.moveToInsertRow();
  updateRow(rset, inr, true);
}
```

The update feature simply updates the row at which the cursor is currently positioned. Since the same methods are used for updating or inserting columns, the code for changing a column or inserting new column values is contained in a separate method named updateRow(). When the user selects update or insert, the program calls the updateRow() method. The method prompts the user for the data for each column; when the user enters the information, the program calls the updateString() or updateInt() method as appropriate to change the column. When the user has finished, the method calls updateRow() for an update, calls insertRow() for an insert, or does nothing if the user does not want to save the change.

```
public static void updateRow(ResultSet rset, BufferedReader inr,
                             boolean insert) throws SQLException,
                             IOException {
  System.out.print("Enter Recording Id: ");
  String recordId = inr.readLine();
  rset.updateInt("RECORDINGID", Integer.parseInt(recordId));

  System.out.print("Enter Track Number: ");
  String trackNumber = inr.readLine();
  rset.updateInt("TRACKNUMBER", Integer.parseInt(trackNumber));

  System.out.print("Enter Track Title: ");
  String trackTitle = inr.readLine();
  rset.updateString("TRACKTITLE", trackTitle);

  System.out.print("Enter Y to commit the change, "
                 + "or any other key to stop the update: ");
  String choice = inr.readLine();
  if (choice.equalsIgnoreCase("Y")) {
    if (insert) {
      rset.insertRow();
      rset.moveToCurrentRow();
    } else {
      rset.updateRow();
    }
```

```
        }
      }
    }
```

If you insert a row using the program, spend some time scrolling the rows. As I noted earlier in the section, the inserted row is *not* in the `ResultSet`. When you rerun the program, you will see the new row.

New in JDBC 3.0 – ResultSet Holdability

At the beginning of the *Modifying Data Using a ResultSet* section, I said that executing another SQL string with the `Statement` object closes the `ResultSet`. Calling the `Connection` method `commit()` also closes the `ResultSet`. JDBC 3.0 adds a new `ResultSet` feature called **holdability**, which refers to whether or not a `ResultSet` is closed when changes to the database are committed. When `commit()` is called with a JDBC 2.0 or 1.0 driver, the `ResultSet` is closed. JDBC 3.0 gives you the capability to keep the `ResultSet` open after changes are committed.

Two class constants were added to the `ResultSet` interface to provide parameters for the `createStatement()` method:

- `ResultSet.HOLD_CURSORS_OVER_COMMIT` – This specifies that the `ResultSet` should ***not*** be closed when changes are committed.
- `ResultSet.CLOSE_CURSORS_AT_COMMIT` – The driver can close `ResultSet` when changes are committed.

A new `createStatement()` method was added to the `Connection` class to support this feature:

```
createStatement(int resultSetType, int resultSetConcurrency,
                intresultSetHoldability)
```

At the time this chapter was written, Sun listed no drivers that provide this capability. You can check the current listing of drivers at http://industry.java.sun.com/products/jdbc/drivers.

Summary

In this chapter we have examined two very closely related objects in the JDBC world: `Statements` and `ResultSets`. `Statements` are used to send SQL to the database; SQL query results are returned in the form of `ResultSets`. In this chapter, you should have learned:

- `Statements` are created from `Connection` objects.
- `Statements` are used to send SQL to the database for execution. In this chapter we looked at using a `Statement` object to send a SQL `UPDATE` to the database.
- `ResultSets` are the rows returned from a database by a query.
- The column values in a `ResultSet` are obtained using methods that can return Java primitive types as well as Java objects.
- We can use the `Statement` to control how the `ResultSet` returns data.

- `ResultSets` can be forward-only (the default) or can be scrollable.
- `ResultSets` can be read-only (the default) or they can be updatable.

akarta JAVA

Java

Using Meta Data

Up until this point, we have assumed that you, the developer of JDBC applications, know the structure of the data you are dealing with. In other words, you know how your data is built up, how the tables are structured, what columns are in the tables, and how they are all related. When you query the database, you can use the exact SQL needed to extract the desired columns from the desired tables. The same is true for inserting, deleting, and updating data.

It is possible, however, that you may be in a situation in which you have no knowledge about the structure of a database, or the contents of the tables in a database. Information *about* a database (as contrasted with information *stored in* a database) can be obtained through meta data objects. In this chapter we will look at:

- What exactly is meta data
- What information we can learn about the database
- A practical use for database meta data
- What information can we learn about a resultset

What is Meta Data?

With a little bit of experimenting with your database, you may have found a tool that shows you the tables and data in it. Cloudscape provides such a tool, called **Cloudview**, or `cview` as it is specified on the command line, and you can try it out by executing the following commands:

```
> set classpath=c:\cloudscape\lib\tools.jar;c:\cloudscape\lib\cloudscape.jar
> java COM.cloudscape.tools.cview
```

Oracle provides a similar tool called Oracle Navigator. If you are using MySQL on Windows, you have WinMySQLadmin. Other databases will have similar tools.

When the Cloudview program is running, click on File, then Open, and navigate to the Music Store database using the file chooser. (If you are using a different tool, you will need to use the appropriate procedure for your tool to open a connection to a database.) In the left-hand pane of Cloudview, the program shows a tree of information about the database. If you expand the Tables node, you will see a list of tables. Click the Stores node, and then select the Data tab in the right-hand pane. You should see a window that looks like this:

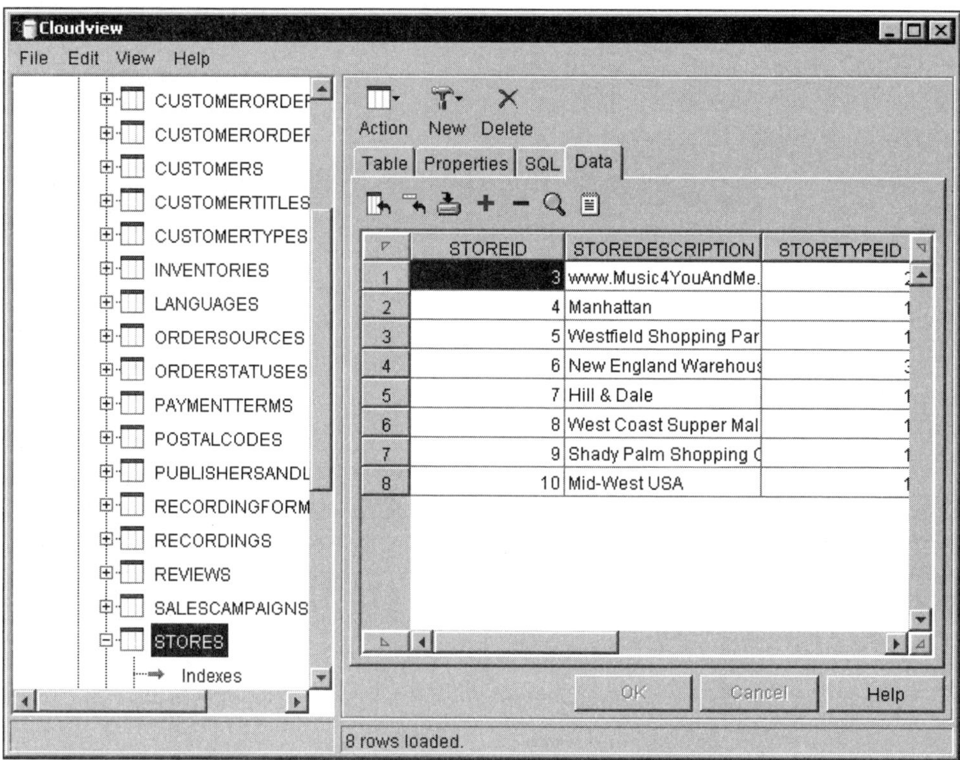

How did the tool know to display columns labeled `STOREID`, `STOREDESCRIPTION`, `STORETYPEID`, and so on? How could the developers at Informix, the company behind the Cloudscape database, know that someday, someone would create a table named `Stores` with these columns?

The answer is that they didn't. The `cview` application is able to dynamically show the database structure and dynamically create queries to show the table data using the **meta data**. Meta data is data that describes the sort of functionality an RDBMS provides and the types of data in the database – effectively, it is 'data about the database'. Meta data is collectively known as the **data dictionary**. In this section of this chapter, we will take a brief look at the `DatabaseMetaData` and `ResultSetMetaData` objects.

In general, you won't need to use these classes much when you are developing against a specific database, as they are used mostly by tool and driver developers. JDBC 3.0 introduces another kind of meta data, `ParameterMetaData`, which we will cover briefly in Chapter 13 on *Prepared Statements.*

DatabaseMetaData

As its name suggests, the `DatabaseMetaData` object provides information about the database. You get a `DatabaseMetaData` object from a `Connection` using:

```
DatabaseMetaData dbmd = connection.getMetaData();
```

By calling the methods of the `DatabaseMetadata` object, code can dynamically learn about a database, and adjust its actions accordingly. There are over 150 methods in the interface; therefore we don't have space to review them all. We will just look at a small sample. A few other methods will be presented in other chapters. You can check the Java documentation to see the complete list of all the methods that are available.

The `DatabaseMetaData` interface provides methods to gather information in the following general areas:

- The database and the user, database identifiers, and functions and stored procedures
- The features that are supported and not supported by the database
- The database limits, such as the maximum length of names in the database
- The schemas, catalogs, tables, and columns

Try It Out – Getting Database Meta Data

Here's a simple program that uses some of the methods from the first and second groups. This class connects to a database, and then gets a `DatabaseMetaData` object. Using this object, the class gets and prints information about the database and driver, and also information about whether the database driver supports updatable `ResultSet` objects or not. Save this program as `C:\BegJavaDB\Ch10\metadata\ShowDatabaseMetaData.java`:

```
package metadata;

import java.sql.*;
import connections.*;

public class ShowDatabaseMetaData {
  public static void main(String[] args) {
    Connection conn = null;

    try {
      conn = ConnectionFactory.getConnection();
      DatabaseMetaData dbmd = conn.getMetaData();

      System.out.println("Information about the database: ");
      System.out.println("Database name=[" + dbmd.getDatabaseProductName()
                         + "]");
      System.out.println("Database version=["
                         + dbmd.getDatabaseProductVersion() + "]");
      System.out.println("Driver name=[" + dbmd.getDriverName() + "]");
      System.out.println("Driver version=[" + dbmd.getDriverVersion()
                         + "]");
```

```
      System.out
        .println("Supports forward only ResultSet=["
                 + dbmd.supportsResultSetType(ResultSet.TYPE_FORWARD_ONLY)
                 + "]");
      System.out
        .println("Supports scroll sensitive ResultSet=["
               + dbmd.supportsResultSetType(ResultSet.TYPE_SCROLL_SENSITIVE)
                 + "]");
      System.out
        .println("Supports scroll insensitive ResultSet=["
             + dbmd.supportsResultSetType(ResultSet.TYPE_SCROLL_INSENSITIVE)
                 + "]");

      System.out
        .println("Supports updatable ResultSet=["
                 +
        dbmd.supportsResultSetConcurrency(ResultSet.TYPE_SCROLL_INSENSITIVE,
        ResultSet.CONCUR_UPDATABLE)
                 + "]");
      System.out.println("Supports ANSI92 entry=["
                         + dbmd.supportsANSI92EntryLevelSQL() + "]");
      System.out.println("Supports ANSI92 intermediate=["
                         + dbmd.supportsANSI92IntermediateSQL() + "]");
      System.out.println("Supports ANSI92 full=["
                         + dbmd.supportsANSI92FullSQL() + "]");
    } catch (Exception e) {
      e.printStackTrace();
    }
    finally {
      ConnectionFactory.close(conn);
    }
  }
}
```

This program uses the `ConnectionFactory` class to get a database connection. The `ConnectionFactory` class is shown next. This source should be saved as `C:\BegJavaDB\Ch10\connections\ConnectionFactory.java`:

```
package connections;

import java.sql.*;

public class ConnectionFactory {
  private static ConnectionFactory ref = new ConnectionFactory();
  private ConnectionFactory() {
    try {
      Class.forName("COM.cloudscape.core.JDBCDriver");
    } catch (ClassNotFoundException e) {
      System.out.println("ERROR: exception loading driver class");
    }
  }
```

```
    public static Connection getConnection() throws SQLException {
      String url = "jdbc:cloudscape:c:/BegJavaDB/Wrox4370.db";
      return DriverManager.getConnection(url);
    }

    public static void close(ResultSet rs) {
      try {
        rs.close();
      } catch (Exception ignored) {}
    }

    public static void close(Statement stmt) {
      try {
        stmt.close();
      } catch (Exception ignored) {}
    }

    public static void close(Connection conn) {
      try {
        conn.close();
      } catch (Exception ignored) {}
    }
  }
```

After compiling the Java code, we can execute the class against the Cloudscape database. Assuming that Cloudscape is installed into `C:\Cloudscape`, and the `ShowDatabaseMetaData` program is installed in `C:\BegJavaDB\Ch10\metadata`, you can use the following commands to execute the program from your `C:\BegJavaDB\Ch10` working directory:

```
> set classpath=C:\cloudscape\lib\cloudscape.jar;C:\BegJavaDB\Ch10
> java metadata.ShowDatabaseMetaData
```

If you are using a different database or driver, you may need to modify the classpath statement above to use the correct driver library. When the program runs, you should see output similar to the following:

```
Information about the database:
Database name=[DBMS:cloudscape]
Database version=[3.6.4]
Driver name=[Cloudscape Embedded JDBC Driver]
Driver version=[3.6]
Supports forward only ResultSet=[true]
Supports scroll sensitive ResultSet=[false]
Supports scroll insensitive ResultSet=[true]
Supports updatable ResultSet=[false]
Supports ANSI92 entry=[false]
Supports ANSI92 intermediate=[false]
Supports ANSI92 full=[false]
```

How It Works

The `ConnectionFactory` provides our connection to the database. The two methods of interest here are the constructor and `getConnection()`. The class has a static reference to an instance of itself. By coding a call to the constructor as part of the variable declaration, we ensure that the constructor is called before anything else occurs:

```
private static ConnectionFactory ref = new ConnectionFactory();
```

The JVM is required to initialize static members when the class is loaded, and before any methods are called. The initialization calls the constructor, which loads the driver class. If you are using this with a different database, you will need to change the driver name used in the constructor. The `getConnection()` method calls the `DriverManager.getConnection()` method with the database URL. Again, you will need to change this URL if you are using a different database. Any class that needs a connection simply calls the `ConnectionFactory.getConnection()` method.

The `ShowDatabaseMetaData` program calls the `getConnection()` method to get a connection to the database. It then calls the `Connection.getMetaData()` method to get the `DatabaseMetaData` object. With the meta data object, the program first calls some of the methods that provide information about the database and JDBC driver, and prints that information. Then it calls some of the methods that show what features the database and driver support. The program shows the information about whether the database supports scrolling and updating `ResultSets`, and which level of SQL-92 is supported.

Scrolling and updating `ResultSet` *objects are covered in Chapter 9,* Using Statements and ResultSets.

Getting a Table List

When I wrote the JDBC chapter for *Professional Oracle 8i Application Programming, ISBN 1-861004-84-2,* for Wrox Press, I developed an application for browsing the tables in a database. This was partly because I needed a meta data sample for the chapter, but also because, although I was frequently doing database work, I was often using a computer that did not have a tool such as `SQL*Plus` or Cloudview available for querying the database.

Here is a screenshot of the original user interface:

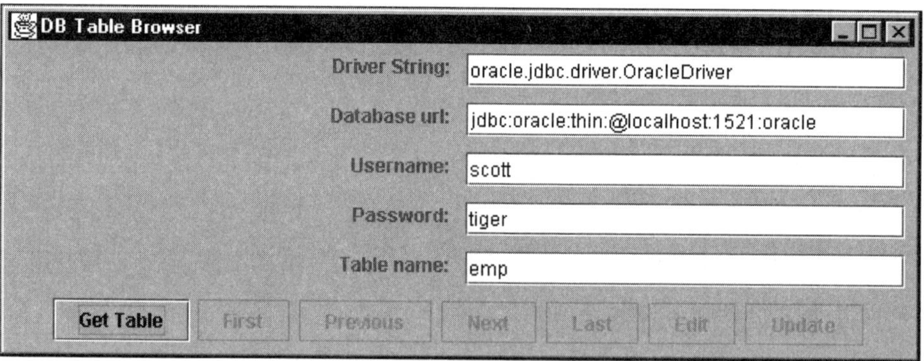

The original application required the user to enter the table name for viewing. After the book was published, I realized that this was not very user-friendly. If you tried to use the tool with an unfamiliar database, how would you know what tables were in the database? So, I updated the application to dynamically get the table names from the database. The revised user interface presents this list of tables to the user, and the user selects a table for viewing. Here is what the new user interface looks like:

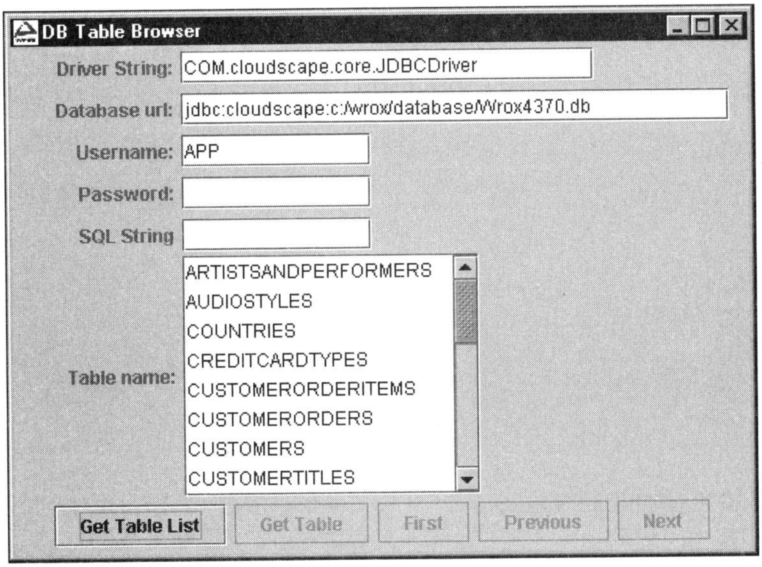

If you want to try the original application, you can download the sourcecode for Professional Oracle 8i Application Programming from http://www.wrox.com/.

Try It Out – Getting a List of Tables

We can create a small program that shows how any database browser tool can get the list of tables in a database. The program that follows does this through a `DatabaseMetaData` object. Save the program as `C:\BegJavaDB\Ch10\metadata\GetTableList.java`.

```
package metadata;

import java.sql.*;
import java.util.*;
import connections.*;

public class GetTableList {
  public static void main(String[] args) {
    Connection conn = null;
    ResultSet rset = null;

    try {
      conn = ConnectionFactory.getConnection();
      DatabaseMetaData dbmd = conn.getMetaData();

      String[] types = {
        "TABLE"
      };
      rset = dbmd.getTables(null, "APP", null, types);
      Vector v = new Vector();

      while (rset.next()) {
        String name = rset.getString("TABLE_NAME");
```

```
            v.add(name);
          }
          Collections.sort(v);
          System.out.println("All tables in schema APP:");
          System.out.println(v.toString());

        } catch (Exception e) {
          e.printStackTrace();
        }
        finally {
          ConnectionFactory.close(rset);
          ConnectionFactory.close(conn);
        }
      }
    }
```

Like the first program in this chapter, this program uses the `ConnectionFactory` class. Refer to the earlier *Try It Out – Getting Database Meta Data* section for details on this class. You should be able to run this program with the following commands:

```
> set classpath=C:\cloudscape\lib\cloudscape.jar; C:\BegJavaDB\Ch10
> java metadata.GetTableList
```

If you are using a different database or driver, you may need to modify the classpath statement above to use the correct driver library. When the program runs, you should see output similar to the following:

```
All tables in schema APP:

[ARTISTSANDPERFORMERS, AUDIOSTYLES, COUNTRIES, CREDITCARDTYPES,
CUSTOMERORDERITEMS, CUSTOMERORDERS, CUSTOMERS, CUSTOMERTITLES, CUSTOMERTYPES,
INVENTORIES, LANGUAGES, ORDERSOURCES, ORDERSTATUSES, PAYMENTTERMS, POSTALCODES,
PUBLISHERSANDLABELS, RECORDINGFORMATS, RECORDINGS, REVIEWS, SALESCAMPAIGNS,
STORES, STORETYPES, TRACKS]
```

How It Works

After getting a connection from the `ConnectionFactory`, the program gets a `DatabaseMetaData` object. The `DatabaseMetaData` object provides the `getTables()` method for getting the list of tables in a database. This method takes four parameters as follows:

- `String catalog` – indicates that the method should get tables from the given catalog. Empty String ("") means no catalog; Null means all catalogs.
- `String schema` – indicates that the method should get tables from the given schema. Empty String ("") means no schema; Null means all schemas. The parameter can include single character wildcards (underscore) or multi-character wildcards (percent sign).
- `String tableName` – indicates that the method should return tables where the table Name matches the parameter. The parameter can include single character wildcards (underscore) or multi-character wildcards (percent sign).

- `String[]` types – an array indicating what types of tables are returned. Possible array entries are `"TABLE"`, `"VIEW"`, `"SYSTEM TABLE"`, `"GLOBAL TEMPORARY"`, `"LOCAL TEMPORARY"`, `"ALIAS"`, `"SYNONYM"`.

Catalog and schema are ways that the database can provide a namespace. Users in one namespace cannot see objects in other namespaces, unless they have been granted permission or access. The schema usually corresponds to the login name; the catalog is a grouping of schemas.

The program called the `getTables()` method like this:

```
String[] types = {
  "TABLE"
};
rset = dbmd.getTables(null, "APP", null, types);
```

The catalog parameter was `null`, so the method gets tables from all catalogs. However, we supplied the String "`APP`" for the schema, so the method gets tables from only the APP schema. The third parameter was `null`, so the method gets tables with any name. The final parameter was the array with the single entry "`TABLE`", so the method gets only tables that have type `TABLE`.

The `getTables()` method is a little different from the methods we saw earlier. Instead of returning a `boolean` or a `String`, the method returns a `ResultSet`. Each row in the `ResultSet` has information about one table. Here are the columns in the `ResultSet` returned by the `getTables()` method.

- `TABLE_CAT` – The name of the catalog to which the table belongs
- `TABLE_SCHEM` – The name of the schema to which the table belongs
- `TABLE_NAME` – The name of the table
- `TABLE_TYPE` – The type of the table
- `REMARKS` – An explanatory comment

The program goes through the `ResultSet` and gets the table name from each row. The name is stored in a `Vector`. After all the table names are retrieved, the `Vector` is sorted and the contents are printed.

Printing the list of table names might be interesting, but by itself, it isn't particularly useful. It is in combining it with other actions that it becomes useful. In a database browser application, value is created by showing the user the table list and allowing the user to select a table for viewing. Another practical application for `DatabaseMetaData` is to reverse-engineer the SQL for a table. If you are in a situation where you need the SQL that creates a database (perhaps you need to recreate the database), but all you have is the database itself, you can use `DatabaseMetaData` to generate the SQL.

Using Meta Data for Schema Reverse-Engineering

In this part of the chapter, we will pull together many concepts that we have learned so far in the book and see how to use JDBC and JDBC meta data to reverse-engineer an existing database to find out what tables and columns make it up.

Suppose that you had been assigned to a project with a functional specification and an existing database to which the application needs to be adapted. Without the benefit of up-to-date documentation on the schema for the database, you will need some means of finding out its structure.

Luckily for us, the JDBC API was designed to support both the development of applications and the development of tools to support databases. It provides powerful mechanisms for introspection into data sources that allow you to discover database architectures on the fly.

You saw earlier that a `ResultSet` interface provided a method called `getMetaData`. This method returned an object implementing the `ResultSetMetaData` interface. That object stored information about the structure of the results of a query. The `Connection` interface also defines a method called `getMetaData`. This method returns an object that implements the `DatabaseMetadata` interface, which in turn can yield a wealth of information about the underlying database.

The `DatabaseMetaData` interface provides a number of methods that provide information about the database and the JDBC driver that connects our application to it. You can get information about the name and version of the driver, specific limitations of the driver (such as maximum number of simultaneous connections, any limitations on size of rows, and so on). Take a look at the documentation for `DatabaseMetaData` – there is a lot of useful (and for most of us, somewhat obscure) information available.

The information that we are interested in right now is the tables in the database and their structure. In fact, what we'd like to do is be able to feed the database to a Java program and have that program analyze the `DatabaseMetaData` to reverse-engineer the database. That is, to generate the SQL statements that would be used to create the database.

The first thing that this program needs to do is to find out what tables are in the database. As we saw earlier, the `DatabaseMetaData` interface defines a method called `getTables` that returns a `ResultSet` containing information for each column defined in the table. We can, in turn, use that information to examine the column names and their types.

Working with the meta data is no different from what you have seen in the previous examples in this book so far. The program simply has to iterate through the `ResultSet` and request information using the `getXXX( columnname )` methods. The only difference is that the column names are not defined by a table definition, but by the JDBC specification. Let's take a look at a code snippet that illustrates this:

```
DatabaseMetaData dbmd = databaseConnection.getMetaData();
String[] tableTypes = new String[] {"TABLE"};
ResultSet tables = dbmd.getTables( null,null,null,tableTypes);
Vector vtables = new Vector();

String aTable;

//build up a list of tables
while(tables.next()) {
  aTable = tables.getString("TABLE_NAME");
  vtables.add(aTable);
}
```

Note that inside the loop iterating through the `ResultSet`, the code is requesting a `String` for the column named `TABLE_NAME`. This is one of a number of column names that are defined for the meta data. Each method of the `DatabaseMetaData` that returns a `ResultsSet` defines the column names that you can query – all of these names are listed in the JDBC API documentation for each method.

Our application to reverse engineer the database is built on this pattern of looping through meta data `ResultSets` and extracting data. We shall use that data to build up SQL `CREATE TABLE` statements. Our strategy will be:

1. Get the names of all of the tables in the database.

2. For each table, get the name and type for each column. If the column type is size-constrained, get that information. If the column is required (that is, it can't be Null), we'll need that information too.

3. For each table identify which, if any, columns compose a primary key.

4. Use the information extracted in steps 1 to 3 to generate a statement in the form:

```
CREATE TABLE tablename ( colname coltype {NOT NULL}, ..., PRIMARY KEY (pkey1,
pk2...))
```

Try It Out – Generating SQL from Meta Data

Here is the sourcecode for the next example, which will generate SQL to create the tables from meta data. Save this source code as `C:\BegJavaDB\Ch10\metadata\GenSql.java`:

```
package metadata;

import java.util.*;
import java.sql.*;
import connections.*;

public class GenSql {
  public static void main(String args[]) {
    Connection conn = null;

    try {
      conn = ConnectionFactory.getConnection();
      DatabaseMetaData dbmd = conn.getMetaData();

      String[] tableTypes = new String[] {
        "TABLE"
      };
      ResultSet tables = dbmd.getTables(null, "APP", null, tableTypes);
      Vector vtables = new Vector();

      String aTable;

      // build up a list of tables
      while (tables.next()) {
        aTable = tables.getString("TABLE_NAME");
        vtables.add(aTable);
      }

      ConnectionFactory.close(tables);
```

```
Iterator iterator = vtables.iterator();

// for each table in the list...
String separator;
while (iterator.hasNext()) {
  aTable = (String) iterator.next();

  // print the create table...
  System.out.print("create table " + aTable + " (");

  // print the columns
  ResultSet columns = dbmd.getColumns(null, null, aTable, null);
  separator = "";
  while (columns.next()) {
    String aColumn;

    System.out.print(separator);
    System.out.print(columns.getString("COLUMN_NAME"));

    int dataType = columns.getInt("DATA_TYPE");
    System.out.print(" " + columns.getString("TYPE_NAME"));

    if (dataType == java.sql.Types.CHAR
            || dataType == java.sql.Types.VARCHAR) {
      System.out.print("(" + columns.getString("COLUMN_SIZE") + ")");
    }

    String isNullable = columns.getString("IS_NULLABLE");
    if (isNullable.equalsIgnoreCase("no")) {
      System.out.print(" NOT NULL");
    }

    separator = ", ";
  }

  // print the primary keys
  ResultSet pkeys = dbmd.getPrimaryKeys(null, null, aTable);
  String pkInfo = ", primary key(";

  separator = "";
  int pkCount = 0;
  while (pkeys.next()) {
    pkInfo = pkInfo.concat(separator
                          + pkeys.getString("COLUMN_NAME"));
    separator = ", ";
    pkCount++;
  }
  pkInfo = pkInfo.concat(")");

  // if there were primary keys defined, add the pk statement
  if (pkCount > 0) {
    System.out.print(pkInfo);

  }
```

```
          System.out.println(")\n");
        }
      } catch (Exception e) {
        e.printStackTrace();
      }
      finally {
        ConnectionFactory.close(conn);
      }
    }
  }
```

Like the other programs in this chapter, this program again uses the `ConnectionFactory` class to get a connection. Refer to the first *Try It Out* section for details on the `ConnectionFactory` class. You should be able to run this program with the following commands.

```
> set classpath=C:\cloudscape\lib\cloudscape.jar;C:\BegJavaDB\Ch10
> java metadata.GenSql
```

If you are using a different database or driver, you may need to modify the `ConnectionFactory` and `classpath` statement above to use the correct driver library. When the program runs, it should produce the output:

```
create table ARTISTSANDPERFORMERS (ARTISTID INT NOT NULL, ARTISTNAME VARCHAR(50)
NOT NULL, ARTISTIMAGEFILESPEC VARCHAR(50), ARTISTBIOTEXT VARCHAR(5000), primary
key(ARTISTID))

create table AUDIOSTYLES (AUDIOSTYLEID INT NOT NULL, AUDIOSTYLEDESCRIPTION
VARCHAR(25) NOT NULL, primary key(AUDIOSTYLEID))

create table COUNTRIES (COUNTRYID INT NOT NULL, COUNTRYABBREV VARCHAR(3),
COUNTRYNAME VARCHAR(50) NOT NULL, primary key(COUNTRYID))

create table CREDITCARDTYPES (CREDITCARDTYPEID INT NOT NULL, CREDITCARDDESCRIPTION
VARCHAR(30) NOT NULL, primary key(CREDITCARDTYPEID))

create table CUSTOMERORDERITEMS (ORDERID INT NOT NULL, LINENUMBER INT NOT NULL,
PRODUCTID INT NOT NULL, QUANTITY INT NOT NULL, PRICEPERITEM DOUBLE PRECISION NOT
NULL, PROVIDINGSTORE INT NOT NULL, primary key(LINENUMBER, ORDERID))

...
```

How It Works

This program uses three methods of the `DatabaseMetaData` object to reverse engineer the table:

- `getTables()`
- `getColumns()`
- `getPrimaryKeys()`

Each of these methods returns a resultset, which contains information about the relevant database feature.

The program first loops through the table's resultset to build up a vector of all of the table names. It does this by calling `getString("TABLE_NAME")` on the ResultSet object. The `TABLE_NAME` column contains the names of all the tables in the database that match the criteria used in the `getTables()` method call. We will need these to query the meta data for each table.

Next, the program calls the `getColumns()` method of the `DatabaseMetaData` object. This returns a `ResultSet` that contains all of the information needed for each column's definition. The name and data type are extracted by calling `getString("COLUMN_NAME")` and `getString("TYPE_NAME")` and concatenated onto the SQL statement. The program also calls `getInt("DATA_TYPE")`. If the data type is `CHAR` or `VARCHAR`, the program checks the value for the column's `COLUMN_SIZE` property to append to the data type. If the `IS_NULLABLE` property of the column is `False`, this indicates that a value is mandatory. A `NOT NULL` expression is concatenated to the column definition to reflect that.

For each table, the program calls the `getPrimaryKeys()` method of the `DatabaseMetaData` object. This produces a `ResultSet` object containing information about the primary key, if one has been specified for the table.

After all of the column definitions have been generated, we are just about done. If the primary key column count is greater than zero (we kept track of this while walking the `ResultSet` obtained from `getPrimaryKeys()`), then we'll concatenate a `PRIMARY KEY` expression to the table definition. After the program outputs the full SQL statement for the table, the process starts again for the next table.

The `DatabaseMetaData` object provides a lot of information about the database, the tables in the database, and the features supported by the database. However, there is also information that it can't provide. For instance, if you look at the SQL created by the example program above, you will notice that it doesn't show that the ID fields are autoincrement fields. Other information it can't provide is whether the column is searchable, is writeable, or is read-only. This information can be obtained, but not from the `DatabaseMetaData` object; it is only available through a different meta data object – `ResultSetMetaData`.

ResultSetMetaData

As you might guess from the title of this section, you can also get meta data information about a resultset. `ResultSetMetaData` contains information about the types and properties of the columns in the resultset. Even though the columns in a `ResultSet` usually contain column data from tables in the database, `ResultSetMetaData` represents more than just information about a table or tables. A resultset can contain information derived from tables (sum, count, and so on), so `ResultSetMetaData` can contain information about columns in the `ResultSet` that do not appear as columns in any table.

A `ResultSetMetaData` object is obtained by a call to a `ResultSet` object:

```
ResultSet rs = statement.executeQuery(sql);
ResultSetMetaData rsmd = rs.getMetaData();
```

Since you can also obtain a `ResultSet` from `PreparedStatements` and `CallableStatements`, you can get meta data about the queries executed by any kind of statement object. By calling methods of the `ResultSetMetData` interface, you can get information about the table and columns returned by a query. Let's have a look at this in action.

Try It Out – Using ResultSet Meta Data

The class below gets a ResultSetMetaData object and uses it to learn about the columns in a ResultSet. Save this file as C:\BegJavaDB\Ch10\metadata\GetResultSetMetaDataOne.java.

```
package metadata;

import java.sql.*;
import java.util.*;
import connections.*;

public class GetResultSetMetaDataOne {
  public static void main (String[] args) {
    Connection conn = null;
    Statement stmt = null;
    ResultSet rset = null;

    try {
      conn = ConnectionFactory.getConnection();
      stmt = conn.createStatement();
      String sql = "select artistid, artistname, artistimagefilespec,
artistbiotext from artistsandperformers";
      rset = stmt.executeQuery(sql);
      ResultSetMetaData rsmd = rset.getMetaData();

      int cols = rsmd.getColumnCount();
      for (int i = 1; i <= cols; i++) {
        System.out.println("Column " + i);
        System.out.println("Name: " + rsmd.getColumnName(i));
        System.out.println("Table Name: " + rsmd.getTableName(i));
        System.out.println("Schema Name: " + rsmd.getSchemaName(i));
        System.out.println("Class: " + rsmd.getColumnClassName(i));
        System.out.println("Type: " + rsmd.getColumnType(i));
        System.out.println("Type name: " + rsmd.getColumnTypeName(i));
        System.out.println("Auto increment: " + rsmd.isAutoIncrement(i));
        System.out.print("Is nullable: ");
        switch (rsmd.isNullable(i)) {
          case ResultSetMetaData.columnNoNulls:
            System.out.println("No Nulls");
            break;
          case ResultSetMetaData.columnNullable:
            System.out.println("Nullable");
            break;

          case ResultSetMetaData.columnNullableUnknown:
            System.out.println("Unknown");
            break;
        }
        System.out.println();
      }
    } catch (Exception e) {
      e.printStackTrace();
    } finally {
      ConnectionFactory.close(rset);
```

```
            ConnectionFactory.close(stmt);
            ConnectionFactory.close(conn);
          }
        }
      }
```

This class uses a `ConnectionFactory` to get a database connection. Refer to the first example in this chapter for details about the `ConnectionFactory` class. Executing the program using something similar to the following:

```
  > java metadata.GetResultSetMetaDataOne
```

results in this output:

```
Column 1
Name: ARTISTID
Table Name: ARTISTSANDPERFORMERS
Schema Name:
Class: java.lang.Integer
Type: 4
Type name: INT
Auto increment: true
Is nullable: No Nulls

Column 2
Name: ARTISTNAME
Table Name: ARTISTSANDPERFORMERS
Schema Name:
Class: java.lang.String
Type: 12
Type name: VARCHAR
Auto increment: false
Is nullable: No Nulls

Column 3
Name: ARTISTIMAGEFILESPEC
Table Name: ARTISTSANDPERFORMERS
Schema Name:
Class: java.lang.String
Type: 12
Type name: VARCHAR
Auto increment: false
Is nullable: Nullable

Column 4
Name: ARTISTBIOTEXT
Table Name: ARTISTSANDPERFORMERS
Schema Name:
Class: java.lang.String
Type: 12
Type name: VARCHAR
Auto increment: false
Is nullable: Nullable
      " " " " " "
```

How It Works

After getting the `Statement` object from the `Connection`, the program executes a query. Note that the query does *not* need to return any rows. The query we executed does not return any rows from the database, yet the `ResultSetMetadata` object is still created with information about the columns that are in the resultset.

The program then uses some of the `ResultSetMetaData` methods to reveal information about the `ResultSet`. It starts by getting the number of columns in the `ResultSet`. Then for each column, it retrieves the column name, the table name, and the schema name. For this query we selected from a single table, so the table name and schema name information is not very interesting. However, if we had performed a join query where we selected columns from two or more tables, the schema name and table name information would help us determine where each column came from. For example, if we change the query to select from two tables like this:

```
      stmt = conn.createStatement();
      String sql =
        " select recordings.recordingid, tracks.tracknumber from" +
        "recordings, tracks where recordings.recordingid=-1";
      rset = stmt.executeQuery(sql);
```

and save it as `C:\BegJavaDB\Ch10\metadata\GetResultSetMetaDataTwo.java`, as well as changing the name of the public class to `GetResultSetMetaDataTwo`, then the table information becomes more useful:

```
> java metadata.GetResultSetMetaDataTwo


Column 1
Name: RECORDINGID
Table Name: RECORDINGS
Schema Name:
Class: java.lang.Integer
Type: 4
Type name: INT
Auto increment: true
Is nullable: No Nulls

Column 2
Name: TRACKNUMBER
Table Name: TRACKS
Schema Name:
Class: java.lang.Integer
Type: 4
Type name: INT
Auto increment: false
Is nullable: No Nulls
```

After the table and schema information, the program prints information about the Java type of the column data, and the SQL type code and type name. The last information it prints is whether the column is an `autoincrement` field (the `artistid` field is) and whether the column can be Null.

Summary

In this chapter we have quickly touched upon some of the features of meta data:

- `DatabaseMetaData` is created by the `getMetaData()` method of the `Connection` object.
- `DatabaseMetaData` provides information about the database and the JDBC driver, information about the features supported by a database and driver, and information about the tables and other objects in the database.
- `ResultSetMetaData` provides information about the columns in a `ResultSet` object.
- Meta data can be used to dynamically discover the structure of databases and tables. Meta data can also be used to reverse-engineer databases. Any time your application needs information about a database, but that information is only available at run time, you can use meta data to obtain the information.

akarta
JAVA
Java

Using Rowsets

As we have seen, the ResultSet is a very useful object for data retrieval. However, one limitation of the ResultSet is that it must remain connected to the data source, and is therefore not serializable for passing across a network. Fortunately, starting with JDBC 2.0, you can implement a new RowSet interface, javax.sql.rowset, in your JDBC code that will allow you to do just this.

An implementation of RowSet can be serializable and, in addition, the RowSet interface extends the ResultSet interface, defining new capabilities. The RowSet can be scrollable and updatable, even when the database or driver does not support scrolling or updating. A RowSet can be connected to the database (like a ResultSet) or it can cache the query results and disconnect from the database once it has the data.

In this chapter, we will introduce rowsets and the RowSet interface and then explore three specific rowset implementations:

- The CachedRowSet class
- The JdbcRowSet class
- The WebRowSet class

An Introduction to RowSets

Simply stated, a RowSet is a collection of rows. The RowSet package implements a custom reader for accessing any data in tabular format, thus making it possible to connect to virtually any tabular data source, including files and spread sheets, not just data in a relational database.

Unlike a ResultSet object, a RowSet object is a JavaBeans component. Therefore, it has the same model for properties and event notification. Additionally, unlike the ResultSet, a RowSet may operate without being connected to its data source. Programmers can use it as part of a development tool to create a RowSet object and set its properties.

A RowSet implementation can be serialized and therefore sent across a network, which is particularly useful for small-footprint clients that want to operate on tabular data without incurring the overhead of a JDBC driver and data source connection. Basically a disconnected RowSet gets a connection to a data source in order to fill itself with data, and can then close the connection.

A `RowSet` object can also update its rows while it is disconnected from its data source, and its implementation can include a custom writer that writes those updates back to the underlying data source, but most of the time it does not have a connection open. While it is disconnected, it does not need a JDBC driver or the full JDBC API, so its footprint is very small. Thus a `RowSet` is an ideal format for sending data over a network to a thin client.

Since it is not continually connected to its data source, a disconnected `RowSet` stores its data in memory. It needs to maintain meta data about the columns it contains, and information about its internal state. It also needs a facility for making connections, for executing commands, and for reading and writing data to and from the data source. A connected `RowSet`, by contrast, opens a connection and keeps it open for as long as the `RowSet` is in use.

A `RowSet` can provide scrollable resultsets or updatable resultsets even when the underlying JDBC driver does not support them.

A `RowSet` is derived from the class `BaseRowSet`, which provides the basic functionality that makes all `RowSet` objects JavaBeans components. A `RowSet` has `setXXX()` methods to set the properties that supply what is necessary for making a connection to a database and executing a query. A `RowSet` that does not need to establish a connection and execute a command, such as one that gets its data from a tabular file instead of a relational database, does not need to have these properties set.

Once a `RowSet` gets populated on the execution of a query or from some other data source, its column values can be updated, and its rows can be inserted or deleted. Since we can add listeners to the `RowSet`, any method that causes a change in the `RowSet`'s values or cursor position automatically notifies the object that has been registered as a listener with the `RowSet`.

As the `RowSet` object is implemented on top of a driver and, like drivers, anyone could implement a `RowSet`. However, they are generally implemented by a driver vendor. Sun, for example, provides three sample implementations of the `RowSet` interface:

- `CachedRowSet` – A disconnected `RowSet` that keeps its data in memory. A `CachedRowSet` is scrollable and serialize. It is thus ideal for a sending tabular data to a thin java client like a Personal Digital Assistant or a browser.
- `JDBCRowSet` – An example of a `RowSet` that always maintains a connection to its data source while it is in use. It can be used to provide a thin layer around a JDBC `ResultSet` object at run-time and thereby make a JDBC technology-based driver look like a JavaBeans component. Thus, a `JDBCRowSet` object could be one of the components a visual development tool makes available for assembling an application.
- `WebRowSet` – A `RowSet` that can produce a representation of its contents in an XML format. Since `WebRowSet` is an extension of `CachedRowSet`, they are quite similar in implementation. `WebRowSet` is an excellent vehicle for providing data to a thin client, using the HTTP/XML for communication and transmission.

Do bear in mind that the features provided by a `RowSet` object are implementation-dependent, so always check the documentation for your particular `RowSet` object for details.

The following simple class diagram illustrates the relationship between these `RowSet` implementations:

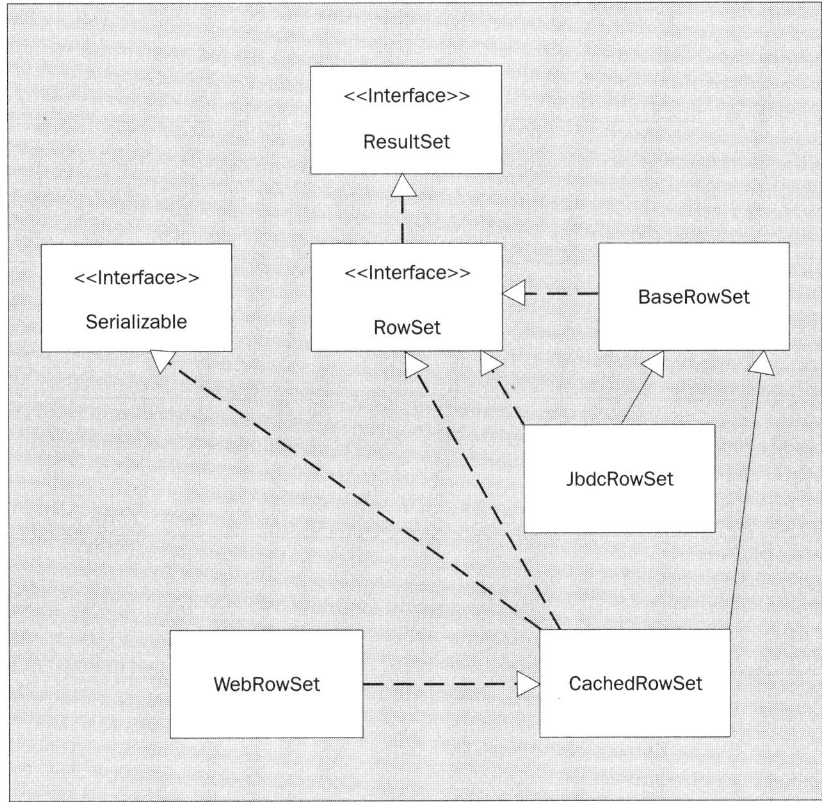

Note that this diagram is intentionally simple, and doesn't show any information about methods or variables.

To use these implementations in the code in this chapter, you will need to download the classes from Sun's early access web site at http://developer.java.sun.com/developer/earlyAccess/crs/index.html.

To access this site, you will need to be a registered member of the Java Developer Connection, but this is both free and a simple process. The classes are contained in a `.zip` file that you will download from Sun. After the file is downloaded, you need to extract the `rowset.jar` file to your file system, and adjust the classpath to include the JAR file. For example, if you extract `rowset.jar` to the directory `c:\java\jdbc\lib`, you would set the classpath like this:

```
set classpath=%classpath%;c:\java\jdbc\lib\rowset.jar
```

If you are using an IDE or are developing in a UNIX environment, you will need to set the classpath in a manner that is appropriate for your environment. Several other libraries are needed for the examples in this chapter:

- `jndi.jar` (http://java.sun.com/products/jndi/#download).
- `jdbc2_0-stdext.jar` (http://java.sun.com/products/jdbc/download.html).

- The library containing the JDBC driver for your database (should come with the database).
- `crimson.jar`, which is available as part of the JAXP (Java API for XML Processing). You can download the JAXP from Sun (http://java.sun.com/xml/download.html – note that this file is 1.5 MB in size).

After downloading the JNDI, JDBC Standard Extension, and JAXP libraries, extract the JAR files to your file system and set the classpath to include those libraries. You may find it helpful to place all the JAR files in a common directory such as `c:\java\lib`.

The RowSet Interface

The `javax.sql.RowSet` interface extends the `java.sql.ResultSet` interface, so right off the bat, a `RowSet` class can do everything that a `ResultSet` class can do because it inherits all the `ResultSet` methods. We can navigate through a `RowSet` using the `next()` and `previous()` methods, and the other navigation methods presented in the earlier chapter. When the `RowSet` contains the results of a query as opposed to being empty or holding information for updating the table, we can get the column values using the same `getXXX()` methods of the `ResultSet`. This is illustrated in the following class diagram:

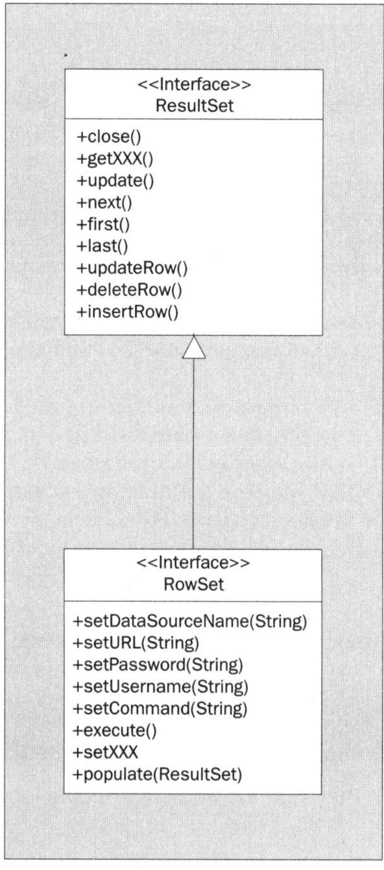

So, once a RowSet has been populated with data (and we'll see how below), we call the next() method to advance to the next row in the RowSet. We call a getXXX() method to get a column value. Examples of getXXX() methods are getArray(), getBigDecimal(), getBinaryStream(), getDate(), getObject(), etc. If we want to update a row we call updateRow(); and when we are finished with the RowSet, we call the close() method.

But wait... there's more! A RowSet can also be used to connect to a database and execute a SQL statement. So even though it does not extend the Connection or Statement interface (because Java classes and interfaces can only extend a single other class or interface), it does have some behavior that is similar to the Connection and Statement objects.

If we look at the class diagram, we'll see that the RowSet has methods named setDataSourceName(), setURL(), setUsername(), and setPassword(). These methods are used to prepare a RowSet object to make a connection to a data source. It also has a setCommand() method for setting the SQL string to be executed, and an execute() method to execute the SQL. When setting the command, you can use a SQL string with placeholders, just like the SQL string you would use with a PreparedStatement (see the PreparedStatement chapter for more information on placeholders). The RowSet interface provides the setXXX() methods to set the values of the placeholders.

The CachedRowSet Class

A RowSet could hold a connection to the data source or could be disconnected depending on the implementation and application demands. In case the client has limited resources, the CachedRowSet becomes an ideal format to send information over the network and helps to keep the memory footprint small.

Since it implements the RowSet interface (and hence the ResultSet interface), we can navigate through a CachedRowSet using the next() and previous() methods, and the other navigation methods. When the CachedRowSet contains the results of a query, we can get the column values using the same get() methods of the ResultSet.

Since the CachedRowSet is a JavaBean it has a simple default constructor to create an instance. Now the application programmer can set the instance properties to suit the application requirements.

The CachedRowSet is a **disconnected** RowSet. The advantages of a CachedRowSet are that it does not need a permanent connection to the database, because it caches the data in the memory. It is not suitable for very large data sets, but very useful for sending tabular data to thin clients. CachedRowSets even enable storing data on a disconnected client and using it offline later. This means that once the RowSet reads the data, the connection to the data source can be closed, and the RowSet will retain the results. Also, the CachedRowSet is serializable. Although the CachedRowSet implements the RowSet interface, it also extends the BaseRowSet class as show in the following diagram:

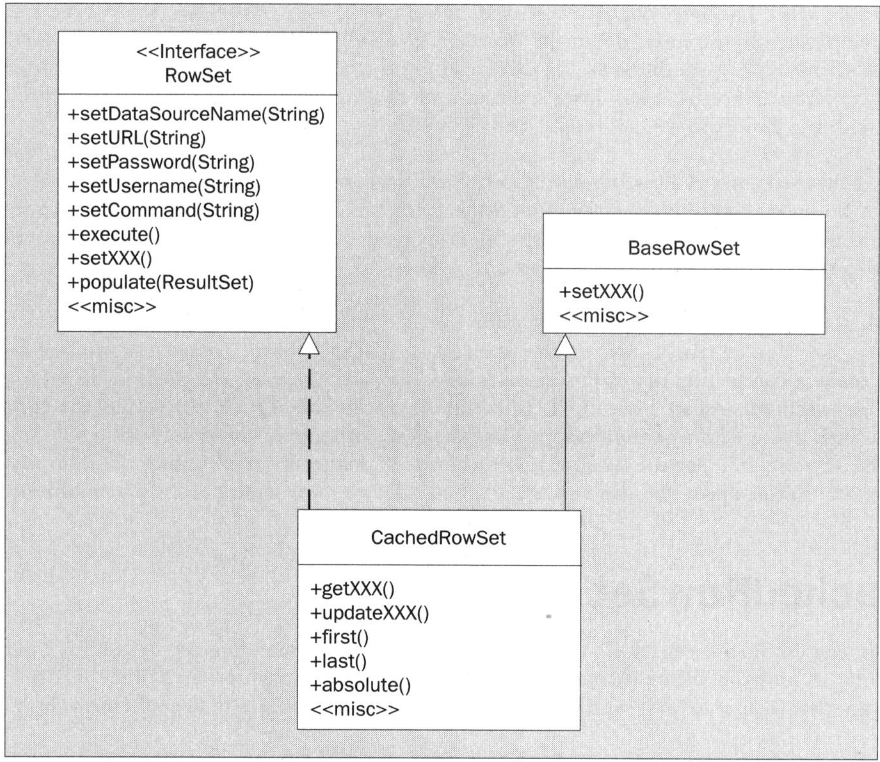

The BaseRowSet is an abstract class that, as the name implies, provides the base functionality for the RowSet implementations. Even though the BaseRowSet does not implement the RowSet interface, it provides method bodies for many of the methods required by the RowSet interface. The CachedRowSet provides the implementation for all the getXXX(), updateXXX(), and row movement methods required by the RowSet and ResultSet interfaces. Examples of updateXXX() include updateBigDecimal(), updateBinaryStream(), updateDate(), updateLong(), updateObject(), and so on.

The CachedRowSet defines three types of ResultSet: forward-only, scroll-insensitive, and scroll-sensitive. As the name suggests, a forward-only ResultSet can only move the cursor forward. A scroll-insensitive ResultSet can move both backward and forward but is insensitive to changes committed by other transactions or other statements within the same transaction. A scroll-sensitive ResultSet can move both backward and forward, and is sensitive to changes committed by other transactions, or other statements within the same transaction.

For each ResultSet type, an application may choose from two different concurrency types for a ResultSet: read-only or updateable. A read-only ResultSet does not support update of its contents; an updateable ResultSet supports updating its contents through the ResultSet. The following lines of code make the CachedRowSet instance scrollable and updateable:

```
CachedRowSet cacheRowSet = new CachedRowSet();
cacheRowSet.setType(ResultSet.TYPE_SCROLL_INSENSITIVE);
cacheRowSet.setConcurrency(ResultSet.CONCUR_UPDATABLE);
```

After a query has been executed, we can verify the ResultSet type and concurrency type that the JDBC driver actually used, by calling one of the following methods on the ResultSet object:

```
int getType() throws SQLException
```

This method returns an int value for the ResultSet type used for the query. The possible values are ResultSet.TYPE_FORWARD_ONLY, ResultSet.TYPE_SCROLL_SENSITIVE, or ResultSet.TYPE_SCROLL_INSENSITIVE.

```
int getConcurrency() throws SQLException
```

This method returns an int value for the concurrency type used for the query. Possible values are ResultSet.CONCUR_READ_ONLY or ResultSet.CONCUR_UPDATABLE.

In a scrollable ResultSet, we can use several ResultSet methods to move to a desired position and to check the current position. The following ResultSet methods are available for moving to a new position in a scrollable ResultSet:

- beforeFirst() – Positions to before the first row of the ResultSet, or has no effect if there are no rows in the ResultSet.
- afterLast() – Positions to after the last row of the ResultSet, or has no effect if there are no rows in the ResultSet.
- first() – Positions to the first row of the ResultSet, or returns False if there are no rows in the ResultSet.
- Last() – Positions to the last row of the result set, or returns False if there are no rows in the ResultSet.
- absolute() – Positions to an absolute row from either the beginning or end of the ResultSet. If we input a positive number, it positions from the beginning; if we input a negative number, it positions from the end. This method returns False if there are no rows in the ResultSet. Calling absolute(1) is equivalent to calling first(); calling absolute(-1) is equivalent to calling last().
- relative() – Moves to a position relative to the current row, either forward if you input a positive number or backward if we input a negative number, or returns false if there are no rows in the ResultSet.

In a scrollable resultset we can iterate backward instead of forward as you process the ResultSet. The following methods are available:

```
boolean next() throws SQLException
boolean previous() throws SQLException
```

The previous() method works similarly to the next() method, in that it returns True as long as the new current row is valid, and False as soon as it runs out of rows (has passed the first row).

There is more than one way to get data into a RowSet object; the easiest is by using the RowSet to connect to and query a database. There is another way to get query data into a RowSet implementation. This other technique is to pass a ResultSet object to the RowSet through the populate() method. When using this technique, you, as the developer, must make the connection, execute the query, and pass the ResultSet object to the RowSet. Here's a code snippet using a CachedRowSet that shows this technique:

```
    Statement statement = connection.createStatement();
    String sql = "select * from Stores";
    ResultSet resultSet = statement.executeQuery(sql);
    CachedRowSet cachedRs = new CachedRowSet();
    cachedRs.populate(resultSet);
```

Try It Out – CachedRowSet

The first example will be accessing the Music Store Cloudscape database for this book; you will need `cloudscape.jar` to run the example. If you are using a different database, you will need the appropriate JAR file for your database.

This example will use the `CachedRowSet` implementation.

The following program creates a connection, and passes that connection to the `CachedRowSet`. The `CachedRowSet` uses the connection to send a query the database. The connection is closed immediately after the `CachedRowSet` queries the database and acquires the data. After the connection is closed, the query results are read and displayed.

```
// rowset/CachedRowSetExample.java
package rowset;

import java.io.*;
import java.sql.*;
import javax.sql.*;
import sun.jdbc.rowset.*;

public class CachedRowSetExample {
  CachedRowSet cachedRs;

  public static void main(String[] args) {
    CachedRowSetExample crse = new CachedRowSetExample();
    try {
      crse.populateRowSet();
      boolean done = false;
      BufferedReader in =
        new BufferedReader(new InputStreamReader(System.in));
      while (!done) {
        System.out.print("Enter a row number (0 to exit) : ");
        String s = in.readLine();
        int result = new Integer(s).intValue();
        if (result == 0) {
          done = true;
        } else {
          crse.showRow(result);
        }
      }
    } catch (Exception e) {
      e.printStackTrace();
    }
  }

  void populateRowSet() throws ClassNotFoundException, SQLException {
    Class.forName("COM.cloudscape.core.JDBCDriver");
    String url = "jdbc:cloudscape:c:/wrox/database/Wrox4370.db";
    String username = "wrox";
    String password = "jdbc";
```

```
      Connection connection =
        DriverManager.getConnection(url, username, password);

      cachedRs = new CachedRowSet();
      String sql = "SELECT * from Stores";
      cachedRs.setCommand(sql);
      cachedRs.execute(connection);
      connection.close();
    }

    void showRow(int row) throws SQLException {
      try {
        cachedRs.absolute(row);
      } catch (SQLException e) {
        System.out.println("Caught exception. Row =[" + row +
                           "], message=[" + e.getMessage() + "]");
        String message = e.getMessage().toLowerCase();
        if (message.indexOf("invalid cursor position") == -1) {
          // If it is not an invalid position, re-throw the exception
          throw e;
        }
      }

      if (cachedRs.isBeforeFirst()) {
        System.out.println("Index " + row + " is before first row");
      } else if (cachedRs.isAfterLast()) {
        System.out.println("Index " + row + " is after last row");
      } else {
        System.out.println("StoreId : " + cachedRs.getInt("StoreID") +
                           " :: StoreDescription : " +
                           cachedRs.getString("StoreDescription"));
      }
    }
  }
```

Assuming you have extracted all the required libraries to the directory `c:\java\lib`, and the class file is in `c:\BegJavaDB\Ch11\rowset`, you can use the following batch file to execute the program:

```
set classpath=%CLASSPATH%;c:\java\lib\cloudscape.jar;c:\java\lib\jdbc2_0-
stdext.jar;c:\java\lib\rowset.jar;c:\java\lib\jndi.jar;c:\java\examples

java rowset.CachedRowSetExample
```

Note that the first two lines are really one continuous line that is too long to fit on a single line. IDE users or users with a different OS will need to adjust the commands for their environment.

When you run the program, the output will look something like this:

```
Enter a row number (0 to exit) : 4
StoreId : 6 :: StoreDescription : New England Warehouse
Enter a row number (0 to exit) : 2
StoreId : 4 :: StoreDescription : Manhattan
Enter a row number (0 to exit) : -1
Index -1 is before first row
Enter a row number (0 to exit) : 0
```

How It Works

The `main()` method creates an instance of the class and calls the `populateRowSet()` method. This method creates a connection to the database using the common `Class.forName()` and `DriverManager.getConnection()` technique. The example uses the Music Store Cloudscape database from this book. If you use a different database, you will need to adjust the driver name and connection URL for your database.

```
void populateRowSet() throws ClassNotFoundException, SQLException {
  Class.forName("COM.cloudscape.core.JDBCDriver");
  String url = "jdbc:cloudscape:c:/wrox/database/Wrox4370.db";
```

Then an instance of `CachedRowSet` is created and the SQL string is passed to the `setCommand()` method as shown in the snippet below. When the `execute(Connection)` method is called, the `RowSet` sends the SQL string to the database.

```
  cachedRs = new CachedRowSet();
  String sql = "select * from Stores";
  cachedRs.setCommand(sql);
  cachedRs.execute(connection);
```

Since a `Connection` object was passed as a parameter to the method, the `CachedRowSet` uses the given connection to interact with the database. If on the other hand, the no-argument version `execute()` had been called, the `CachedRowSet` would have tried to establish its own connection.

It would do this by looking up a `DataSource` using the name provided by a call to `setDataSourceName(String)` and JNDI. More information on using `DataSources` can be found in Chapter 18, *JDBC Data Sources.*

Finally, the connection is closed. Closing the connection also closes any `ResultSet` obtained through the connection. When this occurs, the `ResultSet` can no longer be used to get the column and row data. However, the `CachedRowSet` reads all the data into memory so it can be used to get the data:

```
  connection.close();
```

> **Since the `CachedRowSet` reads all the data into memory, it is unsuitable for use with queries that will return large numbers of rows. The exact value of that large number will vary depending on your database and operating environment.**

Back in the `main()` method, the code goes into a loop to accept user input. The code asks the user for a row number. If the user enters a valid non-zero number, the code calls the `showRow()` method to show the desired row. The `showRow()` method uses only one of the scrolling methods defined in the `ResultSet` interface: `absolute(int)`. The `RowSet` interface inherits this method from the `ResultSet` interface. This method moves the position of the `RowSet` to the row given by the `int` parameter in the method call. Only positive row numbers are accepted by this `CachedRowSet` implementation. Negative row numbers move the `RowSet` to a position before the first row.

The Javadoc for `CachedRowSet` states that calling `absolute()` with a negative row number `n` will move the `RowSet` to the `n`th row from the end. However, when this was tested with the `CachedRowSetExample` program, the behavior was as described in the previous paragraph: only positive row numbers move to the correct row.

```
void showRow(int row) throws SQLException {
  try {
    cachedRs.absolute(row);
  } catch (SQLException e) {
    String message = e.getMessage().toLowerCase();
    if (message.indexOf("invalid cursor position") == -1) {
//if it's not an invalid position, rethrow the exception
throw e;
    }
  }
```

If the call to `absolute(int)` throws an exception, the exception is checked. If it is an invalid position exception, we trap the exception. The invalid position will be handled later in the method. If the exception is anything else, it is rethrown.

The code in the `showRow()` method then calls the `isBeforeFirst()` and `isAfterLast()` methods to determine if the call to `absolute()` moved the `CachedRowSet` to an invalid row. This also ensures that the `CachedRowSet` is on a valid row before the code gets the column data. The code gets two pieces of data from the query results, the store ID, and the store description. It uses the `getInt()` and `getString()` method calls for this. These are two more `ResultSet` methods inherited by the `RowSet` interface.

```
    if (cachedRs.isBeforeFirst()) {
      System.out.println("Index " + row + " is before first row");
    } else if (cachedRs.isAfterLast()) {
      System.out.println("Index " + row + " is after last row");
    } else {
      System.out.println("StoreId : " + cachedRs.getInt("StoreID") +
       " :: StoreDescription : " +
       cachedRs.getString("StoreDescription"));
    }
  }
}
```

As mentioned, there are other ways to populate a `RowSet` with data. In the example above, the `CachedRowSet` sent the SQL string to the database and parsed the `ResultSet`. Another way is for the calling code to get a `ResultSet`, and pass the `ResultSet` to the `RowSet`. The `CachedRowSetExample` code can be easily modified to populate the `RowSet` with an existing `ResultSet` using the `populate()` method. To try this out, modify the `populateRowSet()` method like this:

```
void populateRowSet() throws ClassNotFoundException, SQLException {
  Class.forName("COM.cloudscape.core.JDBCDriver");
  String url = "jdbc:cloudscape:c:/wrox/database/Wrox4370.db";
  String username = "wrox";
  String password = "jdbc";
  Connection connection =
    DriverManager.getConnection(url, username, password);
  cachedRs = new CachedRowSet();
  String sql = "select * from Stores";
  Statement statement = connection.createStatement();
```

```
        ResultSet resultSet = statement.executeQuery(sql);
        cachedRs.populate(resultSet);
        connection.close();
    }
```

Instead of passing a SQL string to the RowSet for execution, the code above gets a ResultSet from the database and passes it to the CachedRowSet. The CachedRowSet then parses the ResultSet, just as in the original example.

The JdbcRowSet Class

The JdbcRowSet is similar in many ways to the CachedRowSet of the previous section. You can see in the following class diagram that, like the CachedRowSet, the JdbcRowSet implements the RowSet and extends the BaseRowSet:

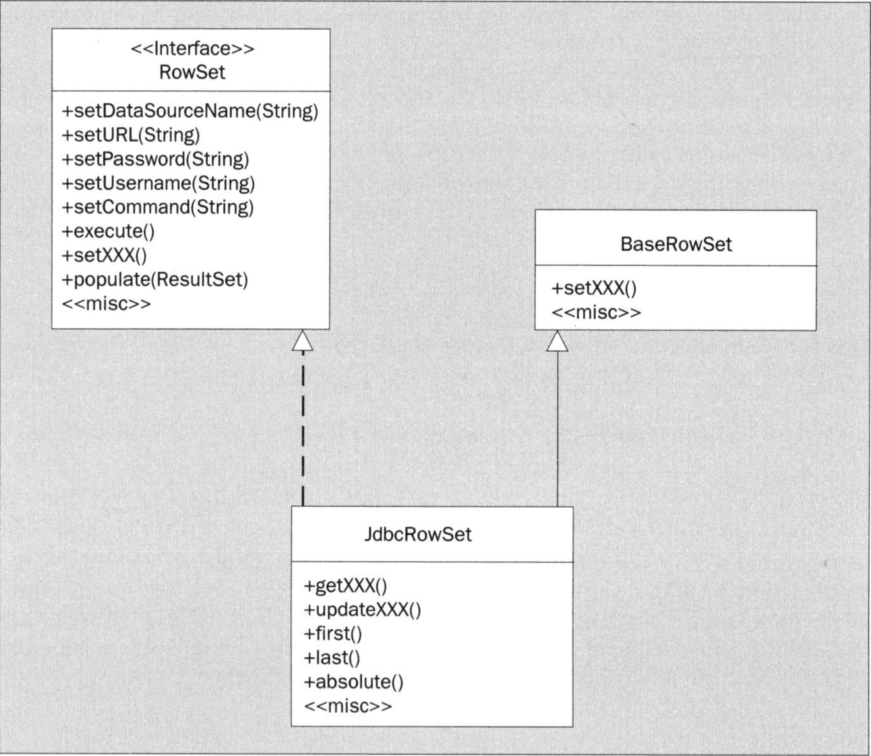

Like the CachedRowSet, the JdbcRowSet can be used to query, read, and update database tables. The big difference between the two classes is that the JdbcRowSet remains connected to the database, while the CachedRowSet is a disconnected RowSet. Since the JdbcRowSet keeps a connection to the database open, it cannot be serialized like the CachedRowSet, or the WebRowSet later in this chapter. Thus, the JdbcRowSet acts as a wrapper around a ResultSet, which makes a JBDC driver look like a JavaBean.

All of the `RowSet` implementations are designed so that they can be used as JavaBeans. A JavaBean is simply a class that follows the JavaBean specification. JavaBeans are self-contained, reusable software components. They can be composed in applications, applets, servlets, or composed components. JavaBeans expose their features to builder tools through introspection. They have properties, appearance, and behavior characteristics that can be changed at design time. Beans communicate with other beans through events. They can even save and restore their state. JavaBeans methods are not different from Java methods. Since `RowSets` are JavaBeans, they work well for visual programming since the developer can 'drag & drop' `RowSets` onto their visual design and attach them directly to their UI forms.

You can get the Java Bean specification at http://java.sun.com/products/javabeans/.

There are several different requirements for JavaBeans. Delving into them all is beyond the scope of this chapter. For our purposes, though, the two important features are:

- JavaBeans expose their properties (member variables) using a specific format for the method names. For example, The specification recommends that methods for accessing and setting properties be named `getXXX()` and `setXXX()`. These methods are referred to as accessor and mutator methods.
- JavaBeans can notify listeners when something occurs in the bean. For example, a Java object can be registered as a listener to a `RowSet`. When a column value in the `RowSet` changes, the `RowSet` notifies the listener and the listener can then take some action. The listener events can for example be used to trigger refreshes to the data fields in the user interface.

Although all three `RowSet` implementations can be JavaBean components, we will look at that aspect of the `RowSet` using the `JdbcRowSet` implementation. The example program in this section will show how to create and use a listener with a `RowSet`.

Event listeners are 'monitorable' behaviors a source publishes using interfaces. The interfaces prescribe one or more methods that the source will invoke when the appropriate event occurs. The target implements the interface and the source notifies the target of the significant event by invoking the target's method. You have to choose the events for which the Bean will issue notifications, as well as the structure and syntax for the event objects and event notification methods.

Try It Out – JdbcRowSet

A listener class thus implements one of the listener interfaces defined in the Java language. The class `ExampleListener` shows a very simple implementation of the listener. The interface in this case is the `RowSetEventListener`. This interface specifies that implementing classes implement three methods:

- `void cursorMoved(RowSetEvent)`
- `void rowChanged(RowSetEvent)`
- `void rowSetChanged(RowSetEvent)`

The class `ExampleListener` indeed implements all three methods by simply printing out information about the event that caused the listener to be notified:

```
package rowset;

import javax.sql.*;

public class ExampleListener implements RowSetListener {
  public void cursorMoved(RowSetEvent event) {
    System.out.println("ExampleListener notified of cursorMoved event");
    System.out.println(" " + event.toString());
  }

  public void rowChanged(RowSetEvent event) {
    System.out.println("ExampleListener notified of rowChanged event");
    System.out.println(" " + event.toString());
  }

  public void rowSetChanged(RowSetEvent event) {
    System.out.println("ExampleListener notified of rowSetChanged event");
    System.out.println(" " + event.toString());
  }
}
```

The listener above will be added to a `JdbcRowSet` in the following class:

```
// rowset/JdbcRowSetExample.java
package rowset;

import java.io.*;
import java.sql.*;
import javax.sql.*;
import sun.jdbc.rowset.*;

public class JdbcRowSetExample {
  JdbcRowSet jdbcRs;

  public static void main(String[] args) {
    JdbcRowSetExample jrse = new JdbcRowSetExample();
    try {
      jrse.populateRowSet();
      jrse.createEvents();
    } catch (SQLException e) {
      e.printStackTrace();
      while ((e = e.getNextException()) != null) {
        e.printStackTrace();
      }
    } catch (Exception e) {
      e.printStackTrace();
    } finally {
      try { jrse.jdbcRs.close(); }
      catch (Exception ignored) {}
    }
  }

  void populateRowSet() throws ClassNotFoundException,
                               SQLException {
    Class.forName("COM.cloudscape.core.JDBCDriver");
    String url = "jdbc:cloudscape:c:/wrox/database/Wrox4370.db";
    String username = "wrox";
    String password = "jdbc";
```

```
    jdbcRs = new JdbcRowSet();
    jdbcRs.setType(ResultSet.TYPE_SCROLL_INSENSITIVE);
    String sql = "SELECT * FROM stores ORDER BY storeid";
    jdbcRs.setCommand(sql);
    jdbcRs.setUrl(url);
    jdbcRs.setUsername(username);
    jdbcRs.setPassword(password);
    jdbcRs.execute();

    // this is where we register the listener class we created
    jdbcRs.addRowSetListener(new ExampleListener());
  }

  void createEvents() throws SQLException, ClassNotFoundException {
    while (jdbcRs.next()) {
      //each call to next, generates a cursorMoved event
    }
  }
}
```

The program above can be run with a batch file similar to the one used in the previous section:

```
set classpath=c:\java\lib\cloudscape.jar;c:\java\lib\jdbc2_0-
stdext.jar;c:\java\lib\rowset.jar;c:\java\lib\jndi.jar;c:\java\examples

java rowset.JdbcRowSetExample
```

As the program iterates through the `ResultSet`, each call to `next()` will generate a `cursorMoved` event, which is sent to all the `RowSetListeners` that have registered with the `JdbcRowSet`. If you run this program with the Cloudscape driver, you can expect an exception stack trace when you run the program because the Cloudscape driver does not implement some required features. However, the rest of the output of the program will look like this:

```
ExampleListener notified of cursorMoved event
 javax.sql.RowSetEvent[source=sun.jdbc.rowset.JdbcRowSet@5d62e409]
ExampleListener notified of cursorMoved event
 javax.sql.RowSetEvent[source=sun.jdbc.rowset.JdbcRowSet@5d62e409]

...additional events not shown
```

How It Works

The `populateRowSet()` method here looks much the same as it does in the `CachedRowSetExample` class in the previous section. However, the `JdbcRowSet` does not have a `populate()` method, so we must set the properties of the `JdbcRowSet` and allow it to make the connection and query the database. Notice that each of the methods for setting a property follows the JavaBean convention of `setXXX()`:

```
    jdbcRs = new JdbcRowSet();
    jdbcRs.setType(ResultSet.TYPE_SCROLL_INSENSITIVE);
    String sql = "SELECT * FROM stores ORDER BY storeid";
    jdbcRs.setCommand(sql);
    jdbcRs.setUrl(url);
    jdbcRs.setUsername(username);
    jdbcRs.setPassword(password);
```

```
    jdbcRs.execute();

    // this is where we register the listener class we created
    jdbcRs.addRowSetListener(new ExampleListener());
```

After the SQL is executed and the RowSet populated, the code adds an instance of the ExampleListener to the RowSet. This is accomplished by calling the addRowSetListener() with an instance of the ExampleListener.

In the createEvents() method, the code simply steps through each row in the RowSet. Each time the RowSet moves to another row, this generates a cursorMoved event. The RowSet object sends this event to the cursorMoved() method of each RowSetListener that was added to the RowSet:

```
void createEvents() throws SQLException,
  ClassNotFoundException
{
  while (jdbcRs.next()) {
    //each call to next, generates a cursorMoved event
  }
}
```

In this example, there is only one listener, the ExampleListener instance. When its cursorMoved() method is called, it prints two lines of output. First, the message that indicates which method was called; then a String representation of the event object that was sent to the method.

```
public void cursorMoved(RowSetEvent event) {
  System.out.println("ExampleListener notified of cursorMoved event");
  System.out.println(" " + event.toString());
}
```

If the test code had changed a row, we would expect a row-changed event to be generated and passed to the rowChanged() method of the listener. Using this approach a user interface can react to changes in the database and refresh itself, for example. If all the data in the RowSet is changed, for instance if the RowSet executes another query, the rowSetChanged() method of the listener is called.

WebRowSet

The third RowSet implementation provided by Sun is the WebRowSet. This RowSet implementation extends the CachedRowSet class; thus, it is a disconnected RowSet. Recall that this means the RowSet iterates through the ResultSet and caches the data in memory. The connection to the database can then be closed while the RowSet will still be able to use the row and column data. The relationship between CachedRowSet and WebRowSet, and the new functions provided by the WebRowSet are illustrated in the following class diagram:

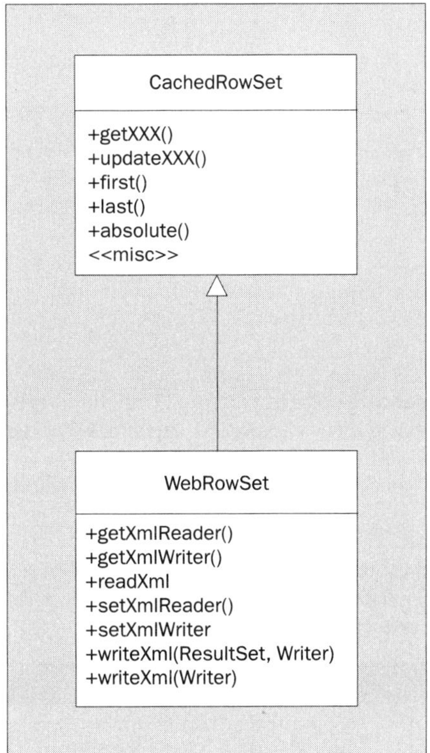

As you can see, all of the new functionality in the `WebRowSet` involves either reading or writing XML data. XML data is data with special markup tags similar to HTML tags. One of the differences, though, is that HTML tags indicate how to display the data; XML tags indicate the meaning of the data.

What this means is that, like its superclass, its set of rows can be sent across a network to a client, and, in addition, the rows can be sent as an XML document. A `WebRowSet` object, like other `RowSet` objects, consists of its rows of data, its meta data, and its properties. As an XML document, these are presented in a format that is specified in a file called a **Document Type Definition (DTD)**. A DTD lists the tags that can be used, the order in which they are to occur, and what is to be included within a tag. The DTD for `WebRowSet` objects is specified in the file `WebRowSet.dtd`. Because all instances of a `WebRowSet` can be represented as XML documents using this pre-specified format, an XML parser can use the DTD to parse the XML document into its constituent parts.

The `WebRowSet` class uses various other classes and interfaces behind the scenes to read and write itself as an XML document.

> *For more information about XML, refer to the XML chapter in this book, Chapter 20.*

Using the `WebRowSet`, data can be read from a database and written in XML; likewise, an XML document containing the proper data can be read and the data in the document written to a database. The figure overleaf shows this interaction between database, `WebRowSet`, and XML document.

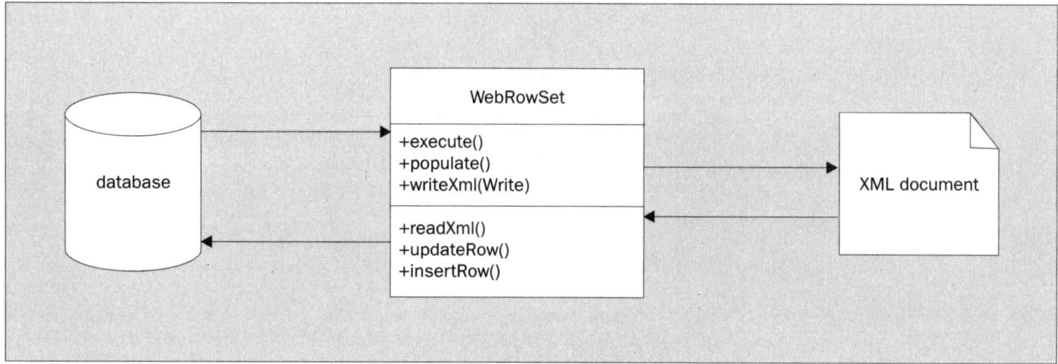

The WebRowSet, through the execute() or populate() methods, gets data from a database. This data can be written to an XML document using the writeXml() method. Given an XML document, the WebRowSet can read the XML using the readXml() method; that data can then be written to the database using the updateRow() or insertRow() and the various updateXXX() methods of the ResultSet interface.

For the XML document to WebRowSet to database path, the XML document must be formatted in a manner that can be understood by the WebRowSet. When you see the XML document created by the writeXml() method in the *Try It Out* section below, you will understand why the XML document read by the WebRowSet, should be one created by a WebRowSet.

Try It Out – WebRowSet

The class below uses a WebRowSet to read track data from the Tracks table of the MusicStore Cloudscape database.

This example queries the database for the track data, and then uses the ResultSet to populate a WebRowSet instance. The WebRowSet writes the data to an XML document that is stored as a file in the file system.

```
// rowset/WebRowSetExample.java
package rowset;

import java.io.*;
import java.sql.*;
import javax.sql.*;
import sun.jdbc.rowset.*;

public class WebRowSetExample {
  WebRowSet webRs;
  int recordingid;

  public static void main(String[] args) {
    WebRowSetExample wrse = new WebRowSetExample();
    try {
      boolean done = false;
      BufferedReader in =
        new BufferedReader(new InputStreamReader(System.in));
      while (!done) {
        wrse.recordingid = 0;
```

```
        System.out.print("Enter a RecordingId (0 to exit) : ");
        String s = in.readLine();
        int result = new Integer(s).intValue();
        if (result == 0) {
          done = true;
        } else {
          wrse.recordingid = result;
          wrse.populateRowSet();
          wrse.writeXml();
        }
      }
    } catch (Exception e) {
      e.printStackTrace();
    }
  }

  void populateRowSet()throws ClassNotFoundException, SQLException {
    Connection connection = null;
    try {
      Class.forName("COM.cloudscape.core.JDBCDriver");
      String url = "jdbc:cloudscape:c:/wrox/database/Wrox4370.db";
      String username = "wrox";
      String password = "jdbc";
      connection = DriverManager.getConnection(url, username, password);
      Statement statement = connection.createStatement();
      String sqlCount = "SELECT COUNT(*) FROM tracks WHERE " +
                        "recordingid=" + recordingid;
      ResultSet rset = statement.executeQuery(sqlCount);
      int count = 0;
      if (rset.next()) {
        count = rset.getInt(1);
      }

      webRs = null;
      if (count > 0) {
        System.out.println("Found " + count +
                           " tracks for recordingid " + recordingid);
        System.out.println("Querying database for track data...");
        String sqlQuery = "SELECT * FROM tracks WHERE " +
                          "recordingid=" + recordingid;
        webRs = new WebRowSet();
        webRs.setCommand(sqlQuery);
        webRs.execute(connection);
      }
    } finally {
      try { connection.close(); } catch (Exception ignored) {}
    }
  }

  void writeXml() throws SQLException, IOException {
    if (webRs == null) {
      System.out.println("No track data found for recording id");
      return;
    }
    FileWriter fw = null;
    try {
      File file = new File("recording" + recordingid + "Tracks.xml");
      fw = new FileWriter(file);
      System.out.println("Writing track data to file " +
                         file.getAbsolutePath());
```

```
            webRs.writeXml(fw);
        } finally {
            fw.flush();
            fw.close();
        }
    }
}
```

Assuming you have extracted all the required libraries to the directory `c:\java\lib`, and the class file is in `c:\BegJavaDB\rowset`, you can use the following batch file to execute the program:

```
set classpath=c:\java\lib\cloudscape.jar;c:\java\lib\jdbc2_0-
stdext.jar;c:\java\lib\rowset.jar;c:\java\lib\jndi.jar;c:\java\lib\parser.jar;c:\j
ava\examples

java rowset.WebRowSetExample
```

Note that the first three lines are really one continuous line that is too long to fit on a single line. IDE users or users with a different OS will need to adjust the commands for their environment.

When you run the program, the output will look something like this:

```
Enter a RecordingId (0 to exit) : 1002
Found 12 tracks for recordingid 1002
Querying database for track data...
Writing track data to file C:\BegJavaDB\rowset\recording1002Tracks.xml
```

The filename for your system may vary depending on your environment. If you open the file in an editor, you will see an XML-formatted document. Here is part of that XML document, edited for space (the full version is 240 lines long):

```
<?xml version="1.0" encoding="UTF-8"?>
<!DOCTYPE RowSet PUBLIC
    '-//Sun Microsystems, Inc.//DTD RowSet//EN'
    'http://java.sun.com/j2ee/dtds/RowSet.dtd'>

<RowSet>
  <properties>

  <!-- data deleted for space -->

  </properties>
  <metadata>
    <column-count>6</column-count>
    <column-definition>
      <column-index>1</column-index>
      <auto-increment>false</auto-increment>
      <case-sensitive>false</case-sensitive>
      <currency>false</currency>
      <nullable>0</nullable>
      <signed>true</signed>
      <searchable>true</searchable>
      <column-display-size>15</column-display-size>
      <column-label>RECORDINGID</column-label>
```

```
      <column-name>RECORDINGID</column-name>
      <schema-name></schema-name>
      <column-precision>10</column-precision>
      <column-scale>0</column-scale>
      <table-name>TRACKS</table-name>
      <catalog-name></catalog-name>
      <column-type>4</column-type>
      <column-type-name>INT</column-type-name>
    </column-definition>

  <!-- data deleted for space -->

  </metadata>
  <data>

  <!-- data deleted for space -->

    <row>
      <col>1002</col>
      <col>11</col>
      <col>Me And A Gun</col>
      <col>121</col>
      <col>17</col>
      <col><null/></col>
    </row>
    <row>
      <col>1002</col>
      <col>12</col>
      <col>Little Earthquakes</col>
      <col>121</col>
      <col>17</col>
      <col><null/></col>
    </row>
  </data>
</RowSet>
```


In addition to the actual column values from the rows in the ResultSet, you can see that the XML document also includes information about the database and the columns retrieved by the query.

How It Works

This class works very much like the CachedRowSetExample presented earlier in the chapter. In the main() method, the code executes a loop in which the user is asked for a recording ID. If the user enters a nonzero ID, then the code calls the populateRowSet() method to query the database. That method first counts the number of tracks in the database for the recording ID:

```
String sqlCount = "SELECT COUNT(*) FROM tracks WHERE " +
                  "recordingid=" + recordingid;
ResultSet rset = statement.executeQuery(sqlCount);
int count = 0;
if (rset.next()) {
  count = rset.getInt(1);
}
```

If the count of tracks is nonzero, then the SQL string is passed to the WebRowSet and the execute() method is called to signal the WebRowSet to execute the SQL:

```
String sqlQuery = "SELECT * FROM tracks WHERE " +
                  "recordingid=" + recordingid;
webRs = new WebRowSet();
webRs.setCommand(sqlQuery);
webRs.execute(connection);
```

The main() method then calls the writeXml() method. This method simply creates a FileWriter instance from a file, and then passes the FileWriter to the writeXml() method of the WebRowSet. The WebRowSet writes the data to the file as an XML document:

```
void writeXml() throws SQLException, IOException {
  if (webRs == null) {
    System.out.println("No track data found for recording id");
    return;
  }
  FileWriter fw = null;
  try {
    File file = new File("recording" + recordingid + "Tracks.xml");
    fw = new FileWriter(file);
    System.out.println("Writing track data to file " +
     file.getAbsolutePath());
    webRs.writeXml(fw);
  } finally {
    fw.flush();
    fw.close();
  }
}
```

Although this example used a FileWriter, the writeXml() method takes a parameter of type Writer. Thus, you could pass any of the Writer subclasses to the writeXml() method, and the code would work the same. The WebRowSet could write the XML document directly to an OutputStream with an OutputStreamWriter. Or it could write to a String or char array with a StringWriter or CharArrayWriter. The WebRowSet can be used to take any database data, and easily convert it to XML and write it to almost any possible output destination.

Summary

RowSet objects extend the functionality of the ResultSet by providing different ways of looking at and using database data. In this chapter we have looked at the following RowSet implementations:

- The CachedRowSet, a disconnected RowSet that can be used to create a scrollable, updatable view of the database even if the driver does not support scrolling and updating.
- The JdbcRowSet, which connects to a database much like a ResultSet, and stays connected. Because of this, it cannot be serialized, although it can, like its companions, be implemented as a JavaBean.
- TheWebRowSet, a disconnected RowSet that creates a translation path between databases and XML documents.

akarta
JAVA
Java

12

Prepared Statements

In the code from previous chapters, a `Statement` object was obtained and used to insert, query, update, and delete data from the database. As we will shortly see, this requires that the driver send the entire SQL string to the database every time the class wants to execute a particular SQL statement. The database then compiles and executes the SQL and returns the result to the caller, regardless of whether the SQL has been passed before. Often, however, the SQL you send to a database will use the same columns in the same tables, and only the data will vary. In the first section, we will look at the `PreparedStatement` interface. This interface provides a means to create a reusable statement that can be precompiled by the database.

After learning the methods of the `PreparedStatement` interface and how to get a prepared statement in the code, in this chapter we will create a class for the `MusicStore` application that uses a prepared statement. We will develop a class to enter track information into the database. Track data is related to the information for a Recording. The `PreparedStatement` object is ideal here because most of the information stored for the tracks in the `Tracks` table is constant for a recording.

When using the `PreparedStatement` with our `MusicStore` application, we already know the SQL string that is being used. Since we know what the string looks like, it is easy to set its parameters before executing the SQL string. Database applications that can be used with any arbitrary database may need to deal with a prepared statement for a database that is unknown to them when the code is developed. With JDBC 2.0, there is no way to determine information about the number of parameters in a `PreparedStatement` and their types using only a `PreparedStatement` object and without the original SQL string used to create the `PreparedStatement`. JDBC 3.0 introduces another meta data class, `ParameterMetaData`, through which a database application or tool can learn the structure of a prepared statement at run-time.

In the final section of the chapter, we take a brief look at some of the advanced data types that are accessible through JDBC. While this may seem like a change of topic, it is actually relevant. When entering some kinds of data into a database, you can simply enter the value of the data directly into an SQL statement and execute the statement. With the advanced data types, however, the only way to use them with JDBC is through a `PreparedStatement`. In the final section, we look at some code that uses a prepared statement to insert and retrieve binary data from the database.

The PreparedStatement Interface

In Chapter 8, a `Store` class was created that had methods for creating, retrieving, updating, and deleting store data from the `Stores` table. For example, this snippet of code is in the `create()` method of the `Store` class:

```
String sql = "INSERT INTO stores " +
    "(StoreDescription, StoreTypeID, StoreAddress1, " +
    "StoreAddress2, StoreCity, StorePostalCode) " +
    "VALUES ('" + storeDescription + "', " +
    storeTypeId + ", " +
    "'" + storeAddress1 + "', " +
    "'" + storeAddress2 + "', " +
    "'" + storeCity + "', " +
    "'" + storePostalCode + "')";
result = statement.executeUpdate(sql);
```

When the code is executed, the SQL string that is created by the code will look something like this (whitespace has been added to make the SQL easy to read):

```
INSERT INTO stores
       (StoreDescription, StoreTypeID, StoreAddress1,
        StoreAddress2, StoreCity, StorePostalCode)
VALUES
       ('Independent Records and Tapes', 1, '123 E. Bijou St.',
        '', 'Colorado Springs', '80903')
```

When a new `Store` entry is needed, we execute another SQL string:

```
INSERT INTO stores
       (StoreDescription, StoreTypeID, StoreAddress1,
        StoreAddress2, StoreCity, StorePostalCode)
VALUES
       ('Mid-West USA', 1, '600 West Central Rd.',
        '', 'Roselle', '60172')
```

Notice that the two SQL strings are very similar. The SQL strings insert data into the same columns in the same table. The only thing that changes is the value of the data being inserted. Yet, every time new store data is inserted, the code will send the entire SQL string to the database where the string is processed and executed.

The processing time consists of parsing the SQL string, checking the syntax and semantics, and generating code. Often the processing time is longer than the actual time needed to execute the statement. Wouldn't it be nice if we could improve performance by telling the database, 'Here is some SQL that needs to be executed multiple times with different data values. Get this SQL ready for execution and I'll send you the data.' The database processes the SQL string once, even though the statement may be executed multiple times.

The `PreparedStatement` interface does just that. A `PreparedStatement` is used to pass an SQL string to the database, where it can be pre-processed for execution. The SQL string includes placeholders for the data. The `PreparedStatement` interface provides methods that you can use to set the data for the SQL, after which you tell the database to execute the SQL.

The PreparedStatement interface extends the Statement interface. It inherits all the methods of the Statement interface, and adds additional methods as shown in the class diagram below:

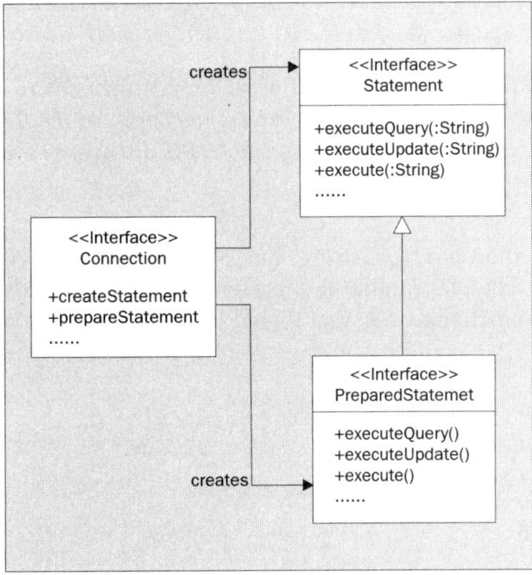

The PreparedStatement interface includes many methods; the diagram only shows three of them because we're going to focus on the basics first. The other methods will be presented later in this chapter. A PreparedStatement object is created in much the same way as the Statement object is created, by calling a method of the Connection object. In the same way that createStatement(String) creates a Statement object, the prepareStatement(String) method creates a PreparedStatement object. There are additional forms of the prepareStatement() method. The table below lists all of the overloads of the prepareStatement method of the Connection interface:

Method	Description
prepareStatement(String sql)	Creates a prepared statement for the given SQL. If the prepared statement returns a, the ResultSet has a type of forward only, is not updatable, and is not holdable.
prepareStatement(String sql, int resultSetType, int resultSetConcurrency)	Creates a prepared statement for the given SQL. If the prepared statement returns a ResultSet, the ResultSet has the given result set type and concurrency, and is not holdable.
prepareStatement(String sql, int resultSetType, int resultSetConcurrency, int resultSetHoldability)	**JDBC 3.0 only**: Creates a prepared statement for the given SQL. If the prepared statement returns a ResultSet, the ResultSet has the given ResultSet type, concurrency, and holdability.

> *In the table above, `ResultSet` type refers to whether a `ResultSet` is forward-only, or if the rows in the `ResultSet` can be read in any order. Concurrency is the ability to update a `ResultSet`. Holdability refers to whether a `ResultSet` is closed when changes are committed. Refer to Chapter 9, Using Statements and `Resultsets`, for more details on these concepts.*

> *As indicated in the description, the third method above is only available in drivers that are JDBC 3.0-compliant. At the time this was written, no drivers implemented the JDBC 3.0 specification. However, the specification was in final draft stage, so JDBC 3.0 drivers should be available by the time you read this, or shortly thereafter.*

The first argument in each method is a SQL string. The SQL string can have **placeholders** that represent data that will be set at a later time. The placeholder is represented by the question mark symbol (`?`). Let's take the SQL string presented above and change it so that it could be used as part of a prepared statement:

```
INSERT INTO stores
       (StoreDescription, StoreTypeID, StoreAddress1,
        StoreAddress2, StoreCity, StorePostalCode)
VALUES
       (?, ?, ?, ?, ?, ?)
//      1  2  3  4  5  6
```

Looking at the SQL above, you can see six numbers immediately below the placeholders. These are the index numbers of each placeholder in the string. Placeholders are consecutively indexed starting with 1 at the beginning of the SQL string. The placeholders correspond to variables in the database known as **bind variables**. Bind variables are similar to variables used in Java code. They can be set with a value, and used in SQL statements, procedures, and functions in the database.

When the SQL in the `PreparedStatement` is sent to the database, the database compiles the SQL. Before you execute a `PreparedStatement`, you must set the placeholders with data. The driver sends the data to the database when the `PreparedStatement` is executed. The database sets the bind variables with the data, and executes the SQL.

> **Placeholders can only be used to take the place of data that will be used as part of the SQL string. You cannot use a placeholder to change the table or columns in the SQL. That is, you can't have a prepared statement that uses placeholders in place of the table name or column name in a SQL string like this:**
>
> **`DELETE FROM ? WHERE ?=1`**

Now that the general form of a SQL string used to create a `PreparedStatement` is known, we can look at the code for creating a `PreparedStatement`. Taking the SQL string example from above and putting it into the `Store` class would result in this code:

```
String sql = "INSERT INTO stores " +
             "(StoreDescription, StoreTypeID, StoreAddress1, " +
             "StoreAddress2, StoreCity, StorePostalCode) " +
             "VALUES (?, ?, ?, ?, ?, ?)";
PreparedStatement ps = connection.prepareStatement(sql);
```

The code snippet above creates a SQL string that includes placeholders for data that will be set later. The string is then passed to one of the `prepareStatement()` methods.

After creating the prepared statement, but before the statement can be executed, the placeholders in the statement must be set. The `PreparedStatement` interface defines various methods for doing this. The methods take the form of `setXXX` where `XXX` is a Java data type name. Here are the methods for the Java primitives and a few Java objects:

```
void setBigDecimal(int parameterIndex, BigDecimal x)
void setBoolean(int parameterIndex, boolean x)
void setByte(int parameterIndex, byte x)
void setBytes(int parameterIndex, byte[] x)
void setDate(int parameterIndex, Date x)
void setDate(int parameterIndex, Date x, Calendar cal)
void setDouble(int parameterIndex, double x)
void setFloat(int parameterIndex, float x)
void setInt(int parameterIndex, int x)
void setLong(int parameterIndex, long x)
void setNull(int parameterIndex, int sqlType)
void setNull(int parameterIndex, int sqlType, String typeName)
void setShort(int parameterIndex, short x)
void setString(int parameterIndex, String x)
void setTime(int parameterIndex, Time x)
void setTime(int parameterIndex, Time x, Calendar cal)
void setTimeStamp(int parameterIndex, TimeStamp x)
void setTimeStamp(int parameterIndex, TimeStamp x, Calendar cal)
void setObject(int parameterIndex, Object x)
void setObject(int parameterIndex, Object x, int TargetJdbcType)
void setObject(int parameterIndex, Object x,
              int TargetJdbcType, int scale)
```

There are additional `setXXX` methods not shown in the table above. We will see them later in the chapter when we look at using prepared statements with SQL99 data types.

The first argument in each method above is the index of the parameter in the SQL string. Each placeholder is referenced by its position in the SQL string. Starting from the beginning of the string, the first placeholder is at index 1, the second at 2, and so on.

The second argument is the data value that replaces the placeholder. So, using the SQL `INSERT` from above, here's how a few of the data values would be set:

```
String sql = "INSERT INTO stores " +
             "(StoreDescription, StoreTypeID, StoreAddress1, " +
             "StoreAddress2, StoreCity, StorePostalCode) " +
             "VALUES (?, ?, ?, ?, ?, ?)";
//parameter index:     1  2  3  4  5  6
PreparedStatement ps = connection.prepareStatement(sql);
ps.setString(1, "Black Hole Music");
ps.setInt(2, 2);
ps.setString(6, "98036");
ps.executeUpdate();
```

The code uses the `setString()` and the `setInt()` methods to set some of the data values. The data values can be set in any order, as long as you get the index correct. That is, you do not need to set the parameters in the order they appear in the string. You can set the fourth parameter before the second, the last one before the first one, and so on, as long as all the parameters are set before the statement is executed.

> **If you do not set all the parameters before executing the SQL, the driver will throw a `SQLException`.**

You might think that you can insert a `NULL` into a database table by not setting the placeholder that corresponds to the column that will have the `NULL` value. As the note above states, however, this will cause the driver to throw an `SQLException`. `NULL` values are inserted into the database by using one of the `setNull()` methods listed in the table above.

Once a placeholder has been set with data, that data remains set for that placeholder until the code explicitly changes the value for the placeholder. In other words, you are not required to set the placeholder every time you want to execute some SQL using the same `PreparedStatement`. If you set the placeholder at some point in the code, and that placeholder uses the same value every time you use the same `PreparedStatement` instance, you only need to set the placeholder the first time. All the placeholders can be cleared by calling the `PreparedStatement` method `clearParameters()`. The value of a placeholder is changed by calling one of the `setXXX()` methods again with the appropriate index like this:

```
ps.setString(6, "98036");
ps.executeUpdate();

// somewhere later in the code
ps.executeUpdate();  //parameter 6 still set to 98036

// somewhere later in the code, we need a new postal code
ps.setString(6, "20101");
// or if we want to clear all the parameter values
ps.clearParameters();
```

After the placeholders in the `PreparedStatement` are set, the SQL can be executed. The class diagram above showed the three methods of `PreparedStatement` used for executing the SQL statement. The methods have the same names (`executeQuery()`, `executeUpdate()`, and `execute()`) as the methods in `Statement`, but they do not take the SQL string as a parameter. The SQL string does not need to be sent with the execute call because it is sent to the database with the `prepareStatement()` method call. In the code snippet above, `executeUpdate()` was used because the code was inserting data into the database.

> **Even though `PreparedStatement` extends `Statement`, it is an error to use the `execute` methods of the `Statement` object with a prepared statement. If you call any of the methods `executeQuery(String)`, `executeUpdate(String)`, or `execute(String)`, the driver will throw a `SQLException`. You must call the no parameter versions of those methods with a prepared statement.**

Try It Out – Using a Prepared Statement

Let's look at one possible use for the `PreparedStatement` object. In Chapter 6, *Designing the Music Store Database*, we listed some of the requirements for the Music Store application. One of those requirements is:

- Provide the ability to search the database by a variety of criteria (by artist, song title, album name, and so on). Ultimately, this search facility will be self-service in the store, with a facility for customers to be able to post reviews of recordings.

If you look at the Music Store database, you will see a `Recordings` table and a `Tracks` table. The `Recordings` table is used to store information about a recording, in other words, a CD, cassette tape, and so on. Data about each selection on the recording is kept in the `Tracks` table. The `Tracks` table also has foreign keys that create a relationship between a row in the `Tracks` table and other tables.

A foreign key is a value in one table row that links the row to one or more rows in another table.

For example, the `Tracks` table contains an entry for the song Happy Phantom. The row for this track has foreign keys that link it to other tables, including the entry for Tori Amos in the `ArtistsAndPerformers` table.

We'll follow the same basic mapping strategy that we've used with other classes in this book to develop a `Track` class. The `Track` class can be used to represent a row in the `Tracks` table; we will also see how it can represent multiple rows in the table. The class will implement three retrieve functions, using a `PreparedStatement` to send the SQL to the database.

```
package statements;

import java.sql.*;
import java.util.*;
import connections.ConnectionFactory;

public class Track {

  // track data
  int recordingId;
  String recordingTitle;
  int trackNumber;
  String trackTitle;
  int artistId;
  String artistName;
  int styleId;
  String styleName;
```

```
String sampleFilespec;

// JDBC variables
PreparedStatement preparedStmt;
ResultSet resultSet;
Vector results;

// CRUD flags
boolean create;
boolean retrieve;
boolean update;
boolean delete;

static String sqlSelect = "SELECT " + "recordings.recordingid, " +
                          "recordings.recordingtitle, " +
                          "tracks.tracknumber, " +
                          "tracks.tracktitle, " + "tracks.artistid, " +
                          "artistsandperformers.artistname, " +
                          "tracks.styleid, " +
                          "audiostyles.audiostyledescription, " +
                          "tracks.samplefilespec ";

static String sqlFrom =
  "FROM tracks, recordings, artistsandperformers, audiostyles ";

static String sqlWhere = "WHERE ";

static String sqlWhereCont =
       "LIKE ? AND recordings.recordingid = tracks.recordingid AND " +
       "artistsandperformers.artistid = tracks.artistid AND " +
       "audiostyles.audiostyleid = tracks.styleid";

// constructor
public Track() {}

// methods to return different SQL strings for searching
public static String getFindTrackTitleSql() {
  return sqlSelect + sqlFrom + sqlWhere + "tracks.tracktitle " +
         sqlWhereCont;
}
public static String getFindRecordTitleSql() {
  return sqlSelect + sqlFrom + sqlWhere + "recordings.recordingtitle " +
         sqlWhereCont;
}

public static String getFindArtistSql() {
  return sqlSelect + sqlFrom + sqlWhere +
         "artistsandperformers.artistname " + sqlWhereCont;
}

// Prepare the class to query for rows in the database. The
// PreparedStatement should be created using the SQL string obtained
// by calling one of the getFindXXXSql() methods in this class.
public void setQueryStatement(PreparedStatement ps) {
```

```
    preparedStmt = ps;
    create = false;
    retrieve = (ps != null ? true : false);
    update = false;
    delete = false;
  }

  // execute the PreparedStatement
  private boolean executeSql() throws SQLException {
    if (create || update || delete) {
      int result = preparedStmt.executeUpdate();
      return (result == 1);
    } else if (retrieve) {
      resultSet = preparedStmt.executeQuery();
      results = new Vector();
      if (resultSet.next()) {
        Track track = new Track();
        track.populate(resultSet);
        results.add(track);
        return true;
      }
      return false;
    } else {
      throw new SQLException("No PreparedStatement has been set.");
    }
  }

  // Find tracks that match a TrackTitle search string
  public Vector findByTrackTitle(String trackTitle) throws SQLException {
    preparedStmt.setString(1, "%" + trackTitle + "%");
    if (executeSql()) {
      parseResultSet();
    }
    return results;
  }

  // Find tracks that match a Recording Title search string
  public Vector findByRecordingTitle(String recordingTitle)
                                    throws SQLException {
    preparedStmt.setString(1, "%" + recordingTitle + "%");
    if (executeSql()) {
      parseResultSet();
    }
    return results;
  }

  // Find tracks that match an Artist name search string
  public Vector findByArtistName(String artistName) throws SQLException {
    preparedStmt.setString(1, "%" + artistName + "%");
    if (executeSql()) {
      parseResultSet();
    }
    return results;
  }
```

```
// Read each row in the ResultSet and create a Track instance from
// the row
private void parseResultSet() throws SQLException {
  try {
    while (resultSet.next()) {
      Track track = new Track();
      track.populate(resultSet);
      results.add(track);
    }
  } finally {
    ConnectionFactory.close(resultSet);
  }
}

// initialize the datamembers of this class using data from the
// current row of the ResultSet
public void populate(ResultSet rset) throws SQLException {
  setRecordingId(rset.getInt("RECORDINGID"));
  setRecordingTitle(rset.getString("RECORDINGTITLE"));
  setTrackNumber(rset.getInt("TRACKNUMBER"));
  setTrackTitle(rset.getString("TRACKTITLE"));
  setArtistId(rset.getInt("ARTISTID"));
  setArtistName(rset.getString("ARTISTNAME"));
  setStyleId(rset.getInt("STYLEID"));
  setStyleName(rset.getString("AUDIOSTYLEDESCRIPTION"));
  setSampleFilespec(rset.getString("SAMPLEFILESPEC"));
}

// Setters and Getters for the member variables

public int getRecordingId() {
  return recordingId;
}
public void setRecordingId(int v) throws SQLException {
  recordingId = v;
}

public int getTrackNumber() {
  return trackNumber;
}
public void setTrackNumber(int v) throws SQLException {
  trackNumber = v;
}

public String getTrackTitle() {
  return trackTitle;
}
public void setTrackTitle(String v) throws SQLException {
  trackTitle = v;
}

public int getArtistId() {
  return artistId;
```

```
  }
  public void setArtistId(int v) throws SQLException {
    artistId = v;
  }

  public int getStyleId() {
    return styleId;
  }
  public void setStyleId(int v) throws SQLException {
    styleId = v;
  }

  public String getSampleFilespec() {
    return sampleFilespec;
  }
  public void setSampleFilespec(String v) throws SQLException {
    sampleFilespec = v;
  }

  public String getRecordingTitle() {
    return recordingTitle;
  }
  public void setRecordingTitle(String v) {
    recordingTitle = v;
  }

  public String getStyleName() {
    return styleName;
  }
  public void setStyleName(String v) {
    styleName = v;
  }

  public String getArtistName() {
    return artistName;
  }
  public void setArtistName(String v) {
    artistName = v;
  }
}
```

Save this file as `C:\BegJavaDB\Ch12\statements\Track.java`, and compile it with the following command from the `Ch12` directory:

```
> javac -classpath . statements/Track.java
```

In this case, we've also copied the `ConnectionFactory.java` file to `C:\BegJavaDB\Ch12\connections\ConnectionFactory.java`, where the compile command above will find it. Alternatively, you can leave the file where it is and use this command to compile:

```
> javac -classpath .;C:\BegJavaDB\Ch08 statements/Track.java
```

Below is the test class, `TestTrack`, that demonstrates the features of the `Track` class above. The class gets a connection and a prepared statement, and uses them to exercise two of the `findXXX()` methods in the `Track` class.

```
package statements;

import java.sql.*;
import java.util.*;
import connections.ConnectionFactory;

public class TestTrack {
  public static void main(String[] args) {
    Connection connection = null;
    PreparedStatement ps = null;

    try {
      connection = ConnectionFactory.getConnection();
      String sql = Track.getFindTrackTitleSql();
      ps = connection.prepareStatement(sql);
      Track track = new Track();
      track.setQueryStatement(ps);

      String subs = "ee";
      System.out.println("\nSearch track titles for " + subs);
      Vector v = track.findByTrackTitle(subs);
      Iterator iterator = v.iterator();
      while (iterator.hasNext()) {
        Track t = (Track) iterator.next();
        checkForSubstring(t.getTrackTitle(), subs);
      }

      subs = "You";
      System.out.println("\nSearch track titles for " + subs);
      v = track.findByTrackTitle(subs);
      iterator = v.iterator();
      while (iterator.hasNext()) {
        Track t = (Track) iterator.next();
        checkForSubstring(t.getTrackTitle(), subs);
      }

      sql = Track.getFindRecordTitleSql();
      ps = connection.prepareStatement(sql);
      track.setQueryStatement(ps);
      subs = "ac";
      System.out.println("\nSearch recording titles for " + subs);
      v = track.findByTrackTitle(subs);
      iterator = v.iterator();
      while (iterator.hasNext()) {
        Track t = (Track) iterator.next();
        checkForSubstring(t.getRecordingTitle(), subs);
      }

    } catch (Exception e) {
      e.printStackTrace();
```

```
        } finally {
          ConnectionFactory.close(ps);
          ConnectionFactory.close(connection);
        }
      }

      static void checkForSubstring(String fullString, String substring) {
        System.out.print("Checking '" + fullString + "' for '" + substring +
                         "' : ");
        if (fullString.indexOf(substring) != -1) {
          System.out.println("OK");
        } else {
          System.out.println("ERROR!");
        }
      }
    }
```

Save this file as `C:\BegJavaDB\Ch12\statements\TestTrack.java`, and compile it with the following command from the `Ch12` directory:

```
> javac -classpath . statements/TestTrack.java
```

Run the class using the following command:

```
> java -classpath .;%JLIB%\<database> statements/TestTrack
```

Where *<database>* is the library file that contains the JDBC drivers for the database your `ConnectionFactory` class connects to (`cloudscape.jar` for Cloudscape, `classes12.zip` for Oracle). When you execute the test class, you should see output that looks like the following screenshot:

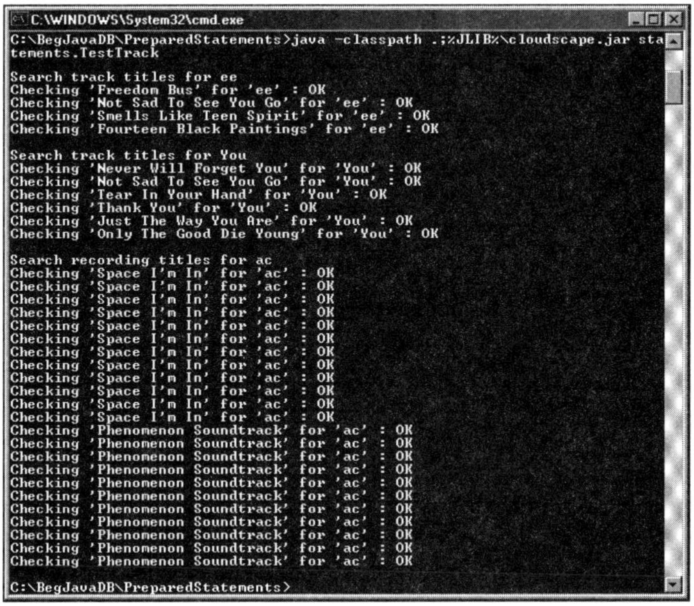

```
C:\WINDOWS\System32\cmd.exe
C:\BegJavaDB\PreparedStatements>java -classpath .;%JLIB%\cloudscape.jar sta
tements.TestTrack

Search track titles for ee
Checking 'Freedom Bus' for 'ee' : OK
Checking 'Not Sad To See You Go' for 'ee' : OK
Checking 'Smells Like Teen Spirit' for 'ee' : OK
Checking 'Fourteen Black Paintings' for 'ee' : OK

Search track titles for You
Checking 'Never Will Forget You' for 'You' : OK
Checking 'Not Sad To See You Go' for 'You' : OK
Checking 'Tear In Your Hand' for 'You' : OK
Checking 'Thank You' for 'You' : OK
Checking 'Just The Way You Are' for 'You' : OK
Checking 'Only The Good Die Young' for 'You' : OK

Search recording titles for ac
Checking 'Space I'm In' for 'ac' : OK
Checking 'Space I'm In' for 'ac' : OK
Checking 'Space I'm In' for 'ac' : OK
Checking 'Space I'm In' for 'ac' : OK
Checking 'Space I'm In' for 'ac' : OK
Checking 'Space I'm In' for 'ac' : OK
Checking 'Space I'm In' for 'ac' : OK
Checking 'Space I'm In' for 'ac' : OK
Checking 'Space I'm In' for 'ac' : OK
Checking 'Space I'm In' for 'ac' : OK
Checking 'Space I'm In' for 'ac' : OK
Checking 'Space I'm In' for 'ac' : OK
Checking 'Phenomenon Soundtrack' for 'ac' : OK
Checking 'Phenomenon Soundtrack' for 'ac' : OK
Checking 'Phenomenon Soundtrack' for 'ac' : OK
Checking 'Phenomenon Soundtrack' for 'ac' : OK
Checking 'Phenomenon Soundtrack' for 'ac' : OK
Checking 'Phenomenon Soundtrack' for 'ac' : OK
Checking 'Phenomenon Soundtrack' for 'ac' : OK
Checking 'Phenomenon Soundtrack' for 'ac' : OK
Checking 'Phenomenon Soundtrack' for 'ac' : OK
Checking 'Phenomenon Soundtrack' for 'ac' : OK
Checking 'Phenomenon Soundtrack' for 'ac' : OK

C:\BegJavaDB\PreparedStatements>
```

How It Works

We'll begin by importing the needed packages and defining class members to hold the track data. The `ConnectionFactory` class from Chapter 8 is used to provide database connections, and tidy up after they've been used. You may notice that the `Track` class actually defines three more data members than columns in the table. Recall that the `Tracks` table contains foreign keys to other tables; this is fine for the database, but human users will be able to use the name of something more easily than the ID. So, we include fields for recording title, artist name, and style description.

Now that we have seen the above two pieces of code in action, we turn our attention to how they actually work. As usual, we define variables for the `ResultSet` and `PreparedStatement` that the class will use, and a `Vector` to hold query results. The next four variables (`create`, `retrieve`, `update`, and `delete`) are flags that the class will use to track which CRUD (create, retrieve, update, or delete) action will be executed. Finally we define a number of strings that will be used to help construct SQL strings:

```
static String sqlSelect = "SELECT " +
  "recordings.recordingid, " +
  "recordings.recordingtitle, " +
  "tracks.tracknumber, " +
  "tracks.tracktitle, " +
  "tracks.artistid, " +
  "artistsandperformers.artistname, " +
  "tracks.styleid, " +
  "audiostyles.audiostyledescription, " +
  "tracks.samplefilespec ";

static String sqlFrom =
  "FROM tracks, recordings, artistsandperformers, audiostyles ";

static String sqlWhere = "WHERE ";

static String sqlWhereCont =
  "LIKE ? AND recordings.recordingid = tracks.recordingid AND " +
  "artistsandperformers.artistid = tracks.artistid AND " +
  "audiostyles.audiostyleid = tracks.styleid";
```

We want to ensure that anyone using this class uses the correct SQL string. Since this class represents the `Tracks` table, it should be responsible for providing the SQL used with the `Tracks` table. Other classes should not have to know the structure of the `Tracks` table or the SQL needed for it. Therefore, the `sqlSelect`, `sqlFrom`, `sqlWhere`, and `sqlWhereCont` strings above are used to create a SQL query string. Here is the method that provides the SQL string to find a recording by track title:

```
//methods to return different SQL strings for searching
public static String getFindTrackTitleSql()
{
  return sqlSelect + sqlFrom + sqlWhere +
    "tracks.tracktitle " + sqlWhereCont;
}
```

The `FROM` clause identifies the four tables from which we will get information for the class. Each column obtained from a table is identified in the `SELECT` clause. The `WHERE` clause uses the foreign key in the `Tracks` table to match the correct row in the other tables for the query.

Following the no-argument constructor are three methods that return an SQL string to the caller. These strings are created from the static SQL strings defined in the class above.

```
//methods to return different SQL strings for searching
public static String getFindTrackTitleSql()
{
  return sqlSelect + sqlFrom + sqlWhere +
    "tracks.tracktitle " + sqlWhereCont;
}
```

The method above and the remaining two (`getFindRecordTitleSql()` and `getFindArtistSql()`) are very similar. Each method takes the SQL string fragments defined in the class, and add a column name to the SQL. This class uses a `LIKE` comparison to search for titles or names that match the user's criteria. So for example, the `getFindTrackTitleSql()` method above will return a SQL string with the following form:

```
SELECT ... FROM ... WHERE tracks.tracktitle LIKE ? AND ...
```

The other two methods return strings that are the same except for the column name used with the `LIKE` phrase.

The `Track` class does not get its own `Connection` or `Statement` objects. These are passed to the class from another class (`TestTrack` in this instance). The class that creates the `PreparedStatement` uses the `setQueryStatement()` method to pass the `PreparedStatement` to the `Track` class; the method also sets the CRUD flags so that the query flag is set, and the others are cleared:

```
public void setQueryStatement(PreparedStatement ps) {
  preparedStmt = ps;
  create = false;
  retrieve = (ps != null ? true : false);
  update = false;
  delete = false;
}
```

To use the `Track` class, we would first call the `getFindTrackTitleSql()` method. The string returned by this method would be used to create a prepared statement, and then that prepared statement would be passed back to this class with the `setQueryStatement()` method. Note that this really doesn't stop a user of the class from passing an arbitrary prepared statement, but if the `Track` class is used properly, it does reduce potential errors and makes it easier to use the class.

The `TestTrack` class follows this procedure to test the `Track` class. `TestTrack` gets a connection, gets a SQL string from the `Track` class, calls the `Connection` method `prepareStatement()` with the SQL string to create a `PreparedStatement`, and lastly passes the `PreparedStatement` back to the `Track` class. Here is the code from the `TestTrack` class that performs those steps:

```
connection = ConnectionFactory.getConnection();
String sql = Track.getFindTrackTitleSql();
ps = connection.prepareStatement(sql);
Track track = new Track();
track.setQueryStatement(ps);
```

If the `setQueryStatement()` method above is called, and the prepared statement is not `null`, the code sets a flag named `retrieve` to `true`, and sets other flags to `false`. The flags are defined as instance variables at the beginning of the source code. The flags are used by the class to determine which execute method to call.

These next three methods are the primary searching methods. They set the placeholder in the `PreparedStatement`, call the `executeSql()` method, and then parse the `ResultSet`:

```
public Vector findByTrackTitle(String trackTitle)
                              throws SQLException {
  preparedStmt.setString(1, "%" + trackTitle + "%");
  if (executeSql()) {
    parseResultSet();
  }
  return results;
}

//Find tracks that match a Recording Title search string
public Vector findByRecordingTitle(String recordingTitle)
                                  throws SQLException {
  preparedStmt.setString(1, "%" + recordingTitle + "%");
  if (executeSql()) {
    parseResultSet();
  }
  return results;
}

//Find tracks that match an Artist name search string
public Vector findByArtistName(String artistName) throws SQLException {
  preparedStmt.setString(1, "%" + artistName + "%");
  if (executeSql()) {
    parseResultSet();
  }
  return results;
}
```

These methods first set the single placeholder in the `PreparedStatement` with a `String`; it does this by calling the `setString()` method that was introduced earlier in the chapter. The `trackTitle` that was passed to the method is wrapped with percentage `%` signs. In a SQL string, `%` is a wildcard; it matches zero or more characters in the column. Then the method calls the `executeSql()` method:

```
private boolean executeSql() throws SQLException {
  if (create || update || delete) {
    int result = preparedStmt.executeUpdate();
    return (result == 1);
  } else if (retrieve) {
    resultSet = preparedStmt.executeQuery();
    results = new Vector();
    if (resultSet.next()) {
      Track track = new Track();
      track.populate(resultSet);
      results.add(track);
      return true;
```

```
        }
        return false;
      } else {
        throw new SQLException("No PreparedStatement has been set.");
      }
    }
```

The `executeSql()` method uses an `if` block to determine whether to call `executeUpdate()` or `executeQuery()`. Since we are testing the retrieve functionality, the `else` block should execute every time. This block calls the `executeQuery()` method of the `PreparedStatement`; it then checks to see if any rows were returned by calling `next()`. Since the call to `next()` will position the cursor on the first row, this method also creates a `Track` object from the first row and adds it to a `Vector` of all the `Track` objects that will be created. If the `executeSql()` returns a True to the `findByTrackTitle()` method, then one or more rows were returned from the database. The first row was processed by the `executeSql()` method.

The `findByTrackTitle()` method then calls the `parseResultSet()` method to process the rest of the rows in the `ResultSet`. Since we have three methods that can get a `ResultSet`, we put the code for reading each row of the `ResultSet` and creating a `Track` object into its own method.

```
    private void parseResultSet() throws SQLException {
      try {
        while (resultSet.next()) {
          Track track = new Track();
          track.populate(resultSet);
          results.add(track);
        }
      } finally {
        ConnectionFactory.close(resultSet);
      }
    }
```

The `parseResultSet()` method moves through the rows of the `ResultSet`, and passes the `ResultSet` to the `populate()` method of each `Track` object being created. The `populate()` method reads the columns from the current row and sets the member data for the object. The `Track` object is then added to a `Vector` of results. After all the rows have been read, the class returns the results `Vector` to the caller:

```
    //initialize the datamembers of this class using data from the
    //current row of the ResultSet
    public void populate(ResultSet rset) throws SQLException {
      setRecordingId(rset.getInt("RECORDINGID"));
      setRecordingTitle(rset.getString("RECORDINGTITLE"));
      setTrackNumber(rset.getInt("TRACKNUMBER"));
      setTrackTitle(rset.getString("TRACKTITLE"));
      setArtistId(rset.getInt("ARTISTID"));
      setArtistName(rset.getString("ARTISTNAME"));
      setStyleId(rset.getInt("STYLEID"));
      setStyleName(rset.getString("AUDIOSTYLEDESCRIPTION"));
      setSampleFilespec(rset.getString("SAMPLEFILESPEC"));
    }
```

Using the `getInt()` and `getString()` methods, the `populate()` method reads the data from the current row of the `ResultSet` and uses the data in the row to populate the member variables of the object.

Finally, the class has setter and getter methods for each member variable of the class.

```
    //Setters and Getters for the member variables

    public int getRecordingId() { return recordingId; }
    public void setRecordingId(int v) throws SQLException {
      recordingId = v;
    }
    // Remaining Setters and Getters not shown
  }
```

Now let's look at the test class, `TestTrack`, which starts by getting a connection from the `ConnectionFactory`. You should be able to use the same `ConnectionFactory` that was originally developed in Chapter 8. This test program is going to use the Cloudscape database; if you are using a different database you may need to modify the `ConnectionFactory` to provide connections to your database.

The code that does the real work that we haven't discussed yet is as follows:

```
        String subs = "ee";
        System.out.println("\nSearch track titles for " + subs);
        Vector v = track.findByTrackTitle(subs);
        Iterator iterator = v.iterator();
        while (iterator.hasNext()) {
          Track t = (Track) iterator.next();
          checkForSubstring(t.getTrackTitle(), subs);
        }
```

The other two sections like this work in much the same way. We declare a `String` to search for, get a `Vector` full of track titles, get an `Iterator`, step through the `Vector`, and for each object in the `Vector` we call the `checkForSubstring()` method on it. Here is the `checkForSubstring()` method:

```
    static void checkForSubstring(String fullString, String substring)
    {
      System.out.print("Checking '" + fullString + "' for '" +
                       substring + "' : ");
      if (fullString.indexOf(substring) != -1) {
        System.out.println("OK");
      } else {
        System.out.println("ERROR!");
      }
    }
  }
```

This method uses the `indexOf()` method to check that the substring is contained within the track title (`fullString`).

New in JDBC 3.0 – ParameterMetaData

The JDBC 3.0 specification adds a new meta data object to the `java.sql` package. This class is the `ParameterMetaData` class. It provides information about a `PreparedStatement` object.

At the time this was written, no drivers implemented the JDBC 3.0 specification. However, the specification was in final draft stage, so JDBC 3.0 drivers should be available by the time you read this, or shortly thereafter.

The `ParameterMetaData` object is obtained by calling a new method of the `PreparedStatement` class, `getParameterMetaData()`:

```
String sql = "INSERT INTO tracks (trackid, tracknumber, tracktitle, " +
             "artistid, styleid, samplefilespec) VALUES (?, ?, ?, ?, ?, ?)";
PreparedStatement ps = connection.prepareStatement(sql);
ParameterMetaData pmd = ps.getParameterMetaData();
```

The methods of the `ParameterMetaData` class are:

Method	Description
`String getParameterClassName(int param)`	Gets the fully qualified name of the class to be passed to the `PreparedStatement.setObject()` method
`int getParameterCount()`	Returns the number of parameters
`int getParameterMode(int param)`	Returns the mode of the specified parameter
`int getParameterType(int param)`	Returns the SQL type of the specified parameter
`String getParameterTypeName(int param)`	Returns the database specific type name of the specified parameter; returns the fully qualified type name if the parameter is user-defined
`int getPrecision(int param)`	Returns the precision (number of decimal digits) for the specified parameter
`int getScale(int param)`	Returns the scale (number of digits to the right of the decimal point) for the specified parameter
`int isNullable(int param)`	Checks to see if the specified parameter is nullable (returns one of three values: `nullable`, `notnullabale`, or `nullableunknown`)
`boolean isSigned(int param)`	Returns True if the specified parameter can be a signed number

Given the SQL in the snippet above (`INSERT INTO tracks...`), the `ParameterMetaData` methods should return the following values:

Method	Return value
`getParameterClassName(1)`	`java.lang.Integer`
`getParameterClassName(3)`	`java.lang.String`
`getParameterCount()`	6 (there are 6 placeholders in the SQL)
`getParameterMode(1)`	`ParameterMetaData.parameterModeIn`
`getParameterType(1)`	`java.sql.Types.INTEGER`
`getParameterType(3)`	`java.sql.Types.VARCHAR`
`getParameterTypeName(1)`	Name of the database type for the parameter; value depends on database
`getPrecision(1)`	`10` (track ID has precision 10 according to the Cloudscape `cview` tool. There is no way to verify that `getPrecision()` would return this value until Cloudscape implements `ParameterMetaData`)
`getScale(1)`	`0` (track ID has scale 0)
`isNullable(1)`	`ParameterMetaData.parameterNoNulls` (track ID is not allowed to be `null`)
`isNullable(3)`	`ParameterMetaData.parameterNullable` (track title can be `null`)
`isSigned(1)`	`false`

The purpose of most of the methods should be clear from the method name. For full details, you can refer to the current Javadoc for JDK1.4 at http://java.sun.com/j2se/1.4/docs/api/index.html and the JDBC 3.0 specification at http://java.sun.com/products/jdbc/download.html.

One method above that we will comment on briefly is the `getParameterClassName()` method. In the `Track` class, the code explicitly called the `setInt()` and `setString()` methods. However, you can set a parameter using the `setObject()` methods. The `setObject()` methods can be used to set parameters that would normally be Java primitives such as `int`, `float`, and `double`. In these cases, the `setObject()` methods take a Java object such as `Integer` and convert the object to the correct JDBC type. For example, suppose you had a placeholder in the first position that could be set with the `setInt()` method. You could use either of the two lines of code below to set that placeholder:

```
//assume x is an int and has been initialized to some value
ps.setInt(1, x);
ps.setObject(1, new Integer(x));
```

In the call to `setObject()`, the `Integer` object is converted to a JDBC `INTEGER` and the placeholder is set with the correct `int` value. The `getParameterClassName()` method returns the Java class name of the object that would be used to set the placeholder using the `setObject()` methods. That is why `getParameterClassName(1)` returns the name `java.lang.Integer` when the column is of type `int`.

In actuality, if you are developing an application against a specific database, you are unlikely to need to use the `ParameterMetaData` object. You will already know the structure of the database, and the prepared statement will reflect that structure. So, there won't be any need for your code to dynamically learn about the `PreparedStatement` object. For example, when the `Track` class was presented in the previous section, we knew the structure of the table and the SQL string for inserting a row into the table. We knew which placeholder represented which column, and the values that needed to be set for that column.

The `ParameterMetaData` object will most likely be used by tool developers or developers of applications that can be used against an arbitrary database.

In Chapter 10, *Using Meta Data*, we looked briefly at an application that could be used to browse an arbitrary database. The `dbbrowser` application used `DatabaseMetaData` to determine which tables were in the database. Then, the application executes the fixed SQL string `SELECT * FROM` *tablename*. It uses `ResultSetMetaData` to learn the number of columns and the column names in the `ResultSet` and uses that information to dynamically build the display for the data. The application uses a scrollable `ResultSet` to allow the table entries to be navigated. However, even though the application allows a user to scroll forwards and backwards through the table, there is no easy way to jump to a specific entry in the table.

The application presented in Chapter 9, *Using Statements and Resultsets*, retrieves all the rows in a given table. If the row that the user wants to examine is in the middle of the `ResultSet`, the user will need to scroll through half the rows to get to the desired row. This might be OK for a table with 10 rows, but not for anything much larger.

Suppose we wanted to allow the user to enter an arbitrary SQL statement that the `dbbrowser` tool would execute using a prepared statement. The user would be able to enter a SQL statement with a `WHERE` clause that returns only a subset of the rows. The tool could create a prepared statement using the SQL string entered by the user, and then use `ParameterMetaData` to dynamically build an interface with fields for each of the parameters in the SQL. For example, we could implement GUI code in the tool to display this dialog box for entering the SQL. The user might enter the SQL string that is shown:

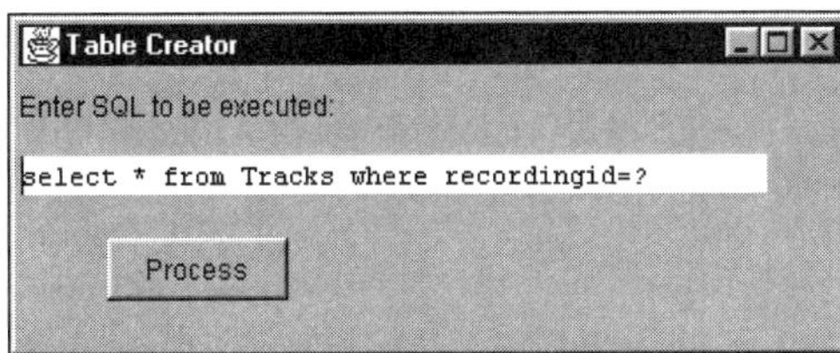

After clicking the Process button, the code would evaluate the prepared statement using `ParameterMetaData`, determine the statement contained a single placeholder (`getParameterCount()`) that represented a number (`getParameterType()`), and finally change the display:

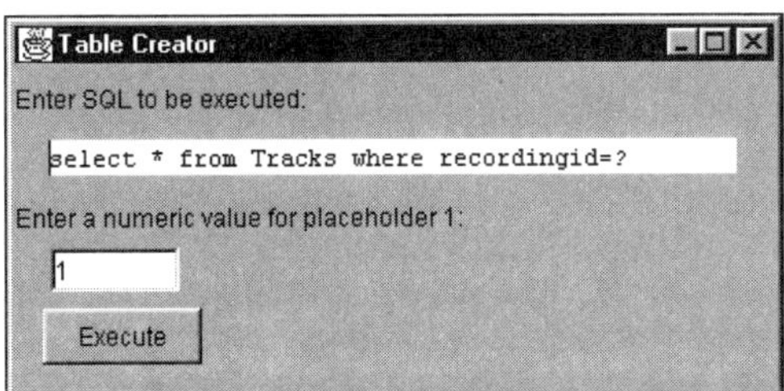

The user would enter the data, and then click the **Execute** button. The application would read the entered value, validate the value, and then execute the SQL. The data display in the application would then show the results of executing the SQL. By leaving the dialog visible on the desktop, the user could enter different values for the placeholder, and then re-execute the SQL.

If the user entered a different SQL string and pressed **Process**, the dialog could be dynamically changed to show the appropriate prompt:

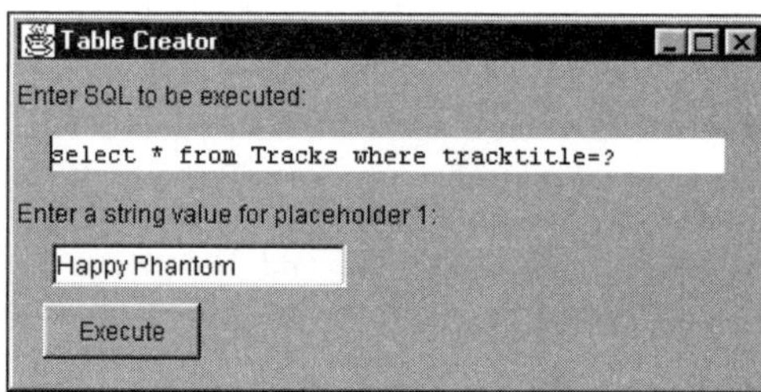

By examining the `ParameterMetaData`, the dialog could be changed to show any number of text fields, one for each placeholder, and adjust the prompt string according to the data type needed.

Although this dynamically adjusting dialog would be a useful addition to the browser application, it can only be implemented if the database and driver implement JDBC 3.0 functionality. Also, this dialog method for entering SQL into the database browser application can't be used to set the placeholders with objects; it can be used only for primitive data types, `Strings`, `Dates`, or any data that can be entered through a text input box. Even though the dialog does not support advanced data types, the `PreparedStatement` object does provide the capability to enter objects or other advanced data types into a database. The next section of the chapter will examine this functionality.

SQL-99 Data Types

While the original JDBC specification only mandated support for SQL-92, JDBC 2.0 and JDBC 3.0 have moved the specification towards support of SQL-99. To support SQL-99, JDBC 2.0 introduced a number of new objects that correspond to data types in SQL-99. Among those new objects are the `BLOB`, `CLOB`, `ARRAY`, `REF`, structured types, distinct types, and `LOCATOR`s. JDBC 3.0 adds the `Boolean` and `Datalink` objects.

When you are inserting simple data types into a database, you can often just insert the literal value into the SQL statement. For example, this code snippet will insert the value 10 into a column in a database:

```
String sql = "INSERT INTO mytable (INT_COL) VALUES (10)";
Statement statement = connection.createStatement();
statement.executeUpdate(sql);
```

However, with advanced data types, we can't just enter the data into an SQL string. For example, suppose we had an array. How do we insert an array into a table?

```
int[] intArray = new int[5][5];
//assume intArray has been initialized
String sql = "INSERT INTO mytable (ARRAY_COL) VALUES (" + intArray + ")";
Statement statement = connection.createStatement();
statement.executeUpdate(sql);
```

The above code will not work. When you concatenate a reference with a `String`, the `toString()` method of the object is called. In the case of the `int` array, this will not insert the array values, but the `String` value of the variable reference. Even if the `toString()` method did return a representation of the data in the array, this would then not fit the SQL because the SQL string is written to insert a single value.

The primary means for inserting an advanced data type into a database is to use a `PreparedStatement`. In the rest of this chapter we briefly cover the various advanced SQL types. There is not time or space to provide examples for all the advanced types, but we will look at two examples of reading and writing advanced data types in a database.

Built-in Types

A **BLOB** is a **B**inary **L**arge **OB**ject, that is, a sequence of bytes (for example, an MP3 file could be stored as a `BLOB`). A **CLOB** is a **C**haracter **L**arge **OB**ject, that is, a string of characters that is too large for a `VARCHAR` or similar column. `BLOB` or `CLOB` data from the database can be manipulated entirely through the `java.sql.Blob` and `java.sql.Clob` objects. The methods provided by the `ResultSet` and `PreparedStatement` objects for handling `BLOB` and `CLOB` data are shown in the table below:

ResultSet	**PreparedStatement**
`Blob getBlob(int)`	`void setBlob(int, Blob)`
`Blob getBlob(String)`	
`Clob getClob(int)`	`void setClob(int, Clob)`
`Clob getClob(String)`	

For example, if you perform a query that returns a `BLOB` column, the `ResultSet` object can call the `getBlob(String)` method. This method does not return the actual data, but rather a reference to the data. Using the `PreparedStatement.setBlob(int, Blob)` method, you can set a placeholder in a prepared statement with the `BLOB` data and 'write' the data into another table by executing the SQL. All this occurs without your code actually reading or writing the binary data. The code to do this might look like this:

```
//assume a table named blob_table with columns blob_col and id
String sql = "select blob_col from blob_table where id=?";
PreparedStatement ps = connection.prepareStatement(sql);
//set the first placeholder with value 1
ps.setInt(1, 1);

ResultSet rset = ps.executeQuery();
//declare variable of type java.sql.Blob
Blob blob = null;
if (rset.next()) {
  blob = rset.getBlob(1);
}
```

The variable `blob` now references `BLOB` data in the database. The binary data has not been sent to the Java program; the variable `blob` does not hold the actual binary data, but rather a reference to the binary data in the database. You can then use this same reference to write the data to another table:

```
//assume another table with a blob column
sql = "insert into blob_table_2 (blob_col) values (?)";
ps = connection.prepareStatement(sql);
ps.setBlob(1, blob);
ps.executeUpdate();
```

The code above "retrieved" binary data from one table and inserted it into another table. At no time, however, was the binary data materialized in the Java code. The Java code dealt with a reference to the binary data.

It is only when you need to materialize the data in your program that the `Blob` and `Clob` objects will be used differently from the other `getXXX` methods of the `ResultSet` object.

The `Blob` and `Clob` interfaces in JDBC 2.0 only provided a means to get the data from the database. This is accomplished by getting an `InputStream` class from the database and reading the data from the stream. Inserting `BLOB` or `CLOB` data into the database relied on database specific functionality. The JDBC 3.0 specification provides additional methods in the `Blob` and `Clob` interfaces for setting the data type of the `BLOB` or `CLOB`. Details of those methods can be found at http://java.sun.com/j2se/1.4/docs/api/index.html.

Try It Out – Storing a Blob Object

In the Music Store database, several of the tables contain data relating to files stored in the file system. The `Tracks` table is one of these tables. It contains a column named `SAMPLEFILESPEC`. This column is intended to hold the path to a file in the file system. That file is a sample of the track, for example, an MP3 file that contains a small sample of the song.

Suppose, however, that the MusicStore application is going to store the track samples in the database itself. We would store the sample as a `BLOB` object in the database. Let's look at the code needed to do this.

The Cloudscape driver does not support the `Blob` object. For this example we will be using an Oracle database. Since this example relies on Oracle specific extensions for storing binary data into a database, this example will only work with an Oracle database.

This example uses the `ConnectionFactory` that was first introduced in Chapter 8. You may need to change it so that it returns a connection to the correct database (Oracle, for this example).

We will implement a class named `TrackSample` that reads and writes binary data into an Oracle table. Here is the complete `TrackSample` class:

```
package sql99;

import javax.swing.*;
import java.io.*;
```

```
import java.sql.*;
import connections.*;

public class TrackSample {
  private int recordingid;
  private int tracknumber;
  private File sampleFile;

  Connection connection;
  Statement statement;
  ResultSet resultset;

  public TrackSample(int id, int number, File file) {
    recordingid = id;
    tracknumber = number;
    sampleFile = file;
  }

  void getConnection(boolean autocommit) throws SQLException {
    connection = ConnectionFactory.getConnection();
    connection.setAutoCommit(autocommit);
  }

  Statement getStatement(boolean autocommit) throws SQLException {
    getConnection(autocommit);
    return connection.createStatement();
  }

  PreparedStatement getPreparedStatement(String sql, boolean autocommit)
                                         throws SQLException {
    getConnection(autocommit);
    return connection.prepareStatement(sql);
  }

  public void create() {
    BufferedInputStream in = null;
    OutputStream out = null;

    try {

      // insert a row into the BLOB table, use the empty_blob()
      // construct for the BLOB field. empty_blob() creates the
      // BLOB locator for Oracle
      statement = getStatement(false);
      statement.executeUpdate("insert into tracksamples " +
                              "(recordingid, tracknumber, sample) " +
                              "values (1, 1, empty_blob())");

      // Retrieve the row that was just inserted
      resultset =
        statement.executeQuery("select sample from tracksamples " +
                               "where recordingid=1 and tracknumber=1 " +
                               "for update");

      if (resultset.next()) {
```

```
      // Get the BLOB locator
      Blob blob = resultset.getBlob(1);

      // Get the output stream which will be used to send
      // data to the table. Use Oracle extension because
      // JDBC 2.0 does not support writing data to BLOB
      out = ((oracle.sql.BLOB) blob).getBinaryOutputStream();

      // Let driver compute buffer size for writing to BLOB
      int bufferSize = (int) ((oracle.sql.BLOB) blob).getBufferSize();

      // Create a buffered stream to read from the file
      in = new BufferedInputStream(new FileInputStream(sampleFile),
                                   bufferSize);

      // Create a byte buffer and start reading from the file
      byte[] b = new byte[bufferSize];
      int count = in.read(b, 0, bufferSize);

      // write the bytes using the OutputStream
      // loop until all bytes are written to the table
      System.out.print("Storing data in database.");
      while (count != -1) {
        out.write(b, 0, count);
        System.out.print(".");
        count = in.read(b, 0, bufferSize);
      }

      System.out.println("Complete");

      // Close the Input and Output Streams
      // The Output stream MUST be closed before the commit
      out.close();
      out = null;
      in.close();
      in = null;

      // And finally, commit the changes
      connection.commit();
    }
  } catch (Exception e) {
    e.printStackTrace();
    try {
      connection.rollback();
    } catch (Exception ignored) {}
  } finally {

    // if an exception occurred, the streams may not have been closed
    // so close them here if needed
    if (out != null) {
      try {
        out.close();
      } catch (Exception ignored) {}
```

```
      }
      if (in != null) {
        try {
          in.close();
        } catch (Exception ignored) {}

      }
      close();
    }
    return;
  }

  public void retrieve() {
    int bufferSize;
    BufferedOutputStream out = null;
    InputStream in = null;

    try {
      statement = getStatement(false);

      // Retrieve the row that has the selected name
      resultset =
        statement.executeQuery("select sample from tracksamples " +
                               "where tracknumber= "+ tracknumber +
                               "and recordingid=" + recordingid);

      if (resultset.next()) {

        // Get the BLOB locator
        Blob blob = resultset.getBlob(1);

        // Get the input stream which will be used to read
        // data from the table.
        in = blob.getBinaryStream();

        bufferSize = (int) ((oracle.sql.BLOB) blob).getBufferSize();

        // Create a buffered stream to write to the file
        out = new BufferedOutputStream(new FileOutputStream(sampleFile),
                                       bufferSize);

        // Create a byte buffer and start reading from the file
        byte[] b = new byte[bufferSize];
        int count = in.read(b, 0, bufferSize);

        // write the bytes using the OutputStream
        // loop until all bytes are written to the table
        System.out.print("Writing file.");
        while (count != -1) {
          System.out.print(".");
          out.write(b, 0, count);
          count = in.read(b, 0, (int) bufferSize);
        }
        System.out.println("Complete");
```

```
        }

        // Close the Input and Output Streams
        out.flush();
        out.close();
        out = null;
        in.close();
        in = null;

      } catch (Exception e) {
        e.printStackTrace();
      } finally {
        if (out != null) {
          try {
            out.close();
          } catch (Exception ignored) {}
        }
        if (in != null) {
          try {
            in.close();
          } catch (Exception ignored) {}

        }
        close();
      }
      return;
    }

    void close() {
      ConnectionFactory.close(resultset);
      ConnectionFactory.close(statement);
      ConnectionFactory.close(connection);
    }
  }
```

Save this as `C:\BegJavaDB\Ch12\sql99\TrackSample.java`, and compile it with the following command:

```
> javac -classpath .;%JLIB%\classes12.zip sql99/TrackSample.java
```

As before, `connections.ConnectionFactory` needs to be in the classpath, and set to establish a connection to an Oracle database. Before looking at the test class, we will first need to create a table to store the track sample. Here is the SQL to do this in Oracle:

```
create table TRACKSAMPLES (RecordingId int,
                           TrackNumber int,
                           Sample Blob);
```

The class to test the `TrackSample` class follows:

```
package sql99;

import javax.swing.*;
import java.io.*;
import java.sql.*;
import connections.*;

public class TestTrackSample {
  public static void main(String[] args) {
    String filename =
      chooseFile("Select the file to be stored in the database");
    System.out.println("Filename=[" + filename + "]");

    TrackSample ts = null;
    if (!filename.equals("")) {
      File file = new File(filename);
      ts = new TrackSample(1, 1, file);
      ts.create();
    }

    filename = chooseFile("Select the file where the binary data " +
                          "will be written");
    System.out.println("Filename=[" + filename + "]");
    if (!filename.equals("")) {
      File file = new File(filename);
      ts = new TrackSample(1, 1, file);
      ts.retrieve();
    }

    System.exit(0);
  }

  static String chooseFile(String title) {

    // Use a JFileChooser to let the user select the file to be
    // read and written to the media table
    JFileChooser chooser = new JFileChooser();
    chooser.setDialogTitle(title);
    int returnVal = chooser.showOpenDialog(null);
    String pathname = "";
    if (returnVal == JFileChooser.APPROVE_OPTION) {
      pathname = chooser.getSelectedFile().getAbsolutePath();
    } else {
      System.out.println("No file selected");
    }

    chooser = null;
    return pathname;
  }
}
```

Save this as `C:\BegJavaDB\Ch12\sql99\TestTrackSample.java`, and compile using the following command:

```
> javac -classpath .;%JLIB%\classes12.zip sql99/TestTrackSample.java
```

When the test program is run with the following command, you will first see a FileChooser dialog:

```
> java -classpath .;%JLIB%\classes12.zip sql99.TestTrackSample
```

Select a file in the file system that the program can write to the database:

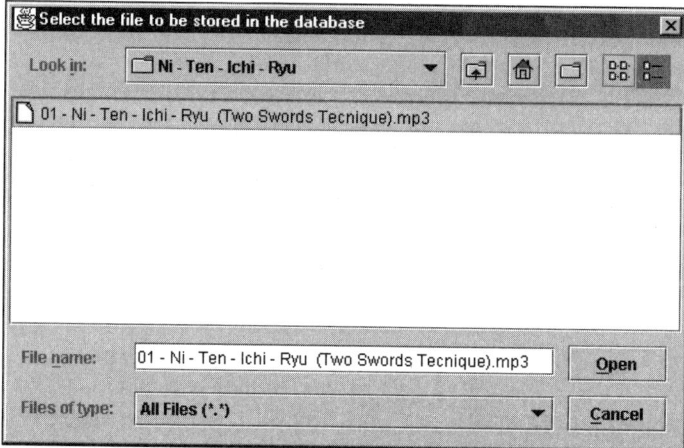

The program displays the progress of writing the data with a series of dots ... as each buffer is written to the database. When the write is complete, another FileChooser dialog is displayed; use this dialog to select a location and file name to write the data from the database back to the file system. You will want to choose an unused file name and path:

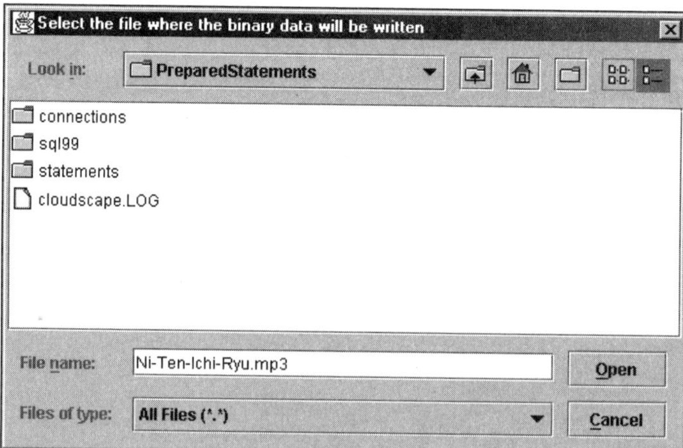

After getting the data from the database and writing it to the file system, the program copies the data from one row in the table to another row. Your output will look something like this:

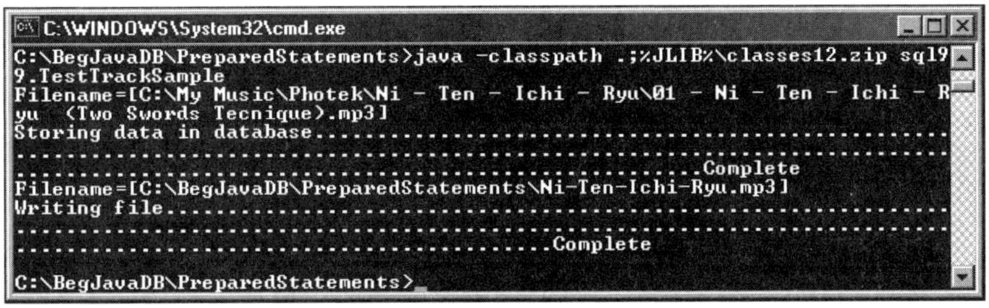

```
C:\WINDOWS\System32\cmd.exe
C:\BegJavaDB\PreparedStatements>java -classpath .;%JLIB%\classes12.zip sql9
9.TestTrackSample
Filename=[C:\My Music\Photek\Ni - Ten - Ichi - Ryu\01 - Ni - Ten - Ichi - R
yu (Two Swords Tecnique).mp3]
Storing data in database..................................................
..........................................................................
.......................................................Complete
Filename=[C:\BegJavaDB\PreparedStatements\Ni-Ten-Ichi-Ryu.mp3]
Writing file..............................................................
..........................................................................
..........................................Complete

C:\BegJavaDB\PreparedStatements>_
```

How It Works

Now let's look at how `TrackSample` works. As mentioned above, JDBC 2.0 does not provide a standard way to insert `BLOB` data into a database, so our example relies on Oracle-specific code to insert a track sample. Like the `Store` class in previous chapters, the `TrackSample` class has a data member for each of the table columns. The one difference is that a `File` object will represent the track sample. The constructor for the class has a parameter for each data member.

Also familiar should be the `getConnection()`, `getStatement()`, and `getPreparedStatement()` methods. One new aspect is that the `getConnection()` method takes a `boolean` parameter.

```
void getConnection(boolean autocommit) throws SQLException {
  connection = ConnectionFactory.getConnection();
  connection.setAutoCommit(autocommit);
}
```

This parameter is used to change the commit setting of the `Connection` object. As you will see soon, we are using a stream to send the binary data to the database. As a result of this, the code must not commit any data until *all the data* has been written to the database. The `getConnection()` method is called from either `getStatement()` or `getPreparedStatement()`. Here is the `getPreparedStatement()` method:

```
PreparedStatement getPreparedStatement(String sql, boolean autocommit)
                                       throws SQLException {
  getConnection(autocommit);
  return connection.prepareStatement(sql);
}
```

The methods in the class that do the bulk of the work are the `create()` and `retrieve()` methods. After getting a `Statement` object, the `create()` method inserts a row into the table. Since we can't pass a `BLOB` in the SQL `INSERT`, the SQL uses a special Oracle parameter, `empty_blob()`, to indicate that the row should be created without `BLOB` data:

```
statement.executeUpdate("insert into tracksamples " +
                        "(recordingid, tracknumber, sample) " +
                        "values (1, 1, empty_blob())");
```

Then, the code queries the database for the newly inserted row, and gets a `BLOB` reference from the `ResultSet`. Using this reference, the code obtains an `OutputStream` object, which can be used to write data to the `BLOB` column in the database:

```
Blob blob = rs.getBlob(1);

out = ((oracle.sql.BLOB)blob).getBinaryOutputStream();
```

When the constructor was called, the calling code passed a `File` object to the class. This file object is opened, and the data is read from the file and written to the database:

```
in = new BufferedInputStream(
  new FileInputStream(sampleFile), bufferSize);

//Create a byte buffer and start reading from the file
byte[] b = new byte[bufferSize];
int count = in.read(b, 0, bufferSize);

//write the bytes using the OutputStream
//loop until all bytes are written to the table
while (count != -1) {
  out.write(b, 0, count);
  count = in.read(b, 0, bufferSize);
}
```

The last thing the method does is to close all the resources that were used by the method.

The `retrieve()` method is similar, except that no database-specific functionality is needed to read `BLOB` data from the database. `BLOB` data can be read by getting a `BLOB` reference from a `ResultSet`, obtaining an input stream from the `BLOB`, and then materializing the data. In the `TrackSample` class, we chose to write the `BLOB` data to a file:

```
Blob blob = rs.getBlob(1);

//Get the input stream which will be used to read
//data from the table.
in = blob.getBinaryStream();

bufferSize = (int) ((oracle.sql.BLOB)blob).getBufferSize();

//Create a buffered stream to write to the file
out = new BufferedOutputStream(
        new FileOutputStream(sampleFile), bufferSize);

//Create a byte buffer and start reading from the file
byte[] b = new byte[bufferSize];
int count = in.read(b, 0, bufferSize);

//write the bytes using the OutputStream
//loop until all bytes are written to the table
System.out.print("Writing file.");
while (count != -1) {
  System.out.print(".");
  out.write(b, 0, count);
  out.flush();
  count = in.read(b, 0, (int)bufferSize);
}
```

The `create()` and `retrieve()` methods need to use streams to send data to or get data from the database. If, however, the data is merely being moved from one table to another, no streams are needed. If we had simply needed to move the `BLOB` from one table to another in the same database, we could have used pure JDBC code. After performing a query of a table with `BLOB` data, the code can get a `BLOB` reference with the `getBlob()` method. Using the `PreparedStatement setBlob(int Blob)` method, the code sets the `BLOB` data for the SQL `INSERT`, and executes the SQL. This is shown in the code snippet below; notice that the code does not need to read or write a binary stream to get `BLOB` data from one table and insert it into another table:

```
blob = rs.getBlob(1);

String sql = "insert into tracksamples " +
  "(recordingid, tracknumber, sample) values (?, ? , ?)";
ps = getPreparedStatement(sql, true);
ps.setInt(1, newRecordingId);
ps.setInt(2, newTrackNumber);
ps.setBlob(3, blob);

int result = ps.executeUpdate();
```

That's it for the `TrackSample` class.

Now, the `TestTrackSample` test class starts by using a `JFileChooser` to allow the user to select a file in the file system. The `JFileChooser` is a Swing class that creates a dialog for choosing a file from the file system. This file will be written into the database. That action is performed by creating a `TrackSample` instance and calling the `create()` method:

```
if (!filename.equals("")) {
  File file = new File(filename);
  ts = new TrackSample(1, 1, file);
  ts.create();
}
```

Next, to demonstrate that the data from the file was actually written to the database, another `JFileChooser` is presented to the user. This time, the user is selecting a location to write the new file. Again, the code creates a `TrackSample` instance, and this time calls the `retrieve()` method:

```
File file = new File(filename);
ts = new TrackSample(1, 1, file);
ts.retrieve();
```

If you are running this code with an Oracle database, you can use SQL*PLUS to verify that a new row has been added to the database. Of course, to verify that this new row does indeed contain a copy of some other track sample, you will need to retrieve the `BLOB` data and examine it. Alternatively, you can play the file that we've just moved to prove to yourself that it works.

User-Defined Types

The other types of data we'll be looking at are user-defined data types.

Structured type

A **structured type** is a way to create new types in the database that more fully define the data being stored in them. The structured type is analogous to a Java object. For example, if a given database supported structured types (like Oracle), we might define a `Track` type like this:

```
CREATE TYPE TRACK_TYPE AS (recordingid int, tracknumber int, tracktitle)
```

Now `TRACK_TYPE` could be used in a SQL `CREATE TABLE` statement as a column type, or in any other place where we might use a built-in data type:

```
CREATE TABLE samples (sample_id NUMBER,
                      sample_track TRACK_TYPE,
                      sample BLOB);
```

In the SQL above, we've created a table with a column that is the structured type `TRACK_TYPE`.

You could even create a Java object that could be mapped to the new type in the database. These types can be manipulated using the `getObject()` and `setObject()` methods:

ResultSet	PreparedStatement
`Object getObject(int)`	`void setObject(int, Object)`
`Object getObject(String)`	

Try It Out

The example in this section was developed and tested against an Oracle database. While the Java portions of the example should work with any database that supports structured types, you may need to modify the SQL for your database. You may also need to modify the `ConnectionFactory` class (see Chapter 8) so that it returns a connection to the correct database.

First, here is the SQL that was used to create a structured type in an Oracle database:

```
CREATE OR REPLACE TYPE artist AS OBJECT (name VARCHAR2(50),
                                         imagespec VARCHAR2(200),
                                         bio VARCHAR2(2000));
```

And we need a table that uses the type. Here's a table with a single column of type `artist`:

```
CREATE TABLE artists (id integer, performer artist);
```

We now need a Java class that can map to this new type. The class will have a member variable for each column in the table, and it must implement an interface named `java.sql.SQLData`. The `SQLData` interface defines two methods: `readSQL()` and `writeSQL()`.

```
package sql99;

import java.sql.*;
import java.io.*;

public class Artist implements SQLData, Serializable {
  public String name;
  public String imagespec;
  public String bio;

  private String sql_type;

  public Artist() {}
  public Artist(String type, String aName, String image, String bioText) {
    sql_type = type;
    name = aName;
    imagespec = image;
    bio = bioText;
  }

  public String getSQLTypeName() {
    return sql_type;
  }

  public void readSQL(SQLInput stream, String type) throws SQLException {
    sql_type = type;
    name = stream.readString();
    imagespec = stream.readString();
    bio = stream.readString();
  }

  public void writeSQL(SQLOutput stream) throws SQLException {
    stream.writeString(name);
    stream.writeString(imagespec);
    stream.writeString(bio);
  }
}
```

Save this code as `C:\BegJavaDB\PreparedStatements\sql99\Artist.java`, and compile it with the following command:

```
> javac -classpath . sql99/Artist.java
```

Then we'll create a class to test this functionality:

```
package sql99;

import java.sql.*;
import connections.ConnectionFactory;
import java.util.Map;

public class TestArtist {
  public static void main(String[] args) {
```

```
    Connection connection = null;
    PreparedStatement ps = null;
    ResultSet resultSet = null;

    try {
      connection = ConnectionFactory.getConnection();
      Map map = connection.getTypeMap();
      map.put("ARTIST", Artist.class);

      String sql = "INSERT INTO artists (id, performer) VALUES (?, ?)";
      ps = connection.prepareStatement(sql);
      Artist artist = new Artist("ARTIST", "John Hiatt", "link to picture",
                                 "Singer-songwriter");
      ps.setInt(1, 1);
      ps.setObject(2, artist);
      int result = ps.executeUpdate();

      if (result != 1) {
        System.out.println("Insert failed!");
        return;
      }

      artist = new Artist("ARTIST", "", "", "");
      System.out.println("Created new artist object, name is [" +
                         artist.name + "]");
      sql = "SELECT * FROM artists WHERE id=1";
      ps = connection.prepareStatement(sql);
      resultSet = ps.executeQuery();
      if (resultSet.next()) {
        artist = (Artist) resultSet.getObject(2);
        System.out.println("Retrieved artist, name = " + artist.name);
      } else {
        System.out.println("Error retrieving artist");
      }
    } catch (Exception e) {
      e.printStackTrace();
    } finally {
      ConnectionFactory.close(resultSet);
      ConnectionFactory.close(ps);
      ConnectionFactory.close(connection);
    }
  }
}
```

Save this file as `C:\BegJavaDB\Ch12\sql99\TestArtist.java`, and compile it with the following command:

```
> javac -classpath . sql99/TestArtist.java
```

We can run this program with the following command:

```
> java -classpath .;%JLIB%\classes12.zip sql99.TestArtist
```

Running this program will result in output like this:

```
C:\WINDOWS\System32\cmd.exe
C:\BegJavaDB\PreparedStatements>java -classpath .;%JLIB%\classes12.zip sql9
9.TestArtist
Created new artist object, name is []
Retrieved artist, name = John Hiatt

C:\BegJavaDB\PreparedStatements>
```

How It Works

The `Artist` class is relatively straightforward. It must have a member variable for every column in the table. It must also have a `getSQLTypeName()`, `readSQL()`, and `writeSQL()` method because it implements `SQLData`. The member variables are initialized in the same order in which they appear in the type definition. The class also writes the member data to the `SQLOutput` stream in the same order as they appear in type definition.

The first step to use the user-defined type is to get the mapping of types to classes from the `Connection`. This is done with a call to `getTypeMap()`. Then we add the mapping from the database type `"ARTIST"` to the class `Artist`:

```
Map map = connection.getTypeMap();
map.put("ARTIST", Artist.class);
```

The next step is to insert a row into the artist table that was created above. The code gets a `PreparedStatement` object, creates an `Artist` object, and then uses the `setObject()` method call to set the object. Calling `executeUpdate()` inserts and commits the new data. Notice that after the table and type have been defined in the database, the driver and the `Artist` class automatically write all the member data to the database:

```
String sql = "INSERT INTO artists (id, performer) VALUES (?, ?)";
ps = connection.prepareStatement(sql);
Artist artist = new Artist("ARTIST", "John Hiatt",
                           "link to picture", "Singer-songwriter");
ps.setInt(1, 1);
ps.setObject(2, artist);
int result = ps.executeUpdate();

if (result != 1) {
  System.out.println("Insert failed!");
  return;
}
```

The same automatic mapping occurs when the object is read from the database. The parsing and initializing of the data members of the `Artist` object is handled automatically. When the driver gets the object from the database, the type map indicates that the data is an `Artist` object. The driver instantiates an `Artist` object and initializes the member variables from the data. It then returns the object. The only special step that the code needs to take is to cast the object to the correct type because `getObject()` returns an `Object` reference:

```
artist = new Artist("ARTIST", "", "", "");
System.out.println("Created new artist object, name is [" +
```

```
                    artist.name + "]");
sql = "SELECT * FROM artists WHERE id=1";
ps = connection.prepareStatement(sql);
resultSet = ps.executeQuery();
if (resultSet.next()) {
  artist = (Artist) resultSet.getObject(2);
```

Distinct Type

The **Distinct type** is like an alias to a built-in type. For example, suppose you wanted to have an alias for a date that more fully defined the function of a particular column. You might define this type like this:

```
CREATE TYPE BIRTHDATE AS DATE
```

Since this new type is simply an alias to an existing built-in type, you would use the existing getXXX and setXXX methods for columns of this new type. In the specific case of the BIRTHDATE type, you would use getDate() and setDate().

Constructed Types

The **Array** is a new type added to the java.sql package to deal with arrays. When getting an array from a database, Array methods can access the row and column values by specifying the row index and column index, or the Array object can return the array as a ResultSet. (Recall that a ResultSet is just a way to access the column values in a set of rows.)

A **Ref object** is the representation of an instance of a structured type in the database. For instance, suppose we had a table that stored an instance of a TRACK_TYPE object in a column (the TRACK_TYPE type was defined above). If we executed a query that returned the TRACK_TYPE column, we would get a reference to that object in the column with getRef().

ResultSet	PreparedStatement
Array getArray(int)	void setArray(int, Array)
Array getArray(String)	
Ref getRef(int)	void setRef(int, Ref)
Ref getRef(String)	

Locator Types

A **LOCATOR** is a reference or a pointer to data that resides in the database. This is data that would normally be expensive to materialize in the client for every value that is accessed. For example, if you had a table of BLOB data and each BLOB entry was 2 GB, you wouldn't want to get the bytes for every entry when you called getBlob(). You would deal with a reference to the BLOB, and only get the bytes if you really needed them.

You will not normally deal directly with a LOCATOR, but rather with a class that uses one. For example, the Blob and Clob interfaces provide a convenient way to deal with BLOB and CLOB data. As mentioned previously, these objects are really references to the actual data. The classes use a LOCATOR internally to provide their functionality.

New for JDBC 3.0

New in JDBC 3.0 is the built-in type `Boolean`. The `Boolean` type represents `true` or `false` values in the database. You get a `Boolean` from a `ResultSet` object using `getBoolean(int)` or `getBoolean(String)` and set a `Boolean` in a `PreparedStatement` object using `setBoolean(int, boolean)`:

ResultSet	PreparedStatement
`boolean getBoolean(int)`	`void setBoolean(int, boolean)`
`boolean getBoolean(String)`	

Also new in JDBC 3.0 is the **Datalink**. The `Datalink` represents data that is stored externally to the database. For example, the Music-Store database has columns in some tables for a file name (for example, the `SAMPLEFILESPEC` column in the `Tracks` table). The data is stored externally to the database in the file system and the table has data that tells us how to access the data in the file system. In JDBC 3.0 this could be represented as a JDBC `Datalink`. `Datalink` values are handled using `setURL()` and `getURL()` methods.

ResultSet	PreparedStatement
`URL getURL(int)`	`void setURL (int, URL)`
`URL getURL(String)`	

PreparedStatement Interface Methods

Many of the methods used to deal with the SQL-99 data types have been mentioned above. Here is the complete list of `setXXX` methods that were added with to the JDBC 2.0 `PreparedStatement` interface. Just as with the `setXXX` methods that were presented earlier in the chapter, the first parameter is the placeholder index in the `PreparedStatement` SQL. The second parameter is the object to be set.

- `void setArray(int parameterIndex, Array x)`
- `void setBlob(int parameterIndex, Blcob x)`
- `void setCharacterStream(int parameterIndex, Reader reader, int length)`
- `void setClob(int parameterIndexc Clob x)`
- `void setDate(int parameterIndex, Date x, Calendar cal)`
- `void setRef(int parameterIndex, Ref x)`
- `void setTime(int parameterIndex, Time x, Calendar cal)`
- `void setTimestamp(int parameterIndex, Timestamp x, Calendar cal)`

Summary

In this chapter we learned one way to improve the efficiency of our JDBC application. The prepared statement provides a means to send a SQL string with placeholders to the database where the database can pre-process the string. Another way to simplify development or improve efficiency is to let the database perform some processing in the application. If you are working with a legacy database, the database may already have procedures stored to perform some processing. We'll look at how to call those procedures in Chapter13, *Callable Statements and Stored Procedures.*

You saw how to use the `PreparedStatement` object when we developed the `Track` class. One scenario for using the `PreparedStatement` object with this class is when we expect to perform many queries for tracks where the only thing that changes is the search value. The chapter did not demonstrate the `create()` function, although the same reasoning applies there as well: much of the data for an entry in the `Tracks` table was the same from track to track.

Suppose that we had used a different design and implementation, one that called for a separate `Track` instance for each track and that as each instance inserted its data, the insert was committed. If we then had a problem executing the code, we might end up with some track information in the database and some track information not present. In Chapter 14, *Transactions*, we'll look at transactions and how a transaction solves the problem of data not being correctly added to the database. We'll also see that the design choice we made for the `Tracks` class helps with transaction management.

We also briefly looked at some SQL-99 data types. Unlike literal values, you will often need to use a `PreparedStatement` to read and write advanced data types in a database. We looked at two examples showing how to use `BLOB` data and a user-defined type with a database. Different databases may handle advanced types differently; you should consult your database documentation for more information.

akarta
JAVA

Callable Statements and Stored Procedures

One way of improving the productivity of database developers has been to provide a means to store commonly executed SQL statements in the database so they can be reused. These stored statements are often called procedures or functions and they provide code reusability and other advantages to database developers. The *Stored Procedures* section provides a brief overview of this functionality.

Since the classes and methods we've seen earlier in the book can be used to execute almost any kind of SQL statement, they can also be used to create stored procedures. In the *Procedure Examples* section we'll look at some simple stored procedures and show one example of using a Java class to create a stored procedure.

The `DatabaseMetaData` interface, which is part of the `java.sql` package, provides methods for determining the support provided for stored procedures by the database and driver. The `ShowDatabaseMetaData` class is modified again to demonstrate how to call these methods.

Next we look at how to actually call stored procedures from JDBC code. This capability is provided through the `CallableStatement` interface, which is again part of the `java.sql` package. In the *Callable Statements* section, we look at how to create a `CallableStatement` object, how to set or register the parameters, and how to get a return value from a `CallableStatement` object.

In the final section of this chapter, *New in JDBC 3.0*, we look at new functionality for callable statements provided by the JDBC 3.0 specification.

Stored Procedures

The first part of this chapter provides an introduction to stored procedures. If you already have experience with stored procedures, you may want to skip the first part of this chapter and go directly to the Java material.

Stored procedures are, as the name might suggest, procedures that are stored in the database. They consist of some set of SQL statements and procedural language (PL) statements that can be called by name to perform some work in the database. The stored procedure may take some input parameters as arguments, or it may take no parameters. It can also return a value to the caller, or it can return nothing. In this sense, stored procedures are similar to methods in Java classes; Java class methods are called by name, they can take some or no parameters, and they can return a value or nothing (void).

In this chapter, the term 'stored procedure' is used generically to refer to both procedures and functions. The main difference between the two is that a function returns a value and a procedure does not return a value. If your database supports storing procedural and SQL statements in the database for execution, but uses a different term, you should consider 'stored procedure' to be a synonym for the term used by your database.

There are many reasons why we would use stored procedures. Some of the services provided by stored procedures are encapsulation and reuse of functionality, control of transactions, and standardization of business rules.

Encapsulation and Reuse

Different parts of our Music Store application will probably need to perform similar functions. For example, out application will probably have code that performs a query of recordings for inventory control; at the same time, there will be a query of recordings for customers to purchase. Rather than have two places in the application with code that queries the `Recordings` table, we could put the query functionality into a stored procedure. This allows any part of the application to have the ability to perform this query. Yet, no part of the application has to know how to structure the query because we've encapsulated the SQL into a procedure that can be called by a simple name.

If you are working with a legacy database that supports stored procedures, the chances are good that many stored procedures have already been written. These stored procedures have probably been well exercised over the years, so we are fairly confident they are bug free. Why should we redevelop this capability when we can reuse something that's already in place? By reusing existing stored procedures, we can concentrate on new functionality.

Transaction Control

Basically, transactions are a way to treat a set of SQL statements as one indivisible (atomic) unit of work. If all the statements succeed, then the changes made by the procedure during the transaction can be committed (saved); if the one of the statements in the transaction fails, the changes can be undone. Because stored procedures provide a means to group SQL statements together, they fit well with transaction control. The procedure is a natural unit of work. We can start a transaction, call a stored procedure, and then either save or undo the change when the procedure ends. Further, we can group multiple procedures together and build larger transactions (as long as none of the procedures saves changes in its body).

We look at transactions and transaction control in greater detail in Chapter 14.

Standardization

If three different developers are providing the same functionality in different parts of the application, it is a certainty that they will each develop the functionality in different ways. Further, if at some point in the future this functionality needs to change, there are three places in the application where the change must be applied. By providing this functionality in a stored procedure we can be sure that every part of the application that uses the functionality does so in the same way. More importantly, when the functionality is changed, there is only one place to make the fix, and then everyone who uses the procedure automatically gets the change.

As a stored procedure in a database, this procedure also becomes accessible to any code that can connect to the database. This is helpful in a distributed application. In a distributed application, we might have application components running on half a dozen or more servers. If the functionality were implemented as a Java class library, or a shared library in another language, the library would have to be physically accessible, either directly or through a mapped drive, to all the components that needed it. By having a procedure in a database, the code exists in one place only, yet is accessible to anyone who can connect to the database.

Even though they provide useful features, not all databases implement stored procedures. The MySQL database is one of those. Other databases may provide similar functionality in a different manner. Cloudscape, for example, doesn't support storing SQL statements, but does support storing and executing Java classes. In the next section, we'll examine some of the general requirements that apply to creating and using stored procedures.

Procedure Requirements

Each stored procedure must follow certain rules for it to be a valid procedure that the database can store. While some of these rules will be database-specific, there are some requirements that will be generally true for all stored procedures. These requirements apply to:

- Names
- Parameter modes
- Parameter types

Names

To be able to call a stored procedure, the procedure must be given a name. Since the procedure is stored in the database, the name used for the procedure must be a legal name in the database. Thus, if your database constrains names to be a certain number of characters long, the procedure name has the same constraint. If only certain characters are legal in a name, the same set of legal characters must be used for the procedure name.

The parameters that are used by the procedure must also have legal database names. In addition, the parameters will have one of three modes: `IN`, `OUT`, or `INOUT` and they will have a valid SQL or database-specific type.

IN Parameters

IN parameters are parameters that are used to pass a value into a stored procedure for the procedure to use. The stored procedure uses but does not change the value of the IN parameter. The stored procedure will be able to accept any legal SQL type as an IN parameter. Further, your database will also allow database-specific types as parameters.

OUT Parameters

An OUT parameter is a parameter that is returned from the procedure. The caller might or might not be able to set the variable used in the procedure call with a value, but the procedure will not use that value in any way. In the course of execution, the procedure will assign a value to the OUT parameter, and the caller can read this value when the procedure completes.

INOUT Parameters

INOUT parameters are parameters that are used to pass information into a stored procedure, and are set by the stored procedure with a new value. That is, the procedure uses the value that is passed into the procedure just like an IN parameter, and it may assign a new value to this parameter just like an OUT parameter.

Parameter Usage

IN parameters can be used with both procedures and functions. OUT and INOUT parameters are usually used with procedures. This is more a matter of good programming than of requirement. A stored function already returns a value; while you can write a function to return multiple values using OUT or INOUT parameters, it is not the best programming style. While there may be situations where it makes sense to have a function return multiple values, returning multiple values is generally a sign that the stored function is trying to do too much, and it should be re-factored into two or more functions or procedures.

Parameter Type

Just as with a Java method, each parameter used by a stored procedure will be of a specific SQL or database type. And, just as with Java methods, it would be an error to pass a value of an incorrect type for one of the parameters. For example, if an IN parameter were defined to be an SQL DOUBLE, it would be an error to call the procedure with a VARCHAR value for that parameter. Likewise, if the procedure were defined to accept three parameters, it would be an error to pass two parameters, four parameters, or any number of parameters other than three.

Procedure Examples

In the real world, you may never need to develop your own stored procedures or stored functions. They may already exist in the database and you will use what is available, or a database expert will provide them for you. Anything else you need you can probably accomplish just as easily with JDBC code sending SQL to the database. On the other hand, because of the advantages of using stored procedures, you may decide that you want to implement or use stored procedures in your application.

For example, suppose our Music Store application was actually developed as a database application in a legacy database. In this case, the original developers probably developed numerous stored procedures that were used by the application. As we redevelop the application using JDBC, rather than re-implementing all that functionality, we could reuse the existing stored procedures. In this section, we'll look at some illustrative stored procedures.

Since the techniques of stored procedure development are different for every database, we will only look at some simple examples of stored procedures. The examples will be written using Oracle's PL/SQL language. I use a real language rather than pseudo-code because this allows me to test and verify that the procedure is correct. You will need to modify this example if you want to try it in a different database. Consult your database documentation for stored procedure information specific to your database.

Try It Out – Using Stored Procedures

First, we'll look at a stored procedure that takes two `IN` parameters and returns nothing. The procedure takes a recording ID and a price, and then updates the `Recordings` table by setting the price of the recording with the given recording ID.

This procedure is used to update the price of a given recording in the database. Before we can create the stored procedure in the database, the `recordings` table must exist. This SQL will create the table in Oracle and insert one row of data if you do not have a `recordings` table. This code is available in the code download as `create_recordings.sql`.

```
CREATE TABLE recordings(
  recordingid INT NOT NULL ,
  recordingtitle VARCHAR(50),
  publisherid INT,
  catalognumber VARCHAR(20),
  recordingformatid INT DEFAULT 1 NOT NULL,
  releasedate DATE,
  languageid INT DEFAULT 1 NOT NULL,
  listprice DOUBLE PRECISION,
  coverimagefilespec VARCHAR(50)
);
```

Later, in our final example, we will be using a table named tracks, which should have been previously created in earlier chapters. If not, you can create it here with the following code (which is available in the code download as `create_tracks.sql`):

```
CREATE TABLE tracks (
recordingid INT NOT NULL,
tracknumber INT NOT NULL,
tracktitle VARCHAR(50)
);
```

This snippet will populate our recordings table with one row (`create_recordings_rows.sql`):

```
INSERT INTO recordings VALUES (
1000,'So',112,2064-24370-2,1,'23-MAY-91',1,14.99,'');
```

And this snippet will populate our tracks table with three rows (`create_tracks_rows.sql`):

```
INSERT INTO tracks VALUES (
1000, 1, 'Red Rain'
);
INSERT INTO tracks VALUES (
1000, 2, 'Sledgehammer'
);
INSERT INTO tracks VALUES (
1000, 3, 'Don''t Give Up'
);
```

Below is the SQL that will create this procedure in an Oracle database; the procedure was entered using Oracle's SQL*Plus tool. A script file with the SQL code in it and named `set_price.sql` can be downloaded as part of the sourcecode for the book. You may need to change the SQL for your specific database; consult your database documentation for information on how to create stored procedures in your system:

```
SQL> CREATE OR REPLACE PROCEDURE set_price (
  2  id IN NUMBER,
  3  price IN NUMBER)
  4  AS
  5  BEGIN
  6  UPDATE recordings
  7  SET listprice = price
  8  WHERE recordingid = id;
  9  END;
 10  /
```

The Java code to call this procedure and the other examples in this section will be shown later in the chapter.

With the procedure in place, we can try it out using SQL*Plus.

```
SQL> SELECT recordingtitle, listprice FROM recordings
  2  WHERE recordingid = 1000;

RECORDINGTITLE                                    LISTPRICE
-------------------------------------------------- ---------
So                                                 14.99

SQL> call set_price(1000, 16.99);

Call completed.

SQL> COMMIT;

Commit complete.

SQL> SELECT recordingtitle, listprice FROM recordings
  2  WHERE recordingid = 1000;
```

```
RECORDINGTITLE                                     LISTPRICE
-------------------------------------------------- ---------
So                                                 16.99

SQL>
```

How It Works

With Oracle PL/SQL you normally `CREATE OR REPLACE a` procedure. If the procedure does not exist, it is created; if a procedure with the given name already exists, the new one replaces the old one. This allows you to easily modify or fix an existing procedure. So, we create a procedure named `set_price.` It has two parameters. There is an IN parameter for the recording ID, and an `IN` parameter for the new price. The body of the procedure is a standard SQL UPDATE statement. The SQL `UPDATE` sets the listprice of a recording with the given `recordingid` to the value that was passed in the procedure call.

After inserting a row, we call the procedure with two arguments. Notice that the procedure call is very similar to a Java method call. We call the procedure by name, passing the arguments inside a set of parentheses. After calling the procedure, we commit the changes, and then select the row to show that the change was made.

I used SQL*Plus to enter and test the procedure above. Alternatively, since the procedure consists of SQL statements, I could use a Java program to send the SQL statements to the database to create the stored procedure.

Try It Out – Calling Stored Procedures from Java

If you are developing stored procedures, you will almost always have an SQL tool such as Oracle SQL*Plus for entering stored procedures into the database. However, if for some reason you don't, the stored procedure presented above can be created using Java code. The program below creates the `set_price` procedure.

This program uses the `ConnectionFactory` class to get a database connection. The class was presented in an earlier chapter. Here it is again for reference:

```
package connections;

import java.sql.*;

public class ConnectionFactory {
  private static ConnectionFactory ref = new ConnectionFactory();
  private ConnectionFactory() {
    try {
      Class.forName("oracle.jdbc.driver.OracleDriver");
    } catch (ClassNotFoundException e) {
      System.out.println("ERROR: exception loading driver class");
    }
  }

  public static Connection getConnection() throws SQLException {
    String url = "jdbc:oracle:thin:@dbserver:1521:ORCL";
    return DriverManager.getConnection(url, "beg", "java");
```

```
  }

  public static void close(ResultSet rs) {
    try {
      rs.close();
    } catch (Exception ignored) {}
  }

  public static void close(Statement stmt) {
    try {
      stmt.close();
    } catch (Exception ignored) {}
  }

  public static void close(Connection conn) {
    try {
      conn.close();
    } catch (Exception ignored) {}
  }
}
```

The `ConnectionFactory` class loads the driver in the constructor, and provides a `getConnection()` method for obtaining a connection. The class above has been modified to load an Oracle driver and return a connection to an Oracle database. If you are connecting to a different database, you will need to modify the `ConnectionFactory` to load the correct driver and use the appropriate database URL.

The `CreateSetPrice` class is next:

```
package procedures;

import java.sql.*;
import java.util.*;
import connections.*;

public class CreateSetPrice {
  public static void main(String[] args) {
    Connection conn = null;
    Statement stmt = null;

    try {
      conn = ConnectionFactory.getConnection();
      stmt = conn.createStatement();

      String sql = "create or replace procedure set_price ( "
                 + "id in number, price in number)" + "as begin "
                 + "update recordings set listprice = price "
                 + "where recordingid = id; end;";
      int result = stmt.executeUpdate(sql);

      // expected value of result is 0 for create procedure
      // if no exception is thrown, assume the procedure was created
      System.out.println("Procedure created successfully");
```

```
      } catch (Exception e) {
        System.out.println("Procedure NOT created");
        e.printStackTrace();
      }
      finally {
        ConnectionFactory.close(stmt);
        ConnectionFactory.close(conn);
      }
    }
  }
```

Save the program as `C:\BegJavaDB\Ch13\procedures\CreateSetPrice.java`. On my system, I've put the driver into the `C:\java\lib` directory. Setting the classpath appropriately, compiling and running the program should result in this output:

```
> set classpath=C:\java\lib\classes12.zip;c:\wrox

> java procedures.CreateSetPrice
```

How It Works

This class uses the `ConnectionFactory` class to get a connection to a database. The `ConnectionFactory` was first introduced in Chapter 8. The class was modified to create a connection to an Oracle database.

The program creates a `Statement` from the `Connection`. The `Statement` is used to send the SQL string that creates the stored procedure. Since the SQL is not a `SELECT` statement, the program uses the `executeUpdate()` method. However, since this SQL does not update any rows, we expect the return value from the `executeUpdate()` method to be `0`.

If no exception is thrown, the program assumes the procedure was created.

Example: Stored Function

Another function developed for the legacy Music Store application was a function that returned the list price for a given recording. Recall that we use the term "function" here because the procedure returns a value:

```
FUNCTION get_price (
  id in number)
RETURN NUMBER IS price NUMBER;
  BEGIN
    SELECT listprice INTO price
      FROM recordings
    WHERE recordingid = id;
    RETURN (price);
  END;
```

Again, the SQL in this function is relatively simple. It uses the `SELECT INTO` syntax to read a column value from a given row and save that value in a variable that was declared at the beginning of the function. This variable is then returned by the function.

Try It Out – Using Stored Functions

Using SQL*Plus you can create this function in an Oracle database. After creating the function, we enter SQL to test it out. If you have not yet done so, you will need to create the `recordings` table and insert a row as shown in the previous section. This function can also be created with the `create_get_price.sql` file available in the code download.

```
SQL> CREATE OR REPLACE FUNCTION get_price (
     id IN NUMBER)
     RETURN NUMBER IS price NUMBER;
     BEGIN
     SELECT listprice INTO price
     FROM recordings
     WHERE recordingid = id;
     RETURN (price);
     END;
     /

Function created.

SQL> VARIABLE sprice NUMBER;
     BEGIN
     :sprice := get_price(1000);
     END;
     /

PL/SQL procedure successfully completed.

SQL> print sprice

   SPRICE
---------
    14.99

SQL> call set_price(1000, 16.99);

Call completed.

SQL> print sprice;

   SPRICE
---------
    14.99

SQL>  begin
      :sprice := get_price(1000);
      end;
      /

PL/SQL procedure successfully completed.

SQL>  print sprice
```

```
   SPRICE
---------
    16.99
```

How It Works

Creating this stored function in Oracle is similar to creating a stored procedure. One difference is that the function must declare the return value before it BEGINs the function. This is analogous to the return value declaration of a Java method:

```
public double getPrice(int id) { … }
```

The body of the function selects the desired column value from the row with the matching recordingid. The column value is saved into a variable. At the end of the SQL block, the function returns the variable.

Then we called the function and printed out the return value. After doing this, we called the set_price() procedure from the previous section to change the price of the recording.

Then we printed out the sprice variable again. This shows that the variable has not been changed even though the row has. I call get_price() again to get the new listprice, and print it out.

As we've seen many times in this section, using stored procedures is very database-dependent. SQL Server handles it differently from Oracle, which handles it differently from PointBase, which handles it differently...etc. You should consult the documentation for your database to learn if it supports stored procedures, and the syntax of the statements for stored procedures. You can also learn a little bit about how the database supports stored procedures through database meta data. We will explore that in the next section.

Database Support for Stored Procedures

While you will most likely already know whether your database supports stored procedures, you can also programmatically determine information about stored procedure support using the DatabaseMetaData interface, part of the java.sql package. The DatabaseMetaData interface defines methods for determining if a database supports procedures, and what procedures are already stored in the database.

These methods are shown in the table overleaf:

ReturnType	Method	Description
boolean	allProceduresAreCallable()	Returns true if the current user is allowed to call all the procedures returned by the getProcedures() method (see below).
boolean	supportsStoredProcedures()	Returns true if the database supports stored procedures.
ResultSet	getProcedures(String catalog, String schema, String namePattern)	Returns a ResultSet object containing information about the procedures that are in the given catalog and schema, and match the name pattern.
ResultSet	getProcedureColumns(String catalog, String schema, String namePattern, String columnPattern)	Returns a ResultSet object containing information about the input parameters, output parameters, and return value for procedures that are in the given catalog and schema, and match the name pattern and column pattern.
String	getProcedureTerm()	Returns the term used by the database vendor for 'procedure'.

catalog and schema are ways of providing separation between users of a database. A schema generally equates to a database user. When you log into a database, all the tables you create belong to your schema. They are not visible to other users unless you grant permission to them to see the objects in your schema. Schemas are then grouped into catalogs.

Two of the methods listed above deserve some comment. Most meta data methods return simple values: true or false for supported features, numeric values for the size of things like names, Strings for information like the driver name. However, some methods return a ResultSet. As shown above, information about the procedures and procedures parameters are returned in a ResultSet.

The method getProcedures() returns a row for each procedure in the database. The columns provide information about the procedure. The complete list of columns returned by getProcedures() is shown opposite:

Column Name	Meaning
PROCEDURE_CAT	The catalog that contains the procedure
PROCEDURE_SCHEM	The schema that contains the procedure
PROCEDURE_NAME	The name of the procedure
reserved	
reserved	
reserved	
REMARKS	Procedure information
PROCEDURE_TYPE	One of three DatabaseMetaData constants describing whether the procedure returns a value: procedureResultUnknown procedureNoResult procedureReturnsResult

The method getColumns() returns a row for each parameter of a stored procedure. The columns provide information about the parameter. For information about what each column in this ResultSet represents, consult the Java documentation for the method.

Try It Out – Accessing Meta Data

By adding some of the methods above to the ShowDatabaseMetaData class, you can explore the stored procedure support of your database. The ShowDatabaseMetaData class was originally presented in Chapter 10. To run this program, you will also need the ConnectionFactory class. That class was shown earlier in this chapter. Here is the ShowDatabaseMetaData class with the new methods that were presented above:

```
package metadata;

import java.sql.*;
import connections.*;
import java.util.*;

public class ShowDatabaseMetaData {
  public static void main(String[] args) {
    Connection conn;

    try {
      conn = ConnectionFactory.getConnection();
      DatabaseMetaData dbmd = conn.getMetaData();

      System.out.println("Information about the database: ");
      System.out.println("Database name=[" + dbmd.getDatabaseProductName()
                         + "]");
      System.out.println("Database version=["
                         + dbmd.getDatabaseProductVersion() + "]");
```

```
        System.out.println("Driver name=[" + dbmd.getDriverName() + "]");
        System.out.println("Driver version=[" + dbmd.getDriverVersion()
                          + "]");

        System.out.println("\nInformation about stored procedure support:");
        System.out.println("Vendors name for \'procedure\'=["
                          + dbmd.getProcedureTerm() + "]");
        System.out.println("All procedures are callable: ["
                          + dbmd.allProceduresAreCallable() + "]");
        System.out.println("Supports stored procedures: ["
                          + dbmd.supportsStoredProcedures() + "]");
        ResultSet rs = dbmd.getProcedures(null, null, null);
        System.out.println("Procedures stored in the database: ");
        int count = 0;
        while (rs.next()) {
          System.out.print(rs.getString("PROCEDURE_NAME") + " ");
          if (count++ > 25) {
            break;
          }
        }
        System.out.println();

      } catch (Exception e) {
        e.printStackTrace();
      }
    }
  }
```

Save the program as `C:\BegJavaDB\Ch13\metadata\ShowDatabaseMetaData.java`. On my system, I've put the driver into the `C:\java\lib` directory. Setting the classpath appropriately, compiling and running the program should result in this output:

```
> set classpath=c:\java\lib\classes12.zip;c:\BegJavaDB

> java metadata.ShowDatabaseMetaData
```

and the following (edited) output results:

```
Information about the database:
Database name=[Oracle]
Database version=[Oracle8i Personal Edition Release 8.1.5.0.0 - Production
With the Java option
PL/SQL Release 8.1.5.0.0 - Production]
Driver name=[Oracle JDBC driver]
Driver version=[8.1.7.0.0]

Information about stored procedure support:
Vendors name for 'procedure'=[procedure]
All procedures are callable: [false]
Supports stored procedures: [true]
Procedures stored in the database:
GET_DISCHARGE LIST_PATIENT LIST_PATIENTS SET_DISCHARGE SHOW_ADMIT SHOW_EMP
SHOW_PATIENT SP_LISTEMP  SYS$DSINTERVALSUBTRACT  SYS$DSINTERVALSUBTRACT
SYS$DSINTERVALSUBTRACT  SYS$DSINTERVALSUBTRACT  SYS$DSINTERVALSUBTRACT
```

My Oracle database already has quite a few stored procedures. In fact, there are so many, I wrote the program to stop displaying the list of procedures after 25 had been displayed. Some of the procedures, such as `GET_DISCHARGE` and `LIST_PATIENT`, are procedures that I have added while doing other projects. Other procedures are provided by Oracle as part of the database. Also, you can see that although many procedure names are returned, the call to `allProceduresAreCallable()` returned a `false`, which indicates that the login used with the connection does not have the privilege to call all the procedures.

How It Works

In the latest version of the `ShowDatabaseMetaData` class is a method that returns something other than a `true` or `false` value. Many of the `DatabaseMetaData` methods return a simple `true` or `false` to indicate whether or not a feature is supported. This time we also used a method that returned a `ResultSet` object, the `getProcedures()` method. There are other methods in the `DatabaseMetaData` interface that return `ResultSet` objects. The `getProcedureColumns()` method shown in the table earlier (but not used in the new `ShowDatabaseMetaData` class) is another of these methods.

The `getProcedures()` method returns a `ResultSet` in which each column provides some information about the stored procedures in the database. This particular method takes three parameters:

- The first parameter is the `catalog` to be matched. An empty string, `''`, means match procedures with no catalog. The code above passed a `null`, which means match all catalogs.
- The second parameter is the `schema` to be matched. Similarly to `catalog`, an empty string means match procedures with no schema; the code above passed a `null`, which means match all schemas.
- The third parameter is a name pattern to be matched. Again, we passed a `null`, which means match all names.

The `ResultSet` that is returned by `getProcedures()` contains seven columns for each row. One of those columns contains the name of the procedure. In the `ShowDatabaseMetaData` class, we called the `ResultSet` method `getString(String)` with the column name `"PROCEDURE_NAME"` to get the value from that column and print it.

For any other method of the `DatabaseMetaData` interface that returns a `ResultSet` object, you should consult the API JavaDoc for the valid input parameters and the definition of the columns returned in the resultset.

You may recall from above that the login name used by the connection did not have the privileges to access all the stored procedures returned by the `getProcedures()` call. There is no easy way to determine the complete list of all the procedures that *can* be called, since that information is not available from the database meta data.

There is a way, however, to get a subset of the procedures that are callable. The login name will always have permission to call stored procedures that belong to the schema of the login name. The list of procedures that are callable is the list of procedures that belong to the login, plus any procedures in other schemas to which the owner has granted access. So, one could either call `getProcedures()` for the procedures that belong to the appropriate login, or check the schema of each row in the resultset for the appropriate schema. For my Oracle database, the `ShowDatabaseMetaData` class uses the login name `wrox`. To get all the procedures for that schema, the code would look like this:

```
System.out.println("Supports stored procedures: [" +
                   dbmd.supportsStoredProcedures() + "]");
ResultSet rs = dbmd.getProcedures(null, "WROX", null);
System.out.println("Procedures stored in the database: ");
```

When I login to my database, my login name is case-insensitive. However, when you pass the schema to a method, that is generally case-sensitive and should be passed as all upper case.

The list returned this time is much smaller. I first ensure that there are procedures in my schema by creating the `set_price()` and `get_price()` methods shown earlier in the chapter. Then when I query for all the procedures in my schema, I get this list:

```
Procedures stored in the database:
GET_PRICE SET_PRICE
```

Callable Statements

The `CallableStatement` interface provides the means for Java code to call stored procedures. The `CallableStatement` interface extends the `PreparedStatement` interface by providing methods to help call stored procedures. Just as with a prepared statement, the SQL string used with a `CallableStatement` object can contain placeholders for `IN` parameters passed to the stored procedure. It can also have placeholders for `OUT` parameters set by the stored procedure, and `INOUT` parameters. Lastly, it can have a placeholder for values returned by the stored procedure.

The relationship between the `CallableStatement` interface, the `PreparedStatement` interface, and the `Connection` interface is shown in the class diagram below:

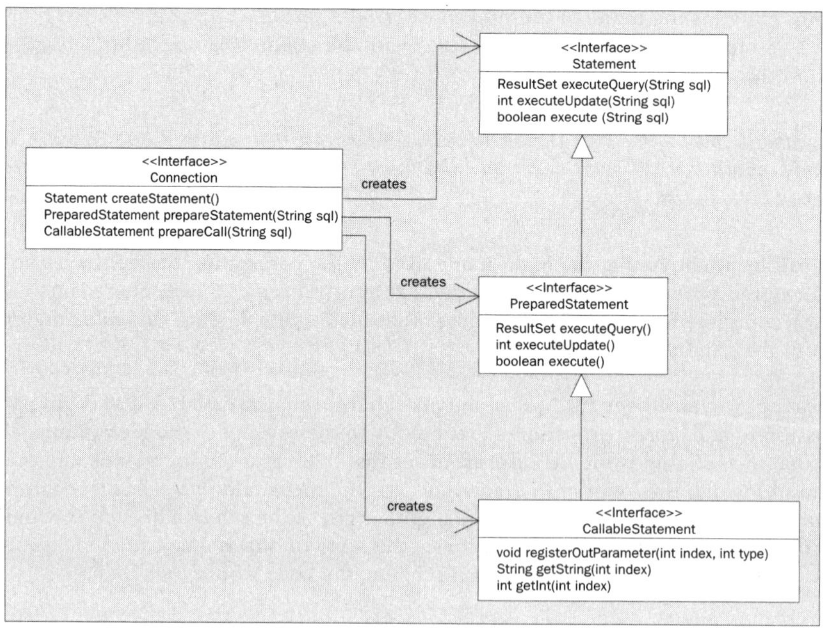

The diagram above only shows a few of the methods in the `CallableStatement` interface. The additional methods will be presented later in this section. The `CallableStatement` interface inherits all the methods of the `PreparedStatement` interface, so the callable statement uses the same methods used by the prepared statement to execute SQL statements. Those methods are the `executeQuery()`, `executeUpdate()`, and `execute()` methods. The SQL string for calling the stored procedure is passed to the `create()` method when the `CallableStatement` object is created.

Creating a CallableStatement

A `CallableStatement` object is created in much the same way as the `PreparedStatement` object is created; by calling a method of the `Connection` object. Looking at the diagram above, you can see that the `prepareCall(String sql)` method creates a `CallableStatement` object. The table below lists all the `Connection` interface methods for creating a `CallableStatement` object.

Method	Description
`prepareCall(String sql)`	Creates a `CallableStatement` object for the given SQL. If the `CallableStatement` returns a `ResultSet` object, the `ResultSet` has a **type** of forward only, is not **updatable**, and is not **holdable**.

`prepareCall(`
`String sql,`
`int resultSetType,`
`int resultSetConcurrency)`
	Create a `CallableStatement` object for the given SQL. If the `CallableStatement` returns a `ResultSet`, the `ResultSet` has the given `ResultSet` type and concurrency, and is not holdable.

`prepareCall(`
`String sql, int resultSetType,`
`int resultSetConcurrency,`
`int resultSetHoldability)`
	JDBC 3.0: Create a `CallableStatement` object for the given SQL. If the `CallableStatement` returns a `ResultSet`, the `ResultSet` has the given `ResultSet` type, concurrency, and holdability.

`ResultSet` type, updatability, and holdability are defined fully in Chapter 9. Type refers to how you can traverse a `ResultSet`. Updatability refers to the ability to change a database through the `ResultSet`. Holdability refers to whether a `ResultSet` is closed with the `commit()` method is called.

As indicated in the description, the third method above is only available in drivers that are JDBC 3.0-compliant. At the time this was written, no drivers implement the JDBC 3.0 specification.

The first argument in each `prepareCall()` method is a SQL String. The SQL string for calling a stored procedure can take one of several forms. Common between all the forms is the SQL keyword `call` that appears before the procedure name, and the curly braces that surround the SQL. This signals the driver that the SQL is not an ordinary SQL statement and that the SQL must be converted into the correct form for calling a procedure in the target database. The most basic form is the SQL for calling a stored procedure that takes no parameters. The SQL string looks like this:

```
{ call procedure_name }
```

For example, suppose the database had a stored procedure named `adjust_prices` that took no parameters and returned no value. The code to create a `CallableStatement` object for this stored procedure would look like:

```
String sql = "{ call adjust_prices }";
CallableStatement cs = connection.prepareCall(sql);
```

When a procedure or function takes parameters, the SQL will look something like this:

```
String sql = "{ call set_price(?, ?) }";
CallableStatement cs = connection.prepareCall(sql);
```

The `set_price` procedure created earlier in the chapter takes two parameters and returns no value. Placeholders mark each parameter in the procedure call. We have already looked at placeholders in detail in Chapter 12 on *Prepared Statements.*

Finally, the SQL for calling a stored function would look like this:

```
String sql = "{ ? = call get_price(?) }";
CallableStatement cs = connection.prepareCall(sql);
```

The return value of the function is marked by a placeholder, as is the parameter sent to the function.

Using Placeholders

Like the `PreparedStatement` object, the placeholders are numbered consecutively, starting with number 1 for the placeholder that appears in the leftmost position in the string. Moving from left to right, each placeholder is given the next number in sequence.

After preparing the callable statement, but before the statement can be executed, the placeholders for any `IN` and `INOUT` parameters in the statement must be set. If you fail to set one of the `IN` or `INOUT` placeholders, the driver will throw a `SQLException` when you attempt to execute the SQL.

In my Oracle database, the exception contains the message, "`not all variables bound`". The `CallableStatement` interface inherits the `setXXX()` methods of the `PreparedStatement` interface for doing this. As a reminder, here is a list of a few of the methods. Refer to Chapter 12 or the API Java documentation for the complete list:

```
void setDouble(int parameterIndex, double x)

void setFloat(int parameterIndex, float x)
```

void setInt(int parameterIndex, int x)
void setLong(int parameterIndex, long x)
void setString(int parameterIndex, String x)

Recall that the first argument in each method above is the index of the parameter in the SQL string. The second argument is the data value that replaces the placeholder.

If any of the parameters are `OUT` parameters, the JDBC type of the `OUT` parameter must also be registered before the call can be executed. If you do not register an `OUT` parameter you will get a `SQLException`. This must also be done for the placeholder that represents the return value of a stored function. This is done with the methods shown in the next table:

void registerOutParameter(int parameterIndex, int jdbcType)
void registerOutParameter(int parameterIndex, int jdbcType, int scale)

Unlike the `setXXX()` methods for the `IN` parameters, the `registerOutParameter()` method only has two forms. The first parameter in the method is the position of the placeholder in the SQL string. The second parameter is one of the constants defined in the `java.sql.Types` class. The `Types` class defines a constant for each generic SQL type.

Here is a partial list of the constants:

- `int SMALLINT`
- `int INTEGER`
- `int FLOAT`
- `int DOUBLE`
- `int NUMERIC`
- `int DECIMAL`
- `int CHAR`
- `int VARCHAR`
- `int DATE`

Notice that each constant is an `int`, which is the data type required for the second parameter in the `registerOutParameter()` method. So, for example, if an `OUT` parameter of a stored procedure is the second parameter and it was type `VARCHAR` in the database, you would register the parameter like this:

```
cs.registerOutParameter(2, java.sql.Types.STRING);
```

If the return value of a function was a `Double`, you could use this:

```
cs.registerOutParameter(1, java.sql.Types.DOUBLE);
```

For the complete list of the available constants, consult the API Java documentation.

When registering an `OUT` parameter that is one of the numeric types such as `FLOAT`, `DOUBLE`, `NUMERIC`, or `DECIMAL`, you could also use the second form of the `registerOutParameter()` method. This method takes a third parameter that defines the scale of the `OUT` parameter. Previously in the chapter, we created a `get_price()` stored function. This function returns the price of a recording, and prices have a scale of 2 (2 digits are to the right of the decimal point.) To register the `OUT` parameter for this stored function, we could use:

```
cs.registerOutParameter(1, java.sql.Types.DOUBLE, 2);
```

If any of the placeholders represent an `INOUT` parameter, the code must call both a `setXXX()` method and a `registerOutParameter()` method prior to executing the callable statement. Just as with `IN` or `OUT` parameters, if you fail to set the value or register the parameter, the driver will throw a `SQLException`.

As with the `PreparedStatement` object, once a placeholder has been set with data, or registered as an `OUT` parameter, that placeholder remains set until the code explicitly changes the placeholder. All the placeholders can be cleared by calling the method `clearParameters()`. The value of a placeholder is changed by calling one of the `setXXX()` or `registerOutParameter()` methods again with the appropriate index.

After the data values are set, the code calls one of the `execute()` methods to tell the database to execute the stored procedure.

> **Even though `CallableStatement` extends `PreparedStatement`, which in turn extends `Statement`, it is an error to use the `execute()` methods of the `Statement` with a `CallableStatement`. If you call any of the methods `executeQuery(String)`, `executeUpdate(String)`, or `execute(String)`, the driver will throw a `SQLException`. You must call the no-parameter versions of those methods with a `CallableStatement`.**

After executing the `CallableStatements`, the values of any `OUT` or `INOUT` parameters are retrieved with `getXXX()` methods, similar to those used to retrieve the column values from a row in a `ResultSet`. Here are is a partial list of the `CallableStatement` methods for getting the value of `OUT` parameters:

```
getBoolean(int index)
getByte(int index)
getShort(int index)
getLong(int index)
getFloat(int index)
getDouble(int index)
getBigDecimal(int index)
getBytes(int index)
getDate(int index)
```

```
getTime(int index)
getTimeStamp(int index)
getObject(int index)
```

These methods allow you to access the value of the `OUT` parameter in the same way that you access the column values of a `ResultSet`. The difference is that with these methods, the parameter is not the column number, but the index of the placeholder in the `CallableStatement`.

Try It Out – Using Callable Statements and Stored Procedures

Earlier in this chapter, we created a stored procedure that set the price of a recording in the `recordings` table, and a function that returned the price of a recording. In this section we'll look at two Java classes that call the stored procedures using some of the methods presented above.

These examples were run against an Oracle database and not the Cloudscape database that has been used for most other examples. Since creating and calling stored procedures can be database-specific, this code may or may not work with your database.

First, here is the `SetPrice` class, which naturally calls the `set_price` stored procedure:

```
package procedures;

import java.sql.*;
import connections.*;
import java.util.*;

public class SetPrice {
  public static void main(String[] args) {
    Connection conn = null;
    CallableStatement stmt = null;

    try {
      conn = ConnectionFactory.getConnection();

      String sql = "{ call set_price(?, ?) }";
      stmt = conn.prepareCall(sql);
      stmt.setInt(1, Integer.parseInt(args[0]));
      stmt.setDouble(2, Double.parseDouble(args[1]));

      stmt.executeUpdate();

      // if no exception is thrown, the update succeeded
      System.out.println("SetPrice succeeded");
    } catch (Exception e) {
      System.out.println("SetPrice failed");
      e.printStackTrace();
    }
    finally {
      ConnectionFactory.close(stmt);
      ConnectionFactory.close(conn);
    }
```

```
    }
}
```

Save the program as `C:\BegJavaDB\Ch13\procedures\SetPrice.java`. On my system, I've put the driver into the `C:\java\lib` directory. Setting the classpath appropriately, and compiling,the code can be accomplished with the following commands:

```
> set classpath=c:\java\lib\classes12.zip;c:\BegJavaDB
> javac procedures\SetPrice.java
```

The first argument on the command line (`1000`) is the recording ID; the second argument (`11.99`) is the new price we are setting through the stored procedure. Assuming the code executes properly, the following output is displayed:

```
> java procedures.SetPrice 1000 11.99
SetPrice succeeded
```

We can check that the price was set with the `GetPrice` class:

```
package procedures;

import java.sql.*;
import connections.*;
import java.util.*;

public class GetPrice {
  public static void main(String[] args) {
    Connection conn = null;
    CallableStatement stmt = null;
    try {
      conn = ConnectionFactory.getConnection();

      String sql = "{ ? = call get_price(?) }";
      stmt = conn.prepareCall(sql);
      stmt.setInt(2, Integer.parseInt(args[0]));
      stmt.registerOutParameter(1, Types.DOUBLE);

      stmt.executeUpdate();

      // if no exception is thrown, the update succeeded
      System.out.println("Price is " + stmt.getDouble(1));
    } catch (Exception e) {
      System.out.println("GetPrice failed");
      e.printStackTrace();
    }
    finally {
      ConnectionFactory.close(stmt);
      ConnectionFactory.close(conn);
    }
  }
}
```

Save the program as `C:\BegJavaDB\Ch13\procedures\GetPrice.java`. On my system, I've put the driver into the `C:\java\lib` directory. Setting the classpath appropriately, compiling, and running the program should result in this output:

```
> set classpath=c:\jdbc\lib\classes12.zip;c:\BegJavaDB
> javac procedures\GetPrice.java
```

```
> java procedures.GetPrice 1000
Price is 11.99
```

How It Works

Both classes use the `prepareCall()` method of the `Connection` interface to get a `CallableStatement` object. The actual SQL passed in the `prepare` method is different for each class since they call different stored procedures. Here again is the code from `SetPrice`:

```
String sql = "{ call set_price(?, ?) }";
CallableStatement stmt = conn.prepareCall(sql);
```

After the `CallableStatement` object is prepared, the placeholders need to be set. The `setXXX()` methods used to set the placeholders are the same methods used to set the placeholders in a `PreparedStatement` object. For the `SetPrice` class, the code needs to set the placeholders for the recording ID and the new price. After the parameters are set, the `executeUpdate()` method is called. The program uses the `executeUpdate()` method because the procedure does not query the database.

```
stmt.setInt(1, Integer.parseInt(args[1]));
stmt.setDouble(2, Double.parseDouble(args[2]));

stmt.executeUpdate();
```

The `GetPrice` class is a little different. Since one of its placeholders is the function return value, it must register the type of the return value:

```
String sql = "{ ? = call get_price(?) }";
CallableStatement stmt = conn.prepareCall(sql);
stmt.setInt(2, Integer.parseInt(args[1]));
stmt.registerOutParameter(1, Types.DOUBLE);

stmt.executeUpdate();
```

After the callable statement is executed, the return value is read using the `getDouble(int)` method. As with the `setXXX()` methods, the `int` parameter in the `getXXX()` methods is the index of the placeholder in the `CallableStatement` object. The placeholder for the function return value is the first placeholder in the SQL string, so its index is 1.

```
System.out.println("Price is " + cs.getDouble(1));
```

Batch Updates

Batching is a process where the CallableStatement does not immediately send the SQL to the database, but rather holds it internally, and then when instructed by the program, sends all the SQL to the database in a batch. Batching is supported by each of the three statement interfaces, Statement, PreparedStatement, and CallableStatement. In this section we briefly look at batch updates with a CallableStatement.

Each time you execute a CallableStatement the "normal" way, the SQL is sent to the database and executed. With batch updates, you prepare the CallableStatement in the normal way. However, after setting the IN parameters, instead of calling executeQuery() or executeUpdate() you call addtoBatch(). This instructs the CallableStatement to store the values in preparation for a batch update. When the program is ready for all the values to be sent to the database for execution in the stored procedure, it calls the executeBatch() method. All the data is sent to the database and used to call the stored procedures. The database returns the update counts of the SQL in an int array.

There are certain restrictions on the types of stored procedures that can be called with batch updates. Stored procedures called in a batch update with a CallableStatement must:

- Take IN parameters only, or no parameters
- Return an update count

Let's suppose that we wanted to update a number of prices in the database using the set_price() procedure defined earlier in the chapter. The code that did this using batch updates would look something like this:

```
String sql = "{ call set_price(?, ?) }";
stmt = conn.prepareCall(sql);
stmt.setInt(1, 1000);
stmt.setDouble(2, 11.99);
stmt.addBatch();

stmt.setInt(1, 1001);
stmt.addBatch();

//...after all the data has been added

int[] results = stmt.executeBatch();
```

Batch updating does not imply that all the stored procedures calls belong to their own transaction or the same transaction. This will depend entirely on the commit mode that is in effect when the executeBatch() method is called. If autocommit is enabled, then each procedure call in the batch will be its own transaction and will be automatically committed. If the program disables autocommit, then the entire batch is one transaction. It is then up to the application to decide whether to commit or rollback.

Getting a ResultSet

The examples above for `CallableStatements` have shown how to use `OUT` parameters to get the basic JDBC types such as `ints`, `floats`, `Strings`, and so on. Stored functions can return other kinds of objects that you can retrieve from an `OUT` parameter. One common JDBC question is whether a `ResultSet` object can be retrieved using a `CallableStatement` object. The answer is yes, but the answer is highly-database dependent. In this section we will see how to get a `ResultSet` from an Oracle stored function. This may or may not be possible to do with other databases. You should check the stored procedure documentation for your database to determine how to do this for your database.

One reason for doing this is to hide the details of the database structure from users. We might want to hide the details so that the system is easier for users to use (they don't need to know table or columns names to get the details they need). Or, we might want to hide the details for security: we don't want the users to know the structure of the database.

Try It Out: – Returning a ResultSet from a Stored Procedure

By creating a stored function that returns a cursor, we can demonstrate how get a `ResultSet`. Like all the examples in this chapter so far, we will be executing this example against an Oracle database.

We start by defining a type to represent a **cursor**:

```
SQL> CREATE OR REPLACE PACKAGE types AS
     TYPE cursorType IS ref cursor;
     END;
     /
```

Cursor is a database term. It generally refers to the set of rows returned by a query. When a cursor is positioned at a row, we mean that we are accessing a particular row in the set.

The name of the new type is `cursorType` and it belongs to the package named `types`. The new type is an object of type `ref cursor`. The term `"ref"` is an abbreviation of reference. We can now declare variables in the database to be of this new type, `cursorType`. Here is the PL/SQL for a function that will return the tracks for a given recording ID:

```
SQL> CREATE OR REPLACE FUNCTION list_tracks (id IN NUMBER)
     RETURN types.cursorType IS tracks_cursor types.cursorType;
     BEGIN
     OPEN tracks_cursor FOR
     SELECT r.recordingid, t.tracknumber,
     t.tracktitle
     FROM recordings r, tracks t
     WHERE r.recordingid = id
     AND t.recordingid = r.recordingid;
     RETURN tracks_cursor;
     END;
     /
```

The JDBC code for retrieving the `ResultSet` object is similar to the code that has already been presented:

```
package procedures;

import java.sql.*;
import connections.*;
import oracle.jdbc.driver.*;
import java.util.*;

public class GetResultSet {
  public static void main(String[] args) {
    Connection conn = null;
    CallableStatement stmt = null;

    try {
      conn = ConnectionFactory.getConnection();
      String sql = "{ ? = call list_tracks(?) }";
      stmt = conn.prepareCall(sql);

      // Use OracleTypes.CURSOR as the OUT parameter type
      stmt.registerOutParameter(1, OracleTypes.CURSOR);
      stmt.setInt(2, Integer.parseInt(args[0]));

      // Execute the function and get the return object from the call
      stmt.executeQuery();
      ResultSet rset = (ResultSet) stmt.getObject(1);

      while (rset.next()) {
        System.out.print(rset.getString(1) + " ");
        System.out.print(rset.getString(2) + " ");
        System.out.println(rset.getString(3) + " ");
      }
    } catch (Exception e) {
      System.out.println("GetResultSet failed");
      e.printStackTrace();
    }
    finally {
      ConnectionFactory.close(stmt);
      ConnectionFactory.close(conn);
    }
  }
}
```

Since the code above is Oracle-specific, you will need an Oracle database with the Music Store data, or you will need to modify the code so that it works with your database.

This is how we would execute the script:

```
> set classpath=c:\java\lib\classes12.zip;c:\BegJavaDB

> javac procedures\GetResultset.java

> java procedures.GetResultSet 1000
```

I only have three tracks in my Oracle Music Store `Tracks` table. After executing the program with the commands above, this is the output I got:

```
1000 1 Red Rain
1000 2 Sledgehammer
1000 3 Don't Give Up
```

How It Works

Other than the fact that the code used an Oracle-specific feature, the `GetResultSet` class is exactly like the other classes in this chapter that access stored procedures.

After the callable statement is prepared, the parameter for the return value is registered just as we did in the `GetPrice` class:

```
cs.registerOutParameter(1, OracleTypes.CURSOR);
cs.setInt(2, Integer.parseInt(args[1]));
```

To get this to work properly, we had to register a database-specific `OUT` parameter, `OracleTypes.CURSOR`. We also set the second placeholder with the `recordingid` that was passed to the program. After the parameters are set and registered, the code calls the `executeQuery()` method. The return value is read using the method `getObject()` and then cast to type `ResultSet`.

```
//Execute the function and get the return object from the call
cs.executeQuery();
ResultSet rset = (ResultSet) cs.getObject(1);
```

Once the code has the `ResultSet` object, it can use the object exactly like any `ResultSet` obtained from a `Statement` or `PreparedStatement`. Each row of the `ResultSet` is traversed, and the `getInt(int)` or `getString(int)` method obtains each column value.

New in JDBC 3.0

As we saw earlier, there are several methods for setting the placeholders and getting the value of placeholders in a `CallableStatement` object. You may have noticed that all of those methods used the `int` index of the placeholder to identify which placeholder was being set or read.

Starting with JDBC 3.0, you will be able to refer to placeholders by using the name of the parameter, as specified by the stored procedure instead of the index in the `CallableStatement` object. One way to get the parameter name is by using the `getProcedureColumns()` method of the `DatabaseMeta Data` interface. This method was mentioned but not demonstrated at the beginning of this chapter. If you already know the name, then you can just use it in the `setXXX()` or `registerOutParameter()` methods without retrieving the metadata.

The `getProcedureColumns()` method returns a `ResultSet` with information about the parameters used by a stored procedure. Each row in the `ResultSet` contains information about a stored procedure parameter. After positioning the cursor at a row, you can get the procedure name by calling `getString("PROCEDURE_NAME")` and the name of the parameter represented by the row with `getString("COLUMN_NAME")`.

Yes, I know it's confusing. We want to get information about the parameters for a stored procedure and the meta data refers to the parameters as columns. Remember, getProcedureColumns gets information about the parameters in a procedure. The method getString("COLUMN_NAME") gets the parameter name in the procedure. One reason for this is that if the procedure in question returns a ResultSet, information about the ResultSet columns is also returned by getProcedureColumns().

By reading through the ResultSet, one can obtain all the names of the parameters used by the stored procedure. These names can then be used in one of the new setXXX(), getXXX(), or registerOutParameter() methods.

Earlier in the chapter, we created a set_price() procedure that had two parameters named "id" and "price." Here's that procedure definition again:

```
PROCEDURE set_price (
  id IN NUMBER,
  price IN NUMBER)
AS
  BEGIN
    UPDATE recordings
       SET listprice = price
     WHERE recordingid = id;
  END;
```

So, given the procedure definitions from earlier in the chapter and using a JDBC 3.0 driver, the SetPrice code could be rewritten like so:

```
cs.setInt("id", Integer.parseInt(args[1]));
cs.setDouble("price", Double.parseDouble(args[2]));
```

The GetPrice code would look like this:

```
cs.setInt("id", Integer.parseInt(args[1]));
cs.registerOutParameter("price", Types.DOUBLE);

cs.executeUpdate();
System.out.println("Price is " + cs.getDouble("price"));
```

Summary

In this chapter we have looked at stored procedures and CallableStatement objects. You have learned that:

- Stored procedures and stored functions are blocks of procedural code and SQL statements stored in a database. They are used to store commonly executed procedures in the database that any application can call.
- Stored functions have return values whereas stored procedures do not (although they can have OUT parameters).

- Stored procedures can be created through standard JDBC programs.
- JDBC, through the `CallableStatement` interface, provides facilities for calling stored procedures.
- `IN` and `INOUT` parameters are set using the `setXXX()` methods that the `CallableStatement` interface inherits from `PreparedStatement`.
- Before executing a `CallableStatement` the `OUT` and `INOUT` parameter types must be registered with a call to `registerOutParameter()`.
- `CallableStatements` can perform batch processing.

akarta
JAVA
Java

Transactions

Transactions should be very familiar to you. Many of the daily interactions in which you engage involve transactions. You exchange time and work for pay. You exchange money for goods and services. Those transactions may span a small number of actions. For example, you pick up a newspaper and give money to the vendor. Or they may span many actions; you place an order, a broker accepts the order and debits your account, the goods or services are purchased, the seller delivers the goods or services, and the broker forwards them to you.

In application terms, however, transactions are more precisely defined. As we'll see in more depth through this chapter, a transaction is an event, or more commonly a series of events that must all complete successfully before their results are made permanent. In a transaction, if one event fails, all must fail, and their results be undone, or rolled back. We'll see why this is so important as we progress through the chapter. We will cover the following aspects of transactions:

- We'll describe what a transaction is, and how to control the number of statements in a transaction.
- In the *Transaction Requirements* section, we look at four properties of a transaction: **a**tomicity, **c**onsistency, **i**solation, and **d**urability (known as ACID properties).
- To determine whether, and to what extent, a JDBC driver provides transaction support, we will enhance the `ShowDatabaseMetaData` class from Chapter 10, *Using Meta Data*, to get transaction support information from `DatabaseMetaData`.
- The JDBC specification defines several methods for controlling transactions. These methods are presented in the *Transaction Control in JDBC* section. In this section we also briefly look at distributed transactions, which are transactions that span more than one database or database connection. Finally, the section provides a preview of another JDBC 3.0 feature: savepoints.
- We conclude the chapter with another class in the Music Store application that demonstrates how transactions could be used in the application.

What are Transactions?

If there is one thing that sets the database apart from a file system, it is the ability to support transactions. If you are in the middle of writing a file and the operating system crashes, this file is likely to be corrupted. If you are writing to a database file, with correct use of transactions, you can ensure that either the process completes successfully, or the database is returned to the state it was in before you began writing.

This is the main purpose of transactions in the database – they take the database from one consistent state to the next. That is their job. When you commit work in the database, you are assured that either all of your changes have been saved, or none of them are. Further, you are assured that data integrity, all of your rules and checks, is fulfilled.

Let's look at the two main transaction control statements that are available to us:

- Commit – Makes permanent in the database all changes made except the current transaction.
- Rollback – Returns the database to the state that existed after the last successful commit, usually prior to the start of the current transaction.

There is actually a third transaction control statement that will be supported in JDBC 3.0, which is the **savepoint**. Savepoints are already supported in many databases, and will soon be available through JDBC. A savepoint marks a place in a transaction; once you have created a savepoint, you can rollback to that marked place rather than rolling back the entire transaction. We will return to the subject of savepoints in the *Transaction Control in JDBC* section of the chapter.

Try It Out – Commit and Rollback

We can see the effects of commit and rollback by interactively executing SQL statements in a database. If you have Oracle installed on your system, you can use the SQL*PLUS tool to execute SQL statements. Other databases will provide similar tools. For example, Cloudscape provides a tool named `ij` for the same purpose. For other databases, you should consult your database documentation to determine if such a tool is provided, and how to use the tool.

If you have access to SQL*PLUS and an Oracle database, start the SQL*PLUS program and connect to your database. Generally, selecting **SQL Plus** from the **Start** menu (Windows) will do this. In UNIX, typing `sqlplus` at the command line (assuming your path has been configured) will start the tool.

If you have Cloudscape, the following batch file can be used to start the `ij` tool. This batch file assumes the Cloudscape `.jar` files have been installed into `c:\cloudscape\lib` and your database is `c:\BegJavaDB\Wrox4370.db`. Note that the third and fourth lines of the listing below are really one single line in the batch file. If you have installed Cloudscape into a different directory or have a different database, you will need to change the batch file to use the paths for your system:

```
rem ij.bat
set classpath=c:\cloudscape\lib\tools.jar;c:\cloudscape\lib\cloudscape.jar
java -Dij.database=jdbc:cloudscape:c:/wrox/database/Wrox4370.db
COM.cloudscape.tools.ij
```

With SQL*PLUS running, enter the sequence of SQL statements shown below:

```
SQL> create table t1 (x int);

Table created.

SQL> insert into t1 values (1);

1 row created.

SQL> commit;
```

```
Commit complete.

SQL> update t1 set x=x+1;

1 row updated.

SQL> select * from t1;

         X
----------
         2

SQL> rollback;

Rollback complete.

SQL> select * from t1;

         X
----------
         1
```

These same commands should work in any SQL tool, although you may need to add one command. The Cloudscape `ij` tool starts with **autocommit** enabled by default; every statement is a transaction, and the transaction is automatically committed. For the example to work with the Cloudscape tool, the first command you issue should be:

```
ij> autocommit off
```

Consult the documentation for your tool to determine whether or not you need to disable autocommit.

*The autocommit mode defines whether the changes are automatically written to the database (autocommit on, or enabled), or if the user must explicitly commit or roll back changes (autocommit off, or disabled). SQL*PLUS defaults to autocommit disabled; Cloudscape `ij` defaults to autocommit enabled. JDBC drivers default to autocommit enabled.*

The first few commands above will look like this with the Cloudscape `ij` tool:

```
ij> autocommit off;
ij> create table t1 (x int);
0 rows inserted/updated/deleted
ij> insert into t1 values (1);
1 row inserted/updated/deleted
ij> commit;
ij>
```

How It Works

The SQL above is trivial, but it does serve nicely to demonstrate commit and rollback. Also, as mentioned above, the same commands should work in any tool you use, although the output from the tool will vary.

Although the SQL syntax used for Oracle was the same as for Cloudscape, that won't always be the case. For example, in Cloudscape we had to disable autocommit using `autocommit off`. That same action in Oracle is `set autocommit off`. Any questions about the correct SQL syntax should be directed to the database documentation.

After connecting to a database, the first step in the example above is to create a temporary table for the demonstration. After the table is created, we disable autocommit for Cloudscape `ij`; we don't need to do this for SQL*PLUS, because it defaults to autocommit disabled.

After the table is created, the first row, containing the single value `1`, is inserted into the table, and committed. Next, we update the row by incrementing the value in the column named `X`. When we perform a `SELECT` on the table, we see the updated value for the row. However, as soon as we issue the `ROLLBACK` command, the changes are discarded. When we perform the `SELECT` again, we see the original row value.

The ability to roll back a transaction is provided using some type of transaction logging. Different databases will implement the log in different ways. In general, as each change is made to a row or table, the database writes enough information to a log to undo that change. If you issue a `ROLLBACK` command, the database uses the information from the log to undo the changes.

Transaction Size

So, how does the programmer know where and when in their programs to commit the changes to the database? A good rule is that transactions should always span:

- As few statements as possible
- As many statements as necessary

While this sounds like conflicting goals, what it really says is 'your transaction should be as big as it needs to be to satisfy your business rules – no more, no less'. For example, consider an ATM transaction to move money from a savings account to a checking account:

```
update accounts
   set balance = balance - 100
 where account = 55 and type = 'Savings';

update accounts
   set balance = balance + 100
 where account = 55 and type = 'Checking';
```

One option here is to issue a commit after each statement. However, if the system crashed after the first statement had been committed, but before the second had been executed, then the customer would have just lost $100 – not acceptable. You would want both of these statements to execute successfully, or neither. If one failed, you would want the other to fail as well. At the same time, there is probably nothing else that needs to be included in the transaction. At the start of the transaction, the database is in a consistent state, with each account having some balance. In between the two statements, the database is not consistent. The total sum of the two accounts is short of $100. After both statements have executed, the database is again in a consistent state. The total balance between the two accounts is correct. With this in mind, let's take the definition presented at the start of this section and formalize it a little more.

A transaction should span as many SQL statements as are needed to move the database from one consistent state, to another. A 'consistent state' should only depend on your business requirements.

The way to achieve this is by using properly coded transactions. You would wrap both of these statements into a transaction and, only commit the changes to the database after both have successfully executed. If one failed, you would programmatically roll back the transaction.

This ability to have all the statements complete successfully, or have them all rolled back, is actually the first important property of a transaction. Transactions must provide four different properties, known as the ACID properties. The next section looks at these properties in detail.

Transaction Requirements

At the beginning of the chapter, we said that a transaction takes a database from one consistent state to another. To be able to do this, a transaction must have four properties. These four properties are

- **Atomicity** – The transaction, whether it consists of one SQL statement or many, is treated as one unit of execution.
- **Consistency** – When it completes, the transaction leaves the database in a valid state.
- **Isolation** – The transaction interacts with other transactions in a well-defined way.
- **Durability** – When the transaction completes, the changes it made are persistent.

These four properties are often referred to by the acronym formed from their first letters: the **ACID** properties. In the next few pages, we'll look at these properties in more detail. After an overview of the ACID properties, we'll look at two issues in more detail: database concurrency (including locking), and levels of isolation.

Let's take a look at these four properties in a little more detail.

Atomicity

Atomicity means that all of the statements in the transaction are treated as one unit. The entire unit must complete successfully, or the transaction is considered to have failed and must be rolled back. This means that each statement in the transaction must complete successfully for the transaction to be committed to the database. If even a single statement fails, the transaction cannot be committed to the database, and all the statements that were executed must be rolled back. In the `TrackSample` class, all the data had to be written to the database, or the transaction was rolled back.

Later in this chapter we'll look at a new JDBC feature that allows you to take an atomic transaction, and perform a partial, rather than a complete, rollback.

Consistency

A database that provides consistency means that the state of the database is valid both before, and after, a transaction. For example, in the Music Store application, if a customer purchases a product, we would expect a number of changes in the database. The `Inventories` table would change to show one less product; the database would show that the store received a payment from the customer. If the transaction is committed but either of those changes did not occur, then the database would not be in a valid state. Either the inventory would be wrong, or even worse the store's financial condition would be in error.

Isolation

Isolation refers to the separation between changes to the database that occur in different transactions. This is an issue that obviously only relates to concurrent database access – in other words, when multiple users are performing transactions against the database at the same time. To illustrate this point, consider a simplified `Inventories` table for our Music Store, with just four rows (the left-hand column is included for ease of reference, it is not an actual column in the `Inventories` table):

	ProductID	QtyOnHand
Row 1	1001	10
Row 2	1002	20
Row 3	1003	15
Row 4	1004	5

Now, say a transaction is being run against this table that calculates the total number of items in stock for a given store:

```
select sum(QtyOnHand) from Inventories where storeid=XXX;
```

and then inserts that value into a column in another table, or uses it for some further calculation. The above query starts reading through the rows, summing the value of each entry in the `QtyOnHand` column, but while it is reading row 2, a second transaction registers the delivery of 5 units of product `1004`. When our first transaction reaches row 4, should it read 5 or 10 units? Your initial conclusion might be that the first transaction should recognize the change and count 10 units. However, what happens if the `UPDATE` statement on row 4 has been executed but not committed? In this case, if the first transaction reads 10 units, you run the risk that the second transaction will later be rolled back. If this happens, your first transaction will report a value that actually never existed at any point in time in the database.

Clearly, the above situation is undesirable. In an ideal situation, no transaction would have any impact on any other transaction. That is, there would be complete isolation between transactions. However, operating at this level of isolation may have a large impact on the performance of the system (depending on the database you are using – this is discussed in the next section). Normally, databases support and operate at a lower level of isolation, with the ability to change isolation when a higher level is needed. We will look at this in much more detail over the coming sections.

Durability

A database that provides durability ensures that as soon as a transaction is committed, the change to the database is made permanent. Even if there is a complete system failure the second after the commit, when the system is restarted, the database still shows the result of the transaction.

Database Concurrency

When multiple users are interacting with the database simultaneously, there will be multiple concurrent transactions in the database. If transactions never needed to access the same database resource, there would never be a problem. As you can guess, that is not the case. Transactions will often need to access the same resource, at the same time. In this section we will discuss one of the mechanisms that will be employed, to a greater or lesser extent, depending on your specific RDBMS, to provide concurrency controls and isolate your transactions: **locking**.

Locks are a mechanism used to regulate concurrent access to a shared resource in a database. Normally this shared resource will be a table or a row in a table, but it does extend beyond that. Locks can be used at many different levels to provide concurrent access to various resources. A database will likely lock a table definition while a transaction is using the table. While an update to a table is occurring, the definition of the table cannot be changed. In another example, Oracle locks a stored procedure while it is executing– the procedure is 'locked' in a mode that allows others to execute it, but will not permit another user to alter it in any fashion. A database can also use locks when accessing memory or system files. Locks are used in the database to permit concurrent access to these shared resources while at the same time providing data integrity and consistency by preventing destructive interference between transactions.

It is difficult to have a discussion on locking without getting very database specific – and this in itself is a very important point. There are as many ways to implement locking in a database, as there are databases. Almost every database implements locking and uses it for concurrency control, but the differences in their implementations are fundamental. Just because you are experienced with locking in one RDBMS, it does not mean you know how it should, or will, work in another.

All we can really do here is provide a good general coverage of locking concepts. You MUST check the documentation for your particular RDBMS to understand how it locks data, or otherwise provides transaction control and isolation.

There are many different types of locks. Locking can be performed at the **row-level**, **page-level**, or **table-level**; locks can be **shared** or **exclusive**. There are **read** locks and there are **write** locks. There is a particular type of lock that is applied to ensure that only one user at a time modifies data in a row (or table), and another type that is applied to a database object during DDL operations (SQL `CREATE` and `ALTER` commands) to protect the definition of the structure of that object from being concurrently changed by another session.

Another important point to understand is that most of this happens transparently in the database. You do not need to tell your database which type of lock to apply – it will make that decision for you depending on the operation you are performing in the database, and the degree of isolation you have specified for your transactions.

The aim of this section is to provide a general explanation of these concepts. Then, when we reach the section on *Transaction Isolation Levels*, we will see how some of these types of locks are applied in order to achieve the required degree of isolation.

Exclusive and Shared Locks

When an exclusive lock is applied to a row or table, it means that only a single transaction at a time can hold a lock on that row or table. If one transaction holds an exclusive lock on a row, no other transaction can get any sort of lock on the same row. Another user may (or may not) be able to read data from that row, but no other user will be able to make any modifications to that row.

Shared locks can be placed on a resource by any number of users. Any number of transactions can have shared locks on the same row or table. The only time you will not be able to place a shared lock is if an exclusive lock is already in place. Conversely, if a shared lock is in place on a row or table, it will not be possible for a user to get an exclusive lock on that row or table (so while the shared lock is in place, the table or row cannot be modified).

Read Locks and Write Locks

A read lock is a lock placed on a resource that is being read or accessed by a transaction. The effect of this lock on other transactions is database-dependent. Read locks usually do not prevent other reads. If you read a row from a table in one transaction, it probably doesn't matter if another transaction reads the same row. In some databases, a read lock may prevent other transactions from changing the rows that are being read by a transaction. In the illustration below, we show this situation using two transactions attempting to access the same table concurrently:

Time	Transaction A	Transaction B
T0	Reads a row from table `T`, database places a read lock on the row.	
T1		Reads the same row from table `T`, the read lock on the row does not prevent the read.
T2		Attempts to update the row, but because the row is locked, the transaction cannot write to it, and blocks until the read lock is released.
T3	Transaction is committed, the database releases the lock.	Updates the row.

Note that this is *not* the situation for every database. For the illustration above, we assumed that a read lock would block a write. However, since locking is database-dependent, read locks in some databases do not block writes. Oracle, for example, has structured its database so that read locks do not block writes, yet they can still provide a consistent view of the data to the reader.

Write locks are used by a database when a transaction is writing to a row or table. A write lock prevents other transactions from changing the same row or table until the transaction holding the lock commits or rolls back the changes.

Table versus Row-Level Locking

Most databases now support row-level as well as page-level and table-level locking.

> *Page-level generally refers to a page in memory or other storage that holds part of a table.*

Version 4.0 of MySQL has row-level locking, although earlier versions had only table-level. Cloudscape supports both types of locking, although it gives the option to disable row-level locking. When a system is configured for row-level locking in Cloudscape, the database then decides whether a lock is applied to a row, a set of rows, or a table, depending on the operation that is taking place and on the isolation level. For example, if we execute a query that selects a single row, the database will be likely to use a read lock applied to the row. Other transactions could then read other rows from the same table with no impact. However, if we execute a query that returns many rows, the database could apply a read lock to only the row that is currently being read, it could apply a row-level lock to each row in the result, or it could apply a table-level lock to the entire table. Enterprise databases such as Oracle use row-locking exclusively.

Again, it is important to remember that every database is likely to deal with a given situation in a slightly different manner. Let's reconsider out `Inventories` example. Say we decide that we would like our:

```
select sum(QtyOnHand)
```

query to give an answer consistent with the data that was in the database at the time the query began, regardless of the actions of other transactions. One way for a database, such as Cloudscape, to achieve this would be to place an exclusive lock on the whole table. This would prevent any other updates from taking place against the `Inventories` table for the entire duration of the query. This would do the job, but at the expense of inhibiting concurrency. If you have many transactions waiting to use that table, then performance would be poor. Bear in mind that for a table of four rows, other transactions would be locked out only for a very short period, but for tables of hundreds of thousands of rows, the effect will be far more significant. If you are using Oracle – a far more versatile enterprise database – then the same results could be achieved with no locking of resources. Oracle implements a complex **multi-versioning** scheme, which basically means that it is able to simultaneously maintain multiple versions of the data in the database.

> *This is such an important point that we repeat it again: EVERY database will implement locking differently. It is important that you consult your database's documentation to understand how locking works for it.*

So, in an Oracle database, the query in our first transaction could proceed without locking a single row to other users. If it hits a locked row, indicating that the row may be modified, it simply 'reads through' that lock, retrieving the value that existed when the query started from a data area known as a **rollback segment**.

> *For more information on locking and concurrency control in Oracle, refer to* Expert One-on-One Oracle *by Thomas Kyte, 1-861004-82-6, by Wrox Press.*

Optimistic and Pessimistic Locking

We have said in this section that the type of lock a database applies is very much determined by, and dependent upon, the database. It will make the appropriate choice of lock depending on the circumstances. However, the programmer can have some say on *when* resources are locked, and this will vary depending on whether you follow a **pessimistic** or an **optimistic** locking scheme.

Suppose you have a JDBC application that performs the following actions:

```
// Queries a table for data.
rset = stmt.executeQuery("SELECT * FROM Stores WHERE storied=123");

// Performs other actions, perhaps displays the query results to the user
// and accepts changes from the user.

//Sometime later... update the row in the database.
stmt.executeUpdate("update stores set ...");
```

Now, assume Transaction A is executing the code. There is a relatively large amount of time between the `SELECT` and the `UPDATE` – enough time for another transaction, Transaction B, to update the same row. Now when the Transaction A commits its changes, the other updates made by Transaction B will be lost. This is illustrated overleaf:

Time	Transaction A	Transaction B
T0	Reads a row from `Stores` table.	Reads the same row from `Stores` table.
T1		Updates the row from the `Stores` table. Transaction committed.
T2	Updates the same row from the `Stores` table. Transaction committed. Any changes made by Transaction B are lost.	

This situation is known as the **lost update**. Both pessimistic and optimistic locking can prevent this situation, but in different ways.

In pessimistic locking, the application can lock the row for writing as soon as it is ready to update the row. First, the transaction will select some or all of the columns from the table. Here's how it would look using just SQL:

```
SELECT storied, storedescription, storecity
  FROM Stores
 WHERE storied=123
```

After displaying the results to the user, and accepting updates from them, the application submits a slightly different SQL `SELECT` statement:

```
SELECT storied, storedescription, storecity
  FROM Stores
 WHERE storied = nn AND
       storedescription = sss1 AND
       storecity = sss2
FOR UPDATE
```

In the SQL above, `nn`, `sss1`, *and* `sss2` *would be replaced by the values obtained in the original query.*

If no other transaction has changed the row, the `SELECT` returns the row for updating, and the `FOR UPDATE` clause tells the database to lock the row so the application can update it with a SQL `UPDATE` statement. No other transaction can then update the row.

If another transaction is already updating the row, then this transaction will block. When the other transaction commits, this transaction will attempt to select the row. If the values that this transaction wants to update are unchanged, the query returns the row and locks it for updating. If the other transaction did change the row such that it doesn't match the query criteria, no row will be returned. The application will then need to perform the original query again.

This locking is called pessimistic because the application attempts to lock the row before actually sending the SQL `UPDATE`. We expect that some other transaction will change the row, so we lock it before sending the `UPDATE`.

Optimistic locking expects (and hopes) that no other transaction has changed the row. The application checks the state of the row and locks it for update at the same time as it sends the SQL UPDATE statement. The application saves the original row data, and then structures the SQL UPDATE like this:

```
UPDATE stores
   SET storied = nn, storedescription = sss1, storecity = sss2
 WHERE storied = old_nn AND
       storedescription = old_sss1 AND
       storecity = old_sss2
```

If no other transaction has changed the row, the UPDATE above will proceed without a problem. If another transaction is updating the row, the update will block until that transaction completes. If another transaction has changed the row such that the WHERE clause fails, then the UPDATE fails.

Deadlocks

Deadlocks occur when two transactions are each blocked waiting for the other transaction to complete. For example, recall the ATM example from earlier in the chapter. Here again are the two SQL statements:

```
update accounts
   set balance = balance - 100
 where account = 55 and type = 'Savings';

update accounts
   set balance = balance + 100
 where account = 55 and type = 'Checking';
```

Suppose someone is attempting to transfer funds from savings to checking as shown above. Through some bizarre twist of fate, someone else decides to transfer from checking to savings at the same time. Here's what happens:

Time	Transaction A	Transaction B
T0	Updates the row for `account = 55` and `type = savings`. This row is now blocked to further updates.	
T1		Updates the row for `account = 55` and `type = checking`. This row is now blocked to further updates.
T2	Attempts to update the row for `account = 55` and `type = checking`. Transaction blocks, waiting for Transaction B to commit or rollback.	
T3		Attempts to update the row for `account = 55` and `type =` savings.

The transactions are now deadlocked. Transaction A is waiting for B to release a resource and will not complete until that occurs. Transaction B can't release the resource until A completes which cannot occur. What happens next depends on the database. If you have a well-designed database, it will detect that the transactions are locked, and select one transaction to be automatically rolled back.

The Performance Impact of Locks

There are two issues to consider here. The first is the obvious observation that the more resources that are locked in the database, the less concurrency our application can support. This in turn means the worse the performance will be in terms of the time users have to wait to receive answers, since transactions are waiting longer and longer for the resources they need to be able to return the answer.

The second issue concerns the expense to the database, in terms of time and memory, of implementing the locks. In some databases the expense is quite high – it takes the database considerable time to acquire and release a lock, and the actual lock may take up quite a bit of memory. As more and more locks are acquired, the performance of the database will degrade. In such databases, row-level locking, although more desirable in that it locks fewer resources, is prohibitively expensive to the database beyond a certain point. For example, in the Cloudscape developer's guide, it states:

> ...row-level locking uses a lot of resources and may have a negative impact on performance...

In such cases, locks are a scarce resource and the database permits lock 'escalation' (whereby, say, 100 row-level locks will be converted into one table-level lock). In Oracle, on the other hand, there is no extra overhead involved in row-level locking and the database will never escalate a lock.

While we have little control over the type or granularity of lock that our database uses, we do have considerable control over the transaction isolation level. So far, we have discussed isolation in broad terms, as being the degree to which one transaction is isolated from the effects of others. In general, it is true that the higher degree of isolation you require, the more resources and locks that will require in the database, so it is important to choose the isolation level carefully to match the needs of your application. The next section looks at his issue in more detail and shows how certain types of locking may be used to achieve a certain isolation level.

Transaction Isolation Levels

Isolation, as you know, refers to the degree to which actions taken in one transaction can be seen by other transactions. At the highest level of isolation, any actions taken in a transaction cannot be seen by any other transaction. This applies to both reads and writes. That is, if one transaction reads a row or rows of data, no other transaction is impacted by the first transaction. At the lowest level of isolation (as defined by the SQL specification) everything done in any transaction, whether committed or not, can be seen by any other transaction.

The ANSI/ISO SQL-92 standard identifies three different types of interactions between transactions. From the lowest to the highest levels of isolation, these types are **dirty reads**, **non-repeatable reads**, and **phantom reads**. The specification also identifies four isolation levels that indicate which interactions are allowed or prevented. Those levels are **read uncommitted**, **read committed**, **repeatable read**, and **serializable**.

Over the following sections, we will examine the types of interaction that are allowed, and the consequences they could have for your applications.

Read Uncommitted

This is the only isolation level that permits dirty reads. A **dirty read** occurs when a database allows uncommitted changes made in one transaction to be seen in other transactions. In other words, any given transaction sees the database the same way as every other transaction. As soon as any transaction makes any change to the database, that change is visible to all other transactions.

You may be wondering why dirty reads would ever be allowed (and, in fact databases such as Oracle do not allow them). The basic goal of a read-uncommitted isolation-level is to provide a standards-based definition that caters for non-blocking reads. Let's go back again to our `Inventories` example. We'll keep the 'querying' transaction the same, but this time the 'updating' transaction will subtract five units from row 1, and add those five units on to row 4 (perhaps to correct a stock discrepancy that has come to light). So at the end of our update transaction, the `Inventories` table will look as follows (initial values in brackets):

	ProductID	QtyOnHand
Row 1	1001	(10) 5
Row 2	1002	(20) 20
Row 3	1003	(15) 15
Row 4	1004	(5) 10

So, consider the following chain of events:

Time	Query	Update
T1	Reads row 1, sum = 10.	
T2	Reads row 2, sum = 30 so far.	
T3		Updates row 1, puts an exclusive lock on row 1 preventing other updates. Row 1 now has 5 units.
T4	Reads row 3, sum = 45 so far.	
T5		Updates row 4, puts an exclusive lock on row 4 preventing other updates. Row 4 now has 10 units.
T6	Reads row 4 and discovers that it has a lock on it.	

So what happens next? Remember that the update transaction has not yet committed so, on the face of it, our query is 'blocked' and must wait for this update to be resolved. In fact, this may well be what would happen in your database if you had a higher isolation level set. However, one way to skirt round this blocking issue is to allow dirty reads. In this case the query will be allowed to read whatever value happens to be there when it reaches that row, whether or not the value is committed. So, in this case, it would read a value of 10, and present a final answer of 55. Unfortunately, this is the 'wrong' answer. The total number of units hasn't changed (it is still 50).

As discussed earlier, if you have a smart database like Oracle, it will skirt the blocking issue altogether and in a way that still guarantees consistent results with regard to certain a point in time.

Read Committed

Databases or drivers that prevent dirty reads, but allow phantom reads and non-repeatable reads are operating at the read committed isolation level. At this level, a transaction can only read changes that have been committed to the database. When one transaction reads a row from the database at this level, the database does not prevent other transactions from writing to the same row. However, when a transaction writes to a row, other transactions do not see the change until it has been committed.

Let's consider the case of the **non-repeatable read**. This occurs when one transaction reads a row from the database, and a different transaction changes the same row in the database. If the first transaction then tries to repeat the read, it gets different data from the database. However, this change is not visible until the second transaction commits the change.

Suppose we have a customer, Lori, logged into the Music Store application and browsing the recordings looking for something to buy. After one particular search, she sees the search result screen showing the recording 'The Essential Miles Davis', and this is apparently in stock.

Before she can put the recording into her shopping cart though, Dave, who is also logged into the application from his computer performs the same search and puts the same recording into his shopping cart. What is not shown to either Lori or Dave is that even though the item is in stock, there is only one copy available. When Dave clicks the Buy Now button and completes his purchase, the application updates the inventory table to show that there are no copies of the recording available. Lori now attempts to put the same recording into her cart, the application checks the inventory table, finds that there are no copies left, and returns a message to Lori saying that the item is now out of stock. Ironically, in the illustration below, the message is displayed in a way such that Lori can still see her search result screen that claims the item is in stock:

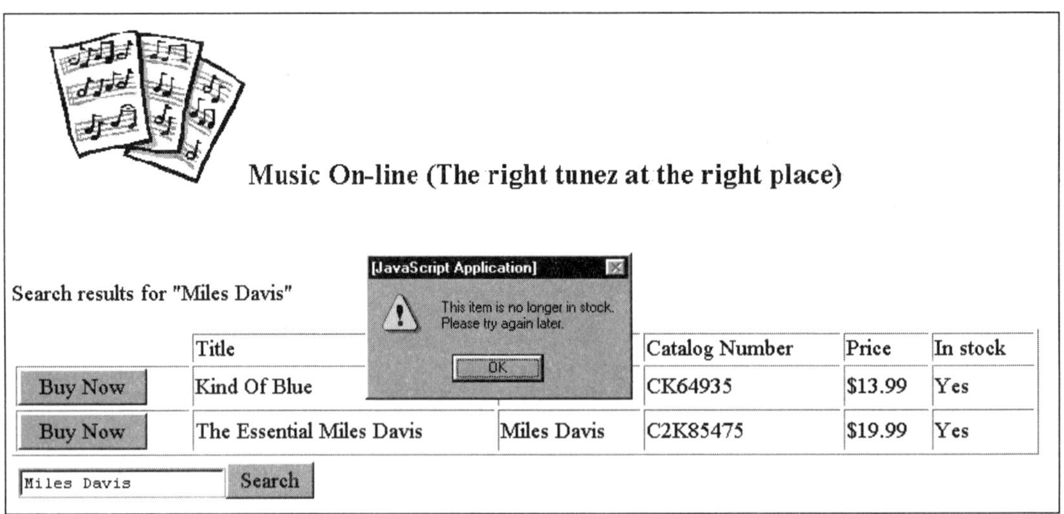

While this might be considered a problem with the application, it does not indicate a problem with the database. If Lori and Dave had both been in a brick-and-mortar store, only one of them would be able to buy the recording. The same is true of our web application. Only one of them can buy the recording. The database was operating at the read, committed isolation level, which means that just because Lori reads a particular row, the database does not stop someone else from reading or changing that row.

Read committed is perhaps the most commonly used isolation level in database applications everywhere. It is rare to see a different isolation level used. However, you should be aware of the potential problems with this level in certain application scenarios – it is not suitable in *all* cases. Let's pick up our `Inventories` example where we left off, and see what might happen if we were working in read-committed mode:

Time	Query	Update
T1	Reads row 1, sum = 10.	
T2	Reads row 2, sum = 30 so far.	
T3		Updates row 1, puts an exclusive lock on it preventing other updates. Row 1 now has 5 units.
T4	Reads row 3, sum = 45 so far.	
T5		Updates row 4, puts an exclusive lock on row 4 preventing other updates. Row 4 now has 10 units.
T6	Reads row 4 and discovers that it has a lock on it. Processing on the query stops and we wait for the lock to be released.	
T7		Commits transaction.
T8	Reads row 4, sees a value of 10 and presents a final answer of 55.	

In this particular scenario, the answer is still wrong, but this time we had to wait longer to get it! Again the behavior of Oracle would be as for read uncommitted – it would simply read through the lock and retrieve the original value of 5.

Repeatable Read

Databases or drivers that allow phantom reads (but not non-repeatable reads or dirty reads) are operating at the repeatable-read isolation level.

By definition, if we have repeatable read enabled, then a re-read of any row at any point in time after the transaction starts would return the same data. So, in our `Inventories` example, if we had read row 4 at T1, when the transaction started, it would have returned a value of 5. So, under repeatable read, it should still return a value of 5 at time T8. The way many databases achieve repeatable read (not Oracle, again) is through use of shared read locks, as follows:

Time	Query	Update
T1	Reads row 1, sum = 10. Places a shared read lock on row 1.	
T2	Reads row 2, sum = 30 so far. Places a shared read lock on row 2.	
T3		Tries to update row 1, but is blocked. Transaction is suspended until it can get an exclusive lock.
T4	Reads row 3, sum = 45 so far.	
T5	Reads row 4, sees a value of 5 and presents a final answer of 50.	
T6		Updates row 1, puts an exclusive lock on row 1 preventing other updates. Row 1 now has 5 units.
T7		Updates row 4, puts an exclusive lock on row 4 preventing other updates. Row 4 now has 10 units.
T8		Commits transaction.

Here, we get the correct answer, but we may have had to make our update transaction wait a long time in order to perform its work.

The repeatable-read isolation level does still allow **phantom reads**. A phantom read occurs when a transaction performs two identical queries on a database, and the second query returns a different result. This occurs when, after the first query and before the second, some other transaction inserts or modifies a new row into the database that satisfies the constraints of the query. When the first transaction performs the query a second time, it finds the new row. This differs from the non-repeatable read in that in this case, data you have already read has not been changed, but *more* data satisfies your query criteria than before.

As an example, suppose someone is performing a search of the database for recordings. After performing a search the result screen looks like this:

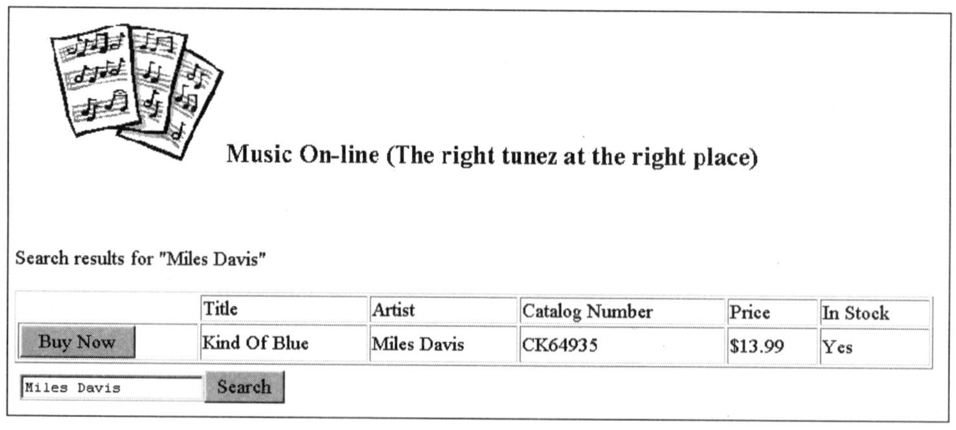

Right after the search, a new recording is entered into the database. This new recording matches the search criteria of the earlier search. When the user clicks the Search button using the same criteria, the second search returns additional records as shown below:

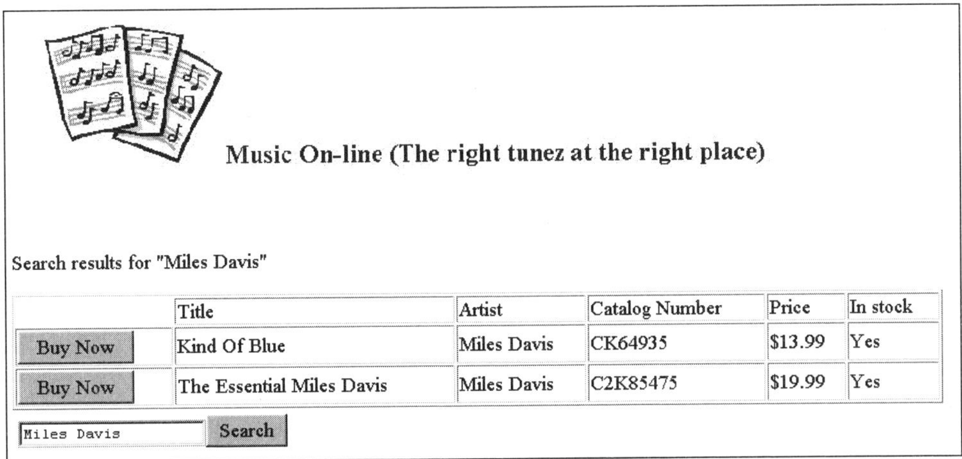

In this particular example, it doesn't matter that the customer got new rows with the second query. The customer probably wanted to get the new rows as soon as they were available. However, there may be other situations where this is not desirable. In the situation where we want to prevent all interactions, dirty reads, non-repeatable reads, and phantom reads, we can use the isolation level serializable.

Serializable

A database or driver that prevents all interactions is operating at the transaction isolation level **serializable**. At this level, all transactions with the database are executed as though each transaction is the only transaction active in the database at any given time. It does *not* mean that each transaction executes serially. In fact, many transactions could be concurrently active in the database. However, the database does not allow any interaction between the transactions.

Suppose we had an application that computed the interest on bank savings accounts. Interest is computed daily on the balance in the account at some fixed point in time. At that point in time, the application queries the table and starts computing the interest. Further, let's assume that it takes an hour to compute and deposit the interest for all the accounts. We would not want this application to prevent customers from making deposits or withdrawals during this hour. Neither do we want the interest to be computed from a balance that did not exist (either through a deposit or withdrawal) when the transaction started. By making the transaction serializable, the transaction executes as though it were the only transaction in the database. While it is computing interest, other transactions are allowed to change the database, but for the duration of its transaction, the interest application sees the database as it existed when the transaction started.

Isolation Summary

The most appropriate isolation level will depend upon the database and the needs of the application. Ideally, we want to execute transactions at the lowest isolation level that does not cause problems for the application. For most applications, this means that you can operate at the read-committed isolation level. This allows non-repeatable reads and phantom reads, but prevents transactions from reading uncommitted changes. In order to get the right answer in our `Inventories` example, most databases would use repeatable-read isolation level, with shared read locks, or completely block one of the two transactions. Both have the drawback that resources are locked in the database and performance will often be affected. An enterprise database such as Oracle would be able to provide a correct, consistent answer with minimal locking of resources.

In the table below, we summarize the various isolation levels and which interactions they allow:

Isolation Level	Dirty Read	Non-Repeatable Read	Phantom Read
Read Uncommitted	Permitted	Permitted	Permitted
Read Committed		Permitted	Permitted
Repeatable Read			Permitted
Serializable			

As we move down the table, the degree of isolation increases, from the read-uncommitted isolation level that allows all the defined types of interaction, to the serializable level, which allows none of them.

Which Isolation Levels are Supported?

Using the `ShowDatabaseMetaData` class from Chapter 10, you can investigate the transaction isolation levels supported by any particular database and JDBC driver. The `ShowDatabaseMetaData` class used a few methods of the `DatabaseMetaData` interface to reveal information such as the name and version of the database. The `DatabaseMetaData` interface also has methods for revealing the transaction support provided by the database and the JDBC driver. Those methods are as follows:

Method	Description
`boolean supportsTransactions()`	Indicates whether or not transactions are supported.
`boolean supportsTransactionIsolationLevel(int)`	Indicates which levels of transaction isolation are supported.

The valid values for the `supportsTransactionIsolationLevel(int)` method are provided as static constants by the `Connection` interface. The following table lists the definitions of the constants according to the `java.sql.Connection` JavaDoc (http://java.sun.com/j2se/1.3/docs/api/index.html).

Constant	Description
`static int TRANSACTION_NONE`	Indicates that transactions are not supported.
`static int TRANSACTION_READ_UNCOMMITTED`	Dirty reads, non-repeatable reads, and phantom reads can occur.
`static int TRANSACTION_READ_COMMITTED`	Dirty reads are prevented; non-repeatable reads and phantom reads can occur.
`static int TRANSACTION_REPEATABLE_READ`	Dirty reads and non-repeatable reads are prevented; phantom reads can occur.
`static int TRANSACTION_SERIALIZABLE`	Dirty reads, non-repeatable reads, and phantom reads are prevented.

Notice that four of the five constants in the table above correspond to the isolation levels defined in the previous section. Since the constants are static member variables of the `Connection` interface, they can be used in code by referencing the variable with the class name like this:

```
Connection.TRANSACTION_READ_UNCOMMITTED);
```

There is one other method that provides information about the transaction level supported by a driver, however, and this method is defined by the `Connection` interface:

`int getTransactionIsolation()`	Returns the current isolation level of transactions. Returns one of the static constants defined by the `Connection` interface.

Try It Out – Determining Isolation Level Support

The `ShowDatabaseMetaData` class has been modified below to include calls to the methods above:

```
package metadata;

import java.sql.*;
import connections.*;

public class ShowDatabaseMetaData {
  public static void main(String[] args) {
    try {
      Connection connection = ConnectionFactory.getConnection();
      DatabaseMetaData dbmd = connection.getMetaData();

      System.out.println("Information about the database: ");
      System.out.println("Database name=[" + dbmd.getDatabaseProductName()
                         + "]");
      System.out.println("Database version=["
                         + dbmd.getDatabaseProductVersion() + "]");
      System.out.println("Driver name=[" + dbmd.getDriverName() + "]");
      System.out.println("Driver version=[" + dbmd.getDriverVersion()
                         + "]");

      System.out.println("Supports transactions=["
                         + dbmd.supportsTransactions() + "]");

      String s = "Supports transaction isolation level ";
      String value = "TRANSACTION_NONE";
      int level = Connection.TRANSACTION_NONE;
      System.out.println(s + value + "=["
                         + dbmd.supportsTransactionIsolationLevel(level)
                         + "]");

      value = "TRANSACTION_READ_UNCOMMITTED";
      level = Connection.TRANSACTION_READ_UNCOMMITTED;
      System.out.println(s + value + "=["
                         + dbmd.supportsTransactionIsolationLevel(level)
                         + "]");

      value = "TRANSACTION_READ_COMMITTED";
      level = Connection.TRANSACTION_READ_COMMITTED;
      System.out.println(s + value + "=["
                         + dbmd.supportsTransactionIsolationLevel(level)
                         + "]");

      value = "TRANSACTION_REPEATABLE_READ";
      level = Connection.TRANSACTION_REPEATABLE_READ;
```

```
        System.out.println(s + value + "=["
                           + dbmd.supportsTransactionIsolationLevel(level)
                           + "]");

        value = "TRANSACTION_SERIALIZABLE";
        level = Connection.TRANSACTION_SERIALIZABLE;
        System.out.println(s + value + "=["
                           + dbmd.supportsTransactionIsolationLevel(level)
                           + "]");


        int dbLevel = connection.getTransactionIsolation();
        System.out.println("Default database isolation level is " + dbLevel);
        System.out.println(Connection.TRANSACTION_NONE
                           + " is TRANSACTION_NONE");
        System.out.println(Connection.TRANSACTION_READ_UNCOMMITTED
                           + " is TRANSACTION_READ_UNCOMMITTED");
        System.out.println(Connection.TRANSACTION_READ_COMMITTED
                           + " is TRANSACTION_READ_COMMITTED");
        System.out.println(Connection.TRANSACTION_REPEATABLE_READ
                           + " is TRANSACTION_REPEATABLE_READ");
        System.out.println(Connection.TRANSACTION_SERIALIZABLE
                           + " is TRANSACTION_SERIALIZABLE");

      } catch (Exception e) {
        e.printStackTrace();
      }
    }
  }
```

The class above gets a connection from the `ConnectionFactory` class that was first developed in *Connecting to a Database*, Chapter 8. When we compile the class above, we'll need to include the `connections` package in the classpath. Suppose you've installed the classes in the directories `C:\BegJavaDB\Ch14\connections` and `C:\BegJavaDB\Ch14\metadata`. Then, you can set the classpath and compile the program like this:

```
C:\BegJavaDB\Ch14>set classpath=%classpath%;c:\BegJavaDB\Ch14
C:\BegJavaDB\Ch14>javac metadata\ShowDatabaseMetaData.java
```

If you've saved the source files to a different location, or you are using something other than Windows, you should adjust the classpath to point to the correct location. To run the class, we need the classpath to point at the appropriate JDBC library. Recall that connections are obtained from the `ConnectionFactory` class.

The `ShowDatabaseMetaData` class file is located in a directory rooted at `C:\BegJavaDB\Ch14\`. Thus, the full path to the `ShowDatabaseMetaData` class is `C:\BegJavaDB\Ch14\metadata\ShowDatabaseMetaData.class`. Assuming the `ConnectionFactory` is returning connections to the Cloudscape database, here is the command to run the program on our system, and get the meta data for the Cloudscape driver:

```
C:\BegJavaDB\Ch14> java -classpath
                     %CLASSPATH%;.;%CLOUDSCAPE_HOME%\lib\cloudscape.jar
                     metadata.ShowDatabaseMetaData
```

If you are using an IDE, you will need to set the classpath and execute the program using the procedure for your IDE. The program produces something similar to the following output:

```
Information about the database:
Database name=[DBMS:cloudscape]
Database version=[3.6.1]
Driver name=[Cloudscape Embedded JDBC Driver]
Driver version=[3.6]
Supports transactions=[true]
Supports transaction isolation level TRANSACTION_NONE=[false]
Supports transaction isolation level TRANSACTION_READ_UNCOMMITTED=[false]
Supports transaction isolation level TRANSACTION_READ_COMMITTED=[true]
Supports transaction isolation level TRANSACTION_REPEATABLE_READ=[true]
Supports transaction isolation level TRANSACTION_SERIALIZABLE=[true]
Default database isolation level is 2
0 is TRANSACTION_NONE
1 is TRANSACTION_READ_UNCOMMITTED
2 is TRANSACTION_READ_COMMITTED
4 is TRANSACTION_REPEATABLE_READ
8 is TRANSACTION_SERIALIZABLE
```

Looking at the output, you can see that the Cloudscape driver supports three isolation levels, and the default level is `TRANSACTION_READ_COMMITTED`. The Cloudscape database always prevents dirty reads; other interactions may or may not be allowed, depending upon the isolation level at which the database is operating.

By changing the `ConnectionFactory` and changing the `-classpath` option above to point to the appropriate JDBC library, you can run the program with a different database. I also have an Oracle development database on my system. I can run the program with the Oracle driver by using these commands:

```
C:\BegJavaDB\Ch14> java -classpath
                    %CLASSPATH%;.;%ORACLE_HOME%\jdbc\lib\classes12.zip
                    metadata.ShowDatabaseMetaData
```

Running the program produces output similar to that shown below:

```
Information about the database:
Database name=[Oracle]
Database version=[Oracle8i Personal Edition Release 8.1.5.0.0 - Production
With the Java option
PL/SQL Release 8.1.5.0.0 - Production]
Driver name=[Oracle JDBC driver]
Driver version=[8.1.7.0.0]
Supports transactions=[true]
Supports transaction isolation level TRANSACTION_NONE=[false]
Supports transaction isolation level TRANSACTION_READ_UNCOMMITTED=[false]
Supports transaction isolation level TRANSACTION_READ_COMMITTED=[true]
Supports transaction isolation level TRANSACTION_REPEATABLE_READ=[false]
Supports transaction isolation level TRANSACTION_SERIALIZABLE=[true]
Default database isolation level is 2
```

Oracle supports two isolation levels, and the default level is `TRANSACTION_READ_COMMITTED`. Like Cloudscape, Oracle always prevents dirty reads.

How It Works – Determining Isolation Level Suppport

The revised ShowDatabaseMetaData class uses the DatabaseMetaData methods presented earlier. However, instead of printing the int value of the isolation level, the new version of the program prints descriptions of the various levels with the result of the DatabaseMetaData method call.

The main method of the class is the same as presented in Chapter 10. The class calls the getConnection() method of the ConnectionFactory class. The connection is then used to get a DatabaseMetaData object. The code prints out some basic database information such as the database name and version:

```
Connection connection = ConnectionFactory.getConnection();
DatabaseMetaData dbmd = connection.getMetaData();

System.out.println("Information about the database: ");
System.out.println("Database name=[" + dbmd.getDatabaseProductName()
                   + "]");
```

The new code in the class is shown below. First, the supportsTransactions() method is called and the results are printed:

```
System.out.println("Supports transactions=["
                   + dbmd.supportsTransactions() + "]");
```

Then the code calls the supportsTransactionIsolationLevel(level) method with each possible isolation value from the Connection interface. The value returned by the method call is printed out along with the string description of which level is being checked. Here is the code that checks the TRANSACTION_NONE level:

```
String s = "Supports transaction isolation level ";
String value = "TRANSACTION_NONE";
int level = Connection.TRANSACTION_NONE;
System.out.println(s + value + "=["
                   + dbmd.supportsTransactionIsolationLevel(level)
                   + "]");
```

The support for each transaction level is checked in a similar manner. The last new piece of code is a call to the getTransactionIsolation() method of the connection:

```
int dbLevel = connection.getTransactionIsolation();
System.out.println("Default database isolation level is " + dbLevel);
```

Transaction Control in JDBC

In some languages, the code can, or must, explicitly tell the database that a transaction is beginning before it sends the SQL to the database. In SQL Server, for example, the BEGIN TRAN command starts a transaction. JDBC does not require you to explicitly begin a transaction (and thus, does not provide any class or methods for you, the application programmer, to perform this action). The JDBC driver you are using will start a transaction for you automatically. If autocommit is enabled, the driver will also end the transaction for you. When autocommit is disabled, the driver still begins the transaction; you only need to end the transaction by issuing the commit or rollback.

Connection Methods for Transaction Control

The connection class provided by the JDBC driver provides transaction control. When your code gets a connection from the `DriverManager`, `DataSource`, or some other source such as a `ConnectionPool`, JDBC requires that the connection be in autocommit mode (autocommit enabled). If you leave this mode enabled in your JDBC applications, then this means that each SQL statement is treated as a transaction, and the transaction is committed when the statement is complete. When a SQL statement is sent to the database, the driver starts a new transaction. The transaction is committed when the statement has finished executing and any results have been returned to the caller. This varies depending on the type of SQL statement as shown in the table:

Statement type	Transaction committed when...
SQL `INSERT`, `UPDATE`, or `DELETE`	The statement has finished executing.
SQL `QUERY`	All the rows in the `ResultSet` have been retrieved, or a `Statement` object is executed on the same connection.

Having the driver in autocommit mode may be acceptable when you are learning JDBC or when you are using a single-user database. However, the fact that the JDBC (and ODBC) API defaults to autocommit enabled is problematic for any type of real-world application. Database applications are almost always multi-user applications.

In previous chapters, most of the transactions between our JDBC code and the database have been single-statement transactions. For example, looking back to Chapters 8 and 9, when the `Store` class inserted a row of data into the database, the transaction consisted of the single SQL `INSERT` statement. As soon as the statement was executed, the transaction was automatically committed to the database by the connection. With single statement transactions, this is not a problem. However, if you look back to the multi-statement ATM transaction example in the previous section, it is clear that if we work with autocommit enabled here, then we are in danger of corrupting our data. JDBC will (silently) place a commit after *each* update and if the system fails between the two statements, the unlucky customer could lose $100.

Many programmers do not understand why this behavior was carried over from ODBC into JDBC, an API that is supposed to be in support of the 'Enterprise', and believe that the very next line of code after opening a connection in JDBC should always be:

```
Connection conn = DriverManager.getConnection
                  ("jdbc:oracle:oci8:@ora8idev","scott","tiger");

conn.setAutoCommit (false);
```

This is a strong argument. It returns control over the transaction back to the developer, which is where it belongs. You can then safely code your account transfer transaction, and commit it after both statements have succeeded.

There are other cases where we must disable the `autocommit` mode and we encountered one in Chapter 12, *Prepared Statements,* when we looked at a `TrackSample` class that sent binary data to an Oracle table. For the `TrackSample` class to work correctly, we turned `autocommit` mode off.

If autocommit had been enabled, the code would not have worked. The binary data was written to the table using a stream. Within the driver, the stream is obtained from a locator (locators are covered briefly in the SQL-99 Data Types *section of Chapter 12, Prepared Statements). While writing to the stream, the locator must remain locked. As soon as the driver commits, the lock is released and the stream cannot be written to. By disabling autocommit, the code could explicitly control the commit.*

Here's a snippet of code from Chapter 12 showing the code that disabled the autocommit mode:

```
void getConnection(boolean autocommit)
  throws SQLException
{
  connection = ConnectionFactory.getConnection();
  connection.setAutoCommit(autocommit);
}
```

When the `getConnection()` method is called by in the `TrackSample` class, it is called with the argument `false`. In the second line of the method, calling `setAutocommit()` with the argument `false` disables autocommit.

When the `autocommit` mode is set to `false`, transaction management must now be performed explicitly by the code, by making calls to the appropriate methods of the connection object at the appropriate times. SQL statements sent to the database will still be executed, but the transaction is not committed when the statement is complete. The transaction will not be committed until the code calls the `commit()` method of the `Connection`. Alternatively, the transaction could be rolled back if the code calls the `rollback()` method.

In the `TrackSample` class, after all the data was written to the database, the streams were closed and the transaction was committed. The code also contained a `catch` block that called the `rollback()` method if an exception was caught while trying to write the data to the database:

```
      //Close the Input and Output Streams
      out.close();
      out = null;
      in.close();
      in = null;
      //And finally, commit the changes
      conn.commit();
    }
  } catch (Exception e) {
    e.printStackTrace();
    try {
      conn.rollback();
    } catch (Exception ignored) {}
```

Summarized in the table below are all the methods of the `Connection` interface that are related to transaction control:

Method	Description
`void setAutoCommit(boolean)`	Sets the autocommit mode to `true` (commit transaction automatically, the default setting) or `false` (require explicit transaction commit).
`boolean getAutoCommit()`	Returns the current autocommit mode.

Method	Description
`void commit()`	Commits the current transaction. All changes made since the last commit or rollback are made permanent. Any database locks are released.
`void rollback()`	Returns the database to the state that existed after the last successful commit, usually prior to the start of the current transaction. Any database locks are released.
`void close()`	Close the `Connection`. This also closes any `Statements` and `ResultSets` that have not been closed. Whether this commits or rolls back the transaction is database-dependent. The JDBC specification does not require a particular behavior.
`boolean isClosed()`	Returns `true` if the method `close()` has been called on the `Connection`.

Transactions and Stored Procedures

I mentioned in the previous section that transaction control belongs in the hands of the programmer. The developers of the system will know the business rules for the application and will be able to make the best decision on what the transactions are, and when those transactions should be committed. While you can perform this control while executing SQL from your application, another way to provide this control is to put all the statements that constitute a transaction into a stored procedure.

Stored procedures are covered in more detail in Chapter 13, Callable Statements and Stored Procedures.

Stored procedures are perhaps the easiest and most accessible method to ensure correct transactions. If you follow a programming paradigm that says, *a stored procedure call is a transaction*, you will have an easier time controlling your transactions and building new ones. You would code stored procedures that received all of the necessary inputs to perform their work. They would take the database from one consistent state to the next. When you invoked their these procedures , you would wrap the procedure call in transaction control statements:

```
// Disable autcommit.
connection.setAutoCommit(false);

String sql = "{ call Procedure }";
CallableStatement cs = connection.prepareCall(sql);

// Call procedure.
cs.executeUpdate();
connection.commit();
```

Now, if PROCEDURE completes successfully, we will commit all of the work it did. If it fails we will roll back the work (although that is not shown in the snippet above). The reason we would not put the commit directly into PROCEDURE itself is because at some later date we might need to combine two or three transactions into one transaction. For example, let's go back to our Inventories example from earlier on in the chapter. Assume we implemented a stored procedure to perform our update. This procedure takes as input the StoreID, the ProductID, and the amount to adjust the QtyOnHand column by. We need to process two calls to this procedure as one call. If this routine did its own commit, we could not do both calls as one transaction. By leaving it up to the client to commit (which is where the choice belongs) we can assemble larger transactions as a collection of smaller ones. We can code:

```
// Disable autocommit.
connection.setAutoCommit(false);

String sql = "{ call Update_Qty(?, ?, ?) }";
```

The question marks (?) above are placeholders that must be set with data before the statement is executed. Chapter 13, Callable Statements and Stored Procedures *shows how to do this.*

```
CallableStatement cs = connection.prepareCall(sql);

// Set the placeholders with data for row 1001.
cs.executeUpdate();
// Set the placeholders with data for row 1004.
cs.executeUpdate();

connection.commit();
```

and we can be assured that they either both happen or neither happens.

Enterprise Java Beans (EJBs) are another viable method for doing this sort of operation without using stored procedures. Stored procedures are nice in that they are callable from many dozens of environments (SQL*PLUS, ODBC, JDBC, EJBs themselves, and so on) but some people want to avoid using them for whatever reason. The implementation of EJBs (effectively a remote procedure call – just like a stored procedure) makes them candidates for encapsulating your transactions as well. Given that EJBs have transaction semantics and features that are compatible with the database, they are also a nice way to encapsulate the transaction. We cover this in more detail in Chapter 19, *J2EE and Java Database Applications.*

Batch Updates

Even when you use multiple statements in a transaction, each statement is still sent to the database, and executed, individually. However, there is a way to send statements to the database in batches. All three statement interfaces, Statement, PreparedStatement, and CallableStatement, support **batch updates**. Here are the methods that are used to perform batch processing:

Method	Description
`void addBatch(String)`	Adds an SQL statement to the batch. `SELECT` statements are not allowed.
`int[] executeBatch()`	Sends the statements to the database for execution. The return value of executing each statement is an element in the `int` array.
`void clearBatch()`	Removes all SQL statements from the batch. Does not affect statements that have already been sent to the database. Statements that have already been sent to the database can only be undone by calling `rollback()`.

Here is a code snippet showing how the batch update would be used as part of a transaction. Assume we have a data file that contains many rows of data to be inserted into a table:

```
connection.setAutoCommit(false);
String sql = "INSERT INTO stores values (?, ?, ?, ?, ?, ?)";
PreparedStatement ps = connection.prepareStatement(sql);
while (!done) {
  // Read a line of data from the data file.
  // Set the parameters of the prepared statement.
  ps.addBatch();
}

// When all data has been read and all statements added to the batch...
int[] result = ps.executeBatch();
connection.commit();
```

The code above does not change how the transaction is managed. What it does is change the way the SQL is sent to the database. Rather than sending the statements one at a time, they are stored in the `PreparedStatement` object until `executeBatch()` is called. At that time, they are all sent to the database.

Distributed Transactions

For most of this chapter, we have been looking at transactions involving a single connection to a single database. In this section we will take a *brief* introductory look at **distributed transactions**. These are transactions that span multiple data sources as shown in this illustration:

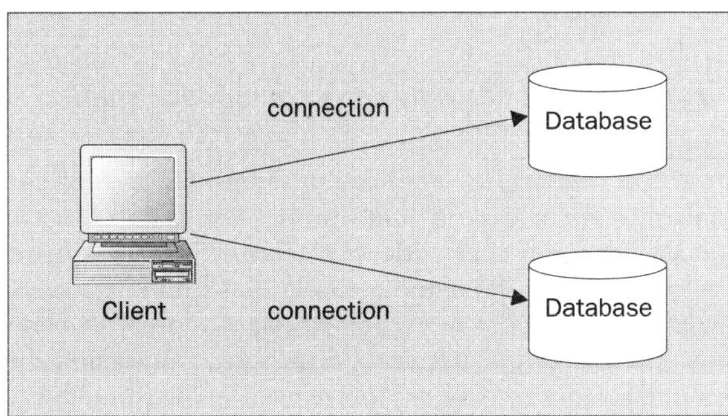

or transactions that span multiple connections to the same data source:

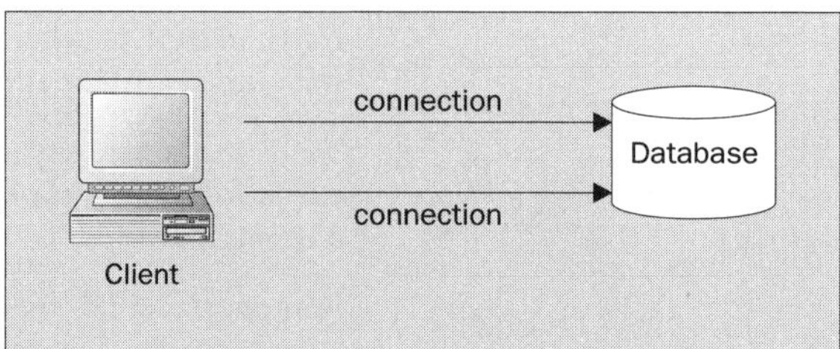

In either case, for the transaction to be successful, all the changes made by each connection must be successful. Discussing all the details of distributed transaction is beyond the scope of this book. However, from the client's point of view, coding a distributed transaction is almost the same as coding for a single connection transaction, so we will be able to look at distributed transactions from that perspective.

While you can use multiple data sources or connections within your JDBC application, the term 'distributed transactions' usually applies to applications or classes that run inside an **application server**. Application servers are programs that provide a working environment for special kinds of Java classes. These 'special' Java classes that use distributed transactions are usually Enterprise JavaBeans (EJBs) that run inside an EJB server such as Bea WebLogic, JBOSS, or Sybase Enterprise Application Server. These are not the only servers available, and this discussion applies to any application server, whether it was just listed or not.

In many ways, EJBs are like any other Java class. What is different between an EJB and a non-EJB Java class is that the server provides many of the low-level services needed by the EJB. These services include thread control (EJBs in particular are prohibited from creating or using threads), communications support, security and authorization control, and transaction control. The EJB developer can concentrate on providing business logic in the EJB, while leaving distributed computing support such as network connections, authentication and authorization, transaction control, database connections, and so on, to the application server.

EJBs usually provide a single service, or coherent set of services, to clients, while the application server provides network services. In addition, different EJBs on the network may provide different services that are all needed by a client to complete a transaction. As part of the service they provide, the EJBs might talk to one or more databases. Since separate EJBs will use separate connections, whether they use the same data source or different data sources, these EJBs will need to be part of a distributed transaction.

When separate EJBs provide part of a transaction, no single component can determine when or how to commit or roll back changes. This then becomes the responsibility of the transaction manager. Since we're working in the Java world, that manager will be an implementation of the **Java Transaction API** (**JTA**).

> *You can learn more about the JTA at http://java.sun.com/products/jta.*

As part of providing transaction support, the application server will use special JDBC classes. Those classes will implement the interfaces `XADataSource`, `XAConnection`, and `XAResource`. The application server vendor or the database vendor will provide these classes. At least one of these classes might look vaguely familiar – the `XAConnection`. Its name is similar to `Connection`, but it has an `XA` at the beginning. As its name suggests, the `XAConnection` interface represents connections. However, in this case, it represents a connection that can be used in a distributed transaction. Likewise, `XADataSource` and `XAResource` represent data sources and resources used in distributed transactions.

However, the developer of the EJB will not need to use or be aware of these classes. At the client level, the code will use the same interfaces that we have seen throughout this book; `Connection`, `Statement`, `ResultSet`. The EJB code used to talk to the database will not look very different from code we have been using in this and previous chapters. For example, the code an EJB will use to get a connection might look like this:

```
Context context = new InitialContext();
DataSource dataSource = context.lookup("jdbc/oracle");
Connection connection = dataSource.getConnection();
```

If you look at Chapter 18 on *JDBC Data Sources*, you will see that the code used to get a 'normal' data source is essentially the same that an application involved in a distributed transaction will use. Under the covers, the application server will likely use an `XAConnection` implementation to get the `Connection` that is passed to the EJB, but in the EJB, the object will be referenced as a `Connection`. After getting the connection, the code would use one of the `Statement` objects to send SQL to the data source. The difference between a non-distributed and a distributed transaction is in how the transaction is committed or rolled back.

Since the transaction is being controlled by a transaction manager outside the EJB, any class involved in a distributed transaction is prohibited from calling any of these methods:

- `commit()`
- `rollback()`
- `setSavepoint()`
- `setAutoCommit(true)`

Committing or rolling back a transaction is entirely under the control of the transaction manager. The EJB does not need to do anything special other than call the `close()` method of the `Connection` interface when it has completed its work. After all the components involved in the transaction have completed, the transaction manager will commit or rollback the transaction.

This commit (or roll back) is called a **two-phase commit**. It has two phases because the transaction manager must poll all the data sources before deciding to commit or roll back. As each data source is polled, it throws an exception if it cannot commit its changes. Suppose we have two clients involved in a distributed transaction. Here is an illustration of how the two-phase commit would proceed.

Time	Description
T0	Both clients have called `close()` to signal that they have completed their work.
T1	Transaction manager calls the `prepare()` method of `XAResource`. There is an `XAResource` for each data source.
T2	If neither `XAResource` throws an exception, then each is ready to commit.
T3	Transaction manager calls the `commit()` method of each `XAResource`. This message is passed to each data source, which then commits.

Note that the above would all occur outside the client code. It is entirely handled by the transaction manager. If no data sources throw an exception, the transaction manager tells all the data sources to commit their changes. If any data source throws an exception, all the data sources are notified to roll back the changes.

New for JDBC 3.0 – Savepoints

JDBC 3.0 introduces a new concept to Java database programming; the **savepoint**. Even though they are new for JDBC, savepoints already exist in many databases. They allow you to take the concept of the atomic transaction and perform a partial rollback of the transaction. Using savepoints, you can mark one or more places in the transaction; at some later time (before you commit) you can perform a rollback to one of those saved places.

`Savepoint` is a new interface in the `java.sql` package. A driver that is JDBC 3.0-compliant will provide a concrete implementation of this interface that implements two methods:

Method	Description
`int getSavepointId()`	Retrieves the generated ID for the savepoint that this `Savepoint` object represents.
`String getSavepointName()`	Retrieves the name of the savepoint that this `Savepoint` object represents.

Your code will create, get references to, and use savepoints by calling new methods of the `Connection` interface:

Method	Description
`Savepoint setSavepoint(String)`	Creates a savepoint with the given name in the current transaction and returns the new `Savepoint` object that represents it.
`Savepoint setSavepoint()`	Creates an unnamed savepoint in the current transaction and returns the new `Savepoint` object that represents it.
`void releaseSavepoint(Savepoint savepoint)`	Removes the given `Savepoint` object from the current transaction.
`void rollback(Savepoint savepoint)`	Undoes all changes made after the given `Savepoint` object was set.

Suppose we had some code that inserted multiple rows into two tables in one transaction. One table is important, but the second is not as vital. If we can't insert data into the first table, we want to do a complete rollback, but if we can't insert into the second table, we still want to commit the changes in the first table.

We could use the new savepoint functionality to do a partial rollback and commit. That code might look like this:

```
boolean needCommit = false;
Savepoint recordSavepoint = null;
try {
  // Data is an object that holds the data for the table.
  insertIntoTable1(data);
  // If no exception, then the insert succeeded.
  needCommit = true;
  // Connection is a class member.
```

```
        recordSavepoint = connection.setSavepoint("Insert complete");
        insertIntoTable2(data);
      } catch (Exception e) {
        e.printStackTrace();
        try {
          // If savepoint is NOT Null, then insertIntoTable1 was good
          // but insertIntoTable2 failed, do partial rollback.
          if (recordSavepoint != null) {
            connection.rollback(recordSavepoint);
          } else {
            // insertIntoTable1 failed, do complete rollback.
            needCommit = false;
            connection.rollback();
          }
        } catch (SQLException e2) {
          e2.printStackTrace();
        }
      } finally {
        if (needCommit) {
          connection.commit();
        }
        close(connection);
      }
```

In the code above, two new variables are declared, one of type `boolean` and one of type `Savepoint`. The `boolean` variable will act as a flag indicating whether the transaction needs to be committed. In the `try` block, if the `insertRecording()` method returns without throwing an exception, then the recording data was successfully inserted and the flag and savepoint are set. Execution then continues to the other method calls in the `try` block.

If an exception is thrown somewhere in the `create()` method, execution will pass immediately into the `catch` block. Inside the `catch` block, if the `Savepoint` variable is not Null, then the `insertRecordingData()` method completed successfully, and since there was an exception, one of the other methods threw the exception. The transaction is rolled back to the savepoint by calling the `rollback(Savepoint)` method. If the `Savepoint` variable is Null, then there was an exception in the `getConnection()` method or the `insertedRecordingData()` method, and the transaction is completely rolled back by calling the `rollback()` method.

In the `finally` block, the changes are committed as needed. The `boolean` variable, `needCommit` was set to `true` when the recording data was successfully inserted into the database. It is only set to `false` when the entire transaction is rolled back. The recording data needs to be committed; track data may have been inserted as well. So, the transaction is committed.

There are three actions that can invalidate savepoints. Attempting to use a savepoint as a parameter to `releaseSavepoint(Savepoint)` or `rollback(Savepoint)` after it has been invalidated causes a `SQLException`.

- Calling `commit()` or `rollback()` invalidates all savepoints created since the transaction started.
- Calling `releaseSavepoint(Savepoint)` invalidates the given savepoint.
- Calling `rollback(Savepoint)` invalidates any savepoints that had been created after the given savepoint.

One additional method will be added to the DatabaseMetaData interface for savepoints. It will indicate whether the database and driver supports savepoints:

Method	Description
boolean supportsSavepoints()	Returns true if the driver supports savepoints.

Using Transactions in the Music Store

In the Music Store application, there are some tables where we would not want each insert of a row into the table to be automatically committed to the database. One such table is the Tracks table that we looked at in Chapter 12, *Prepared Statements.*

In our application we would probably want all the tracks to be successfully inserted before we committed any of the inserts. If you look back at the previous chapter, however, we actually did the opposite. The test class that we used to demonstrate the Track class did not control the transaction at all. It left the Connection in autocommit mode so that every row that was inserted through the Track class was immediately committed to the database. The test class inserted only four tracks from the recording, which was not the complete set of tracks. So, when the test class completed executing, it left the database in an inconsistent state.

While it might be OK to leave a development database in an inconsistent state while code is being tested, this would not be good for a production system. Let's look at a new class that will control the transaction for inserting tracks, and commit or roll back the changes as necessary.

Try It Out

The *Prepared Statements* chapter presented a class for inserting track data into the Tracks table. This class used a PreparedStatement object to insert the track data into the table. The code that demonstrated how to use the Track class was shown in the TestTrack class. Before the TestTrack class could insert the track data, it had to insert a row into the Recordings table. In this chapter, we will look at a Recording class that will represent the Recordings table.

The implementation of the Recording class will be similar to some of the other classes that have been presented in previous chapters. The class will have a create() method for creating an entry in the database. The Recording class will make use of the Track class from the *Prepared Statements* chapter to insert the track data.

We will also need a way to get all the data for a recording and the tracks into the class so the data can be inserted into the database. For the purposes of this example program, the data will be stored in a properties file that the test driver will read and pass to the Recording class. To run this program, you can start by creating the data file. Here is what it should look like:

```
recordingtitle=The Stranger
publisherid=101
catalognumber=CK34987
recordingformatid=1
releasedate=1977-07-01
languageid=1
price=12.99
coverimagefilespec=
```

```
numberoftracks=9
track0=Movin' Out (Anthony's Song),104,12
track1=The Stranger,104,12
track2=Just The Way You Are,104,12
track3=Scenes From An Italian Restaurant,104,12
track4=Vienna,104,12
track5=Only The Good Die Young,104,12
track6=She's Always A Woman,104,12
track7=Get It Right The First Time,104,12
track8=Everybody Has A Dream,104,12
```

The data file should be created with the name `Recording.dat`. For the program to locate the property file, the file must be located in the same directory from where the program is executed. For example, if we execute the program from the root directory like this:

```
C:\>java transactions.TestRecording
```

then the data file will need to be located in the root directory. If we execute the program from some other directory, the data file will need to be in the same directory. If you are executing the program in an IDE, the data file may need to be in the same directory as the source or the class file, depending on your IDE.

Each piece of data needed for the `Recordings` table is present as a name/value pair in the data file, and an equals sign (=) delimits each name and value. When the `java.util.Properties` class reads this file, each line in the file becomes a property with the given name and value. The data for each track is contained in a single line of data, with each field delimited by commas.

The procedure needed to insert recording data into the database has been divided into four steps in the `Recording` class:

- Get a `Connection`
- Insert data into the recording table
- Get the recording ID
- Insert data into the `Tracks` table

Each of these steps is implemented in a separate method, all four of which are called in turn by the `create()` method. Here is the complete source for the `Recording` class:

```
package transactions;

import java.sql.*;
import java.math.*;
import java.util.*;
import statements.*;
import connections.*;

public class Recording {
  int recordingId;
  String recordingTitle;
  int publisherId;
  String catalogNumber;
```

```
  int recordingFormatId;
  String releaseDate;
  int languageId;
  BigDecimal price;
  String coverImageFileSpec;

  Connection connection;

  static String insertSql =
    "INSERT INTO RECORDINGS "
    + "(RECORDINGTITLE, PUBLISHERID, CATALOGNUMBER, RECORDINGFORMATID, "
    + "RELEASEDATE, LANGUAGEID, LISTPRICE, COVERIMAGEFILESPEC) "
    + "VALUES (?, ?, ?, ?, ?, ?, ?, ?)";
  static String queryIdSql = "SELECT RECORDINGID FROM RECORDINGS "
                           + "WHERE CATALOGNUMBER=?";

  public boolean create(Properties data) {
    boolean result = true;
    try {
      getConnection(false);
      insertRecording(data);
      recordingId = getRecordingId();
      insertTracks(data);
      connection.commit();
      System.out.println("All data has been entered and committed");
    } catch (Exception e) {
      e.printStackTrace();
      try {
        connection.rollback();
      } catch (SQLException e2) {
        e2.printStackTrace();
      }
      result = false;
    }
    finally {
      ConnectionFactory.close(connection);
    }
    return result;
  }

  void insertRecording(Properties data)
          throws SQLException, NumberFormatException {
    PreparedStatement ps = getPreparedStatement(insertSql);

    recordingTitle = data.getProperty("recordingtitle");
    ps.setString(1, recordingTitle);

    publisherId = Integer.parseInt(data.getProperty("publisherid"));
    ps.setInt(2, publisherId);

    catalogNumber = data.getProperty("catalognumber");
    ps.setString(3, catalogNumber);

    recordingFormatId =
      Integer.parseInt(data.getProperty("recordingformatid"));
    ps.setInt(4, recordingFormatId);

    releaseDate = data.getProperty("releasedate");
    ps.setString(5, releaseDate);
```

```
    languageId = Integer.parseInt(data.getProperty("languageid"));
    ps.setInt(6, languageId);

    price = new BigDecimal(data.getProperty("price"));
    ps.setDouble(7, price.doubleValue());

    coverImageFileSpec = data.getProperty("coverimagefilespec");
    ps.setString(8, coverImageFileSpec);

    ps.executeUpdate();
    ConnectionFactory.close(ps);
  }

  int getRecordingId() throws SQLException {
    PreparedStatement ps = getPreparedStatement(queryIdSql);
    ps.setString(1, catalogNumber);
    ResultSet rs = ps.executeQuery();
    rs.next();
    int result = rs.getInt(1);
    ConnectionFactory.close(rs);
    ConnectionFactory.close(ps);
    return result;
  }

  void insertTracks(Properties data) throws SQLException {
    int numTracks = Integer.parseInt(data.getProperty("numberoftracks"));
    Track track = new Track();
    PreparedStatement ps = getPreparedStatement(track.getCreateSql());
    track.setCreateStatement(ps);
    track.setRecordingId(recordingId);
    for (int i = 0; i < numTracks; i++) {
      System.out.println("Entering data for track " + (i + 1));
      String trackData = data.getProperty("track" + i);
      StringTokenizer st = new StringTokenizer(trackData, ",");
      track.setTrackNumber(i + 1);
      track.setTrackTitle(st.nextToken());
      track.setArtistId(Integer.parseInt(st.nextToken()));
      track.setStyleId(Integer.parseInt(st.nextToken()));
      track.setSampleFilespec("");
      track.executeSql();
    }
  }

  void getConnection(boolean autocommit) throws SQLException {
    connection = ConnectionFactory.getConnection();
    connection.setAutoCommit(autocommit);
  }

  PreparedStatement getPreparedStatement(String sql) throws SQLException {
    return connection.prepareStatement(sql);
  }
}
```

The test class is shown below. The test class starts by creating a `Properties` object and loading it with the data from the data file. Notice that the code uses the simple name of the data file when creating the `FileInputStream`. If you have problems getting the code to read the data file on your system, you can replace the simple filename with the absolute path to the file, and the `Properties` object should be able to load the file. After loading the data, a `Recording` object is instantiated, and the `create()` method is called:

```
package transactions;

import java.io.*;
import java.util.*;

public class TestRecording {
  public static void main(String[] args) {
    try {
      Properties props = new Properties();
      File file = new File("Recording.dat");
      FileInputStream fis = new FileInputStream(file);
      props.load(fis);
      fis.close();

      Recording recording = new Recording();
      recording.create(props);
    } catch (Exception e) {
      e.printStackTrace();
    }
  }
}
```

To run the test program, you will need to ensure the classpath is set correctly, and then execute the class using the `java` command. Here is the command:

```
C:\BegJavaDB\Ch14> java -classpath
                    %CLASSPATH%;.%CLOUDSCAPE_HOME%\lib\cloudscape.jar
                    transactions.TestRecording
```

If you are using an IDE, you will need to set the classpath and run the program using the correct procedure for your IDE. When the program is executed, you should see output similar to this:

```
Entering data for track 1
Entering data for track 2
Entering data for track 3
Entering data for track 4
Entering data for track 5
Entering data for track 6
Entering data for track 7
Entering data for track 8
Entering data for track 9
All data has been entered and committed
```

How It Works

As mentioned above, the work of inserting recording data into the database is controlled through the `create(Properties)` method:

```
  public boolean create(Properties data) {
    boolean result = true;
    try {
      getConnection(false);
      insertRecording(data);
      recordingId = getRecordingId();
      insertTracks(data);
      connection.commit();
      System.out.println("All data has been entered and committed");
```

```
      } catch (Exception e) {

        e.printStackTrace();
        try {
          connection.rollback();
        } catch (SQLException e2) {
          e2.printStackTrace();
        }
        result = false;
      }
      finally {
        ConnectionFactory.close(connection);
      }
      return result;
    }
```

This method calls four helper methods in turn to insert all of the data. The `create(Properties)` method calls:

- `getConnection(boolean)` method to get a connection.
- `insertRecording(Properties)` method to insert into the `Recordings` table.
- `getRecordingId()` method to query the database for the ID of the newly created recording.
- `insertTracks(Properties)` method to insert the track data.

If all the methods complete successfully without throwing an exception, the data is committed. If an exception is thrown, `rollback()` is called in the `catch` block. The `getConnection(boolean)` method is very similar to versions of this method seen in other classes. You can see it in the source code above. It uses an instance of `ConnectionFactory` to get a connection. After getting a connection, the code disables autocommit mode.

The `insertRecording(Properties)` method gets a `PreparedStatement` object from the connection and sets the data in the statement with data from the `Properties` object. After all the data has been set, the `executeUpdate()` method is called:

```
    void insertRecording(Properties data)
            throws SQLException, NumberFormatException {
      PreparedStatement ps = getPreparedStatement(insertSql);

      recordingTitle = data.getProperty("recordingtitle");
      ps.setString(1, recordingTitle);

      // ...

      ps.executeUpdate();
      ConnectionFactory.close(ps);
    }
```

In the Cloudscape database for the Music Store, the `RecordingId` has been defined as an auto-incremented field. As each row is entered, the ID is generated and inserted by the database. So, after the `Recording` data has been inserted, the code queries the database for the newly created `RecordingId` using another prepared statement.

With the `RecordingId` set in the class, the last method is called to insert the track data:

```
void insertTracks(Properties data) throws SQLException {
  int numTracks = Integer.parseInt(data.getProperty("numberoftracks"));
  Track track = new Track();
  PreparedStatement ps = getPreparedStatement(track.getCreateSql());
  track.setCreateStatement(ps);
  track.setRecordingId(recordingId);
  for (int i = 0; i < numTracks; i++) {
    System.out.println("Entering data for track " + (i + 1));
    String trackData = data.getProperty("track" + i);
    StringTokenizer st = new StringTokenizer(trackData, ",");
    track.setTrackNumber(i + 1);
    track.setTrackTitle(st.nextToken());
    track.setArtistId(Integer.parseInt(st.nextToken()));
    track.setStyleId(Integer.parseInt(st.nextToken()));
    track.setSampleFilespec("");
    track.executeSql();
  }
}
```

The `insertTracks(Properties)` method is similar to the test class used in the *Prepared Statements* chapter to test the `Track` class. It gets the SQL from the `Track` class and uses that to create a `PreparedStatement` object. Then it gets each set of track data from the `Properties` object and sets the `Track` object with the data. After all the data for a track has been set, the `executeSql()` method of the `Track` class is called to insert the data.

Unlike the `TestTrack` class from Chapter 12, the code above explicitly sets the artist ID and style ID for each track. Recall that since we are using a `PreparedStatement` object to insert the data, we do not need to set a given parameter it if the parameter has already been set. However, the `Recording` class does not test to see if the artist ID or style ID changes from track to track. One reason for that is because it would require more code and make the class slightly more complicated than just simply setting the parameters every time.

After all the tracks are inserted, the transaction is committed. However, if there was some error in the transaction, the entire transaction will be rolled back. You can demonstrate this by purposely inserting an error into the data file. Start by deleting the entire track and recording data that was just inserted from the database. After that has been accomplished, delete one of the entries for track data so that there are only eight tracks instead of nine (but leave the `numberoftracks` property set to `9`). When you run the program, a `NullPointerException` will be thrown. If you then examine the database, you will see that none of the data has been committed to the database.

Summary

Whether explicit or not, all interactions with the database are part of a transaction. The transaction may span a single SQL statement, or it may span many statements. In this chapter, you should have learned:

- Setting the autocommit mode controls the number of statements included in a transaction. When disabled, transactions must be explicitly committed or rolled back. When enabled, each transaction consists of a single statement that is committed immediately.
- Transactions have four properties. These four properties are atomicity, consistency, isolation, and durability.
- There are three kinds of interactions (phantom reads, non-repeatable reads, and dirty reads) and four isolation levels (serializable, read repeatable, read committed, and read uncommitted). The isolation level determines what interactions are allowed.
- Databases provide concurrency control using locks. However, each database will implement locking in its own way. Understanding how your database performs locking is important for the success of your database application.
- The `DatabaseMetaData` interface provides the `supportsTransactions()` and `supportsIsolationLevel(int)` methods for determining the amount of transaction support provided by a database.
- When JDBC 3.0 is implemented, the `Connection` interface will provide support for savepoints, which can be used to perform a partial rollback of a transaction.
- Application coding for a distributed transaction looks much like coding for a non-distributed transaction. The difference is that the application is prohibited from executing any transaction control methods such as `commit()` or `rollback()`.

Object-Relational Mapping Concepts

As your Java database application grows, you will encounter a problem where your Java code and your relational database design 'clash'. This is because Java is an object-oriented software development language using a set of objects to accomplish work. Relational databases run off a relational or table-based model, where each table has a set of column definitions for data that can be held in the table. The table can contain any number of rows, each row containing values for each of the columns in the table. Java objects do the work in your Java application, yet store and retrieve their persistent data using relational database tables. Since the two models (object and relational) are so different, you will need to spend time in the design of both your Java code and your relational database to make sure you efficiently 'map' the two technologies to each other.

To illustrate the clash between the two technologies, we will 'grow' an application from an easy map between Java objects and relational databases, to a complex map. As the application grows in complexity, you will see the clash between the two technologies. You will also get an idea of how complex the code becomes to efficiently resolve the clash. In the next chapter, we will discover how an object-relational mapping framework will help you execute the complex mapping, minimizing the impact of the map on your code.

A Simple Recording Database Application

For our example database application, we will continue with the theme of the book to work on a database of music recordings. Imagine if you will, a small store stocking eclectic music. The store is owned, managed, and staffed entirely by one person and operates in a desirable location. The store does well, and the owner decides to expand in both size and staff. The expansion suddenly presents a problem for the owner. She knows all the music the store stocks by heart, as she ordered all of it. Her new employees do not, so she decides to put together a searchable database of the music she stocks. Sometimes the owner forgets from whom she ordered some recordings, so the database will also help *her*, as she grows the inventory of her store. Being a bit of a Java buff, she also decides to write a user interface to the database in Java.

Object-Relational Mapping

The owner starts simple; one table containing all of the recordings in the store. Likewise, the Java code is simple; one class that directly corresponds to the recordings. The mapping looks like the following diagram:

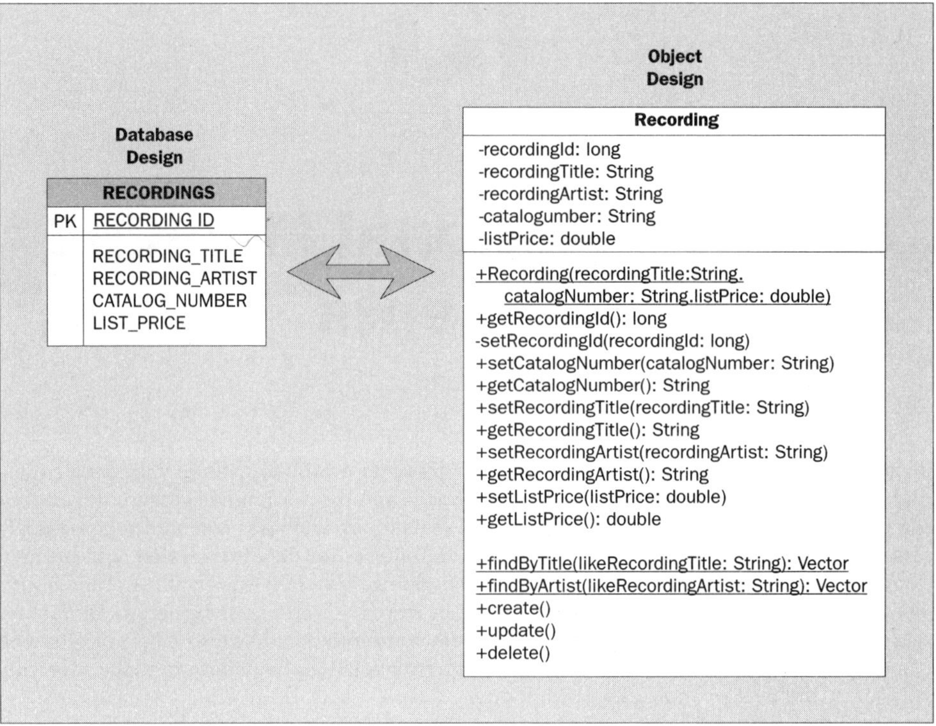

The `RECORDINGS` table contains a synthetic primary key, recording ID, along with a recording title, artist, catalog number, and list price. The **ERD** (**E**ntity **R**elationship **D**iagram) for the database design is shown on the left side of the diagram above.

> *A synthetic primary key is one that is not a natural part of the data in the table; recording ID is an arbitrary number that is assigned based on the order in which the recordings are input to the table.*

Good object design requires a bit more in the way of the object model as compared to the database model. The object model on the right side of the diagram is shown in **UML** (**U**nified **M**odeling **L**anguage) notation. UML is the standard modeling notation for object models, just as the ERD is the standard modeling notation for relational databases. As you may be less familiar with UML, let's walk through the model on the right in detail. See Chapter 7 for a more detailed explanation of UML notation if necessary.

A box with up to three compartments represents each Java class. The top-most box is the name of the class, `Recording`. Note that the class name is singular, as opposed to the relational table name, which is plural. This is because the relational table holds multiple instances of recordings (many data modelers prefer to keep their table names singular as well, and that is just fine). However, an object of the Java class `Recording` can hold at most one recording. This is the most basic difference between the object and relational models.

One relational table almost always holds many rows or instances, where an object typically holds only one instance. There are classes in Java, like `ArrayList`, `Vector`, and of course arrays, that hold multiple instances, but we rarely design such classes due to not knowing how many rows we'll need to store. Instead, we simply use the classes provided by the language and design classes that hold only one instance of related data.

Another minor difference between the two models is capitalization. In the database model, we use commonly accepted database naming standards. These standards have both table and column names in all upper case, with underscores (_) between words. In Java, we use commonly accepted Java naming standards. For a class name, we capitalize the first letter of each word of the class, with no underscores.

The middle box of a UML class contains the variable definitions of the class. Good object design practice is to protect access to the variables of an object. Only the methods of an object should be able to access the data inside that object. We signify this protection by putting a minus (`-`) sign before all the variables, which is UML notation for the Java `private` keyword. Some designers prefer to use the Java `protected` keyword instead, and if so use the pound sign (#) instead of the minus sign. Along with the protection and name of the variable, we include the variable type after a colon (`:`). Variable names have the first word of the variable all lowercase, followed by any other words with the first letter capitalized.

The bottom box of a UML class holds the method definitions for the class. Methods are where the action is in Java. The methods execute code to construct new objects, get and set variables, and communicate to the database via the JDBC API. Method names in Java follow the same capitalization rules and naming conventions as variable names. In the example above, (almost) all methods are `public`, signified by the plus (+) sign before the method name. At least some of your methods must be public, or the class wouldn't be very useful at all. Other objects (for example, your user interface objects) could not make use of the class if all its methods were private. It is a good idea to scrutinize setter methods in your design.

The design above does not allow external objects to set the `recordingId` variable. This variable reflects the primary key of the table, which of course, cannot be changed once the object is saved to the database. An alternative design is to not have a `setRecordingId` method at all, but most designers prefer to have it and make it private. That way you limit the modification of the `recordingId` variable to one method in the entire class, the `setRecordingId()` method, rather than have the variable directly accessed and modified in any number of methods in the code.

Methods may have input parameters, and these are placed inside the parentheses of the method call. If the method returns a variable, the type of the variable being returned is placed at the end of the method definition following a colon. One final note on UML notation is the underlining of some method definitions. All constructors and static methods should be underlined so they stand out from regular instance methods. These methods are special methods to create or retrieve instances of the object, whereas instance methods are used to manipulate an instance of an object that is already created or retrieved from the database.

A Sample Mapping Implementation

Now that we understand the design of the database and the Java class, let's dig into a sample implementation of the mapping, done in Java code for the `Recording.java` class. To make the sample program self-contained, the class has a few extra methods in it that are not shown in the design above. This is so that it can run from a command line and connect to an Oracle database.

Try It Out – Recording Java Class to RECORDINGS Database Table

In an Oracle database instance, create the following table and sequence:

```
create table OR_RECORDINGS (RECORDING_ID INT not null,
                            RECORDING_TITLE VARCHAR2(50) not null,
                            RECORDING_ARTIST VARCHAR2(50) not null,
                            CATALOG_NUMBER VARCHAR2(20) not null,
                            LIST_PRICE DECIMAL(7,2) not null,
                            constraint OR_RECORDINGS_PK primary key (RECORDING_ID) );

create sequence RECORDINGS_SEQ;
```

The `Recording.java` class below maps `Recording` objects to the above database definition. The program is split into three sections for the explanation that follows. The first section is typical JavaBean coding, where you create instance variables, a constructor, and getter and setter methods. The second section comprises the methods that map the class to the relational database using the JDBC API. The third section comprises the extra methods required to make the class self-contained, and to test the capabilities of the class from the static main method.

```
import java.util.*;
import java.sql.*;

/**
 * This class connects to an Oracle database with a simple
 * Recording table and maps the data in this class to/from
 * that table. One instance of this class corresponds to one
 * row in the OR_RECORDINGS table.
 */
public class Recording {

  // ------------------------------------------------------------
  // Section 1: JavaBean methods
  // ------------------------------------------------------------

  /**
   * Holds the synthetic primary key of the OR_RECORDINGS table.
   */
  private long recordingId;

  /**
   * Holds the title of the Recording.
   */
  private String recordingTitle;

  /**
   * Holds the artist that made the Recording.
   */
  private String recordingArtist;

  /**
   * Holds the catalog number of the Recording for ordering.
   */
```

```
private String catalogNumber;

/**
 * Holds the selling price of the Recording.
 */
private double listPrice;

/**
 * Main constructor for the class.
 */
public Recording(String recordingTitle, String recordingArtist,
                 String catalogNumber, double listPrice) {
  setRecordingTitle(recordingTitle);
  setRecordingArtist(recordingArtist);
  setCatalogNumber(catalogNumber);
  setListPrice(listPrice);
}

/**
 * Retrieves the database ID of the Recording.
 */
public long getRecordingId() {
  return recordingId;
}

/**
 * Sets the database ID of the Recording.
 */
private void setRecordingId(long recordingId) {
  this.recordingId = recordingId;
}

/**
 * Retrieves the title of the Recording.
 */
public String getRecordingTitle() {
  return recordingTitle;
}

/**
 * Sets the title of the Recording.
 */
public void setRecordingTitle(String recordingTitle) {
  this.recordingTitle = recordingTitle;
}

/**
 * Retrieves the artist that made the Recording.
 */
public String getRecordingArtist() {
  return recordingArtist;
}

/**
```

```
   * Sets the artist that made the Recording.
   */
  public void setRecordingArtist(String recordingArtist) {
    this.recordingArtist = recordingArtist;
  }

  /**
   * Retrieves the catalog number of the Recording.
   */
  public String getCatalogNumber() {
    return catalogNumber;
  }

  /**
   * Sets the catalog number of the Recording.
   */
  public void setCatalogNumber(String catalogNumber) {
    this.catalogNumber = catalogNumber;
  }

  /**
   * Retrieves the selling price of the Recording.
   */
  public double getListPrice() {
    return listPrice;
  }

  /**
   * Sets the selling price of the Recording.
   */
  public void setListPrice(double listPrice) {
    this.listPrice = listPrice;
  }


  // -------------------------------------------------------------
  // Section 2: Methods to map the class to the database
  // -------------------------------------------------------------

  /**
   * Helper method to iterate through a result set and create
   * one Recording object for each row, returning them in a Vector.
   */
  private static Vector resultSetToRecordings(ResultSet resultSet)
          throws SQLException {
    Vector recordings = new Vector();
    Recording recording;

    while (resultSet.next()) {

      // Retrieve values from the resultset
      long recordingId = resultSet.getLong(1);
      String recordingTitle = resultSet.getString(2);
      String recordingArtist = resultSet.getString(3);
```

```
      String catalogNumber = resultSet.getString(4);
      double listPrice = resultSet.getDouble(5);

      // Construct and populate all variables
      recording = new Recording(recordingTitle, recordingArtist,
                                catalogNumber, listPrice);
      recording.setRecordingId(recordingId);

      // Add to output vector
      recordings.addElement(recording);
    }

    return recordings;
  }

  /**
   * Helper method to find zero to many Recording objects given
   * a SQL query, returning them in a Vector.
   */
  private static Vector findRecordingsBySQLQuery(String sqlQuery)
          throws Exception {

    Connection databaseConnection = null;
    Statement statement = null;
    ResultSet resultSet = null;

    try {

      // Get a new connection and statement
      databaseConnection = getConnection();
      statement = databaseConnection.createStatement();

      // Run the query
      resultSet = statement.executeQuery(sqlQuery);

      // Translate the result set into Recording objects
      return resultSetToRecordings(resultSet);

    } finally {

      // If we got a result set, close it
      if (resultSet != null) {
        resultSet.close();
      }

      // If we got a statement, close it
      if (statement != null) {
        statement.close();
      }

      // If we got a connection, close it
      if (databaseConnection != null) {
        databaseConnection.close();
      }
```

```
    }
  }

  /**
   * Finds zero to many Recording objects that have a title
   * like the input string, returning them in a Vector.
   */
  public static Vector findByTitle(String likeRecordingTitle)
          throws Exception {
    String sqlQuery = "select * from OR_RECORDINGS " +
                      "where RECORDING_TITLE like '" + likeRecordingTitle +
                      "'";

    return findRecordingsBySQLQuery(sqlQuery);
  }

  /**
   * Finds zero to many Recording objects that have an artist
   * like the input string, returning them in a Vector.
   */
  public static Vector findByArtist(String likeRecordingArtist)
          throws Exception {
    String sqlQuery = "select * from OR_RECORDINGS " +
                      "where RECORDING_ARTIST like '" +
                      likeRecordingArtist + "'";

    return findRecordingsBySQLQuery(sqlQuery);
  }


  /**
   * Inserts a new Recording object in the database. Uses an
   * Oracle sequence to get a unique identifier for the table key.
   */
  public void create() throws Exception {

    Connection databaseConnection = null;
    Statement statement = null;
    Statement statement2 = null;
    ResultSet resultSet = null;

    try {

      // Get a new connection and statements
      databaseConnection = getConnection();

      // Set up a transaction for the two SQL statements
      databaseConnection.setAutoCommit(false);

      statement = databaseConnection.createStatement();
      statement2 = databaseConnection.createStatement();

      // Insert the row
      String insertSQL = "insert into OR_RECORDINGS ( " + " RECORDING_ID, " +
```

```
                    " RECORDING_TITLE, " + " RECORDING_ARTIST, " +
                    " CATALOG_NUMBER, " + " LIST_PRICE) " +
                    "values ( " + " RECORDINGS_SEQ.NEXTVAL, " + "'" +
                    getRecordingTitle() + "', " + "'" +
                    getRecordingArtist() + "', " + "'" +
                    getCatalogNumber() + "', " + getListPrice() +
                    ") ";

    statement.executeUpdate(insertSQL);

    // execute query to get recordingId
    String idSQL = "select RECORDINGS_SEQ.CURRVAL from DUAL";
    resultSet = statement2.executeQuery(idSQL);

    // retrieve from result set
    resultSet.next();
    setRecordingId(resultSet.getLong(1));

    // Commit the transaction
    databaseConnection.commit();

  } finally {

    // If we got a result set, close it
    if (resultSet != null) {
      resultSet.close();
    }

    // If we got a statement, close it
    if (statement != null) {
      statement.close();
    }
    if (statement2 != null) {
      statement2.close();
    }


    // If we got a connection, close it
    if (databaseConnection != null) {
      databaseConnection.close();
    }
  }

}

/**
 * Updates the non-key values of the current Recording object
 * in the database.
 */
public void update() throws Exception {

  Connection databaseConnection = null;
  Statement statement = null;
```

```
    try {

      // Get a new connection and statement
      databaseConnection = getConnection();
      statement = databaseConnection.createStatement();

      // Update the row
      String updateSQL = "update OR_RECORDINGS" + " set RECORDING_TITLE = '" +
                         getRecordingTitle() + "', " +
                         " RECORDING_ARTIST = '" + getRecordingArtist() +
                         "', " + " CATALOG_NUMBER = '" +
                         getCatalogNumber() + "', " + " LIST_PRICE = " +
                         getListPrice() + " where RECORDING_ID = " +
                         getRecordingId();

      statement.executeUpdate(updateSQL);

    } finally {

      // If we got a statement, close it
      if (statement != null) {
        statement.close();
      }

      // If we got a connection, close it
      if (databaseConnection != null) {
        databaseConnection.close();
      }
    }

  }

  /**
   * Deletes the current Recording object from the database.
   */
  public void delete() throws Exception {

    Connection databaseConnection = null;
    Statement statement = null;

    try {

      // Get a new connection and statement
      databaseConnection = getConnection();
      statement = databaseConnection.createStatement();

      // Insert the row
      String deleteSQL = "delete from OR_RECORDINGS " +
                         " where RECORDING_ID = " + getRecordingId();

      statement.executeUpdate(deleteSQL);

    } finally {
```

```
      // If we got a statement, close it
      if (statement != null) {
        statement.close();
      }

      // If we got a connection, close it
      if (databaseConnection != null) {
        databaseConnection.close();
      }
    }

  }


  // ----------------------------------------------------------------
  // Section 3: Methods to make the class self-contained
  // ----------------------------------------------------------------

  /**
   * Prints the contents of all variables.
   */
  public String toString() {
    return "Recording: " + getRecordingId() + "\n  Title: " +
           getRecordingTitle() + "\n  Artist: " + getRecordingArtist() +
           "\n  Catalog Number: " + getCatalogNumber() +
           "\n  List Price: " + getListPrice();
  }

  /**
   * Constant for the name of the JDBC Driver class connecting
   * to the Oracle demo database.
   */
  private static final String ORACLE_JDBC_DRIVER_CLASS_NAME =
    "oracle.jdbc.driver.OracleDriver";

  /**
   * Constant for the name of the URL for where the Oracle
   * JDBC driver will connect to the database.
   */
  private static final String ORACLE_DEMO_DB_URL =
    "jdbc:oracle:thin:@dbserver:1521:database";

  /**
   * Constants for the user to log into the Oracle demo database.
   */
  private static final String ORACLE_DEMO_DB_USERID_PROPERTY = "user";
  private static final String ORACLE_DEMO_DB_USERID = "beg";

  /**
   * Constants for the password to log into the Oracle demo database.
   */
  private static final String ORACLE_DEMO_DB_PASSWORD_PROPERTY = "password";
  private static final String ORACLE_DEMO_DB_PASSWORD = "java";
```

```
/**
 * Helper method to retrieve a JDBC connection from
 * the Oracle demo database. Note, this code must be called
 * in a try block with a finally block which closes the connection.
 *
 * @throws Exception if the connection cannot be created
 *
 * @return JDBC Connection to the Oracle demo database if successful
 */
private static Connection getConnection() throws Exception {

  // Create a new instance of the driver manager class, so
  // it initializes itself for use and registers with the
  // JDBC DriverManager
  Class.forName(ORACLE_JDBC_DRIVER_CLASS_NAME).newInstance();

  // Create connection properties object
  Properties connectionProperties = new Properties();

  connectionProperties.put(ORACLE_DEMO_DB_USERID_PROPERTY,
                           ORACLE_DEMO_DB_USERID);

  connectionProperties.put(ORACLE_DEMO_DB_PASSWORD_PROPERTY,
                           ORACLE_DEMO_DB_PASSWORD);

  // create a connection
  return DriverManager.getConnection(ORACLE_DEMO_DB_URL,
                                     connectionProperties);
}

/**
 * Helper method to output a set of Recording objects
 * in a Vector to System.out.
 */
private static void outputRecordings(Vector recordings) {

  Recording recording;
  Enumeration e = recordings.elements();

  while (e.hasMoreElements()) {
    recording = (Recording) e.nextElement();

    // Print to output stream
    System.out.println("\n" + recording);
  }

}

/**
 * Main method to test the capabilities above. CRUDs the
 * database by creating 4 recordings, reading them back,
 * updates the price on one and reads it back, and
 * deletes all 4.
```

```
  */
  public static void main(String[] args) {
    Recording rec1, rec2, rec3, rec4;

    try {
      rec1 = new Recording("Cuts Like A Knife", "Bryan Adams",
                           "392-0000022", 11.99);

      rec2 = new Recording("Working Class Dog", "Rick Springfield",
                           "RS-32-1133", 10.99);

      rec3 = new Recording("Come And Join Us", "Petra", "303-9388293",
                           11.99);

      rec4 = new Recording("Lucky Town", "Bruce Springsteen",
                           "BK-30-23993", 13.99);

      // Create the recordings in the database
      rec1.create();
      rec2.create();
      rec3.create();
      rec4.create();

      // Read the recordings back and output
      System.out.println("\nYou should see 4 recordings:");

      Vector springArtistRecordings = Recording.findByArtist("%Spring%");
      outputRecordings(springArtistRecordings);

      Vector recordingsStartWithC = Recording.findByTitle("C%");
      outputRecordings(recordingsStartWithC);

      // Update recording 1 price
      rec1.setListPrice(7.99);
      rec1.update();

      // Read record back and make sure update made it
      System.out.println("\nThis recording should have a price of 7.99");
      Vector updatedRecording = Recording.findByArtist("Bryan Adams");
      outputRecordings(updatedRecording);

      // Delete all recordings
      rec1.delete();
      rec2.delete();
      rec3.delete();
      rec4.delete();

      // Read all recordings back, shouldn't be any
      System.out.println("\nDeleted all, shouldn't be any recordings:");
      Vector allRecordings = Recording.findByArtist("%");
      outputRecordings(allRecordings);

    } catch (Exception e) {
      e.printStackTrace();
```

```
            }
        }
    }
```

Now you need to edit the constants in code section 3 above to connect to the Oracle database instance where you created the OR_RECORDINGS table and sequence. Compiling and executing the program should achieve the following results:

```
C:\BegJavaDB\ORConcepts>javac Recording.java

C:\BegJavaDB\ORConcepts>java -classpath .;%JLIB%\classes12.zip Recording

You should see 4 recordings:

Recording: 2
  Title: Working Class Dog
  Artist: Rick Springfield
  Catalog Number: RS-32-1133
  List Price: 10.99

Recording: 4
  Title: Lucky Town
  Artist: Bruce Springsteen
  Catalog Number: BK-30-23993
  List Price: 13.99

Recording: 1
  Title: Cuts Like A Knife
  Artist: Bryan Adams
  Catalog Number: 392-0000022
  List Price: 11.99

Recording: 3
  Title: Come And Join Us
  Artist: Petra
  Catalog Number: 303-9388293
  List Price: 11.99

This recording should have a price of 7.99

Recording: 1
  Title: Cuts Like A Knife
  Artist: Bryan Adams
  Catalog Number: 392-0000022
  List Price: 7.99

Deleted all, shouldn't be any recordings:

C:\BegJavaDB\ORConcepts>_
```

How It Works

As we saw, the first section of the code is straightforward – we declare our variables, the class constructor, and the get and set methods for the variable. Section 2 is where things start to get interesting. Here we **CRUD** (**C**reate, **R**ead, **U**pdate, **D**elete) `Recording` objects as rows in the database.

Helper methods are used to eliminate any redundancy in the public methods of the class. So, if more than one public method needs the same code, we create private helper methods instead of duplicating the code in the public methods. The `resultSetToRecordings()` and `findRecordingsBySQLQuery()` methods are helper methods for the two *read* methods named `findByTitle()` and `findByArtist()`. These methods read the database to try to find `Recording` objects by recording title or artist, respectively. We name them `find` instead of `read` to mimic the trend of EJBs in the J2EE specification. The method that does the *create* part of CRUD is more appropriately named `create()`, *update* is `update()`, and *delete* is of course `delete()`.

The code in these helper methods is similar to code seen several times already, so we'll not concentrate on its workings here. Compare these methods to code performing a similar task earlier in the book.

Section 3 contains helper methods to get a connection to the database, to output data to `System.out` so we can see whether the program works or not, and finally a main method to exercise all of the CRUD capabilities of the class.

The main method of the program creates four recording objects as follows:

```
rec1 = new Recording("Cuts Like A Knife", "Bryan Adams",
                     "392-0000022", 11.99);

rec2 = new Recording("Working Class Dog", "Rick Springfield",
                     "RS-32-1133", 10.99);

rec3 = new Recording("Come And Join Us", "Petra", "303-9388293",
                     11.99);

rec4 = new Recording("Lucky Town", "Bruce Springsteen",
                     "BK-30-23993", 13.99);

// Create the recordings in the database
rec1.create();
rec2.create();
rec3.create();
rec4.create();
```

Each new object calls its `create()` method. The `Recording.create()` method responds by executing two SQL statements, one to insert a row into the database, and another to retrieve the ID of the new row just inserted.

The database generates a unique identifier, via an Oracle sequence (the part of the `INSERT` SQL statement that references `RECORDINGS_SEQ.NEXTVAL`), when we insert the row. We need to retrieve that ID in case the object is to be updated or deleted later (which it is). So before we return to the caller of the `create()` method, we set the `recordingId` instance variable with the value returned from the following SQL statement:

```
select RECORDINGS_SEQ.CURRVAL from DUAL
```

This SQL statement is a bit confusing on two accounts. First of all, we need to retrieve the same `RECORDING_ID` value that was generated in the previous SQL statement. If we use `RECORDINGS_SEQ.NEXTVAL` as in the first SQL statement, that will increment the counter and we will not get the same value back. So on the subsequent select statement, we use the current value instead of a new value.

Second, the `SELECT` statement gets the value from some table named `DUAL`. Oracle requires all `SELECT` statements to reference a table, so when you do not have one (in this case, we are retrieving a value from a sequence, not a table), then use a pre-defined table in Oracle called `DUAL`.

The following diagram shows a graphical depiction of events to create the `rec1` object:

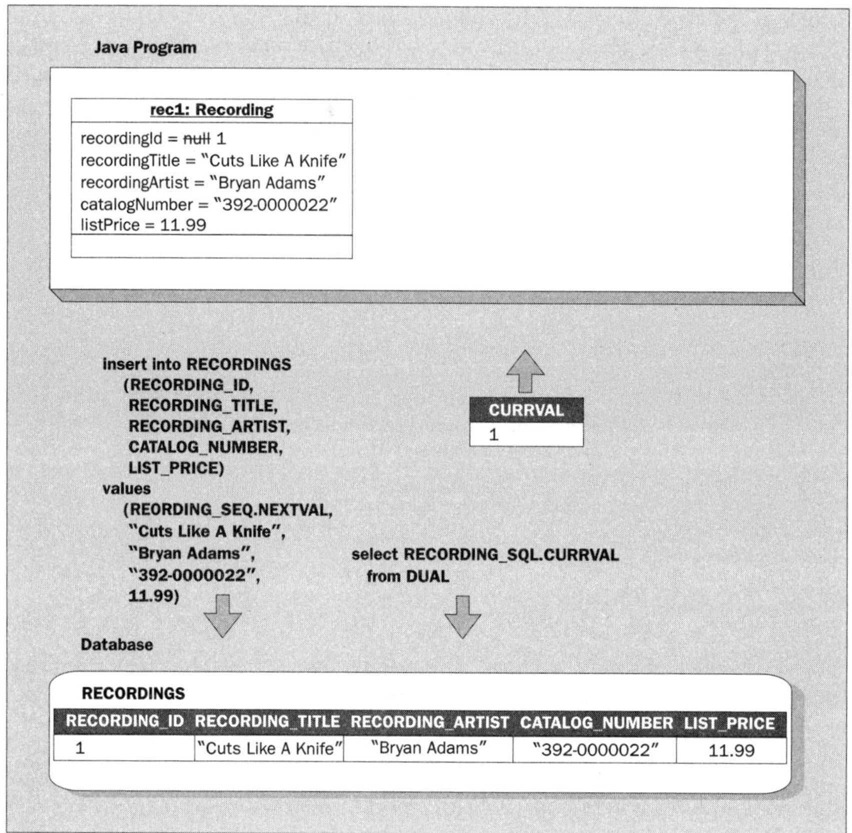

When the `create()` method is initially called, it doesn't have a `recordingId` value. It retrieves it from `CURRVAL` and calls the `setRecordingId()` method before it returns to caller. This is why the diagram above shows null crossed out and replaced with 1. The `rec2`, `rec3`, and `rec4` objects are created in the same manner.

Next, the program proceeds to read and output the four objects just created in the database. To do this, it calls the static finder methods as shown below:

```
Vector springArtistRecordings = Recording.findByArtist("%Spring%");

Vector recordingsStartWithC = Recording.findByTitle("C%");
```

Two of the four recordings created have `Spring` somewhere in the recording artist column, so these two should be found by the first finder method. The other two recordings have a title that starts with `C`, and these two should be found by the second finder method. You can see the two `ResultSets` retrieved from the database in the following diagram:

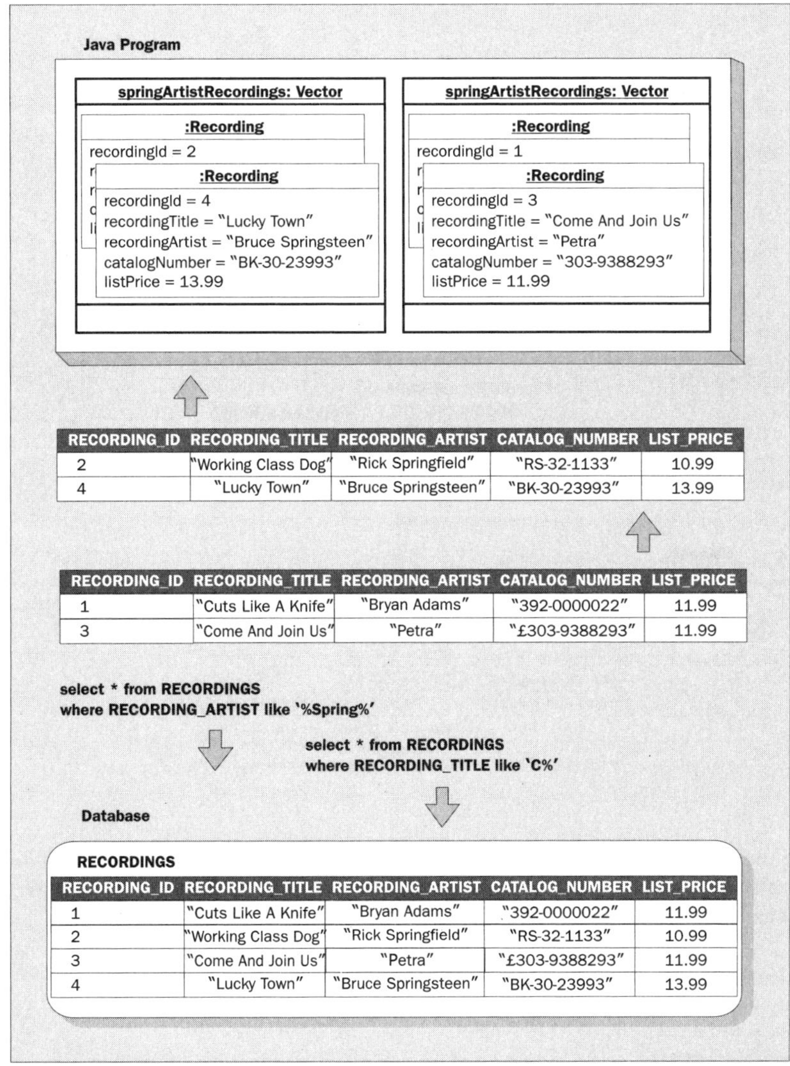

The program prints the results of the finder methods so you can be sure all four objects are found. Next, the program updates the `rec1` object by changing its list price from `11.99` to `7.99` as follows:

```
rec1.setListPrice(7.99);
rec1.update();
```

The program sends an update SQL statement to the database, to reflect the change made to the Java object, shown in the following diagram:

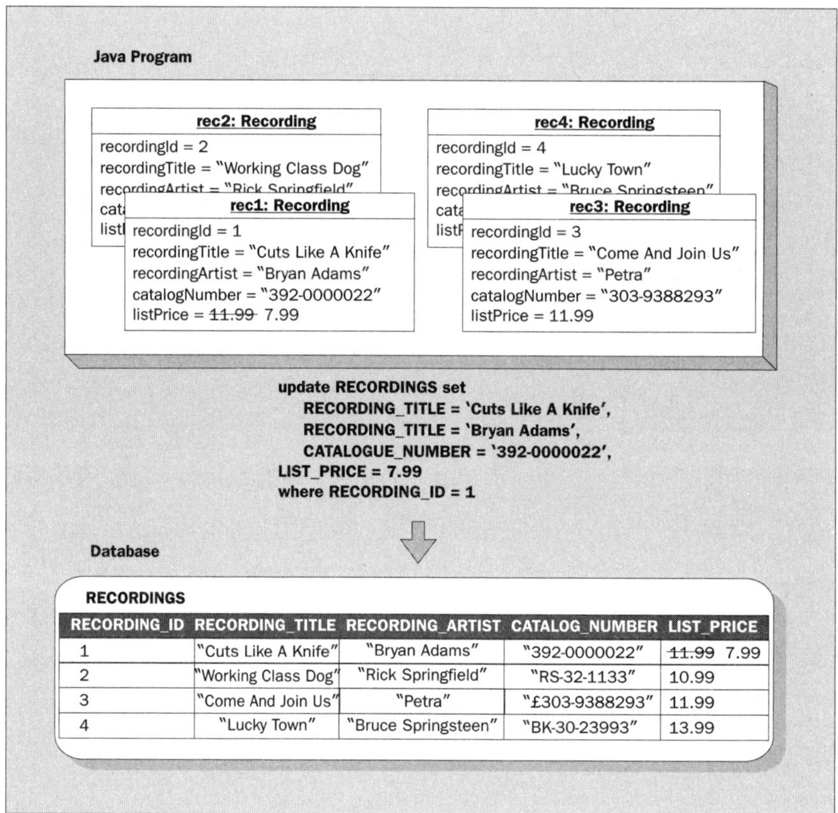

After sending the SQL statement update, the program reads a new object for that recording back and prints it to `System.out`, just to make sure the price change made it into the database. It then deletes all recordings as follows:

```
rec1.delete();
rec2.delete();
rec3.delete();
rec4.delete();
```

The following diagram concentrates on the delete for the `rec1` record:

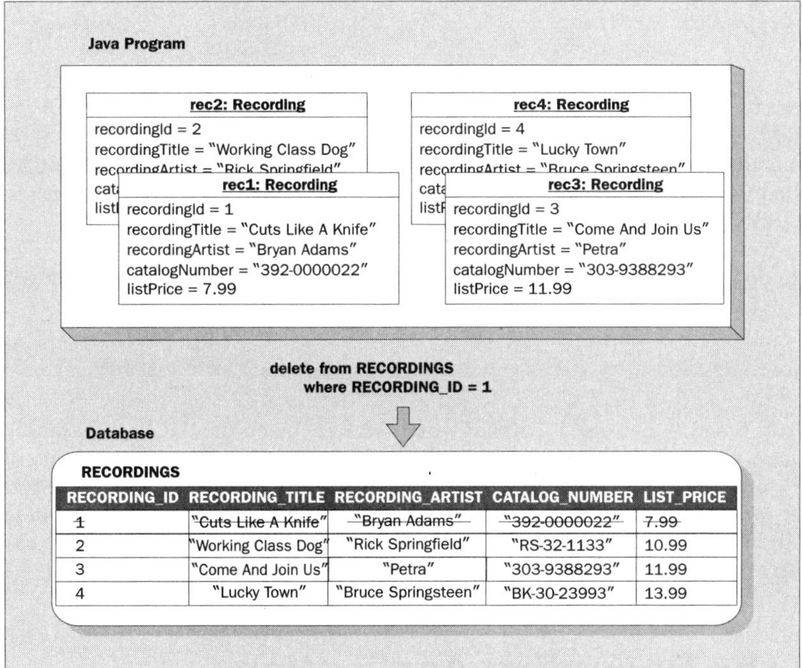

Finally, the program tries to read all objects from the database and outputs any that it finds. Since no other programs have inserted rows in the table, it finds and reports no `Recording` objects, and then exits. All four letters of the CRUD acronym are exercised and working properly.

The simple `Recording` class above fully maps to the `OR_RECORDINGS` database table in a one-Java-class-to-one-relational-database-table scenario. This is about the simplest type of object-relational map there is, and it required a good deal of code to carry out. Of the 524 lines of code in the class, 120 were the JavaBean methods in section one, 250 were used to do the CRUD object-relational mapping in section two, and the remaining 154 were used to make the class self-contained in section three. Ignoring section three, we have 68 percent of the program devoted to executing the object-relational map. One other note to point out is that the map demonstrated above is only safe for one database user at a time. If multiple users want access to the same database, you will need to enhance the mapping with extra code to make sure that two users don't try to update the same column at the same time. We address this locking problem in the next chapter.

Using the Recording Class with Autonumber Columns in Cloudscape

To get the right `autoincrement` value, you have to use database-specific SQL. So you will need to work on the SQL statement:

```
// execute query to get recordingId
String idSQL = " select RECORDINGS_SEQ.CURRVAL from DUAL";
```

Unfortunately, each database is completely different here, so you need to read the database-specific documentation. If you read the documentation for Cloudscape on `autoincrement` fields, you get the value through a statement something like:

```
VALUES ConnectionInfo.lastAutoincrementValue('schemaName', 'tableName',
                                              'columnName')
```

where *schemaName* is the name of your database, *tableName* is RECORDINGS, and *columnName* is RECORDING_ID. There is one slight problem with this – it's not standard SQL, it's SQL-J. SQL-J is a means for embedding SQL into Java statements, but is unfortunately not easily compatible with the JDBC code that we use here. For more information on using SQL-J, consult *Professional Java Data*, from Wrox Press, ISBN 1861004109.

If you want to do this the wrong way (that is, technically incorrect but will still work with the example as it is written), use:

```
String idSQL = "select max(RECORDING_ID) from RECORDINGS";
```

This is **very** bad practice, because it will not work correctly when the database has multiple users at the same time, but it will work for a database like Access, which isn't really designed for concurrent access, and will also work for Cloudscape. What we do here is get the largest value in the RECORDING_ID column; there is nothing, however, to stop another piece of code inserting a record in the table between our insert and this call. If this happened, we would have the wrong RECORDING_ID value, and would end up deleting the wrong record.

Growing the Recording Application

As things rarely stay simple in Java database applications, let's go on to examine some typical application enhancement scenarios. In the following two sections, we are going to expand the application we have been looking at. First we will add relationships to the present model, and then add a Java class hierarchy. We will not show the Java code implementation of these two sections because of the great deal of complexity they introduce to the application. The actual execution of the two scenarios will be explored in the following chapter where we use an O-R mapping framework to help us execute the design.

Adding Relationships

The recent addition of floor space and personnel to the eclectic music store makes it even more successful. Customers are intrigued by the owner's use of computers to locate recordings they desire. They ask the owner to notify them when new releases become available, which they may be interested in.

The owner thinks about this request for a moment, deciding it would be a lot of work to put out postcards to customers as new recordings come in. If she enhanced the Java database application by tracking customer e-mail addresses, purchases, and interests, she could easily send out e-mail notifications via the JavaMail API. Knowing that her customers are very concerned with privacy, she decides to keep minimal personal information on them (that is, a nickname and an e-mail address). The owner also decides that tracking purchases and interests should be a completely voluntary, or 'opt-in', service to her customers. She enhances her database design as follows to track this information:

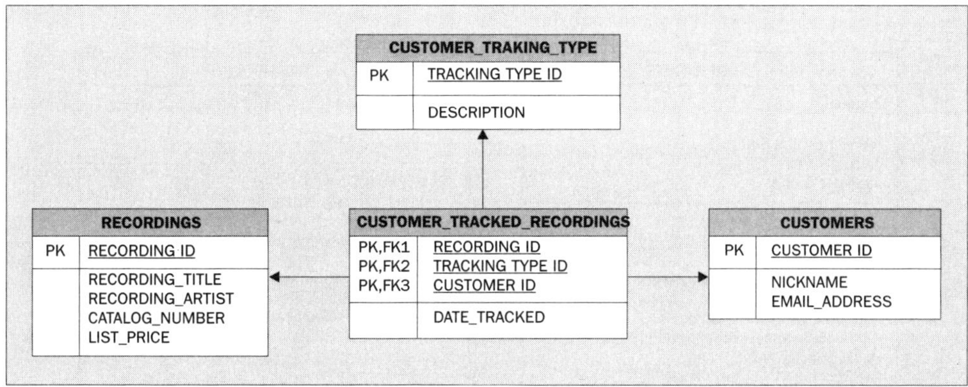

The design above adds three tables, namely CUSTOMERS, CUSTOMER_TRACKING_TYPE, and CUSTOMER_TRACKED_RECORDINGS.

- The CUSTOMERS table contains the customer's nickname and e-mail address so the owner can automate the process of sending out e-mail notifications to interested customers.
- The CUSTOMER_TRACKING_TYPE table contains two rows; one to designate customer interests, and another to designate customer purchases. In the future, this table could be expanded to track recordings on back order or for any number of other tracking reasons.
- The CUSTOMER_TRACKED_RECORDINGS table keeps relationships to the other three tables in the diagram. It also contains the date the relationship was created. That way, the owner can record customer purchases or interests in particular recordings.

The database design is pretty straightforward (we'll create these tables in the next chapter), so let's move on to design the Java classes that map to these tables. Your first shot at a Java class design may be to continue with the simple mapping pattern of one Java class to one relational table. This design would look something like the following:

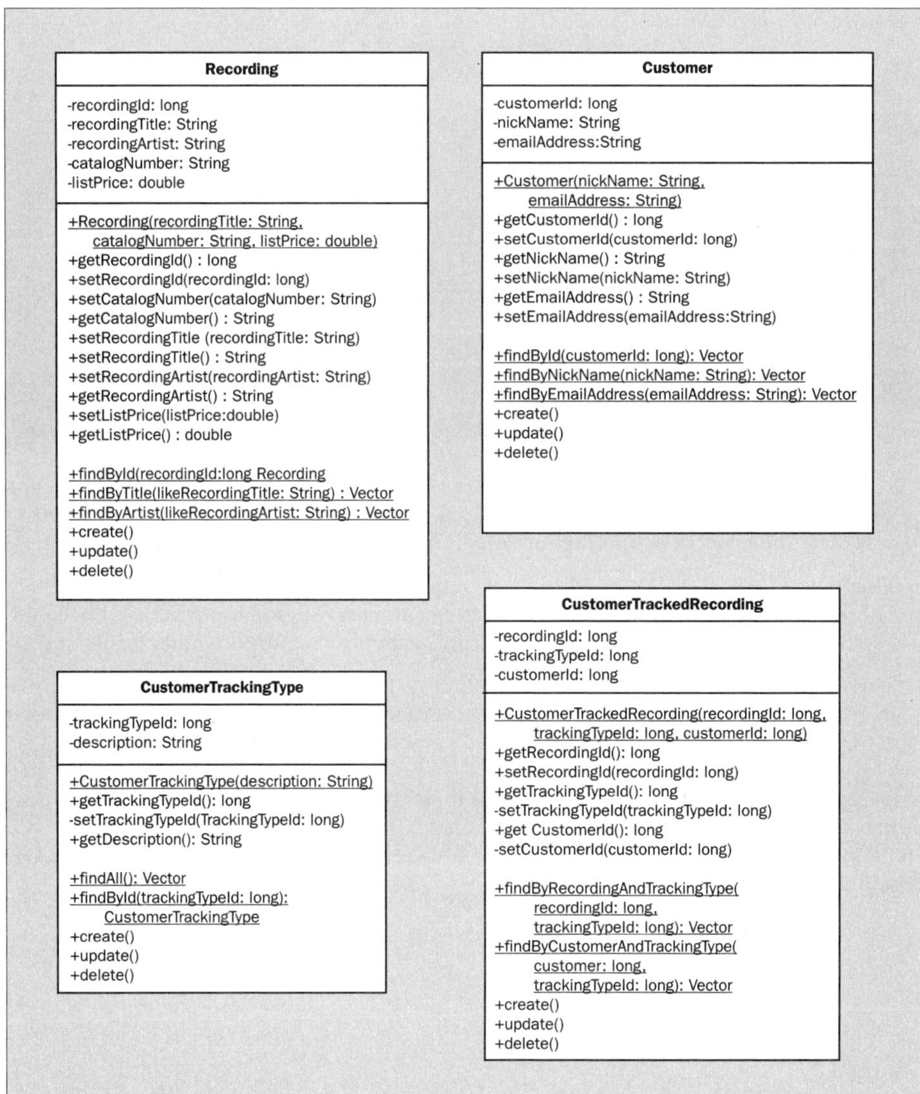

Unfortunately, this design doesn't accomplish all the tasks the owner wishes to carry out, or at least does not do it efficiently. For example, a new recording from an artist becomes available. The owner wants to know which customers have registered an interest in any previous recordings from that same artist. Then, the owner wants to send e-mail to each of these customers. The Java code, according to the design above, would have to go through the following steps:

1. Execute the `findByArtist()` method of the `Recording` class to retrieve a `Vector` of all recordings by that artist.

2. For each recording in the `Vector`, execute the `findByRecordingAndTrackingType()` method on the `CustomerTrackedRecording` class. This will retrieve a `Vector` of all relationships in the `CUSTOMER_TRACKED_RECORDINGS` table showing the customers interested in that particular recording.

3. For each object in the `Vector` returned in step 2 above, retrieve the customer ID. Add the customer ID to a set of IDs, eliminating any duplicates as you go along. You do not want to send multiple e-mails to the same customer, and it is possible that that a customer registered an interest in several recordings of the same artist.

4. Now that you have iterated through all of the tracked recording records and filtered out any duplicates, you can retrieve the customer information for each customer ID. This will require a series of calls to the `findById()` method in the `Customer` class; one call for each customer ID.

5. Send e-mail to each of the resulting `Customers`.

Say that you have a new recording by an artist who has five other recordings in the database. Among these recordings, a hundred people have registered an interest in this artist. Besides the amount of Java code required to implement the process above, how many queries of the database are needed to get customer information for e-mail messages? Step 1 requires one `select` statement, step 2 requires five `select` statements, and step 4 requires a hundred `select` statements. That is a total of 106 database queries to get information that could be equally well be returned by the following single SQL statement:

```
SELECT DISTINCT c.NICKNAME, c.EMAIL_ADDRESS
       FROM RECORDINGS r,
            CUSTOMER_TRACKED_RECORDINGS ctr,
            CUSTOMERS c
       WHERE r.RECORDING_ARTIST = 'artist name'
             AND r.RECORDING_ID = ctr.RECORDING_ID
             AND ctr.TRACKING_TYPE_ID = 2
             AND ctr.CUSTOMER_ID = c.CUSTOMER_ID
```

To solve this problem more efficiently, and many others like it, somehow the Java class design must utilize the relationships between the relational database tables. SQL does this by joining tables in the `FROM` and `WHERE` clauses, but Java has no such concept. Experienced Java database application designers use several tricks to efficiently address problems like this, some of which will be covered in the next chapter. For now, we just want to make sure you are aware of the problem in dealing with relationships between relational database tables and Java classes. Another problem to watch out for as you increase the capabilities and complexity of your Java database application is the problem of mapping inheritance hierarchies to relational database tables.

See Chapter 3, SQL Queries and Data Manipulation, *for more on joins.*

Adding a Java Class Hierarchy

What used to be a small, eclectic music store is starting to become a booming business. Even the owner is surprised at the success of the business, in no small part due to the simple Java database application she wrote. Customers are becoming very loyal. Over half of her business is repeat customers, and most of these purchases resulted from the e-mail notifications she sent out when they registered an interest.

The owner decides to start a customer loyalty program to reward those repeat customers. In a trade for a bit more personal information, specifically their full name and address, the owner is willing to give discounts on volume purchases. Volume customers who have purchased more than five recordings get a 5 percent discount on all future purchases. Volume customers who are for-profit corporations and purchase more than 100 recordings get a 10 percent discount on all future purchases. Volume customers who are non-profit corporations get a really special deal, they get a 15 percent discount just for registering (they must bring their non-profit tax ID for proof), and as such we can't charge them sales tax.

Business rules translate well into Java code, so let's start there first. We can take advantage of all of the previous work done to capture customer purchases if we think about a volume customer being a 'specialization' of a customer, which it certainly is. We model this relationship using the UML generalization relationship (a solid line between the two classes with a hollow arrowhead pointing from the specialized class to the generalized class).

In Java, this relationship is coded with the `extends` keyword, where the specialized class extends the capabilities of the generalized class. Specialized classes 'inherit' all the variables and methods of generalized classes. That is, generalized class variables and methods are available for use in the specialized classes without any other effort than to declare the generalized class via the `extends` keyword. So, a volume customer has a nickname, e-mail address, and the customer-tracked recording relationships for purchases and interests. For all volume customers, we add new instance variables and accessor methods to keep their name and mailing address.

Now that we have a design for volume customers, we keep on with that pattern to add frequent buyers and corporations. Frequent buyers get a 5 percent discount after five purchases. For corporations, we need a company name plus previous purchases of at least 100 recordings for their 10 percent discount. Non-profit corporations are specializations of corporations with a non-profit tax ID. They have no volume requirements but receive a 15 percent discount.

Notice here that we're adding to an existing class; we are **not** redesigning from scratch. In UML notation, a class diagram for the customer hierarchy is shown in the following diagram:

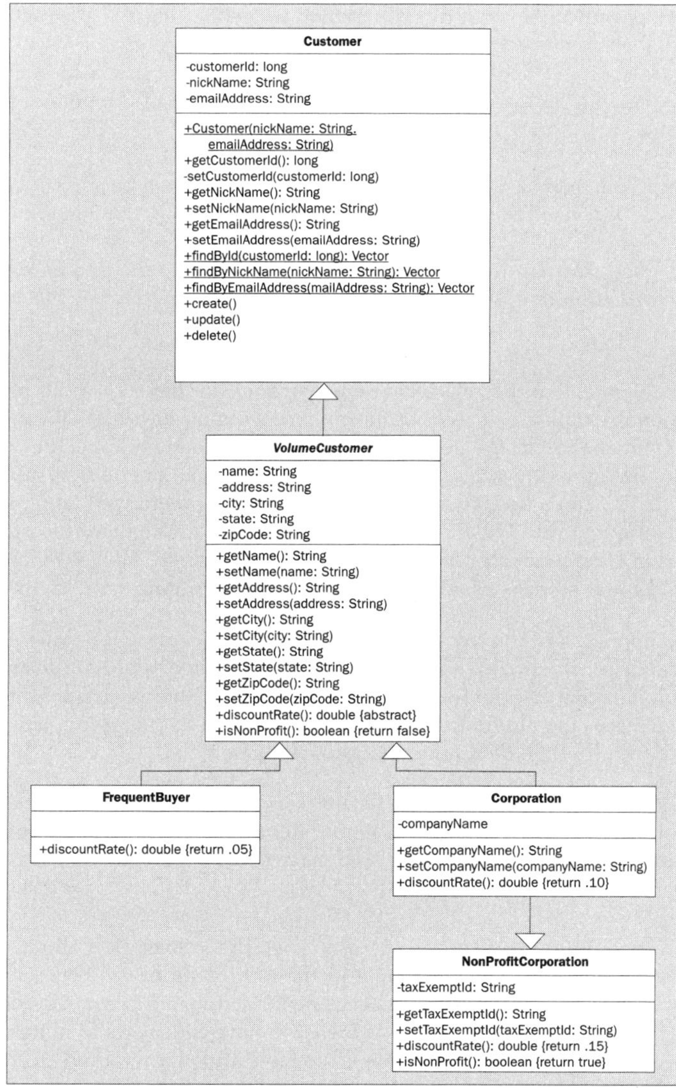

The `Customer` class is unchanged from the previous section. `VolumeCustomer` is a new class that extends `Customer`. It is also an **abstract** class (hence the name in *italics*), which means that we will not instantiate objects of this class. Instead, it serves as a place to put variables and methods in common to classes that extend it. It contains instance variables for a volume customer's name and mailing address, accessor methods for those variables, and two business logic methods.

The first business logic method, `discountRate()`, is the amount of discount the volume customer should receive, according to its classification. This method is an abstract method, which means classes that extend `VolumeCustomer` must provide an implementation specific to their class. The second method, `isNonProfit()`, returns a default implementation of `false`. The `NonProfitCorporation` subclass later overrides this method to return `true` for all of its instances.

`VolumeCustomer` has two classes that directly extend it. Neither class is abstract, so they must provide implementations of all abstract methods above. `FrequentBuyer` returns a 5% (0.05) rate of discount, and `Corporation` returns a 10% (0.10) rate of discount. `Corporation` also includes a new instance variable to keep the name of the company, as opposed to the name of the person from that corporation who set up the account.

`NonProfitCorporation` extends `Corporation`. It overrides the two business logic methods to give a discount rate of 15% (0.15) and tell the caller that it is indeed a non-profit company, so it should not be taxed.

Now that we have a good start on the Java design, we should turn to the database and see where we are going to keep the information the Java objects need to operate properly. We have two difficult problems to deal with.

1. The first problem is that the relational database does not have a way to model the generalization relationship. Tables do not inherit from other tables. We either need to put the specialized information in the generalized table as optional columns (because it may not be there depending upon the subclass instantiated), or we can create new tables for each specialized class, with a foreign key relationship to the generalized table. Neither approach is ideal for several reasons. The first approach is contrary to the database normalization rules you learned in Chapter 5, *Relational Database Design Concepts.* However, having one larger table with optional fields is usually more efficient than joining several smaller tables.

   The second approach of having specialized tables keeps a parallel between your Java classes and your database. It will also keep your database architect and administrators happy because optional columns that are not used still take up space in the database. Unfortunately, this approach increases the amount of Java code needed for the mapping, and also requires table joins to retrieve all of the data for a specialized Java object.

   Since we have a small number of specialized variables, we choose the first approach and add optional columns to the `CUSTOMER` table for all variables added in the specialized classes. The more variables you have in the specialized classes, the more likely you are to use the second approach.

2. The second problem to deal with is where to keep the information about which Java class to create when a customer is read from the database. It could be an instance of `Customer`, `FrequentBuyer`, `Corporation`, or `NonProfitCorporation`. The design opposite creates a new `CUSTOMER_TYPE` table, which will have four rows to match the types of Java objects we can create (types of customer). We have added a required `CUSTOMER_TYPE_ID` column in the `CUSTOMERS` table so that when we read any customer from the database, we know which
   class to instantiate:

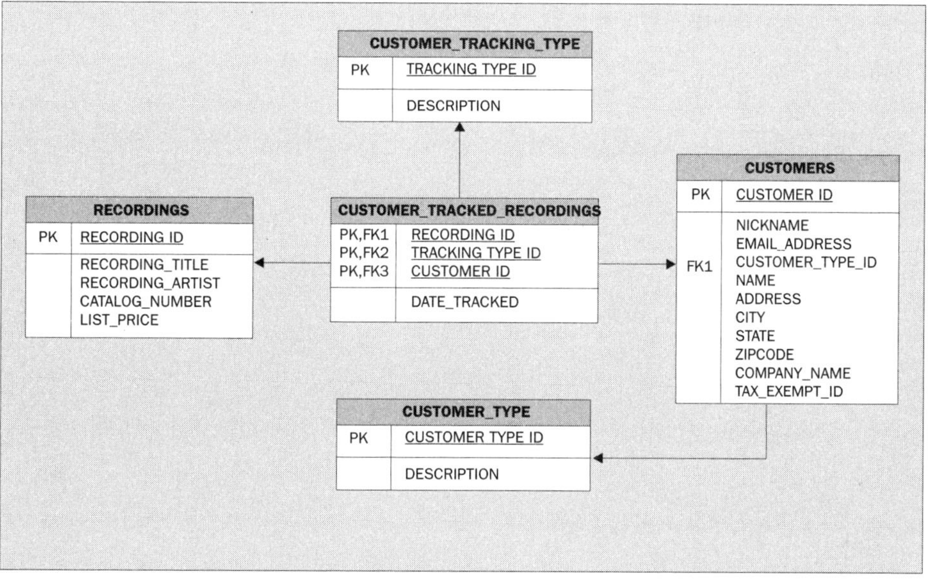

For the first time so far, we have a Java class design and a relational database design that do not exhibit the pattern of one class to one table. Instead, we have five Java classes (the `Customer` hierarchy) mapping to two relational database tables (`CUSTOMERS` and `CUSTOMER_TYPE`). The code required to implement this map is quite complex. If you do decide to tackle this kind of mapping, you must take care to implement it in such a way that you can add additional subclasses into the `Customer` class hierarchy. Many designers hard-code the mapping to the current class hierarchy, which makes it difficult to enhance the Java design at a later date. The object-relational mapping framework in the next chapter requires very little code to implement such a map. It also uses a table for the mapping, so you can easily extend the inheritance hierarchy by adding entries into the hierarchy table.

Summary

Mapping Java objects to a relational database for a simple application is usually straightforward. One Java class usually maps to one relational database table. You CRUD the Java object by creating public `create`, `read` (or `finder`), `update`, and `delete` methods. The SQL used in these methods is also straightforward, as no database table joins are required.

Unfortunately, this blissful period of simple mapping rarely lasts. As you add Java classes and relational database tables to your design, you invariably add relationships between the various classes, and of course the various relational database tables. You are also likely to create inheritance hierarchies in your Java class design. Both relationships and inheritance hierarchies are particularly problematic when mapping to relational database tables. It is quite difficult to implement the map efficiently, and the mapping consumes quite a bit of code in your application. In fact, the lines of code needed to map your objects to the database can easily exceed all the other lines of code in your entire application. For this reason, many people, and even entire companies, have created object-relational mapping frameworks for you to use. The next chapter explores the use of an open source mapping framework to minimize the amount of mapping code in your application.

akarta
JAVA
Java

Using an Object-Relational Mapping Framework

In the last chapter, we 'grew' an application from a simple object and data model into a fairly complex one. It was easy to see how to map a single Java class directly to a single relational table – the effort required little JDBC API code to do so. However, as we added many objects with relationships to each other and created class inheritance hierarchies, the amount of code you would need to do the mapping between the objects, particularly to do this task efficiently, quickly gets out of hand. This problem is so challenging (and important) that there are companies doing little else than creating and selling object-relational mapping products for a variety of programming languages. In this chapter, we will use the data mapping portion of an open source framework called **JLF** (**J**ava **L**ayered **F**rameworks) from http://jlf.sourceforge.net/ This object-relational mapping framework works to minimize the amount of code in your application needs to map your Java objects to the relational database. It also helps you to execute complex mappings in an efficient way, reducing the number of SQL statements you send to the database. We will start off by describing the high-level design of the JLF data mapping framework and executing a simple mapping from a single table to one Java class. We will then move on to review the most complex Java database application design from the previous chapter, and implement the entire design with the help of JLF. You will need an intimate understanding of the previous chapter in order to proceed with the discussion below.

JLF Data Mapping Overview

JLF is a set of frameworks, layered one on top of another, designed to help Java application developers develop their database applications more quickly, and with less code. These frameworks include the following capabilities:

1. Configuration framework

2. Logging framework

3. Utility library

4. Data mapping framework

5. HTTP request processing framework

The **configuration framework** basically initializes JLF by identifying where property files are located. Java property files configure the operation of the remainder of the frameworks in JLF, and the configuration framework helps the other frameworks to find those property files. We will not need to discuss this framework in this book, as it is simply a service provider for the other JLF frameworks.

In Chapter 17, *Debugging and Logging*, we will discuss the **logging framework** portion of JLF in detail. This portion of the framework helps you instrument your application to more quickly find and fix defects. The frameworks that follow the logging framework are all instrumented according to the standards described in Chapter 17.

The **utility library** portion of JLF contains code to do some of the more difficult but common coding tasks in Java. Examples include properly creating hash values for complex objects and using the `Reflection` API. We will not discuss the utility library in this book either. Like the configuration framework, it is a service provider to the other frameworks in JLF.

The **data mapping framework** is the main framework in JLF and the one we will explore in detail in this chapter. The data mapping framework is designed to help you map data in your Java objects to any number of different data source/sink technologies. We will concentrate on relational databases and the JDBC API in this book, but JLF accommodates other types of data sources and sinks as well (for example, XML documents, or parameters from HTTP requests).

The framework layers described above are shown graphically in the following architectural layer diagram. Each framework layer shows the Java package where it is implemented in parentheses, so you know which package to import in your code. In the diagram, the top packages are dependent upon the bottom packages:

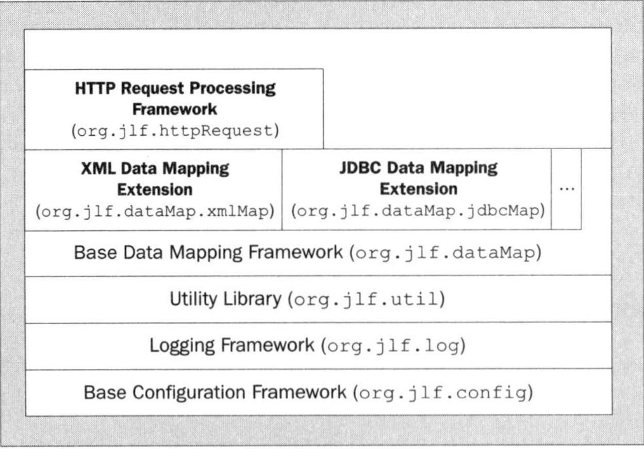

For the remainder of the chapter, we are going to concentrate on the JDBC portion of the data mapping framework. This framework will help us accomplish the goals of this chapter to easily perform complex object-relational data mappings in an efficient manner.

In order to use the data mapping framework in JLF, you must understand three core concepts:

1. Da ta mapped objects

2. Data mappers

3. Data location property files

Data-mapped objects are the Java classes you create for your database application. These objects hold the data you want to map to your database. Data mappers are objects the JLF framework provides for you to do the work of mapping your data to, and from, a relational database. Data location property files are Java property files you create. They tell the data mappers how to map data between your data-mapped objects and your database. So, all three concepts go hand-in-hand to accomplish object-relational data mapping. We will go through each concept in detail below.

Data-Mapped Objects

Any Java classes that you want JLF to map to the relational database must be subclasses of JLF's `DataMappedObject` class. This class contains all the core code to help you define and access variables, relationships, and inheritance hierarchies, so that the framework can map these for you. Instead of defining instance variables in your object, you define `DataAttributeDescriptors`. When you want to create relationships between `DataMappedObjects` in your design, you create `RelationshipDescriptors`. If you have an inheritance hierarchy in your `DataMappedObject` subclasses, you create a hierarchy table so JLF can instantiate the proper types of objects automatically. See the UML class diagram below for the primary classes in the JLF framework you use to define your `DataMappedObjects`:

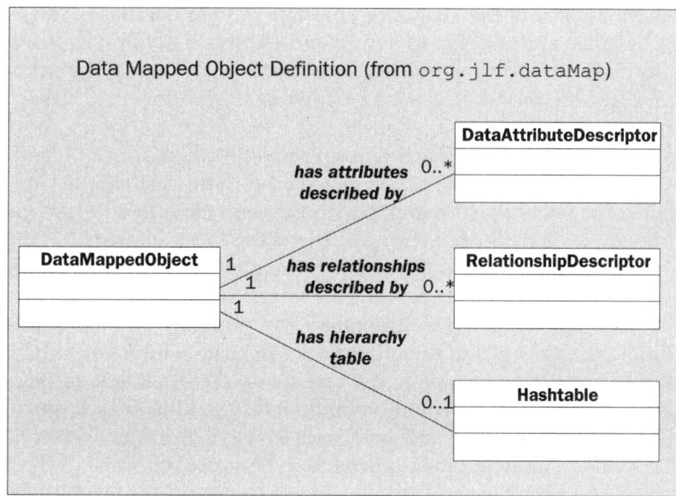

Once you have defined your `DataMappedObject` subclasses with the proper attributes, relationships, and an optional hierarchy table, the data mapped object framework goes to work. It creates `DataAttributes` and `Relationships` as it maps data back and forth between your Java objects and the database. These two classes of objects help the data mapping framework coordinate the data flowing from and to the database.

DataAttributes are used to replace instance variables in your classes. You may wonder why you cannot simply use instance variables like any other JavaBean class would. The answer is two-fold. DataAttributes help the data mapping framework efficiently map the data to the database, and they also help to do optimistic locking. In the first case, if you do not change a value in your object after it is read from the database, then there is no need to send an update SQL statement when you store your object back to the database. Since you have made no change to the object, sending a SQL statement to the database would just take up database resources, changing a row to the same values it already contains. Not only would this consume precious database resources, it would also delay application response time to the application user. So the data mapping framework, in the execution of an update() method, will first check to see if anything has really changed in the object before it executes the SQL UPDATE statement. If you use simple instance variables in your design, the JLF data mapping framework would have a much more difficult time discovering if you have updated your object. Secondly, in previous chapters we have already discussed that the most efficient way to use a database in a very high-volume, transactional system is to use **optimistic locking**. To recap from Chapter 14 on *Transactions*, optimistic locking is when you execute a locking query before you update or delete an object in the database. The locking query makes sure another process hasn't modified the object since you originally read it from the database. There are several ways to do this locking query, and one of the common ways is to check the values of the object in the database and make sure they haven't changed since the original query. With a simple instance variable in your objects, there is no initial value to do the locking query, before you update the row with the new value. DataAttributes keep the original value read from the database, as well as the new value to which you wish to change the object.

DataAttributes have different subclasses to help overcome the limitations of Java native types. As an example of one of these limitations, Java String variables do not have a limit on the number of characters you can store in them. When using a relational database, you almost always define a maximum string length for any of the character columns in your database. The StringAttribute subclass of DataAttribute allows you to define and enforce a maximum string length. Use LongAttribute for int and long variables, DoubleAttribute for float and double variables, DateAttribute for Dates, and of course StringAttribute for Strings.

Relationship objects help you to efficiently map related DataMappedObjects to the database. If you remember back to one of the problems we discovered in the last chapter, it took 106 SQL queries to populate the right set of Java objects using the simple, one table to one Java class data mapping pattern. We could design a single SQL query to retrieve the same information, but we would have a very difficult time mapping the query to the already designed and implemented Java objects. The data mapping framework does this 'heavy lifting' for you when you designate a relationship to be read in the same query as its originating object. Then, one query can populate any number of Java objects when you deem that to be more efficient. On the other hand, in cases where you rarely traverse a relationship, you do not want to take the time to populate the objects on the other side of the relationship until you know you need them. Otherwise, you would be inefficiently pulling back large quantities of unused data from the database. The data mapping framework uses Relationship objects to 'lazy read', or read on demand, such objects when you deem that approach to be more efficient.

The UML class diagram opposite shows how the DataAttribute and Relationship objects described above work with DataMappedObjects:

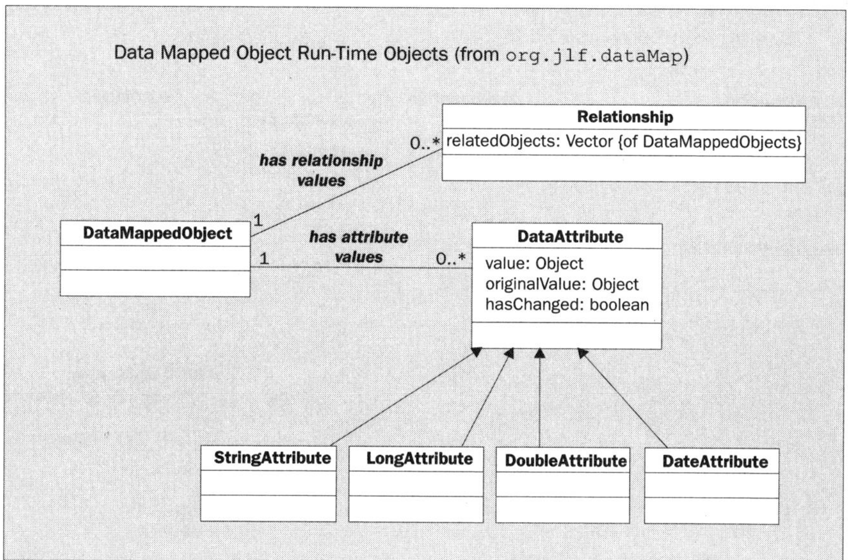

DataMappers

The data mapping framework uses a data mapping 'plug-in' called a **DataMapper**. `DataMappers` map objects to and from a particular data source/sink technology. The goal behind the data mapping plug-in design is to hide the complexity of mapping data to, and from, that technology. For example, say that your Java application needs to map data in its objects to a relational database using the JDBC API, to XML documents using an XML parsing API, from HTML input forms via the Servlet API, and then send messages to queues using the JMS API. You would have to learn the complexities of four different and complex APIs to get your work done. You would also need to write a *lot* of code, as each API is very different, requiring completely different code to execute the mapping. The data mapping framework hides this complexity from you. The code to map your objects to a relational database looks practically identical to code mapping your objects to an XML document or to the input parameters of a servlet. The `DataMapper` plug-in deals with the appropriate Java API, so under ideal circumstances, your code has no technology-specific API code in it at all. There are always going to be cases where the framework doesn't do what you need to do when using, for example, the `JDBCDataMapper`. In those cases you hopefully write a little bit of JDBC code and let the `JDBCDataMapper` do the rest of the work for you.

The `JDBCDataMapper` is shown in the UML class diagram overleaf:

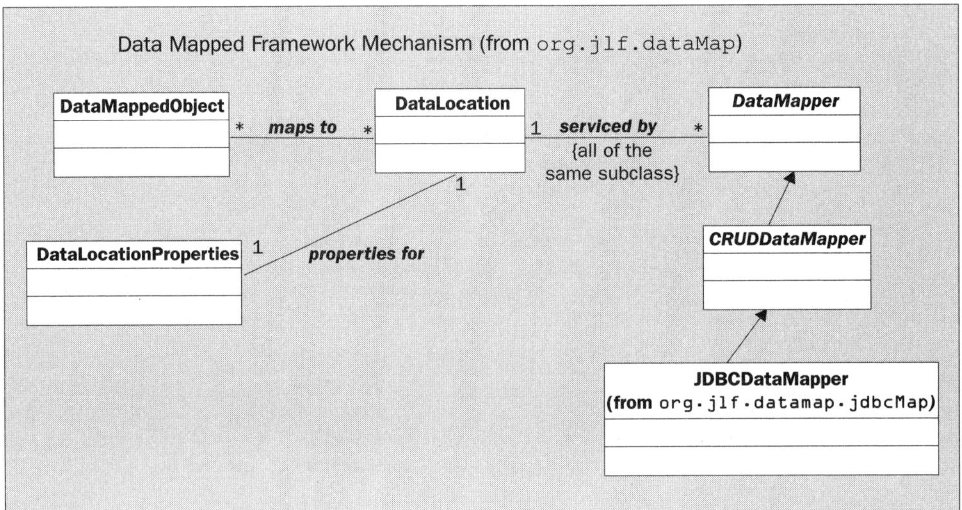

Data Location Property Files

Each `DataMapper` looks to a property file for information on how to map your objects to the data source/sink technology it supports. These property files are called **data locations**. They describe how to get to a particular data location, and map the data between Java objects and that data location. To open a connection to a JDBC data location, the `DataMapper` needs information such as the database URL, the appropriate JDBC driver, and perhaps a user ID and password. Once the connection is established, the `DataMapper` needs to know what SQL statements to send to CRUD (create, read, update, delete) the data. You also tell the `DataMapper` how you want to efficiently map your relationships, reading them in the same query as the original object, or perhaps lazy-reading them on demand.

Now that we understand the basic concepts of the data mapping framework, lets execute a simple CRUD mapping of the `Recordings` table from the previous chapter.

Mapping the Recordings Table

In the last chapter, we illustrated a simple mapping between one Java class and one relational database table. The code to execute the mapping was straightforward, but was a bit cumbersome. As our first venture into using the JLF mapping framework, let's attempt that same mapping, but enhance the design to support optimistic locking of that data as well. The object-relational mapping looks as follows:

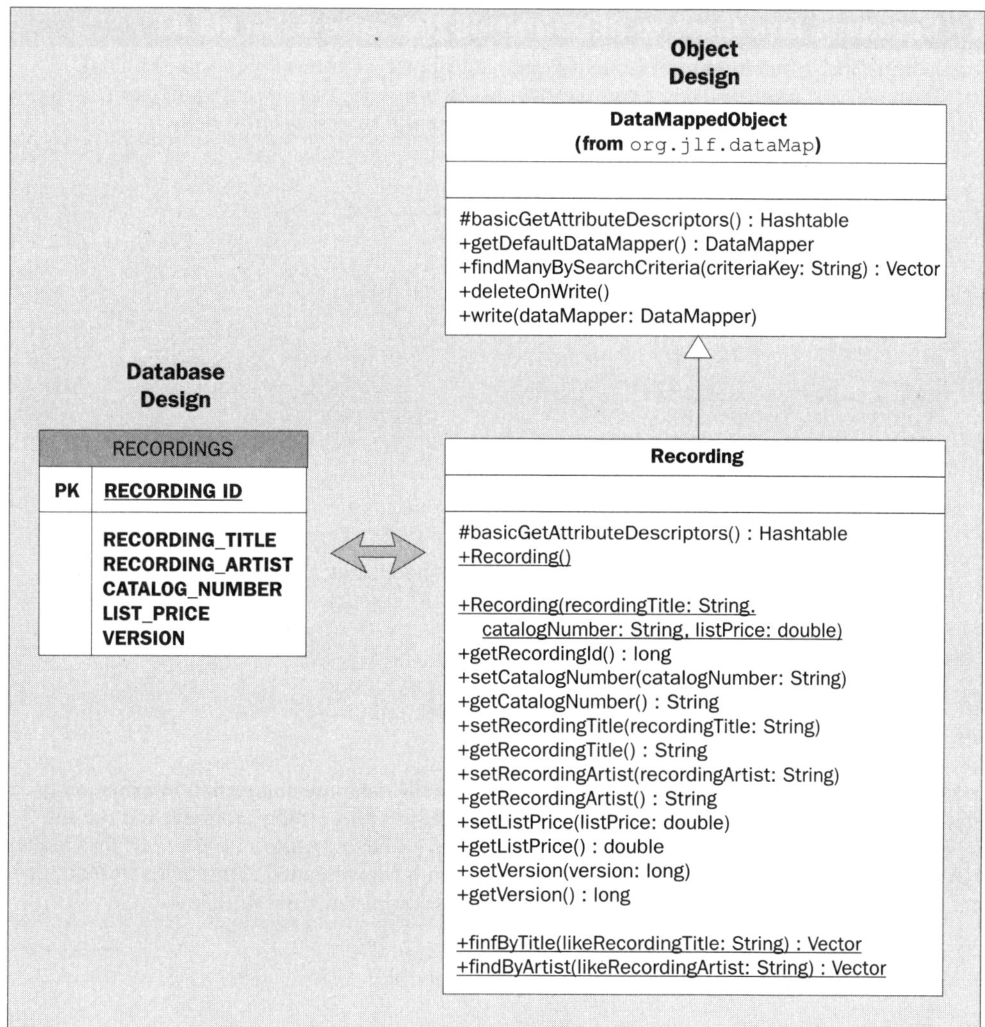

The `Recording` class design above changes to extend the `DataMappedObject` class and replaces instance variables with `DataAttributeDescriptors`. We also remove almost all the CRUD methods and inherit them from `DataMappedObject`. The only two CRUD methods left are the `findByArtist()` and `findByTitle()` methods, and the implementation of these methods is fairly trivial as shown in the next section.

Try It Out – Recording Java Class to RECORDINGS Database Table via JLF

In an Oracle SQL*PLUS session in the Oracle database instance of your choice, run the DDL statements in the `SimpleRecordingsTable.DDL` file in the `simpleRecordingExample` directory for this chapter. A successful run should look something like the screen capture below:

```
SQL> drop table RECORDINGS;

Table dropped.

SQL> drop sequence RECORDINGS_SEQ;

Sequence dropped.

SQL> create table RECORDINGS (
  2      RECORDING_ID INT not null,
  3      RECORDING_TITLE VARCHAR2(50) not null,
  4      RECORDING_ARTIST VARCHAR2(50) not null,
  5      CATALOG_NUMBER VARCHAR2(20) not null,
  6      LIST_PRICE DECIMAL(7,2) not null,
  7      VERSION INT not null,
  8      constraint RECORDINGS_PK primary key (RECORDING_ID) );

Table created.

SQL> create sequence RECORDINGS_SEQ;

Sequence created.
```

Next, update the `RecordingDB.properties` file to change the database connection information to the Oracle database instance you have prepared for the `Recordings` table. Finally, compile and run the `Recording.java` program. This program requires the JDBC jar file (`classes12_01.zip` for Oracle) and the JLF JAR file (available with the code for this chapter or can be downloaded at http://jlf.sorceforge.net) to be in your Java `CLASSPATH`. A partial screen capture for a successful run looks as follows:

```
C:\WINNT\System32\cmd.exe
C:\BegJavaDB\Ch16\simpleRecordingExample> set CLASSPATH=..\classes12.zip;..\jlf.jar;.

C:\BegJavaDB\Ch16\simpleRecordingExample>javac *.java

C:\BegJavaDB\Ch16\simpleRecordingExample>java Recording
Log org.jlf.log.AppLog opened on 19/07/01 at 21:07:31:553
org.jlf.log.AppLog|L4|21:07:31:563|main|Loading application property file at ./App.properties
Log org.jlf.dataMap.DataMapLog opened on 19/07/01 at 21:07:31:573
org.jlf.dataMap.DataMapLog|L3|21:07:31:573|main|Cannot find data mapping property file setting for D
ata Location RecordingDB in main application property file under key org.jlf.dataMap.DataLocation.Re
cordingDB.DataMapPropertyFile, trying a default property file name RecordingDB.properties
org.jlf.log.AppLog|L4|21:07:31:583|main|Loading application property file at ./RecordingDB.propertie
s
Log org.jlf.log.SQLLog opened on 19/07/01 at 21:07:32:464
org.jlf.log.SQLLog|L4|21:07:32:464|main|Executing Update Statement for Class Recording with criteria
 key createStatement:
  insert into RECORDINGS ( RECORDING_ID, RECORDING_TITLE, RECORDING_ARTIST, CATALOG_NUMBER, LIST_PRI
CE, VERSION) values ( RECORDINGS_SEQ.NEXTVAL, 'Cuts Like A Knife', 'Bryan Adams', '392-0000022', 11.
99, 1 )
org.jlf.log.SQLLog|L4|21:07:32:474|main|Executing Query  to update an object of Class Recording with
 criteria key createStatement2:
  select RECORDINGS_SEQ.CURRVAL as RECORDING_ID from DUAL
org.jlf.log.SQLLog|L4|21:07:32:524|main|Executing Update Statement for Class Recording with criteria
 key createStatement:
  insert into RECORDINGS ( RECORDING_ID, RECORDING_TITLE, RECORDING_ARTIST, CATALOG_NUMBER, LIST_PRI
CE, VERSION) values ( RECORDINGS_SEQ.NEXTVAL, 'Working Class Dog', 'Rick Springfield', 'RS-32-1133',
 10.99, 1 )
org.jlf.log.SQLLog|L4|21:07:32:534|main|Executing Query  to update an object of Class Recording with
 criteria key createStatement2:
  select RECORDINGS_SEQ.CURRVAL as RECORDING_ID from DUAL
org.jlf.log.SQLLog|L4|21:07:32:544|main|Executing Update Statement for Class Recording with criteria
 key createStatement:
  insert into RECORDINGS ( RECORDING_ID, RECORDING_TITLE, RECORDING_ARTIST, CATALOG_NUMBER, LIST_PRI
CE, VERSION) values ( RECORDINGS_SEQ.NEXTVAL, 'Come And Join Us', 'Petra', '303-9388293', 11.99, 1 )

org.jlf.log.SQLLog|L4|21:07:32:544|main|Executing Query  to update an object of Class Recording with
 criteria key createStatement2:
  select RECORDINGS_SEQ.CURRVAL as RECORDING_ID from DUAL
org.jlf.log.SQLLog|L4|21:07:32:564|main|Executing Update Statement for Class Recording with criteria
 key createStatement:
  insert into RECORDINGS ( RECORDING_ID, RECORDING_TITLE, RECORDING_ARTIST, CATALOG_NUMBER, LIST_PRI
CE, VERSION) values ( RECORDINGS_SEQ.NEXTVAL, 'Lucky Town', 'Bruce Springsteen', 'BK-30-23993', 13.9
9, 1 )
org.jlf.log.SQLLog|L4|21:07:32:564|main|Executing Query  to update an object of Class Recording with
 criteria key createStatement2:
  select RECORDINGS_SEQ.CURRVAL as RECORDING_ID from DUAL

You should see 4 recordings:
org.jlf.log.SQLLog|L4|21:07:32:775|main|Executing Query  to retrieve objects of Class Recording with
 criteria key findByArtist:
  select * from RECORDINGS where RECORDING_ARTIST like '%Spring%'

Recording: 2
  Title: Working Class Dog
  Artist: Rick Springfield
  Catalog Number: RS-32-1133
  List Price: 10.99

Recording: 4
  Title: Lucky Town
  Artist: Bruce Springsteen
  Catalog Number: BK-30-23993
  List Price: 13.99
org.jlf.log.SQLLog|L4|21:07:32:975|main|Executing Query  to retrieve objects of Class Recording with
 criteria key findByTitle:
  select * from RECORDINGS where RECORDING_TITLE like 'C%'

Recording: 1
  Title: Cuts Like A Knife
  Artist: Bryan Adams
  Catalog Number: 392-0000022
  List Price: 11.99

Recording: 3
  Title: Come And Join Us
```

You will see output identical to the previous chapter, with the addition of several instrumented output statements. Note that the JLF framework is fully instrumented according to the guidelines set forth in Chapter 17. That way, you can easily debug your Java database program as it uses the JLF framework, without even writing a single line of code to instrument your application. JLF reports every SQL statement it executes, puts a timer around each SQL statement so you can see how many milliseconds it takes to execute, and traps any exceptions in its execution, outputting a stack trace as well as a detailed error message for such exceptions. If you turn the logging level to `TRACE` level, JLF outputs all resource allocation and de-allocation information for database `Connection`, `Statement`, and `ResultSet` resources.

How It Works

Executing the object-relational mapping in the example program above was a three-step process:

1. Prepare the database schema
2. Code the `Recording` class
3. Define the data location `.properties` file

Database Schema for Recording Class

We enhanced the schema we developed from the previous chapter to add in an optimistic locking version identifier. The Oracle DDL statements in the `SimpleRecordingsTable.DDL` file below drop the table and sequence, and recreate them with the new version column, as follows:

```
drop table RECORDINGS;

drop sequence RECORDINGS_SEQ;

create table RECORDINGS (
        RECORDING_ID INT not null,
        RECORDING_TITLE VARCHAR2(50) not null,
        RECORDING_ARTIST VARCHAR2(50) not null,
        CATALOG_NUMBER VARCHAR2(20) not null,
        LIST_PRICE DECIMAL(7,2) not null,
        VERSION INT not null,
        constraint RECORDINGS_PK primary key (RECORDING_ID) );

create sequence RECORDINGS_SEQ;
```

Recording Class Implementation

The `Recording.java` class shown below is an implementation of the detailed design we discussed above. For explanation, it is split into four sections. The first section prepares the class as a `DataMappedObject` by extending that class, creates a `DataAttributeDescriptor` for each variable, and implements a public default constructor that the framework uses. The second section is typical JavaBean programming, but with a twist that you access data attributes instead of instance variables. The third section implements the finder methods, as methods inherited from the framework does all of the other CRUD work. Finally, the fourth section adds methods to make the class self-contained so we can easily test it.

```
import java.util.*;
import java.sql.*;

import org.jlf.dataMap.*;

/**
 * This class connects to an Oracle database with a simple
 * Recording table and maps the data in this class to/from
 * that table. One instance of this class corresponds to one
```

```
 * row in the RECORDINGS table.
 */
public class Recording extends DataMappedObject {
```

Above is the first change you should take notice of, as compared to the Recording.java program in the last chapter. We must extend the DataMappedObject class so the framework can map our data.

```
  // -------------------------------------------------------------
  // Section 1: DataMappedObject descriptors
  // -------------------------------------------------------------

  // Constants for attributes
  public static final String ID_ATTRIBUTE = "RECORDING_ID";
  public static final String TITLE_ATTRIBUTE = "RECORDING_TITLE";
  public static final String ARTIST_ATTRIBUTE = "RECORDING_ARTIST";
  public static final String CATALOG_NUMBER_ATTRIBUTE = "CATALOG_NUMBER";
  public static final String LIST_PRICE_ATTRIBUTE = "LIST_PRICE";

  // Used for optimistic locking
  public static final String VERSION_ATTRIBUTE = "VERSION";
```

In the start of section 1, we define constants for our attributes. Remember that instead of instance variables, the JLF mapping framework uses DataAttributeDescriptors. We use the constants above to help us define the DataAttributeDescriptors below. You override the basicGetAttributeDescriptors() method from DataMappedObject to add in the attributes/data you want to be able to map. Then, the framework maps the data attributes you define to SQL columns received in the various SQL queries you execute. In this example, we define data attributes for each of the columns in the Recordings table (that is, RECORDING_ID, RECORDING_TITLE, RECORDING_ARTIST, CATALOG_NUMBER, LIST_PRICE, and VERSION). Then later, when we put SQL statements in the data mapping property file (for example, reading Recording objects according to their title via select * from RECORDINGS where RECORDING_TITLE like RECORDING_TITLE), the JDBC data mapper retrieves all of the columns and data returned in the query and places the data in the correct object attributes according to column name.

The basicGetAttributeDescriptors() method is shown below, followed by a detailed explanation:

```
  /**
   * Sets up a table of attribute descriptors for the Recording
   * object.
   */
  protected Hashtable basicGetAttributeDescriptors() {

    // Always call the superclass!
    Hashtable descriptors = super.basicGetAttributeDescriptors();
    DataAttributeDescriptor descriptor;

    // Then add recording-specific attributes
    descriptor = new DataAttributeDescriptor(ID_ATTRIBUTE,
                                             LongAttribute.class, true);
    descriptor.setIsKeyField(true);
    descriptors.put(ID_ATTRIBUTE, descriptor);

    descriptor = new DataAttributeDescriptor(TITLE_ATTRIBUTE,
                                             StringAttribute.class, false);
```

```
        descriptor.setMaximumLength(50);
        descriptors.put(TITLE_ATTRIBUTE, descriptor);

        descriptor = new DataAttributeDescriptor(ARTIST_ATTRIBUTE,
                                                StringAttribute.class, false);
        descriptor.setMaximumLength(50);
        descriptors.put(ARTIST_ATTRIBUTE, descriptor);

        descriptor = new DataAttributeDescriptor(CATALOG_NUMBER_ATTRIBUTE,
                                                StringAttribute.class, false);
        descriptor.setMaximumLength(20);
        descriptors.put(CATALOG_NUMBER_ATTRIBUTE, descriptor);

        descriptor = new DataAttributeDescriptor(LIST_PRICE_ATTRIBUTE,
                                                DoubleAttribute.class, false);
        descriptors.put(LIST_PRICE_ATTRIBUTE, descriptor);

        descriptor = new DataAttributeDescriptor(VERSION_ATTRIBUTE,
                                                LongAttribute.class, false);
        descriptors.put(VERSION_ATTRIBUTE, descriptor);

        return descriptors;
    }
```

This method is kind of long, so let's step through it one chunk of code at a time. The first chunk of code calls the superclass (`DataMappedObject` in this case) method that we override. This is not only good object-oriented design practice, but is also vital when we define an inheritance hierarchy later in the chapter. Any time you extend another class and override one of its methods, good practice is to design the override in such a way that you call the superclass method either before, or after, you do the work in your method override. That way, if you revise the superclass method, you 'inherit' the changes. If you override a method without calling the superclass, the code in the superclass will not be available to your subclass hierarchy, which may cause the superclass code to fail.

Once you call the superclass to retrieve any of its data attribute descriptors, the remaining chunks in the method simply add their own `Recording` class-specific descriptors. There is one chunk of code for each descriptor. The first descriptor is the primary key of the table with an attribute name `RECORDING_ID`, precisely matching the column name in the database. It is an `INT` type in the database, which maps pretty well to the framework `LongAttribute` implementation class. So, we create the `DataAttributeDescriptor` with the name `RECORDING_ID`, the type `LongAttribute`, and we set a flag to true telling the framework this attribute is allowed to be Null. The framework automatically checks your attributes to make sure you populate them before it allows you to save them to the database. In the case of a synthetic primary key, this key field is not populated when we create the object in the database; it is retrieved as a result of the creation process. So, we tell the framework it is allowed to be Null before we create the data. Next, we tell the framework that named attribute is a key field by the `setIsKeyField()` method. Now that the descriptor is fully defined, we add it to the hash table and move on to the next descriptor. All other attributes defined must be populated and cannot be Null before any interaction with the database.

The second descriptor added is the RECORDING_TITLE descriptor, to match the same named column in the database. This column is not a key field, cannot be Null, and is of StringAttribute type. Additionally, we set a maximum length to match the database definition, in this case 50 characters long. Now the framework knows to expect to map this attribute to a column named RECORDING_TITLE in the database, to expect that field to be required (not Null), and to be no longer than 50 characters. If you attempt to write a Recording Java object to the database violating any of these constraints, the JLF data mapping framework will raise an exception.

The third (RECORDING_ARTIST) and fourth (CATALOG_NUMBER) descriptors are similar to the second; mapping StringAttributes to VARCHAR2 Oracle columns of a maximum character string length.

The fifth descriptor maps the LIST_PRICE column to a DoubleAttribute rather than a LongAttribute, as the information in this column is decimal format. The sixth descriptor maps the VERSION column to a LongAttribute. We didn't tell the framework that this column is a special optimistic locking attribute, which comes later in the mapping property file.

Now that we have all of the data for our object defined, we need to define one other method for the framework to work properly. We must define a default (that is, no input parameter) constructor so the framework can create new instances of this object. Typically, this is poor object design practice, which is why we did not do this in the last chapter. Hopefully in a future version of the framework, this restriction will be eliminated. Code you write should not use this constructor, it should use the parameterized constructor in Section 2 below:

```
/**
 * Default constructor must be public for the data mapping
 * framework!  However, when creating a new object, look to use
 * a paramterized constructor.
 */
public Recording() {}

// ----------------------------------------------------------------
// Section 2: Java Bean methods
// ----------------------------------------------------------------

/**
 * Main constructor for the class.
 */
public Recording(String recordingTitle, String recordingArtist,
                 String catalogNumber, double listPrice) {
  setRecordingTitle(recordingTitle);
  setRecordingArtist(recordingArtist);
  setCatalogNumber(catalogNumber);
  setListPrice(listPrice);

  // Set initial object version to 1, increment every time the
  // object is saved
  setVersion(1);
}
```

As you can imagine, Section 2 needs a good bit of changing to provide the typical Java bean get and set methods. Instead of using instance variables, you need to use DataAttribute subclasses. Fortunately, the data mapping framework understands your needs for these, and makes it easy to make the transition.

The first change you should notice is in the public constructor above. We simply added a method call to set the `VERSION` attribute to an initial value of `1`. So, the first time we create a row in the database for a `Recording` object, it has a version identifier set to `1`. Every subsequent write to the object increments the version identifier after checking to make sure some other process didn't update it between the time the current process read it from the database, and tried to update or delete it.

Next, we removed the `setRecordingId()` method as it is no longer needed. The framework will handle this for us, whereas before we had to manually code retrieving the synthetic key from the database when we created or read the object.

Finally, we changed all the other JavaBean `get` and `set` methods to use framework methods for getting and setting attributes. For attributes of type `LongAttribute`, use `getLongAttribute()` and `setLongAttribute()`. For `StringAttribute` types, use `getStringAttribute()` and `setStringAttribute()`. And for `DoubleAttribute`, use `getDoubleAttribute()` and `setDoubleAttribute()`.

```
  /**
   * Retrieves the database id of the Recording.
   */
  public long getRecordingId() {
    return getLongAttribute(ID_ATTRIBUTE);
  }

  /**
   * Retrieves the title of the Recording.
   */
  public String getRecordingTitle() {
    return getStringAttribute(TITLE_ATTRIBUTE);
  }

  /**
   * Sets the title of the Recording.
   */
  public void setRecordingTitle(String recordingTitle) {
    setStringAttribute(TITLE_ATTRIBUTE, recordingTitle);
  }

  /**
   * Retrieves the artist that made the Recording.
   */
  public String getRecordingArtist() {
    return getStringAttribute(ARTIST_ATTRIBUTE);
  }

  /**
   * Sets the artist that made the Recording.
   */
  public void setRecordingArtist(String recordingArtist) {
    setStringAttribute(ARTIST_ATTRIBUTE, recordingArtist);
  }

  /**
   * Retrieves the catalog number of the Recording.
```

```
  */
  public String getCatalogNumber() {
    return getStringAttribute(CATALOG_NUMBER_ATTRIBUTE);
  }

  /**
   * Sets the catalog number of the Recording.
   */
  public void setCatalogNumber(String catalogNumber) {
    setStringAttribute(CATALOG_NUMBER_ATTRIBUTE, catalogNumber);
  }

  /**
   * Retrieves the selling price of the Recording.
   */
  public double getListPrice() {
    return getDoubleAttribute(LIST_PRICE_ATTRIBUTE);
  }

  /**
   * Sets the selling price of the Recording.
   */
  public void setListPrice(double listPrice) {
    setDoubleAttribute(LIST_PRICE_ATTRIBUTE, listPrice);
  }

  /**
   * Retrieves the version of the Recording object.
   */
  public long getVersion() {
    return getLongAttribute(VERSION_ATTRIBUTE);
  }

  /**
   * Sets the version of the Recording object.
   */
  private void setVersion(long version) {
    setLongAttribute(VERSION_ATTRIBUTE, version);
  }
```

So far we haven't seen the positive impact of the data mapping framework. We actually had more work to do in the previous sections because we had to define data attribute descriptors. Section 3 is where we see the benefit. We do not even need to code a `create()`, `update()`, or `delete()` method. All three of these methods are replaced by a call to the `write()` method defined in `DataMappedObject`, discussed in Section 4 later. The framework knows when to execute `CREATE`, `UPDATE`, or `DELETE` SQL statements because it keeps track of whether the object has been read or written to the database in previous method calls.

We still need to define methods to read the object, but they are fairly simple 'pass through' methods to the superclass, as shown below:

```
  // ------------------------------------------------------------------
  // Section 3: Methods to map the class to the database
  // ------------------------------------------------------------------
```

```
/**
 * Finds zero to many Recording objects that have a title
 * like the input string, returning them in a Vector.
 */
public static Vector findByTitle(String likeRecordingTitle) {

  // Create a new recording and populate the title to look for
  Recording recording = new Recording();
  recording.setRecordingTitle(likeRecordingTitle);

  // Have the framework execute the query
  return recording.findManyBySearchCriteria("findByTitle");
}

/**
 * Finds zero to many Recording objects that have an artist
 * like the input string, returning them in a Vector.
 */
public static Vector findByArtist(String likeRecordingArtist) {

  // Create a new recording and populate the title to look for
  Recording recording = new Recording();
  recording.setRecordingArtist(likeRecordingArtist);

  // Have the framework execute the query
  return recording.findManyBySearchCriteria("findByArtist");
}
```

To read a set of objects from the database, you execute the `findManyBySearchCriteria()` method defined in `DataMappedObject`. This method looks for a SQL `SELECT` statement in the data mapping property file, parameterizes the SQL statement with any attribute values you may have set in the object, executes the query, and creates `Recording` objects for each row in the resultset. The methods above execute a different SQL statement query with a different parameter, to match the type of read query you want to do. The `findByTitle()` method uses the `RECORDING_TITLE` attribute and the `findByTitle` key in the property file to execute the read. The `findByArtist()` method uses the `RECORDING_ARTIST` attribute and the `findByArtist` key in the property file to execute the read. You do not have to do any of the work to create or populate `Recording` objects; the framework does that for you and returns them in a vector, just as we coded manually in the last chapter.

Section 4 below is also simplified. It does not contain any code to retrieve a connection from the database, nor to clean it up when you are finished with it; the framework handles that for you. In order to apply optimistic locking to the object, however, we need to introduce a small bit of complexity called a `DataMapper`, described below:

```
// ------------------------------------------------------------
// Section 4: Methods to make the class self-contained
// ------------------------------------------------------------

/**
 * Prints the contents of all variables.
 */
public String toString() {
```

```
    return "Recording: " + getRecordingId() + "\n  Title: "
           + getRecordingTitle() + "\n  Artist: " + getRecordingArtist()
           + "\n  Catalog Number: " + getCatalogNumber()
           + "\n  List Price: " + getListPrice();
  }

  /**
   * Helper method to output a set of Recording objects
   * in a Vector to System.out.
   */
  private static void outputRecordings(Vector recordings) {

    Recording recording;
    Enumeration e = recordings.elements();

    while (e.hasMoreElements()) {
      recording = (Recording) e.nextElement();

      // Print to output stream
      System.out.println("\n" + recording);
    }

  }

  /**
   * Main method to test the capabilities above.  CRUDs the
   * database by creating 4 recordings, reading them back,
   * updates the price on one and reads it back, and
   * deletes all 4.
   */
  public static void main(String[] args) {
    Recording rec1, rec2, rec3, rec4;

    DataMapper dataMapper = null;

    try {
      rec1 = new Recording("Cuts Like A Knife", "Bryan Adams",
                           "392-0000022", 11.99);

      rec2 = new Recording("Working Class Dog", "Rick Springfield",
                           "RS-32-1133", 10.99);

      rec3 = new Recording("Come And Join Us", "Petra", "303-9388293",
                           11.99);

      rec4 = new Recording("Lucky Town", "Bruce Springsteen",
                           "BK-30-23993", 13.99);

      dataMapper = rec1.getDefaultDataMapper();
```

The code above retrieves a `DataMapper` from the object you want map to the database. The `DataMapper` helps us to batch up requests to the database, and commits them as part of a whole unit of work or commit scope. So, you can CRUD any number of objects as part of one or many different transactions. When you want to end your transaction and commit it, you simply call `commitWrites()` on the `DataMapper` object. In the code overleaf, we create all four new recording objects before we commit the transaction:

```
// Create the recordings in the database
rec1.write(dataMapper);
rec2.write(dataMapper);
rec3.write(dataMapper);
rec4.write(dataMapper);

dataMapper.commitWrites();

// Read the recordings back and output
System.out.println("\nYou should see 4 recordings:");
```

Now that we have all four new `Recording` objects in the database, we move on to verify their existence. We read two of them by artist and two by title, echoing all four to `System.out` for program verification.

```
Vector springArtistRecordings = Recording.findByArtist("%Spring%");
outputRecordings(springArtistRecordings);

Vector recordingsStartWithC = Recording.findByTitle("C%");
outputRecordings(recordingsStartWithC);
```

Next, we test the ability to update an object by lowering its list price. You reset the attribute, write the object out (remember that the framework understands when to create or update an object), and commit it as shown below. The program also re-reads it from the database and echoes it out to verify the update succeeded:

```
// Update recording 1 price
rec1.setListPrice(7.99);
rec1.write(dataMapper);
dataMapper.commitWrites();

// Read record back and make sure update made it
System.out.println("\nThis recording should have a price of 7.99");
Vector updatedRecording = Recording.findByArtist("Bryan Adams");
outputRecordings(updatedRecording);
```

The only part of CRUD left to test is the `DELETE`, so the following code does that. For each object you want to delete, you set a flag in the object by calling the `deleteOnWrite()` method defined in `DataMappedObject`. The framework then executes a SQL statement you defined in the property file to delete it from the database. All four objects are written in the same commit scope. Then the program tries to read and report any objects in the database, of which there should be none after the deletes take effect:

```
// Delete all recordings
rec1.deleteOnWrite();
rec1.write(dataMapper);

rec2.deleteOnWrite();
rec2.write(dataMapper);

rec3.deleteOnWrite();
rec3.write(dataMapper);

rec4.deleteOnWrite();
rec4.write(dataMapper);
```

```
      dataMapper.commitWrites();

      // Read all recordings back, shouldn't be any
      System.out.println("\nDeleted all, shouldn't be any recordings:");
      Vector allRecordings = Recording.findByArtist("%");
      outputRecordings(allRecordings);

    } catch (Exception e) {
      e.printStackTrace();
    }
    finally {
      if (dataMapper != null) {
        dataMapper.close();
      }
    }
  }
}
```

If you compare the implementation of the `Recording.java` code above with that of the last chapter, you will notice a reduction of nearly 40 percent in the lines of code required to implement the class, even though we added optimistic locking to our design. Most of the reduction came from the ability to use `DataMappedObject` methods to CRUD the data, reducing Section 2 from 285 lines of code to a much more manageable 31. Of course, we pay for that reduction just a bit by introducing an 80-line property file in the next section.

Data Location Property File

A data location in our case represents a database. In a data location property file, you define how to connect to that database (that is, the JDBC driver, connection URL, username, and password), as well as the SQL statements to CRUD your objects in that database. In the `RecordingDB.properties` file below, you will see the database connection properties first, followed by SQL statements for the `Recording` class:

```
##########################################################
# Properties to map Recording objects in the
# to an Oracle database

####################
# These properties define the connection

DataMapperClass=org.jlf.dataMap.jdbcMap.JDBCDataMapper

ConnectionProperties.DriverClass=oracle.jdbc.driver.OracleDriver
ConnectionProperties.DatabaseURL=jdbc:oracle:thin:@dbserver:1521:database
ConnectionProperties.user=scott
ConnectionProperties.password=tiger
```

The properties above define the connection to a test database we use; you should have changed them to connect to your Oracle database instance.

The properties below should not change, however, as they map specifically to the Oracle database schema defined earlier. We defined the properties below in CRUD order; first the create SQL statements, next the read (which are used by the finder methods), then update, and finally the delete. You will notice backslash (\) characters at the end of most lines. They are used to split a single property file entry into multiple lines for readability. So, the `createStatement` property is one entire property divided into several lines so you can more easily read the statement. When the property is complete, the last line of the property does not have the backslash:

```
# SQL statements to create a recording
Recording.criteriaKey.createStatement.sqlStatement=\
    insert into RECORDINGS ( \
        RECORDING_ID, \
        RECORDING_TITLE, \
        RECORDING_ARTIST, \
        CATALOG_NUMBER, \
        LIST_PRICE, \
        VERSION) \
    values ( \
        RECORDINGS_SEQ.NEXTVAL, \
        {RECORDING_TITLE}, \
        {RECORDING_ARTIST}, \
        {CATALOG_NUMBER}, \
        {LIST_PRICE}, \
        {VERSION} )

Recording.criteriaKey.createStatement2.sqlStatement=\
    select RECORDINGS_SEQ.CURRVAL as RECORDING_ID \
      from DUAL
Recording.criteriaKey.createStatement2.isQuery=true
```

All CRUD properties for a `DataMappedObject` subclass begin with a prefix of the class name followed by `.criteriaKey`. That way, you can define any number of different Java classes in the same data location property file. The next part of the key tells us which criteria key you are defining. The framework provides several default criteria keys for you, namely `createStatement`, `updateStatement`, and `deleteStatement` for the 'C', 'U', and 'D' letters respectively in CRUD. To create a `Recording` object in the database, we need to execute two SQL statements, so we define `createStatement.sqlStatement` and `createStatement2.sqlStatement`. The second SQL statement is a `SELECT` statement, which is not the default behavior for a `CREATE` activity. You need to tell the framework this, or it will assume that it is another create SQL statement and will not retrieve any data. Set the `createStatement2.isQuery=true` so the framework can retrieve the all-important `RECORDING_ID` as the object's primary key.

You will notice some non-standard SQL in the first `CREATE` statement. There are braces `{}` around values inserted into the table. The framework scans for braces as replaceable parameters. The text inside the braces must be an attribute defined as an attribute descriptor of the object. Before the execution of the SQL statement, the framework encounters an entry like `{RECORDING_TITLE}`, looks up the `RECORDING_TITLE` attribute, finds a value like 'Reckless' for the 'Bryan Adams' recording, and replaces the text with that value in the SQL statement. It does this process for each of the remaining braced parameters, and then it executes the statement.

Next, we define SQL statements for the `find` methods. If you remember in the last section, for the `findByTitle()` method we told the framework we wanted to find many objects in the database by executing `findManyBySearchCriteria("findByTitle")`. The framework looks for a user-defined criteria key with the name `findByTitle` as shown below. Likewise in the `findByArtist()` method, JLF looks for the `findByArtist` criteria key:

```
# SQL statement for a "findByTitle" search criteria
Recording.criteriaKey.findByTitle.sqlStatement=\
    select * \
      from RECORDINGS \
     where RECORDING_TITLE like {RECORDING_TITLE}

# SQL statement for a "findByArtist" search criteria
Recording.criteriaKey.findByArtist.sqlStatement=\
    select * \
      from RECORDINGS \
     where RECORDING_ARTIST like {RECORDING_ARTIST}
```

Before we define `UPDATE` or `DELETE` statements, we need to determine if we want to do an optimistic locking query. The framework defines a special criteria key called `optimisticLockingStatement`. If you populate that criteria key with one or more SQL statements, the framework executes those statements and expects one row of data as output for a successful optimistic locking check. In our case, we are using a special column called `VERSION`, so our optimistic locking query is very simple. We do a `SELECT` on the `RECORDINGS` table to make sure we have a row in the database where our object's version matches that in the database for the `RECORDING_ID` we are using. If not, some other process updated or deleted the same object after we read it and the optimistic lock fails with a 'dirty' read:

```
# SQL statement to optimistic lock a recording
Recording.criteriaKey.optimisticLockingStatement.sqlStatement=\
    select VERSION \
      from RECORDINGS \
     where RECORDING_ID = {RECORDING_ID} \
       and VERSION = {VERSION}
```

Now that we have a safe optimistic locking query, we can define `UPDATE` and `DELETE` criteria keys below that assume the object is locked. `UPDATE` and `DELETE` SQL statements will not be executed if the optimistic lock fails (that is, the `SELECT` statement does not return a row), and any other SQL statements in the same unit of work or commit scope will be rolled back as well:

```
# SQL statement to update a recording
Recording.criteriaKey.updateStatement.sqlStatement=\
    update RECORDINGS set \
        RECORDING_TITLE = {RECORDING_TITLE}, \
        RECORDING_ARTIST = {RECORDING_ARTIST}, \
        CATALOG_NUMBER = {CATALOG_NUMBER}, \
        LIST_PRICE = {LIST_PRICE}, \
        VERSION = VERSION + 1 \
    where RECORDING_ID = {RECORDING_ID}

# Retrieves the reset VERSION
Recording.criteriaKey.updateStatement2.sqlStatement=\
```

```
      select VERSION \
        from RECORDINGS \
       where RECORDING_ID = {RECORDING_ID}
Recording.criteriaKey.updateStatement2.isQuery=true

# SQL statement to delete a recording
Recording.criteriaKey.deleteStatement.sqlStatement=\
    delete from RECORDINGS \
          where RECORDING_ID = {RECORDING_ID}
```

The JLF framework needs a main property file called `App.properties` (by default). This file is used to adjust how the framework runs your code. For example, you can define logging framework overrides to output log messages at a higher or lower level of detail. For our purposes, we need to tell the framework the name of the default data mapping property file above, for each class we intend to map to the database. `App.properties` in our example consists only of the following:

```
##########################################################
# JLF Properties

# Default data locations/property files for Recording database objects
Recording.defaultDataLocation=RecordingDb
```

Given this entry in the main application property file, the JLF data mapping framework looks for a property file named `RecordingDb.properties` when asked to create a default `DataMapper` for the object. The `RecordingDb.properties` file above told the framework to use a `JDBCDataMapper` for its data source/sink interaction. That `DataMapper` plug-in connects to your Oracle database and executes the SQL statements in the property file to CRUD your object.

Now that we have our feet wet with the JLF data mapping framework, we will move on to implement the most complex object and database model from the previous chapter. In doing so, we will take advantage of several features available in the data mapping framework to optimize our mapping to the database.

A Complex JLF Data Mapping Application

The last chapter showed the evolution of a Java database application as it grew from a very simple application with one table and one Java class, to a relatively complex application. In the most complex version of the application, we wished to track customer purchases, and interests in recordings,that the store made available for sale. We also implemented a customer loyalty discount program where we reduced the price of our recordings under certain circumstances. In this section, we will implement the key Java classes that map to that database, using the JLF data mapping framework to help us do so.

The following relational database data model is the most complex data model from the last chapter, with the addition of optimistic locking columns for all tables we are going to CRUD. Note that the `CUSTOMER_TRACKING_TYPE` and `CUSTOMER_TYPE` tables do not have optimistic locking columns. For simplicity, we will not CRUD these tables. They will contain static reference data only, so the Java objects will read these tables, but will not create, update, or delete them. When we create the tables in the next section, we will populate them with the correct data at the same time:

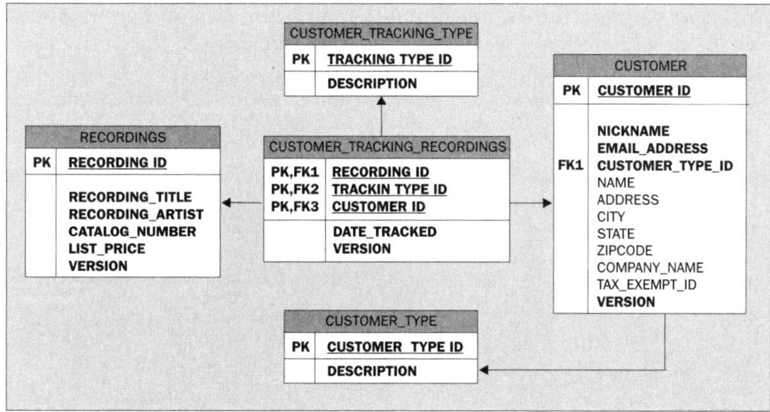

The following object model is split into two UML class diagrams so you can more easily read the classes and relationships in the model. Also, all the variables and methods are hidden for better readability. In complex applications, it is often more important to understand the main classes and relationships of an application, and leave the detail in the code. We will take that approach and explore the code in detail in sections to follow.

The first UML class diagram shows the key classes involved in the Java design. Each of these classes map one-to-one with Oracle database tables of similar name:

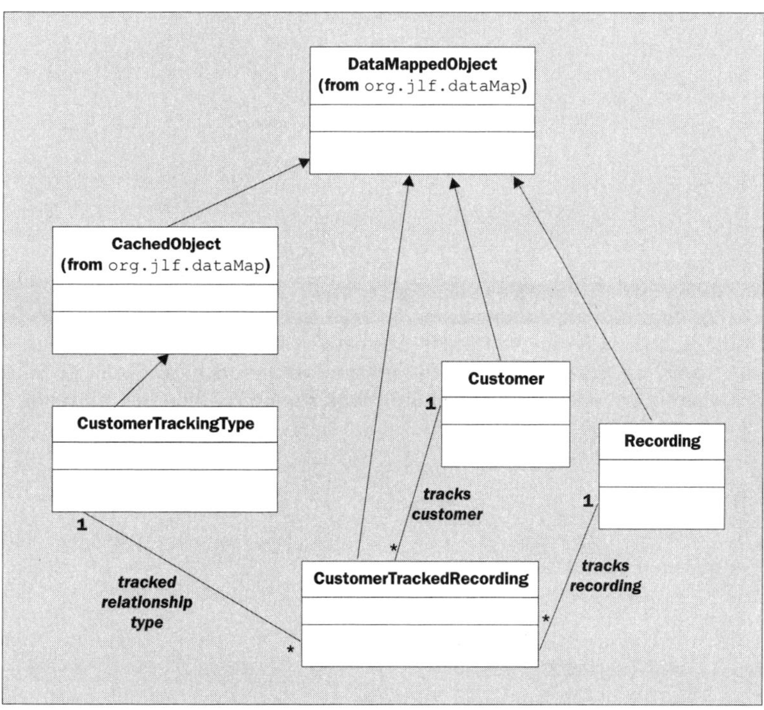

The second UML class diagram shows the complete `Customer` class hierarchy discussed in the previous chapter. As described there, we will map all the subclasses in the `Customer` class hierarchy to the `CUSTOMERS` database table:

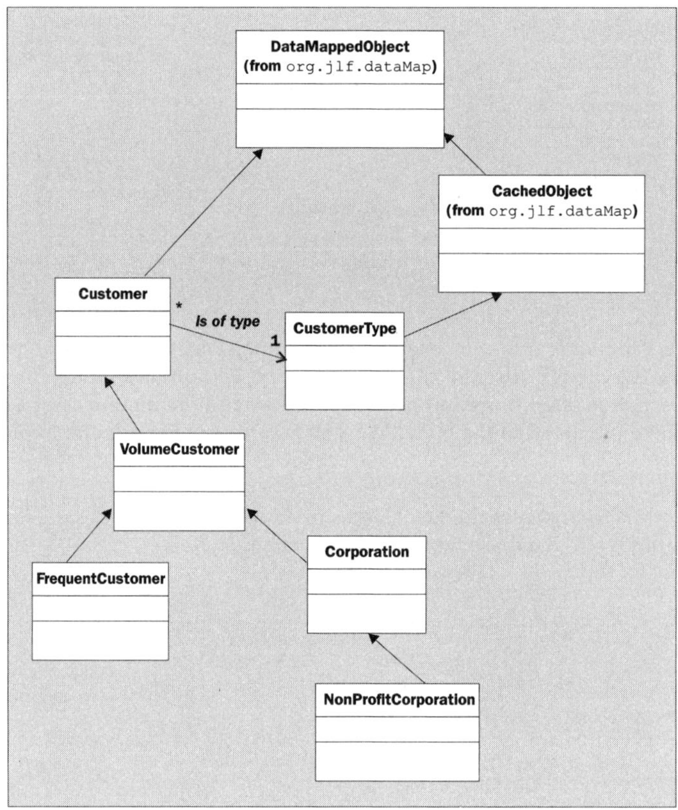

Try It Out – Complex Application Mapping Example

In an Oracle SQL*PLUS session in the Oracle database instance of your choice, run the DDL statements in the `ComplexDatabase.DDL` file (located in the `complexRecordingExample` directory for this chapter). A successful run should look something like the following screen capture:

```
SQL> drop table RECORDINGS;

Table dropped.

SQL> drop sequence RECORDINGS_SEQ;

Sequence dropped.

SQL> create table CUSTOMER_TYPE (
  2          CUSTOMER_TYPE_ID INT not null,
  3          DESCRIPTION VARCHAR2(50) not null,
  4          constraint CUSTOMER_TYPE_PK primary key (CUSTOMER_TYPE_ID) );
```

```
Table created.

SQL> create table CUSTOMER_TRACKING_TYPE (
  2         TRACKING_TYPE_ID INT not null,
  3         DESCRIPTION VARCHAR2(50) not null,
  4         constraint CUSTOMER_TRACKING_TYPE_PK primary key (TRACKING_TYPE_ID)
);

Table created.

SQL> create table CUSTOMERS (
  2         CUSTOMER_ID INT not null,
  3         NICKNAME VARCHAR2(20) not null,
  4         EMAIL_ADDRESS VARCHAR2(50) not null,
  5         CUSTOMER_TYPE_ID INT not null,
  6         NAME VARCHAR2(50) null,
  7         ADDRESS VARCHAR2(50) null,
  8         CITY VARCHAR2(20) null,
  9         STATE CHAR(2) null,
 10         ZIPCODE CHAR(10) null,
 11         COMPANY_NAME VARCHAR2(50) null,
 12         TAX_EXEMPT_ID VARCHAR2(50) null,
 13         VERSION INT not null,
 14         constraint CUSTOMERS_PK primary key (CUSTOMER_ID),
 15         constraint CUSTOMER_TYPE_CUSTOMERS_FK1 foreign key (CUSTOMER_TYPE_ID)
 16             references CUSTOMER_TYPE (CUSTOMER_TYPE_ID) );

Table created.

SQL> create table RECORDINGS (
  2         RECORDING_ID INT not null,
  3         RECORDING_TITLE VARCHAR2(50) not null,
  4         RECORDING_ARTIST VARCHAR2(50) not null,
  5         CATALOG_NUMBER VARCHAR2(20) not null,
  6         LIST_PRICE DECIMAL(7,2) not null,
  7         VERSION INT not null,
  8         constraint RECORDINGS_PK primary key (RECORDING_ID) );

Table created.

SQL> create table CUSTOMER_TRACKED_RECORDINGS (
  2         RECORDING_ID INT not null,
  3         TRACKING_TYPE_ID INT not null,
  4         CUSTOMER_ID INT not null,
  5         DATE_TRACKED DATE not null,
  6         VERSION INT not null,
  7         constraint CUSTOMER_TRACKED_RECORDINGS_PK
  8         primary key (RECORDING_ID, CUSTOMER_ID, TRACKING_TYPE_ID),
  9     constraint RECORDINGS_ID_FK1 foreign key (RECORDING_ID)
 10             references RECORDINGS (RECORDING_ID),
 11         constraint CUSTOMER_TRACKING_ID_FK1 foreign key (TRACKING_TYPE_ID)
 12         references CUSTOMER_TRACKING_TYPE (TRACKING_TYPE_ID),
 13     constraint CUSTOMERS_ID_FK1 foreign key (CUSTOMER_ID)
```

```
             references CUSTOMERS (CUSTOMER_ID) );

Table created.

SQL> create sequence RECORDINGS_SEQ;

Sequence created.

SQL> create sequence CUSTOMERS_SEQ;

Sequence created.

SQL> insert into CUSTOMER_TYPE
          values (1, 'Generic Customer');

1 row created.

SQL> insert into CUSTOMER_TYPE
          values (2, 'Frequent Buyer');

1 row created.

SQL> insert into CUSTOMER_TYPE
          values (3, 'Corporate Customer');

1 row created.

SQL> insert into CUSTOMER_TYPE
          values (4, 'Non-Profit Corporation');

1 row created.

SQL> insert into CUSTOMER_TRACKING_TYPE
          values (1, 'Customer Purchase');

1 row created.

SQL>
SQL> insert into CUSTOMER_TRACKING_TYPE
          values (2, 'Customer Interest');

1 row created.

SQL> commit;

Commit complete.
```

The `ComplexDatabase.DDL` file, which you can download from the Wrox web site, will drop the table and sequence from the last example, create all the tables and sequences for the complex application design above, and finally populate the `CUSTOMER_TRACKING_TYPE` and `CUSTOMER_TYPE` static reference tables, as demonstrated above.

Next, update the `RecordingDB.properties` file to change the database connection information to the Oracle database instance you have prepared above. Compile all the classes in the `complexRecordingExample` directory and run the `TestCustomerTracking` class, with the proper JDBC driver and JLF framework JAR file in the Java `CLASSPATH`. The partial screen capture below shows a successful run:

```
C:\WINNT\System32\cmd.exe
C:\BegJavaDB\Ch16\complexRecordingExample>set CLASSPATH=..\classes12.zip;..\jlf.jar;.

C:\BegJavaDB\Ch16\complexRecordingExample>javac *.java

C:\BegJavaDB\Ch16\complexRecordingExample>java TestCustomerTracking
Log org.jlf.log.AppLog opened on 20/07/01 at 09:43:51:327
org.jlf.log.AppLog|L4|09:43:51:327|main|Loading application property file at ./App.properties
Log org.jlf.dataMap.DataMapLog opened on 20/07/01 at 09:43:51:337
org.jlf.dataMap.DataMapLog|L3|09:43:51:337|main|Cannot find data mapping property file setting for D
ata Location RecordingDb in main application property file under key org.jlf.dataMap.DataLocation.Re
cordingDb.DataMapPropertyFile, trying a default property file name RecordingDb.properties
org.jlf.log.AppLog|L4|09:43:51:337|main|Loading application property file at ./RecordingDb.propertie
s
Log org.jlf.log.SQLLog opened on 20/07/01 at 09:43:53:560
org.jlf.log.SQLLog|L4|09:43:53:560|main|Executing Query  to retrieve objects of Class CustomerType w
ith criteria key findByPrimaryKey:
  select * from CUSTOMER_TYPE where CUSTOMER_TYPE_ID = 1
org.jlf.log.SQLLog|L4|09:43:53:790|main|Executing Query  to retrieve objects of Class CustomerType w
ith criteria key findByPrimaryKey:
  select * from CUSTOMER_TYPE where CUSTOMER_TYPE_ID = 2
org.jlf.log.SQLLog|L4|09:43:53:920|main|Executing Query  to retrieve objects of Class CustomerType w
ith criteria key findByPrimaryKey:
  select * from CUSTOMER_TYPE where CUSTOMER_TYPE_ID = 3
org.jlf.log.SQLLog|L4|09:43:54:071|main|Executing Query  to retrieve objects of Class CustomerType w
ith criteria key findByPrimaryKey:
  select * from CUSTOMER_TYPE where CUSTOMER_TYPE_ID = 4
org.jlf.log.SQLLog|L4|09:43:54:271|main|Executing Update Statement for Class Customer with criteria
key createStatement:
  insert into CUSTOMERS ( CUSTOMER_ID, CUSTOMER_TYPE_ID, NICKNAME, EMAIL_ADDRESS, VERSION) values (
CUSTOMERS_SEQ.NEXTVAL, 1, 'shiney', 'shiney@yahoo.com', 1 )
org.jlf.log.SQLLog|L4|09:43:54:281|main|Executing Query  to update an object of Class Customer with
criteria key createStatement2:
  select CUSTOMERS_SEQ.CURRVAL as CUSTOMER_ID from DUAL
org.jlf.log.SQLLog|L4|09:43:54:291|main|Executing Update Statement for Class FrequentBuyer with crit
eria key createStatement:
  insert into CUSTOMERS ( CUSTOMER_ID, CUSTOMER_TYPE_ID, NICKNAME, EMAIL_ADDRESS, NAME, ADDRESS, CIT
Y, STATE, ZIPCODE, VERSION) values ( CUSTOMERS_SEQ.NEXTVAL, 2, 'charlemange', 'charle@hotmail.com',
'Charlie Charlemange', '123 Main Street', 'Minneapolis', 'MN', '55132', 1 )
org.jlf.log.SQLLog|L4|09:43:54:341|main|Executing Query  to update an object of Class FrequentBuyer
with criteria key createStatement2:
  select CUSTOMERS_SEQ.CURRVAL as CUSTOMER_ID from DUAL
org.jlf.log.SQLLog|L4|09:43:54:381|main|Executing Update Statement for Class Corporation with criter
ia key createStatement:
  insert into CUSTOMERS ( CUSTOMER_ID, CUSTOMER_TYPE_ID, NICKNAME, EMAIL_ADDRESS, NAME, COMPANY_NAME
, ADDRESS, CITY, STATE, ZIPCODE, VERSION) values ( CUSTOMERS_SEQ.NEXTVAL, 3, 'choo', 'choo@aol.com',
 'Chester Sunshine', 'Trains And More...', '431 Broadway', 'Minneapolis', 'MN', '55332', 1 )
org.jlf.log.SQLLog|L4|09:43:54:441|main|Executing Query  to update an object of Class Corporation wi
th criteria key createStatement2:
  select CUSTOMERS_SEQ.CURRVAL as CUSTOMER_ID from DUAL
org.jlf.log.SQLLog|L4|09:43:54:481|main|Executing Update Statement for Class NonProfitCorporation wi
th criteria key createStatement:
  insert into CUSTOMERS ( CUSTOMER_ID, CUSTOMER_TYPE_ID, NICKNAME, EMAIL_ADDRESS, NAME, COMPANY_NAME
, ADDRESS, CITY, STATE, ZIPCODE, TAX_EXEMPT_ID, VERSION) values ( CUSTOMERS_SEQ.NEXTVAL, 4, 'honey',
 'honey@yahoo.com', 'Honey Princess', 'Princess For a Day', '3390 3rd Ave. North', 'Minneapolis', 'M
N', '55133', '3390-honey-USMN', 1 )
org.jlf.log.SQLLog|L4|09:43:54:541|main|Executing Query  to update an object of Class NonProfitCorpo
ration with criteria key createStatement2:
  select CUSTOMERS_SEQ.CURRVAL as CUSTOMER_ID from DUAL
org.jlf.log.SQLLog|L4|09:43:54:591|main|Executing Update Statement for Class Recording with criteria
 key createStatement:
  insert into RECORDINGS ( RECORDING_ID, RECORDING_TITLE, RECORDING_ARTIST, CATALOG_NUMBER, LIST_PRI
CE, VERSION) values ( RECORDINGS_SEQ.NEXTVAL, 'Cuts Like A Knife', 'Bryan Adams', '392-0000022', 11.
99, 1 )
org.jlf.log.SQLLog|L4|09:43:54:632|main|Executing Query  to update an object of Class Recording with
 criteria key createStatement2:
```

The `TestCustomerTracking` class will create several customers and recordings, and then add some tracking relationships to the database. It will test the capabilities of the application by querying the database for interesting tracking information and report the results to `System.out`. Finally, it deletes all the relationships and rows it created. You should see something like the following output:

```
Should have found 2 customers below, one Frequent Buyer and one Non-Profit Corp.


Customer: 2
  Nickname: charlemange
```

```
   Email: charle@hotmail.com
   Name: Charlie Charlemange
   Address: 123 Main Street
            Minneapolis, MN  55132
   Discount Rate: 0.05
   Is Non-Profit: false

Customer: 4
   Nickname: honey
   Email: honey@yahoo.com
   Name: Honey Princess
   Address: 3390 3rd Ave. North
            Minneapolis, MN  55133
   Discount Rate: 0.15
   Is Non-Profit: true
   Company Name: Princess For a Day
   Tax Exempt Id: 3390-honey-USMN

Should have found 1 Corporate customer below

Customer: 3
   Nickname: choo
   Email: choo@aol.com
   Name: Chester Sunshine
   Address: 431 Broadway
            Minneapolis, MN  55332
   Discount Rate: 0.1
   Is Non-Profit: false
   Company Name: Trains And More...

Should have found 1 non-volume Customer below

Customer: 1
   Nickname: shiney
   Email: shiney@yahoo.com
   .
   .
   .
```

Recall from the last example that the JLF frameworks perform heavy instrumentation during the course of their execution, and all that output will go to `System.err` by default. You can redirect that output to a file if you like so you can more easily see the results of the program as follows:

```
C:\BegJavaDB\Ch16\complexRecordingExample> java TestCustomerTracking 2> jlf.log
```

How It Works

To best understand how the application works, let's slowly introduce complexity to the application, starting by adding a one-to-one relationship, then a one-to-many relationship, and finally the object hierarchy. We wrap things up by walking through the test program, which shows the usefulness of the system we developed.

Adding a One-to-One Relationship

The `Customer` class looks and functions very similarly to the `Recording` class, with two exceptions. `Customer` objects have a one-to-one relationship to their `CustomerType`, and the `Customer` class is not only a functional concrete class, but is also a base class in a non-trivial class hierarchy. We will revisit the class to explore its class hierarchy in a following section. In this section, we will concentrate on the relationship between `Customer` and `CustomerType`. The implementation of the `Customer` class, omitting details on its hierarchy, is shown below. The `Customer` class looks very similar in nature to the `Recording` class in the last example, but with different attributes of course:

```
import java.util.*;

import org.jlf.log.*;
import org.jlf.dataMap.*;

/**
 * This class hold information for a customer so we can track their
 * recording purchases and interests.
 */
public class Customer extends DataMappedObject {

  // ------------------------------------------------------------------
  // Section 1: DataMappedObject descriptors
  // ------------------------------------------------------------------

  // Constants for attributes
  public static final String ID_ATTRIBUTE = "CUSTOMER_ID";
  public static final String CUSTOMER_TYPE_ID_ATTRIBUTE =
    "CUSTOMER_TYPE_ID";
  public static final String NICKNAME_ATTRIBUTE = "NICKNAME";
  public static final String EMAIL_ADDRESS_ATTRIBUTE = "EMAIL_ADDRESS";

  // Used for optimistic locking
  public static final String VERSION_ATTRIBUTE = "VERSION";

  // Constants for relationships
  public static final String CUSTOMER_TYPE_RELATIONSHIP = "customerType";
  public static final String CUSTOMER_TRACKED_RECORDINGS_RELATIONSHIP =
    "customerTrackedRecordings";

  /**
   * Sets up a table of attribute descriptors for the Customer
   * object.
   */
  protected Hashtable basicGetAttributeDescriptors() {

    // Always call the superclass!
    Hashtable descriptors = super.basicGetAttributeDescriptors();
    DataAttributeDescriptor descriptor;

    // Then add class-specific attributes
    descriptor = new DataAttributeDescriptor(ID_ATTRIBUTE,
                                          LongAttribute.class, true);
    descriptor.setIsKeyField(true);
```

```
    descriptors.put(ID_ATTRIBUTE, descriptor);

    descriptor = new DataAttributeDescriptor(CUSTOMER_TYPE_ID_ATTRIBUTE,
                                             LongAttribute.class, true);
    descriptors.put(CUSTOMER_TYPE_ID_ATTRIBUTE, descriptor);

    descriptor = new DataAttributeDescriptor(NICKNAME_ATTRIBUTE,
                                             StringAttribute.class, false);
    descriptor.setMaximumLength(20);
    descriptors.put(NICKNAME_ATTRIBUTE, descriptor);

    descriptor = new DataAttributeDescriptor(EMAIL_ADDRESS_ATTRIBUTE,
                                             StringAttribute.class, false);
    descriptor.setMaximumLength(50);
    descriptors.put(EMAIL_ADDRESS_ATTRIBUTE, descriptor);

    descriptor = new DataAttributeDescriptor(VERSION_ATTRIBUTE,
                                             LongAttribute.class, false);
    descriptors.put(VERSION_ATTRIBUTE, descriptor);

    return descriptors;
  }
```

The code above should look familiar to you. It prepares the class to be mapped to the database by extending the `DataMappedObject` class, and defining data attribute descriptors. The method immediately below is new to you. It creates relationship descriptors instead of attribute descriptors. If you recall from earlier in the chapter, data attribute descriptors are used to define simple Java types like `long`, `String`, and `Date` data. These types map directly to columns in a database table. Anything more complex than a simple type is a relationship between two `DataMappedObject` subclasses. The first relationship descriptor below relates the `Customer` class to the `CustomerTrackedRecording` class, and the second descriptor relates the `Customer` class to the `CustomerType` class:

```
  /**
   * Sets up the relationships from this object to its
   * customer, recording, and tracking type.
   */
  protected Hashtable basicGetRelationshipDescriptors() {

    // Always call the superclass!
    Hashtable descriptors = super.basicGetRelationshipDescriptors();

    // Add new relationships for this class
    descriptors
      .put(CUSTOMER_TRACKED_RECORDINGS_RELATIONSHIP,
           new RelationshipDescriptor(CUSTOMER_TRACKED_RECORDINGS_RELATIONSHIP,
                                      CustomerTrackedRecording.class));

    descriptors.put(CUSTOMER_TYPE_RELATIONSHIP,
                    new RelationshipDescriptor(CUSTOMER_TYPE_RELATIONSHIP,
                                               CustomerType.class));

    return descriptors;
```

```
}

/**
 * This class has a subclass hierarchy!
 */
protected boolean hasHierarchyTable() {
  return true;
}

/**
 * This method defines the attributes used in the hierarchy table.
 */
protected Vector basicGetHierarchyTableKeyAttributes() {
  Vector hierarchyTableAttributes =
    super.basicGetHierarchyTableKeyAttributes();

  hierarchyTableAttributes.addElement(CUSTOMER_TYPE_ID_ATTRIBUTE);
  return hierarchyTableAttributes;
}

/**
 * This method defines the hierarchy mappings for this
 * class and any subclasses.  Use
 * the <code>DataMappedObjectKey</code> as the key and a
 * <code>Class</code> object as the value.<p>
 *
 * At this level in the hierarchy, no hierarchy table members
 * are known.  Return an empty hash table that can be populated
 * by the subclass(es).
 */
protected Hashtable basicGetHierarchyTable() {
  Hashtable hierarchyTable = super.basicGetHierarchyTable();

  // Customer Type "Generic Customer" is this class.
  // Construct an object key as such.
  DataMappedObjectKey dmoKey =
    new DataMappedObjectKey(CUSTOMER_TYPE_ID_ATTRIBUTE,
                            CustomerType.GENERIC_CUSTOMER_ID);
  hierarchyTable.put(dmoKey, Customer.class);

  // Customer Type "Frequent Buyer" is subclass FrequentBuyer.
  // Construct an object key as such.
  dmoKey = new DataMappedObjectKey(CUSTOMER_TYPE_ID_ATTRIBUTE,
                                   CustomerType.FREQUENT_BUYER_ID);
  hierarchyTable.put(dmoKey, FrequentBuyer.class);

  // Customer Type "Corporate Customer" is subclass Corporation.
  // Construct an object key as such.
  dmoKey = new DataMappedObjectKey(CUSTOMER_TYPE_ID_ATTRIBUTE,
                                   CustomerType.CORPORATE_CUSTOMER_ID);
  hierarchyTable.put(dmoKey, Corporation.class);

  // Customer Type "Non-Profit Corp." is subclass NonProfitCorporation.
```

```
    // Construct an object key as such.
    dmoKey = new DataMappedObjectKey(CUSTOMER_TYPE_ID_ATTRIBUTE,
                                     CustomerType.NON_PROFIT_CUSTOMER_ID);
    hierarchyTable.put(dmoKey, NonProfitCorporation.class);

    return hierarchyTable;
  }

  /**
   * Default constructor must be public for the data mapping
   * framework!  However, when creating a new object, look to use
   * a paramterized constructor.
   */
  public Customer() {}

  // ---------------------------------------------------------------
  // Section 2: JavaBean methods
  // ---------------------------------------------------------------

  /**
   * Main constructor for the class.  Takes a nickname and
   * email address, categorizes the customer as a generic customer
   * type.
   */
  public Customer(String nickname, String emailAddress) {
    setNickname(nickname);
    setEmailAddress(emailAddress);

    setCustomerType(CustomerType.GENERIC_CUSTOMER);

    // Set initial object version to 1, increment every time the
    // object is saved
    setVersion(1);
  }

  /**
   * Retrieves the database id of the Customer.
   */
  public long getCustomerId() {
    return getLongAttribute(ID_ATTRIBUTE);
  }

  /**
   * Retrieves the customer's nickname.
   */
  public String getNickname() {
    return getStringAttribute(NICKNAME_ATTRIBUTE);
  }

  /**
   * Sets the customer's nickname.
   */
  public void setNickname(String nickname) {
    setStringAttribute(NICKNAME_ATTRIBUTE, nickname);
```

```
  }

  /**
   * Retrieves the customer's email address.
   */
  public String getEmailAddress() {
    return getStringAttribute(EMAIL_ADDRESS_ATTRIBUTE);
  }

  /**
   * Sets the customer's email address.
   */
  public void setEmailAddress(String emailAddress) {
    setStringAttribute(EMAIL_ADDRESS_ATTRIBUTE, emailAddress);
  }

  /**
   * Retrieves the version of the Customer object.
   */
  public long getVersion() {
    return getLongAttribute(VERSION_ATTRIBUTE);
  }

  /**
   * Sets the version of the Customer object.
   */
  private void setVersion(long version) {
    setLongAttribute(VERSION_ATTRIBUTE, version);
  }
```

The code above should look familiar to you as well. The `Recording` class in the previous example used JavaBean methods just like the ones above to get and set data attributes instead of instance variables.

The code below is new to you. For one-to-one relationships, you get the object involved in the relationship by using the `getRelatedObject()` method from the `DataMappedObject` superclass. To set the object involved in the relationship, you use `addRelatedObject()` as long as another object is not already involved in the relationship. If it is, you violate the one-to-one constraint you desire on the relationship, so the `setCustomerType()` method throws an error if you attempt to do so, and the `resetCustomerType()` method eliminates an existing `CustomerType` object from the relationship before it sets a new one.

```
  /**
   * Retrieves the Customer Type.
   */
  public CustomerType getCustomerType() {
    return (CustomerType) getRelatedObject(CUSTOMER_TYPE_RELATIONSHIP);
  }

  /**
   * Sets the Customer Type.
   */
  public void setCustomerType(CustomerType customerType) {
    if (getRelatedObject(CUSTOMER_TYPE_RELATIONSHIP) != null) {
```

```
      throw new DataMapError("Customer Type already set!" +
                             "Use resetCustomerType() method instead",
                             null, Log.ERROR_LEVEL);
    }     addRelatedObject(CUSTOMER_TYPE_RELATIONSHIP, customerType);
    setLongAttribute(CUSTOMER_TYPE_ID_ATTRIBUTE,
                     customerType.getCustomerTypeId());
  }

  /**
   * Resets the Customer Type once set.
   */
  protected void resetCustomerType(CustomerType customerType) {
    Vector customerTypes = getRelatedObjects(CUSTOMER_TYPE_RELATIONSHIP);

    customerTypes.removeAllElements();
    setCustomerType(customerType);
  }
```

The remaining methods of the class are finder methods for different customer search criteria, similar in nature to the finder methods in the `Recording` class.

```
  // --------------------------------------------------------------
  // Section 3: Methods to map the class to the database
  // --------------------------------------------------------------

  /**
   * Finds zero to many Customer objects that have a nickname
   * like the input string, returning them in a Vector.
   */
  public static Vector findByNickname(String likeNickname) {

    // Create a new customer and populate the nickname to look for
    Customer customer = new Customer();
    customer.setNickname(likeNickname);

    // Have the framework execute the query
    return customer.findManyBySearchCriteria("findByNickname");
  }

  /**
   * Finds zero to many Customer objects that have an email address
   * like the input string, returning them in a Vector.
   */
  public static Vector findByEmailAddress(String likeEmailAddress) {

    // Create a new customer and populate the email address
    // to look for
    Customer customer = new Customer();
    customer.setEmailAddress(likeEmailAddress);

    // Have the framework execute the query
    return customer.findManyBySearchCriteria("findByEmailAddress");
  }
```

```
   /**
    * Finds zero to many Customer objects that have customer tracking
    * records in the system that match the CustomerTrackedRecording
    * object with a Recording artist and title like the title and artist in
    * CustomerTrackedRecording's recording object, and a tracking type
    * like the one in the CustomerTrackedRecording's tracking type object.
    */
   public static Vector findByTrackingCriteria(CustomerTrackedRecording
customerTrackedRecording) {

     // Create a new customer and populate the title to look for
     Customer customer = new Customer();
     customer.addCustomerTrackedRecording(customerTrackedRecording);

     // Have the framework execute the query
     return customer.findManyBySearchCriteria("findByTrackingCriteria");
   }
```

The data mapping property file entries for the `Customer` class are shown below. All entries should be of similar nature to the `Recording` class:

```
##########################################################
# Customer class data mapping

# SQL statements to create a customer
Customer.criteriaKey.createStatement.sqlStatement=\
    insert into CUSTOMERS ( \
        CUSTOMER_ID, \
        CUSTOMER_TYPE_ID, \
        NICKNAME, \
        EMAIL_ADDRESS, \
        VERSION) \
    values ( \
        CUSTOMERS_SEQ.NEXTVAL, \
        {CUSTOMER_TYPE_ID}, \
        {NICKNAME}, \
        {EMAIL_ADDRESS}, \
        {VERSION} )

Customer.criteriaKey.createStatement2.sqlStatement=\
    select CUSTOMERS_SEQ.CURRVAL as CUSTOMER_ID \
      from DUAL
Customer.criteriaKey.createStatement2.isQuery=true

# SQL statement for a "findByPrimaryKey" search criteria
Customer.criteriaKey.findByPrimaryKey.sqlStatement=\
    select * \
      from CUSTOMERS \
     where CUSTOMER_ID = {CUSTOMER_ID}

# SQL statement for a "findByNickname" search criteria
Customer.criteriaKey.findByNickname.sqlStatement=\
```

```
    select * \
      from CUSTOMERS \
     where NICKNAME like {NICKNAME}

# SQL statement for a "findByEmailAddress" search criteria
Customer.criteriaKey.findByEmailAddress.sqlStatement=\
    select * \
      from CUSTOMERS \
     where EMAIL_ADDRESS like {EMAIL_ADDRESS}

# SQL statement to find customers by tracking criteria
Customer.criteriaKey.findByTrackingCriteria.sqlStatement=\
select distinct c.CUSTOMER_ID, \
       c.NICKNAME, c.EMAIL_ADDRESS, c.CUSTOMER_TYPE_ID, \
       c.NAME, c.ADDRESS, c.CITY, c.STATE, c.ZIPCODE, \
       c.COMPANY_NAME, c.TAX_EXEMPT_ID, c.VERSION \
  from RECORDINGS r, \
       CUSTOMER_TRACKED_RECORDINGS ctr, \
       CUSTOMERS c \
 where r.RECORDING_ARTIST like
{customerTrackedRecordings.recording.RECORDING_ARTIST} \
   and r.RECORDING_TITLE like
{customerTrackedRecordings.recording.RECORDING_TITLE} \
   and r.RECORDING_ID = ctr.RECORDING_ID \
   and ctr.TRACKING_TYPE_ID =
{customerTrackedRecordings.customerTrackingType.TRACKING_TYPE_ID} \
   and ctr.CUSTOMER_ID = c.CUSTOMER_ID

# SQL statement to optimistic lock a customer
Customer.criteriaKey.optimisticLockingStatement.sqlStatement=\
    select VERSION \
      from CUSTOMERS \
     where CUSTOMER_ID = {CUSTOMER_ID} \
       and VERSION = {VERSION}

# SQL statement to update a customer
Customer.criteriaKey.updateStatement.sqlStatement=\
    update CUSTOMERS set \
        NICKNAME = {NICKNAME}, \
        EMAIL_ADDRESS = {EMAIL_ADDRESS}, \
        VERSION = VERSION + 1 \
    where CUSTOMER_ID = {CUSTOMER_ID}

# Retrieves the reset VERSION
Customer.criteriaKey.updateStatement2.sqlStatement=\
    select VERSION \
      from CUSTOMERS \
     where CUSTOMER_ID = {CUSTOMER_ID}
Customer.criteriaKey.updateStatement2.isQuery=true

# SQL statement to delete a customer
Customer.criteriaKey.deleteStatement.sqlStatement=\
    delete from CUSTOMERS \
```

```
        where CUSTOMER_ID = {CUSTOMER_ID}

# Define relationship between Customer and CustomerTrackedRecording objects
Customer.relationship.customerTrackedRecordings.lazyReadRelationship=true
```

Now that we have a solid `Customer` class to relate to a `CustomerType`, let's move on to the `CustomerType` implementation below. It is a fairly simple class, as it has few attributes and no relationships (it is involved in a relationship with `Customer` objects, but the relationship is in one direction only, from a `Customer` to its `CustomerType`).

```
import java.util.*;

import org.jlf.log.*;
import org.jlf.dataMap.*;


/**
 * This class holds the different types of Customers in
 * the system.  One instance of this class corresponds to one
 * row in the CUSTOMER_TYPE table.
 */
public class CustomerType extends CachedObject {
```

First off, you will notice above that the `CustomerType` class extends `CachedObject` instead of `DataMappedObject`. Since the data this class maps to is so small in terms of the number of rows, and the data in the table is very static (that is, we only read it from Java), we tell the framework to cache instances of this object. So, the first time an object with a particular primary key is read, it is put into an object cache. The next time an object with the same primary key is read, instead of issuing a `SELECT` query to the database, the JLF data mapping framework retrieves it from the cache. In large applications, this type of optimization can save a great deal of time. Of course, the drawback of this optimization is that any time you update the table this class maps to, you must stop and restart the program to clear out the cache, otherwise you will be dealing with stale data. Commercial object-relational mapping frameworks have more sophisticated caching strategies to reduce the drawbacks of caching.

Sections 1 and 2 below should come as no surprise to you by now, they simply introduce attributes and JavaBean methods for those attributes:

```
  // ---------------------------------------------------------------
  // Section 1: DataMappedObject descriptors
  // ---------------------------------------------------------------

  // Constants for attributes
  public static final String ID_ATTRIBUTE = "CUSTOMER_TYPE_ID";
  public static final String DESCRIPTION_ATTRIBUTE = "DESCRIPTION";

  /**
   * Sets up a table of attribute descriptors for the
   * object.
   */
  protected Hashtable basicGetAttributeDescriptors() {
```

```
    // Always call the superclass!
    Hashtable descriptors = super.basicGetAttributeDescriptors();
    DataAttributeDescriptor descriptor;

    // Then add recording-specific attributes
    descriptor = new DataAttributeDescriptor(ID_ATTRIBUTE,
                                             LongAttribute.class, true);
    descriptor.setIsKeyField(true);
    descriptors.put(ID_ATTRIBUTE, descriptor);

    descriptor = new DataAttributeDescriptor(DESCRIPTION_ATTRIBUTE,
                                             StringAttribute.class, false);
    descriptor.setMaximumLength(50);
    descriptors.put(DESCRIPTION_ATTRIBUTE, descriptor);

    return descriptors;
  }

  /**
   * Default constructor must be public for the data mapping
   * framework!  However, when creating a new object, look to use
   * a paramterized constructor.
   */
  public CustomerType() {}

  // ---------------------------------------------------------------
  // Section 2: Java Bean methods
  // ---------------------------------------------------------------

  /**
   * Retrieves the database id of the object.
   */
  public long getCustomerTypeId() {
    return getLongAttribute(ID_ATTRIBUTE);
  }

  /**
   * Retrieves the description of the type.
   */
  public String getDescription() {
    return getStringAttribute(DESCRIPTION_ATTRIBUTE);
  }
```

About the only tricky part to this class is Section 3. For convenience in the `Customer` class hierarchy, the `CustomerType` class creates some public static final variables to hold each of the `CustomerType` objects in the database. The `Customer` class above specifically uses the `CustomerType.GENERIC_CUSTOMER` variable as the default `CustomerType`, and later, when we go into the `Customer` class hierarchy, we will see the remaining three variables:

```
  // ---------------------------------------------------------------
  // Section 3: Convenience accessors for types
  // ---------------------------------------------------------------
  public static final long GENERIC_CUSTOMER_ID = 1;
```

```
  /**
   * Type of customer that has no volume discount.
   */
  public static final CustomerType GENERIC_CUSTOMER =
    CustomerType.findById(GENERIC_CUSTOMER_ID);

  public static final long FREQUENT_BUYER_ID = 2;

  /**
   * Type of customer that has purchased enough
   * recordings to receive a volume discount.
   */
  public static final CustomerType FREQUENT_BUYER =
    CustomerType.findById(FREQUENT_BUYER_ID);

  public static final long CORPORATE_CUSTOMER_ID = 3;

  /**
   * Type of customer that is a corporation with a volume discount.
   */
  public static final CustomerType CORPORATE_CUSTOMER =
    CustomerType.findById(CORPORATE_CUSTOMER_ID);

  public static final long NON_PROFIT_CUSTOMER_ID = 4;

  /**
   * Type of customer that is a non-profit corporation
   * and has a volume discount.
   */
  public static final CustomerType NON_PROFIT_CUSTOMER =
    CustomerType.findById(NON_PROFIT_CUSTOMER_ID);

  /**
   * Tries to find a CustomerType by its primary key, its id.
   * Returns the CustomerType if found in the database, null if not.
   */
  public static CustomerType findById(long id) {
    CustomerType customerType = new CustomerType();
    customerType.setAttributeValue(ID_ATTRIBUTE, new Long(id));
    return (CustomerType) customerType.findByPrimaryKey();
  }

}
```

The `CustomerType` class requires only one entry in the data mapping property file; the entry to tell the data mapping framework how to read an object by its primary key. As we discussed earlier, because the data in the `CUSTOMER_TYPE` table is very static, we do not need to `CREATE`, `UPDATE`, or `DELETE` it. We load the data when we create the table and read it with the following mapping property:

```
############################################################
# CustomerType class data mapping

# SQL statement for a "findByPrimaryKey" search criteria
```

```
CustomerType.criteriaKey.findByPrimaryKey.sqlStatement=\
     select * \
       from CUSTOMER_TYPE \
      where CUSTOMER_TYPE_ID = {CUSTOMER_TYPE_ID}
```

Implementing a one-to-one relationship is straightforward with the JLF data mapping framework. You simply define a relationship descriptor, a couple of JavaBean methods, and `findByPrimaryKey` search criteria on the object on the other side of the relationship. The framework takes care of the rest for you by spanning the relationship using primary key data from the current object to populate a read on the related object. In simpler terms, when you read a `Customer` class, it finds its associated `CustomerType` and populates it from the cache. The framework does this by seeing that the `CUSTOMERS` table has a `CUSTOMER_TYPE_ID` column, which is the primary key in the `CustomerType` attribute descriptors, and also a parameter used in the `findByPrimaryKey` search criteria SQL statement.

Unfortunately, one-to-many relationships are not quite as easy to implement, especially if you want to implement them efficiently. We will attempt to use the JLF framework in the next section to implement a one-to-many relationship efficiently.

Adding a One-to-Many Relationship

Both `Customer` objects and `Recording` objects have one-to-many relationships to `CustomerTrackedRecording` objects. A customer can certainly purchase more than one recording (we sure hope they do), and different customers can purchase or show interest in the same recording. Any time you introduce a one-to-many relationship, you need to be concerned about performance. In the implementation below, we use two features of the data mapping framework that minimize the performance impact of one-to-many relationships, namely reading the relationship in the same query and lazy-reading the relationship at the time it is first referenced. Let's begin with the `CustomerTrackedRecording` class below, and then move on to the `Customer`, `Recording`, and `CustomerTrackingType` classes to which it is related.

CustomerTrackedRecording Class Implementation

Now, let's take a look at the `CustomerTrackedRecording` class:

```
import java.util.*;

import org.jlf.log.*;
import org.jlf.dataMap.*;

/**
 * This class is used to track Customer purchases
 * and interests in Recordings.  It maps to the
 * CUSTOMER_TRACKED_RECORDINGS table in the database and has
 * relationships to Customer, Recording, and CustomerTrackingType
 * objects.
 */
public class CustomerTrackedRecording extends DataMappedObject {

  // ----------------------------------------------------------------
  // Section 1: DataMappedObject descriptors
  // ----------------------------------------------------------------
```

```
// Constants for attributes
public static final String CUSTOMER_ID_ATTRIBUTE = "CUSTOMER_ID";
public static final String RECORDING_ID_ATTRIBUTE = "RECORDING_ID";
public static final String CUSTOMER_TRACKING_TYPE_ID_ATTRIBUTE =
  "TRACKING_TYPE_ID";

public static final String DATE_TRACKED_ATTRIBUTE = "DATE_TRACKED";

// Used for optimistic locking
public static final String VERSION_ATTRIBUTE = "VERSION";

// Relationships
public static final String CUSTOMER_RELATIONSHIP = "customer";
public static final String RECORDING_RELATIONSHIP = "recording";
public static final String CUSTOMER_TRACKING_TYPE_RELATIONSHIP =
  "customerTrackingType";

/**
 * Sets up a table of attribute descriptors for the
 * object.
 */
protected Hashtable basicGetAttributeDescriptors() {

  // Always call the superclass!
  Hashtable descriptors = super.basicGetAttributeDescriptors();
  DataAttributeDescriptor descriptor;

  // Then add class-specific attributes, starting with primary key
  descriptor = new DataAttributeDescriptor(CUSTOMER_ID_ATTRIBUTE,
                                           LongAttribute.class, true);
  descriptor.setIsKeyField(true);
  descriptors.put(CUSTOMER_ID_ATTRIBUTE, descriptor);

  descriptor = new DataAttributeDescriptor(RECORDING_ID_ATTRIBUTE,
                                           LongAttribute.class, true);
  descriptor.setIsKeyField(true);
  descriptors.put(RECORDING_ID_ATTRIBUTE, descriptor);

  descriptor =
    new DataAttributeDescriptor(CUSTOMER_TRACKING_TYPE_ID_ATTRIBUTE,
                                LongAttribute.class, true);
  descriptor.setIsKeyField(true);
  descriptors.put(CUSTOMER_TRACKING_TYPE_ID_ATTRIBUTE, descriptor);

  // Add non-key attributes
  descriptor = new DataAttributeDescriptor(DATE_TRACKED_ATTRIBUTE,
                                           DateAttribute.class, false);
  descriptors.put(DATE_TRACKED_ATTRIBUTE, descriptor);

  descriptor = new DataAttributeDescriptor(VERSION_ATTRIBUTE,
                                           LongAttribute.class, false);
  descriptors.put(VERSION_ATTRIBUTE, descriptor);
```

```
    return descriptors;
  }
```

The `CustomerTrackedRecording` object maps to the `CUSTOMER_TRACKED_RECORDINGS` table in the database. This table has a composite primary key composed of foreign keys to the `CUSTOMERS`, `RECORDINGS`, and `CUSTOMER_TRACKING_TYPE` tables. On the Java side, the `CustomerTrackedRecording` object has three primary key attribute descriptors above, and three one-to-one relationships below. The one-to-one relationships to the `Customer`, `Recording`, and `CustomerTrackingType` objects are all handled the same way the one-to-one relationship between `Customer` and `CustomerType` was handled in the last section, with one slight twist we will get into when we examine the data mapping property file.

```
  /**
   * Sets up the relationships from this object to its
   * customer, recording, and tracking type.
   */
  protected Hashtable basicGetRelationshipDescriptors() {

    // Always call the superclass!
    Hashtable descriptors = super.basicGetRelationshipDescriptors();

    // Add new relationships for this class
    descriptors.put(CUSTOMER_RELATIONSHIP,
                    new RelationshipDescriptor(CUSTOMER_RELATIONSHIP,
                                               Customer.class));

    descriptors.put(RECORDING_RELATIONSHIP,
                    new RelationshipDescriptor(RECORDING_RELATIONSHIP,
                                               Recording.class));

    descriptors
      .put(CUSTOMER_TRACKING_TYPE_RELATIONSHIP,
           new RelationshipDescriptor(CUSTOMER_TRACKING_TYPE_RELATIONSHIP,
                                      CustomerTrackingType.class));

    return descriptors;

  }
```

Now comes the tricky part. As we discussed before, the framework easily handles one-to-one relationships where foreign keys span the relationship in the database. Unfortunately, we do not have that situation in a one-to-many relationship, and we have two such relationships to worry about in the Java design model. `Customer` objects can have several `CustomerTrackedRecording` objects related to them, so a single-valued foreign key won't do the trick. The default implementation of the `DataMappedObject's` `findByRelationship` method assumes you are attempting to populate a one-to-one relationship using a single-valued foreign key. When that is not the case, you must override that method and provide your own implementation to populate the relationship when you span it. Since two different Java classes are related to a `CustomerTrackedRecording`, the `findByRelationship` method for this class must accommodate both possibilities, as shown next:

```
/**
 * Override to perform lazy-read relationships.
 */
public Vector findByRelationship(Relationship relationship,
                                 DataMapper dataMapper) {
  DataMappedObject dmo = relationship.getPrimaryObject();

  // If primary object is a Customer, find all objects
  // by Customer.
  if (dmo instanceof Customer) {

    // Look into the primary object for a customer.
    // Set the customer and execute find by customer criteria.
    Customer customer = (Customer) dmo;
    setCustomer(customer);

    return findManyBySearchCriteria("findByCustomer", dataMapper);
  } else {

    // Not a customer, must be a recording.  Give it a try
    // and execute find by recording criteria.
    Recording recording = (Recording) dmo;
    setRecording(recording);

    return findManyBySearchCriteria("findByRecording", dataMapper);
  }

}
```

The code above first checks to see which of the two classes that can be related to a `CustomerTrackedRecording` is currently being accessed. If it is a `Customer` class, then we populate our search object with that `Customer` object, and tell the framework to execute and return `CustomerTrackedRecording` objects according to the `"findByCustomer"` search criteria. If the class is a `Recording` class, then we populate our object with the `Recording` and use the `"findByRecording"` search criteria. This will become clearer when we go through the data mapping property file for this class in just a bit.

The remainder of the code in this class should look familiar to you, it looks pretty much like the other Java classes we have implemented that use data attributes and relationships from the JLF data mapping framework:

```
/**
 * Default constructor must be public for the data mapping
 * framework!  However, when creating a new object, look to use
 * a paramterized constructor.
 */
public CustomerTrackedRecording() {}

// ----------------------------------------------------------------
// Section 2: Java Bean methods
// ----------------------------------------------------------------

/**
 * Main constructor for the class.  Sets customer,
```

```
     * recording, and tracking type as input, and sets
     * the date tracked to the current date/time.
     */
    public CustomerTrackedRecording(Customer customer, Recording recording,
                                    CustomerTrackingType trackingType) {
      setCustomer(customer);
      setRecording(recording);
      setCustomerTrackingType(trackingType);
      setDateTracked(new Date());

      // Set initial object version to 1, increment every time the
      // object is saved
      setVersion(1);
    }

    /**
     * Retrieves the Recording.
     */
    public Recording getRecording() {
      return (Recording) getRelatedObject(RECORDING_RELATIONSHIP);
    }

    /**
     * Sets the Recording.
     */
    public void setRecording(Recording recording) {
      if (getRelatedObject(RECORDING_RELATIONSHIP) != null) {
        throw new DataMapError("Cannot reset a Recording once set!", null,
                               Log.ERROR_LEVEL);
      }
      addRelatedObject(RECORDING_RELATIONSHIP, recording);
    }

    /**
     * Retrieves the Customer.
     */
    public Customer getCustomer() {
      return (Customer) getRelatedObject(CUSTOMER_RELATIONSHIP);
    }

    /**
     * Sets the Customer.
     */
    public void setCustomer(Customer customer) {
      if (getRelatedObject(CUSTOMER_RELATIONSHIP) != null) {
        throw new DataMapError("Cannot reset a Customer once set!", null,
                               Log.ERROR_LEVEL);
      }
      addRelatedObject(CUSTOMER_RELATIONSHIP, customer);
    }

    /**
     * Retrieves the CustomerTrackingType.
```

```
     */
    public CustomerTrackingType getCustomerTrackingType() {
      return (CustomerTrackingType)
  getRelatedObject(CUSTOMER_TRACKING_TYPE_RELATIONSHIP);
    }

    /**
     * Sets the CustomerTrackingType.
     */
    public void setCustomerTrackingType(CustomerTrackingType customerTrackingType) {
      if (getRelatedObject(CUSTOMER_TRACKING_TYPE_RELATIONSHIP) != null) {
        throw new DataMapError("Cannot reset a CustomerTrackingType once set!",
                               null, Log.ERROR_LEVEL);
      }
      addRelatedObject(CUSTOMER_TRACKING_TYPE_RELATIONSHIP,
                       customerTrackingType);
    }

    /**
     * Retrieves the date this relationship was tracked.
     */
    public Date getDateTracked() {
      return (Date) getAttributeValue(DATE_TRACKED_ATTRIBUTE);
    }

    /**
     * Sets the date this relationship was tracked.
     */
    public void setDateTracked(Date dateTracked) {
      setAttributeValue(DATE_TRACKED_ATTRIBUTE, dateTracked);
    }

    /**
     * Retrieves the version of the Recording object.
     */
    public long getVersion() {
      return getLongAttribute(VERSION_ATTRIBUTE);
    }

    /**
     * Sets the version of the Recording object.
     */
    private void setVersion(long version) {
      setLongAttribute(VERSION_ATTRIBUTE, version);
    }

  }
```

The data mapping properties for the `CustomerTrackedRecording` object is shown below. The `CREATE`, `UPDATE`, and `DELETE` statements should look familiar to you, but you may scratch your head a bit for the read statements, so we will go through that in more detail:

```
###########################################################
# CustomerTrackedRecording class data mapping

# SQL statements to create a tracking relationship
CustomerTrackedRecording.criteriaKey.createStatement.sqlStatement=\
    insert into CUSTOMER_TRACKED_RECORDINGS ( \
        CUSTOMER_ID, \
        RECORDING_ID, \
        TRACKING_TYPE_ID, \
        DATE_TRACKED, \
        VERSION) \
    values ( \
        {customer.CUSTOMER_ID}, \
        {recording.RECORDING_ID}, \
        {customerTrackingType.TRACKING_TYPE_ID}, \
        to_date({DATE_TRACKED}, 'MM/DD/YYYY HH24:MI:SS'), \
        {VERSION} )

CustomerTrackedRecording.criteriaKey.createStatement2.sqlStatement=\
    select CUSTOMER_ID, RECORDING_ID, TRACKING_TYPE_ID \
      from CUSTOMER_TRACKED_RECORDINGS \
     where CUSTOMER_ID = {customer.CUSTOMER_ID} \
       and RECORDING_ID = {recording.RECORDING_ID} \
       and TRACKING_TYPE_ID = {customerTrackingType.TRACKING_TYPE_ID}

CustomerTrackedRecording.criteriaKey.createStatement2.isQuery=true

# SQL statement for a "findByCustomer" search criteria
CustomerTrackedRecording.criteriaKey.findByCustomer.sqlStatement=\
    select ctr.RECORDING_ID, ctr.TRACKING_TYPE_ID, ctr.CUSTOMER_ID, \
           ctr.DATE_TRACKED, ctr.VERSION, \
           c.NICKNAME, c.EMAIL_ADDRESS, c.CUSTOMER_TYPE_ID, \
           c.NAME, c.ADDRESS, c.CITY, c.STATE, c.ZIPCODE, \
           c.COMPANY_NAME, c.TAX_EXEMPT_ID, c.VERSION as CUST_VERSION, \
           r.RECORDING_TITLE, r.RECORDING_ARTIST, r.CATALOG_NUMBER, \
           r.LIST_PRICE, r.VERSION as REC_VERSION \
      from CUSTOMER_TRACKED_RECORDINGS ctr, \
           CUSTOMERS c, \
           RECORDINGS r \
     where ctr.CUSTOMER_ID = {customer.CUSTOMER_ID} \
       and r.RECORDING_ID = ctr.RECORDING_ID \
       and c.CUSTOMER_ID = ctr.CUSTOMER_ID
```

The `findByCustomer` (above) and `findByRecording` (below) `SELECT` statements do a lot more than simply read the data in the `CUSTOMER_TRACKED_RECORDING` table – and for good reason. We are going to take advantage of a JLF data mapping feature called `readRelationshipInSameQuery`. There are two ways to efficiently span a one-to-one relationship. The first way we already explored, reading the relationship object from a cache. That works fine for the `CustomerType` and `CustomerTrackingType` classes because the data those classes map to in the database is very small and static. Not so for `Customer` and `Recording` classes. We hope to have thousands of recordings and perhaps even millions of customers, so the data in the tables is not small. Customer and recording data certainly isn't static either; we plan to `CREATE` and `UPDATE` `Customers` and `Recordings` quite often. So, caching the data probably isn't the best idea, but thankfully, it is not the only way to efficiently span the relationship.

The second way to populate the data on the other side of the relationship is to read it in the same query as the primary object. So when we read a `CustomerTrackedRecording` object, we also read its related `Customer` and `Recording` objects. We do not read the `CustomerTrackingType` object, as that object is likely to be already cached, and we would be transferring redundant data from the database. Caching the data is always going to be more efficient, but often not applicable. When caching is not a good fit for your design, you may be able to read the relationship in the same query as the primary object.

So far, we have explained the need for a read of the `RECORDINGS` and `CUSTOMERS` table, but we did not discuss why we alias the `VERSION` columns in those tables. Since we use the same column name in all three tables, we must somehow tell the data mapping framework which `VERSION` column goes to which class. We do this easily by aliasing the column in `SELECT` statement using `c.VERSION as CUST_VERSION` and `r.VERSION as REC_VERSION`. The columns are un-aliased when we define relationship mapping properties in a moment:

```
# SQL statement for a "findByRecording" search criteria
CustomerTrackedRecording.criteriaKey.findByRecording.sqlStatement=\
    select ctr.RECORDING_ID, ctr.TRACKING_TYPE_ID, ctr.CUSTOMER_ID, \
           ctr.DATE_TRACKED, ctr.VERSION, \
           c.NICKNAME, c.EMAIL_ADDRESS, c.CUSTOMER_TYPE_ID, \
           c.NAME, c.ADDRESS, c.CITY, c.STATE, c.ZIPCODE, \
           c.COMPANY_NAME, c.TAX_EXEMPT_ID, c.VERSION as CUST_VERSION, \
           r.RECORDING_TITLE, r.RECORDING_ARTIST, r.CATALOG_NUMBER, \
           r.LIST_PRICE, r.VERSION as REC_VERSION \
      from CUSTOMER_TRACKED_RECORDINGS ctr, \
           CUSTOMERS c, \
           RECORDINGS r \
     where ctr.RECORDING_ID = {recording.RECORDING_ID} \
       and r.RECORDING_ID = ctr.RECORDING_ID \
       and c.CUSTOMER_ID = ctr.CUSTOMER_ID

# SQL statement to optimistic lock a tracking relationship
CustomerTrackedRecording.criteriaKey.optimisticLockingStatement.sqlStatement=\
    select VERSION \
      from CUSTOMER_TRACKED_RECORDINGS \
     where CUSTOMER_ID = {CUSTOMER_ID} \
       and RECORDING_ID = {RECORDING_ID} \
       and TRACKING_TYPE_ID = {TRACKING_TYPE_ID} \
       and VERSION = {VERSION}

# SQL statement to update a tracking relationship
CustomerTrackedRecording.criteriaKey.updateStatement.sqlStatement=\
    update CUSTOMER_TRACKED_RECORDINGS set \
        DATE_TRACKED = to_date({DATE_TRACKED}, 'MM/DD/YYYY HH24:MI:SS'), \
        VERSION = VERSION + 1 \
    where CUSTOMER_ID = {CUSTOMER_ID} \
      and RECORDING_ID = {RECORDING_ID} \
      and TRACKING_TYPE_ID = {TRACKING_TYPE_ID}

# Retrieves the reset VERSION
CustomerTrackedRecording.criteriaKey.updateStatement2.sqlStatement=\
    select VERSION \
      from CUSTOMER_TRACKED_RECORDINGS \
    where CUSTOMER_ID = {CUSTOMER_ID} \
      and RECORDING_ID = {RECORDING_ID} \
```

```
      and TRACKING_TYPE_ID = {TRACKING_TYPE_ID}
CustomerTrackedRecording.criteriaKey.updateStatement2.isQuery=true

# SQL statement to delete a tracking relationship
CustomerTrackedRecording.criteriaKey.deleteStatement.sqlStatement=\
    delete from CUSTOMER_TRACKED_RECORDINGS \
    where CUSTOMER_ID = {CUSTOMER_ID} \
      and RECORDING_ID = {RECORDING_ID} \
      and TRACKING_TYPE_ID = {TRACKING_TYPE_ID}
```

The optimistic locking query, UPDATE, and DELETE statements should look familiar, but the relationship mappings below are new. The first property tells the framework to read the relationship between a CustomerTrackedRecording object and its Customer object in the same query as reading the CustomerTrackedRecording primary object. Likewise for the second property in its relationship to a Recording object. The third key un-aliases the REC_VERSION column for the Recording object, and likewise for the fourth key to un-alias the CUST_VERSION column for the Customer object. Therefore, when the data mapping framework reads a CustomerTrackedRecording object, it tries to populate a Recording object from the same SELECT statement, mapping the REC_VERSION column to the VERSION attribute in the Recording object rather than the CustomerTrackedRecording or Customer object. The SELECT statements in the findByRecording and findByCustomer search criteria above read all attributes of not only the CustomerTrackedRecording object, but also the Customer and Recording objects as well.

```
# Define relationships to CustomerTrackedRecording objects
CustomerTrackedRecording.relationship.customer.readRelationshipInSameQuery=true
CustomerTrackedRecording.relationship.recording.readRelationshipInSameQuery=true

CustomerTrackedRecording.relationship.recording.attributeAlias.VERSION=REC_VERSION
CustomerTrackedRecording.relationship.customer.attributeAlias.VERSION=CUST_VERSION
```

So far, we still haven't implemented the one-to-many relationship. We have the basic building blocks in the form of the CustomerTrackedRecording class, and now we need to enhance the Customer and Recording classes to implement a one-to-many relationship in each of those classes.

Customer Class Implementation Enhancement

To enhance the Customer class to implement the one-to-many relationship between a Customer and any number of CustomerTrackedRecording objects, we simply tell the framework to lazy-read the relationship for efficiency. Below is the data mapping property file entry:

```
# Define relationship between Customer and CustomerTrackedRecording objects
Customer.relationship.customerTrackedRecordings.lazyReadRelationship=true
```

By default, at the time an object is read from the database, the JLF framework attempts to populate any, and all, attributes and relationships defined in the object. Typically, this involves a separate read of the database for each relationship involved. This is not efficient, though. For example, say we query the database for all Customer objects that have an interest in a very popular recording. That query returns 100 customers in one query. All of the Customer attributes are in that same query, so we do not need to execute any more queries to populate the Customer object's attributes. Now for each of those customers, we have a CustomerType relationship and a CustomerTrackedRecording relationship. If we do not do any optimizations, it would require 100 separate queries of the database, one query for each Customer object, to populate the one CustomerType object it is related to, and another 100 queries to populate the (possibly many) CustomerTrackedRecording objects it is related to.

Since we cache the `CustomerType` object, that relationship will rarely be read from the database. Unfortunately, the `CustomerTrackedRecording` object is not a good candidate to be cached, as there are many of these in the database and we frequently create new ones. The next optimization we learned is reading the relationship in the same query. This is a fine optimization and we could certainly take advantage of it, but let's take one more moment to examine the scenario. When we read large numbers of `Customer` objects from the database, are we always concerned with the `CustomerTrackedRecordings` that are related to it? That answer is definitely no. Often, we just want to know something like the customer's nickname and e-mail address so we can send out an e-mail to them, and notify them that a new recording has come available, which they may be interested in. So instead of going to the trouble to read all that data from the database in the same query, taking time to populate data we may not be interested in at the moment, we can tell the data mapping framework to lazy-read it, or read it only when the code spans the relationship (in our case, uses the `getCustomerTrackedRecordings()` method).

Recording Class Implementation Enhancement

The `Recording` class is enhanced in the same way as the `Customer` class, using a lazy-read for the one-to-many relationship as shown in the property file entry below.

```
# Define relationship between Recording and CustomerTrackedRecording objects
Recording.relationship.customerTrackedRecordings.lazyReadRelationship=true
```

We have now implemented the one-to-many relationships in the system, but haven't discussed the `CustomerTrackingType` class yet. For `CustomerTrackedRecording` to function, it needs this class to record the type of tracking record it creates (in our case, either customer interests or customer purchases).

CustomerTrackingType Class Implementation

The `CustomerTrackingType` class is virtually identical to `CustomerType` in nature. It maps to a very static database table so it can be cached. For completeness, its implementation is below:

```
import java.util.*;

import org.jlf.log.*;
import org.jlf.dataMap.*;

/**
 * This class holds the different types of CustomerTrackedRecording
 * relationships in the system.  One instance of this class
 * corresponds to one row in the CUSTOMER_TRACKING_TYPE table.
 */
public class CustomerTrackingType extends CachedObject {

  // ------------------------------------------------------------
  // Section 1: DataMappedObject descriptors
  // ------------------------------------------------------------

  // Constants for attributes
  public static final String ID_ATTRIBUTE = "TRACKING_TYPE_ID";
  public static final String DESCRIPTION_ATTRIBUTE = "DESCRIPTION";

  /**
```

```
   * Sets up a table of attribute descriptors for the
   * object.
   */
  protected Hashtable basicGetAttributeDescriptors() {

    // Always call the superclass!
    Hashtable descriptors = super.basicGetAttributeDescriptors();
    DataAttributeDescriptor descriptor;

    // Then add recording-specific attributes
    descriptor = new DataAttributeDescriptor(ID_ATTRIBUTE,
                                            LongAttribute.class, true);
    descriptor.setIsKeyField(true);
    descriptors.put(ID_ATTRIBUTE, descriptor);

    descriptor = new DataAttributeDescriptor(DESCRIPTION_ATTRIBUTE,
                                            StringAttribute.class, false);
    descriptor.setMaximumLength(50);
    descriptors.put(DESCRIPTION_ATTRIBUTE, descriptor);

    return descriptors;
  }

  /**
   * Default constructor must be public for the data mapping
   * framework!  However, when creating a new object, look to use
   * a paramterized constructor.
   */
  public CustomerTrackingType() {}

  // ----------------------------------------------------------------
  // Section 2: Java Bean methods
  // ----------------------------------------------------------------

  /**
   * Retrieves the database id of the object.
   */
  public long getCustomerTrackingTypeId() {
    return getLongAttribute(ID_ATTRIBUTE);
  }

  /**
   * Retrieves the description of the type.
   */
  public String getDescription() {
    return getStringAttribute(DESCRIPTION_ATTRIBUTE);
  }

  // ----------------------------------------------------------------
  // Section 3: Convenience accessors for types
  // ----------------------------------------------------------------
  public static final long CUSTOMER_PURCHASE_ID = 1;

  /**
```

```
     * This is a convenience accessor for tracking customer
     * purchases of recordings.
     */
    public static final CustomerTrackingType CUSTOMER_PURCHASE =
      CustomerTrackingType.findById(CUSTOMER_PURCHASE_ID);

    public static final long CUSTOMER_INTEREST_ID = 2;

    /**
     * This is a convenience accessor for tracking customer
     * interests of recordings.
     */
    public static final CustomerTrackingType CUSTOMER_INTEREST =
      CustomerTrackingType.findById(CUSTOMER_INTEREST_ID);

    /**
     * Tries to find a CustomerTrackingType by its primary key, its id.
     * Returns the CustomerTrackingType if found in the database, null if not.
     */
    public static CustomerTrackingType findById(long id) {
      CustomerTrackingType customerTrackingType = new CustomerTrackingType();
      customerTrackingType.setAttributeValue(ID_ATTRIBUTE, new Long(id));
      return (CustomerTrackingType) customerTrackingType.findByPrimaryKey();
    }

  }
```

The Java implementation above requires the `findByPrimaryKey` search criteria to span the relationship between a `CustomerTrackedRecording` and its `CustomerTrackingType`. The data mapping property file entry is shown below:

```
##########################################################
# CustomerTrackingType class data mapping

# SQL statement for a "findByPrimaryKey" search criteria
CustomerTrackingType.criteriaKey.findByPrimaryKey.sqlStatement=\
    select * \
      from CUSTOMER_TRACKING_TYPE \
     where TRACKING_TYPE_ID = {TRACKING_TYPE_ID}
```

We have now discussed the implementation of simple data attribute mapping, one-to-one relationship mapping, one-to-many relationship mapping, and three different optimizations (object caching, reading relationships in the same query, and lazy-reading relationships) that can be used to minimize or eliminate executing additional SQL statements when spanning relationships. We have covered all the complexities of the recording database problem of the last chapter except for mapping the `Customer` class hierarchy, which comes next.

Adding an Object Hierarchy

When we discussed the implementation of the `Customer` class above, we deliberately left out the complexity of its inheritance hierarchy. This is a luxury you cannot afford, unless you use a very good object-relational mapping framework. With JLF, you can create, enhance, or destroy inheritance hierarchies with ease. To add an inheritance hierarchy, you need to define three methods as shown overleaf:

```
/**
 * This class has a subclass hierarchy!
 */
protected boolean hasHierarchyTable() {
  return true;
}
```

The first method, `hasHierarchyTable()`, simply tells the framework that there is indeed an inheritance hierarchy the framework needs to worry about when instantiating objects of this type. The default implementation of this method in `DataMappedObject` returns False so the framework can map objects that do not have a hierarchy more efficiently.

```
/**
 * This method defines the attributes used in the hierarchy table.
 */
protected Vector basicGetHierarchyTableKeyAttributes() {
  Vector hierarchyTableAttributes =
    super.basicGetHierarchyTableKeyAttributes();

  hierarchyTableAttributes.addElement(CUSTOMER_TYPE_ID_ATTRIBUTE);
  return hierarchyTableAttributes;
}
```

The `basicGetHierarchyTableKeyAttributes()` method tells the framework what attributes serve as the key to determining what class of object to create. In our case, the `CUSTOMER_TYPE_ID` column in the database tells us what type of customer we are dealing with.

```
/**
 * This method defines the hierarchy mappings for this
 * class and any subclasses.  Use
 * the <code>DataMappedObjectKey</code> as the key and a
 * <code>Class</code> object as the value.<p>
 *
 * At this level in the hierarchy, no hierarchy table members
 * are known.  Return an empty hash table that can be populated
 * by the subclass(es).
 */
protected Hashtable basicGetHierarchyTable() {
  Hashtable hierarchyTable = super.basicGetHierarchyTable();

  // Customer Type "Generic Customer" is this class.
  // Construct an object key as such.
  DataMappedObjectKey dmoKey =
    new DataMappedObjectKey(CUSTOMER_TYPE_ID_ATTRIBUTE,
                            CustomerType.GENERIC_CUSTOMER_ID);
  hierarchyTable.put(dmoKey, Customer.class);

  // Customer Type "Frequent Buyer" is subclass FrequentBuyer.
  // Construct an object key as such.
  dmoKey = new DataMappedObjectKey(CUSTOMER_TYPE_ID_ATTRIBUTE,
                                   CustomerType.FREQUENT_BUYER_ID);
  hierarchyTable.put(dmoKey, FrequentBuyer.class);
```

```
    // Customer Type "Corporate Customer" is subclass Corporation.
    // Construct an object key as such.
    dmoKey = new DataMappedObjectKey(CUSTOMER_TYPE_ID_ATTRIBUTE,
                                     CustomerType.CORPORATE_CUSTOMER_ID);
    hierarchyTable.put(dmoKey, Corporation.class);

    // Customer Type "Non-Profit Corp." is subclass NonProfitCorporation.
    // Construct an object key as such.
    dmoKey = new DataMappedObjectKey(CUSTOMER_TYPE_ID_ATTRIBUTE,
                                     CustomerType.NON_PROFIT_CUSTOMER_ID);
    hierarchyTable.put(dmoKey, NonProfitCorporation.class);

    return hierarchyTable;
  }
```

The last method to define is `basicGetHierarchyTable()`. This method adds entries into a hash table to tell the framework when the `CUSTOMER_TYPE_ID` column has the value `GENERIC_CUSTOMER_ID (1)`, to instantiate a `Customer` object. When it has the value `FREQUENT_BUYER_ID (2)`, to instantiate a `FrequentBuyer` object, and so on.

Now for the magic; once the framework knows this information, any time you read a `Customer` object from the database, as long as you remember to read the `CUSTOMER_TYPE_ID` column, it will instantiate the right object class. Say you read 100 customers from the database to satisfy a query such as finding all customers who bought a particular 'Pearl Jam' recording. Some of the customers are just plain `Customer` objects, some are `FrequentBuyers`, some `Corporations`, and others `NonProfitCorporations`. They are all intermixed in the resultset from the query, but this doees not matter to the framework. Each row will have a `CUSTOMER_TYPE_ID` value and the framework uses that to instantiate the correct class for you.

To round out the design, we show implementations of the `VolumeCustomer`, `FrequentBuyer`, `Corporation`, and `NonProfitCorporation` classes below. It may be helpful to you to refer back to the previous chapter for a detailed design discussion of this class hierarchy as you walk through the code.

VolumeCustomer Class Implementation

If you recall the design from the previous chapter, the `VolumeCustomer` class holds additional information for customers we give a volume discount to, in order to minimize fraud. The source code for the `VolumeCustomer` class follows:

```
import java.util.*;

import org.jlf.log.*;
import org.jlf.dataMap.*;

/**
 * This class is an abstract class used to hold
 * information for a volume customer
 * to give discounts in reward for their loyalty.
 */
public abstract class VolumeCustomer extends Customer {
```

```
// -----------------------------------------------------------------
// Section 1: DataMappedObject descriptors
// -----------------------------------------------------------------

// Constants for attributes
public static final String NAME_ATTRIBUTE = "NAME";
public static final String ADDRESS_ATTRIBUTE = "ADDRESS";
public static final String CITY_ATTRIBUTE = "CITY";
public static final String STATE_ATTRIBUTE = "STATE";
public static final String ZIP_CODE_ATTRIBUTE = "ZIPCODE";

/**
 * Adds attribute descriptors for the current class.
 */
protected Hashtable basicGetAttributeDescriptors() {

  // Always call the superclass!
  Hashtable descriptors = super.basicGetAttributeDescriptors();
  DataAttributeDescriptor descriptor;

  // Then add class-specific attributes
  descriptor = new DataAttributeDescriptor(NAME_ATTRIBUTE,
                                           StringAttribute.class, false);
  descriptor.setMaximumLength(50);
  descriptors.put(NAME_ATTRIBUTE, descriptor);

  descriptor = new DataAttributeDescriptor(ADDRESS_ATTRIBUTE,
                                           StringAttribute.class, true);
  descriptor.setMaximumLength(50);
  descriptors.put(ADDRESS_ATTRIBUTE, descriptor);

  descriptor = new DataAttributeDescriptor(CITY_ATTRIBUTE,
                                           StringAttribute.class, true);
  descriptor.setMaximumLength(20);
  descriptors.put(CITY_ATTRIBUTE, descriptor);

  descriptor = new DataAttributeDescriptor(STATE_ATTRIBUTE,
                                           StringAttribute.class, true);
  descriptor.setMaximumLength(2);
  descriptors.put(STATE_ATTRIBUTE, descriptor);

  descriptor = new DataAttributeDescriptor(ZIP_CODE_ATTRIBUTE,
                                           StringAttribute.class, true);
  descriptor.setMaximumLength(10);
  descriptors.put(ZIP_CODE_ATTRIBUTE, descriptor);

  return descriptors;
}

/**
 * Default constructor must be public for the data mapping
 * framework! However, when creating a new object, look to use
 * a paramterized constructor.
```

```
   */
  public VolumeCustomer() {}

  // ----------------------------------------------------------------
  // Section 2: Java Bean methods
  // ----------------------------------------------------------------

  /**
   * Main constructor for the class.  Populates all
   * attributes of the class.
   */
  public VolumeCustomer(String nickname, String emailAddress, String name,
                        String address, String city, String state,
                        String zipcode) {
    super(nickname, emailAddress);
    setName(name);
    setAddress(address);
    setCity(city);
    setState(state);
    setZipCode(zipcode);
  }

  /**
   * Retrieves the Customer's name.
   */
  public String getName() {
    return getStringAttribute(NAME_ATTRIBUTE);
  }

  /**
   * Sets the Customer's name.
   */
  public void setName(String name) {
    setStringAttribute(NAME_ATTRIBUTE, name);
  }

  /**
   * Retrieves the Customer's address.
   */
  public String getAddress() {
    return getStringAttribute(ADDRESS_ATTRIBUTE);
  }

  /**
   * Sets the Customer's address.
   */
  public void setAddress(String address) {
    setStringAttribute(ADDRESS_ATTRIBUTE, address);
  }

  /**
   * Retrieves the Customer's city.
   */
  public String getCity() {
```

```
    return getStringAttribute(CITY_ATTRIBUTE);
  }

  /**
   * Sets the Customer's city.
   */
  public void setCity(String city) {
    setStringAttribute(CITY_ATTRIBUTE, city);
  }

  /**
   * Retrieves the Customer's state.
   */
  public String getState() {
    return getStringAttribute(STATE_ATTRIBUTE);
  }

  /**
   * Sets the Customer's state.
   */
  public void setState(String state) {
    setStringAttribute(STATE_ATTRIBUTE, state);
  }

  /**
   * Retrieves the Customer's zip code.
   */
  public String getZipCode() {
    return getStringAttribute(ZIP_CODE_ATTRIBUTE);
  }

  /**
   * Sets the Customer's zip code.
   */
  public void setZipCode(String zipCode) {
    setStringAttribute(ZIP_CODE_ATTRIBUTE, zipCode);
  }

  /**
   * Add to superclass to output additional
   * volume customer attributes
   */
  public String toString() {
    return super.toString() + "\n  Name: " + getName() + "\n  Address: "
           + getAddress() + "\n            " + getCity() + ", " + getState()
           + "  " + getZipCode() + "\n  Discount Rate: " + discountRate()
           + "\n  Is Non-Profit: " + isNonProfit();
  }

  // ---------------------------------------------------------------
  // Section 3: Business logic methods
  // ---------------------------------------------------------------

  /**
```

```
   * Return the amount of discount applicable to the volume
   * customer.  The value returned is multiplied by the purchase
   * price to determine discount.
   */
  public abstract double discountRate();

  /**
   * Tell if the customer is a non-profit corporation.
   */
  public boolean isNonProfit() {
    return false;
  }

}
```

The VolumeCustomer class is an abstract class, so it has no data mapping property file keys to worry about. The remaining classes in this section are concrete and have both Java implementations and corresponding data mapping property file entries.

FrequentBuyer Class Implementation

The FrequentBuyer class represents a volume customer who has purchased enough recordings to entitle them to a 5 percent discount:

```
import java.util.*;

import org.jlf.log.*;
import org.jlf.dataMap.*;

/**
 * This class hold information for a customer who is a
 * frequent buyer, to give discounts in reward for their loyalty.
 */
public class FrequentBuyer extends VolumeCustomer {

  /**
   * Main constructor for the class.  Populates all
   * attributes of the class and sets the type accordingly.
   */
  public FrequentBuyer(String nickname, String emailAddress, String name,
                       String address, String city, String state,
                       String zipcode) {
    super(nickname, emailAddress, name, address, city, state, zipcode);
    resetCustomerType(CustomerType.FREQUENT_BUYER);
  }

  /**
   * Default constructor must be public for the data mapping
   * framework!  However, when creating a new object, look to use
   * a paramterized constructor.
   */
  public FrequentBuyer() {}

  /**
```

```
    * Return the amount of discount applicable to the volume
    * customer.  Give a 5% discount to all frequent buyers.
    */
   public double discountRate() {
     return 0.05;
   }

 }
```

The `FrequentBuyer` class above is mapped to the database as follows:

```
###########################################################
# FrequentBuyer class data mapping

# SQL statements to create a frequent buyer
FrequentBuyer.criteriaKey.createStatement.sqlStatement=\
    insert into CUSTOMERS ( \
        CUSTOMER_ID, \
        CUSTOMER_TYPE_ID, \
        NICKNAME, \
        EMAIL_ADDRESS, \
        NAME, \
        ADDRESS, \
        CITY, \
        STATE, \
        ZIPCODE, \
        VERSION) \
    values ( \
        CUSTOMERS_SEQ.NEXTVAL, \
        {CUSTOMER_TYPE_ID}, \
        {NICKNAME}, \
        {EMAIL_ADDRESS}, \
        {NAME}, \
        {ADDRESS}, \
        {CITY}, \
        {STATE}, \
        {ZIPCODE}, \
        {VERSION} )

FrequentBuyer.criteriaKey.createStatement2.sqlStatement=\
    select CUSTOMERS_SEQ.CURRVAL as CUSTOMER_ID \
      from DUAL
FrequentBuyer.criteriaKey.createStatement2.isQuery=true

# SQL statement for a "findByPrimaryKey" search criteria
FrequentBuyer.criteriaKey.findByPrimaryKey.sqlStatement=\
    select * \
      from CUSTOMERS \
     where CUSTOMER_ID = {CUSTOMER_ID}

# SQL statement to optimistic lock a frequent buyer
FrequentBuyer.criteriaKey.optimisticLockingStatement.sqlStatement=\
    select VERSION \
      from CUSTOMERS \
```

```
     where CUSTOMER_ID = {CUSTOMER_ID} \
       and VERSION = {VERSION}

# SQL statement to update a frequent buyer
FrequentBuyer.criteriaKey.updateStatement.sqlStatement=\
    update CUSTOMERS set \
        NICKNAME = {NICKNAME}, \
        EMAIL_ADDRESS = {EMAIL_ADDRESS}, \
        NAME = {NAME}, \
        ADDRESS = {ADDRESS}, \
        CITY = {CITY}, \
        STATE = {STATE}, \
        ZIPCODE = {ZIPCODE}, \
        VERSION = VERSION + 1 \
    where CUSTOMER_ID = {CUSTOMER_ID}

# Retrieves the reset VERSION
FrequentBuyer.criteriaKey.updateStatement2.sqlStatement=\
    select VERSION \
      from CUSTOMERS \
     where CUSTOMER_ID = {CUSTOMER_ID}
FrequentBuyer.criteriaKey.updateStatement2.isQuery=true

# SQL statement to delete a frequent buyer
FrequentBuyer.criteriaKey.deleteStatement.sqlStatement=\
    delete from CUSTOMERS \
          where CUSTOMER_ID = {CUSTOMER_ID}

# Define relationship between FrequentBuyer and CustomerTrackedRecording objects
FrequentBuyer.relationship.customerTrackedRecordings.lazyReadRelationship=true
```

Corporation Class Implementation

According to the business rules defined in the previous chapter, corporate customers receive an automatic 10 percent discount on all their purchases. The `Corporation` class below is used to track these volume customers:

```
import java.util.*;

import org.jlf.log.*;
import org.jlf.dataMap.*;

/**
 * This class hold information for a corporate
 * customer to give volume discounts for their purchases.
 */
public class Corporation extends VolumeCustomer {

  // ----------------------------------------------------------------
  // Section 1: DataMappedObject descriptors
  // ----------------------------------------------------------------

  // Constants for attributes
```

```
public static final String COMPANY_NAME_ATTRIBUTE = "COMPANY_NAME";

/**
 * Adds attribute descriptors for the current class.
 */
protected Hashtable basicGetAttributeDescriptors() {

  // Always call the superclass!
  Hashtable descriptors = super.basicGetAttributeDescriptors();
  DataAttributeDescriptor descriptor;

  // Then add class-specific attributes
  descriptor = new DataAttributeDescriptor(COMPANY_NAME_ATTRIBUTE,
                                           StringAttribute.class, false);
  descriptor.setMaximumLength(50);
  descriptors.put(COMPANY_NAME_ATTRIBUTE, descriptor);

  return descriptors;
}

/**
 * Default constructor must be public for the data mapping
 * framework!  However, when creating a new object, look to use
 * a paramterized constructor.
 */
public Corporation() {}


// ---------------------------------------------------------------
// Section 2: Java bean and business logic methods
// ---------------------------------------------------------------

/**
 * Main constructor for the class.  Populates all
 * attributes of the class and sets the type accordingly.
 */
public Corporation(String nickname, String emailAddress, String name,
                   String companyName, String address, String city,
                   String state, String zipcode) {
  super(nickname, emailAddress, name, address, city, state, zipcode);
  setCompanyName(companyName);
  resetCustomerType(CustomerType.CORPORATE_CUSTOMER);
}

/**
 * Retrieves the Corporation's name.
 */
public String getCompanyName() {
  return getStringAttribute(COMPANY_NAME_ATTRIBUTE);
}

/**
 * Sets the Corporation's name.
 */
public void setCompanyName(String name) {
```

```
    setStringAttribute(COMPANY_NAME_ATTRIBUTE, name);
  }

  /**
   * Return the amount of discount applicable to the volume
   * customer.  Give a 10% discount to all corporations.
   */
  public double discountRate() {
    return 0.10;
  }

  /**
   * Add to superclass to output additional
   * volume customer attributes
   */
  public String toString() {
    return super.toString() + "\n  Company Name: " + getCompanyName();
  }

}
```

The `Corporation` class above is mapped to the database as follows:

```
############################################################
# Corporation class data mapping

# SQL statements to create a corporation
Corporation.criteriaKey.createStatement.sqlStatement=\
    insert into CUSTOMERS ( \
        CUSTOMER_ID, \
        CUSTOMER_TYPE_ID, \
        NICKNAME, \
        EMAIL_ADDRESS, \
        NAME, \
        COMPANY_NAME, \
        ADDRESS, \
        CITY, \
        STATE, \
        ZIPCODE, \
        VERSION) \
    values ( \
        CUSTOMERS_SEQ.NEXTVAL, \
        {CUSTOMER_TYPE_ID}, \
        {NICKNAME}, \
        {EMAIL_ADDRESS}, \
        {NAME}, \
        {COMPANY_NAME}, \
        {ADDRESS}, \
        {CITY}, \
        {STATE}, \
        {ZIPCODE}, \
        {VERSION} )

Corporation.criteriaKey.createStatement2.sqlStatement=\
```

```
    select CUSTOMERS_SEQ.CURRVAL as CUSTOMER_ID \
      from DUAL
Corporation.criteriaKey.createStatement2.isQuery=true

# SQL statement for a "findByPrimaryKey" search criteria
Corporation.criteriaKey.findByPrimaryKey.sqlStatement=\
    select * \
      from CUSTOMERS \
     where CUSTOMER_ID = {CUSTOMER_ID}

# SQL statement to optimistic lock a corporation
Corporation.criteriaKey.optimisticLockingStatement.sqlStatement=\
    select VERSION \
      from CUSTOMERS \
     where CUSTOMER_ID = {CUSTOMER_ID} \
       and VERSION = {VERSION}

# SQL statement to update a corporation
Corporation.criteriaKey.updateStatement.sqlStatement=\
    update CUSTOMERS set \
        NICKNAME = {NICKNAME}, \
        EMAIL_ADDRESS = {EMAIL_ADDRESS}, \
        NAME = {NAME}, \
        COMPANY_NAME = {COMPANY_NAME}, \
        ADDRESS = {ADDRESS}, \
        CITY = {CITY}, \
        STATE = {STATE}, \
        ZIPCODE = {ZIPCODE}, \
        VERSION = VERSION + 1 \
    where CUSTOMER_ID = {CUSTOMER_ID}

# Retrieves the reset VERSION
Corporation.criteriaKey.updateStatement2.sqlStatement=\
    select VERSION \
      from CUSTOMERS \
     where CUSTOMER_ID = {CUSTOMER_ID}
Corporation.criteriaKey.updateStatement2.isQuery=true

# SQL statement to delete a corporation
Corporation.criteriaKey.deleteStatement.sqlStatement=\
    delete from CUSTOMERS \
          where CUSTOMER_ID = {CUSTOMER_ID}

# Define relationship between Corporation and CustomerTrackedRecording objects
Corporation.relationship.customerTrackedRecordings.lazyReadRelationship=true
```

NonProfitCorporation Class Implementation

If you recall from the previous chapter, non-profit corporations receive two wonderful benefits. First of all, we give them a generous 15 percent discount, and secondly, they don't get charged sales tax, but we must make sure to note their tax-exempt ID in case we get audited. The `NonProfitCorporation` class below fulfills all of these requirements:

```
import java.util.*;

import org.jlf.log.*;
import org.jlf.dataMap.*;

/**
 * This class hold information for a non-profit corporate
 * customer to give volume discounts for their purchases
 * and also not charge them sales tax.
 */
public class NonProfitCorporation extends Corporation {

  // -------------------------------------------------------------
  // Section 1: DataMappedObject descriptors
  // -------------------------------------------------------------

  // Constants for attributes
  public static final String TAX_EXEMPT_ID_ATTRIBUTE = "TAX_EXEMPT_ID";

  /**
   * Adds attribute descriptors for the current class.
   */
  protected Hashtable basicGetAttributeDescriptors() {

    // Always call the superclass!
    Hashtable descriptors = super.basicGetAttributeDescriptors();
    DataAttributeDescriptor descriptor;

    // Then add class-specific attributes
    descriptor = new DataAttributeDescriptor(TAX_EXEMPT_ID_ATTRIBUTE,
                                             StringAttribute.class, false);
    descriptor.setMaximumLength(50);
    descriptors.put(TAX_EXEMPT_ID_ATTRIBUTE, descriptor);

    return descriptors;
  }

  /**
   * Default constructor must be public for the data mapping
   * framework!  However, when creating a new object, look to use
   * a paramterized constructor.
   */
  public NonProfitCorporation() {}


  // -------------------------------------------------------------
  // Section 2: Java bean and business logic methods
  // -------------------------------------------------------------

  /**
   * Main constructor for the class.  Populates all
   * attributes of the class and sets the type accordingly.
   */
  public NonProfitCorporation(String nickname, String emailAddress,
```

```
                          String name, String companyName,
                          String address, String city, String state,
                          String zipcode, String taxExemptId) {
    super(nickname, emailAddress, name, companyName, address, city, state,
          zipcode);
    setTaxExemptId(taxExemptId);
    resetCustomerType(CustomerType.NON_PROFIT_CUSTOMER);
  }

  /**
   * Retrieves the tax exempt id.
   */
  public String getTaxExemptId() {
    return getStringAttribute(TAX_EXEMPT_ID_ATTRIBUTE);
  }

  /**
   * Sets the tax exempt id.
   */
  public void setTaxExemptId(String id) {
    setStringAttribute(TAX_EXEMPT_ID_ATTRIBUTE, id);
  }

  /**
   * Return the amount of discount applicable to the volume
   * customer.  Give a 15% discount to all non-profit groups.
   */
  public double discountRate() {
    return 0.15;
  }

  /**
   * This customer is a non-profit corporation.
   */
  public boolean isNonProfit() {
    return true;
  }

  /**
   * Add to superclass to output additional
   * volume customer attributes
   */
  public String toString() {
    return super.toString() + "\n  Tax Exempt Id: " + getTaxExemptId();
  }
}
```

The `NonProfitCorporation` class above is mapped to the database as follows:

```
#########################################################
# NonProfitCorporation class data mapping

# SQL statements to create a non-profit
NonProfitCorporation.criteriaKey.createStatement.sqlStatement=\
```

```
    insert into CUSTOMERS ( \
        CUSTOMER_ID, \
        CUSTOMER_TYPE_ID, \
        NICKNAME, \
        EMAIL_ADDRESS, \
        NAME, \
        COMPANY_NAME, \
        ADDRESS, \
        CITY, \
        STATE, \
        ZIPCODE, \
        TAX_EXEMPT_ID, \
        VERSION) \
    values ( \
        CUSTOMERS_SEQ.NEXTVAL, \
        {CUSTOMER_TYPE_ID}, \
        {NICKNAME}, \
        {EMAIL_ADDRESS}, \
        {NAME}, \
        {COMPANY_NAME}, \
        {ADDRESS}, \
        {CITY}, \
        {STATE}, \
        {ZIPCODE}, \
        {TAX_EXEMPT_ID}, \
        {VERSION} )

NonProfitCorporation.criteriaKey.createStatement2.sqlStatement=\
    select CUSTOMERS_SEQ.CURRVAL as CUSTOMER_ID \
      from DUAL
NonProfitCorporation.criteriaKey.createStatement2.isQuery=true

# SQL statement for a "findByPrimaryKey" search criteria
NonProfitCorporation.criteriaKey.findByPrimaryKey.sqlStatement=\
    select * \
      from CUSTOMERS \
     where CUSTOMER_ID = {CUSTOMER_ID}

# SQL statement to optimistic lock a non-profit
NonProfitCorporation.criteriaKey.optimisticLockingStatement.sqlStatement=\
    select VERSION \
      from CUSTOMERS \
     where CUSTOMER_ID = {CUSTOMER_ID} \
       and VERSION = {VERSION}

# SQL statement to update a non-profit
NonProfitCorporation.criteriaKey.updateStatement.sqlStatement=\
    update CUSTOMERS set \
        NICKNAME = {NICKNAME}, \
        EMAIL_ADDRESS = {EMAIL_ADDRESS}, \
        NAME = {NAME}, \
        COMPANY_NAME = {COMPANY_NAME}, \
        ADDRESS = {ADDRESS}, \
        CITY = {CITY}, \
        STATE = {STATE}, \
```

```
        ZIPCODE = {ZIPCODE}, \
        TAX_EXEMPT_ID = {TAX_EXEMPT_ID}, \
        VERSION = VERSION + 1 \
    where CUSTOMER_ID = {CUSTOMER_ID}

# Retrieves the reset VERSION
NonProfitCorporation.criteriaKey.updateStatement2.sqlStatement=\
    select VERSION \
      from CUSTOMERS \
     where CUSTOMER_ID = {CUSTOMER_ID}
NonProfitCorporation.criteriaKey.updateStatement2.isQuery=true

# SQL statement to delete a non-profit
NonProfitCorporation.criteriaKey.deleteStatement.sqlStatement=\
    delete from CUSTOMERS \
          where CUSTOMER_ID = {CUSTOMER_ID}

# Define relationship between NonProfitCorporation and CustomerTrackedRecording
objects
NonProfitCorporation.relationship.customerTrackedRecordings.lazyReadRelationship=t
rue
```

TestCustomerTracking Walkthrough

The `TestCustomerTracking.java` class below tests the Java database application we developed above to make sure it accomplishes all the system requirements in the last chapter. If you examine the output of the system, including the JLF instrumentation output to `System.err`, you will see that not only does the system fulfill all its requirements, but it also does so very efficiently. The main test of the application is to find customers in the system, who have an interest in a particular kind of recording. In the last chapter, we discussed how difficult it is to map this kind of query efficiently to the database, and how it could take hundreds of SQL queries if you do not deliberately design your classes to accommodate this type of query. With the JLF framework, there was no need to redesign the classes for the query. The query simply required one new finder method and one new search criterion for the `Customer` class. The query is performed in only one SQL statement, as it should be:

```
import java.util.*;

import org.jlf.log.*;
import org.jlf.dataMap.*;

/**
 * This class tests the objects of the Recording Java
 * database application ability to track customer purchases
 * and interests in recordings.
 */
public class TestCustomerTracking {

  /**
   * Main method to kick off the tests.
   */
  public static void main(String[] args) {
    Customer cust1, cust2, cust3, cust4;
```

```
    Recording rec1, rec2, rec3, rec4, findRec;
    CustomerTrackedRecording ctr1, ctr2, ctr3, ctr4, ctr5, findCtr;

    DataMapper dataMapper = null;

    try {
```

The test program begins by putting some customers and recordings into the database, so it can later create tracking relationships between the two. For customers, it creates one of each type, so we can see how effectively the JLF data mapping framework deals with inheritance hierarchies:

```
      cust1 = new Customer("shiney", "shiney@yahoo.com");

      cust2 = new FrequentBuyer("charlemange", "charle@hotmail.com",
                                "Charlie Charlemange", "123 Main Street",
                                "Minneapolis", "MN", "55132");

      cust3 = new Corporation("choo", "choo@aol.com", "Chester Sunshine",
                              "Trains And More...", "431 Broadway",
                              "Minneapolis", "MN", "55332");

      cust4 = new NonProfitCorporation("honey", "honey@yahoo.com",
                                       "Honey Princess",
                                       "Princess For a Day",
                                       "3390 3rd Ave. North",
                                       "Minneapolis", "MN", "55133",
                                       "3390-honey-USMN");

      rec1 = new Recording("Cuts Like A Knife", "Bryan Adams",
                           "392-0000022", 11.99);

      rec2 = new Recording("Working Class Dog", "Rick Springfield",
                           "RS-32-1133", 10.99);

      rec3 = new Recording("Come And Join Us", "Petra", "303-9388293",
                           11.99);

      rec4 = new Recording("Lucky Town", "Bruce Springsteen",
                           "BK-30-23993", 13.99);

      dataMapper = cust1.getDefaultDataMapper();

      // Create the customers in the database
      cust1.write(dataMapper);
      cust2.write(dataMapper);
      cust3.write(dataMapper);
      cust4.write(dataMapper);

      // Create the recordings in the database
      rec1.write(dataMapper);
      rec2.write(dataMapper);
```

```
    rec3.write(dataMapper);
    rec4.write(dataMapper);

    dataMapper.commitWrites();
```

The test program has four customers and four recordings in the database. Next, it proceeds to track five relationships. Four of the relationships are customer interests in recordings, and one is a customer purchase. The test program wants to make sure the system knows the difference between the two different tracking relationship types, so we don't pull back information on customer purchases when we are going after customer interests and vice versa:

```
    // Add some customer trackings.
    // Customer 1 has an interest in Petra recording 3
    ctr1 =
      new CustomerTrackedRecording(cust1, rec3,
                                   CustomerTrackingType
                                     .CUSTOMER_INTEREST);
    ctr1.write(dataMapper);

    // Customer 4 has interest in Springfield (2) and Springsteen (4)
    ctr2 =
      new CustomerTrackedRecording(cust4, rec2,
                                   CustomerTrackingType
                                     .CUSTOMER_INTEREST);
    ctr2.write(dataMapper);

    ctr3 =
      new CustomerTrackedRecording(cust4, rec4,
                                   CustomerTrackingType
                                     .CUSTOMER_INTEREST);
    ctr3.write(dataMapper);

    // Customer 2 has interest in Springsteen (4)
    ctr4 =
      new CustomerTrackedRecording(cust2, rec4,
                                   CustomerTrackingType
                                     .CUSTOMER_INTEREST);
    ctr4.write(dataMapper);

    // Customer 3 has purchased in Springfield (2)
    ctr5 =
      new CustomerTrackedRecording(cust3, rec2,
                                   CustomerTrackingType
                                     .CUSTOMER_PURCHASE);
    ctr5.write(dataMapper);

    dataMapper.commitWrites();
```

After the customers, recordings, and tracking relationships are present in the database, the program tests the system's ability to query that information. The first query asks for any customers that have registered an interest in any recordings with a `Spring` somewhere in the artist's name. There are two recordings and three relationships pertinent to this query. However, two of the pertinent relationships both point to customer 4, and one points to customer 3. The output shows one copy of customer 3 and one copy of customer 4, just as it should. The output also shows something else very interesting. Customer 3 is a corporation, which receives a 10 percent discount. Customer 4 is a non-profit corporation, which receives a 15 percent discount and non-profit status. The output reflects all of these characteristics, showing the JLF data mapping framework indeed instantiates the correct object instances for an inheritance hierarchy, even within the same query.

```
      // Now for the real test.  Let's see if we can find
      // all customers that have registered an interest
      // in any recording with artist %Spring%, any title.
      // The result should be customer 3 and 4

      // Build Recording object to find artist and title
      findRec = new Recording();
      findRec.setRecordingArtist("%Spring%");
      findRec.setRecordingTitle("%");

      // Build CustomerTrackedRecording object to
      // find the recording above with a tracking type
      // of customer interest
      findCtr = new CustomerTrackedRecording();
      findCtr.setRecording(findRec);
      findCtr
        .setCustomerTrackingType(CustomerTrackingType.CUSTOMER_INTEREST);

      // Find customers by tracking criteria built above
      Vector customersInterestedInSpringArtists =
        Customer.findByTrackingCriteria(findCtr);

      System.out.println("\nShould have found 2 customers below, one "
                         + "Frequent Buyer and one Non-Profit Corp.");
      Customer.outputCustomers(customersInterestedInSpringArtists);
```

The next test below shows that the system can distinguish between customer purchases and customer interests. It also shows that the system properly reads objects of type `FrequentBuyer`:

```
      // Next let's find any customers with purchases.
      // The result should be corporate customer 2 only

      // Build Recording object to find any artist and title
      findRec = new Recording();
      findRec.setRecordingArtist("%");
      findRec.setRecordingTitle("%");

      // Build CustomerTrackedRecording object to
      // find the recording above with a tracking type
      // of customer purchase
      findCtr = new CustomerTrackedRecording();
      findCtr.setRecording(findRec);
```

```
findCtr
  .setCustomerTrackingType(CustomerTrackingType.CUSTOMER_PURCHASE);

// Find customers by tracking criteria built above
Vector customersWithPurchases =
  Customer.findByTrackingCriteria(findCtr);

System.out.println("\nShould have found 1 Corporate customer below");
Customer.outputCustomers(customersWithPurchases);
```

The final test below makes sure the system can properly query for, and instantiate objects, of type `Customer`. The output confirms this by showing an object that has only a nickname and e-mail address, with no discount:

```
// Wrap it up with a query to find non-volume
// customer 1, who is interested in Petra's
// "Come And Join Us" recording

// Build Recording object to find any artist and title
findRec = new Recording();
findRec.setRecordingArtist("%");
findRec.setRecordingTitle("Come%");

// Build CustomerTrackedRecording object to
// find the recording above with a tracking type
// of customer interest
findCtr = new CustomerTrackedRecording();
findCtr.setRecording(findRec);
findCtr
  .setCustomerTrackingType(CustomerTrackingType.CUSTOMER_INTEREST);

// Find customers by tracking criteria built above
Vector customers = Customer.findByTrackingCriteria(findCtr);

System.out.println("\nShould have found 1 non-volume Customer below");
Customer.outputCustomers(customers);
```

Every good test program should try to clean up its activity, so this program deletes all database rows it created. It also tests the system capability to remove information as well as create it:

```
// Delete all tracking relationships
ctr1.deleteOnWrite();
ctr1.write(dataMapper);

ctr2.deleteOnWrite();
ctr2.write(dataMapper);

ctr3.deleteOnWrite();
ctr3.write(dataMapper);

ctr4.deleteOnWrite();
ctr4.write(dataMapper);
```

```
        ctr5.deleteOnWrite();
        ctr5.write(dataMapper);

        // Delete all customers
        cust1.deleteOnWrite();
        cust1.write(dataMapper);

        cust2.deleteOnWrite();
        cust2.write(dataMapper);

        cust3.deleteOnWrite();
        cust3.write(dataMapper);

        cust4.deleteOnWrite();
        cust4.write(dataMapper);

        dataMapper.commitWrites();

        // Delete all recordings
        rec1.deleteOnWrite();
        rec1.write(dataMapper);

        rec2.deleteOnWrite();
        rec2.write(dataMapper);

        rec3.deleteOnWrite();
        rec3.write(dataMapper);

        rec4.deleteOnWrite();
        rec4.write(dataMapper);

        dataMapper.commitWrites();

      } catch (Exception e) {
        e.printStackTrace();
      }
      finally {
        if (dataMapper != null) {
          dataMapper.close();
        }
      }
    }
  }
```

Where to Go from Here: O-R Mapping Options

Experts in the O-R mapping field are working hard to help you in this all-important design and implementation activity. You have some other options at your disposal; below is a list ordered according to the amount of time and effort required for you to implement them, with the least amount listed first.

1. For smaller and simpler applications, use JDBC to directly map your classes to relational database tables. Limit the use of relationships and inheritance hierarchies that cause mapping difficulties. The JDBC API does not take very long to learn and use, but as your application grows in size and complexity, this approach will be problematic as shown in the previous chapter.

2. Look for a commercial object-relational mapping framework like TopLink (www.webgain.com) or CocoBase (www.thoughtinc.com). These products specialize in mapping Java classes to relational databases, but will take a bit of time to understand and use effectively.

3. See if Java technologies like JDO (Java Data Objects) and EJB (Enterprise JavaBeans) are applicable to your problem. Both of these technologies contain significant object-relational mapping capabilities in their latest releases. We take a look at the EJB framework in Chapter 19, *J2EE and Java Database Applications.*

4. Try to reuse or enhance someone else's already-built O-R mapping framework. Chances are, a previous Java development effort in your organization built a custom framework that you can use and enhance. If not, you can try the open source JLF data mapping framework (http://jlf.sourceforge.net/). Beware that this alternative is likely to involve a significant time investment; but you will learn a lot in the process.

Summary

Bridging the chasm between an object and a relational database model is a significant chore. We hope the two examples in this chapter gave you some insight into the problems you will encounter when you add size and complexity to your Java database application. With the use of a good O-R mapping framework, you can minimize the mapping impact on your code. However, you will never be able to totally eliminate it because object and relational technologies are so different from each other. An O-R mapping framework will also introduce a number of optimization features you can take advantage of to efficiently map your Java objects to relational database tables. We showed how the JLF data mapping framework caches static data, reads relationships in the same query as the parent object, lazy-reads relationships you do not use very often, and maps object hierarchies, all with little additional code added to your application. As your application grows, O-R mapping frameworks reduce the amount of time, effort, and code required to map your Java objects to a relational database, when compared to coding the mapping yourself.

akarta
JAVA

Debugging and Logging

The typical Java database application starts small. You begin with a few tables and Java classes, maybe add reports with a report generation tool, and all of sudden envision new possibilities for enhancing the application. Users see the usefulness of the system and start requesting all kinds of new capabilities. Of course, adding each new capability grows the application in terms of size. That is, the number of database tables and Java classes the application relies on. As the application grows in size, it also grows in complexity.

Each new database table probably adds a relationship to one or more existing tables. Java objects call methods on other Java objects in new, and more complex ways. User interfaces get more elaborate. Your application, which was once small, well defined, and well designed, has grown to be large and complex. You have forgotten all of the different relationships between the tables in your database and likewise, within your Java code. Perhaps you are not the only one involved in its development any longer; other developers enhance the database and Java code as well.

The number of users of your application has grown to be many times the number you originally planned. You get more volume going through your application, and it starts to fail intermittently under load. You get errors/exceptions you have never seen before, like JDBC connection failures, database deadlocks, queries that take too long or time out, and Java out-of-memory errors. The simple techniques you have used in the past to debug your application are not as effective as they were when you understood every detail of the database and application.

The purpose of this chapter is to inform you of different problems you may encounter as your application grows. We will discuss:

- Common techniques for debugging such problems
- Implementing each technique on a very simple Java database application
- Analyzing each technique's applicability and effectiveness, so you can determine which technique will be most appropriate to your situation
- Using the logging portion of the JLF framework, from the previous chapter

Before we evaluate and implement the techniques, however, we need to understand the kind of information we should have at our disposal to fix the common problems identified above.

Effective Debugging

Now, let's talk through some typical problems you will encounter when developing Java database applications. In the course of this discussion, we will list the information you need to detect and correct these problems.

Exception Handling

The first problem any programmer using the JDBC API will encounter is dealing with the dreaded `SQLException`. `SQLException` is an exception that many JDBC API method calls potentially generate. It usually signifies a pretty significant error in communicating with the database. For example, database connection failure, improper SQL statement, violation of database security or integrity constraints, and so on. `SQLException` is a checked exception, so all calls to methods that throw such an exception must be surrounded with a `try/catch` block expecting that the exception could be generated (or you could also in turn throw the `SQLException` back to the caller of your method).

The problem with exceptions, however, is dealing with the fact that you received one, and doing so in a manner where you can rapidly detect and address the situation when possible. In most cases, you will not be able to code anything in the exception handling `catch` block to resolve problem situations. For example, if a database connection cannot be made, it is likely the database or the network is down and there probably isn't much your Java code can do to restart the database or fix a network router. Instead, you should be looking to report information on the exception you detected. That way you can debug the problem when it happens (instead of just seeing your application fail and now knowing why) and then be able to address the problem outside the context of your application. When debugging exceptions, you will need to know the following, in order of importance:

- What exception was generated (the exception name).
- The message contained in the exception (almost all exceptions give you a text message with information about why the exception was generated).
- The data being passed to the method that generated the exception.
- Where in the code the exception was generated.
- The context of the method call. That is, what were you doing before (and potentially after) you called the method that generated the exception. You will need this information so you can debug problems where the current JDBC call is dependent upon a previous JDBC call in the same transaction or commit scope. Problem context is the most important information you need to debug difficult problems. Unfortunately, it is also the most challenging information to report. If you report too much problem context, you are overloaded with information and you fail to quickly identify the problem. If you do not report enough information, you will not be able to identify the problem at all.

In practice, you will rarely report all of the information in the list above, as this involves significant time and effort to code. However, when you do take the time, it is usually pretty easy to detect and correct the cause of the exception. The next problem, proper resource disposal, is not nearly as easy to detect and correct.

Forgetting to Clean Up Resources

A major language feature of Java is its **garbage collector**. The idea behind a garbage collector is that the JVM, the process that runs your Java code, periodically 'cleans up' for you as you run your program. You, as a programmer, don't have to spend much time or energy remembering to tell the JVM to free every object you allocate. When you don't need it any more, you just stop using it. The JVM detects when you are not using the object any longer, and it frees the memory taken by up by that object. Your software development effort goes much faster because you don't have to write code to tell the JVM when to clean up.

Garbage collection works fine and dandy for objects that only occupy memory inside the JVM. Unfortunately, when dealing with a database and using the JDBC API, you are doing much more than allocating memory in the JVM. You are opening connections to the database, executing queries (which allocate `ResultSets`), updating rows in a table (which start transactions and create database locks), and doing a whole lot more that we don't really need to comprehend. Unless we tell the database, again via the JDBC API, that we are finished with a database resource (for example, commit a transaction, close a `ResultSet`, or close a `Connection`), the database is going to keep that resource open or row locked for an extended period of time. Databases generally have time out periods that clean up for us when we forget, but these time out periods can take anywhere from minutes to hours. During this time, other processes cannot use these resources, and you may get a `SQLException` generated when you run out of resources that should have been freed.

To be a good steward of your database resources (and keep your friendly neighborhood database administrator from knocking on your door), you need to code the cleanup of any JDBC resource you allocate. As stated before though, you are probably used to the JVM doing this for you so you forget. You need to have an effective debugging mechanism at your disposal to help you detect when you do forget.

Tracking resource allocation and cleanup is such a challenging problem that companies release software tools to help resolve it. The tools are called **code profilers**, as they watch over and monitor your code as it executes.

Code profilers accumulate statistics on the number of resources you allocate over time, such as memory usage (which can let you know if you have a memory leak), or CPU usage. If you run your code for a while and you forget to free resources, they track where in the code you allocated resources you didn't free. Then you can pretty easily figure out where you should have freed the resource, knowing where you allocated it. Code profilers are beyond the scope of this book as they do a number of other things besides finding where you forgot to free resources. Instead, we will discuss a couple of simpler, albeit less effective, techniques for finding resources you have forgotten about. Examples of tools on the market to do code profiling are:

- Optimizeit (http://www.vmgear.com)
- JProbe (http://www.jprobe.com)
- DevPartner Java Edition (http://www.numega.com)

Regardless of the technique used to debug resource problems, though, the information you need is a trace of every resource you allocate and free, so that you can match them up and see which ones you haven't freed. The trace information needs to have in it the following:

- The place in the code where it was allocated
- The time it was allocated or freed
- Its unique resource identifier

Performance Problems

As your application, and the number of users, grows it is almost inevitable that you run into performance problems in dealing with your database. What used to take a fraction of a second may now always, or worse intermittently, take a minute or an hour or more. Any number of problems can contribute to query or update delays.

If the delay is pretty consistent, the most common reason is that your tables have grown over time, as users add volumes of data to your database. You may need to enhance your database design to add indexes, redesign your queries to be more efficient, repartition your data, or perform any number of other remedies that a good database administrator can help you with. Alternatively, the delays could be due to network latency, but dealing with that is outside the scope of this book.

The main difficulty in tracking performance problems, though, is how you can know which queries or updates are slow. One user interface screen often results in many queries and updates on the database. Simply having the user tell you which screen is slow does not accurately pinpoint the problem. You need to be able to trace every interaction with the database, telling what that interaction is (for example, what SQL statement is being executed), where in the code you are executing that interaction, and how long that interaction takes (that is, capture the time it takes to execute the JDBC API method to perform that interaction). Again, this is a very challenging problem that some code profilers address for you, so you may want to look to a commercial code profiler to help you here. We will discuss less sophisticated techniques to address this class of problem.

Debugging Techniques

Now that we understand the information we need for debugging typical Java database application problems, we must find techniques for getting at this information. The following techniques are very common and widely available at little or no cost:

- Logging to `System.out` and `System.err`
- Running a **local interactive debugger**
- Running a **remote interactive debugger**
- Instrumenting your application

Let's implement each technique in a small, but complete program, in order to analyze their effectiveness for the problems at hand.

Logging to System.out and System.err

The most pervasive, and simplest, approach to debugging and logging errors in your application is through calls to Java's `System.out` and `System.err` print streams. These streams are a native part of the Java language, contained in the `java.lang` package that is implicitly imported into every class file you develop. You can write output to either stream in a single line of code. `System.err` is meant to output errors from your application, and `System.out` for all other textual output. If you get many errors, or you are executing your code for a long period of time, say over 24 hours, then you might want to write this information to a file.

These output streams are so convenient that most Java developers never go beyond their use to other debugging techniques. Unfortunately, as your application grows, this technique also becomes the least effective of all.

Try It Out – Logging to System.out and System.err

The following example program, `LogCustomerNames.java`, logs all of the information you need to debug the problems discussed above. It logs all exceptions to `System.err`, logs all JDBC resource allocations and de-allocations to `System.out`, and times and logs the only database query to `System.out` as well. The comments in the code are shown unhighlighted:

```
import java.util.*;
import java.sql.*;

/**
 * This class connects to the Oracle demo database and reads
 * customer names from the CUSTOMER table, outputing
 * them to System.out.  Along the way,
 * it logs information to System.out and errors to System.err
 * so you can debug the program should something go wrong.
 */
public class LogCustomerNames {

  /**
   * Constant for the name of the JDBC Driver class connecting
   * to the Oracle demo database.
   */
  private static final String ORACLE_JDBC_DRIVER_CLASS_NAME =
    "oracle.jdbc.driver.OracleDriver";

  /**
   * Constant for the name of the URL for where the Oracle
   * JDBC driver will connect to the database.
   */
  private static final String ORACLE_DEMO_DB_URL =
    "jdbc:oracle:thin:@dbserver:1521:database";

  /**
   * Constants for the user to log into the Oracle demo database.
   */
  private static final String ORACLE_DEMO_DB_USERID_PROPERTY = "user";
  private static final String ORACLE_DEMO_DB_USERID = "beg";

  /**
   * Constants for the password to log into the Oracle demo database.
   */
  private static final String ORACLE_DEMO_DB_PASSWORD_PROPERTY = "password";
  private static final String ORACLE_DEMO_DB_PASSWORD = "java";

  /**
   * Constant for the SQL Query to execute
   */
```

```
  private static final String SQL_QUERY = "select CUSTOMERFIRSTNAME from
CUSTOMERS";

  /**
   * Helper method to retrieve a JDBC connection from
   * the Oracle demo database.  Note, this code must be called
   * in a try block with a finally block which closes the connection.
   *
   * @throws Exception if the connection cannot be created
   *
   * @return JDBC Connection to the Oracle demo database if successful
   */
  private Connection getConnection() throws Exception {

    // Create a new instance of the driver manager class, so
    // it initializes itself for use and registers with the
    // JDBC DriverManager
    Class.forName(ORACLE_JDBC_DRIVER_CLASS_NAME).newInstance();

    // Create connection properties object
    Properties connectionProperties = new Properties();

    connectionProperties.put(ORACLE_DEMO_DB_USERID_PROPERTY,
                             ORACLE_DEMO_DB_USERID);

    connectionProperties.put(ORACLE_DEMO_DB_PASSWORD_PROPERTY,
                             ORACLE_DEMO_DB_PASSWORD);

    // create a connection
    return DriverManager.getConnection(ORACLE_DEMO_DB_URL,
                                       connectionProperties);
  }

  /**
   * Outputs the customer names from the result set to System.out.
   */
  private void printResultSet(ResultSet resultSet) {

    // Output a header for the data
    System.out.println("Customer Name");
    System.out.println("-------------");

    try {
      while (resultSet.next()) {

        // Retrieve and print the first column
        System.out.println(resultSet.getString(1));
      }
    } catch (SQLException e) {

      // Something went wrong retrieving result set, log it
      System.err.println("Error retrieving result set rows from '" +
                         resultSet + "', caught exception " + e);
      e.printStackTrace();
    }
```

```
  }

  /**
   * Given an opened JDBC connection, reads customer names
   * from the CUSTOMER table.
   */
  private void readCustomers(Connection connection) {
    Statement statement = null;
    ResultSet resultSet = null;

    // Get a new statement and run the query
    try {
      statement = connection.createStatement();

      // Log the fact we got a connection so we remember to clean up
      System.out.println("Opened JDBC Statement " + statement +
                         " at LogCustomerNames.readCustomers()");

      // Log that we are trying to execute the query
      System.out.println("Executing SQL Query: '" + SQL_QUERY +
                         "' on database " + ORACLE_DEMO_DB_URL);

      // Start a timer
      long queryStartTime = System.currentTimeMillis();

      // Execute query
      resultSet = statement.executeQuery(SQL_QUERY);

      // Calculate time to execute and log
      long queryTime = System.currentTimeMillis() - queryStartTime;
      System.out.println("SQL Query: '" + SQL_QUERY + "' took " +
                         queryTime + " milliseconds to execute");

      // Log that we aquired a result set to clean up
      System.out.println("Retrieved JDBC ResultSet " + resultSet +
                         " at LogCustomerNames.readCustomers()");

      // Print result set
      printResultSet(resultSet);

    } catch (SQLException e) {

      // Something went wrong with query, log it
      System.err.println("Error querying database '" + ORACLE_DEMO_DB_URL +
                         "', caught exception " + e);
      e.printStackTrace();
    }
    finally {

      // If we got a result set, close it
      if (resultSet != null) {
        try {
          resultSet.close();

          // Log the fact we closed the connection
```

```
          System.out.println("Closed JDBC ResultSet " + resultSet);
        } catch (SQLException e) {

          // Something went wrong closing result set, log it
          System.err.println("Error closing result set " + resultSet +
                             ", caught exception " + e);
          e.printStackTrace();
        }
      }

      // If we got a statement, close it
      if (statement != null) {
        try {
          statement.close();

          // Log the fact we closed the statement
          System.out.println("Closed JDBC Statement " + statement);
        } catch (SQLException e) {

          // Something went wrong closing statement, log it
          System.err.println("Error closing statement " + statement +
                             ", caught exception " + e);
          e.printStackTrace();
        }
      }
    }
  }

  /**
   * Main method for the simple program.  Creates a connection
   * to the database, reads customer names from the database,
   * and cleans up.
   */
  public void runQuery() {
    Connection databaseConnection = null;

    try {

      // Get the connection
      databaseConnection = getConnection();

      // Log the fact we got a connection so we remember to clean up
      System.out.println("Opened JDBC Connection " + databaseConnection +
                         " at LogCustomerNames.runQuery()");

      // Read customers with that connection
      readCustomers(databaseConnection);

    } catch (Exception e) {

      // Something went wrong with connection, log it
      System.err.println("Error opening connection to database '" +
                         ORACLE_DEMO_DB_URL + "', caught exception " + e);
      e.printStackTrace();
    } finally {
```

```
        // If we got a connection, close it
        if (databaseConnection != null) {
          try {
            databaseConnection.close();

            // Log the fact we closed the connection
            System.out.println("Closed JDBC Connection "
                               + databaseConnection);
          } catch (SQLException e) {

            // Something went wrong closing connection, log it
            System.err.println("Error closing connection to database '" +
                               ORACLE_DEMO_DB_URL + "', caught exception " +
                               e);
            e.printStackTrace();
          }

        }
      }
    }

    /**
     * Main method to run the simple program.  Creates a new instance
     * of this class to read and log customer names.
     */
    public static void main(String[] args) {
      LogCustomerNames logCustomerNames = new LogCustomerNames();

      logCustomerNames.runQuery();
    }
  }
```

Save this as C:\BegJavaDB\Ch17\LogCustomerNames.java, and compile with the following command:

```
> javac LogCustomerNames.java
```

We can then run the class with the following command:

```
> java -classpath .;%JLIB%\classes12.zip LogCustomerNames
```

Running the class should produce results like those shown in the following screenshot:

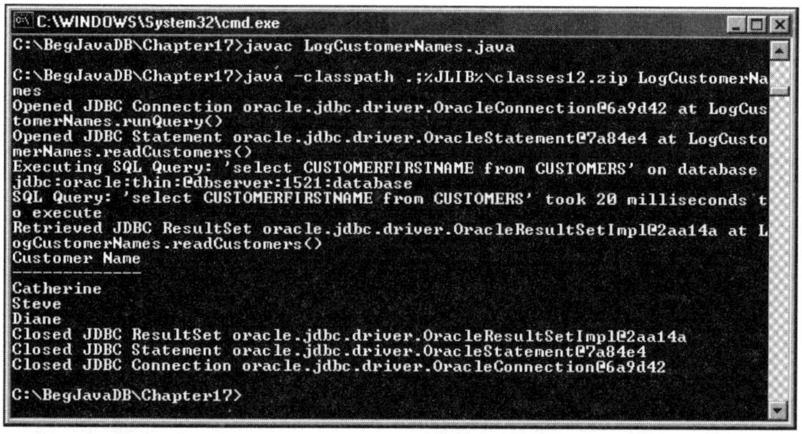

```
C:\WINDOWS\System32\cmd.exe
C:\BegJavaDB\Chapter17>javac LogCustomerNames.java

C:\BegJavaDB\Chapter17>java -classpath .;%JLIB%\classes12.zip LogCustomerNa
mes
Opened JDBC Connection oracle.jdbc.driver.OracleConnection@6a9d42 at LogCus
tomerNames.runQuery()
Opened JDBC Statement oracle.jdbc.driver.OracleStatement@7a84e4 at LogCusto
merNames.readCustomers()
Executing SQL Query: 'select CUSTOMERFIRSTNAME from CUSTOMERS' on database
jdbc:oracle:thin:@dbserver:1521:database
SQL Query: 'select CUSTOMERFIRSTNAME from CUSTOMERS' took 20 milliseconds t
o execute
Retrieved JDBC ResultSet oracle.jdbc.driver.OracleResultSetImpl@2aa14a at L
ogCustomerNames.readCustomers()
Customer Name
-------------
Catherine
Steve
Diane
Closed JDBC ResultSet oracle.jdbc.driver.OracleResultSetImpl@2aa14a
Closed JDBC Statement oracle.jdbc.driver.OracleStatement@7a84e4
Closed JDBC Connection oracle.jdbc.driver.OracleConnection@6a9d42

C:\BegJavaDB\Chapter17>
```

As you can see above, this simple program takes quite a few lines of code to implement the logging technique (although 80 lines of the above 'code' are in fact comments and Javadoc comments to help understand what is happening).

How It Works

Let's dig into exactly what parts of the program above address which typical Java database program problems.

Exception Logging

When you catch an exception in your code, you will probably want to know the information discussed in the previous section, in order to debug why you received the exception. Say you are having problems connecting to the database. The following code, extracted from the program above, will log all the information previously discussed. This information includes the name of the exception and its error message, which database instance you are trying to connect to, and finally, a stack trace showing exactly where in the code the exception was thrown.

```
    try {

      // Get the connection
      databaseConnection = getConnection();

// make use of the connection
    } catch (Exception e) {

      // Something went wrong with connection, log it
      System.err.println("Error opening connection to database '" +
                         ORACLE_DEMO_DB_URL + "', caught exception " + e);
      e.printStackTrace();
    }
```

Every time an exception is generated, the JVM records a **stack trace** inside the exception. A stack trace is a record of the nested method calls (including the class name and even the line of code inside that class!) on the current execution thread. The method that generated the exception is the first method reported on the stack trace (at the top), followed by the method which called that method, and so on. This continues until the JVM traces the method call stack back to the original method that created the thread and started the whole process (shown at the bottom of the trace). Executing the `printStackTrace()` method of the exception prints the exception's stack trace out to the `System.err` output stream.

Here is an example program execution, showing the output of the above program encountering an error:

```
Error opening connection to database 'jdbc:oracle:thin:@dbserver:1521:database',
caught exception java.sql.SQLException: ORA-01033: ORACLE initialization or
shutdown in progress

java.sql.SQLException: ORA-01033: ORACLE initialization or shutdown in progress

        at oracle.jdbc.dbaccess.DBError.throwSqlException(DBError.java:114)
        at oracle.jdbc.ttc7.TTIoer.processError(TTIoer.java:208)
        at oracle.jdbc.ttc7.O3log.receive1st(O3log.java, Compiled Code)
        at oracle.jdbc.ttc7.TTC7Protocol.logon(TTC7Protocol.java:224)
        at oracle.jdbc.driver.OracleConnection.<init>(OracleConnection.java:198)
        at oracle.jdbc.driver.OracleDriver.getConnectionInstance(OracleDriver.ja
va:251)
        at oracle.jdbc.driver.OracleDriver.connect(OracleDriver.java:224)
        at java.sql.DriverManager.getConnection(DriverManager.java:457)
        at java.sql.DriverManager.getConnection(DriverManager.java:106)
        at LogCustomerNames.getConnection(LogCustomerNames.java:73)
        at LogCustomerNames.runQuery(LogCustomerNames.java:212)
        at LogCustomerNames.main(LogCustomerNames.java:264)
```

As you can see from the output, it is very easy to debug the source of the problem. The program was trying to connect to the Oracle database, which was in the process of an initialization or shutdown sequence, so it could not connect. You can see precisely where in the code the error was encountered. The first stack frames reported are methods executed inside the JDBC driver, so keep going down the stack trace until you find the first class you wrote (`LogCustomerNames`). A `SQLException` was generated from line 73 of Java class `LogCustomerNames.java`, inside method `getConnection()`. Too easy to identify the problem? Sure, but it is nice to start with easy errors to get used to the way Java outputs a stack trace.

One quick note before we move on; very few developers actually output all of this information for every exception they capture. Most just dump the stack and move on. When you do so, you risk not having all the information needed to rapidly debug the error. In the above example, we can see the machine name and port of the database instance to which we were trying to connect, so in an environment where you have many databases running, you know which database is having the problem. The stack trace does not give this information, so weigh the risk of not having all the information necessary to debug the problem against the time it takes to code the output of that information.

Another thing to note about stack traces like this is that they shouldn't be presented to the user of the program ever. Not only are they not helpful, but they can also be off-putting. Additionally, if a malicious user sees the stack trace, it could reveal secrets about the workings of your code that you don't want made public. For a production environment, we would replace the somewhat ugly (but useful) stack trace with a more presentable error message for the user.

Resource Tracking

Database connections are by far the most precious resources to track. If you can't get a database connection because previous executions of your program acquired connections, but did not free them, you will be unable to run your application until these resources are timed out by the database. As an example, we will log database connection resources, but remember there are several other JDBC resources to track as well. In the following code snippet, we connect to an Oracle database and log this fact in a message to `System.out`:

```
// Get the connection
databaseConnection = getConnection();

// Log the fact we got a connection so we remember to clean up
System.out.println("Opened JDBC Connection " +
    databaseConnection + " at LogCustomerNames.runQuery()");
```

Note that in the output message we record the class and method we are in, and the resource identifier (printing the `databaseConnection` object typically causes the memory location of the resource to be printed, which is a unique identifier for the resource). Next we put out a log message after we close this resource (using the same format as above), as follows:

```
databaseConnection.close();

// Log the fact we closed the connection
System.out.println("Closed JDBC Connection " + databaseConnection);
```

Running the program, we get output similar to the following:

```
Opened JDBC Connection oracle.jdbc.driver.OracleConnection@f4974841 in method
LogCustomerNames.runQuery()
...
Closed JDBC Connection oracle.jdbc.driver.OracleConnection@f4974841
```

If you put this type of logging in your code, every time you open or close a resource, you can easily find which resources you have forgotten to clean up. In cases where you have not properly freed all your resources, the quantity of close log messages will be less than the quantity of open log messages. You can match open messages to close messages by resource identifier (`f4974841` in the above example) and trace unclosed resources back to where they were opened by the class and method name in the logging statement.

Another addition we could make, but don't here, is the time the connection is established. Although we could provide this functionality, we'll leave this for a logging framework to implement for us.

Logging Performance Timings

It seems as though developers of large database applications are constantly bombarded by complaints of performance problems. To track down the cause of performance problems, you either need a good code profiler, as discussed earlier, or you need to log how long it takes to perform actions in your code. Even if you do use a code profiler, you probably don't want to run it in production, as most slow your code down considerably since they gather statistics on execution. If you want to use `System.out` to output timings from your code, you can easily do this by capturing the system time, in milliseconds, right before an action you think may be slow, then performing the action, then capturing the system time in milliseconds again immediately afterward. Given the two timestamps, write the difference between them to `System.out` as the time it took to perform that event, in milliseconds. The following code snippet does this when executing a SQL query:

```
// Start a timer
long queryStartTime = System.currentTimeMillis();

// Execute query
resultSet = statement.executeQuery(SQL_QUERY);

// Calculate time to execute and log
long queryTime = System.currentTimeMillis() - queryStartTime;
System.out.println("SQL Query: '" +
    SQL_QUERY + "' took " + queryTime +
    " milliseconds to execute");
```

Running the program, we get output something like:

```
SQL Query: 'select NAME from CUSTOMER' took 261 milliseconds to execute
```

As you can see, the code to do this timing is a bit cumbersome, but the end result is very valuable when analyzing performance problems.

Given all the above knowledge of how to log typical Java database problems, you are now equipped to do some analysis of the advantages and disadvantages of using `System.out` and `System.err`.

Advantages of System.out and System.err Logging

The main advantage of using `System.out` and `System.err` to log errors, traces, and timings, is that the output streams are very easy for programmers to use. They are available to all Java code statements through an implicit language import, and require no configuration work. They are *convenient* for programmers to use.

In both cases, we can specify to where the message gets written. The standard output for `System.out` is the command line; for `System.err` it is the same. This latter print stream is the one most likely to be changed, using the `System.setErr(PrintStream err)` method. We need a `PrintStream` object; for the purposes of `System.err` it is commonly a log file. After the call to `setErr()`, all further `System.err.println()` method calls send the message to that file.

Limitations of System.out and System.err Logging

The main limitation of the `System.out` and `System.err` logging approach is scaling it for large, long-running applications. There are only two output streams – log all errors to `System.err`, and all other messages to `System.out`. Large systems need the ability to segregate error and trace logs by function (for example, write HTML log files in one place, database access logs in a second place, security logs in a third place, and so on). They also need to write logs to files and keep them for a system execution history. Additionally, critical errors should not just get written to files, but rather, someone should be automatically notified to correct the error as soon as possible thereafter it first appears.

Another problem with logging to output streams is the large amount of code involved in this approach. Most programmers do not take the time to log all errors, resources, and timings necessary to debug all the different problems that may happen in the code. In their defense, doing so would probably result in more code doing the work of logging than doing the real work of the system, and it would of course slow the system down considerably. Instead, programmers will take a guess as to the most critical sections of code and log them more aggressively, hoping that this investment will pay off. When they don't log a particular section of code that has a problem in it, the programmer must go back to that section, insert log statements, recompile the code, and re-execute the program to recreate the error. This process takes quite some time, but with the newly added logging code, they could hopefully find the defect right away. If they don't, they repeat the cycle again and again until they log the correct source of the defect, getting valuable information needed to resolve it. Of course, the larger the program, the less likely you are to guess the correct portion of the code to log.

You will find two nasty side effects when you insert logging statements into a problematic program. Developers typically have a more advanced, but less stable, test version of the program, where they work on enhancements to the system. This version does not match the version (say in production) having the problems. Developers must remember to reload the code that exactly matches the version having problems, insert logging statements, and then try to reproduce the error with that one-off version of the production code. You need a very mature configuration management process to do this correctly. The second side effect is even more problematic. When you insert logging statements into a program, you change the program by definition. Your change may mask the defect, move it, or create new ones.

One other problem to note with logging to `System.err` and `System.out` is that often you need the context of the error, or information about what the system is doing before, and sometimes after, the error. As we discussed previously, in a database transaction where you execute several SQL statements, and the error isn't in the first SQL statement (it could be five or ten statements down the line), you probably need to know all the previous SQL statements executed in order to debug the failing statement. If you unconditionally log all your SQL statements to `System.out`, along with other context information, you will quickly find that output stream cluttered with information you do not need most of the time. This makes it much more difficult to find the information you do need when the time comes to debug a problem.

A final problem comes into play if your Java code is running in a threaded environment (pretty much all application servers are heavily threaded for performance and throughput) or is itself multi-threaded. The statements we logged above did not take into account the thread of execution. Therefore, log statements from one thread can be intermixed with any number of other threads. The output streams will be gibberish if you don't have a way to segregate one thread's output from another. You can do so easily by appending the name of the thread to each output statement, but programmers rarely remember to do this.

In summary, if you are lucky enough to guess the right sections of code to log, and you are thorough in the information you are logging, the technique of using `System.err` and `System.out` works pretty well. However, if you don't guess correctly (and chances are you won't in a large program), inserting logging statements after the fact is a very inefficient and error-prone process. Interactive debuggers were invented precisely to be able to debug a program without having to insert new logging statements.

Running a Local Interactive Debugger

Interactive debuggers have been commonplace in the software industry for many years now. Several companies provide interactive debuggers in their commercial Java development environments, and there is at least one freely available development environment with an excellent interactive debugger. Developers can set breakpoints in the code to stop the code in its tracks at a particular line.

After setting breakpoints, you then tell the debugger to launch the application and execute the code until it hits a breakpoint. Once the debugger halts system execution on a breakpoint, the developer can examine (and sometimes even alter) the values of pretty much any variable actively in use. So the limitations when logging output to mechanisms like `System.out` above do not apply. The developer can step through the execution of their code and view almost anything the system is doing, without having to make any changes to or recompilations of the code.

Let's go on to see how an interactive debugger can help us with the typical Java database application problems we may encounter.

Try It Out – Interactive Debugging

The following program, `BareCustomerNames.java`, is a version of the customer name program we discussed in the last section, stripped of almost all logging statements.

```
import java.util.*;
import java.sql.*;

/**
 * This class connects to the Oracle demo database and reads
 * customer names from the CUSTOMER table, outputing
 * them to System.out.  It does very little logging, only
 * catching a single exception in the main program so you know
 * what to catch in an interactive debugger,
 * should something go wrong.
 */
public class BareCustomerNames {

  /**
   * Constant for the name of the JDBC Driver class connecting
   * to the Oracle demo database.
   */
  private static final String ORACLE_JDBC_DRIVER_CLASS_NAME =
    "oracle.jdbc.driver.OracleDriver";

  /**
```

```
     * Constant for the name of the URL for where the Oracle
     * JDBC driver will connect to the database.
     */
    private static final String ORACLE_DEMO_DB_URL =
      "jdbc:oracle:thin:@dbserver:1521:database";

    /**
     * Constants for the user to log into the Oracle demo database.
     */
    private static final String ORACLE_DEMO_DB_USERID_PROPERTY = "user";
    private static final String ORACLE_DEMO_DB_USERID = "beg";

    /**
     * Constants for the password to log into the Oracle demo database.
     */
    private static final String ORACLE_DEMO_DB_PASSWORD_PROPERTY = "password";
    private static final String ORACLE_DEMO_DB_PASSWORD = "java";

    /**
     * Constant for the SQL Query to execute
     */
    private static final String SQL_QUERY = "select CUSTOMERFIRSTNAME from
  CUSTOMERS";

    /**
     * Helper method to retrieve a JDBC connection from
     * the Oracle demo database.  Note, this code must be called
     * in a try block with a finally block which closes the connection.
     *
     * @throws Exception if the connection cannot be created
     *
     * @return JDBC Connection to the Oracle demo database if successful
     */
    private Connection getConnection() throws Exception {

      // Create a new instance of the driver manager class, so
      // it initializes itself for use and registers with the
      // JDBC DriverManager
      Class.forName(ORACLE_JDBC_DRIVER_CLASS_NAME).newInstance();

      // Create connection properties object
      Properties connectionProperties = new Properties();

      connectionProperties.put(ORACLE_DEMO_DB_USERID_PROPERTY,
                               ORACLE_DEMO_DB_USERID);

      connectionProperties.put(ORACLE_DEMO_DB_PASSWORD_PROPERTY,
                               ORACLE_DEMO_DB_PASSWORD);

      // create a connection
      return DriverManager.getConnection(ORACLE_DEMO_DB_URL,
                                         connectionProperties);
    }

    /**
```

```
     * Outputs the customer names from the result set to System.out.
     *
     * @throws SQLException if a JDBC API fails
     */
    private void printResultSet(ResultSet resultSet) throws SQLException {

      // Output a header for the data
      System.out.println("Customer Name");
      System.out.println("-------------");

      while (resultSet.next()) {

        // Retrieve and print the first column
        System.out.println(resultSet.getString(1));
      }
    }

    /**
     * Given an opened JDBC connection, reads customer names
     * from the CUSTOMER table.
     */
    private void readCustomers(Connection connection) throws SQLException {
      Statement statement = null;
      ResultSet resultSet = null;

      // Get a new statement and run the query
      try {
        statement = connection.createStatement();

        // Execute query
        resultSet = statement.executeQuery(SQL_QUERY);

        // Print result set
        printResultSet(resultSet);
      } finally {

        // If we got a result set, close it
        if (resultSet != null) {
          resultSet.close();
        }

        // If we got a statement, close it
        if (statement != null) {
          statement.close();
        }
      }
    }

    /**
     * Main method for the simple program.  Creates a connection
     * to the database, reads customer names from the database,
     * and cleans up.
     *
     * @throws Exception on failure
```

```
   */
  public void runQuery() throws Exception {
    Connection databaseConnection = null;

    try {

      // Get the connection
      databaseConnection = getConnection();

      // Read customers with that connection
      readCustomers(databaseConnection);

    } finally {

      // If we got a connection, close it
      if (databaseConnection != null) {
        databaseConnection.close();
      }
    }
  }

  /**
   * Main method to run the simple program.  Creates a new instance
   * of this class to read and log customer names.
   */
  public static void main(String[] args) {
    BareCustomerNames logCustomerNames = new BareCustomerNames();

    try {
      logCustomerNames.runQuery();
    } catch (Exception e) {
      e.printStackTrace();
    }
  }
}
```

Edit the program above to connect to your database and query your table of choice, then save it as `C:\BegJavaDB\Chapter17\BareCustomerNames.java`. Using an interactive debugger (these come in virtually all Java development environments), set a breakpoint in the `readCustomers()` method. The following screenshot shows an interactive debugger in action, specifically the one that comes as part of Forte for Java, Community Edition. It shows the debugger stopped at a breakpoint, where you can examine the values of any of the variables at hand, including the JDBC connection, statement, and result set:

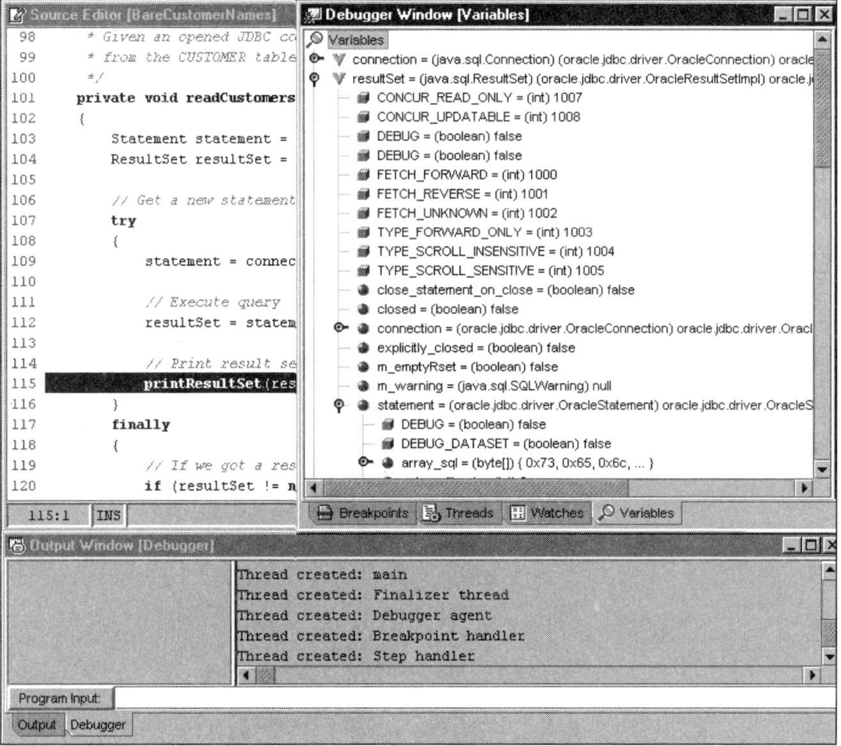
Source Editor [BareCustomerNames]
98 * Given an opened JDBC co
99 * from the CUSTOMER table
100 */
101 private void readCustomers
102 {
103 Statement statement =
104 ResultSet resultSet =
105
106 // Get a new statement
107 try
108 {
109 statement = connec
110
111 // Execute query
112 resultSet = statem
113
114 // Print result se
115 printResultSet(res
116 }
117 finally
118 {
119 // If we got a res
120 if (resultSet != n
115:1 INS
Debugger Window [Variables]
Variables
connection = (java.sql.Connection) (oracle.jdbc.driver.OracleConnection) oracle
resultSet = (java.sql.ResultSet) (oracle.jdbc.driver.OracleResultSetImpl) oracle.j
CONCUR_READ_ONLY = (int) 1007
CONCUR_UPDATABLE = (int) 1008
DEBUG = (boolean) false
DEBUG = (boolean) false
FETCH_FORWARD = (int) 1000
FETCH_REVERSE = (int) 1001
FETCH_UNKNOWN = (int) 1002
TYPE_FORWARD_ONLY = (int) 1003
TYPE_SCROLL_INSENSITIVE = (int) 1004
TYPE_SCROLL_SENSITIVE = (int) 1005
close_statement_on_close = (boolean) false
closed = (boolean) false
connection = (oracle.jdbc.driver.OracleConnection) oracle.jdbc.driver.Oracl
explicitly_closed = (boolean) false
m_emptyRset = (boolean) false
m_warning = (java.sql.SQLWarning) null
statement = (oracle.jdbc.driver.OracleStatement) oracle.jdbc.driver.OracleS
DEBUG = (boolean) false
DEBUG_DATASET = (boolean) false
array_sql = (byte[]) { 0x73, 0x65, 0x6c, ... }
Breakpoints
Threads
Watches
Variables
Output Window [Debugger]
Thread created: main
Thread created: Finalizer thread
Thread created: Debugger agent
Thread created: Breakpoint handler
Thread created: Step handler
Program Input:
Output
Debugger

How It Works

You will note that the program above is over 30 percent smaller than `LogCustomerNames.java`. It is also much easier to read and understand. You won't need to log all that information, as the interactive debugger or code profiler can get to any of it, and more! In the sections below, we will discuss how the `BareCustomerNames.java` program is significantly reduced in complexity while still being able to use an interactive debugger to quickly detect problems in the code.

Exception Handling

When running your Java database application under an interactive debugger (whether as part of an IDE, or as a standalone application), you have a few choices to find and analyze exceptions in your code. Most programmers set breakpoints, or targeted lines of code at which the debugger will stop program execution, near code that generates the exception. Then they can interactively view program variables and step through the code until the exception is thrown.

Many debuggers allow you to stop the program when a particular exception is thrown, which is a much better method than setting breakpoints. You just tell the debugger which exception(s) you are interested in, and the debugger will keep executing the code until one of the watched exceptions is thrown or a breakpoint is encountered. The debugger then shows you the code that generated the exception, and as usual, you can view program variables, the method call stack, and other threads of execution if your program is multi-threaded.

In order to effectively debug your program, you will probably only need to log the stack trace from any exceptions generated. The above program propagates all checked exceptions so you can do this in one place, the main method of the program, and this is shown below:

```
try {
  logCustomerNames.runQuery();
} catch (Exception e) {
  e.printStackTrace();
}
```

The simple output trace generated when any exception is encountered gives you enough information to set breakpoints or exception watches in the debugger.

Resource Tracking

Most debuggers won't be able to help you track resources to make sure that all the resources you create you also freed. You generally have to use code profilers for this instead, as discussed previously. Only a few debuggers include profiling features. If they do, just activate those features during your debugging session and the debugger will track them for you. You don't have to write any code to do this; the profiler monitors resource allocations and de-allocations, and can pinpoint resources you forgot to free. Good profilers (like those mentioned in the *Forgetting to Clean Up Resources* section) allow you to select a resource that hasn't been freed, and then direct you to the sourcecode that allocated the resource. Once you know where in the code you allocate a resource, it is usually a simple matter to figure out where to free it.

Logging Performance Timings

In general, an interactive debugger will not help you with performance timings either. You need to move to a code profiler with performance analysis features. Look in particular for code profilers that monitor JDBC API calls. Most profilers only time the code executing in the JVM, which doesn't account for the time it takes to communicate with an external database. You are likely be very concerned with the time it takes to execute a query or update, retrieve a `ResultSet`, or create a connection to the database, so make sure your profiler tracks the time the JVM waits on the database performing such actions.

Advantages of Local Interactive Debugging

The main advantage of an interactive debugger is that you do not need to modify your program in order to debug it. The debugger just runs your code under your control, and allows you to see pretty much anything going on in your system. If you forgot to log some data needed to debug the problem at hand – no problem. You just stop the code and navigate through debugger screens to find the data you need to see. Also, you don't have to be concerned about data overload. You target the data you want to look at, and ignore the rest. No more sifting through hundreds of lines of logging output, either. If you have a debugger that can stop on thrown exceptions, you can debug these types of errors more effectively with this technique than any other.

Another advantage with this technique is that your code is not cluttered with logging statements, as compared with the previous technique. The program will run faster without those statements, as it takes time for Java to construct the log messages and output them to the output streams. Your code will be smaller and easier to read without logging statements.

Limitations of Local Interactive Debugging

There are several limitations to using a local interactive debugger. The most problematic limitation is that you must be able to recreate the problem locally, that is, where the interactive debugger is installed (typically on your development computer). Many Java database application problems cannot be recreated on a developer test machine; they only fail in a high-volume production environment. You will not want to install and use an interactive debugger in a production environment, as the debugger slows performance, and of course entirely stops the system when you hit a breakpoint or watched exception. However, when you can recreate the problem on a developer test machine, you should be able to find the problem much more quickly with this technique compared to inserting calls to `System.out` and recompiling the code.

A second limitation of this technique is one we discussed in the last technique as well. Since you run a local debugging session on your test machine, and not in production, you must make sure you are running the same version of the code as the system having the problem. If the problem is in a production system, developers rarely have this version on their computer. If your version control procedures are lacking, you may not be able to reliably reproduce the correct version of the code. You could be debugging a version of the code that doesn't have the problem at all, or you could be wasting time debugging defects in your version only, and not in the problematic system.

A third limitation in using this technique is that of problem context. You may want to see, for example, previous SQL statements executed as a context for what is happening when an exception or performance problem is encountered. If you interactively step through the code before the problem, you can sort of see the context of the problem. This is often cumbersome though, as interactive debuggers step through many lines of code (for example, getters and setters) that you are most likely not interested in. You can usually tell the debugger to step over methods you do not care about (that is, the debugger executes the entire method, it just doesn't stop on each line for you to view its execution). However, this process can easily distract you from the problem at hand.

Most debuggers have limits on the amount of code profiling they do. Traditional debuggers without profiling options really only help us deal with the first common application error; debugging exceptions. Tracing resources and performance problems generally require a different tool or approach.

A final limitation of the local interactive debugger is that often this technique will not work. If your code runs inside an application server, you will run into a problem where most application servers have a variety of options and configuration settings. If you try to start the application server within an interactive debugging environment, you may have great difficulty configuring the JVM to start correctly. You could spend more time trying to get the application server to run inside the debugger than it takes to insert a couple of logging statements to `System.out` (or even debugging *your* code). This is where running a remote debugging session can help a great deal.

Running a Remote Interactive Debugger

Many of the limitations of a local interactive debugger above are addressed with an architectural enhancement to the debugger and the JVM. Instead of only being able to debug code locally started and controlled by the debugger, what if you could communicate with any JVM, anywhere network-accessible, to establish a debugging session just when that system has problems? You wouldn't have to go through all the work to reproduce the error on a test machine under the control of a local debugger, which can be a significant or in some cases impossible effort. **JPDA** (**J**ava **P**latform **D**ebugger **Ar**chitecture) is a new Java standard put in place precisely for this reason. Any debugger supporting this standard should be able to dynamically (that is, while the JVM is running) attach to any JVM supporting this standard, as shown below:

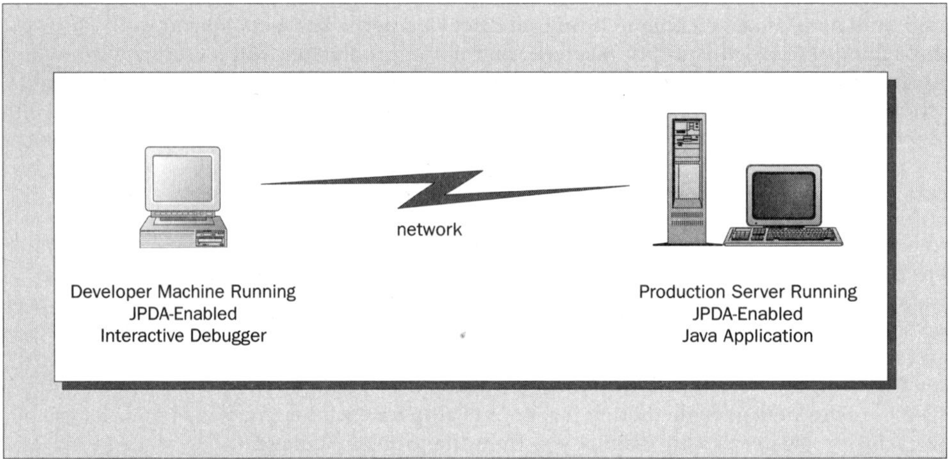

No changes whatsoever are necessary in your code to use a remote interactive debugger over a local interactive debugger.

For more information on the JPDA, take a look at http://java.sun.com/products/jpda/. JDK1.3 comes with the JPDA as standard.

Try It Out – Remote Interactive Debugging

Instead of running the `BareCustomerNames.java` program from within an interactive debugger, run the very same program from a command line using a JDK that is JPDA-enabled for debugging. Sun's JDK version 1.3 or above has JPDA features installed automatically. Using such a JDK, you start the program as follows (the command is all one line):

```
java -Xdebug -Xnoagent -Xrunjdwp:transport=dt_socket,server=y,address=8000
                       -Djava.compiler=NONE BareCustomerNames
```

The Java program above was started with a JPDA socket listener on port 8000. With the options above, no code in the `BareCustomerNames` program is executed until you attach the debugger. See your JDK documentation for other JPDA start options.

The screenshot opposite shows an interactive debugger tracing the execution of the remote JVM we started, with a breakpoint set in the `printResultSet()` method.

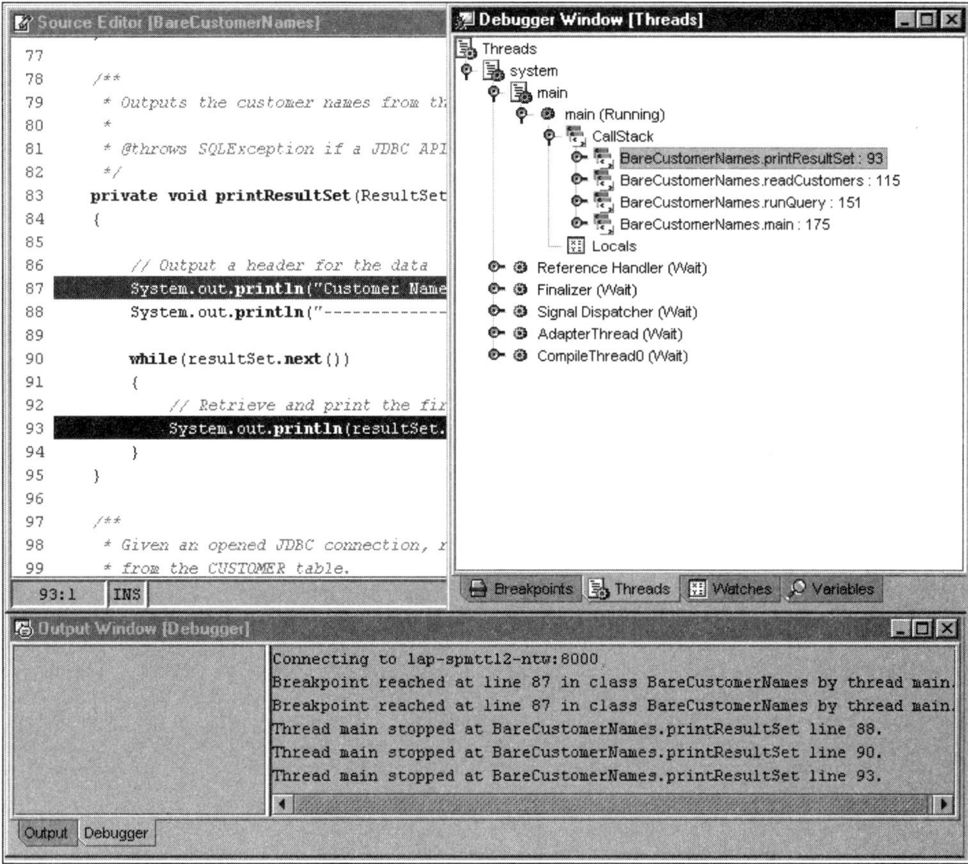

Using a JPDA-enabled debugger, you next attach to this process and interactively debug it just as if it were running locally. Simply tell the debugger to attach to the machine running the process above, tell it to use the socket listener type (`dt_socket`), and give it port 8000.

Remote Debugging Typical Java Database Application Problems

A remote debugging session (such as may be provided by a JPDA-compliant debugger) addresses program defects in the same manner as a local debugging session. See the previous section for a discussion of how interactive debuggers can be used to debug exceptions, trace resources, and detect performance problems. The same test program (`BareCustomerNames.java`) applies.

Advantages of Remote Interactive Debugging

Remote interactive debugging has the same advantages as using a local interactive debugger. The only difference is that a remote debugger removes many of the limitations of an interactive debugger restricted to local execution. See below for remaining limitations.

Limitations of Remote Interactive Debugging

Remote interactive debugging does little to address problem context, having the same limitation discussed in the last section with local interactive debugging.

Enabling remote debugging also has side effects. You can only attach to a JVM that is running with remote debugging enabled. To start a JVM in a JPDA-enabled mode (as we saw above), not only do you start a JPDA listener (to receive the remote debuggers order), but you also must turn off JVM optimizations so the remote debugger can correctly step through your code.

High-performance JVMs, like Sun's HotSpot, optimize your code in a variety of ways during its execution. The JVM may inline method calls, compress class hierarchies, and use a variety of other optimization techniques. The results of code execution are the same optimized, as non-optimized; it just takes less time to run the optimized code. If a remote debugger tried to step through the execution of optimized code, it wouldn't make sense to you, the programmer. That defeats the purpose of interactive debugging, so you need to turn *all* optimizations off. You will want to be very selective in the JVMs you enable for JPDA remote debugging, as they will then run significantly slower.

An even more detrimental side effect of remote debugging a production Java application is that breakpoints will stop the system dead in its tracks. You generally do not want to stop production applications, even if they have problems here and there.

A final problem to note is that remote debugging is slower than local debugging. Quite a bit of information is needed to coordinate the remote debugger and the JVM. That information needs to go between two machines across the network, instead of just between two processes on the same machine. If you are going to conduct a prolonged interactive debugging session, you may want to try to recreate and debug the problem locally.

Instrumenting Your Application

Instrumenting your application is like putting the `System.out` and `System.err` debugging technique on steroids. You use a logging or instrumentation framework to remove many of the limitations of simple output streams.

For example, a good logging framework allows you to segregate logging for different portions of your large application. It remembers to record the date and time of each log entry, as well as the thread of execution. It can output log entries to more than one place at a time, so you can log important errors to a file, as well as notify someone via pager or e-mail. Logging frameworks know to dump the stack of an exception and record this information in the log entry, along with the exception name and error message.

The Java programming environment is just now starting to develop standards for application logging. Until those standards are widely adopted and incorporated into released and supported development environments, we have to turn to proprietary solutions. There are several open source alternatives you can use for free.

One of those is the logging framework that is part of the open source project called Java Layered Frameworks (**JLF**), which can be found at http://jlf.sourceforge.net/, which we discussed in Chaper 16. If you have not already done so, you will need to download the full implementation ZIP file (`jlfDistribution.zip`), and extract it to a convenient directory (`JLF2_0`, say).

We will show how you can use JLF to address each of the three typical Java database application problems. Before we can do this though, we need to step back and prepare to instrument the entire application. It is not until you properly instrument your whole application that you achieve the true benefits of this technique.

Steps to Application Instrumentation

Previous techniques for debugging Java database applications did not address problem context. What interesting events (that is, interesting from the perspective of being able to rapidly detect and correct defects) took place before and after the error? A well-instrumented application will precisely answer that question. Here are some steps you should follow to instrument your application properly:

1. Determine system event criticalities
2. Determine interesting events you will log and at what granularity
3. Document and enforce the standards above
4. Use a good logging/instrumentation framework to instrument your application

System Event Criticalities

Say a significant event happens in your Java code. This event could be any of several different types and conditions. Before you start instrumenting your application, you must categorize and document what you perceive as interesting events so that all developers log events consistently. The first categorization is the **criticality** of the event.

The JLF logging framework, by default, uses the six system event criticalities shown in the following table. You may tailor these to your needs, as long as the more important the event, the lower the number (high numbers are for less critical events):

Level	Name	Purpose
1	`CRITICAL_ERROR`	The system encountered a critical error at this logging level, which affects the overall accuracy, integrity, reliability, or capability of the system. Someone should be paged to address the error as soon as possible.
2	`ERROR`	The system encountered an unexpected error at this logging level, which means the code intercepted an error it cannot handle. This error is not of a critical nature and can be typically recovered from automatically. Future requests into the system should be able to be processed without error. Someone should be e-mailed to resolve the error in the near future to increase the reliability of the product.

Table continued on following page

Level	Name	Purpose
3	`WARNING`	The system encountered an expected error situation. The system recovered from it, but the fact that it happened should be recorded to see how *frequently* it happens.
4	`INFORMATION`	Normal logging level. All interesting periodic events should be logged at this level, so someone looking through the log can see the amount and type of processing happening in the system (this forms the context for helping to resolve any problems in the system).
5	`DETAIL`	Moderately detailed logging level to be used to help debug typical problems in the system. Not so detailed that the big picture gets lost.
6	`TRACE`	Most detailed logging level. Everything sent to the log will be logged. Use this level to trace system execution for really nasty problems. At this level, the logging will typically be so verbose that the system performance will be affected.

Logging Granularity

Once you have agreed upon a set of event criticalities and documented them in your coding standards, you need to determine the **granularity** to which you will log those events. For example, an application may have a thread pool, a database connection pool, and a request processing framework. It executes lots of SQL statements, using many JDBC resources in the process.

Now, when debugging a thread pool problem say, you will not want the log to be cluttered with SQL log statements or resource traces. Create one log for the thread pool, a second for SQL statements, and a third for resource tracing. If the application is very large, create separate logs for the different subsystems of the application. If not, just have one log for the non-specific parts of the application.

The following table shows a sample logging granularity for a fictitious system:

Log Name	Purpose
`AppLog`	General application event logging
`SQLLog`	Logs all SQL-related processing activities
`ThreadLog`	Logs all events related to managing the thread pool
`RequestLog`	Logs all requests into the system, including the time to fulfill the request
`DbPoolLog`	Logs events related to managing the database connection pool

You will need to look over your application, decide how many logs you want, and what information they will log. Too few logs and they will get flooded with information, thus causing difficulties sorting through a log file in order to debug a problem. Too many logs and you will spend a lot of time managing and correlating problems between them all.

Next, document and enforce logging granularity standards for your application. If you do not take this step, your logs will become inconsistent, and you will not be able to debug your application as quickly. For example, say you have a `SQLLog` and an `AppLog` in your application and someone logs a SQL statement to `AppLog`. Or maybe someone doesn't log the SQL statement at all. Either way, when you try to debug a problem querying the database, you look in the `SQLLog` to see what SQL statements your system is processing and not all the information is there. If the errant SQL statement is not logged according to your standards, you will not be able to find the problem as quickly.

Instrumentation Standards

This is another reminder for you to make sure you document how you are going to log events in your code. Sorry to be redundant, but it is so important that we need to discuss it again. If you don't document logging standards and enforce them somehow (for example, through code reviews, code inspections, or other approaches), this technique will only be as effective as logging to `System.out` and `System.err`.

You will have to go back and insert logging statements into your code when the logs don't contain the information you need to resolve the problem. You will have to recompile and re-deploy your code, then recreate the problem. A well-instrumented application will help you pinpoint defects without *any* modifications to the code, whether that code be in production, or on your development computer.

Logging Framework Implementation

Once you have thought through the issues above and developed standards for instrumentation, you are ready to implement them with a logging or instrumentation framework. Since this is a common technique for debugging programs, especially large and complex ones, several frameworks are freely available. JDK release 1.4 and above will have logging capabilities standardized and built into the language libraries. For now though, you need to use a proprietary solution. As discussed previously, we will demonstrate the logging framework portion of the open source JLF package in the remainder of the chapter.

We will instrument just about the simplest Java database application possible, though rarely will you encounter such a trivial task. You probably have an existing application with thousands of lines of code to deal with. Most projects move to instrumentation techniques as they have outgrown simpler debugging techniques. Just about any size project can be instrumented, but you don't get there overnight. You should start instrumenting your problem areas first.

For example, if you are having query performance problems, search through your entire application for all SQL queries. Add instruments for each query, and don't concern yourself about all the other things you are supposed to instrument – at least not yet. Run your application, see the benefits of that simple instrumentation addition, and then move on systematically to instrument other problems in your application in order of problem criticality. Refrain from trying to instrument everything in your application from day one, or you are likely to get frustrated and lose the discipline needed to maintain the technique.

Instrumenting with JLF

The following Java program, `InstrumentCustomerNames.java`, is another version of the same customer name test program we have been using, but applying the instrumentation technique instead. This program logs all output to the `SQLLog` log. Larger applications will need more logs of the granularity discussed in the previous section.

Try It Out – Application Instrumentation via JLF

```
import java.util.*;
import java.sql.*;

import org.jlf.log.*;

/**
 * This class connects to the Oracle demo database and reads
 * customer names from the CUSTOMER table, outputting
 * them to System.out.  Along the way,
 * it logs information to the JLF Logging Framework,
 * so you can debug the program should something go wrong.
 */
public class InstrumentCustomerNames {

  /**
   * Constant for the name of the JDBC Driver class connecting
   * to the Oracle demo database.
   */
  private static final String ORACLE_JDBC_DRIVER_CLASS_NAME =
    "oracle.jdbc.driver.OracleDriver";

  /**
   * Constant for the name of the URL for where the Oracle
   * JDBC driver will connect to the database.
   */
  private static final String ORACLE_DEMO_DB_URL =
    "jdbc:oracle:thin:@dbserver:1521:database";

  /**
   * Constants for the user to log into the Oracle demo database.
   */
  private static final String ORACLE_DEMO_DB_USERID_PROPERTY = "user";
  private static final String ORACLE_DEMO_DB_USERID = "beg";

  /**
   * Constants for the password to log into the Oracle demo database.
   */
  private static final String ORACLE_DEMO_DB_PASSWORD_PROPERTY = "password";
  private static final String ORACLE_DEMO_DB_PASSWORD = "java";

  /**
   * Constant for the SQL Query to execute
   */
  private static final String SQL_QUERY = "select CUSTOMERFIRSTNAME from
CUSTOMERS";

  /**
   * Helper method to retrieve a JDBC connection from
   * the Oracle demo database.  Note, this code must be called
   * in a try block with a finally block which closes the connection.
   *
   * @return JDBC Connection to the Oracle demo database if successful
```

```
 */
private Connection getConnection() {

  try {

    // Create a new instance of the driver manager class, so
    // it initializes itself for use and registers with the
    // JDBC DriverManager
    Class.forName(ORACLE_JDBC_DRIVER_CLASS_NAME).newInstance();

    // Create connection properties object
    Properties connectionProperties = new Properties();

    connectionProperties.put(ORACLE_DEMO_DB_USERID_PROPERTY,
                             ORACLE_DEMO_DB_USERID);

    connectionProperties.put(ORACLE_DEMO_DB_PASSWORD_PROPERTY,
                             ORACLE_DEMO_DB_PASSWORD);

    // create a connection
    return DriverManager.getConnection(ORACLE_DEMO_DB_URL,
                                       connectionProperties);
  } catch (Exception e) {

    // Something went wrong with connection, log it
    throw new AppError("Error opening connection to database " +
                       ORACLE_DEMO_DB_URL, e, SQLLog.getInstance(),
                                          Log.CRITICAL_ERROR_LEVEL);
  }
}

/**
 * Outputs the customer names from the result set to System.out.
 */
private void printResultSet(ResultSet resultSet) {

  // Output a header for the data
  System.out.println("Customer Name");
  System.out.println("-------------");

  try {
    while (resultSet.next()) {

      // Retrieve and print the first column
      System.out.println(resultSet.getString(1));
    }
  } catch (SQLException e) {

    // Something went wrong retrieving result set, log it
    throw new AppError("Error retrieving result set rows from '" +
                       resultSet + "'", e, SQLLog.getInstance(),
                                          Log.CRITICAL_ERROR_LEVEL);
  }
}
```

```
/**
 * Given an opened JDBC connection, reads customer names
 * from the CUSTOMER table.
 */
private void readCustomers(Connection connection) {
  Statement statement = null;
  ResultSet resultSet = null;

  // Get a new statement and run the query
  try {
    statement = connection.createStatement();

    // Log the fact we got a connection so we remember to clean up
    SQLLog.trace("Opened JDBC Statement " + statement +
                 " at InstrumentCustomerNames.readCustomers()");

    // Log that we are trying to execute the query
    SQLLog.info("Executing SQL Query: '" + SQL_QUERY + "' on database " +
                ORACLE_DEMO_DB_URL);

    // Start a timer
    AppInstrument queryInstrument =
      new AppInstrument("executing SQL Query '" + SQL_QUERY,
                        SQLLog.getInstance());

    // Execute query
    resultSet = statement.executeQuery(SQL_QUERY);

    // Log time to execute query
    queryInstrument.logTime();

    // Log that we aquired a result set to clean up
    SQLLog.trace("Retrieved JDBC ResultSet " + resultSet +
                 " at InstrumentCustomerNames.readCustomers()");

    // Print result set
    printResultSet(resultSet);

  } catch (SQLException e) {

    // Something went wrong with query, log it
    throw new AppError("Error querying database " + ORACLE_DEMO_DB_URL,
                       e, SQLLog.getInstance(), Log.CRITICAL_ERROR_LEVEL);
  }
  finally {

    // If we got a result set, close it
    if (resultSet != null) {
      try {
        resultSet.close();

        // Log the fact we closed the result set
        SQLLog.trace("Closed JDBC ResultSet " + resultSet);
```

```
        } catch (SQLException e) {

          // Something went wrong closing result set, log it
          throw new AppError("Error closing result set " + resultSet, e,
                             SQLLog.getInstance(), Log.ERROR_LEVEL);
        }
      }

      // If we got a statement, close it
      if (statement != null) {
        try {
          statement.close();

          // Log the fact we closed the statement
          SQLLog.trace("Closed JDBC Statement " + statement);
        } catch (SQLException e) {

          // Something went wrong closing statement, log it
          throw new AppError("Error closing statement " + statement, e,
                             SQLLog.getInstance(), Log.ERROR_LEVEL);
        }
      }
    }
  }

  /**
   * Main method for the simple program.  Creates a connection
   * to the database, reads customer names from the database,
   * and cleans up.
   */
  public void runQuery() {
    Connection databaseConnection = null;

    try {

      // Get the connection
      databaseConnection = getConnection();

      // Log the fact we got a connection so we remember to clean up
      SQLLog.trace("Opened JDBC Connection " + databaseConnection +
                   " at InstrumentCustomerNames.runQuery()");

      // Read customers with that connection
      readCustomers(databaseConnection);
    }
    finally {

      // If we got a connection, close it
      if (databaseConnection != null) {
        try {
          databaseConnection.close();

          // Log the fact we closed the connection
          SQLLog.trace("Closed JDBC Connection " + databaseConnection);
```

```
        } catch (SQLException e) {

          // Something went wrong closing connection, log it
          throw new AppError("Error closing connection to database '" +
                             ORACLE_DEMO_DB_URL, e, SQLLog.getInstance(),
                                                    Log.ERROR_LEVEL);
        }

      }
    }
  }

  /**
   * Main method to run the simple program.  Creates a new instance
   * of this class to read and log customer names.
   */
  public static void main(String[] args) {
    InstrumentCustomerNames InstrumentCustomerNames =
      new InstrumentCustomerNames();

    InstrumentCustomerNames.runQuery();
  }
}
```

Edit the program above to connect to your database and query your table of choice, then save it as `C:\BegJavaDB\Chapter17\InstrumentCustomerNames.java`. Compile the program with the following command, issued form the `Chapter17` directory:

```
> javac -classpath .;%JLIB%\jlf.jar InstrumentCustomerNames.java
```

Note that we've stored the `jlf.jar` file that contains all the JLF classes we need in the `C:\java\lib` directory (as referenced by the variable `JLIB`). Before we run the class, we need to add a properties file `App.properties`. This file can go anywhere in the classpath, although the directory we're running `InstrumentCustomerNames` from is the easiest.

The `App.properties` file contains a list of property settings that the JLF uses to determine the level of logging. Here is a simple `App.properties` file that we will use for our example:

```
LoggingLevel = 6
LoggingMechanism = org.jlf.log.StandardErrLoggingMechanism
LogFieldSeparator = |
```

Run the program from the same directory, using the following command:

```
> java -classpath .;%JLIB%\jlf.jar;%JLIB%\classes12.zip
                  InstrumentCustomerNames
```

The initial results should look something like this:

```
C:\BegJavaDB\Chapter17>java -classpath .;%JLIB%\classes12.zip;%JLIB%\jlf.ja
r InstrumentCustomerNames
Log org.jlf.log.SQLLog opened on 17/07/01 at 10:27:41:399
org.jlf.log.SQLLog|L6|10:27:41:399|main|Opened JDBC Connection oracle.jdbc.
driver.OracleConnection@2aa14a at InstrumentCustomerNames.runQuery()
org.jlf.log.SQLLog|L6|10:27:41:419|main|Opened JDBC Statement oracle.jdbc.d
river.OracleStatement@6fd552 at InstrumentCustomerNames.readCustomers()
org.jlf.log.SQLLog|L4|10:27:41:429|main|Executing SQL Query: 'select CUSTOM
ERFIRSTNAME from CUSTOMERS' on database jdbc:oracle:thin:@dbserver:1521:dat
abase
org.jlf.log.SQLLog|L5|10:27:41:459|main|Event: 'executing SQL Query 'select
 CUSTOMERFIRSTNAME from CUSTOMERS' took 0 milliseconds to execute
org.jlf.log.SQLLog|L6|10:27:41:469|main|Retrieved JDBC ResultSet oracle.jdb
c.driver.OracleResultSetImpl@b4b2f at InstrumentCustomerNames.readCustomers
()
Customer Name
-------------
Catherine
Steve
Diane
org.jlf.log.SQLLog|L6|10:27:41:529|main|Closed JDBC ResultSet oracle.jdbc.d
river.OracleResultSetImpl@b4b2f
org.jlf.log.SQLLog|L6|10:27:41:549|main|Closed JDBC Statement oracle.jdbc.d
river.OracleStatement@6fd552
org.jlf.log.SQLLog|L6|10:27:41:559|main|Closed JDBC Connection oracle.jdbc.
driver.OracleConnection@2aa14a

C:\BegJavaDB\Chapter17>
```

Some new and valuable information being reported in this program execution, as explained below.

How It Works

The `InstrumentCustomerNames.java` program is about the same size as the first program, `LogCustomerNames.java`, which is a good bit larger than `BareCustomerNames.java`. However, `InstrumentCustomerNames.java` has a number of advantages to it, discussed in the next section, for roughly the same or fewer lines of code as in the first debugging technique. Let's dig into exactly how these advantages are implemented in the code, again using the JLF logging framework to do all the hard work.

Explaining how the framework does the logging is too complicated for this book; however, we will explain the `App.properties` file a little more:

```
LoggingLevel = 6
LoggingMechanism = org.jlf.log.StandardErrLoggingMechanism
LogFieldSeparator = |
```

The first value, `LoggingLevel`, sets the detail level for event criticality. As it stands, the value 6 will mean that all logging of `Trace` or higher will be shown in the log. If we change this value to 2, we will only get unexpected errors written to the log:

```
C:\BegJavaDB\Chapter17>java -classpath .;%JLIB%\classes12.zip;%JLIB%\jlf.ja
r InstrumentCustomerNames
Customer Name
-------------
Catherine
Steve
Diane

C:\BegJavaDB\Chapter17>
```

Note here the power and convenience of using a logging framework – we make a change to a flat properties file, and the amount of logging information our application produces changes, **without** having to recompile the code.

Any of the above property tags can be overridden for a particular log, by prefixing the property key by the log name. Also note that because you may have more than one logging mechanism open for the same log, you should append a consecutive integer to the property starting at 2. For example:

```
AppLog.LoggingLevel = 3
AppLog.LogFieldSeparator = >
```

In this case, any logging carried out by the `AppLog` would only appear in the log if it was level 3 (warning) or worse, and the fields of the log would be separated by greater than signs.

The `LoggingMechanism` in our example is one provided by the framework, and again is beyond the scope of this chapter to explain. The key thing in this example is that the framework is configurable without changing the code we're running.

Exception Logging

The example program above uses the `AppError` object from the JLF logging framework to wrap and throw exceptions. In the process of re-throwing an exception, it is logged to the logging framework. `AppError` was written purely for convenience. You can use whatever exception-handling strategy you want and log errors manually. However, `AppError` was designed to handle typical error scenarios and minimize the amount of code you need to do so.

The following code snippet from the program creates a new connection to the database. If anything goes wrong, it logs it as a critical error.

```
try {

  // create a connection
  return DriverManager.getConnection(ORACLE_DEMO_DB_URL,
                                     connectionProperties);
} catch (Exception e) {

  // Something went wrong with connection, log it
  throw new AppError("Error opening connection to database " +
                     ORACLE_DEMO_DB_URL, e, SQLLog.getInstance(),
                                          Log.CRITICAL_ERROR_LEVEL);
}
```

In the constructor for the `AppError` object above, there are four parameters:

- The first parameter is a detailed error message, giving data involved in the action that resulted in the error. In our case, we were trying to open a connection to an Oracle database URL, so we state that fact along with the URL we are trying to get to.
- Next we give the exception we caught, so `AppError` can dump its stack trace to the log.
- The third parameter is the log to which we want the error message and stack trace to be logged. The log you use should be determined from the documented coding standards we discussed, and in our case it is `SQLLog` because we are performing a SQL-related operation.

- The final parameter is the logging-level constant. We choose critical error in this situation, as opposed to error or warning, because if you cannot get a connection to the database, nothing else of substance in the program will work, so it is indeed a critical error and someone needs to take a look at it right away to salvage any value in the program.

You will of course choose the logging level to match your documented coding standards, as discussed previously.

The following output is generated when the Oracle database instance we are trying to connect to is unavailable:

```
org.jlf.log.SQLLog|L1|18:01:55:919|main|Application Error: Message: Error opening
connection to database jdbc:oracle:thin:@dbserver:1521:database
Original thrown object message: java.sql.SQLException: Io exception: The Network
 Adapter could not establish the connection
Stack trace:java.sql.SQLException: Io exception: The Network Adapter could not
establish the connection
        at oracle.jdbc.dbaccess.DBError.throwSqlException(DBError.java:114)
        at oracle.jdbc.dbaccess.DBError.throwSqlException(DBError.java:156)
        at oracle.jdbc.dbaccess.DBError.throwSqlException(DBError.java:269)
        at oracle.jdbc.driver.OracleConnection.<init>(OracleConnection.java:210)

        at
oracle.jdbc.driver.OracleDriver.getConnectionInstance(OracleDriver.java:251)
        at oracle.jdbc.driver.OracleDriver.connect(OracleDriver.java:224)
        at java.sql.DriverManager.getConnection(DriverManager.java:517)
        at java.sql.DriverManager.getConnection(DriverManager.java:146)
        at InstrumentCustomerNames.getConnection(InstrumentCustomerNames.java:75)
        at InstrumentCustomerNames.runQuery(InstrumentCustomerNames.java:220)
        at InstrumentCustomerNames.main(InstrumentCustomerNames.java:264)
```

The output above looks very familiar. It is pretty much the same output you receive when executing the `printStackTrace()` method on an exception. The major difference is in the power of the framework to direct log traces when and where you need them. Also, the trace above includes the name of the log (`SQLLog`), the logging level (`L1` meaning `CRITICAL_ERROR`), the time the trace was logged (`18:01:55:919` or just after 6 p.m.), and the thread of execution (`main`). You can configure the logging framework to segregate logs into different files by log name, date them, and/or send out e-mails or pages. You can also extend the logging framework to work the way you want it to, by customizing logging levels, adding logs, developing new logging mechanisms, and so on.

Resource Tracking

Tracking resources works just like tracing resources to an output stream. Simply replace the call to `System.out.println()` with a call to the logging framework. See below for cross-sections of the `InstrumentCustomerNames` program to trace opening and closing a `ResultSet`:

```
        // Execute query
        resultSet = statement.executeQuery(SQL_QUERY);

        // Log that we aquired a result set to clean up
        SQLLog.trace("Retrieved JDBC ResultSet " + resultSet +
                     " at InstrumentCustomerNames.readCustomers()");...
...
```

```
        resultSet.close();

        // Log the fact we closed the result set
        SQLLog.trace("Closed JDBC ResultSet " + resultSet);
```

The traces above were logged at the most detailed level of logging, `TRACE` level. The only time you want to see this information is when you have an idea that your program is forgetting to free some JDBC resources. If you run the program above at the default logging level, `INFORMATION` level, you will not see any of these traces. This shows some of the power of the logging framework.

When you do not want to see very low-level debugging information, instead of removing or commenting out the code to do this (very cumbersome), you simply tell the framework (via a property file setting) that you don't want to see that level of information. You do not change your code one bit, the framework decides if it should log the event during system execution, depending upon the log's logging level setting. Later, when you are having a problem in this area, you tell the framework you want to see `SQLLog` entries at trace level and above. Again, no changes to your code, but this time when it is executed, the following output appears:

```
org.jlf.log.SQLLog|L6|18:46:04:728|main|Retrieved JDBC ResultSet
oracle.jdbc.driver.OracleResultSetImpl@34a1fc at
InstrumentCustomerNames.readCustomers()
...
org.jlf.log.SQLLog|L6|18:46:04:818|main|Closed JDBC ResultSet
oracle.jdbc.driver.OracleResultSetImpl@34a1fc
```

As with exception logging, all traces have the name of the log, level, time, and thread of execution.

Logging Performance Timings

The JLF logging framework uses an `AppInstrument` object to help you time and log events in your application. In the example program above, we chose to time the one and only query in the application. Here is code extracted from the program:

```
    // Start a timer
    AppInstrument queryInstrument =
      new AppInstrument("executing SQL Query '" + SQL_QUERY,
                        SQLLog.getInstance());

    // Execute query
    resultSet = statement.executeQuery(SQL_QUERY);

    // Log time to execute query
    queryInstrument.logTime();
```

The framework starts the timer (that is, records the current time in milliseconds) when you construct an `AppInstrument` object. `AppInstrument`, provided by the JLF, has a number of different constructors you can choose from to customize how the instrument runs. We use a simple one where we give the log message and log instance only. `DETAIL` logging level is assumed.

You proceed with the event while the timer is running. After the event is finished, you tell the instrument to stop the timer and log an entry with that time. The framework does the time calculation for you and reports it to the log you told it to (`SQLLog`), at the `DETAIL` (`L5`) logging level, as shown below:

```
org.jlf.log.SQLLog|L5|12:25:12:053|main|Event: 'executing SQL Query 'select NAME
from CUSTOMER' took 10 milliseconds to execute
```

`AppInstrument` also allows you to set a time threshold and raise the criticality of the log message if the threshold is exceeded. For example, if you want to be e-mailed for any query that takes longer than one second, you can tell `AppInstrument` to log the event at `ERROR` level, simply by using a different constructor.

You are now equipped with all the different debugging and logging techniques we will discuss. Let's analyze the instrumentation approach in detail and wrap up with an overall analysis of the techniques.

Advantages of Application Instrumentation

The main advantage to the application instrumentation technique is that, when done properly, it requires no code changes to detect problems in your code. You instrument your application with information you think will pinpoint you to problems. Then, when your code is running, in test or even in production, you tell the logging framework what events you are interested in viewing. If your application is working fine, you typically tell the framework to log errors and only the most interesting events (that is, `INFO` level or more critical).

When having a problem with a particular part of the application, you tell the framework to log more events of less criticality (for example, set one or two logs to `TRACE` level). At this level, you get a lot more of the problem context that is so important to debug difficult problems. No other debugging technique has this ability to hide or reveal problem context with such ease.

Another advantage to this technique is the speed with which you detect problems. In previous techniques, you typically have to go through quite a bit of work to get the information you need. When debugging a well-instrumented application, you simply look through the log files after you receive a page or e-mail that your production application is having problems. When dealing with exceptions, you may not even need to look at the logs! Your e-mail notification will have a stack trace and tell you the exception name and error message. Often, this is enough to tell you, for example, when a database is down or having problems, so you can contact a database administrator for resolution.

Good logging and instrumentation frameworks also minimize the lines of logging code you insert into your application. The ideal would be none at all, taking the approach of the interactive debugger or code profiler. However, because of the side effects of these tools, you can rarely run them on a production application. Therefore, you will have to put logging statements in your code, and a logging framework minimizes that code compared to directly writing to `System.err` or `System.out`. With one line of code, you can log detailed information on a caught exception, including its stack trace, the thread on which it was executed, and the time and date it happened. That exception can be logged to a file, a page, an e-mail message, or any combination thereof. Resources can be traced with one line of code as well, and taking performance timings only requires two lines of code.

Limitations of Application Instrumentation

Application instrumentation requires developer discipline, often in the form of coding standards and their enforcement. If you forget to instrument something, or instrument it inconsistently, the logged information will be either missing or, worse, misleading. You have access to virtually all information in your application with little or no effort using an interactive debugger.

Instrumentation requires additional lines of code and complexity in your application. We have shown this to be the same as, or less than, the lines of code generally required to log to `System.out` and `System.err`. However, you need practically none when using an interactive debugger.

Instrumentation in Java is 'always on'. That is, code in your system is executed to do instrumentation even when you do not want to see its output. This will slow the overall performance of the system to some degree. Good logging frameworks minimize this performance impact, but cannot eliminate it. This tradeoff comes, however, to achieve the great benefit that you do not need to change, recompile, re-deploy, and retest your code to debug it.

When developing real-time applications, you may have a performance concern here. Java database applications, however, rarely have such aggressive performance requirements. If they did, they would not be using an external database. In the time it takes to execute one query of an external database, you can instrument anywhere from hundreds to millions of events in your application.

Summary

There are numerous advantages and limitations to each debugging technique discussed above. As such, you are not likely to get by using just one to debug your large, complex Java database application.

We looked in this chapter at several means for debugging applications:

- Simple logging to `System.out` and `System.err`, requires no additional classes but a lot of extra lines of code.
- Although using an interactive debugger to step through problem code; has the advantage of lots of information about your code, it does require an interactive debugging program such as are found in IDEs.
- We saw that interactive debugging can potentially be performed on a remote computer, as well as the local computer; attaching a remote debugger to a production application can cause many problems for the users of said application.
- Finally, we looked at instrumenting your application using a logging framework; this has the advantage of being able to provide as much information as you would want without either recompiling the code or using intrusive interactive debugging techniques.

Hopefully you are now well informed on the different techniques and can use the one most appropriate for the situation. For large, complex Java database applications, we have found the instrumentation technique very effective. It allows you to see what is going wrong with your production application without the side effects of changing the code to add logging statements or running it under a debugger. If you do decide to use the instrumentation technique, do it *slowly* and *methodically*. Happy debugging!

akarta
JAVA

JDBC DataSources

While using JDBC through internet-standard URLs offers a standard means for identifying a database connection, the introduction of JDBC 2.0 adds a new feature, a `DataSource`. This Java object encapsulates the information required to establish a database connection, which makes your code more portable and easier to maintain than if a URL was used. In this chapter, we aim to take a closer look at `DataSource` objects. We've seen briefly (in Chapter 8) that they can be used as a convenient means of storing connection information, but they also simplify deployment and are the foundation for other advanced features such as connection pooling and distributed transactions.

However, to make any use of `DataSource` objects, we need to explain how they work and how to use them, and that is the purpose of this chapter. So, we will:

- Cover basic `DataSource` concepts and the services `Datasources` can provide (although we will not go into detail on the latter here)
- Give a step-by-step guide to setting up a `DataSource`
- Re-architect our `Store` class from Chapter 8 to use a `DataSource` object
- Demonstrate how, when using a `DataSource` object, we can take advantage of the performance benefits of connection pooling

DataSource Concepts and Terminology

They say that pictures speak a thousand words, so let's look at an architecture diagram for JDBC:

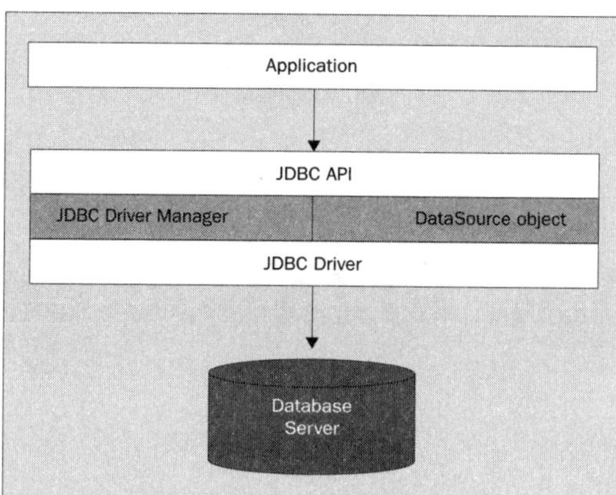

The diagram shows that an application will access a database server through a set of software layers, the first layer being JDBC. This API abstracts (or hides) the details of how a database connection is established and used but will involve the use of a JDBC Driver of one type or another (more on JDBC driver types in Chapter 7).

The diagram shows that the `DataSource` assumes responsibility for the connection between the application and the JDBC driver, a role that would normally have been assumed by the `DriverManager` (and still can) when using JDBC URLs for a connection.

DataSources

In Chapter 8, we looked at a way to make your JDBC classes more flexible by providing a single source for connections, and optionally storing the connection parameters in a configuration file. However, our connection class was still very much part of our application code. If we wished to change the connection parameters, we only had to do so in one place, but we would still have to recompile our application to take account of these changes. There is a similar method of providing connections that uses a class called a `DataSource`. The `DataSource` interface – introduced as part of the `javax.sql` optional package of JDBC 2.0 – attempts to provide a more flexible architecture for creating and using database connections.

> *Note, again, that the `DataSource` itself is an interface. That is, it cannot be instantiated, only implemented.*

A `DataSource` object is created and managed separately from your application. You can modify the `DataSource` to access different databases without making a single change in your application code. The `DataSource` hides the connection details so that you, as the client programmer, never need to worry about the connection URL, host, port, and so on.

The `DataSource` is an interface so, like the other interfaces in the JDBC API (`Connection`, `Statement`, `ResultSet`, and so on), your client code will use variables of the interface type. So, for example, when we get a connection from the `DriverManager`, the variable is of type `Connection`:

```
Connection conn = DriverManager.getConnection(...)
```

But the actual object that is returned by the DriverManager is instantiated from a class that is provided by the driver vendor. When using Oracle, for example, this class is OracleConnection. When the client code calls getConnection(), the DriverManager finds the correct driver, and then asks the driver for the connection. The Oracle driver creates an instance of OracleConnection, which gets passed to the DriverManager and is returned to the client.

The same argument applies for the DataSource. When creating a data source for an Oracle database, the code that creates the data source on the server side will need the following imports:

```
import java.sql.*;
import javax.sql.*;
import oracle.jdbc.pool.OracleDataSource;
```

The first two imports are probably familiar to you. The first import is the standard Java SQL package. The second import is the Java SQL standard extension package. The final import is needed to create a specific DataSource instance. Since javax.sql.DataSource is an interface, you can't create an instance of DataSource. When you deploy a DataSource, you will need to create an instance of a class that implements DataSource. The driver vendor will provide this class. For Oracle, that specific class is the oracle.jdbc.pool.OracleDataSource class (provided with the Oracle driver library, classes12.zip). We import it in the source so that we can create an instance of that class.

On the client side, the client just needs the java.sql and javax.sql packages. When the client looks up the data source, the variable that references the object is a variable of type DataSource even though the actual object is a specific class such as OracleDataSource.

Types of DataSource

As well as providing a single source for connections, DataSource objects also enable the use of enterprise-level features such as connection pooling and distributed transactions, both of which are essential in such an environment. In a traditional, two-tier architecture, it is likely that if you are required to store information, a database will play a part somewhere and so a database connection will need to be established between the two parties (client and server). In a multi-tiered environment, however, it is theoretically possible for many "clients" to want a database connection, for example applets, servlets, Enterprise JavaBeans, and so on; these would all required hard-coded URLs in a JDBC URL environment or some other storage mechanism such as configuration files.

In order to make use of these enterprise services, you will need to create a type of DataSource that supports them. There are three different ways to implement a DataSource object:

- A **basic** DataSource object, which will implement the javax.sql.DataSource interface. A basic DataSource implementation produces Connection objects that are not pooled or used in a distributed transaction. This is the most costly in terms of processing; such a Connection must be established from scratch each time and would typically be used in a single-tier environment where the application and the database are not separated. This is the level of DataSource we will be using in the chapter

- A `DataSource` class with **connection pooling** support allows `Connection` objects to be reused, thereby offering better performance. This sort of `DataSource` will implement the `javax.sql.ConnectionPoolDataSource` interface. Again your database driver vendor will provide the class that implements this interface. Once a `ConnectionPooledDataSource` object is instantiated, calls to its `getPooledConnection()` method will return a `PooledConnection` object – a physical connection that can be cached in memory. On the client side, the application programmer will use variables of type `DataSource`. When they call `getConnection()`, they will not know whether the actual underlying object is a `DataSource` or a `ConnectionPoolDataSource`. We discuss connection pooling in more detail later in this chapter.

- A `DataSource` class that supports **distributed transactions** produces `Connection` objects that may participate in a distributed transaction; this is where a transaction may involve more than one DBMS server. This sort of `DataSource` will implement the `javax.sql.XADataSource` interface and will return a `Connection` object of type `XAConnection`. The topic of distributed transactions was discussed in Chapter 14, *Transactions*, and is not considered in further detail here.

How does a DataSource Work?

As we've mentioned, a `DataSource` is the information required to establish a database connection, encapsulated in a Java object that is then stored within a directory service. The client then establishes a physical database connection through this 'named' `DataSource`:

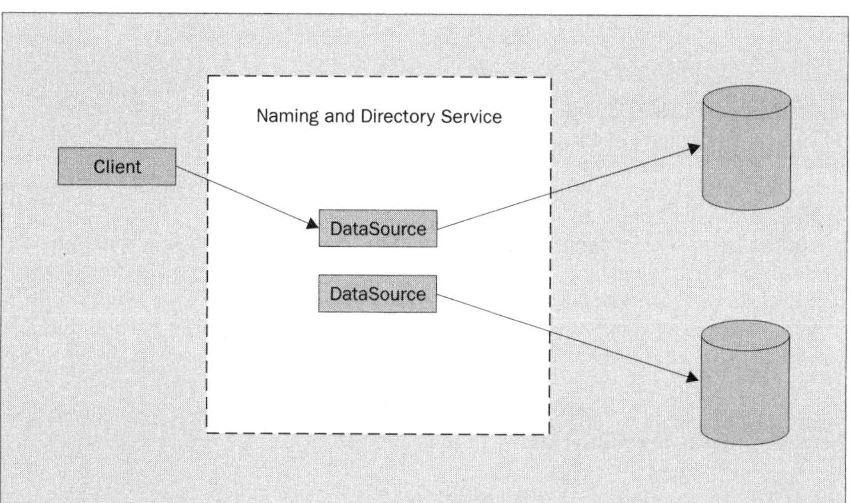

A client may be an Enterprise JavaBean, a servlet, or a Java application, either way, the `DataSource` may be looked up using the JNDI as can any other Java object stored in a Directory Service. The `getConnection()` method may then be used on the `DataSource` object to establish a database connection. The JNDI interface handles the lookup; the `DataSource` object handles the database connection.

Using a DataSource

There are two ways in which you may create a DataSource, either programmatically using the Java Programming Language and various API's or using one of the tools that are often supplied with an application server. The latter will automatically create and register the DataSource but the former relies on these actions being performed manually, and it is these that we will be concentrating on.

A DataSource is similar to the DriverManager in that it provides methods for obtaining a connection to a database. In fact, the basic method for obtaining a connection has the same name: getConnection().

Before any client code can get a connection from a DataSource, however, a DataSource object must be created and bound to a directory. The exact steps will be different for every directory and database. The database administrator will likely perform this step. The DataSource will be created with parameters for connecting to the database, and then the DataSource will be bound to a directory.

Here is a code snippet showing how that might be accomplished programmatically for a Cloudscape database:

```
//create the context, env is an object which contains information
//about the particular context
Context context = new InitialContext(env);

//Create a Cloudscape BasicDataSource object
BasicDataSource csDataSource = new BasicDataSource();

//set the connection parameters
csDataSource.setDatabaseName("c:/wrox/database/Wrox4370.db");

//bind the DataSource with the name
context.bind("jdbc/cloudscape", csDataSource);
```

Now, whatever directory the Context object refers to, has associated the name "jdbc/cloudscape" with the Cloudscape BasicDataSource object that knows how to connect to the database "c:/wrox/database/Wrox4370.db". Any client that has access to the same directory context and knows the correct name can then obtain a DataSource by performing a lookup in the directory, as shown in the following snippet:

```
Context context = new InitialContext(env);
DataSource dataSource = (DataSource) context.lookup(bindName);
Connection connection = dataSource.getConnection();
```

Using a DataSource to get a connection, the JDBC client code doesn't need to know anything about the database. It simply performs a directory lookup and obtains a connection from the DataSource it gets from the directory. Using a DataSource, a database administrator could change anything about the database such as the connection URL, username, and password. By simply changing and rebinding the DataSource, the change would be completely transparent to the JDBC client code. As soon as the client code performs a lookup, it will automatically get the connection without knowing that anything about the connection has changed.

In the rest of this chapter, we're going to present enough information to set up and use a DataSource.

Directory Overview

A `DataSource` is usually obtained by performing a lookup in a **context**. At its simplest, a context is just a means to associate a name with a resource. One implementation of a context is a directory. There are numerous implementations of directory services and protocols. There is Active Directory, X.500, Lightweight Directory Access Protocol (LDAP), and your computer's directory (which associates a name with a file resource).

On the server side of the connection, some code will create a `DataSource` instance, and then **bind** that instance in the directory. Binding is the action that tells a directory that a particular name is associated with a particular resource. For example, in a telephone directory, information (a resource) about your address and phone number is associated with your name.

Another example is when you created the `Store01.java` file in the file system of your computer. When you did that, you caused a collection of bytes to be written to some media such as the hard drive; at the same time, you told the operating system to associate (bind) that collection of bytes with the name `Store01.java`. Thus, anyone who has access to the hard drive can get the collection of bytes by giving the name "`Store01.java`" to the operating system.

Just as JDBC provides a vendor-neutral interface to numerous databases, Java has provided a vendor-neutral interface to directory services: the Java Naming and Directory Interface (JNDI). This API provides a common set of functions for accessing directories. The details of talking to a particular directory are provided by directory-specific libraries, in a similar fashion to JDBC drivers.

In this section, we will create a `DataSource` in the file system. To make use of the `DataSource` in this manner, we need some extra files to deal with the directory.

Try It Out – Setting up to use a DataSource

The libraries, which can be downloaded from http://java.sun.com/products/jndi/, are:

- `jndi1_2_1.zip`, the JNDI 1.2.1 class libraries and sample code
- `fscontext1_2beta3.zip` , the File system service provider, 1.2 beta 3 release

1. You'll need to select the Continue button next to Download JNDI 1.2.1 & More, towards the bottom of the page, then accept the terms of the license, and finally select the files you need. Each of these downloads is less than 100KB.

2. After downloading the archives, extract the library files `jndi.jar` from the `jndi1_2_1.zip` file, and `fscontext.jar` and `providerutil.jar` from the `fscontext1_2beta3.zip` file.

3. Copy the JAR files to the `C:\java\lib` directory, or elsewhere if you prefer; wherever you put them, make sure they will be in the classpath when you come to run the following code.

Creating and Using a DataSource

We're going to create a `DataSource` that can be used with our `Store` classes and an Oracle database. This `DataSource` can be used as a replacement for the static `ConnectionFactory` class we created in Chapter 8.

If you don't have an Oracle database, don't worry. We will change the code later in the chapter to use a `DataSource` for a Cloudscape database. Following these examples, you should be able to implement a data source for any other driver that provides a `DataSource` implementation.

In order to be able to take advantage of using a `DataSource`, let's first look at what we'll need to produce, and how it all fits together:

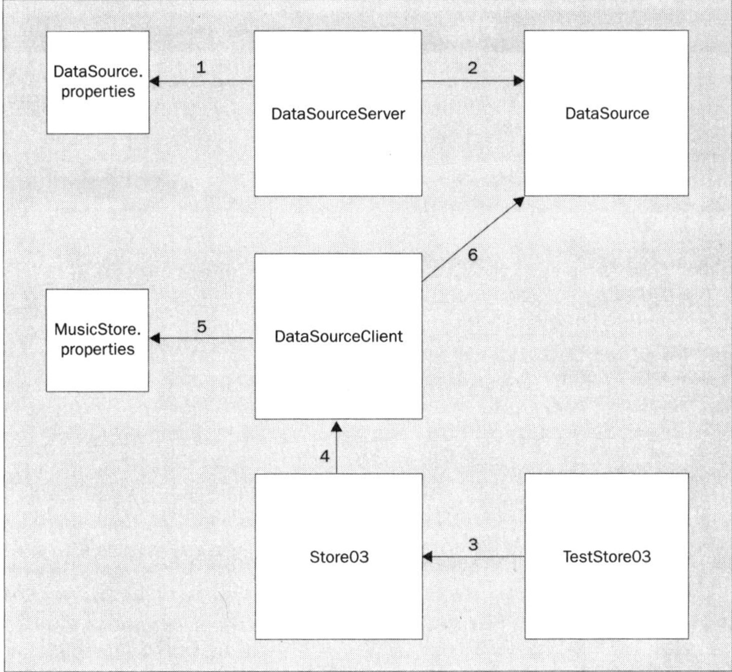

The numbers on the diagram indicate the sequence in which events will happen (but not necessarily the order in which we'll create the files).

1. The `DataSourceServer` class (which we'll see soon) is run, and looks up values in the `DataSource.properties` file (which we'll see next.)

2. These values enable the `DataSourceServer` class to create the `DataSource`.

3. The `TestStoreDS` class (which we'll create when we've created the `StoreDS` class) calls the `StoreDS` class and asks for some information from the database.

4. The `StoreDS` class (which we'll create after we've created the `DataSourceClient` class) instantiates a `DataSourceClient` (which we'll create after we've created the `DataSourceServer` class) in order to get a connection to the database.

5. The `DataSourceClient` object looks up values in the `MusicStore.properties` file, so it knows where to find the `DataSource`.

6. The `DataSourceClient` finds and instantiates the `DataSource`, thus allowing the `StoreDS` class to get its connection to the database, and extract the information it requires.

Let's get started with this array of components we need to create in order to demonstrate the use of a `DataSource`.

Try It Out – Creating a Properties File

1. Start by creating a properties file called `DataSource.properties`, which will hold the various parameters used to bind the `DataSource` in the directory and parameters used by the `DataSource` object to create a connection. Here's an example file that was created for an Oracle database:

```
# DataSource.properties
datasource.factory=com.sun.jndi.fscontext.RefFSContextFactory
datasource.url=file:/C:/temp/jndi
datasource.bindname=jdbc/MusicStore
datasource.username=beg
datasource.password=java
datasource.server=dbserver
datasource.port=1521
datasource.drivertype=thin
datasource.netprotocol=tcp
datasource.databasename=database
```

2. Save this properties file in the directory `C:\BegJavaDB\DataSource\`, which is where our code will be placed (or at least the package structure will start there). Alternatively, you can place this file anywhere you like on your system as long as you make sure it is included in your classpath; since the code it is associated with will be in the classpath, storing this file in the directory from which the code is compiled and run makes sense.

3. This file will require the creation of a directory `C:\temp\jndi`.

How It works – The Properties File

Let's start with the property file:

```
# DataSource.properties
datasource.factory=com.sun.jndi.fscontext.RefFSContextFactory
datasource.url=file:/C:/temp/jndi
datasource.bindname=jdbc/MusicStore
datasource.username=beg
datasource.password=java
datasource.server=dbserver
datasource.port=1521
datasource.drivertype=thin
datasource.netprotocol=tcp
datasource.databasename=database
```

The first line is a comment telling us the name of the file – this comment has no bearing on the way the process works.

The first three properties contain information used by JNDI to create the directory entry. In this simple example, the name of each property we are setting is prefixed with `datasource.`; thus the `url` property is listed as `datasource.url`. In a more complicated example, we could provide more properties in one file, and we would need to make sure that properties were well differentiated. We could do this by prefixing the property name with something like `oracle.datasource.url`, and `cloudscape.datasource.url`. This is like packaging our classes; it helps us to keep things tidy and distinct.

In creating the directory entry, JNDI requires a name to bind it to (the value of `bindname`: `jdbc/MusicStore`; this will be used by the client to retrieve the `DataSource`), a place to create the binding (the value of `url`: `C:/temp/jndi`; this is where JNDI will create a `.bindings` file that lists the bindings made), and finally a factory class to do the work (the value of factory: `com.sun.jndi.fscontext.RefFSContextFactory`; this is the piece of code that takes the other pieces of information, along with the remaining entries in the properties file, and turns them into a `DataSource` reference).

The remaining seven properties provide the information needed to create a connection: username, password, server, port, driver type, protocol, and database name.

Try It Out – Implementing the DataSourceServer Class

1. Next, we implement a class that will create a `DataSource` object and bind that object to a name in the directory. In this case, we will use the file system of your computer as the directory. Any client that needs a connection will connect to the directory and look up the `DataSource` in the directory. The client can then get a connection from the `DataSource`. Here is the complete source for such a class, called `DataSourceServer`:

```
package datasource;

import java.sql.*;
import javax.sql.*;
import oracle.jdbc.pool.OracleDataSource;
import javax.naming.*;
import java.util.*;

/**
 * A class to create a DataSource and bind it to a directory.
 */
public class DataSourceServer {
  static ResourceBundle bundle = null;

  public static void main(String[] args) {
    bundle = ResourceBundle.getBundle("DataSource");
    try {

      // create and store parameters which are used to create the context
      Hashtable env = new Hashtable();
      env.put(Context.INITIAL_CONTEXT_FACTORY,
              bundle.getString("datasource.factory"));
```

```
      env.put(Context.PROVIDER_URL, bundle.getString("datasource.url"));

      // create the context
      Context context = new InitialContext(env);

      // Create a DataSource object
      OracleDataSource dataSource = new OracleDataSource();

      // set the connection parameters
      String s = bundle.getString("datasource.username");
      dataSource.setUser(s);
      s = bundle.getString("datasource.password");
      dataSource.setPassword(s);
      s = bundle.getString("datasource.drivertype");
      dataSource.setDriverType(s);
      s = bundle.getString("datasource.netprotocol");
      dataSource.setNetworkProtocol(s);
      s = bundle.getString("datasource.server");
      dataSource.setServerName(s);
      dataSource.setPortNumber(getPort());
      s = bundle.getString("datasource.databasename");
      dataSource.setDatabaseName(s);

      // get the name
      String bindName = bundle.getString("datasource.bindname");

      // bind the DataSource with the name
      context.rebind(bindName, dataSource);
      System.out.println("DataSource completed");
    } catch (Exception e) {
      e.printStackTrace();
    }
  }

  static int getPort() throws NumberFormatException {
    String s = bundle.getString("datasource.port");
    return Integer.parseInt(s);
  }
}
```

2. Save the file as `C:\BegJavaDB\DataSource\datasource\DataSourceServer.java`, and compile it using the following command:

```
> javac -classpath %CLASSPATH%;.;%JLIB%/classes12.zip
                   datasource/DataSourceServer.java
```

Notice the inclusion of `%JLIB%\classes12.zip` in the `-classpath` option. This is the file that contains the `OracleDataSource` class.

3. Next, we run the class using the following command:

```
> java -classpath
  %CLASSPATH%;.;%JLIB%/classes12.zip;%JLIB%\fscontext.jar;%JLIB%\providerutil.jar
            datasource.DataSourceServer
```

Make sure that the three archive files listed in the `-classpath` option (`classes12.zip`, `fscontext.jar`, and `providerutil.jar`) are available in the `%JLIB%` directory) You should see results like the following screenshot:

```
C:\WINDOWS\System32\cmd.exe
C:\BegJavaDB\DataSource>java  -classpath %CLASSPATH%;.;%JLIB%\classes12.zip
;%JLIB%/fscontext.jar;%JLIB%\providerutil.jar datasource.DataSourceServer
DataSource completed

C:\BegJavaDB\DataSource>_
```

Although this class does what we want, we'll need more code to make any demonstrable use of it. Let's explain what we've got first.

How It Works

All of the work in our `DataSourceServer` class occurs in the `main()` method. Here's a snapshot of what is occurring:

A reference to the properties file `DataSource.properties` is obtained through a resource bundle:

```
bundle = ResourceBundle.getBundle("DataSource");
```

The directory parameters are read from the `ResourceBundle` and stored in a `Hashtable`.

```
Hashtable env = new Hashtable();
env.put(Context.INITIAL_CONTEXT_FACTORY,
        bundle.getString("datasource.factory"));
env.put(Context.PROVIDER_URL,
        bundle.getString("datasource.url"));
```

A `Context` is created using the `Hashtable`. A context simply represents a set of name-to-object bindings. In this example, the set of bindings is a file system:

```
Context context = new InitialContext(env);
```

A `DataSource` object is created and connection parameters are read from the `ResourceBundle` and stored:

```
OracleDataSource dataSource = new OracleDataSource();

//set the connection parameters
String s = bundle.getString("datasource.username");
dataSource.setUser(s);
```

Finally the `DataSource` is bound to a name in the directory (the code uses `rebind()` so that the new object replaces any object that was previously bound):

```
context.rebind(bindName, dataSource);
```

By binding the `DataSource` object to a name in the local file system, the `DataSource` is accessible only to clients running on the local computer.

The code above uses the Oracle `DataSource` class. If you are using a different database, you will need to change the import statements to use the appropriate `DataSource` class. After compiling and executing the class above, you can inspect the bound object by navigating to the `C:\temp\jndi` directory. In this directory you will find a file that contains the connection parameters; this file is created by the code, and will be called `.bindings`. When a client does a lookup for a `DataSource` object, the JNDI classes recreate the `DataSource` object using the information in the file resource. As long as the connection parameters do not change, the `DataSourceServer` class only needs to be run once.

Try It Out – A DataSourceClient

Next, we provide a class that uses JNDI to look up the `DataSource` and provide a connection to any clients in our system that need a connection:

```
package datasource;

import java.sql.*;
import javax.sql.*;
import javax.naming.*;
import java.util.*;
import oracle.jdbc.pool.OracleDataSource;

public class DataSourceClient {
  Connection conn;
  static ResourceBundle bundle = ResourceBundle.getBundle("MusicStore");
  OracleDataSource dataSource;

  public DataSourceClient() {
    Context context;

    try {

      // create and store parameters which are used to create the context
      Hashtable env = new Hashtable();
      env.put(Context.INITIAL_CONTEXT_FACTORY,
              bundle.getString("datasource.factory"));
      env.put(Context.PROVIDER_URL, bundle.getString("datasource.url"));

      // create the context
      context = new InitialContext(env);

      // call method to get DataSource and Connection
      String bindName = bundle.getString("datasource.bindname");
      dataSource = (OracleDataSource) context.lookup(bindName);
    } catch (Exception e) {
      e.printStackTrace();
    }
  }

  public Connection getConnection() throws SQLException {
    return dataSource.getConnection();
  }
}
```

Save this as C:\BegJavaDB\DataSource\datasource\DataSourceClient.java, and compile it using the following command:

```
> javac -classpath .;%JLIB%/classes12.zip datasource/DataSourceClient.java
```

To use the DataSourceClient, you need to do the following:

- Make sure you have created a directory c:\temp\jndi
- Run the DataSourceServer class
- Use the DataSourceClient class in JDBC code, which we'll show in the next *Try It Out*

The property file must be located somewhere on the classpath. So if the classpath includes c:\BegJavaDB\Ch18, the properties file can be located in the Ch18 directory and the JVM will be able to find it. You can try using the absolute path to the property file, which should work also.

Here is the properties file we will use, MusicStore.properties:

```
# MusicStore.properties
datasource.factory=com.sun.jndi.fscontext.RefFSContextFactory
datasource.url=file:/C:/temp/jndi
datasource.bindname=jdbc/MusicStore
```

How It Works

Notice that the constructor in the client class is very similar to the constructor of the DataSourceServer class. Using a properties file (MusicStore.properties), it fills a Hashtable with directory parameters and then creates a Context object.

```
static ResourceBundle bundle = ResourceBundle.getBundle("MusicStore");

public DataSourceClient() {
  Context context;

  try {

    Hashtable env = new Hashtable();
    env.put(Context.INITIAL_CONTEXT_FACTORY,
            bundle.getString("datasource.factory"));
    env.put(Context.PROVIDER_URL, bundle.getString("datasource.url"));

    // create the context
    context = new InitialContext(env);
```

The difference is that in this class, instead of rebind(), the code calls lookup() to locate the DataSource in the directory.

```
    String bindName = bundle.getString("datasource.bindname");
    dataSource = (DataSource) context.lookup(bindName);
```

The other method in the class is the getConnection() method.

```
public Connection getConnection() throws SQLException {
  return dataSource.getConnection();
}
```

Notice that because the DataSource creates the connection, the DataSourceClient does not need to know any of the database connection parameters. It simply needs to know how to connect to the directory and get a DataSource object. So the MusicStore.properties file for the client contains just three properties:

```
# MusicStore.properties
datasource.factory=com.sun.jndi.fscontext.RefFSContextFactory
datasource.url=file:/C:/temp/jndi
datasource.bindname=jdbc/MusicStore
```

Because of the way ResourceBundle looks up resources, save the MusicStore.properties class in a directory above the datasource directory. Therefore, we will put the properties file in the C:\BegJavaDB\DataSource directory.

Try It Out – Using the DataSource with the Store Class

The last class in this section is the Store class again. This version of the class (StoreDS) uses the DataSourceClient class. This class creates a DataSourceClient and asks it for a DataSource. Using the DataSource, the StoreDS class can get a Connection without needing to know the database URL, host, username, and so on. The DataSource handles all those details.

```
package connections;

import java.sql.*;
import javax.sql.*;
import datasource.*;

/**
 * A class to represent a retail store in the Music system.
 */
public class StoreDS {
  int storeId;
  String storeDescription = "";
  int storeTypeId;
  String storeAddress1 = "";
  String storeAddress2 = "";
  String storeCity = "";
  String storePostalCode = "";

  DataSourceClient client;
  Connection connection;
  Statement statement;
  ResultSet resultSet;

  public StoreDS() {
    this("", 0, "", "", "", "");
  }
```

```
  public StoreDS(String description, int typeId, String address1,
                 String address2, String city, String postalCode) {
    client = new DataSourceClient();
    storeDescription = description;
    storeTypeId = typeId;
    storeAddress1 = address1;
    storeAddress2 = address2;
    storeCity = city;
    storePostalCode = postalCode;
  }

  private Statement getStatement() throws SQLException {
    connection = client.getConnection();
    return connection.createStatement();
  }

  public boolean create() {
    int result = 0;
    try {
      statement = getStatement();
      String sql = "insert into stores " +
                   "(StoreId, StoreDescription, StoreTypeID, StoreAddress1, " +
                   "StoreAddress2, StoreCity, StorePostalCode) " + "values (" +
                   "Storeid_SEQ.NEXTVAL, " + "'" + storeDescription + "', " +
                   storeTypeId + ", " + "'" + storeAddress1 + "', " + "'" +
                   storeAddress2 + "', " + "'" + storeCity + "', " + "'" +
                   storePostalCode + "')";
      result = statement.executeUpdate(sql);
    } catch (Exception e) {
      errorMessage = e.getMessage();
      e.printStackTrace();
    } finally {
      close(statement);
      close(connection);
    }

    return (result == 1);
  }

  public boolean findByPrimaryKey(String id) {
    if (id == null || id.equals("")) {
      return false;
    }
    boolean result = false;
    try {
      statement = getStatement();
      String sql = "select * from stores " + "where StoreID=" + id;
      resultSet = statement.executeQuery(sql);
      if (resultSet.next()) {
        result = true;
        setStoreId(resultSet.getInt("StoreID"));
        storeDescription = resultSet.getString("StoreDescription");
        storeTypeId = resultSet.getInt("StoreTypeID");
        storeAddress1 = resultSet.getString("StoreAddress1");
```

```
            storeAddress2 = resultSet.getString("StoreAddress2");
            storeCity = resultSet.getString("StoreCity");
            storePostalCode = resultSet.getString("StorePostalCode");
          }
        } catch (Exception e) {
          e.printStackTrace();
        } finally {
          close(resultSet);
          close(statement);
          close(connection);
        }
        return result;
      }

      private void close(ResultSet resultSet) {
        try {
          if (resultSet != null) {
            resultSet.close();
          }
        } catch (Exception ignored) {
          ignored.printStackTrace();
        }
      }

      private void close(Statement statement) {
        try {
          if (statement != null) {
            statement.close();
          }
        } catch (Exception ignored) {
          ignored.printStackTrace();
        }
      }

      private void close(Connection connection) {
        try {
          if (connection != null) {
            connection.close();
          }
        } catch (Exception ignored) {
          ignored.printStackTrace();
        }
      }

      public String toString() {
        return "Name      : " + storeDescription + "\n" + "Store Id : " +
               storeId + "\n" + "Address   : " + storeAddress1 + "\n" +
               "          : " + storeAddress2 + "\n" + "          : " +
               storeCity + ", " + storePostalCode;
      }

      public int getStoreId() {
        return storeId;
      }
      public void setStoreId(int v) {
```

```
      this.storeId = v;
    }

    // get and set methods for the other member variables
    // are not shown here. They are unchanged from Store02 in Chapter 8
}
```

Save this file as `C:\BegJavaDB\DataSource\connections\StoreDS.java`, and compile it from the `C:\BegJavaDB\DataSource` directory using the following command:

```
> javac -classpath .;%JLIB%\jdbc2_0-stdext.jar connections\StoreDS.java
```

Note that we include the `-classpath` option in order to include the `datasource` package in the classpath, and the `jdbc2_0-stdext.jar` file, which contains the `javax.sql` package.

Next, we can make a few modifications to the last test class we used, as shown below:

```
package connections;

public class TestStoreDS {
  public static void main(String[] args) {
    String id = "4";
    StoreDS store = new StoreDS();
    boolean result = store.findByPrimaryKey(id);
    if (result) {
      System.out.println("Store retrieved");
      System.out.println("Store details: \n" + store.toString());
    } else {
      System.out.println("Store NOT retrieved");
    }
  }
}
```

As you can see, the changes are minimal. Save this file as `C:\BegJavaDB\DataSource\connections\TestStoreDS.java`, and compile it using the following command issued from the `C:\BegJavaDB\DataSource` directory:

```
> javac -classpath .;%JLIB%\fscontext.jar;%JLIB%\providerutil.jar;
                   %JLIB%\jdbc2_0-stdext.jar;%JLIB%\classes12.zip
                                                  connections/TestStoreDS.java
```

Finally, we can run the example as follows:

```
>java -classpath .;%JLIB%\fscontext.jar;%JLIB%\providerutil.jar;
                 %JLIB%\jdbc2_0-stdext.jar;%JLIB%\classes12.zip
                                                connections.TestStoreDS
```

This should produce the same results as `TestStore02` did in Chapter 8. For a bit of variety, we changed the value of the `String` variable `id` in `TestStoreDS`, recompiled and ran it again. Here are the results:

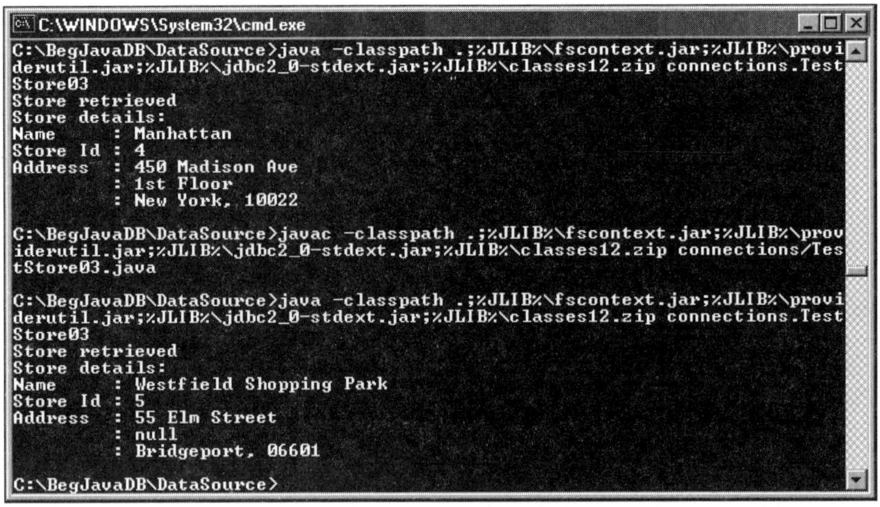

```
C:\WINDOWS\System32\cmd.exe
C:\BegJavaDB\DataSource>java -classpath .;%JLIB%\fscontext.jar;%JLIB%\provi
derutil.jar;%JLIB%\jdbc2_0-stdext.jar;%JLIB%\classes12.zip connections.Test
Store03
Store retrieved
Store details:
Name      : Manhattan
Store Id  : 4
Address   : 450 Madison Ave
          : 1st Floor
          : New York, 10022

C:\BegJavaDB\DataSource>javac -classpath .;%JLIB%\fscontext.jar;%JLIB%\prov
iderutil.jar;%JLIB%\jdbc2_0-stdext.jar;%JLIB%\classes12.zip connections/Tes
tStore03.java

C:\BegJavaDB\DataSource>java -classpath .;%JLIB%\fscontext.jar;%JLIB%\provi
derutil.jar;%JLIB%\jdbc2_0-stdext.jar;%JLIB%\classes12.zip connections.Test
Store03
Store retrieved
Store details:
Name      : Westfield Shopping Park
Store Id  : 5
Address   : 55 Elm Street
          : null
          : Bridgeport, 06601

C:\BegJavaDB\DataSource>
```

How It Works

Now for the fun part, explaining what's happening. The `StoreDS` class has only a few slight changes from `Store02`.

The first and most important change is the use of the `DataSourceClient` class to get a `DataSource` for establishing a connection, instead of using the `ConnectionFactory` class. Thus, we need to import the `datasource` package, and declare a `DataSourceClient` variable:

```
package connections;

import java.sql.*;
import datasource.*;

public class StoreDS {
  // other variables
  DataSourceClient client;
```

The next change we make is how we establish a connection to the database. Since we're using a `DataSource`, we can write the `getStatment()` method to use the `DataSourceClient` to create a `Connection` and then return us a `Statement`, as follows:

```
  private Statement getStatement() throws SQLException {
    connection = client.getConnection();
    return connection.createStatement();
  }
```

The next major change we've made is in how we tidy up the JDBC objects once we've finished using them. Since we're not using the `ConnectionFactory`, we can't rely on its `close()` methods. Instead, we implement three `close()` methods ourselves, once for each type of object:

```
void close(ResultSet resultSet) {
  try {
    if (resultSet != null) {
      resultSet.close();
    }
  } catch (Exception ignored) {
    ignored.printStackTrace();
  }
}
```

Each of the `close()` methods (we'll only show `close(ResultSet)` here, but the other two work the same way) checks to see if the object it has been passed is already null; if it isn't, it closes it. If we catch an exception, we simply print the stack trace to the standard output.

Other than the changes to how we make the connection to the database, the class does the same job as before.

Making Changes for Cloudscape

After testing the class, you might try changing the `DataSourceServer` class to create a `DataSource` for a different database. If you have a Cloudscape database on your system, you can use a Cloudscape `DataSource`. Here are the changes to be made to the properties file for the Cloudscape database:

```
# CloudDataSourceProps.properties
datasource.factory=com.sun.jndi.fscontext.RefFSContextFactory
datasource.url=file:/C:/temp/jndi
datasource.bindname.cloudscape=jdbc/cloudscape
datasource.databasename.cloudscape=c:/wrox/database/Wrox4370.db
```

How It Works

The only change really required above was to change the database name to match the name used in Cloudscape. The `DataSourceServer` class needs to be changed to import and instantiate a different `DataSource` class, and to remove some `setXXX` methods that are not used by the Cloudscape `DataSource`:

```
// datasource.CloudDataSource.java
package datasource;

import java.sql.*;
import javax.sql.*;
import COM.cloudscape.core.*;
import javax.naming.*;
import java.util.*;

/**
 * A class to create a DataSource and bind it to a directory.
 */
public class CloudDataSource {
  static ResourceBundle bundle = null;

  public static void main(String[] args)
```

```
    {
      bundle = ResourceBundle.getBundle("CloudDataSourceProps");
      try {
        //create and store parameters which are used to create the context
        Hashtable env = new Hashtable();
        env.put(Context.INITIAL_CONTEXT_FACTORY,
           bundle.getString("datasource.factory"));
        env.put(Context.PROVIDER_URL,
           bundle.getString("datasource.url"));
        //create the context
        Context context = new InitialContext(env);

        //Create a DataSource object
        BasicDataSource csDataSource = new BasicDataSource();

        s = bundle.getString("datasource.databasename.cloudscape");
        csDataSource.setDatabaseName(s);

        //get the name
        String bindName = bundle.getString("datasource.bindname.cloudscape");
        //bind the DataSource with the name
        context.rebind(bindName, csDataSource);
        System.out.println("DataSource completed");
      } catch (Exception e) {
        e.printStackTrace();
      }
    }

  }
```

We'll also need to make a couple of little changes to the `DataSourceClient` class, to account for the different type of `DataSource` being created. Here are those changes:

```
package datasource;

import java.sql.*;
import javax.sql.*;
import javax.naming.*;
import java.util.*;
import COM.cloudscape.core.*;

public class DataSourceClient {
  Connection conn;
  static ResourceBundle bundle = ResourceBundle.getBundle("MusicStore");
  BasicDataSource dataSource;

  public DataSourceClient() {
    Context context;

    try {

      // create and store parameters which are used to create the context
      Hashtable env = new Hashtable();
      env.put(Context.INITIAL_CONTEXT_FACTORY,
```

```
            bundle.getString("datasource.factory"));
      env.put(Context.PROVIDER_URL, bundle.getString("datasource.url"));

      // create the context
      context = new InitialContext(env);

      // call method to get DataSource and Connection
      String bindName = bundle.getString("datasource.bindname");
      dataSource = (BasicDataSource) context.lookup(bindName);
    } catch (Exception e) {
      e.printStackTrace();
    }
  }

  public Connection getConnection() throws SQLException {
    return dataSource.getConnection();
  }
}
```

We can continue to use `TestStoreDS` to check this, although we might want to change the value of `id` again:

```
C:\WINDOWS\System32\cmd.exe
C:\BegJavaDB\DataSource>java -classpath .;%JLIB%\fscontext.jar;%JLIB%\provi
derutil.jar;%JLIB%\jdbc2_0-stdext.jar;%JLIB%\cloudscape.jar connections.Tes
tStore03

Store retrieved
Store details:
Name      : Westfield Shopping Park
Store Id  : 5
Address   : 55 Elm Street
          : null
          : Bridgeport, 06601

C:\BegJavaDB\DataSource>javac -classpath .;%JLIB%\fscontext.jar;%JLIB%\prov
iderutil.jar;%JLIB%\jdbc2_0-stdext.jar;%JLIB%\cloudscape.jar connections/Te
stStore03.java

C:\BegJavaDB\DataSource>java -classpath .;%JLIB%\fscontext.jar;%JLIB%\provi
derutil.jar;%JLIB%\jdbc2_0-stdext.jar;%JLIB%\cloudscape.jar connections.Tes
tStore03

Store retrieved
Store details:
Name      : Independent Records and Tapes
Store Id  : 14
Address   : 123 E. Bijou St.
          :
          : Colorado Springs, 80903

C:\BegJavaDB\DataSource>
```

Connection Pooling

One of the most expensive operations using JDBC will be establishing your database connection; this involves a number of steps such as locating the server, submitting authentication requests, which in turn need to be validated. Eventually, after any internal connection work has been performed, the connection details are returned. As a result the process of connection pooling was provided to help remove such overheads. Typically, pools of connections are made available and when a client requests a connection, they are assigned one from the pool. When the connection is no longer required, instead of being disconnected, it is returned to the pool, ready for reuse.

Custom Connection Pooling

In order to clearly demonstrate the performance benefits of using connection pooling, we're going to create a custom class that can provide a pool of connections. The Sun Microsystems Java web site has a nice article on connection pooling on which we will base our custom code, although our example will be simplified, and will use a `DataSource` to get the connections. The article can be found at:

http://developer.java.sun.com/developer/onlineTraining/Programming/JDCBook/conpool.html.

In order that you can actually see the potential benefits, in terms of actual timings, we're first going to define a profiling class that can capture and record how long a piece of code takes to execute using the internal system clock.

Try It Out – Example Profiler Class, Profiler.java

The profiler class is a fairly simple affair:

```
package profiler;

public class Profiler {
  private long m_startTime;
  private long m_stopTime;
  private String m_routineName;

  public void Start(String routineName) {
    m_startTime = System.currentTimeMillis();
    m_routineName = routineName;
  }

  public void Stop() {
    m_stopTime = System.currentTimeMillis();
    System.out.println("Routine [" + m_routineName + "] took " +
                       (m_stopTime - m_startTime) +
                       " msecs to execute.\n");
  }
}
```

Save the class as `C:\BegJavaDB\Chapter18\profiler\Profiler.java`, and compile it with the following command from the `Chapter18` directory:

```
> javac -classpath . profiler/Profiler.java
```

How It Works

This is a very simple class, which times how long a section of code takes to run. Before the code we want to time starts executing, we make a call to the `Start()` method:

```
public void Start(String routineName) {
  m_startTime = System.currentTimeMillis();
  m_routineName = routineName;
}
```

Here we set two variables; the first contains the name of the method (or some descriptive text about the set of code we're profiling), and the second starts the timer. After the block of code we are interested in finishes, we call the `Stop()` method:

```
public void Stop() {
  m_stopTime = System.currentTimeMillis();
  System.out.println("Routine [" + m_routineName + "] took " +
                     (m_stopTime - m_startTime) +
                     " msecs to execute.\n");
}
```

Here we take the current system time, and print out a message indicating how long the timer has been running (we do the calculation during the `System.out.println()` call.

Typical usage might be:

```
package profiler;

public class ProfilerTest {

  public static void main(String args[]) {

    Profiler p = new Profiler();

    // Start the profiler
    p.Start("A routine");


    for (long nCounter = 0; nCounter < 100; nCounter++) {
      System.out.println(nCounter);
    }

    p.Stop();

  }
}
```

The output would look something like this:

```
1
.
.
.
99
Routine [A Routine] took 20 msecs to execute.
```

This is represents simple class that can be used around a section of code that you wish to profile. Of course, you could extend this to keep a count of the number of times this is executed or allow a stack of profiling requests to be collated but these are simple to implement and are left as a task for yourself. This approach is best used in conjunction with the internal performing features of the Java run-time, when you are developing on a budget. For more industrial strength performance tuning, especially important when developing larger applications, often across multiple tiers, you should review the commercial or shareware profiling tools available to see which best fits your needs.

OK, let's now move on and create our connection pool class. You'll notice that we've added a method to dump information on the pool size and the status of all slots within the pool.

Try It Out – DataSourceConnectionPool.java

The first task is to define our class object that will hold a number of database connections and provide the user the ability to request or return connections from the available pool.

```
package pooling;

import java.sql.*;
import java.util.*;
import datasource.*;

public class DataSourceConnectionPool {

  private Vector connections;
  private boolean inUse[];
  final private int poolsize = 10;

  // ////////////////////////////////////////////////////////////////////
  // Name     DataSourceConnectionPool
  // Description  Constructor
  // ////////////////////////////////////////////////////////////////////
  public DataSourceConnectionPool() {
    connections = new Vector(poolsize);
    inUse = new boolean[poolsize];

    try {
      SetupConnectionsPool();
    } catch (Exception e) {
      e.printStackTrace();
    }
  }

  // ////////////////////////////////////////////////////////////////////
  // Name     SetupConnectonsPool
  // Description  Pre-Create our pool of connections
  // ////////////////////////////////////////////////////////////////////
  private void SetupConnectionsPool() throws SQLException {
    for (int i = 0; i < poolsize; i++) {
      Connection conn = new DataSourceClient().getConnection();
      connections.addElement(conn);
      inUse[i] = false;
    }
  }

  // ////////////////////////////////////////////////////////////////////
  // Name     freeConnection
  // Description  Release resource
  // ////////////////////////////////////////////////////////////////////
  public void freeConnection(int connectionIdx) {
    inUse[connectionIdx] = false;
  }
```

```
  // /////////////////////////////////////////////////////////////////
  // Name    getConnection
  // Description  Obtain a connection from the pool (if available)
  // /////////////////////////////////////////////////////////////////
  public Connection getConnection() {
    Connection c = null;
    for (int idx = 0; idx < connections.size(); idx++) {
      if (inUse[idx] == false) {
        c = (Connection) connections.elementAt(idx);
        inUse[idx] = true;
      }
    }
    return c;
  }

  // /////////////////////////////////////////////////////////////////
  // Name    dumpConnectionStatus
  // Description  Dump the status of pool and connections
  // /////////////////////////////////////////////////////////////////
  public void dumpConnectionStatus() {
    System.out.println("\nConnection Pool Status");
    System.out.println("\nPool Size is " + connections.size());
    for (int i = 0; i < connections.size(); i++) {
      System.out.println("Pool Index [" + i + "] In Use status = " + inUse[i]);
    }
  }
}
```

Save this as `C:\BegJavaDB\Chapter18\pooling\DataSourceConnectionPool.java`, and compile with the following command from the `Chapter18` directory:

```
> javac -classpath
        .;%JLIB%\fscontext.jar;%JLIB%\providerutil.jar;%JLIB%\jdbc2_0-stdext.jar
        pooling/DataSourceConnectionPool.java
```

How It Works

First we need to establish our connection pooling class. We declare some variables, including a `Vector` in which we will be storing our pool of connections. Now we can load the JDBC driver and setup our pool of connections:

```
  public DataSourceConnectionPool() {
    connections = new Vector(poolsize);
    inUse = new boolean[poolsize];

    try {
      SetupConnectionsPool();
    } catch (Exception e) {
      e.printStackTrace();
    }
  }
```

We define the connection pool setup in a different method for clarity; this method runs through a loop for as many items we wish to exist in the pool and requests a connection from a new `DataSourceClient`, storing this within our `Vector` list and marking the connection as not in use.

```
private void SetupConnectionsPool() throws SQLException {
  for (int i = 0; i < poolsize; i++) {
    Connection conn = new DataSourceClient().getConnection();
    connections.addElement(conn);
    inUse[i] = false;
  }
}
```

To facilitate obtaining and releasing connections from the pool, we provide opposite methods called `getConnection()` and `freeConnection()` to request and release connections accordingly. First, we'll take a look at the `getConnection()` method:

```
public Connection getConnection() {
  Connection c = null;
  for (int idx = 0; idx < connections.size(); idx++) {
    if (inUse[idx] == false) {
      c = (Connection) connections.elementAt(idx);
      inUse[idx] = true;
    }
  }
  return c;
}
```

This code is fairly straightforward in that we scan through the array used to hold the connection status, and when a slot is found as available, we return this `Connection`. If not slots are available, that is all connections in the pool have been requested, we merely return null for action on the client end. Once obtained, we mark the `Connection` as in use so that it is not obtained again without first being released.

This sets the stage for the `freeConnection()` method, used to release a connection back into the pool (note, its released back but *not* closed). Lets take a look at this method:

```
public void freeConnection(int connectionIdx) {
  inUse[connectionIdx] = false;
}
```

Finally, we can display the status of our connection pool by calling the `dumpConnectionStatus()` method:

```
public void dumpConnectionStatus() {
  System.out.println("\nConnection Pool Status");
  System.out.println("\nPool Size is " + connections.size());
  for (int i = 0; i < connections.size(); i++) {
    System.out.println("Pool Index [" + i + "] In Use status = " + inUse[i]);
  }
}
```

This method simply loops through the `inUse[]` array and prints the values, representing which connections are in use.

A straightforward implementation; all we need do is mark the connection as no longer being in use, ready for the next request.

Next, let's take a look at some code that uses this class to see what performance merits are obtained. First, we'll write a small class that establishes 10 connections, and time this using our `Profiler` class.

Try It Out - NonPoolTest.java

Create the following `NonPoolTrest.java` class:

```
package pooling;

import java.sql.*;
import profiler.Profiler;
import datasource.DataSourceClient;

public class NonPoolTest {

  private static ConnectionPool pool;

  public static void main(String args[]) {

    // Create an instance of our profiling tool
    Profiler p = new Profiler();

    try {

      // Lets Get 10 Connections
      Connection c[] = new Connection[10];

      // Obtain 10 connections and profile this section of code
      // .. START
      p.Start("main() in NON PoolTest");
      for (int i = 0; i < 10; i++) {
        c[i] = new ClientDataSource().getConnection();
      }
      p.Stop();

      // .. END

    } catch (Exception e) {
      e.printStackTrace();
    }
  }
}
```

Save this as `C:\BegJavaDB\Chapter18\pooling\NonPoolTest.java`, and compile it with the following command:

```
> javac -classpath . pooling/NonPoolTest.java
```

Next, we can run it with the following command (all on one line):

```
> java -classpath
       .;%JLIB%\cloudscape.jar;%JLIB%\fscontext.jar;%JLIB%\providerutil.jar;
       %JLIB%\jdbc2_0-stdext.jar pooling.NonPoolTest
```

You should see results similar to this:

```
Routine [main() in NON PoolTest] took 4816 msecs to execute.
```

How It Works

The crux of the code is the loop that establishes 10 connections and stores them in an array; this is the code we are profiling as you can see below:

```
p.Start("main() in NON PoolTest");
for (int i = 0; i < 10; i++) {
  c[i] = new ClientDataSource().getConnection();
}
p.Stop();
```

We start the profiler, create 10 `Connection` instances from our `DataSourceClient`, and stop the timer.

Now we can test similar code but using the `DataSourceConnectionPool` class we've developed; this will request a connection from the pool instead of establishing the connection in-line. Let's take a look at this example:

Try It Out – PoolTest.java

Here is the code for the `PoolTest.java` class:

```
package pooling;

import java.sql.*;
import profiler.Profiler;

public class DataSourcePoolTest {

  private static DataSourceConnectionPool pool;
  private static String url = "jdbc:cloudscape:c:/wrox/database/Wrox4370.db";

  public static void main(String args[]) {

    // Create an instance of our profile
    Profiler p = new Profiler();

    try {

      // Establish our Connection
      System.out.println("Establish a connection [" + url + "]");
      pool = new DataSourceConnectionPool();

      // Lets Get 10 Connections
      Connection c[] = new Connection[10];
```

```
        // Obtain 10 connections and profile this section of code
        // .. START
        p.Start("main() in PoolTest");
        for (int i = 0; i < 10; i++) {
          c[i] = pool.getConnection();
        }
        p.Stop();

        // .. END

      } catch (Exception e) {
        e.printStackTrace();
      }
    }
  }
```

Save this as `C:\BegJavaDB\Chapter18\pooling\DataSourcePoolTest.java`, and compile it with the following command from the `Chapter18` directory:

```
> javac -classpath . pooling/DataSourcePoolTest.java
```

Then we can run it with the following command:

```
> java -classpath
      .;%JLIB%\cloudscape.jar;%JLIB%\fscontext.jar;%JLIB%\providerutil.jar;
      %JLIB%\jdbc2_0-stdext.jar pooling.DataSourcePoolTest
```

The code is similar to our previous example except that the connections are obtained from the `DataSourceConnectionPool` class, the instance of which is called `pool` in our example. The results should be similar to those below:

```
Routine [main() in PoolTest] took 0 msecs to execute.
```

Of course, the output is a little misleading. Getting 10 connections from a pool will take some time, but the granularity of our `Profiler` class (milliseconds) is not fine enough to record the time taken. If we log the time taken to create the connection pool in the first place, however, we get a different result. Make the following changes to `DataSourcePoolTest.java`:

```
        // Establish our Connection
        System.out.println("Establish a connection [" + url + "]");
        p.Start("creating a pool of 10 connections");
        pool = new DataSourceConnectionPool();

        // Lets Get 10 Connections
        Connection c[] = new Connection[10];
        p.Stop();
```

Save the file, recompile it, and then run it. The result should be something like this:

```
Routine [creating a pool of 10 connections] took 4637 msecs to execute.

Routine [main() in PoolTest] took 0 msecs to execute.
```

Creating the pool of connections takes a similar time to getting the connections the other way, so why would we want to employ connection pooling? The simple answer is that we create the pool of connections when we fire up the application, rather than creating individual connections when the user demands. This way, we trade some extra startup time for less time when the customer is actually using the application.

Connection Pooling in the Enterprise

We've looked at the concept of connection pooling, how creating our own 'pool' of connections offers us some performance increase, albeit it small on examples of our size. However, in the enterprise, imagine thousands of transactions a second all requiring a database connection! In this environment, the accumulative performance increase can be substantial. So, how do we take advantage of this without have to code our own connection pooling as in the previous example?

The answer is that we would make use of vendor-provided classes that implement the `ConnectionPoolDataSource` interface and let our database or application server take care of the connection pooling for us.

Lets take a look at a code snippet that demonstrates how we might go about this if we were using an Enterprise JavaBean to establish a database connection. Note, this code will only run within the context of an application server and the Enterprise JavaBean interface definitions.

> *Enterprise JavaBeans are discussed in Chapter 19,* J2EE and Java Database Applications, *and Appendix B shows how to configure a connection pool for the JBoss Application Server.*

```
import java.sql.*;
import javax.sql.*;
// import any vendor specific JDBC drivers here

public MyEJB ejbCreate()
{
      try
      {
        // initialize JNDI context
        Context ctx = new InitialContext();
        // ...as per our JNDI examples

        // Obtain our connection
        ConnectionPoolDataSource ds =
(ConnectionPoolDataSource)ctx.lookup("<DataSource name>");

        PooledConnection pc = ds.getPooledConnection();
        Connection conn = pc.getConnection();

        //
        // Your database manipulation code goes here
        //

        // Close the connection
        conn.close();
      }
       catch(Exception e)
```

```
        {
            e.printStackTrace();
        }
    }
```

Some of this will look familiar, we still establish our `InitialContext` so that we can look up our `DataSource` object. This is done in two stages: first we establish our `InitialContext` object, the root for all directory operations:

```
            // initialize JNDI context
            Context ctx = new InitialContext();
```

And then we perform our lookup, which if successful will return our `DataSource` object previously stored:

```
            // Obtain our connection
            ConnectionPoolDataSource ds =
    (ConnectionPoolDataSource)ctx.lookup("<DataSource name>");
```

We're now in a position to establish our connection; we do this by using the `ConnectionPoolDataSource` `getConnection()` method which, in the case of our `ConnectionPoolDataSource` interface, will return a connection from the established pool. The database driver vendor provides the interface implementation; this is because implementation details will change depending on the vendor concerned:

```
            PooledConnection pc = ds.getPooledConnection();
            Connection conn = pc.getConnection();
```

Using the above code will ensure the fastest possible database connection method when dealing with Enterprise applications with many clients. Finally, we close the connection when it is no longer required. This will cause the connection to be released back into the pool, ready for the next connection request:

```
            // Close the connection
            conn.close();
```

When you are developing outside an Application Server, some Database Management Systems offer their own flavor of connection pooling but the implementation of this is very specific to each vendor. Even if such a feature isn't available to you, there is no reason why you cannot manage your own database connections on the client via a custom-built class as we have demonstrated earlier on in the chapter.

What Else Can We Do with a DataSource?

As presented in this chapter, the `DataSource` is not available to classes running on other machines. If we can't use our `DataSource` from a remote computer, what good is it? Well, as we said earlier, this chapter is about the basics, and using a `DataSource` from a remote computer is a complicated job. Let's take a little look at what we would need:

- A way of identifying the `DataSource` across a network
- A way of communicating the search for that `DataSource` across the network

Much as we have done with tying the `DataSource` to a point on the local computer, we can tie a `DataSource` to a point in a directory listing that is independent of its location. In order to do this, we need a directory service. Fortunately, Java provides one in the form of **Java Naming and Directory Interface** (**JNDI**). We have used some of the power of JNDI to work with the `DataSource` on the local computer; however, by understanding JNDI more, we can make the location of the `DataSource` transparent to the class that wants to use it.

Great, we can use our `DataSource` on remote computers! Unfortunately, describing JNDI sufficiently is beyond the scope of this book, so we won't be showing you how to take full advantage. If you want to find out more about JNDI, a good start is *Professional Java Data* from Wrox Press, ISBN 1-861004-10-9. Alternatively, you could try *JNDI API Tutorial and Reference: Building Directory-Enabled Java Applications*, from Addison-Wesley Pub Co, ISBN 0-201705-02-8 if you want something that focuses solely on JNDI (and is quite complicated).

Summary

Hopefully this chapter has given you a good feel for what a `DataSource` object is, how to set one up and obtain a connection from it, and the benefits that using a `DataSource` can bring. These include the ability to use connection pooling and to provide support for distributed transactions. Towards the end of the chapter we hinted at how we can use `DataSources` with enterprise technologies such as Enterprise JavaBeans (EJBs) to produce highly scaleable applications. EJBs are a component that forms part of the Java 2 Enterprise Edition – a platform for the development of powerful, scaleable Java applications. In the next chapter, we will see how the Java and JDBC programming skills that we have covered in this book can be used in this J2EE environment.

J2EE and Java Database Applications

In Chapter 15 we examined *Object-Relational Mapping Concepts* and established that the difference between a relational/tabular data model and an object-oriented data model could prove a formidable obstacle for application developers. As you gain experience developing Java database-enabled applications of increasing size you will no doubt begin to address a host of other database-related complexities.

In this chapter we will discuss how the **Java 2 Platform Enterprise Edition** (**J2EE**) provides a robust, standard framework of services, which can eliminate several common complexities of enterprise application development, or at least remove them from the developer. In this chapter we will:

- Give a brief overview of J2EE including the major components and their value propositions
- Describe what a **container** is and examine its relationship to the services available in J2EE
- Give a brief overview of **JavaServer Pages** and **Servlet** technologies and show how to reuse the `Track` class from Chapter 12, in a JSP-bean pattern
- Discuss the benefits that the J2EE framework – services that are provided for free, and that can remove complexity from the code that you, the Java developer, have to write we will focus on the area of connection pooling, since this has particular relevance for database-driven development;
- Walk through an Enterprise JavaBean (EJB) example, whereby we convert the `Recording` class from Chapter 15 into an entity bean that uses container-managed persistence

It is important to note, right at the start, that this chapter is *not* intended to be a tutorial on all aspects of J2EE – that is well beyond the scope of this book. Rather, the goal is to give a good feel for how your Java/JDBC skills can be put to use in this environment, the benefits it can bring, and how you can reuse some of the classes you have developed previously in this book in this environment. Hopefully it will give you a good feel for the sort of issues that the J2EE framework sets out to tackle and why you might consider using it, and will provide a good platform from which to move on to a dedicated J2EE book, such as *Professional Java Server J2EE Edition* (Wrox Press ISBN: 1-861004-65-6).

The Development Environment

You should be able to gain considerable benefit from simply reading through this chapter. However, if you want to see the examples in action then you will need the following software:

- Java 2 Platform, Enterprise Edition SDK 1.2.1 (or you can go for the J2EE 1.3 beta 2 if you prefer, although its stability won't be guaranteed). They are available from http://java.sun.com/products/j2ee/.
- An application server in which to host an Enterprise JavaBean. We have chosen to use the open source application server **JBoss** (http://www.jboss.org/).
- A JSP and servlet container to host JavaServer Pages and servlets. We have chosen to use **Tomcat** (http://jakarta.apache.org/tomcat/).

Installation instructions are given for a version of the JBoss application server that integrates the Tomcat Web Server in Appendix B.

An Introduction to J2EE

Sun introduced the Java 2 Enterprise Edition in response to an overwhelming demand for a standardized enterprise application development platform. The J2EE specification is available at http://java.sun.com/products/j2ee/.

Realizing that several pieces of enterprise software such as databases, directory services, and transaction processing monitors were disjointed and duplicated in the large applications across an enterprise, Sun collaborated with many software companies and application developers to devise a strategy to turn commonly used enterprise application components into infrastructure and weave them together through a set of common APIs.

Meet the J2EE Components

At a high level, J2EE divides mainly into a group of **container-managed components** (more on this in a moment) and a group of **Service APIs** . The APIs provide the actual service and a container is a run-time environment that manages the use of services by the components it contains. This is of benefit to developers since experts in each field can develop the containers, the services, and the components that use them, thus leaving us more time to concentrate on producing the business logic.

Component Technologies

The most important elements in any programming framework are the components that it provides for us to write well-defined, reusable business logic. J2EE provides two types of container each of which provides a specific run time environment for application components. A **Web Container** provides a run-time environment for Servlets and JavaServer Pages, and an **EJB Container** provides run-time support for Enterprise JavaBeans.

- **Servlets** – server-side programs that allow application logic to be embedded in the request-response process of the HTTP. Servlets provide a means to extend the functionality of the web server to enable us to generate dynamic content in HTML, XML, or other web languages. With the release of J2EE 1.2, the servlets specification reached version 2.2

- **JavaServer Pages** (**JSP**) – provide a way to embed components in a page, and to have them do their work to generate the page that is eventually sent to the client. A JavaServer Page can contain HTML, Java code, and JavaBean components. JavaServer Pages is an extension of the servlet-programming model – when a user requests a JSP page, the web server compiles the JSP page into a servlet. The Java-enabled web server then invokes the servlet and returns the resulting content to the web browser

- **Enterprise JavaBeans** (**EJBs**) – The much talked about EJB specification provides a standard model for developing distributed business application components that are scalable, multi-user safe, and transaction aware. EJBs allow you to distribute business functionality on the server and can provide an object representation of persistent data.

The Service API

J2EE comprises the following service APIs and component extensions to the Java 2 Platform Standard Edition:

- **JDBC 2.0 API** – As you've already learned, JDBC is a rich API that allows you to interact with database management systems. The JDBC 2.0 API included as part of J2EE provides additional feature enhancements such as `DataSource` objects, which handle the pooling of database resources, and distributed transactions support, allowing several different, possibly distributed, enterprise components to participate in a single transaction. More about these two important enhancements is coming later in this chapter.

- **Java Naming and Directory Interface** (**JNDI**) – JNDI is an API that provides access to enterprise naming and directory services. A naming service server, such as for the Domain Name System (DNS), is used to manage the scope (or "context") of names and to provide translations between systems of names.

  For example, you can ask a DNS server to tell you that the name www.wrox.com corresponds to the IP address 204.148.170.161. Directory services (such as Novell Directory Services, or Microsoft Active Directory) are a special kind of read-optimized database that allow data to be stored in a hierarchical fashion with associated attributes that you can use for searching. JNDI is used as the central mechanism for locating many of the other J2EE components such as `DataSource` objects, message queues, and Enterprise JavaBeans.

- **Java Transaction API** (**JTA**) – While J2EE defines a specification for the automation of transaction management for components like Enterprise JavaBeans, the JTA allows enterprise components to explicitly manage their own transactions. In addition, the JTA can be used inside the container to provide the ability for transactions to span across multiple components and data sources.

- **Java Message Service** (**JMS**) – JMS provides a standard API through which components can send and receive asynchronous, fault-tolerant application messages. JMS is usually implemented by software called a **message queue**, which acts like a hub for inter-component messages. Instead of the components communicating directly in real time, the message queue is an intermediary that makes sure that the message gets transmitted. The message queue can ensure the integrity of this communication even if it doesn't happen in real-time (which is often the case). Much as JNDI sits atop naming and directory service software, you use JMS to interact with a variety of off-the-shelf message queuing solutions such as MQSeries and SonicMQ.
- **JavaMail API** – Since a good number of large applications require the ability to send and view e-mail messages, J2EE includes the JavaMail API. JavaMail encapsulates a service that handles the underlying complexities of sending or receiving mail messages from applications whether they are simple e-mails, faxes, or wireless messages.
- **eXtensible Markup Language** (**XML**) – a powerful technology for describing and structuring data (described in Chapter 20). J2EE uses XML as its native format for specifying **deployment descriptors,** which are used to configure J2EE application components. Descriptors serve the same purpose as Java properties files, but since they are stored in XML they can be used to represent more powerful configuration options than the simple name-value pairs the properties file provides.

As you can see, the J2EE platform provides a wide umbrella of development support for the intricacies of large, complicated pieces of software. Because the containers provide the environment that allows us to take advantage of database-related services, we now focus our attention to the web and EJB containers.

Exploiting J2EE Container Features

Under the J2EE specification, both web and EJB containers can implement the full suite of service APIs. It may be helpful to explain a little more about the containers themselves before talking about their common features for database support.

A container is a vendor-implemented piece of software that provides a host environment for the component type it supports. The host environment consists of the standard Java runtime (J2SE), and an optional set of services. By using services and own implementation code, the container is able to manage the lifecycle of its contained objects from instantiation, to use, persistence, and eventual destruction. The following simple diagram shows the general contents of the two types of container:

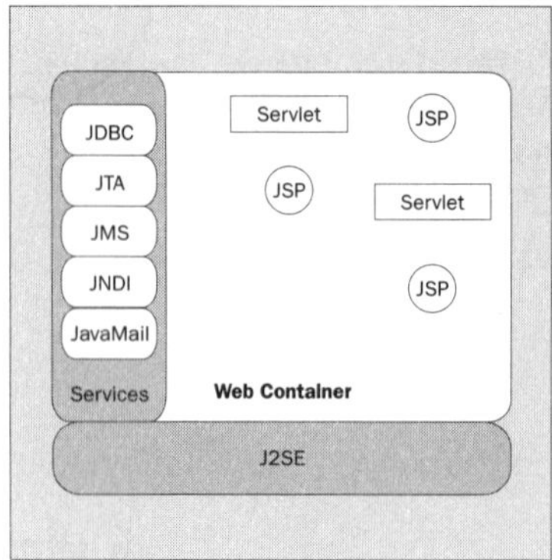

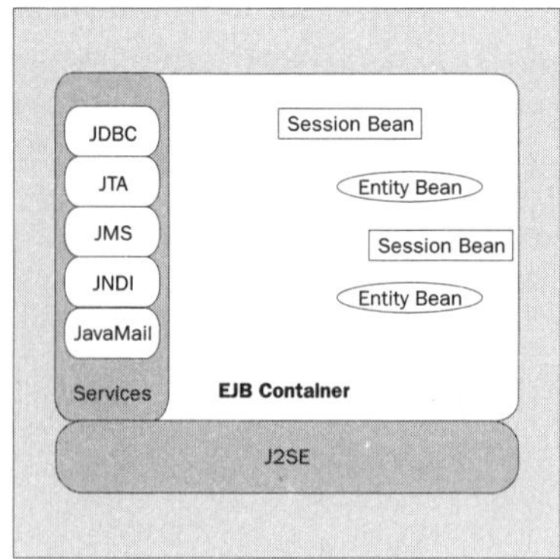

Some containers provide connectors through which components can access separate, standalone implementations of the services APIs (directory servers, message queues, etc.) and other containers are included as part of an **application server**, which bundles the container along with service implementations. An example of this product is the open source application server JBoss, which provides an EJB container along with implementations of the core service components, and optionally includes Tomcat or Jetty, web container implementations.

The main difference between the two types of containers is that the web container is typically used to host components that render the view (or user interface) of an application. The EJB container will host components that represent the data and the bulk of the logic code for an application.

Later in this chapter, we'll use JBoss to demonstrate a neat feature of EJB servers that can simplify the work done in the previous chapter on object-relational mapping. Right now, let's take a look at how a web container can simplify database development for web-based applications.

Database Applications on the Web

The basic goal of this section is to show you how you can use the components of J2EE to make your database-driven applications available on the Web. We will briefly introduce the Servlet and JSP technologies and, as part of this process, we will show you how to 'web-enable' the `Track` class that we developed in Chapter 12. However, what we will purposefully do **not** do, is delve into the specifics of each API: you will not find details of the `javax.servlet` and `javax.servlet.http` packages that compose the Servlet API. Neither will we explore in detail the JSP API. What we will attempt to do is explain how these components fit in to the basic structure of database-driven web applications and how they can be used to provide content from our Music Store database on the Web.

> *Note: The specification details of both the Servlet and JSP API are available at* http://java.sun.com/products/servlet/ *and* http://java.sun.com/products/jsp/ *respectively.*

The first thing we want to do is look at the sort of application architecture that we are considering when we move to a J2EE environment. J2EE explicitly promotes the breaking down of an application's business logic along well-defined logical units of work. We have coded our Java classes in this book to adhere to this philosophy. In a J2EE web environment, our application architecture may look something like the following:

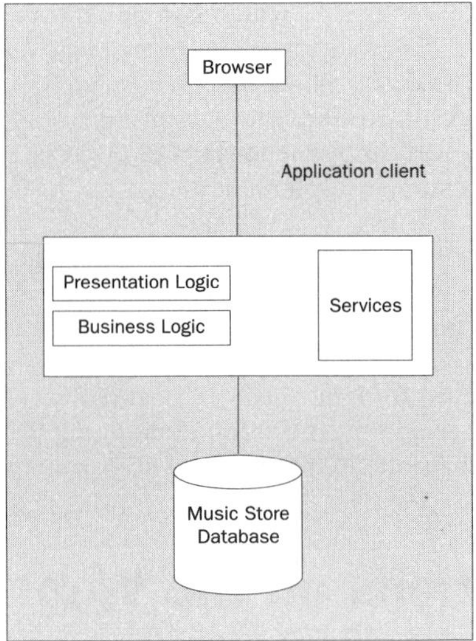

We can see that the architecture breaks down as follows:

- A **user interface**, in this case a web browser, handles the user's interaction with the application.
- **Presentation logic** defines what the user interface displays and how a user's requests are handled. In a J2EE environment we would generally encapsulate presentation logic in a JSP.
- **Business logic** models the application's business rules. Here we might use a Servlet, a JavaBean or an Enterprise JavaBean. After reading this chapter you should have some ideas about when each technique might be appropriate.
- **Infrastructure services** provide additional functionality required by the application components, such as connection pooling, transactional support, as described previously.
- The **data layer** is where the enterprise's data resides. In this case, our Music Store database.

In fact, applications based on this architecture are employing the **Model-View-Controller (MVC)** pattern. What this ultimately means is that the data (the model) is separated from how the information is presented (the view). In between this is the application/business logic (the controller) that controls the flow of the information. Therefore, an application is designed based on these three functional components (model, view, and controller) interacting with each other. We discuss this model in much more detail in Chapter 22.

Let's now take a look at the use of Servlets with our Music Store application.

Using Servlets

Java servlets allow application logic to be embedded in the HTTP request-response process. Java servlets are specified in the Java Servlet API Specification 2.2 available at http://java.sun.com/products/servlet/.

The HTTP (Hypertext Transfer Protocol) is the underlying communication protocol on the Web. It is a stateless protocol based on requests and responses. In this paradigm, client applications (such as your web browser) send requests to the servers (such as the web server of our online music store) to receive information (such as downloading a catalog), or to initiate specific processing on the server (such as placing an order).

HTTP does not define a standard means for embedding application logic during the response-generation phase. There is no programming model specified for such tasks. HTTP defines how clients can request information, and how servers can respond. HTTP is not concerned with how the response could be generated.

This is where server-side technologies such as Java servlets and JavaServer Pages come into the picture. With these technologies you can *embed* custom application logic during one or more stages of the request processing and response generation.

Java servlets are not applications we can invoke ourselves. Instead, the web container in which the web application containing the servlets is deployed invokes the servlets. When a servlet has been invoked, the web container exchanges the incoming request information with the servlet, such that the servlet can analyze the incoming request, and generate responses dynamically. The web container in turn interfaces with the web server by accepting requests for servlets, and transmitting responses back to the web server.

In order to better understand how a servlet interacts with a web server via a web container, consider the basic invocation process with the web server receiving an HTTP request. As we've seen, the HTTP protocol is based on a request-response paradigm. In this paradigm, a browser (or client) connects to a web server and sends an HTTP request over the connection. Based on the request URL, the following sequence of events happens. Note that this sequence is not 'all inclusive', but only demonstrates a typical sequence.

This sequence is illustrated below. In this figure, the rightward arrows indicate requests, while leftward arrows indicate responses:

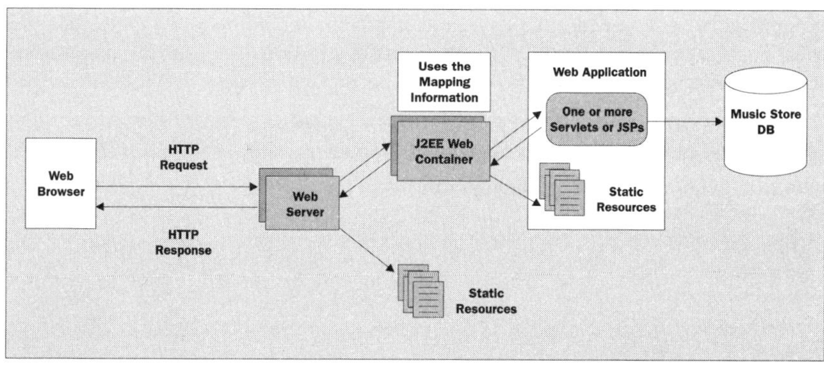

- Firstly, the web server has to figure out if the incoming request corresponds to a web application in the web container. This requires an implicit understanding between the web server and the web container. Web containers use the notion of a **servlet context** to identify web applications. You can specify the context when you're deploying the application onto the container via the deployment descriptor.

- Once the application figures out that the web container should handle the request, the web server delegates the request to the web container. You can think of this process as the web server invoking a local/remote method on the web container, with the request information.
- Once the web container receives the request, it will decide which application should handle this request. In a J2EE web application, an HTTP request can be mapped to a servlet, or a JSP page, or any static resource based on certain text being present in the requested URL. Static resources include HTML/XML pages, images, applet class/JAR files, etc. Note that all these are part of the web application. When you package and deploy a web application, you also specify this mapping information. The web container uses this mapping information to map each incoming request to a servlet, a JSP, or a static resource. If the resource is mapped to a static resource, all that the web container has to do is to pass that resource to the web server, and this forms the body of the response that the web server sends to the browser.
- However, based on the mapping information, if the web container determines that the request should be handled by a servlet, the container creates or locates a servlet instance, and delegates the request.
- When the container delegates the request to a servlet, the container also passes objects encapsulating the HTTP request and HTTP response to the servlet instance. For a servlet instance, these objects represent the request and response streams from the browser. The servlet can read the request information, and write its response to these streams. For writing response, the servlet can use the `java.io.PrintWriter` object associated with the response stream, and write content (using `println()` methods) to the response. This is equivalent to writing content to the already opened connection from the web browser.

In order to build and deploy a servlet based application, there are two steps that you'll be required to do:

- Write the servlet with the required application logic. This is part of the development phase.
- Provide a context and optional URL mapping information during the deployment phase. This mapping information is used in identifying the appropriate servlet from a web application to handle the request. The Tomcat web container has a feature whereby it can automatically create a web application context without a developer explicitly including it in a deployment descriptor. At startup, Tomcat scans its `%TOMCAT_HOME%/webapps` directory, and any directories underneath this one are automatically set up as contexts. This is what we do in the following example.

Try It Out – Displaying a List of Customers Using a Servlet

1. Create the `CustomerList` servlet as follows:

```
import java.io.*;
import java.sql.*;
import java.text.*;
import java.awt.*;
import javax.servlet.*;
import javax.servlet.http.*;

public class CustomerList extends HttpServlet {
  Connection db;     // The connection to the database
  Statement stmt;    // Our statement to run queries with
  String url, usr, pwd;

  public void init(ServletConfig config) throws ServletException {
```

```
    super.init(config);
    url = "jdbc:oracle:thin:@dbserver:1521:database";
    usr = "beg";
    pwd = "java";

    // Load the driver
    try {
      Class.forName("oracle.jdbc.driver.OracleDriver");
    } catch (Exception ex) {
      System.err.println("Problem loading Oracle Driver");
      ex.printStackTrace();
    }
  }

  public void doGet(HttpServletRequest request,
                    HttpServletResponse response) throws ServletException,
                    IOException {
    PrintWriter out;

    response.setContentType("text/html");
    out = response.getWriter();

    out.println("<HTML><HEAD><TITLE>");
    out.println("Servlet Example Connecting to the Oracle Database");
    out.println("</TITLE></HEAD>");

    out.println("<BODY BGCOLOR=\"#FFCCFF\">");
    out.println("<P><B>Customer List:</B></P>");
    out.println("Connecting to Database URL = " + url + "<br>");
    try {
      db = DriverManager.getConnection(url, usr, pwd);
    } catch (Exception ex) {
      out.println("Error connecting to database");
      ex.printStackTrace();
    }

    if (db == null) {
      out.println("<p>Error getting connection</p>");
    } else {
      out.println("<p>Connected...</p>");
      try {
        stmt = db.createStatement();

        // Now run tests using JDBC methods
        getCustomers(out);

        // Finally close the database
        out.println("<p>Closing database connection<p>");
        stmt.close();
        db.close();
      } catch (Exception ex) {
        out.println("Exception! ");
        ex.printStackTrace();
      }
```

```
    }
    out.println("</BODY></HTML>");

    out.close();
  }  // doGet

  /*
   * This gets the customer list:
   */
  public void getCustomers(PrintWriter out) throws SQLException {

    // Perform a query on the table
    String sqlQuery = "";

    sqlQuery = "select ct.CustomerTitleAbbrev || ' ' || "+
               "c.CustomerFirstName || ' ' || c.CustomerLastName Customer ";
    sqlQuery += " from Customers c, CustomerTitles ct where " +
                "c.CustomerTitleID = ct.CustomerTitleID";

    ResultSet rs = stmt.executeQuery(sqlQuery);
    if (rs != null) {

      // Now we run through the result set, printing out the result.
      // Note, we must call .next() before attempting to read any results

      out
        .println("<TABLE BORDER COLS=2 WIDTH=\"45%\" BGCOLOR=\"#FFFFCC\">");
      out.println("<TD WIDTH=\"50%\"></TD>");

      while (rs.next()) {
        String cust = rs.getString("Customer");
        out.println("<TR>");

        // don't repeat module names
        out.println("<TD>" + cust + "</TD>");
      }
      out.println("</TR>");
    }
    out.println("</TABLE>");
    rs.close();
  }
}
```

2. Save this file as `C:\BegJavaDB\Chapter19\CustomerList.java`, and compile it from the `Chapter19` directory with the following command:

```
> javac CustomerList.java
```

Note that in order to be able to compile the class using this command, you need the `javax.servlet` package in your classpath. This package is available in the `servlet.jar` file that can be found in the `%TOMCAT_HOME%\common\lib` directory; you can either reference the file there, or copy (**DON'T MOVE**) it to the `C:\java\lib` directory along with all our other library files.

To actually run the servlet, we need a servlet engine such as Tomcat. There are two things we need to do:

3. Copy the compiled servlet file to the `webapps\list\WEB-INF\classes` folder (create these directories first). The `webapps` folder is where Tomcat looks for web applications to deploy and run; the `list` folder is the folder we create for this example (it can be called pretty much anything we like); the `WEB-INF` folder is one in which we store deployment descriptors for web applications; the `classes` folder is the root folder for our classes and servlets – if our servlet were in a package, it would be in a directory structure matching the package structure, starting at `classes`.

4. Copy (again, **DON'T MOVE**) the `classes12.zip` file into the `webapps\list\WEB-INF\lib` folder, and rename it `classes12.jar`. The `lib` directory is where Tomcat looks for archive files used by our application; we have to change `classes12.zip` to `classes12.jar` because Tomcat only looks for files ending in `.jar`. If you're using Cloudscape (or any other database), put the JAR file containing the driver classes in `lib`.

5. Next, we need to start Tomcat (using the `%TOMCAT_HOME% \bin\startup.bat` file), and call the servlet from your browser, using the following URL:

   http://localhost:8080/list/servlet/CustomerList

   If everything is working properly, you should see the following screen:

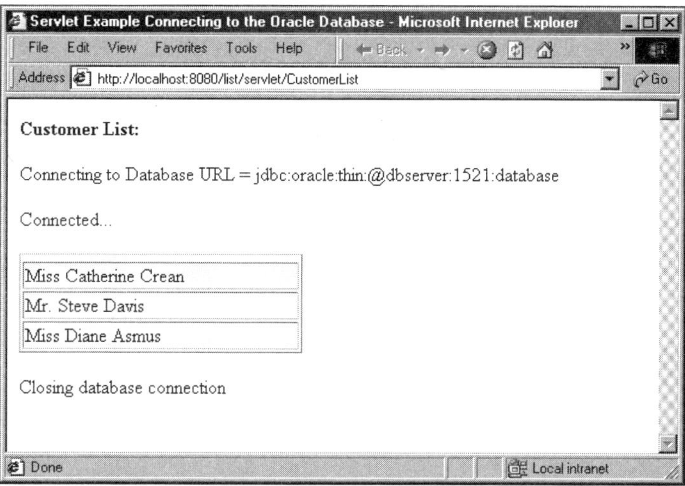

How It Works

The order of execution of a servlet is dictated by the servlet specification. While the specification details all execution flows possible, we will focus on the one present in our example. The first thing the container does when it receives a request for the servlet is call the `init()` method of the servlet:

```
public void init(ServletConfig config) throws ServletException {
  super.init(config);
  url = "jdbc:oracle:thin:@dbserver:1521:database";
```

```
    usr = "beg";
    pwd = "java";

    // Load the driver
    try {
      Class.forName("oracle.jdbc.driver.OracleDriver");
    } catch (Exception ex) {
      System.err.println("Problem loading Oracle Driver");
      ex.printStackTrace();
    }
  }
```

The init() method is called before the servlet begins servicing any web requests, and is only called once for each instance of the servlet. A web container will typically send multiple requests to a single servlet instance, so this method performs set up operations (such as initializing database drivers) to prepare the servlet for the following requests. In response to a request for a servlet, the container will call our doGet() method.

It is in our doGet() method that we do the necessary processing to respond to the web request.

```
    PrintWriter out;

    response.setContentType("text/html");
    out = response.getWriter();
```

First we declare and initialize a PrintWriter for the response stream. Note that in this example we set the content of the page to be text/html. Next we start writing the HTML page, and then try to get a connection to our database:

```
    out.println("<HTML><HEAD><TITLE>");
  ...
    out.println("Connecting to Database URL = " + url + "<br>");
    try {
      db = DriverManager.getConnection(url, usr, pwd);
```

Once we have our connection, we can create a Statement and call the getCustomers() method to execute a statement against the database:

```
    if (db == null) {
      out.println("<p>Error getting connection</p>");
    } else {
      out.println("<p>Connected...</p>");
      try {
        stmt = db.createStatement();

        // Now run tests using JDBC methods
        getCustomers(out);
```

In the getCustomers() method, the list of customers is retrieved from the database by building and executing a SQL statement:

```
String sqlQuery = "";
...
    sqlQuery = "select ct.CustomerTitleAbbrev || ' ' || "+
               "c.CustomerFirstName || ' ' || c.CustomerLastName Customer ";
    sqlQuery += " from Customers c, CustomerTitles ct where " +
                "c.CustomerTitleID = ct.CustomerTitleID";
```

After executing the statement, a `ResultSet` is created. We look through the `ResultSet` and print the customer names on the web page. This is simple code that we've seen many times already

To keep this example simple, we just placed all of the logic in the servlet – not a particularly OO approach. We're going to take a look now at how to use a JSP with a JavaBean, with the bean encapsulating the business logic and the JSP taking care of presentation.

Simplifying Database Development with JSP

In Chapter 12, we saw several examples that used a `Track` class to represent music information from the database in object form. The `Track` class also contained all of its database-mapping information, and given a `Connection` and `PreparedStatement`, could be used not only to search for tracks based on artist, recording, and title, but could also convey that result.

Most of our examples so far have retrieved information from the database and dumped it to `System.out` for display. Of course this just won't do in the modern age of web-enabled applications, and luckily for us, there is a Java technology for developing Web presentation that you have already heard about: **Java Server Pages (JSP)**.

A Brief Overview of JSP

Dynamic content generation can be achieved in two ways: programmatic content generation, or template-based content generation. While Java servlets fall into the first category, **JavaServer Pages (JSP)** belong to the second category. JavaServer Pages technology is an extension of the Java servlet technology. However, when compared to servlets, which are pure Java programs, JSP pages are text-based documents. To say this another way, in servlets we typically embed HTML in Java whereas in JSP we typically embed Java in HTML. A JSP page contains two parts:

- HTML or XML for the static content
- JSP tags and scriptlets written in the Java programming language to encapsulate the logic that generates the dynamic content

Since a JSP page provides a general representation of content that can produce multiple views depending on the results of JSP tags and scriptlets, a JSP page acts like a template for producing content.

A template is basically an HTML/XHTML/XML page with special placeholders (JSP tags and scriptlets) embedded. These placeholders contain special processing information for the underlying template processor (or content generator). In a JSP page, the usual XML/HTML/XHTML tags allow you to define the static structure and content of a page. The additional JSP tags and scriptlets embedded in the page let you include programming logic to be executed during page generation.

The key advantage of this technology is that it enables you to keep the content design and development activities separated from the design and development of the application logic. This in turn allows visual designers to focus on layout and Java developers to focus on the application logic. On the contrary, if you choose to develop the content purely with Java servlets, the above two activities would be coupled strongly. This is undesirable because such lumped applications do not lead to easy maintenance.

The JSP technology is based on page-compilation. The web container converts the JSP page into a servlet class, and compiles it. This process typically happens when the web container invokes a JSP page for the first time in response to a request or at container startup. Web containers also allow you to precompile JSPs into servlets. Most of the containers available today automatically repeat this process whenever the page is modified. This is called the page translation phase. The container invokes the generated/compiled servlet for subsequent requests to the JSP. This is the request-processing phase as indicated in the following diagram:

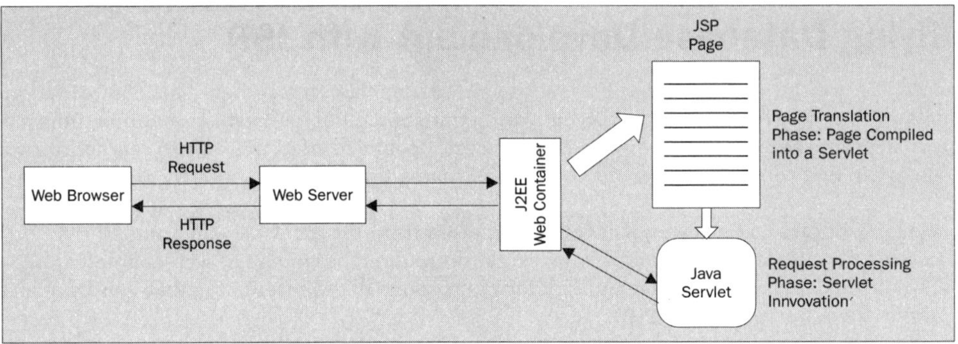

In this figure, the white arrows represent the page compilation process. Once the JSP page is compiled into a servlet, the rest of the request processing and response generation is the same as described in the previous section.

The above architecture leads to very useful and flexible applications using JSPs and servlets:

- You can use servlets alone for application logic and content generation.
- You can also use JSP pages alone for application logic and content generation.
- You can combine these, with application logic handled by the servlet, and content generation handled by JSP pages.

JSP allows us to harness the power of the Java language to build HTML for web browser display. We have access to the entire Java API, and any custom classes we create. Many application-building firms employ web designers who are wizards when it comes to making HTML come to life with various dynamic scripting technologies such as PHP, Active Server Pages, and JSP. Unfortunately, some Java API's can be too complex in this case, and JDBC is no exception.

Sure, most scripters understand looping constructs and given a `ResultSet` object, would be able to extract the data they need via method calls, but they also need to obtain the `ResultSet`. (And get the `Connection`, and prepare the `PreparedStatement`, and so on.) Furthermore, as we discussed in Chapter 7, there are some very compelling reasons for centralizing your database access and not letting the clients work with `ResultSet` objects. Wouldn't it be great if we could somehow provide the data in an easy-to-use form and hide the complexities of how that data was obtained? We're going to show that with JSP and a little help from JavaBeans, this is no sweat!

JavaBeans

JavaBeans is a specification from Sun Microsystems (available at http://java.sun.com/products/javabeans/) that defines a design pattern for creating discrete components that have accessible properties and perform a set function.

We can use beans to store data and then retrieve it at a later date. For instance, we might have a bean that modeled a bank account. This bean might have account number and balance properties. Formally, a JavaBean is really nothing more than a class that maintains some data (the properties) and follows certain coding conventions such as exposing private data via accessor and mutator methods. These conventions provide a mechanism for automated support. This automated support means that the JSP engine, for example Tomcat, can inspect the bean and discover what properties it has.

JavaBeans were originally conceived of to allow developers to create standalone components that could be dropped into the GUI of an integrated development environment like JBuilder or VisualAge and configured visually. These components could be visual, such as tables, progress bars, etc. or non-visual components used to simplify access to things like network services. JavaBeans functioned well in IDEs and were so useful as a common way of interacting with a project's state (or properties) that they were eventually supported in other environments, including JSP.

Part of what makes JavaBeans so useful is that they allow you to package complex or unwieldy code into a simpler interface. In the case of the JSP, this is particularly useful since it allows us to centralize some of our database access code, and simplify its use for people who may not be familiar with JDBC, but still need the data to get their job done. JSP even provides special tags to create instances of JavaBeans and interact with their properties.

If we return to our `Track` example, let's suppose that the manager of our music store has just hired an 18-year-old web developer to build a web-based system that allows her customers to search for the tracks of any music artist. This kid is really handy when it comes to building user interfaces with script, but couldn't parse a `ResultSet` to save his life. Because of our experience writing the `Track` class, our boss has asked us to provide a simpler interface to our novice co-worker. Let's take a look at a diagram of how the entire process will flow, using a JavaBean to connect to the database.

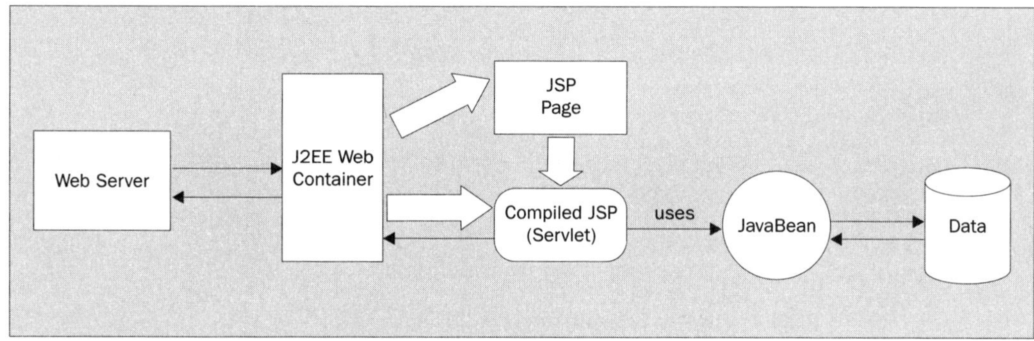

As you can see, flow is quite similar to the diagram above with the exception that once execution gets to our JSP page, we're going to use a JavaBean to do all of the processing and interaction with the database, and merely use the JSP to render an interface.

Knowing that JavaBeans are a good way to simplify our tricky `Track` class, we'll get to our task.

Try It Out – Building a JavaBean

Let's take a look at the entire code listing for our JavaBean, and then we'll look at it step-by-step to see what's going on:

```
package javabean;

import connections.ConnectionFactory;
import statements.Track;

import java.util.Vector;
import java.sql.*;

public class ArtistSearchBean {

  private String searchCriteria;

  public ArtistSearchBean() {
    searchCriteria = "";
  }

  public String getSearchCriteria() {
    return searchCriteria;
  }

  public void setSearchCriteria(String searchCriteria) {
    if (searchCriteria == null) {
      this.searchCriteria = "";
    } else {
      this.searchCriteria = searchCriteria;
    }
  }

  /**
   * Execute the search and return the results of our search
   * as a Track array
   */
  public Track[] executeSearch() {
    Track t = new Track();
    Track[] searchResult = null;

    Connection conn = null;
    PreparedStatement ps = null;
    try {
      conn = ConnectionFactory.getConnection();
      ps = conn.prepareStatement(t.getFindArtistSql());
      t.setQueryStatement(ps);
      Vector v = t.findByArtistName(searchCriteria);
      searchResult = (Track[]) v.toArray(new Track[0]);
    } catch (SQLException sqle) {
      sqle.printStackTrace();
    } finally {
      try {
        if (ps != null) {
```

```
          ps.close();
        }
        if (conn != null) {
          conn.close();
        }
      } catch (SQLException sqle) {
        throw new java.lang.InternalError("Something really bad happened.");
      }
    }
    return searchResult;
  }

}
```

How It Works

Let's have a look at some of the key points to our JavaBean. First, we import the necessary classes. Note that if we weren't creating a JavaBean, this code would be inserted in *every* place where we wanted to utilize the `Track` class. This could quickly make our JSP pages and Java Swing GUIs very difficult to understand and maintain. By encapsulating the code in a JavaBean, we write it once, and let other pieces of code use the bean when they need this kind of functionality:

```
package javabean;

import connections.ConnectionFactory;
import statements.Track;

import java.util.Vector;
import java.sql.*;
```

We then declare our class. The JavaBean specification doesn't dictate a name for the class, but you will often see the word `Bean` appended to the end of the class name as a convention. We also declare a variable that will hold the `string` we will try to match against the artist's name in the database. In the JavaBean specification, all properties should be accessed through getter and setter methods and thus will be made `private`:

```
public class ArtistSearchBean {

  private String searchCriteria;
```

Next we create a constructor with no parameters, which initializes the search criteria to an empty string. This is necessary because it eventually becomes part of a SQL statement fed to the database:

```
  public ArtistSearchBean() {
    searchCriteria = "";
  }
```

Then we provide a `get` method to access our property. This method is part of the JavaBean specification and is named `get` followed by the name of our property:

```
  public String getSearchCriteria() {
    return searchCriteria;
  }
```

The JavaBean specification also defines the need for a `set()` method for each property we want to expose. Here, as in the constructor, we also guarantee that the value won't be set to `null`:

```
public void setSearchCriteria(String searchCriteria) {
  if (searchCriteria == null) {
    this.searchCriteria = "";
  }
  else this.searchCriteria = searchCriteria;
}
```

Now we are ready to begin our search method, which will return an array of `Track` objects. While a `Track` object can be used to interact with the database, it also provides JavaBean-like storage and access for all of the data fields associated with the `Track`. Because the data in a `Track` can be accessed with `get` methods, it should be simple enough for our web developer to work with.

While there are no hard and fast rules for where a Java developer's capabilities end and a page designer's begin, encapsulating logic in a JavaBean provides a better separation between these roles, which makes web applications much easier to develop and maintain.

Going into our `executeSearch()` method we create a `Track` so that we can use it to aid our interaction with the database, and an array of tracks that will hold our search result.

```
public Track[] executeSearch() {
  Track t = new Track();
  Track[] searchResult = null;

  Connection conn = null;
  PreparedStatement ps = null;
```

Note in the following code that when we call upon the `Track` object `t` to perform a search, we pass it our internal search criteria. The `findByArtistName()` method returns a vector, but we use a special method of the vector class to convert it to an array of type `Track`.

```
  try {
    conn = ConnectionFactory.getConnection();
    ps = conn.prepareStatement(t.getFindArtistSql());
    t.setQueryStatement(ps);
    Vector v = t.findByArtistName(searchCriteria);
    searchResult = (Track[]) v.toArray(new Track[0]);
```

Several methods we are calling potentially throw `SQLException` errors, so we dutifully catch them and, finally close our resources before we return our result:

```
  } catch (SQLException sqle) {
    sqle.printStackTrace();
  } finally {
    try {
      if (ps != null) {
        ps.close();
      }
```

```
          if (conn != null) {
            conn.close();
          }
        } catch (SQLException sqle) {
          throw new java.lang.InternalError("Something really bad happened.");
        }
      }
      return searchResult;
    }
```

As you can see, creating the JavaBean was just a little extra work and we have greatly simplified the process of searching for a `Track` list for our new friend, the web developer. Let's take a look at how he can use a JSP to take advantage of what we've done.

Integrating a JavaBean into JSP

While a complete look at the details of JavaServer Pages is the subject of another book, for example *Beginning JSP Web Development* (Wrox Press, ISBN: 1-861002-09-2), we will cover some of the basic points needed to understand what our web developer is implementing. The first matter of business is to create an input form through which users can submit their search criteria.

The search.html page

We'll start out little trip with a simple HTML page to get information from the user:

```
<html>
  <head>
    <title>Search for tracks by an Artist</title>
  </head>
  Please enter as much of the artist's name as possible
  and press the search button.
  <P>
  <form action="DoArtistSearch.jsp">
    Artist Name: <input type="text" name="searchCriteria"><BR><BR>
                 <input type="submit" name="Search">
  </form>
</html>
```

The following screenshot shows what the page looks like when viewed through a browser:

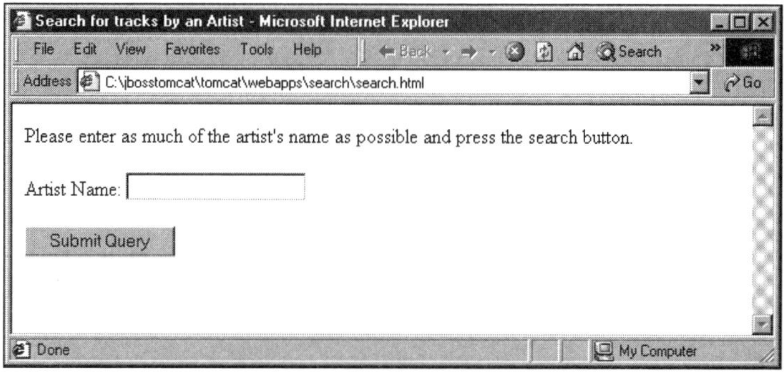

Our web developer is no slouch and certainly knows to keep it simple. The simple form that he's created in HTML will provide the user with one input field to enter their search criteria, and a button to submit their request. You will notice that the `action` attribute of the form tag is set to `DoArtistSearch.jsp`. This is the JSP that will process the user's request and display the search results. That is our web developer's next task.

Try It Out – DoArtistSearch.jsp

Our JSP page is slightly more complex and more likely to have unfamiliar elements. Let's take a quick look at the file in its entirety and then discuss what's happening:

```
<%@ page import="statements.Track" %>
<HTML>
<HEAD>
<jsp:useBean id="searchBean" scope="page"
             class="javabean.ArtistSearchBean" />
<jsp:setProperty name="searchBean" property="*" />
<%
  Track[] t = searchBean.executeSearch();
%>
<TITLE>
Search for tracks by "<jsp:getProperty name="searchBean"
                                        property="searchCriteria"/>"
</TITLE>
</HEAD>
<b><i>Your search returned <%= t.length %> results.</i></b>
<P>
<%
  if (t.length > 0) {
%>
<TABLE BORDER='1'>
  <TR>
    <TD><b>Track Title:</b></TD>
    <TD><b>Artist:</b></TD>
    <TD><b>Track #:</b></TD>
    <TD><b>Album:</b></TD>
    <TD><b>Style:</b></TD>
  </TR>
<%
  for (int i = 0; i < t.length; i++) {

%>
  <TR>
    <TD><%= t[i].getTrackTitle() %></TD>
    <TD><%= t[i].getArtistName() %></TD>
    <TD><%= t[i].getTrackNumber() %></TD>
    <TD><%= t[i].getRecordingTitle() %></TD>
    <TD><%= t[i].getStyleName() %></TD>
  </TR>
<%
    }
  }
%>
</TABLE>
```

```
</BODY>
</HTML>
```

This JSP is saved to the same directory as `search.html`, namely `tomcat\webapps\search`.

How It Works

As you can see, a JSP bears some resemblance to an HTML document. This is because a JSP *is* HTML with Java tags interspersed to perform processing before the page is delivered. The server interprets the tags, executing the Java code, and returns the resulting HTML to the user's web browser. Let's have a look at how that's done.

The very first line we see is a Java import directive. Similar to an import statement in a class file, we are telling this JSP which classes we will need that are not part of the standard JDK. This import statement is enclosed in a special `<%@...%>` tag, which lets the JSP parser know that it's a program setup instruction:

```
<%@ page import="statements.Track" %>
```

Next we have some standard opening HTML tags, followed by two tags that you probably haven't seen before. The first unusual tag, `<jsp:useBean>` tells the page processor that we'd like to create an instance of a JavaBean. We include an attribute called `id`, with a value `searchBean`, which is how we declare the reference name of this bean. Then we include a "scope" attribute, which says how long this bean will exist. We can make it just live for a single viewing of this page, or allow it to persist for the entire length of the user session. Finally, we tell the JSP compiler what type of class to instantiate for our JavaBean:

```
<HTML>
<HEAD>
<jsp:useBean id="searchBean" scope="page"
             class="javabean.ArtistSearchBean" />
```

The second tag, `<jsp:setProperty>`, is how we set the value of our bean's properties. The first attribute we include is `name`. This corresponds to the `id` we declared in the `<jsp:useBean>` tag. Next we declare which property we would like to set. Normally this would be a `String` corresponding to the name of one of our bean setter methods minus the word "set". By using an asterisk, we are indicating that we would like the bean to have all of its properties reset with the incoming request values:

```
<jsp:setProperty name="searchBean" property="*" />
```

This tells the container to look for any parameter values in the incoming request and try to match them up with the `searchBean`. In our case, there will be an incoming form parameter called `searchCriteria` whose value will be used to set the `searchCriteria` property of our bean. This feature is made available to us by the specification since we are using a JavaBean.

In the next lines, you will notice another new tag, `<%...%>`. This tag encloses actual Java code. The tag is a directive, which tells the JSP processor to wake up and start evaluating the code.

After we have set the user's search criteria, we then call upon the bean to execute the search:

```
<%
  Track[] t = searchBean.executeSearch();
%>
```

Does that seem to be too easy? Well, that's how easy it is! And now all that's left is to loop through the returned array and create some HTML to display to the user:

```
<TITLE>
Search for tracks by "<jsp:getProperty name="searchBean"
                                       property="searchCriteria"/>"
</TITLE>
</HEAD>
<b><i>Your search returned <%= t.length %> results.</i></b>
<P>
<%
  if (t.length > 0) {
%>
<TABLE BORDER='1'>
  <TR>
    <TD><b>Track Title:</b></TD>
    <TD><b>Artist:</b></TD>
    <TD><b>Track #:</b></TD>
    <TD><b>Album:</b></TD>
    <TD><b>Style:</b></TD>
  </TR>
<%
  for (int i = 0; i < t.length; i++) {

%>
  <TR>
    <TD><%= t[i].getTrackTitle() %></TD>
    <TD><%= t[i].getArtistName() %></TD>
    <TD><%= t[i].getTrackNumber() %></TD>
    <TD><%= t[i].getRecordingTitle() %></TD>
    <TD><%= t[i].getStyleName() %></TD>
  </TR>
<%
    }
  }
%>
</TABLE>
</BODY>
</HTML>
```

Notice that we have used conditional statements here that actually affect whether or not the enclosed HTML is displayed. The same holds true for the HTML displayed when looping through the `ResultSet`. The ability to omit and repeat blocks of HTML based on Java conditions is only a small demonstration of the power of JSP. Let's now put the whole thing together.

Try it Out – Getting it up and Running

To get this example up and running we need to complete the following steps:

1. Make sure that `search.html` is located in the `%TOMCAT_HOME%/webapps/search` directory. Remember from our servlet example that this will automatically create an application context called "search" when Tomcat is started.

2. Make sure that `DoArtistSearch.jsp` is also in the `%TOMCAT_HOME%/webapps/search/` directory. In `search.html` we set the action to this page. When the `search.html` page form gets submitted, this is the JSP that will process it.

3. Compile `ArtistSearchBean.java` with the following command (note that the `Track` and `ConnectionFactory` classes will need to be present in your classpath):

```
>javac -classpath . javabeans/ArtistSearchBean.java
```

   Here we assume that the connections and statements packages are below the directory we're compiling from.

4. Copy the resulting class file, `ArtistSearchBean.class`, to `%TOMCAT_HOME%/webapps/search/WEB-INF/classes/javabeans/`.

5. Copy the `Track` class to `%TOMCAT_HOME%/webapps/search/WEB-INF/classes/statements`.

6. Copy the `ConnectionFactory` class to `webapps\WEB-INF\classes\connections`.

7. Make sure your database driver JAR file is copied to the `search/WEB-INF/lib` directory.

8. Start Tomcat and point your web browser to http://localhost:8080/search/search.html, and you should see the following:

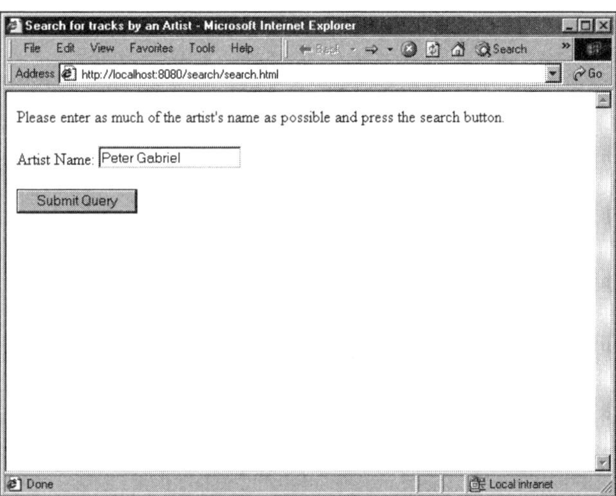

Enter a value for the Artist Name field and press the Submit Query button. You will then see a list of search results like the following:

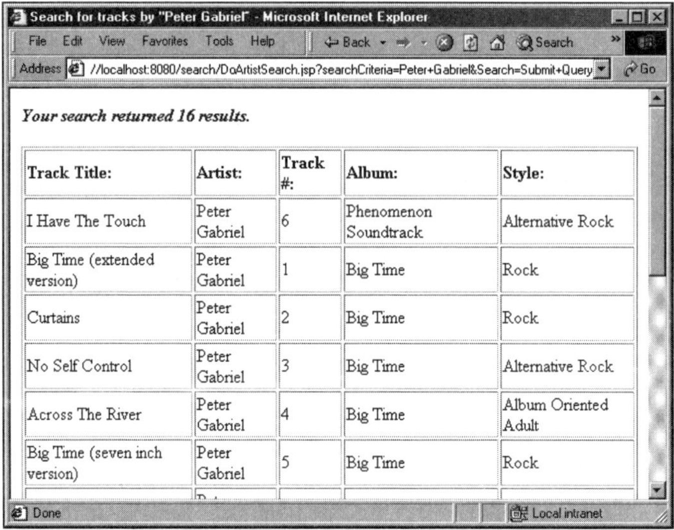

If no tracks match the artist name you entered, you will see the following screen:

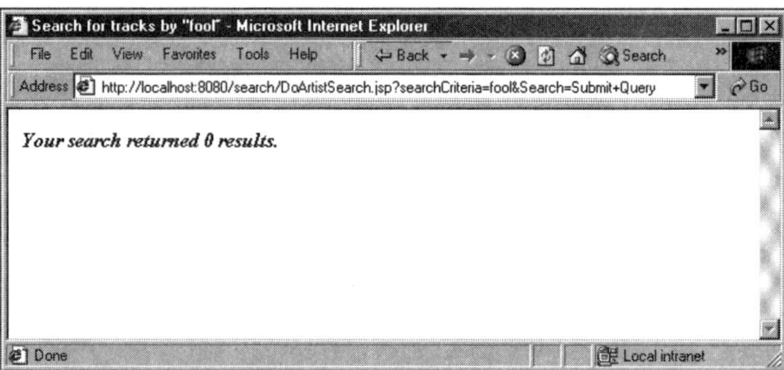

Although the capabilities of JSP go far beyond the scope of this example, we have now seen how JSP paired with JavaBeans can help bring information out of the database simply for a dynamic presentation.

And of course, JSP and JavaBeans are only two container-accessible J2EE technologies that can make database development easier. One of those most basic services bundled with J2EE containers is a convenient mechanism for managing database resources: the connection pool.

Connection Pools

As part of the JDBC 2.0 implementation most containers includes a method for getting hold of a `DataSource`. Recall from Chapter 18, that a `DataSource` object is a factory for obtaining database connections. The `DataSource` encapsulates connection information like the database URL, username, and password, and is usually bound as an object in the directory service the container provides access to.

> ***Binding*** *is how a Java object becomes associated with a location in the directory service hierarchy. You access a bound object via JNDI by providing the appropriate name for the object. For instance, an object you bind into the directory service at the name* `"java:comp/env/myObject"` *can be retrieved by performing a lookup using JNDI at the location* `"java:comp/env/myObject"`*. A* `DataSource` *is typically bound into an application server's JNDI tree.*

We have seen that database resources, particularly `Connection` objects, can be time-consuming to instantiate and limited by resources like database licenses and system memory. Also, database connections often make heavy use of network resources. In an effort to make more efficient use of these precious resources, `DataSource` objects are usually implemented to pool database connections. What this means is that the connection pool maintains a certain number of instantiated database `Connection` objects and when the `getConnection()` method of a `DataSource` is called, the pool passes one of the connections out.

The pool keeps track of which connections are in use, and when connections get returned. Because the container is managing all of this work for you, getting a pooled connection is as easy to do as looking up a `DataSource` object and calling `getConnection()`.

Something you'll discover is that pooled connections don't need to be explicitly returned to the `DataSource`. If we don't return the `connection` to the pool, how will the pool know that the connection is no longer in use and make it available for another client?

Recall that the `Connection` class defines an interface, not a concrete object. Most database vendors will provide an implementation for this interface that can be used to access their database. This also means that the `DataSource` can pass back its own implementation of `Connection` from the `getConnection()` method. Most often this Connection implementation will have two internal references, one to the connection pool, and one to a database vendor-provided implementation of `Connection`.

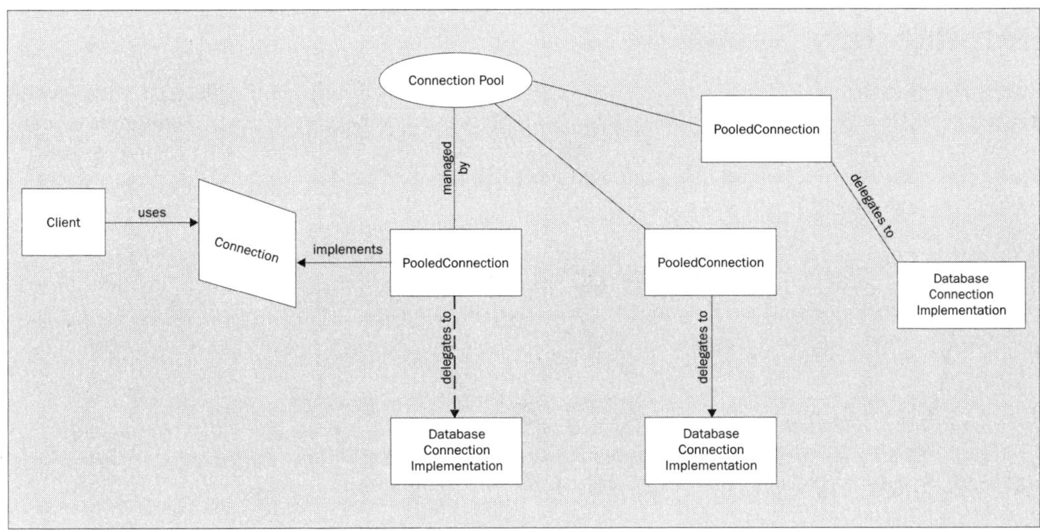


```
public class PooledConnection implements java.sql.Connection {
  private ConnectionPool _pool;
  private Connection _vendorConnection;
```

```
  ...
}
```

In this case, the `PooledConnection` is called a **proxy** because it sits in between an interface and another implementation of the interface. Because of its position, `PooledConnection` can intercept calls to the methods in the `Connection` interface and decide whether to perform any processing or to forward the call to the vendor connection, or both:

```
public class PooledConnection implements java.sqlConnection {
  private ConnectionPool _pool;
  private Connection _vendorConnection;

  public PreparedStatement prepareStatement(String sql) throws SQLException{
    // forward this call to the vendor connection
    return _vendorConnection.prepareStatement(sql);
  }

  public void close() {
    // intercept this call and notify the pool that the connection is free
    _pool.releaseConnection(this);
  }
}
```

As you can see, a connection provided by a pool will typically be a proxy that returns itself to the pool when you invoke the `close()` method in your code. This proxy-delegation setup is a very common way for a container to manage the interaction between your components (be they Servlet or JSP), and the service APIs of the J2EE platform. As we will see with EJB, this technique can be quite powerful.

Enterprise JavaBeans

Enterprise JavaBeans (EJBs) are network-aware, transaction-aware, distributed objects with several useful properties. We introduce EJBs as a way to highlight advanced persistence techniques available under the J2EE platform. EJBs can help a high-traffic production application use precious system resources more effectively, and allow a team of application developers to operate without concern for the type of persistence layer data is stored in.

A complete treatment of EJBs is beyond the scope of this book so this section will cover the basics of implementing and deploying a bean and walk through a small application that demonstrates how EJBs can exploit transaction and persistence functions that are managed by the container. First, an introductory look at EJBs is required.

A note on versions: as of the time of this book's release the EJB specification versions 1.0 and 1.1 are currently available to the public. The EJB version 2.0 specifications are still under review, and most popular EJB containers currently conform to the EJB 1.1 specification. This chapter assumes EJB 1.1, with a few notes concerning changes made where appropriate.

EJB Overview

EJBs are deployable components that together make up part of an enterprise application. EJBs are flexible enough to be used as connectors to legacy data sources via CORBA and implementations of J2EE connector architecture. For the purposes of our example, we will demonstrate their more common use as business components and object representations of persistent data.

We have used the terms "network-aware" and "distributed" as adjectives describing EJB. What does this mean? EJBs are network-aware in that they are able to communicate with client applications over a network. Client applications can be inside the same Java virtual machine or in a different JVM that may be on a local area network or distributed across the world through the Internet.

This capability is hidden from client code using beans, as well as from the bean supplier (the developer who writes the EJB). The bean supplier need not worry about the complications of how to make method calls across a network or access distributed objects that may exist in different JVMs. The user of the bean has to make some accommodations based on the possibility that the bean could be in a different location, but this just entails catching a few EJB-specific exceptions.

EJBs must be deployed in a container, which will manage the process of using the bean. As we'll see, any method calls a client wants to make to a given EJB are in fact made to the container, which passes the call to the bean. There are currently two main classifications of EJBs. Let's have a look.

EJB Classification

A detailed discussion of the types of EJBs is out of scope for this text, (it is in fact the subject of a rather large specification, see *Professional EJB*, from Wrox Press ISBN 1-861005-08-3) but for now, please keep the following generalizations in mind concerning types of EJB:

- **Session beans** are components that contain useful business logic. A session bean might calculate sales tax on an order or determine if a requested item is in stock. They are typically a server-side extension of functionality that would appear on the client. Session beans come in two flavors:
    - **Stateless** session beans do not maintain any internal data state between method calls.
    - **Stateful** session beans are capable of storing their internal state between method calls, and can be used when your application must remember some part of its state in between a client's method calls.
- **Entity beans** are components that represent the pieces of data that make up a business entity. A car, a record, and an employee could be entity beans within an application. A specific reference to an entity bean represents a specific, unique object in a persistent store, often a database. Persistence for entity beans can be handled in two ways:
    - **Container-Managed Persistence** requires that the bean developer define rules for which fields in an entity bean should be persisted and to what parts of the database. The container then creates and executes the appropriate SQL to perform the persistence operation when needed.
    - **Bean-Managed Persistence** requires that the developer implement the persistence by writing code. Bean Managed Persistence closely resembles and builds upon the techniques used in the object-relational chapter.

One thing that may not be completely clear yet is that both entity and session beans can be used to interact with persistent data. Session beans interact with persistent data in a service-like fashion. They can retrieve it and operate on it. Entity beans, on the other hand, are meant to be an object representation of the actual data itself.

For example, a table in the database may be represented to your application as an entity bean with getter and setter methods that correspond to the columns of data. In this case, there would be one entity bean for each row in the database. Luckily, this does not mean that your application would have an object in memory for each row in the database. The EJB container manages the lifecycle of both types of beans: creating them, pooling them, and in the case of entity beans, loading data into them from the database at appropriate times.

Let's have a closer look at the EJB container's relationship to the beans.

EJB Containers

An Enterprise JavaBean needs to operate within a special environment. This environment is the **EJB container**. An EJB container is often part of a J2EE application server. This container/application server provides the following services for the bean including those we discussed earlier:

- Generating additional classes needed to facilitate the distributed nature of EJBs
- Managing a bean's persistence when using CMP
- Managing a bean's transactional state
- Notifying the bean before and after significant events in the bean's lifecycle
- Facilitating instance pooling for beans, if instance pooling is used
- Managing bean security
- Managing bean concurrency
- Managing any other J2EE service resources (application servers only)

In order to provide the services described above, the container will intercept the method calls between the client and the EJB, (in a similar fashion to the way a pooled connection intercepts calls to a database-provided connection object). By inserting proxy objects the container is allowed to perform any additional processing required before forwarding a client's method call to the intended EJB. The entire lifecycle model for an EJB is detailed in the EJB 1.1 specifications.

Transaction Management

J2EE specifies the Java Transaction API to allow components and containers to manage distributed transactions. This means that in the context of our container, we can co-ordinate a transaction between several different databases at the same time. We can even include legacy systems in the scope of our transaction. With EJB, transaction management couldn't get any easier!

The reason transaction management is so easy to implement is that it can be specified in a deployment descriptor. Recall that XML is used in J2EE to specify application properties. Our EJB container makes use of some special entries in the deployment descriptor to determine which methods of an EJB must be called in the context of a transaction. It is possible to dictate that a bean method must never be used in a transaction, can be used in a transaction, or must be used in a transaction. This means that your method can be implemented to do whatever is required and its transactional involvement can be specified at dictated at deployment time, even when interacting with a database.

Remember how a database connection pool creates a delegating proxy to intercept method calls? EJB containers employ a similar strategy to make sure that the appropriate JTA methods get called. The container also coordinates with the connection pool to make sure the `commit()` method is called at exactly the correct time. The container also uses this interception technique to coordinate transactions across different databases.

The relationship between an EJB and its interface is somewhat different from that of a `Connection` and its implementation (in fact, the EJB provides ***two*** interfaces.)

EJB Structure

EJBs are distributed objects. In order to create a deployable Bean we need to do a little more work than just creating one class or implementing an interface. An Enterprise JavaBean has four parts:

- A **Remote Interface**
- A **Home Interface**
- The **Bean implementation**
- The **Deployment Descriptor**

Remote Interface

Each bean must provide two interfaces, a remote and a home interface. The remote interface extends `javax.ejb.EJBObject`. An EJB's remote interface is the means by which clients of the bean gain access to the bean's business methods. Whereas the home interface is used to create and search for beans, the remote interface is used to make the bean do tasks, or expose its data. Typically, the remote interface of an EJB bears the name of the bean it belongs to, thus the remote interface for an EJB named Recording would be called `Recording`.

Home Interface

Every EJB will also have an interface that extends `javax.ejb.EJBHome`. The home interface defines methods that allow the container to manage each bean's lifecycle: finding beans, creating, or destroying beans. The home interface can declare one or more `create()` methods which create an instance of the bean implementation class on the server and return a remote reference. The home interface is typically named after the remote interface, but with `Home` added to the end, thus the home interface for our Recording bean would be `RecordingHome`.

Bean Implementation

This is where you define the implementation of your bean. Place here any data or business logic that the bean will need to utilize. Session beans must implement the `javax.ejb.SessionBean` interface; entity beans must implement the `javax.ejb.EntityBean` interface. It may seem like the bean implementation should implement the home or remote interfaces, but we don't so that a very important step can take place when the bean is deployed.

You see, it is actually the EJB container that provides an implementation of the home and remote interfaces. Sometimes this occurs dynamically at run time, and some containers provide a tool to generate the classes. This generated `EJBObject` implementation becomes a delegating proxy, much like our earlier `PooledConnection`. The following diagram illustrates this dependency:

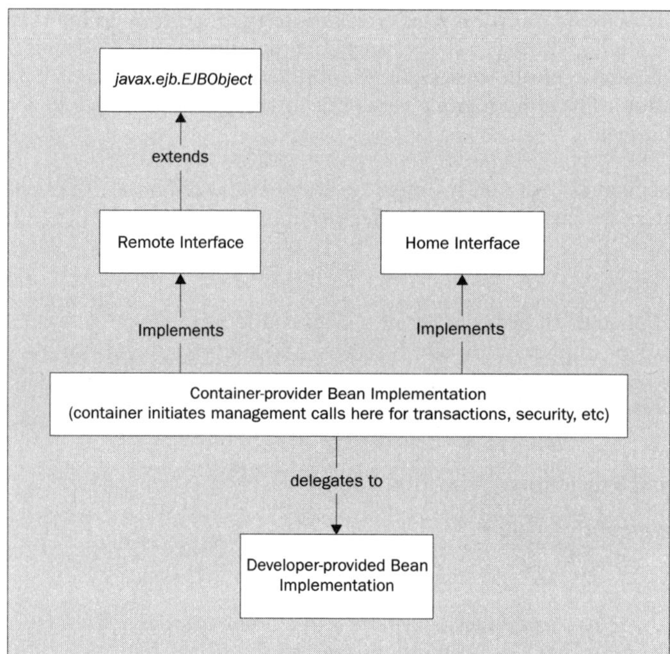

It is in this proxy object that the container is able to seamlessly manage your transactions and provide any other services your bean needs. The implementation class for an EJB generally bears the name of the remote interface, with `EJB` or `Bean` added to the end, thus the implementation of our Recording bean would be named `RecordingEJB` or `RecordingBean`. As with other Java classes, the name isn't important but it does make life a lot easier if we give our code sensible names – calling the components of our EJB Fred, Ethel, and Mary wouldn't be very helpful to other developers, including ourselves when we come back to our code later.

Deployment Descriptor

The deployment descriptor is an XML file, as we've already seen. For an EJB, the deployment descriptor identifies the home and remote interfaces, together with the implementation class. Depending on the type of EJB we have, the deployment descriptor will contain other information, specifying which methods require transactions, which variables are to be persisted, and which variable represents the primary key for the bean. The deployment descriptor must be called `ejb-jar.xml` – there is no getting away from this name.

We have one more feature particular to entity beans to discuss and then we'll get to see an example of this simple coding (but complicated infrastructure) in action!

Container-Managed Persistence

As we have already discussed, an EJB container is typically provided by an application server to support the services required by the EJB specification. The EJB specification requires that our bean classes (remote and home interfaces, and implementation class) implement various callback methods to allow our bean to react to significant events that have happened or are about to happen. Remember also that these methods are never directly accessed by client code but instead are intercepted by the container first. Business methods exposed to client code through the bean's remote interface are passed through the proxy object as well.

Because of this situation, an EJB container is in a unique position to provide additional value-added services. One of these services is Container-Managed Persistence (CMP). CMP is the process by which significant events in the lifecycle of an entity bean are intercepted by a container-provided persistence mechanism and acted upon. For instance, calling an EJB `findByPrimaryKey()` method (a method required in entity beans) will result in the container doing a lookup against a persistent store in an effort to locate an object in that store. Performing an EJB `remove()` action causes the container to look up the entity bean in the persistent store and remove the object from that store. Create and update events can be tracked by the container as well: after any business method is called on an entity bean the bean has an opportunity to reconcile its state with a persistent store.

As you may have already guessed, one very common way of implementing CMP is for the container to *automatically* generate SQL statements to perform the CRUD (Create, Retrieve, Update, and Delete) operations for entity beans when significant events occur. While this process is automated you have to do some work up front to tell the container how to persist your Java objects to a relational database. This usually involves:

- Giving the CMP mechanism database connection information.
- Giving the CMP mechanism information about how the data in the database maps to the entity bean. This is effectively setting up an Object-Relational Map. Some application vendors provide tools to do this.

Now that we see one of the database benefits the J2EE platform gives us for almost free, we should take a look at the alternative, Bean-Managed Persistence.

Bean-Managed Persistence

BMP, or Bean-Managed Persistence assumes that the supplier of the entity bean knows best how the data contents of the beans should be loaded, saved, and removed from a persistent store. This means the person implementing the bean's business methods must also provide implementations that:

- Load the bean's state from the database in response to the EJB-specified `ejbLoad()` method
- Remove the bean's state from the database in response to the EJB-specified `ejbRemove()` method
- Create the bean's state in the database in response to the EJB-specified `ejbCreate()` method

There is one final topic to cover before we get to see an example of CMP in action.

Deploying a Bean

Once the Enterprise Bean's home and remote interfaces, and implementation class are complete, the bean is ready to be deployed. Deployment is the process whereby the bean is registered with the container and the container begins managing the bean.

Each bean you wish to deploy must have a **deployment descriptor**. Most application server vendors supply a tool to create the deployment descriptor, but it can be created by hand if necessary. In EJB 1.1 the deployment descriptor takes the form of an XML file. The deployment descriptor, as we said earlier, must be called `ejb-jar.xml`. This XML file contains data about the bean such as the fully qualified class name of the bean, and the name of the bean's home and remote interfaces. There are different attributes to be specified in deployment descriptors for entity and session beans.

For example a deployment descriptor for a session bean may have tags that alert the container as to the type of session and transactional properties the bean should have, whereas a deployment descriptor for an entity bean will have tags telling the container what type of persistence the bean uses and its primary key class. In an entity bean, the primary key is used to uniquely identify an object, much like a primary key is used to uniquely identify a table's row in a relational database. In EJB, we have the ability to specify a type of object used to hold this key.

The XML file is packaged with the EJB JAR as part of the bean. We will see an example of a deployment descriptor in a moment.

EJBs in the Music Store Application

In the object-relational chapter we grew an application using basic object-relational mapping concepts. We directly determined in the application when we would save, update, delete, or create an object in the underlying database by calling methods on various Java objects.

In the object-relational chapter our record-store owner experienced quite a growth in business and found that she could no longer manage all her titles by remembering the details for each recording she ordered. To combat this problem a Java user interface to the database was built and the CRUD services for the Java objects were built using JDBC and SQL. We will continue to use the record store data as an example in this chapter.

Let us say now that our enterprising record-store owner wishes to branch out and do some advertising in a unique way. There is a shopping complex close to the record store; contained within this mall are numerous kiosks used by the stores as advertisements. Some of these kiosks contain computers where shoppers can access the Internet to view web sites.

> **Note: this example ignores possible complications such as firewalls. Also, this would be an ideal situation in which to implement a more complicated enterprise solution using the entire J2EE platform, but we assume a command-line program for simplicity.**

The `Recording` class created in Chapter 15 demonstrated object-relational mapping techniques allowing the application to work with the `Recordings` database table. In the distributed application scenario mentioned above, the `Recording` object makes a perfect candidate for an Entity Bean.

What Persistence Method is most Appropriate?

Assume the recording application in the object-relational chapter was indeed redesigned to incorporate entity beans. Which persistence method is most appropriate in this situation?

CMP most likely works best in this situation. There is a single database table that maps cleanly to a single Java class. Rather than perform the sometimes-tedious work of writing the SQL for CRUD operations it is safe in this situation to allow the container to do the dirty work for us.

Let's say that we added an `ArrayList` of tracks to the `Recording` object and the `recordingArtist` gained enough attributes to warrant a table of its own. As the object model becomes more complex the container must become smarter. For large applications, a thorough evaluation of the container and its tools is a must. If the deployment tools are not adequate, or cannot map complex joins, BMP must be used.

However, in this simple one-to-one mapping, we are going to use CMP.

Implementing the Recording Class as an EJB

We could choose to create a recording class as follows, very similar to the `Recording` object in Chapter 15. You should be somewhat familiar with the UML notation introduced in that chapter as well. We introduce one new UML concept here, the stereotype. Our stereotype here is *Interface* because as you will see in the next section `Recording` is not a concrete class.

Before we show specific program code to create the application, we should understand the sequence of events that will occur in the program.

It basically works like this:

1. The server is started and the bean is deployed according to the parameters specified in the `ejb-jar.xml` deployment descriptor for each bean:

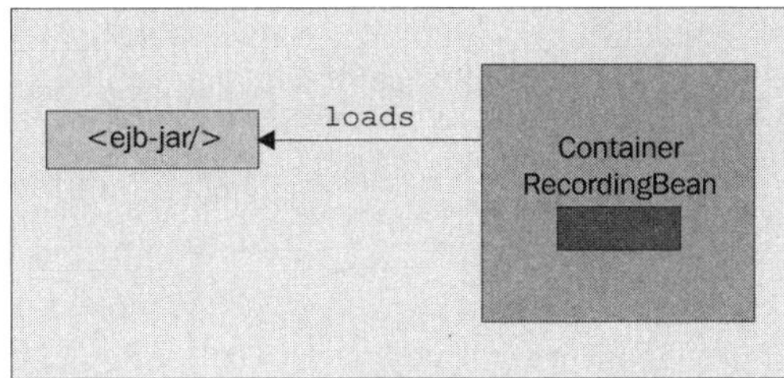

2. A client program wishes to use a bean. It uses JNDI to look up the location of the container and obtains a reference to the bean's home interface:

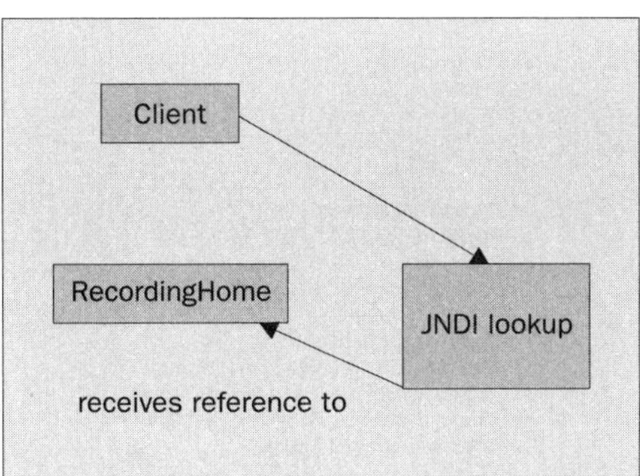

3. The home interface is used to get a reference to a bean on the server. Since the JNDI lookup in Step 2 returns an `Object` reference, we need to cast this to the class we actually want. This is commonly performed as seen here:

```
RecordingHome home =
  (RecordingHome) PortableRemoteObject.narrow(reference,
                                              RecordingHome.class);
```

Here we have a reference to an `Object`, and we narrow it down (using `PortableRemoteObject.narrow()` because we're dealing with a remote object) to be a reference to the type of object we actually want. Then, we can use this to call methods on the bean, and create a bean instance:

```
Recording rec = home.create();
```

4. The remote interface can now be used to interact with an instance of the bean on the server:

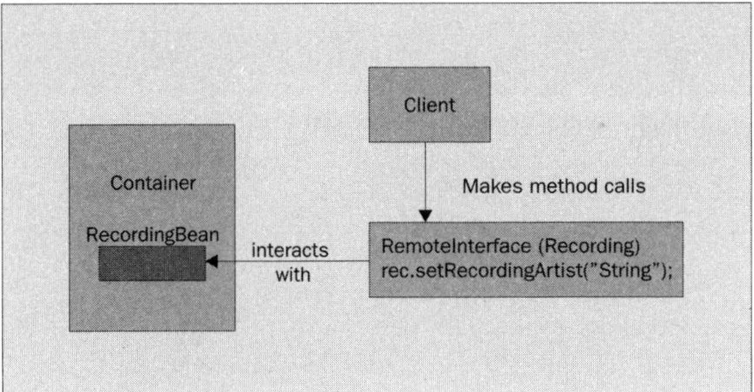

Let's look at a class diagram for what will become our new `Recoding` bean:

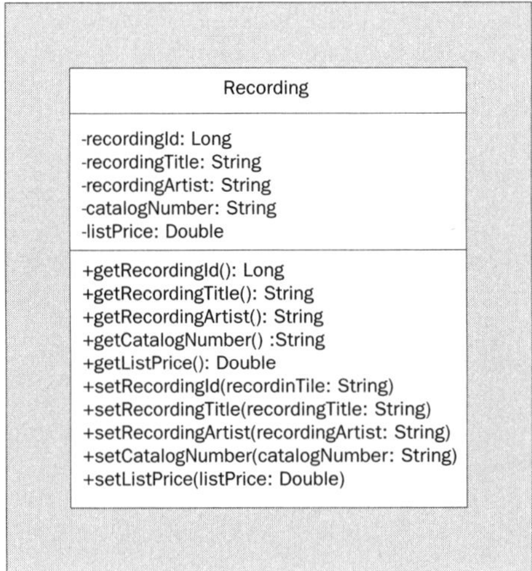

You may notice two differences between the Recording presented here and the Recording presented in the object-relational chapter. First, Java primitives represented recordingId and listPrice; long and double respectively. Here, they have been replaced by their respective object wrappers, Long and Double. Remember that Java object wrappers are capitalized names similar to the primitive name. Second, CRUD operations are missing from the Recording interface here. How does an application perform these operations? Read on.

The Client Application

In the object-relational chapter we developed an application to perform CRUD operations for a Recording object. In the object-relational chapter we had a Recording object that represented a row of data in an Oracle database, and a simple driver program to test the CRUD operations. This model is repeated here for clarity. We will use the same database design and the Java class shown above.

Try It Out – Writing the Client Application

1. Build the client application, called SimpleEJB, as follows:

```
import java.sql.*;
import java.util.Properties;
import java.util.Collection;
import java.util.Iterator;
import javax.rmi.PortableRemoteObject;
import java.rmi.RemoteException;
import javax.naming.*;
import javax.ejb.CreateException;

import ejb.recording.*;


/**
 * A driver program for EJB examples
 */
public class SimpleEJB {

  public static void main(String[] args) {

     /**
      * We need these properties to connect with the container
      */
     Properties containerEnvironment = new Properties();
     containerEnvironment
       .setProperty("java.naming.factory.initial",
                    "org.jnp.interfaces.NamingContextFactory");
     containerEnvironment.setProperty("java.naming.provider.url",
                                     "localhost:1099");
     containerEnvironment.setProperty("java.naming.factory.url.pkgs",
                                     "org.jboss.naming");

     InitialContext jndiContext = null;
     Object reference = null;
     try {
```

```
      // naming context comment
      jndiContext = new InitialContext(containerEnvironment);

      // Get a reference to the Recording Bean
      reference = jndiContext.lookup("Recording");
    } catch (NamingException ne) {
      System.out.println("Naming exception:");
      ne.printStackTrace();
    }

    // Narrow
    RecordingHome home =
      (RecordingHome) PortableRemoteObject.narrow(reference,
            RecordingHome.class);

    // Use the home interface to get a recording object

    Recording rec1 = null;
    Recording rec2 = null;
    Recording rec3 = null;
    Recording rec4 = null;

    // Create the same Recordings as the OR chapter:
    try {
      rec1 = home.create(new Integer(1), "392-000022", new Double(11.99),
                         "Bryan Adams", "Cuts Like A Knife");
      rec2 = home.create(new Integer(2), "RS-32-1133", new Double(10.99),
                         "Rick Springfield", "Working Class Dog");
      rec3 = home.create(new Integer(3), "303-9399293", new Double(11.99),
                         "Petra", "Come And Join Us");
      rec4 = home.create(new Integer(4), "BK-30-23993", new Double(13.99),
                         "Bruce Springsteen", "Lucky Town");

      /**
       * The code for the client application looks very similar to the
       * driver program in the object-relational chapter, doesn't it?
       * The way the Recording class is implemented is a bit different
       */

    } catch (RemoteException re) {
      re.printStackTrace();
    } catch (CreateException ce) {
      ce.printStackTrace();
    }

    /**
     * Now try to find a recording using EJB
     */
    try {
      Collection c = home.findByArtist("Bryan%");
      Iterator iter = c.iterator();
      while (iter.hasNext()) {
        Recording temp = (Recording) iter.next();
        System.out.println("Found: " + temp.getRecordingTitle() + " by "
```

```
                          + temp.getRecordingArtist());
      }
    } catch (Exception e) {
      System.out.println("No Recordings found!");
    }

    /**
     * Get rid of the Recordings
     */
    try {
      rec1.remove();
      rec2.remove();
      rec3.remove();
      rec4.remove();
    } catch (Exception e) {
      e.printStackTrace();
    } // Note, these methods really throw
      // RemoteException and RemoveException

  }

}
```

2. Save this as `C:\BegJavaDB\Chapter19\SimpleEJB.java`. We can't compile this until we have written the component classes of our bean.

How It Works

This application is an example of how we might make use of an entity bean from a basic Java application. In the following sections we will look at an implementation of the `Recording` entity bean we use above.

Let's step through the code. First we import the required classes:

```
import java.util.Properties;
import java.util.Collection;
import java.util.Iterator;
import javax.rmi.PortableRemoteObject;
import java.rmi.RemoteException;
import javax.naming.*;
import javax.ejb.CreateException;

import ejb.recording.*;
```

The `java.util` packages should be familiar already, and `ejb.recording` contains the classes needed for the client to use our bean (which we'll create shortly). The rest could use some explaining. The `java.rmi.RemoteException` class must be imported so the driver application can recognize and handle the remote exceptions that may be passed back from the server. The `javax.naming` package is necessary to do lookups against a JNDI name, which must be done to locate the EJB home interface for the Recording bean. Finally, `javax.ejb.CreateException` will be thrown if a problem arises while attempting to create a new instance of the bean.

Now, the first bit of unfamiliar code involves setting up the program environment to use the JBoss EJB container. Behind the scenes code will use these settings to connect for us. For example, the "`java.naming.provider.url`" property is set to "`localhost:1099`" – this tells the program that we should look at the computer called *localhost* on port 1099 for JNDI lookups:

```
Properties containerEnvironment = new Properties();
containerEnvironment
  .setProperty("java.naming.factory.initial",
               "org.jnp.interfaces.NamingContextFactory");
containerEnvironment.setProperty("java.naming.provider.url",
                                 "localhost:1099");
containerEnvironment.setProperty("java.naming.factory.url.pkgs",
                                 "org.jboss.naming");
```

Now we must go about obtaining a reference to the EJB `home` interface for the `Recording` bean. First we set up a JNDI context with the properties specified earlier:

```
    InitialContext jndiContext = null;

 // start of try-catch block

      jndiContext = new InitialContext(containerEnvironment);
```

Now we are ready to get a reference to the `RecordingHome`. We do this as follows:

```
      // Get a reference to the Recording Bean
      reference = jndiContext.lookup("Recording");

 // catch block

    RecordingHome home =
      (RecordingHome) PortableRemoteObject.narrow(reference,
                                             RecordingHome.class);
```

"`Recording`" is the JNDI name we will give the `Recording` EJB home. We will see more of this when the deployment descriptor is built below. Don't worry about the `narrow()` function, consider it an additional step in doing a class cast to cast the object reference to a `RecordingHome`.

Now the home interface's `create()` method is used to create four remote references to `Recording` entity beans. Here is how we declare the first (the others work the same way, using different values for the `create()` method though):

```
    Recording rec1 = null;

 // try-catch block

      rec1 = home.create(new Integer(1), "392-000022", new Double(11.99),
                         "Bryan Adams", "Cuts Like A Knife");
```

Once the recordings are created, we can search for titles:

```
      Collection c = home.findByArtist("Bryan%");
```

Note that we specify the wildcard character (%) after the name so that we get all artists with Bryan as their first name. Then we iterate through the collection, just as we did before, Finally, we can get rid of the recordings we have created by calling the `remove()` method:

```
rec1.remove();
```

The next section shows how to build the remote interface.

The Remote Interface

Here is the implementation for the remote interface, where we expose business methods to the client code that will use our beans. Our EJB container will create classes that implement this interface and serve as a remote reference.

Try It Out – Building the Remote Interface

1. Build the remote interface, called `Recording.java`, as follows:

```
package ejb.recording;

import javax.ejb.EJBObject;
import java.rmi.RemoteException;

/**
 * This is the Remote Interface, where we expose business methods to the
 * client code which will use our beans. Our EJB container will create
 * classes that implement this interface and serve as a remote reference
 *
 */
public interface Recording extends EJBObject {

  /**
   * Accessors
   */
  public Integer getRecordingId() throws RemoteException;

  public String getRecordingTitle() throws RemoteException;

  public String getRecordingArtist() throws RemoteException;

  public String getCatalogNumber() throws RemoteException;

  public Double getListPrice() throws RemoteException;

  /**
   * Mutators
   */
  public void setRecordingId(Integer inId) throws RemoteException;

  public void setRecordingTitle(String inTitle) throws RemoteException;

  public void setRecordingArtist(String inArtist) throws RemoteException;
```

```
    public void setCatalogNumber(String inNumber) throws RemoteException;

    public void setListPrice(Double inPrice) throws RemoteException;
}
```

2. Save this code as C:\BegJavaDB\Chapter19\ejb\recording\Recording.java. We can compile this class now, using the following command from the Chapter19 directory:

```
> javac -classpath .;%JBOSS%\lib\ext\ejb.jar ejb\recording\Recording.java
```

Where %JBOSS% points to the jboss directory of your JBoss installation (C:\JBoss-2.2.2_Tomcat-3.2.2\jboss).

How It Works

There is one new class to import in the remote interface Java file:

```
import javax.ejb.EJBObject;
```

All EJB remote interfaces extend EJBObject, which itself extends java.rmi.Remote. The EJBObject interface defines five methods: getEJBHome(), getHandle(), getPrimaryKey(), isIdentical(), and remove(). It is not actually necessary to provide the implementation to these methods assuming the container is managing persistence, implementation will be provided at deployment or run time depending on how the container is implemented. The only method from EJBObject our example uses is remove() in the SimpleEJB client class above.

The remote interface class exposes our business methods to the outside world. The methods in the Recording remote interface are simple getters and setters but any type of method could be exposed.

Note that all of our exposed business methods can throw a RemoteException. Remember that Recording is the interface that a container-created class will implement to serve as a remote reference to a RecordingBean that exists in the container. A RemoteException is thrown if anything goes wrong at the EJB container.

The Home Interface

Like the remote interface, the home interface exposes methods that can be called from clients of the bean. Most of these methods deal with helping manage the lifecycle of the bean or locating beans.

Try It Out – Building the Home Interface

1. Build the home interface, called RecordingHome.java, as follows:

```
package ejb.recording;

import java.rmi.RemoteException;
import javax.ejb.CreateException;
import javax.ejb.FinderException;
import javax.ejb.EJBHome;
import java.util.Collection;
```

```
public interface RecordingHome extends EJBHome {

  /**
   * Create a new Recording with the given data
   */
  public Recording create(Integer key, String catalogNumber,
                          Double listPrice, String recordingArtist,
                          String recordingTitle) throws RemoteException,
                          CreateException;


  // Both of these find methods are implemented by the container at runtime.
  // If we used BMP we have to implement these in the bean class...

  /**
   * Find a Recording matching the target primary key
   */
  public Recording findByPrimaryKey(Integer target)
          throws RemoteException, FinderException;

  /**
   * Find Recordings with recordingArtist field same as the artist parameter
   */
  public Collection findByArtist(String artist) throws RemoteException,
                                                        FinderException;
}
```

2. Save this file as `C:\BegJavaDB\Chapter19\ejb\recording\RecordingHome.java`. We can compile this class now as well, using the following command issued from the `Chapter19` directory:

```
> javac -classpath .;%JBOSS%\lib\ext\ejb.jar
        ejb\recording\RecordingHome.java
```

If this doesn't work, you need to find the `java.rmi.RemoteException` class and add it to your classpath.

How It Works

The `RecordingHome` class imports three previously unseen classes:

- `CreateException` will be thrown by any EJB create method if there is a problem with instantiating an entity
- `FinderException` is likewise thrown when the container fails to find an entity matching the criteria supplied
- `EJBHome` is imported, as our `RecordingHome` must extend this interface
- The `java.util.Collection` class is imported to support our `findByArtist()` method, which may return zero or more objects

EJB 1.1 CMP allows for returning `Collections`; the specific implementing class is usually configurable using the container's assembly/deployment tools. The `findByArtist()` method is similar to the `findByArtist(String sqlQuery)` method found in the `Recording` class from Chapter 15.

The methods within the EJB home interface shown here can be the same for container- or bean-managed persistence. However, with CMP we merely describe how these operations should work and implementation is delayed until runtime/deployment. With BMP, the bean developer must provide the implementation for each method inside the bean implementation class.

The Bean Implementation

Here is the implementation for the `RecordingBean`, assuming CMP. The business methods exposed to client applications by the remote interface are implemented here; in the case of the `Recording` bean the remote interface has exposed accessors and mutators so you can see the interaction with the data members of the bean.

There are methods in the bean implementation here that are very similar to some methods on the `Recording` class created in Chapter 15. The `ejbCreate()` and `ejbPostCreate()` methods are very similar to the constructor provided by the earlier `Recording` class. The getters and setters are almost identical.

While many similar methods are *shown* here, what are not shown are these methods getting *called.* Also, many of the method implementations are empty. There is far less code here than in the `Recording` class found in Chapter 15. Still, the work must get done somewhere. The container does part of this work automatically; the rest is done by indicating how certain aspects of the bean should function using the deployment descriptor. This will be discussed in detail in the deployment descriptor section.

Try It Out – Building the Bean

1. Build the bean implementation class, called `RecordingBean`, as follows:

```
package ejb.recording;

import java.rmi.RemoteException;
import javax.ejb.EntityBean;
import javax.ejb.EntityContext;


/**
 * This class is our bean implementation where the business methods
 * are implemented. Note that the RecordingBean does not implement
 * the Recording interface.
 */
public class RecordingBean implements EntityBean {

  /**
   * Member variables
   */
  public Integer recordingId;
  public String recordingTitle;
  public String recordingArtist;
  public String catalogNumber;
```

```
  public Double listPrice;

  /**
   * These are our business methods that do our work.
   * These should be exposed by our remote interface.
   */

  /**
   * Accessors
   */
  public Integer getRecordingId() {
    return recordingId;
  }

  public String getRecordingTitle() {
    return recordingTitle;
  }

  public String getRecordingArtist() {
    return recordingArtist;
  }

  public String getCatalogNumber() {
    return catalogNumber;
  }

  public Double getListPrice() {
    return listPrice;
  }


  /**
   * Mutators
   */
  public void setRecordingId(Integer inId) {
    recordingId = inId;
  }

  public void setRecordingTitle(String inTitle) {
    recordingTitle = inTitle;
  }

  public void setRecordingArtist(String inArtist) {
    recordingArtist = inArtist;
  }

  public void setCatalogNumber(String inNumber) {
    catalogNumber = inNumber;
  }

  public void setListPrice(Double inPrice) {
    listPrice = inPrice;
  }
```

```
  /**
   * Create an instance of a Recording.
   * In BMP this method would return the key.
   * The EJB container manages creation.
   * Notice the parameters match those for create() in the Home interface
   */
  public Integer ejbCreate(Integer newId, String newCatalogNumber,
                           Double newListPrice, String newRecordingArtist,
                           String newRecordingTitle) {
    recordingId = newId;
    catalogNumber = newCatalogNumber;
    listPrice = newListPrice;
    recordingArtist = newRecordingArtist;
    recordingTitle = newRecordingTitle;

    return null;
  }

  /**
   * Each ejbCreate must have a matching ejbPostCreate.
   */
  public void ejbPostCreate(Integer newId, String newCatalogNumber,
                            Double newListPrice, String newRecordingArtist,
                            String newRecordingTitle) {}

  /**
   * These are the EJB methods, which we must define as
   * an entity bean.
   * Empty implementations for our simple CMP example
   */
  public void ejbActivate() {}

  public void ejbLoad() {}

  public void ejbPassivate() {}

  public void ejbRemove() {}

  public void ejbStore() {}

  public void setEntityContext(EntityContext ctx) {}

  public void unsetEntityContext() {}

}
```

2. Save this file as `C:\BegJavaDB\Chapter19\ejb\recording\RecordingBean.java`. We can compile this class using the following command issued from the `Chapter19` directory:

```
> javac -classpath .;%JBOSS%\lib\ext\ejb.jar
        ejb\recording\RecordingBean.java
```

3. We can also now compile our `SimpleEJB` test program, using the following command from the `Chapter19` directory:

```
> javac -classpath .;%JBOSS%\lib\ext\ejb.jar SimpleEJB.java
```

We'll see how to run this code shortly, after we've explained a little of what's going on.

How It Works

We begin the bean implementation by importing the following new classes:

```
import javax.ejb.EntityBean;
import javax.ejb.EntityContext;
```

`EntityBean` is the interface that must be implemented by all entity beans. The `EntityContext` interface provides the container-provided run-time context of the entity bean. We won't be using this but it is required for the `setEntityContext()` method.

The accessors and mutators (getters and setters) are fairly self explanatory, and there is no persistence code provided in this bean implementation since the container is managing that for us. Because the container is managing persistence in the example program and there is no special processing to do in this case, there are empty implementations for all of the `EntityBean` methods. A brief description of what these methods are intended to do couldn't hurt though.

- `ejbActivate()` – This method is called by the container to associate this bean with a specific entity instance.
- `ejbLoad()` – The container calls this method to instruct the entity bean to load its state from an underlying store, most often a relational database. When using BMP this method would contain code with SQL `SELECT` statements to populate the data members.
- `ejbPassivate()` – The container calls this method to disassociate this bean instance from any specific entity. Before the bean is passivated it will be asked to synchronize its state with the underlying store.
- `ejbRemove()` – The entity associated with this bean instance is removed from the underlying store. In a BMP scenario this method might contain a SQL DELETE FROM statement to remove the database row represented by this entity. The EJB home interface has a similar method that takes a primary key or `Handle` as argument.
- `ejbStore()` – The container calls this method to instruct the entity bean to synchronize its state with the underlying store. In a BMP scenario this method might contain a SQL `update` statement.
- `setEntityContext()` – The container calls this method when a bean instance becomes associated with a particular entity. The `EntityContext` is the bean's environmental information.
- `unsetEntityContext()` – Called to remove the bean's environmental information when the bean is no longer associated with a particular entity.

The bean implementation presented here differs greatly from the `Recording` class supplied in the object-relational chapter. The most obvious difference is the lack of SQL code in any methods. Given that these objects are represented in the same database as those in the object-relational chapter the class presented here might appear to be missing something. SQL code *does* get generated and will execute, but this is hidden from us. The container uses the information about the entities supplied to it to generate the necessary SQL at important points in the entity bean's lifecycle.

The Deployment Descriptor

Finally, here's the deployment descriptor or our `Recording` bean using CMP. Remember that the deployment descriptor provides information about a bean to the container the bean is deployed to.

Try It Out – Building the Deployment Descriptor

1. Build the deployment descriptor, called `ejb-jar.xml`, as follows:

```
<?xml version="1.0" encoding="UTF-8"?>
<!DOCTYPE ejb-jar PUBLIC
        "-//Sun Microsystems, Inc.//DTD Enterprise JavaBeans 1.1//EN"
        "http://java.sun.com/j2ee/dtds/ejb-jar_1_1.dtd">
<ejb-jar>
  <description>Simple Recording EJB app</description>
  <display-name>Recording</display-name>
  <enterprise-beans>
    <entity>
      <ejb-name>Recording</ejb-name>
      <home>ejb.recording.RecordingHome</home>
      <remote>ejb.recording.Recording</remote>
      <ejb-class>ejb.recording.RecordingBean</ejb-class>
      <persistence-type>Container</persistence-type>
      <prim-key-class>java.lang.Integer</prim-key-class>
      <reentrant>False</reentrant>
      <cmp-field>
        <field-name>recordingId</field-name>
      </cmp-field>
      <cmp-field>
        <field-name>recordingTitle</field-name>
      </cmp-field>
      <cmp-field>
        <field-name>recordingArtist</field-name>
      </cmp-field>
      <cmp-field>
        <field-name>catalogNumber</field-name>
      </cmp-field>
      <cmp-field>
        <field-name>listPrice</field-name>
      </cmp-field>
      <primkey-field>recordingId</primkey-field>
    </entity>
  </enterprise-beans>
  <assembly-descriptor>
    <container-transaction>
      <method>
```

```
        <ejb-name>Recording</ejb-name>
        <method-name>*</method-name>
      </method>
      <trans-attribute>Required</trans-attribute>
    </container-transaction>
  </assembly-descriptor>
</ejb-jar>
```

2. This file should be saved as `C:\BegJavaDB\Chapter19\META-INF\ejb-jar.xml`.

How It Works

The XML shown in the `ejb-jar` file is very human-readable and should make sense. The information concerning the `Recording` class is contained between the `<entity>` beginning and end tags.

```
<entity>
  <ejb-name>Recording</ejb-name>
  <home>ejb.recording.RecordingHome</home>
  <remote>ejb.recording.Recording</remote>
  <ejb-class>ejb.recording.RecordingBean</ejb-class>
  <persistence-type>Container</persistence-type>
  <prim-key-class>java.lang.Integer</prim-key-class>
  <reentrant>False</reentrant>
```

The `<ejb-name>` serves as a default to identify the entity bean.

The `<home>`, `<remote>`, and `<ejb-class>` tags tell the container which classes compose which parts of the bean; home and remote interfaces, and bean implementation class respectively.

The next part that deserves mention is the `<cmp-field>` tags:

```
  <cmp-field>
    <field-name>recordingId</field-name>
  </cmp-field>
  <cmp-field>
    <field-name>recordingTitle</field-name>
  </cmp-field>
  <cmp-field>
    <field-name>recordingArtist</field-name>
  </cmp-field>
  <cmp-field>
    <field-name>catalogNumber</field-name>
  </cmp-field>
  <cmp-field>
    <field-name>listPrice</field-name>
  </cmp-field>
  <primkey-field>recordingId</primkey-field>
</entity>
```

Here are listed all of the fields of the bean class for which the container should manage persistence. In this example we have chosen to persist all fields, but this is not a rule. The `<primkey-field>` tag tells the container which field uniquely identifies this entity, and based on this the container can create the implementation of the `findByPrimaryKey()` method.

Note that even though we are assuming that the `Recording` beans are saved to the same Oracle database as the one used in the object-relational chapter there is no SQL shown here. In fact, there is no JDBC code at all. However, the deployment descriptor lists `recordingId`, `recordingTitle`, `recordingArtist`, `catalogNumber`, and `listPrice` within <cmp-field> tags.

Don't worry about the syntax of the `ejb-jar.xml` file. As with other parts of this example, we don't want to spend too long on the details – just enough for you to see what's happening. If you want more information on EJBs, look at *Professional EJB* from Wrox Press, ISBN 1-0861005-08-3.

What about transactions? The container manages transactions as well.

```
<assembly-descriptor>
  <container-transaction>
    <method>
      <ejb-name>Recording</ejb-name>
      <method-name>*</method-name>
    </method>
    <trans-attribute>Required</trans-attribute>
  </container-transaction>
</assembly-descriptor>
```

In the final part of the `ejb-jar.xml` file we mandate that the server take care of transactions for us. By specifying a star in the <method-name> tag under <container-transaction>, we tell the server that all methods for the bean named in <ejb-name> should have transactional management from the server.

The container will begin a transaction when making an attempt at updating this entity bean in the database. Exception situations occurring while the container attempts to update this bean in the database will cause the transaction to be rolled back.

For example, assume in the test application above that the programmer was unaware of the nature of the underlying database, as could well happen. The programmer calls the `setCatalogNumber()` method on a `Recording`, passing in a catalog number 21 characters long (the database specifies `VARCHAR2(20)`). When the container attempted to update the database representation, the database would complain that the inserted value is too large for the column, and the container would roll the transaction back.

Try It Out – Bringing it all Together

The last part in getting the sample application running is configuring JBoss to persist the `Recording` bean. The CMP piece of JBoss is called JAWS.

1. Copy the Oracle JDBC driver JAR or zip file to the `jboss/lib/ext` directory. The file must be here for JBoss to find it upon startup.

2. Replace the JDBC driver code in `jboss\conf\default\jboss.jcml` with that shown below:

```
<!-- JDBC -->
<mbean code="org.jboss.jdbc.JdbcProvider"
       name="DefaultDomain:service=JdbcProvider">
  <attribute name="Drivers">oracle.jdbc.driver.OracleDriver</attribute>
</mbean>
```

If we leave the JDBC driver code already present in `jboss.jcml`, we run the risk of having conflicting database settings.

3. Add the JDBC connection pooling code shown below to `jboss/conf/default/jboss.jcml`, just after the above code:

```
<mbean code="org.jboss.jdbc.XADataSourceLoader"
       name="DefaultDomain:service=XADataSource,name=OracleDS">
  <attribute name="PoolName">OracleDS</attribute>
  <attribute name="DataSourceClass">
    org.opentools.minerva.jdbc.xa.wrapper.XADataSourceImpl
  </attribute>
  <attribute name="Properties"></attribute>
  <attribute name="URL">jdbc:oracle:thin:@dbserver:1521:database</attribute>
  <attribute name="GCMinIdleTime">1200000</attribute>
  <attribute name="JDBCUser">beg</attribute>
  <attribute name="MaxSize">10</attribute>
  <attribute name="Password">java</attribute>
  <attribute name="GCEnabled">false</attribute>
  <attribute name="InvalidateOnError">false</attribute>
  <attribute name="TimestampUsed">false</attribute>
  <attribute name="Blocking">true</attribute>
  <attribute name="GCInterval">120000</attribute>
  <attribute name="IdleTimeout">1800000</attribute>
  <attribute name="IdleTimeoutEnabled">false</attribute>
  <attribute name="LoggingEnabled">false</attribute>
  <attribute name="MaxIdleTimeoutPercent">1.0</attribute>
  <attribute name="MinSize">0</attribute>
</mbean>
```

4. Create the `jaws.xml` file as shown below, and save it in the `C:\BegJavaDB\Chapter19\META-INF` directory along with the `ejb-jar.xml` file:

```
<?xml version="1.0" encoding="UTF-8"?>
<jaws>
  <default-entity>
  <!-- don't try to create the table, assume we've already created it -->
    <create-table>false</create-table>
    <!-- don't delete the table when we're done either -->
    <remove-table>false</remove-table>
    <tuned-updates>false</tuned-updates>
    <read-only>false</read-only>
    <time-out>300</time-out>
    <select-for-update>false</select-for-update>
  </default-entity>
<!-- these values must match the names defined in the ejb-jar.xml file -->
  <enterprise-beans>
    <!-- This should be familiar now that you know JDBC.
         These cmp-field XML tags map an object field
         to a jdbc type, to a database type.
         The jdbc-type and sql-type tags should not be necessary
```

```
        since JBoss is configured to work with Oracle,
        but are shown for illustration purposes
    -->
    <entity>
      <ejb-name>Recording</ejb-name>
      <table-name>or_recordings</table-name>
      <cmp-field>
        <field-name>recordingId</field-name>
        <column-name>RECORDING_ID</column-name>
        <jdbc-type>INTEGER</jdbc-type>
        <sql-type>int</sql-type>
      </cmp-field>
      <cmp-field>
        <field-name>recordingTitle</field-name>
        <column-name>RECORDING_TITLE</column-name>
        <jdbc-type>VARCHAR</jdbc-type>
        <sql-type>VARCHAR(50)</sql-type>
      </cmp-field>
      <cmp-field>
        <field-name>recordingArtist</field-name>
        <column-name>RECORDING_ARTIST</column-name>
        <jdbc-type>VARCHAR</jdbc-type>
        <sql-type>VARCHAR(50)</sql-type>
      </cmp-field>
      <cmp-field>
        <field-name>catalogNumber</field-name>
        <column-name>CATALOG_NUMBER</column-name>
        <jdbc-type>VARCHAR</jdbc-type>
        <sql-type>VARCHAR(50)</sql-type>
      </cmp-field>
      <cmp-field>
        <field-name>listPrice</field-name>
        <column-name>LIST_PRICE</column-name>
          <jdbc-type>DOUBLE</jdbc-type>
            <sql-type>NUMBER(38,15)</sql-type>
      </cmp-field>

      <!-- the container needs to know how this finder should work,
           note that we are almost writing some SQL here -->

      <finder>
        <name>findByArtist</name>
        <query>recording_artist like {0}</query>
        <order>recording_artist DESC</order>
      </finder>
    </entity>
  </enterprise-beans>
</jaws>
```

Note: more general information about JAWS can be found in the JAWS section of the JBoss documentation at http://www.jboss.org/documentation/HTML/ch05.html.

5. Build the `Recording.jar` file. This is done issuing the following command from the `Chapter19` directory:

```
> jar cvf Recording.jar ejb META-INF
```

Here we create a new JAR file called `Recording.jar`, and it will have the contents of the `ejb` and `META-INF` directories (that is, all the code for the bean, and all the deployment descriptors).

6. Now that we have built this JAR file, we merely copy it into the `jboss\deploy` directory and start JBoss using the `jboss\bin\run.bat` file to deploy the bean. Run the `SimpleEJB` class with the following statement:

```
> java -classpath %JB%\ejb.jar;%JB%\jbosssx-client.jar;
      %JB%\jboss-client.jar;%JB%\jndi.jar;%JB%\jnp-client.jar;. SimpleEJB
```

Where `%JB%` points to the `jboss\client` directory. These JAR files contain the necessary packages to deal with the interaction between our client code and the server. We should see something like the following as our results:

```
C:\WINDOWS\System32\cmd.exe
C:\BegJavaDB\Chapter19>java -classpath %JB%\ejb.jar;%JB%\jbosssx-client.jar
;%JB%\jboss-client.jar;%JB%\jndi.jar;%JB%\jnp-client.jar;. SimpleEJB
Found: Cuts Like A Knife by Bryan Adams

C:\BegJavaDB\Chapter19>
```

How It Works

Let's examine the pieces that have just been built one by one in order to see what's going to happen when the client program runs.

The remote and home interfaces, and bean implementation classes each do part of the work of the EJB. The `Recording` class serves as the interface that the client program uses to interact with an instance of `RecordingBean` on the server. The client application used a JNDI lookup with the `ejb-name` `"Recording"` in order to gain a reference to the `RecordingHome`, which was then used to make calls to create four `Recording` references that in turn caused four `RecordingBean` instances to be activated on the server.

The three classes and the XML files were packaged as an application using the `jar` command. JBoss then deployed this JAR file, using the information found in the XML files in the `META-INF` directory. Based on the information in `ejb-jar.xml` and `jaws.xml` the container was able to determine how to manage the lifecycle of the `Recording` entity bean when the client application (`SimpleEJB`) ran. One visible result of this lifecycle management is JBoss generating SQL to manage the state of the `RecordingBean`, as shown below. Some of the logging messages have been removed to more clearly show the SQL being created.

```
[JAWS] Create, id is 1
[JAWS] Exists command executing: SELECT COUNT(*) FROM recordings WHERE
RECORDING_ID=?
[JAWS] Set parameter: idx=1, jdbcType=INTEGER, value=1
```

```
[JAWS] Create command executing: INSERT INTO recordings
(LIST_PRICE,RECORDING_ID,RECORDING_ARTIST,CATALOG_NUMBER,RECORDING_TITLE) VALUES
(?,?,?,?,?)
[JAWS] Set parameter: idx=1, jdbcType=DECIMAL, value=11.99
[JAWS] Set parameter: idx=2, jdbcType=INTEGER, value=1
[JAWS] Set parameter: idx=3, jdbcType=VARCHAR, value=Bryan Adams
[JAWS] Set parameter: idx=4, jdbcType=VARCHAR, value=392-000022
[JAWS] Set parameter: idx=5, jdbcType=VARCHAR, value=Cuts Like A Knife
[JAWS] Rows affected = 1

. . .

[JAWS] findByArtist command executing: SELECT RECORDING_ID, recording_artist FROM
recordings WHERE recording_artist like ? ORDER BY recording_artist DESC
[JAWS] Set parameter: idx=1, jdbcType=VARCHAR, value=Bryan%
[JAWS] Store command executing: UPDATE recordings SET
LIST_PRICE=?,RECORDING_ID=?,RECORDING_ARTIST=?,CATALOG_NUMBER=?,RECORDING_TITLE=?
WHERE RECORDING_ID=?
[JAWS] Set parameter: idx=1, jdbcType=DECIMAL, value=11.99
[JAWS] Set parameter: idx=2, jdbcType=INTEGER, value=1
[JAWS] Set parameter: idx=3, jdbcType=VARCHAR, value=Bryan Adams
[JAWS] Set parameter: idx=4, jdbcType=VARCHAR, value=392-000022
[JAWS] Set parameter: idx=5, jdbcType=VARCHAR, value=Cuts Like A Knife
[JAWS] Set parameter: idx=6, jdbcType=INTEGER, value=1
[JAWS] Rows affected = 1

. . .

[JAWS] Remove command executing: DELETE FROM recordings WHERE RECORDING_ID=?
[JAWS] Set parameter: idx=1, jdbcType=INTEGER, value=1
[JAWS] Rows affected = 1
```

JAWS creates JDBC prepared statements based on the fields listed in `jaws.xml` as container managed fields. JAWS uses the field specified as primary key to uniquely identify entities and their corresponding database rows. The simple one-table-to-one-entity mapping results in easy to read SQL that performs as expected. The container, using the JDBC connection information and driver specified in `jboss.jcml`, handles the business of obtaining and using JDBC connections automatically.

Summary

The J2EE provides a robust platform of service APIs and components that can be used to simplify the development of database applications. The bulk of these services are usually hosted by application servers and brokered to our components: JSP, Servlets, pages and EJBs, via the container in which they live. Some services particularly relevant to database development are connection pooling and distributed transaction management.

JavaBeans provide us with a centralized way to manage the data coming into and going out of our application. They are powerfully simple, and can be presented by JSP pages to give the user a rich visual interaction with the application's data.

Enterprise Java Beans provide a way to tackle computing problems in a distributed environment. EJBs can increase the scalability of your application by providing object instance pooling thereby decreasing the frequency with which your application will need to create new objects.

The second sample application focused on the use of entity beans with a relational database. As was demonstrated, the application was able to leverage the same logic without changing when the Bean's persistence mechanism changed. The example could have been even more extreme in many ways. With Container-Managed Persistence an entirely different database or database schema could be used behind the scenes and the only change necessary to the application would be reconfiguring JBoss to use the new database. With Bean-Managed Persistence even more radical changes could take place. The data entities represented by the entity beans might have been moved to XML files, or perhaps they existed as some type of file structure on a legacy mainframe system? The EJB component architecture allows the application to be almost completely ignorant of these implementation details.

In the next chapter we will look at another enterprise technology, XML, and how it can be used to revolutionize the way data is represented and shared.

Exporting Relational Data to XML

We live in a world surrounded by data. We are exposed to it every minute of every day. This data comes in a multitude of forms ranging from the chill we feel when our feet touch a cold bedroom floor in the morning to the processing and understanding of the text you are reading right now. Human beings are incredible computational machines. They can receive data from a wide variety of sources, turn that data into information, and use it almost instantaneously. What is even more impressive is that this data can be presented in multiple, often unstructured, formats. Even the fastest and most powerful computers are incapable of processing the plethora of unstructured data that the "human machine" is confronted with on a daily basis.

The data to be processed by a software application must be structured in a specific manner. If it is not structured in the way the application is expecting it, the application will fail or produce unexpected results. So what happens when two applications have to share data?

Often, getting applications to communicate requires writing code that takes data from one application and transforms it into a format that the other application understands. The other application has to then 'decipher' the data and store or use it. This does not sound too hard when you have to integrate only two applications, but what if you need to integrate three or four applications? What about 10 or 20 applications? As you can see, the more applications that need to be integrated together the greater the task of integrating them. Complicating all of this are the following:

- Many enterprise application vendors often give little thought to providing tools that can easily import (push) and export (pull) data to and from their applications. They provide primitive tools for data integration, but usually it is up to a company's development staff to use these tools to build the more complex solutions that meet the needs of their organizations. The application vendor's focus is on delivering functionality to its customers and not on building robust solutions for integrating their applications. Note that we're not talking about simple word processing applications here, but rather large scale enterprise resource planning applications.
- The lack of integration tools forces many companies to write numerous homegrown integration solutions or use proprietary third-party integration products that tie their applications directly together. Both homegrown and third-party solutions are expensive. Their expense is not just in terms of development costs, but also the significant cost of maintaining these proprietary integration points over the life of an application.

- Data for applications is often stored in different formats using different database technologies. While there are some common APIs for accessing the different databases available, specifically Microsoft's Open Database Connectivity (ODBC) and Sun's JDBC standard, there have been up to this point, few options for representing data independently of the database it is being stored in.

What is needed is a standard means of describing both the syntax of how data is to be packaged and the semantics of what the different data elements mean, independent of any of the applications that might use the data. This is where the **eXtensible Markup Language** (**XML**) standard can be used to allow applications to communicate in a common language.

Where does XML fit in a book on Java database development? Java is a platform-neutral language that can access relational and non-relational databases through a common API (JDBC). XML is a platform-neutral standard for representing data independently of how the application is using or storing the data. Combining these two technologies give us an extremely powerful arsenal of tools for integrating applications.

This chapter will not provide an in-depth examination of all the details involved with developing XML-based applications. Instead, this chapter will introduce you to the basics of using XML within the context of Java database development. The topics that will be covered in this chapter include:

- XML Parsers
- Mapping XML to relational databases. This topic will cover:
    - Mapping a single table to XML
    - Mapping a one-to-many relationship in XML
    - Mapping a many-to-many relationship in XML

This chapter assumes you already know a little about how to write XML documents. If you don't yet know anything about XML, there is an XML primer included as Appendix C.

XML Parsers

In order to work with XML in our Java code, we need an XML parser that can read the XML syntax and understand what it means. The parser will enable us to break an XML document down into its component elements and search/retrieve data from it.

Since XML is standardized it should be a straightforward process to write an XML parser in a language like Visual Basic, Java, or C.

Fortunately, there is no need for developers to write their own XML parsers. With the widespread adoption of XML as a data interchange standard, there are now many open source and non-open source XML parsers freely available for download from of the Internet. Some of the freely available Java XML parsers are:

Vendor and Parser	Download From	Comment
Apache Software Foundation's Xerces XML Parser	http://xml.apache.org	Open-source parser
Oracle Corporation's XML Parser Version 2	http://www.oracle.com/xml	Freely available for download. Must register.
SAX2 Parser	http://www.megginson.com/SAX	Freely available SAX parser.

Note, not all parsers are created equaly. Different parsers offer different features, levels of XML support, and algorithms for parsing an XML document. Understanding the different types of XML parsers and the algorithms they use is important because the parser you choose can have an impact on the performance of your applications and the development approach you take. The next section will explore the different types (but not implementations) of XML parsers and what their strengths and weaknesses are.

The Different Types of XML Parsers

Currently there are two types of XML parsers: the **DOM** (**Document Object Model**) parser and the **SAX** (**Simple API** for **XML**) parser. The major difference between the DOM and the SAX parser is the algorithm they use for parsing an XML document.

The DOM parser loads all of the elements within an XML document as a tree in physical memory. Since the document is represented as a tree it is very easy to reorder, add, and delete elements in the document. However, loading the XML document into memory is not always advantageous. Large XML documents in a high transaction environment can quickly eat up memory on even the largest server. The more memory used to hold these XML documents, the less memory is available for processing user requests.

The SAX parser does not load entire XML document into memory and avoids the scalability problem that the DOM parser can have. The SAX parser is an **event-based** parser. It will parse pieces of the XML document as the user requests it. This means that as we request information from the XML document, the parser will start searching the document until it finds the data we are looking for. As soon as the data is found a callback is made and we are notified. The SAX parser can be very fast when used to perform a simple, linear search for an element within the XML document. However, one significant disadvantage of using the SAX parser is it cannot be used to modify the structure of an XML document.

The decision to use the DOM or SAX parser is going to be based on need. If you have an XML document that will have its structure added to, deleted from or modified then use the DOM parser. Remember though, a document parsed by a DOM parser is represented in its entirety within the physical memory of the machine. Having to parse even a small number of large XML documents concurrently with a DOM parser can incur a significant amount of overhead on even large servers. If you need a parser that can quickly parse large documents and you do not need to modify their underlying structure, use the SAX parser.

The code examples that follow use the Apache Software Foundation's (ASF) Xerces Parser for building and parsing XML documents. The Xerces parser was chosen because of the significant functionality supported by the parser, its open source origins, and its support for both the SAX and DOM parsing models.

Downloading the Xerces Parser

The Apache Software Foundation (ASF) is membership-based organization dedicated to the creation of high-quality, commercial-level open source software. It has a number of projects currently underway and one these projects is the **Apache XML Project**. The Apache XML Project has built a number of powerful XML-based tools. One of these tools is the Xerces XML Parser. The Xerces XML parser is available for the Java, C++, and Perl programming language. It is XML 1.0-compliant and supports the following features:

- DOM Level 1 and 2 compliance
- SAX 1.0 and 2.0 compliance
- XML Schema support

The Xerces XML parser is a production-level parser that is freely available for download. The parser can be downloaded from the Apache-XML web site at: http://xml.apache.org/xerces-j/index.html. While you're at the Apache web site, you'll need to download Xalan as well. Xalan is an XSLT processor, but we only want the download for the XPath classes in the `xalan.jar` file. Xalan can be found at the following site: http://xml.apache.org/xalan-j/.

The download for Xalan also includes the latest version of Xerces, so you can save yourself some time by just downloading Xalan; this way of obtaining Xerces means you don't get any documentation.

It is important to note that the Xerces parser is freely available for download, but there are restrictions on its use and distribution. The **Apache Software License** governs its use. This license states how the Xerces parser may be used and distributed. The Apache Software License can be viewed at or downloaded from: http://xml.apache.org/dist/LICENSE.txt.

Installing the Xerces XML Parser

The Xerces XML Parser can be installed in the following steps:

1. Download the latest version of Xerces from the ASF web site. If you want to use Xerces on Windows, download the ZIP version of the application. If you want to use Xerces on Unix, download the Gzipped version. This version will have a `.gz` on the end of the file.

2. Unpack the compressed file to a directory of your choice.

3. After uncompressing the Xerces Parser from the ASF web site, you should have a directory containing all of the Xerces files. While writing this book, the author downloaded version 1.4.0 of the Xerces parser. The directory structure for the parser looked something like:

```
\xerces-1_4_0
             \data                 (Data used for some of the samples)
             \docs                 (JavaDocs for the Xerces Parser)
             \samples              (Example Xerces Parser code)
             LICENSE               (File containing the ASF Software License)
             Readme.html           (Opening page to the Xerces Documentation)
             xerces.jar            (Jar file containing the Xerces Java Classes)
             xercesSamples.jar     (Class files for the sample code)
```

After performing the above steps, you should be ready to run the code examples in the rest of the chapter.

Mapping XML to Relational Databases

Much of the work found within an Information Technology (IT) department in any organization often involves application integration, which usually involves moving data around, from one system to another. This data may reside in multiple databases on different hardware platforms. By far the most common type of database that is used for IT applications is the relational database.

XML is a data transfer medium that facilitates this integration process. Integration applications can either pull data out of a relational database or push data into a relational database, using XML as packaging tool for the data as it passes between the databases. An XML document can contain not only the data that is to be imported or exported from an application, but can also represent the relationships that exist between different data elements.

The following sections will look at how to use Java and XML not only to pull data out of a relational database, but also to represent that data in an XML document. Specifically, these sections will focus on building XML documents that can adequately reflect the common relationships that exist between data elements within a table. The mapping techniques discussed will include:

- Mapping data from a single database table to XML
- Mapping one-to-many relationships to XML
- Mapping many-to-many relationships to XML

Relational Theory Revisited

By now, you should be familiar with the concept of relational databases. As you recall, relational databases store data as groups of tables joined together by "keyed" values. These "keyed" values can come in two forms:

- A primary key, which uniquely represents a row of data within a table.
- A foreign key, which is used to establish a relationship that exists between different data sets. Typically, a foreign key links two different database tables via a common key in both tables.

Let's take another lok at thr Entity-Relationship (E-R) diagram for the Customer Orders subject area of our Music Store schema:

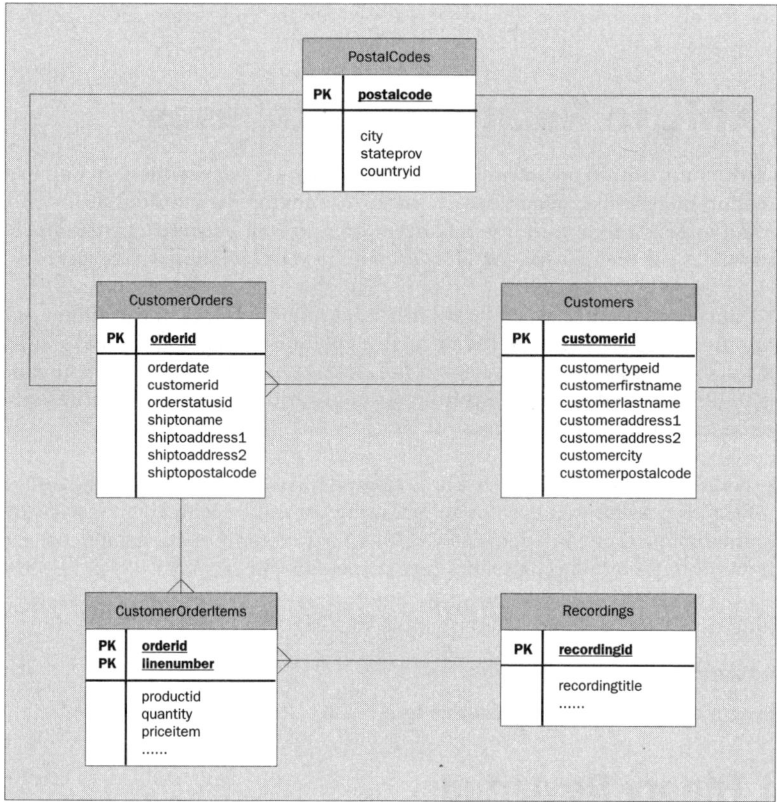

From this diagram, you can see that the following database relationships exists between the customer order tables:

- A customer order contains one or more line items (represented in the `CustomerOrderItems` table)
- A customer order belongs to one and only one customer
- A customer must have one or more invoices; in our system a customer does not exist until they purchase something
- A postal code belongs to one or more customer
- A postal code belongs to one or more customer order
- A record item can be on one or more customer order line items (`productid` links to `recordingid`)

The previous chapters in this book have shown you how to use JDBC and SQL to retrieve data from the above database. However, the data retrieved is usually contained within a Java object known as `ResultSet`. The problem with a `ResultSet` object is that the data can only be retrieved and manipulated by another application written in Java. What if you want to send the data in the Java `ResultSet` to a Visual Basic application? In previous years, the most common solution would be to write the data out into some kind of proprietary text format.

> **A proprietary format is a format that is specific to your application and does not conform to any recognized parsing standard.**

Then, after the data was written to a flat file, we would send the data to another application that would parse the data out of the text file and write the results to the Visual Basic application.

Fortunately, the XML standard has removed much of the 'grunt' work associated with doing this kind of integration. Using XML, you could pull the data out of the first application with JDBC, create an XML document to hold this data, and then send the data to the Visual Basic application. Once the Visual Basic application received the data, it could use the Microsoft XML Parser to parse and process the data.

XML is ideal for moving data between applications that run across a wide spectrum of heterogenous platforms. Furthermore, XML can very easily capture the relationships that exist between different entities within a relational database. Lets walk through several different examples of how to use XML to model the common relationships found within a relational database.

There are tools available to perform this type of work for you. These tools will generate an XML document containing all of the data returned from a given SQL statement. These tools are very powerful, but using them will not teach you how to properly model and build relationships using XML. For this reason, all of the examples shown in this chapter are built by hand.

Mapping a Single Table to XML

Let's start with a simple example of pulling all of the data from the `Customer` table using SQL and JDBC. We will take the data contained within the JDBC `ResultSet` and use the Xerces XML parser to build our XML document. The action the code will be taking will look something like this:

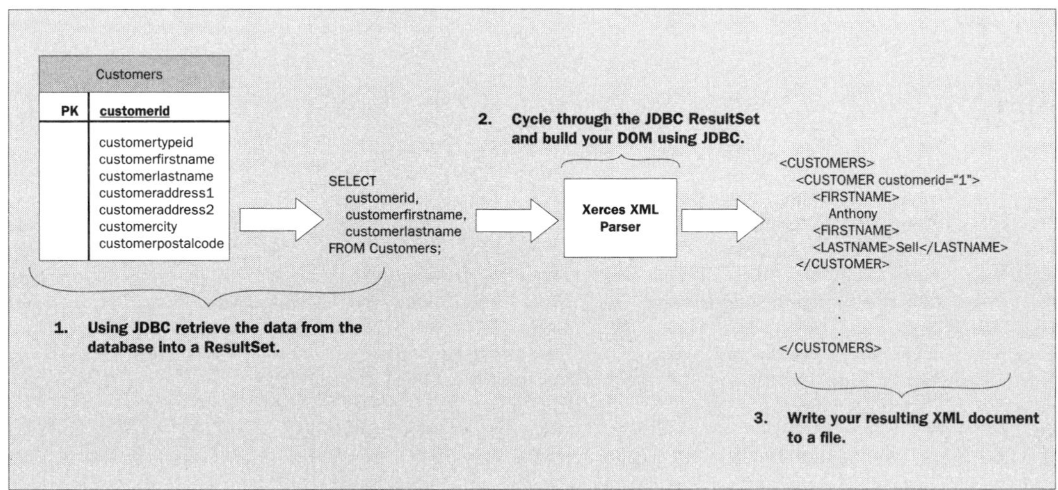

In the above diagram, JDBC and SQL are used to retrieve a Java `ResultSet` containing customer data. We loop through the `ResultSet` and each record is extracted. Each extracted record is then built into an XML document using the Xerces parser. Let's show how this can be done using an example that you can run.

Try it Out: Mapping XML to a Single Table

Here is the Java class that will pull data out of the `Customers` table in the database and convert the output to an XML DOM:

```
import java.sql.*;                      /* JDBC Classes */
import org.w3c.dom.*;                   /* W3C Interfaces */
import org.apache.xerces.dom.*;         /* Xerces DOM Classes */
import org.apache.xml.serialize.*;      /* Xerces serializer */
import java.io.*;                       /* Java io classes for file access */

public class SimpleXMLData {

  public static final String JDBCURL =
    "jdbc:cloudscape:c:/BegJava DB/Wrox4370.db";
  public static final String JDBCDRIVER = "COM.cloudscape.core.JDBCDriver";
  public static final String SQL = "SELECT customerid, customerfirstname, " +
                                   " customerlastname " +
                                   "FROM customers";
  public static final String OUTPUTFILE = "c:\\customer.xml";


  /**
   * ***************************************************************************
   * This class has purposely been written as a set of static methods
   * because at this point I want to focus on the XML code and not
   * necessarily the OO features of Java.
   * ***************************************************************************
   */

  public static void main(String args[]) {

    try {

      /**
       * ****Step 1 - Making my JDBC Connection to Cloudscape****
       */
      Class.forName(JDBCDRIVER).newInstance();
      Connection conn = DriverManager.getConnection(JDBCURL);

      /**
       * ****Step 2 - Retrieve my customer data from the database****
       */
      Statement statement = conn.createStatement();
      ResultSet customerRS = statement.executeQuery(SQL);

      /**
       * ****Step 3 - Build customer XML DOM.****
       */
      Document xmlDoc = buildCustomerXML(customerRS);

      /**
       * ****Step 4 - Writing the output to a file ****
       */
```

```
      File outputFile = new File(OUTPUTFILE);
      printDOM(xmlDoc, outputFile);

      conn.close();   /* Closing my connection */
    } catch (Exception e) {
      System.out.println("Really poor exception handling: " + e.toString());
    }
  }

  /**
   * ******************************************************************
   *
   * The buildCustomerXML will build a simple XML document based on the
   * records retrieved from SQL statement defined in the SQL constant.
   *
   * The XML document object will then be passed back to the main
   * method where it will be written to a flat file.
   *
   * ******************************************************************
   */
  private static Document buildCustomerXML(ResultSet _customerRS)
                          throws Exception {
    Document xmlDoc = new DocumentImpl();

    /* Creating the root element */
    Element rootElement = xmlDoc.createElement("CUSTOMERS");
    xmlDoc.appendChild(rootElement);

    while (_customerRS.next()) {
      Element customer = xmlDoc.createElement("CUSTOMER");

      /* Building the id attribute for the DOM */
      customer.setAttribute("customerid", _customerRS.getString("customerid"));

      /* Creating the elements within my customer DOM */
      Element firstName = xmlDoc.createElement("FIRSTNAME");
      Element lastName = xmlDoc.createElement("LASTNAME");

      /* Populating my customer DOM with data */
      firstName.appendChild(xmlDoc.createTextNode(
                          _customerRS.getString("customerfirstname")));

      lastName.appendChild(xmlDoc.createTextNode(
                         _customerRS.getString("customerlastname")));

      /*
       * Appending the customer elements to the customer element declared at
       * the beginning of the while loop.
       */
      customer.appendChild(firstName);
      customer.appendChild(lastName);

      /* Appending the customer to the root class */
      rootElement.appendChild(customer);
    }
```

```
        return xmlDoc;
    }

    /**
     * ***********************************************************************
     *
     * The printDOM method below will write the contents of the XML document
     * passed into it out to the a file. The method will that the XML
     * document will be written out is defined by the File object passed into
     * it.
     * ***********************************************************************
     */
    private static void printDOM(Document _xmlDoc,
                                 File _outputFile) throws Exception {
      OutputFormat outputFormat = new OutputFormat("XML", "UTF-8", true);
      FileWriter fileWriter = new FileWriter(_outputFile);

      XMLSerializer xmlSerializer = new XMLSerializer(fileWriter,
                                                      outputFormat);
      xmlSerializer.asDOMSerializer();

      xmlSerializer.serialize(_xmlDoc.getDocumentElement());
    }
}
```

Running the SimpleXMLData Example

Save this as `C:\BegJavaDB\Chapter 20\SimpleXMLData.java`, and compile the file using the following command:

```
> javac -classpath %JLIB%\xerces.jar SimpleXMLData.java
```

To run the `SimpleXMLData`, issue the following command from the `C:\BegJavaDB\Chapter 20:` directory

```
> java -classpath .;%JLIB%\xerces.jar;%JLIB%\cloudscape.jar SimpleXMLData
```

When the `SimpleXMLData` example is run, it will take the data stored in the customer table of our relational database and build an XML document that looks something like this:

```
<?xml version="1.0" encoding="UTF-8"?>
<CUSTOMERS>
    <CUSTOMER customerid="1000">
        <FIRSTNAME>Catherine</FIRSTNAME>
        <LASTNAME>Crean</LASTNAME>
    </CUSTOMER>
    <CUSTOMER customerid="1001">
        <FIRSTNAME>Steve</FIRSTNAME>
        <LASTNAME>Davis</LASTNAME>
    </CUSTOMER>
    <CUSTOMER customerid="1002">
        <FIRSTNAME>Villiage DJ</FIRSTNAME>
```

```
        <LASTNAME/>
    </CUSTOMER>
    <CUSTOMER customerid="1003">
        <FIRSTNAME>Diane </FIRSTNAME>
        <LASTNAME>Asmus</LASTNAME>
    </CUSTOMER>
</CUSTOMERS>
```

The document will be saved as `C:\customer.xml`.

How It Works

Let's walk through the code and see exactly what actions are being performed. The first section of code that we are going to examine is in the `main()` method of the `SimpleXMLData` class listed above. Step 1 of the code example loads the JDBC driver and establishes a connection with the target database:

```
Class.forName(JDBCDRIVER).newInstance();
Connection conn = DriverManager.getConnection(JDBCURL);
```

The required database driver and the URL used to connect to the database are defined as class-level properties. These properties are:

```
public static final String JDBCURL =
  "jdbc:cloudscape:c:/wrox/database/Wrox4370.db";
public static final String JDBCDRIVER = "COM.cloudscape.core.JDBCDriver";
```

In Step 2 of the `main()` method, two things are happening. First, a `Statement` object is created from the `Connection` object instantiated in Step 1. After the `Statement` object has been created, it will be used to execute the SQL statement defined in the constant `SQL` (as seen in the call `statement.executeQuery()`). The SQL statement stored in this constant retrieves all of the customer information in the customer table. The customer data retrieved is stored inside a `ResultSet` object called `customerRS`:

```
Statement statement = conn.createStatement();
ResultSet customerRS = statement.executeQuery(SQL);
```

None of the above should be new to you, but the next step is where the code becomes interesting. We have the `ResultSet` returned from the `statement.executeQuery()`. This `ResultSet` object is passed to the `buildCustomerXML()` method. The first thing that happens inside this method is that a `Document` object called `xmlDoc`, is created. The `xmlDoc` object is going to be used to build and hold all of the elements within our XML document:

```
Document xmlDoc= new DocumentImpl();
```

Once the `Document` object is created, a document root is established. In the code example below, the document root is called `CUSTOMERS`:

```
Element rootElement = xmlDoc.createElement("CUSTOMERS");
xmlDoc.appendChild(rootElement);
```

The xmlDoc.appendChild() method call will append the rootElement object to the xmlDoc object as a child element. This is an important step to remember because often when people are learning how to build an XML document, they forget to attach the rootElement object to the "parent" document object. At this point, if you were to print out the contents of the XML document being built, it would look something like this:

```
<CUSTOMERS>
</CUSTOMERS>
```

Now, as the rest of the XML document is being built, all of the elements being created will be appended to rootElement element. After the rootElement has been created, the _customerRS object passed into the method call is iterated through using a while loop. As the method iterates through the rows, each single customer row from the customer table is converted to XML. Then after the row has been created, it is appended to the rootElement object. The first step in converting the database row to XML is to create an Element object called CUSTOMER.

After the CUSTOMER element has been created an ID attribute called customerid is added to establish the unique identity of the customer:

```
      while (_customerRS.next()) {
        Element customer = xmlDoc.createElement("CUSTOMER");

        /* Building the id attribute for the DOM */
        customer.setAttribute("customerid", _customerRS.getString("customerid"));
```

An attribute, rather then an element, is used to establish the identity of the customer within an XML document. Attributes are used to provide additional meta data about a particular data element, so in this case it makes sense to put the customerid as an attribute because it is providing very specific additional information about the <CUSTOMER></CUSTOMER> tag.

> **The customerid attribute in our example is considered the equivalent of a primary key within a database table.**

Always remember to use the ID attribute to establish the uniqueness of the record. At this point the rest of the data from the database row can be converted to XML:

```
        /* Creating the elements within my customer DOM */
        Element firstName = xmlDoc.createElement("FIRSTNAME");
        Element lastName = xmlDoc.createElement("LASTNAME");

        /* Populating my customer DOM with data */
        firstName.appendChild(xmlDoc.createTextNode(
                              _customerRS.getString("customerfirstname")));

        lastName.appendChild(xmlDoc.createTextNode(
                             _customerRS.getString("customerlastname")));
```

In the above code snippet, an `Element` object is created for each of the different elements that are going to be attached to the `Element` object called `customer`. The `xmlDoc` object is being used to create a `TextNode` for the each of the different fields being attached. These `TextNodes` hold the value retrieved from the `_customerRS` object passed into the `buildCustomerXML()` method. Each `TextNode` is attached to its corresponding `Element` object. After each of the elements have been created and populated with their values they are appended to the `customer` object via the `appendChild()` method. The `customer` object is then appended to the `rootElement` object:

```
        customer.appendChild(firstName);
        customer.appendChild(lastName);

        /* Appending the customer to the root class */
        rootElement.appendChild(customer);
      }
```

It is important to note that you do not have to explicitly declare an `Element` object for each field within a database row. We did this in our code example in order to explictly show how customer data was added to the XML document.

Once the XML document is completed, it is returned to the main `method()`.The `printDOM()` method is then used to write the document to a file.

```
  private static void printDOM(Document _xmlDoc,
                               File _outputFile) throws Exception {
    OutputFormat outputFormat = new OutputFormat("XML", "UTF-8", true);
    FileWriter fileWriter = new FileWriter(_outputFile);

    XMLSerializer xmlSerializer = new XMLSerializer(fileWriter,
                                                    outputFormat);
    xmlSerializer.asDOMSerializer();

    xmlSerializer.serialize(_xmlDoc.getDocumentElement());
  }
```

To print the contents of the XML document to a file, the `printDOM()` method first creates a `OutputFormat` object called `outputFormat`:

```
    OutputFormat outputFormat = new OutputFormat("XML", "UTF-8", true);
```

The `XMLSerializer` class uses the `outputFormat` object in order to control how the data within the XML document is written to a file. The `OutputFormat` constructor takes three parameters that tell the `OutputFormat` that the format of the data will be XML, that it will be a UTF-8 encoding, and that the output should be indented (as indicated by the `true` value being passed in as the third parameter).

After the `outputFormat` has been created, a `FileWriter` object is instantiated. This object tells the `XMLSerializer` object which file the contents of the XML document should be written out to:

```
    FileWriter fileWriter = new FileWriter(_outputFile);
```

The `XMLSerializer` object is used to serialize the contents of the XML document to an `OutputWriter` object. In this example, the contents of the XML document are being dumped from its in-memory, hierarchical tree representation to a `FileWriter` object. The `XMLSerializer` is instantiated by passing in the `outputFormat` and `fileWriter` objects created earlier.

```
XMLSerializer xmlSerializer = new XMLSerializer(fileWriter,
                                                outputFormat);
```

Once the `XMLSerializer` object is created, it is told what kind of parser is being used in the serialization. It does this by calling the `xmlSerializer.asDOMSerializer()` method:

```
xmlSerializer.asDOMSerializer();
```

To carry out the serializing of the XML document to a file, the `serialize()` method on the `xmlSerializer` object is called, passing in the root element of the XML document:

```
xmlSerializer.serialize(_xmlDoc.getDocumentElement());
```

Mapping a One-to-Many Relationship in XML

The above example is extremely simplistic. Often when a developer retrieves records from a relational database they are retrieving data that has a one-to-many relationship. A one-to-many relationship is a relationship where one record acts as the parent (header) record to other children (detail) records.

The `customerorder` and `customerorderitems` tables in our `MusicStore` database are an example of a one-to-many relationship. If you wanted to design an application that would extract invoice and line-item data from our `MusicStore` database, while still maintaing the one-to-many relationship between the data, the application would have to perform the following steps:

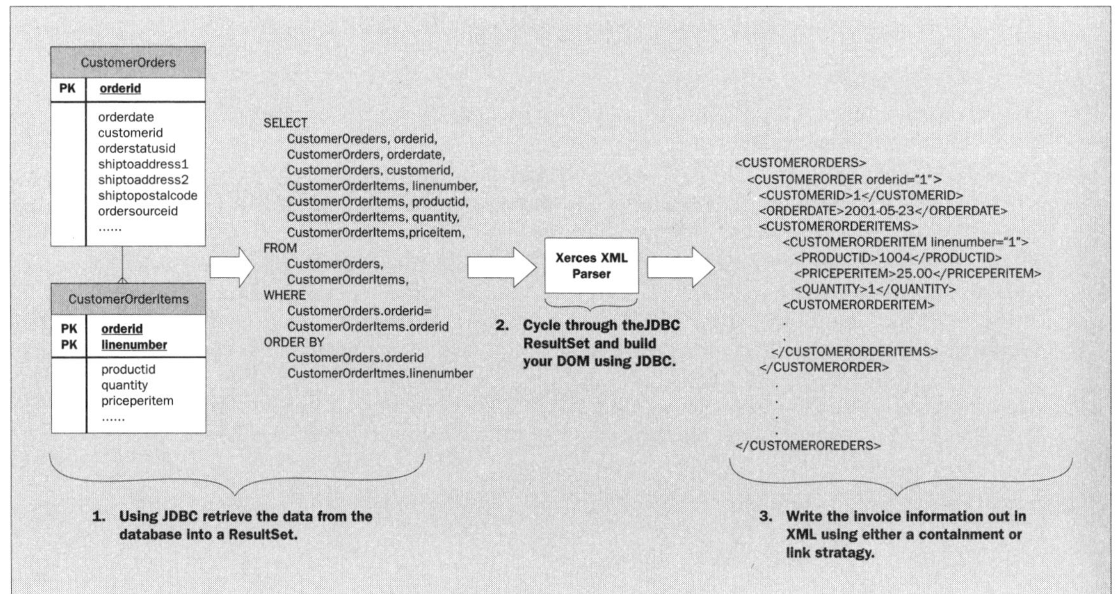

There are two different strategies to building an XML document that contains database relationships. These two strategies are:

- Containing
- Linking

Each of these strategies has advantages and disdvantages. In addition, each strategy requires a different approach to building XML documents. In the following section, the 'Containing' strategy is going to be explored in detail. In the section *Mapping a Many-to-Many Relationship in XML* in this chapter, the 'Linking' strategy will be discussed.

Using a Containing Strategy

The **containing** strategy puts the child information as part of a hierarchy of elements underneath the parent. The diagram above illustrates a containing strategy that is being used to illustrate the customer order XML document. Remember, the data from the `customerorder` table is the "one" part of the relationship and the data from the `customerOrderItems` table is the "many" part of the relationship.

```
<?xml version="1.0" encoding="UTF-8"?>
<CUSTOMERORDERS>
    <CUSTOMERORDER orderid="1001"> <-- Master Record -->
        <CUSTOMERID>1000</CUSTOMERID>
        <ORDERDATE>2001-05-23</ORDERDATE>
        <CUSTOMERORDERITEMS>
            <CUSTOMERORDERITEM linenumber="1"> <-- Detail Record -->
                <PRODUCTID>1004</PRODUCTID>
                <PRICEPERITEM>15.65</PRICEPERITEM>
                <QUANTITY>1</QUANTITY>
            </CUSTOMERORDERITEM>
            <CUSTOMERORDERITEM linenumber="2"> <-- Detail Record -->
                <PRODUCTID>1002</PRODUCTID>
                <PRICEPERITEM>9.99</PRICEPERITEM>
                <QUANTITY>1</QUANTITY>
            </CUSTOMERORDERITEM>
        </CUSTOMERORDERITEMS>
    </CUSTOMERORDER>
```

Try It Out: Mapping a One-to-Many Relationship in XML

In the above example, the relationship between the `CUSTOMERORDER` data and the `CUSTOMERORDERITEM` data is hierarchical. Let's walk through the code example that builds the above XML document:

```
import java.sql.*;                      /* JDBC Classes */
import org.w3c.dom.*;                   /* W3C Interfaces */
import org.apache.xerces.dom.*;         /* Xerces DOM Classes */
import org.apache.xml.serialize.*;      /* Xerces serializer */
import java.io.*;                       /* Java io classes for file reading/writing
*/

public class OneToManyXmlData {
  public static final String JDBCURL =
    "jdbc:cloudscape:c:/wrox/database/Wrox4370.db";
```

```
public static final String JDBCDRIVER = "COM.cloudscape.core.JDBCDriver";
public static StringBuffer SQL = new StringBuffer("");
public static final String OUTPUTFILE = "c:\\customerOrder.xml";

/*
 * The intializeSQL method builds the SQL statement using a StringBuffer.
 */
public static void initializeSQL() {
  SQL.append("SELECT                              ");
  SQL.append("  CustomerOrders.orderid,           ");
  SQL.append("  CustomerOrders.orderdate,         ");
  SQL.append("  CustomerOrders.customerid,        ");
  SQL.append("  CustomerOrderItems.linenumber,    ");
  SQL.append("  CustomerOrderItems.productid,     ");
  SQL.append("  CustomerOrderItems.quantity,      ");
  SQL.append("  CustomerOrderItems.priceperitem   ");
  SQL.append("FROM                                ");
  SQL.append("  CustomerOrders,                   ");
  SQL.append("  CustomerOrderItems                ");
  SQL.append("WHERE                               ");
  SQL.append("  CustomerOrders.orderid=           ");
  SQL.append("  CustomerOrderItems.orderid        ");
  SQL.append("ORDER BY                            ");
  SQL.append("  CustomerOrders.orderid        asc,          ");
  SQL.append("  CustomerOrderItems.linenumber asc   ");
}

/*
 * The following is an example of how to capture a one-to-many relationship
 * using XML. The data being pulled is invoice and line item data being pulled
 * from the invoice and line item tables.
 */

public static void main(String args[]) {
  try {

    /**
     * ****Step 1 - Making my JDBC Connection to Cloudscape****
     */
    Class.forName(JDBCDRIVER).newInstance();
    Connection conn = DriverManager.getConnection(JDBCURL);

    /**
     * ****Step 2 - Retrieve my order data from the database****
     */
    initializeSQL();
    Statement statement = conn.createStatement();
    ResultSet customerOrderRS = statement.executeQuery(SQL.toString());

    /**
     * ****Step 3 - Build CustomerOrder XML DOM.****
     */
    Document xmlDoc = buildCustomerOrderXML(customerOrderRS);
```

```
      /**
       * ****Step 4 - Writing the output to a file ****
       */
      File outputFile = new File(OUTPUTFILE);
      printDOM(xmlDoc, outputFile);

      customerOrderRS.close();   /* Closing my result set */
    } catch (Exception e) {
      System.out.println("Really poor exception handling: " + e.toString());
    }
  }

  /*
   * The buildCustomerOrderXML method will build an XML document containing
   * CustomerOrder information.
   */
  private static Document buildCustomerOrderXML(ResultSet _customerOrderRS)
                                              throws Exception {
    Document xmlDoc = new DocumentImpl();

    /* Creating the root element */
    Element rootElement = xmlDoc.createElement("CUSTOMERORDERS");
    xmlDoc.appendChild(rootElement);

    /* Declaring the different Elements found within the invoice */
    Element customerOrder = null;
    Element customerOrderItems = null;
    Element customerOrderItem = null;

    /* Initializing order id holders */
    String currentOrderId = "";   /* Order ID of the current resultset record */
    String holderOrderId = ""; /* Holder for the order ID being currently built */

    /* Cycling through all of the records within the resultset */
    while (_customerOrderRS.next()) {

      /* Getting the order ID of the current record being looked at */
      currentOrderId = _customerOrderRS.getString("orderid");

      /*
       * If the current order id does not match the holder invoice ID
       * (which will be an empty string when we process the first record
       * in the resultset) then we are dealing with a new customer order and will
       * have to build the customer order header information. Otherwise,
       * the record is for the same customer order.
       */
      if (!(currentOrderId.equals(holderOrderId))) {

        /* Set the holder order ID to be the current invoice ID */
        holderOrderId = new String(currentOrderId);

        /* Initialize the different elements found within an invoice record */
        customerOrder = xmlDoc.createElement("CUSTOMERORDER");
        customerOrderItems = xmlDoc.createElement("CUSTOMERORDERITEMS");
```

```
      customerOrderItem = xmlDoc.createElement("CUSTOMERORDERITEM");

      /* Setting up my primary key for my invoice */
      customerOrder.setAttribute("orderid",
                               _customerOrderRS.getString("orderid"));

      /* Adding my different elements to the invoice header */
      customerOrder.appendChild(buildDBElement(xmlDoc, "CUSTOMERID",
                                  _customerOrderRS.getString("customerid")));
      customerOrder.appendChild(buildDBElement(xmlDoc, "ORDERDATE",
                                   _customerOrderRS.getString("orderdate")));

      /* Appending my lines element */
      customerOrder.appendChild(customerOrderItems);
    }

    /* Building my line item data */
    customerOrderItem.setAttribute("linenumber",
                              _customerOrderRS.getString("linenumber"));
    customerOrderItem.appendChild(buildDBElement(xmlDoc, "PRODUCTID",
            _customerOrderRS.getString("productid")));
    customerOrderItem.appendChild(buildDBElement(xmlDoc, "PRICEPERITEM",
            _customerOrderRS.getString("priceperitem")));
    customerOrderItem.appendChild(buildDBElement(xmlDoc, "QUANTITY",
            _customerOrderRS.getString("quantity")));

    /* Appending everything together */
    customerOrderItems.appendChild(customerOrderItem);

    customerOrderItem = xmlDoc.createElement("CUSTOMERORDERITEM");

    customerOrder.appendChild(customerOrderItems);
    rootElement.appendChild(customerOrder);
  }

  return xmlDoc;
}

/*
 * The printDOM method below will write the contents of the xml document
 * passed into it out to the a file. The method will that the xml document
 * will be written out is defined by the File object passed into it.
 */
private static void printDOM(Document _xmlDoc,
                             File _outputFile) throws Exception {
  OutputFormat outputFormat = new OutputFormat("XML", "UTF-8", true);
  FileWriter fileWriter = new FileWriter(_outputFile);

  XMLSerializer xmlSerializer = new XMLSerializer(fileWriter, outputFormat);
  xmlSerializer.asDOMSerializer();

  xmlSerializer.serialize(_xmlDoc.getDocumentElement());
}
```

```
  /*
   * The buildDBElement will add a text node onto an element and return it back to
   * the method that calls it. This is simply a helper method that makes it easier
   * to add elements to another element.
   */
  private static Element buildDBElement(Document _xmlDoc, String _elementName,
                                         String _elementValue) throws Exception {

    Element item = _xmlDoc.createElement(_elementName);
    item.appendChild(_xmlDoc.createTextNode(_elementValue));

    return item;
  }
}
```

Running the OneToManyXmlData Example

Save this as `C:\BegJavaDB\Chapter 20\OneToManyXMLData.java`, and compile with the following command:

```
> javac -classpath .;%JLIB%\xerces.jar OneToManyXmlData.java
```

We can run the code with the following command:

```
> java -classpath .;%JLIB%\xerces.jar;%JLIB%\cloudscape.jar OneToManyXmlData
```

After the `OneToManyXmlData` example has been run, a file called `c:\customerOrder.xml` will be created. The contents of that file will be as follows:

```
<?xml version="1.0" encoding="UTF-8"?>
<CUSTOMERORDERS>
    <CUSTOMERORDER orderid="1001">
        <CUSTOMERID>1000</CUSTOMERID>
        <ORDERDATE>2001-05-23</ORDERDATE>
        <CUSTOMERORDERITEMS>
            <CUSTOMERORDERITEM linenumber="1">
                <PRODUCTID>1004</PRODUCTID>
                <PRICEPERITEM>15.65</PRICEPERITEM>
                <QUANTITY>1</QUANTITY>
            </CUSTOMERORDERITEM>
            <CUSTOMERORDERITEM linenumber="2">
                <PRODUCTID>1002</PRODUCTID>
                <PRICEPERITEM>9.99</PRICEPERITEM>
                <QUANTITY>1</QUANTITY>
            </CUSTOMERORDERITEM>
        </CUSTOMERORDERITEMS>
    </CUSTOMERORDER>
    <CUSTOMERORDER orderid="1003">
        <CUSTOMERID>1001</CUSTOMERID>
        <ORDERDATE>2001-05-24</ORDERDATE>
        <CUSTOMERORDERITEMS>
            <CUSTOMERORDERITEM linenumber="1">
                <PRODUCTID>1002</PRODUCTID>
```

```
                    <PRICEPERITEM>9.99</PRICEPERITEM>
                    <QUANTITY>1</QUANTITY>
                </CUSTOMERORDERITEM>
            </CUSTOMERORDERITEMS>
        </CUSTOMERORDER>
    </CUSTOMERORDERS>
```

How It Works

The above example looks in some ways very similar to the code in our first example. It is connecting to the database and executing a SQL statement. The difference comes in how the actual document is built. The `SimpleXMLData` example took the `customer` database table and converted its contents to an XML document. The `OneToManyXmlData` example here builds an XML document containing data that has a master-detail relationship (invoice header to invoice line items). Capturing this master-detail relationship within an XML document is going to take a lot more work.

The database code in the `main()` method of the `OneToManyXmlData` class looks very much like the code from the previous example. The `MusicStore` database is connected to, a SQL statement is executed, and the data is put into a `ResultSet` object called `customerOrderRS`. The real difference between this code and the `SimpleXMLData` class is how the XML document is built in the `buildCustomerOrderXML()` method.

The `buildCustomerOrderXML()` method loops through the `_customerOrderRS ResultSet` and build an XML document containing all of the data within it. Furthermore, the `buildCustomerOrderXML()` method rebuilds the master-detail relationship that existed between the customer order and customer order items.

When using SQL, JDBC, and a relational database, we are taking data from multiple locations using SQL and returning the data as a JDBC `ResultSet`. This `ResultSet` flattens the parent-child relationship into a tabular format. The hierarchical structure that existed between the `customerorder` and `customerorderitems` tables has been lost. Thus, when the customer order XML document is being built, the code will have to recreate this parent-child relationship.

Let's walk through the `buildCustomerOrderXML()` method. The first piece of code in this method creates a new `Document` object called `xmlDoc` and also creates the root element for the customer order XML document being created.

```
private static Document buildCustomerOrderXML(ResultSet _customerOrderRS)
                                              throws Exception {
  Document xmlDoc = new DocumentImpl();

  /* Creating the root element */
  Element rootElement = xmlDoc.createElement("CUSTOMERORDERS");
  xmlDoc.appendChild(rootElement);
```

If the contents of the XML document were written out to a file after the above code fragment ran, the result would be as follows:

```
<CUSTOMERORDERITEMS>
</CUSTOMERORDERITEMS>
```

After the root element is created, all of the XML elements that make up a customer order are declared within the code:

```
Element customerOrder = null;
Element customerOrderItems = null;
Element customerOrderItem = null;
```

This is different from the SimpleXMLData example. In the SimpleXMLData example, all of the Element objects needed to create a specific customer were declared inside the while{} loop. In the SimpleXMLData example, every row in the ResultSet was treated as an individual customer. Our SimpleXMLData example did not have a parent-child relationship to worry about.

In this example, we cannot make such an assumption. There has to be some way of determining whether a record currently being returned by the ResultSet is an invoice (CustomerOrder), in which case it would be a parent record, or is a line item (CustomerOrderItems), in which case it would be a child record.

To make this determination two steps are being undertaken. The first step uses a SQL ORDER BY statement to make sure that all of the records retrieved into customerOrderRS are ordered by customerOrder.orderid and then customerOrderItem.linenumber.

```
ORDER BY
  CustomerOrder.invoiceid          asc,
  CustomerOrderItems.linenumber    asc
```

The second step is to compare the current record being retrieved from _customerOrderRS with the current customer order element being built for our XML document. To do this we need to store the current order ID being processed by the code and order ID of the customer order being built into our XML document. This is done by declaring two variables:

```
String currentOrderId = "";   /* Order ID of the current resultset record */
String holderOrderId = ""; /* Holder for the order ID being currently built */
```

We'll discuss how these two variables are used as we walk through the code in the while loop. The first part of the while loop initializes the currentOrderId variable with the order ID of the record being returned from _currentOrderRS:

```
while (_customerOrderRS.next()) {

  /* Getting the order ID of the current record being looked at */
  currentOrderId = _customerOrderRS.getString("orderid");
```

Once the currentOrderId variable has been set, it will be checked against the holderOrderId variable to see if they are equal. The holderOrderId variable is used to hold the order ID of the current order being built in our XML document. Remember, the ResultSet has "flattened" the relationship between the CustomerOrder and CustomerOrderItems tables. Let's look at the following code segment and see how the relationship between the CustomerOrder and CustomerOrderItems tables can be un-flattened:

```
  if (!(currentOrderId.equals(holderOrderId))) {
```

In the code above, if the `currentOrderId` and `holderOrderId` variable do not match then a new order must be created. This involves several steps, the first of which is to populate the `holderOrderId` variable with the value in `currentOrderId`:

```
holderOrderId = new String(currentOrderId);
```

This is done so that when `_customerOrderRS` is processing other records, our application will be able to determine whether the record is a new order or a line item. The second step initializes each `Element` object needed to build an order element for our orders XML document:

```
customerOrder = xmlDoc.createElement("CUSTOMERORDER");
customerOrderItems = xmlDoc.createElement("CUSTOMERORDERITEMS");
customerOrderItem = xmlDoc.createElement("CUSTOMERORDERITEM");
```

After these elements have been initialized, the order header information is retrieved from the current record of the `_customerOrderRS` `ResultSet` object. The data from this current record is used to build the different pieces of the order header:

```
customerOrder.setAttribute("orderid",
                           _customerOrderRS.getString("orderid"));

customerOrder.appendChild(buildDBElement(xmlDoc, "CUSTOMERID",
                                _customerOrderRS.getString("customerid")));
customerOrder.appendChild(buildDBElement(xmlDoc, "ORDERDATE",
                                _customerOrderRS.getString("orderdate")));
```

The last step in this process is to append the `customerOrderItems` element to the `customerOrder` element:

```
customerOrder.appendChild(customerOrderItems);
```

This step is done to make sure all of the order items for the order being processed have something to 'hook' on to. If a snapshot were taken after the first record in `ResultSet` were processed, the resulting XML would look something like this:

```
<?xml version="1.0" encoding="UTF-8"?>
<CUSTOMERORDERS>
    <CUSTOMERORDER orderid="1001">
        <CUSTOMERID>1000</CUSTOMERID>
        <ORDERDATE>2001-05-23</ORDERDATE>
        <CUSTOMERORDERITEMS>
            <CUSTOMERORDERITEM linenumber="1">
                <PRODUCTID>1004</PRODUCTID>
                <PRICEPERITEM>15.65</PRICEPERITEM>
                <QUANTITY>1</QUANTITY>
            </CUSTOMERORDERITEM>
            <CUSTOMERORDERITEM linenumber="2">
                <PRODUCTID>1002</PRODUCTID>
                <PRICEPERITEM>9.99</PRICEPERITEM>
                <QUANTITY>1</QUANTITY>
            </CUSTOMERORDERITEM>
```

```
        </CUSTOMERORDERITEMS>
    </CUSTOMERORDER>
</CUSTOMERORDERS>
```

Now, if the currentOrderId and the holderOrderId variables do match, then the row retrieved from the _customerOrderRS ResultSet object will be used to build a line item for the customer order being added to the customer orders XML document. This is done via the code below:

```
customerOrderItem.setAttribute("linenumber",
                               _customerOrderRS.getString("linenumber"));
customerOrderItem.appendChild(buildDBElement(xmlDoc, "PRODUCTID",
        _customerOrderRS.getString("productid")));
customerOrderItem.appendChild(buildDBElement(xmlDoc, "PRICEPERITEM",
        _customerOrderRS.getString("priceperitem")));
customerOrderItem.appendChild(buildDBElement(xmlDoc, "QUANTITY",
        _customerOrderRS.getString("quantity")));
```

After all of the logic is executed for building a new order, or an order item for an existing customer order, all of the different Element objects for the customer order must be appended. This is done with the following code:

```
customerOrderItems.appendChild(customerOrderItem);
customerOrderItem = xmlDoc.createElement("CUSTOMERORDERITEM");
customerOrder.appendChild(customerOrderItems);
rootElement.appendChild(customerOrder);
```

It is important to notice that the customerOrderItem variable is being re-initialized after each iteration through the while loop. This re-initialization is being done to make sure that on the next iteration through the while loop, there will be a clean customerOrderItem variable. Failure to re-initialize Element variables like customerOrderItem can cause the XML document being built to be improperly formed.

The containing strategy is easy to implement when dealing with simple one-to-many relationships like the one seen between the CustomerOrder and CustomerOrderItems tables. However, this strategy can be wasteful to use when trying to capture more complicated table relationships like a many-to-many relationship. The next section will explain how to use a linking strategy, which uses XML to build this more complicated relationship.

Mapping a Many-to-Many Relationship in XML

As we saw in the previous example, an invoice can have one or more line items associated with it. A line item can belong to only one invoice. Let's change the scenario. What happens if we have two or more customers who might share the same address? We cannot use a one-to-many relationship to model this because in a one-to-many relationship the address row would have to belong to one and only one customer. We could theoretically set up multiple rows with the same address information with each one pointing back to a specific customer. This is not a good solution to implement within a relational database. There are two reasons for this:

- This is a waste of space within a database. The redundant data for the one-to-many solution might seem trivial, until you have a database that has several million rows of customer and address information. Space and performance become a critical concern.

- If a change has to occur for an address, that change would have to be applied to several different records within the `address` table. Lets say the zip code changes for an address. If there are several instances of the same address in a table, it is very easy to not update all of the addresses. Over time, these multiple instances of the same address can result in a significant amount of garbage data being accumulated within the `MusicStore` database.

In the current `MusicStore` database model, we cannot support this because address data is embedded in both the `customerorder` and `customers` tables. The address must be normalized out into a many-to-many relationship that looks like this:

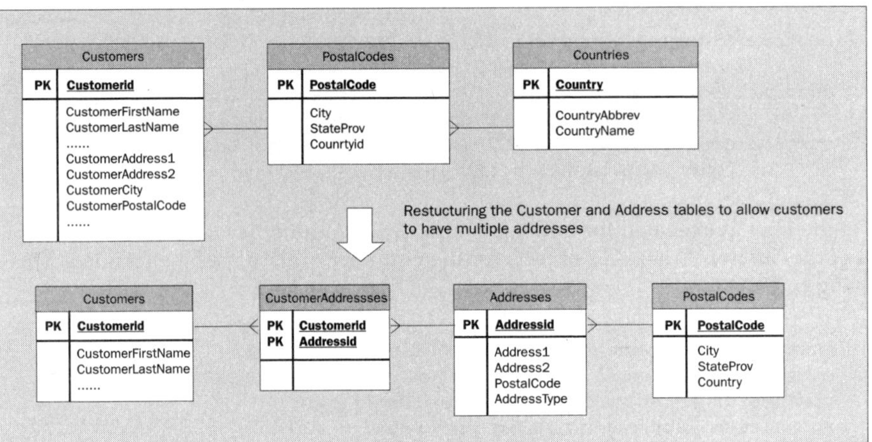

A many-to-many relationship solves the problems described above by adding a table between the customer and address tables. This table, which we will call `CustomerAddresses`, acts as a road map that maps a specific customer with a specific address. If multiple customers share the same address, this table can capture this by having multiple rows, one for each customer, that point to the same address in the address table:

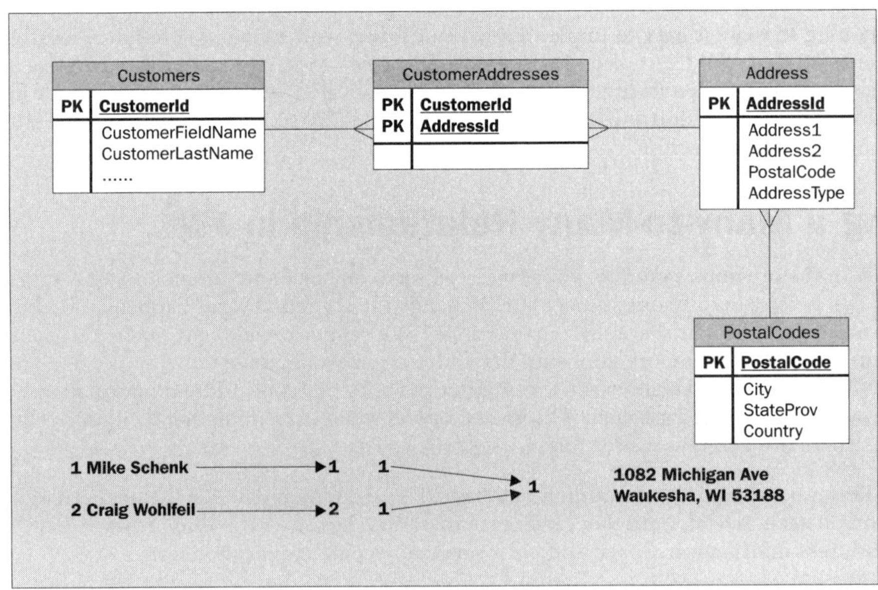

As you can see in the above diagram, the `CustomerAddresses` table links the `Customers` and `Address` tables together. It does this by storing the primary key of a customer with the primary key of an address. This pairing allows an address record stored in the `address` table to be linked with multiple customers.

Before you rush off to change the `Wrox4370.db` database to match this new schema, we've already done it for you. For the purposes of this example, we've created a small database, `BegJDB`. This database (available with the code download) has the four tables listed above, along with some example data.

The above relationship can easily be represented within an XML document. A many-to-many relationship can be modeled using a containing strategy. However, a containing strategy is not the most efficient means of storing data for many-to-many relationships. The inefficiencies of this strategy are the same problems found with trying to store multiple copies of the same record within a database:

- A containing strategy would require a separate copy of the same address information be stored as child element beneath each customer element. This is wasteful and bloats the document. This additional bloat requires more memory to parse and can significantly add to the amount of time required to search and locate data within an XML document.
- A containing strategy would replicate the same address information across multiple customer elements. If the address has to be updated or deleted within the XML document, it would have to be done in multiple places.

There is a better solution than the containing strategy; we can use a **linking** strategy. A linking strategy stores an `ID` within one part of the XML document and uses it to link to another element within the same document. A linking strategy uses less space in the XML document because one record can be associated with multiple records by the use of links. Let's look at how the linking strategy can be used to pull data out of the `Customer` and `Address` tables.

Using a Linking Strategy

A simplified diagram showing the process for extracting data from the `Customer` and `Address` tables when using a linking strategy would look like this:

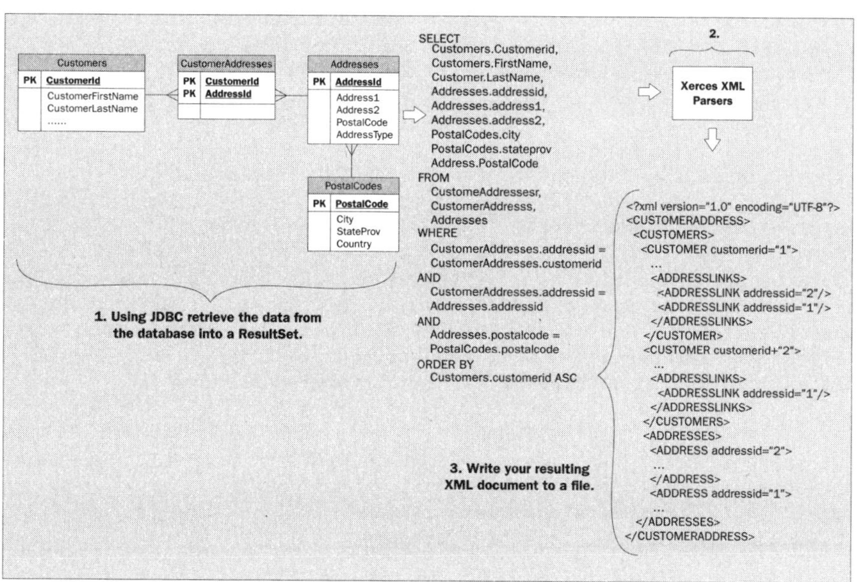

The process shown above is nothing new. The application is using SQL, Java, and JDBC to pull the data out of the `Customer`, `CustomerAddresses`, and the `Address` tables and build an XML document via the Xerces parser. The major difference between this and the one-to-many example is that a linking strategy is being used to build the relationship between the customers and their addresses.

This example requires the `xalan-j_2_2_D6.zip` file we downloaded earlier, or more specifically the `xalan.jar` file it contains. The `ManyToManyXmlData` example uses the `XPathAPI` class. The `XPathAPI` class provides a number of convenience methods that wrap the low-level XPath APIs. All of the Xalan examples in this book use version 2.2.0 of the Xalan XSLT processor.

While the `XPathAPI` class is part of the official distribution for version 2.2D6 of Xalan, the `XPathAPI` class is not part of the distribution in earlier Xalan releases (releases below version 2.0). To compile the `ManyToManyXmlData` class with earlier versions of the Xalan XSLT processor you will need to compile the `XPathAPI.java` source file.

For earlier Xalan releases, this XPathAPI file is typically located in the `\`*`Xalan Directory`*`\samples\ApplyXPath` directory.

For example to compile the `XPathAPI` class for Xalan version 1.2.2, you must issue the following command from a DOS window:

```
javac -classpath c:\xalan-j_1_2_2\xalan.jar;c:\xerces-1_3_0\xerces.jar
      XPathAPI.java
```

Make sure you change the Xalan and Xerces references in the classpath parameter shown above to point to the proper location of these JAR files.

Try It Out – Mapping a Many-to-Many Relationship in XML

The code for the application looks like this:

```
import java.sql.*;                   /* JDBC Classes */
import org.w3c.dom.*;                /* W3C Interfaces */
import org.apache.xerces.dom.*;      /* Xerces DOM Classes */
import org.apache.xml.serialize.*;   /* Xerces serializer */
import java.io.*;                    /* Java io classes for file reading/writing
*/
import org.apache.xpath.XPathAPI;    /* Xalan XPath Classes */

public class ManyToManyXmlData {

  /* Note we are connecting to a different database then the previous examples */
  public static final String JDBCURL = "jdbc:cloudscape:c:/wrox/database/BegJDB";
  public static final String JDBCDRIVER = "COM.cloudscape.core.JDBCDriver";
  public static StringBuffer SQL = new StringBuffer("");
  public static String OUTPUTFILE = "c:\\customerAddress.xml";

  private static void initializeSQL() {
    SQL.append("SELECT                          ");
    SQL.append("  Customers.customerid,         ");
    SQL.append("  Customers.customerfirstname,  ");
    SQL.append("  Customers.customerlastname,   ");
```

```
    SQL.append("  Addresses.addressid,          ");
    SQL.append("  Addresses.address1,           ");
    SQL.append("  Addresses.address2,           ");
    SQL.append("  Addresses.addresstype,        ");
    SQL.append("  PostalCodes.city,             ");
    SQL.append("  PostalCodes.stateprov,        ");
    SQL.append("  Addresses.PostalCode          ");
    SQL.append("FROM                            ");
    SQL.append("  Customers,                    ");
    SQL.append("  CustomerAddresses,            ");
    SQL.append("  Addresses,                    ");
    SQL.append("  PostalCodes                   ");
    SQL.append("WHERE                           ");
    SQL.append("  Customers.customerid =        ");
    SQL.append("  CustomerAddresses.customerid  ");
    SQL.append("AND                             ");
    SQL.append("  CustomerAddresses.addressid = ");
    SQL.append("  Addresses.addressid           ");
    SQL.append("AND                             ");
    SQL.append("  Addresses.postalcode=         ");
    SQL.append("  PostalCodes.postalcode        ");
    SQL.append("ORDER BY                        ");
    SQL.append("  Customers.customerid  ASC      ");
  }

  public static void main(String args[]) {
    try {

      /**
       * ****Step 1 - Making my JDBC Connection to Cloudscape****
       */
      Class.forName(JDBCDRIVER).newInstance();
      Connection conn = DriverManager.getConnection(JDBCURL);

      /**
       * ****Step 2 - Retrieve my customer address data from the database****
       */
      initializeSQL();
      Statement statement = conn.createStatement();
      ResultSet customerAddressRS = statement.executeQuery(SQL.toString());

      /**
       * ****Step 3 - Build invoice XML DOM.****
       */
      Document xmlDoc = buildCustomerAddressXML(customerAddressRS);

      /**
       * ****Step 4 - Writing the output to a file ****
       */
      File outputFile = new File(OUTPUTFILE);
      printDOM(xmlDoc, outputFile);

      customerAddressRS.close();   /* Closing my result set */
    } catch (Exception e) {
```

```
      System.out.println("Really poor exception handling: " + e.toString());
    }
  }

  /*
   * The buildCustomerAddressXML method build the Customer section of the
   * XML document. It will build a link, called AddressLink, to the
   * Addresses the customer is currently associated with.
   */
  private static Document buildCustomerAddressXML(ResultSet _customerAddressRS)
                                                          throws Exception {
    Document xmlDoc = new DocumentImpl();

    /* Creating the root element */
    Element rootElement = xmlDoc.createElement("CUSTOMERADDRESS");
    Element customers = xmlDoc.createElement("CUSTOMERS");
    Element addresses = xmlDoc.createElement("ADDRESSES");

    xmlDoc.appendChild(rootElement);
    rootElement.appendChild(customers);
    rootElement.appendChild(addresses);

    /* Declaring the different Elements found within a customer record */
    Element customer = null;
    Element addressLinks = null;
    Element addressLink = null;

    /* Initializing customer ID holders */
    String currentCustomerId = "";
    String holderCustomerId = "";

    /* Cycling through all of the records within the resultset */
    while (_customerAddressRS.next()) {

      /* Getting the customer ID of the current record being looked at */
      currentCustomerId = _customerAddressRS.getString("customerid");

      if (!(currentCustomerId.equals(holderCustomerId))) {

        holderCustomerId = new String(currentCustomerId);

        /* Initialize the different elements found within an invoice record */
        customer = xmlDoc.createElement("CUSTOMER");
        addressLinks = xmlDoc.createElement("ADDRESSLINKS");
        addressLink = xmlDoc.createElement("ADDRESSLINK");

        /* Setting up my primary key for my customer */
        customer.setAttribute("customerid",
                              _customerAddressRS.getString("customerid"));

        /* Adding my different elements to the customers header */
        customer.appendChild(buildDBElement(xmlDoc, "FIRSTNAME",
                              _customerAddressRS.getString("customerfirstname")));
        customer.appendChild(buildDBElement(xmlDoc, "LASTNAME",
```

```
                                    _customerAddressRS.getString("customerlastname")));

          /* Appending my addresslinks element */
          customer.appendChild(addressLinks);
        }

        /* Building my address link data */
        addressLink.setAttribute("addressid",
                                    _customerAddressRS.getString("addressid"));

        /* Appending everything together */
        addressLinks.appendChild(addressLink);

        addressLink = xmlDoc.createElement("ADDRESSLINK");

        /* Builds the actual address information */
        buildAddressesXML(_customerAddressRS, addresses, xmlDoc);

        customer.appendChild(addressLinks);
        customers.appendChild(customer);
      }

      return xmlDoc;
    }

    /*
     * The buildAddressesXML will build the Addresses section of the
     * CustomerAddress XML document. The method uses XPath to see if the address
     * being passed in already exists. If the address exists nothing further
     * is done with the Addresses element. If the address does not exist, a new
     * Address element is added as a child to the Addresses element.
     */
    private static void buildAddressesXML(ResultSet _customerAddressRS,
                                          Element _addresses,
                                          Document _xmlDoc) throws Exception {
      StringBuffer queryString =
              new StringBuffer("/CUSTOMERADDRESS/ADDRESSES/ADDRESS[@addressid='");
      queryString.append(_customerAddressRS.getString("addressid"));
      queryString.append("']");


      /*
       * Use XPath to see if the   an address with the target address ID we are
       * Looking for, already exists as part of the Addresses element.
       */
      Node queryResult = XPathAPI.selectSingleNode(_xmlDoc,
                                                   queryString.toString());

      /*
       * If a match is not found, add the address as a new element
       */
      if (queryResult == null) {
        Element address = _xmlDoc.createElement("ADDRESS");
        address.setAttribute("addressid",
```

```
                                    _customerAddressRS.getString("addressid"));

        address.appendChild(buildDBElement(_xmlDoc, "ADDRESS1",
                                    _customerAddressRS.getString("address1")));
        address.appendChild(buildDBElement(_xmlDoc, "ADDRESS2",
                                    _customerAddressRS.getString("address2")));
        address.appendChild(buildDBElement(_xmlDoc, "CITY",
                                    _customerAddressRS.getString("city")));
        address.appendChild(buildDBElement(_xmlDoc, "STATE",
                                    _customerAddressRS.getString("stateprov")));
        address.appendChild(buildDBElement(_xmlDoc, "ZIP",
                                    _customerAddressRS.getString("postalcode")));
        address.appendChild(buildDBElement(_xmlDoc, "ADDRESSTYPE",
                                    _customerAddressRS.getString("addresstype")));

        _addresses.appendChild(address);
      }
    }

    /*
     * The printDOM method below will write the contents of the xml document
     * passed into it out to the a file. The method will that the xml document
     * will be written out is defined by the File object passed into it.
     */
    private static void printDOM(Document _xmlDoc,
                                 File _outputFile) throws Exception {
      OutputFormat outputFormat = new OutputFormat("XML", "UTF-8", true);
      FileWriter fileWriter = new FileWriter(_outputFile);

      XMLSerializer xmlSerializer = new XMLSerializer(fileWriter,
                                                       outputFormat);
      xmlSerializer.asDOMSerializer();

      xmlSerializer.serialize(_xmlDoc.getDocumentElement());
    }

    /*
     * The buildDBElement will add a text node onto an element and return it back to
     * the method that calls it. This is simply a helper method that makes it easier
     * to add elements to another element.
     */
    private static Element buildDBElement(Document _xmlDoc, String _elementName,
                                          String _elementValue) throws Exception {

      Element item = _xmlDoc.createElement(_elementName);
      item.appendChild(_xmlDoc.createTextNode(_elementValue));

      return item;
    }
  }
```

Running the ManyToManyXmlData Example

Save this code as `C:\BegJavaDB\Chapter 20\ManyToManyXmlData.java`, and compile it using the
following command:

```
> javac -classpath .;%JLIB%\xerces.jar;%JLIB%\xalan.jar ManyToManyXmlData.java
```

Notice the two JAR files in the `-classpath` option: `xerces.jar` for parsing the XML, and `xalan.jar` for the XPath functions. The command to run the program looks like this:

```
> java -classpath .;%JLIB%\xerces.jar;%JLIB%\xalan.jar;%JLIB%\cloudscape.jar
      ManyToManyXmlData
```

After this program has been executed the following output will be written out to the file located at `C:\customerAddress.xml`. The contents of this file will be:

```
<?xml version="1.0" encoding="UTF-8"?>
<CUSTOMERADDRESS>
    <CUSTOMERS>
        <CUSTOMER customerid="1">
            <FIRSTNAME>Mike</FIRSTNAME>
            <LASTNAME>Schenk</LASTNAME>
            <ADDRESSLINKS>
                <ADDRESSLINK addressid="2"/>
                <ADDRESSLINK addressid="1"/>
            </ADDRESSLINKS>
        </CUSTOMER>
        <CUSTOMER customerid="2">
            <FIRSTNAME>Craig</FIRSTNAME>
            <LASTNAME>Wohlfeil</LASTNAME>
            <ADDRESSLINKS>
                <ADDRESSLINK addressid="1"/>
            </ADDRESSLINKS>
        </CUSTOMER>
    </CUSTOMERS>
    <ADDRESSES>
        <ADDRESS addressid="2">
            <ADDRESS1>1532 West Meyer Avenue</ADDRESS1>
            <ADDRESS2/>
            <CITY>Waukesha</CITY>
            <STATE>WI</STATE>
            <ZIP>53188</ZIP>
            <ADDRESSTYPE>Billing</ADDRESSTYPE>
        </ADDRESS>
        <ADDRESS addressid="1">
            <ADDRESS1>1534 West Meyer Avenue</ADDRESS1>
            <ADDRESS2/>
            <CITY>Waukesha</CITY>
            <STATE>WI</STATE>
            <ZIP>53188</ZIP>
            <ADDRESSTYPE>Shipping</ADDRESSTYPE>
        </ADDRESS>
    </ADDRESSES>
</CUSTOMERADDRESS>
```

How It Works

We are not going to walk through the entire code example above. The first half of the application is similar to the two previous examples, except that we connect to a different database and extract slightly different data. The real interest is when the `buildCustomerAddressXML()` method is called. The method behaves very similarly to the `buildCustomerOrderXML()` method in the one-to-many example:

```
private static Document buildCustomerAddressXML(ResultSet _customerAddressRS)
                                                throws Exception {
  Document xmlDoc = new DocumentImpl();

  /* Creating the root element */
  Element rootElement = xmlDoc.createElement("CUSTOMERADDRESS");
  Element customers = xmlDoc.createElement("CUSTOMERS");
  Element addresses = xmlDoc.createElement("ADDRESSES");

  xmlDoc.appendChild(rootElement);
  rootElement.appendChild(customers);
  rootElement.appendChild(addresses);
```

The above code builds the base elements of the `customerAddress` XML document. The code first creates the root element <CUSTOMERADDRESS>. After the root element has been created two more `Elements` are created and appended to the `rootElement` object: <CUSTOMERS> and <ADDRESSES>. At this point the `customerAddress.xml` document looks like this:

```
<CUSTOMERADDRESS>
   <CUSTOMERS>
    </CUSTOMERS>
   <ADDRESSES>
   </ADDRESSES>
</CUSTOMERADDRESS>
```

After the base XML document has been built, the following `Element` objects (`customer`, `addressLinks`, and `addressLink`) are declared, along with a pair of variables for tracking where which address we're dealing with (`currentCustomerId` and `holderCustomerId`):

```
/* Declaring the different Elements found within a customer record */
Element customer = null;
Element addressLinks = null;
Element addressLink = null;

/* Initializing customer ID holders */
String currentCustomerId = "";
String holderCustomerId = "";
```

As you can see from the code, pulling data for a many-to-many relationship from JDBC and SQL still has the same challenges as the one-to-many relationship. The data has been flattened and the hierarchical structure of the data will need to be "rebuilt". This rebuilding of the data hierarchy will be done in a similar fashion to the one-to-many code example shown earlier in the chapter:

```
while (_customerAddressRS.next()) {
```

```
/* Getting the customer ID of the current record being looked at */
currentCustomerId = _customerAddressRS.getString("customerid");

if (!(currentCustomerId.equals(holderCustomerId))) {
  holderCustomerId = new String(currentCustomerId);
  /* Initialize the different elements found within an invoice record */
  customer = xmlDoc.createElement("CUSTOMER");
  addressLinks = xmlDoc.createElement("ADDRESSLINKS");
  addressLink = xmlDoc.createElement("ADDRESSLINK");
  /* Setting up my primary key for my customer */
  customer.setAttribute("customerid",
                      _customerAddressRS.getString("customerid"));
  /* Adding my different elements to the customers header */
  customer.appendChild(buildDBElement(xmlDoc, "FIRSTNAME",
                      _customerAddressRS.getString("customerfirstname")));
  customer.appendChild(buildDBElement(xmlDoc, "LASTNAME",
                       _customerAddressRS.getString("customerlastname")));
  /* Appending my addresslinks element */
  customer.appendChild(addressLinks);
}
```

The customer records retrieved from the SQL statement are ordered by the customer's `customerid`. As the `_customerAddressRS` `ResultSet` object is iterated through, a new `<CUSTOMER><CUSTOMER/>` element is created as the `customerid` on the record changes. When this occurs the customer's first name and last name are appended as elements to the newly created `<CUSTOMER></CUSTOMER>` element. In addition the `<ADDRESSLINKS></ADDRESSLINKS>` element is created and appended to the `<CUSTOMER></CUSTOMER>` element. The `<ADDRESSLINKS></ADDRESSLINKS>` element will contain zero or more `<ADDRESSLINK></ADDRESSLINK>` elements.

The code below builds an `<ADDRESSLINK></ADDRESSLINK>` element for each of the addresses that belong to that particular customer.

```
/* Building my address link data */
addressLink.setAttribute("addressid",
                       _customerAddressRS.getString("addressid"));

/* Appending everything together */
addressLinks.appendChild(addressLink);

addressLink = xmlDoc.createElement("ADDRESSLINK");
```

The `<ADDRESSLINK></ADDRESSLINK>` element being built does not have a text value associated with it. It only has an attribute called `addressid`. This attribute serves as a link to an `<ADDRESS></ADDRESS>` element located later in the XML document. If you were to look at the first customer and address being processed after the above code has run, your `customerAddress.xml` document would look like this:

```
<CUSTOMERADDRESS>
  <CUSTOMERS>
```

```
        <CUSTOMER customerid="1">
            <FIRSTNAME>Mike</FIRSTNAME>
            <LASTNAME>Schenk</LASTNAME>
            <ADDRESSLINKS>
                <ADDRESSLINK addressId="1"/>
            </ADDRESSLINKS>
        </CUSTOMER>
    </CUSTOMERS>
    <ADDRESSES>
    </ADDRESSES>
</CUSTOMERADDRESS>
```

At this point the `<ADDRESSLINK></ADDRESSLINK>` element has been established. It is now time to see if the address already exists as a child element within the `<ADDRESSES></ADDRESS>` element. This is done by calling the `buildAddressesXML()` method:

```
/* Builds the actual address information */
buildAddressesXML(_customerAddressRS, addresses, xmlDoc);
```

The `buildAddressesXML()` method checks the `Addresses` element to see if the address currently being examined from `_customerAddressRS` already exists as a child element. To see if the address exists, the `buildAddressesXML()` method uses the XPath standard to search the `customerAddress.xml` document.

XPath is a W3C recommendation that defines syntax for querying and searching XML documents. The Apache Software Foundation currently provides an XPath implementation with its Xalan XLST processor, which we downloaded earlier in the chapter when we obtained Xerces.

We are not going to go into a great detail about the XPath query language in this chapter. For more information on XPath and how to use it, please refer to *XSLT Programmer's Reference*, by Michael Kay, from Wrox Press ISBN 1-861005-06-7. This book explores XSLT and XPath in great deal and is a must have for any XML developer's bookshelf.

The code below gives a very simple example of using XPath to query an XML document to locate all addresses whose `ID` attribute match the address `ID` being passed into the `buildAddressesXML()` method.

```
private static void buildAddressesXML(ResultSet _customerAddressRS,
                                      Element _addresses,
                                      Document _xmlDoc) throws Exception {
  StringBuffer queryString =
          new StringBuffer("/CUSTOMERADDRESS/ADDRESSES/ADDRESS[@addressid='");
  queryString.append(_customerAddressRS.getString("addressid"));
  queryString.append("']");
```

The first thing being done in the above example is to populate a `StringBuffer`, called `queryString`, with an XPath search query. The XPath query string used for our code looks like this once we locate the value for `addressid`:

```
/CUSTOMERADDRESS/ADDRESSES/ADDRESS[@addressid='1']
```

As you can see from the example above, an XPath query navigates down the hierarchy found within the customerAddresses XML document. The above query is specifically searching for an ADDRESS element whose attribute "ID" is equal to 1. The query string above is very simplistic. XPath can be used to write very sophisticated queries.

Once our query string has been constructed, it is passed to the XPathAPI.selectSingleNode() method.

```
Node queryResult = XPathAPI.selectSingleNode(_xmlDoc,
                                             queryString.toString());
```

The XPathAPI call is a convenience class that is part of the Xalan XSLT processor. This class wraps much of the gory detail needed to execute an XPath query. The selectSingleNode() is a static method that takes a Document object to be searched and an XPath query string. Two things can happen when this method is called:

- The data being searched in the XML document will be returned. If there is more then one element being returned from the query string, the first element matching the query will be returned in a Node object.
- If no data is retrieved from the selectSingleNode() method, a null value will be returned.

After the XPath query is executed, the code will check to see if the address being requested has been found. We do this by checking if the queryResult object is null. If the queryResult object is null, a new <ADDRESS></ADDRESS> element will be created, populated with data from _customerAddressRS, and then appended to <ADDRESSES></ADDRESSES> element:

```
    /*
     * If a match is not found, add the address as a new element
     */
    if (queryResult == null) {
      Element address = _xmlDoc.createElement("ADDRESS");
      address.setAttribute("addressid",
                           _customerAddressRS.getString("addressid"));

      address.appendChild(buildDBElement(_xmlDoc, "ADDRESS1",
                                  _customerAddressRS.getString("address1")));
      address.appendChild(buildDBElement(_xmlDoc, "ADDRESS2",
                                  _customerAddressRS.getString("address2")));
      address.appendChild(buildDBElement(_xmlDoc, "CITY",
                                  _customerAddressRS.getString("city")));
      address.appendChild(buildDBElement(_xmlDoc, "STATE",
                                  _customerAddressRS.getString("stateprov")));
      address.appendChild(buildDBElement(_xmlDoc, "ZIP",
                                  _customerAddressRS.getString("postalcode")));
      address.appendChild(buildDBElement(_xmlDoc, "ADDRESSTYPE",
                                  _customerAddressRS.getString("addresstype")));

      _addresses.appendChild(address);
    }
  }
```

Finally, once all the Elements have been created, they are all appended together in the `buildCustomerAddressXML()` method:

```
        customer.appendChild(addressLinks);
        customers.appendChild(customer);
      }

      return xmlDoc;
    }
```

Containing vs. Linking

The containing and linking strategies have their advantages and disadvantages. The containing strategy is easy to use and most accurately reflects the natural hierarchical relationship that often exists between different pieces of data. The containing strategy is the easier to implement of the two strategies and is the better suited when working with data entities that have a one-to-many relationship. The containing strategy also performs better when trying to parse through the children elements of a particular record. Because child elements are located within the structure of the parent element, it often takes less time for the a child element to be located and parsed with an XML document built using a containing strategy vs. an XML document built using a linking strategy.

The containing strategy, when used to express a many-to-many relationship, can significantly increase the size of an XML document. The same data for an element will be replicated across multiple sections of the XML document. This might not seem like a big problem when dealing with small XML documents, but when the XML document being parsed is several thousand records long, this can significantly increase the amount of memory and resources being used by the XML parser. The linking strategy is a better fit for many-to-many relationships because it minimizes the amount of data being replicated within the XML document. The trade off with the linking strategy is that it can add a significant amount of overhead when searching for an element's child records. For instance, in the example above, every time an address needs to be located for a customer, the `ADDRESSLINKS` elements for the customer must be parsed and then the `ADDRESSES` element must be searched for those elements.

Elements vs. Attributes

There is a fierce debate within the XML community as to whether elements or attributes should be used when packaging database information. The element advocates think all data should be modeled using primarily XML elements. Element advocates believe attributes should only be used to provide primary key ID, foreign key ID, and type information. Our customer example shown in the *Mapping a simple Table to XML* section earlier gave an example of this. In the customer example the `customerid` is declared as an attribute, while all other customer data is declared as elements:

```
<CUSTOMER customerid="1000">
  <FIRSTNAME>Catherine</FIRSTNAME>
  <LASTNAME>Crean</LASTNAME>
</CUSTOMER>
```

The attribute advocates argue that all customer address information should be added as attributes. They would rewrite the above XML fragment as:

```
<CUSTOMER customerid="1000" firstname="Catherine" lastname="Crean"/>
```

The element method more clearly defines and segments the different pieces of the XML document and clearly shows the hierarchical relationships that exist between the elements. However, with large XML documents, the element method can make the document unreadable. Almost every database field has to be spelled out as an XML element.

In addition, when building large XML documents using the DOM API, the more deeply nested the elements are the more space the document will take up in memory. Remember, the DOM API parses the entire tree in memory. If your application is going to need to deal with very large XML documents or a large number of them you might want to consider the attribute method.

The attribute method makes for a cleaner looking, leaner XML document. However, attributes are limited in their use. An attribute can be used once within an XML element only. Thus, it cannot be used to express a master-detail relationship like customers and their addresses. In these situations a combination of elements and attributes are used:

```
<CUSTOMER customerid="1000" firstname="Catherine" lastname="Crean">
   <ADDRESSES>
      <ADDRESS type="Shipping" street="1509 Michigan Avenue"
               city="Madison" state="WI"/>
      <ADDRESS type="Billing" street="1438 Melbour Place"
               city="Waukesha" state="WI"/>
   </ADDRESSES>
<CUSTOMER>
```

Another thing to consider with the attribute method is that there are several XML parser operations not covered in this chapter that deal with sub-strings and manipulation of data within a tree hierarchy. Creating an element using attributes to store data retrieved from a database precludes you from using these operations.

Personally, the author prefers the element method of building XML documents. The element method clearly shows the hierarchy between data elements and lets the reader quickly pick the primary and foreign key IDs out of the document. While this method can use more system resources, it does provide more options for building and manipulating the XML document via the DOM API.

Summary

The last five years have been a truly exciting time to be an application developer. The Internet has provided us with a global highway in which data and processes can be integrated on a larger scale then ever imagined. XML is positioned to become the *lingua franca* of the Internet. It will allow applications to integrate on a global scale. This level of integration could never have been imagined five years ago when so many hardware and software vendors were jockeying for market share by trying to lock their customers into proprietary standards.

This chapter has focused on several basic topics, including:

- ❑ The different types of XML partners:
  - ❑ DOM parser
  - ❑ SAX parser

- How XML can be used to represent the different data relationships found within a relational database:
  - XML and a single table
  - XML and the one-to-many relationship
  - XML and the many-to-many relationship
- What the different strategies are for representing relationships between entities within a relational database:
  - Using a Containing strategy for one-to-many relationships
  - Using a Linking strategy for many-to-many relationships

This chapter was not designed to give you in-depth knowledge of XML. Instead, its purpose was to provide basic examples of how to use Java, JDBC, and XML to build data extracts from a relational database. This chapter is only an introduction to the most basic material.

There is a lot of hype surrounding XML. This hype can often confuse what XML is and how it can be used for a good application development. Whenever you come across the *nth* standard that claims to be XML based just remember this basic concept:

The XML standard provides a mechanism by which the structure and content of data can be described independently of how it is used or stored. Everything else is just implementation detail.

Using XSLT

As we saw at the end of the last chapter, XML is all very well for wrapping up data in a readily portable format, but it does have limitations. The answer to many of XML's limitations is **XSL**, the e**X**tensible **S**tylesheet **L**anguage. XSL is a way of defining a mapping from one XML document to another XML document. As we'll see in this chapter, the process isn't as hideously complicated as it might at first seem.

A full introduction to XSL would (and indeed, does) take a whole book to do it justice. For the purposes of this chapter, we're going to take you on a whirlwind tour of the very basics of XSL, focusing on XSLT (XSL Transformations, the process of transforming an XML document). We'll show you just enough to whet your appetite for more (hopefully), and also to demonstrate some of the power of XSLT.

In this chapter, we will be covering the following topics:

- An introduction to XSLT
- Examples of different XSLT structures and constructs. Some of the topics that will be covered include:
    - How to search for data within an XML document using XSLT
    - How to loop through different parts of an XML document using XSLT
    - Using conditional logic (`IF...THEN`) within XSLT to provide different types of presentation based on the data being returned
- The use of Java and the Apache Xalan parser to perform the transformation of XSLT/XML to some other format
- Examples of how to use XSLT to build HTML pages

> **If you are unfamiliar with XML it is highly recommended you read the previous chapter and the XML primer, provided as Appendix C, before diving into the material. Much of the material presented here relies on information covered in the previous chapter.**

An Introduction to XSLT

XSLT, which stands for **eXtensible Stylesheet Language: Transformations**, is a language which, according to the very first sentence in the specification (found at http://www.w3.org/TR/xslt), is primarily designed for transforming one XML document into another. However, XSLT is more than capable of transforming XML to HTML and many other text-based formats, so a more general definition might be as follows:

> **XSLT is a language for transforming the structure of an XML document.**

Why should you want to do that? Well, we saw in the last chapter that XML is a simple, standard way to interchange structured textual data between computer programs. Part of its success comes because it is also readable and writable by humans using nothing more complicated than a text editor, but this doesn't alter the fact that it is primarily intended for communication between software systems. As such, XML satisfies two compelling requirements:

- **Separating data from presentation**. The need to separate information from details of the way it is to be presented on a particular device. This need is becoming ever more urgent as the range of internet-capable devices grows. Organizations that have invested in creating valuable information sources need to be able to deliver them not only to the traditional PC-based web browser (which itself now comes in many flavors), but also to TV sets and WAP phones, not to mention the continuing need to produce print-on-paper.
- **Transmitting data between applications**. The need to transmit information (such as orders and invoices) from one organization to another without investing in bespoke software integration projects. As electronic commerce gathers pace, the amount of data exchanged between enterprises increases daily and this need becomes ever more urgent.

Of course, these two ways of using XML are not mutually exclusive. An invoice can be presented on the screen as well as being input to a financial application package, and weather forecasts can be summarized, indexed, and aggregated by the recipient instead of being displayed directly. Another of the key benefits of XML is that it unifies the worlds of documents and data, providing a single way of representing structure regardless of whether the information is intended for human or machine consumption. The main point is that, whether the XML data is ultimately used by people or by a software application, it will very rarely be used directly in the form it arrives: it first has to be transformed into something else.

In order to communicate with a human reader, this something else might be a document that can be displayed or printed: for example an HTML file, a PDF file, or even audible sound. Converting XML to HTML for display is probably the most common application of XSLT today but that is far from the end of the story.

In order to transfer data between different applications we need to be able to transform data from the data model used by one application to the model used in another. To load the data into an application, the required format might be a comma-separated-values file, a SQL script, an HTTP message, or a sequence of calls on a particular programming interface. Alternatively, it might be another XML file using a different vocabulary from the original. As XML-based electronic commerce becomes widespread, so the role of XSLT in data conversion between applications also becomes ever more important.

How does XSLT work?

By now you are probably wondering exactly how XSLT goes about processing an XML document in order to convert it into the required output. There are usually two aspects to this process:

- The first stage is a structural transformation, in which the data is converted from the structure of the incoming XML document to a structure that reflects the desired output.
- The second stage is formatting, in which the new structure is output in the required format such as HTML or PDF.

The second stage covers the ground we discussed in the previous section; the data structure that results from the first stage can be output as HTML, a text file and so on. XSLT is primarily concerned with the first stage – the transformation that makes it possible to provide output in all of these formats. This stage might involve selecting data, aggregating and grouping it, sorting it, or performing arithmetic conversions such as changing centimeters to inches.

XSLT performs this transformation according to a set of declarative "rules". These rules are based on defining what output should be generated when particular patterns occur in the input. The language is declarative, in the sense that you describe the transformation you require, rather than providing a sequence of procedural instructions to achieve it. XSLT describes the required transformation and then relies on the XSLT processor to decide the most efficient way to go about it.

XSLT still relies on an XML parser – be it a DOM parser or a SAX-compliant one – to convert the XML document into a tree structure. It is the structure of this tree representation of the document that XSLT manipulates, not the document itself.

XSLT and SQL

It is interesting to think of an analogy between XSLT and SQL. In a relational database, the data consists of a set of tables. The true power of a relational database doesn't come so much from this data structure as from the language that processes the data, SQL. It's when we get a high-level language expressly designed to manipulate the data structure that we start to find we've got something interesting on our hands, and for XML data that language is XSLT.

Superficially, SQL and XSLT are very different languages. But if you look below the surface, they actually have a lot in common. For starters, in order to process specific data, be it in a relational database or an XML document, the processing language must incorporate a declarative query syntax for selecting the data that needs to be processed. In SQL, that's the `SELECT` statement. In XSLT, the equivalent is the **XPath expression**, which we will introduce in this chapter.

The XPath expression language forms an essential part of XSLT, though it is actually defined in a separate W3C Recommendation (http://www.w3.org/TR/xpath) because it can also be used independently of XSLT. The XPath query syntax is designed to retrieve nodes from an XML document, based on a path through the XML document or the context in which the node appears. It allows access to specific nodes, while preserving the hierarchy and structure of the document. XSLT is then used to manipulate the results of these queries (rearranging selected nodes, constructing new nodes, etc).

OK, it's time to start taking a look at some examples of how XSLT can be used to transform your data.

XSLT, XML, and the Transformation

The best way to understand how to use XSLT is to try it out through using a simple set of examples and walk through the process of what happens when an XSLT stylesheet is merged with an XML document. All XSLT development begins with the creation of an XSLT stylesheet, which is a plain text file that contains special processing instructions, in the form of template rules and elements, what I like to call "XSLT meta-tags".

XSLT meta-tags describe how the data in an XML document is to be formatted. However, these meta-tags are more than just a markup language; they provide some basic programmatic functionality that allows the XSLT developer to search and manipulate data within an XML document.

To demonstrate the flexibility of XSLT, we are going to transform customer address data into two different formats using two different XSLT stylesheets. These output formats are:

- HTML
- Plain Text

First things first though, we will need to get ourselves an XSLT processor.

XSLT Processors

There are many XSLT processors available and they support different types of output formats. In general, most processors support the ability to transform XSLT and XML into either HTML or plain text. The table below lists the three most common XSLT processors. All of the XSLT processors shown below have a Java version of the processor.

XLST Processor	Download From	Comment
Xalan	http://xml.apache.org/	Open source XSLT processor
Oracle Corporation's XSL Processor	http://www.oracle.com/	Freely available for download – must register to download
Saxon	http://saxon.sourceforge.net/	Open source XSLT processor written by Michael Kay

For the examples in this chapter, we are going to be using the Xalan XSLT processor.

Downloading the Xalan XSLT Processor

The Xalan XSLT processor is available for free download from the ASF's web site. The URL for this is http://xml.apache.org/xalan-j/. For the code examples in this chapter, version 2.2.D6 of the Xalan XSLT processor was used. This version of the Xalan processor supports the following features:

- Full support for the XSLT Version 1.0 draft
- Full support the XML Path Language (XPath) version 1.0 draft
- Full support for the SAX 1 standard
- Compliance with the DOM Level 2 standard
- Transformation capabilities for transforming XML data to HTML, text, or another XML document

All in all, the Xalan XSLT processor is a powerful XSLT open source processor and as such is one of the most popular XSLT processors available.

Installing the Xalan XSLT Processor

The Xalan XSLT processor can be installed in the following steps:

1. Download version 2.2.D6 of the Xalan XSLT processor from the ASF web site. (http://xml.apache.org/xalan-j/) This is was the most stable version of the XSLT processor at the time the text was written. If you want to use Xalan on Windows, download the ZIP version of the application. If you want to use Xalan on UNIX, download the Gzipped version. This version will have a `.gz` on the end of the file.

   NOTE: You should be aware that the Xalan distribution is very large (over 10MB in size) and can take a long time to download over a slow Internet connection.

2. Unpack the compressed file to a directory of your choice.

3. After uncompressing the Xalan XSLT Parser from the ASF web site, you should have a directory containing all of the Xalan files. Some important parts of the directory structure of the Xalan XSLT processor are:

```
\xalan-j_2_2_D6
              \docs        (Javadocs for the Xalan XSLT Processor)
              \src         (Source code for the Xalan Processor)
              \samples     (Example XSL and Xalan code)
              License      (File containing the ASF Software License)
              Readme.html  (Opening page to the Xalan Documentation)
              \bin         (Contains all of the Jar files used by Xalan)
```

Once the Xalan XSLT processor has been unzipped and installed, let's run the `customerAddress.xsl` and `customerAddess.xml` files through the processor and look at the result.

You do not need to learn the ins and outs of the Xalan Java API immediately in order to begin experimenting with XSLT. Xalan provides a command line interface that lets you transform an XSLT and XML file into HTML, XML, or plain text. To use the XSLT parser you need to set up your `CLASSPATH` environment variable to point to the `xalan.jar` and `xerces.jar` files. Once these JAR files have been added to your classpath, the Xalan command line interface can be invoked.

To simplify this process, I've written a simple MS-DOS batch file called `transformIt.bat`. This batch file can easily be converted to a shell script that runs within a UNIX environment. The `transformIt.bat` file is shown overleaf:

```
@echo off
REM ********************************************************************
REM *                                                                  *
REM *  The transformIT script is a simple MS-DOS script that will      *
REM *  kick off the Xalan processor.                                   *
REM *                                                                  *
REM ********************************************************************

REM ********************************************************************
REM *                                                                  *
REM * Setting my Path for my Java executable and the location of       *
REM * my Xalan bin directory.                                          *
REM *                                                                  *
REM ********************************************************************
set JAVA=c:\jdk1.3\bin\java
set XALANHOME=c:\xalan-j_2_2_D6

REM ********************************************************************
REM *                                                                  *
REM * Add in the xalan and xerces jars. Note:  You need the Xerces Jar *
REM * files to use Xalan.                                              *
REM *                                                                  *
REM ********************************************************************
set CLASSPATH=%XALANHOME%\bin\xalan.jar
set CLASSPATH=%CLASSPATH%;%XALANHOME%\bin\xerces.jar

REM ***********************************************************************
REM *                                                                     *
REM *  Reading my command line parameter into my local variables.       *
REM *                                                                     *
REM *  XMLFILE - Path and name of the XML file to be processed.          *
REM *  XSLFILE - Path and name of the XSL file to be processed.          *
REM *  OUTFILE - Output file name for the results of the XSLT            *
REM *            transformation.                                          *
REM *                                                                     *
REM ***********************************************************************

set XMLFILE=%1%
set XSLFILE=%2%
set OUTFILE=%3%

REM **************************************
REM *                                    *
REM * Invoking the Xalan XSLT processor. *
REM *                                    *
REM **************************************
%JAVA% -cp %CLASSPATH% org.apache.xalan.xslt.Process -IN %XMLFILE% -XSL %XSLFILE%
-OUT %OUTFILE%
```

Example 1: Transforming XML to HTML

In our first example, two files will be created. One file, `customerAddress.xml`, is an XML document containing some customer address data. The other file, `customerAddressHTML.xsl`, is an XSLT stylesheet that contains HTML and XSLT meta-tags. However, these two files by themselves are not enough to produce HTML. What is needed is some mechanism for transforming these two files from XML and XSLT into an HTML document. This transformation occurs by taking the two files and running them through an XSLT processor. Graphically, the transformation process of XSLT and XML using an XSLT processor looks like this:

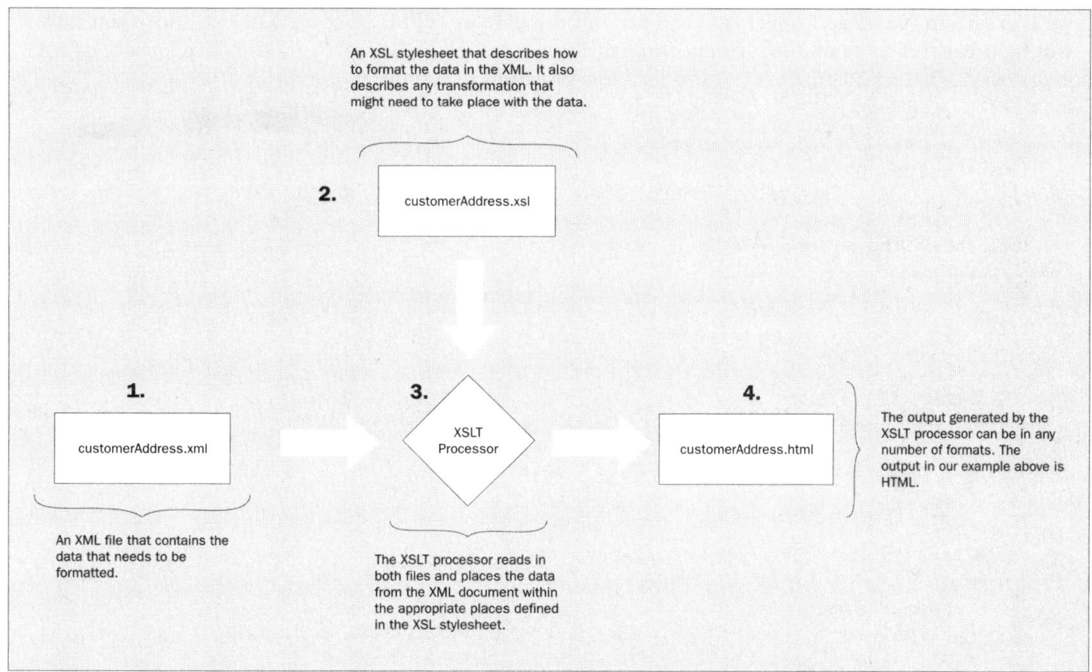

The figure shows an XML document and XSLT stylesheet being fed into an XSLT processor (items 1 and 2). The XSLT processor (item 3) takes the format defined in an XSLT stylesheet and 'plugs' in data from the XML document. However, as we will see in later sections of this chapter, XSLT is more than just a markup language for doing text replacement. It is a sophisticated programming language that allows you to transform how data is to be presented based on the data being passed in via an XML document.

Try It Out – Transforming XML to HTML

Let's start with a simple XML document called `customerAddress.xml`. This XML document contains customer address data for a single customer from our Music Store database.

```
<CUSTOMER customerid = "109">
  <CUSTOMERNAME>
    <FIRSTNAME>Jeff</FIRSTNAME>
    <LASTNAME>Dooley</LASTNAME>
  </CUSTOMERNAME>
  <ADDRESS>
```

```
      <CUSTOMERADDRESS1>1509 Westbrook Avenue</CUSTOMERADDRESS1>
      <CUSTOMERADDRESS2></CUSTOMERADDRESS2>
      <CUSTOMERCITY>Framingham</CUSTOMERCITY>
      <CUSTOMERSTATE>MA</CUSTOMERSTATE>
      <ZIP>53188</ZIP>
    </ADDRESS>
  </CUSTOMER>
```

Once the above file has been created, you are going to need a file called an XSLT **stylesheet** that describes how the data in the `customerAddress.xml` file is to be presented to the end user. For now we'll create an XSLT stylesheet that can present the data as HTML, but we will also show you how it can be presented as plain text. To accomplish this we are going to create an XSLT stylesheet called `customerAddressHTML.xsl`. – the contents of which looks like:

```
<?xml version="1.0" encoding="UTF-8"?>
<xsl:stylesheet version="1.0"
                xmlns:xsl="http://www.w3.org/1999/XSL/Transform">
<xsl:output method="html"/>
<xsl:template match="/">
  <HTML>
  <TITLE>Beginning Java Databases - XSL Example</TITLE>
  <BODY>
  <TABLE align="left">
    <TR>
    <TD>
      <IMG src="musicstore.gif" width="74" height="72"/>
    </TD>
    <TD><H2>Customer Lookup Results</H2></TD>
    </TR>
  </TABLE>
  <BR/><BR/><BR/><BR/><BR/><BR/><BR/><HR/>
  <P>
    Customer Name:
    <xsl:value-of select="CUSTOMER/CUSTOMERNAME/FIRSTNAME"/> 
    <xsl:value-of select="CUSTOMER/CUSTOMERNAME/LASTNAME"/>
  </P>

  <HR/>
  <BR/>
    <xsl:value-of select="CUSTOMER/ADDRESS/CUSTOMERADDRESS1"/><BR/>
    <xsl:value-of select="CUSTOMER/ADDRESS/CUSTOMERCITY"/>, 
    <xsl:value-of select="CUSTOMER/ADDRESS/CUSTOMERSTATE"/> 
    <xsl:value-of select="CUSTOMER/ADDRESS/CUSTOMERZIP"/> 
  </BODY>
  </HTML>
</xsl:template>
</xsl:stylesheet>
```

To invoke the `transformationIT.bat` batch file, you need to open a DOS window and then execute the following call:

```
> transformit customerAddress.xml customerAddressHTML.xsl
  customerAddress.html
```

If the transformation has taken place you should see a new file called customerAddress.html. When the file is opened in a web browser it will look like this:

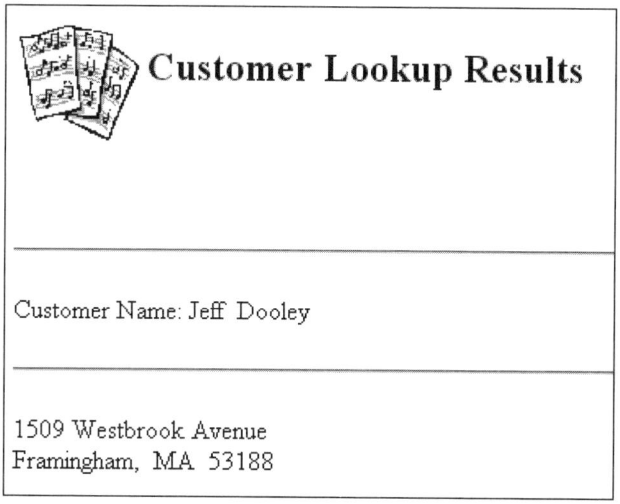

Before we jump into the details of XSLT, let's examine the customerAddressHTML.xsl stylesheet and make a few observations:

- The customerAddressHTML.xsl stylesheet is an XML document. It meets all the requirements of an XML document. It is a well-formed XML document that follows all the basic rules of XML. This means that for every XSLT stylesheet:
  - There must be a root element called <xsl:stylesheet></xsl:stylesheet>
  - All element tags must have a start and end tag. If the element is an empty tag it must follow the <Element/> convention.
  - All special characters in the document must be properly encoded in the document. For example, any '&' characters within the XSL stylesheet must be properly encoded (that is, using `&` or `&`).
- In the example above, XSLT has been used to display an XML document as HTML. However, XSLT is not limited to just output formats. XSLT can format data as any number of formats including Adobe's Personal Document Format (PDF) and Microsoft Word.
- There are a number of tags within the customerAddressHTML.xsl file that begin with the text xsl. As we will discuss in the section below, these tags are the XSL meta-tags that allow various operations to be performed on data that is going to be 'merged' into the XSLT stylesheet.

How It Works

As you can see above, the web page generated contains all of the HTML tags from within the customerAddressHTML.xsl file. The data from the customerAddress.xml file has been transformed into the HTML tags via the customerAddressHTML.xsl file. The customerAddress.html file looks like this:

```
<HTML>
  <TITLE>Beginning Java Databases - XSL Example</TITLE>
  <BODY>
    <TABLE align="left">
      <TR>
        <TD><IMG height="72" width="74" src="musicstore.gif"></TD><TD>
          <H2>Customer Lookup Results</H2>
        </TD>
      </TR>
    </TABLE>
    <BR>
    <BR>
    <BR>
    <BR>
    <BR>
    <BR>
    <BR>
  <HR>
    <P>
      Customer Name:
                  Jeff 
                  Dooley</P>
      <HR>
      <BR>1509 Westbrook Avenue<BR>Framingham, 
           MA 
           53188 
  </BODY>
</HTML>
```

The majority of the HTML shown above was taken line for line out of the `customerAddressHTML.xsl` file. However, the HTML fragment that shows the customer's name and address was populated with data from the `customerAddress.xml` file. The HTML fragment with the customer name and address is shown below:

```
<P>
  Customer Name:
     Jeff 
     Dooley</P>
  <HR>
  <BR>1509 Westbrook Avenue<BR>Framingham, 
      MA 
      53188 
```

The XSLT processor, when transforming the `customerAddress.xml` and `customerAddressHTML.xsl` files, used the following XSLT code to search the XML in the `customerAddress.xml` file and pull out the customer's first name, last name and address information from it. The XSLT code that does this is simple to understand.

```
<P>
  Customer Name:
    <xsl:value-of select="CUSTOMER/CUSTOMERNAME/FIRSTNAME"/> 
    <xsl:value-of select="CUSTOMER/CUSTOMERNAME/LASTNAME"/>
```

```
</P>

<HR/>
<BR/>
  <xsl:value-of select="CUSTOMER/ADDRESS/CUSTOMERADDRESS1"/><BR/>
  <xsl:value-of select="CUSTOMER/ADDRESS/CUSTOMERCITY"/>, 
  <xsl:value-of select="CUSTOMER/ADDRESS/CUSTOMERSTATE"/> 
  <xsl:value-of select="CUSTOMER/ADDRESS/CUSTOMERZIP"/> 
```

The `<xsl:value-of/>` tag tells the XSLT processor to replace the `<xsl:value-of/>` tag with data retrieved from an XML element or attribute. The exact element or attribute to be retrieved is defined by the `<xsl:value-of/>` tag's select attribute. So, the `<xsl:value-of/>` tag:

```
<xsl:value-of select="CUSTOMER/ADDRESS/CUSTOMERADDRESS1"/><BR/>
```

would, when transformed with the `customerAddress.xml` file, produce the following HTML fragment:

```
1509 Westbrook Avenue<BR>Framingham, 
```

The address data shown in the above HTML is retrieved from the `<CUSTOMERADDRESS1></CUSTOMERADDRESS1>` element shown below:

```
<CUSTOMER customerid = "109">
      <CUSTOMERNAME>
            . . .
      </CUSTOMERNAME>
      <ADDRESS>
         <CUSTOMERADDRESS1>1509 Westbrook Avenue</CUSTOMERADDRESS1>
            . . .
      </ADDRESS>
</CUSTOMER>
```

Example 2: Transforming XML to a Text File

As we know, HTML is far from the only format to which an XML document can be transformed. Let's take a look at a text file example.

Try It Out – Transforming XML to a CDF Text File

For the text file example, we are going to create an XSLT stylesheet called `customerAddressCDF.xsl`. This XSLT stylesheet will format the data in the `customerAddress.xml file` into a Comma-Delimited Format (CDF). As many software developers are aware, the CDF file format is still a very common way to share data between applications, particularly among older legacy applications. The CDF file formats a data record so that each record is a row of data and each data element in the record is enclosed with quotes and delineated from other data elements using a comma. The `customerAddressCDF.xsl` file is shown below:

```
<?xml version="1.0" encoding="UTF-8"?>
<xsl:stylesheet version="1.0"
      xmlns:xsl="http://www.w3.org/1999/XSL/Transform">
  <xsl:output method="text"/>
  <xsl:template match="/">
    &#34;<xsl:value-of select="CUSTOMER/CUSTOMERNAME/FIRSTNAME"/>&#34;,
    &#34;<xsl:value-of select="CUSTOMER/CUSTOMERNAME/LASTNAME"/>&#34;,
    &#34;<xsl:value-of select="CUSTOMER/ADDRESS/CUSTOMERADDRESS1"/>&#34;,
    &#34;<xsl:value-of select="CUSTOMER/ADDRESS/CUSTOMERCITY"/>&#34;,
    &#34;<xsl:value-of select="CUSTOMER/ADDRESS/CUSTOMERSTATE"/>&#34;,
    &#34;<xsl:value-of select="CUSTOMER/ADDRESS/CUSTOMERZIP"/>&#34;
  </xsl:template>
</xsl:stylesheet>
```

The code above is not the most readable XSLT stylesheet, however, what it is doing is pulling the different data elements out of the `customerAddress.xml` file, enclosing the elements in quotes and separating them with a comma.

Invoke the `transformationIT.bat` batch file with the following command line:

```
> transformit customerAddress.xml customerAddressCDF.xsl customerAddress.cdf
```

If the transformation has taken place you should see a new file called `customerAddress.cdf` `containing` a single line of comma-separated data. When the file is opened in a text editor, such as Notepad, it should look like this:

```
"Jeff","Dooley","1509 Westbrook Avenue","Framingham","MA","53188"
```

How It Works

As you can see above, the text file generated contains all of the address information from the `customerAddress.xml` file, which has been transformed into the comma-delimited format via the `customerAddressCDF.xsl` file.

An important note to make is that apart from the lack of HTML tags, the only difference between `customerAddressCDF.xsl` and `customerAddressHTML`.xsl is the output method tag:

```
<xsl:output method="text"/>
```

The customer address example shown is a very simple example of how XSLT can be used to format and present data from an XML document. However, XSLT has more than just 'search and replace' capabilities. XSLT has a multitude of robust programming constructs that allow the developer a great deal of flexibility in defining how their data is to be presented to an end-user.

Let's move on to the next step and look at a more sophisticated XSLT page. In this XSLT page we will:

- Take a more in-depth look at basic XSLT syntax
- Search an XML document using XSLT
- Perfom looping using XSLT
- Apply conditional logic within XSLT

Basic XSLT Syntax

All XSLT stylesheets have to start with a few basic elements. Let's strip out all of the detail in the `customerAdressHTML.xsl` file shown above and start with the minimum number of elements needed to create a valid XSLT stylesheet.

```
<xsl:stylesheet version="1.0"
                xmlns:xsl="http://www.w3.org/1999/XSL/Transform">
  <xsl:output method="html"/>
</xsl:stylesheet>
```

This document root is all that is required to begin writing an XSLT stylesheet. Inside the example, <xsl:stylsheet></xsl:stylesheet> are two attributes. These attributes are used to communicate information to the XSLT processor that is going to process the document. What the XSLT processor does with the information provided by the attributes is entirely up to the developers who wrote the XSLT processor.

The first attribute tells the XSLT processor that the XSLT version that this document is going to use is version 1.0. The second attribute is used to declare the `xsl:` namespace. Namespaces provide a mechanism for grouping related tags together to avoid ambiguity and name collisions within an XML document.

Why are the <xsl:stylesheet></xsl:stylesheet> tags important? Because XSLT is only a standard and how it is implemented is entirely up to the organization writing the XSLT processor. Often, when a developer moves their XSLT stylesheet from one vendor's XSLT processor to another, they will encounter errors.

XSLT is a standard, but every vendor's interpretation of the standard can be slightly different. Keep this in mind and carefully review example stylesheets provided with the XSLT processor being used – this can end up saving you a significant amount of time and energy.

Searching an XML Document using XPath

From almost all of the XSLT stylesheet examples shown in previous sections, we can see that the XSLT processor has the capability to pull data from the XML document being merged with the XSLT stylesheet. In both the customer address and customer order examples, data is 'pulled' from an XML document using the **XPath query language**. XPath allows the developer to query an XML document for data using text-based query string.

XPath uses the location path to describe how to find specific elements, attributes, processing instructions, etc. in a document. A location path is simply a description of how to get from one place in the document to someplace else. To use a crude analogy, the location path is similar to a set of instructions for finding a specific location within a city. If we wanted to find a particular office tower, a guide might tell us "Go to the second set of lights, turn left and you'll find the office tower two blocks ahead on your right". In the same way, we can use the location path to find what we are looking for in an XML document. The location path describes a path from one point in an XML document to another point, and it provides a way for each of the items within the document to be addressed. In other words, it describes the address of one of the document's nodes, in relationship to another node.

Just as our guide's set of instructions starts with where we currently are in the city, so the location path also is relative to the starting location. This concept is called the context node, which is where the addressing starts. We'll examine the general issue of context in greater detail in a later section.

XPath treats the XML document as a logical tree, with a root node as well as nodes for elements, attributes, character data (text), processing instructions, comments, and namespaces. The root node is the root of the document. Every XML document has one, and it contains an optional prolog and the document element. A location path that begins with a slash (/) is considered relative to the root node, while a path that begins with two slashes (//) relates to descendants of the root node.

XPath is seen in several places throughout the examples in this chapter. The most common usage for XPath queries in XSLT stylesheets is the <xsl:value-of/> tag .

The <xsl:value-of/>tag tells the XSLT parser to retrieve a value from the XML document. The value to be retrieved is defined by the XPath query, defined in the <xsl:value-of> tag's `select` attribute. An example XPath query string, taken from the customer address example, is shown below in bold:

```
<xsl:value-of select="CUSTOMER/CUSTOMERNAME/FIRSTNAME"/>
```

The above query, when issued against the `customerAddress.xml` file, tells the XSLT processor to locate the customer's first name.

XPath is an extremely rich query language. This section will walk you through some simple examples that will enable a beginning developer to very quickly pick up XPath and use it for their XSLT stylesheet development. It will not cover the full XPath specification. For more information on XPath you can use the following online resources:

URL	Comment
http://www.w3.org/TR/xpath	W3C Specification for XPath
http://xml.coverpages.org/xll.html	Link to an online magazine with several articles on XPath and other XSL querying technologies
http://www.xml.com	An excellent site with a number of articles on XPath and other XSL and XML-related topics

Let's build on the skeleton XSLT stylesheet from the start of this section. The most common task performed in XSLT stylesheet development is to pull data out of an XML document. Let's add a new tag called <xsl:template></xsl:template> to our skeleton stylesheet:

```
<?xml version="1.0" encoding="UTF-8"?>
<xsl:stylesheet version="1.0"
                xmlns:xsl="http://www.w3.org/1999/XSL/Transform">
  <xsl:output method="html"/>

  <xsl:template match="*"></xsl:template>
</xsl:stylesheet>
```

The <xsl:template></xsl:template> tag is used to set the scope of searching an XML document. An XML document is structured as a hierarchical tree. The <xsl:template></xsl:template> tag tells the XSLT processor where to begin searching for the data within the XML document. For instance, using the <xsl:template match="*"></xsl:template> tag will cause all queries coded in the XSLT stylesheet to:

- Search the entire document for the query requested
- Finds all elements within the XML document that match the query requested

Using the "*" for the match parameter can be useful when you want to use XPath queries in your XSLT stylesheet to search the entire XML document for data. However, using the "*" parameter for searching an XML document from within an XSLT stylesheet can be an expensive operation. Every query in the XSLT stylesheet will search the entire XML document even if you know the data you are searching for is located only within one specific part of the document.

To limit the scope of queries within an XML document, we can use different patterns within the <xsl:template> tag's match attribute. For example, to enforce that all queries are searched from the root element of an XML document (as in our earlier examples), you would use the following pattern in your <xsl:template></xsl:template> tag's match attribute:

```
<xsl:template match="/">
</xsl:template>
```

Because the above code was used within the customerAddressText.xsl stylesheet, all XPath queries began searching at the root element of the customerAddress.xml document. The root element of the customerAddress.xml file is:

```
<CUSTOMER>
.
.
.
</CUSTOMER>
```

Essentially, using the "/" for the match attribute forced all queries to begin at the top element, <CUSTOMER></CUSTOMER> within the customerAddress.xml file to begin searching for the requested query. For example, if the following XSLT stylesheet:

```
<?xml version="1.0" encoding="UTF-8"?>
<xsl:stylesheet version="1.0"  xmlns:xsl="http://www.w3.org/1999/XSL/Transform">
<xsl:output method="text"/>
<xsl:template match="/">
   Customer First Name : <xsl:value-of
                             select="CUSTOMER/CUSTOMERNAME/FIRSTNAME"/>
  </xsl:template>
</xsl:stylesheet>
```

were to be merged with customerAddress.xml, shown previously in this chapter, it would produce the output:

```
Customer First Name :  Jeff
```

You can limit which part of an XML document you want by providing more path information in your `match` attribute. In the XSLT stylesheet below, all queries for within the XML document will begin at the `<HEADER>` element of the XML document.

```
<?xml version="1.0" encoding="UTF-8"?>
<xsl:stylesheet version="1.0"  xmlns:xsl="http://www.w3.org/1999/XSL/Transform">
<xsl:output method="text"/>
<xsl:template match="/CUSTOMER/CUSTOMERNAME">
   Customer First Name : <xsl:value-of select="FIRSTNAME"/>
  </xsl:template>
</xsl:stylesheet>
```

Changing the match attribute to begin searching at the `<CUSTOMER></CUSTOMER>` element of the XML document also means that the `<xsl:value-of></xsl:value-of>` tag's `select` attribute has to be changed. Since the `match` attribute has been changed from `"/"` to `"/CUSTOMER/CUSTOMERNAME"` the `select` attribute in the above XSLT no longer has to include the entire path for the `<FIRSTNAME></FIRSTNAME>` element.

Common Problems with XPath Queries in XSLT

There are two common problems to watch for when learning XPath for the first time. These can be very frustrating and can often result in several hours of intense debugging before you realize what is wrong. The first is the `<xsl:value-of></xsl:value-of>` tag. This will retrieve the value of the first element encountered in the XML document that matches the query string, ignoring all other elements. The template will control the scope of where the query searches the XML document. This means that:

```
<xsl:value-of select="CUSTOMER/CUSTOMERNAME/FIRSTNAME"/>
```

when run against a `customerAddress.xml` file containing multiple customer records:

```
<CUSTOMER customerid = "109">
  <CUSTOMERNAME>
    <FIRSTNAME>Jeff</FIRSTNAME>
    <LASTNAME>Dooley</LASTNAME>
  </CUSTOMERNAME>
  <ADDRESS>
    ...
  </ADDRESS>
</CUSTOMER>
<CUSTOMER customerid = "110">
  <CUSTOMERNAME>
    <FIRSTNAME>Anna</FIRSTNAME>
    <LASTNAME>Woolston</LASTNAME>
  </CUSTOMERNAME>
  <ADDRESS>
    ...
  </ADDRESS>
</CUSTOMER>
```

will retrieve only the first `<FIRSTNAME></FIRSTNAME>` tag's value. The `<FIRSTNAME></FIRSTNAME>` tag's value, `Anna`, will not be returned. Retrieving multiple element values from an XML document will be discussed in the next section on using XSLT to loop through collections of elements within the XML document.

The second problem is misunderstanding how to build XPath query strings when the `"/"` pattern is used for the `<xsl:template></xsl:template>` tag's `match` attribute. Searching from the root element using `<xsl:template match="/">` does not require all of the queries to use the actual root element tag in the XPath query string. For example, using the following example will not give the expected results:

```
<xsl:template match="/">
<H1>
   <xsl:value-of
select="CUSTOMER/CUSTOMERNAME/FIRSTNAME"/>
</xsl:template>
```

The XPath query string shown above will not return the customer's first name from the `customerOrder.xml` document. The reason for this is because it is looking for a match within the `customerOrder.xml` file that matches the following XML document structure:

```
<CUSTOMER>
  <CUSTOMER>
         <CUSTOMERNAME>
           <FIRSTNAME>
           </FIRSTNAME>
         </CUSTOMERNAME>
  </CUSTOMER>
</CUSTOMER>
```

The proper query string to use is:

```
<xsl:template match="/">
<H1>
   <xsl:value-of
select="CUSTOMERNAME/FIRSTNAME"/>
</xsl:template>
```

When using "/" for the `match` attribute, the root element for the XML document is not included in any of the XPath query strings in the XSLT stylesheet. In the `customerOrder.xml` file, the root element is the `<CUSTOMER></CUSTOMER>` element.

This section is by no means meant to cover every single aspect of searching an XML document from within an XSLT stylesheet. It is a very basic introduction to what can be a very complex topic. At this point, you should be able to do the following:

- Build a simple XSLT stylesheet that will format data as HTML
- Use XPath, the `<xsl:template></xsl:template>` and the `<xsl:value-of></xsl:value-of>` tags to instruct an XSLT processor to pull data from an XML document and merge it with an XSLT stylesheet
- Use the Xalan XSLT command line tools to merge an XSLT stylesheet and XML document to produce an HTML document

Looping Through an XML Document

Almost any relational database application written will have to be able to support data with a one-to-many relationship. A customer order example is a perfect example of one these situations as an order may have one or more individual order lines.

All of the XPath query examples shown up to this point have been used to pull back a single data element, such as the customer's first name. The following question then arises, 'How does XSLT support looping through a set of data elements, like order lines?' XSLT supports this through a looping meta-tag called `<xsl:for-each></xsl:for-each>`.

The `<xsl:for-each></xsl:for-each>` tag has an attribute called `select`. This attribute is used to set an XPath query string that will search the `multicustomerOrder.xml` file for all of the elements underneath the `CUSTOMERORDERS` element. The XSLT processor will then loop through each of the `CUSTOMERORDERITEM` elements and process all XSLT instructions between the `<xsl:for-each></xsl:for-each>` tag.

An XSLT stylesheet can support nested `<xsl:for-each></xsl:for-each>` tags. For instance, the `customerOrders.xml` document could easily contain multiple customer orders retrieved from the Music Store database. To loop through each of these customer orders records from within an XSLT stylesheet requires the ability to nest `<xsl:for-each></xsl:for-each>`. The `multiOrderCustomer.xsl` stylesheet shown below demonstrates how to embed `<xsl:for-each></xsl:for-each>` tags:

```
<?xml version="1.0" encoding="UTF-8"?>
<xsl:stylesheet version="1.0"  xmlns:xsl="http://www.w3.org/1999/XSL/Transform">
<xsl:output method="html"/>
<xsl:template match="/">
  <HTML>
    <Title>Music On-line</Title>
    <BODY>
    <TABLE align="left">
       <TR>
         <TD>
           <H2>
             <IMG src="musicStore.gif"/>
              Music OnLine (The right tunez at the right place)
           </H2>
         </TD>
       </TR>
    </TABLE>
    <BR></BR>
```

This is where the outer `for-each` loop begins. It cycles through each order item, displaying them in an HTML table:

```
             <xsl:for-each select="CUSTOMERORDERS/CUSTOMERORDER">
                   <BR/><BR/><BR/><BR/><BR/><BR/><BR/><BR/><BR/><HR/>
                   <TABLE border="0" align="left">
                       <TR>
                        <TD align="left"><B>Customer Order Number:</B></TD>
```

```
            <TD align="left">
              <xsl:value-of select="@orderid"/>
            </TD>
          </TR>
          <TR>
            <TD align="left"><B>Customer Name:</B></TD>
             <TD align="left">
               <xsl:value-of select="HEADER/CUSTOMERFIRSTNAME"/> 
               <xsl:value-of select="HEADER/CUSTOMERLASTNAME"/>
             </TD>
          </TR>
          <TR>
            <TD align="left"><B>Address:</B></TD>
             <TD align="left">
               <xsl:value-of select="HEADER/SHIPTOADDRESS1"/>
             </TD>
          </TR>
          <TR>
            <TD align="left"></TD>
             <TD align="left">
               <xsl:value-of select="HEADER/SHIPTOCITY"/>,
               <xsl:value-of select="HEADER/SHIPTOSTATE"/> 
               <xsl:value-of select="HEADER/SHIPTOZIPCODE"/>
             </TD>
          </TR>
          <TR>
             <TD align="left"><B>Order Date:</B></TD>
             <TD align="left">
               <xsl:value-of select="HEADER/ORDERDATE"/>
             </TD>
          </TR>
          <TR>
             <TD align="left"><B>Order Status:</B></TD>
             <TD align="left">
               <xsl:value-of select="HEADER/ORDERSTATUS"/>
                <xsl:choose>
                  <xsl:when test="HEADER/ORDERSTATUS='Order Cancelled'">
                        
                    <FONT color="red" size="2">
***Warn the customer their order has been canceled
                    </FONT>
                </xsl:when>
                <xsl:when test="HEADER/ORDERSTATUS='Waiting for Backorder'">
                           
                        <FONT color="red" size="2">

***Tell the customer the back order will be cleared in 3-5 business days.
                        </FONT>
                    </xsl:when>
                    <xsl:otherwise>
                           
                        <FONT color="blue" size="2">

*** No additional information to provide
```

```
                        </FONT>
                    </xsl:otherwise>
               </xsl:choose>
               </TD>
          </TR>
     </TABLE>
     <BR></BR><BR></BR><BR></BR><BR></BR><BR></BR><BR></BR><BR></BR><BR></BR><BR>

     <TABLE border="1">
       <TBODY>
          <TR>
            <TD align="center" bgcolor="#C0C0C0"><B>Line #</B></TD>
            <TD align="center" bgcolor="#C0C0C0"><B>Product Description</B></TD>
            <TD align="center" bgcolor="#C0C0C0"><B>Quantity</B></TD>
            <TD align="center" bgcolor="#C0C0C0"><B>Price Per Item</B></TD>
          </TR>
```

This is where the inner `for-each` loop begins that cycles through each order item. The `<xsl:for-each></xsl:for-each>` tag instructs the XSLT processor to search for a set of nodes within an XML document and then loop through them. In our `multiCustomerOrder.xsl` stylesheet, the `<xsl:for-each></xsl:for-each>` tag is used to cycle through each of the order lines found within the `customerOrder.xml` file and print the results out in an HTML table:

```
                 <xsl:for-each select="CUSTOMERORDERITEMS/CUSTOMERORDERITEM">
                <TR>
                  <TD align="center">
                     <xsl:value-of select="@linenumber"/>
                  </TD>
                  <TD align="center">
                     <xsl:value-of select="PRODUCTDESCR"/>
                  </TD>
                  <TD align="center">
                     <xsl:value-of select="QUANTITY"/>
                  </TD>
                  <TD align="center">
                     <xsl:value-of select="PRICEPERITEM"/>
                  </TD>
                </TR>
                </xsl:for-each>
```

We've reached the end of the inner `for-each` loop which can be seen by the `</xsl:for-each>` tag.

```
                 <TR></TR>
                 <TR>
                         <TD>Total:</TD>
                         <TD></TD>
                         <TD></TD>
                         <TD align="center">
                                 <xsl:value-of
   select="sum(CUSTOMERORDERITEMS/CUSTOMERORDERITEM/PRICEPERITEM)"/>
```

```
                    </TD>
                </TR>
                </TBODY>
            </TABLE>
                    <xsl:if test  =
"sum(CUSTOMERORDERITEMS/CUSTOMERORDERITEM/PRICEPERITEM) &gt; 50">
                    <FONT size="4" color="blue">
                        <BR/>
                            ** Elite Music Member
                    </FONT>
                </xsl:if>
            </xsl:for-each>
```

The </xsl:for-each> tag here denotes the end of the outer loop.

```
            <BR></BR>
    </BODY>
  </HTML>
  </xsl:template>
</xsl:stylesheet>
```

You will have seen a lot of processing elements in the above multiCustomerOrder.xsl style sheet, such as <xsl:choose>, <xsl:if>, and so on. We'll now go on to examine some of them.

Applying Conditional Logic within XSLT

Any modern programming language provides support for conditional logic. Conditional logic allows a piece of code to determine if a condition is True or False and act according to that outcome. Conditional logic in most programming languages is expressed in terms of IF...THEN or IF...THEN...ELSE statements.

XSL provides conditional logic through two different xsl tags; <xsl:if></xsl:if> and <xsl:choose></xsl:choose>. While the two tags are both used for conditional logic, they are slightly different. The multiCustomerOrder.xsl stylesheet includes examples of the <xsl:if></xsl:if> and <xsl:choose></xsl:choose> tags.

Let's take a look at the two different conditional tags and see how they work.

Try It Out – <xsl:if>

The <xsl:if></xsl:if> tag is the equivalent of an IF...THEN statement. This means that there can only be one outcome to an expression evaluated with the <xsl:if></xsl:if> tag.

For example, our multiCustomerOrder.xsl stylesheet prints a special message on the page for all orders over $50, by using this code:

```
<xsl:if test="sum(CUSTOMERORDERITEMS/CUSTOMERORDERITEM/PRICEPERITEM) &gt; 50">
   <FONT size="4" color="blue">
            <BR/>
      ** Elite Music Member
   </FONT>
```

```
</xsl:if>
```

If the `multiCustomerOrder.xsl` file is merged with the `multiCustomerOrder.xml`, by typing this command line:

```
> transformit multiCustomerOrder.xml multiCustomerOrder.xsl
              multiCustomerOrder.html
```

The output looks like this:

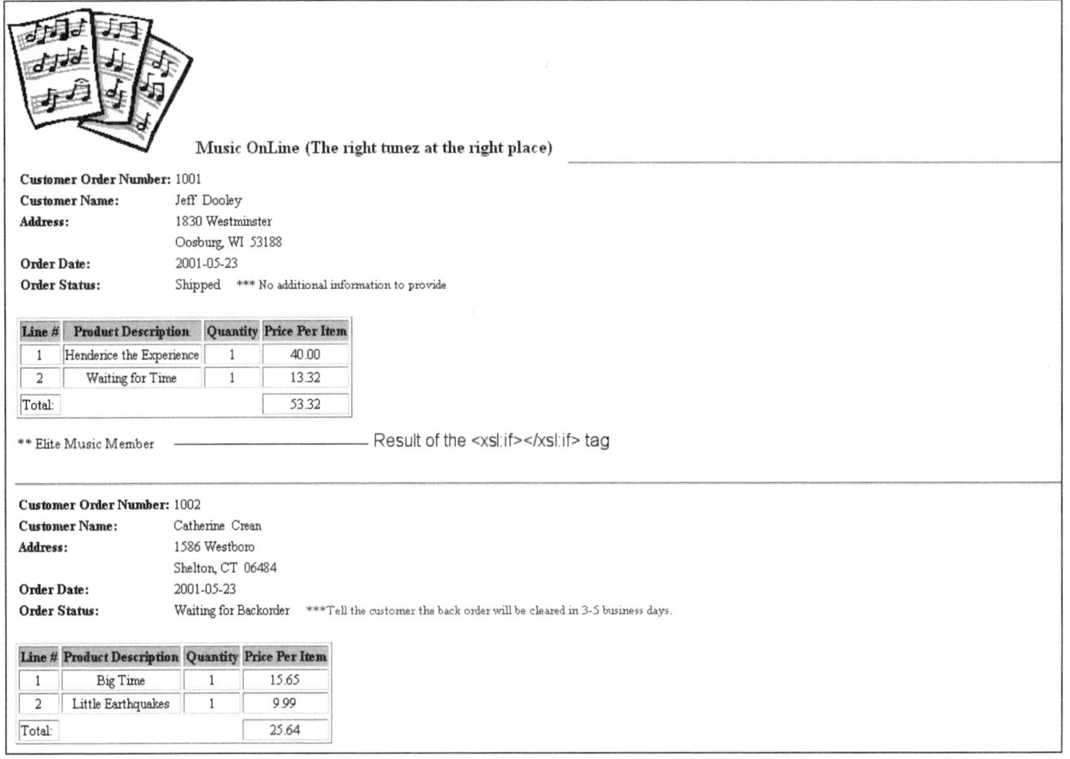

Music OnLine (The right tunez at the right place)

Customer Order Number: 1001
Customer Name: Jeff Dooley
Address: 1830 Westminster
Oosburg, WI 53188
Order Date: 2001-05-23
Order Status: Shipped *** No additional information to provide

Line #	Product Description	Quantity	Price Per Item
1	Henderice the Experience	1	40.00
2	Waiting for Time	1	13.32
Total:			53.32

** Elite Music Member — Result of the <xsl:if></xsl:if> tag

Customer Order Number: 1002
Customer Name: Catherine Crean
Address: 1586 Westboro
Shelton, CT 06484
Order Date: 2001-05-23
Order Status: Waiting for Backorder ***Tell the customer the back order will be cleared in 3-5 business days.

Line #	Product Description	Quantity	Price Per Item
1	Big Time	1	15.65
2	Little Earthquakes	1	9.99
Total:			25.64

How It Works

Both of the customer orders found in the `multiCustomerOrder.xml` file were evaluated. However, only the first order had line items that totaled to over $50 dollars. The second order did not meet the condition set forth in the `<xsl:if></xsl:if>` tag and thus did not have the additional message attached to it.

The `<xsl:if></xsl:if>` tag does not allow you to build the `IF...THEN...ELSE` structure found in most programming languages. If you want to provide an `ELSE` situation or check an XML document for more then one condition you must use the `<xsl:choose></xsl:choose>` tag.

Using XSLT

As we saw at the end of the last chapter, XML is all very well for wrapping up data in a readily portable format, but it does have limitations. The answer to many of XML's limitations is **XSL**, the e**X**tensible **S**tylesheet **L**anguage. XSL is a way of defining a mapping from one XML document to another XML document. As we'll see in this chapter, the process isn't as hideously complicated as it might at first seem.

A full introduction to XSL would (and indeed, does) take a whole book to do it justice. For the purposes of this chapter, we're going to take you on a whirlwind tour of the very basics of XSL, focusing on XSLT (XSL Transformations, the process of transforming an XML document). We'll show you just enough to whet your appetite for more (hopefully), and also to demonstrate some of the power of XSLT.

In this chapter, we will be covering the following topics:

- An introduction to XSLT
- Examples of different XSLT structures and constructs. Some of the topics that will be covered include:
  - How to search for data within an XML document using XSLT
  - How to loop through different parts of an XML document using XSLT
  - Using conditional logic (`IF...THEN`) within XSLT to provide different types of presentation based on the data being returned
- The use of Java and the Apache Xalan parser to perform the transformation of XSLT/XML to some other format
- Examples of how to use XSLT to build HTML pages

> **If you are unfamiliar with XML it is highly recommended you read the previous chapter and the XML primer, provided as Appendix C, before diving into the material. Much of the material presented here relies on information covered in the previous chapter.**

Music OnLine (The right tunez at the right place)

Customer Order Number: 1001
Customer Name: Jeff Dooley
Address: 1830 Westminster
Oosburg, WI 53188
Order Date: 2001-05-23
Order Status: Shipped *** No additional information to provide

Line #	Product Description	Quantity	Price Per Item
1	Henderice the Experience	1	40.00
2	Waiting for Time	1	13.32
Total:			53.32

** Elite Music Member

Customer Order Number: 1002
Customer Name: Catherine Crean
Address: 1586 Westboro
Shelton, CT 06484
Order Date: 2001-05-23
Order Status: Waiting for Backorder ***Tell the customer the back order will be cleared in 3-5 business days.

Result of the <xsl:choose></xsl:choose> tag

Line #	Product Description	Quantity	Price Per Item
1	Big Time	1	15.65
2	Little Earthquakes	1	9.99
Total:			25.64

How it Works

Embedded inside the `<xsl:choose></xsl:choose>` tags are two additional tags, `<xsl:when></xsl:when>` and `<xsl:otherwise></xsl:otherwise>`. The `<xsl:when></xsl:when>` tag is checking to see if the condition being examined is `True`. In our `multiCustomerOrder.xsl` stylesheet, the `<xsl:choose></xsl:choose>` tags are being used to check a customer's order status. If the order status for the customer is either '`Order Cancelled`' or '`Waiting for Back Order`', then a red message containing additional text information is placed next to the order status.

The `<xsl:otherwise><xsl:/otherwise>` tag is used to tell the XSLT processor what actions should take place if none of the `<xsl:when></xsl:when>` conditions are met within the `<xsl:choose></xsl:choose>` tags. In the XSLT fragment shown above, if the order status conditions are neither '`Order Cancelled`', or '`Waiting for Back Order`' then a text message indicating that there is no additional information is displayed in blue.

The `<xsl:if></xsl:if>` and `<xsl:choose></xsl:choose>` tags provide a powerful set of tools for controlling how data is going to be formatted and presented. A developer using these conditional logic tags can customize their web pages based upon the data being retrieved. This means that one end user's experience on a web site built using XSLT can be completely different from another user's.

Practical XSLT Applications

So far, we have dissected the different parts of the `multiCustomerOrder.xsl` stylesheet. While this has been an interesting exercise, it does not show how we can use XSLT for any practical applications.

This part of the chapter is going to demonstrate how to use XSL to build a simple web page. This web page will retrieve a summarized list of all of the customer orders within the music record database and present it back to the end user as HTML. XSLT is not the only technology used to build this page; this example will also use these other technologies:

- JavaServer Pages (JSP) – When the end user makes a request for the web page, it will be processed by a simple JSP.
- Cloudscape – Our Music Store database used in this chapter will be running on the Cloudscape database platform.
- Java and JDBC – We are going to build a Java class to retrieve customer order data from the Music Store database. This class will also build an XML document containing customer order data. This XML document will be merged with a XSLT stylesheet to produce the HTML the end user will see.
- The Xalan Java APIs – Our example will show how to programmatically transform our XSLT documents using Xalan Java's APIs.

The Customer Order Summary Screen

The web page we are going to build is called the customer order summary page. This screen will list of all of the customer orders within the database as a table containing a row for each customer order. Each row will contain the following information:

- Customer order number
- Customer name
- Total order amount in dollars

The customer order number will be a hyperlink that allows the customer to bring up the detail information for that order.

This customer order summary screen will be built using a combination of JSP, Java, XSL, and XML. When this screen is requested by the end user, the following actions take place:

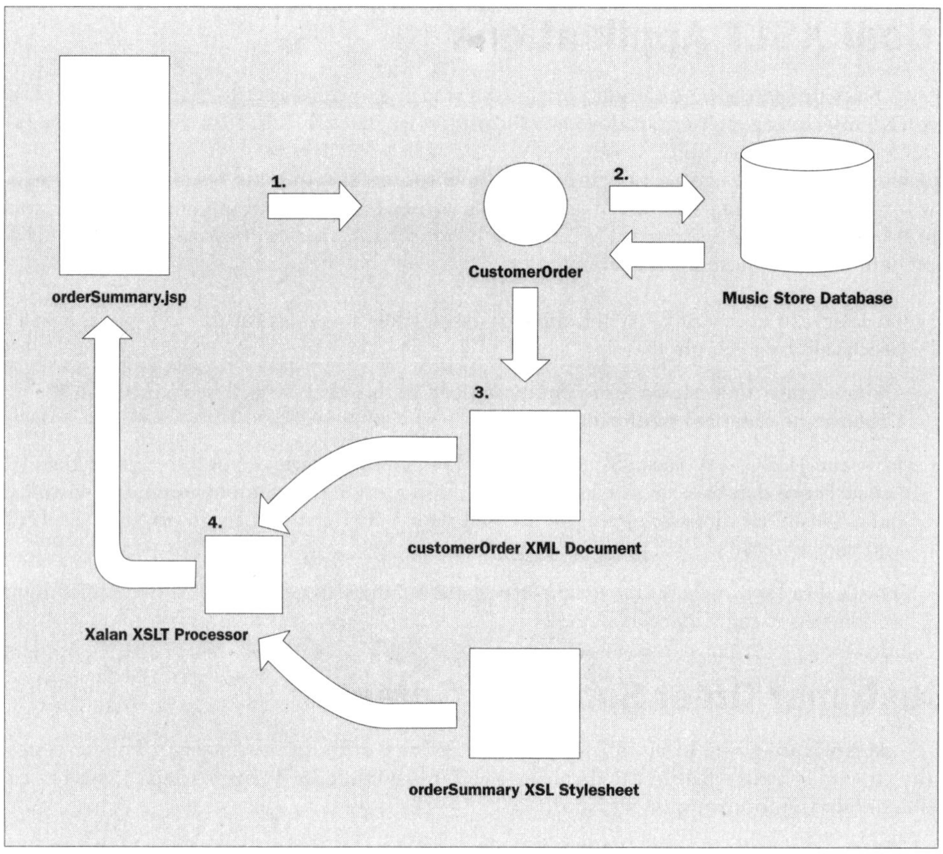

Let's walk through the diagram step-by-step:

1. The `orderSummary.jsp` page has been requested by the end user. The first thing the `orderSummary.jsp` page does is to create an instance of the `CustomerOrder` class.

2. The `CustomerOrder` class will use JDBC to execute a SQL statement against the music record database and retrieve all of the customer orders within the database/

3. Once a JDBC `ResultSet` has been retrieved from the music record database, the `CustomerOrder` class will create an XML document containing all of the customer orders. The XML document created will be the same structure as the `customerOrder.xml` file used in earlier examples.

4. After the XML document containing all of the customer orders has been created, it will be returned back to the `orderSummary.jsp` page. The `orderSummary.jsp` page will then transform the returned XML document and the `orderSummary.xsl` stylesheet through the Xalan processor to generate HTML, which will be written out to the end user.

Let's explore the `orderSummary.jsp`, `CustomerOrder.java`, and `orderSummary.xsl` files in more detail.

OrderSummary.jsp

The `orderSummary.jsp` file is a simple piece of JSP code that creates a `CustomerOrder` class, retrieves all of the customer order information from the database as an XML document, and then using XSLT produces an HTML table containing a summarized view of all of the customer records in the application. The `orderSummary.jsp` page will be hosted by the Apache Tomcat server. The Tomcat server is an open source web server used to host servlet and JSP pages and is available for download from http://jakarta.apache.org/tomcat/index.html. Setting up Tomcat will be covered in Appendix B.

The code for this Try It Out can be found in the code download for this chapter, available from http://www.wrox.com/. This example is ready packaged in a folder called `begjdb` that needs to be placed in your Tomcat `webapps` directory so that it will look something like this:

```
C:\jakarta-tomcat-3.2.2\webapps\
                                   \begjdb\etc\orderSummary.xsl
                                           \WEB-INF\web.xml
                                                   \classes\CustomerOrder.class
                                            \musicStore.gif
                                            \orderSummary.jsp
```

To get this example to work you will need to place `xalan.jar`, `xerces.jar` and `cloudpath.jar` in your classpath and also in your Tomcat `lib` directory. Due to some XML parsers not supporting SAX 2 you may also need to remove `jaxp.jar`, `parser.jar` and `xt.jar` from your classpath.

Try It Out – Creating OrderSummary.jsp

The `orderSummary.jsp` code is a very simple JSP page. It will use the `CustomerOrder` class to retrieve an XML document containing customer order information, and then transform it with the Xalan processor using the `orderSummary.xsl` stylesheet. The `orderSummary.jsp` file is shown below:

```
<%@page import="java.util.*"%>
<%@page import="java.io.*"%>
<%@page import="org.w3c.dom.*"%>
<%@page import="javax.xml.transform.*"%>
<%@page import="javax.xml.transform.stream.StreamResult"%>
<%@page import="javax.xml.transform.stream.StreamSource"%>
<%@page import="org.apache.xalan.processor.*"%>
<%@page import="javax.xml.transform.dom.DOMSource"%>


<%
    String xslFileName =
       new String("file:///k://JBoss-2.2.2_Tomcat-
3.2.2//tomcat//webapps//begjdb//etc//orderSummary.xsl");

      try{
        /*Step 1 Getting a Transformation Factory*/
       TransformerFactory tFactory = new TransformerFactoryImpl();

        /*Step 2 Getting a transformer and passing in the XSL file name*/
        Transformer transformer =
           tFactory.newTransformer(new StreamSource(xslFileName));
```

```
        /*Step 3 Creating the customer order object and retrieving data*/
        CustomerOrder   customerOrder = new CustomerOrder();

        /*Step 4 Getting an XML document using the customer order class*/
        Document xmlCustomerDoc = customerOrder.retrieveCustomerOrders();

        /*Loading the XML document return from the customerOrder call into
          a DOMSource class
        */
        DOMSource domSource = new DOMSource(xmlCustomerDoc);

        /*Step 5 Perform the transformation of XML/XSL to HTML*/
        transformer.transform(domSource, new StreamResult(out));

      }
      catch(Exception e){
        out.write(e.toString());
      }
  %>
```

The previous XSLT examples in this chapter produced their HTML output by using the Xalan command line interface for merging the XSLT stylesheet and XML document together. The `orderSummary.jsp` page, uses the Xalan Java APIs to do the same thing. Using the Xalan API for merging XSLT and XML documents together is a very straightforward process.

How It Works

The Xalan XSLT processor is using the TraX (Transformation API for XML) to carry out the transformation of XSLT and XML to another format. This API enables a developer to plug in different XML and XSLT processors without having to change code. However, for the purposes of this example we will not be using this functionality and instead use the default XML parser and XSLT processor, Xerces and Xalan respectively, used by the TraX API.

The first step in using the Xalan API is to create a `Transformer` object. This object is created by using the `TransformerFactoryImpl` class to create the `Transformer` on your behalf:

```
/*Step 1 Getting a Transformation Factory*/
TransformerFactory tFactory = new TransformerFactoryImpl();

/*Step 2 Getting a transformer and passing in the XSL file name*/
Transformer transformer =
   tFactory.newTransformer(new StreamSource(xslFileName));
```

The `TranformerFactory` returns a `Transformer` object. The Xalan XSLT processor is built so that XML parsers other than the Apache Xerces XML parser can be used with it. After a `Transformer` class has been created, the JSP page is going to instantiate a `CustomerOrder` object and retrieve customer order data as an XML `Document` object:

```
/*Step 3 Creating the customer order object and retrieving data*/
CustomerOrder     customerOrder = new CustomerOrder();
```

```
/*Step 4 Getting an XML document using the customer order class*/
Document xmlCustomerDoc = customerOrder.retrieveCustomerOrders();
```

Don't worry about the details of the `customerOrder` class right now. This class will be examined in the next section. The `customerOrder` class uses JDBC to retrieve customer order records from the music record database and build an XML `Document` object containing these records.

After a `Document` object is returned, a `DOMSource` called `domSource` will be instantiated. The `domSource` object is used to hold the `Document` object (`xmlCustomerDoc`) returned by the `Customer` object. To instantiate the `DOMSource` object, the `xmlCustomerDoc` object is passed into its constructor:

```
/*Loading the XML document return from the customerOrder call into
  a DOMSource class
*/
DOMSource domSource = new DOMSource(xmlCustomerDoc);
```

At this point we are ready to perform the transformation. The XSLT stylesheet has been loaded into the transformer object and the XML document containing the customer order information has been used to create a `DOMSource` object. The `DOMSource` object is used to hold the XML document as a hierarchical tree in memory. To actually carry out the transformation of XSLT and XML to HTML the JSP calls the transform method of the transformer class:

```
/*Step 5 Perform the transformation of XML/XSL to HTML*/
transformer.transform(domSource, new StreamResult(out));
```

The `StreamResult` object is used by the transformer to write out the HTML results of the transformation. In the call above, the results of the transformation are written out to the JSP page via the JSP's `out` variable. The `out` parameter passed into the `StreamResult` constructor is an implicit variable that is used by the JSP to write information back to the end user.

Let's now walk through the `CustomerOrder.java` file and look at how the XML `Document`, called `xmlCustomerDoc`, is built.

CustomerOrder.java

The `CustomerOrder.java` class was written to help abstract away all of the data-retrieval and XML document-building code out of the `orderSummary.jsp` page.

Try It Out – Creating the Data retrieval Class

The `CustomerOrder.java` code is presented below:

```
import java.sql.*;                    /*JDBC Classes              */
import COM.cloudscape.core.*;         /*Cloudscape JDBC classes   */
import org.w3c.dom.*;                 /*W3C Interfaces            */
import org.apache.xerces.dom.*;       /*Xerces DOM Classes        */
import org.apache.xml.serialize.*;    /*Xerces serializer         */
import java.io.*;                     /*Java io classes for file
                                        reading/writing*/
```

```
public class CustomerOrder {

   public static final String JDBCURL="jdbc:cloudscape:m:/BegJDBMusic/Wrox4370.db";
   public static final String JDBCDRIVER="COM.cloudscape.core.JDBCDriver";
   public static final String OUTPUTFILE="c://temp//customerOrder.xml";
   public StringBuffer sql = new StringBuffer();
```

The `CustomerOrder()` constructor has only one task. To build the SQL statement that will be used to retrieve the customer order data from the Cloudscape database.

```
   public CustomerOrder() {
     sql.append("SELECT                                                     ");
     sql.append("   CustomerOrders.orderId,                                 ");
     sql.append("   Customers.customerFirstName,                            ");
     sql.append("   Customers.customerLastName,                             ");
     sql.append("   CustomerOrderItems.linenumber,                          ");
     sql.append("   CustomerOrderItems.quantity,                            ");
     sql.append("   CustomerOrderItems.pricePerItem,                        ");
     sql.append("   Recordings.recordingtitle                               ");
     sql.append("FROM                                                       ");
     sql.append("   CustomerOrders,                                         ");
     sql.append("   CustomerOrderItems,                                     ");
     sql.append("   Customers,                                              ");
     sql.append("   OrderStatuses,                                          ");
     sql.append("   PostalCodes,                                            ");
     sql.append("   Recordings                                              ");
     sql.append("WHERE                                                      ");
     sql.append("   CustomerOrders.orderId=CustomerOrderItems.orderId       ");
     sql.append("AND                                                        ");
     sql.append("   CustomerOrders.customerId = Customers.customerId        ");
     sql.append("AND                                                        ");
     sql.append("   CustomerOrders.shipToPostalCode =                       ");
     sql.append("   PostalCodes.postalCode                                  ");
     sql.append("AND                                                        ");
     sql.append("   CustomerOrders.OrderStatusId =                          ");
     sql.append("   OrderStatuses.OrderStatusId                             ");
     sql.append("AND                                                        ");
     sql.append("   CustomerOrderItems.productId =                          ");
     sql.append("   Recordings.recordingId                                 ");
     sql.append("ORDER BY                                                  ");
     sql.append("   CustomerOrders.orderId          asc,                   ");
     sql.append("   CustomerOrderItems.lineNumber asc                      ");
}
```

The `retrieveCustomerOrders()` method will retrieve all of the customer order data from our Music Store database. It will then take the returned resultset, build an XML document out of it, and return it back to the method that called it.

```
   public Document retrieveCustomerOrders(){
     Document xmlDoc = null;
     try{
       /*Retrieves the resultset containing all of the customer order data.*/
```

```
      ResultSet customerOrderRS = retrieveCustomerOrderRS();

      /*
       Builds the XML document that will be returned to whoever called this
       method.
      */
      xmlDoc = buildCustomerOrderXML(customerOrderRS);

      /*Creates a file that the XML file will be written to*/
      File outputFile = new File(OUTPUTFILE);

      /*Dumps the output to that file*/
      printDOM(xmlDoc, outputFile);

      /*Closes the ResultSet*/
      customerOrderRS.close();
    }
    catch(Exception e){System.out.println(e.toString());}

      return xmlDoc;
  }
```

This method will connect to the cloudscape database and execute the SQL query defined in the constructor:

```
  private ResultSet retrieveCustomerOrderRS(){
    ResultSet customerOrderRS = null;
    try{
      /*Making my JDBC Connection to Cloudscape*/
      Class.forName(JDBCDRIVER).newInstance();
      Connection conn= DriverManager.getConnection(JDBCURL);

      /*Retrieve my customer order data from the database*/
      Statement statement = conn.createStatement();
      customerOrderRS = statement.executeQuery(sql.toString());
    }
    catch(Exception e){
      System.out.println("Error occurred in retrieveCustomerOrderRS: " +
           e.toString());
    }
    return customerOrderRS;
  }
```

The `buildCustomerOrderXML()` method will build an XML document containing customer order information:

```
  private Document buildCustomerOrderXML(ResultSet _customerOrderRS)
    throws Exception{
    Document xmlDoc= new DocumentImpl();

    /*Creating the document root*/
    Element documentRoot      = xmlDoc.createElement("CUSTOMERORDERS");
```

```
    Element customerOrder    = xmlDoc.createElement("CUSTOMERORDER");

    xmlDoc.appendChild(documentRoot);

    /*Declaring the different Elements found within a customer record*/
    Element header                  = null;
    Element customerOrderItems      = null;
    Element customerOrderItem       = null;

    /*Initializing customer Order id holders*/
    String currentCustomerOrderId = "";
    String holderCustomerOrderId  = "";


    /*Cycling through all of the records within the resultset*/
    while (_customerOrderRS.next()){

      /*Getting the customer id of the current record being looked at*/
      currentCustomerOrderId = _customerOrderRS.getString("orderId");
      if (!(currentCustomerOrderId.equals(holderCustomerOrderId))){

        holderCustomerOrderId = new String(currentCustomerOrderId);
```

This is where we initialize the different elements found within a customer order record:

```
        header                = xmlDoc.createElement("HEADER");
        customerOrderItems    = xmlDoc.createElement("CUSTOMERORDERITEMS");
        customerOrder         = xmlDoc.createElement("CUSTOMERORDER");

        /*Setting up my primary key for my customer order*/
        customerOrder.setAttribute("orderid", holderCustomerOrderId);

        /*Adding my different elements to the order header*/
        header.appendChild(buildDBElement(xmlDoc, "CUSTOMERFIRSTNAME",
          _customerOrderRS.getString("customerFirstName")));
        header.appendChild(buildDBElement(xmlDoc, "CUSTOMERLASTNAME",
          _customerOrderRS.getString("customerLastName")));

        /*Appending my lines element*/
        customerOrder.appendChild(header);
        customerOrder.appendChild(customerOrderItems);
      }

      customerOrderItem = xmlDoc.createElement("CUSTOMERORDERITEM");
      customerOrderItem.setAttribute("linenumber",
        _customerOrderRS.getString("lineNumber"));
      customerOrderItem.appendChild(buildDBElement(xmlDoc,"PRODUCTDESCR",
        _customerOrderRS.getString("recordingTitle")));

      Double lineItemQuantity =
        new Double(_customerOrderRS.getString("quantity"));
      Double pricePerItem     =
        new Double(_customerOrderRS.getString("pricePerItem"));
```

```
        Double lineItemPrice     =
        new Double(lineItemQuantity.doubleValue()*pricePerItem.doubleValue());

        customerOrderItem.appendChild(
          buildDBElement(xmlDoc,"LINEITEMPRICE", lineItemPrice.toString()));

        /*Appending everything together*/
        customerOrderItems.appendChild(customerOrderItem);
        customerOrderItem = xmlDoc.createElement("CUSTOMERORDERITEM");

        customerOrder.appendChild(customerOrderItems);
        documentRoot.appendChild(customerOrder);
      }

      return xmlDoc;
    }
```

The `printDOM()` method will take the XML document and the `File` object passed into the method and dump its contents out to a file. This is only here for debugging purposes and should not be used in production code.

```
    private static void printDOM(Document _xmlDoc, File _outputFile)
      throws Exception{
       OutputFormat     outputFormat   = new OutputFormat("XML", "UTF-8", true);
       FileWriter       fileWriter     = new FileWriter(_outputFile);

       XMLSerializer    xmlSerializer = new XMLSerializer( fileWriter,
                                                           outputFormat );
       xmlSerializer.asDOMSerializer();

       xmlSerializer.serialize( _xmlDoc.getDocumentElement() );
    }
```

The `buildDBElement` will add a text node onto an element and return it back to the method that calls it. This is simply a helper method that makes it easier to add elements to another element.

```
    private static Element buildDBElement(Document _xmlDoc,
                                          String _elementName,
                                          String _elementValue)
      throws Exception{

      Element item      = _xmlDoc.createElement(_elementName);
      item.appendChild( _xmlDoc.createTextNode(_elementValue));
      return item;
    }
  }
```

How It Works

This is a lot of code to try to process all at once, which is why we've broken it into chunks. Let's take a look at the `retrieveCustomerOrders()` method to get a feel for what is going on. When the `retrieveCustomerOrders()` method is called, the first action that is performed is to retrieve a `ResultSet` object containing all of the customer orders in the Music Store database:

```
/*Retrieves the resultset containing all of the customer order data.*/
ResultSet customerOrderRS = retrieveCustomerOrderRS();
```

The `retrieveCustomerOrderRS()` method connects to our Cloudscape music store database and executes the SQL query defined in the class-level variable `sql`. After the `retrieveCustomerOrderRS()` method has retrieved the data, it will return it back to the `retrieveCustomerOrders()` method. This `ResultSet` object is then passed into the `buildCustomerOrderXML()` method:

```
/*
  Builds the XML document that will be returned to whoever called this
  method.
*/
xmlDoc = buildCustomerOrderXML(customerOrderRS);
```

The `buildCustomerOrder()` method takes the `ResultSet` object, called `customerOrderRS`, and builds an XML document out of the `resultset`. The details of how the XML document is built from the `ResultSet` object are covered in detail in the previous chapter.

The XML document created from the `buildCustomerOrderXML()` method looks like this:

```
<?xml version="1.0" encoding="UTF-8"?>
<CUSTOMERORDERS>
   <CUSTOMERORDER orderid="1001">
      <HEADER>
         <CUSTOMERFIRSTNAME>Catherine</CUSTOMERFIRSTNAME>
         <CUSTOMERLASTNAME>Crean</CUSTOMERLASTNAME>
      </HEADER>
      <CUSTOMERORDERITEMS>
         <CUSTOMERORDERITEM linenumber="1">
            <PRODUCTDESCR>Big Time</PRODUCTDESCR>
            <LINEITEMPRICE>15.65</LINEITEMPRICE>
         </CUSTOMERORDERITEM>
         <CUSTOMERORDERITEM linenumber="2">
            <PRODUCTDESCR>Little Earthquakes</PRODUCTDESCR>
            <LINEITEMPRICE>9.99</LINEITEMPRICE>
         </CUSTOMERORDERITEM>
      </CUSTOMERORDERITEMS>a
   </CUSTOMERORDER>
   <CUSTOMERORDER orderid="1003">
      <HEADER>
         <CUSTOMERFIRSTNAME>Steve</CUSTOMERFIRSTNAME>
         <CUSTOMERLASTNAME>Davis</CUSTOMERLASTNAME>
      </HEADER>
      <CUSTOMERORDERITEMS>
         <CUSTOMERORDERITEM linenumber="1">
```

```
            <PRODUCTDESCR>Little Earthquakes</PRODUCTDESCR>
            <LINEITEMPRICE>9.99</LINEITEMPRICE>
         </CUSTOMERORDERITEM>
      </CUSTOMERORDERITEMS>
   </CUSTOMERORDER>
</CUSTOMERORDERS>
```

This XML document is returned to the `orderSummary.jsp` page. The `orderSummary.jsp` page merges this XML document with `orderSummary.xsl` stylesheet.

orderSummary.xsl

The `orderSummary.xsl` file is a very straightforward XSLT file based on earlier examples in this chapter. There is nothing new in the `orderSummary.xsl` file. All of the XSLT used here has been explained in earlier examples.

Try It Out – Building the XSLT Stylesheet

The `orderSummary.xsl` file looks like this:

```
<?xml version="1.0" encoding="UTF-8"?>
<xsl:stylesheet version="1.0"  xmlns:xsl="http://www.w3.org/1999/XSL/Transform">
<xsl:output method="html"/>
<xsl:template match="/">
  <HTML>
    <Title>Music On-line</Title>
    <BODY>
    <TABLE align="left">
       <TR>
         <TD><H2><IMG src="musicStore.gif"/>Music OnLine (The right tunez at the
right place)</H2></TD>
       </TR>
    </TABLE>
    <BR/><BR/><BR/><BR/><BR/><BR/><BR/><BR/><BR/><HR/>

      <H3>Customer Order Summary:</H3>
      <TABLE border="1">
              <TBODY>
                  <TR>
                   <TD align="center" bgcolor="#C0C0C0">
         <B>Order Number</B>
        </TD>
                   <TD align="center" bgcolor="#C0C0C0">
        <B>Customer Name</B>
        </TD>
                   <TD align="center" bgcolor="#C0C0C0">
        <B>Total Dollar Amount</B>
        </TD>
                  </TR>
                    <xsl:for-each select="CUSTOMERORDERS/CUSTOMERORDER">
                          <TR>
                             <TD align="center">
                               <a>
```

```
                                    <xsl:attribute name="href">
                                       orderDetail.jsp&amp;orderNumber=
                                       <xsl:value-of select="@orderid"/>
                                    </xsl:attribute>
                                    <xsl:value-of select="@orderid"/>
                                  </a>
                                </TD>
                                <TD align="center">
                                   <xsl:value-of
                                      select="HEADER/CUSTOMERFIRSTNAME"/> 
                                   <xsl:value-of
                                      select="HEADER/CUSTOMERLASTNAME"/>
                                </TD>
                                <TD align="center">
                    $<xsl:value-of select="
                    "sum(CUSTOMERORDERITEMS/CUSTOMERORDERITEM/LINEITEMPRICE)"/>
                                </TD>
                             </TR>
                        </xsl:for-each>
               </TBODY>
          </TABLE>
          <BR></BR>

           <P>
               <FONT size="3">
                 Welcome to music on-line, the world's leading on-line music
                 record database. <BR/>
                 Please click on the hyperlink
                above to select the details of a specific customer order.
              </FONT>
           </P>
        </BODY>
     </HTML>
     </xsl:template>
  </xsl:stylesheet>
```

How It Works

The `orderSummary.xsl` stylesheet used in the case study loops through each of the customer orders within the XML document returned by the `customerOrder.retrieveCustomerOrder()` method call:

```
<xsl:for-each select="CUSTOMERORDERS/CUSTOMERORDER">
        .
        .
        .
</xsl:for-each>
```

The `orderSummary.xsl` stylesheet takes each invoice found within the XML document and creates a line in an HTML table. There are three pieces of information within this table:

- The customer order number
- The customer's name
- The sum of all of the line items for that customer invoice

How the customer order number and the order totals are built is of particular interest.

The order number on an invoice with the table is a hyperlink. If you click on the link, it will take you to the `orderDetail.jsp` page. The `<xsl:attribute></xsl:attribute>` used in the `orderSummary.xsl` page is used to build the hypertext link to the `orderDetail.jsp` page:

```
<a>
  <xsl:attribute name="href">
     orderDetail.jsp&amp;orderNumber=
    <xsl:value-of select="@orderid"/>
  </xsl:attribute>
  <xsl:value-of select="@orderid"/>
</a>
```

The `<xsl:attribute></xsl:attribute>` sets an attribute for a particular tagged element. The XSLT snippet above is adding the `href` attribute to the anchor tag (`<a></a>`). When the `<xsl:attribute></xsl:attribute>` element for the above code is processed by the XSLT parser it produces the following output:

```
<a href="orderDetail.jsp&amp;orderNumber=1001">1001</a>
```

The second area of interest in the `orderSummary.xsl` stylesheet is how the total value of a customer order is calculated. The XML document returned by the `customerOrder.retrieveCustomerOrder()` method call does not contain a total dollar amount for an invoice. Instead, the total dollar amount for each invoice is calculated using the XSLT `sum` function:

```
<TD align="center">
  $<xsl:value-of select=
            "sum(CUSTOMERORDERITEMS/CUSTOMERORDERITEM/LINEITEMPRICE)"/>
</TD>
```

When the above line is processed in our example, it will calculate the sum for the price-per-item node and then produce the following HTML:

```
<TD align="center">$25.64</TD>
```

Once the directory structure is set up as described above and you have Tomcat running, point your web browser to:

http://localhost:8080/begjdb/orderSummary.jsp

and you should get the following page:

Music OnLine (The right tunez at the right place)

Customer Order Summary:

Order Number	Customer Name	Total Dollar Amount
1001	Catherine Crean	$25.64
1003	Steve Davis	$9.99

Welcome to music on-line, the world's leading on-line music record database.
Please click on the hyperlink above to select the details of a specific customer order.

XSLT – What's the Big Deal?

So, why all of this work just to produce the above web page? Why not write the screen using just JSP pages? It is definitely more complicated to develop and debug an application using XSLT than pounding the code out in JSP.

The answer has everything to do with the size and complexity of writing web-based applications. Very few applications consist of just one or two screens. A complex application can consist of over a hundred screens. Technology like JSP and Java Servlets often make it too easy to quickly write applications without long-term maintenance in mind. In particular, most developers will often fall into the trap of mixing their presentation logic (the code that defines what the end user sees) with their business logic (the code that defines how to carry out what the user wants).

XSLT allows the developer to write their presentation code and cleanly separate it from the business logic. This separation of the presentation and business logic has four benefits:

- The presentation of an application can be changed very quickly. By writing all of the presentation logic in XSLT, we can quickly give an application an entirely new look and feel without having to hack through presentation logic embedded within several dozen (hundred) pages of JSP or Java servlet code.
- An application written using XSLT can be quickly ported to multiple presentation platforms. By putting all of the presentation code within XSLT, an application can have its user interface very quickly rewritten to support such platforms as Personal Digital Assistants or even cellular phones.

- XSLT promotes business logic reuse. By separating the presentation logic from the business logic we can start reusing that code in other applications. One of the primary problems with early client-server development tools like Visual Basic or Powerbuilder is that these tools encouraged the developer to place all of their code within the user interface. This meant that the only reuse options many endusers had was through the time-honored tradition of cut and paste.
- XSLT is platform-independent. XSLT written on for use on another development platform, like Microsoft's .NET framework, can very easily be ported over to an application written in Java. This kind of flexibility and portability was unheard of only a few years ago.

XSLT is a very powerful tool for writing flexible and reusable applications. However, it is also easy to try to over-use XSLT. Many developers who discover the power and flexibility of XSLT too often embed too much logic into their XSLT stylesheets. Remember, XSLT is a tool for describing how data should be presented. A good XSLT stylesheet might have some simple logic in it to control presentation or offer different types of formatting, but some would say that's as far as it should go.

If you as a developer are finding that the XSLT stylesheet you are working on is becoming over-complicated or is carrying out complex business logic, take a step back. Examples of over-complicated stylesheets include:

- Heavily nested <xsl:if></xsl:if>, <xsl:choose></xsl:choose>, or <xsl:for-each></xsl:for-each> tags
- Complicated mathematical computations being performed in the stylesheet
- Over-use of XSLT functions within the stylesheet (such as `substring` functions)

The point here is to keep it simple. XSLT is only supposed to describe how data is to be formatted. When your code begins to look like it's doing too much programmatic work, It's probably a good idea to take a look at how you are writing the code. Push as much of your business logic as possible back out of the XSLT and into the more robust Java development language.

Summary

This chapter has provided a very brief overview of XSLT and how to use it to build data-driven web applications. This chapter should have provided you with enough information to be able to begin experimenting and building simple XSLT stylesheets for use within your Java applications. Some of the major topics covered in this chapter include:

- An introduction to what an XSLT stylesheet is
- How XSLT and XML are used to transform an XML document into another format (in this chapter, we looked at the transformation of XSLT and XML into an HTML document)
- How to use the Apache Xalan XSLT processor's command line interface to perform XSLT/XML transformation
- The basic syntax and programming constructs found within an XSLT stylesheet. The specific areas covered include:
  - How to search for data within an XML document using XSLT

    - How to loop through different parts of an XML document using XSLT
    - Using conditional logic (equivilant to `IF...THEN`) within XSL to provide different types of presentation based on the data being returned

- A simple example that demonstrates how to build a data-driven web page using the Xalan XSLT processor to programmatically perform the XSLT/XML transformation.

This chapter is not meant to be an in-depth coverage of the XSLT. Fortunately there are several books devoted exclusively to the topic of XSLT. By far the most comprehensive is Michael Kay's *XSLT Programmers Reference ISBN 1861005067*, from Wrox Press. For anyone interested in learning about XSLT in greater detail, this is a must-have book for your bookshelf.

This chapter and the previous chapter have both dealt with the topic of using Java and XML as part of an application. The next chapter is going to focus on using Java, JDBC, XML, and XSLT to build a framework for application development, shifting the focus from building a single application to building a foundation that multiple applications can be built upon.

akarta JAVA

The Model-View-Controller Framework

Developing an application is rarely a finite process. Project plans are developed showing the beginning and end points of the development process, but rarely reflect the amount of time and energy that is put into maintaining and extending an application after it is built. This lack of foresight of the project manager is often repeated and propagated by the application architect.

The application architect is the individual responsible for designing and building the framework in which the business logic of the application can be built and executed. If you were to use the analogy of the human body, an application's architecture is the equivalent of the skeleton, while the pieces of code that carry out the business tasks of the application are the equivalent of the body's internal organs.

Application architects are under considerable pressure to build the application as quickly as possible. This pressure often translates into the application architect taking a very tactical and often short-term approach to designing the application's core architecture. The application architect will focus on the immediate functional business requirements the application must support, while often ignoring the long-term technical and business ramifications of their design.

This short-term approach comes at a price. Most software is written to support and enhance a set of business processes within a company. An accounting package will support the managing of a company's financial transactions. A customer relationship management package will help an organization streamline the management and use of their customer data. However, the environment in which a company operates and does business in is constantly evolving. This means that their internal processes must be able to change quickly and as a result, the software that supports these processes must be extensible and adaptable.

Extensibility and adaptability must be designed from the beginning into an application. It must be done with the strategic foresight that businesses change and the software must change with them. However, as any experienced application architect will tell you:

> *Extensibility and adaptability are too often sacrificed upon the altar of expedience and compressed project delivery time lines.*

So what does this have to do with an introductory book on Java and database development? Most applications you will write will have to interact with a database of one kind or another. Database-driven applications are unique because of the relationship between how an application stores data within a database, how an application is designed to retrieve data, and the mechanisms used by the application to present data to an end-user all have profound impact on the long-term extensibility and adaptability of the application.

This chapter will look at the following topics and how they relate to the building of a solid application architecture:

- Common design problems involved with building an application
- The common types of application architectures
- How to use XSL (also referred to as XSLT), XML, and Java to build a simple, but elegant **Model-View-Controller framework** to build scalable and pluggable n-tier applications
- Examples of how you can use freely available open source projects to build your applications; some of the technologies covered will include:
  - The **Tomcat** JSP and servlet container
  - The **JBoss** application server
  - The **Xalan** XSLT processor and the **Xerces** XML parser

The material in this chapter relies heavily on concepts discussed in Chapter 20, *Exporting Relational Data to XML*, and Chapter 21, *Using XSLT*. If you have not read these chapters yet, please review them carefully before reading the material presented in this chapter.

The Flaws of a Typical Application

Before diving into the different types of application architectures, it is best to look at some of the common design flaws found in a typical application. Let's say you are a consultant asked to come into an organization's IT department, and audit how well the development groups build their applications. You have selected a small set of screens from the company's web-based Music OnLine application to audit. You have been asked to look at the overall design of the application, specifically focusing on the areas of:

- Application **extensibility** – Can additional functionality be added to the application without rewriting it?
- Application **reusability** – Can the logic in the application be generalized and reused in other applications?

The Music OnLine application is an e-commerce application that allows the customer to purchase music albums and CDs via the Internet. The application also provides the end-users the ability to search for information on a desired artist or album. Employees of the record store can also go into the application and look up and edit a customer's personal information.

The application you have chosen to audit is the customer maintenance application, specifically looking at the design and implementation of the customer address maintenance module. This module allows an end-user to edit and maintain a customer's address information. It consists of two web screens. The first screen, called the customer list screen, retrieves a list of all of the customers and their addresses. This web page uses JavaServer Pages and JDBC to retrieve a list of all of the customers and their addresses.

The JSP code for the customer address maintenance page is simple, but represents some common design flaws. The JDBC and SQL code closely resemble some of the examples seen in the previous two chapters. However, the similarity ends there, and it is recommended that you do not use the code example below as model for building JSP-database applications. The JSP example (`customerList.jsp`) pulled from the customer address maintenance application is shown below:

```
<%@page import ="java.sql.*"%>
<%@page import ="java.util.*"%>
<%@page import ="COM.cloudscape.core.*"%>

<HTML>
  <Title>Music OnLine</Title>
  <BODY>
    <TABLE align="left">
      <TR>
        <TD>
          <H2>
          <IMG src="musicStore.gif"/>
          Music OnLine (The right tunez at the right place)
          </H2>
        </TD>
      </TR>
    </TABLE>
  <BR/><BR/><BR/><BR/><BR/><BR/><BR/><BR/><BR/><HR/>
    <P>
      <FONT size="3">
        Welcome to Music OnLine's Customer Address Maintenance Application.
        Please select the customers whose address you want to edit by
        clicking on their customer id.
      </FONT>
    </P>
    <HR/>
      <H3>Customer Address List:</H3>
        <TABLE border="1">
          <TBODY>
            <TR>
              <TD align="center" bgcolor="#C0C0C0"><B>Customer Id</B></TD>
              <TD align="center" bgcolor="#C0C0C0">
                <B>Customer Name and Address</B>
              </TD>
            </TR>

    <%
      /*CALLOUT # 1*/
      String JDBCURL = "jdbc:cloudscape:c:/wrox/database/Wrox4370.db";
      String JDBCDRIVER = "COM.cloudscape.core.JDBCDriver";
      StringBuffer sql = new StringBuffer("");

      /*CALLOUT # 2*/
      sql.append("SELECT                                          ");
      sql.append("  customers.CustomerId              ,           ");
      sql.append("  customers.CustomerFirstName       ,           ");
```

```
      sql.append("  customers.CustomerLastName     ,          ");
      sql.append("  customers.CustomerAddress1     ,          ");
      sql.append("  customers.CustomerAddress2     ,          ");
      sql.append("  customers.CustomerCity         ,          ");
      sql.append("  postalcodes.StateProv          ,          ");
      sql.append("  postalcodes.postalcode         ,          ");
      sql.append("  countries.CountryName                     ");
      sql.append("FROM                                        ");
      sql.append("  customers                      ,          ");
      sql.append("  postalcodes                    ,          ");
      sql.append("  countries                                 ");
      sql.append("WHERE                                       ");
      sql.append("  customers.customerpostalcode=postalcodes.postalcode " );
      sql.append("AND                                         ");
      sql.append("  postalcodes.countryid=countries.countryid ");

      /******Step 1 - Making my JDBC Connection to Cloudscape******/
      Class.forName(JDBCDRIVER);
      Connection conn= DriverManager.getConnection(JDBCURL);

      Statement statement = conn.prepareStatement(sql.toString());

      /*Executing the results*/
      ResultSet rs = statement.executeQuery(sql.toString());

      while (rs.next()){
    %>

    <TR>
      <TD align="center">
        <a href="customer.jsp?customerid="<%=rs.getString("customerid")%>">
          <%=rs.getString("CustomerId")%>
        </a>
      </TD>
      <TD align="left">
        <%=rs.getString("CustomerFirstName")%> 
        <%=rs.getString("CustomerLastName")%><BR/>
           <%=rs.getString("CustomerAddress1")%><BR/>

        /*CALLOUT # 3*/
        <%if (rs.getString("CustomerAddress2")!=null){%>
             <%=rs.getString("CustomerAddress2")%><BR/>
        <%}%>

           <%=rs.getString("CustomerCity")%>, 

        <%=rs.getString("StateProv")%> 

        <%=rs.getString("postalCode")%><BR/>
           <%=rs.getString("CountryName")%>
      </TD>
    </TR>
    <%
      }

      rs.close();
    %>
      </TBODY>
    </TABLE>
  </BODY>
</HTML>
```

From a short-term perspective, the JSP above does exactly what it is required to do. When the `customerList.jsp` page is accessed, it builds a web page and displays the customer address results from the SQL query in an HTML table:

Music OnLine (The right tunez at the right place)

Welcome to Music OnLine's Customer Address Maintenance Application. Please select the customers whose address you want to edit by clicking on their customer id.

Customer Address List:

Customer Id	Customer Name and Address
1000	Catherine Crean 62 Windsor Drive Shelton, CT 06484 United States
1001	Steve Davis 567 Captain's Bluff Unit 4A West Haven, CT 06877 United States
1002	Villiage DJ null 125 Stanford Road Trumbull, CT 06628 United States
1003	Diane Asmus 324 White Street Shelton, CT 06484 United States

However, just because the application has been written, it does not mean the code will be frozen in place and no changes are ever going to be made to it. From a long-term extensibility and adaptability perspective, the code example above is a very ugly piece of code. Two immediate problems include:

- Database connectivity information is embedded directly in code for the JSP
- The SQL statement for the application is embedded directly within the JSP

The first call-out shown in the above code (designated by the bolded text and `CALLOUT # 1` in the comments) is that the application developer has embedded database connection information within the application. The JDBC connection parameters (the URL of the database and the JDBC driver to be used) are embedded directly within the JSP page.

```
/*CALLOUT # 1*/
String JDBCURL = "jdbc:cloudscape:c:/wrox/database/Wrox4370.db";
```

This does not seem like a major development flaw until we consider the following:

- A large application with 40 or 50 screens/pages has been written and now has to be changed. If any of the database connection parameters used in the application change (the database user ID or password, say), that change will have to be propagated to possibly 40 to 50 screens. It is extremely easy to miss one screen and end up spending a significant amount of time trying to find the one problem screen. In the worst-case scenario, it can result in data corruption as the application writes its data to the wrong database.
- During the course of the application lifecycle, the database the application is running on is migrated from one vendor's database software to another. This migration could occur for any number of reasons. Maybe scalability was an issue. Originally the application might have been developed to run on Microsoft's SQL Server and for performance reasons has to be ported to Oracle 8i. With the porting of the application to Oracle 8i, every screen in the application with connection information embedded within has to be ported to the new database.
- Your database's security has been compromised. JSP pages are stored on a server as text files. Anyone who can see the JSP files will see the user ID and passwords for your databases. Embedding user IDs and passwords within the JSP is an invitation for trouble.

The second call-out, seen by the comment `CALLOUT # 2`, in `customerList.jsp` deals with not abstracting away the physical structure of the database from the application code that is using it. The above code has the SQL statement directly embedded within the JSP page using it:

```
/*CALLOUT # 2*/
sql.append("SELECT                                        ");
sql.append("  customers.CustomerId            ,           ");
sql.append("  customers.CustomerFirstName     ,           ");
sql.append("  customers.CustomerLastName      ,           ");
sql.append("  customers.CustomerAddress1      ,           ");
sql.append("  customers.CustomerAddress2      ,           ");
sql.append("  customers.CustomerCity          ,           ");
sql.append("  postalcodes.StateProv           ,           ");
sql.append("  postalcodes.postalcode          ,           ");
sql.append("  countries.CountryName                       ");
sql.append("FROM                                          ");
sql.append("  customers                       ,           ");
sql.append("  postalcodes                     ,           ");
sql.append("  countries                                   ");
sql.append("WHERE                                         ");
sql.append("  customers.customerpostalcode=postalcodes.postalcode " );
sql.append("AND                                           ");
sql.append("  postalcodes.countryid=countries.countryid ");
```

This is a very common development mistake. Like the first callout, embedding SQL code in the application makes for a maintenance nightmare. The above example is querying the Music Store database for customer address information. Almost all of the data for the customer's address data is coming from the `Customers` table, as shown in the following diagram:

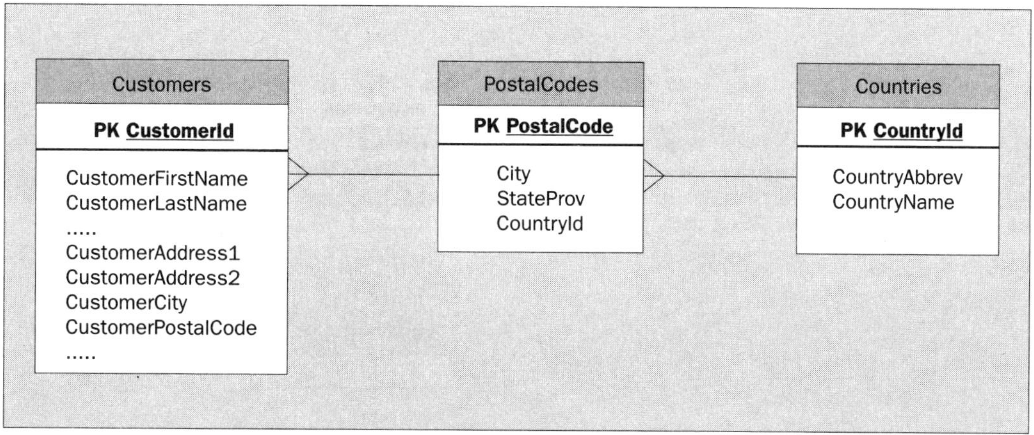

In the Entity-Relationship diagram shown above we can see the following things:

- A customer has one and only one associated postal code
- A postal code can have or more customers
- A postal code can belong to one and only one country
- A country can have one or more postal codes

There is a one-to-one relationship that exists between the `Customers` and `PostalCodes` table, and the `PostalCodes` and `Countries` table. The above data model is very limiting for two reasons:

- If multiple customers share the same address (it happens more often then you might think), each address needs to be redundantly stored within the same table.
- The database above only allows a customer to store one address. A customer might have multiple addresses. These addresses include billing and shipping addresses.

To address the two items above, you are going to need to restructure the Music Store database. The data model has been revised to support multiple customers sharing an address and allow the storing of multiple address types for a customer. It does this by pulling the address data out of the customer table and creating a many-to-many relationship. By creating a many-to-many relationship between the Customers and Addresses tables, we can have multiple customers sharing the same address and can indicate what the address type is for the address.

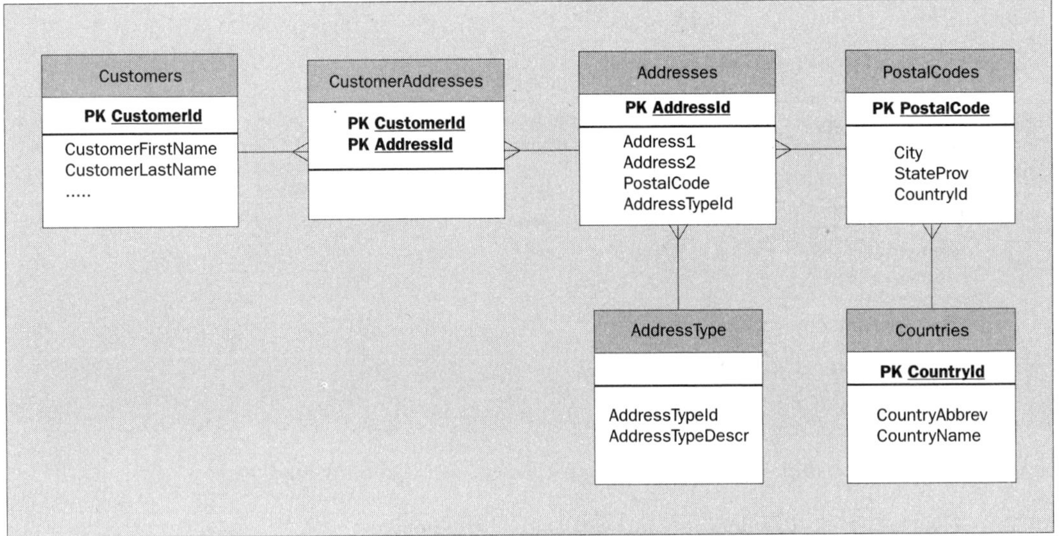

Unfortunately, with the way the `customerList.jsp` screen is currently designed, the restructuring of the Music Store database will force the `customerList.jsp` screen to be almost completely rewritten. Any SQL statements in the customer address maintenance application that use the customer or addresses table will need to be revisited.

The third callout highlights the fundamental problem with the manner in which the customer address maintenance application has been written:

```
/*CALLOUT # 3*/
<%if (rs.getString("CustomerAddress2")!=null){%>
     <%=rs.getString("CustomerAddress2")%><BR/>
<%}%>
```

This example shows Java code determining whether or not the second line of the address should be displayed, while also embedding the specific name of the database field inside the HTML tags that are going to format the code. When taken in context of the entire application this is bad design. The application is not cleanly separating the presentation, business, and data access logic. What happens if you want to port the application over to a PDF or cell-phone? You are going to need to rewrite the application because all of the different types of logic are mixed together.

Also, the code example is again tying the database's structure (the column name) to the presentation code. If the database is changed, all of the underlying code also has to change. What the customer address maintenance application is lacking is an application architecture that will cleanly separate the different types of logic and present.

Application Architectures Revisited

Earlier in the book, the three most common application architectures were discussed. These application architectures are:

- 2-tier
- 3-tier
- n-tier

All of the architectures shown involve partitioning the application's presentation, business, and data logic into distinct pieces, known as **tiers**.

2-Tier Architecture

A 2-tier architecture splits the application up into two pieces. Presentation logic and business logic are often partitioned so that the end-user interacts with a GUI client on their desktop. This GUI client will access its application data from a centralized database server. This architecture is shown in the following diagram:

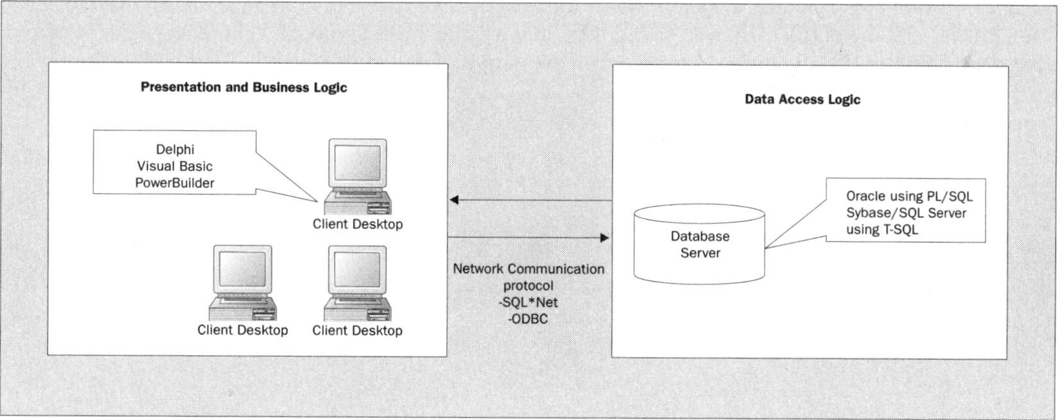

Often, the 2-tier application's database code (usually in the form of SQL) is embedded directly within a GUI application residing on the end-user's desktop. 2-tier architectures were quite common before the Internet became one of the platforms of choice for application development. These 2-tier applications were usually written within a development tool like Delphi, Visual Basic, or PowerBuilder. They often communicated directly with a database using a proprietary network protocol such as Oracle's SQL*Net or Sybases's Client lib API, or indirectly via a Windows-centric API like Microsoft's Open DataBase Connectivity (ODBC) standard.

The 2-tier application architecture is a poor architecture of choice for large (enterprise-type) applications with many end-users. 2-tier applications in these situations often do not scale because a majority of the application code will be embedded on the end-user's desktop. An end-user's desktop computer is often limited in two ways:

- Capacity – Most companies do not buy their employees big machines with lots of processing. Instead they opt for the often older or cheaper (interpreted as more cost-effective) PCs that have a limited amount of memory and disk. 'Fat' client applications with a great deal of code will often outstrip the capacity of the machine they are running on.
- Competition – End-user's rarely have one application installed or running on their machine at any given time. 2-tier applications often find themselves under-performing because they are competing for the same computing resources as other desktop applications (word processing, e-mail, and so on).

In addition, applications built on a 2-tier architecture become a maintenance headache because any change within the application's presentation, business, or database layers often results in the entire application having to be redeployed to the end-users desktop.

This is not to say that a 2-tier application architecture does not have merit. For applications that are only going to run within a small workgroup or be used by a small number of people, 2-tier architectures are a preferable model for application development. They are easy to implement and can be deployed quickly to a small user-base.

3-Tier Architecture

A 3-tier application architecture refined the 2-tier model by cleanly separating the presentation, business, and data sources into three distinct tiers. Each tier in a 3-tier architecture can only talk with the tiers immediately adjacent to it. This means that in a 3-tier architecture, the presentation tier could only communicate with the business-logic tier. The presentation tier would issue a request from the end-user to a piece of code that executed it. The business tier was the only piece of code that was allowed to speak to the database. Some of the early web-based three-tier architectures involved technologies like JavaServer Pages (JSP) and JDBC. Below is a typical implementation of one of these early 3-tier architectures:

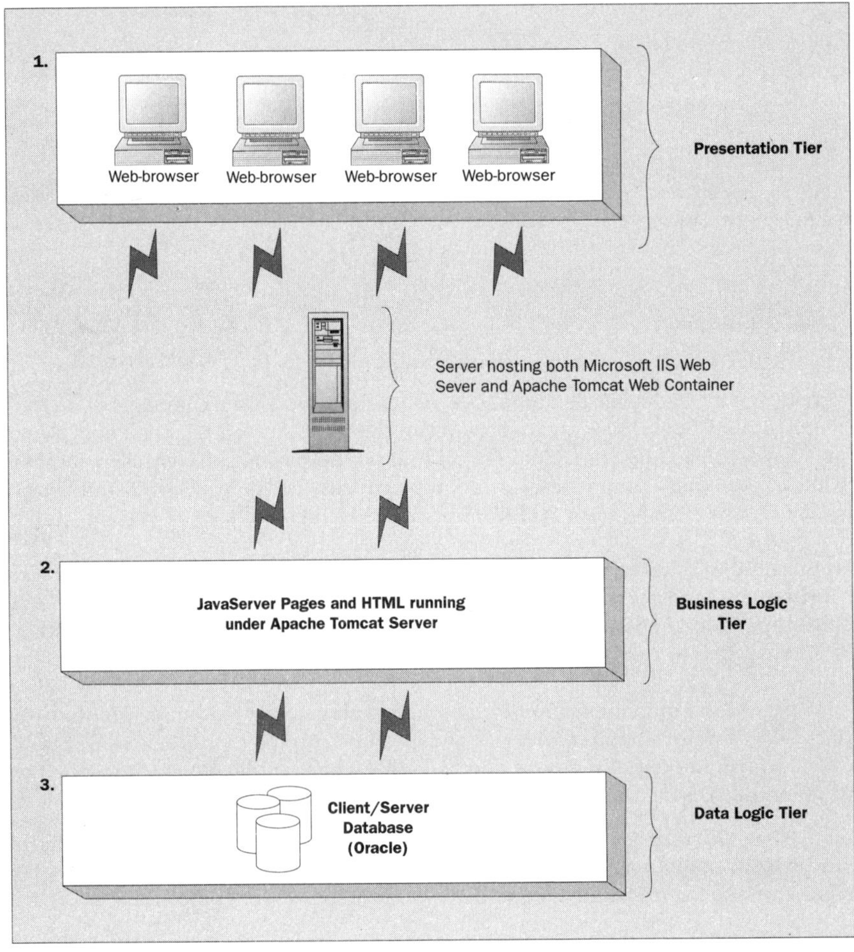

Let's walk through each of the pieces of the illustration shown above and discuss what happens when an end-user makes a request:

1. A user makes a request for a page via a web browser. The end-user's request is processed by a web server.

2. The web server passes the request to a Java ServerPage running within a JSP container. The illustration above shows the JSP running in the Apache Tomcat server. The JSP is considered the business logic-tier. The JSP processes the user's request, applies any business rules that are needed and generates HTML. The web browser, which in the diagram above is the presentation tier-takes the HTML returned by the JSP and renders the page.

3. The JSP instantiates a Java class that contains all of the business logic the user is requesting for their transaction. This Java class, along with any other classes it uses, would be considered the business-logic tier. The Java classes in our example need to retrieve data from a database and perform actions on that data. In order to perform actions against the database, the Java classes will manipulate the data using JDBC.

4. The database in our graphic is a client-server database, such as Oracle or Microsoft's SQL Server. The database is responsible for properly storing, retrieving, and maintaining transactional integrity of the data. In addition, the database in our graphic might also control what actions can take place with data in the database via stored procedures and/or database triggers.

Many believe a 3-tier architecture implies that each of the three tiers of an application must reside on completely separate servers. This is not true.

The focus of the 3-tier, and the n-tier architecture for that matter, is on separating the application into logical pieces that can only communicate through well-defined interfaces.

While each tier of the architecture is clearly defined and can only communicate with the tier immediately below or above it, it is quite possible to have a 3-tier architecture that has the presentation, business, and data logic separated into tiers, but physically deployed on one server.

n-Tier Architecture

The n-tier architecture expands on the concept of the 3-tier architecture. The 3-tier architecture focused on splitting an application apart into its three logical pieces of business logic. The n-tier architecture also splits an application into three logical tiers, but also adds the concept of **location transparency**.

Location transparency is when an application is built by using small pieces of code called **components** that are capable of being deployed and invoked on different application servers on different physical servers. The application uses the code, but has no idea of where the code is physically residing. Location transparency offers several advantages, including:

- **Load balancing** – The processing load for an application can be split into small pieces running across multiple servers within an organization. If more processing power is needed for an application, the application's software components can be distributed to another server. This server can then be added to a group of servers already running (commonly referred to as a **server cluster**) and begin processing end-user transactions.
- **Fault tolerance** – Location transparency also enables an application to be fault-tolerant. If one of the servers running the application goes down, the other servers can pick up the slack without the application having to be aware that there was any kind of disruption in services.

In the Java 2 Platform, Enterprise Edition (J2EE), the distributable software components that make the code of an n-tier architecture are called **Enterprise JavaBeans** (**EJBs**) and run within a piece of software called an **application server**. The following diagram gives an example of n-tier architecture:

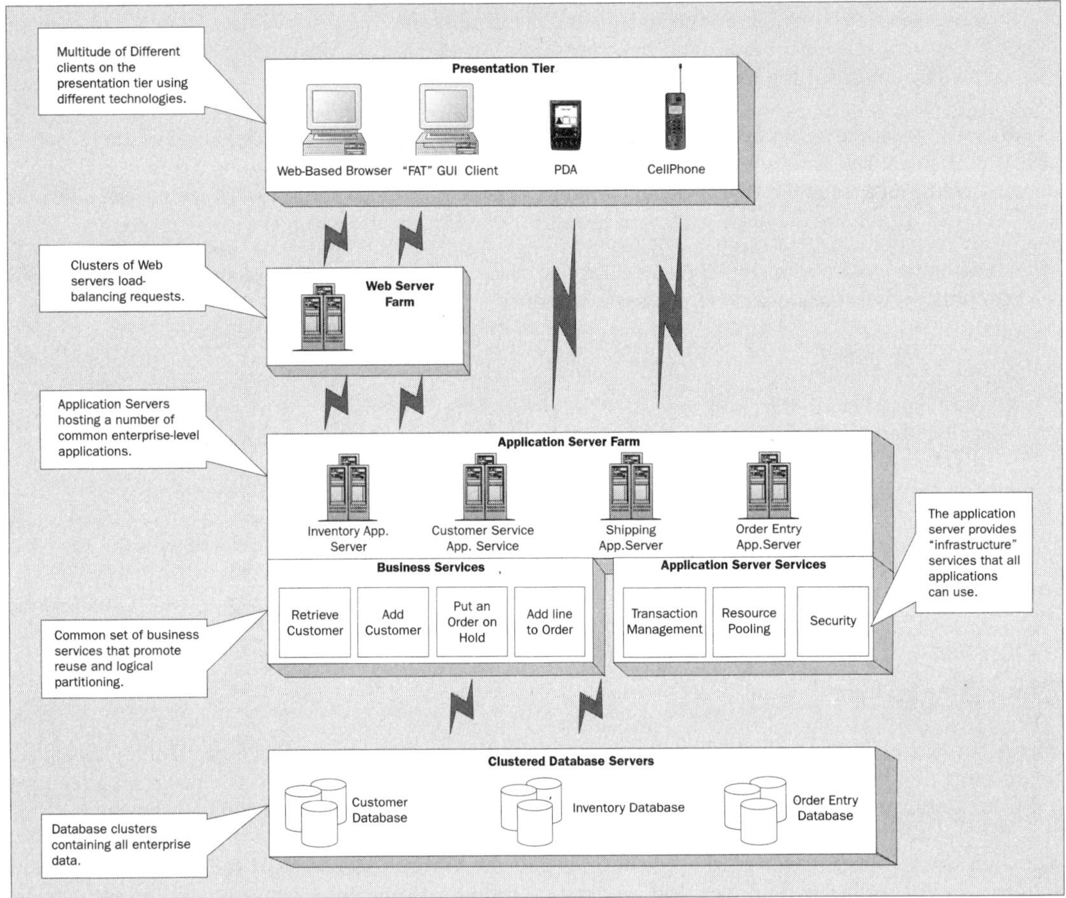

One of the driving principals behind n-tier architectures is that applications are not meant to be monolithic chunks of code that are locked within one code-base residing on one set of servers. Instead, applications are built on the concept of **services**. Typically within n-tier architecture there are two kinds of services:

- **Business services**
- **Infrastructure services**

Business services consist of software components that reside on application servers throughout a company's information systems (IS). These components enforce business rules and provide access to corporate data stores. For instance, in the figure above, the Customer Service application server hosts software components that would allow an application to retrieve, edit, and update customer information.

Infrastructure services are provided by the application server. Examples of infrastructure services include:

- Transaction management
- Security
- Resource-pooling of heavily used components

Infrastructure services represent services that an application developer should not have to re-write every time they produce an application. Using infrastructure services provided by the application servers allows the developer to focus more time on developing business logic and less time on writing 'plumbing' code.

Application Architecture: Lessons Learned

Building a database-driven application that does not have a well-designed architecture is like building a house on a foundation of sand. Sooner or later, the application, like the house, will collapse under the pressure of its own weight. Well-written application architecture allows the developer to quickly build solutions while:

- Generalizing common business and development tasks into software services that can be reused in other applications.
- Abstracting away implementation details so that when something internal within a particular software services changes it will not disrupt the applications that utilize the service
- Extending the application beyond its original capabilities. The developer must be able to leverage the application architecture so that new software services offering new functionality can be snapped into place without have to rewrite a significant portion of any existing applications built on the architecture.

These three characteristics are important for applications that have heavy database development involved. The three principals of application architecture when applied to building database-based applications should produce the following:

- A set of generalized services for accessing the database. These services will allow the user to access and manipulate (view, insert, delete, and so on) data uniformly across all applications that utilize the services. Changes to the service's logic will automatically be propagated to all applications that use it.
- The physical structure of the database and the tools for accessing the database will be abstracted away from the application. An application will never know the JDBC URL for a database connection, nor will the application use SQL calls embedded directly within its code. Instead, it will use some other source to retrieve the data on its behalf.
- New functionality and access to new data stores can be plugged into the framework. Well-designed application architecture will allow the developer to plug in new database code without disrupting existing architectures.

So far the application architectures presented have all been discussed in pure generalities. The following sections of this chapter will explore how to use what is known as a **Model-View-Controller** (**MVC**) framework to build an application architecture that will mitigate many of the problems seen in our sample application.

Introducing the MVC Framework

The Model-View-Controller framework allows the user to quickly build 3-tier and n-tier applications. It does this by clearly defining distinct interfaces that each piece of the application must communicate with in order to work.

The following diagram depicts the general flow of user requests built on MVC architecture:

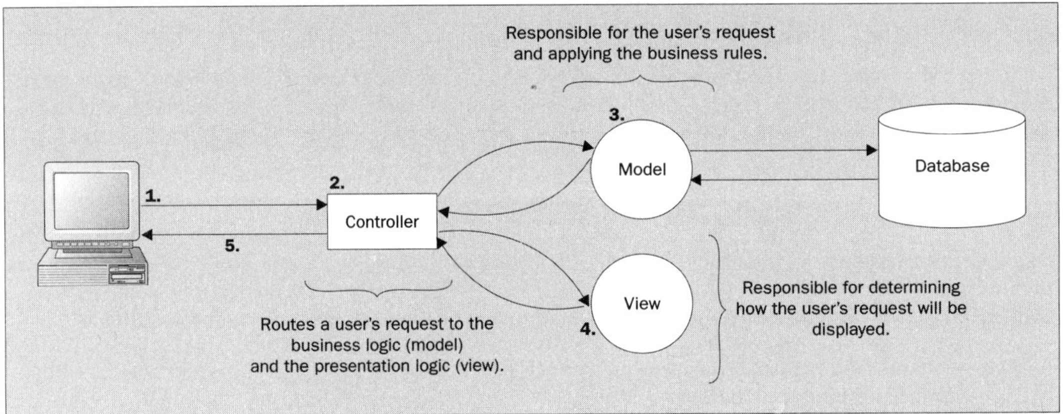

Let's examine step by step what happens when an MVC-based application processes a request:

1. An **end-user** makes a request via the application. The request is forwarded to the Controller software service.

2. The **controller** acts as a traffic cop. It examines the user's request and then decides what piece of business logic to use to process the request. It then forwards the request to a business component for processing. This business component is called the Model. The controller will determine what business component will be invoked to process a user's request.

3. The **model** contains all of the business rules that process the user's request and also performs all of the data access needed by the end-user. Any data retrieved on behalf of the end-user is packaged up and returned to the controller.

4. The controller takes the data returned from the model and selects the mechanism in which the data is to be presented to the end-user. This presentation mechanism is referred to as the **view**. The view is a software service for actually displaying the database back to the end-user.

5. The controller then returns the results to the end-user after processing the request.

As you begin studying the MVC architecture, we will rewrite the customer address maintenance application that we showed earlier in the chapter. During this rewrite, you are going to leverage many of the tools and technologies shown throughout this text. These technologies include:

- JavaServer Pages (JSP)
- eXtensible Markup Language (XML)
- eXtensible Stylesheet Language (XSL)
- JDBC API
- Enterprise JavaBeans (EJB)
- Cloudscape

Let's revisit the MVC figure and identify where all of the technologies described above are going to be used:

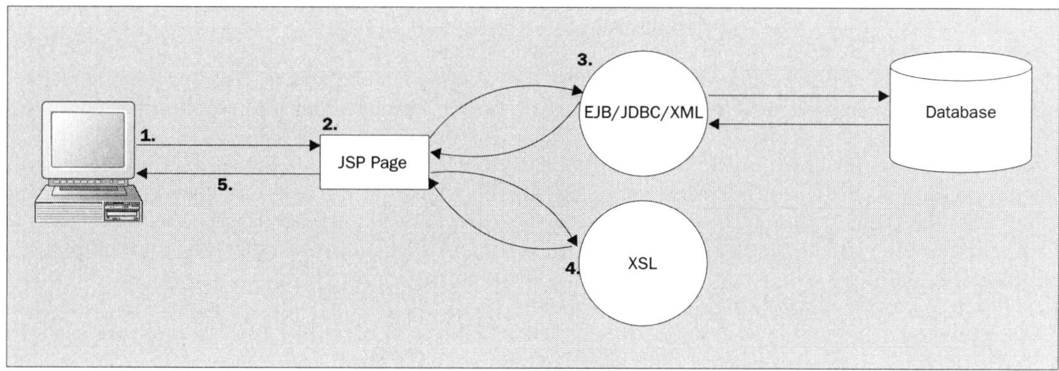

1. A user makes a request to a JavaServer Page via a web browser. Embedded within the request are two variables passed as HTTP Parameters: `Request` and `Action`.

2. The JSP page reads the `Request` and `Action` parameters and performs the following actions:

   - The JSP page instantiates a session EJB whose name was passed in the HTTP parameter called `Request`. This business object is the 'model' piece of our MVC architecture.
   - The JSP page invokes one of two methods on the session EJB: `retrieve()` or `post()`. The `retrieve()` method is invoked when the user only wants to retrieve data and does not want to do anything else. The `post()` method is used when the user wants to submit data to the application. The `Action` parameter indicates whether the `retrieve()` or `post()` method is to be invoked the EJB.

3. After a session EJB is instantiated it will process the user's request. In the case of the customer address maintenance application, the EJB retrieves customer address data from the database and performs some processing on the data. Once the EJB processes the user's request, the data returned from the EJB will be packaged as an XML document and returned to the JSP page.

4. Once the JSP page has retrieved an XML document from the EJB, it uses XSL to transform and format the data contained within the XML document into HTML.

5. The JSP page returns this HTML to the end-user's web browser.

The above diagram demonstrates how the Java 2 Platform, Enterprise Edition technologies can be used to build an MVC architecture. Let's dive down into the implementation and look at the code used to build an MVC-based customer address maintenance application.

Details of the MVC Architecture

In order to actually implement the MVC architecture shown above we will need to include two pieces of technology that have not been shown in any of our diagrams. These two technologies are:

- A JavaServer Pages container that will host our controller JSP
- An application server that will host any EJBs used by the applications

For the MVC architecture being built in this chapter, we will be using the Tomcat JSP/Servlet container and the JBoss application server. Both of these 'products' are open source projects that are freely available for download.

JBoss is available for download from http://jboss.org/. A bundled JBoss/Tomcat distribution is available from the JBoss web site. This distribution contains both JBoss and Tomcat and already has the necessary configuration done to launch JBoss and Tomcat together. For the purposes of the discussion here, we are going to use version 2.2.2 of JBoss and version 3.2.2 of Tomcat. Instructions for setting up and configuring the JBoss and Tomcat server can be found in Appendix B.

The following diagram has been updated to reflect where the Tomcat and JBoss servers are used. It also breaks out the key Java classes used for our MVC implementation:

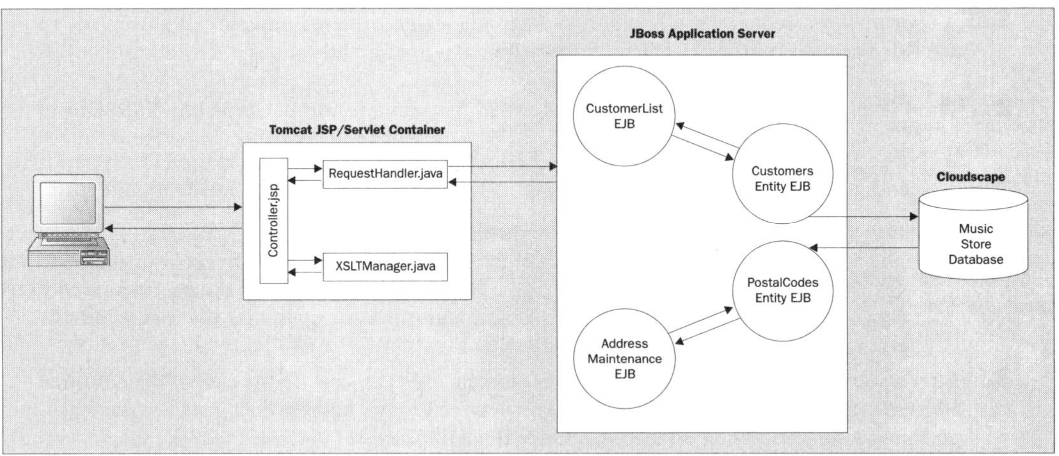

The following sections will examine the code behind each of the pieces of the MVC architecture shown above. Following the flow of all of the diagrams shown so far, the controller piece of the MVC architecture will be the starting point for our discussion.

Controller

The 'controller' piece of our MVC architecture consists of two parts. These are: the `controller.jsp` and the `RequestHandler.java` class, as shown in the following diagram:

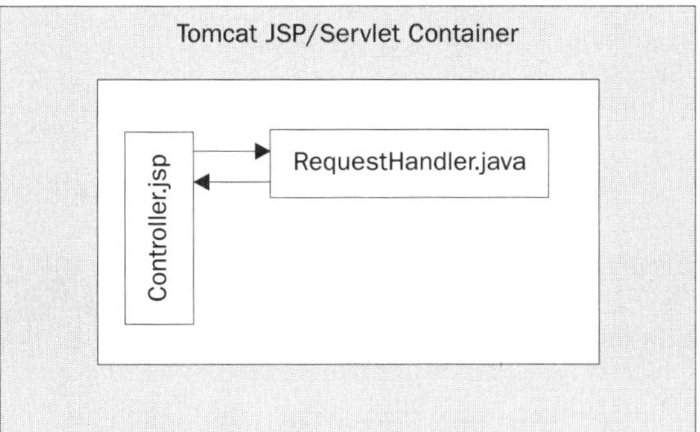

The `controller.jsp` is the entry point for all user requests; having decided what action is to be taken, it uses `RequestHandler.java` as a helper class to instantiate the EJB for processing the user request.

controller.jsp

This JSP page receives all requests for the customer address maintenance application and decides what EJB to instantiate to process the end-user's request. Once the request has been processed the `controller.jsp` routes the request to the 'view' piece of the MVC architecture. The 'view' piece of this MVC implementation uses XSL to present the results of a user's request.

Try It Out – controller.jsp

Write the JSP as shown here:

```
<%@page import="java.util.*"%>
<%@page import="java.io.*"%>
<%@page import="org.w3c.dom.Document"%>
<%@page import="mvc.*"%>

<%

    /*
      The MVC framework shown for this chapter use the Xalan XSLT
      processor and Xerces XML parser. Xalan and Xerces are freely
      available from the http://xml.apache.org. The MVC framework built
      in this chapter uses version 2.2.D6 of the Xalan XSLT processor and
      version 1.3 of the Xerces XML parser. In controller.jsp the
      org.w3c.dom.Document class comes from the Xerces jar file
      (xerces.jar).
    */


    /*
      The controller JSP is the controller piece of the MVC Framework.
      This piece will first try and retrieve the name of the XSL file the
      user wants to view. After the xslFileName is retrieved it will
      instantiate the Request handler. The request handler will invoke the
      appropriate model. The model will return an XML document with all of
```

```
        the data to be presented to the end-user. The controller.jsp will
        then return the JspWriter out variable, the data returned from the
        RequestHandler, and the name of the XSL file that will be used to
        present the data. The XSLTManager will carry out the merging of the
        XSL and XML document.
      */
   try{
     String requestValue = request.getParameter("Request");
     String actionValue  = request.getParameter("Action");

    /*Step 1 - Retrieve the name of the XSL file that is going to be used*/
     String  xslFileName =
                       MVCHelper.getXSLFileName(requestValue,actionValue);

     if (xslFileName == null){
       throw new Exception("Unable to locate an XSL file that matches the " +
                           "request and action requested. Request: " +
                            requestValue + " , Action: " + actionValue);
     }

     /*Step 2 - Instantiate the RequestHandler and process the user's request
     */
     RequestHandler requestHandler = new RequestHandler();
     Document returnedData = requestHandler.process(request);

     /*Step 3 - Take the Document retrieved from the requesthandler and
                transform it to HTML
     */
     XSLTManager xsltManager = new XSLTManager();
     xsltManager.transformOutput(out, returnedData, xslFileName);
   } catch(Exception e){
     MVCHelper.buildErrorPage(e, out);
   }
   %>
```

How It Works

When a user makes a request in the customer address maintenance application, the first thing the JSP server does is retrieve the name of the XSL file that will be used to present the screen to the end-user.

```
     String requestValue = request.getParameter("Request");
     String actionValue  = request.getParameter("Action");

    /*Step 1 - Retrieve the name of the XSL file that is going to be used*/
     String  xslFileName =
                       MVCHelper.getXSLFileName(requestValue,actionValue);

     if (xslFileName == null){
       throw new Exception("Unable to locate an XSL file that matches the " +
                           "request and action requested. Request: " +
                            requestValue + " , Action: " + actionValue);
     }
```

The `controller.jsp` does this by retrieving the `Request` and `Action` parameters out of the JSP `request` object and passing them in the `getXSLFileName()` method on the `MVCHelper` class. The `MVCHelper` class is a Java class that contains a set of utility methods that are used in different places throughout the MVC architecture. These methods do not fit nicely into classes so they have been grouped together under the `MVCHelper` class. The `getXSLFileName()` method for the `MVCHelper` class is shown below:

```
/*
 * This method will retrieve the name of an XSL file from the xslFileNames
 * object. It does this by appending the _request and _action parameters
 * into a string that looks like this:
 * Request.Action
 * This string created from the two method parameters is used as a key
 * to search xslFileNames for the appropriate file names.
 */
public static String getXSLFileName(String _request,
                                    String _action) throws Exception {

  /* If the xslFileNames object is empty, load the data from the
     configuration file */
  if (xslFileNames.isEmpty()) {
    xslFileNames.load(new FileInputStream(XSLCONFIGPROPERTIES));
  }

  /* Building the lookup key */
  StringBuffer key = new StringBuffer(_request);
  key.append(".");
  key.append(_action);

  /* Retrieving the string */
  String xslFileName = xslFileNames.getProperty(key.toString());

  /* If no file name was retrieved throw an exception */
  if (xslFileName == null) {
    throw new Exception("MVCHelper.getXSLFileName: " +
                        "Unable to locate XSL file based on the request" +
                        " and action passed. Key=" + key.toString());
  }

  return xslFileName;
}
```

This method will retrieve the path and name of the XSL stylesheet that will be processed by the request. The XSL stylesheet file returned is based on a string key that is made up of the request name, a dot (.), and the action name. For the customer list screen, the following entry exists in the `xslConfig.properties` file:

```
CustomerList.Retrieve=file:///c://jbosstomcat//tomcat//webapps//begjdb//etc//custo
merList.xsl
```

The above entry tells the 'controller' piece of the MVC architecture that the `customerList.xsl` file should be used for all end-user's requests that have a request of `CustomerList` and an action of `Retrieve`. If the XSL file name is not found for the request being made an exception is raised. This file will be stored in the `tomcat\webapps\begjdb\etc` directory.

Before we move on to the rest of the JSP, let's take a quick look at the `MVCHelper`:

```
package mvc;

/* Standard Java Packages */
import java.util.Properties;
import java.io.File;
import java.io.FileWriter;
import java.io.FileInputStream;
```

```
/* Imported from the J2EE or JBoss servlet.jar */
import javax.servlet.jsp.JspWriter;

/* Imported from xerces.jar */
import org.w3c.dom.Document;
import org.w3c.dom.Element;
import org.apache.xml.serialize.OutputFormat;
import org.apache.xml.serialize.XMLSerializer;

public class MVCHelper {

  /* Properties object containing all of the XSL File Names and the
     Request.Action key */
  private static Properties xslFileNames = new Properties();

  /* Location of the XSL Configuration Information File */
  private static String XSLCONFIGPROPERTIES =
    new
String("c:\\jbosstomcat\\tomcat\\webapps\\begjdb\\etc\\xslConfig.properties");

  /*
   * This method will retrieve the name of an XSL file from the xslFileNames
   * object. It does this by appending the _request and _action parameters
   * into a string that looks like this:
   * Request.Action
   * This string created from the two method parameters is used as a key
   * to search xslFileNames for the appropriate file names.
   */
  public static String getXSLFileName(String _request,
                                      String _action) throws Exception {

    /* If the xslFileNames object is empty, load the data from the
       configuration fiel */
    if (xslFileNames.isEmpty()) {
      xslFileNames.load(new FileInputStream(XSLCONFIGPROPERTIES));
    }

    /* Building the lookup key */
    StringBuffer key = new StringBuffer(_request);
    key.append(".");
    key.append(_action);

    /* Retrieving the string */
    String xslFileName = xslFileNames.getProperty(key.toString());

    /* If no file name was retrieved throw an exception */
    if (xslFileName == null) {
      throw new Exception("MVCHelper.getXSLFileName:
                          "Unable to locate XSL file based on the request"
                          + "and action passed. Key=" + key.toString());
    }

    return xslFileName;
  }

  /*
   * The printDOM method will take the XML document and the File object
   * passed into the method and dump its contents out to a file. This is
   * only here for debugging purposes and should not be used in production
   * code.
```

```
  */
  public static void printDOM(Document _xmlDoc,
                              File _outputFile) throws Exception {
    OutputFormat outputFormat = new OutputFormat(_xmlDoc);
    FileWriter fileWriter = new FileWriter(_outputFile);

    XMLSerializer xmlSerializer = new XMLSerializer(fileWriter,
            outputFormat);
    xmlSerializer.asDOMSerializer();

    xmlSerializer.serialize(_xmlDoc.getDocumentElement());
  }


  /*
   * The buildDBElement will add a text node onto an element and return it
   * back to the method that calls it. This is simply a helper method that
   * makes it easier to add elements to another element.
   */
  public static Element buildDBElement(Document _xmlDoc, String _elementName,
                                       String _elementValue) throws Exception {

    Element item = _xmlDoc.createElement(_elementName);

    if (_elementValue == null) {
      item.appendChild(_xmlDoc.createTextNode(""));
    } else {
      item.appendChild(_xmlDoc.createTextNode(_elementValue));
    }
    return item;
  }


  /*
   * Builds a generic help screen.
   */
  public static void buildErrorPage(Exception _e, JspWriter _out) {
    try {
      _out.write("<H1>We are currently unable to process your request. : "
                 + _e.toString() + "</H1>");
      System.out.println(_e.toString());
    } catch (Exception e) {
      System.out.println(_e.toString());
    }
  }
}
```

The only method in here that is particularly new or complicated is `getXSLFileName()`, which we've already explained. The others are just convenience methods that perform simple tasks.

After the XSL file name has been retrieved a `RequestHandler` class is instantiated. The `RequestHandler`, in our example called `requestHandler`, creates the EJB that will carry out the end-user's request. This process of creating the EJB and carrying out the user's request is started when the `controller.jsp` calls the `process()` method. When calling the `process()` method the `controller.jsp` passes in its `request` object. This `request` object will contain all of the HTTP parameters passed in when the user made their request to the web server.

```
/*Step 2 - Instantiate the RequestHandler and process the user's request
*/
RequestHandler requestHandler = new RequestHandler();
Document returnedData = requestHandler.process(request);
```

After the `requestHandler` object has completed processing the user's request it will return an XML `Document` object (`returnedData`). The XML `Document` returned by the `requestHandler` will contain all of the data that is to be presented to the end-user.

Once the XML `Document` object has been returned from the `process()` method, the end-user's request is ready to be transformed into HTML. To carry out the transformation, the `controller.jsp` page will use the `XSLTManager` class to carry out the transformation:

```
/*Step 3 - Take the Document retrieved from the requesthandler and
           transform it to HTML
*/
XSLTManager xsltManager = new XSLTManager();
xsltManager.transformOutput(out, returnedData, xslFileName);
```

To perform the transformation, the `XSLTManager.transformOutput()` method is called. The `controller.jsp`'s `out` object, the `returnedData` object and `xslFileName` object are all passed into this method.

The `XSLTManager` class is the 'view' piece of our MVC architecture. It acts as a wrapper around the XSLT classes that transform the XSL stylesheet and the XML document retrieved within the `RequestHandler`'s `process()` method.

The `XSLTManager` class is a helper class that is responsible only for transforming the XML and XSL into HTML. The `XSLTManager` class is based on the Xalan code examples found in Chapter 21. The only real difference between the code presented below and the code from Chapter 21 is that it has been made into a class:

```
package mvc;

/* These classes are found in the Xerces jar file (Xerces.jar) */
import org.w3c.dom.Document;

/*
 * These classes are part of the J2EE jar file or if you are using
 * JBoss/tomcat the servlet.jar file found in your Tomcat/lib directory.
 */
import javax.servlet.jsp.JspWriter;

/* Imported from the Xalan.jar */
import javax.xml.transform.TransformerFactory;
import javax.xml.transform.Transformer;
import javax.xml.transform.stream.StreamResult;
import javax.xml.transform.stream.StreamSource;
import org.apache.xalan.processor.TransformerFactoryImpl;
import javax.xml.transform.dom.DOMSource;


public class XSLTManager {
```

```
    /*
     * The transformOutput method will transform an XML Document and XSL
     * stylesheet into HTML and then write the HTML out to the JspWrite passed
     * into the method call.
     */
    public void transformOutput(JspWriter _out, Document _xmlDoc,
                                String _xslFileName) throws Exception {

      TransformerFactory tFactory = new TransformerFactoryImpl();

      Transformer transformer =
        tFactory.newTransformer(new StreamSource(_xslFileName));

      DOMSource domSource = new DOMSource(_xmlDoc);

      transformer.transform(domSource, new StreamResult(_out));
    }
  }
```

Save this file as `C:\BegJavaDB\Ch22\mvc\XSLTManager.java`, and compile it with the following command from the `Ch22` directory:

```
> javac -classpath
  .;%JLIB%\xerces.jar;%JLIB%\xalan.jar;c:\jbosstomcat\tomcat\lib\servlet.jar
  mvc/XSLTManager.java
```

Now we can examine the second half of the controller software service, the `RequestHandler` class.

RequestHandler.java

The `RequestHandler` class is used by the `controller.jsp` to instantiate the EJB that will process the end-user's request. The `RequestHandler` class contains all of the code for connecting to the JBoss application server, asking JBoss to create the EJB for it, and invoking the `retrieve()` or `post()` method to process the end-user's request.

Try It Out – RequestHandler.java

The code for the `RequestHandler`, like the `controller.jsp`, is a simple, but elegant piece of code:

```
package mvc;

import java.io.*;
import java.util.*;

/*
 * The two classes imported can be found as part of the J2EE v1.2.2
 * distribution available from Sun's web site. These classes are part of the
 * J2EE.jar that comes with the distribution. If you have not downloaded
 * this Jar you can also find the classes in JBoss/Tomcat distributions. For
 * the bundled JBoss/Tomcat distribution these jars were located in:
 * javax.servlet.http.HttpServletRequest
 *                              - %JBOSS DIRECTORY%/tomcat/lib/servlet.jar
 * javax.naming.InitialContext - %JBOSS DIRECTORY%/jboss/lib/ext/ejb.jar
 */
import javax.servlet.http.HttpServletRequest;
import javax.naming.InitialContext;
```

```
/*
 * The org.w3c.dom.Document class is located in the Xalan jar.
 */
import org.w3c.dom.Document;

import mvc.templates.*;

public class RequestHandler {

  /*
   * The process method is used to process a request sent by the end-user.
   * It reads the request and action variables from the HttpServletRequest
   * parameter passed in. The request parameter returned from the
   * HttpServletRequest object is used to instantiate our EJB. The action
   * parameter is used to define whether the retrieve or post method of the
   * instantiated bean is called.
   */
  public Document process(HttpServletRequest _request) throws Exception {

    /* Step 1 - Retrieving the class parameters
     * from the HttpServletRequest object
     */
    String requestValue = _request.getParameter("Request");
    String actionValue = _request.getParameter("Action");

    /* Step 2 - Looking up and retrieving the desired EJB from JBoss */
    InitialContext ctx = new InitialContext();
    MVCHome home = (MVCHome) ctx.lookup(requestValue);
    MVCObject mvcComponent = home.create();

    /* Step 3 - Decide to invoke the Retrieve or Post Method on the Bean */
    if (actionValue.equals("Retrieve")) {
      return mvcComponent.retrieve(_request);
    }

    if (actionValue.equals("Post")) {
      System.out.println("I am in the post");
      return mvcComponent.post(_request);
    }

    /* Step 4 - If the value is neither Retrieve or Post throw an exception */
    throw new Exception("RequestHandler.process: " +
                        "Action passed is not a Retrieve or a Post");
  }
}
```

Save this file as `C:\BegJavaDB\Ch22\mvc\RequestHandler.java`. We'll compile this class later, since it is dependent upon other classes we haven't developed yet.

How It Works

The first thing the `RequestHandler` does is pull the `Request` and `Action` parameter values out of the `_request` object passed into the application.

```
String requestValue = _request.getParameter("Request");
String actionValue = _request.getParameter("Action");
```

The `RequestHandler` uses the value stored in the `requestValue` variable to instantiate the EJB the user has requested.

```
InitialContext ctx = new InitialContext();
MVCHome home = (MVCHome) ctx.lookup(requestValue);
MVCObject mvcComponent = home.create();
```

At this point do not look too deeply into the EJB details. These details will be covered when the 'model' piece of the MVC architecture is discussed. For now, take at face value that the above code instantiates an EJB for the end-user. We will look into how the EJB actually carries out the end-user's request.

After the EJB has been instantiated, it is time to decide which method in our EJB is to be invoked. Every EJB within the MVC architecture presented in this chapter must have two public methods:

```
Document retrieve(HttpServletRequest _request)
Document post(HttpServletRequest _request)
```

As stated earlier, the `retrieve()` method is used when the user wants to retrieve data from a database and the `post()` method is used when the user wants to actually insert, update, or delete data. The `RequestHandler` class decides what method to invoke by looking at the value set in the `actionValue` variable.

```
if (actionValue.equals("Retrieve")) {
  return mvcComponent.retrieve(_request);
}

if (actionValue.equals("Post")) {
  System.out.println("I am in the post");
  return mvcComponent.post(_request);
}
```

Each of these methods will return an XML `Document` object containing data that is to be displayed to the end-user. If the `actionValue` variable is *not* set to either `Retrieve` or `Post`, an exception will be thrown:

```
throw new Exception("RequestHandler.process: " +
                    "Action passed is not a Retrieve or a Post");
```

Looking at the code for the `RequestHandler`, one might ask why this code was not directly embedded into the `controller.jsp`. The `RequestHandler` code has been broken apart from the `controller.jsp` page for the purposes of abstraction. The 'controller' service in the MVC architecture should act like a traffic cop directing traffic. Its sole purpose is to figure out what tasks the user is trying to accomplish. It does not care about how the task is actually carried out.

Putting the code that carries out the end-user's request in the controller over-complicates it. It makes the code more difficult to understand because unnecessary detail is being included in the `controller.jsp`. In addition it is tightly coupling the routing code with the code that executes the user's tasks. This means if you want to change how a task is executed you have to modify the controller service. An example of this might be changing the controller to use web services instead of EJBs to process an end-user's request.

Remember this simple rule:

> **When you touch code, you break the code. By centralizing your code into a set of discrete business components you lessen the number of times you have to touch your code to make changes.**

Model

The 'model' piece of this chapter's MVC architecture is used to process an end-user's request. The 'model' has three responsibilities:

1. Apply any business rules that need to be applied for the end-user request

2. Retrieve, update, delete, insert any data in the database

3. Return an XML document containing all of the data to be returned to the end-user

All of the 'model' services built for this chapter are Enterprise JavaBeans (EJB). Developed by Sun Microsystems, an EJB is a server-side software component that is based completely on the Java programming language. EJBs give software developers the ability to write small pieces of distributable code that can be placed on any server that supports a Sun Microsystems-compliant JVM.

There are two basic EJB types: **Session EJBs** and **Entity EJBs**. Session EJBs are used to carry out end-user transactions. Session EJBS can be stateless or stateful. A **stateless** session bean holds the state of its internal variables for the length of one method call. As soon as the method call has been completed, all internal variable states in the bean are 'forgotten'. A stateless session bean can possess only methods.

Stateful session beans are the opposite of stateless session beans. A stateful session bean will hold its state across multiple method invocations. A stateful session bean can have properties that can be retrieved and set by the consumer of the bean. A stateful session bean's properties and variables will not be lost between invocations of methods on the EJB. A stateful session bean is often used to capture complex business processes with multiple data transactions that cannot be performed in a linear fashion inside one method call.

Entity EJBs are used to provide a data persistence layer to 'hide' the messy physical database structures (tables, views, and so on) of a database. Entity beans were covered briefly in Chapter 19. If you have not read that chapter, it is highly recommended you review it before continuing. The customer address maintenance application uses two CMP-based entity beans called: `Customers` and `PostalCode`.

For the purposes of the customer address maintenance application, the 'model' piece of the MVC is implemented using stateless session beans. The customer address application is a web-based application that could potentially service a large number of users. Stateless beans work better for web-based applications because they use fewer resources and naturally fit into the request/response model web-based applications support.

Anatomy of a Model

Every 'model' within the customer address maintenance application MVC architecture must be a stateless session EJB. Stateless session EJBs consist of three pieces: a remote interface, a home interface and the bean class.

- The **remote interface** is the one that the user interacts with, this interface also hides from the user the location of the actual bean
- The **home interface** is used to create a bean and hides whether the EJB is created on the same machine as the application or on a separate machine
- The EJB implementation class does the actual work of the bean

Just having an EJB does not mean it can be placed into our MVC architecture. Every EJB used in our architecture has to have two methods: `retrieve()` and `post()`. To enforce this rule, we are going to extend each of the three interfaces that normally make up a session EJB. These extended interfaces are called `MVCHome`, `MVCObject` and `MVCBean`.

The MVCHome interface extends the EJBHome. The MVCHome interface defines the create() method which is used by the application to instantiate the EJB and return the EJB's remote interface. For those familiar with Enterprise JavaBeans, you might ask why we need a MVCHome and MVCObject class for our MVC implementation.

A standard EJB extends its home interface from the `EJBHome` interface. The home interface knows how to create and return a remote interface for that specific EJB. However, in our MVC framework we need the flexibility to create an EJB and always be guaranteed that there is a standard interface and set of methods on the EJB to invoke. The `MVCHome` and `MVCObject` interfaces enable us to do this for two reasons:

- The `MVHome` interface always guarantees that when a create method is called on one of the EJBs in our framework an `MVCObject` interface will be returned. This way we know that we will always have a standard interface for our MVC to interact with.
- The `MVCObject` interface ensures that every EJB in our MVC framework has a `retrieve()` and `post()` method defined. This is absolutely critical because having these methods ensures existing EJBs can be modified and new EJBs be added without having to do a significant amount of code rewrite. These EJBs just have to implement the `MVCObject` interface.

The additional work of the `MVCHome`, `MVCObject`, and `MVCBean` artifacts ensure that every 'model' in our MVC framework has a single well-defined interface for the `RequestHandler` to interact with. The code for the `MVCHome` interface is shown below:

Try It Out – The MVCHome Interface

```
package mvc.templates;

import java.io.Serializable;
import javax.ejb.EJBHome;
import java.rmi.RemoteException;
import javax.ejb.CreateException;

public interface MVCHome extends EJBHome{
  MVCObject create() throws RemoteException, CreateException;
}
```

Try It Out – The MVCObject Interface

The `MVCObject` interface extends the `EJBObject` interface. This interface is the EJB remote interface. The end-user interacts with this interface when they want to make method calls on the EJB. Thus, to enforce the rule that every EJB in the MVC architecture has a `retrieve()` and `post()` method, we are going to define these two methods in the `MVCObject` interface.

```
package mvc.templates;

import javax.ejb.EJBObject;
import java.rmi.RemoteException;

import org.w3c.dom.*;
import org.xml.sax.*;
```

```
import org.apache.xerces.parsers.*;
import javax.servlet.http.HttpServletRequest;

public interface MVCObject extends EJBObject{

  public Document retrieve(HttpServletRequest _request)
                         throws RemoteException, Exception;

  public Document post(HttpServletRequest _request) throws RemoteException,
                                                          Exception;
}
```

Try It Out – The MVCBean Interface

The `MVCBean` interface extends the `SessionBean` interface. The `MVCBean` interface will be implemented by the Java class that carries out the end-user's request. In the case of our MVC architecture, the class that implements the `MVCBean` interface implements the `retrieve()` and `post()` methods required by the MVC architecture.

```
package mvc.templates;

import java.rmi.RemoteException;
import javax.ejb.SessionBean;
import javax.ejb.SessionContext;

import org.w3c.dom.*;
import org.xml.sax.*;
import org.apache.xerces.parsers.*;
import javax.servlet.http.HttpServletRequest;
import xsl.*;

public interface MVCBean extends SessionBean {
  public Document retrieve(HttpServletRequest _request)
                        throws RemoteException, Exception;
  public Document post(HttpServletRequest _request)
                      throws RemoteException, Exception;
}
```

The `retrieve()` and `post()` methods shown in the above interface are used by our MVC architecture to facilitate the two most common tasks within an application: retrieving data from an application and posting data a user has keyed in. The `retrieve()` method is used by the 'model' to query a database and package the retrieved data in an XML document that will be processed by the rest of the MVC architecture. The `post()` method is invoked when the user wants to insert, update, or delete a record from a database. The `post()` method will also package any data that needs to be displayed to the end-user as an XML document.

Any 'model' implemented within our MVC architecture needs to implement these three classes. Lets look at an example.

The CustomerList EJB

The `CustomerList` EJB is used to retrieve a list of all of the customers and their addresses within the Music Store database. This EJB implements the `MVCHome`, `MVCObject`, and `MVCBean` interfaces defined in the previous section.

The `CustomerList` EJB will also provide a simple example of how data is retrieved from the Music Store database using JDBC and then packaged as an XML document. Since the customer list screen in the customer address maintenance application does not save any data, a `post()` method will be defined in the EJB, but there will be no code present in it.

Try It Out – The CustomerList EJB

The first piece of the `CustomerList` EJB to look at is the `CustomerListHome` interface. This interface extends the `MVCHome` interface. You will notice that in the `CustomerListHome` and `CustomerList` interfaces show in this section do not explicitly define any of the standard EJB methods (such as the `create()` method found on the home interface). This is because these methods have been defined in the parent interfaces `MVCHome` and `MVCObject`. `CustomerListHome` and `CustomerList` extend these interfaces and thus do not need to explicitly define any additional methods.

You will also find that by creating parent interfaces for your EJB interfaces, and then sub-classing all of the EJBs for your application with these interfaces, you will save yourself some typing. The code below shows the code for the `CustomerListHome` interface for our `CustomerList` EJB:

```
package mvc.custlist;

import java.io.Serializable;
import javax.ejb.EJBHome;
import java.rmi.RemoteException;
import javax.ejb.CreateException;
import mvc.templates.*;

public interface CustomerListHome extends MVCHome{

}
```

Save this file as `C:\BegJavaDB\Ch22\mvc\custlist\CustomerListHome.java`.

The second piece of the `CustomerList` EJB is the remote interface, `CustomerList`. The `CustomerList` interface extends the `MVCObject` interface and is the conduit through which the application and EJB communicate. An application is never allowed direct access to the EJB methods that carry out the actual work. Instead, the EJB's remote interface (the `CustomerList` interface) sits between the application and the EJB. An EJB's remote interface allows an application to use it without having to know where the EJB is physically located:

```
package mvc.custlist;

import mvc.templates.*;

public interface CustomerList extends MVCObject{

}
```

Save this file as `C:\BegJavaDB\Ch22\mvc\custlist\CustomerList.java`.

The final piece of the `CustomerList` EJB is the `CustomerListBean`. This class contains the code that will process the end-user's request. It also implements the `MVCBean` interface.

```
package mvc.custlist;

/* Standard Java class package */
import java.rmi.RemoteException;
import java.io.File;
import java.util.Collection;
import java.util.Iterator;

/* Pulled from the J2EE or JBoss servlet.jar */
import javax.servlet.http.HttpServletRequest;

/* Pulled from the J2EE or JBoss ejb.jar */
import javax.naming.InitialContext;
import javax.ejb.SessionContext;

/* Classes pulled from the xerces.jar */
import org.w3c.dom.Document;
import org.w3c.dom.Element;
import org.apache.xerces.dom.DocumentImpl;

import mvc.templates.*;
import mvc.*;
import mvc.entitybeans.customers.*;
import mvc.entitybeans.postalcodes.*;


public class CustomerListBean implements MVCBean {

  /*
   * The retrieve method for CustomerListBean retrieves all of the customers
   * and their addresses from the Music Record database. The data is
   * packaged as XML and returned to the application invoking the
   * CustomerList EJB.
   */
  public Document retrieve(HttpServletRequest _request)
                            throws RemoteException, Exception {

    InitialContext ctx = new InitialContext();
    CustomersHome customersHome = (CustomersHome) ctx.lookup("Customers");

    Collection customersCollections = customersHome.findAll();

    /* Building the XML Document that contains the customerRS data */
    Document xmlDocReturned = buildXML(customersCollections, ctx);

    return xmlDocReturned;
  }

  /*
   * The post() method is returning null because the CustomerList screen
   * does not actually save any data.
   */
  public Document post(HttpServletRequest _request)
                        throws RemoteException, Exception {
    return null;
  }

  /*
   * The buildXML method builds an XML document containing the customer
   * address data retrieved from the music record database.
   */
```

```
private Document buildXML(Collection _customerCollections,
                          InitialContext _ctx) throws Exception {
  Document xmlDoc = new DocumentImpl();

  /* Creating the rootElement */
  Element rootElement = xmlDoc.createElement("CUSTOMERS");
  Element customerElement = xmlDoc.createElement("CUSTOMER");

  xmlDoc.appendChild(rootElement);

  Iterator iterator = _customerCollections.iterator();

  /* Cycling through all of the records within the resultset */
  while (iterator.hasNext()) {

    /* Retrieve my customer object from my iterator */
    Customers customer = (Customers) iterator.next();

    /* Setting up my primary key for my customer order */
    customerElement.setAttribute("customerid",
                             customer.getCustomerId().toString());

    /* Adding my different elements to the order header */
    customerElement.appendChild(MVCHelper.buildDBElement(xmlDoc,
            "CUSTOMERFIRSTNAME", customer.getCustomerFirstName()));

    customerElement.appendChild(MVCHelper.buildDBElement(xmlDoc,
            "CUSTOMERLASTNAME", customer.getCustomerLastName()));

    customerElement.appendChild(MVCHelper.buildDBElement(xmlDoc,
            "CUSTOMERADDRESS1", customer.getCustomerAddress1()));

    customerElement.appendChild(MVCHelper.buildDBElement(xmlDoc,
            "CUSTOMERADDRESS2", customer.getCustomerAddress2()));

    customerElement.appendChild(MVCHelper.buildDBElement(xmlDoc,
            "CUSTOMERCITY", customer.getCustomerCity()));

    /* Retrieving my postal code information */
    PostalCodesHome postalCodesHome =
      (PostalCodesHome) _ctx.lookup("PostalCodes");
    PostalCodes postalCodes =
      postalCodesHome.findByPrimaryKey(customer.getCustomerPostalCode());

    customerElement.appendChild(MVCHelper.buildDBElement(xmlDoc,
            "CUSTOMERSTATE", postalCodes.getStateProv()));

    customerElement.appendChild(MVCHelper.buildDBElement(xmlDoc,
            "CUSTOMERZIP", postalCodes.getPostalCode()));

    rootElement.appendChild(customerElement);
    customerElement = xmlDoc.createElement("CUSTOMER");

    MVCHelper.printDOM(xmlDoc, new File("c:\\temp\\output.xml"));
  }

  return xmlDoc;
}
```

```
    /*
     * Standard EJB Methods. For simplicity's sake these methods have
     * been implemented as empty methods.
     */
    public void ejbCreate() {}
    public void ejbRemove() {}
    public void ejbActivate() {}
    public void ejbPassivate() {}
    public void setSessionContext(SessionContext sessionCtx) {}
}
```

Save this file as `C:\BegJavaDB\Ch22\mvc\custlist\CustomerListBean.java`. Again, we can't compile this class yet because there are other as yet unwritten classes it depends on. We'll also show the `ejb-jar.xml` file when we come to compile and package this EJB.

How It Works

The `retrieve()` method is the most appropriate place to begin the discussion. The first action the `retrieve()` method performs is to retrieve all of the customers from the Music Store database. The `retrieve()` method does this by instantiating a `Customers` entity EJB and calling its `findAll()` method. The `findAll()` method returns a `Collection` object, called `customerCollections`, that contains a `Customers` object for each customer in the Music Store database.

```
InitialContext ctx = new InitialContext();
CustomersHome customersHome = (CustomersHome) ctx.lookup("Customers");

Collection customersCollections = customersHome.findAll();
```

Don't worry about the details of the `Customers` entity EJB just yet; we will be covering this EJB, along with the `PostalCodes` entity EJB, later on in the chapter.

Using the `Customers` entity EJB instead of a SQL statement is an extremely powerful method for retrieving data. First, we don't have to tie our business logic (the `CustomerList` session EJB) to the actual database tables in the Music Store database. The physical structure of the database is completely abstracted away by the `Customers` entity EJB. Secondly, because the `Customers` entity EJB is a Container-Managed Persistence (CMP) entity bean, no SQL or JDBC code needs to be rewritten to retrieve customer information. If the `CustomerList` EJB had been written using SQL, you would have had to embed the following code into your `CustomerListBean.retrieve()` method:

```
/*Building the SQL statement for retrieving CustomerAddress data*/
StringBuffer sql = new StringBuffer("");

sql.append("SELECT                                       ");
sql.append("  customers.CustomerId          ,             ");
sql.append("  customers.CustomerFirstName   ,             ");
sql.append("  customers.CustomerLastName    ,             ");
sql.append("  customers.CustomerAddress1    ,             ");
sql.append("  customers.CustomerAddress2    ,             ");
sql.append("  customers.CustomerCity        ,             ");
sql.append("  postalcodes.StateProv         ,             ");
sql.append("  postalcodes.postalcode        ,             ");
sql.append("  countries.CountryName                      ");
sql.append("FROM                                         ");
sql.append("  customers                     ,             ");
sql.append("  postalcodes                  ,             ");
```

```
    sql.append("  countries                                    ");
    sql.append("WHERE                                          ");
    sql.append("  customers.customerpostalcode=postalcodes.postalcode " );
    sql.append("AND                                            ");
    sql.append("  postalcodes.countryid=countries.countryid ");

    DataSourceClient client = new DataSourceClient();
    Connection connection = client.getConnection("jdbc/oracle");

    /*Retrieve the customer order data from the database*/
   Statement statement  = conn.createStatement();
   ResultSet customerRS = statement.executeQuery(sql.toString());
```

As you can see, using a CMP entity EJB like `Customers` takes significantly less code than the SQL and JDBC code shown above.

After the `customersCollection` object has been filled via the `Customers.findAll()` method, it will be passed along with the `ctx` object to the `buildXML()` method. The `buildXML()` method builds the XML `Document` object that will be returned to the `RequestHandler` class.

The `buildXML()` method builds an XML document using the one-to-one mapping techniques discussed earlier in Chapter 20. There are two differences between the `buildXML()` method shown here and the code XML shown in Chapter 20:

- The data for the XML document being built is retrieved via an individual `Customers` entity EJB. It is not being retrieved from a JDBC `ResultSet`.
- The `Customers` entity EJB does not contain postal code information. Inside the `buildXML()` method a `PostalCodes` entity EJB is instantiated and used to populate the individual customer's postal code and state information.

The `buildXML()` method is shown below, with the two items discussed in the bullet points above, highlighted:

```
  private Document buildXML(Collection _customerCollections,
                            InitialContext _ctx) throws Exception {
    Document xmlDoc = new DocumentImpl();

    /* Creating the rootElement */
    Element rootElement = xmlDoc.createElement("CUSTOMERS");
    Element customerElement = xmlDoc.createElement("CUSTOMER");

    xmlDoc.appendChild(rootElement);

    Iterator iterator = _customerCollections.iterator();

    /* Cycling through all of the records within the resultset */
    while (iterator.hasNext()) {

      /* Retrieve my customer object from my iterator */
      Customers customer = (Customers) iterator.next();

      /* Setting up my primary key for my customer order */
      customerElement.setAttribute("customerid",
                                   customer.getCustomerId().toString());
```

```
      /* Adding my different elements to the order header */
      customerElement.appendChild(MVCHelper.buildDBElement(xmlDoc,
              "CUSTOMERFIRSTNAME", customer.getCustomerFirstName()));

      customerElement.appendChild(MVCHelper.buildDBElement(xmlDoc,
              "CUSTOMERLASTNAME", customer.getCustomerLastName()));

      customerElement.appendChild(MVCHelper.buildDBElement(xmlDoc,
              "CUSTOMERADDRESS1", customer.getCustomerAddress1()));

      customerElement.appendChild(MVCHelper.buildDBElement(xmlDoc,
              "CUSTOMERADDRESS2", customer.getCustomerAddress2()));

      customerElement.appendChild(MVCHelper.buildDBElement(xmlDoc,
              "CUSTOMERCITY", customer.getCustomerCity()));

      /* Retrieving my postal code information */
      PostalCodesHome postalCodesHome =
        (PostalCodesHome) _ctx.lookup("PostalCodes");
      PostalCodes postalCodes =
        postalCodesHome.findByPrimaryKey(customer.getCustomerPostalCode());

      customerElement.appendChild(MVCHelper.buildDBElement(xmlDoc,
              "CUSTOMERSTATE", postalCodes.getStateProv()));

      customerElement.appendChild(MVCHelper.buildDBElement(xmlDoc,
              "CUSTOMERZIP", postalCodes.getPostalCode()));

      rootElement.appendChild(customerElement);
      customerElement = xmlDoc.createElement("CUSTOMER");

      MVCHelper.printDOM(xmlDoc, new File("c:\\temp\\output.xml"));
    }

    return xmlDoc;
  }
```

The XML `Document` object built by the `buildXML()` method will retrieve the following data from the music record database:

```
<CUSTOMERS>
  <CUSTOMER customerid="1000">
    <CUSTOMERFIRSTNAME>Catherine</CUSTOMERFIRSTNAME>
    <CUSTOMERLASTNAME>Crean</CUSTOMERLASTNAME>
    <CUSTOMERADDRESS1>62 Windsor Drive</CUSTOMERADDRESS1>
    <CUSTOMERADDRESS2/>
    <CUSTOMERCITY>Shelton</CUSTOMERCITY>
    <CUSTOMERSTATE>CT</CUSTOMERSTATE>
    <CUSTOMERZIP>06484</CUSTOMERZIP>
  </CUSTOMER>
  <CUSTOMER customerid="1001">
    <CUSTOMERFIRSTNAME>Steve</CUSTOMERFIRSTNAME>
    <CUSTOMERLASTNAME>Davis</CUSTOMERLASTNAME>
    <CUSTOMERADDRESS1>567 Captain&apos;s Bluff</CUSTOMERADDRESS1>
    <CUSTOMERADDRESS2>Unit 4A</CUSTOMERADDRESS2>
    <CUSTOMERCITY>West Haven</CUSTOMERCITY>
    <CUSTOMERSTATE>CT</CUSTOMERSTATE>
    <CUSTOMERZIP>06877</CUSTOMERZIP>
    <CUSTOMERCOUNTRY>United States</CUSTOMERCOUNTRY>
  </CUSTOMER>
```

```
    <CUSTOMER customerid="1002">
      <CUSTOMERFIRSTNAME>Villiage DJ</CUSTOMERFIRSTNAME>
      <CUSTOMERLASTNAME/>
      <CUSTOMERADDRESS1>125 Stanford Road</CUSTOMERADDRESS1>
      <CUSTOMERADDRESS2/>
      <CUSTOMERCITY>Trumbull</CUSTOMERCITY>
      <CUSTOMERSTATE>CT</CUSTOMERSTATE>
      <CUSTOMERZIP>06628</CUSTOMERZIP>
    </CUSTOMER>
    <CUSTOMER customerid="1003">
      <CUSTOMERFIRSTNAME>Diane </CUSTOMERFIRSTNAME>
      <CUSTOMERLASTNAME>Asmus</CUSTOMERLASTNAME>
      <CUSTOMERADDRESS1>324 White Street</CUSTOMERADDRESS1>
      <CUSTOMERADDRESS2/>
      <CUSTOMERCITY>Shelton</CUSTOMERCITY>
      <CUSTOMERSTATE>CT</CUSTOMERSTATE>
      <CUSTOMERZIP>06484</CUSTOMERZIP>
    </CUSTOMER>
  </CUSTOMERS>
```

After the above XML `Document` has been built, it will be returned to the `RequestHandler`. The `RequestHandler` then forwards the XML `Document` to the `XSLTManager`. The `XSLTManager` will take the data in the `Document` object and format HTML out of it.

View

The 'view' piece of this chapter's MVC framework is encapsulated in the `XSLTManager` class:

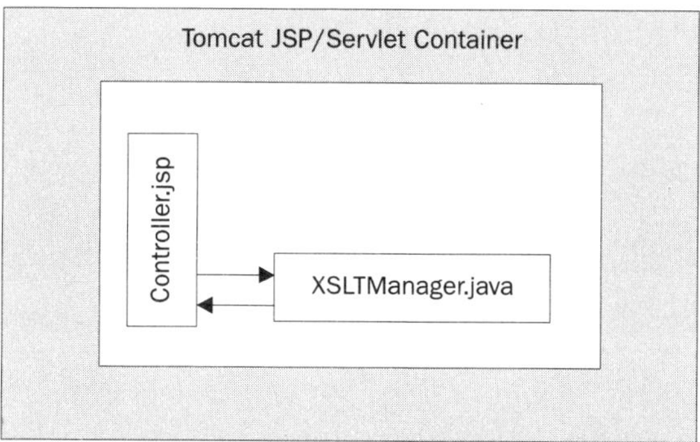

Why go through all of the work of wrapping the XSLT processor code into a class? The primary reason is that you can switch XSL processors without having to rewrite major pieces of any of your applications. As a developer writing applications based on the MVC framework presented here, you do not care what XSL processor is being used. Instead, you care that there is a service out there called a 'view' that will transform your XML and XSL into HTML.

This power of abstraction is extremely useful. For instance, suppose you want to use the Oracle XSL processor rather than the Xalan XSL processor. The `XSLTManager` can be changed to use the new processor. As long as your XSL stylesheets use standard XSL and do not leverage any of the proprietary extensions an XSLT vendor might add to their XSLT processor implementation, your applications would never know the difference. This ability to easily switch XSL processors highlights one of the main keys to solid application architecture.

Abstract away the implementation details of any task to the point that the actual task being carried out can be changed without affecting the rest of the application.

The customerList.xsl Stylesheet

The first screen in the customer address maintenance application is formatted and presented by the `customerAddress.xsl` stylesheet. This stylesheet formats the data returned into an HTML table and creates a hyperlink for each of the customer addresses in the Music Store database. The `customerAddress.xsl` looks very much like the stylesheets presented in Chapter 21.

Try It Out – The customerList.xsl Stylesheet

```
<?xml version="1.0" encoding="UTF-8"?>
<xsl:stylesheet version="1.0"
                xmlns:xsl="http://www.w3.org/1999/XSL/Transform">
<xsl:output method="html"/>
<xsl:template match="/">
  <HTML>
    <Title>Music On-line</Title>
    <BODY>
    <TABLE align="left">
      <TR>
        <TD>
          <H2>
            <IMG src="musicStore.gif"/>Music OnLine (The right tunez at the
              right place)
          </H2>
        </TD>
      </TR>
    </TABLE>
    <BR/><BR/><BR/><BR/><BR/><BR/><BR/><BR/><BR/><BR/><HR/>
    <P>
      <FONT size="3">
        Welcome to Music OnLine's Customer Address Maintenance
        Application. Please select the customer's whose
        address you want to edit by clicking on their customer id.
      </FONT>
    </P>
    <HR/>
      <H3>Customer Address List:</H3>
      <TABLE border="1">
        <TBODY>
          <TR>
          <TD align="center" bgcolor="#C0C0C0"><B>Customer Id</B></TD>
          <TD align="center" bgcolor="#C0C0C0"><B>Customer Name and Address
          </B></TD>
          </TR>

          <xsl:for-each select="CUSTOMERS/CUSTOMER">
            <TR>
              <TD align="center">
                <a>
                  <xsl:attribute name="href">
controller.jsp&amp;Request=CustomerAddressMaintenance&amp;Actiond=select&amp
;customerId=<xsl:value-of select="@customerid"/>
```

```
                    </xsl:attribute>
                    <xsl:value-of select="@customerid"/>
                  </a>
                </TD>
                <TD align="left">
                  <xsl:value-of select="CUSTOMERFIRSTNAME"/> 
                  <xsl:value-of select="CUSTOMERLASTNAME"/><BR/>

                     
                  <xsl:value-of select="CUSTOMERADDRESS1"/><BR/>

                     
                  <xsl:value-of select="CUSTOMERADDRESS2"/><BR/>

                     
                  <xsl:value-of select="CUSTOMERCITY"/>, 
                  <xsl:value-of select="CUSTOMERSTATE"/> 
                  <xsl:value-of select="CUSTOMERZIP"/><BR/>

                </TD>
              </TR>
            </xsl:for-each>
          </TBODY>
      </TABLE>
      </BODY>
    </HTML>
  </xsl:template>
  </xsl:stylesheet>
```

Save this as `tomcat\webapps\begjdb\etc\customerList.xsl`. We'll add more stylesheets here soon.

How It Works

After the above XSL stylesheet is used to transform the XML document returned from the `CustomerList` EJB, the following HTML screen will be generated and returned back to the end-user's browser:

Music OnLine (The right tunez at the right place)

Welcome to Music OnLine's Customer Address Maintenance Application. Please select the customer's whose address you want to edit by clicking on their customer id.

Customer Address List:

Customer Id	Customer Name and Address
1000	Catherine Crean 62 Windsor Drive Shelton, CT 06484
1001	Steve Davis 567 Captain's Bluff Unit 4A West Haven, CT 06877
1003	Diane Asmus 324 White Street Shelton, CT 06484

At this point you should be seeing a pattern. Most of the code and concepts presented in this chapter have been built directly on the previous chapters. The JDBC code presented in the `CustomerList` EJB is based on examples from Chapter 19. The code used to build the XML `Document` object is taken directly from Chapter 20. The `XSLTManager` and the `customerList.xsl` file are built on examples from Chapter 21. Developing architecture does not mean writing, or even rewriting, code from the ground up.

Building Further Screens

Our previous code examples have focused more on the MVC architecture and less on how to actually build a screen and deploy it within the MVC architecture. This section is going to strip away all of the architectural detail and look at building the second half of the customer address maintenance application: the customer address maintenance screen. This screen lets the user modify address information for a selected customer. The customer address maintenance screen looks like this:

Music OnLine (The right tunez at the right place)

Welcome to Music OnLine's Customer Address Maintenance Application. Please make your customer edits and hit the save button on the screen. After the save button has been hit, you will be returned back to the customer list.

Customer Address Information

Customer Name: Steve Davis

Street Address 1 :	567 Captain's Bluff
Street Address 2 :	Unit 4A
City:	West Haven
Zip Code:	06877

Save

To build and deploy this application in our MVC architecture requires four steps:

1. Building the EJBs (both the session and entity beans) that will process the end-users request.

2. Building the XSL that will present the address maintenance screen to the end-user.

3. Modifying the `xslConfig.properties` file to include the new XSL stylesheet. We have not introduced how the `xslConfig.properties` file is used. This will be covered in a later section.

4. Deploying the EJB to the JBoss application server.

The customer address maintenance screen consists of three pieces of Java code and one XSL stylesheet:

1. The `AddressMaintenance` EJB. This EJB consists of three files:

    - `AddressMaintenance.java` – The remote interface for the EJB
    - `AddressMaintenanceHome.java` – The home interface for the EJB
    - `AddressMaintenanceBean.java` – The bean class containing all of the implementation code for the EJB

2. The `Customers` entity EJB. This EJB consists of three files:

   - `Customers.java` – The remote interface for the EJB
   - `CustomersHome.java` – The home interface for the EJB
   - `CustomersBean.java` – The bean class containing all of the implementation code for the EJB

3. The `PostalCodes` entity EJB. This EJB consists of three files:

   - `PostalCodes.java` – The remote interface for the EJB
   - `PostalCodesHome.java` – The home interface for the EJB
   - `PostalCodesBean.java` – The bean class containing all of the implementation code for the EJB

4. The `AddressMaintenance.xsl` file

Building the AddressMaintenance EJB

The `AddressMaintenance` EJB will be used to retrieve and post individual customer address records from the Music Store database. The `AddressMaintenance` EJB has the same basic structure as the `CustomerList` EJB. It has `retrieve()` and `post()` methods, and will return an XML document after a call to one of these methods.

Both the `CustomerList` and the `AddressMaintenance` EJBs are explicitly written so that they never interact directly with the Music Store database. These EJBs do not know where the database is located (via the JDBC URL) or how the tables are physically structured (a SQL statement). The customer address maintenance application has completely decoupled the business logic and data logic within the application.

This decoupling of the business logic and data logic is called **data abstraction**. Data abstraction is a very powerful concept that helps shield application developers from the complexity of writing SQL code to manipulate a database.

For the purposes of this discussion we are going to use two CMP entity EJBs, `Customers` and `PostalCodes`, to hide the details of how we access the customer record database. Entity EJBs provide a portable means of isolating the 'model' services from the database. They can be complex to write for the new developer. Entity beans offer the highest level of data abstraction; they hide the process of managing database transactions and they provide a standard mechanism for building an object interface over corporate data sources.

AddressMaintenance EJB

The `AddressMaintenance` EJB consists of three classes:

- `AddressMaintenance.java` – The EJB's remote interface
- `AddressMaintenanceHome.java` – The EJB's home interface
- `AddressMaintenanceBean.java` – The EJB's bean class that has all of the implemented code

The `AddressMaintenance` and `AddressMaintenanceHome` interfaces look very much like the `CustomerList` remote and home interfaces defined in the earlier sections of this chapter. These two interfaces are presented opposite, but will not be discussed.

Try It Out – The AddressMaintenance EJB

The AddressMaintenance.java Remote Interface

```
package mvc.addressmaintenance;

import mvc.templates.*;

public interface AddressMaintenance extends MVCObject{

}
```

The AddressMaintenanceHome.java Home Interface

```
package mvc.addressmaintenance;

import mvc.templates.*;

public interface AddressMaintenanceHome extends MVCHome{

}
```

The AddressMaintenanceBean.java Implementation Class

The `AddressMaintenanceBean` is where the really interesting code is located. The `AddressMaintenanceBean` EJB has both the `retrieve()` and `post()` methods fully implemented:

```
package mvc.addressmaintenance;

/* Standard Java Classes */
import java.rmi.RemoteException;
import java.util.Collection;
import java.util.Iterator;
import java.io.File;

/* Imported from the J2EE or JBoss ejb.jar and servlet.jar files */
import javax.ejb.SessionBean;
import javax.ejb.SessionContext;
import javax.naming.InitialContext;
import javax.servlet.http.HttpServletRequest;

/* Imported from the xerces.jar file */
import org.w3c.dom.Document;                     /* W3C Interfaces */
import org.w3c.dom.Element;
import org.apache.xerces.dom.DocumentImpl;   /* Xerces DOM Classes */

/* Class files for the chapter */
import mvc.templates.*;
import mvc.MVCHelper;
import mvc.entitybeans.customers.*;
import mvc.entitybeans.postalcodes.*;
import mvc.custlist.*;


public class AddressMaintenanceBean implements MVCBean {
```

```
/*
 * The retrieve method for the AddressMaintenanceBean is using the
 * Customers and PostalCodes entity beans to retrieve a customer address
 * record and build an XML document to return back to the calling
 * application.
 */
public Document retrieve(HttpServletRequest _request)
                            throws RemoteException, Exception {
  Integer customerId = new Integer(_request.getParameter("customerId"));

  InitialContext ctx = new InitialContext();
  CustomersHome customersHome = (CustomersHome) ctx.lookup("Customers");
  Customers customers = customersHome.findByPrimaryKey(customerId);

  PostalCodesHome postalCodesHome =
                 (PostalCodesHome) ctx.lookup("PostalCodes");
  PostalCodes postalCodes =
      postalCodesHome.findByPrimaryKey(customers.getCustomerPostalCode());

  return buildXML(customers, postalCodes, ctx);
}

/*
 * The buildXML method will build an XML document based on the values
 * stored in the internal class variables. It will then query the
 * music record database and retrieve a list of all of the Postal Codes
 * stored within the postal codes table. These postal codes are used to
 * populate the dropdown box seen in the address maintenance screen.
 */
private Document buildXML(Customers _customers, PostalCodes _postalCodes,
                           InitialContext _ctx) throws Exception {
  Document xmlDoc = new DocumentImpl();

  /* Creating the root element */
  Element rootElement = xmlDoc.createElement("CUSTOMERS");
  Element customer = xmlDoc.createElement("CUSTOMER");

  xmlDoc.appendChild(rootElement);
  customer.setAttribute("customerid",
                        _customers.getCustomerId().toString());

  /* Adding my different elements to the customer record */
  customer.appendChild(MVCHelper.buildDBElement(xmlDoc,
          "CUSTOMERFIRSTNAME", _customers.getCustomerFirstName()));

  customer.appendChild(MVCHelper.buildDBElement(xmlDoc,
          "CUSTOMERLASTNAME", _customers.getCustomerLastName()));

  customer.appendChild(MVCHelper.buildDBElement(xmlDoc,
          "CUSTOMERADDRESS1", _customers.getCustomerAddress1()));

  customer.appendChild(MVCHelper.buildDBElement(xmlDoc,
          "CUSTOMERADDRESS2", _customers.getCustomerAddress2()));

  customer.appendChild(MVCHelper.buildDBElement(xmlDoc, "CUSTOMERCITY",
          _customers.getCustomerCity()));
```

```
    customer.appendChild(MVCHelper.buildDBElement(xmlDoc, "CUSTOMERSTATE",
            _postalCodes.getStateProv()));

    customer.appendChild(MVCHelper.buildDBElement(xmlDoc, "CUSTOMERZIP",
            _postalCodes.getPostalCode()));

    rootElement.appendChild(customer);

    /*
     * Retrieving all of the postal codes stored within the
     * music record database and
     * appending them onto the customer's document root object.
     */
    rootElement.appendChild(buildPostalCodes(xmlDoc, _ctx));
    return xmlDoc;
  }

  /*
   * The buildPostCodes method will build the <POSTALCODES></POSTALCODES>
   * piece of the <CUSTOMERS>...</CUSTOMERS> XML DOM that is returned to
   * the code calling the toXML() method on this class.
   */
  private Element buildPostalCodes(Document _xmlDoc,
                                   InitialContext _ctx) throws Exception {
    PostalCodesHome postalCodesHome =
               (PostalCodesHome) _ctx.lookup("PostalCodes");
    Collection postalCodeCollections = postalCodesHome.findAll();

    /* Appending individual <POSTALCODE> elements to <POSTALCODES> */
    Iterator iterator = postalCodeCollections.iterator();

    /* Building the <POSTALCODES> XML Element */
    Element postalCodesElement = _xmlDoc.createElement("POSTALCODES");
    Element postalCodeElement = null;

    while (iterator.hasNext()) {
      PostalCodes postalCodes = (PostalCodes) iterator.next();

      postalCodeElement = _xmlDoc.createElement("POSTALCODE");
      postalCodeElement.setAttribute("postalcodeid",
                                 postalCodes.getPostalCode());
      postalCodesElement.appendChild(postalCodeElement);
    }

    return postalCodesElement;
  }

  /*
   * The post method populates an AddressMaintenanceHelper class with
   * data returned from the music record database.
   * Since this screen returns to the CustomerList
   * screen after updating the record, it instantiates the CustomerList EJB
   * and performs a retrieve.
   */
  public Document post(HttpServletRequest _request)
          throws RemoteException, Exception {
    Integer customerId = new Integer(_request.getParameter("customerId"));

    InitialContext ctx = new InitialContext();
    CustomersHome customersHome = (CustomersHome) ctx.lookup("Customers");
```

```
      Customers customers = customersHome.findByPrimaryKey(customerId);

      /*
       * Populating the addressMaintenanceHelper class with data posted when
       * the user hit the Save button on the Address Maintenance screen.
       */
     customers.setCustomerAddress1(_request.getParameter("customerAddress1"));
     customers.setCustomerAddress2(_request.getParameter("customerAddress2"));
     customers.setCustomerCity(_request.getParameter("customerCity"));
     customers.setCustomerPostalCode(_request.getParameter("postalCode"));

      /*
       * Instantiating the CustomerList class and using it to return a
       * refreshed list of the Customer Records.
       */
      MVCHome customerListHome = (MVCHome) ctx.lookup("CustomerList");
      MVCObject mvcComponent = customerListHome.create();

      return mvcComponent.retrieve(_request);
    }

    /*
     * Standard EJB Methods. For simplicity's sake these methods have
     * been implemented as empty methods.
     */
    public void ejbCreate() {}
    public void ejbRemove() {}
    public void ejbActivate() {}
    public void ejbPassivate() {}
    public void setSessionContext(SessionContext sessionCtx) {}
}
```

Save this as `C:\BegJavaDB\Ch22\mvc\addressmaintenance\AddressMaintenanceBean.java`. We'll compile this when we've written the other classes this depends upon.

How It Works

The `retrieve()` method in the `AddressMaintenanceBean` classes uses the `Customers` and `PostalCodes` entity EJBs to retrieve the customer address record from the Music Store database:

```
      Integer customerId = new Integer(_request.getParameter("customerId"));

      InitialContext ctx = new InitialContext();
      CustomersHome customersHome = (CustomersHome) ctx.lookup("Customers");
      Customers customers = customersHome.findByPrimaryKey(customerId);
```

In the code above, the customer selected by the end-user is retrieved by instantiating a `Customers` entity EJB and calling its `findPrimaryKey()` method. The customer ID selected by the end-user is passed into the `findByPrimaryKey()` method.

Once the specific customer has been retrieved, the postal code information for the customer is retrieved by instantiating a `PostalCodes` object, called `postalCodes`. The postal code that is to be retrieved will be determined by the value inside the `customers.getPostalCode()` method call:

```
PostalCodesHome postalCodesHome =
                (PostalCodesHome) ctx.lookup("PostalCodes");
PostalCodes postalCodes =
     postalCodesHome.findByPrimaryKey(customers.getCustomerPostalCode());
```

Once the `Customers` and `PostalCodes` entity EJBs have been created they are passed to the `buildXML()` method. The `buildXML()` method will pull the customer address information from the two beans and build an XML document object. This XML document is then returned to `RequestHandler` class. Part of the code for the `buildXML()` method is shown below, although it should be familiar by now:

```
private Element buildPostalCodes(Document _xmlDoc,
                                 InitialContext _ctx) throws Exception {
  Document xmlDoc = new DocumentImpl();

  /* Creating the root element */
  Element rootElement = xmlDoc.createElement("CUSTOMERS");
  Element customer = xmlDoc.createElement("CUSTOMER");

  xmlDoc.appendChild(rootElement);
  customer.setAttribute("customerid",
                        _customers.getCustomerId().toString());

  /* Adding my different elements to the customer record */
  customer.appendChild(MVCHelper.buildDBElement(xmlDoc,
          "CUSTOMERFIRSTNAME", _customers.getCustomerFirstName()));

// Other elements missed

  rootElement.appendChild(customer);

  rootElement.appendChild(buildPostalCodes(xmlDoc, _ctx));
  return xmlDoc;
}
```

The `buildPostalCodes()` method called in the above code will build a list of all of the postal codes stored in the music record database as an XML element. It will then append the returned postal codes to the `rootElement` object.

```
rootElement.appendChild(buildPostalCodes(xmlDoc, _ctx));
```

The `buildPostCodes()` methods is a very straightforward piece of code:

```
private Element buildPostalCodes(Document _xmlDoc,
                                 InitialContext _ctx) throws Exception {
  PostalCodesHome postalCodesHome =
                (PostalCodesHome) _ctx.lookup("PostalCodes");
  Collection postalCodeCollections = postalCodesHome.findAll();
```

The `buildPostalCodes()` method builds an XML document by retrieving a `Collection` of `PostalCodes` entity beans from the Music Store database.

The method then loops through the collection and builds an element containing all of the postal codes based on the data retrieved from a `PostalCode` entity bean.

```
    /* Appending individual <POSTALCODE> elements to to <POSTALCODES> */
    Iterator iterator = postalCodeCollections.iterator();

    /* Building the <POSTALCODES> XML Element */
    Element postalCodesElement = _xmlDoc.createElement("POSTALCODES");
    Element postalCodeElement = null;

    while (iterator.hasNext()) {
      PostalCodes postalCodes = (PostalCodes) iterator.next();

      postalCodeElement = _xmlDoc.createElement("POSTALCODE");
      postalCodeElement.setAttribute("postalcodeid",
                                     postalCodes.getPostalCode());
      postalCodesElement.appendChild(postalCodeElement);
    }

    return postalCodesElement;
  }
```

As the process involved with building an XML document should be well understood by now, we will not be walking through the XML generated by the `buildPostalCode()` method in any further detail. Let's look at the `AddressMaintenance` EJBs `post()` method.

The `post()` method for the `AddressMaintenance` bean uses two different EJBs to carry out its work. The first bean, the `Customers` bean, is instantiated and used to update the customer record submitted by the user:

```
Integer customerId = new Integer(_request.getParameter("customerId"));

InitialContext ctx = new InitialContext();
CustomersHome customersHome = (CustomersHome) ctx.lookup("Customers");
Customers customers = customersHome.findByPrimaryKey(customerId);

customers.setCustomerAddress1(_request.getParameter("customerAddress1"));
customers.setCustomerAddress2(_request.getParameter("customerAddress2"));
customers.setCustomerCity(_request.getParameter("customerCity"));
customers.setCustomerPostalCode(_request.getParameter("postalCode"));
```

Once the user's data has been set in the `customers` entity EJB, the end-user should be returned to the customer list screen. To accomplish this the `post()` method uses the code already found in the `CustomerList` EJB.

```
MVCHome customerListHome = (MVCHome) ctx.lookup("CustomerList");
MVCObject mvcComponent = customerListHome.create();

return mvcComponent.retrieve(_request);
```

The `AddressMaintenanceBean.post()` method, upon successfully saving the updated customer address information will instantiate the `CustomerList` EJB and invoke its `retrieve()` method. The `Document` object returned from the `mvcComponent.retrieve()` method will then be passed right back from the `AddressMaintenanceBean.post()` method.

Building the Customers and PostalCodes Entity Beans

The `Customers` and `PostalCodes` entity beans abstract away the `Customers` and `PostalCode` tables in the Music Store database. As stated earlier in the chapter, we are using entity beans to abstract away the implementation details of our database. Our rewritten customer address maintenance application does not know how the tables are physically laid out in the database.

Why use entity beans? After all there are other methods of data abstraction that should not be discounted out of hand. These methods include:

- Helper classes. Helper classes perform the database transaction and if necessary build the XML document for the 'model'. This method is very easy to implement, but does not provide all of the built-in transactional support found within more robust technologies like entity EJBs.
- Database stored procedures. This method allows extremely fast transaction times with the database, but also ties the data logic to a proprietary format. In addition, many older applications are written using stored procedures. Using these stored procedures in your EJBs can significantly cut down on application development time.

We use entity beans for two reasons. First, entity beans abstract away all of the gory development details a typical developer goes through when writing a database application. Using entity EJBs, a developer does not have to worry about database connection information or when to commit or rollback a transaction. These "plumbing" details are abstracted away by a familiar, object-based model of development. Furthermore, depending on whether or not you are using container-managed persistence or bean-managed persistence, you can eliminate the need for your development team writing SQL code.

The second reason why entity beans were chosen as our database abstraction method is that they are database-platform-vendor independent. Writing an entity EJB does not tie you to a particular database vendor's database. Using entity EJBs, you can move your entire database and the code that accesses it to another database platform without a significant amount of effort. Other methods of data abstraction, like stored procedures, do not offer this flexibility. Stored procedures, while offering better performance than an entity EJB, are vendor-specific. Code written in Oracle's PL/SQL stored procedure language cannot be moved over to Microsoft's SQL server without a complete rewrite of the code.

The examples in this chapter were written using Container-Managed Persistence (CMP) rather then Bean Managed Persistence (BMP). Using CMP-based entity beans means we do not have to write SQL code for either the `Customers` or `PostalCodes` EJBs. Instead, the **JAWS** (**Just Another Web Storage**) object-relational (O-R) mapping tool is used to build both the `Customers` and `PostalCodes` entity Beans. JAWS comes with JBoss, so we don't have to rush off to get yet more downloads.

Let's review the code from the `Customers` entity EJB.

Try It Out – Customers Entity EJB

The `Customers` entity EJB is used to retrieve data from the `customers` table in the Music Store database. Like all EJBs the Customers entity bean has a remote interface, a home interface, and a bean class.

The `Customers.java` file is the `Customers` EJB's remote interface and looks like this:

```
package mvc.entitybeans.customers;

import javax.ejb.EJBObject;
import java.rmi.RemoteException;

public interface Customers extends EJBObject {

  /* Accessors */
  public Integer getCustomerId() throws RemoteException;
  public String getCustomerFirstName() throws RemoteException;
  public String getCustomerLastName() throws RemoteException;
  public String getCustomerAddress1() throws RemoteException;
  public String getCustomerAddress2() throws RemoteException;
  public String getCustomerCity() throws RemoteException;
  public String getCustomerPostalCode() throws RemoteException;

  /* Mutators */
  public void setCustomerId(Integer inCustomerId) throws RemoteException;
  public void setCustomerFirstName(String inCustomerFirstName)
                                     throws RemoteException;
  public void setCustomerLastName(String inCustomerLastName)
                                    throws RemoteException;
  public void setCustomerAddress1(String inCustomerAddress1)
                                    throws RemoteException;
  public void setCustomerAddress2(String inCustomerAddress2)
                                    throws RemoteException;
  public void setCustomerCity(String inCustomerCity) throws RemoteException;
  public void setCustomerPostalCode(String inCustomerPostalCode)
                                      throws RemoteException;
}
```

The `Customers.java` remote interface defines all of the getter and setter methods for the `Customer` EJB.

The home interface, `CustomersHome.java`, for the `Customers` entity EJB defines three methods: `create()`, `findByPrimaryKey()`, and `findAll()`:

```
package mvc.entitybeans.customers;

import java.rmi.RemoteException;
import javax.ejb.CreateException;
import javax.ejb.FinderException;
import javax.ejb.EJBHome;
import java.util.Collection;

public interface CustomersHome extends EJBHome {

  public Customers create(Integer customerId)
                         throws RemoteException, CreateException;
  public Customers findByPrimaryKey(Integer target)
                                  throws RemoteException, FinderException;
  public Collection findAll() throws RemoteException, FinderException;
}
```

The `create()` method is used to create a customer record in the `customers` table. The author has to admit a bit of laziness on his part. The `create()` method above only passes in one field. In reality you want to pass in all of the fields that would make up a new record. So, if you wanted to build an entity EJB outside of this chapter your `create()` method might look like:

```
public Customers create(Integer customerId, String customerFirstName,
                        String CustomerLastName, etc...)
                        throws RemoteException, CreateException;
```

The `findByPrimaryKey()` method will retrieve a single customer record from the Music Store database. The record retrieved will match the customer ID passed into the method. The `findAll()` method will retrieve a collection containing all of the customer records in the customers table.

The `CustomersBean` class implements all of the methods defined in the remote interface. However, as you will see from the code below, there is no SQL code present to actually retrieve the data:

```
package mvc.entitybeans.customers;

import java.rmi.RemoteException;
import javax.ejb.CreateException;
import javax.ejb.EntityBean;
import javax.ejb.EntityContext;

public class CustomersBean implements EntityBean {

  public Integer customerId;
  public String customerFirstName;
  public String customerLastName;
  public String customerAddress1;
  public String customerAddress2;
  public String customerCity;
  public String customerPostalCode;

  /* Accessors */
  public Integer getCustomerId() {
    return customerId;
  }
  ;

  public String getCustomerFirstName() {
    return customerFirstName;
  }
  ;

  public String getCustomerLastName() {
    return customerLastName;
  }
  ;

  public String getCustomerAddress1() {
    return customerAddress1;
  }
  ;

  public String getCustomerAddress2() {
    return customerAddress2;
  }
  ;

  public String getCustomerCity() {
    return customerCity;
  }
  ;
```

```
  public String getCustomerPostalCode() {
    return customerPostalCode;
  }
  ;

  /* Mutators */
  public void setCustomerId(Integer inCustomerId) {
    customerId = inCustomerId;
  }
  ;

  public void setCustomerFirstName(String inCustomerFirstName) {
    customerFirstName = inCustomerFirstName;
  }
  ;

  public void setCustomerLastName(String inCustomerLastName) {
    customerLastName = inCustomerLastName;
  }
  ;

  public void setCustomerAddress1(String inCustomerAddress1) {
    customerAddress1 = inCustomerAddress1;
  }
  ;

  public void setCustomerAddress2(String inCustomerAddress2) {
    customerAddress2 = inCustomerAddress2;
  }
  ;

  public void setCustomerCity(String inCustomerCity) {
    customerCity = inCustomerCity;
  }
  ;

  public void setCustomerPostalCode(String inCustomerPostalCode) {
    customerPostalCode = inCustomerPostalCode;
  }
  ;

  public Integer ejbCreate(Integer newId)
          throws CreateException, RemoteException {
    customerId = newId;
    return null;
  }

  public void ejbPostCreate(Integer newId) {}

  public void ejbStore() {}
  public void ejbRemove() {}
  public void ejbActivate() {}
  public void ejbLoad() {}
  public void ejbPassivate() {}
  public void setEntityContext(EntityContext ctx) {}
  public void unsetEntityContext() {}
}
```

Save this as `C:\BegJavaDB\Ch22\mvc\entitybeans\customers\CustomersBean.java`.

Once you have all the Java code for this bean in the `mvc\entitybeans\customers` directory, you can compile it using the following command issued from the `Ch22` directory:

```
>javac -classpath .;%JBOSS%\ejb.jar;%JBOSS%\jnpserver.jar;
  %JBOSS%\jboss.jar;%JBOSS%\jbosssx.jar;%JBOSS%\jaas.jar
  mvc/entitybeans/customers/*.java
```

Where `%JBOSS%` points to the `jboss\client` directory.

How It Works

At this point you might be wondering how the data is actually retrieved from the database. There is no SQL code shown above. The SQL code is generated by JAWS. JAWS uses a file called `jaws.xml` that maps the fields in the `CustomerHome.java` class to the fields in the database. The `jaws.xml` file for the `Customers` entity EJB is shown below:

```
<jaws>
  <default-entity>
  <!-- don't try to create the table, assume we've already created it -->
    <create-table>false</create-table>
    <!-- don't delete the table when we're done either -->
    <remove-table>false</remove-table>
    <tuned-updates>false</tuned-updates>
    <read-only>false</read-only>
    <time-out>300</time-out>
    <select-for-update>false</select-for-update>
  </default-entity>
<!-- these values must match the names defined in the ejb-jar.xml file -->
  <enterprise-beans>
    <entity>
      <ejb-name>Customers</ejb-name>
      <table-name>Customers</table-name>
      <cmp-field>
        <field-name>customerId</field-name>
        <column-name>customerid</column-name>
        <jdbc-type>INTEGER</jdbc-type>
        <sql-type>NUMBER(10)</sql-type>
      </cmp-field>
      <cmp-field>
        <field-name>customerFirstName</field-name>
        <column-name>customerfirstname</column-name>
        <jdbc-type>VARCHAR</jdbc-type>
        <sql-type>VARCHAR(255)</sql-type>
      </cmp-field>
      <cmp-field>
        <field-name>customerLastName</field-name>
        <column-name>customerlastname</column-name>
        <jdbc-type>VARCHAR</jdbc-type>
        <sql-type>VARCHAR(255)</sql-type>
      </cmp-field>
      <cmp-field>
        <field-name>customerAddress1</field-name>
        <column-name>customeraddress1</column-name>
        <jdbc-type>VARCHAR</jdbc-type>
        <sql-type>VARCHAR(255)</sql-type>
      </cmp-field>
      <cmp-field>
        <field-name>customerAddress2</field-name>
```

```
        <column-name>customeraddress2</column-name>
        <jdbc-type>VARCHAR</jdbc-type>
        <sql-type>VARCHAR(255)</sql-type>
      </cmp-field>
      <cmp-field>
        <field-name>customerCity</field-name>
        <column-name>customercity</column-name>
        <jdbc-type>VARCHAR</jdbc-type>
        <sql-type>VARCHAR(255)</sql-type>
      </cmp-field>
      <cmp-field>
        <field-name>customerPostalCode</field-name>
        <column-name>customerpostalcode</column-name>
        <jdbc-type>VARCHAR</jdbc-type>
        <sql-type>VARCHAR(255)</sql-type>
      </cmp-field>
    </entity>
  </enterprise-beans>
</jaws>
```

The <cmp-field></cmp-field> tags above map the field in the `CustomersBean` class with a field in the `customers` table. For example, to map the `customerId` variable in the `CustomersBean` class and the `customerid` column in the `customers` table we would use the following declaration in the `jaws.xml` file:

```
<cmp-field>
  <field-name>customerId</field-name>
  <column-name>customerid</column-name>
  <jdbc-type>INTEGER</jdbc-type>
  <sql-type>NUMBER(10)</sql-type>
</cmp-field>
```

The <field-name></field-name> and <column-name></column-name> tags map the customer ID in the `CustomersBean` class. The <jdbc-type></jdbc-type> tags define what type of Java field is being passed in the code and the <sql-type></sql-type> tag maps to the SQL data type of the column in the database (which in this case are values specific to Oracle).

Deploying the Customers Entity EJB

The Customers EJB needs three deployment descriptor files in order to be deployed to JBoss: an `ejb-jar.xml` file, `jboss.xml` file, and the `jaws.xml` file. The `ejb-jar.xml` file for the `Customers` entity EJB contains additional information in it that defines the database fields the entity EJB maps to. Here is the `ejb-jar.xml` file:

```
<?xml version="1.0" encoding="UTF-8"?>
<!DOCTYPE ejb-jar PUBLIC "-//Sun Microsystems, Inc.//DTD Enterprise
JavaBeans 1.1//EN" "http://java.sun.com/j2ee/dtds/ejb-jar_1_1.dtd">
<ejb-jar>
  <description>Customers Entity EJB</description>
  <display-name>Customers</display-name>
  <enterprise-beans>
    <entity>
      <ejb-name>Customers</ejb-name>
      <home>
        mvc.entitybeans.customers.CustomersHome
      </home>
      <remote>
```

```
        mvc.entitybeans.customers.Customers
      </remote>
      <ejb-class>
        mvc.entitybeans.customers.CustomersBean
      </ejb-class>
      <persistence-type>Container</persistence-type>
      <prim-key-class>java.lang.Integer</prim-key-class>
      <reentrant>False</reentrant>
      <cmp-field>
        <field-name>customerId</field-name>
      </cmp-field>
      <cmp-field>
        <field-name>customerFirstName</field-name>
      </cmp-field>
      <cmp-field>
        <field-name>customerLastName</field-name>
      </cmp-field>
      <cmp-field>
          <field-name>customerAddress1</field-name>
      </cmp-field>
      <cmp-field>
      <field-name>customerAddress2</field-name>
    </cmp-field>
          <cmp-field>
      <field-name>customerCity</field-name>
    </cmp-field>
    <cmp-field>
       <field-name>customerPostalCode</field-name>
    </cmp-field>
    <primkey-field>customerId</primkey-field>
  </entity>
  </enterprise-beans>
  </ejb-jar>
```

Like the <cmp-field></cmp-field> tags shown in the `jaws.xml` field these tags are used by the JBoss application server to identity the fields in the entity EJB that are going to be mapped to fields in the `customers` table.

This should be saved in a `META-INF` directory at the same level as the `mvc` directory. Since we are going to be repeating this procedure a few times, we'll create another directory structure in which to put the class files for our EJBs and the `META-INF` folder. This could be a directory named after the bean. So, for this Customers EJB, we will create a new directory structure as follows:

```
Ch22/
    Customers/
             mvc/entitybeans/customers
             META-INF/
```

It is in the `Ch22/Customers/META-INF` directory that we shall save all three deployment descriptors for the Customers EJB; `ejb-jar.xml`, `jaws.xml`, and `jboss.xml`. We will be repeating this pattern, with modifications, for the other EJBs we create.

> **An EJB will only deploy properly if it has the correct deployment descriptors in the JAR file.**

The third deployment descriptor in the `META-INF` directory is the `jboss.xml` file. The `jboss.xml` file tells the JBoss application server what JNDI (Java Naming and Directory Interface) name to use when a user wants to connect to the application server. Here is the `jboss.xml` file for the Customers entity bean:

```
<?xml version="1.0" encoding="UTF-8"?>
<jboss>
  <enterprise-beans>
     <session>
       <ejb-name>Customers</ejb-name>
       <jndi-name>Customers</jndi-name>
     </session>
  </enterprise-beans>
</jboss>
```

Now that we have all the class files in the right place (the `Ch22/Customers/mvc/entitybeans/customers` directory), and all the deployment descriptors in the right place (the `Ch22/Customers/META-INF directory`), we can create a JAR file ready to deploy. From the `Ch22/Customers` directory, issue the following command:

```
> jar -cvf CustomersEJB.jar mvc META-INF
```

This will create a JAR file called `CustomersEJB.jar`, with the three class files and the three deployment descriptors.

Try It Out – PostalCodes Entity EJB

The `PostalCodes` entity EJB is used to retrieve and save data to the `postalcodes` table. Like, the `Customers` EJB, the `PostalCodes` EJB is using container-managed persistence to generate the SQL to retrieve, insert, update, and delete data in the `postalcodes` table. Shown below are the listings for the `PostalCodes.java`, `PostalCodesHome.java`, and `PostalCodesBean.java` files. Since there is no ground-breaking material presented in the bean, we will not be walking through the code.

PostalCodes.java

```
package mvc.entitybeans.postalcodes;

import javax.ejb.EJBObject;
import java.rmi.RemoteException;

public interface PostalCodes extends EJBObject{

  /*Accessors*/
  public String  getPostalCode() throws RemoteException;
  public String  getCity()       throws RemoteException;
  public String  getStateProv()  throws RemoteException;
  public Integer getCountryId()  throws RemoteException;

  /*Mutators*/
  public void  setPostalCode(String inPostalCode) throws RemoteException;
  public void  setCity(String inCity)       throws RemoteException;
  public void  setStateProv(String inStateProv)  throws RemoteException;
  public void  setCountryId(Integer inCountryId)  throws RemoteException;
}
```

PostalCodesHome.java

```
package mvc.entitybeans.postalcodes;

import java.rmi.RemoteException;
import javax.ejb.CreateException;
import javax.ejb.FinderException;
import javax.ejb.EJBHome;
import java.util.Collection;

public interface PostalCodesHome extends EJBHome{
   public PostalCodes create(String postalCode)
  throws RemoteException, CreateException;
   public PostalCodes findByPrimaryKey(String target)
  throws RemoteException, FinderException;
   public Collection  findAll() throws RemoteException, FinderException;
}
```

PostalCodesBean.java

```
package mvc.entitybeans.postalcodes;

import java.rmi.RemoteException;
import javax.ejb.CreateException;
import javax.ejb.EntityBean;
import javax.ejb.EntityContext;


public class PostalCodesBean  implements EntityBean{
  public String  postalCode;
  public String  city;
  public String  stateProv;
  public Integer countryId;

  /*Accessors*/
  public String  getPostalCode() throws RemoteException{
    return postalCode;
  }

  public String  getCity()       throws RemoteException{
    return city;
  }

  public String  getStateProv()  throws RemoteException{
    return stateProv;
  }

  public Integer getCountryId()  throws RemoteException{
    return countryId;
  }

  /*Mutators*/
  public void  setPostalCode(String inPostalCode) throws RemoteException{
    postalCode = inPostalCode;
  }
  public void  setCity(String inCity)       throws RemoteException{
    city = inCity;
  }
```

```
    public void  setStateProv(String inStateProv)  throws RemoteException{
      stateProv = inStateProv;
    }

    public void  setCountryId(Integer inCountryId)  throws RemoteException{
      countryId = inCountryId;
    }

    public String ejbCreate(String newPostalCode) throws CreateException,
  RemoteException{
      postalCode = newPostalCode;
      return null;
    }

    public void ejbPostCreate(String newPostalCode) {

    }

    public void ejbStore(){}
    public void ejbRemove(){}
    public void ejbActivate(){}
    public void ejbLoad(){}
    public void ejbPassivate(){}
    public void setEntityContext(EntityContext ctx){}
    public void unsetEntityContext(){}
  }
```

Save these files to the `C:\BegJavaDB\Chapter22\mvc\entitybeans\postalcode` directory, and compile them all with the following command run from the `Ch22` directory:

```
> javac -classpath .;%JBOSS%\ejb.jar;%JBOSS%\jnpserver.jar;
  %JBOSS%\jboss.jar;%JBOSS%\jbosssx.jar;%JBOSS%\jaas.jar
  mvc/entitybeans/postalcodes/*.java
```

Deploying the PostalCodes Entity EJB

Like the `Customers` entity EJB, the `PostalCodes` entity EJB requires `ejb-jar.xml`, `jaws.xml`, and `jboss.xml` files. Again, like the Customers EJB, we will create a new directory structure from which to create our JAR file. This structure will be like the following:

```
Ch22/
     PostalCodes/
                mvc/entitybeans/postalcodes/
                META-INF/
```

Copy all the class files for the PostalCodes EJB into the `Ch22/PostalCodes/mvc/entitybeans/postalcodes` directory.

PostalCodes ejb-jar.xml

```
<?xml version="1.0" encoding="UTF-8"?>
<!DOCTYPE ejb-jar PUBLIC "-//Sun Microsystems, Inc.//DTD Enterprise
JavaBeans 1.1//EN" "http://java.sun.com/j2ee/dtds/ejb-jar_1_1.dtd">
<ejb-jar>
  <description>PostalCodes Entity EJB</description>
  <display-name>PostalCodes</display-name>
  <enterprise-beans>
```

```
    <entity>
      <ejb-name>PostalCodes</ejb-name>
      <home>mvc.entitybeans.postalcodes.PostalCodesHome</home>
      <remote>mvc.entitybeans.postalcodes.PostalCodes</remote>
      <ejb-class>mvc.entitybeans.postalcodes.PostalCodesBean
      </ejb-class>
      <persistence-type>Container</persistence-type>
      <prim-key-class>java.lang.String</prim-key-class>
      <reentrant>False</reentrant>
      <cmp-field>
        <field-name>postalCode</field-name>
      </cmp-field>
      <cmp-field>
        <field-name>city</field-name>
      </cmp-field>
      <cmp-field>
        <field-name>stateProv</field-name>
      </cmp-field>
      <cmp-field>
        <field-name>countryId</field-name>
      </cmp-field>
      <primkey-field>postalCode</primkey-field>
    </entity>
  </enterprise-beans>
</ejb-jar>
```

PostalCodes jaws.xml

```
<jaws>
  <default-entity>
    <!-- don't try to create the table, assume we've already created it -->
    <create-table>false</create-table>
    <!-- don't delete the table when we're done either -->
    <remove-table>false</remove-table>
    <tuned-updates>false</tuned-updates>
    <read-only>false</read-only>
    <time-out>300</time-out>
    <select-for-update>false</select-for-update>
  </default-entity>
  <!-- these values must match the names defined in the ejb-jar.xml file -->
  <enterprise-beans>
    <entity>
      <ejb-name>PostalCodes</ejb-name>
        <table-name>PostalCodes</table-name>
      <cmp-field>
        <field-name>postalCode</field-name>
        <column-name>postalcode</column-name>
          <jdbc-type>VARCHAR</jdbc-type>
          <sql-type>VARCHAR(255)</sql-type>
      </cmp-field>
      <cmp-field>
        <field-name>city</field-name>
        <column-name>city</column-name>
          <jdbc-type>VARCHAR</jdbc-type>
          <sql-type>VARCHAR(255)</sql-type>
      </cmp-field>
      <cmp-field>
        <field-name>stateProv</field-name>
        <column-name>stateprov</column-name>
          <jdbc-type>VARCHAR</jdbc-type>
```

```
          <sql-type>VARCHAR(255)</sql-type>
        </cmp-field>
        <cmp-field>
          <field-name>countryId</field-name>
          <column-name>countryid</column-name>
            <jdbc-type>INTEGER</jdbc-type>
            <sql-type>NUMBER(10)</sql-type>
        </cmp-field>
      </entity>
    </enterprise-beans>
  </jaws>
```

PostalCodes jboss.xml

```
<?xml version="1.0" encoding="UTF-8"?>
<jboss>
  <enterprise-beans>
    <session>
      <ejb-name>PostalCodes</ejb-name>
      <jndi-name>PostalCodes</jndi-name>
    </session>
  </enterprise-beans>
</jboss>
```

Once these are all in place in the `Ch22/PostalCodes/META-INF` directory, we can create another JAR file. From the `Ch22/PostalCodes` directory, issue the following command:

```
> jar -cvf PostalCodesEJB.jar mvc META-INF
```

As before, this creates our JAR file. Now, we can compile and package the other EJBs.

Deploying the CustomerList EJB

Remember when we wrote the `CustomerListBean` class and said that we wouldn't be able to compile it yet? Now that we have created and compiled the necessary classes, we can compile the `CustomerList` EJB components. Since we're effectively going to be compiling the `MVCHelper` class as well, we need to include the `xerces.jar` file as well; plus the `CustomerListBean` imports classes from the `servlet.jar` file, so we'll need that in the classpath as well. The following command run from the `Ch22` directory should compile all the Java code we're after:

```
> javac -classpath
        .;%JBOSS%\ejb.jar;%JBOSS%\jnpserver.jar;%JBOSS%\jboss.jar;
        %JBOSS%\jbosssx.jar;%JBOSS%\jaas.jar;%JLIB%\xerces.jar;
        c:\jbosstomcat\tomcat\lib\servlet.jar
        mvc/custlist/*.java
```

Again, `%JBOSS%` points to the `jboss\client` directory, `%JLIB%` points to `c:\java\lib`, and `c:\jbosstomcat\tomcat\lib` is where the `servlet.jar` file that comes with Tomcat can be found. This command will compile the following Java files:

- `custlist/CustomerList`
- `custlist/CustomerListHome`
- `custlist/CustomerListBean`

You can also change the command line so that the following files are compiled:

- `templates/MVCObject`
- `templates/MVCHome`
- `templets.MVCBean`
- `mvc/MVCHelper`

Next, we can begin to create another JAR file. Start by creating a new directory structure as follows:

```
Ch22/
    CustomerList/
                mvc/custlist/
                META-INF/
```

Copy the `CustomerList` EJB class files into the `Ch22/CustomerList/mvc/custlist` directory. Now, we need some deployment descriptors for this EJB. Let's start with the `ejb-jar.xml` file:

```
<?xml version="1.0" encoding="UTF-8"?>
<ejb-jar>
  <description>Beginning Java Databases CustomerList Example</description>
  <display-name>CustomerList Example</display-name>
  <enterprise-beans>
    <session>
      <ejb-name>CustomerList</ejb-name>
      <home>mvc.custlist.CustomerListHome</home>
      <remote>mvc.custlist.CustomerList</remote>
      <ejb-class>mvc.custlist.CustomerListBean</ejb-class>
      <session-type>Stateless</session-type>
      <transaction-type>Bean</transaction-type>
    </session>
  </enterprise-beans>
</ejb-jar>
```

Next, because we're deploying on JBoss, the `jboss.xml` file:

```
<?xml version="1.0" encoding="UTF-8"?>
<jboss>
  <enterprise-beans>
    <session>
      <ejb-name>CustomerList</ejb-name>
    </session>
  </enterprise-beans>
</jboss>
```

Since we're deploying a session bean here, we don't need the `jaws.xml` file to establish CMP mappings. Once both of these deployment descriptors are saved in the `Ch22\CustomerList\META-INF` directory (with nothing else), we can create the JAR file using the following command issued from the Ch22\CustomerList directory:

```
> jar -cvf CustomerListEJB.jar mvc META-INF
```

That's all we need to deploy the `CustomerList` EJB. Next, we'll deploy the `AddressMaintenance` EJB and test the application.

AddressMaintenance EJB

To deploy the AddressMaintenance EJB in this chapter's MVC framework five tasks need to be carried out:

1. The code needs to be compiled
2. An ejb-jar.xml must be written
3. A jboss.xml file needs to be written
4. A JAR file must be created containing all of the AddressMaintenance EJB class files and the ejb-jar.xml and jboss.xml files
5. The newly created EJB file must be deployed to the JBoss application server

The first task in deploying the AddressMaintenance EJB to the JBoss application server is to compile all of the AddressMaintance Java files. The following command issued from Ch22 directory will do the job:

```
> javac -classpath
        .;%JBOSS%\ejb.jar;%JBOSS%\jnpserver.jar;%JBOSS%\jboss.jar;
        %JBOSS%\jbosssx.jar;%JBOSS%\jaas.jar;%JLIB%\xerces.jar;
        c:\jbosstomcat\tomcat\lib\servlet.jar
        mvc/addressmaintenance/*.java
```

Now we can create a new directory structure, as follows:

```
Ch22/
    AddressMaintenance/
                          mvc/addressmaintenance/
                          META-INF/
```

Next, as before, we need two deployment descriptors, ejb-jar.xml and jboss.xml, both of which will be saved in the Ch22/AddressMaintenance/META-INF directory. Here is the ejb-jar.xml file:

```
<?xml version="1.0" encoding="UTF-8"?>
<ejb-jar>
  <description>
     Beginning Java Databases CustomerList Example
  </description>
  <display-name>AddressMaintenance Example</display-name>
  <enterprise-beans>
    <session>
      <ejb-name>AddressMaintenance</ejb-name>
        <home>
          mvc.addressmaintenance.AddressMaintenanceHome
        </home>
        <remote>
          mvc.addressmaintenance.AddressMaintenance
        </remote>
```

```
        <ejb-class>
          mvc.addressmaintenance.AddressMaintenanceBean
        </ejb-class>
      <session-type>Stateless</session-type>
      <transaction-type>Bean</transaction-type>
    </session>
  </enterprise-beans>
</ejb-jar>
```

and jboss.xml:

```
<?xml version="1.0" encoding="UTF-8"?>
<jboss>
  <enterprise-beans>
    <session>
      <ejb-name>AddressMaintenance</ejb-name>
    </session>
  </enterprise-beans>
</jboss>
```

Now we can create a JAR file for our EJB, using the following command from the Ch22\AddressMaintenance directory:

```
> jar -cvf AddressMaintenanceEJB.jar mvc META-INF
```

This AddressMaintenanceEJB.jar file, along with all the other JAR files we've created (CustomerListEJB.jar, CustomersEJB.jar, and PostalCodesEJB.jar), must now be deployed to the JBoss application server. Deploying an EJB in JBoss is extremely easy. All you have to do is copy the JAR file for the EJB to JBoss's deploy directory. If JBoss is already running, the new EJB will automatically be detected. If JBoss is not running, then the next time the JBoss application server is run, it will pick up the new EJB.

This section has provided a brief overview for deploying EJBs within the JBoss application server. For more detail and an excellent tutorial that covers specifically writing and deploying EJBs within the JBoss application server please refer to the JBoss tutorial located at http://www.jboss.org/documentation/HTML/index.html.

Building addressMaintenance.xsl

The addressMaintenance.xsl file we need for the application uses all of the XSL syntax and structures discussed in Chapter 21. The addressMaintenance.xsl stylesheet is listed below:

Try It Out – addressMaintenance.xsl

```
<?xml version="1.0" encoding="UTF-8"?>
<xsl:stylesheet version="1.0"
              xmlns:xsl="http://www.w3.org/1999/XSL/Transform">
<xsl:output method="html"/>
<xsl:template match="/">
  <HTML>
    <Title>Music On-line</Title>
    <BODY>
    <TABLE align="left">
      <TR>
```

```
    <TD>
<H2>
  <IMG src="musicStore.gif"/>
  Music OnLine (The right tunez at the right place)
</H2>
  </TD>
  </TR>
</TABLE>
<BR/><BR/><BR/><BR/><BR/><BR/><BR/><BR/><BR/><HR/>
<P>
  <FONT size="3">
    Welcome to Music On-Line's Customer Address Maintenance Application.
    Please make your customer edits and hit the save button on the
    screen. After the save button has been hit, you will be returned
    back to the customer list.
  </FONT>
</P>
<HR/>
<H3>Customer Address Information </H3>

<P>
  Customer Name:
  <xsl:value-of select="CUSTOMERS/CUSTOMER/CUSTOMERFIRSTNAME"/> 
  <xsl:value-of select="CUSTOMERS/CUSTOMER/CUSTOMERLASTNAME"/><BR/>
</P>
<HR/>

<FORM method="post" action="controller.jsp">
  <INPUT type="hidden" name="Request" value   ="AddressMaintenance"/>
  <INPUT type="hidden" name="Action"    value   ="Post"/>
  <INPUT type="hidden" name ="customerId">
    <xsl:attribute name="value">
      <xsl:value-of select="CUSTOMERS/CUSTOMER/@customerid"/>
    </xsl:attribute>
  </INPUT>

  <TABLE border="1" align="center">
    <TBODY>
      <TR>
        <TD align="center" bgcolor="#C0C0C0">
          <B>Street Address 1 :</B>
        </TD>
        <TD align="center" bgcolor="#C0C0C0">
          <INPUT name="customerAddress1" type="text">
          <xsl:attribute name="value">
            <xsl:value-of select="CUSTOMERS/CUSTOMER/CUSTOMERADDRESS1"/>
          </xsl:attribute>
          </INPUT>
        </TD>
      </TR>

      <TR>
        <TD align="center" bgcolor="#C0C0C0">
          <B>Street Address 2 :</B>
        </TD>
        <TD align="center" bgcolor="#C0C0C0">
          <INPUT name="customerAddress2" type="text">
            <xsl:attribute name="value">
            <xsl:value-of select="CUSTOMERS/CUSTOMER/CUSTOMERADDRESS2"/>
            </xsl:attribute>
          </INPUT>
```

```
          </TD>
        </TR>

        <TR>
          <TD align="center" bgcolor="#C0C0C0"><B>City:</B></TD>
          <TD align="center" bgcolor="#C0C0C0">
            <INPUT name="customerCity" type="text">
              <xsl:attribute name="value">
                <xsl:value-of select="CUSTOMERS/CUSTOMER/CUSTOMERCITY"/>
              </xsl:attribute>
            </INPUT>
          </TD>
        </TR>

        <TR>
          <TD align="center" bgcolor="#C0C0C0"><B>Zip Code:</B></TD>
          <TD align="center" bgcolor="#C0C0C0">
            <SELECT name="postalCode">
              <OPTION>
                <xsl:value-of select="CUSTOMERS/CUSTOMER/CUSTOMERZIP"/>
              </OPTION>
              <xsl:for-each select="CUSTOMERS/POSTALCODES/POSTALCODE">
              <OPTION>
                <xsl:value-of select="@postalcodeid"/>
              </OPTION>
              </xsl:for-each>
            </SELECT>
          </TD>
        </TR>
      </TBODY>
    </TABLE>
    <TABLE border="0" align="center">
      <TR align="center">
        <TD align="center">
        <INPUT align ="center" name="submit" type="submit" value="Save"/>
        </TD>
        <TD align="center"> </TD>
      </TR>
    </TABLE>
  </FORM>
 </BODY>
 </HTML>
</xsl:template>
</xsl:stylesheet>
```

Save this file in your `\tomcat\webapps\begjdb\etc` directory.

How It Works

The key elements in the `addressMaintenance.xsl` are the hidden fields used in the `<FORM></FORM>` tags:

```
<FORM method="post" action="controller.jsp">
  <INPUT type="hidden" name="Request" value   ="AddressMaintenance"/>
  <INPUT type="hidden" name="Action"    value   ="Post"/>
  <INPUT type="hidden" name ="customerId">
    <xsl:attribute name="value">
      <xsl:value-of select="CUSTOMERS/CUSTOMER/@customerid"/>
    </xsl:attribute>
```

```
        </INPUT>
      .
      .
      .
    </FORM>
```

These Request and Action input fields tell the controller.jsp what actions to take when the user presses the Save button on the customer address maintenance screen. The customerId hidden field is populated with the customer ID. Any data that is not actively used in an <INPUT></INPUT> tag and is needed by the targeted EJB for carrying out its tasks should be placed inside the <FORM></FORM> tags as a hidden <INPUT></INPUT> tag.

Deploying the addressMaintenance.xsl File

To deploy the addressMaintenance.xsl file into the MVC architecture a modification to the xslConfig.properties file is needed. Remember from earlier in this chapter, the xslConfig.properties file defines the location and filename of each XSL stylesheet associated with a request and action.

To set up the AddressMaintenance EJB for use by the controller two additional entries have to be added to the tomcat\webapps\begjdb\etc\xslConfig.properties file:

```
AddressMaintenance.Retrieve=file:///c://jbosstomcat//tomcat//webapps//begjdb//etc/
/addressMaintenance.xsl

AddressMaintenance.Post=file:///c://jbosstomcat//tomcat//webapps//begjdb//etc//cus
tomerList.xsl
```

Once these lines have been added to the xslConfig.properties file, the JBoss application server has to be restarted. The MVCHelper class caches these entries in the xslConfig.properties file into a static Properties object. This way the xslConfig.properties file does not have to be re-parsed with each user's request. Unfortunately, this cache is not dynamically refreshed each time a new entry is added to the xslConfig.properties. To read these new entries, JBoss must be restarted.

Now, finally, we can compile the RequestHandler class, using the following command from the Ch22 directory:

```
> javac -classpath .;%JLIB%\xerces.jar;%JLIB%\xalan.jar
        ;c:\jbosstomcat\tomcat\lib\servlet.jar;%JBOSS%\ejb.jar
        mvc/RequestHandler.java
```

Running the Address Maintenance MVC Application

Before we run the application, let's just check that we have all the files we need in the right places. The following table shows where all the files we have created go:

File	Location
controller.jsp	C:\jbosstomcat\tomcat\webapps\begjdb\jsp
addressMaintenance.xsl	C:\jbosstomcat\tomcat\webapps\begjdb\etc
customerList.xsl	C:\jbosstomcat\tomcat\webapps\begjdb\etc

File	Location
`orderSummary.xsl`	`C:\jbosstomcat\tomcat\webapps\begjdb\etc`
`xslConfig.properties`	`C:\jbosstomcat\tomcat\webapps\begjdb\etc`
AddressMaintenance EJB files	`C:\BegJavaDB\Ch22\mvc\addressmaintenance`
`AddressMaintenanceEJB.jar`	`C:\jbosstomcat\jboss\deploy`
CustomerList EJB files	`C:\BegJavaDB\Ch22\mvc\custlist`
`CustomerListEJB.jar`	`C:\jbosstomcat\jboss\deploy`
Customers EJB files	`C:\BegJavaDB\Ch22\mvc\entitybeans\customers`
`CustomersEJB.jar`	`C:\jbosstomcat\jboss\deploy`
PostalCodes EJB files	`C:\BegJavaDB\Ch22\mvc\entitybeans\postalcodes`
`PostalCodesEJB.jar`	`C:\jbosstomcat\jboss\deploy`
`MVCHelper.class`	`C:\BegJavaDB\Ch22\mvc`
`RequestHandler.class`	`C:\BegJavaDB\Ch22\temp\mvc`
`XSLTManager.class`	`C:\BegJavaDB\Ch22\temp\mvc`

As we saw in Chapter 19, JBoss needs JDBC configuration information in the `jboss.jcml` file. Since we're going to be running JBoss and Tomcat together this time, we'll have to use the `jboss\conf\tomcat\jboss.jcml` file. We should make the same changes we did in Chapter 19, which are as follows:

Replace the contents of the section marked `<!-- JDBC -->` with the following text, remembering to change the URL property (shown in bold) of your Oracle connection string (and the username and password as well):

```
<!-- JDBC -->
<mbean code="org.jboss.jdbc.JdbcProvider"
      name="DefaultDomain:service=JdbcProvider">
  <attribute name="Drivers">oracle.jdbc.driver.OracleDriver</attribute>
</mbean>

<mbean code="org.jboss.jdbc.XADataSourceLoader"
       name="DefaultDomain:service=XADataSource,name=OracleDS">
  <attribute name="PoolName">OracleDS</attribute>
  <attribute
name="DataSourceClass">org.opentools.minerva.jdbc.xa.wrapper.XADataSourceImpl</att
ribute>
  <attribute name="Properties"></attribute>
  <attribute name="URL">jdbc:oracle:thin:@dbserver:1521:database</attribute>
  <attribute name="GCMinIdleTime">1200000</attribute>
  <attribute name="JDBCUser">beg</attribute>
  <attribute name="MaxSize">10</attribute>
  <attribute name="Password">java</attribute>
  <attribute name="GCEnabled">false</attribute>
  <attribute name="InvalidateOnError">false</attribute>
  <attribute name="TimestampUsed">false</attribute>
  <attribute name="Blocking">true</attribute>
```

```
    <attribute name="GCInterval">120000</attribute>
    <attribute name="IdleTimeout">1800000</attribute>
    <attribute name="IdleTimeoutEnabled">false</attribute>
    <attribute name="LoggingEnabled">false</attribute>
    <attribute name="MaxIdleTimeoutPercent">1.0</attribute>
    <attribute name="MinSize">0</attribute>
  </mbean>
```

This will enable our CMP entity beans, or rather JBoss, to connect to the database. Before we start JBoss and Tomcat by using the `run_with_tomcat` command, we should edit the script file (`.bat` or `.sh`, depending on your operating system) to include the following JAR files in the classpath:

- `xalan.jar`
- `xerces.jar`
- Cloudscape's `client.jar`, `cloudscape.jar`, and `tools.jar` files
- `servlet.jar`

Also, we need to have the `mvc` package in the classpath, which we can do by including `C:\BegJavaDB\Ch22` in the classpath as well. When we've finished adding these JAR files and directories to the file, it should look as follows:

```
@echo off
set JBOSS_CLASSPATH=
set WROX_CLASSPATH=
set WROX_CLASSPATH=C:\BegJavaDB\Ch22
set WROX_CLASSPATH=%WROX_CLASSPATH%;%JLIB%\xalan.jar;%JLIB%\xerces.jar
set
WROX_CLASSPATH=%WROX_CLASSPATH%;%JLIB%\client.jar;%JLIB%\cloudscape.jar;%JLIB%\too
ls.jar
set WROX_CLASSPATH=%WROX_CLASSPATH%;c:\jbosstomcat\tomcat\lib\servlet.jar

set JBOSS_CLASSPATH=%JBOSS_CLASSPATH%;%WROX_CLASSPATH%;%JAVA_HOME%/lib/tools.jar
    .\run.bat tomcat
```

Now, we should be able to run the file and see the application working! If you look at the command window where the `run_with_tomcat` command has been issued, you'll probably find the following warnings:

```
Bean   : CustomerList
Method : public abstract MVCObject create() throws RemoteException,
CreateException
Section: 6.8
Warning: The create method of a stateless session bean home interface must return
the session bean's remote interface.

[Verifier]
Bean   : CustomerList
Method : public abstract MVCObject create() throws RemoteException,
CreateException
Section: 6.10.6
Warning: The return type for a create(...) method must be the session bean's
remote interface type.
```

Don't worry about these – this is because we are using our own extensions to the standard EJB objects. JBoss, and our application, will still run properly. Once JBoss and Tomcat are running without errors, point your browser at the following URL:

http://localhost:8080/begjdb/jsp/controller.jsp?Request=CustomerList&Action=Retrieve

you should see the following page:

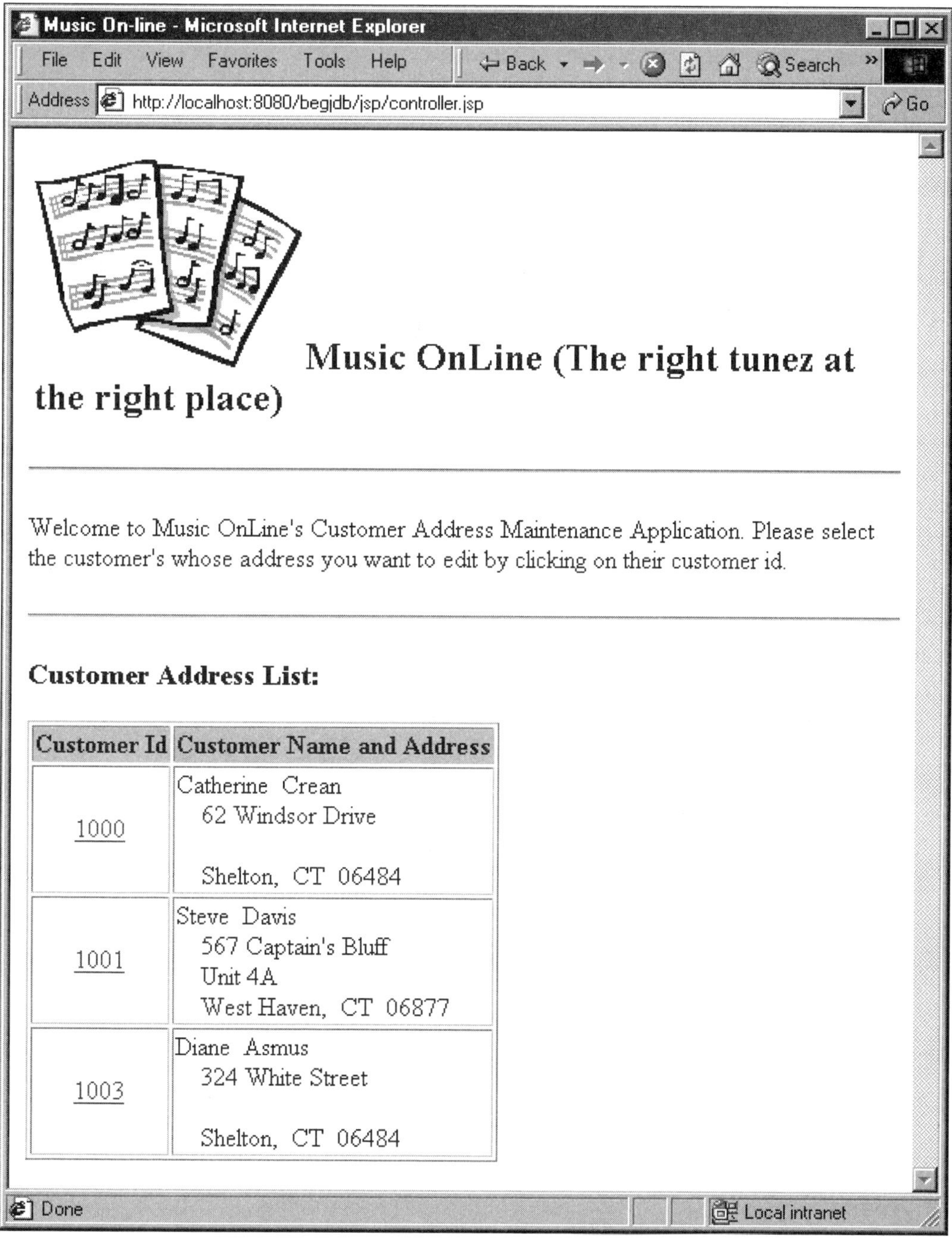

Click on one of the Customer Id links, and you'll be taken to a screen like the following:

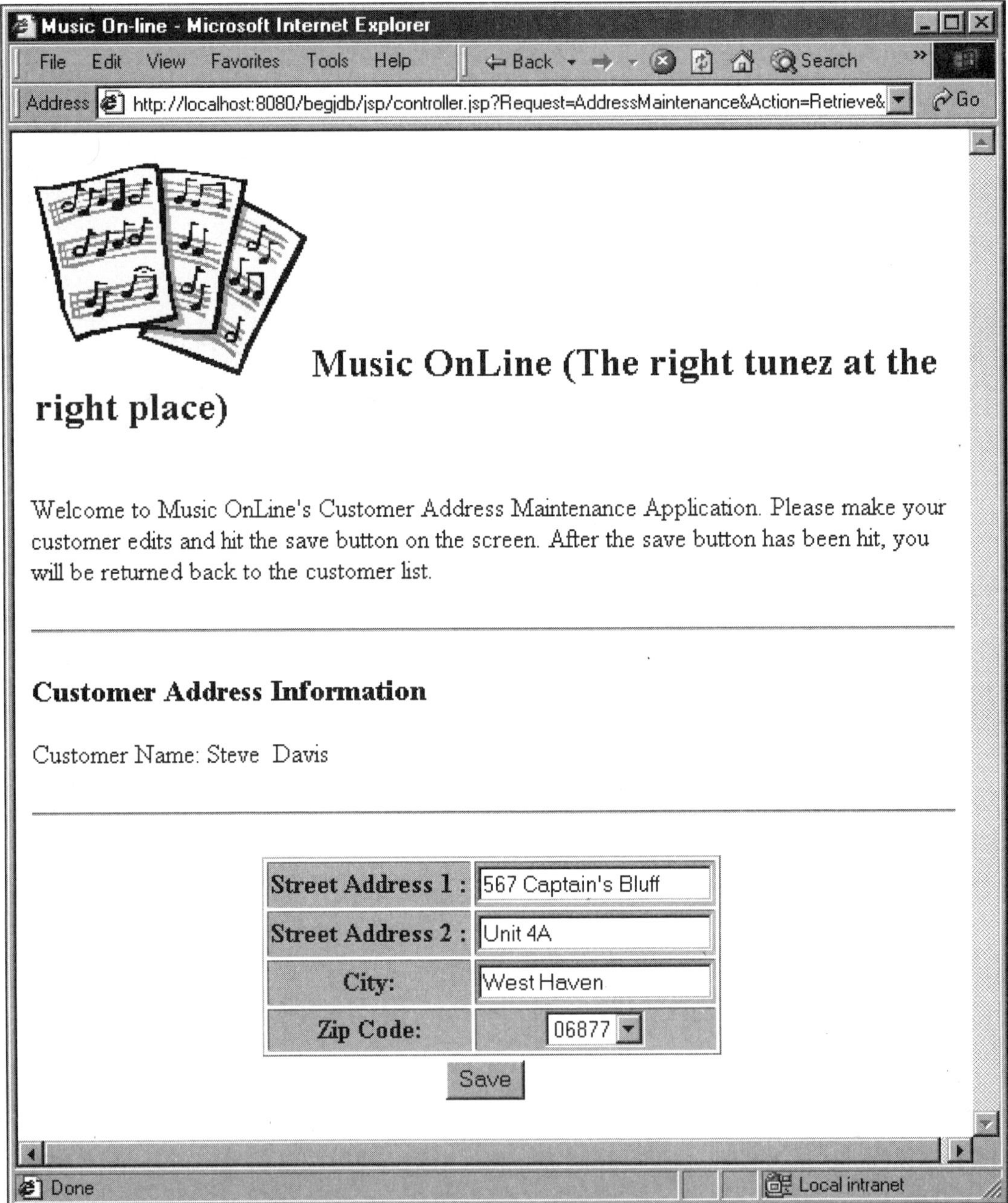

As you can see, we have textboxes for the customer address. Let's change Steve's address to Unit 10A by editing the textbox for Street Address 2:

Now, click on the Save button and return to the initial screen:

Music On-line - Microsoft Internet Explorer

Address http://localhost:8080/begjdb/jsp/controller.jsp

Customer Address List:

Customer Id	Customer Name and Address
1000	Catherine Crean 62 Windsor Drive Shelton, CT 06484
1001	Steve Davis 567 Captain's Bluff Unit 10A West Haven, CT 06877
1003	Diane Asmus 324 White Street Shelton, CT 06484

Done — Local intranet

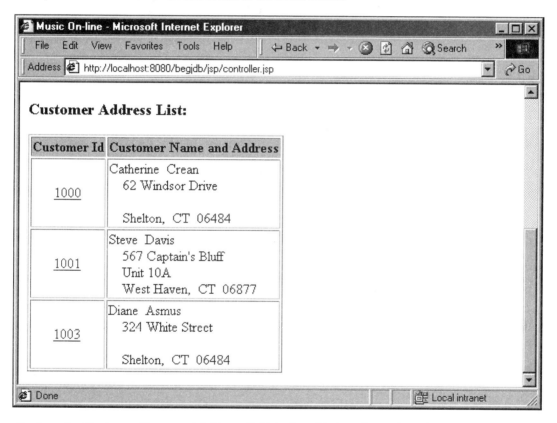

See how the Customer Name and Address field in the table has changed? Let's confirm that it has changed in the database as well by using SQL*PLUS. After connecting to the database, we can issue the following commands and see the changes:

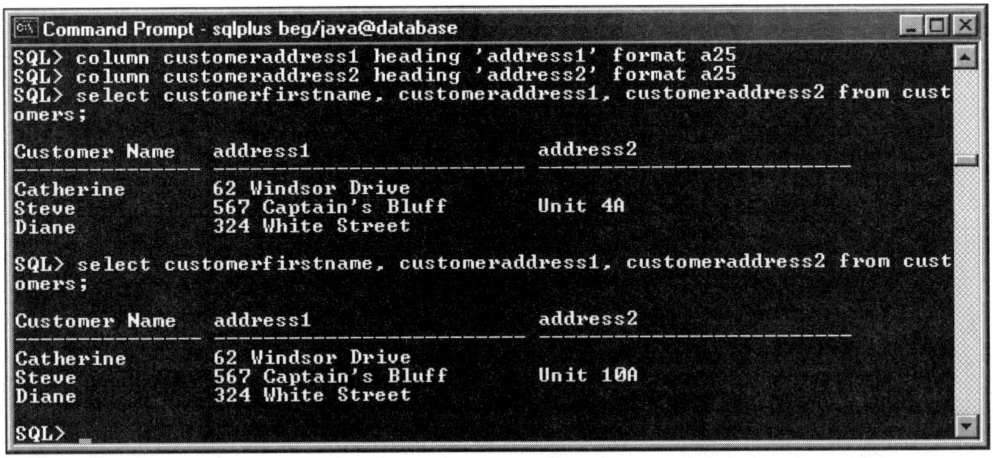

```
Command Prompt - sqlplus beg/java@database
SQL> column customeraddress1 heading 'address1' format a25
SQL> column customeraddress2 heading 'address2' format a25
SQL> select customerfirstname, customeraddress1, customeraddress2 from cust
omers;

Customer Name   address1                  address2
--------------- ------------------------- -------------------------
Catherine       62 Windsor Drive
Steve           567 Captain's Bluff       Unit 4A
Diane           324 White Street

SQL> select customerfirstname, customeraddress1, customeraddress2 from cust
omers;

Customer Name   address1                  address2
--------------- ------------------------- -------------------------
Catherine       62 Windsor Drive
Steve           567 Captain's Bluff       Unit 10A
Diane           324 White Street

SQL> _
```

In fact, what we did here was to check the data before clicking the Save button on the web application, and check it again afterwards. The value has changed: our application works!

Some Final Thoughts

The MVC architecture presented within this chapter is a powerful structure for building applications. However, the implementation of this architecture is very stripped down and simplistic. Good application architecture will provide more then just the three services provided by the MVC architecture.

Robust application architecture will provide such additional services as:

- **Security** – There is no code within the architecture that enforces what actions the user can or cannot take. Security is something that should be part of an application's architecture and not embedded within the application code itself. An application should be able to authenticate that a user is who they say they are and authorize that the action the user is undertaking is allowed. The current application architecture allows any user to perform any action. Ideally, we should not even have to write security code into the application architecture. Instead, we should be able to use the security services offered by an application server.
- **Error handling** – There is no consistent method of handling application -pecific errors in the application. Right now, each screen built within our architecture can implement different mechanisms for tracking and dealing with errors within the application – this is poor development practice. Error handling should be a service that is offered by the application architecture so that every application handles application and run-time errors in the same manner.
- **Flexibility** – The MVC architecture presented here could be more flexible. The EJB that is to be invoked for each screen within that customer address maintenance application is hard-coded into the XSL stylesheet. A better practice would be to embed a key within the XSL that would map to an EJB name and the method to be called. This mapping could then be stored apart from the application in either an XML file or a database table. This way, the EJB and the method that gets invoked could be changed without having to touch the XSL.

The author challenges the reader to review the three 'gaps' shown above and think of how such services could be plugged into the basic MVC framework.

Summary

Building application architecture is not about re-inventing code and is, frankly, not restricted to the computer science types who sit in research facilities pontificating about the 'pure' way to write software.

> **Good application architecture is about looking for patterns within your applications and generalizing them into a framework that all of your applications can share.**

If you feel as if you are designing the architecture from the ground up then chances are you are trying too hard. Take a step back, look at code that you have previously written and ask yourself:

> *What, from each of these applications, could be generalized, reused, and shared across all of my applications?*

This statement is the essence of application architecture. Architecture is not about inventing something new, but generalizing and reusing what has already been written.

This chapter has reviewed some of the common design flaws found within many database-based applications. The design flaws reviewed ranged from the bad coding practices, like embedding database connectivity information directly into the application, to the more serious architectural issues, like not cleanly delineating the application into discernible and discrete units of presentation, business, and data logic.

This chapter also examined the three basic types of generic application architectures: 2-tier, 3-tier, and n-tier. Specifically we discussed how to build a 3-tier/n-tier architecture using a Model-View-Controller framework. This architecture provides three basic services:

- Model Service – The model service allowed the developer to build components that, when following a specific set of standards, could be plugged into the MVC architecture for immediate use by other applications. The EJBs used as models in our implementation of an MVC architecture must follow two basic rules:
  - The EJB has to be built using the `MVCHome`, `MVCObject`, and `MVCBean` interfaces. These interfaces guarantee that the EJB can be plugged into our MVC architecture and that it will have:
    - A public `retrieve()` method for retrieving data from the Music Store database
    - A public `post()` method for saving data to the Music Store database
  - The EJB's `retrieve()` and `post()` methods return an XML Document

  Any EJBs that do not follow these rules can still be used within the application, but they cannot be plugged into our framework.
- **View Service** – The view service allowed a developer to declare what XSL stylesheet was going to be used to present user information. The View service would use the XSL stylesheet and any data returned from the Model to present information to the end-user. Some important things to remember about the view service are that:
  - The View service allows the developer to define how the data is to be presented **declaratively** rather than **programmatically**.

- The View service acts as a firewall between changes within the business and data logic for the application. The presentation piece of the application is completely independent of the other layers.

- **Controller Service** – The Controller service acts as a traffic cop routing the end-user's request to the appropriate business logic (EJB) and the appropriate presentation logic (XSL Stylesheet). The three pieces of information are needed for a controller to carry out an end-user's request:
  - The name of the Enterprise JavaBean that is going to carry out the end-user's business request
  - The action the EJB is to carry out, whether it is a `post()` or `retrieve()` method, on behalf of the end-user
  - The name of the XSL file that will be used to present the data to the end-user; the XSL filename is retrieved by using searching an entry within the `xslConfig.properties` files that matches the `Request` and `Action` submitted by the end-user

Finally, there are two last thoughts to consider when building the architecture for your applications. Data is the lifeblood of an organization. Firstly, bear in mind that the way that data is stored and distributed will frequently, and sometimes radically, change, as the application is forced to adapt within the competitive jungle most businesses operate in. The way in which corporate data needs to be routed, handled and displayed can change literally overnight. Architect your applications to smoothly and quickly embrace change. Secondly, extensibility and adaptability can rarely be retrofitted into an application. Trying to build architecture for an application after it is deployed is difficult and complicated at best, disastrous at worse. Build the base architecture before building the application – it will save a significant amount of rework and headache later on down the road.

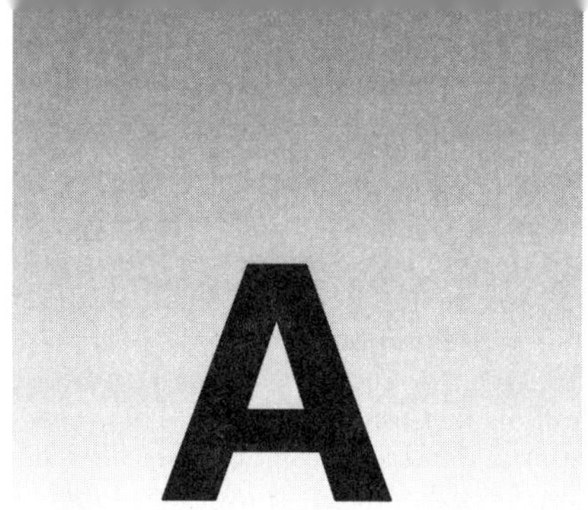

Connecting to the Music Store Database

The two databases that we have used extensively in this book are Cloudscape and Oracle. In this appendix we will:

- Step through the process of installing a copy of Personal Oracle 8i on your machine, run the SQL scripts to create the Music Store database and then demonstrate connecting to the database through various driver types
- Show how to connect to the Music Store on the Cloudscape database, through the RMI-JDBC driver
- Show how to set up and access the Music Store database on Microsoft Access

Connecting to Oracle

Some of the examples in the book rely on are more advanced features of a relational database than is provided for by Cloudscape, especially enterprise-level applications spanning the Web. Generally, it is assumed that the reader most interested in these sections will be developing Java applications against an enterprise version of the database, that has been set up and configure by their DBA team.

However, in order that you may work through this code regardless, we provide a step-by-step guide for setting up Personal Oracle 8i on your own computer. This installation guide is for the NT/Windows2000 version of the product.

A Brief Note on Oracle Versions

The most recent version of Oracle's powerful Internet database is 9i. However, at the time of writing the personal edition of 9i was unavailable, so the 8i version is used (8.1.7).

There are four distributions of Oracle 9i. Each distribution has it own unique niche within the corporate Information Technology (IT) environment. We will start with the smallest Oracle distribution, Oracle Lite, and work our way up to the largest, Oracle Enterprise Edition.

Oracle 9i Lite

Oracle 9i Lite is designed for the mobile computing environments. It is used to develop applications that have to be disconnected and reside in a device as small as a Palm Pilot or other PDA device. Oracle 9i Lite consists of two different components:

- A stripped down version of the Oracle database. This version of the Oracle database is a lightweight object-relational database designed specially for mobile computers and devices. The database has minimal overhead, yet allows developers to write database application code using both PL/SQL and Java.
- A set of synchronization and replication tools called **iConnect**. iConnect empowers application developers to write applications that that can easily synchronize and Oracle 9i Lite database with any of the other Oracle 9i distributions. (Oracle 9i Personal Edition all the way up to Oracle 9i Enterprise Edition).

Oracle 9i Lite was never meant to be a full-blown, fully functional DBMS. Instead Oracle has positioned this distribution to be the link between the mobile user and corporate Oracle databases.

Personal Oracle 9i

Personal Oracle 9i provides a single-user development license. This edition was designed with the student, consultant, and developer in mind. Personal Oracle 9i provides the same features as the standard Oracle 9i edition except that it only provides a single user license. One of Personal Oracle 9i's greatest strengths is the ability for developers to develop their applications on their own desktop or notebook computer. This minimizes development conflict between developers. We have all been in those situations before. Developer A just overwrote six hours of Developer B's work and it now appears as if Developer B is going to get physically violent with Developer A.

Using Personal Oracle 9i, developers can completely write and test their code locally and then easily deploy their work to any other Oracle environments.

Oracle 9i Standard Edition

Oracle 9i is the departmental/small-business version of the Oracle database. Applications written using Oracle 9i Standard Edition do not have the performance and fault tolerance found in their enterprise-level brethren. Oracle 9i standard edition lacks the data partitioning and parallel server features of Oracle 9i. However, this Oracle distribution includes the most commonly used options and features that Oracle 9i has to offer. The Oracle 9i Standard Edition includes easy-to-use management tools for common database management tasks (like backing up and restoring an Oracle database), Oracle's Web Server, and many of the web development tools need to develop robust Internet, and Intranet applications.

Oracle 9i Enterprise Edition

This is the most feature-rich version of Oracle 9i. The Oracle 9i Enterprise Edition is designed for large scale, high-end data processing. Oracle 9i Enterprise Edition is perfect for data applications that require query-intensive data warehousing. Furthermore, Oracle 9i Enterprise Edition should be considered when business criteria demand large-scale Web applications as well as data intense online transaction processing (OLTP).

Downloading Personal Oracle 8i

Firstly, a central point of information for useful Oracle resources is the URL, http://technet.oracle.com/ Here, you can find out all the information about Oracle, from products, to downloads, to jobs, and so on. One of the initial things you will have to do before you can get your hands on Personal Oracle is to sign up for membership of Technet. To do this, go to the aforementioned URL, click on Membership on the top row of buttons, and follow the instructions to sign up.

After you have received your password by e-mail and logged yourself into Technet, you can now click on the Downloads button on the left-hand side under Software. On the next screen you can select to download 8i Personal Edition under the products list. A word of warning before you proceed is that the download for this file is around 600 MB! Even on a very fast T1 connection, this will take around three hours to download. You have been warned.

If, on the other hand, you would rather just pay a fee and get a package of software on CD delivered straight your door, you can click on the Technology Track link, and be taken to a useful menu. Here, you can select the appropriate bundle of software for your needs. Click on the relevant buttons, pay your money, and your software will be with you soon. Getting the software this way means that you will be supplied with a whole suite of applications, not just Personal Oracle, and it will save you a lot of time downloading it from the Internet.

Once you have downloaded the ZIP file, unzipping it to an appropriate place will present you with the following directory structure:

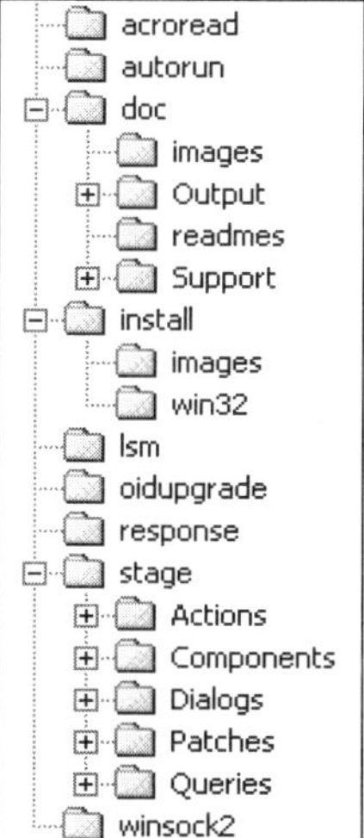

Installing Personal Oracle 8i 8.1.7.0.0

What you need to do next depends on whether you downloaded Personal Oracle, or are setting it up from a CD. From the CD all you need to do is find the `setup.exe` file and execute it. If you are installing from a downloaded ZIP file (and obviously do not have the CD) then you need to go to the `install` directory, then `win32` and execute the `setup.exe` that is found there. What you will see next is the Oracle Universal Installer. As its name suggests, this is a 'central' program with which you install components from the Oracle Corporation:

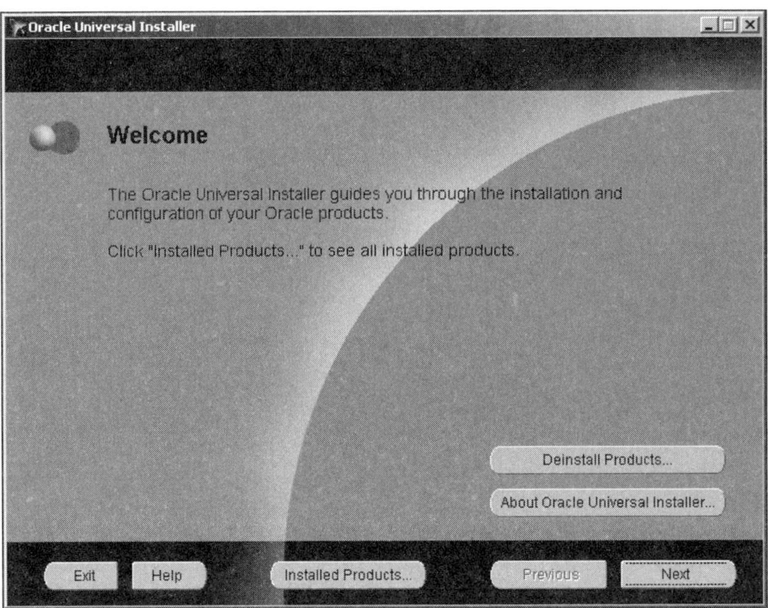

You can click on Installed Products... at the bottom of the screen to see what, if any, Oracle products are already installed on your system. Otherwise, hit Next to move on. The following screen will ask you for the source and destination of the installation, in other words, where the program should look to find the products you want to install, and where to place them on installation:

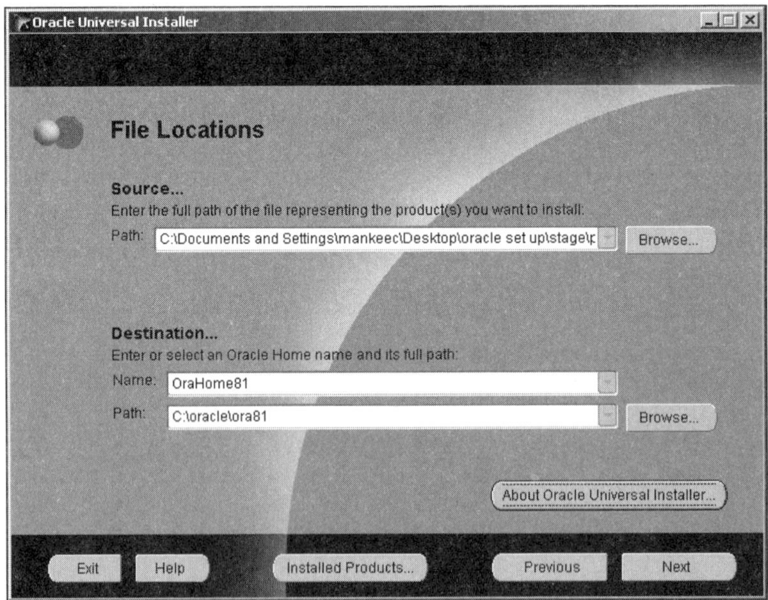

The install is 'intelligent' in that it will already have filled in the fields for you by default. It is up to you whether you keep these defaults or alter them and install the products wherever you please. Hit Next if you are happy with your options and proceed. The next thing to happen is for the program to load some information about the product you are installing. This will take a few moments.

The real fun begins now. The next screen you will be presented with is the one where you get to choose what gets put on your system. The option we are interested in is Oracle8i Personal Edition 8.1.7.0.0, so select that and click Next. More options on the next screen and this is where you get to choose how much of your hard disk space is eaten up. A typical install is 778 MB, with a minimal install being 591 MB. Either way, it will take up plenty of space:

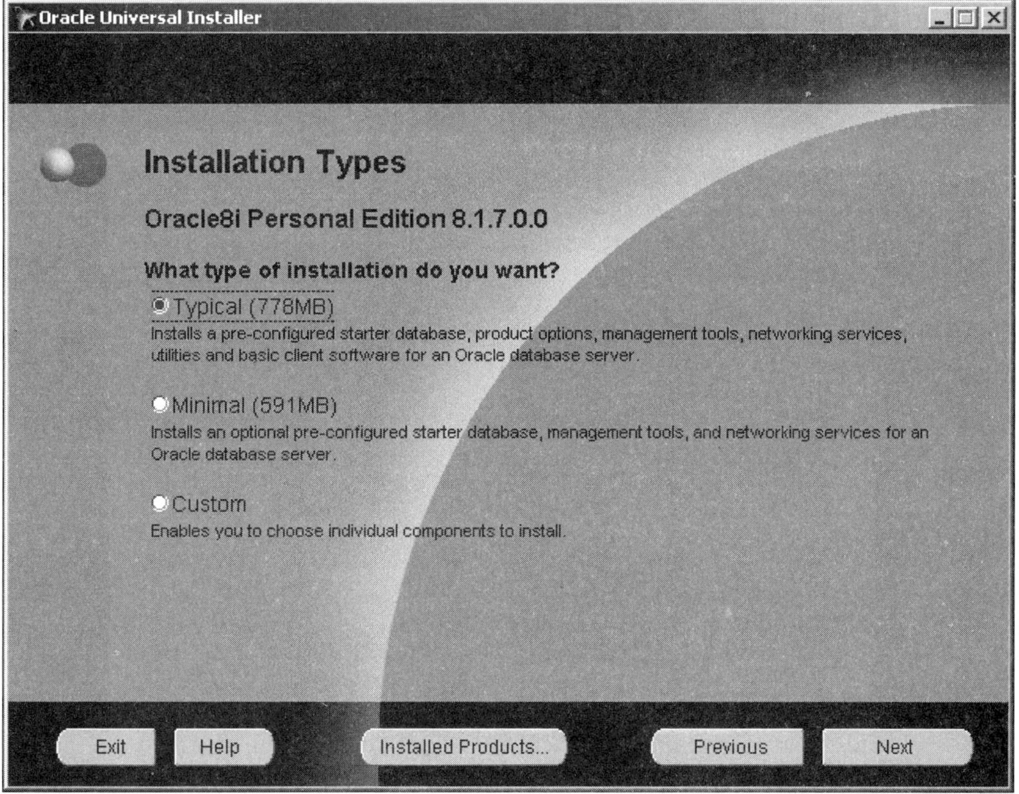

The next screen will ask you to identify the database you are about to create. It requires two inputs:

- A global database name
- An Oracle **S**ystem **ID**entifier (SID)

The global database name is of the form, `name.domain`, and it is recommended that the `domain` mirrors the network domain that your machine is connected to. This uniquely identifies the database from any other on the network domain. The SID identifies the specific database instance on the computer, and is unique on the machine in question.

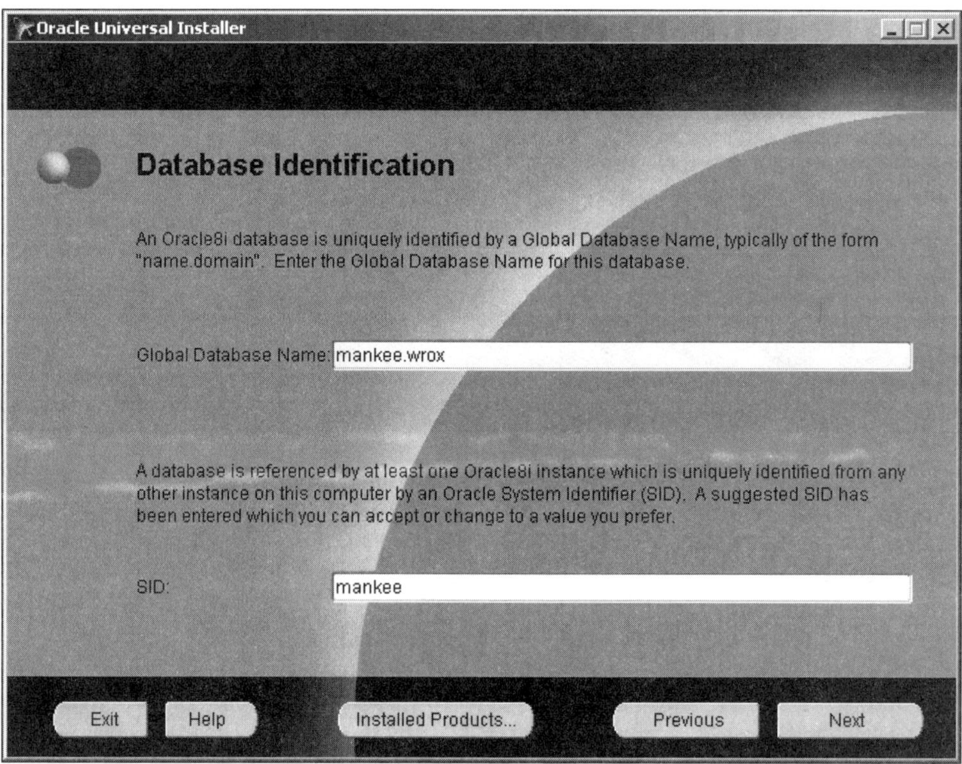

The next screen will be summary of the options you have selected, the amount of space required, components that will be installed, already installed components, and so on. Finally, you can click Install and sit back and watch Oracle Universal Installer do its job.

After the installation has completed, you will be shown a Configuration Tools screen. The Oracle Database Configuration Assistant will now help you set up a new database, according to the parameters you gave in the previous screen. After configuration is complete, you will get a summary indicating the database name, system identifier, and various passwords for the `INTERNAL`, `SYS`, and `SYSTEM` accounts.

The Oracle HTTP Service will also be set up and started at the same time. This means that you can go to your web browser and type in the URL http://localhost to make sure that it is working OK. While there, you can also have a play around with some of Oracle's HTTP server component demonstrations, courtesy of the Apache Web Server.

Setting Up a Listener

What you need to do next is to set up a **listener** for your database so that other clients can connect to it, and access and manipulate the data stored in it. To do this, go to Start | Programs | Oracle - OraHome81 | Network Administration | Net8 Assistant. As you are configuring your listener, it would also be useful to have the Net8 Configuration Assistant open. This is located in the same place: Start | Programs | Oracle - OraHome81 | Network Administration:

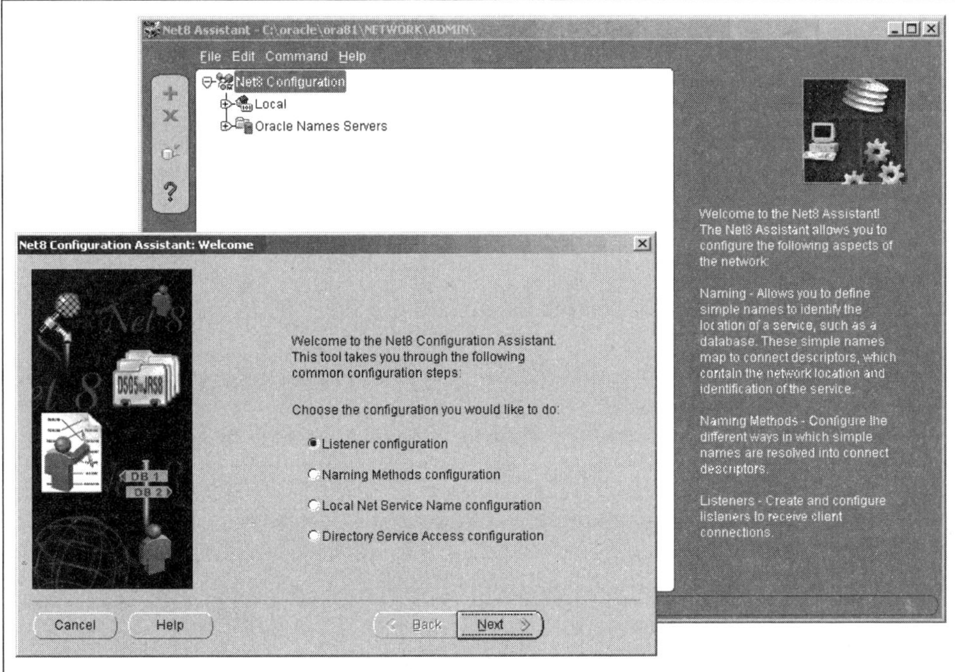

The first thing that we will do is to set up a new Net8 Listener so that connections can be made to our newly created database. Select Listener configuration from the options screen, click on Next, select Add, click Next, and enter the name of the listener you want to add. The next set of screens enable you to select the protocols you require and set them up as you please. You will be asked if you would like to set up any more listeners. If not then you can select the appropriate option, click on Next and then you will be given a message that Listener configuration complete! Finally, click on Finish to quit.

Testing the Personal Oracle Installation

Now that you have installed Personal Oracle, set up a database, and configured a listener, you can test it out on same machine on which the database is situated. To check that the setup of your system will enable you to connect to the database, go to the file located at `C:\oracle\ora81\network\ADMIN\tnsnames.ora`. This is an Oracle configuration file that will let you identify, locate, and connect to a chosen database on a network. According to the above database configurations in the screenshots, the global database name in this case is `mankee.wrox` and the SID is `mankee`, so there will be an entry in the `tnsnames.ora` like this.

```
MANKEE =
  (DESCRIPTION =
    (ADDRESS_LIST =
      (ADDRESS = (PROTOCOL = TCP)(HOST = JFGELSW)(PORT = 1521))
    )
    (CONNECT_DATA =
      (SERVICE_NAME = mankee.wrox)
    )
  )
```

The important settings in this entry are highlighted and are pretty self-explanatory:

tnsnames.ora Entry	Meaning
`MANKEE`	The SID of the database instance we are connecting to
`TCP`	The type of protocol to be used
`JFGELSW`	The name of the host machine where the database is situated
`1521`	The port number used in the connection
`mankee.wrox`	Global database name

If all is well, you can now use an Oracle tool called SQL*PLUS to connect to the database and execute an example query. First you need to start SQL*PLUS and this is done by going to Start | Programs | Oracle - OraHome81 | Application Development | SQL Plus. Now enter the relevant UserName, Password, and Host String. If successful, you will now encounter the following screen:

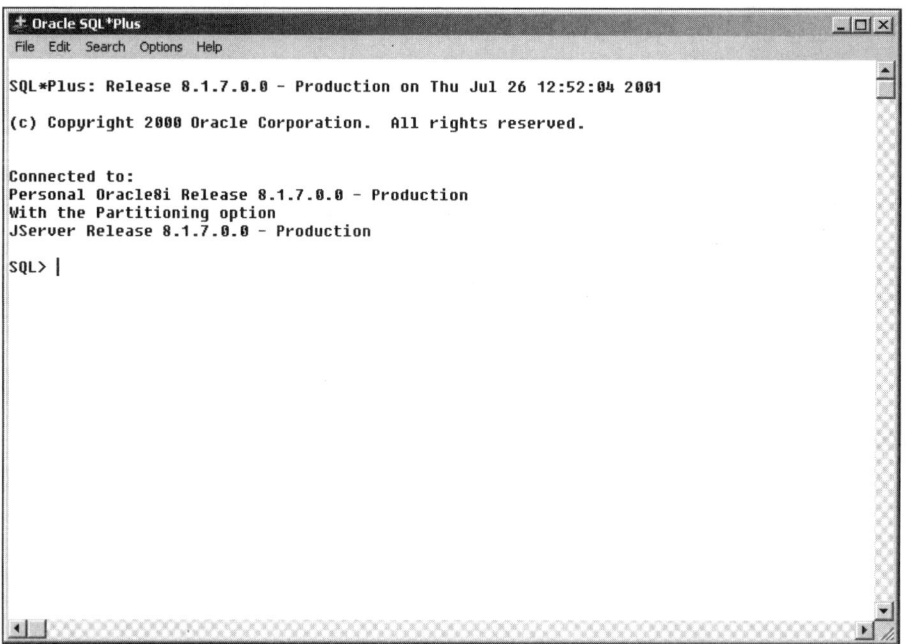

Congratulations! You have now successfully connected up to the database and are ready to query, modify, access, and generally change the data to your heart's content. As an example of a first query, you can log in as `SYS`, with the default password of `change_on_install`, and execute the following query:

```
SELECT *
  FROM scott.emp
```

Assuming that you selected to install the sample database in the installation of the Personal Oracle 8i product, this will select all of the data contained in the table `emp`, which is in the `scott` schema.

Now that you have connected to the database on a local machine, the next step would be to connect via a remote connection. We can follow pretty much the same set of procedures to install a client on another, 'clean' machine. Locate the `setup.exe` from either the downloaded ZIP file or from the CD, and then select to install the Oracle Client 8.1.7.0.0. The next screen will enable you to select different types of installation, depending on what you intend to use the client for.

After the installation of the client is complete, you can do exactly as before:

1. Locate the file `C:\oracle\ora81\network\ADMIN\tnsnames.ora`.
2. Add an entry pointing to the correct SID, protocol, host, port, and global database name.
3. Start SQL*PLUS.
4. Enter the relevant username, password, and host string.

and hey presto. You have a remote connection to your database ready to be used.

Loading the Music Store Database

To make a connection to the Oracle database we first have to decide where the Music Store schema is to be installed. This is best done under a new user's schema, this way there will be a 'clean slate' for you to test the code in the book. To create a new user, start up SQL*PLUS (this can done by clicking on the SQL*PLUS icon or typing `sqlplus` in a command prompt window).

We need DBA (Database Administrator) privileges to create a new user so connect to your database (in our case, called `Mankee`) as the user `system` (with the password `manager`) or as any other user with a DBA **role** (roles are used by Oracle to give different levels of privileges to users in the database). Once you are connected, you will need to issue the following command:

```
SQL> grant connect, resource to beg identified by java;
```

This will create a new user `beg` with the password `java`. The `grant` gives the user `beg` various roles. The `connect` role is the most basic in Oracle, it allows a user just to connect to the database and not much else. The `resource` role allows a user to create their tables, views, and so on in the database. Once the user is created, the Music Store database can be installed by running scripts supplied in the source code download.

The Oracle Scripts

In order to create and populate the Music Store tables on Oracle we have provided the following four SQL scripts. In order to run each of these scripts, simply open up SQL*PLUS and enter a command like the following:

```
@"C:\BegJavaDB\OracleScripts\Oracle_Create.sql";
```

This command will execute the `Oracle_Create.sql` script, stored in the directory `C:\BegJavaDB\OracleScripts`.

The Oracle_Create.sql Script

This script creates all of the tables, sequences and constraints for our Music Store database. For example, the code in the script to create the `Stores` table looks as follows:

```
CREATE TABLE Stores (
       StorePostalCode       VARCHAR2(12) NOT NULL,
       StoreID               NUMBER NOT NULL,
       StoreDescription      VARCHAR2(30) NOT NULL,
       CountryID             NUMBER DEFAULT 1 NOT NULL,
       StoreTypeID           NUMBER DEFAULT 1 NOT NULL,
       StoreAddress1         VARCHAR2(50),
       StoreAddress2         VARCHAR2(50),
       StoreCity             VARCHAR2(30)
);

ALTER TABLE Stores
       ADD CONSTRAINT PK_Stores Primary Key (StoreID);

ALTER TABLE Stores
       ADD CONSTRAINT FK_Stores_StoreTypes Foreign Key (StoreTypeID)
       REFERENCES StoreTypes(StoreTypeID);

ALTER TABLE STORES
      ADD CONSTRAINT
      FK_Stores_PostalCodes Foreign Key (StorePostalCode, CountryID)
      REFERENCES PostalCodes(PostalCode, CountryID);
The Oracle_ClearIt.sql Script
```

The Oracle_Populate Script

This script creates all sequences, which will supply unique values for our numerical primary key columns, and populates all of our tables with sample data. For example, the following extract from the script creates a sequence for the `Stores` table and then populates it with two rows of data:

```
CREATE SEQUENCE seqStores INCREMENT BY 1 START WITH 1 NOCYCLE;

INSERT INTO Stores (StoreID,StoreDescription,StoreTypeID
,StoreAddress1,StoreAddress2,StoreCity,StorePostalCode) VALUES
(seqStores.NextVal,'www.Music4YouAndMe.com',2,'190 Grunge Way','Suite
100','Manhatten','10022');

INSERT INTO Stores (StoreID,StoreDescription,StoreTypeID
,StoreAddress1,StoreAddress2,StoreCity,StorePostalCode) VALUES
(seqStores.NextVal,'Manhattan',1,'450 Madison Ave','1st Floor','New
York','10022');
```

The Oracle_Clear Script

This script contains the SQL to drop all of the tables and sequences. The following extract drops the `Stores` table and sequence:

```
DROP Table Stores;
...
DROP SEQUENCE seqStores;
```

The Oracle_init Script

This script embeds the previous three scripts into one:

```
REMARK We're running the Drop script
@"c:\BegJavaDB\OracleScripts\Oracle_Clear.sql";

REMARK Now we create the Music Store tables
@"c:\BegJavaDB\OracleScripts\Oracle_Create.sql";

REMARK Now we populate the tables
@"c:\BegJavaDB\OracleScripts\Oracle_Populate.sql";
```

This script will allow you to "start again from scratch". It will drop all of the tables (and sequences), recreate then and then re-populate the tables. To run this script, simply issue the following command from the SQL*PLUS prompt:

```
@"c:\BegJavaDB\OracleScripts\Oracle_init.sql";
```

Oracle JDBC Drivers

You can now try out connecting to the Music Store databases through Oracle's type 2 and type 4 drivers. A discussion of the different JDBC driver types is given in Chapter 7. Before you proceed, make sure that you move the class file archive (`classes12.zip`) to the `C:\java\lib` directory, where we are storing all of our external Java libraries (see the *Setting up you Java Environment* section, at the start of this book).

Oracle's JDBC/OCI Driver

Oracle's JDBC/OCI is a Type 2 JDBC driver that converts JDBC invocations to calls to the **Oracle Call Interface** (**OCI**), which are then sent over SQL*Net to the Oracle database server. SQL*Net is Oracle's format and protocol, and is the base level of communication between Oracle clients, middleware products, and data servers. Through the use of SQL*Net, the JDBC/OCI Driver can achieve much higher throughput than competing JDBC solutions that interface to ODBC.

The JDBC/OCI driver transforms calls from Java to C (since the driver must use a layer of C in order to make calls to the OCI), and is written in a combination of the two languages, which precludes it from being downloadable. Further, the JDBC/OCI driver also requires installation of the OCI libraries, SQL*Net, CORE libraries, and other support files on the machine on which the JDBC driver is installed, in other words, on each of the client machines, or the middle-tier Java application server. It is therefore suited for client-server Java applications and middle tiers, but not for Java applets.

The JDBC/OCI driver benefits from a number of different features of the Oracle Call Interface including:

- **Globalization support** – It provides complete support for globalized character sets allowing Java applications to access databases that use any Oracle character set. This is achieved by converting the characters to Unicode 1.2.

- **Performance optimizations** – The JDBC/OCI driver leverages a number of the OCI's performance optimizations including reductions in the number of client-to-server round trips for binds, defines, and describes. It also allows batched statement execution, row pre-fetching, and use of the array interface.
- **SQL*Net version support** – Since it is targeted to support client-server Java applications, the JDBC/OCI driver supports all SQL*Net adapters including SQL*Net Adapters, IPC, Named Pipes, DECNet, TCP/IP, and others. It also supports all features of Oracle's Advanced Networking Option including encrypted SQL*Net.
- **Database version support** – The JDBC/OCI driver supports all Oracle 7 database versions and can also access Oracle 8 databases.

Try It Out – Connecting to Oracle through the JDBC/OCI Driver

1. The complete code listing that retrieves a connection and iterates a `ResultSet` using Oracle JDBC/OCI Driver is given below:

```
import java.sql.*;

class RecordingOCI
{
  public static void main (String args [])
        throws SQLException
  {
    DriverManager.registerDriver(new oracle.jdbc.driver.OracleDriver());

    // In the URL, database is of the form (description=(address=(host=
    // <mc-name>)(protocol=tcp)(port=<port-no>))(connect_data=(sid=<sid>))
    Connection conn = DriverManager.getConnection
("jdbc:oracle:oci8:@(description=(address=(host=dbserver)(protocol=tcp)(port=1521)
)(connect_data=(sid=database)))", "beg","java");

    // Create a Statement object.
    Statement stmt = conn.createStatement ();

    // Select the RecordingTitle column from the Recordings table.
    ResultSet rset = stmt.executeQuery ("select RecordingTitle from Recordings");

    // Iterate through the result and print the recordings.
    while (rset.next ())
      System.out.println (rset.getString ("RecordingTitle"));

    rset.close();
    stmt.close();
    conn.close();
  }
}
```

2. Save and compile the class, then run it as follows:

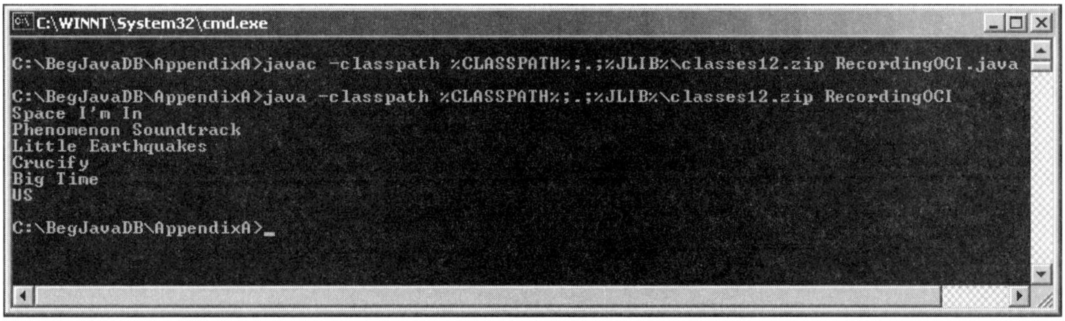

```
C:\WINNT\System32\cmd.exe

C:\BegJavaDB\AppendixA>javac -classpath %CLASSPATH%;.;%JLIB%\classes12.zip RecordingOCI.java

C:\BegJavaDB\AppendixA>java -classpath %CLASSPATH%;.;%JLIB%\classes12.zip RecordingOCI
Space I'm In
Phenomenon Soundtrack
Little Earthquakes
Crucify
Big Time
US

C:\BegJavaDB\AppendixA>_
```

Oracle's Thin JDBC Driver

Oracle comes with a thin JDBC Type 4 driver that is designed for Java applet developers. This driver is completely written in Java, and is fully compliant with the JDBC standard. The thin JDBC driver was designed to be about 150 KB in size (300 KB uncompressed) so that it can be downloaded with the Java applet. The JDBC driver then establishes a direct connection to the Oracle database server over Java sockets. It provides its own lightweight implementation of a TCP/IP version of Oracle's SQL*Net/Net8 protocol. The thin JDBC Driver has the following important features:

- **No library installation** – Unlike the JDBC/OCI driver, which requires pre-installation of the SQL*Net, `CORE`, and other support files, the thin JDBC driver was designed to be completely downloadable and does not require any pre-installation of software on the client desktops.
- **Globalization support** – It also provides complete support for globalized character sets allowing Java applications to access databases that use any Oracle character set. This is achieved by converting the characters to Unicode 1.2.
- **Performance optimizations** – The thin JDBC driver also provides a number of performance optimizations including reductions in the number of client-to-server round trips for binds, defines, and describes; batched statement execution, and so on.

In contrast to the JDBC/OCI driver, the thin JDBC driver has two restrictions on its usage:

- **SQL*Net version support** – Unlike the JDBC/OCI driver, the thin JDBC driver only works with TCP/IP-based networks. Users who are running applications on non-TCP/IP networks are encouraged to use the JDBC/OCI driver.
- **Database version support** – The thin JDBC driver only supports Oracle 7.2 database versions and upward. Like the Oracle JDBC/OCI driver, it can also access Oracle 8 databases.

Using the Oracle Thin JDBC Driver

The Oracle thin JDBC driver can be used in the following manner:

- Installing and setting the classpath
- Using JDBC classes
- Loading the driver
- Retrieving the connection

Let's see an example of how a Type 4 driver can be used with the above steps

Installing and Setting the Classpath

Install the Oracle thin driver and add `[ORACLE_HOME]\jdbc\lib\classes111.zip` to your `CLASSPATH`. (If using JDK-1.0.2 add `classes102.zip` instead.)

Using JDBC Classes

Import the JDBC classes in your programs that use JDBC, using the following statement:

```
import java.sql.*;
```

Loading the Driver

The JDBC program must register the Oracle driver before being able to use it. To do that, include the following line at the beginning of the `main` function:

```
DriverManager.registerDriver (new oracle.jdbc.driver.OracleDriver ());
```

Retrieving the Connection

A connection to the database can be opened with the `getConnection` call. The connection URL is of the format `jdbc:oracle:thin:@`*`<database>`*, where *`<database>`* is either a string of the form *`<host>:<port>:<sid>`* or a SQL*Net name/value pair.

```
Connection conn = DriverManager.getConnection
                  ("jdbc:oracle:thin:@<database>", "scott", "tiger");
```

Try It Out – Connecting to Oracle through the Thin Driver

1. The complete code listing that retrieves a connection and iterates a `ResultSet` using Oracle thin driver is given below:

```
import java.sql.*;

class RecordingThin {
  public static void main(String args[]) throws SQLException {
    DriverManager.registerDriver(new oracle.jdbc.driver.OracleDriver());

    // In the URL, database is of the form <host>:<port>:<sid>.
    Connection conn =
```

```
        DriverManager.getConnection("jdbc:oracle:thin:@dbserver:1521:database",
                                    "beg", "java");

      // Create a Statement object.
      Statement stmt = conn.createStatement();

      // Select the RecordingTitle column from the Recordings table.
      ResultSet rset = stmt.executeQuery("select RecordingTitle from Recordings");

      // Iterate through the result and print the recordings.
      while (rset.next()) {
        System.out.println(rset.getString("RecordingTitle"));
      }

      rset.close();
      stmt.close();
      conn.close();
    }
  }
```

2. Compile and run the class as previously.

Connecting to Cloudscape Using the RMI-JDBC Driver

Throughout the chapters in the book, we develop Java applications that need to access a Cloudscape database, so we've been using the JDBC driver supplied with Cloudscape. However, we've also been accessing the database on our local computer. In order to be able to access a Cloudscape database on another computer, we need to use the RMI-JDBC driver.

In order to use a Cloudscape database in a multi-user environment, Cloudscape provides two options. You could either purchase the CloudConnector product, or you can use the free RMI-JDBC server that is provided with the database. The RMI-JDBC server is a daemon (program listening on a port) that boots an instance of the database and then manages multiple connections to that single instance. For testing and development purposes, the RMI-JDBC server will meet our needs just fine. However, if you use Cloudscape in a production environment, then I would recommend purchasing the CloudConnector product.

Try It Out – Starting the RMI-JDBC Server

1. Open a command prompt window.

2. Set the classpath to include the `RmiJdbc.jar` and `cloudscape.jar` files (or add these files to your existing `C:\java\lib` directory). The `RmiJdbc.jar` file will be in the `Cloudscape\Frameworks\RmiJdbc\classes` directory. You might want to move this to the `c:\java\lib` directory along with all the other JAR files we've been using in the book.

3. Add the path to the `C:\cloudscape\demo\programs\tours` directory to your classpath. (This is necessary for our example since the objects we are retrieving from the database rely on class definitions that are stored under this directory.)

```
set CLASSPATH=
    %CLASSPATH%; set classpath=%CLASSPATH%;C:\cloudscape\demo\programs\tours
```

4. Start the server.

```
>java -classpath %CLASSPATH%;%JLIB%\RmiJdbc.jar;%JLIB%\cloudscape.jar
      -Dcloudscape.system.home=C:\cloudscape\demo\databases
       RmiJdbc.RJJdbcServer COM.cloudscape.core.JDBCDriver
```

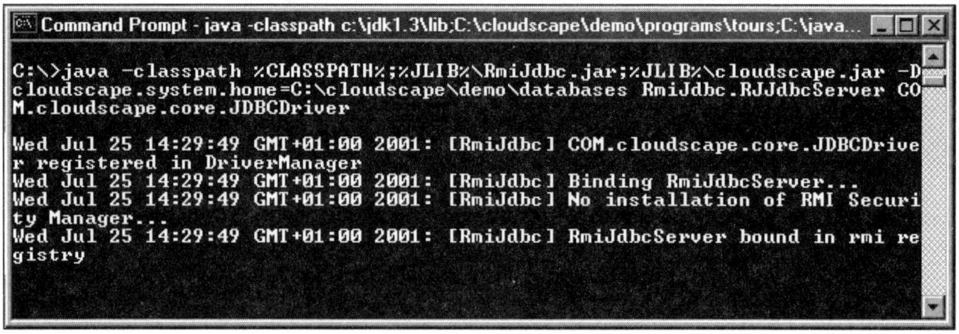

```
Command Prompt - java -classpath c:\jdk1.3\lib;C:\cloudscape\demo\programs\tours;C:\java...

C:\>java -classpath %CLASSPATH%;%JLIB%\RmiJdbc.jar;%JLIB%\cloudscape.jar -D
cloudscape.system.home=C:\cloudscape\demo\databases RmiJdbc.RJJdbcServer CO
M.cloudscape.core.JDBCDriver

Wed Jul 25 14:29:49 GMT+01:00 2001: [RmiJdbc] COM.cloudscape.core.JDBCDrive
r registered in DriverManager
Wed Jul 25 14:29:49 GMT+01:00 2001: [RmiJdbc] Binding RmiJdbcServer...
Wed Jul 25 14:29:49 GMT+01:00 2001: [RmiJdbc] No installation of RMI Securi
ty Manager...
Wed Jul 25 14:29:49 GMT+01:00 2001: [RmiJdbc] RmiJdbcServer bound in rmi re
gistry
```

To access a database through the RMI-JDBC server, you would use the `COM.cloudscape.core.RmiJdbcDriver` class. Again, this driver is located in the `cloudscape.jar` file, which should be located in your classpath. Here's a code snippet that shows how to access a database in this manner:

```
Class.forName("COM.cloudscape.core.RmiJdbcDriver");
Connection db = DriverManager.getConnection(
                "jdbc:cloudscape:rmi://localhost:1099/toursDB");
```

The first line of code registers the driver in the same manner as we did in the previous example. The second line, however, has a slightly different format. The database URL now includes a subprotocol telling the `DriverManager` that we are accessing the database through RMI.

To access a database through RMI, you need to identify the hostname and port that the RMI-JDBC server is running on. By default, the RMI-JDBC server for Cloudscape listens to port 1099. In this case, we're pointing the code at the localhost computer. For a remote computer, we would supply the name or IP address, just like for a web site.

Finally, we pass in the name of the database we wish to connect to.

In order to give you a taste of how to use the `RmiJdbcDriver`, the following simple program connects to a (potentially remote) Cloudscape database.

Try It Out – Using the RMI Drivers for Cloudscape

Here's what our program looks like:

```
import java.sql.*;

public class Example {
```

```
  public Example() {

    Connection db = null;
    Statement s = null;
    ResultSet rs = null;

    try {

      /* Register Driver */
      Class.forName("COM.cloudscape.core.RmiJdbcDriver");

      /* Connect to toursDB */
      db = DriverManager.getConnection(
        "jdbc:cloudscape:rmi://localhost:1099/toursDB");

      /* Create statement */
      s = db.createStatement();

      /* Execute SQL */
      String sql ="select * from countries where region='Africa'";
      rs = s.executeQuery(sql);
      System.out.println("SQL Query: " + sql + "\n");

      /* Loop through results */
      while (rs.next()) {
        System.out.println(rs.getString(1));
      }

    } catch (ClassNotFoundException e) {
      System.err.println("Error locating database driver");
      e.printStackTrace();
    } catch (SQLException e) {
      /*
        Loop through exception 'stack'
        (There can be many nested exceptions
        within a SQLException object)
      */
      while (e != null) {
        System.err.println(e.toString());
        e = e.getNextException();
      }
    } finally {
      /*
        Close all database objects
        (The statement object will automatically
        close the ResultSet object)
      */
      try {
        s.close();
        db.close();
      } catch (SQLException e) {
        e.printStackTrace();
      }
    }
```

```
    }

    public static void main(String[] args) {
      Example1 example11 = new Example1();
    }

  }
```

Save this file as `Example.java`, and compile it. Notice that you don't need to include anything other than your standard Java classes in the classpath. When we come to run this, we will need to include both the `RmiJdbc.jar` and `cloudscape.jar` files in the classpath:

To run the program, first be sure to start the `RmiJdbc` server (see previous section). Then, open a new command window and execute it like so:

```
> java -classpath %JLIB%\cloudscape.jar;.;%JLIB%\RmiJdbc.jar Example1
```

Here's a sample of what you should see when you run the program:

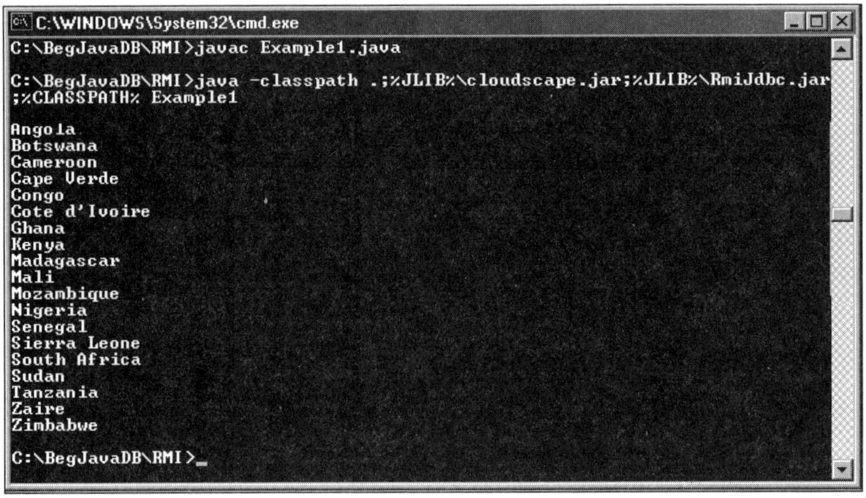

```
C:\WINDOWS\System32\cmd.exe
C:\BegJavaDB\RMI>javac Example1.java

C:\BegJavaDB\RMI>java -classpath .;%JLIB%\cloudscape.jar;%JLIB%\RmiJdbc.jar
;%CLASSPATH% Example1

Angola
Botswana
Cameroon
Cape Verde
Congo
Cote d'Ivoire
Ghana
Kenya
Madagascar
Mali
Mozambique
Nigeria
Senegal
Sierra Leone
South Africa
Sudan
Tanzania
Zaire
Zimbabwe

C:\BegJavaDB\RMI>_
```

How It Works

For this example, we will be using a table from the 'toursDB' database that is packaged with the Cloudscape DBMS. Here's the DDL (Database Definition Language) that was used to create the table:

```
CREATE TABLE COUNTRIES(COUNTRY VARCHAR(26) ,
                       COUNTRY_ISO_CODE CHAR(2) NOT NULL,
                       REGION VARCHAR(26)
                       )
```

Before we can use the Cloudscape JDBC driver, we must first register it with the `DriverManager`. This can be done using the `Class.forName()` method. Remember, we're using the `RmiJdbc` server, so we need to register the appropriate driver.

```
Class.forName("COM.cloudscape.core.RmiJdbcDriver");
```

All of our interactions with the database will occur through a `Connection` object. This can be obtained through the `DriverManager.getConnection()` method, passing in the URL to the database.

```
db = DriverManager.getConnection(
  "jdbc:cloudscape:rmi://localhost:1099/toursDB");
```

If you have a network connection to a computer with the Cloudscape `toursDB` database on, you can substitute `localhost` with the name of that computer.

Once we have a connection to the database, we can create and use a `Statement` object just like elsewhere. In this case, we populate a `ResultSet` with African countries, loop through it, and print them to the screen. Then we tidy up after ourselves.

Connecting to Access

In the sourcecode download for this book you will also find a `Music_Access.mdb` file for the Microsoft Access database.

Setting Up the Database

The first thing we need to do is set up an Access database driver for the database. In Windows, navigate to the ODBC Data Source Administrator dialog box, which can be found via Start | Settings | Control Panel, and then double-clicking on the ODBC Data Sources icon (it may be in the Administrative Tools folder). Select the System DSN tab at the top of the dialog box, and click on the Add... button at the right. In the listbox that comes up, select Microsoft Access Driver (*.mdb), and then click on Finish. A further dialog box will then come up with the title ODBC Microsoft Access Setup. In the Data Source Name textbox at the top of the dialog, type in Music_Access. Type in a suitable description in the Description text field if you wish. In the Database section of the dialog, click on the Select button, and in the file browsing dialog box that comes up, find and select your saved version of technical_library.mdb, then click OK. Now click on OK in the ODBC Microsoft Access Setup dialog. The System DSN section of the initial ODBC Data Source Administrator dialog should now have technical_library in the list of system data sources available. Click on the OK button at the bottom of the dialog to exit.

Using JDBC-ODBC Bridge

We need to install and configure the ODBC driver with which the Bridge is supposed to work. The Bridge is used by opening a JDBC connection using a URL with the `ODBC` sub-protocol. URLs for this sub-protocol are of the form:

```
jdbc:odbc:<data-source-name>[;<attribute-name>=<attribute-value>]
```

For example:

```
jdbc:odbc:MyDb;UID=me;PWD=secret
jdbc:odbc:Oracle1234;Cachesize=300
```

Before establishing a connection, the Bridge driver class, `sun.jdbc.odbc.JdbcOdbcDriver`, must be loaded. The driver class could either be added to the `java.lang.System` property named `jdbc.drivers`, or explicitly loaded using the Java class loader. Explicit loading is done with the following line of code:

```
Class.forName("sun.jdbc.odbc.JdbcOdbcDriver");
```

When loaded, the JDBC-ODBC driver creates an instance of itself, registers this with the JDBC DriverManager, and makes itself available for providing connections and executing SQL statements.

ODBC drivers are available for Oracle, Sybase, Informix, Microsoft SQL Server, MS Access, and Ingres.

Try It Out – Connecting to the Music Store on Access

1. Here is the code for our `RecordingAccess` class:

```
import java.sql.*;

class RecordingAccess {
  public static void main(String args[]) throws SQLException {
    DriverManager.registerDriver(new sun.jdbc.odbc.JdbcOdbcDriver());


 // This defines the data source for the driver

    String sourceURL = "jdbc:odbc:Music_Access";


// Create connection through the DriverManager

   Connection conn = DriverManager.getConnection(sourceURL);


    // Create a Statement object.
    Statement stmt = conn.createStatement ();

    // Select the RecordinTitle column from the Recordings table.
   ResultSet rset = stmt.executeQuery ("select RecordingTitle from RECORDINGS");

    // Iterate through the result and print the recordings.
    while (rset.next ())
      System.out.println (rset.getString ("RecordingTitle"));

    rset.close();
    stmt.close();
    conn.close();
  }
}
```

You can compile and run this in the usual fashion. The code assumes that the `mdb` file is stored in the same directory as the above class.

Debugging

The Bridge provides extensive tracing when DriverManager tracing is enabled. Tracing allows you to debug the application and determine the point of execution of the program that might have caused any errors. The following line of code enables tracing and sends it to standard output:

```
java.sql.DriverManager.setLogStream(java.lang.System.out);
```

A snapshot of the output of the JDBC-ODBC Bridge while retrieving a JDBC connection with tracing enabled, is given below:

```
Going to register JDBC driver
Going to get connection
DriverManager.getConnection("jdbc:odbc:myDSN")
    trying driver[className=sun.jdbc.odbc.JdbcOdbcDriver,
                            sun.jdbc.odbc.JdbcOdbcDriver@5d87b2]
*Driver.connect (jdbc:odbc:myDSN)
JDBC to ODBC Bridge: Checking security
Going to make a query
```

A snapshot of the output of the JDBC-ODBC Bridge while making a query with tracing enabled, is given below:

```
Going to make a query
*Connection.createStatement
Allocating Statement Handle (SQLAllocStmt), hDbc=150409832
hStmt=150413912
Setting statement option (SQLSetStmtOption),
                            hStmt=150413912, fOption=6, vParam=0
Setting statement option (SQLSetStmtOption),
                            hStmt=150413912, fOption=7, vParam=1
Registering Statement sun.jdbc.odbc.JdbcOdbcStatement@712c4e
*Statement.executeQuery ( SELECT  NAME  FROM  myTable )
```

akarta JAVA
Java

Installing the JBoss Application Server and Tomcat Web Container

JBoss 2 is an open source, 100 percent pure Java implementation of the J2EE platform. The brainchild of Marc Fleury, a Sun Microsystems expatriate, JBoss utilizes several innovations that make it among the most attractive options for J2EE development.

The entire application is built using Java's plug-in services component architecture JMX (http://java.sun.com/products/JavaManagement/). This means that virtually every component in the application server is replaceable. Everything, from the database connection pool, to the container managed persistence engine, can be swapped out with a commercial component, or one that you have written yourself.

JBoss also gains a great deal of strength from its participation in the open source movement. The application server is both free, and freely available. Anyone who wants to view the source code and see how a particular feature is implemented is welcome to, provided that they have the source control client tool for **CVS**, a free **Concurrent Versioning System** (available from http://cvshome.org/). Also, any developer is free to join the project and submit new features and feature enhancements.

JBoss currently lacks a few critical features found in commercial application server products. Most notable are support for clustering and failover. These features allow multiple instances of the application server to serve the same requests when the system is under load, and also allow the application to remain running even if one of the servers in a cluster goes down. Their current absence in the 2.2.2 release makes JBoss an unlikely candidate for most production environments. Fortunately, these features are at the top of list for the upcoming JBoss 3.0 release; in the meantime, the standards supportease of use, and the wide user base make JBoss 2.0 an ideal choice for developing J2EE applications. Due to standards support, it is entirely possible to develop an application with JBoss, and then deploy it to a commercial application server for production with minimal changes.

Installing the JBoss Application Server

We will now take a look at step-by-step instructions for locating, installing, and configuring the JBoss application server to support the development of the database examples in this book. The following software is needed to install and run JBoss:

- Sun's Java Development Kit (JDK) version 1.3. (http://java.sun.com/j2se/1.3/). The documentation states that the application server will also work with JDK 1.2.2, but several users have had difficulty in getting certain features such as hot-deployment of EJBs to work without the JDK 1.3. Hot deployment allows you to deploy new and/or modified EJBs to the server without shutting it down or restarting it.
- A web browser to download the binary distribution.
- An un-archiving utility such as WinZip or UNIX tar and gunzip/bzip2 to unpack the distribution.

Locating the JBoss Installation Program

JBoss is currently maintained in two locations. The first location is at the official JBoss web site (http://www.jboss.org/). The second is at SourceForge (http://sourceforge.net/), an online repository for a multitude of open source projects. SourceForge maintains more detailed information about the current development status of JBoss, but it is easier to locate the binary distribution on the JBoss web site, so the instructions will focus there.

1. Point your web browser to http://www.jboss.org/binary.jsp:

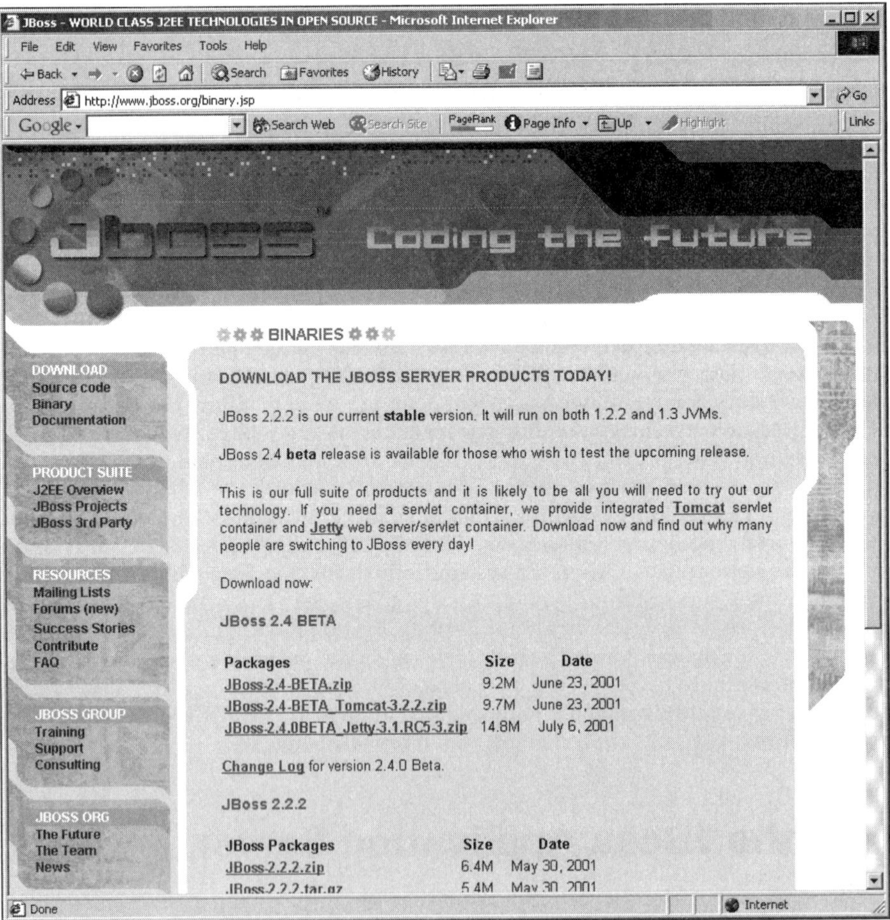

2. Locate the latest stable release version of JBoss. At the time of writing, this was version 2.2.2:

JBoss - WORLD CLASS J2EE TECHNOLOGIES IN OPEN SOURCE - Microsoft Internet Explorer

Address http://www.jboss.org/binary.jsp

RESOURCES
Mailing Lists
Forums (new)
Success Stories
Contribute
FAQ

JBOSS GROUP
Training
Support
Consulting

JBOSS ORG
The Future
The Team
News

people are switching to JBoss every day!

Download now:

JBoss 2.4 BETA

Packages	Size	Date
JBoss-2.4-BETA.zip	9.2M	June 23, 2001
JBoss-2.4-BETA_Tomcat-3.2.2.zip	9.7M	June 23, 2001
JBoss-2.4.0BETA_Jetty-3.1.RC5-3.zip	14.8M	July 6, 2001

Change Log for version 2.4.0 Beta.

JBoss 2.2.2

JBoss Packages	Size	Date
JBoss-2.2.2.zip	6.4M	May 30, 2001
JBoss-2.2.2.tar.gz	5.4M	May 30, 2001
JBoss-2.2.2.tar.bz2	5.1M	May 30, 2001

JBoss + Tomcat Packages	Size	Date
JBoss-2.2.2_Tomcat-3.2.2.zip	9.7M	May 30, 2001
JBoss-2.2.2_Tomcat-3.2.2.tar.gz	8.3M	May 30, 2001
JBoss-2.2.2_Tomcat-3.2.2.tar.bz2	7.7M	May 30, 2001

JBoss + Jetty Packages	Size	Date
JBoss-2.2.2_Jetty-3.1.RC5.zip	10.9M	June 6, 2001
JBoss-2.2.2_Jetty-3.1.RC5.tar.gz	9.0M	June 6, 2001
JBoss-2.2.2_Jetty-3.1.RC5.tar.bz2	8.4M	June 6, 2001

Change Log for version 2.2.2.

The older JBoss versions (2.2 and 2.2.1) are available here.

Oh, and remember we love you.

Designed by NeoLine   JBoss™ is a trademark of Marc Fleury. Copyright © 1999-2001, jboss.org. All rights reserved.

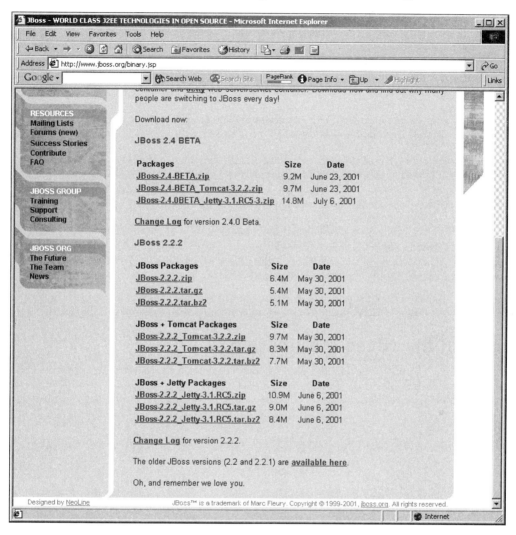

You should notice three different types of packages listed for the current version: JBoss Packages, JBoss + Tomcat Packages, and JBoss + Jetty Packages. As a convenience, JBoss comes optionally packaged with either the Tomcat (JBoss + Tomcat Packages) or Jetty (JBoss + Jetty Packages) web server integrated. You can also download JBoss without a web server (JBoss Packages).

Both Tomcat (see online documentation at http://jakarta.apache.org/tomcat/) and Jetty (http://jetty.mortbay.com/) are open source **web containers** (web servers that can also execute servlets and JSPs). We will choose the Tomcat package since Sun is now shipping Tomcat with the Servlet Development Kit and examples.

The integration between Tomcat/Jetty and JBoss is tight, and ensures that calls between the two happen at the JVM layer instead of the network layer, which results in a dramatic performance increase. This embedding requires a special type of sourcecode compilation which is already done for you in the 'JBoss + Tomcat' and 'JBoss + Jetty' releases. If you are interested in doing this compilation on your own, instructions are available at: http://www.jboss.org/documentation/HTML/ch11.html#howtotomcat.

Note that it is possible to integrate another web container into JBoss to provide a complete J2EE stack. Doing so requires extending a special class provided by JBoss that hooks the web container into the application deployment process. This is a step that is meant to be taken by web container provider (or ambitious developers). Full instructions for doing so are available at http://www.jboss.org/documentation/HTML/ch11s172.html.

With the exception of web server-specific items, the JBoss configuration will be identical for any of the packages. Only one step remains:

3. Select the type of archive you want and download by clicking on the appropriate link.

   The file with the `.zip` extension will require a ZIP application such as WinZip (http://www.winzip.com/). The file with the `.tar.gz` will require applications like gunzip and tar (common UNIX utilities) to unpack. The file with the `.tar.bz2` extension will require the `bzip2` utility to unpack (http://sources.redhat.com/bzip2/).

Once you have clicked the link, your web browser should begin downloading the file. The location you save this file in is not important; just make sure you remember it so that you can unpack the archive.

Unpacking the JBoss Distribution

The specific method for unpacking the JBoss distribution will depend on your development platform, and the archiving type of the distribution you downloaded. You will want to turn on any options necessary to preserve the file names and folder structure of the archive. When unpacked, you should see the following folder hierarchy:

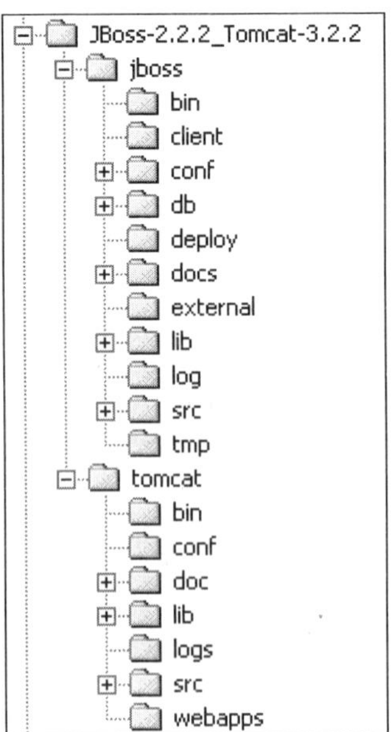

You'll notice that both JBoss and Tomcat ship with various documentation and sourcecode. This is stored in the `docs` and `src` folder under `jboss`, and in the `doc` and `src` folder under `tomcat`. This is not complete application documentation, which is available on their web sites, but rather miscellaneous information meant to supplement the use of the software. A brief description of the contents for the remaining folders under `/jboss` follows below:

Directory	Purpose
`/jboss/bin`	Contains JBoss 'executable' shell scripts (for UNIX platforms) and batch files (for Windows platforms). Also contains the EJX deployment descriptor editor.
`/jboss/client`	Contains the JAR files needed by client applications to access JBoss.
`/jboss/conf`	Contains configuration files for JBoss and its components.
`/jboss/db`	Contains files for the Hypersonic and instantdb database products included with JBoss, as well as files to support the JBossMQ, the message queue shipped with JBoss. Some features of JBoss utilize this internally, but you will not interact with this directory as the examples in this book rely on external databases such as Cloudscape and Oracle.
`/jboss/deploy`	JBoss' default deployment directory. Enterprise ARchive (EAR) files copied here will be deployed to JBoss, as will JAR files.
`/jboss/docs`	Contains JavaDoc documentation for JBoss.
`/jboss/external`	Contains JAR files for external extensions to the JBoss application server.
`/jboss/lib`	Contains JARs that are automatically included in the classpath of the server.
`/jboss/log`	Contains the log files for the application server and its components.
`/jboss/src`	Contains the JBoss source code.
`/jboss/tmp`	A directory used to store temporary files.

And the folders under `/tomcat`:

Directory	Purpose
`/tomcat/bin`	Contains startup and shutdown scripts for Tomcat.
`/tomcat/conf`	Contains the main Tomcat configuration file and configuration files for various applications deployed to Tomcat.
`/tomcat/doc`	Contains documentation for Tomcat.
`/tomcat/lib`	Contains JARs used by Tomcat
`/tomcat/logs`	This is where Tomcat places its log files.
`/tomcat/src`	The servlet API interface sourcecode.
`/tomcat/webapps`	Contains sample web applications, and is where we place our web applications.

In the course of your development you will never touch most of these directories. When using the JBoss-Tomcat distribution, most of your interaction will be with the JBoss configuration files under `/jboss/conf` and with deploying applications to the `/jboss/deploy` directory.

Running JBoss

Now comes the easy part. In order to get JBoss running initially, you only need to make sure that one environment variable is set. You need to make sure the directory containing `java.exe` is included in you system `PATH` environment variable. To check this simply type the following at a command prompt:

```
> java
```

If you have the proper path set, you should see a brief explanation of the usage of the `java` command like the following:

```
C:\WINNT\System32\cmd.exe

C:\>java
Usage: java [-options] class [args...]
           (to execute a class)
   or  java -jar [-options] jarfile [args...]
           (to execute a jar file)

where options include:
    -cp -classpath <directories and zip/jar files separated by ;>
                  set search path for application classes and resources
    -D<name>=<value>
                  set a system property
    -verbose[:class|gc|jni]
                  enable verbose output
    -version      print product version and exit
    -showversion  print product version and continue
    -? -help      print this help message
    -X            print help on non-standard options

C:\>_
```

If you do not see an explanation of the java command and get a message such as File Not Found, or 'java' is not recognized as an internal variable..., your `PATH` variable is probably not set correctly. Double-check your `PATH` setting and try the command again. If it fails, consult your operating system documentation on how to set operating system environment variables.

Once this is taken care of, change to the `/jboss/bin` directory where you unpacked your distribution. From a command prompt, type:

```
> run
```

If you are using a Windows system, this will invoke the `run.bat` file. If you are in a UNIX-based shell, this will execute the `run.sh` shell script. You should then see a great deal of information scrolling by on the screen. This is logging, indicating the startup of all the components in JBoss. When JBoss is finished booting up, you should see a message indicating that JBoss has been started, like the following:

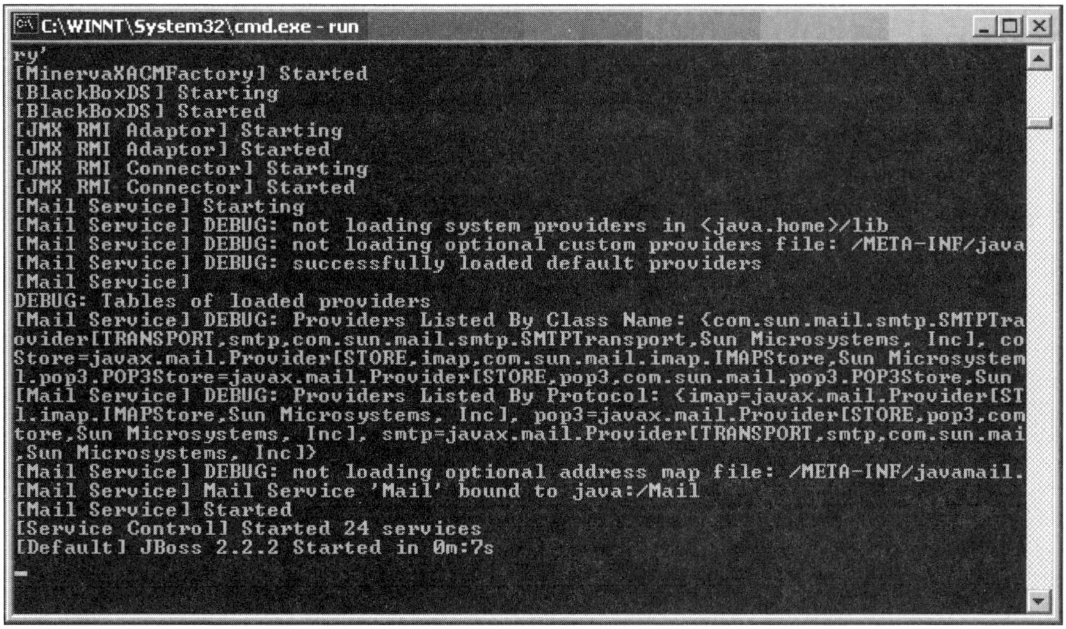

```
C:\WINNT\System32\cmd.exe - run
ry'
[MinervaXACMFactory] Started
[BlackBoxDS] Starting
[BlackBoxDS] Started
[JMX RMI Adaptor] Starting
[JMX RMI Adaptor] Started
[JMX RMI Connector] Starting
[JMX RMI Connector] Started
[Mail Service] Starting
[Mail Service] DEBUG: not loading system providers in <java.home>/lib
[Mail Service] DEBUG: not loading optional custom providers file: /META-INF/java
[Mail Service] DEBUG: successfully loaded default providers
[Mail Service]
DEBUG: Tables of loaded providers
[Mail Service] DEBUG: Providers Listed By Class Name: {com.sun.mail.smtp.SMTPTra
ovider[TRANSPORT,smtp,com.sun.mail.smtp.SMTPTransport,Sun Microsystems, Inc], co
Store=javax.mail.Provider[STORE,imap,com.sun.mail.imap.IMAPStore,Sun Microsystem
l.pop3.POP3Store=javax.mail.Provider[STORE,pop3,com.sun.mail.pop3.POP3Store,Sun
[Mail Service] DEBUG: Providers Listed By Protocol: {imap=javax.mail.Provider[ST
l.imap.IMAPStore,Sun Microsystems, Inc], pop3=javax.mail.Provider[STORE,pop3,com
tore,Sun Microsystems, Inc], smtp=javax.mail.Provider[TRANSPORT,smtp,com.sun.mai
,Sun Microsystems, Inc]}
[Mail Service] DEBUG: not loading optional address map file: /META-INF/javamail.
[Mail Service] Mail Service 'Mail' bound to java:/Mail
[Mail Service] Started
[Service Control] Started 24 services
[Default] JBoss 2.2.2 Started in 0m:7s
_
```

Congratulations! You have successfully installed the JBoss application server. When you are ready to shut the server down, you may do so my pressing *Ctrl-C*, at which point the server will display several logging messages indicating the shutdown of the components:

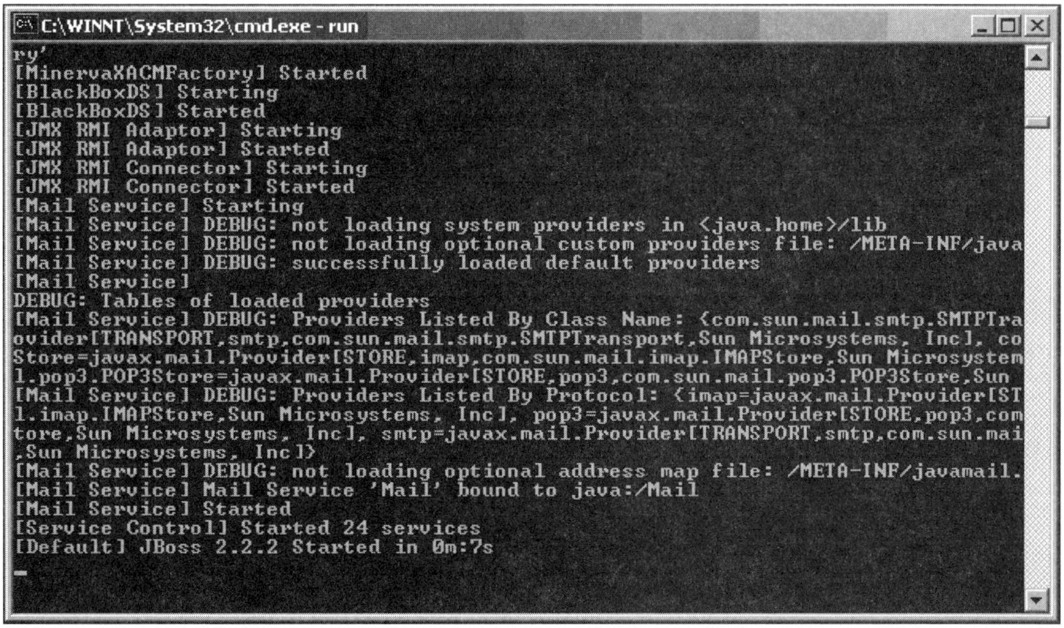

```
C:\WINNT\System32\cmd.exe - run
ry'
[MinervaXACMFactory] Started
[BlackBoxDS] Starting
[BlackBoxDS] Started
[JMX RMI Adaptor] Starting
[JMX RMI Adaptor] Started
[JMX RMI Connector] Starting
[JMX RMI Connector] Started
[Mail Service] Starting
[Mail Service] DEBUG: not loading system providers in <java.home>/lib
[Mail Service] DEBUG: not loading optional custom providers file: /META-INF/java
[Mail Service] DEBUG: successfully loaded default providers
[Mail Service]
DEBUG: Tables of loaded providers
[Mail Service] DEBUG: Providers Listed By Class Name: {com.sun.mail.smtp.SMTPTra
ovider[TRANSPORT,smtp,com.sun.mail.smtp.SMTPTransport,Sun Microsystems, Inc], co
Store=javax.mail.Provider[STORE,imap,com.sun.mail.imap.IMAPStore,Sun Microsystem
l.pop3.POP3Store=javax.mail.Provider[STORE,pop3,com.sun.mail.pop3.POP3Store,Sun
[Mail Service] DEBUG: Providers Listed By Protocol: {imap=javax.mail.Provider[ST
l.imap.IMAPStore,Sun Microsystems, Inc], pop3=javax.mail.Provider[STORE,pop3,com
tore,Sun Microsystems, Inc], smtp=javax.mail.Provider[TRANSPORT,smtp,com.sun.mai
,Sun Microsystems, Inc]}
[Mail Service] DEBUG: not loading optional address map file: /META-INF/javamail.
[Mail Service] Mail Service 'Mail' bound to java:/Mail
[Mail Service] Started
[Service Control] Started 24 services
[Default] JBoss 2.2.2 Started in 0m:7s
_
```

Starting JBoss with Tomcat

Recall that the JBoss distribution we downloaded also comes bundled with the Tomcat web server. To utilize the Tomcat web server for JSP and Servlet deployment, you will want to start up JBoss with Tomcat enabled. To do this, JBoss makes use of special Tomcat configuration files located in `/jboss/conf/tomcat`. There is another batch file in the `/jboss/bin` directory that ensures the proper configuration file is loaded up. To start up JBoss with Tomcat enabled, simply execute the following in the `/jboss/bin` directory as in the previous `run` command:

```
> run_with_tomcat
```

Again, in a Windows environment, this will be a batch file, and under UNIX, it will be a shell script. After executing the batch file or shell script, you will see a flood of logging similar to when you started up JBoss by itself. To verify that JBoss was started with Tomcat, open up a web browser and go to http://localhost:8080. You should then see the default web page for Tomcat:

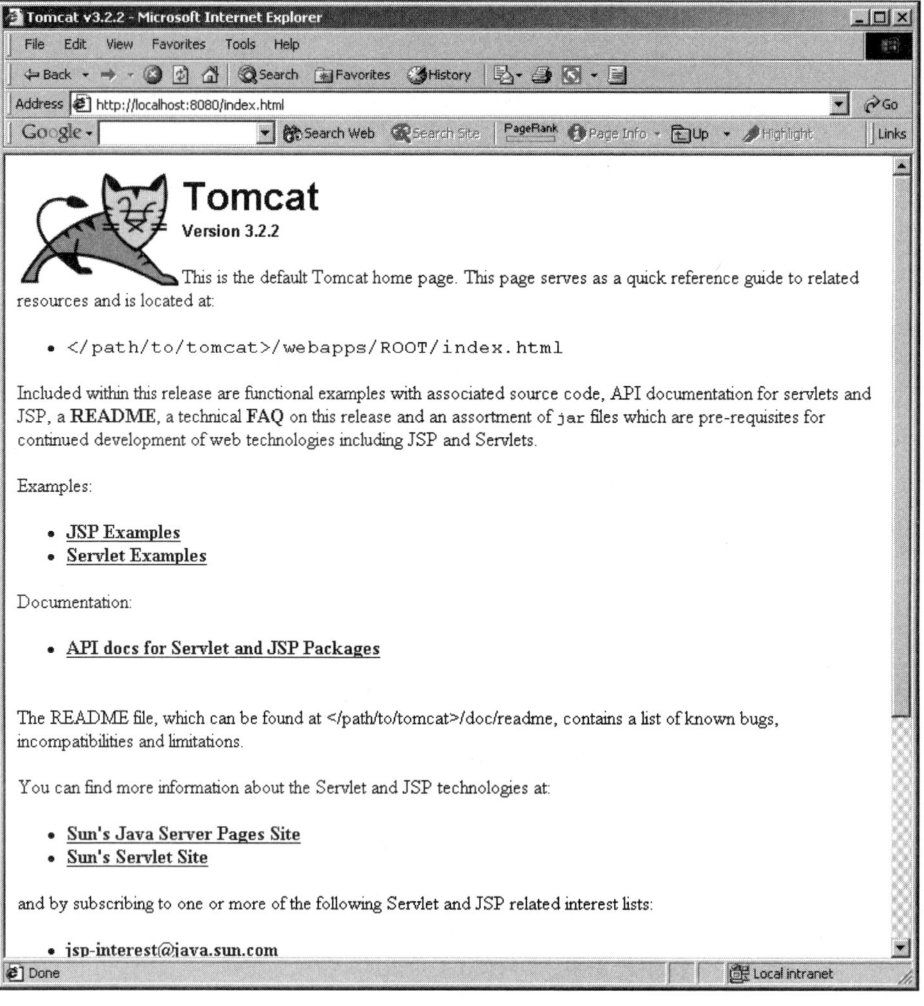

The shutting down of JBoss and Tomcat is identical to that of JBoss running alone. Simply go to the command window where JBoss is running, and press *Ctrl-C*.

Configuring the JDBC in JBoss

While information regarding configuration of all features of JBoss and Tomcat would be well beyond the scope of this book, there is some configuration that will be necessary to run the examples in this book. One of the most important features will be the configuration of a `DataSource` in JBoss to use the driver and settings for your database.

JBoss ships with the **Minerva** database connection pooling component. Minerva allows you to create several pools, even for the same driver. This is useful if you have cases where certain pools need to be more available than others when under load.

In order to set up JBoss for database access, there are two steps that must be completed:

- Installation of the database driver
- Configuration of the connection pool

Installing a JDBC Driver in JBoss

There are two steps that must take place to install a database driver in JBoss:

1. Copy the driver JAR file for your database into `/jboss/lib/ext`

   Files in JBoss's `/lib/ext` directory are added into the classpath of the application server

2. Add a database driver entry to the `/jboss/conf/default/jboss.jcml` configuration file

Once the database driver is available in the classpath, we must add a configuration instruction to JBoss to instruct it to load and register our driver. We do this by creating a **JdbcProvider MBean**. MBeans are a type of component in Sun's **Java Management Extensions** (**JMX**) framework. While a full discussion of JMX is out of scope for this book, consider MBeans to be a kind of software 'plug-in' that allows an application to be easily extended.

We will be adding our `JdbcProvider` MBean to the file under the section commented by:

```
<!-- JDBC -->
```

The `JdbcProvider` tag looks like this:

```
<mbean code="org.jboss.jdbc.JdbcProvider"
       name="DefaultDomain:service=JdbcProvider">
  <attribute
    name="Drivers">org.hsql.jdbcDriver,org.enhydra.instantdb.jdbc.idbDriver
  </attribute>
</mbean>
```

The database driver will always have an mbean code element attribute value of org.jboss.jdbc.JdbcProvider. There is another element called attribute enclosed by the mbean element. The attribute element has an attribute called name that will always have the value Drivers. The opening and closing tags for the attribute element should contain the fully qualified class name of the database driver you are registering. So if you were registering the Oracle driver, your mbean element would look like this:

```
<mbean code="org.jboss.jdbc.JdbcProvider"
       name="DefaultDomain:service=JdbcProvider">
  <attribute
    name="Drivers">oracle.jdbc.driver.OracleDriver
  </attribute>
</mbean>
```

You will only need to create one JdbcProvider mbean element for each database driver, even if multiple pools will use the same driver.

Creating a JBoss Connection Pool

Configuration of a JBoss connection pool requires the addition of an org.jboss.jdbc.XADataSourceLoader MBean to the jboss.jcml configuration file. What you need to do next is insert an MBean just after the code above. A sample of the kind of mbean element required is listed below:

```
<mbean code="org.jboss.jdbc.XADataSourceLoader"
       name="DefaultDomain:service=XADataSource,name=InstantDS">
  <attribute name="PoolName">InstantDS</attribute>
  <attribute
    name="DataSourceClass">org.opentools.minerva.jdbc.xa.wrapper.XADataSourceImpl
  </attribute>
  <attribute name="Properties"></attribute>
  <attribute
    name="URL"> jdbc:HypersonicSQL:hsql://localhost:1476</attribute>
  <attribute name="GCMinIdleTime">1200000</attribute>
  <attribute name="JDBCUser">sa</attribute>
  <attribute name="MaxSize">10</attribute>
  <attribute name="Password" />
  <attribute name="GCEnabled">false</attribute>
  <attribute name="InvalidateOnError">false</attribute>
  <attribute name="TimestampUsed">false</attribute>
  <attribute name="Blocking">true</attribute>
  <attribute name="GCInterval">120000</attribute>
  <attribute name="IdleTimeout">1800000</attribute>
  <attribute name="IdleTimeoutEnabled">false</attribute>
  <attribute name="LoggingEnabled">false</attribute>
  <attribute name="MaxIdleTimeoutPercent">1.0</attribute>
  <attribute name="MinSize">0</attribute>
</mbean>
```

This looks like a lot of data to be entered, but fortunately, only a few attributes need to be specified. The connection pooling component will provide defaults for the rest. The attributes that must be specified are:

Attribute name	Purpose
`PoolName`	The name by which this datasource will be registered in the JBoss directory service.
`DatasourceClass`	The fully-qualified class name of a datasource implementation. In most cases, the Minerva implementation, `org.opentools.minerva.jdbc.xa.wrapper.XADataSourceImpl`, will suffice.
`URL`	The JDBC URL for the datasource.
`JDBCUser`	The database username for this connection pool.
`Password`	The database password for the username specified for this connection pool.

A sample connection pool MBean for connecting to Oracle with the minimum attributes might look like the following:

```
<mbean code="org.jboss.jdbc.XADataSourceLoader"
       name="DefaultDomain:service=XADataSource,name=OracleDB">
  <attribute name="PoolName">OracleDB</attribute>
  <attribute
    name="DataSourceClass">org.opentools.minerva.jdbc.xa.wrapper.XADataSourceImpl
  </attribute>
  <attribute name="URL">jdbc:oracle:thin:@serverhostname:1521:ORCL</attribute>
  <attribute name="JDBCUser">scott</attribute>
  <attribute name="Password">tiger</attribute>
</mbean>
```

Your driver and connection pool are now configured for use with JBoss.

Installing Standalone Tomcat

In the previous section of this appendix, we have looked at how JBoss can be downloaded as a bundle with the Tomcat web server. Here, we will look at how Tomcat can be obtained and set up on its own, independently of JBoss.

Tomcat is implemented in Java and needs the Java development environment to be available, so you should install the Java SDK first. Once you have done that, you can obtain the latest build of Tomcat from http://jakarta.apache.org/builds/jakarta-tomcat/release/v3.2.3/bin/, and just unpack the Tomcat archive to a convenient place on your hard drive. This will be a `.zip` archive for Windows or a `tar.gz` archive for UNIX.

At the time of writing, the latest production-quality build of Tomcat is version 3.2.3.

When you unpack the `jakarta-tomcat-3.2.3` archive, it will generate the following directory structure:

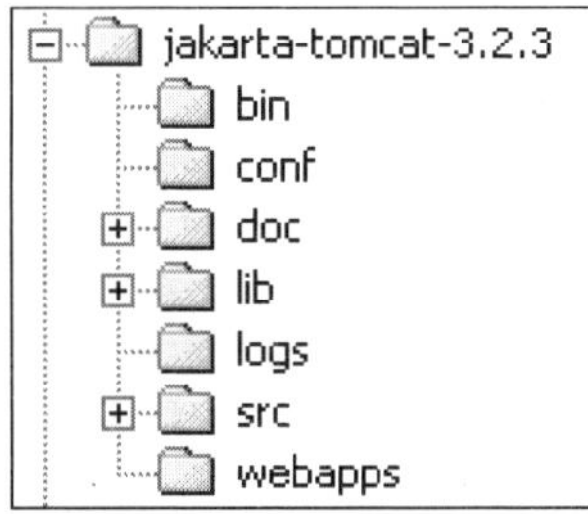

The table below summarizes the contents of the directories:

Directory	Purpose
`jakarta-tomcat-3.2.3`	The Tomcat home directory.
`bin`	Contains the scripts to start up and shut down the Tomcat server.
`conf`	Contains the Tomcat configuration files.
`doc`	Contains FAQ and readme files plus directories containing Tomcat documentation files.
`lib`	Contains JAR files used by Tomcat.
`logs`	Contains Tomcat log files.
`src`	Contains Java source files for the servlet interfaces and abstraction classes.
`webapps`	Contains sample web applications.

You now need to define two environment variables, `TOMCAT_HOME` and `JAVA_HOME`. `TOMCAT_HOME` should have a value corresponding to the home directory for Tomcat, and `JAVA_HOME` should be set to the Java SDK home directory. For instance, if you are running Windows and you have installed the Java 2 SDK 1.3 to `C:\`, then `JAVA_HOME` should be set to `C:\jdk1.3`. If you also unpacked the Tomcat zip to `C:\`, then `TOMCAT_HOME` should be set to `C:\jakarta-tomcat-3.2.3`. You should also have added the path to the Java SDK `bin` directory to the paths specified in the `PATH` environment variable.

Starting Tomcat

You are now ready to run Tomcat by executing the startup script that you will find in the `bin` directory. This will be `startup.bat` if you are running under Windows or `startup.sh` for UNIX. If you are running under Windows 2000, don't close the window where the `startup` command was executed, otherwise you will stop the Tomcat server. You can see whether Tomcat is running by opening your browser and specifying the URL http://localhost:8080, much like in the previous section. Again, your browser should display the following page:

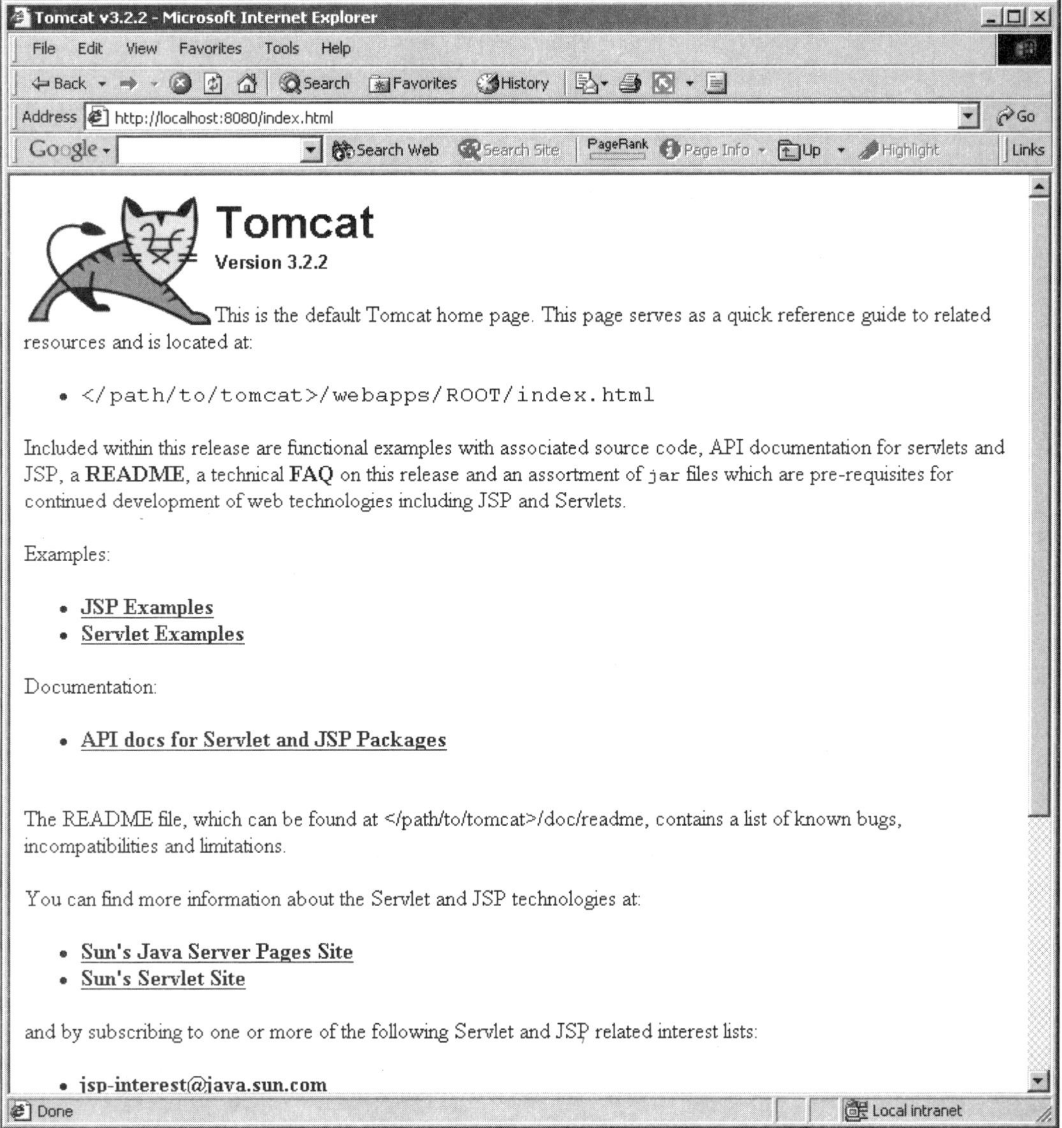

If the page doesn't display, look at the contents of the `tomcat.log` file in the Tomcat `logs` directory. This will contain information about any errors that were identified during startup. There are two likely reasons why Tomcat fails to start. Either you have not set up the environment variables correctly, or the Java SDK is not installed properly. If the page does display, you can click on the JSP Examples link and try out some JSP pages. If the JSP examples don't work, the most likely reason is that Tomcat is not finding the Java 2 SDK. This may be because you have not installed it properly, or because the `JAVA_HOME` environment variable is not defined correctly. Don't forget that if you set environment variables under Windows 9x by modifying `autoexec.bat`, you need to reboot your machine for the changes to take effect.

When Tomcat executes a web application it will generate a further directory in the Tomcat home directory. This is the work directory that is used by Tomcat to store compiled JSP files.

Stopping Tomcat

To stop Tomcat you just have to execute the `shutdown` script from the Tomcat `bin` directory – `shutdown.bat` for Windows or `shutdown.sh` for UNIX.

akarta
JAVA

XML Primer

In this appendix, we're going to take a quick look at the basics of XML. If you use XML on a daily basis already, you can skip this. For those of you who are coming from a pure relational-database background, or if you can't remember the difference between an element and an attribute, read on.

We will be looking at:

- Basics of XML Markup
- Well-formed and valid documents
- Related technologies and how they fit in

Of course, there are whole books devoted to teaching XML, such as *Beginning XML, ISBN 1861003412* from Wrox Press, and this is just intended to get you up to speed with what you need to know for this book.

The first thing to make clear is that, assuming you are familiar with HTML, XML offers a new way of tagging (or marking up) your data that is so straightforward you will wonder why it is making such big waves. Yet, while HTML and XML may look very similar, they are in fact quite different.

Before we dive into using XML and showing you how it can be used, it would be helpful to have a quick look at markup languages in general and what markup is.

What is a Markup Language?

While you may not realize it, we come across markup every day. Quite simply, markup refers to anything put on a document that adds special meaning or provides extra information. For example, highlighted or bolded text is a form of markup.

But unless others understand our markup it is of little use, so we need a set of rules encompassing the following points for it to be understood:

- To declare what constitutes markup
- To declare exactly what our markup means

A markup language is such a set of rules. A familiar example is HTML – which is a markup language that enables you to write a document for display on the Web.

Tags and Elements

Even those of us who are familiar with HTML still often get the meaning of tags and elements mixed up. Just to clarify, tags are the angled brackets (known as delimiters), and the text between them. Here are some examples of tags used in HTML:

- `<P>` is a tag that marks the beginning of a new paragraph
- `<I>` is a tag indicating that the following text should be rendered in italic type
- `</I>` is a tag that indicates the end of a section of text to be rendered in italic type

Elements, however, refer to the tags *plus* their content. So the following is an example of an element:

```
<B>Here is some bold text</B>
```

In general terms, tags are labels that tell a user agent (such as a browser or parser) to do something to whatever is encased in the tags.

A user agent is anything that acts on your behalf. You are a user agent working for your boss, your computer is a user agent working for you, your browser is a user agent working for you and your computer, and so it goes on.

Empty elements which don't have closing tags, such as the `<IMG>` element in HTML, have to be treated differently in XML to make up for them not having a closing tag, but don't worry about that for now, we will come back to them later.

The following diagram illustrates the parts of an element:

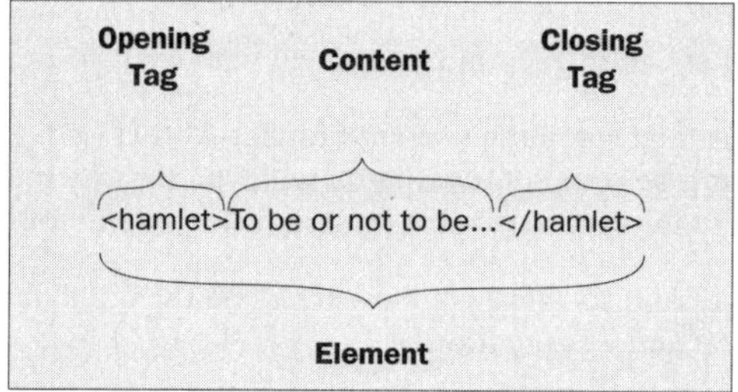

Attributes

Any tag can have an attribute as long as it is defined. They take the form of name/value pairs (also referred to as attribute/value pairs), in that the element can be given an attribute (with a name), and the attribute must carry a text value surrounded in quotation marks. They take the form:

```
<tagname attribute="value">
```

For example, in HTML 4.0 the `<BODY>` tag can take the following attributes:

```
CLASS ID   DIR           LANG     STYLE   TITLE
BACKGROUND BGCOLOR       ALINK    LINK    VLINK   TEXT
```

So, for example, in HTML, <BODY> could take the following attributes:

```
<BODY BGCOLOR="#000000" ALINK="#999999" LINK="#990099" VLINK="#888888"
TEXT="#999999">
```

As we shall see shortly there are other types of markup, but these are the two most used parts.

What is XML?

XML, or Extensible Markup Language to give its full name, is an example of a markup language, and just like HTML it makes extensive use of tags and attributes.

With HTML you have a fixed set of markup you can use – there is a prescribed set of tags and attributes with which you can write web pages.

XML, however, is a lot more flexible. You can make up your own tags and attributes, and its uses go beyond displaying information in a web browser. Because you can create your own tags and attributes in XML you can use markup that actually describes the content of the element, rather than just using tags that tell you how to present the data on a web page.

Because you can use tags that describe the content of an element, XML has become a general format for marking up all kinds of data – not just data that will be for presented on the web. Let's dive straight in and look at an example so that we get a feel for it.

At its simplest level XML is just a way of marking up data so that it is **self-describing**. What do we mean by this? Well, imagine that you were running an e-commerce system, and that part of this system generates invoices. If a customer wanted to check their invoice over the web, it may be displayed to them marked up in HTML, and the HTML could look something like this:

```
<DOCTYPE HTML PUBLIC "-//W3C//DTD HTML 4.0 //EN">
<HTML>
   <HEAD><TITLE>Invoice</TITLE></HEAD>

<BODY>
   <H3>Invoice: Kevin Williams</H3>

<TABLE>
   <TR>
      <TD valign="top">
         <H4>Billing Address</H4>
            <UL>
               <LI>Kevin Williams</LI>
               <LI>742 Evergreen Terrace</LI>
               <LI>Springfield</LI>
               <LI>KY</LI>
               <LI>12345</LI>
```

```
            </UL>
         </TD>

      <TD valign="top">
         <H4>Shipping Address</H4>
            <UL>
               <LI>742 Evergreen Terrace</LI>
               <LI>Springfield</LI>
               <LI>KY</LI>
               <LI>12345</LI>
               <LI><B>Shipping Company</B> Fed Ex</LI>
            </UL>
      </TD>
   </TR>
</TABLE>

Item
   <UL>
      <LI><B>Item Description </B>Widget (3 inch)</LI>
      <LI><B>Item Code </B>1A2A3AB</LI>
      <LI><B>Quantity </B>17</LI>
      <LI><B>Price </B> 0.10</LI>
</UL>

Item
   <UL>
      <LI><B>Item Description </B>Grommet (0.5 inch)</LI>
      <LI><B>ItemCode </B>1A2A3AB</LI>
      <LI><B>Quantity </B>22</LI>
      <LI><B>Price </B>0.05</LI>
   </UL>

</BODY>
</HTML>
```

While this may be fine for display on a web page, and we will see the result in the next screenshot, tags like `<LI>` don't tell you that here they are containing information about a product you just ordered. There is nothing in the HTML markup to tell you that this is an invoice.

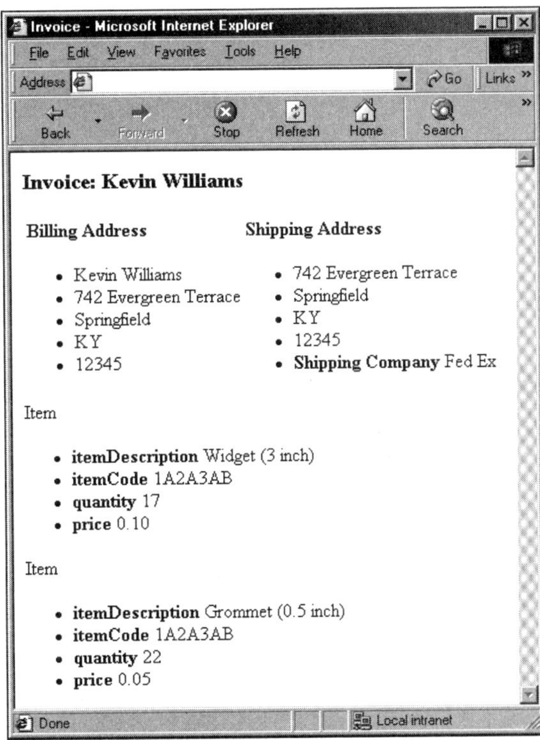

This is all very good for display on the web, but remember that we are running an e-commerce system here. Now, imagine that this e-commerce system is written in PHP, and that once it has generated the invoice information other parts of the company may need the same data:

- The packing department might need a copy to send the items out – but they run a UNIX-based system written in C.
- The customer support team who can track the package may need it if there is a problem with delivery – but their system is written in Visual Basic.
- The service department may need to check it if the product is returned because it is faulty – and they run an application written in Java.

The potential number of uses for the data goes on, accounts, marketing, etc.; all of these users may need a copy of it. This means that there are a lot of uses for the same data, but the different departments that need the data use software written in different programming languages, and run on different operating systems. Wouldn't it be great if we could have a platform-independent way of passing this data between programs, and of telling the programs what each piece of data that was marked up did?

Well, let's change the markup language and use XML instead of HTML. As I said, we can create our own tags with XML, so how about we use tags that describe what we are trying to say about the document – that it represents an invoice, and what the invoice contains. Let's make up some of our own tags and we can re-create this information with tags that describe the data we are marking up:

```
<?xml version="1.0" ?>

<Invoice
   customerName="Kevin Williams"
   billingAddress="742 Evergreen Terrace"
   billingCity="Springfield"
   billingState="KY"
   billingPostalCode="12345"
   shippingAddress="742 Evergreen Terrace"
   shippingCity="Springfield"
   shippingState="KY"
   shippingPostalCode="12345"
   shippingCompany="FedEx">
   <LineItem
      itemCode="1A2A3AB"
      itemDescription="Widget (3 inch)"
      quantity="17"
      price="0.10" />
   <LineItem
      itemCode="2BC3DCB"
      itemDescription="Grommet (0.5 inch)"
      quantity="22"
      price="0.05" />
</Invoice>
```

OK, if you opened this up in a browser, it would not look like a web page, it would look like this:

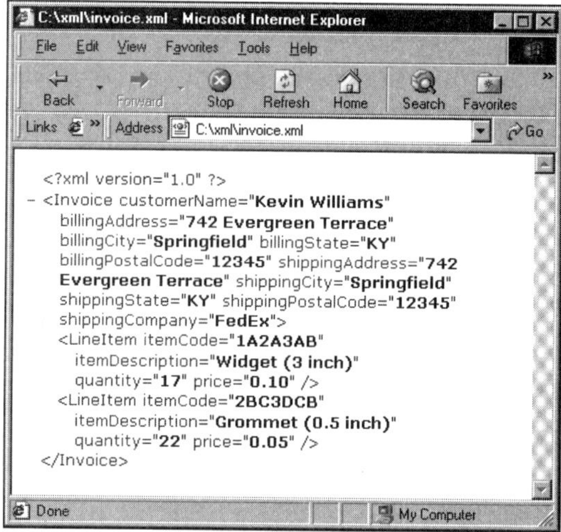

But, we do know that in the `Invoice` element, we will find an invoice, and that in the `customerName` attribute, we will find out the customer whose invoice it is.

Furthermore, this XML file is just plain text, so the data in an XML file would be available for any programming language, and it would be available on any platform, and it can easily be passed over HTTP. So, we could actually use this data we had marked up in XML in a lot more ways that we could the HTML version. Because it is just text, and because we know that every time there is an `invoice` element there will be details about an invoice inside, the data becomes a lot more flexible.

Now you have to move your thoughts away from just displaying data in a web browser – think about anywhere that you need to exchange information, or you need to store information, and there *may* be a use for XML.

Let's just look at one last example so that you can really see why this is important. Pick a programming language, any programming language in which you may write an object. If you had to represent the invoice we have just seen in an object as part of the e-commerce system, we could pass the state into and out of the object as XML. Take a look at this:

```
<? xml version="1.0" ?>
 <ObjectData id="customer125" classname="Invoice.Customer">
        <string name="sCustomerName">Kevin Williams</string>
        <string name="sAddress">744 Evergreen Terrace</string>
        <string name="sCity">Springfield</string>
        <string name="sState">KY</string>
        <string name="sPostalCode">12345</string>
   </Object>

   <Object id="order9876" classname="Invoice.Order">
        ...
   </Object>
</ObjectData>
```

Again, we are using markup that describes its content, it is simple text, it will be available to any programming language and any platform, and we can pass it easily in this form across a network. (In fact, we could even translate this into the invoice we saw earlier using a language called extensible stylesheet language.)

This set of tags and attributes that we have written to mark up the invoice data are what we call an XML **vocabulary**. Vocabularies have already been created for a number of purposes, and it is always worth checking whether one has already been created for the task that you need to perform. But if one does not exist, you can always create your own and share it with others.

As you are able to create you own tags and attributes in XML, we obviously need some way to define a vocabulary in order for us to be able to share it with others, and get them using the same syntax. The XML 1.0 specification uses **Document Type Definitions** or **DTDs** to do this. The DTD defines what markup can be used in a document that is supposed to conform to that vocabulary. For example, it can set out which elements a document can contain, how many instances of an element can occur, and in which order they should appear. It can set out which attributes an element can take, whether they must appear on a given element, if there is a default value should none be specified, and so on. So, in our invoice example we might have defined our markup in a way that says that every `invoice` element must contain a `customerName` attribute, a `billingAddress` attribute, and so on.

There is an interesting distinction to note here. When an XML document, using any vocabulary, conforms to the rules laid down in the XML 1.0 specification, it is said to be a **well-formed** document. When a well-formed document correctly corresponds to the rules laid out in a DTD describing that vocabulary, it is also said to be **valid**.

How XML Documents are Processed

XML documents are processed by a piece of software called a **parser**, which reads the XML document as plain text. Furthermore, parsers implement one or more **application programming interface**(s) (or **APIs**), such as the **Document Object Model** (**DOM**) or the **Simple API for XML** (**SAX**) either of which you may have heard of – if not do not worry, we will introduce them later. The API offers programmers a set of functionality that they can call from a program to request information from the parser as it processes the document. For example, a program can ask the parser for the first child of the root element, and the text in it. Of course, there is a lot more you can do with an API implemented by a parser, but this gives you the idea of how the XML documents are actually made use of by processing applications.

Some parsers are able to check an instance of an XML document against the DTD that is used to describe the vocabulary, to check whether the markup used conforms to the intended markup. Parsers that have this functionality are known as **validating** parsers (although most validating parsers allow you to specify that they validate as an option, because validation takes up extra processing time and resources).

We now know that you can use XML to create your own markup language, and you can tell others how to use it. So, let's take a closer look at how we really structure an XML file, and then at how we declare the language we create.

The Basic Building Blocks of XML

We have seen that we can create tags and attributes that describe their content – and these usually constitute the majority of our markup – but there are also some other forms of markup available in our XML toolbox. In all we have:

- The XML Declaration
- Elements
- Attributes
- Character Data (CDATA)
- Processing Instructions
- Comments
- Entity References

Let's look at each of these in turn.

The XML Declaration

You might have noticed this at the start of the earlier examples. The **XML declaration** is actually optional, although you are strongly advised to use it so that the receiving application knows that it is an XML document and also the version used (although there is only one version of XML at the moment, it does future proof your documents as well as indicate their format).

```
<?xml version="1.0"?>
```

If you use the XML declaration, also known as the **XML prolog**, it must be right at the start of the document (there should be nothing before it, not even whitespace), and the `xml` should be in lowercase

In this declaration, you can also define the language in which you have written your XML data. This is particularly important if your data contains characters that aren't part of the English ASCII character set. You can specify the language encoding using the optional encoding attribute:

```
<?xml version="1.0" encoding="iso-8859-1"?>
```

The most common ones are shown in the following table:

Language	Character set
Unicode (8 bit)	UTF-8
Latin 1 (Western Europe, Latin America)	ISO-8859-1
Latin 2 (Central/Eastern Europe)	ISO-8859-2
Latin 3 (SE Europe)	ISO-8859-3
Latin 4 (Scandinavia/Baltic)	ISO-8859-4
Latin/Cyrillic	ISO-8859-5
Latin/Arabic	ISO-8859-6
Latin/Greek	ISO-8859-7
Latin/Hebrew	ISO-8859-8
Latin/Turkish	ISO-8859-9
Latin/Lappish/Nordic/Eskimo	ISO-8859-10
Japanese	EUC-JP or Shift_JIS

Elements

The most important components of XML documents are elements. Every XML document must have at least one in which all other markup is nested. In the following document there is just one element, `SampleDoc`:

```
<?xml version="1.0"?>
<SampleDoc>
   This is a simple sample XML document.
</SampleDoc>
```

The highest-level element is termed the document element (although you may also see it referred to as the root element).

Elements may be used in one of two ways:

- As shown in this example with an opening tag and a closing tag where the element has three parts:
  - A start-tag (`<SampleDoc>`)
  - Followed by some content (the string 'This is a simple XML document.')

- Followed by an end-tag (</SampleDoc>). End-tags always start with a forward slash, followed by the name of the start-tag to which they correspond.

or

- As an **empty element**. These are used where there is no content between a start and end tag, instead a single tag is used with a forward slash before the closing bracket, for example:

```
<?xml version="1.0"?>
<SampleDoc />
```

At first, this seems pretty silly – what's the point of having an element without any content? However, it could be that in your document the presence of the element is all that's significant – think about how the <BR> element is used in HTML. Also, additional information can be attached to the empty element by using attributes, which we'll talk about next.

> **Note that XML is case-sensitive, so apart from the forward slash, the elements must be exactly the same; <SampleDoc> and <sampledoc> are different tags.**

Tag names can start with a letter, an underscore (_), or a colon character (:), followed by any combination of letter, digits, hyphens, underscores, colons, and periods. The only exception is that you cannot start a tag with the letters XML in any combination of upper or lowercase letters. You are also advised not to start a tag with a colon, in case it gets treated as a namespace (something we shall meet later on).

All tags must nest properly; this means that there must be no **overlapping elements**. For example, this is correct:

```
<SampleDoc>
   <SomeData>Some character data</SomeData>
</SampleDoc>
```

while this would be incorrect:

```
<SampleDoc>
      <SomeData>
            Some character data
</SampleDoc>
      </SomeData>
```

This is because the closing </SomeData> tag is after the closing </SampleDoc> tag.

Attributes

You've probably used attributes before in HTML – for example, when using the HREF attribute on the <A> element to define a hyperlink:

```
<A HREF="http://www.wrox.com">Go to Wrox's web site</A>
```

They work exactly the same way in XML. Attributes are included in an element's start-tag, and are expressed as **name-value pairs**. The value must always be wrapped in single or double quotes (it doesn't matter which ones, as long as you use the same quote before and after the value). For example:

```
<?xml version="1.0"?>
<SampleDoc Author="Ron Obvious">
   This is a simple XML document.
</SampleDoc>
```

In this sample document, the `SampleDoc` element has one attribute associated with it. The attribute **name** is Author, and the **value** is Ron Obvious.

Also, each attribute name may only appear once for a particular start-tag. So, the following is not allowed in XML:

```
<?xml version="1.0"?>
<SampleDoc Author="Ron Obvious" Author="Ken Shabby">
   This is a simple XML document.
</SampleDoc>
```

However, the following is perfectly acceptable:

```
<?xml version="1.0"?>
<SampleDoc>
   <Sentence Author="Ron Obvious">
      This is a simple XML document.
   </Sentence>
   <Sentence Author="Ken Shabby">
      This is the second sentence of the document.
   </Sentence>
</SampleDoc>
```

It should go without saying that attributes are always associated with elements (since they appear only in start-tags or empty-element-tags, which are always part of elements). Also, attributes may not contain the characters `<`, `&`, `'`, or `"`.

Finally, it does not matter which order you put your attributes in an element – so the following two documents are semantically identical:

```
<?xml version="1.0"?>
<SampleDoc Author="Ron Obvious" CreateDate="7/23/2000">
   This is a simple XML document.
</SampleDoc>
```

and

```
<?xml version="1.0"?>
<SampleDoc CreateDate="7/23/2000" Author="Ron Obvious">
   This is a simple XML document.
</SampleDoc>
```

Character Data

In the examples we have been looking at so far, the element `SampleDoc` contains the text `This is a simple XML document.` It is the **element content**, although it has a special name in XML and is called **character data**. If you remember back to the section on how XML documents are processed, we said that they are processed by an application called a parser; the parser can read the content of the elements and pass it to applications that request it. We make this distinction now, because, as you will soon see, it is also possible to have data that is not parsed by the parser in this way.

As you'll see when looking further into XML technologies, contiguous blocks of text within an element are treated as one unit when being parsed or manipulated. Let's take a look at a slightly more complex example.

```
<?xml version="1.0"?>
<AlarmProcedure>
   This is a <alarmtype>test</alarmtype> of the Emergency Broadcast System.
</AlarmProcedure>
```

In this example, the element `AlarmProcedure` contains three pieces of data:

- The text block `This is a`
- The `alarmtype` element
- The text block `of the Emergency Broadcast System`

In turn, the `alarmtype` element contains one piece of data:

- The text block `test`

This character data can appear anywhere inside elements, or as values of attributes. However, there are some special characters that are not allowed in text blocks: the ampersand symbol (&) and the less-than symbol (<). This is because these symbols are interpreted by XML parsers as the start of markup; specifically, as the start of an entity instance and as the start of element start-, end-, or empty-element-tags. If you need to include these characters in your XML document (either in attribute values or in text blocks), you need to either use a CDATA section or entities (which we will deal with next).

CDATA Section

If you want to embed markup in your XML document, one way to do so is by wrapping the markup in a **CDATA section**. XML parsers ignore any characters wrapped in a CDATA section declaration when they are attempting to determine whether markup is present. For example, the following document will not produce the desired result:

```
<?xml version="1.0"?>
<MarkupSample>
   To start an element, use a start-element tag: <myTag>
</MarkupSample>
```

When a parser attempts to process this document, it will identify the string `<myTag>` as the beginning of a new element, and then complain when it doesn't find the matching end-tag `</myTag>`. One solution would be to embed the relevant text in a CDATA section:

```
<?xml version="1.0"?>
<MarkupSample>
   <![CDATA[To declare an element, use a start-element tag: <myTag>]]>
</MarkupSample>
```

As you can see, CDATA sections start with the CDATA start marker:

```
<![CDATA[
```

and end with the CDATA end marker:

```
]]>
```

When the parser encounters the CDATA start marker, it turns off all scanning for markup except for the detection of the CDATA end marker. In the above document, the `MarkupSample` element contains one CDATA section item with the value `'To declare an element, use a start-element tag: <myTag>'`.

It's important to remember that CDATA section items and text items are treated as two separate beasts by XML parsers. For example, the following two documents would seem to contain the same information:

```
<?xml version="1.0"?>
<MarkupSample>
   <![CDATA[To declare an element, use a start-element tag: <myTag>]]>
</MarkupSample>
```

```
<?xml version="1.0"?>
<MarkupSample>
   To declare an element, use a start-element tag: <![CDATA[<myTag>]]>
</MarkupSample>
```

In the second document, the parser will report the `MarkupSample` element as containing two items: the text string "To declare an element, use a start-element tag:" and the CDATA section item `<myTag>`. This can throw off a parser that is specifically looking for one item contained in the `MarkupSample` element.

This approach is good if you want to escape a number of characters that a parser might treat as markup, however, if you only want to escape occasional characters, you may be better off using an entity reference.

Entity References

As we mentioned before, CDATA sections are only one way to include characters like < and `&` in your XML documents. The other way is by using an **entity reference**. Before we dive into how entities work, let's take a look at an example.

```
<?xml version="1.0"?>
<MarkupSample>
   To declare an element, use a start-element tag: &lt;myTag>
</MarkupSample>
```

In this example, the string < is an entity reference; specifically, it's an instance of the entity called lt. Entity references in XML documents (as opposed to in document type definitions) always begin with an ampersand and end with a semicolon. When a parser encounters an entity reference, it goes to the symbol table created when the document type declaration was parsed (we'll take a look at document type declarations later) and extracts the relevant string, if it's present (it might not be, as we'll see a little later). It then substitutes that string in place of the entity instance. Entities that are treated this way are known as parsed entities. It is also possible to declare unparsed entities in an XML document – we'll see how this is done a little later.

There are two types of parsed entities that may be instanced in an XML document:

- Internal entities, which actually have their replacement content embedded in the document type declaration for the document
- External entities, which point to some external resource (via a URI) that contains the replacement text

A non-validating processor is not necessarily obligated to resolve external parsed entity references to their replacement content (although most do), and this can lead to the non-substituted value for an entity reference alluded to above.

There are some standard entities that are defined for XML documents:

Entity	Character
<	<
>	>
&	&
'	'
"	"

Any conforming XML parser will automatically recognize these entities and expand them to their proper values.

Additionally, you may include character references in your documents – they look almost like entities, but they are treated differently by the processor (that is, they are immediately resolved without resorting to an entity lookup). Any decimal code, preceded by &# and followed by ;, is treated as a character reference; the Unicode character with the stated decimal character code is substituted for the reference. Similarly, any hex code preceded by &#x and followed by ; is treated as a character reference stated in hex. So the following two character references:

```
&#38;
&#x26;
```

both correspond to the ampersand character.

Another frequently needed character in XML documents is the non-breaking space – in HTML, this is represented by the entity reference . You can specify this in your XML document by using the numeric equivalent:

```
 
```

You could also declare an entity called nbsp to have the value   and then reference that entity in your document using the name rather than the number. We'll see how this is done a little later in this appendix.

Processing Instructions

If you want a processing application to take some action when it reaches a certain point in a document, you can embed a processing instruction to indicate that some action needs to take place where it was reported. The parser indicates this – either by showing a processing instruction node at the appropriate place in the node tree (in the case of DOM parsers), or by firing a processing instruction event (in the case of SAX parsers). The code that is driving the processor may then take some action on the document based on the type and value of the processing instruction. Processing instructions start with the processing instruction markup start string <?, and end with the string ?>.

```
<?xml version="1.0"?>
<Book>
   <Author>
      <?archive 17?>
      <Name>Kevin Williams</Name>
      <Address>742 Evergreen Terrace</Address>
      <City>Springfield</City>
      <State>KY</State>
      <PostalCode>12345</PostalCode>
   </Author>
</Book>
```

In this example, the string <?archive 17?> is a processing instruction declaration. For example, this processing instruction might indicate that the author information presented is the authoritative copy of that information, and older versions of the data should be stored to an archive for the author whose primary key is 17. Processing instruction declarations always come in two parts: the processing instruction target (in this case, the string archive) and the string to be operated upon (in this case, 17). Everything in the processing instruction declaration before the first whitespace is considered to be the processing instruction target, and everything after that whitespace is the string used to govern the processor's behavior. So, in the following example:

```
<?xml-stylesheet type="text/xml" href="#style1"?>
```

the target would be xml-stylesheet, and the additional information string would be the rest of the text up to, but not including, the question mark at the end of the tag declaration – in other words, the entire string type="text/xml" href="#style1". Note that if you want to access the contents of this string, you'll need to parse it manually – it's not returned as name-value pairs.

> **The processing instruction target may not begin with the string XML, in upper, lower, or mixed cases – these targets are reserved by the W3C for future extensions to the XML specification.**

Comments

Comments may be added to an XML document, using exactly the same syntax as comments in HTML. They always begin with the comment markup start string `<!--` and end with the comment markup end string `-->`:

```
<?xml version="1.0"?>
<!-- Created on 8/8/2000 -->
<DocumentElement/>
```

Note that you can't embed the string `--` in a comment – the parser will think you are indicating the end of the comment and become confused. It's important to note that comments may or may not be retained by an XML parser. When developing processing strategies, make sure to avoid processing based on statements like 'the text I want is always the first item in the Foo element' – because it might not always be, unless you exclusively control the source of the XML documents. For example, say you had the following document fragment:

```
<Book>
  <!-- This is an updated book element -->
  <Author>Kevin Williams</Author>
</Book>
```

Some processors will return two child nodes of the Book node – one for the comment, and one for the Author element. Other processors will only return one node – the Author element. Thus, if you were relying on the Author element to be the second child node of the Book element, you might or might not see it where you were expecting it. It's a good practice to always use names when navigating your XML structures.

Namespaces

In a distributed web environment, we must assume that the same type or element name may mean different things to different people. One XML document may use Address elements to specify where people live, and another may use Address elements to describe locations of computer memory. An XML application has no way of knowing how to process an Address element unless it has some additional information about whose definition we are dealing with.

In XML 1.0, element type names and attribute names are considered **local names.** The W3C (World Wide Web Consortium) XML Namespaces Recommendation tries to improve this situation by extending the data model to allow element type names and attribute names to be qualified with a **URI** (Universal Resource Identifier) that identifies the namespace. This URI should be unique and persistent over time. Note that the URI doesn't actually have to point to anything – although sometimes navigating to the URI using a web browser will bring you to a specification describing that namespace, nothing is obliged to be found at the URI for the namespace. In our example, then, the `wrox:` namespace prefix is declared to map to the namespace http://www.wrox.com/oracle. The combination of a local name and a qualifying URI creates **universal names**. The role of the URI in a universal name is purely to allow applications to recognize the name.

Except in very unusual circumstances, you should declare all of the namespaces for your document as attributes of the root element to ensure that they are in scope for the entire document. It is also worth noting that an XML document can contain many namespaces. In XSLT (you will encounter XSLT in Chapter 21) the namespaces are very important – XSLT matches both the local name and the namespace, so you need to declare the namespaces properly in your XSLT stylesheet to have it recognize the corresponding elements in your documents.

Here is an example of namespaces:

```
<document  xmlns:wrox:"http://www.wrox.com/oracle"
<wrox:address wrox:addressingSystem="US">
        <wrox:name> Kevin Williams </wrox:name>
        <wrox:street>744 Evergreen Terrace </wrox:street>
        <wrox:city> Springfield </wrox:city>
        <wrox:state> KY </wrox:state>
        <wrox:postcode>12345</wrox:postcode>
</wrox:address>
</document>
```

Here, we declare a **namespace** `wrox`, which is the local name for this namespace to be associated with the URI http://www.wrox.com/oracle. This immediately distinguishes these addresses from those developed by others. Having defined the namespace, we qualify all elements and attributes with `wrox:`, thus distinguishing them from identically named elements and attributes in other namespaces.

Document Type Definitions

In the XML 1.0 specification, a mechanism is provided for (loosely) constraining the content that may appear in an XML document. This is done by means of a document type definition, or DTD, which is basically a set of rules that any XML document it is applied to should follow. Some XML parsers are able to validate an XML document against its respective DTD, and if it doesn't follow the rules imposed on it by the DTD, it will throw up an error. These kinds of parsers are referred to as validating parsers. If the XML is found to conform to the rules of a DTD, then it can be referred to as **valid** XML, rather than merely well-formed.

The Document Type Definition can be either an external file or it can be included in the XML document. If the DTD is in an external file it is referred to in the XML document using a **Document Type Declaration** which is written using the syntax `<!DOCTYPE... >`:

```
<!DOCTYPE MyXMLDoc SYSTEM "http://www.yoursite.com/xml/MyXMLDoc.dtd">
```

Here we are pointing to a DTD called `MyXMLDoc`, note that the name of your DTD must correspond to the root element of the XML document, so the root element of XML documents written according to this DTD must be `<MyXMLDoc>`. The use of the `SYSTEM` keyword indicates that the DTD is in an external file, whose location is referenced in the quotation marks. This type of DTD is known as an **external** DTD, because it is in an external file. It is also possible to declare a DTD with the `PUBLIC` keyword – this allows you to specify the location of the DTD in some way that is understood by many different processors, eliminating the need for an always-on connection to the Internet to validate the documents. However, there isn't one well-defined way to resolve DTDs declared as `PUBLIC`, so you're better off using the system identifiers to point to your DTDs.

The name of the DTD does not have to be the same as the name of the root element. The DTD itself can be called anything you want, as long as it is declared in the `!DOCTYPE` declaration to match the root element name.

The DTD can also be written inside the document type declaration, in which case it is known as an **internal** document type definition, like so:

```
<!DOCTYPE MyXMLDoc [
   <!ELEMENT MyXMLDoc (#PCDATA)>
]>
```

Here, all the constraints on the content of the document are provided as declarations inside the square brackets [...]. (Don't worry too much about the element declaration just yet – we'll be getting to that soon enough.)

When a validating parser encounters an external document type definition, it accesses the resource indicated in the URI and pulls the document constraints from it; it then behaves as if these constraints were declared in-line.

If you have a situation where you can benefit from it, you can also mix the two declaration modes:

```
<!DOCTYPE MyXMLDoc SYSTEM "MyXMLDoc.dtd" [
   <!ELEMENT MyXMLDoc (#PCDATA)>
]>
```

For example, this technique would allow you to customize the allowable content of the Bar element. Note that in the above example, only the file name is included, rather than the whole path as well. This would only be suitable if the external file is in the same location as this one.

It's usually more helpful to have the document type definition be external to the document itself – this allows multiple documents to use the same rules without having to include the set of constraints in each document.

> **Note: it is easy to get confused between the terms document type declaration and document type definition. To clarify, the document type definition constrains the markup and this is either contained in, or referenced to, a document type declaration.**

The Standalone Declaration

There is an attribute on the XML declaration that indicates whether a document type definition is standalone or not; that is, whether all of the declarations for the XML document are stated in the `!DOCTYPE` declaration, or whether some external URI needs to be accessed to obtain all the declarations (either through an external parameter entity, which we'll talk about later, or an external DTD). This attribute should also be used when your document declares namespaces. You don't have to explicitly declare this, but it might be useful to help streamline workflow and the transmission of XML documents.

To declare that a document stands alone, use this XML declaration:

```
<?xml version="1.0" standalone="yes"?>
```

If the declaration is omitted, the assumed default is that the document is not standalone.

Next, let's take a look at the various declarations you can use within a DTD to constrain the types of content an XML document conforming to that DTD may contain.

Element Declarations

The most important type of declaration in a DTD is the element declaration. Each DTD will have at least one of these (the declaration of the root element).

We saw how to simply declare an element in the previous example, but we did not explain what it was doing there:

```
<!ELEMENT MyXMLDoc (#PCDATA)>
```

We declare an element using the syntax:

```
<!ELEMENT elementName (contentModel)>
```

Where `elementName` is the name of the element, and the `contentModel` is what that element can contain. This is the basic declaration that we need to start, so in our example we were declaring an element called `MyXMLDoc`. This element contains text-only content – defined using the syntax `#PCDATA`.

There are five different types of element content that may be declared with an element declaration:

- Element content
- Mixed content
- Text-only content
- The `EMPTY` content model
- The `ANY` content model

Let's take a look at each, in turn.

Element Content

In the first type of element declaration, the element is defined as only containing other elements. The declaration specifies the order and cardinality with which each contained element may appear. For example, the declaration:

```
<!ELEMENT Foo (A, B, C)>
```

States that, within the Foo element, the elements A, B, and C must each appear exactly once, in that order. So for the following DTD:

```
<!ELEMENT Foo (A, B, C)>
<!ELEMENT A (#PCDATA)>
<!ELEMENT B (#PCDATA)>
<!ELEMENT C (#PCDATA)>
```

This example XML document conforms to the DTD:

```
<?xml version="1.0" standalone="no"?>
<!DOCTYPE Foo SYSTEM "Foo.DTD">
<Foo>
   <A> Some content <A />
   <B> Some more content <B />
   <C> Even more content <C />
</Foo>
```

But the following three examples do not. The first is missing a `C` element:

```
<?xml version="1.0" standalone="no"?>
<!DOCTYPE Foo SYSTEM "Foo.DTD">
<Foo>
   <A> Some content <A />
   <B> some more content <B />
</Foo> <!-- the C element is missing -->
```

The next one does not contain the elements in the correct order:

```
<?xml version="1.0" standalone="no"?>
<!DOCTYPE Foo SYSTEM "Foo.DTD">
<Foo>
   <B> Some more content <B />
   <A> Some content<A />
   <C> Even more content <C />
</Foo> <!-- the elements are not in the right order -->
```

And the final one uses too many `A` elements:

```
<?xml version="1.0" standalone="no"?>
<!DOCTYPE Foo SYSTEM "Foo.DTD">
<Foo>
   <A> Some content <A />
   <A> Some content <A />
   <B> Some more content <B />
   <C> Even more content <C />
</Foo> <!-- too many A elements -->
```

It is also possible to define a set of elements, only one of which may be present. This is indicated by separating the possibilities with the pipe character `|`. So the declaration:

```
<!ELEMENT Foo (A | B | C)>
```

states that the Foo element should contain either an A element, a B element, or a C element – but only one of the above.

Child elements declared in the element declaration may also take cardinality suffixes. These suffixes indicate how many of each element (or element group, which we'll talk about later) may occur at that location in the element content. The following four cardinality operators exist:

Operator	Meaning
?	Optional (may occur 0 or 1 times)
*	Optional multiple (may occur 0 or more times)
(no suffix)	Required (must occur exactly once)
+	Required multiple (must occur 1 or more times)

Additionally, child elements may be grouped together in the element declaration. They may be grouped in either a sequence or a choice list. These groupings may also have the cardinality operators specified in the previous table applied to them. At this point, some examples are probably in order.

Example 1:

This states that zero or more A elements may appear as child elements of the Foo element, followed by one or more B elements; the B element or elements may then be followed by no more than one C element.

```
<!ELEMENT Foo (A*, B+, C?)>
```

The following XML fragments for the Foo element are all valid:

```
<Foo>
   <A> Some content <A />
   <B> Some more content <B />
</Foo>
```

```
<Foo>
   <B> Some more content <B />
   <B> Some more content<B />
   <B> Some more content<B />
</Foo>
```

```
<Foo>
   <A> Some content <A />
   <A> Some content <A />
   <B> Some more content <B />
   <C> even more content <C />
</Foo>
```

Example 2:

This states that either an A element or a B element comes first in the Foo element; that element must then be followed by a C element.

```
<!ELEMENT Foo ((A | B), C)>
```

So the following two examples are the only possible examples of valid content for `Foo`:

```
<Foo>
   <A> Some content <A />
   <C> Even more content <C />
</Foo>
```

```
<Foo>
   <B> Some more content <B />
   <C> Even more content <C />
</Foo>
```

Example 3:

In this example, Foo must contain either one or more A elements followed optionally by a B element, or this group can all be replaced by zero or more C elements.

```
<!ELEMENT Foo ((A+, B?) | C*)>
```

Again, the following is valid:

```
<Foo>
   <A> Some content <A />
   <A> Some content <A />
   <A> Some content <A />
</Foo>
```

as is this:

```
<Foo>
   <A> Some content <A />
   <B> Some more content <B />
</Foo>
```

and also this:

```
<Foo>
   <C> Even more content <C />
   <C> Even more content <C />
   <C> Even more content <C />
</Foo>
```

For the purposes of the XML structures we'll be creating, in elements that have all element content we'll avoid the choice operator and stick to sequences with cardinality:

```
<!ELEMENT Foo (A?, B*, C?, D, E+)>
```

Mixed Content

Elements may also be declared as having mixed content. Elements declared this way may contain any of the elements included in the content list, in any order, with text interspersed anywhere in between. A mixed-content element declaration looks like this:

```
<!ELEMENT Foo (#PCDATA | A | B | C)*>
<!ELEMENT A (#PCDATA)>
<!ELEMENT B (#PCDATA)>
```

The #PCDATA is required to be the first thing in the pipe-delimited list – it indicates that text may be present in the element. The other listed elements may or may not appear. Note that no constraint is imposed on the order in which the elements may appear, or how many times. This is the only allowable declaration for mixed content – you are not allowed to constrain the location or number of the various sub-elements in a mixed-content element. Thus, the following fragments are all valid:

```
<Foo>
   Here is some <A>text</A> with interspersed <B>elements</B>.
</Foo>
```

```
<Foo>
   <C /><C /><C />Why so many C elements?
</Foo>
```

```
<Foo>
   There are no child elements in this element at all.
</Foo>
```

```
<Foo />
```

Text-only Content

If you're familiar with relational databases, you're probably wincing right now, and you have a right to be – representing mixed content in a relational database is a real headache. A special case of the mixed content model, however, may prove quite useful – that case where an element may contain only text. Elements that are defined to contain only text look like this:

```
<!ELEMENT Foo (#PCDATA)>
```

This is one of the two major ways that a data point (a value) should be represented in XML for data:

```
<!ELEMENT Author (Name, Address, City, State, PostalCode)>
<!ELEMENT Name (#PCDATA)>
<!ELEMENT Address (#PCDATA)>
<!ELEMENT City (#PCDATA)>
<!ELEMENT State (#PCDATA)>
<!ELEMENT PostalCode (#PCDATA)>
```

```
<Author>
   <Name>Kevin Williams</Name>
```

```
    <Address>742 Evergreen Terrace</Address>
    <City>Springfield</City>
    <State>KY</State>
    <PostalCode>12345</PostalCode>
</Author>
```

The EMPTY Content Model

The `EMPTY` content model for elements states that an element may not contain anything. Empty elements are declared as follows:

```
<!ELEMENT Foo EMPTY>
```

Elements declared this way must take one of the two following forms:

```
<Foo />
```

```
<Foo></Foo>
```

However, it is strongly advised that you stick to the first form, as the second can easily get confused with an empty `PCDATA` element.

We talked about the reasons you might want to define an element that has no allowable content earlier in the chapter. For our purposes, however, we will only be defining elements this way if they have attributes associated with them. We'll see how attributes are declared for elements a little later on.

The ANY Content Model

If an element is declared to have a content model of `ANY`, that's just what it may contain – any well-formed XML whatsoever as long as any child elements validate against their own content models as defined elsewhere, in the DTD. Elements of this type are declared like so:

```
<!ELEMENT Foo ANY>
```

The following examples are valid for this declaration:

```
<Foo>
   Here's some random thing.
</Foo>
```

```
<Foo>
   <A><B><C><D><E></E></D></C></B></A>
</Foo>
```

```
<Foo>
   <A>This</A><B>is</B><C>marked</C><D>up</D>
</Foo>
```

Note that the sub-elements do not inherit the 'free content properties' of the Foo element – they must still conform to their own declarations. So in our second example above, a single B element must be acceptable content for the A element, a single C element acceptable for B, and so on.

For the representation of data, this syntax is perilous. Allowing users to simply include whatever elements or text they feel like in an element is another relational database nightmare, worse than that caused by mixed element content declarations because you can't even narrow down the list of elements that might occur. You should avoid using the `ANY` content model for elements when designing XML structures for data.

Attribute Declarations

The next most common type of declaration in DTDs is the attribute declaration. This allows you to define what attributes may or must appear for a given element. The general syntax for an attribute declaration looks like this:

```
<!ATTLIST element-name attribute-definition*>
```

where an attribute definition looks like this:

```
attribute-name attribute-type default-declaration
```

So, let's say we have this pair of definitions in our DTD:

```
<!ELEMENT Foo EMPTY>
<!ATTLIST Foo
   Texture CDATA #REQUIRED>
```

This says that the Foo element, which must be empty, has one required attribute called Texture that may take any string value. So the following document fragment is valid:

```
<Foo Texture="bumpy" />
```

Next, let's take a look at the various attribute types that may be defined in a DTD.

The CDATA Attribute Type

The most commonly encountered attribute type in a DTD is `CDATA`. Attributes that take this type may take any string value. Remember that in all attribute values, the markup characters <, &, >, ", and ' should always be escaped to prevent parser confusion. So for this example:

```
<!ELEMENT Foo EMPTY>
<!ATTLIST Foo
   Texture CDATA #REQUIRED
   Color CDATA #REQUIRED
   Shape CDATA #REQUIRED>
```

the following document fragment follows the rules of the above DTD:

```
<Foo Texture="bumpy" Color="red&amp;blue" Shape="sphere" />
```

The ID Attribute Type

DTDs provide a way to assign unique identifiers to elements. This can be very useful when expressing more complex relationships in XML documents than can be shown by simple nesting, as we'll see later. In order for a document to be valid, every element that has an ID attribute associated with it in a single document must have a unique ID value. Also, the values for ID attributes must be valid XML names – in other words, they must begin with a letter (as defined by the Unicode standard) or an underscore (colons are also allowed, but their use is discouraged because of namespaces) – so simply using an identity or autoincrement value from a relational database is not sufficient. One strategy that works is to prefix that relational value with a string (unique across all elements in your document) that corresponds to the entity.

Let's see some examples. For this document declaration fragment:

```
<!ELEMENT Foo EMPTY>
<!ATTLIST Foo
   FooID ID #REQUIRED>
```

```
<!ELEMENT Bar EMPTY>
<!ATTLIST Bar
   BarID ID #REQUIRED>
```

the following would be valid:

```
<Foo FooID="foo1" />
<Bar BarID="bar1" />
```

but the following examples would not:

```
<Foo FooID="17" /> <!-- ID value is not a proper XML name -->
```

```
<Foo FooID="foo1" />
<Foo FooID="foo1" /> <!-- no two elements may have the same ID value -->
```

```
<Foo FooID="foo1" />
<Bar BarID="foo1" /> <!-- no two elements may have the same ID value -->
```

It is illegal to define more than one ID attribute on the same element.

The IDREF Attribute Type

The `IDREF` attribute type provides a way to 'point' one element to another – in effect, expressing a one-to-one relationship between the two attributes. Values for attributes that are defined as `IDREF` attributes must match an ID attribute found somewhere in the XML document. So for the following DTD fragment:

```
<!ELEMENT Author EMPTY>
<!ATTLIST Author
   AuthorID ID #REQUIRED>
<!ELEMENT Book EMPTY>
<!ATTLIST Book
   BookID ID #REQUIRED
   AuthorIDREF IDREF #REQUIRED>
```

the following would be valid:

```
<Author AuthorID="author1" />
<Book BookID="book1" AuthorIDREF="author1" />
```

```
<Author AuthorID="author1" />
<Book BookID="book1" AuthorIDREF="book1" />
```

The second example makes an important point. `IDREF` attributes do not define the type of element their value points to, so it's equally valid to have an attribute called `AuthorIDREF` match an ID value for a `Book` element. If you want to strictly enforce the types of elements that may be matched by an `IDREF` attribute, you'll need to do so in your processing code.

The following example, of course, is not valid, and a validating processor will throw an error:

```
<Author AuthorID="author1" />
<Book BookID="book1" AuthorIDREF="author2" /> <!-- ID does not exist -->
```

The IDREFS Attribute Type

You can think of the `IDREFS` attribute as a way to include multiple `IDREF` values in one attribute. The value for an `IDREFS` attribute must be a whitespace-separated list of XML names that correspond to one or more ID attribute values defined in the document. Just as `IDREF` can be used to express a one-to-one relationship, so can `IDREFS` be used to express a one-to-many relationship. Here's an example:

```
<!ELEMENT Foo EMPTY>
<!ATTLIST Foo
   FooID ID #REQUIRED>
<!ELEMENT Bar EMPTY>
<!ATTLIST Bar
   BarID ID #REQUIRED
   FooIDREF IDREFS #REQUIRED>
```

For this DTD fragment, the following document fragments are valid:

```
<Foo FooID="foo1" />
<Foo FooID="foo2" />
<Bar BarID="bar1" FooIDREF="foo1" />
```

```
<Foo FooID="foo1" />
<Foo FooID="foo2" />
<Bar BarID="bar1" FooIDREF="foo1 foo2" />
```

```
<Foo FooID="foo1" />
<Foo FooID="foo2" />
<Bar BarID="bar1" FooIDREF="foo1 foo1" />
<!-- uniqueness is not enforced -->
```

but the following examples are not valid:

```
<Foo FooID="foo1" />
<Foo FooID="foo2" />
<Bar BarID="bar1" FooIDREF="" />
<!-- there must be at least one ID value -->
```

```
<Foo FooID="foo1" />
<Foo FooID="foo2" />
<Bar BarID="bar1" FooIDREF="foo1+foo2" />
<!-- not a space-separated list -->
```

The ENTITY Attribute Type

Attributes defined with the ENTITY attribute type must match the name of an unparsed entity declared elsewhere in the DTD. Typically, you'd use this to insert non-text content into your XML document, like an image or a sound file. Here's an example (don't worry too much about the entity and notation declarations – we'll take a look at those later in this appendix):

```
<!NOTATION gif PUBLIC "GIF">
<!ENTITY BlueLine SYSTEM "blueline.gif" NDATA gif>
<!ELEMENT Separator EMPTY>
<!ATTLIST Separator
   img ENTITY #REQUIRED>
```

A valid document would then be:

```
<Separator img="BlueLine" />
```

We won't spend much time talking about this type of attribute in this book, but you might find it useful if you want to build XML documents with embedded non-XML entities.

The ENTITIES Attribute Type

Briefly, ENTITIES is to ENTITY as IDREFS is to IDREF – it's a way to include multiple unparsed entity references in the same attribute by using a space-separated list of entity names. So, for example:

```
<!NOTATION gif PUBLIC "GIF">
<!ENTITY BlueLine SYSTEM "blueline.gif" NDATA gif>
<!ENTITY RedLine SYSTEM "redline.gif" NDATA gif>
<!ELEMENT Separator EMPTY>
<!ATTLIST Separator
   img ENTITIES #REQUIRED>
```

A valid document would then be:

```
<Separator img="BlueLine RedLine" />
```

The NMTOKEN Attribute Type

Attributes with a type of `NMTOKEN` must have a value that contains only letters, digits, underscores, hyphens, colons, periods, and other Unicode characters that are acceptable in XML names. So for the following declaration:

```
<!ELEMENT Foo EMPTY>
<!ATTLIST Foo
   FooToken NMTOKEN #REQUIRED>
```

the following document fragments are valid:

```
<Foo
   FooToken="17" /> <!-- no leading letter or underscore is required -->
```

```
<Foo
   FooToken="____" /> <!-- underscores are fine -->
```

but the following are not:

```
<Foo
   FooToken="red&amp;blue" /> <!-- ampersands are not allowed -->
```

```
<Foo
   FooToken="bad token" /> <!-- whitespace is not allowed -->
```

Attributes with the type `NMTOKEN` (or `NMTOKENS`) give you a little more control over the allowable data in an attribute, by making the value (or each value, in the case of `NMTOKENS`) abide by the rules for proper XML names.

The NMTOKENS Attribute Type

Like `IDREFS` and `ENTITIES`, the `NMTOKENS` attribute type allows one attribute to contain a list of whitespace-separated `NMTOKEN` values. For this example:

```
<!ELEMENT Foo EMPTY>
<!ATTLIST Foo
   FooToken NMTOKENS #REQUIRED>
```

the following fragments are valid:

```
<Foo
   FooToken="17 19 23" />
```

```
<Foo
   FooToken="_ _ - - ." />
```

Enumerated Value Sets

Another great feature of attribute declarations in DTDs is the ability to constrain the possible values that may appear for an attribute. This is very helpful if you have data points that correspond to a well-defined set of values. Let's see how this is done:

```
<!ELEMENT Foo EMPTY>
<!ATTLIST Foo
   Color (Red | Green | Blue) #REQUIRED>
```

As you can see, in an enumerated value set declaration the possible values for an attribute are listed, separated by pipe characters. As with anything else in XML, these values are case-sensitive. For this DTD fragment, the following document fragment is valid:

```
<Foo Color="Red" />
```

but this one is not:

```
<Foo Color="Orange" />
```

This is one of the few ways to strongly constrain the allowable values for a data point in a DTD.

Notation Attribute Declaration

Using this declaration, you can associate a particular notation (or one of a set of notations) with an element. This is useful if the element content, which for all other intents and purposes looks like text, actually needs to be processed another way – say, if it happens to be PostScript or a base-64 encoded block.

```
<!NOTATION ps PUBLIC "PostScript level 3">
<!NOTATION base64 PUBLIC "Base-64 encoded">
<!ELEMENT Foo (#PCDATA)>
<!ATTLIST Foo
   Datatype NOTATION (ps | base64) #REQUIRED>
```

Note that each possible value for the notation attribute must match the name of a notation defined elsewhere in the DTD.

A valid example of a document:

```
<Foo Datatype="ps">gsave 112 75 moveto 112 300 lineto showpage grestore</Foo>
```

Next, we need to look at the various ways in which cardinality and default values may be specified for attributes.

#REQUIRED

You've probably noticed that we've been using the `#REQUIRED` default declaration for all of our examples. This means what you'd expect – that the attribute value must be supplied in the XML document in order for it to be valid. So for this declaration:

```
<!ELEMENT Foo EMPTY>
<!ATTLIST Foo
   Color (Red | Green | Blue) #REQUIRED>
```

this is a valid XML fragment:

```
<Foo Color="Red" />
```

but this is not:

```
<Foo /> <!-- the Color attribute is required! -->
```

#IMPLIED

The #IMPLIED default declaration for an attribute means that the attribute may or may not be supplied. If the attribute is not supplied, then no value is available to the XML parser for that attribute when parsing that document. So in this case, with the declaration:

```
<!ELEMENT Foo EMPTY>
<!ATTLIST Foo
   Color (Red | Green | Blue) #IMPLIED>
```

both of the following are valid document fragments:

```
<Foo Color="Red" />

<Foo /> <!-- the Color attribute does not have to be supplied -->
```

Default Value Declarations

There is a third default declaration that is available when declaring an attribute. In this declaration, a value is provided for the attribute; if the attribute value is not supplied in the XML document, the default value is substituted and available to the XML parser as if it were explicitly stated in the XML document. An example is in order. For the declaration:

```
<!ELEMENT Foo EMPTY>
<!ATTLIST Foo
   Color (Red | Green | Blue) "Red">
```

when the document fragment

```
<Foo Color="Green" />
```

is parsed by the XML processor, the value Green will be returned for the Color attribute of this Foo element. Now, suppose that we have this document fragment:

```
<Foo />
```

In this case, since the Color attribute is missing from the XML fragment, the processor will automatically substitute and return the value Red for the attribute.

#FIXED value declarations

Finally, you may use the `#FIXED` declaration to indicate that the value of the attribute is always taken from the value specified in the attribute declaration. For example, you could have these declarations:

```
<!ELEMENT Foo EMPTY>
<!ATTLIST Foo
  Color CDATA "Red" #FIXED>
```

When an XML parser reads a document created using this set of declarations, the value Red will **always** be provided for the attribute Color on **all** Foo elements – even though the Color attribute is never mentioned in the XML document itself. In fact, it's an error to provide any other value – a document that looks like this will not validate against the declarations above:

```
<Foo Color="Orange" />
```

Instead, you must omit the attribute altogether, or provide the exact value in the attribute declaration:

```
<Foo />
<Foo Color="Red" />
```

One very good use for this technique is to pass version information about the DTD to the XML parser so that it can make intelligent guesses as to the available content in the XML document. You might declare a Version attribute that has a `#FIXED` value of 1.0, for example, and this would be available as if the XML document itself contained this value.

Notation Declarations

If you are going to use notations in your XML document (for unparsed entities, to specify a URI for the target of a processing instruction, or to annotate an element, for example), you need to declare them in the DTD. A notation declaration looks like this:

```
<!NOTATION gif PUBLIC "GIF">
```

It includes the name of the notation, as well as a system and/or public identifier that a processor can use to determine the application or information type to which the notation pertains. For the purposes of this book, we won't be spending much time on notations, but if you come across a notation declaration in an existing DTD you'll be able to figure out what it means. Several of the subsequent sections of this appendix detail various uses of these declarations.

Entity Declarations

There are two types of entities that may be declared: internal entities and external entities.

Internal Entities

Internal entities contain their replacement value in their declaration; when a parser encounters a reference to the specified internal entity, it substitutes the replacement value found in that entity's declaration.

For example:

```
<!ENTITY DocumentStatus "Draft">
<!ELEMENT About (#PCDATA)>
```

```
<About>
   This document is currently in &DocumentStatus; status.
</About>
```

When the parser reads this document, it substitutes the string provided in the entity declaration for the entity reference string "`&DocumentStatus;`" To a processor, the document looks like this:

```
<About>
   This document is currently in Draft status.
</About>
```

External Entities

By contrast, external entities refer to resources outside the context of the XML document. A system identification containing a URI where the external entity content may be found is provided; additionally, some sort of public identifier may be provided so that a processor can attempt to generate an alternative URI. Here are two examples of external entity declarations:

```
<!ENTITY SalesData SYSTEM "sales/summary.xml">
```

```
<!ENTITY SiteMap SYSTEM "http://www.yoursite.com/sitemap.xml"
                 PUBLIC "//yoursite//sitemap.xml">
```

When entities are declared this way, their content is retrieved and substituted in place where they are referenced. They are known as parsed entities because they must conform to the rules of XML. It's also possible to declare external unparsed entities, as we mentioned earlier in the appendix – we'll see how that's done a little later.

Say we have the following DTD, called `invoice.dtd`:

```
<!ENTITY InvoiceLineItems SYSTEM "lineitems.xml">
<!ELEMENT Invoice (CustomerName, LineItem+)>
<!ELEMENT CustomerName (#PCDATA)>
<!ELEMENT LineItem (Item, Quantity, Price)>
<!ELEMENT Item (#PCDATA)>
<!ELEMENT Quantity (#PCDATA)>
<!ELEMENT Price (#PCDATA)>
```

and the following document, called `invoice.xml`:

```
<?xml version="1.0"?>
<!DOCTYPE Invoice SYSTEM "invoice.dtd">
<Invoice>
  <CustomerName>Kevin Williams</CustomerName>
  &InvoiceLineItems;
</Invoice>
```

If the document `lineitems.xml` contains the following:

```
<LineItem>
  <Item>Widget</Item>
  <Quantity>50</Quantity>
  <Price>75.00</Price>
</LineItem>
<LineItem>
  <Item>Sprocket</Item>
  <Quantity>25</Quantity>
  <Price>100.00</Price>
</LineItem>
```

Then the document, after substitution, will be:

```
<?xml version="1.0"?>
<!DOCTYPE Invoice SYSTEM "invoice.dtd">
<Invoice>
  <CustomerName>Kevin Williams</CustomerName>
  <LineItem>
    <Item>Widget</Item>
    <Quantity>50</Quantity>
    <Price>75.00</Price>
  </LineItem>
  <LineItem>
    <Item>Sprocket</Item>
    <Quantity>25</Quantity>
    <Price>100.00</Price>
  </LineItem>
</Invoice>
```

Note that we still had to declare the substructure of the external parsed entity in our DTD. Parsed entities (whether internal or external) must conform to any document type definition provided for the document that references them. So if your `lineitems.xml` was instead formed like this:

```
<LineItem>
  <Item>Widget</Item>
  <Quantity>50</Quantity>
</LineItem>
```

A validating parser would complain because the `Price` sub-lement is missing from the `LineItem` element.

Parameter Entities

It's also possible to declare entities that are substituted into the DTD itself, rather than into the XML document. These are called parameter entities, and here's an example declaration:

```
<!ENTITY % ThirdColorChoice "Blue">
<!ELEMENT Foo EMPTY>
<!ATTLIST Foo (Red | Green | %ThirdColorChoice;)>
```

As you might imagine, substitution works just like it does for other entity references. To the validating parser, the DTD looks like this:

```
<!ELEMENT Foo EMPTY>
<!ATTLIST Foo (Red | Green | Blue)>
```

External parameter entities may also be declared:

```
<!ENTITY % ColorChoiceList SYSTEM "colorchoices.txt">
<!ELEMENT Foo EMPTY>
<!ATTLIST Foo (%ColorChoiceList;)>
```

And in `colorchoices.txt`, we might have:

```
Red | Green | Blue
```

Leading to the substituted DTD looking like this:

```
<!ELEMENT Foo EMPTY>
<!ATTLIST Foo (Red | Green | Blue)>
```

Unparsed Entities

Unparsed entities (entities that do not have their values extracted) may also be declared. These are the entity types we discussed when talking about attribute declarations. They may only appear as the values of attributes that are declared as having the `ENTITY` or `ENTITIES` type. To declare an unparsed entity, you use the same declaration as for an external parsed entity but add a notation declaration to the end of it:

```
<!NOTATION gif PUBLIC "GIF">
<!ENTITY PropertyImage SYSTEM "image.gif" NDATA gif>
```

```
<!NOTATION midi PUBLIC "MIDI 1.0">
<!ENTITY BackgroundMusic SYSTEM "http://www.yoursite.com/music.mid"
                         NDATA midi>
```

The notation name at the end of the unparsed entity declaration must also be declared, in a notation declaration elsewhere in the document type definition, as seen in the above examples.

Conditional Sections

In a DTD, you can choose to include or ignore sections of the DTD by enclosing them in **conditional sections**. External entities may be used to control the inclusion or exclusion of document type declarations in much the same way that `#define` and `#ifdef`/`#ifndef` macros may be used to control the compilation of C++ source code. Let's see how this works.

If you want to include a section of declarations, you wrap them in the conditional section include markers – `<![INCLUDE[` at the beginning and `]]>` at the end. Similarly, to exclude a section of declarations, start with `<![IGNORE[` and end with `]]>`. For example, the first set of declarations in the following DTD will be included (used for validating XML), and the second set will be ignored:

```
<![INCLUDE[
<!ELEMENT Foo (#PCDATA)>
]]>
```

```
<![IGNORE[
<!ELEMENT Foo EMPTY>
]]>
```

To the validating parser, this will look like

```
<!ELEMENT Foo (#PCDATA)>
```

If we add parameter entities to the mix, we can turn on or off sections at will by changing the values of the parameter entities:

```
<!ENTITY % TextContent "INCLUDE">
<!ENTITY % AttributesOnly "IGNORE">

<![&TextContent;[
<!ELEMENT Foo (#PCDATA)>
]]>

<![&AttributesOnly;[
<!ELEMENT Foo EMPTY>
]]>
```

Using parameter entities this way allows us to easily control the structure of our DTD.

Thinking in Trees

Now that we've taken a look at the building blocks that go together to make up XML documents, we need to talk about how these building blocks fit together. To do this, we're going to need to stop thinking about XML documents as serial files and start thinking about them as node trees.

Take this sample XML document:

```
<Invoice>
  <CustomerName>Kevin Williams</CustomerName>
  <ShipTo>
    <Address>742 Evergreen Terrace</Address>
    <City>Springfield</City>
    <State>KY</State>
    <PostalCode>12345</PostalCode>
  </ShipTo>
  <LineItem>
    <Item>Widget</Item>
    <Quantity>15</Quantity>
    <Price>25.00</Price>
  </LineItem>
```

```
    <LineItem>
      <Item>Sprocket</Item>
      <Quantity>22</Quantity>
      <Price>44.00</Price>
    </LineItem>
  </Invoice>
```

If you're used to working with flat files, such as comma-delimited files, you are probably thinking about this file serially: there's the invoice start tag, then the customer name start tag, then the customer name, and so on. However, most XML technologies don't model the information this way. Instead, the information is modelled as a tree:

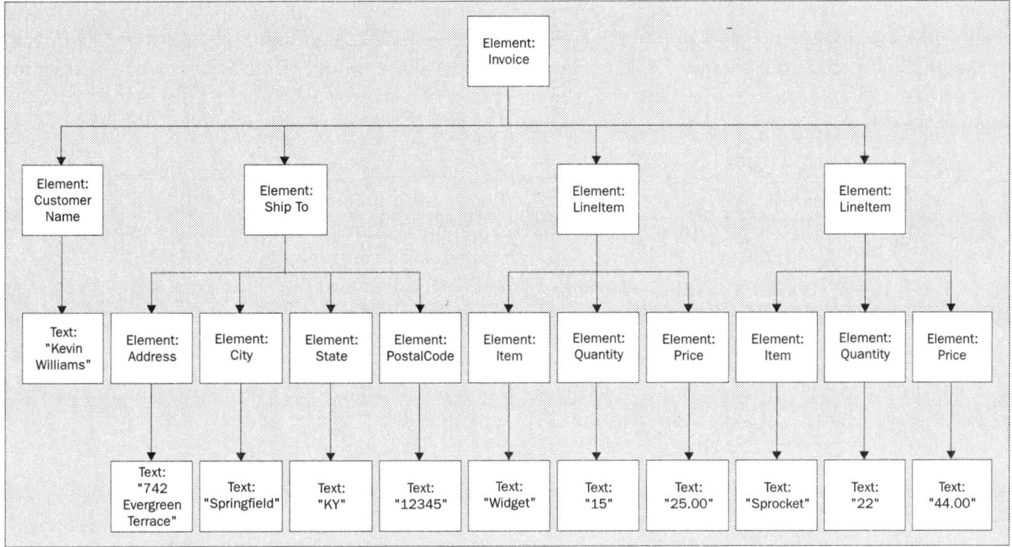

When you're working with XML documents through the DOM or using XPath, described later in this Primer, to specify a particular location in an XML document, everything is expressed in terms of child lists and branch traversals. For example, if you had to apply the following XPath expression:

```
/Invoice/LineItem[position()=2]/Quantity
```

to the serialized document, it's not immediately apparent what's being referenced. However, once you understand that this expression describes a navigation through the node tree in our diagram – "go to the Invoice element, then to the second LineItem child of that element, then to the Quantity child of that element" (which gives us 22). It's obvious what's being requested.

Learning to think of XML documents in terms of node trees, rather than in terms of serialized text, will help you to more easily query and manipulate those documents from code.

Technology Overview

Let's take a quick look at the XML technologies covered in this book. We will see how each of these technologies may be used to facilitate our access to, and manipulation of, data stored in XML documents.

XML Schemas

XML Schemas are a new mechanism that the W3C is working on to define XML Vocabularies, as a replacement for DTDs. As of the time of writing, XML Schemas are in working draft last call status. This means that they are fairly stable, but may still change somewhat before they reach recommendation status.

The Document Object Model (DOM)

You could treat the XML document as just a text file, and write a text file reader that interprets the information in the XML document in a way that your application code can use. This would, however, be quite tedious, and require you to understand all the constructs of XML. Also, such code would have to be written repeatedly by whoever wants to access information in XML documents. W3C realized that this would be a problem, and they created a standard way to create these XML document processors or XML parsers. Typically, XML processors parse an XML document, build a tree model of the elements in the document, and then allow the application to access this tree by means of a standard API called the Document Object Model or DOM.

A DOM XML parser is, quite simply, a program that converts your XML documents into a Java object model. You point a DOM XML parser to an XML document; it parses the document, and gives you a bunch of objects in the memory of your Java Virtual Machine. When you need to manipulate any information stored in the XML document, you can do so through these objects in memory. So, a DOM XML parser creates a Java document object **representation** of your XML document file. There are lots of free DOM XML parsers out there, including one from Oracle as part of the XDK.

The parser also performs some simple text processing as it creates the object model. It expands all entities, compares the structure of the information in the XML document to a DTD or schema (if one is used), and if this processing is successful, the XML document is converted into a tree of nodes in memory. The tree of nodes contains all the data and structure of the information contained in the XML document. This node tree can be accessed and modified using the DOM API.

The DOM API consists of a set of **interfaces**. The XML parser implements these interfaces. If you want to access XML documents from within Java, you need to import the `org.w3c.dom` package in Java, and then simply use these classes to get at the tree of nodes.

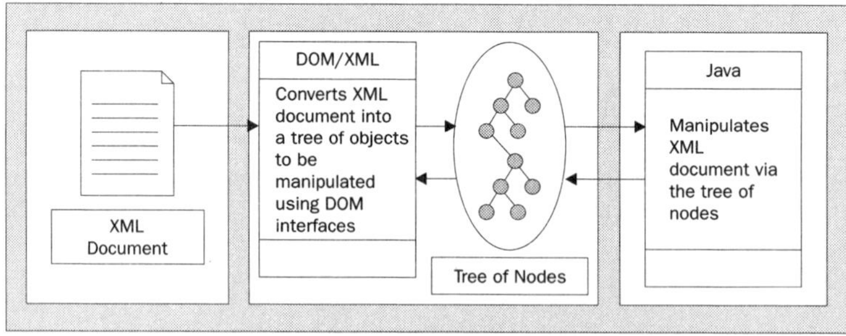

The W3C decided DOM would apply to common constructs like elements, comments, processing instructions, text content and so on. that are present in both HTML and XML, and would, in addition, have some HTML-specific extensions.

In the document object tree, everything is a **node**. A node may have other nodes nested inside it. The node can hold information, like its tag-name, its value, and its child nodes (if any). This hierarchical organization reminds one of a file-system view of data, with the big difference that in a file system, the names name instances, whereas in XML they name types. Items are organized hierarchically, a folder may have files in it or other folders, and everything is descended from one root folder.

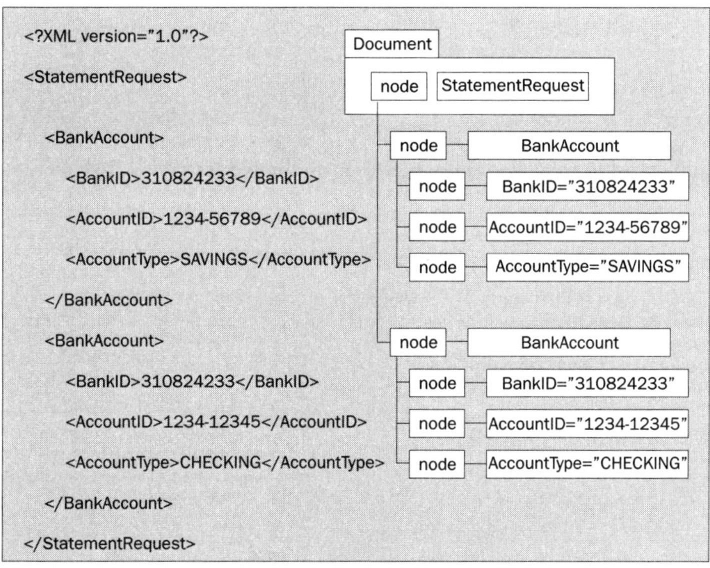

A document object itself is a node, it is descended from one node, and it may have other nodes inside it.

The Node interface is central to DOM – most of the time, you can get by using just this interface. There are also other interfaces like `DocumentType`. Most of the interfaces are, however, subclasses of Node, and extend it to provide specific functionality.

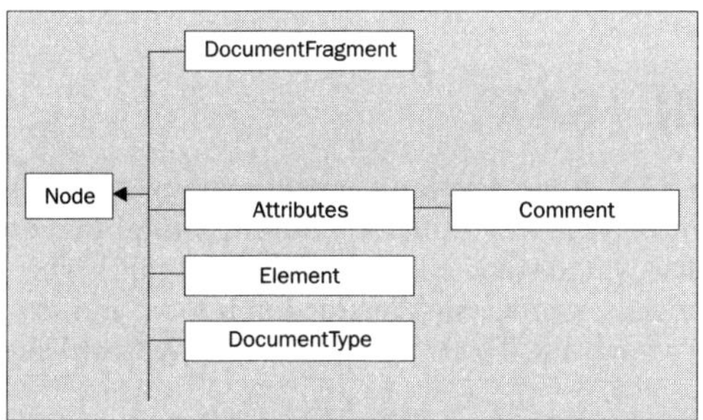

What kinds of behavior or methods do these interfaces have? For the most part, programmers want to get a node's value, its child Nodes and so on, and of course such methods are provided. In other situations, programmers want to know what the type of a node is (for example, whether it is an Element or a piece of Notation), so these methods are provided as well.

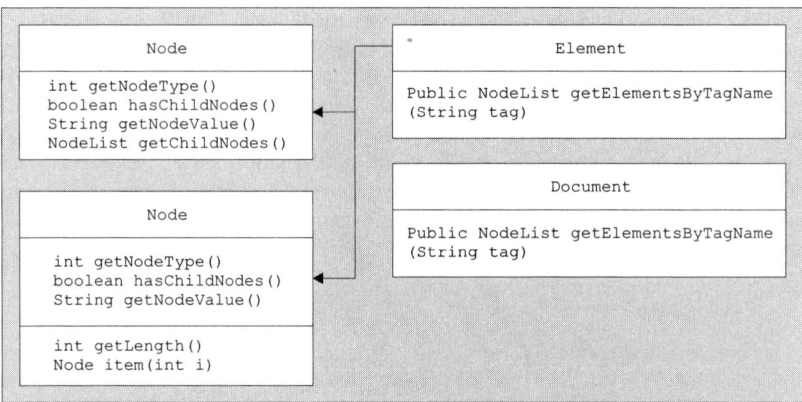

What answers would we get if we called these methods on the Nodes in our XML fragment?

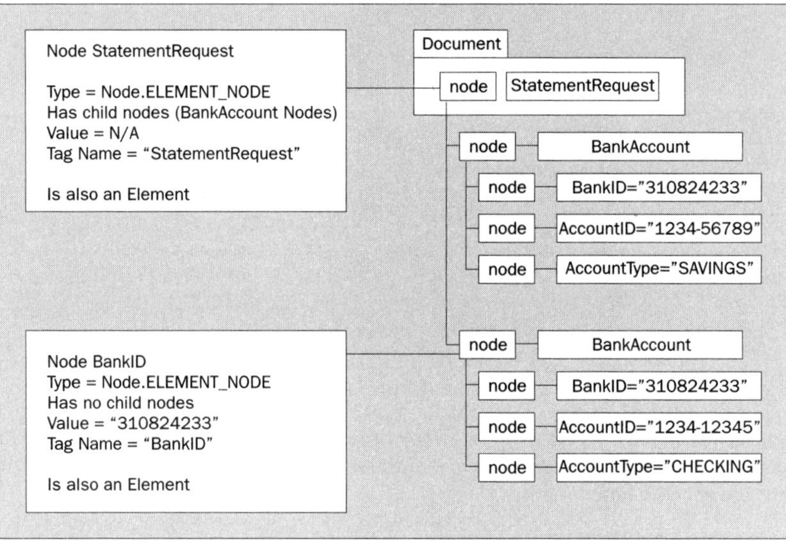

Simple API for XML (SAX)

The Simple API for XML, or SAX, is the development community's response to the DOM. It also parses XML documents, but is **event driven** rather than **document-model driven** like DOM. That is, it streams the document through the parse window and issues events to the caller when parts of the document are found (an element starts, an element ends, a processing instruction is read, and so on). Compared to the DOM, SAX has a very small memory footprint. The event model of SAX works like this:

- The SAX XML parser processes elements serially.
- The XML application registers for those events that it is interested in and provides callback functions to handle the element.
- When the events of interest are encountered, the callback functions are invoked.

The callback functions are defined by the interfaces `DocumentHandler`, `ErrorHandler`, `DTDHandler` and `EntityResolver`. For example, an application might be interested in the `DocumentHandler` interface and hence provide callbacks for the methods in this interface – `StartDocument`, `EndDocument` , `StartElement`, and `EndElement`. The application might also want to implement the methods defined by the `ErrorHandler` interface (for example `Warning` or `FatalError`). The SAX parser then informs the application when it encounters these events, and the application in turn invokes methods to process the events.

The SAX API is a fast API. It has a lighter computational footprint than DOM – that is, it consumes less memory and CPU resources. The DOM API must construct a tree out of the whole document before any processing can be done. DOM is ideal for interactive applications that require an object representation in memory. SAX is more suited for server-side applications that do not need to create a tree structure. SAX may be a good choice for network-oriented programs that send and receive XML documents. SAX is particularly useful for filtering very large XML documents, because DOM uses a lot of memory on these. SAX, in general requires a lot more coding than the DOM interface. Unfortunately, if the XML document is complexly connected (perhaps through the use of `ID` to `IDREF` relationships), using SAX can necessitate either multiple parses of a document or sophisticated buffering to retrieve needed information that has already passed through the parse window.

XPath

XPath is a language that can be used to point to a specific thing or a set of things in an XML document. XPath uses the location path to describe how to find specific elements, attributes, processing instructions, etc. in a document. A location path is simply a description of how to get from one place in the document to someplace else. To use a crude analogy, the location path is similar to a set of instructions for finding a specific location within a city. If we wanted to find a particular office tower, a guide might tell us "Go to the second set of lights, turn left and you'll find the office tower two blocks ahead on your right". In the same way, we can use the location path to find what we are looking for in an XML document. The location path describes a path from one point in an XML document to another point, and it provides a way for each of the items within the document to be addressed. In other words, it describes the address of one of the document's nodes, in relationship to another node.

Just as our guide's set of instructions starts with where we currently are in the city, so the location path also is relative to the starting location. This concept is called the context node, which is where the addressing starts.

XPath treats the XML document as a logical tree, with a root node as well as nodes for elements, attributes, character data (text), processing instructions, comments, and namespaces. The root node is the root of the document; every XML document has one, and it contains an optional prolog and the document element. A location path that begins with a slash (`/`) is considered relative to the root node, while a path that begins with two slashes (`//`) relates to descendants of the root node.

For more information about XPath, look at the following URL: http://www.w3.org/TR/xpath.

Summary

In this appendix, we've spent some time bringing you up to speed (or back up to speed) on the building blocks of XML and how they fit together. We've also taken a quick look at some of the technologies we'll be using to access and manipulate XML documents throughout the remainder of the book. If you found this chapter a little overwhelming, you might find a book like *Beginning XML, ISBN 1861003412* helpful to flesh out some of the details of the subjects we've discussed.

akarta
Java

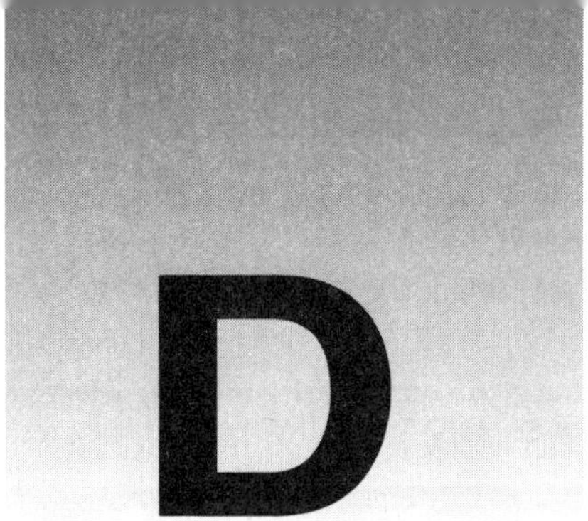

Support, Errata, and p2p.wrox.com

One of the most irritating things about any programming book is when you find that bit of code you've just spent an hour typing simply doesn't work. You check it a hundred times to see if you've set it up correctly, and then you notice the spelling mistake in the variable name on the book page. Of course, you can blame the authors for not taking enough care and testing the code, the editors for not doing their job properly, or the proofreaders for not being eagle-eyed enough, but this doesn't get around the fact that mistakes do happen.

We try hard to ensure no mistakes sneak out into the real world, but we can't promise that this book is 100 percent error-free. What we can do is offer the next best thing by providing you with immediate support and feedback from experts who have worked on the book, and try to ensure that future editions eliminate these gremlins. We also now commit to supporting you, not just while you read the book, but once you start developing applications as well through our online forums where you can put your questions to the authors, reviewers, and fellow industry professionals.

In this appendix we'll look at how to:

- Enroll in the **Programmer To Programmer™** forums at http://p2p.wrox.com
- Post and check for errata on our main site, http://www.wrox.com
- E-mail technical support a query or feedback on our books in general

Between all three of these support procedures, you should get an answer to your problem in no time at all.

The Online Forums at p2p.wrox.com

Join the Java mailing list for author and peer support. Our system provides **Programmer To Programmer™** support on mailing lists, forums, and newsgroups all in addition to our one-to-one e-mail system, which we'll look at in a minute. Be confident that your query is not just being examined by a support professional, but by the many Wrox authors and other industry experts present on our mailing lists.

How to Enroll for Support

Just follow these simple instructions:

1. Go to http://p2p.wrox.com in your favorite browser. Here, you'll find any current announcements concerning P2P – new lists created, any removed, and so on:

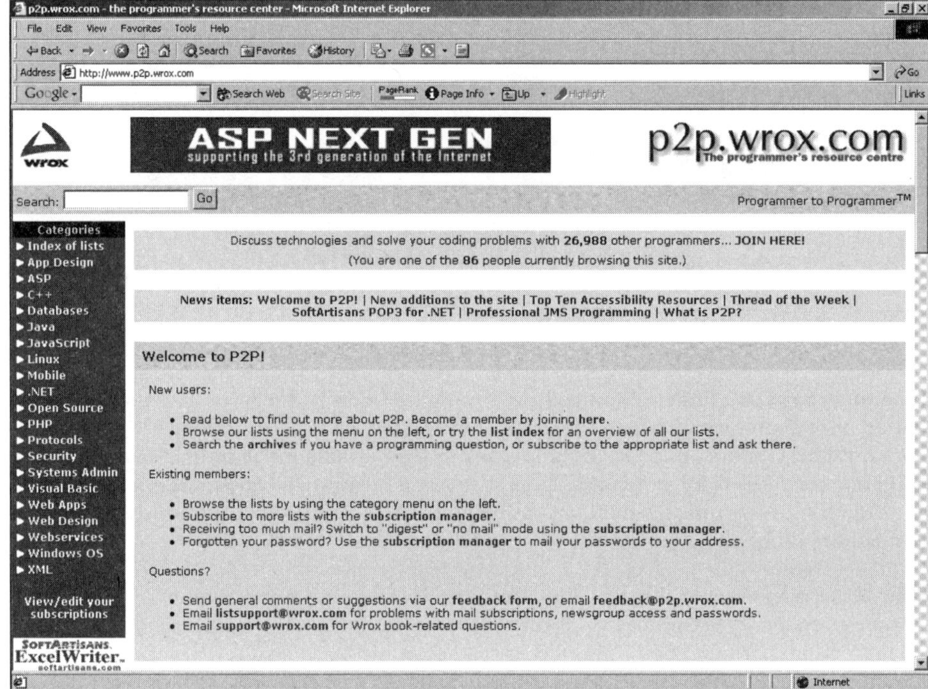

2. Click on the Java link in the left-hand column.

3. Choose to access the beginning_java_databases list.

4. If you are not a member of the list, you can choose to either view the list without joining it or create an account in the list, by hitting the respective buttons.

5. If you wish to join, you'll be presented with a form in which you'll need to fill in your e-mail address, name, and a password (of at least four alpha-numeric characters). Choose how you would like to receive the messages from the list and then hit Subscribe.

6. Congratulations! You're now a member of the beginning_java_databases mailing list.

Why This System Offers the Best Support

You can choose to join the mailing lists to receive mails as they are contributed, or a daily digest, or you can receive them as a weekly digest. If you don't have the time or facility to receive the mailing list, then you can search our online archives. You'll find the ability to search on specific subject areas or keywords. As these lists are moderated, you can be confident of finding good, accurate information quickly. Mails can be edited or moved by the moderator into the correct place, making this a most efficient resource. Junk and spam mail are deleted, and your own e-mail address is protected by the unique Lyris system from web-bots that can automatically hoover up newsgroup mailing list addresses. Any queries about joining, or leaving lists, or any query about the list should be sent to support@wrox.com.

Checking the Errata Online at www.wrox.com

The following section will take you step-by-step through the process of posting errata to our web site to get that help. The sections that follow, therefore, are:

- Finding a list of existing errata on the web site
- Adding your own erratum to the existing list

There is also a section covering how to e-mail a question for technical support. This comprises:

- What your e-mail should include
- What happens to your e-mail once it has been received by us

Finding an Erratum on the Web Site

Before you send in a query, you might be able to save time by finding the answer to your problem on our web site at http://www.wrox.com.

Each book we publish has its own page, and its own errata sheet. You can get to any book's page by clicking on the relevant links underneath the Books heading on the left hand navigation bar. To view the errata for that book, click on the Book Errata link on the right-hand side of the book information pane, underneath the book information.

We update these pages regularly to ensure that you have the latest information on bugs and errors.

Add an Erratum

If you wish to point out an erratum to put up on the web site, or directly query a problem in the book page with an expert who knows the book in detail, then e-mail support@wrox.com with the title of the book and the last four numbers of the ISBN in the subject field of the e-mail. Clicking on the submit errata link on the web site's errata page will send an e-mail using your e-mail client. A typical e-mail should include the following things:

- The **name**, **last four digits of the ISBN**, and **page number** of the problem in the Subject field
- Your **name**, **contact info**, and the **problem** in the body of the message

We won't send you junk mail. We need the details to save both your time and ours. If we need to replace a disk or CD we'll be able to get it to you straight away. When you send an e-mail, it will go through the following chain of support:

Customer Support

Your message is delivered to one of our customer support staff who will be the first people to read it. They have files on most frequently asked questions, and will answer anything general immediately. They answer general questions about the book and the web site.

Editorial

Deeper queries are forwarded to the technical editor responsible for that book. They have experience with the programming language or particular product, and are able to answer detailed technical questions on the subject. Once an issue has been resolved, the editor can post the erratum to the web site.

The Authors

Finally, in the unlikely event that the editor can't answer your problem, they will forward the request to the author. We try to protect the author from any distractions from writing. However, we are quite happy to forward specific requests to them. All Wrox authors help with the support on their books. They'll mail the customer and the editor with their response, and again all readers should benefit.

What We Can't Answer

Obviously with an ever-growing range of books and an ever-changing technology base, there is an increasing volume of data requiring support. While we endeavor to answer all questions about the book, we can't answer bugs in your own programs that you've adapted from our code. So, while you might have loved the chapters on file handling, don't expect too much sympathy if you cripple your company with a routine that deletes the contents of your hard drive, but do tell us if you're especially pleased with the routine you developed with our help.

How to Tell Us Exactly What You Think

We understand that errors can destroy the enjoyment of a book and can cause many wasted and frustrated hours, so we seek to minimize the distress that they can cause.

You might just wish to tell us how much you liked or loathed the book in question. Or you might have ideas about how this whole process could be improved. If this is the case, you should e-mail feedback@wrox.com. You'll always find a sympathetic ear, no matter what the problem is. Above all you should remember that we do care about what you have to say and we will do our utmost to act upon it.

Index

Symbols

A

B

C

D

E

F

J

K

L

M

N

S

T